Cleveland School of the Arts
2064 Stearns Road
Cleveland, Ohio 44106

HOLT

Elements of
LITERATURE

Fourth Course

correlated to

Ohio

Academic Content Standards
for Language Arts

CONTENTS

HOLT, RINEHART AND WINSTON

ISBN-13:
ISBN-10:0
2 3 4 5 0868

OH2

Ohio
The Buckeye State

State Capitol, Columbus

Cover Picture Credits: (bkgd) Photos.com; (cl), George Marks / Retrofile RF / Getty Images; (inset), Sylvain Grandadam / The Image Bank / Getty Images; (bc), Jo McRyan / Stone / Getty Images; (br), Philip & Karen Smith / Digital Vision / Getty Images.

978-0-55-400552-2
...55-400552-2

...0 09

State flower,
scarlet carnation

State bird,
red male cardinal

<· · · **Unpacking Ohio Academic Content
Standards for Language Arts**

Ohio Academic Content Standards for Language Arts

READING

Acquisition of Vocabulary

>1 Define unknown words through context clues and the author's use of comparison, contrast and cause and effect.

What does it mean? Clues from surrounding words and sentences can help you define new words.

EXAMPLE: Using Context Clues For practice using context clues, see the Language Coach feature on page 61 and the Vocabulary Development lesson on page 228.

>2 Analyze the relationships of pairs of words in analogical statements (e.g., synonyms and antonyms, connotation and denotation) and infer word meanings from these relationships.

What does it mean? Relationships between words—including opposites, or antonyms—help you learn a word's meaning.

EXAMPLE: Understanding Word Analogies For information about word analogies, see Vocabulary Development on pages 336 and 520.

>3 Infer the literal and figurative meaning of words and phrases and discuss the function of figurative language, including metaphors, similes, idioms and puns.

What does it mean? Interpreting figurative language in a work can add to your understanding and enjoyment of it.

EXAMPLE: Understanding Figures of Speech For information about figurative language, including similes, metaphors, personification, and other figures of speech, see pages 274, 284, 443, 645 and 705.

>4 Analyze the ways that historical events influenced the English language.

What does it mean? Migrating groups, invaders, and traders all affected the development of the English language.

*Goldenrod,
rural Ohio*

OH4

EXAMPLE: The History of the English Language

See pages 1034, 1059, and 1077 for information about the development of the English language.

>5 Use knowledge of Greek, Latin and Anglo-Saxon roots, prefixes and suffixes to understand complex words and new subject-area vocabulary (e.g., unknown words in science, mathematics, and social studies).

What does it mean? You will break words into parts—roots and affixes— and use the meanings of those parts to understand science, math, and social studies terms.

EXAMPLE: Roots, Prefixes, and Suffixes

For a chart of common Greek, Latin, and Anglo-Saxon/Old English roots, prefixes, and suffixes, with their meanings and examples, see pages 1214–1215. Memorizing the meanings of the most common word parts will help you read more efficiently.

TOOLS AND RESOURCES

>6 Determine the meanings and pronunciations of unknown words by using dictionaries, glossaries, technology and textual features, such as definitional footnotes or sidebars.

What does it mean? Use reference sources and text features to aid your comprehension and pronunciation of new words.

EXAMPLE: Resources for Unknown Words

The selections in this textbook footnote word definitions and pronunciations as needed. Poems and plays often have sidebar definitions. For help with using a dictionary, see page 129. You will find a glossary on pages 1266–1270 and a Spanish glossary on pages 1271–1274.

Reading Process: Concepts of Print, Comprehension Strategies and Self-Monitoring Strategies

COMPREHENSION STRATEGIES

>1 Apply reading comprehension strategies, including making predictions, comparing and contrasting, recalling and

summarizing and making inferences and drawing conclusions.

What does it mean? Effective readers use a variety of reading comprehension strategies to fully grasp texts.

EXAMPLE: Using Comprehension Strategies See the Reading Focus features on pages 8–9 and 106–107 for comprehension strategies such as making predictions, cause and effect, visualizing, and comparing and contrasting.

>2 Answer literal, inferential, evaluative and synthesizing questions to demonstrate comprehension of grade-appropriate print texts and electronic and visual media.

What does it mean? To truly understand a text, you must not only recall facts, but also draw conclusions, predict outcomes, and evaluate and synthesize what you read.

EXAMPLE: Demonstrating Comprehension Questions appear at the end of most selections. For example, see page 153. For more on drawing conclusions, see page 565. For more about making inferences, see pages 790 and 1209. For more about making predictions, see pages 8 and 790.

SELF-MONITORING STRATEGIES

>3 Monitor own comprehension by adjusting speed to fit the purpose, or by skimming, scanning, reading on, looking back, note taking or summarizing what has been read so far in text.

What does it mean? Your pace for leisure reading is usually much faster than your pace for school reading. If you find yourself getting confused about what you have read, slow down and use as many reading strategies as necessary to get back on track.

EXAMPLE: Monitoring for Comprehension See the self-monitoring directed-reading questions in literary and informational selections (for example, on pages 179–185). Pages 312–313, 564, and 1145 discuss tips for improving comprehension, including asking questions, note taking, re-reading, retelling, summarizing, and using key words.

Columbus skyline

Blue Hen Falls,
Cuyahoga Valley
National Park

INDEPENDENT READING

>4 Use criteria to choose independent reading materials (e.g., personal interest, knowledge of authors and genres or recommendations from others).

What does it mean? Choose other works by an author you enjoyed; choose topics, genres, and types of writing that interest you; or ask for suggestions from others.

EXAMPLE: Independent Reading The Read On features at the end of each collection (for example, pages 1116–1117) provide information about literature you can read independently.

>5 Independently read books for various purposes (e.g., for enjoyment, for literary experience, to gain information or to perform a task).

What does it mean? You may choose books to expand your literary base, to acquire general or specific knowledge, or to find out how to do specific tasks.

EXAMPLE: Independent Reading At the end of each collection, you will find a Read On page that lists fiction and nonfiction books recommended for independent reading (for an example, see page 1116–1117). A short summary of each book is included.

Reading Applications: Informational, Technical and Persuasive Text

>1 Identify and understand organizational patterns (e.g., cause-effect, problem-solution) and techniques, including repetition of ideas, syntax and word choice, that authors use to accomplish their purpose and reach their intended audience.

What does it mean? Recognizing the organization and techniques an author uses can enhance your understanding.

EXAMPLE: Organizational Patterns See "Text Structures" (pages 1212–1213) in the Handbook of Reading and Informational Terms. Other useful entries include "Cause and Effect," "Chronological Order," "Comparison and Contrast," "Logical Order," "Order of Importance," and "Spatial Order."

>2 Critique the treatment, scope and organization of ideas from multiple sources on the same topic.

What does it mean? You will identify, evaluate, and compare the methods several authors have used to examine the same subject.

EXAMPLE: Evaluating and Comparing Sources For evaluating information from multiple sources on the same subject, see the article "R.M.S. Titanic" (pages 398–410), "A Fireman's Story" (page 411), and "From a Lifeboat" (page 412).

>3 Evaluate the effectiveness of information found in maps, charts, tables, graphs, diagrams, cutaways and overlays.

What does it mean? You will analyze graphic information to determine whether it is useful and whether it supplements the text and promotes the author's purpose.

EXAMPLE: Evaluating Graphics See page 1210 for help with reading maps and pages 1224–1225 for reading graphs.

>4 Assess the adequacy, accuracy and appropriateness of an author's details, identifying persuasive techniques (e.g., transfer, glittering generalities, bait and switch) and examples of propaganda, bias and stereotyping.

What does it mean? You will analyze how an author appeals to an audience and examine techniques, details, and evidence that develop an argument or viewpoint.

EXAMPLE: Analyzing Arguments For step-by-step help in analyzing an argument, see "How Do You Evaluate Persuasive Arguments?" (pages 564–565) and the Literary Focus on page 593. See also "Fallacious Reasoning" (pages 1208–1209).

>5 Analyze an author's implicit and explicit argument, perspective or viewpoint in text.

What does it mean? An author's viewpoint may be stated, implied, or hidden. Examine the reasons and evidence—and possibly other sources—to evaluate texts.

EXAMPLE: Analyzing Arguments On pages 606–607, you will evaluate the credibility of the arguments in two opinion pieces. On pages 609–615, you will evaluate the arguments presented in two articles.

>6 Identify appeals to authority, reason and emotion.

What does it mean? To analyze persuasive writing, you must look at the elements that make up the argument—for example, appeals to logic, emotion, ethics, and authority; analogies, and arguments by causation.

EXAMPLE: Analyzing Persuasive Elements On pages 602, 606, and 609, you will find discussions of types of supporting evidence in a persuasive essay. On pages 564–565, you will learn about such persuasive elements as appeals and rhetorical devices.

>7 Analyze the effectiveness of the features (e.g., format, graphics, sequence, headers) used in various consumer documents (e.g., warranties, product information, instructional materials), functional or workplace documents (e.g., job-related materials, memoranda, instructions) and public documents (e.g., speeches or newspaper editorials).

What does it mean? Clear organization is essential in real-world documents, especially those designed to help you complete a task or make an informed decision.

EXAMPLE: Analyzing Consumer Documents You will evaluate the features of consumer documents (pages 1166–1170) and analyze and evaluate a set of technical directions (pages 1150–1154). See also "Consumer Documents" (page 1206) and "Workplace Documents" (page 1213) in the Handbook of Reading and Informational Terms.

>8 Describe the features of rhetorical devices used in common types of public documents, including newspaper editorials and speeches.

What does it mean? Devices used to persuade include emotional, logical, and ethical appeals; diction; allusion; metaphor; repetition; parallelism; and rhetorical questions.

EXAMPLE: Analyzing Rhetorical Devices See pages 564–565 for a discussion of rhetorical devices used in persuasive essays and speeches.

Reading Applications: Literary Text

>1 Compare and contrast an author's use of direct and indirect characterization, and ways in which characters reveal traits about themselves, including dialect, dramatic monologues and soliloquies.

What does it mean? Examine characters, and analyze how authors reveal their characters' personalities and motivations.

EXAMPLE: Analyzing Characterization Read the Literary Focus on pages 102–103 for information about direct and indirect characterization. Many Response and Analysis questions in the collections also focus on characterization. See, for example, question 8 on page 125, which asks you to name a few of a character's traits.

>2 Analyze the features of setting and their importance in a literary text.

What does it mean? The setting details of place, time, weather, sounds, smells, and mood can make a story realistic. You will analyze and compare these and other features.

EXAMPLE: Analyzing Setting Review "What Do You Know About Plot and Setting?" (pages 4–5) to increase your understanding of the features of setting.

>3 Distinguish how conflicts, parallel plots and subplots affect the pacing of action in literary text.

What does it mean? First, identify the parts of the plot. Then, note how authors use the parts to speed up or slow down action, increase tension, foreshadow events, provide comic relief, and create other effects.

EXAMPLE: Analyzing Plot and Conflict Collection 1 focuses on plot and conflict. See the essay "What Do You Know About Plot and Setting?" (pages 4–5). Many Response and Analysis questions examine plot, internal and external conflicts, suspense, climax, and resolution. See also the Handbook of Literary Terms for the entries "Plot" (page 1200) and "Conflict" (page 1195).

>4 Interpret universal themes across different works by the same author and different authors.

What does it mean? Universal themes reflect the common desires, needs, and experiences of people everywhere, so they appear in works from many authors and cultures.

EXAMPLE: Interpreting Universal Themes In Collection 4, "Comparing Themes," you

will interpret, compare, and contrast universal themes in two selections (pages 966–974).

>5 Analyze how an author's choice of genre affects the expression of a theme or topic.

What does it mean? You will analyze how the same topic or theme is treated in such genres as a short story and a newspaper article.

EXAMPLE: Analyzing Genre You will analyze how a topic is examined in more than one genre in "R.M.S. Titanic" (pages 398–410), "A Fireman's Story" (page 411), and "From a Lifeboat" (page 412).

>6 Explain how literary techniques, including foreshadowing and flashback, are used to shape the plot of a literary text.

What does it mean? Authors use foreshadowing and flashback to enrich their stories. You will examine these and other techniques to determine the effect they have on a plot.

EXAMPLE: Explaining Literary Techniques See the essay "What Do You Know About Plot and Setting?" (pages 4–5) as well as the Literary Focus on flashback and foreshadowing (page 37).

>7 Recognize how irony is used in a literary text.

What does it mean? Irony involves the difference between expectation and reality in what people say, how events occur, or what the audience knows. You will determine how authors use irony to create elements of surprise.

EXAMPLE: Examining Irony See the Literary Skills Review on page 257. Also see the essay "How Do Symbolism and Irony Help Writers Tell Stories?" on pages 308–309.

>8 Analyze the author's use of point of view, mood and tone.

What does it mean? Point of view— whether first person, third person, limited, or omniscient—affects what readers learn about events and characters in the test. The author's choice of tone and mood also affect the story.

Cleveland

EXAMPLE: Point of View, Mood, and Tone See the essay "What Do You Need to Know About Narrator and Voice?" on pages 208–209 for a discussion of point of view and tone.

>9 Explain how authors use symbols to create broader meanings.

What does it mean? You must examine how authors make symbols work by association and how readers make sense of the text by building on those associations.

EXAMPLE: Understanding Symbols See the essay "How Do Symbolism and Irony Help Writers Tell Stories?" on pages 308–309.

>10 Describe the effect of using sound devices in literary text (e.g., to create rhythm, to appeal to the senses or to establish mood).

What does it mean? Sound effects used in both prose and poetry can create rhythm, appeal to the senses, and establish mood. You must be able to recognize and describe these sound devices in different types of text.

EXAMPLE: Using Sound Effects See the Literary Focus on page 734 for a discussion of the use of sound in poems. See also the entries for specific sound devices in the Handbook of Literary Terms, pages 1193–1204.

>11 Explain ways in which an author develops a point of view and style (e.g., figurative language, sentence structure and tone) and cite specific examples from the text.

What does it mean? You will examine an author's word choice and techniques and determine how they reveal characters' thoughts and actions.

EXAMPLE: Point of View and Style See the essay "What Do You Need to Know

About Narrator and Voice?" on pages 208–209 for a discussion of point of view. See also the Literary Perspectives "Analyzing Style" on page 355.

WRITING

Writing Processes

PREWRITING

>1 Generate writing ideas through discussions with others and from printed material, and keep a list of writing ideas.

What does it mean? Writing ideas may come from many sources. Keep a list of these ideas to use in writing assignments.

EXAMPLE: Generating Ideas The Writing Workshops in this textbook provide a variety of suggestions for generating writing ideas. See, for example, the Prewriting section on page 425.

>2 Determine the usefulness of and apply appropriate pre-writing tasks (e.g., background reading, interviews, or surveys).

What does it mean? You cannot use every prewriting strategy when developing a new piece of writing. Learn to choose the strategy that best suits a particular assignment.

EXAMPLE: Doing Prewriting Tasks See the Listening and Speaking Workshop "Conducting an Interview" (page 1188) for tips on interviewing. See also page 626–630 for types of evidence used in a persuasive essay. For information about primary and secondary sources, see pages 189 and 397.

>3 Establish and develop a clear thesis statement for informational writing or a clear plan or outline for narrative writing.

What does it mean? Decide first what point your writing will make, either by compos-

OH10

Autumn in Ohio

ing a sentence stating that point or by jotting down crucial events in a narrative.

EXAMPLE: Writing a Thesis Statement
Many of the Writing Workshops in this textbook give advice on writing a thesis statement. See for example, page 768.

>4 Determine a purpose and audience and plan strategies (e.g., adapting focus, content structure, and point of view) to address purpose and audience.

What does it mean? Why are you writing, and who will read what you write? Identify both before you begin writing.

EXAMPLE: Identifying Purpose and Audience The Writing Workshops in this textbook help you pinpoint your specific purpose and audience for each piece you will write. See, for example, page 767.

>5 Use organizational strategies (e.g., notes and outlines) to plan writing.

What does it mean? Different strategies can help you plan different types of writing. For example, you might outline an informative report but make notes in a flowchart for an essay explaining a process.

EXAMPLE: Using Note Cards and Outlines For help with using note cards, taking notes, and creating outlines, see pages 1118–1126 in "Research Paper." See also "Outlining" (page 1211) in the Handbook of Reading and Information Terms.

DRAFTING, REVISING AND EDITING

>6 Organize writing to create a coherent whole with an effective and engaging introduction, body and conclusion, and a closing sentence that summarizes, extends or elaborates on points or ideas in the writing.

What does it mean? As you write, you will need to follow your plan, making that plan and your main idea clear to readers in your introduction and conclusion.

EXAMPLE: Achieving Coherence Each Writing Workshop gives tips about what goes into the essay's introduction, body, and conclusion. For an example, see page 626. For help with paragraph structure, unity, and coherence, see pages 1217–1221.

>7 Use a variety of sentence structures and lengths (e.g., simple, compound and complex sentences; parallel or repetitive sentence structure).

What does it mean? Keep your readers interested by varying the types of sentences you use. Use parallel sentence structures to help your readers follow your ideas.

EXAMPLE: Varying Sentences For practice in varying sentence structures and lengths, see the Grammar Link on page 365 and try the Your Turn practice exercise at the bottom of the page.

>8 Use paragraph form in writing, including topic sentences that arrange paragraphs in a logical sequence, using effective transitions and closing sentences and maintaining coherence across the whole through the use of parallel structures.

What does it mean? Coherence is the interconnectedness of ideas in writing. Topic sentences, transitions, and parallelism can show how ideas are connected.

EXAMPLE: Writing Effective Paragraphs For a detailed description of the elements of a good paragraph and for exercises to strengthen your paragraph writing skills, see pages 1217–1221 in the Writer's Handbook.

>9 Use language, including precise language, action verbs, sensory details and colorful modifiers, and style as appropriate to audience and purpose, and use techniques to convey a personal style and voice.

What does it mean? Vivid, precise words and a distinct voice will keep your readers interested in your ideas.

EXAMPLE: Using Effective Language See "The Writer's Language" (pages 1221–1222) for tips on using precise language, action verbs, sensory details, appropriate modifiers, and the active voice.

>10 Use available technology to compose text.

What does it mean? Technology makes writing and revising very efficient. Moving,

Toledo, Ohio

adding, or deleting text is quick and easy. Graphics, such as bullet points and simple charts, can enhance your message.

EXAMPLE: Using Technology "Designing Your Writing" (pages 1222–1225) will help you enhance the impact and readability of your papers.

>11 **Reread and analyze clarity of writing, consistency of point of view and effectiveness of organizational structure.**

What does it mean? Revising to make ideas clear and easy to follow is an essential step in the writing process.

EXAMPLE: Revising See "Qualities of Paragraphs" (pages 1219–1221). In every Writing Workshop, a section on revising guides you through the many aspects of revising (for example, see page 630).

>12 **Add and delete information and details to better elaborate on a stated central idea and more effectively accomplish purpose.**

What does it mean? For unity, delete details that do not directly support your main idea, and elaborate on those that do.

EXAMPLE: Elaborating Ideas On pages 1219–1221 you will find a discussion of how to bring unity and coherence to your paragraphs. On page 1218 is a list of many kinds of supporting details you can use to elaborate on a paragraph's main idea.

>13 **Rearrange words, sentences and paragraphs, and add transitional words phrases to clarify meaning and maintain consistent style, tone and voice.**

What does it mean? Put your thoughts in a logical sequence, and connect them with helpful transitions.

EXAMPLE: Revising for Clarity See the revising step in every Writing Workshop

(for example, page 700). For style and tone, see pages 186, 209, 443, and 448–451.

>14 **Use resources and reference materials (e.g., dictionaries and thesauruses) to select effective and precise vocabulary that maintains consistent style, tone and voice.**

What does it mean? Choose the exact words to communicate each idea clearly, using a dictionary or thesaurus for help.

EXAMPLE: Using Resources Find the precise word you are looking for by using a dictionary (page 1207) as well as a thesaurus, or book of synonyms (page 58).

>15 **Proofread writing, edit to improve conventions (e.g., grammar, spelling, punctuation and capitalization), identify and correct fragments and run-ons and eliminate inappropriate slang or informal language.**

What does it mean? Careless errors or inappropriate language can detract from the effect of otherwise strong writing.

EXAMPLE: Proofreading Every Writing Workshop has a section on proofreading. For an example, see "Get It Right," page 633. You will find proofreading guidelines and proofreading symbols on page 1217.

>16 **Apply tools (e.g., rubric, checklist and feedback) to judge the quality of writing.**

What does it mean? You can determine how good a piece of writing is by using specific criteria such as items on a rubric.

EXAMPLE: Using Guidelines to Evaluate You will find revision guidelines in every Writing Workshop. See page 428 for an example.

PUBLISHING

>17 **Prepare for publication (e.g., for display or for sharing with others) writing that fol-**

lows a manuscript form appropriate for the purpose, which could include such techniques as electronic resources, principles of design (e.g., margins, tabs, spacing and columns) and graphics (e.g., drawings, charts and graphs) to enhance the final product.

What does it mean? Give your writing every advantage. Use formatting, design, and visuals to appeal to readers.

EXAMPLE: Publishing Publishing— sharing your writing with an audience — is the fun part. Before you post your writing online or create a class anthology or a multi-media display, check out "Designing Your Writing" (pages 1222–1225).

Writing Applications

>1 Write narratives that: (a) sustain reader interest by pacing action and developing an engaging plot (e.g., tension and suspense); (b) use a range of strategies and literary devices including figurative language and specific narration; and (c) include an organized, well-developed structure.

What does it mean? A gripping narrative holds reader attention by building complications and bringing people and places to life.

EXAMPLE: Writing Narratives You will find step-by-step guidance in the narrative Writing Workshop "Writing an Autobiographical Narrative" (page 424).

>2 Write responses to literature that organize an insightful interpretation around several clear ideas, premises or images and support judgments with specific references to the original text, to other texts, authors and to prior knowledge.

What does it mean? After you read a work, you can interpret the author's ideas, add your own ideas to develop generalizations, and evaluate the work's effectiveness.

EXAMPLE: Responding to Literature Throughout the text, you are asked to write brief responses to literature. For example, see the writing prompt for a character analysis on page 139. See also "Writing a Response to Poetry" (page 766) and "Presenting a Response to Literature" (page 776).

>3 Write business letters, letters to the editor and job applications that: (a) address audience needs, stated purpose and context in a clear and efficient manner; (b) follow the conventional style appropriate to the text using proper technical terms; (c) include appropriate facts and details; (d) exclude extraneous details and inconsistencies; and (e) provide a sense of closure to the writing.

What does it mean? Mastering writing skills can help you achieve such real-life goals as getting a job.

EXAMPLE: Writing Functional Documents See pages 1178–1186 for help with the elements and format of a business letter

>4 Write informational essays or reports, including research, that: (a) pose relevant and tightly drawn questions that engage the reader; (b) provide a clear and accurate perspective on the subject; (c) create an organizing structure appropriate to the purpose, audience and context; (d) support the main ideas with facts, details, examples and explanations from sources; and (e) document sources and include bibliographies.

What does it mean? Throughout your school career, you will need to report organized and elaborated information and cite your sources appropriately.

EXAMPLE: Writing Informational Essays See the following Writing Workshops: "Writing an Informative Essay" (page 994), "Writing a Research Paper" (page 1118), and "Writing Business Communications"

OH14

(page 1178), which guide you through every step in the process.

>5 Write persuasive compositions that: (a) support arguments with detailed evidence; (b) exclude irrelevant information; and (c) cite sources of information.

What does it mean? Effective persuasion requires well-supported arguments, a clear focus, and authoritative information.

EXAMPLE: Writing Persuasive Essays For detailed instruction on writing persuasively, see "Writing a Persuasive Essay" (page 626).

>6 Produce informal writings (e.g., journals, notes and poems) for various purposes.

What does it mean? Not everything you write is a formal composition. In fact, some of your strongest insights may shine through in writings such as e-mails, journals, and song lyrics.

EXAMPLE: Writing Informally The writing prompts on Respond and Think Critically pages throughout the text offer many opportunities to write informally. For example, you will write a descriptive paragraph (page 57), a brief dialogue (page 125), and a poem (page 704).

Writing Conventions

SPELLING

>1 Use correct spelling conventions.

What does it mean? Never rely on a computer spell-checker as your only check for spelling errors. Learn to spell the words you use in your writing, or look them up.

EXAMPLE: Using Correct Spelling Every Writing Workshop includes a proofreading step that includes checking your paper for correct spelling. See page 431 for an example. For help in using a dictionary, see page 1207.

PUNCTUATION AND CAPITALIZATION

>2 Use correct punctuation and capitalization.

What does it mean? Correct mechanics make your meaning precise. Consider the potential for confusion not using a comma could cause in the following sentence: According to the French, fries are not acceptable food.

EXAMPLE: Using Correct Punctuation and Capitalization For a review of capitalization and punctuation rules, see pages 1250–1259 in the Language Handbook.

Rhododendron and azalea gardens

GRAMMAR AND USAGE

>3 Use clauses (e.g., main, subordinate) and phrases (e.g., gerund, infinitive, participial).

What does it mean? A **clause** is a group of words with a subject and verb used as part of a sentence. A **phrase** is a group of related words, used as a single part of speech, that does not have both a subject and verb.

EXAMPLE: Using Clauses and Phrases
For detailed information about clauses and phrases, see pages 1238–1241 in the Language Handbook. See also the Grammar Link lessons on clauses (page 155) and phrases (page 1035).

>4 Use parallel structure to present items in a series and items juxtaposed for emphasis.

What does it mean? Parallel structure means having the same grammatical form. In the sentence "I like to sing, playing piano, and reading," the items in the series are not parallel. Can you improve the sentence?

EXAMPLE: Using Parallel Structure
For help with parallel structure, see the Grammar Link on page 581. See also pages 1248–1249 in the Language Handbook.

>5 Use proper placement of modifiers.

What does it mean? A misplaced modifier may be confusing or unintentionally funny, as in this example: My sister talked to her dog, who was combing her hair.

EXAMPLE: Using Modifiers For information about placement of modifiers, see page 1236–1237 in the Language Handbook. See also the Grammar Link on page 1068.

RESEARCH

>1 Compose open-ended questions for research, assigned or personal interest, and modify questions as necessary during inquiry and investigation to narrow the focus or extend the investigation.

What does it mean? You will learn to choose research topics and to adapt and refine them.

EXAMPLE: Writing Research Questions
For help in generating productive research questions, see page 1212. For help with selecting a topic and developing questions for a research paper, see pages 1118–1120.

>2 Identify appropriate sources and gather relevant information from multiple sources (e.g., school library catalogs, online databases, electronic resources and Internet-based resources).

What does it mean? Learn to find and choose appropriate resources.

EXAMPLE: Using Sources See "Find and Evaluate Sources" on page 1120 for resources, including both primary and secondary sources, that you can explore for information for your research paper.

>3 Determine the accuracy of sources and the credibility of the author by analyzing the sources' validity (e.g., authority, accuracy, objectivity, publication date and coverage, etc.).

What does it mean? You will learn how to evaluate research sources.

EXAMPLE: Evaluating Credibility The entry "Credibility" on pages 1206–1207 describes many criteria for evaluating the credibility of sources for a research paper.

>4 Evaluate and systematically organize important information, and select appropriate sources to support central ideas, concepts and themes.

What does it mean? You will find information and support in reliable sources and organize that information well.

EXAMPLE: Analyzing and Organizing Information You will prepare source cards and take notes (pages 1121–1122). Then, you will sort your cards to prepare informal and formal outlines (pages 1124–1125).

>5 Integrate quotations and citations into written text to maintain a flow of ideas.

What does it mean? In your writing, you will use quotations and citations effectively and fluently.

EXAMPLE: Using Quotations On page 1127–1128 are examples of ways to insert direct quotations into your research paper.

>6 Use style guides to produce oral and written reports that give proper credit for sources and include an acceptable format for source acknowledgement.

What does it mean? Use styles guides such as the MLA Handbook for Writers of Research Papers, which provides information on how to cite and credit your research sources.

EXAMPLE: Documenting Sources Follow the format that your teacher requires for documenting sources. See page 1125 for tips on how to credit sources. See also pages 1161–1164 for citing information from the Internet.

>7 Use a variety of communication techniques, including oral, visual, written or multimedia reports, to present information that supports a clear position about the topic or research question and to maintain an appropriate balance between researched information and original ideas.

Steamboat on the Ohio River

What does it mean? You will use written, oral, and multimedia reports to share research findings and ideas.

EXAMPLE: Creating Multimedia Presentations
Show and tell what you have discovered about your topic. Detailed advice on how to present research in a speech is on pages 1132–1133.

COMMUNICATION: ORAL AND VISUAL

LISTENING AND VIEWING

>1 Apply active listening strategies (e.g., monitoring message for clarity, selecting and organizing essential information, noting cues such as changes in pace) in a variety of settings.

What does it mean? To meet this standard for effective communication, you must apply active listening skills.

EXAMPLE: Listening Actively and Critically
You will listen actively as you conduct an interview (page 113) and analyze and evaluate a speech (pages 1004–1005).

>2 Identify types of arguments used by the speaker such as authority and appeals to audience.

What does it mean? Recognizing the types of arguments speakers use will help you analyze the speakers' messages.

EXAMPLE: Analyzing Arguments
The Listening and Speaking Workshop on pages 1004–1005 has sections on analyzing a speaker's argument and analyzing a speaker's use of rhetorical devices.

>3 Evaluate the credibility of the speaker (e.g., hidden agendas, slanted or biased material)

and recognize fallacies of reasoning used in presentations and media messages.

What does it mean? You can become a knowledgeable listener by learning to evaluate and analyze speakers' messages and agendas.

EXAMPLE: Critiquing a Speech
Fallacious reasoning is explained on page 1208. For help in analyzing a speaker's argument, see "Analyzing and Evaluating Speeches" (pages 1004–1005).

>4 Identify how language choice and delivery styles (e.g., repetition, appeal to emotion, eye contact) contribute to meaning.

What does it mean? To meet this indicator, you will learn to recognize rhetorical strategies and understand how they affect an audience or listener.

EXAMPLE: Evaluating a Speech
You will analyze and evaluate a speech in the Listening and Speaking Workshop on pages 1004–1005. You can also use tips on language and delivery style in the Listening and Speaking Workshops (see, for example, pages 434–435).

SPEAKING SKILLS AND STRATEGIES

>5 Demonstrate an understanding of the rules of the English language and select language appropriate to purpose and audience.

What does it mean? Effective communicators know how to use standard English, both formal and informal, and can choose the form that will best suit their audiences and the occasions.

EXAMPLE: Using Standard English
Review the trouble spots: subject-verb agreement (page 259), pronoun usage (pages 35), modifiers (page 1068), and active and passive voice (page 1221).

>6 Adjust volume, phrasing, enunciation, voice modulation and inflection to stress important ideas and impact audience response.

What does it mean? Good speakers use both verbal and nonverbal techniques to engage their listeners.

EXAMPLE: Using Delivery Techniques Instruction on using verbal techniques appears in every Listening and Speaking Workshop.

>7 Vary language choices as appropriate to the context of the speech.

What does it mean? To meet this indicator, you will learn to choose your words to fit different audiences and occasions.

EXAMPLE: Using Appropriate Language Adapt diction to fit your purpose. For example, presenting an argument (pages 636–637) requires formal language, while presenting a description (page 715) uses more informal language.

SPEAKING APPLICATIONS

>8 Deliver informational presentations (e.g., expository, research) that: (a) demonstrate an understanding of the topic and present events or ideas in a logical sequence; (b) support the controlling idea or thesis with well-chosen and relevant facts, details, examples, quotations, statistics, stories and anecdotes; (c) include an effective introduction and conclusion and use a consistent organizational structure (e.g., cause-effect, compare-contrast, problem-solution); (d) use appropriate visual materials and available technology to enhance presentation (e.g., diagrams, c harts, illustrations); and (e) draw from multiple sources, including both primary and secondary sources, and identify sources used.

What does it mean? Effective informational presentations rely on a variety of skills and strategies.

EXAMPLE: Delivering Informational Presentations For step-by-step help in preparing an informational presentation, see the Listening and Speaking Workshop "Presenting Research" (pages 1132–1133).

>9 Deliver formal and informal descriptive presentations that convey relevant information and descriptive details.

What does it mean? To meet this indicator, you will learn to give engaging and informative descriptive presentations.

EXAMPLE: Delivering Descriptive Presentations You will engage in different types of descriptive writing. See, for example, the Writing Focus on page 481.

>10 Deliver persuasive presentations that: (a) establish and develop a logical and controlled argument; (b) include relevant evidence, differentiating between evidence and opinion, to support a position and to address counter-arguments or listener bias; (c) use persuasive strategies, such as rhetorical devices, anecdotes and appeals to emotion, authority and reason; (d) consistently use common organizational structures as appropriate (e.g., cause-effect, compare-contrast, problem-solution); and (e) use speaking techniques (e.g., reasoning, emotional appeal, case studies or analogies).

What does it mean? Persuading others through presentations requires a variety of skills and strategies.

EXAMPLE: Delivering Persuasive Presentations The Listening and Speaking Workshop "Presenting an Argument" (pages 636–637) leads you step-by-step through the stages of planning and delivering a persuasive speech.

Taking the Ohio Graduation Test

In Ohio, passing the **Ohio Graduation Test** (OGT) is an important step toward graduating from high school. The OGT includes separate tests in reading, writing, mathematics, science, and social studies. The OGT measures your mastery of the skills and knowledge described in Ohio's Academic Content Standards.

The OGT in **reading** contains three types of questions (multiple choice, short answer, and extended response) based on several reading passages. The OGT in **writing** includes both objective questions (multiple choice and short answer) and writing prompts that assess your mastery of the elements of good writing.

The tips and practice in this section will help you do your best on the OGT and on other tests you will take in school.

Marblehead Lighthouse, Lake Erie

Tips for Taking the OGT in Reading

TIP 1 **LOOK AHEAD.** Quickly skim the test. On the OGT you will find several reading passages, a mixture of literary and informational texts of varying lengths. Notice which passages have written-response questions. Then, estimate how long you can spend on each passage and set of questions. Plan to spend up to five minutes answering a short-answer question and up to fifteen minutes for an extended-response question. Check often to see if you need to work faster.

TIP 2 **READ EVERYTHING CAREFULLY.** Do not skip anything. Pay careful attention to the directions, the reading passages, and each entire question.

TIP 3 **FOR DIFFICULT MULTIPLE-CHOICE QUESTIONS, MAKE EDUCATED GUESSES.** Read all four choices carefully before you choose your answer. You can usually eliminate one or two answers you know are wrong. If you cannot answer a question, skip it and come back to it later.

TIP 4 **ANSWER ALL PARTS OF THE SHORT-ANSWER AND EXTENDED-RESPONSE QUESTIONS.** A written-response question is worth more points than a multiple-choice question. The test may not label short- and extended-response items, but your answer will be the right length if you answer all parts of the question. Be sure your explanation is logical and clearly related to the question and passage. As support, use examples from the passage rather than from your own knowledge or experience, and write in complete sentences.

TIP 5 **MARK YOUR ANSWER CAREFULLY.** Do not lose your place on the answer document. For multiple-choice questions, match your answer carefully to each question's number. For short-answer and extended-response questions, neatly mark any necessary changes.

TIP 6 **REVIEW YOUR WORK.** If you have time, go back and answer any questions you skipped. Try to answer every question.

Practice OGT in Reading

In this practice test you will find two passages, each followed by sample questions of the kind you will find on the OGT.

Directions: After reading each passage, choose the best answer to each question. You may refer to the passages as often as necessary.

---

from Explorers Say There's Still Lots to Look For

1   NEW YORK—"There is a popular illusion that all corners of the earth have been explored,"[oceanographer Sylvia] Earle says. "The greatest mountain ranges on the planet are underwater, where there is a whole continent waiting to be explored."

2   In the past two years alone, Ian Baker reported discovering the fabled Shangri-La waterfall on Tibet's mighty Tsangpo River; [archaeologist Johan] Reinhard recovered three frozen Inca mummies from an Andean volcano; the body of English climber George Mallory, who disappeared in 1924, was discovered on Mount Everest; and Robert Ballard located the world's oldest shipwrecks—two Phoenician cargo vessels in the Mediterranean. The same trip led him to uncover evidence of a giant flood about 7,000 years ago— perhaps the biblical flood of Noah.

3   Explorers still <u>scale</u> peaks that never have been climbed, crawl through caves to the insides of earth, hurtle into space to walk among the stars. They find ancient tribes and ancient cities. They dig up dinosaurs. They journey to places where no one has reported being before: the jungles of central Congo, the Amazon and Peru, the deserts of Tibet and China, vast underwater caves in Mexico and Belize. They are only beginning to probe the oceans; 5 percent has been explored, though water covers 71 percent of the planet.

4   All of which makes Earle say, "I think the great era of exploration has just begun."

What Sets Them Apart

5   "Men wanted for hazardous journey. Small wages, bitter cold, long months of complete darkness, constant danger, safe return doubtful. Honor and recognition in case of success."—Ernest Shackleton's 1914 advertisement for crew members for *Endurance*.

6   The ship was aptly named. Although Shackleton failed in his quest to cross the Antarctic, his journey became one of the great epics of survival. Marooned for months on an ice floe, his ship crushed by pack ice, Shackleton managed to sail a lifeboat 800 miles, scale an unmapped mountain range, reach a Norwegian whaling station, and return to rescue all of his men.

7   Seventy-five years later, Robert Ballard wants to dig through the ice and find his hero's ship.

8   Ballard is one of the most famous living explorers, and not just because he discovered the world's most famous shipwreck. Long before the lights of his little roaming robot lit up *Titanic's* ghostly bow in 1985, the former naval officer and oceanographer dedicated his life to exploration. *Bismarck*. U.S.S. *Yorktown*. *Lusitania*. Ballard has explored them all.

9   "When I die," Ballard says, "I want one word on my tombstone: Explorer."

10   He is standing in his Institute of Exploration in Mystic, Connecticut, in a replica of the control room from which he discovered *Titanic*. The institute, which opened last year, is packed with videos and displays from Ballard's finds. On one wall, a large chart details his plans: searching for ancient wrecks in the Black Sea, the lost ships of the Franklin expedition in the Canadian Arctic, Shackleton's *Endurance*.

11   "A lot of people do adventure," Ballard says. "They retrace Hannibal's route in a Winnebago. They take a helicopter to the North Pole and have cocktails. That is not exploration."

12   True exploration, he says, is about having a vision and following it, about going where no one has dared go before, about bringing back scientific information and publishing it in journals.

13   "It's about having the heart to push on when you want to turn back," he says. "That is what sets explorers apart."

RA.I.10.1

>1   From the content, vocabulary, and style, you can infer that the author wrote this article for an audience of
A. third-graders.
B. general adult readers.
C. professional explorers.
D. university professors.

EXPLANATION: The article is too difficult for third-graders to read, so you can eliminate A. On the other hand, the article is too easy for professional explorers, who would already be familiar with the information in the article, and for university professors, who would require more specific details. **The correct answer is B.**

RP.10.2A

>2   Which of these statements is a fact that can be found in the selection?
A. Explorers are braver than adventurers.
B. The *Endurance* is the world's most famous shipwreck.
C. Robert Ballard discovered the sunken *Titanic* in 1985.
D. Explorers are happier than most people.

EXPLANATION: A fact is a statement that can be verified or proved true. An opinion is a personal belief that cannot be proved true. A, B, and D are opinions—note that they all make comparisons (*braver, most famous, happier*). Answer C is a fact that can be verified in an encyclopedia or by other sources. **The correct answer is C.**

RA.I.10.1

>3 In the section "What Sets Them Apart," what method does the author use to discuss adventurers and explorers?

A. chronological order
B. cause-effect
C. comparison-contrast
D. problem-solution

EXPLANATION: Answering this question correctly depends on your being able to identify and analyze a method often used in informational material: comparison and contrast. Ballard uses it to show how people who "do adventure" differ from true explorers.
The correct answer is C.

VO.10.1

>4 "Explorers still <u>scale</u> peaks that never have been climbed. . . ." (paragraph 3) Which definition of <u>scale</u> best applies to its use in this sentence?

A. to measure by a scale
B. to climb up or over
C. to remove in thin layers
D. to become covered with scales

EXPLANATION: A, B, C, and D are all definitions of *scale* that you can find in a dictionary. You need to look for context clues to find the meaning of scale in this sentence. The word *peaks* is the first clue; the second clue is climbed, a synonym for *scale* here. The only meaning that fits the context is B, so B is the correct answer.

WA.10.2

>5 According to Robert Ballard, what are the explorers in this passage most interested in doing? Use information from the passage to explain how you came to this conclusion. Write your answer on a separate sheet of paper. Then, read the sample response.

Sample Response

According to Robert Ballard, who found the <u>Titanic</u>, explorers are most interested in bringing back new knowledge and information. They go to places where others have not been to discover new information and bring it back to share with the scientific world.

from Where Have You Gone, Charming Billy?

1   The platoon of twenty-six soldiers moved slowly in the dark, single file, not talking. One by one, like sheep in a dream, they passed through the hedgerow, crossed quietly over a meadow, and came down to the rice paddy. There they stopped. Their leader knelt down, motioning with his hand, and one by one the other soldiers squatted in the shadows, vanishing in the primitive stealth of warfare. For a long time they did not move. Except for the sounds of their breathing, the twenty-six men were very quiet: some of them excited by the adventure, some of them afraid, some of them exhausted from the long night march, some of them looking forward to reaching the sea, where they would be safe. At the rear of the column, Private First Class Paul Berlin lay quietly with his forehead resting on the black plastic stock of his rifle, his eyes closed. He was pretending he was not in the war, pretending he had not watched Billy Boy Watkins die of a heart attack that afternoon. He was pretending he was a boy again, camping with his father in the midnight summer along the Des Moines River. In the dark, with his eyes pinched shut, he pretended. He pretended that when he opened his eyes, his father would be there by the campfire and they would talk softly about whatever came to mind and then roll into their sleeping bags, and that later they'd wake up and it would be morning and there would not be a war, and that Billy Boy Watkins had not died of a heart attack that afternoon. He pretended he was not a soldier.

2   In the morning, when they reached the sea, it would be better. The hot afternoon would be over, he would bathe in the sea, and he would forget how frightened he had been on his first day at the war. The second day would not be so bad. He would learn.

3   There was a sound beside him, a movement, and then a breathed "Hey!"

4   He opened his eyes, shivering as if emerging from a deep nightmare.

5   "Hey!" a shadow whispered. "We're *moving.* Get up."

6   "Okay."

7   "You sleepin', or something?"

8   "No." He could not make out the soldier's face. With clumsy, concrete hands he clawed for his rifle, found it, found his helmet.

9   The soldier shadow grunted. "You got a lot to learn, buddy. I'd shoot you if I thought you was sleepin'. Let's go."

10   Private First Class Paul Berlin blinked.

11   Ahead of him, silhouetted against the sky, he saw the string of soldiers wading into the flat paddy, the black outline of their shoulders and packs and weapons. He was comfortable. He did not want to move. But he was afraid, for it was his first night at the war, so he hurried to catch up, stumbling once, scraping his knee, groping as though blind; his boots sank into the thick paddy water, and he smelled it all around him. He would tell his mother how it smelled: mud and algae and cattle manure and chlorophyll; decay, breeding mosquitoes and leeches as big as mice; the fecund warmth of the paddy waters rising up to his cut knee. But he would not tell how frightened he had been.

12   Once they reached the sea, things would be better. They would have their rear guarded by three thousand miles of ocean, and they would swim and dive into the breakers and hunt crayfish and smell the salt, and they would be safe.

Columbus skyline

RA.L.10.10

>6 In paragraph 1, the repetition of "He was pretending" and "He pretended" emphasizes that Paul Berlin
A. has a good imagination.
B. is trying to calm himself.
C. is a bad soldier.
D. is new to the war.

EXPLANATION: We have no evidence that C is true. We know that D is true, but it does not seem to be related to the repetition. A is possible, but the rhythm of the language points more directly to B. The correct answer is B.

RA.L.10.6

>7 Which of the following is a flashback that is important in the story?
A. Paul goes camping with his father.
B. Paul meets Billy Boy Watkins.
C. Paul marches through the night.
D. Paul talks with another soldier.

EXPLANATION: C and D are not flashbacks; they occur in the present. B does not appear in the passage. The correct answer is A.

RA.L.10.8

>8 The writer chose the third-person-limited point of view because it
A. allows us to know what Paul Berlin thinks and feels.
B. allows us to know what all the characters think and feel.
C. allows the author to reveal his personal thoughts and feelings.
D. is completely objective and reveals no one's thoughts and feelings.

EXPLANATION: B applies to omniscient point of view; C applies to first person. D is wrong: The writer reveals Paul Berlin's thoughts and feelings. The correct answer is A.

Terminal Tower, Cleveland

RA.L.10.8

>9 What methods does the author use to create the dark, ominous tone of the story? Give at least three examples from the passage to support and explain your response. Write your answer on a separate piece of paper. Then, read the sample response.

Sample Response

> The author's choice of words and images is precise, making the reader feel that he or she is in the shadows, too, watching and listening to the soldiers. The words "One by one, like sheep in a dream, they passed through the hedgerow" are especially vivid because images of people counting sheep are common. Later in the story, the author describes the rice paddy, using words that assault our senses and intensify the dark tone: "mud and algae and cattle manure and chlorophyll; decay, breeding mosquitoes and leeches. . . ." The author also uses repetition. He describes the soldiers' mental states, repeating the phrase "some of them" four times. This repetition creates an ominous feeling that something horrible is coming closer, step by step. Harsh dialogue adds to the dark tone. On Paul's first night, a soldier threatens, "I'd shoot you if I thought you was sleepin," thus intensifying the new soldier's fear.

Taking the OGT in Writing

The OGT in writing includes multiple-choice and short-answer questions about the writing process and prompts that assess your mastery of writing applications and conventions. The sample questions and responses that follow will help prepare you for the kinds of questions you will see on the OGT in writing.

Use this excerpt from a draft about success to answer questions 1–4.

(1) What is success? (2) Is it expensive sports cars? a three-story house in the hills? the latest fashions? (3) Sadly, our culture—as portrayed in movies, songs, and TV ads—sometimes seems to say yes. (4) <u>Therefore</u>, I believe that success comes from personal achievement. (5) Because wealth can be a sign of achievement, we sometimes confuse the two.

(6) Society sends messages that might be subtle, but we see and hear them constantly. (7) Own these products, dress this way, or live like these people, and you will be successful. (8) In my opinion, some of the wealthiest people are not very successful. (9) However, there is a problem with that message: Wealth and the things it buys do not make a person a success. (10) Although they might meet our culture's superficial definition of success, it is important to ask what they have achieved—at what have they succeeded?

WP.10.13

>**1** In sentence 4, <u>Therefore</u>, does not correctly link the ideas. Which of these words should be used instead?
A. However,
B. Consequently,
C. Likewise,
D. Thus,

EXPLANATION: In sentence 3, the perspective of "our culture" is expressed. Then in sentence 4, an opposing idea is stated. The only choice that signals contrast is A.

WP.10.12

>**2** Which supporting sentence would be appropriate to add after sentence 7?
A. Along with success come responsibilities, such as being a good role model.
B. Wealth does not equal happiness.
C. I believe we are left with one question: At what cost do we achieve success?
D. One must look beyond the cars, clothes, and lifestyles to see the person within.

EXPLANATION: Unlike the other choices, the words *cars, clothes,* and *lifestyles* in D link directly to ideas in sentence 7. D is correct.

WP.10.13

>3 Sentence 8 is not in the correct sequence. Sentence 8 is best placed directly after

A. sentence 1.
B. sentence 3.
C. sentence 9.
D. sentence 10.

EXPLANATION: Read sentence 8 in each sequence listed. The word *they* in sentence 10 refers to some of *the wealthiest people* in sentence 8. Sentence 8 should directly precede this reference. C is correct.

WA.10.5

>4 The rough draft below is the beginning of a persuasive essay about success. Continue the draft by adding another argument, including supporting information, that will persuade your readers that success comes from personal achievement rather than wealth.

Sample Response:

> True success is less obvious than wealth. On the same street as the one mansion in our town is the small house where Mrs. Cooper, a fifth-grade teacher, lives. Imposing walls and gates surround the lonely mansion. Mrs. Cooper's house, on the other hand, is open to her former students, who grew up in one of the toughest neighborhoods in the state. Many of these students have become community leaders, teachers, and healthcare professionals. They credit Mrs. Cooper for starting them on the path of helping others. Mrs. Cooper may drive an old car, but she is far more successful than the man who lives behind the gates down the road.

Responding To Writing Prompts

This section of the OGT may ask you to write narrative, persuasive, or expository responses to two prompts. Here are steps for writing each response.

STEP 1 **ANALYZE THE PROMPT.** Look for key verbs that define your task, and identify your audience.

STEP 2   **PLAN AND DRAFT YOUR ESSAY.** On scratch paper, use a cluster diagram or other organizer to brainstorm main ideas and support. As you write, make sure each paragraph clearly relates to your main idea or position. Add relevant details to support and elaborate each point. Give your essay a strong introduction and a definite closing.

STEP 3   **REVISE AND EDIT YOUR DRAFT.** Re-read your draft. Look for places where you can add transitions or combine sentences to make ideas flow more smoothly. Eliminate unnecessary repetition and wordiness. Strengthen your paper with additional supporting details and improved order. Finally, find and correct errors in grammar, usage, and mechanics. Mark all corrections neatly.

Sample Writing Prompt

WA.10.1

Write an expository paper that describes one place that is important to you. Use sensory details that help readers experience the place as you do, and give convincing reasons why you treasure this place.

Sample Response

Here is one writer's response to the writing prompt. It would likely receive a top score, according to Ohio's rubric.

> My favorite store, a forest campsite, my bedroom: I love all of these places. None of them, though, is as special to me as my grandmother's attic, which is like my own personal time machine.
> Grandma's attic is dimly lit and spreads above most of her hundred-year-old house. Except for the occasional creaking of the house settling, the attic is a silent refuge. Its rafters are high in the middle, but they angle down low at the edges. Over the years, many mysterious boxes found homes in those dark, low corners. Bicycles stood in the high sections. Skis and ironing boards leaned against the walls.
> As a little child, I loved opening those dusty boxes along the edges. I found so many different objects in those boxes—old

clothes, letters, toys—that exploring the attic was like a day at an amusement park. I still remember lifting the dusty sheet covering one oddly shaped "box" to find a realistic, two-story dollhouse my grandfather built long ago. It always took some effort for my grandmother to coax me out of the attic. She saw it as a cluttered, slightly dangerous place that made me sneeze. I saw it as a magical playground that I ruled.

As I grew older, I began to see the attic as a treasure-trove of family history. For instance, there was the trunk full of mementos of my great-uncle Charlie, who died in Vietnam. It held coins from Navy ports of call all over Asia, diplomas and certificates, reel-to-reel audiotapes, and, best of all, photos that made him real to me.

Writing this essay makes me want to explore Grandma's attic again. All of my aunts and uncles stored things there long ago. Perhaps my "time machine" holds objects they would treasure today.

Evaluating Your Writing

Your OGT essay will receive two scores: an "applications" score from 0 to six (the top score) and a "conventions" score from 0 to 3 (the top score). Here are the Ohio criteria for top scores, with key points in bold:

Applications (top score of 6)
- The paper is clearly **focused** on the prompt and adapted to **the audience and purpose.**
- **Development** of the topic is rich, with sophisticated ideas and examples.
- The **organizational structure** is coherent with a sense of wholeness.
- **Vocabulary** is chosen carefully to achieve the purpose, and **sentence structure** is varied and mature, contributing to a personal **style.**

Conventions (top score of 3)
- Any errors in **mechanics** do not interfere with understanding.
- The paper shows a clear understanding of the **rules of grammar.**

HOLT

Elements of LITERATURE

Fourth Course

How To Use Your

READER/WRITER Notebook

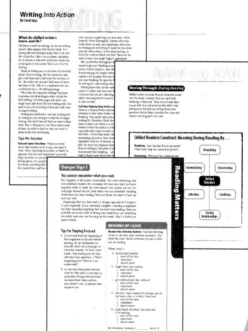

You've been in school long enough to know that you can't write in your textbooks. But, many times, you need a place to capture your thoughts about what you are reading or write your ideas down on paper. Your *Reader/Writer Notebook* is a place where you can do just that.

Want to improve your skills?

By now, you can read and write, but are you as strong as you want to be? In your *Reader/Writer Notebook*, you'll find helpful tips from real experts on how to become a better reader and writer. You can also take a survey to help you see how you think as a reader and as a writer.

Thinking like a Reader

In your notebook, you can track how much you read, what you read, and how you react to each piece. This habit helps you understand what you like or don't like to read, but more importantly, you can chart how reading changes you. Just as musicians can quickly tell you music that they enjoy playing and athletes can reaccount their victories, you can know what makes you a reader.

Your teachers probably tell you to take notes about what you are reading, but that task is easier said than done! A blank piece of paper doesn't tell you how to take notes, but your *Reader/Writer Notebook* outlines space for you to take notes on up to 30 different reading selections.

Thinking like a Writer

When you read, you are also learning how to be a writer, so your *Reader/Writer Notebook* makes space to take your writing notes within your reading notes. There is lots of space for sketching out your ideas and trying out drafts, too. You can work on the Writing Workshops and Your Turn activities from your textbook in your RWN notebook.

Finding the Right Words

You can't read or write without words. As you read, you run across new words or words that you know that are used in a new way. As you write, you try to find the best way to express what you want to say. For both of these reasons, vocabulary is an important part of being a reader/writer. Your notebook helps you increase your personal vocabulary by helping you take better notes as you read and write. It also has a handy reference list of all the word parts and academic vocabulary found in your textbook and graphic organizers to help you tackle new words.

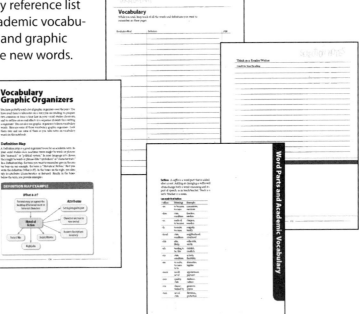

Program Authors

Kylene Beers is the senior program author for *Elements of Literature*. A former middle school teacher, she is now Senior Reading Advisor to Secondary Schools for Teachers College Reading and Writing Project at Columbia University. She is the author of *When Kids Can't Read: What Teachers Can Do* and co-editor (with Linda Rief and Robert E. Probst) of *Adolescent Literacy: Turning Promise into Practice*. The former editor of the National Council of Teachers of English (NCTE) literacy journal *Voices from the Middle*, Dr. Beers assumed the NCTE presidency in 2008. With articles in *English Journal, Journal of Adolescent and Adult Literacy, School Library Journal, Middle Matters,* and *Voices from the Middle,* she speaks both nationally and internationally as a recognized authority on struggling readers. Dr. Beers has served on the review boards of *English Journal, The ALAN Review,* the Special Interest Group on Adolescent Literature of the International Reading Association, and the Assembly on Literature for Adolescents of the NCTE. She is the 2001 recipient of the Richard W. Halley Award given by NCTE for outstanding contributions to middle school literacy.

Carol Jago is a teacher with thirty-two years of experience at Santa Monica High School in California. The author of nine books on education, she continues to share her experiences as a writer and as a speaker at conferences and seminars across the country. Her wide and varied experience in standards assessment and secondary education in general has made her a sought-after speaker. As an author, Ms. Jago also works closely with Heinemann Publishers and with the National Council of Teachers of English. Her longtime association with NCTE led to her June 2007 election to a four-year term on the council's board. During that term she will serve for one year as president of the council. She is also active with the California Association of Teachers of English (CATE) and has edited CATE's scholarly journal *California English* since 1996. Ms. Jago served on the planning committees for the 2009 NAEP Reading Framework and the 2011 NAEP Writing Framework.

Deborah Appleman is professor and chair of educational studies and director of the Summer Writing Program at Carleton College in Northfield, Minnesota. Dr. Appleman's primary research interests include adolescent response to literature, multicultural literature, and the teaching of literary theory in high school. With a team of classroom teachers, she co-edited *Braided Lives,* a multicultural literature anthology. In addition to many articles and book chapters, she is the author of

Linda Rief, Alfred Tatum, Kylene Beers, Patrick Schwarz, and Carol Jago

iii

Critical Encounters in High School English: Teaching Literary Theory to Adolescents and co-author of *Teaching Literature to Adolescents.* Her most recent book, *Reading for Themselves,* explores the use of extracurricular book clubs to encourage adolescents to read for pleasure. Dr. Appleman was a high school English teacher, working in both urban and suburban schools. She is a frequent national speaker and consultant and continues to work weekly in high schools with students and teachers.

Leila Christenbury is a former high school English teacher and currently professor of English education at Virginia Commonwealth University, Richmond. The former

editor of *English Journal,* she is the author of ten books, including *Writing on Demand, Making the Journey, and Retracing the Journey: Teaching and Learning in an American High School.* Past president of the National Council of Teachers of English, Dr. Christenbury is also a former member of the steering committee of the National Assessment of Educational Progress (NAEP). A recipient of the Rewey Belle Inglis Award for Outstanding Woman in English Teaching, Dr. Christenbury is a frequent speaker on issues of English teaching and learning and has been interviewed and quoted on CNN and in the *New York Times, USA Today, Washington Post, Chicago Tribune,* and *US News & World Report.*

Sara Kajder, author of *Bringing the Outside In: Visual Ways to Engage Reluctant Readers* and *The Tech-Savvy English Classroom,* is an assistant professor at Virginia Polytechnic Institute and State University (Virginia Tech). She has served as co-chair of NCTE's Conference on English Education (CEE) Technology Commission and of the Society for Information Technology and Teacher Education (SITE) English Education Committee. Dr. Kajder is the recipient of the first SITE National Technology Leadership Fellowship in English Education; she is a former English and language arts teacher for high school and middle school.

Linda Rief has been a classroom teacher for twenty-five years. She is author of *The Writer's-Reader's Notebook, Inside the Writer's-Reader's Notebook, Seeking Diversity, 100 Quickwrites,* and *Vision and Voice* as well as the co-author (with Kylene Beers and Robert E. Probst) of *Adolescent Literacy: Turning Promise into Practice.* Ms. Rief has written numerous chapters and journal articles, and she co-edited the first five years of *Voices from the Middle.* During the summer she teaches graduate courses at the University of New Hampshire and Northeastern University. She is a national and international consultant on adolescent literacy issues.

Leila Christenbury, Héctor Rivera, Sara Kajder, Eric Cooper, and Deborah Appleman

Program Consultants

Isabel Beck, Harvey Daniels, Margaret McKeown, and Mabel Rivera

Isabel L. Beck is professor of education and senior scientist at the University of Pittsburgh. Dr. Beck has conducted extensive research on vocabulary and comprehension, and has published well over one hundred articles and several books, including *Improving Comprehension with Questioning the Author* (with Margaret McKeown) and *Bringing Words to Life: Robust Vocabulary Instruction* (with Margaret McKeown and Linda Kucan). Dr. Beck's numerous national awards include the Oscar S. Causey Award for outstanding research from the National Reading Conference and the William S. Gray Award from the International Reading Association for lifetime contributions to the field of reading research and practice.

Margaret G. McKeown is a senior scientist at the University of Pittsburgh's Learning Research and Development Center. Her research in reading comprehension and vocabulary has been published extensively in outlets for both research and practitioner audiences. Recognition of her work includes the International Reading Association's (IRA) Dissertation of the Year Award and a National Academy of Education Spencer Fellowship. Before her career in research, Dr. McKeown taught elementary school.

Amy Benjamin is a veteran teacher, literacy coach, consultant, and researcher in secondary-level literacy instruction. She has been recognized for excellence in teaching from the New York State English Council, Union College, and Tufts University. Ms. Benjamin is the author of several books about reading comprehension, writing instruction, grammar, and differentiation. Her most recent book (with Tom Oliva) is *Engaging Grammar: Practical Advice for Real Classrooms,* published by the National Council of Teachers of English. Ms. Benjamin has had a long association and leadership role with the NCTE's Assembly for the Teaching of English Grammar (ATEG).

Eric Cooper is the president of the National Urban Alliance for Effective Education (NUA) and co-founder of the Urban Partnership for Literacy with the IRA. He currently works with the National Council of Teachers of English (NCTE) to support improvements in urban education and collaborates with the Council of the Great City Schools. In line with his educational mission to support the improvement of education for urban and minority students, Dr. Cooper writes, lectures, and produces educational documentaries and talk shows to provide advocacy for children who live in disadvantaged circumstances.

Harvey Daniels is a former college professor and classroom teacher, working in urban and suburban Chicago schools. Known for his pioneering work on student book clubs, Dr. Daniels is author and co-author of many books, including *Literature Circles: Voice and Choice in Book Clubs and Reading Groups* and *Best Practice: Today's Standards for Teaching and Learning in America's Schools.*

Ben Garcia is associate director of education at the Skirball Cultural Center in Los Angeles, California, where he oversees school programs and teacher professional development. He is a board member of the Museum Educators of Southern California and presents regularly at conferences in the area of visual arts integration across curricula. Prior to the Skirball, he worked with classroom teachers for six years in the *Art and Language Arts* program at the J. Paul Getty Museum. Recent publications include *Art and Science: A Curriculum for K–12 Teachers* and *Neoclassicism and the Enlightenment: A Curriculum for Middle and High School Teachers.*

PROGRAM CONSULTANTS continued

Amy Benjamin, Eric Cooper, Ben Garcia, Robin Scarcella, and Judith Irvin

Judith L. Irvin taught middle school for several years before entering her career as a university professor. She now teaches courses in curriculum and instructional leadership and literacy at Florida State University. Dr. Irvin's many publications include *Reading and the High School Student: Strategies to Enhance Literacy* and *Integrating Literacy and Learning in the Content Area Classroom*. Her latest book, *Taking Action: A Leadership Model for Improving Adolescent Literacy,* is the result of a Carnegie-funded project and is published by the Association for Supervision and Curriculum Development.

Victoria Ramirez is the interim education director at the Museum of Fine Arts, Houston, Texas, where she plans and implements programs, resources, and publications for teachers and serves as liaison to local school districts and teacher organizations. She also chairs the Texas Art Education Association's museum division. Dr. Ramirez earned a doctoral degree in curriculum and instruction from the College of Education at the University of Houston and an M.A.T. in museum education from George Washington University. A former art history instructor at Houston Community College, Dr. Ramirez currently teaches education courses at the University of Houston.

Héctor H. Rivera is an assistant professor at Southern Methodist University, School of Education and Human Development. Dr. Rivera is also the director of the SMU Professional Development/ESL Supplemental Certification Program for Math and Science Teachers of At-Risk Middle and High School LEP Newcomer Adolescents. This federally funded program develops, delivers, and evaluates professional development for educators who work with at-risk newcomer adolescent students. Dr. Rivera is also collaborating on school reform projects in Guatemala and with the Institute of Arctic Education in Greenland.

Mabel Rivera is a research assistant professor at the Texas Institute for Measurement, Evaluation, and Statistics at the University of Houston. Her current research interests include the education of and prevention of reading difficulties in English-language learners. In addition, Dr. Rivera is involved in local and national service activities for preparing school personnel to teach students with special needs.

Robin Scarcella is a professor at the University of California at Irvine, where she also directs the Program in Academic English/English as a Second Language. She has a Ph.D. in linguistics from the University of Southern California and an M.A. degree in education-second language acquisition from Stanford University. She has taught all grade levels. She has been active in shaping policies affecting language assessment, instruction, and teacher professional development. In the last four years, she has spoken to over ten thousand teachers and administrators. She has written over thirty scholarly articles that appear in such journals as the *TESOL Quarterly* and *Brain and Language*. Her most recent publication is *Accelerating Academic English: A Focus on the English Learner*.

Patrick Schwarz is professor of special education and chair of the Diversity in Learning and Development department for National-Louis University, Chicago, Illinois. He is author of *From Disability to Possibility* and *You're Welcome* (co-written with Paula Kluth), texts that have inspired teachers worldwide to reconceptualize inclusion to help all children. Other books co-written with Paula

Kluth include *Just Give Him the Whale* and *Inclusion Bootcamp*. Dr. Schwarz also presents and consults worldwide through Creative Culture Consulting.

Alfred W. Tatum is an associate professor in the Department of Curriculum and Instruction at the University of Illinois at Chicago (UIC), where he earned his Ph.D. He also serves as the director of the UIC Reading Clinic. He began his career as an eighth-grade teacher, later becoming a reading specialist. Dr. Tatum has written more than twenty-five articles, chapters, and monographs and is the author of *Teaching Reading to Black Adolescent Males: Closing the Achievement Gap*. His work focuses on the literacy development of African American adolescent males, particularly the impact of texts on their lives.

UNIT INTRODUCTION WRITERS ON WRITING

UNIT 1 SHORT STORIES

Rick Moody

"A story hints at what is beyond its margins, at the enormity of life beyond, without having to include it exhaustively."

UNIT 2 NONFICTION

Azadeh Moaveni

"[Nonfiction] helps us make sense of the larger than life events that define our age…and recognize the humanity we share with people in distant lands."

UNIT 3 POETRY

Jennifer Chang

"We've all experienced it. When doing what you really like becomes the last thing you want to do. You can leave or you can sit there and try. I tried."

UNIT 4 DRAMA

Carl Hancock Rux

"Reading plays (and later, writing them) allowed me to step into the shoes of other characters, and walk around my own neighborhood."

UNIT 5 MYTHS AND LEGENDS

Madeline L'Engle

"Myth is, for me, the vehicle of truth. Myth is where you look for reality."

UNIT 6 WRITING FOR LIFE

Carol Jago

"The newspaper is a public forum. You have a right to be heard. Seize the day."

Critical Reviewers

Noreen L. Abdullah
Chicago Public Schools
Chicago, Illinois

Martha Armenti
Baltimore City College High School
Baltimore, Maryland

Jessica J. Asmis-Carvajal
Coronado High School
El Paso, Texas

Susan Beechum
Apopka High School
Apopka, Florida

Nilda Benavides
Del Rio High School
Del Rio, Texas

Melissa Bowell
Ft. Walton Beach High School
Ft. Walton Beach, Florida

Stacey Chisolm
Meridian High School
Meridian, Mississippi

Vincent Contorno
L. C. Anderson High School
Austin, Texas

Rita Curington
Athens High School
Athens, Texas

Melinda Fulton
Leon High School
Tallahassee, Florida

Holly Hillgardner
South Bronx Preparatory
New York, New York

Anna Yoccabel Horton
Highland Middle School
Gilbert, Arizona

Elizabeth Ignatius
Paul R. Wharton High School
Tampa, Florida

Tim King
Mason High School
Mason, Ohio

Barbara Kimbrough
Kane Area High School
Kane, Pennsylvania

Jennifer Moore Krievs
Midlothian High School
Midlothian, Virginia

Lynn V. Mason
Newark High School
Newark, Ohio

Vivian Nida
University of Oklahoma
Norman, Oklahoma

John Kevin M. Perez
Hampton Bays Secondary
  High School
Hampton Bays, New York

Judd Pfeiffer
Bowie High School
Austin, Texas

Aimee Riordan
Sun Valley High School
Monroe, North Carolina

Celia Rocca
Western High School
Baltimore, Maryland

Kelly L. Self
Alexandria Senior High School
Alexandria, Louisiana

Dr. Rosa Smith-Williams
Booker T. Washington High School
Houston, Texas

Kelly Southern
Ouachita Parish High School
Monroe, Louisiana

Jody Steinke
Quincy Senior High School
Quincy, Illinois

Kelly Swifney
Zeeland West High School
Zeeland, Michigan

Nichole Wilson
Mason High School
Mason, Ohio

Dr. Bernard Zaidman
Greenville Senior High School
  Academy of Academic
  Excellence
Greenville, South Carolina

FIELD-TEST PARTICIPANTS

Linda Brescia
HS for Health Professions and
  Human Services
New York, New York

Katherine Burke
Timber Creek High School
Orlando, Florida

Greg Cantwell
Sheldon High School
Eugene, Oregon

Cheryl Casbeer
Del Rio High School
Del Rio, Texas

Ms. Linda Chapman
Colonel White High School
Dayton, Ohio

Kim Christiernsson
Durango High School
Las Vegas, Nevada

Amanda Cobb
Timber Creek High School
Orlando, Florida

Gwynne C. Eldridge
Royal Palm Beach Community
   High School
Royal Palm Beach, Florida

Marylea Erhart-Mack
University High School
Orlando, Florida

Yolanda Fernandez
Del Rio High School
Del Rio, Texas

Angela Ferreira
Hoover High School
San Diego, California

Dan Franke
Lemont High School
Lemont, Illinois

Ellen Geisler
Mentor High School
Mentor, Ohio

Luanne Greenberg
Coronado High School
El Paso, Texas

Colleen Hadley
Abilene High School
Abilene, Texas

Leslie Hardiman
Hoover High School
San Diego, California

Sandra Henderson
Lemont High School
Lemont, Illinois

Lee Ann Hoffman
Southeast High School
Bradenton, Florida

Jennifer Houston
Timber Creek High School
Orlando, Florida

Eva M. Lazear
Springfield North High School
Springfield, Ohio

Phil Lazzari
Lemont High School
Lemont, Illinois

Jacquelyn McLane
Cypress Creek High School
Orlando, Florida

Kathleen Mims
H. Grady Spruce High School
Dallas, Texas

Julie Moore
Monroe High School
Monroe, Wisconsin

Denise Morris
Rich Central High School
Olympia Fields, Illinois

Bunny Petty
Florence High School
Florence, Texas

Valerie Pfeffer
Durango High School
Las Vegas, Nevada

Bernadette Poulos
Reavis High School
Burbank, Illinois

Jennifer Roberson
Samuel F. B. Morse High School
San Diego, California

Ann L. Rodgers
Currituck County High School
Barco, North Carolina

Narima Shahabudeen
East Orange Campus 9
High School
East Orange, New Jersey

Shari Simonds
Valley High School
Las Vegas, Nevada

Gail Tuelon
University High School
Orlando, Florida

Mandy Unruh
Brownsburg High School
Brownsburg, Indiana

Vanessa Vega
Irving High School
Irving, Texas

Elizabeth Weaver
Cypress Creek High School
Orlando, Florida

Tamera West
McQueen High School
Reno, Nevada

Erica White
Sherando High School
Stephens City, Virginia

Contents in Brief

Ohio Academic Content Standards for Language Arts for each collection can be found in the full Table of Contents on pages A4, A6, A8, A10, A12, A14, A16, A20, A22, and A24.

Short Stories

Writers on Writing ....

COLLECTION **1** Plot and Setting

"There are only two or three human stories, and they go on repeating themselves as fiercely as if they had never happened before." **—Willa Cather**

What Do You Think? What common human experiences do we share?

Ohio Academic Content Standards for Language Arts

Acquisition of Vocabulary   VO.10.3; VO.10.5; VO.10.6
Reading Process   RP.10.1
Reading Applications   RA.I.10.1; RA.I.10.4; RA.I.10.5; RA.L.10.2; RA.L.10.3; RA.L.10.5; RA.L.10.6
Writing Processes   WP.10.1; WP.10.9; WP.10.14; WP.10.15; WP.10.17
Writing Applications   WA.10.1.b; WA.10.1.c; WA.10.2; WA.10.4.c
Communication: Oral and Visual   C.10.9

Short Stories

COLLECTION **2** Character

"For me it's always about complex characters who are somewhat unpredictable, going through some sort of struggle." —Steve Buscemi

What Do You Think? What makes us the way we are?

Ohio Academic Content Standards for Language Arts

Acquisition of Vocabulary VO.10.1; VO.10.3; VO.10.6
Reading Process RP.10.1; RP.10.2; RP.10.4
Reading Applications RA.I.10.2; RA.L.10.1; RA.L.10.2; RA.L.10.3; RA.L.10.8
Writing Processes WP.10.1; WP.10.9; WP.10.14
Writing Applications WA.10.1.b; WA.10.2; WA.10.4.c; WA.10.6
Writing Conventions WC.10.2; WC.10.3
Research R.10.4
Communication: Oral and Visual C.10.8.e

Short Stories

COLLECTION **3** Narrator and Voice

"From a certain point onward there is no longer any turning back. That is the point that must be reached." —Franz Kafka

What Do You Think? How do people react when they are in a situation they cannot change?

Ohio Academic Content Standards for Language Arts

Acquisition of Vocabulary VO.10.1; VO.10.3; VO.10.5; VO.10.6
Reading Process RP.10.1; RP.10.2
Reading Applications RA.I.10.1; RA.L.10.1; RA.L.10.4; RA.L.10.5; RA.L.10.7; RA.L.10.8; RA.L.10.9; RA.L.10.11
Writing Processes WP.10.1; WP.10.15
Writing Applications WA.10.1.a; WA.10.1.b; WA.10.1.c; WA.10.2; WA.10.6

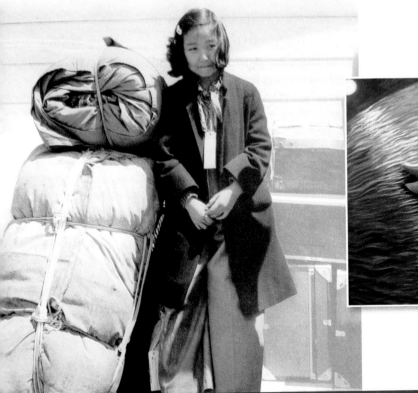

Short Stories

COLLECTION **4** Symbolism and Irony

"It is our choices that show what we truly are, far more than our abilities."
—J. K. Rowling

What Do You Think? What do our choices reveal about who we really are?

Ohio Academic Content Standards for Language Arts

Acquisition of Vocabulary VO.10.1; VO.10.2; VO.10.3; VO.10.5; VO.10.6
Reading Process RP.10.1; RP.10.3; RP.10.4; RP.10.5
Reading Applications RA.I.10.1; RA.I.10.2; RA.I.10.4; RA.I.10.5; RA.L.10.2; RA.L.10.3; RA.L.10.4; RA.L.10.5; RA.L.10.6; RA.L.10.7; RA.L.10.8; RA.L.10.9; RA.L.10.11
Writing Processes WP.10.1; WP.10.2; WP.10.3; WP.10.4; WP.10.6; WP.10.7; WP.10.8; WP.10.10; WP.10.12; WP.10.15; WP.10.16; WP.10.17
Writing Applications WA.10.1.b; WA.10.1.c; WA.10.4.c; WA.10.4.d; WA.10.6
Writing Conventions WC.10.3
Research R.10.2; R.10.3; R.10.4
Communication: Oral and Visual C.10.5; C.10.6; C.10.7; C.10.8.c; C.10.8.d; C.10.8.e; C.10.9

Nonfiction

Writers on Writing

COLLECTION 5 Form and Style

"Life is either a daring adventure or nothing. To keep our faces toward change and behave like free spirits in the presence of fate is strength undefeatable"
—Helen Keller

What Do You Think? What gives an event meaning in our lives?

Ohio Academic Content Standards for Language Arts

Acquisition of Vocabulary VO.10.2; VO.10.3; VO.10.6
Reading Process RP.10.4
Reading Applications RA.I.10.1; RA.I.10.2; RA.I.10.5; RA.L.10.1; RA.L.10.2; RA.L.10.5; RA.L.10.6; RA.L.10.7; RA.L.10.8; RA.L.10.9; RA.L.10.11
Writing Processes WP.10.1; WP.10.8; WP.10.15
Writing Applications WA.10.1.b; WA.10.1.c; WA.10.2; WA.10.4.c; WA.10.4.d; WA.10.5.a; WA.10.6
Writing Conventions WC.10.1
Research R.10.1
Communication: Oral and Visual C.10.8.b; C.10.8.d; C.10.8.e

Nonfiction

COLLECTION **6** Persuasion

*"I can't believe the news today. I can't close my eyes
and make it go away."* — **Bono**

What Do You Think? What do we believe in, and why?

Ohio Academic Content Standards for Language Arts

Acquisition of Vocabulary VO.10.1; VO.10.3; VO.10.5; VO.10.6
Reading Process RP.10.1; RP.10.4; RP.10.5
Reading Applications RA.I.10.2; RA.I.10.4; RA.I.10.5; RA.I.10.6; RA.I.10.8; RA.L.10.8
Writing Processes WP.10.2; WP.10.4; WP.10.7; WP.10.10; WP.10.12; WP.10.16
Writing Applications WA.10.4.b; WA.10.4.c; WA.10.5.a
Writing Conventions WC.10.1; WC.10.2; WC.10.4
Communication: Oral and Visual C.10.2; C.10.3; C.10.5; C.10.7; C.10.8.e; C.10.10.a; C.10.10.b; C.10.10.c; C.10.10.d

Poetry

Writers on Writing

COLLECTION **7** Poetry

*"Ink runs from the corners of my mouth. There is no happiness
like mine. I have been eating poetry."* —**Mark Strand**

What Do You Think? How do we use our imagination to
transform our world?

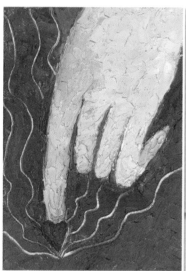

Ohio Academic Content Standards for Language Arts

Acquisition of Vocabulary VO.10.1; VO.10.3; VO.10.4; VO.10.6
Reading Process RP.10.1; RP.10.4; RP.10.5
Reading Applications RA.I.10.1; RA.I.10.4; RA.L.10.1; RA.L.10.2; RA.L.10.4; RA.L.10.5; RA.L.10.8; RA.L.10.9;
RA.L.10.10; RA.L.10.11
Writing Processes WP.10.1; WP.10.2; WP.10.3; WP.10.4; WP.10.9; WP.10.10; WP.10.12; WP.10.14; WP.10.16
Writing Applications WA.10.1.b; WA.10.1.c; WA.10.2; WA.10.4.d; WA.10.6
Writing Conventions WC.10.1
Research R.10.5
Communication: Oral and Visual C.10.5; C.10.7; C.10.8.b; C.10.8.d; C.10.9

Comparing Texts

UNIT 4

Drama

Writers on Writing

COLLECTION **8** Elements of Drama

"There's something about the theater which makes my fingertips tingle." —Wole Soyinka

What Do You Think? How do we know what choice to make—when it is not clear which choice is the right one?

Ohio Academic Content Standards for Language Arts

Acquisition of Vocabulary VO.10.1; VO.10.2; VO.10.3; VO.10.6
Reading Process RP.10.1; RP.10.4; RP.10.5
Reading Applications RA.I.10.4; RA.I.10.5; RA.L.10.1; RA.L.10.2; RA.L.10.3; RA.L.10.4; RA.L.10.5; RA.L.10.6; RA.L.10.7; RA.L.10.8; RA.L.10.9
Writing Processes WP.10.2; WP.10.3; WP.10.4; WP.10.6; WP.10.8; WP.10.9; WP.10.11; WP.10.12; WP.10.16
Writing Applications WA.10.1.b; WA.10.1.c; WA.10.2; WA.10.4.b; WA.10.4.d
Writing Conventions WC.10.1
Research R.10.5
Communication: Oral and Visual C.10.1; C.10.2; C.10.3; C.10.4

Informational Text Focus

Myths and Legends

COLLECTION 9 The Hero's Story

"How important it is for us to recognize and celebrate our heroes and she-roes."
—Maya Angelou

What Do You Think? Why are some stories retold across generations and cultures?

Ohio Academic Content Standards for Language Arts

Acquisition of Vocabulary VO.10.1; VO.10.3; VO.10.5; VO.10.6
Reading Process RP.10.1; RP.10.3; RP.10.5
Reading Applications RA.I.10.1; RA.L.10.1; RA.L.10.3; RA.L.10.5; RA.L.10.7; RA.L.10.8; RA.L.10.11
Writing Processes WP.10.1; WP.10.4; WP.10.6; WP.10.7; WP.10.9; WP.10.10; WP.10.11; WP.10.12; WP.10.14; WP.10.16; WP.10.17
Writing Applications WA.10.1.b; WA.10.1.c; WA.10.2; WA.10.3.c; WA.10.4.a; WA.10.4.b; WA.10.4.c; WA.10.4.e; WA.10.5.c; WA.10.6
Writing Conventions WC.10.3; WC.10.5
Research R.10.1; R.10.2; R.10.4; R.10.5; R.10.6; R.10.7
Communication: Oral and Visual C.10.5; C.10.7; C.10.8.a; C.10.8.c; C.10.8.d; C.10.8.e; C.10.10.d; C.10.10.e

Writing for Life

COLLECTION **10** Reading for Life

"I suppose leadership at one time meant muscles; but today it means getting along with people." —**Indira Gandhi**

What Do You Think? What skills do you need to succeed in the world?

> ### Ohio Academic Content Standards for Language Arts
>
> **Acquisition of Vocabulary** VO.10.1; VO.10.3; VO.10.6
> **Reading Process** RP.10.4; RP.10.5
> **Reading Applications** RA.I.10.1; RA.I.10.3; RA.I.10.7
> **Writing Processes** WP.10.4; WP.10.5; WP.10.7; WP.10.13; WP.10.16
> **Writing Applications** WA.10.3.a; WA.10.3.b; WA.10.3.c; WA.10.3.d; WA.10.3.e; WA.10.4.a; WA.10.4.e; WA.10.5.b; WA.10.5.c
> **Writing Conventions** WC.10.1
> **Research** R.10.6
> **Communication: Oral and Visual** C.10.9

RESOURCE CENTER

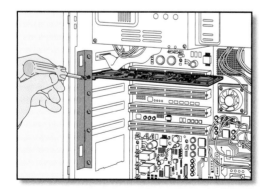

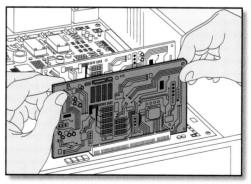

Selections by Alternative Themes

Selections are listed here in alternative theme groupings.

SELECTIONS BY ALTERNATIVE THEMES continued

STRANGE ENCOUNTERS

WISHES AND DREAMS

Skills, Workshops, and Features

SKILLS

LITERARY FOCUS ESSAYS BY CAROL JAGO

INFORMATIONAL TEXT FOCUS ESSAY
BY CAROL JAGO

READING FOCUS ESSAYS BY KYLENE BEERS

LITERARY SKILLS

SKILLS, WORKSHOPS, AND FEATURES continued

SKILLS, WORKSHOPS, AND FEATURES continued

WORKSHOPS
WRITING WORKSHOPS

PREPARING FOR TIMED WRITING

LISTENING AND SPEAKING WORKSHOPS

FEATURES
ANALYZING VISUALS

CROSS-CURRICULAR LINKS

LITERARY PERSPECTIVES

GRAMMAR LINKS

SKILLS REVIEW

LANGUAGE HANDBOOK

WRITER'S HANDBOOK

Why Be a Reader/Writer?

by **Kylene Beers**

Third Time's the Charm

When my daughter, Meredith, was in tenth grade—just as you are right now—her English class read a book titled *Night*. There's nothing too unusual about that. Lots of tenth graders read this book. What *was* unusual was that this was the *third* time she had been assigned this book!

She'd read it in eighth grade and then again in ninth grade. Both of those times, I asked her "What did you think?" Her response? It was an unenthusiastic "*good.*"

Meredith's third time reading *Night* was in tenth grade (she'd transferred schools, and the new school taught the book in tenth grade). This time, I asked her again, "What did you think?" Her response?

"*It was the single most important book I have **ever** read.*" *Why?* She told me that the book had given her insights about how people treat others. "It made me think about myself," she said. "What I like in myself and what I don't."

What had changed?

How did a just "good" book suddenly become the "single most important book she had ever read"? *Night* hadn't changed. It wasn't shorter, longer, or easier to read. Elie Wiesel hadn't written an alternative ending. So what *had* changed? Two things had changed:

1. Meredith had changed.

Three years is a lot of time. It's nearly 20% of your life! How YOU saw the world in eighth grade is *very* different from how you see it now, don't you think? You've grown, experienced a lot of life, and moved to high school. *BIG* changes.

2. This was the third time Meredith had read the book.

You know that the more times you watch your favorite movie, the more you appreciate it:

- You move beyond the basic plot.
- You get inside the characters' heads.

The more you listen to your favorite song, the more deeply you understand it.

- You feel the singer's emotions.
- You catch the artistic use of rhythm and rhyme.

Similarly, if you really want to appreciate and understand what you read—to get to *know* it—you need to re-read it.

visited Holocaust Museum

What Does It Mean?

How does Meredith's story relate to "Why Be a Reader/Writer?" Think about what she said after her *third* reading: "*It was the single most important book I have **ever** read.*"

She didn't say *anything at all* about school.
Night had *changed her life*—her vision of herself and her world.
THAT is why you should be a reader and a writer.

IDENTIFICATION CARD

For the dead and the living we must bear witness

tes
l Museum

Reading and Writing in the Coming Year

We (the writers and editors of this textbook) don't expect you to read *everything* in this book *three times,* but you should stop occasionally and re-read what you've *just* read. Sometimes, *months* later, you ought to return to a text. IT won't have changed, but YOU will have.

In December, look back at what you read in September.
In May, look back at what you read in January.

You'll be surprised how your reactions will change in even a short period of time. Revisiting a text is a powerful way to sharpen your understanding of YOURSELF.

Throughout this book, you'll find many opportunities to *write* about what you've *read.* If you approach these assignments as more than just assignments, but rather as moments to explore what YOU think, you'll find that writing, like reading, is a powerful way to learn about YOURSELF.

Throughout this year, as you learn valuable strategies to help you become a more skillful reader and more effective writer, I hope you'll hear me asking (as I asked Meredith)—

"What do YOU think?"

When your answer is less about what you are reading or writing and more about what YOU are learning about YOURSELF, then you, like Meredith, will have discovered the reason for being a reader and a writer.

Kylene Beers

Senior Author
Elements of Literature

How to Use Your Textbook

Getting to know a new textbook is like getting to know a new video game. In each case, you have to figure out how the game or book is structured, as well as its rules. If you know how your book is structured, you can be successful from the start.

Writers on Writing

If you think about the authors of the selections in your book, you may think they are a rare breed like astronauts or underwater explorers. **Writers on Writing** introduces you to authors whose stories, poems, plays, or articles began with experiences that were transformed by the author's words.

Collection Opener

What is the focus of each collection, or section of the book? What does the image suggest about what the collection will cover? On the right hand side, you'll see a bold heading that says "Plot and Setting" or "Drama." These are the **literary skills** or **types of texts** you will study in the collection. Also in bold type is the **Informational Text Focus** for the collection. These are the skills you use when you read and think about a newspaper or Web site. Keep the **What Do You Think?** question in mind as you go through the collection. Your answers will probably change as you read and think.

Literary Focus

Like a map, the **Literary Focus** shows you how literary elements work in stories and poems, helping you navigate through selections more easily. The Literary Focus will show you the path and help you get to your destination—understanding and enjoying the selection.

Analyzing Visuals

Visuals are all around you: billboards, paintings in museums, video-game graphics. Because you see images daily, you probably know quite a bit about analyzing them. **Analyzing Visuals** helps you apply these skills to understand the literary elements that drive the selections.

Reading Focus

Your mind is working all the time as you read, even if you're not aware of it. Still, all readers, even very good readers, sometimes don't understand what they've read. **Reading Focus** gives you the skills to help you improve your reading.

Reading Model

You tend to do things more quickly and easily if you have a model to follow. The **Reading Model** shows you the literary and reading skills that you will practice in the collection so that you can learn them more quickly and easily.

Wrap Up

Think of **Wrap Up** as a bridge that gives you a chance to practice the skills on which the collection will focus. It also introduces you to the **Academic Vocabulary** you will study in the collection: the language of school, business, and standardized tests. To be successful in school, you'll need to understand and use its language.

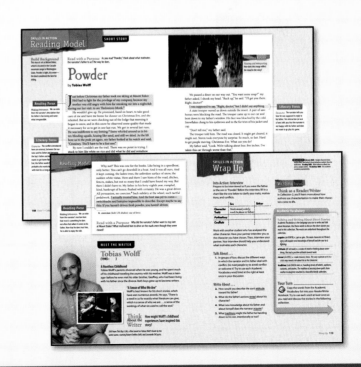

How to Use Your Textbook

Literary Selection Pages
Preparing to Read

If you have ever done something complicated, you know that things go more smoothly with some preparation. It's the same with reading. The **Preparing to Read** page gives you a boost by presenting the literary, reading, and writing skills you'll learn about and use as you read the selection. The list of **Vocabulary** words gives the words you need to know for reading both the selection and beyond the selection. **Language Coach** explains the inner workings of English—like looking at the inside of a clock.

Selection

Meet the Writer gives you all kinds of interesting tidbits about the authors who wrote the selections in this book. **Build Background** provides information you sometimes need when a selection deals with unfamiliar times, places, and situations. **Preview the Selection** presents the selection's main character, like a movie trailer that hints at what is to come. **Read with a Purpose** helps you set a goal for your reading. It helps you answer the question, "What's the point of this selection?"

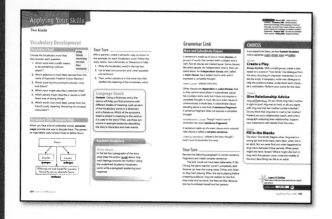

Applying Your Skills

If you have a special talent or hobby, you know that you have to practice to master it. In **Applying Your Skills,** you will apply the reading, literary, vocabulary, and language skills from the Preparing to Read page that you practiced as you read the selection. This gives you a chance to check on how well you are mastering these skills.

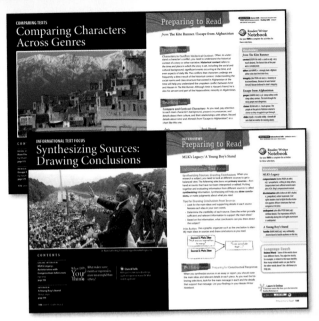

Comparing Texts

You probably compare people, places, and things all the time, such as the special effects in one movie and the acting in another. In **Comparing Texts,** you will compare different works—sometimes by the same author, sometimes by different authors--that have something in common.

Informational Text Focus

If you've ever read an online newspaper or figured out a bus schedule, you've read informational texts. The skills you need for this type of reading are different from the ones you use for literary text. **Informational Text Focus** helps you gain the skills that will enable you to be a more successful reader in daily life and on standardized tests.

Preparing for Standardized Tests

Do you dread test-taking time? Do you struggle over reading the passage and then choosing the correct answer? **Preparing for Standardized Tests** can reduce your "guesses" and give you the practice you need to feel more confident during testing.

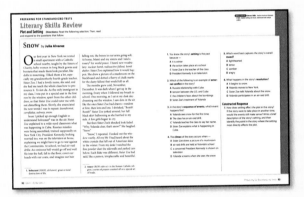

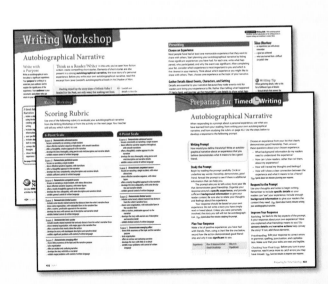

Writing Workshop

Does a blank piece of paper send shivers up your spine? The **Writing Workshop** will help you tackle the page. It takes you step-by-step through developing an effective piece of writing. Models, annotations, graphic organizers, and charts take the "What now?" out of writing for different purposes and audiences.

Preparing for Timed Writing

What's your idea of a nightmare? Maybe it's trying to respond to a writing prompt. **Preparing for Timed Writing** helps you practice for on-demand, or timed, writing so that you can realize your dreams of success.

UNIT 1

Short Stories
Writers on Writing

Rick Moody on Short Stories Rick Moody was born in New York City and grew up in various suburbs in Connecticut, where some of his writing is set. As a child, he felt most at home reading and listening to his grandfather tell tall tales. Today, he is known for his short stories and novels, which often focus on the hardships of contemporary life.

"Short stories are like lemmings—the little furry guys who will run off a cliff in the midst of their migration. That's how I thought about short stories when I was first trying to write them. As a teenager, I had an itch to say something.

I suppose this was because I read a lot. I loved books, and I wanted to contribute something of my own to the bookshelves around me.

Short stories, it seemed, were the way to start. You could write them quickly. You could figure out the beginnings, middles, and ends. You could figure out who was telling the story, what the conflict was, and you were off.

Unfortunately, there was a problem with this way of thinking. There was a problem with imagining that short stories were lemmings that might be expeditiously sacrificed. Upon investigation, I discovered that even though short stories were short, they were not easy.

In fact, it was when I began writing short stories that I truly began reading them. And there is no substitute for reading them. I suppose I'd consumed a few in my early high school years. I remember, for example, encounters with Poe and Hawthorne. Upon beginning to write seriously, though, I read Salinger's short stories, the ones collected in *Nine Stories.* I read some Hemingway. Some John Cheever. Some Flannery O'Connor. I began to see, as both reader and writer, that it was actually a lot harder than it looked to cram a character into this narrow space of the short story.

Something precious and mystical about life gets captured in this brevity. A story hints at what is beyond its margins, at the enormity of life beyond, without having to include it exhaustively. A story is a complex of allusions spinning off in all sorts of directions. Compared to the novel, it's reticent, and yet in terms of its implications, it's outsized. It's grand. It's huge.

The more keenly I read, the more convinced I was that stories were almost mystically subtle. The only easy thing about them is how easy they are to get wrong. You can see when they tail off badly. You can see when the characters haven't been thought out. You can see when a story lacks the necessary commitment. That little shiver of readerly recognition, in which life feels as precious and original as when you are a child seeing, maybe, your first electrical storm—there's nothing better in literature. But rare is the story that manages to capture this.

I'm still trying to write short stories. These days, I write them out of the hope that if I keep at it I will inevitably write a good one now and then. But now they seem less like lemmings to me. More like white tigers.

Think as a Writer

What does Rick Moody tell us about short stories in this essay? When you start a story, does it feel like a lemming or a white tiger—or something else?

Plot and Setting

INFORMATIONAL TEXT FOCUS

Analyzing Main Idea and Supporting Details

"There are only two or three human stories, and they go on repeating themselves as fiercely as if they had never happened before."

—Willa Cather

What Do You Think

What common human experiences do we share?

withinstandstillessence (2005) by John Oswald.   Courtesy the Artist and Jack Shaiman Gallery.

Learn It Online

Meet selections in this collection through the introductory videos online at:

go.hrw.com | L10-3 | **Go**

Literary Focus

by **Carol Jago**

What Do You Know About Plot and Setting?

Engaging storytellers know instinctively how to shape a plot. They draw you in, help you imagine the setting, and build suspense. If you can explain what happens in a story, you understand plot. If you can describe where and when a story happens, you understand setting.

Plot

Plot The **plot** of a story is a series of related events. Plot has several parts: a **basic situation** (sometimes called the **exposition**), a **conflict** (a character's problem or problems), a series of **complications,** a **climax** (the point at which we learn what the outcome of the conflict will be), and a **resolution** (the closing of the story). The plot of most stories is built around characters who experience a problem or conflict that is solved in some way.

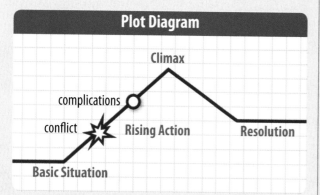

Plot Diagram

Climax

complications

conflict   Rising Action

Resolution

Basic Situation

Time and Sequence When stories present events in the order in which they happen, we refer to their organization as **chronological sequence.** Jack Finney's "Contents of the Dead Man's Pocket" uses a chronological sequence; Finney narrates each event as it happens. He builds suspense by seeming to slow the passage of time.

> Without pause he continued—right foot, left foot, right foot, left—his shoe soles shuffling and scraping along the rough stone, never lifting from it, fingers sliding along the exposed edging of brick.
>
> from "Contents of the Dead Man's Pocket" by Jack Finney

Flashback Writers sometimes interrupt the forward movement of plot with a scene from an earlier time. A scene that occurs out of sequence and tells of events that happened in the past is called a **flashback.** Writers can use flashback to deepen our understanding of a situation or reveal details of a character's past. Louise Erdrich's story "The Leap," for example, contains flashbacks that help us understand the narrator's attitude toward her mother.

> That, I think, was the likely situation on that day in June. . . . As the clouds gathered outside, unnoticed, the ringmaster cracked his whip, shouted his introduction, and pointed to the ceiling of the tent, where the Flying Avalons were perched.
>
> from "The Leap" by Louise Erdrich

RA.L.10.3 Distinguish how conflicts, parallel plots and subplots affect the pacing of action in literary text. **RA.L.10.2** Analyze the features of setting and their importance in a literary text. **RA.L.10.6** Explain how literary techniques, including foreshadowing and flashback, are used to shape the plot of a literary text.

Foreshadowing Writers often pepper their stories with clues that hint at what will happen later in the plot. These clues are called **foreshadowing.** The use of foreshadowing helps to keep readers interested by building suspense.

Suspense When your heart races and you quickly turn a book's pages to find out what will happen next, you are experiencing **suspense.** To create suspense, writers create interesting characters—people you care about—who are involved in conflicts to which you can relate. Writers may vary sentence structure to heighten a reader's anticipation of events to come. Writers may also use foreshadowing clues to hint at upcoming danger or future conflict. Suspense can also be created when writers slow down, speed up, or interrupt plot events through flashback and flash-forward.

Conflict Have you noticed that if your day runs smoothly, you have fewer stories to tell? The reason is that a good plot needs a problem or struggle—a conflict. **Conflict** happens when two forces oppose one another. **Internal conflict** occurs inside a character's mind or heart. **External conflict** occurs when a character faces off against nature, another character, or a group of people—even a whole society.

Conflict Type	Example
Internal	"If I went to the Place of the Gods, I would surely die, but, if I did not go, I could never be at peace with my spirit again." from "By the Waters of Babylon" by Stephen Vincent Benét
External	"The water is still calm, but Murad knows better than to trust the Mediterranean. He's known the sea all his life and he knows how hard it can pull." from "The Trip" by Laila Lalami

Setting

Setting is the time and place in which a story occurs. The setting can also reveal information about the customs of the society in which the story takes place. In addition, setting can contribute to the conflict to a story. For example, in Jack Finney's "Contents of the Dead Man's Pocket," the main character struggles to keep his balance and his fear at bay as he tries to retrieve an important paper from the ledge outside his eleventh-story apartment.

> He lowered his right shoulder and his fingers had the paper by a corner, pulling it loose. At the same instant he saw, between his legs and far below, Lexington Avenue stretched out for miles ahead.
>
> from "Contents of the Dead Man's Pocket" by Jack Finney

Mood Setting also contributes to a story's emotional effect—its **mood,** or atmosphere. A story's mood might be joyful, frightening, or gloomy. For example, a ghost story usually contains specific details (a haunted house) to create a creepy mood.

Your Turn Analyze Plot and Setting

1. Define **plot, setting,** and **mood.**
2. What external forces might create conflict in a story about illegal immigrants crossing a border? What mental or emotional forces might create another kind of conflict?

Learn It Online
To organize your thoughts, use one of the interactive graphic organizers at:

go.hrw.com   L10-5   **Go**

Analyzing Visuals

How Can You Interpret Setting and Mood in Art?

Both artists and writers take great pains to create a particular **setting** for their work. While writers use descriptive language to create setting, artists focus on color choices, lines, and shapes. Artists express **mood,** or atmosphere, by using dark and light contrasts, color, and perspective (the angle at which the viewer sees the subject), in addition to other techniques.

Analyzing a Still Shot from a Movie

Use these guidelines to help you interpret artwork:

1. Find the **focal point**—the most striking point of interest.

2. Look at the setting. When and where does the scene take place?

3. Identify the action. What is happening? Does the action in the scene affect the mood?

4. Look at the colors, lines, and contrasts of dark and light. How do these elements shape the mood?

5. Identify the perspective of the still shot. Are you looking up or down at the subject? How does this angle influence the mood?

Look at the details from the movie still to help you answer the questions on page 7.

RA.L.10.2 Analyze the features of setting and their importance in a literary text.

1. This still shot from a movie is set in a bamboo forest. How does knowing this detail help you understand more about the **setting?**

2. How does the use of color, light, and shadow contribute to the **mood** of the **setting?**

3. The camera angle allows you to see the people in the trees. How does this angle contribute to the **mood?**

4. The central figure is holding a Bo, a staff used in some martial arts. What does this detail tell you about the **setting** and what is taking place?

Still shot from *House of Flying Daggers* (2003), directed by Zhang Yimou.

Your Turn Write About Setting and Mood

Find a painting or photograph in this book that is set in a specific time and place. Study the artwork, and write a description of the setting. Then, explain how the artist uses colors, shapes, and lighting to create a particular mood.

Reading Focus

by **Kylene Beers**

What Reading Skills Help You Analyze Plot and Setting?

Within the pages of a short story lies a whole world. This world is given life through the writer's use of words. To more fully enjoy, participate in, and analyze the plot and setting of a story, make predictions about what actions its characters will take, analyze why characters behave the way they do, and visualize the surroundings the characters inhabit.

Making Predictions

How often have you wondered while reading a good story, "What will happen next?" This kind of guessing about the plot is called **making predictions.** Sound predictions are based on clues in the story, your experiences in real life, and your knowledge of how stories work.

This excerpt from Louise Erdrich's story "The Leap" leads us to make the prediction that something may happen with a fire and someone possibly could be hurt.

> As I sit sewing in the room of the rebuilt house in which I slept as a child, I hear the crackle, catch a whiff of smoke from the stove downstairs, and suddenly the room goes dark, the stitches burn beneath my fingers, and I am sewing with a needle of hot silver, a thread of fire.
>
> from "The Leap" by Louise Erdrich

Understanding Cause and Effect

The plot of a story is made up of a series of events that are strung together like beads on a necklace. The string that holds the beads together is cause and effect. A **cause** is the reason something happens. An **effect** is the result of an event. In a story, one event often leads to a result that, in turn, creates another problem. This series of complications propels the plot forward toward the climax.

> The outboard motor idles. In the sudden silence, everyone turns to look at Rahal, collectively holding their breath. He pulls the starter cable a few times, but nothing happens.
>
> from "The Trip" by Laila Lalami

Filling in a chart like the one below as you read will help you identify cause and effect in a story. It will also help you predict what will happen next.

Cause	Effect	Cause	Prediction
→	→	→	
There was a fire.	The narrator was trapped.	Her mother had a plan.	The narrator will be rescued.

RP.10.1 Apply reading comprehension strategies, including making predictions, comparing and contrasting, recalling and summarizing and making inferences and drawing conclusions. **RA.I.10.1** Identify and understand organizational patterns and techniques, including repetition of ideas, syntax and word choice, that authors use to accomplish their purpose and reach their intended audience.

Visualizing

Have you ever seen a movie based on a book you have read and been disappointed with the movie? When we read a story, novel, poem, or play, our imagination translates the words into images. This process, called **visualizing,** makes literature come alive. As you read the stories in this collection, pay attention to the sensory images your mind creates. Try asking yourself these questions:

- What are the characters doing?
- Where are they?
- What do you hear, taste, touch, and smell as you read?
- What conclusions can you draw based on what you have visualized?

Descriptive details are underlined in the following passage. Notice how these details allow us to step into the story and experience what the character experiences.

He saw, in that instant, the <u>Loew's theater sign</u>, blocks ahead past Fiftieth Street; the <u>miles of traffic signals</u>, all <u>green</u> now; the <u>lights of cars and street lamps</u>; countless <u>neon signs</u>; and the <u>moving black dots of people.</u>
from "Contents of the Dead Man's Pocket" by Jack Finney

Your Turn Apply Reading Skills

Read the following passage from Jack Finney's story "Contents of the Dead Man's Pocket," and complete the activities that follow.

He watched her walk down the hall, flicked a hand in response as she waved, and then he started to close the door, but it resisted for a moment. As the door opening narrowed, the current of warm air from the hallway, channeled through this smaller opening now, suddenly rushed past him with accelerated force. Behind him he heard the slap of the window curtains against the wall and the sound of paper fluttering from his desk, and he had to push to close the door.

Turning, he saw a sheet of white paper drifting to the floor in a series of arcs, and another sheet, yellow, moving toward the window, caught in the dying current flowing through the narrow opening. As he watched, the paper struck the bottom edge of the window and hung there for an instant. . . . Then . . . he saw the yellow sheet drop to the window ledge and slide over out of sight.

1. List the events in the order they occur, and label them "cause" and "effect" as appropriate.
2. Predict what might happen next in the story. Explain your prediction.
3. List the words and phrases that help you visualize the story's plot and setting.

Now go to the Skills in Action: Reading Model

Learn It Online
Try the *PowerNotes* version of this lesson at:
go.hrw.com   L10-9   **Go**

Build Background

In the early 1950s, Ray Bradbury was a young man living in southern California. He did not know how to drive, and he liked walking around his suburban neighborhood at night. Such behavior was so rare that he was once stopped and questioned by the police. If an innocent walk was so suspicious in mid-twentieth-century America, Bradbury wondered how it might be viewed in the future. This story is set in an unnamed American suburb in the year 2053.

Read with a Purpose As you read this short story, think about the comment Bradbury is making about the ways technology influences our lives.

The Pedestrian

by **Ray Bradbury**

To enter out into that silence that was the city at eight o'clock of a misty evening in November, to put your feet upon that buckling concrete walk, to step over grassy seams and make your way, hands in pockets, through the silences, that was what Mr. Leonard Mead most dearly loved to do. He would stand upon the corner of an intersection and peer down long moonlit avenues of sidewalk in four directions, deciding which way to go, but it really made no difference; he was alone in this world of A.D. 2053, or as good as alone, and with a final decision made, a path selected, he would stride off, sending patterns of frosty air before him like the smoke of a cigar.

Sometimes he would walk for hours and miles and return only at midnight to his house. And on his way he would see the cottages and homes with their dark windows, and it was not unequal to walking through a graveyard where only the faintest glimmers of firefly light appeared in flickers behind the windows. Sudden gray phantoms seemed to manifest upon inner room walls where a curtain was still undrawn against the night, or there were whisperings and murmurs where a window in a tomblike building was still open.

Mr. Leonard Mead would pause, cock his head, listen, look, and march on, his feet making no noise on the lumpy walk. For long ago he had wisely changed to sneakers when strolling at night, because the dogs in intermittent squads would parallel his journey with barkings if he wore hard heels, and lights might click on and faces appear and an entire street be startled by the passing of a lone figure, himself, in the early November evening.

Literary Focus

Setting and Mood Notice how this setting creates a mood of foreboding—a feeling that something is wrong. Words like *dark windows, graveyard, gray phantoms,* and *tomblike* suggest ruin and death.

On this particular evening he began his journey in a westerly direction, toward the hidden sea. There was a good crystal frost in the air; it cut the nose and made the lungs blaze like a Christmas tree inside; you could feel the cold light going on and off, all the branches filled with invisible snow. He listened to the faint push of his soft shoes through autumn leaves with satisfaction and whistled a cold, quiet whistle between his teeth, occasionally picking up a leaf as he passed, examining its skeletal pattern in the infrequent lamplights as he went on, smelling its rusty smell.

"Hello, in there," he whispered to every house on every side as he moved. "What's up tonight on Channel 4, Channel 7, Channel 9? Where are the cowboys rushing, and do I see the United States Cavalry over the next hill to the rescue?"

The street was silent and long and empty, with only his shadow moving like the shadow of a hawk in midcountry. If he closed his eyes and stood very still, frozen, he could imagine himself upon the center of a plain, a wintry, windless Arizona desert with no house in a thousand miles, and only dry riverbeds, the streets, for company.

"What is it now?" he asked the houses, noticing his wristwatch. "Eight-thirty p.m.? Time for a dozen assorted murders? A quiz? A revue? A comedian falling off the stage?"

Was that a murmur of laughter from within a moon-white house? He hesitated but went on when nothing more happened. He stumbled over a particularly uneven section of sidewalk. The cement was vanishing under flowers and grass. In ten years of walking by night or day, for thousands of miles, he had never met another person walking, not one in all that time.

He came to a cloverleaf intersection which stood silent where two main highways crossed the town. During the day it was a thunderous surge of cars, the gas stations open, a great insect rustling, and a ceaseless jockeying for position as the scarab beetles,[1] a faint incense puttering from their exhausts, skimmed homeward to the far directions. But now these highways, too, were like streams in a dry season, all stone and bed and moon radiance.

He turned back on a side street, circling around toward his home. He was within a block of his destination when the lone car turned a corner quite suddenly and flashed a fierce white cone of light upon him. He stood entranced, not unlike a night moth, stunned by the illumination and then drawn toward it.

---

1. **scarab beetles:** large, brilliantly colored beetles. Bradbury uses a metaphor to compare the automobiles to beetles.

Reading Focus

Cause and Effect Here, we learn the cause of the buckling sidewalk: No one else has walked on these streets for ten years.

Reading Model

A metallic voice called to him:
"Stand still. Stay where you are! Don't move!"
He halted.
"Put up your hands!"
"But—" he said.
"Your hands up! Or we'll shoot!"

Literary Focus

Plot The conflict is introduced. Leonard Mead is stopped by the police on his nighttime walk.

The police, of course, but what a rare, incredible thing; in a city of three million, there was only *one* police car left, wasn't that correct? Ever since a year ago, 2052, the election year, the force had been cut down from three cars to one. Crime was ebbing; there was no need now for the police, save for this one lone car wandering and wandering the empty streets.

"Your name?" said the police car in a metallic whisper. He couldn't see the men in it for the bright light in his eyes.
"Leonard Mead," he said.
"Speak up!"
"Leonard Mead!"
"Business or profession?"
"I guess you'd call me a writer."
"No profession," said the police car, as if talking to itself. The light held him fixed, like a museum specimen, needle thrust through chest.

Reading Focus

Making Predictions When you read that the police officer has a metallic voice, you might predict that the inhabitants of the car are not human. When the voice says that writing is not a profession, you might predict that this society does not respect artists.

"You might say that," said Mr. Mead. He hadn't written in years. Magazines and books didn't sell anymore. Everything went on in the tomblike houses at night now, he thought, continuing his fancy.[2] The tombs, ill-lit by television light, where the people sat like the dead, the gray or multicolored lights touching their faces, but never really touching them.

Literary Focus

Setting The setting becomes more ominous. The houses are tombs; the people are like the dead.

"No profession," said the phonograph voice, hissing. "What are you doing out?"
"Walking," said Leonard Mead.
"Walking!"
"Just walking," he said simply, but his face felt cold.
"Walking, just walking, walking?"
"Yes, sir."
"Walking where? For what?"
"Walking for air. Walking to *see*."
"Your address!"
"Eleven South Saint James Street."

---

2. **fancy:** here, fantasy or imagination.

"And there is air *in* your house, you have an air *conditioner*, Mr. Mead?"

"Yes."

"And you have a viewing screen in your house to see with?"

"No."

"No?" There was a crackling quiet that in itself was an accusation.

"Are you married, Mr. Mead?"

"No."

"Not married," said the police voice behind the fiery beam. The moon was high and clear among the stars and the houses were gray and silent.

"Nobody wanted me," said Leonard Mead with a smile.

"Don't speak unless you're spoken to!"

Leonard Mead waited in the cold night.

"Just *walking*, Mr. Mead?"

"Yes."

"But you haven't explained for what purpose."

"I explained: for air, and to see, and just to walk."

"Have you done this often?"

"Every night for years."

The police car sat in the center of the street with its radio throat faintly humming.

"Well, Mr. Mead," it said.

"Is that all?" he asked politely.

"Yes," said the voice. "Here." There was a sigh, a pop. The back door of the police car sprang wide. "Get in."

"Wait a minute, I haven't done anything!"

"Get in."

"I protest!"

"Mr. Mead."

He walked like a man suddenly drunk. As he passed the front window of the car, he looked in. As he had expected, there was no one in the front seat, no one in the car at all.

"Get in."

He put his hand to the door and peered into the back seat, which was a little cell, a little black jail with bars. It smelled of riveted steel. It smelled of harsh antiseptic; it smelled too clean and hard and metallic. There was nothing soft there.

"Now, if you had a wife to give you an alibi," said the iron voice. "But—"

"Where are you taking me?"

Reading Focus

Making Predictions This description of the back of the car as a prison leads us to predict that Mead is in big trouble.

The car hesitated, or rather gave a faint, whirring click, as if information, somewhere, was dropping card by punch-slotted card under electric eyes. "To the Psychiatric Center for Research on Regressive Tendencies."

He got in. The door shut with a soft thud. The police car rolled through the night avenues, flashing its dim lights ahead.

They passed one house on one street a moment later, one house in an entire city of houses that were dark, but this one particular house had all of its electric lights brightly lit, every window a loud yellow illumination, square and warm in the cool darkness.

"That's *my* house," said Leonard Mead.

No one answered him.

The car moved down the empty riverbed streets and off away, leaving the empty streets with the empty sidewalks and no sound and no motion all the rest of the chill November night.

Literary Focus

Setting and Mood The repeated use of the word *empty* ends the story with a mood of horror.

MEET THE WRITER

Ray Bradbury
(1920–   )

The Man with the Child Inside

Ray Bradbury calls himself "that special freak—the man with the child inside who remembers all." Bradbury, who started writing at age seven, calls himself a magical realist. When he was a child, his mother often sneaked him into movies. Here he describes his favorites:

> "I was in love, then, with monsters and skeletons and circuses and carnivals and dinosaurs and at last, the red planet, Mars. From these primitive bricks I have built a life and a career."

Think About the Writer Bradbury often uses futuristic settings to comment on the way we live today. What aspects of modern life might he criticize?

RA.L.10.3 Distinguish how conflicts, parallel plots and subplots affect the pacing of action in literary text. *Also covered* **RP.10.1; VO.10.6**

Into Action: Plot Diagram

Using this diagram as a guide, draw a plot diagram of your own for "The Pedestrian." Then, write a sentence describing what happens at each stage of the story.

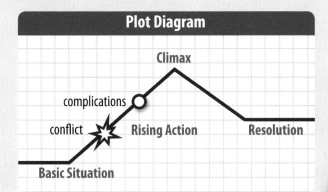

Talk About . . .

1. In groups of three, discuss whether or not the plot and setting of this story are believable. Try to use each Academic Vocabulary word listed at the right at least once in your discussion.

Write About . . .

Answer the following questions about "The Pedestrian."

2. How do the story's plot events build <u>tension</u>?

3. What <u>aspects</u> of modern society could you identify in the story?

4. Do you find Bradbury's portrayal of the future <u>credible</u>? Explain.

5. What <u>evaluation</u> do the police make when they see Leonard Mead?

Writing Focus

Think as a Reader/Writer

Find It in Your Reading Ray Bradbury chooses descriptive words and phrases to turn a familiar setting—the suburbs—into a sinister, threatening environment. In Collection 1, you'll be introduced to ways in which the writers in this collection create interesting and memorable stories. On the Applying Your Skills pages, you will have a chance to practice the writers' techniques in your own writing.

Academic Vocabulary for Collection 1

Talking and Writing About Short Stories

Academic Vocabulary is the language you use to write and talk about literature. Use these words to discuss the stories you read in this collection. The words are underlined throughout the collection.

aspects (AS pehkts) *n. pl.:* parts or features of a subject; facets. *Leonard Mead found many aspects of modern life bewildering.*

credible (KREHD uh buhl) *adj.:* believable; trustworthy. *Bradbury creates a credible, futuristic setting in "The Pedestrian."*

tension (TEHN shuhn) *n.:* strained condition. *The ominous setting of "The Pedestrian" causes tension.*

evaluation (ih val yoo AY shuhn) *n.:* judgment; assessment. *I'm hoping to get a good evaluation on my book report.*

Your Turn

Copy the words from the Academic Vocabulary list into your *Reader/Writer Notebook.* You may be familiar with some of them. As you read and discuss the stories in the following collection, try to use each of these words at least once.

CONTENTS OF THE DEAD MAN'S POCKET

by **Jack Finney**

What Do You Think

What values do you think are most important in people's lives?

QuickTalk

With a partner, list values such as friendship, health, and so on, that you find important. Then, discuss the values you listed.

Reader/Writer Notebook

Use your **RWN** to complete the activities for this selection.

OH **RA.L.10.3** Distinguish how conflicts, parallel plots and subplots affect the pacing of action in literary text. **RA.I.10.1** Identify and understand organizational patterns and techniques, including repetition of ideas, syntax and word choice, that authors use to accomplish their purpose and reach their intended audience.

Literary Focus

Plot: Time and Sequence The series of related events in a story is called the **plot.** Usually the events in a plot are told in **chronological order**—they move in sequence through a series of related events until the conflict is resolved. In "Contents of the Dead Man's Pocket," each event in the plot intensifies our tension. To make the tension even stronger, Jack Finney does something interesting with time: He slows down the action so that you can feel the seconds ticking away. The time it takes to read the story roughly matches the timing of the character's ordeal.

Literary Perspectives Apply the literary perspective described on page 19 as you read this story.

Reading Focus

Understanding Cause and Effect A **cause** is the reason something happens. An **effect** is the result of some event or action. Most causes and effects happen in chains, with a cause leading to an effect that leads to another cause, and so on. Many suspenseful stories rely on edge-of-your-seat causes and effects that keep you guessing.

Into Action As you read "Contents of the Dead Man's Pocket," identify the chain of cause-and-effect events. Use a chart like the one below to record your observations.

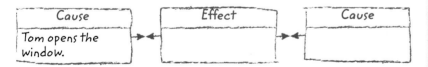

Cause	Effect	Cause
Tom opens the window.		

Writing Focus

Think as a Reader/Writer

Find It in Your Reading **Imagery** is language that appeals to the senses. Most images are visual—that is, they appeal to our sense of sight. But imagery can also appeal to our senses of hearing, smell, touch, and taste. As you read, list images in your *Reader/Writer Notebook* that help you share Tom's hair-raising experience.

Vocabulary

projection (pruh JEHK shuhn) *n.:* something that juts out from a surface. *Tom Benecke stood on a projection high above Lexington Avenue.*

exhalation (ehks huh LAY shuhn) *n.:* breath; something breathed out. *After holding his breath for so long, his exhalation was a relief.*

imperceptibly (ihm puhr SEHP tuh blee) *adv.:* in such a slight way as to be almost unnoticeable. *Tom moved along the ledge almost imperceptibly because he was afraid to move quickly.*

rebounded (rih BOWND ihd) *v.:* bounced back. *After he broke the glass, Tom's body rebounded with the force of the impact.*

irrelevantly (ih REHL uh vuhnt lee) *adv.:* in a way not relating to the point or situation. *Thoughts occurred to Tom irrelevantly as he clung to the narrow ledge.*

Language Coach

Prefixes A word part added to the front of a word to change its meaning is a **prefix.** Identify the prefix in each word above. Then, see if you can figure out the meaning of each prefix by studying the word's definition.

 Learn It Online
There's more to words than just definitions. Get the whole story at:

| go.hrw.com | L10-17 | Go |

Jack Finney
(1911–1995)

Space Aliens and Time Travel

Menacing alien plants hatch from pods, take human form, and gradually replace everyone—or almost everyone—in a small California town. Jack Finney created this science fiction scenario in his second novel, *The Body Snatchers* (1955). The novel was turned into a horror-movie classic, *The Invasion of the Body Snatchers,* in 1956. For years, critics debated the meaning of the story—is it a protest against communism or a criticism of anticommunist hysteria? Finney had his own explanation: "I wrote the story purely as a good read."

From Advertising to Fiction

Finney was an advertising copywriter in New York City in the 1940s. Bored with his job, he began to write short stories. Eventually, he quit the advertising business to write full time. He published eight novels, five of which were made into movies.

"The modern world is full of insecurity, fear, war, worry, and all the rest of it, and . . . I just want to escape. Well, who doesn't?"

Think About the Writer

How did Finney escape from the fear and worry of the modern world?

Build Background

In the 1940s and 1950s, movie theaters often presented double features, two movies for the price of one. A newsreel usually preceded the features, as did a cartoon. Therefore, people could spend a long time at the movies. These facts have frightening implications in the plot of this story.

You'll notice that the main character uses a typewriter and carbon paper to produce his memos. Carbon paper was used in typewriters to make copies of documents. Today this work would be done on a computer; carbon paper has long been a thing of the past. If a computer had been available, we might not have this story.

Preview the Selection

There is basically only one character in this story of suspense. We meet Tom Benecke's wife only briefly, and we spend almost all of the story with **Tom**—a young man with ambitions, who, for a few minutes, is willing to risk his life to further his career.

CONTENTS OF THE DEAD MAN'S POCKET

by **Jack Finney**

At the little living-room desk Tom Benecke rolled two sheets of flimsy[1] and a heavier top sheet, carbon paper sandwiched between them, into his portable. *Interoffice Memo,* the top sheet was headed, and he typed tomorrow's date just below this; then he glanced at a creased yellow sheet, covered with his own handwriting, beside the typewriter. "Hot in here," he muttered to himself. Then, from the short hallway at his back, he heard the muffled clang of wire coat hangers in the bedroom closet, and at this reminder of what his wife was doing he thought: hot—guilty conscience.

He got up, shoving his hands into the back pockets of his gray wash slacks, stepped to the living-room window beside the desk and stood breathing on the glass, watching the expanding circlet of mist, staring down through the autumn night at Lexington Avenue,[2] eleven stories below. He was a tall, lean, dark-haired young man in a pullover sweater, who looked as though he had played not football, probably, but basketball in college. Now he placed the heels of his hands against the top edge of the lower window frame and shoved upward. But as usual the window didn't budge, and he had to lower his hands and then shoot them hard upward to jolt the window open a few inches. He dusted his hands, muttering.

But still he didn't begin his work. He crossed the room to the hallway entrance and, leaning against the doorjamb, hands shoved into his back pockets again, he called, "Clare?"

Literary Perspectives

Analyzing Philosophical Context Philosophy is a conscious search for truth. This perspective asks us to uncover and consider the philosophical ideas of authors as we read their works. Philosophical context refers to an author's underlying assumptions about larger questions about life and its meaning. Although one's philosophy can lead to certain political beliefs or ideologies, a philosophy is much broader or more general. It refers to thought rather than political action. An author's philosophy influences literary texts in a variety of ways, through the credibility of the characters, the form in which the literary text is written, and the overarching themes or messages the author conveys. As you read, use the notes and questions in the text to guide you in using this perspective.

---

1. **flimsy:** thin paper used for making carbon copies.
2. **Lexington Avenue:** a main street in New York City.

When his wife answered, he said, "Sure you don't mind going alone?"

"No." Her voice was muffled, and he knew her head and shoulders were in the bedroom closet. Then the tap of her high heels sounded on the wood floor, and she appeared at the end of the little hallway, wearing a slip, both hands raised to one ear, clipping on an earring. She smiled at him—a slender, very pretty girl with light brown, almost blond, hair—her prettiness emphasized by the pleasant nature that showed in her face. "It's just that I hate you to miss this movie; you wanted to see it, too."

"Yeah, I know." He ran his fingers through his hair. "Got to get this done, though."

She nodded, accepting this. Then, glancing at the desk across the living room, she said, "You work too much, though, Tom—and too hard."

He smiled. "You won't mind, though, will you, when the money comes rolling in and I'm known as the Boy Wizard of Wholesale Groceries?"

"I guess not." She smiled and turned back toward the bedroom.

At his desk again, Tom lighted a cigarette; then a few moments later, as Clare appeared, dressed and ready to leave, he set it on the rim of the ashtray. "Just after seven," she said. "I can make the beginning of the first feature."

He walked to the front-door closet to help her on with her coat. He kissed her then and, for an instant, holding her close, smelling the perfume she had used, he was tempted to go with her; it was not actually true that he had to work tonight, though he very much wanted to. This was his own project, unannounced as yet in his office, and it could be postponed. But then they won't see it till Monday, he thought

once again, and if I give it to the boss tomorrow he might read it over the weekend . . . "Have a good time," he said aloud. He gave his wife a little swat and opened the door for her, feeling the air from the building hallway, smelling faintly of floor wax, stream gently past his face.

He watched her walk down the hall, flicked a hand in response as she waved, and then he started to close the door, but it resisted for a moment. As the door opening narrowed, the current of warm air from the hallway, channeled through this smaller opening now, suddenly rushed past him with accelerated force. Behind him he heard the slap of the window curtains against the wall and the sound of paper fluttering from his desk, and he had to push to close the door.

Turning, he saw a sheet of white paper drifting to the floor in a series of arcs, and another sheet, yellow, moving toward the window, caught in the dying current flowing through the narrow opening. As he watched, the paper struck the bottom edge of the window and hung there for an instant, plastered against the glass and wood. Then as the moving air stilled completely, the curtains swinging back from the wall to hang free again, he saw the yellow sheet drop to the window ledge and slide over out of sight. **Ⓐ**

He ran across the room, grasped the bottom of the window and tugged, staring through the glass. He saw the yellow sheet, dimly now in the darkness outside, lying on the ornamental ledge a yard below the window. Even as he watched, it was moving, scraping slowly along the ledge, pushed by the breeze that pressed steadily against the building wall. He heaved on the window with all his strength, and it shot open with a bang, the window weight rattling

---

Ⓐ **Reading Focus** **Cause and Effect** What causes the sheet of paper to fly out the window?

in the casing. But the paper was past his reach and, leaning out into the night, he watched it scud[3] steadily along the ledge to the south, half plastered against the building wall. Above the muffled sound of the street traffic far below, he could hear the dry scrape of its movement, like a leaf on the pavement.

The living room of the next apartment to the south projected a yard or more further out toward the street than this one; because of this the Beneckes paid seven and a half dollars less rent than their neighbors. And now the yellow sheet, sliding along the stone ledge, nearly invisible in the night, was stopped by the projecting blank wall of the next apartment. It lay motionless, then, in the corner formed by the two walls—a good five yards away, pressed firmly against the ornate corner ornament of the ledge by the breeze that moved past Tom Benecke's face.

He knelt at the window and stared at the yellow paper for a full minute or more, waiting for it to move, to slide off the ledge and fall, hoping he could follow its course to the street, and then hurry down in the elevator and retrieve it. But it didn't move, and then he saw that the paper was caught firmly between a projection of the convoluted corner ornament and the ledge. He thought about the poker from the fireplace, then the broom, then the mop—discarding each thought as it occurred to him. There was nothing in the apartment long enough to reach that paper.

---

3. scud: glide or move quickly.

Vocabulary **projection** (pruh JEHK shuhn) *n.:* something that juts out from a surface.

It was hard for him to understand that he actually had to abandon it—it was ridiculous—and he began to curse. Of all the papers on his desk, why did it have to be this one in particular! On four long Saturday afternoons he had stood in supermarkets, counting the people who passed certain displays, and the results were scribbled on that yellow sheet. From stacks of trade publications, gone over page by page in snatched half hours at work and during evenings at home, he had copied facts, quotations, and figures onto that sheet. And he had carried it with him to the Public Library on Fifth Avenue, where he'd spent a dozen lunch hours and early evenings adding more. All were needed to support and lend authority to his idea for a new grocery-store display method; without them his idea was a mere opinion. And there they all lay, in his own improvised shorthand—countless hours of work—out there on the ledge. **B**

For many seconds he believed he was going to abandon the yellow sheet, that there was nothing else to do. The work could be duplicated. But it would take two months, and the time to present this idea was *now,* for use in the spring displays. He struck his fist on the window ledge. Then he shrugged. Even though his plan was adopted, he told himself, it wouldn't bring him a raise in pay—not immediately, anyway, or as a direct result. It won't bring me a promotion either, he argued—not of itself. But just the same—and he couldn't escape the thought—this and other independent projects, some already done and others planned for the future, would gradually mark him out from

> He stood on the ledge outside in the slight, chill breeze, eleven stories above the street.

the score of other young men in his company. They were the way to change from a name on the payroll to a name in the minds of the company officials. They were the beginning of the long, long climb to where he was determined to be—at the very top. And he knew he was going out there in the darkness, after the yellow sheet fifteen feet beyond his reach. **C**

By a kind of instinct, he instantly began making his intention acceptable to himself by laughing at it. The mental picture of himself sidling along the ledge outside was absurd—it was actually comical—and he smiled. He imagined himself describing it; it would make a good story at the office and, it occurred to him, would add a special interest and importance to his memorandum, which would do it no harm at all.

To simply go out and get his paper was an easy task—he could be back here with it in less than two minutes—and he knew he wasn't deceiving himself. The ledge, he saw, measuring it with his eye, was about as wide as the length of his shoe, and perfectly flat. And every fifth row of brick in the face of the building, he remembered—leaning out, he verified this—was indented half an inch, enough for the tips of his fingers, enough to maintain balance easily. It occurred to him that if this ledge and wall were only a yard aboveground—as he knelt at the window staring out, this thought was the final confirmation of his intention—he could move along the ledge indefinitely.

On a sudden impulse, he got to his feet, walked to the front closet, and took out an old tweed jacket; it would be cold outside. He put

---

B **Literary Focus** **Plot** What problem has been established in the story?

C **Reading Focus** **Cause and Effect** Why does Tom decide to go out the window?

it on and buttoned it as he crossed the room rapidly toward the open window. In the back of his mind he knew he'd better hurry and get this over with before he thought too much, and at the window he didn't allow himself to hesitate.

He swung a leg over the sill, then felt for and found the ledge a yard below the window with his foot. Gripping the bottom of the window frame very tightly and carefully, he slowly ducked his head under it, feeling on his face the sudden change from the warm air of the room to the chill outside. With infinite care he brought out his other leg, his mind concentrating on what he was doing. Then he slowly stood erect. Most of the putty, dried out and brittle, had dropped off the bottom edging of the window frame, he found, and the flat wooden edging provided a good gripping surface, a half inch or more deep, for the tips of his fingers.

Now, balanced easily and firmly, he stood on the ledge outside in the slight, chill breeze, eleven stories above the street, staring into his own lighted apartment, odd and different-seeming now.

First his right hand, then his left, he carefully shifted his fingertip grip from the puttyless window edging to an indented row of bricks directly to his right. It was hard to take the first shuffling sideways step then—to make himself move—and the fear stirred in his stomach, but he did it, again by not allowing himself time to think. And now—with his chest, stomach, and the left side of his face pressed against the rough cold brick—his lighted apartment was suddenly gone, and it was much darker out here than he had thought.

Without pause he continued—right foot, left foot, right foot, left—his shoe soles shuffling and scraping along the rough stone, never lifting from it, fingers sliding along the exposed edging of brick. He moved on the balls of his feet, heels lifted slightly; the ledge was not quite as wide as he'd expected. But leaning slightly inward toward the face of the building and pressed against it, he could feel his balance firm and secure, and moving along the ledge was quite as easy as he had thought it would be. He could hear the buttons of his jacket scraping steadily along the rough bricks and feel them catch momentarily, tugging a little, at each mortared crack. He simply did not permit himself to look down, though the compulsion to do so never left him; nor did he allow himself actually to think. Mechanically—right foot, left foot, over and again—he shuffled along crabwise, watching the projecting wall ahead loom steadily closer. . . .

Then he reached it, and at the corner—he'd decided how he was going to pick up the paper—he lifted his right foot and placed it carefully on the ledge that ran along the projecting wall at a right angle to the ledge on which his other foot rested. And now, facing the building, he stood in the corner formed by the two walls, one foot on the ledging of each, a hand on the shoulder-high indentation of each wall. His forehead was pressed directly into the corner against the cold bricks, and now he carefully lowered first one hand, then the other, perhaps a foot farther down, to the next indentation in the rows of bricks.

Very slowly, sliding his forehead down the trough of the brick corner and bending his knees, he lowered his body toward the paper lying between his outstretched feet. Again he lowered his fingerholds another foot and bent his knees still more, thigh muscles taut, his forehead sliding and bumping down the brick V. Half squatting now, he dropped his left hand to the next indentation and then slowly reached with his right hand toward the paper between his feet.

He couldn't quite touch it, and his knees now were pressed against the wall; he could bend them no farther. But by ducking his head

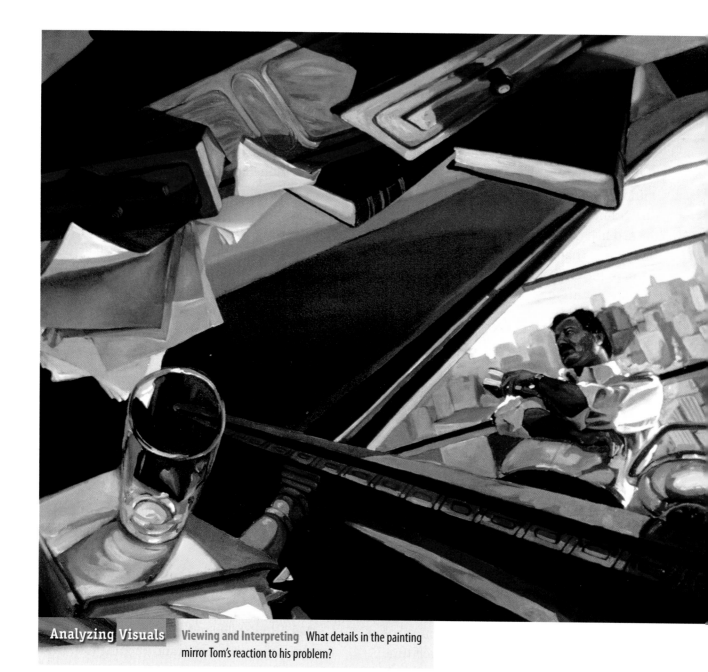

another inch lower, the top of his head now pressed against the bricks, he lowered his right shoulder and his fingers had the paper by a corner, pulling it loose. At the same instant he saw, between his legs and far below, Lexington Avenue stretched out for miles ahead. **D**

He saw, in that instant, the Loew's theater sign, blocks ahead past Fiftieth Street; the miles of traffic signals, all green now; the lights of cars and street lamps; countless neon signs; and the moving black dots of people. And a violent, instantaneous explosion of absolute terror

D **Literary Perspectives** **Philosophical Context** What does Tom's decision suggest about what is most important to him at this point in his life?

Man in Office Standing by the Large Window by Eric Masi.

In the fractional moment before horror paralyzed him, as he stared between his legs at that terrible length of street far beneath him, a fragment of his mind raised his body in a spasmodic jerk to an upright position again, but so violently that his head scraped hard against the wall, bouncing off it, and his body swayed outward to the knife-edge of balance, and he very nearly plunged backward and fell. Then he was leaning far into the corner again, squeezing and pushing into it, not only his face but his chest and stomach, his back arching; and his fingertips clung with all the pressure of his pulling arms to the shoulder-high half-inch indentation in the bricks. **F**

He was more than trembling now; his whole body was racked with a violent shuddering beyond control, his eyes squeezed so tightly shut it was painful, though he was past awareness of that. His teeth were exposed in a frozen grimace, the strength draining like water from his knees and calves. It was extremely likely, he knew, that he would faint, slump down along the wall, his face scraping, and then drop backward, a limp weight, out into nothing. And to save his life he concentrated on holding on to consciousness, drawing deliberate deep breaths of cold air into his lungs, fighting to keep his senses aware.

Then he knew that he would not faint, but he could not stop shaking nor open his eyes. He stood where he was, breathing deeply, trying to hold back the terror of the glimpse he had had of what lay below him; and he knew he had made a mistake in not making himself stare down at the street, getting used to it and accepting it, when he had first stepped out onto the ledge.

It was impossible to walk back. He simply

roared through him. For a motionless instant he saw himself externally—bent practically double, balanced on this narrow ledge, nearly half his body projecting out above the street far below—and he began to tremble violently, panic flaring through his mind and muscles, and he felt the blood rush from the surface of his skin. **E**

E **Reading Focus** Cause and Effect How does Tom react when he looks down at the street below him?

F **Reading Focus** Cause and Effect What causes Tom to lose his balance and almost fall?

could not do it. He couldn't bring himself to make the slightest movement. The strength was gone from his legs; his shivering hands—numb, cold, and desperately rigid—had lost all deftness;[4] his easy ability to move and balance was gone. Within a step or two, if he tried to move, he knew that he would stumble clumsily and fall.

Seconds passed, with the chill faint wind pressing the side of his face, and he could hear the toned-down volume of the street traffic far beneath him. Again and again it slowed and then stopped, almost to silence; then presently, even this high, he would hear the click of the traffic signals and the subdued roar of the cars starting up again. During a lull in the street sounds, he called out. Then he was shouting *Help!* so loudly it rasped his throat. But he felt the steady pressure of the wind, moving between his face and the blank wall, snatch up his cries as he uttered them, and he knew they must sound directionless and distant. And he remembered how habitually, here in New York, he himself heard and ignored shouts in the night. If anyone heard him, there was no sign of it, and presently Tom Benecke knew he had to try moving; there was nothing else he could do. **G**

Eyes squeezed shut, he watched scenes in his mind like scraps of motion-picture film—he could not stop them. He saw himself stumbling suddenly sideways as he crept along the ledge and saw his upper body arc outward, arms flailing. He saw a dangling shoestring caught between the ledge and the sole of his other shoe, saw a foot start to move, to be stopped with a jerk, and felt his balance leaving him. He saw himself falling with a terrible speed as his body revolved in the air, knees clutched tight to his chest, eyes squeezed shut, moaning softly.

Out of utter necessity, knowing that any of these thoughts might be reality in the very next seconds, he was slowly able to shut his mind against every thought but what he now began to do. With fear-soaked slowness, he slid his left foot an inch or two toward his own impossibly distant window. Then he slid the fingers of his shivering left hand a corresponding distance. For a moment he could not bring himself to lift his right foot from one ledge to the other; then he did it, and became aware of the harsh exhalation of air from his throat and realized that he was panting. As his right hand, then, began to slide along the brick edging, he was astonished to feel the yellow paper pressed to the bricks underneath his stiff fingers, and he uttered a terrible, abrupt bark that might have been a laugh or a moan. He opened his mouth and took the paper in his teeth, pulling it out from under his fingers.

By a kind of trick—by concentrating his entire mind on first his left foot, then his left hand, then the other foot, then the other hand—he was able to move, almost imperceptibly, trembling steadily, very nearly without thought. But he could feel the terrible strength of the pent-up horror on just the other side of the flimsy barrier he had erected in his mind; and he knew that if it broke through he would lose this thin artificial control of his body.

During one slow step he tried keeping his eyes closed; it made him feel safer, shutting him

---

4. **deftness:** coordination or skillfulness.

off a little from the fearful reality of where he was. Then a sudden rush of giddiness swept over him and he had to open his eyes wide, staring sideways at the cold rough brick and angled lines of mortar, his cheek tight against the building. He kept his eyes open then, knowing that if he once let them flick outward, to stare for an instant at the lighted windows across the street, he would be past help.

He didn't know how many dozens of tiny sidling steps he had taken, his chest, belly, and face pressed to the wall; but he knew the slender hold he was keeping on his mind and body was going to break. He had a sudden mental picture of his apartment on just the other side of this wall—warm, cheerful, incredibly spacious. And he saw himself striding through it, lying down on the floor on his back, arms spread wide, reveling[5] in its unbelievable security. The impossible remoteness of this utter safety, the contrast between it and where he now stood, was more than he could bear. And the barrier broke then, and the fear of the awful height he stood on coursed through his nerves and muscles.

A fraction of his mind knew he was going to fall, and he began taking rapid blind steps with no feeling of what he was doing, sidling with a clumsy desperate swiftness, fingers scrabbling along the brick, almost hopelessly resigned to the sudden backward pull and swift motion outward and down. Then his moving left hand slid onto not brick but sheer emptiness, an impossible gap in the face of the wall, and he stumbled.

His right foot smashed into his left anklebone; he staggered sideways, began falling,

> For an instant he hung suspended between balance and falling.

and the claw of his hand cracked against glass and wood, slid down it, and his fingertips were pressed hard on the puttyless edging of his window. His right hand smacked gropingly beside it as he fell to his knees; and, under the full weight and direct downward pull of his sagging body, the open window dropped shudderingly in its frame till it closed and his wrists struck the sill and were jarred off.

For a single moment he knelt, knee bones against stone on the very edge of the ledge, body swaying and touching nowhere else, fighting for balance. Then he lost it, his shoulders plunging backward, and he flung his arms forward, his hands smashing against the window casing on either side; and—his body moving backward—his fingers clutched the narrow wood stripping of the upper pane.

For an instant he hung suspended between balance and falling, his fingertips pressed onto the quarter-inch wood strips. Then, with utmost delicacy, with a focused concentration of all his senses, he increased even further the strain on his fingertips hooked to these slim edgings of wood. Elbows slowly bending, he began to draw the full weight of his upper body forward, knowing that the instant his fingers slipped off these quarter-inch strips he'd plunge backward and be falling. Elbows imperceptibly bending, body shaking with the strain, the sweat starting from his forehead in great sudden drops, he pulled, his entire being and thought concentrated in his fingertips. Then suddenly, the strain slackened and ended, his chest touching the windowsill, and he was kneeling on the ledge, his forehead pressed to the glass of the closed window.

Dropping his palms to the sill, he stared into his living room—at the red-brown

---

5. **reveling** (REHV uhl ihng): taking delight or great pleasure in something.

davenport[6] across the room, and a magazine he had left there; at the pictures on the walls and the gray rug; the entrance to the hallway; and at his papers, typewriter, and desk, not two feet from his nose. A movement from his desk caught his eye and he saw that it was a thin curl of blue smoke; his cigarette, the ash long, was still burning in the ashtray where he'd left it—this was past all belief—only a few minutes before. **H**

His head moved, and in faint reflection from the glass before him he saw the yellow paper clenched in his front teeth. Lifting a hand from the sill he took it from his mouth; the moistened corner parted from the paper, and he spat it out.

For a moment, in the light from the living room, he stared wonderingly at the yellow sheet in his hand and then crushed it into the side pocket of his jacket.

He couldn't open the window. It had been pulled not completely closed, but its lower edge was below the level of the outside sill; there was no room to get his fingers underneath it. Between the upper sash and the lower was a gap not wide enough—reaching up, he tried—to get his fingers into; he couldn't push it open. The upper window panel, he knew from long experience, was impossible to move, frozen tight with dried paint. **I**

Very carefully observing his balance, the fingertips of his left hand again hooked to the narrow stripping of the window casing, he drew back his right hand, palm facing the glass, and then struck the glass with the heel of his hand.

His arm rebounded from the pane, his body tottering, and he knew he didn't dare strike a harder blow.

But in the security and relief of his new position, he simply smiled; with only a sheet of glass between him and the room just before him, it was not possible that there wasn't a way past it. Eyes narrowing, he thought for a few moments about what to do. Then his eyes widened, for nothing occurred to him. But still he felt calm; the trembling, he realized, had stopped. At the back of his mind there still lay the thought that once he was again in his home, he could give release to his feelings. He actually *would* lie on the floor, rolling, clenching tufts of the rug in his hands. He would literally run across the room, free to move as he liked, jumping on the floor, testing and reveling in its absolute security, letting the relief flood through him, draining the fear from his mind and body. His yearning for this was astonishingly intense, and somehow he understood that he had better keep this feeling at bay.

He took a half dollar from his pocket and struck it against the pane, but without any hope that the glass would break and with very little disappointment when it did not. After a few moments of thought he drew his leg up onto the ledge and picked loose the knot of his shoelace. He slipped off the shoe and, holding it across the instep, drew back his arm as far as he dared and struck the leather heel against the glass. The pane rattled, but he knew he'd been a long way from breaking it. His foot was cold and he slipped the shoe back on. He shouted again, experimentally, and then once more, but there was no answer.

---

6. **davenport** (DAV uhn pawrt): sofa or couch.

H **Literary Focus** **Plot** What makes Tom suddenly realize that very little time has actually passed?

I **Reading Focus** **Cause and Effect** Why can't Tom get back into his apartment?

Vocabulary **rebounded** (rih BOWND ihd) *v.*: bounced back.

The realization suddenly struck him that he might have to wait here till Clare came home, and for a moment the thought was funny. He could see Clare opening the front door, with-drawing her key from the lock, closing the door behind her, and then glancing up to see him crouched on the other side of the window. He could see her rush across the room, face astounded and frightened, and hear himself shouting instructions: "Never mind how I got here! Just open the wind—" She couldn't open it, he remembered, she'd never been able to; she'd always had to call him. She'd have to get the building superintendent or a neighbor, and he pictured himself smiling and answering their questions as he climbed in. "I just wanted to get a breath of fresh air, so—"

He couldn't possibly wait here till Clare came home. It was the second feature she'd wanted to see, and she'd left in time to see the first. She'd be another three hours or— He glanced at his watch; Clare had been gone eight minutes. It wasn't possible, but only eight min-utes ago he had kissed his wife goodbye. She wasn't even at the theater yet!  **J**

It would be four hours before she could possibly be home, and he tried to picture himself kneeling out here, fingertips hooked to these narrow strippings, while first one movie, preceded by a slow listing of credits, began, developed, reached its climax, and then finally ended. There'd be a newsreel next, maybe, and then an animated cartoon, and then interminable scenes from coming pictures. And then, once more, the beginning of a full-length picture—while all the time he hung out here in the night.

J **Literary Focus** Plot What does this passage tell you about Tom's perception of time?

He might possibly get to his feet, but he was afraid to try. Already his legs were cramped, his thigh muscles tired; his knees hurt, his feet felt numb, and his hands were stiff. He couldn't possibly stay out here for four hours or any-where near it. Long before that his legs and arms would give out; he would be forced to try changing his position often—stiffly, clumsily, his coordination and strength gone—and he would fall. Quite realistically, he knew that he would fall; no one could stay out here on this ledge for four hours.

A dozen windows in the apartment build-ing across the street were lighted. Looking over his shoulder, he could see the top of a man's head behind the newspaper he was reading; in another window he saw the blue-gray flicker of a television screen. No more than twenty-odd yards from his back were scores of people, and if just one of them would walk idly to his window and glance out. . . . For some moments he stared over his shoulder at the lighted rectangles, wait-ing. But no one appeared. The man reading his paper turned a page and then continued his reading. A figure passed another of the win-dows and was immediately gone.

In the inside pocket of his jacket he found a little sheaf of papers, and he pulled one out and looked at it in the light from the living room. It was an old letter, an advertisement of some sort; his name and address, in purple ink, were on a label pasted to the envelope. Gripping one end of the envelope in his teeth, he twisted it into a tight curl. From his shirt pocket he brought out a book of matches. He didn't dare let go the casing with both hands but, with the twist of paper in his teeth, he opened the matchbook with his free hand; then he bent one of the matches in two without tearing it from the folder, its red-tipped end now touching the striking surface. With his thumb, he rubbed the red tip across the striking area.

He did it again, then again, and still again, pressing harder each time, and the match sud-denly flared, burning his thumb. But he kept it alight, cupping the matchbook in his hand and shielding it with his body. He held the flame to the paper in his mouth till it caught. Then he snuffed out the match flame with his thumb and fore-finger, careless of the burn, and replaced the book in his pocket. Taking the paper twist in his hand, he held it flame down, watching the flame crawl up the paper, till it flared bright. Then he held it behind him over the street, moving it from side to side, watching it over his shoulder, the flame flickering and gut-tering in the wind.

There were three letters in his pocket and he lighted each of them, holding each till the flame touched his hand and then dropping it to the street below. At one point, watching over his shoulder while the last of the letters burned, he saw the man across the street put down his paper and stand—even seeming, to Tom, to glance toward his window. But when he moved, it was only to walk across the room and disap-pear from sight. **Ⓚ**

> Quite realistically, he knew that he would fall; no one could stay out here on this ledge for four hours.

Ⓚ **Literary Focus** **Plot** What attempt has Tom made to resolve his problem? What is the result?

There were a dozen coins in Tom Benecke's pocket and he dropped them, three or four at a time. But if they struck anyone, or if anyone noticed their falling, no one connected them with their source, and no one glanced upward.

His arms had begun to tremble from the steady strain of clinging to this narrow perch, and he did not know what to do now and was terribly frightened. Clinging to the window stripping with one hand, he again searched his pockets. But now—he had left his wallet on his dresser when he'd changed clothes—there was nothing left but the yellow sheet. It occurred to him irrelevantly that his death on the sidewalk below would be an eternal mystery; the window closed—why, how, and from where could he have fallen? No one would be able to identify his body for a time, either—the thought was somehow unbearable and increased his fear. All they'd find in his pockets would be the yellow sheet. *Contents of the dead man's pockets,* he thought, *one sheet of paper bearing penciled notations—incomprehensible.*

He understood fully that he might actually be going to die; his arms, maintaining his balance on the ledge, were trembling steadily now. And it occurred to him then with all the force of a revelation that, if he fell, all he was ever going to have out of life he would then, abruptly, have had. Nothing, then, could ever be changed; and nothing more—no least experience or pleasure—could ever be added to his life. He wished, then, that he had not allowed his wife to go off by herself tonight—and on similar nights. He thought of all the evenings he had spent away from her, working; and he regretted them. He thought wonderingly of his fierce ambition and of the direction his life had taken; he thought of the hours he'd spent by himself, filling the yellow sheet that had brought him out here. *Contents of the dead man's pockets,* he thought with sudden fierce anger, *a wasted life.* **L**

He was simply not going to cling here till he slipped and fell; he told himself that now. There was one last thing he could try; he had been aware of it for some moments, refusing to think about it, but now he faced it. Kneeling here on the ledge, the fingertips of one hand pressed to the narrow strip of wood, he could, he knew, draw his other hand back a yard perhaps, fist clenched tight, doing it very slowly till he sensed the outer limit of balance, then, as hard as he was able from the distance, he could drive his fist forward against the glass. If it broke, his fist smashing through, he was safe; he might cut himself badly, and probably would, but with his arm inside the room, he would be secure. But if the glass did not break, the rebound, flinging his arm back, would topple him off the ledge. He was certain of that.

He tested his plan. The fingers of his left hand clawlike on the little stripping, he drew back his other fist until his body began teetering backward. But he had no leverage now—he could feel that there would be no force to his swing—and he moved his fist slowly forward till he rocked forward on his knees again and could sense that his swing would carry its greatest force. Glancing down, however, measuring the distance from his fist to the glass, he saw that it was less than two feet.

It occurred to him that he could raise his arm over his head, to bring it down against the glass. But, experimentally in slow motion, he knew it would be an awkward blow without the force of a driving punch, and not nearly enough to break the glass.

Vocabulary **irrelevantly** (ih REHL uh vuhnt lee) *adv.*: in a way not relating to the point or situation.

L Literary Perspectives **Philosophical Context** What might the author be conveying here about his own values?

Facing the window, he had to drive a blow from the shoulder, he knew now, at a distance of less than two feet; and he did not know whether it would break through the heavy glass. It might; he could picture it happening, he could feel it in the nerves of his arm. And it might not; he could feel that too—feel his fist striking this glass and being instantaneously flung back by the unbreaking pane, feel the fingers of his other hand breaking loose, nails scraping along the casing as he fell.

He waited, arm drawn back, fist balled, but in no hurry to strike; this pause, he knew, might be an extension of his life. And to live even a few seconds longer, he felt, even out here on this ledge in the night, was infinitely better than to die a moment earlier than he had to. His arm grew tired, and he brought it down and rested it.

Then he knew that it was time to make the attempt. He could not kneel here hesitating indefinitely till he lost all courage to act, waiting till he slipped off the ledge. Again he drew back his arm, knowing this time that he would not bring it down till he struck. His elbow protruding over Lexington Avenue far below, the fingers of his other hand pressed down bloodlessly tight against the narrow stripping, he waited, feeling the sick tenseness and terrible excitement building. It grew and swelled toward the moment of action, his nerves tautening. He thought of Clare—just a wordless, yearning thought—and then drew his arm back just a bit more, fist so tight his fingers pained him, and knowing he was going to do it. Then with full power, with every last scrap of strength he could bring to bear, he shot his arm forward toward the glass, and he said "Clare!"

He heard the sound, felt the blow, felt himself falling forward, and his hand closed on the living-room curtains, the shards and fragments of glass showering onto the floor. And then, kneeling there on the ledge, an arm thrust into the room up to the shoulder, he began picking away the protruding slivers and great wedges of glass from the window frame, tossing them in onto the rug. And, as he grasped the edges of the empty window frame and climbed into his home, he was grinning in triumph. **Ⓜ**

He did not lie down on the floor or run through the apartment, as he had promised himself; even in the first few moments it seemed to him natural and normal that he should be where he was. He simply turned to his desk, pulled the crumpled yellow sheet from his pocket, and laid it down where it had been, smoothing it out; then he absently laid a pencil across it to weight it down. He shook his head wonderingly, and turned to walk toward the closet.

There he got out his topcoat and hat and, without waiting to put them on, opened the front door and stepped out, to go find his wife. He turned to pull the door closed and warm air from the hall rushed through the narrow opening again. As he saw the yellow paper, the pencil flying, scooped off the desk and, unimpeded by the glassless window, sail out into the night and out of his life, Tom Benecke burst into laughter and then closed the door behind him. **Ⓝ**

Ⓜ **Literary Focus** Plot How has Tom's problem been resolved?

Ⓝ **Literary Focus** Plot Which earlier event are you reminded of as the paper sails out into the night?

Applying Your Skills

OH **RA.L.10.3** Distinguish how conflicts, parallel plots and subplots affect the pacing of action in literary text. **RA.L.10.2** Analyze the features of setting and their importance in a literary text. *Also covered* **RA.I.10.1; WP.10.9**

Contents of the Dead Man's Pocket

Respond and Think Critically

Reading Focus

Quick Check

1. Why does Tom climb out of his window?

2. How does Tom try to attract attention? Why is he unsuccessful?

Read with a Purpose

3. How does Tom's life change as a result of his ordeal on the ledge?

Reading Skills: Understanding Cause and Effect

4. While reading, you used a chart to record the series of causes and effects that make up the plot. Now, cross out one cause or effect. How does the plot change?

Cause		Effect		Cause
Tom opens the window a few inches.				

Literary Focus

Literary Analysis

5. **Analyze** A conflict is **external** when the character struggles with something outside himself or herself. A conflict is **internal** when the character struggles with inner thoughts and feelings. What conflicts does Tom experience?

6. **Interpret** Based on Tom's actions at the story's end, what can you infer about the story's **theme** (its revelation about life)?

7. **Evaluate** Was the resolution of the story credible? Did you find Tom's actions believable? Why or why not?

8. **Literary Perspectives** The ending of this story reveals a significant shift in Tom's **philosophy,** or stance on the meaning or purpose of life. How is this shift revealed in the contrast between Tom's values at the beginning and his values at the end?

Literary Skills: Plot

9. **Analyze** Even though the events of the story are told in chronological order, Tom and the reader are both shocked to discover on page 29 that only eight minutes have passed. How does Finney make time seem to move slowly?

Literary Skills Review: Setting

10. **Compare and Contrast** A story's **setting** is the time and place in which the story occurs. How does Finney contrast the two settings of the ledge and the apartment?

Writing Focus

Think as a Reader/Writer

Use It in Your Writing Finney's vivid images help us share Tom's ordeal. Write a brief description of a person in a threatening situation. Use images to help your reader see, hear, feel, taste, and smell what your character experiences.

What Do You Think Now

What ordinary experiences can force a person to rethink his or her values and priorities?

Applying Your Skills

Contents of the Dead Man's Pocket

Vocabulary Development

Vocabulary Check

Match each of the following Vocabulary words with its definition.

1. **projection**   a. bounced back
2. **exhalation**   b. almost unnoticeably
3. **imperceptibly** c. something that juts out from a surface
4. **rebounded**   d. in a way not relating to the point or situation
5. **irrelevantly**   e. something breathed out

Vocabulary Skills: Prefixes

A **prefix** is a letter or group of letters placed at the beginning of a word to change its meaning. Changing the meaning of a word can be as simple as changing its prefix. For example, the word *like* can be changed to *dislike* by adding the prefix *dis–*.

Knowing the meaning of prefixes can help you figure out the meanings of some words that might be unfamiliar to you.

The chart below contains some common prefixes and their meanings:

Latin Prefix	Meaning	Example
in–, il–, im–, ir–	no, not; in, into, on	inoperable
inter–	between, among; together	international
pro–	forward; defending	promote
re–	again	reexamine
Greek Prefix	**Meaning**	**Example**
hyper–	above; more than normal	hyperactive
micro–	small	microorganism
mono–	one	monologue
ex–	away from; out	exhale

Your Turn

Using your knowledge of prefixes, answer the following questions.

1. Does a **projection** jut forward or backward?
2. What word is the opposite of **exhale?**
3. What word is the opposite of **imperceptibly?**
4. What does a ball do if it **rebounds** from a basket?
5. How does the meaning of **irrelevantly** change when you remove the prefix?

Language Coach

Prefixes Work with a partner or team to list other example words for each of the prefixes in the chart on this page.

Academic Vocabulary

Write About . . .
Use Academic Vocabulary to answer the following questions.

1. What aspects of the story tell you it is set in a different time period? What details of the story would have to be updated to set it in today's modern world?
2. Describe ways in which Finney creates a credible situation and main character.

OH **RA.L.10.3** Distinguish how conflicts, parallel plots and subplots affect the pacing of action in literary text. *Also covered* **RA.I.10.1; VO.10.5; VO.10.6; WA.10.2; WP.10.15; C.10.9**

Grammar Link

Using Personal Pronouns

Personal pronouns are words used in place of nouns or other pronouns. Because personal pronouns have two forms, or cases, you need to choose the correct form to fit each situation. Look at the following table for the two cases:

Nominative Case	I, you, he, she, it, we, they
Objective Case	me, you, him, her, it, us, them

Use a **nominative-case pronoun** if the pronoun functions as a subject or predicate nominative.

He and **I** read "Contents of the Dead Man's Pocket." *He* and *I* carry out the action; therefore *He* and *I* are subjects.

The main characters are **he** and his wife. *He* identifies the subject after a linking verb; therefore *he* is a predicate nominative.

Use an **objective-case pronoun** if the pronoun functions as a direct object, an indirect object, or the object of a preposition.

Tom went to see **her**. *Her* is a direct object.

The narrator tells **us** the story. *Us* is an indirect object.

The window broke for **him**. *Him* is the object of a preposition.

Your Turn

Writing Applications Rewrite the following paragraph with the correct personal pronouns.

> Julio told Carrie and I about a fabulous trapeze act he saw at the circus. Mary and him went to the circus last night and were astonished by what they saw. They described to the teacher and we the trapeze artists' tricks. Then him and Mary gave Carrie and I two discount tickets to the circus.

CHOICES

As you respond to the Choices, use the **Academic Vocabulary** words as appropriate: aspects, credible, tension, and evaluation.

REVIEW
Analyze Plot and Setting

Timed └Writing Re-read the story, looking for the ways in which Jack Finney uses plot and setting to create tension. Write a brief essay in which you analyze Finney's techniques. Identify specific details from the story to support your ideas.

CONNECT
Retell a Story

Listening and Speaking With a partner, examine the cause-and-effect relationships in "Contents of the Dead Man's Pocket" by taking turns retelling scenes to each other. Identify passages in which multiple causes have single effects, and single causes have multiple effects. Discuss whether you think the plot events create a credible story.

EXTEND
Write the Sequel

By the end of the story, Tom's frightening experience has led him to rethink his values. Write a brief sequel to the story that tells what happens after Tom closes the door behind him. Does he tell his wife what happened on the ledge? How will Clare respond to his sudden appearance at the movie? In your sequel, strive to stay true to the story's characters.

Learn It Online
There's more to this story than meets the eye. Expand your view with these Internet links:

go.hrw.com   L10-35   **Go**

THE
Leap

by **Louise Erdrich**

What Do You Think?

When can taking risks help you do the right thing?

⏱ QuickWrite

What sacrifices do we make for the people we care about? Has anyone ever taken a risk or given up something to help you? Have you ever taken a risk to help someone else? Write a few sentences about that experience.

Circus Heights (2002)
by Carolyn Hubbard-Ford.
Private Collection.

Reader/Writer Notebook

Use your **RWN** to complete the activities for this selection.

OH **RA.L.10.6** Explain how literary techniques, including foreshadowing and flashback, are used to shape the plot of a literary text. **RP.10.1** Apply reading comprehension strategies, including making predictions, comparing and contrasting, recalling and summarizing and making inferences and drawing conclusions.

Literary Focus

Plot: Flashback A **flashback** interrupts the chronological sequence of events in a story to show events that happened earlier. Flashbacks can provide insight into characters' lives, minds, and actions. In "The Leap," Erdrich uses flashbacks to create a fluid, circular style of storytelling, in which what seems to be the beginning of one story is really the end of another.

Reading Focus

Making Predictions Part of the pleasure in reading a story comes from **making predictions,** or guessing what will happen next. You make predictions based on clues in the story that seem to **foreshadow,** or hint at, future events. You can also use what you know about how people behave—and about storytelling. In "The Leap," flashbacks reveal important events in the past. The way those events influence the present is often surprising. Things don't always turn out exactly as you (or the characters) might have predicted.

Into Action As you read, note the details and events that help you predict what is going to happen next. Use a chart like the one below.

Detail / Event	My Prediction
Mother was part of a blindfold trapeze act.	The story might be about a circus.

Writing Focus

Think as a Reader/Writer

Find It in Your Reading Storytellers can jump ahead to the future, as well as back to the past. Some writers start a new chapter to separate time periods. Some start a new paragraph or use italic type. As you read, jot down in your *Reader/Writer Notebook* the words that tell you that a jump backward or forward has taken place.

Vocabulary

generate (JEHN uhr ayt) *v.:* cause to come into being. *The circus owners worried that weather conditions might generate a storm.*

extricating (EHKS truh kayt ihng) *v.* used as *n:* releasing or disentangling from something. *In extricating Anna from the wreckage of the tent, the rescuer broke Anna's arm.*

constricting (kuhn STRIHKT ihng) *v.* used as *adj.:* limiting; confining. *The narrator's father wanted to travel because he found the town constricting.*

complied (kuhm PLYD) *v.:* did as requested. *The man complied with Anna's request to put the broken ladder against the tree.*

tentative (TEHN tuh tihv) *adj.:* uncertain; hesitant. *Even though the house was on fire, Anna's tap on her child's bedroom window was tentative.*

Language Coach

Antonyms An **antonym** is a word that has the opposite or nearly opposite meaning of another word. It is not the same as a **synonym,** which has the same meaning as another word. Which of the words above is an antonym for *generate?* for *tentative?*

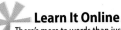 **Learn It Online**
There's more to words than just definitions. Get the whole story at:

go.hrw.com | L10-37 | **Go**

Louise Erdrich
(1954–   )

National Book Award WINNER

Growing Up with Stories

When she was a child, Louise Erdrich was surrounded by a family of storytellers. Her mother was French Chippewa, her father was German American, and her grandfather was the tribal chairman at Turtle Mountain Reservation in North Dakota. Erdrich began telling stories early. Her father paid her a nickel for every story she wrote, and her mother "published" the stories with construction-paper covers.

Mythical Settings

The work that first drew Erdrich critical acclaim was *Love Medicine,* a collection of interrelated stories spanning several generations. This bestseller was followed by two other novels, *The Beet Queen* and *Tracks,* which tell the stories of the same Chippewa families. Erdrich has been compared with the great Southern writer William Faulkner. Both writers created mythical territories and characters that keep appearing and reappearing in stories that readers find hard to put down.

> "There's something particularly strong about a *told* story. You've got your listener right there, you've got to keep him hooked—or her."

Think About the Writer

Louise Erdrich's family valued storytelling. Why do we need stories?

Learn It Online

Learn more about Erdrich at:

go.hrw.com L10-38 Go

Build Background

Erdrich's story is about a woman who long ago performed with her husband in a circus trapeze act. Circuses like the one in the story once traveled all over America and Europe. The circus tents were set up in open areas of towns and cities. The woman in the story is now blind from cataracts, a condition in which the lens of the eye thickens and that, if not treated, will cause blindness.

Preview the Selection

Anna Avalon, the narrator's mother and a skilled trapeze artist in her day, performed a death-defying circus act with her first husband, **Harold Avalon.** The narrator, in contrast to her daring mother, has spent much of her time "where the land is flat." She has recently returned home to New Hampshire to take care of her mother in her old age.

THE Leap

by **Louise Erdrich**

My mother is the surviving half of a blindfold trapeze act, not a fact I think about much even now that she is sightless, the result of encroaching[1] and stubborn cataracts. She walks slowly through her house here in New Hampshire, lightly touching her way along walls and running her hands over knick-knacks, books, the drift of a grown child's belongings and castoffs. She has never upset an object or as much as brushed a magazine onto the floor. She has never lost her balance or bumped into a closet door left carelessly open.

It has occurred to me that the catlike precision of her movements in old age might be the result of her early training, but she shows so little of the drama or flair one might expect from a performer that I tend to forget the Flying Avalons. She has kept no sequined costume, no photographs, no fliers or posters from that part of her youth. I would, in fact, tend to think that all memory of double somersaults and heart-stopping catches had left her arms and legs were it not for the fact that sometimes, as I sit sewing in the room of the rebuilt house in which I slept as a child, I hear the crackle, catch a whiff of smoke from the stove downstairs, and suddenly the room goes dark, the stitches burn beneath my fingers, and I am sewing with a needle of hot silver, a thread of fire. Ⓐ

I owe her my existence three times. The first was when she saved herself. In the town square a replica tent pole, cracked and splintered, now stands cast in concrete. It commemorates the disaster that put our town smack on the front page of the Boston and New York tabloids. It is from those old newspapers, now historical records, that I get my information. Not from my mother, Anna of the Flying Avalons, nor from any of her in-laws, nor certainly from the other half of her particular act, Harold Avalon, her first husband. In one news account it says, "The day was mildly overcast, but nothing in the air or temperature gave any hint of the sudden force with which the deadly gale would strike." Ⓑ

I have lived in the West, where you can see the weather coming for miles, and it is true that out here we are at something of a disadvantage. When extremes of temperature collide, a hot and cold front, winds generate instantaneously behind a hill and crash upon you without warning. That, I think, was the likely situation on that day in June. People probably commented on the pleasant air, grateful that no hot sun beat upon the striped tent that stretched over the

---

1. **encroaching** (ehn KROHCH ihng): advancing.

Ⓐ **Reading Focus** Making Predictions What do you predict might happen in this story based on the first two paragraphs?

Ⓑ **Literary Focus** Plot How does the newspaper account use foreshadowing?

Vocabulary **generate** (JEHN uhr ayt) *v.*: cause to come into being.

entire center green. They bought their tickets and surrendered them in anticipation. They sat. They ate caramelized popcorn and roasted peanuts. There was time, before the storm, for three acts. The White Arabians of Ali-Khazar rose on their hind legs and waltzed. The Mysterious Bernie folded himself into a painted cracker tin, and the Lady of the Mists made herself appear and disappear in surprising places. As the clouds gathered outside, unnoticed, the ringmaster cracked his whip, shouted his introduction, and pointed to the ceiling of the tent, where the Flying Avalons were perched.

They loved to drop gracefully from nowhere, like two sparkling birds, and blow kisses as they threw off their plumed helmets and high-collared capes. They laughed and flirted openly as they beat their way up again on the trapeze bars. In the final vignette[2] of their act, they actually would kiss in midair, pausing, almost hovering as they swooped past one another. On the ground, between bows, Harry Avalon would skip quickly to the front rows and point out the smear of my mother's lipstick, just off the edge of his mouth. They made a romantic pair all right, especially in the blindfold sequence.

That afternoon, as the anticipation increased, as Mr. and Mrs. Avalon tied sparkling strips of cloth onto each other's face and as they puckered their lips in mock kisses—lips destined "never again to meet," as one long breathless article put it—the wind rose, miles off, wrapped itself into a cone, and howled. There came a rumble of electrical energy, drowned out by the sudden roll of drums. One detail not mentioned by the press, perhaps unknown—Anna was pregnant at the time,

seven months and hardly showing, her stomach muscles were that strong. It seems incredible that she would work high above the ground when any fall could be so dangerous, but the explanation—I know from watching her go blind—is that my mother lives comfortably in extreme elements. She is one with the constant dark now, just as the air was her home, familiar to her, safe, before the storm that afternoon. **Ⓒ**

From opposite ends of the tent they waved, blind and smiling, to the crowd below. The ringmaster removed his hat and called for silence, so that the two above could concentrate. They rubbed their hands in chalky powder, then Harry launched himself and swung, once, twice, in huge calibrated[3] beats across space. He hung from his knees and on the third swing stretched wide his arms, held his hands out to receive his pregnant wife as she dove from her shining bar.

It was while the two were in midair, their hands about to meet, that lightning struck the main pole and sizzled down the guy wires, filling the air with a blue radiance that Harry Avalon must certainly have seen through the cloth of his blindfold as the tent buckled and the edifice toppled him forward, the swing continuing and not returning in its sweep, and Harry going down, down into the crowd with his last thought, perhaps, just a prickle of surprise at his empty hands. **Ⓓ**

My mother once said that I'd be amazed at how many things a person can do within the act of falling. Perhaps, at the time, she was teaching me to dive off a board at the town pool, for I associated the idea with midair somersaults. But I also think she meant that even in that

---

2. **vignette** (vihn YEHT): short, memorable scene.

3. **calibrated** (KAL uh brayt ihd): measured.

Ⓒ **Literary Focus** Flashback To what time and place has the narrator flashed back?

Ⓓ **Reading Focus** Making Predictions What do you think will happen to Anna?

awful doomed second one could think, for she certainly did. When her hands did not meet her husband's, my mother tore her blindfold away. As he swept past her on the wrong side, she could have grasped his ankle, the toe end of his tights, and gone down clutching him. Instead, she changed direction. Her body twisted toward a heavy wire and she managed to hang on to the braided metal, still hot from the lightning strike. Her palms were burned so terribly that once healed they bore no lines, only the blank scar tissue of a quieter future. She was lowered, gently, to the sawdust ring just underneath the dome of the canvas roof, which did not entirely settle but was held up on one end and jabbed through, torn, and still on fire in places from the giant spark, though rain and men's jackets soon put that out.

Three people died, but except for her hands my mother was not seriously harmed until an overeager rescuer broke her arm in extricating her and also, in the process, collapsed a portion of the tent bearing a huge buckle that knocked her unconscious. She was taken to the town hospital, and there she must have hemorrhaged,[4] for they kept her, confined to her bed, a month and a half before her baby was born without life.

Harry Avalon had wanted to be buried in the circus cemetery next to the original Avalon, his uncle, so she sent him back with his brothers. The child, however, is buried around the corner, beyond this house and just down the highway. Sometimes I used to walk there just

> When her hands did not meet her husband's, my mother tore her blindfold away.

to sit. She was a girl, but I rarely thought of her as a sister or even as a separate person really. I suppose you could call it the egocentrism[5] of a child, of all young children, but I considered her a less finished version of myself. **Ⓔ**

When the snow falls, throwing shadows among the stones, I can easily pick her out from the road, for it is bigger than the others and in the shape of a lamb at rest, its legs curled beneath. The carved lamb looms larger as the years pass, though it is probably only my eyes, the vision shifting, as what is close to me blurs and distances sharpen. In odd moments, I think it is the edge drawing near, the edge of everything, the unseen horizon we do not really speak of in the eastern woods. And it also seems to me, although this is probably an idle fantasy, that the statue is growing more sharply etched, as if, instead of weathering itself into a porous mass, it is hardening on the hillside with each snowfall, perfecting itself.

It was during her confinement in the hospital that my mother met my father. He was called in to look at the set of her arm, which was complicated. He stayed, sitting at her bedside, for he was something of an armchair traveler and had spent his war quietly, at an air force training grounds, where he became a specialist in arms and legs broken during parachute training exercises. Anna Avalon had been to many of the places he longed to visit—Venice, Rome, Mexico, all through France and Spain. She had no family of her own and was taken in by

---

4. **hemorrhaged** (HEHM uh rihjd): lost a great deal of blood.

5. **egocentrism** (ee goh SEHN trihz uhm): self-centeredness.

Vocabulary **extricating** (EHKS truh kayt ihng) *v.* used as *n.*: releasing or disentangling from something.

Ⓔ **Literary Focus** Flashback What important details have you learned in this long flashback?

the Avalons, trained to perform from a very young age. They toured Europe before the war, then based themselves in New York. She was illiterate.

It was in the hospital that she finally learned to read and write, as a way of overcoming the boredom and depression of those weeks, and it was my father who insisted on teaching her. In return for stories of her adventures, he graded her first exercises. He bought her her first book, and over her bold letters, which the pale guides of the penmanship pads could not contain, they fell in love.

I wonder if my father calculated the exchange he offered: one form of flight for another. For after that, and for as long as I can remember, my mother has never been without a book. Until now, that is, and it remains the greatest difficulty of her blindness. Since my father's recent death, there is no one to read to her, which is why I returned, in fact, from my failed life where the land is flat. I came home to read to my mother, to read out loud, to read long into the dark if I must, to read all night. **F**

Once my father and mother married, they moved onto the old farm he had inherited but didn't care much for. Though he'd been thinking of moving to a larger city, he settled down and broadened his practice in this valley. It still seems odd to me, when they could have gone anywhere else, that they chose to stay in the town where the disaster had occurred, and which my father in the first place had found so constricting. It was my mother who insisted upon it, after her child did not survive. And then, too, she loved the sagging farmhouse with its scrap of what was left of a vast acreage of woods and hidden hayfields that stretched to the game park.

I owe my existence, the second time then, to the two of them and the hospital that brought them together. That is the debt we take for granted since none of us asks for life. It is only once we have it that we hang on so dearly.

I was seven the year the house caught fire, probably from standing ash. It can rekindle, and my father, forgetful around the house and perpetually exhausted from night hours on call, often emptied what he thought were ashes from cold stoves into wooden or cardboard containers. The fire could have started from a flaming box, or perhaps a buildup of creosote[6] inside the chimney was the culprit. It started right around the stove, and the heart of the house was gutted. The baby sitter, fallen asleep in my father's den on the first floor, woke to find the stairway to my upstairs room cut off by flames. She used the phone, then ran outside to stand beneath my window. **G**

When my parents arrived, the town volunteers had drawn water from the fire pond and were spraying the outside of the house, preparing to go inside after me, not knowing at the time that there was only one staircase and that it was lost. On the other side of the house, the superannuated[7] extension ladder broke in half. Perhaps the clatter of it falling against the walls woke me, for I'd been asleep up to that point.

As soon as I awakened, in the small room that I now use for sewing, I smelled the smoke.

---

6. **creosote** (KREE uh soht): oily deposit of tar, a byproduct of burning wood.
7. **superannuated** (soo puhr AN yoo ay tihd): too old or worn-out to be of service.

F **Literary Focus** Plot Why does the narrator return to her childhood home?

G **Literary Focus** Plot How does the narrator explain the cause of the fire?

Vocabulary **constricting** (kuhn STRIHKT ihng) v. used as *adj.*: limiting; confining.

Burning House (2005) by Gregory Lomasveya. Collection of the artist.

Analyzing Visuals

Viewing and Interpreting
In what ways does this painting evoke the mood of the story? Explain.

I followed things by the letter then, was good at memorizing instructions, and so I did exactly what was taught in the second-grade home fire drill. I got up, I touched the back of my door before opening it. Finding it hot, I left it closed and stuffed my rolled-up rug beneath the crack. I did not hide under my bed or crawl into my closet. I put on my flannel robe, and then I sat down to wait.

Outside, my mother stood below my dark window and saw clearly that there was no rescue. Flames had pierced one side wall, and the glare of the fire lighted the massive limbs and trunk of the vigorous old elm that had probably been planted the year the house was built, a hundred years ago at least. No leaf touched the wall, and just one thin branch scraped the roof. From below, it looked as though even a squirrel would have had trouble jumping from the tree onto the house, for the breadth of that small branch was no bigger than my mother's wrist.

Standing there, beside Father, who was preparing to rush back around to the front of the house, my mother asked him to unzip her dress. When he wouldn't be bothered, she made

H **Reading Focus** **Making Predictions** How do you think the narrator will escape?

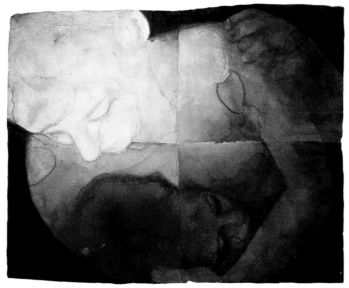

Wound (2004) by Graham Dean. Courtesy the artist and Waterhouse & Dodd, London.

him understand. He couldn't make his hands work, so she finally tore it off and stood there in her pearls and stockings. She directed one of the men to lean the broken half of the extension ladder up against the trunk of the tree. In surprise, he complied. She ascended. She vanished. Then she could be seen among the leafless branches of late November as she made her way up and, along her stomach, inched the length of a bough that curved above the branch that brushed the roof.

Once there, swaying, she stood and balanced. There were plenty of people in the crowd and many who still remember, or think they do, my mother's leap through the ice-dark air toward that thinnest extension, and how she broke the branch falling so that it cracked in her hands, cracked louder than the flames as she vaulted with it toward the edge of the roof, and how it hurtled down end over end without her, and their eyes went up, again, to see where she had flown.

I didn't see her leap through air, only heard the sudden thump and looked out my window. She was hanging by the backs of her heels from the new gutter we had put in that year, and she was smiling. I was not surprised to see her, she was so matter-of-fact. She tapped on the window. I remember how she did it, too. It was the friendliest tap, a bit tentative, as if she was afraid she had arrived too early at a friend's house. Then she gestured at the latch, and when I opened the window she told me to raise it wider and prop it up with the stick so it wouldn't crush her fingers. She swung down, caught the ledge, and crawled through the opening. Once she was in my room, I realized she had on only underclothing, a bra of the heavy stitched cotton women used to wear and step-in, lace-trimmed drawers. I remember feeling lightheaded, of course, terribly relieved, and then embarrassed for her to be seen by the crowd undressed.

I was still embarrassed as we flew out the window, toward earth, me in her lap, her toes pointed as we skimmed toward the painted target of the firefighter's net.

I know that she's right. I knew it even then. As you fall, there is time to think. Curled as I was, against her stomach, I was not startled by the cries of the crowd or the looming faces. The wind roared and beat its hot breath at our back, and flames whistled. I slowly wondered what would happen if we missed the circle or bounced out of it. Then I wrapped my hands around my mother's hands. I felt the brush of her lips and heard the beat of her heart in my ears, loud as thunder, long as the roll of drums. **①**

Vocabulary **complied** (kuhm PLYD) *v.:* did as requested.
tentative (TEHN tuh tihv) *adj.:* uncertain; hesitant.

① **Literary Focus** **Plot** How do the details in this paragraph relate to the beginning of the story?

Applying Your Skills

RA.L.10.6 Explain how literary techniques, including foreshadowing and flashback, are used to shape the plot of a literary text. *Also covered* **RP.10.1; VO.10.3; WA.10.1.c; WP.10.9**

The Leap

Respond and Think Critically

Reading Focus

Quick Check

1. Why has the narrator returned East?

2. The narrator owes her mother her existence "three times." What are those three times?

Read with a Purpose

3. Describe the leaps in this story. Which leaps are literal? Which are figurative?

Reading Skills: Making Predictions

4. Add two columns to your chart. In the third column, note the accuracy of your predictions. If you were inaccurate, note the actual event.

Detail/ Event	Prediction	Accuracy	What Actually Happened
blindfold trapeze act	story might be about a circus	incorrect	story is about trapeze artist who is narrator's mother

5. Find examples of foreshadowing in the story. Did these clues help you make predictions about the outcome? Explain your answer.

✓ Vocabulary Check

Answer the following questions about the Vocabulary words for this story.

6. When you **generate** a plan, are you making or rejecting one?

7. Does **extricating** mean "disentangling" or "tangling"?

8. If a job is **constricting,** is it limited or limitless?

9. Does **complied** mean "obeyed" or "disobeyed"?

10. If a date is **tentative,** is it certain or uncertain?

Literary Focus

Literary Analysis

11. **Analyze** Re-read the second paragraph of the story, in which the narrator describes sewing in her room. What is really happening here?

12. **Evaluate** Do you think the story of the mother's rescue is credible? Explain.

Literary Skills: Plot—Flashback

13. **Explain** Locate places in which the story flashes back and forward. Plot the main events in chronological order on a time line.

Literary Skills Review: Suspense

14. **Evaluate** We describe **suspense** as the anxiety the reader feels about what is going to happen next. What parts of the story are most suspenseful? How do flashback and foreshadowing contribute to the suspense? Give examples.

Writing Focus

Think as a Reader/Writer

Use It in Your Writing In two paragraphs, relate a past experience that affected your life or the life of someone you know. Open in the present, and then flash back to the past. How will you show the shift in time?

What Do You Think Now Would most people take risks to save a child? How would you have responded to the narrator's situation?

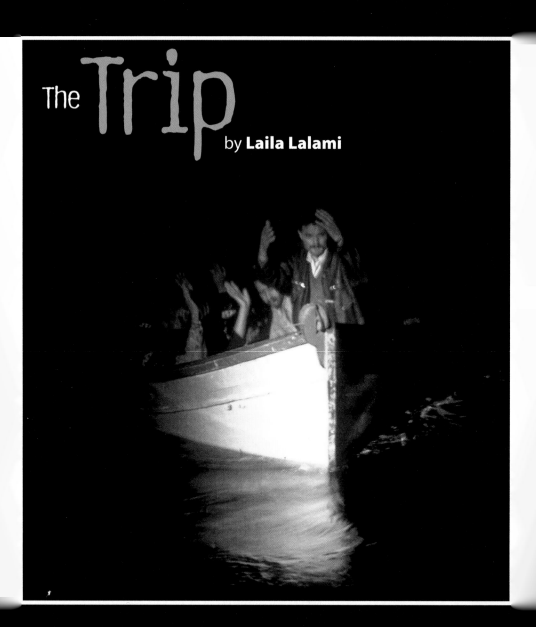

The Trip

by **Laila Lalami**

ʔhat Do You hink?

Why are dangerous journeys sometimes necessary?

QuickTalk

With a classmate, discuss a movie or a television show in whic character undertook a dangerous journey. What compelled th acter to take the risk? How did the journey change his or her l

Reader/Writer Notebook

Use your **RWN** to complete the activities for this selection.

OH **RA.L.10.2** Analyze the features of setting and their importance in a literary text. **RP.10.1** Apply reading comprehension strategies, including making predictions, comparing and contrasting, recalling and summarizing and making inferences and drawing conclusions.

Literary Focus

Setting and Mood The **setting** of a story establishes the time and place of the action. Writers can also use setting to create a **mood,** or atmosphere—a subtle emotional overtone that can strongly affect our feelings. For example, settings can be used to suggest freedom, community, and peace. Settings can also be used to create an atmosphere of danger or anxiety.

Reading Focus

Visualizing Good writers use precise details to help you envision a story's characters and settings. **Visualizing**, or picturing those details as you read, can help you experience a story more fully.

Into Action As you read "The Trip," record descriptive language that helps you visualize the setting. Use a chart like the one below.

Setting	Descriptive Language
Strait of Gibraltar at night	The waves are inky black . . . glistening white under the moon . . . tombstones in a dark cemetery.

Writing Focus

Think as a Reader/Writer

Find It in Your Reading As you read, notice how Lalami uses descriptive language to create a vivid setting and mood. In your *Reader/Writer Notebook,* jot down words or phrases that catch your attention.

TechFocus As you read, think about how a film director might handle aspects of the story's setting and mood. For example, would the film begin with silence or with the sound of water lapping at the sides of the boat?

Vocabulary

pondered (PAHN duhrd) *v.:* thought over; considered carefully. *Murad pondered his decision.*

destinies (DEHS tuh neez) *n.:* what becomes of people or things in the end; fates. *The passengers' destinies were unknown.*

exudes (ehg ZOODZ) *v.:* seems to radiate; oozes. *Murad believes that Aziz exudes confidence and energy.*

putrid (PYOO trihd) *adj.:* foul; decaying or rotten. *The boat had a putrid stench of mold and dead fish.*

prospects (PRAHS pehkts) *n.:* things expected or looked forward to; outlook for the future. *The prospects of a job and shelter were enough to lure him from home.*

Language Coach

Synonyms A **synonym** is a word that has the same or nearly the same meaning as another word. Study the definition for *putrid,* and locate a synonym for that word. What other synonyms for the Vocabulary words can you find?

Laila Lalami
(1968–   )

Moorish Girl

Laila Lalami was born in Morocco and grew up speaking Arabic and French. Now she writes only in English. Her Web site, moorishgirl.com, focuses on Arab culture and literature. In 2006, Lalami received a Fulbright Fellowship. She is currently Assistant Professor of Creative Writing at University of California Riverside.

Hope and Other Dangerous Pursuits

While living in the United States, Lalami came across a report about fifteen Moroccan immigrants who drowned while crossing the Strait of Gibraltar. The victims were *harragas,* poor people who paid a lot of money to enter Spain illegally in hope of a better life. Hungry for news of her native culture, she began research on illegal immigration. "It [the research] didn't tell me what I wanted to know. . . . I thought the answers to my questions might lie in creating a story about a group of *harragas.*" The result was *Hope and Other Dangerous Pursuits* (2005), a collection of intertwined stories.

"There was something in [these] stories . . . that seemed completely familiar to me. Back home, I never had to look very hard or very far to find the kind of misfortune that drives people to desperate acts."

Think About the Writer How do you think Lalami's background influences her choice of subject matter?

Build Background

Morocco is separated from Spain by a narrow waterway called the Strait of Gibraltar. Europe has long been a magnet for Moroccans and other African people who hope to make a better life for themselves and their families. Illegal immigrants cross the strait in large numbers, often in crowded, leaky boats, led by guides who often cheat them or leave them at risk of being caught—or worse.

Preview the Selection

Murad, the main character of this story, is a young man with a college education who is struggling to find work. He attempts to leave his native Morocco for a better life in Spain.

The Trip

by **Laila Lalami**

Fourteen kilometers. Murad has pondered that number hundreds of times in the last year, trying to decide whether the risk was worth it. Some days he told himself that the distance was nothing, a brief inconvenience, that the crossing would take as little as thirty minutes if the weather was good. He spent hours thinking about what he would do once he was on the other side, imagining the job, the car, the house. Other days he could think only about the coast guards, the ice-cold water, the money he'd have to borrow, and he wondered how fourteen kilometers could separate not just two countries but two universes.

Tonight the sea appears calm, with only a slight wind now and then. The captain has ordered all the lights turned off, but with the moon up and the sky clear, Murad can still see around him. The six-meter Zodiac inflatable[1] is meant to accommodate eight people. Thirty huddle in it now, men, women, and children, all with the anxious look of those whose destinies

are in the hands of others—the captain, the coast guards, God.

Murad has three layers on: undershirt, turtleneck, and jacket; below, a pair of thermal underwear, jeans, and sneakers. With only three hours' notice, he didn't have time to get waterproof pants. He touches a button on his watch, a Rolex knockoff he bought from a street vendor in Tangier,[2] and the display lights up: 3:15 A.M. He scratches at the residue the metal bracelet leaves on his wrist, then pulls his sleeve down to cover the timepiece. Looking around him, he can't help but wonder how much Captain Rahal and his gang stand to make. If the other passengers paid as much as Murad did, the take is almost 600,000 dirhams, enough for an apartment or a small house in a Moroccan beach town like Asilah or Cabo Negro.

He looks at the Spanish coastline, closer with every breath. The waves are inky black, except for hints of foam here and there, glisten-

---

1. **Zodiac inflatable:** a small inflatable boat that has a motor.

2. **Tangier** (tan JIHR): a city in northern Morocco, on the Strait of Gibraltar.

Vocabulary **pondered** (PAHN duhrd) *v.*: thought over; considered carefully.
destinies (DEHS tuh neez) *n.*: what becomes of people or things in the end; fates.

(A) Literary Focus Setting and Mood How would you describe the mood in the first part of the story? What details of the setting contribute to this mood?

ing white under the moon, like tombstones in a dark cemetery. Murad can make out the town where they're headed. Tarifa. The mainland point of the Moorish[3] invasion in 711. Murad used to regale tourists with anecdotes about how Tariq Ibn Ziyad had led a powerful Moor army across the Straits and, upon landing in Gibraltar, ordered all the boats burned. He'd told his soldiers that they could march forth and defeat the enemy or turn back and die a coward's death. The men had followed their general, toppled the Visigoths, and established an empire that ruled over Spain for more than seven hundred years. Little did they know that we'd be back, Murad thinks. Only instead of a fleet, here we are in an inflatable boat—not just Moors, but a motley mix of people from the ex-colonies, without guns or armor, without a charismatic leader.

It's worth it, though, Murad tells himself. Some time on this flimsy boat and then a job. It will be hard at first. He'll work in the fields like everyone else, but he'll look for something bet-

ter. He isn't like the others—he has a plan. He doesn't want to break his back for the *spagnol,* spend the rest of his life picking their oranges and tomatoes. He'll find a real job, where he can use his training. He has a degree in English and, in addition, he speaks Spanish fluently, unlike some of the harraga.[4]

His leg goes numb. He moves his ankle around. To his left, the girl (he thinks her name is Faten) shifts slightly, so that her thigh no longer presses against his. She looks eighteen, nineteen maybe. "My leg was asleep," he whispers. Faten nods to acknowledge him but doesn't look at him. She pulls her black cardigan tight around her chest and stares down at her shoes. He doesn't understand why she's wearing a hijab scarf on her hair for a trip like this. Does she imagine she can walk down the street in Tarifa in a headscarf without attracting attention? She'll get caught, he thinks.

Back on the beach, while they all were waiting for Rahal to get ready, Faten sat alone, away from everyone else, as though she were sulking.

---

3. **Moorish** (MUR ihsh): relating to the Moors, a population of Muslim people from northwestern Africa.

4. **harraga:** Moroccan slang term for people fleeing for Spain.

She was the last one to climb into the boat, and Murad had to move to make room for her. He couldn't understand her reluctance. It didn't seem possible to him that she would have paid so much money and not been eager to leave when the moment came.

Across from Murad is Aziz. He's tall and lanky and he sits hunched over to fit in the narrow space allotted to him. This is his second attempt at crossing the Strait of Gibraltar. He told Murad that he'd haggled with Rahal over the price of the trip, argued that, as a repeat customer, he should get a deal. Murad tried to bargain, too, but in the end he still had to borrow almost 20,000 dirhams from one of his uncles, and the loan is on his mind again. He'll pay his uncle back as soon as he can get a job.

Aziz asks for a sip of water. Murad hands over his bottle of Sidi Harazem and watches him take a swig. When he gets the bottle back, he offers the last bit to Faten, but she shakes her head. Murad was told he should keep his body hydrated, so he's been drinking water all day. He feels a sudden urge to urinate and leans forward to contain it.

Next to Aziz is a middle-aged man with greasy hair and a large scar across his cheek, like Al Pacino in *Scarface.* He wears jeans and a short-sleeved shirt. Murad heard him tell someone that he was a tennis instructor. His arms are muscular, his biceps bulging, but the energy he exudes is rough, like that of a man used to trouble with the law. Murad notices that Scarface has been staring at the little girl sitting next to him. She seems to be about ten years old, but the expression on her face is that of an older child. Her eyes, shiny under the moonlight, take up most of her face. Scarface asks her name. "Mouna," she says. He reaches into his

pocket and offers her chewing gum, but the girl quickly shakes her head. **Ⓑ**

Her mother, Halima, asked Murad the time before they got on the boat, as though she had a schedule to keep. She gives Scarface a dark, forbidding look, wraps one arm around her daughter and the other around her two boys, seated to her right. Halima's gaze is direct, not shifty like Faten's. She has an aura of quiet determination about her, and it stirs feelings of respect in Murad, even though he thinks her irresponsible, or at the very least foolish, for risking her children's lives on a trip like this.

On Aziz's right is a slender African woman, her cornrows tied in a loose ponytail. While they were waiting on the beach to depart, she peeled an orange and offered Murad half. She said she was Guinean. She cradles her body with her arms and rocks gently back and forth. Rahal barks at her to stop. She looks up, tries to stay immobile, and then throws up on Faten's boots. Faten cries out at the sight of her sullied shoes.

"Shut up," Rahal snaps.

The Guinean woman whispers an apology in French. Faten waves her hand, says that it's okay, says she understands. Soon the little boat reeks of vomit. Murad tucks his nose inside his turtleneck. It smells of soap and mint and it keeps out the stench, but within minutes the putrid smell penetrates the shield anyway. Now Halima sits up and exhales loudly, her children still huddling next to her. Rahal glares at her, tells her to hunch down to keep the boat balanced.

"Leave her alone," Murad says.

Halima turns to him and smiles for the first time. He wonders what her plans are, whether she's meeting a husband or a brother there or

---

Vocabulary **exudes** (ehg ZOODZ) *v.*: seems to radiate; oozes.
putrid (PYOO trihd) *adj.*: foul; decaying or rotten.

Ⓑ **Reading Focus** Visualizing What details in this paragraph help you visualize the man and the girl?

if she'll end up cleaning houses or working in the fields. He thinks about some of the illegals who, instead of going on a boat, try to sneak in on vegetable trucks headed from Morocco to Spain. Last year the Guardia Civil[5] intercepted a tomato truck in Algeciras and found the bodies of three illegals, dead from asphyxiation,[6] lying on the crates. At least on a boat there is no chance of that happening. He tries to think of something else, something to chase away the memory of the picture he saw in the paper.

The outboard motor idles. In the sudden silence, everyone turns to look at Rahal, collectively holding their breath. He pulls the starter cable a few times, but nothing happens.

"What's wrong?" Faten asks, her voice laden with anxiety.

Rahal doesn't answer.

"Try again," Halima says.

Rahal yanks at the cable.

"This trip is cursed," Faten whispers. Everyone hears her.

Rahal bangs the motor with his hand. Faten recites a verse from the second sura of the Qur'an: "'God, there is no God but Him, the Alive, the Eternal. Neither slumber nor sleep overtaketh Him—'"

"Quiet," Scarface yells. "We need some quiet to think." Looking at the captain, he asks, "Is it the spark plug?"

"I don't know. I don't think so," says Rahal.

Faten continues to pray, this time more quietly, her lips moving fast. "'Unto Him belongeth all that is in the heavens and the earth . . .'"

Rahal yanks at the cable again.

Aziz calls out, "Wait, let me see." He gets on all fours, over the vomit, and moves slowly to keep the boat stable.

Faten starts crying, a long and drawn-out whine. All eyes are on her. Her hysteria is contagious, and Murad can hear someone sniffling at the other end of the boat.

"What are you crying for?" Scarface asks, leaning forward to look at her face.

"I'm afraid," she whimpers.

"Baraka!" he orders.

"Leave her be," Halima says, still holding her children close.

"Why did she come if she can't handle it?" he yells, pointing at Faten.

Murad pulls his shirt down from his face. "Who the hell do you think you are?" He's the first to be surprised by his anger. He is tense and ready for an argument.

"And who are you?" Scarface says. "Her protector?"

A cargo ship blows its horn, startling everyone. It glides in the distance, lights blinking.

"Stop it," Rahal yells. "Someone will hear us!"

Aziz examines the motor, pulls at the hose that connects it to the tank. "There's a gap here," he tells Rahal, and he points to the connector. "Do you have some tape?" Rahal opens his supplies box and takes out a roll of duct tape. Aziz quickly wraps some around the hose. The captain pulls the cable once, twice. Finally the motor wheezes painfully and the boat starts moving.

"Praise be to God," Faten says, ignoring Scarface's glares.

The crying stops and a grim peace falls on the boat.

Tarifa is about 250 meters away now. It'll only take another few minutes. The Guinean woman throws a piece of paper overboard. Murad figures it's her ID. She'll probably pretend she's from Sierra Leone so she can get political asylum. He shakes his head. No such luck for him.

---

5. **Guardia Civil:** Spanish police force with both military and civilian functions.

6. **asphyxiation** (as fihk see AY shuhn): lack of air.

Viewing and Interpreting What emotions might the people in the photograph and in the story share?

The water is still calm, but Murad knows better than to trust the Mediterranean. He's known the sea all his life and he knows how hard it can pull. Once, when he was ten years old, he went mussel picking with his father at the beach in Al Hoceima. As they were working away, Murad saw a dark, beautiful bed of mussels hanging from their beards inside a hollow rock. He lowered himself in and was busy pulling at them when a wave filled the grotto and flushed him out. His father grabbed Murad, still holding the bucket, out of the water. Later, Murad's father would tell his friends at the café an adorned version of this story, which would be added to his repertoire of family tales that he narrated on demand. **C**

"Everyone out of the boat now!" Rahal shouts. You have to swim the rest of the way."

Aziz immediately rolls out into the water and starts swimming.

Like the other passengers, Murad looks on, stunned. They expected to be taken all the way to the shore, where they could easily disperse and then hide. The idea of having to swim the rest of the way is intolerable, especially for those who are not natives of Tangier and accustomed to its waters.

Halima raises a hand at Rahal. "You thief! We paid you to take us to the coast."

Rahal says, "You want to get us all arrested as harraga? Get out of the boat if you want to get there. It's not that far. I'm turning back."

Someone makes an abrupt movement to reason with Rahal, to force him to go all the way to the shore, but the Zodiac loses balance and then it's too late. Murad is in the water now. His clothes are instantly wet, and the shock of the cold water all over his body makes his heart go still for a moment. He bobs, gasps for air, realizes that there's nothing left to do but swim. So he wills his limbs, heavy with the weight of his clothes, to move.

C Literary Focus Setting and Mood What does this description of the setting add to your understanding of the characters' situation?

Around him, people are slowly scattering, led by the crosscurrents. Rahal struggles to right his boat and someone, Murad can't quite tell who, is hanging on to the side. He hears howls and screams, sees a few people swimming in earnest. Aziz, who was first to get out of the boat, is already far ahead of the others, going west. Murad starts swimming toward the coast, afraid he might be pulled away by the water. From behind, he hears someone call out. He turns and holds his hand out to Faten. She grabs it and the next second she is holding both his shoulders. He tries to pull away, but her grip tightens.

"Use one hand to move," he yells.

Her eyes open wider but her hands do not move. He forces one of her hands off him and manages to make a few strokes. Her body is heavy against his. Each time they bob in the water, she holds on tighter. There is water in his ears now and her cries are not as loud. He tries to loosen her grip but she won't let go. He yells out. Still she holds on. The next time they bob, water enters his nose and it makes him cough. They'll never make it if she doesn't loosen her grip and help him. He pushes her away. Free at last, he moves quickly out of her reach. "Beat the water with your arms," he yells. She thrashes wildly. "Slower," he tells her, but he can see that it is hopeless, she can't swim. A sob forms in his throat. If only he had a stick or a buoy that he could hand her so that he could pull her without risking that they both drown. He's already drifting away from her, but he keeps calling out, telling her to calm down and start swimming. His fingers and toes have gone numb, and he has to start swimming or he'll freeze to death.

> He turns around and scans the dark waters, looking for Faten.

He faces the coast. He closes his eyes, but the image of Faten is waiting for him behind the lids. Eyes open again, he tries to focus on the motion of his limbs.

There is a strange quietness in the air. He swims until he feels the sand against his feet. He tries to control his breathing, the beating of his heart in his ears. He lies on the beach, the water licking his shoes. The sun is rising, painting the sand and the buildings far ahead a golden shade of orange. With a sigh, Murad relieves his bladder. The sand around him warms up but cools again in seconds. He rests there for a little while, then pushes himself to his knees.

He stands, legs shaking. He turns around and scans the dark waters, looking for Faten. He can see a few forms swimming, struggling, but it's hard to tell who is who. Aziz is nowhere to be seen, but the Guinean woman is getting out of the water a few meters away. **D**

In the distance, a dog barks.

Murad knows he doesn't have much time before the Guardia Civil come after them. He takes a few steps and drops to his knees on the sand, which feels warmer than the water. With a trembling hand, he opens a side pocket of his cargos and extracts a plastic bag. In it is a mobile phone, with a Spanish SIM card.[7] He calls Rubio, the Spaniard who will drive him north to Catalonia.

"Soy Murad. El amigo de Rahal."
"Espéreme por la caña de azucar."
"Bien."[8]

---

7. **SIM card:** device used in cellular phones.
8. **"Soy Murad. . . . Bien":** "I am Murad. Rahal's friend." "Wait for me by the sugar cane." "Okay."

D **Reading Focus** **Visualizing** How do these visual details help you better understand what Murad is going through?

He takes a few steps forward, but he doesn't see the sugar cane Rubio mentioned. He continues walking anyway. A hotel appears on the horizon. Another dog barks, and the sound soon turns into a howl. He walks toward it and spots the sugar cane. A small path appears on the left side and he sits at its end. He takes his shoes off, curls his frigid toes in the wet socks and massages them. Replacing his shoes, he lies back and takes a deep breath of relief. He can't believe his luck. He made it.

It will be all right now. He comforts himself with the familiar fantasy that sustained him back home, all those nights when he couldn't fall asleep, worrying about how he would pay rent or feed his mother and brothers. He imagines the office where he'll be working; he can see his fingers moving quickly and precisely over his keyboard; he can hear his phone ringing. He pictures himself going home to a modern, well-furnished apartment, his wife greeting him, the TV in the background.

A light shines on him. Rubio is fast. No wonder it cost so much to hire him. Murad sits up. The light is away from his eyes only a moment, but it is long enough to see the dog, a German shepherd, and the infinitely more menacing form holding the leash.

The officer from the Guardia Civil wears fatigues, and a black beret cocked over his shaved head. His name tag reads Martinez. He sits inside the van with Murad and the other illegals, the dog at his feet. Murad looks at himself: his wet shoes, his dirty pants stuck against his legs, the bluish skin under his nails. He keeps his teeth clenched to stop himself from shivering beneath the blanket the officer gave him. It's only fourteen kilometers, he thinks. If they hadn't been forced into the water, if he'd swum faster, if he'd gone west instead of east, he would have made it.

The Strait of Gibraltar

The Strait of Gibraltar figures prominently in this story. Lalami describes it as a body of water separating "not just two countries but two universes." The strait connects the Atlantic Ocean and the Mediterranean Sea by a thin ribbon of water that is 8.7 miles (14 kilometers) wide at its narrowest point. It extends from the southernmost point of Spain to the northernmost point of Africa. For many centuries it has been an important body of water for trading and strategic purposes. The Spanish and Moroccan governments have discussed building a tunnel under the strait, similar to the one connecting England and France beneath the English Channel.

Ask Yourself
If this tunnel connecting Morocco and Spain were built, how might the details of the journey described in the story change?

When he climbs down from the van, Murad notices a wooded area up the hill just a few meters away, and beyond it, a road. The guards are busy helping a woman who seems to have collapsed from the cold. Murad takes off, running as fast as he can. Behind him, he hears a whistle and the sound of boots, but he continues running, through the trees, his feet barely touching the crackled ground. When he gets closer to the road, he sees it is a four-lane highway, with cars whizzing by. It makes him pause. Martinez grabs him by the shirt.

The clock on the wall at the Guardia Civil post shows six in the morning. Murad sits on a metal chair, handcuffed. There are men and women, all wrapped in blankets like him, huddled close together to stay warm. He doesn't recognize many of them; most came on other boats. Scarface sits alone, smoking a cigarette, one leg resting on the other, one shoe missing. There is no sign of Aziz. He must have made it. Just to be sure, he asks the Guinean woman a few seats down from him. "I haven't seen him," she says.

Lucky Aziz. Murad curses his own luck. If he'd landed just a hundred meters west, away from the houses and the hotel, he might have been able to escape. His stomach growls. He swallows hard. How will he be able to show his face again in Tangier? He stands up and hobbles to the dusty window. He sees Faten outside, her head bare, in a line with some of the other boatmates, waiting for the doctors, who wear surgical masks on their faces, to examine them. A wave of relief washes over him, and he gesticulates as best as he can with his handcuffs, calling her name. She can't hear him, but eventually she looks up, sees him, then looks away.

A woman in a dark business suit arrives, her high heels clicking on the tiled floor. "Soy sus abogada,"[9] she says, standing before them. She tells them they are here illegally and that they must sign the paper that the Guardia Civil are going to give them. While everyone takes turns at signing, the woman leans against the counter to talk to one of the officers. She raises one of her legs behind her as she talks, like a little girl. The officer says something in a flirtatious tone, and she throws her head back and laughs.

Murad puts in a false name even though it won't matter. He is taken to the holding station, the sand from the beach still stuck on his pants. On his way there, he sees a body bag on the ground. A sour taste invades his mouth. He swallows but can't contain it. He doubles over and the officer lets go of him. Murad stumbles to the side of the building and vomits. It could have been him in that body bag; it could have been Faten. Maybe it was Aziz or Halima.

The guard takes him to a moldy cell already occupied by two other prisoners, one of whom is asleep on the mattress. Murad sits on the floor and looks up through the window at the patch of blue sky. Seagulls flutter from the side of the building and fly away in formation, and for a moment he envies them their freedom. But tomorrow the police will send him back to Tangier. His future there stands before him, unalterable, despite his efforts, despite the risk he took and the price he paid. He will have to return to the same old apartment, to live off his mother and sister, without any prospects or opportunity. He thinks of Aziz, probably already on a truck headed to Catalonia, and he wonders—if Aziz can make it, why not he? At least now he knows what to expect. It will be hard to convince his mother, but in the end he knows he will prevail on her to sell her gold bracelets. If she sells all seven of them, it will pay for another trip. And next time, he'll make it. **Ⓔ**

___
9. **"Soy sus abogada"**: "I am your lawyer."

Ⓔ **Literary Focus** Setting and Mood What is the mood at the end of the story? How does it compare to the mood at the beginning?

Vocabulary **prospects** (PRAHS pehkts) *n.*: things expected or looked forward to; outlook for the future.

Applying Your Skills

OH **RA.L.10.2** Analyze the features of setting and their importance in a literary text. **RA.L.10.3** Distinguish how conflicts, parallel plots and subplots affect the pacing of action in literary text. *Also covered* **RP.10.1; WP.10.9**

The Trip

Respond and Think Critically

Reading Focus

Quick Check

1. Why does Murad want to leave Morocco? What does he expect his life to be like in Spain?

2. Why do the passengers feel cheated by Rahal?

3. What is Murad planning at the end of the story?

Read with a Purpose

4. What are some obstacles that Murad must overcome? What <u>aspects</u> of Murad's character are revealed as he struggles to achieve his goal?

Reading Skills: Visualizing

5. While reading "The Trip," you recorded details that helped you visualize the story's settings. Now, add a column to your chart. In this column, explain how these details of setting contribute to the mood of the story.

Setting	Descriptive Language	Mood
Strait of Gibraltar at night	The waves are inky black . . . foam here and there . . . glistening white under the moon . . . tombstones in a dark cemetery.	serene but ominous

Literary Focus

Literary Analysis

6. **Compare** Murad is not alone on his journey. How do his actions compare to those of the other passengers?

7. **Draw Conclusions** Why do you think Lalami includes the background information about the Moorish invasion? How does this knowledge contribute to your understanding of the story?

8. **Make Judgments** Even if Murad were to make it to Spain, how realistic do you think his dream is? Do you admire him or think he is foolish for what he is trying to do? Explain.

9. **Analyze** What **theme,** or insight about life, do you think Lalami conveys with this story?

Literary Skills: Setting and Mood

10. **Evaluate** How does the setting contribute to the mood of the story? How would the story change if it had a different setting?

Literary Skills Review: Conflict

11. **Analyze** How does the setting of "The Trip" create **conflict,** or struggle? What kinds of conflict does Murad experience?

Writing Focus

Think as a Reader/Writer

Use It in Your Writing Lalami's precise language in "The Trip" heightens the story's dramatic moments and creates distinct moods. Write a descriptive paragraph about a place or event. Decide on a mood to convey. Choose your words carefully for the most expressive effect.

 What Do You Think Now

Murad endures his journey and risks death because he longs for a better life. Do you think his risk taking is justified? Why or why not?

Applying Your Skills

The Trip

Vocabulary Development

Vocabulary Check

Fill in the blank with the correct Vocabulary word.

pondered
destinies
exudes
putrid
prospect

1. It's obvious that Antoine knows what he is doing, because he _____ confidence.

2. The _____ of food and warm beds cheered the weary travelers.

3. Mark _____ the riddle and knew that the answer was within his grasp.

4. Although Jessica and her sister always expected to become teachers, their _____ were not at all what they had imagined.

5. Shelley took out the garbage to remove the _____ fish scraps from the house.

Vocabulary Skills: Etymologies

Etymology is the study of word origins. Many words in English were originally derived from Greek or Latin. For example, the word *etymology* itself comes from the Latin *etymologia*. Most dictionaries provide the origin of a word as well as the definition of the root word. Origins usually appear in brackets after the word's pronunciation, and the oldest form of the word is listed last. A typical etymology entry looks like this, for the word *parallel*:

par al lel (PAIR uh lehl) [< Latin *parallelus* < Greek *parallēlos* < *para-* "side by side"]

This tells you that the word came into English from Latin but originally came from the Greek *parallēlos*, meaning "side by side."

Your Turn

Use a dictionary to complete a diagram like the one below for each of the Vocabulary words.

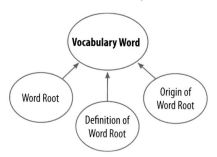

Language Coach

Synonyms Many words have **synonyms,** or words with the same—or almost the same—meaning. For example, *destinies* has the synonyms *fates* and *fortunes*.

Use a thesaurus or dictionary to find synonyms for two more Vocabulary words. Pay special attention to slight differences of meaning. Write a sentence illustrating these differences for each synonym.

Academic Vocabulary

Talk About . . .

Discuss the following questions with a partner.

1. Is Murad a <u>credible</u> character?

2. What <u>aspects</u> of the story do you find most memorable?

Grammar Link

Present Tense

Lalami tells "The Trip" in present tense to create the illusion that the story's events are happening right now, as you read. Use the chart below to compare Lalami's present-tense narrative to the same events told in past tense. Notice that verbs are not the only words that change when you change the tense of a story. Adverbs that give you information about time, such as *now* and *tonight*, change as well.

Past Tense	Present Tense
That night the sea **appeared** calm, with only a slight wind now and then. The captain **had ordered** all the lights turned off, but with the moon up and the sky clear, Murad **could** still see around him. The six-meter Zodiac inflatable **was** meant to accommodate eight people. Thirty **huddled** in it **that night**.	**Tonight** the sea **appears** calm, with only a slight wind now and then. The captain **has ordered** all the lights turned off, but with the moon up and the sky clear, Murad **can** still see around him. The six-meter Zodiac inflatable is meant to accommodate eight people. Thirty **huddle** in it **now**.

Your Turn

Writing Applications Rewrite each of these sentences in present tense. Pay attention to how the events relate to each other in time. You may want to change other words in the sentence as well.

1. Before he had time to think about it, Murad plunged into the icy water.
2. The day before his trip, he had purchased a cheap watch.
3. One man on the boat had a long scar across his face, something he had probably acquired in a fight.
4. Coughing and sputtering, Murad fought to swim.

CHOICES

As you respond to the Choices, use these **Academic Vocabulary** words where appropriate: aspects, credible, tension, and evaluation.

REVIEW
Change the Setting
Timed ⌚ Writing "The Trip" is a fictional story about a real-life situation in present-day Morocco. How might this story be different if it were set somewhere else, in the United States, for example? In a brief essay, outline what details would have to change if the story were set elsewhere.

CONNECT
Film the Story
TechFocus A storyboard is a series of drawings that show the main camera angles, images, and actions in a film. Create a storyboard of the scene in which Murad lands on the beach. Keep in mind that you can use close-ups to show emotion, long shots to establish setting, and moving shots to show action or uncertainty. Share your storyboard with your classmates.

EXTEND
Create a Different Ending
Rewrite the ending of the story so Murad escapes. How would a new ending change the mood of the story? Describe Murad's thoughts, as Lalami does. Also, use imagery to bring the story to life and create a specific mood with your descriptions.

Learn It Online
Find out how media-literate you are—and what more there is to learn—at:

go.hrw.com   L10-59   Go

Comparing Plot and Setting Across Genres

CONTENTS

 What Do You Think? What can we learn about ourselves and the world by going on a journey?

 QuickWrite
Think about a book you've read or a movie you've seen in which the main character undertakes a journey. What lessons did he or she learn on the journey? Jot down your ideas.

Preparing to Read

By the Waters of Babylon / Coyote Kills the Giant

RA.L.10.3 Distinguish how conflicts, parallel plots and subplots affect the pacing of action in literary text. RA.L.10.5 Analyze how an author's choice of genre affects the expression of a theme or topic. *Also covered* RP.10.1

Reader/Writer Notebook

Use your **RWN** to complete the activities for these selections.

Literary Focus

Plot and Setting Across Genres You have learned that **plot** (a series of related events) and **setting** (time and place) play a central role in short stories. Now you will see how these elements work across **genres,** or types of literature. A **folk tale** is an anonymous traditional story originally passed down orally from generation to generation. Folk tales are told in every culture, and similar tales are told throughout the world. Examples of folk tales are fairy tales, fables, legends, ghost stories, and tall tales. Folk tales tend to travel, so the same plot often appears in several cultures.

Reading Focus

Comparing Texts To compare texts, look for similarities and differences between them. As you read the story and the folk tale that follow, think about the journey each of the main characters takes. Visualizing the details of these journeys will help you find their similarities and differences.

Into Action Try using a chart like the one below to track the journey in each selection.

Selection	Basic Situation	Conflict	Resolution
By the Waters of Babylon	John must go on a journey.		
Coyote Kills the Giant			

Vocabulary

ignorant (IHG nuhr uhnt) *adj.:* lacking knowledge; unaware. *I was ignorant of what had happened in the Place of the Gods.*

customs (KUHS tuhmz) *n.:* habits; traditions. *We were not familiar with the customs and practices of the Forest People.*

perplexed (puhr PLEHKST) *adj.:* puzzled; confused. *I was perplexed by what I saw; it was not what I had expected.*

> I was **perplexed**
>
> because
>
> I was **ignorant** — of that country's **customs.**

Language Coach

Context Clues Sometimes writers give clues about a word's meaning by placing a definition nearby. Look at this sentence: *Our customs are very different from the habits and traditions of people in other countries.* Which words tell you what *customs* means?

Writing Focus

Think as a Reader/Writer

Find It in Your Reading Writers create setting with descriptive words and phrases. As you read, write down the details the authors use to develop the settings in your *Reader/Writer Notebook*.

Learn It Online
There's more to words than just definitions. Get the whole story at:

go.hrw.com   L10-61   **Go**

Stephen Vincent Benét (1898–1943)

In Love with History

Benét was the son of a well-known colonel who instilled a love of literature and American history in his children. Stephen Vincent's brother and sister also became writers. With this background it's not surprising that Benét turned to American history, folklore, and legend in his stories and poems. Benét won the Pulitzer Prize for *John Brown's Body* (1928), a book-length narrative poem about the fiery abolitionist who attacked Harper's Ferry in 1859 and was hanged for treason. Benét always emphasized the importance of clear style. He once advised a young writer, "Don't use four adjectives when one will do. Don't use five long words to say, 'It rained.' Write of the simple things simply."

Alfonso Ortiz (1939–1997)

Richard Erdoes (1912–   )

Spotlight on Native American Writers

Dr. Alfonso Ortiz, a native of San Juan Pueblo in New Mexico, was well known for his research on the Tewa Pueblo people. He received his doctorate in anthropology from the University of Chicago and eventually became a professor at the University of New Mexico.

Richard Erdoes was born in Austria and developed an early interest in Native American history. As a writer, a photographer, and an illustrator, Erdoes has authored a number of his own books and collaborated on several more with such important Native American writers as Lame Deer and Alfonso Ortiz.

Think About the Writers

What similar interests might these writers share?

Preview the Selections

John, the narrator of "By the Waters of Babylon," is the son of a priest. He prepares and goes on a journey to a sacred and forbidden place.

Coyote is the traditional trickster of Native American folklore. In "Coyote Kills the Giant," Coyote takes on one of his greatest challenges.

By the Waters of Babylon

by **Stephen Vincent Benét**

Read with a Purpose
Read this story to learn about a young man's journey to find the truth about a destroyed civilization.

Build Background
The title of this story is an **allusion,** or reference, to Psalm 137 in the Bible. The psalm tells of the Israelites' sorrow over the destruction of their temple in Zion (a reference to Jerusalem) and their enslavement in Babylon. The psalm begins, "By the waters of Babylon, there we sat down and wept, when we remembered Zion."

The north and the west and the south are good hunting ground, but it is forbidden to go east. It is forbidden to go to any of the Dead Places except to search for metal, and then he who touches the metal must be a priest or the son of a priest. Afterward, both the man and the metal must be purified. These are the rules and the laws; they are well made. It is forbidden to cross the great river and look upon the place that was the Place of the Gods—this is most strictly forbidden. We do not even say its name though we know its name. It is there that spirits live, and demons—it is there that there are the ashes of the Great Burning. These things are forbidden—they have been forbidden since the beginning of time.

My father is a priest; I am the son of a priest. I have been in the Dead Places near us, with my father—at first, I was afraid. When my father went into the house to search for the metal, I stood by the door and my heart felt small and weak. It was a dead man's house, a spirit house. It did not have the smell of man, though there were old bones in a corner. But it

is not fitting that a priest's son should show fear. I looked at the bones in the shadow and kept my voice still.

Then my father came out with the metal—a good, strong piece. He looked at me with both eyes but I had not run away. He gave me the metal to hold—I took it and did not die. So he knew that I was truly his son and would be a priest in my time. That was when I was very young—nevertheless, my brothers would not have done it, though they are good hunters. After that, they gave me the good piece of meat and the warm corner by the fire. My father watched over me—he was glad that I should be a priest. But when I boasted or wept without a reason, he punished me more strictly than my brothers. That was right. **Ⓐ**

After a time, I myself was allowed to go into the dead houses and search for metal. So I learned the ways of those houses—and if I saw bones, I was no longer afraid. The bones are light and old—sometimes they will fall into dust if you touch them. But that is a great sin.

I was taught the chants and the spells—I

Ⓐ **Reading Focus** **Visualizing** What images strike you as you read the first part of the story? How do those images establish the mood of the story?

was taught how to stop blood from a wound and many secrets. A priest must know many secrets—that was what my father said. If the hunters think we do all things by chants and spells, they may believe so—it does not hurt them. I was taught how to read in the old books and how to make the old writings—that was hard and took a long time. My knowledge made me happy—it was like a fire in my heart. Most of all, I liked to hear of the Old Days and the stories of the gods. I asked myself many questions that I could not answer, but it was good to ask them. At night, I would lie awake and listen to the wind—it seemed to me that it was the voice of the gods as they flew through the air.

We are not ignorant like the Forest People—our women spin wool on the wheel, our priests wear a white robe. We do not eat grubs from the tree, we have not forgotten the old writings, although they are hard to understand. Nevertheless, my knowledge and my lack of knowledge burned in me—I wished to know more. When I was a man at last, I came to my father and said, "It is time for me to go on my journey. Give me your leave." **B**

He looked at me for a long time, stroking his beard, then he said at last, "Yes. It is time." That night, in the house of the priesthood, I asked for and received purification. My body hurt but my spirit was a cool stone. It was my father himself who questioned me about my dreams.

He bade[1] me look into the smoke of the fire and see—I saw and told what I saw. It was

what I have always seen—a river, and, beyond it, a great Dead Place and in it the gods walking. I have always thought about that. His eyes were stern when I told him—he was no longer my father but a priest. He said, "This is a strong dream."

"It is mine," I said, while the smoke waved and my head felt light. They were singing the Star song in the outer chamber and it was like the buzzing of bees in my head.

He asked me how the gods were dressed and I told him how they were dressed. We know how they were dressed from the book, but I saw them as if they were before me. When I had finished, he threw the sticks three times and studied them as they fell.

"This is a very strong dream," he said. "It may eat you up."

"I am not afraid," I said and looked at him with both eyes. My voice sounded thin in my ears but that was because of the smoke.

He touched me on the breast and the forehead. He gave me the bow and the three arrows.

"Take them," he said. "It is forbidden to travel east. It is forbidden to cross the river. It is forbidden to go to the Place of the Gods. All these things are forbidden."

"All these things are forbidden," I said, but it was my voice that spoke and not my spirit. He looked at me again.

"My son," he said. "Once I had young dreams. If your dreams do not eat you up, you may be a great priest. If they eat you, you are still my son. Now go on your journey." **C**

I went fasting, as is the law. My body hurt but not my heart. When the dawn came, I was

---

1. **bade** (bayd): tell someone what to do; command (past tense of *bid*).

B Literary Focus Plot and Setting What do the narrator's comments about the Forest People lead you to understand about his own people?

C Literary Focus Plot and Setting Where is the narrator going, and why?

Vocabulary **ignorant** (IHG nuhr uhnt) *adj.*: lacking knowledge; unaware.

out of sight of the village. I prayed and purified myself, waiting for a sign. The sign was an eagle. It flew east.

Sometimes signs are sent by bad spirits. I waited again on the flat rock, fasting, taking no food. I was very still—I could feel the sky above me and the earth beneath. I waited till the sun was beginning to sink. Then three deer passed in the valley, going east—they did not wind[2] me or see me. There was a white fawn with them— a very great sign.

I followed them, at a distance, waiting for what would happen. My heart was troubled about going east, yet I knew that I must go. My head hummed with my fasting—I did not even see the panther spring upon the white fawn.

> Then I raised my eyes and looked south. It was there, the Place of the Gods.

But, before I knew it, the bow was in my hand. I shouted and the panther lifted his head from the fawn. It is not easy to kill a panther with one arrow but the arrow went through his eye and into his brain. He died as he tried to spring—he rolled over, tearing at the ground. Then I knew I was meant to go east—I knew that was my journey. When the night came, I made my fire and roasted meat. **D**

It is eight suns' journey to the east and a man passes by many Dead Places. The Forest People are afraid of them but I am not. Once I made my fire on the edge of a Dead Place at night and, next morning, in the dead house, I found a good knife, little rusted. That was small to what came afterward but it made my heart feel big. Always when I looked for game, it was

in front of my arrow, and twice I passed hunting parties of the Forest People without their knowing. So I knew my magic was strong and my journey clean, in spite of the law.

Toward the setting of the eighth sun, I came to the banks of the great river. It was half a day's journey after I had left the god-road—we do not use the god-roads now, for they are falling apart into great blocks of stone, and the forest is safer going. A long way off, I had seen the water through trees but the trees were thick.

At last, I came out upon an open place at the top of a cliff. There was the great river below, like a giant in the sun. It is very long, very wide. It could eat all the streams we know and still be thirsty. Its name is Oudis-sun, the Sacred, the Long. No man of my tribe had seen it, not even my father, the priest. It was magic and I prayed. **E**

Then I raised my eyes and looked south. It was there, the Place of the Gods.

How can I tell what it was like—you do not know. It was there, in the red light, and they were too big to be houses. It was there with the red light upon it, mighty and ruined. I knew that in another moment the gods would see me. I covered my eyes with my hands and crept back into the forest.

Surely, that was enough to do, and live. Surely it was enough to spend the night upon the cliff. The Forest People themselves do not come near. Yet, all through the night, I knew that I should have to cross the river and walk in the places of the gods, although the gods ate me up. My magic did not help me at all and yet

---

2. **wind** (wihnd): detect scent of.

D **Literary Focus** Plot and Setting What signs does the narrator encounter on his journey?

E **Reading Focus** Visualizing What details help you visualize the great river?

Pelvis with the Distance (1943)
by Georgia O'Keeffe.

Indianapolis Museum of Art.
Gift of Anne Marmon Greenleaf in
memory of Caroline M. Fesler.
The Georgia O'Keeffe Foundation/
© 2009 Georgia O'Keeffe Museum/
Artists Rights Society (ARS), NY.

there was a fire in my bowels, a fire in my mind. When the sun rose, I thought, "My journey has been clean. Now I will go home from my journey." But, even as I thought so, I knew I could not. If I went to the Place of the Gods, I would surely die, but, if I did not go, I could never be at peace with my spirit again. It is better to lose one's life than one's spirit, if one is a priest and the son of a priest.

Nevertheless, as I made the raft, the tears ran out of my eyes. The Forest People could have killed me without fight, if they had come upon me then, but they did not come. When the raft was made, I said the sayings for the dead and painted myself for death. My heart was cold as a frog and my knees like water, but the burning in my mind would not let me have peace. As I pushed the raft from the shore, I began my death song—I had the right. It was a fine song.

"*I am John, son of John,*" I sang. "*My people are the Hill People. They are the men.*
I go into the Dead Places but I am not slain.
I take the metal from the Dead Places but I am not blasted.
I travel upon the god-roads and am not afraid.E-yah! I have killed the panther, I have killed the fawn!
E-yah! I have come to the great river. No man has come there before.
It is forbidden to go east, but I have gone, forbidden to go on the great river, but I am there.
Open your hearts, you spirits, and hear my song. Now I go to the Place of the Gods, I shall not return.

F **Literary Focus** **Plot and Setting** Why does the narrator decide to continue his journey?

My body is painted for death and my limbs weak, but my heart is big as I go to the Place of the Gods!"

All the same, when I came to the Place of the Gods, I was afraid, afraid. The current of the great river is very strong—it gripped my raft with its hands. That was magic, for the river itself is wide and calm. I could feel evil spirits about me, in the bright morning; I could feel their breath on my neck as I was swept down the stream. Never have I been so much alone—I tried to think of my knowledge, but it was a squirrel's heap of winter nuts. There was no strength in my knowledge anymore and I felt small and naked as a new-hatched bird—alone upon the great river, the servant of the gods.

Yet, after a while, my eyes were opened and I saw. I saw both banks of the river—I saw that once there had been god-roads across it, though now they were broken and fallen like broken vines. Very great they were, and wonderful and broken—broken in the time of the Great Burning when the fire fell out of the sky. And always the current took me nearer to the Place of the Gods, and the huge ruins rose before my eyes. **G**

I do not know the customs of rivers—we are the People of the Hills. I tried to guide my raft with the pole but it spun around. I thought the river meant to take me past the Place of the Gods and out into the Bitter Water of the legends. I grew angry then—my heart felt strong. I said aloud, "I am a priest and the son of a priest!" The gods heard me—they showed me how to paddle with the pole on one side of the raft. The current changed itself—I drew near to the Place of the Gods.

When I was very near, my raft struck and turned over. I can swim in our lakes—I swam to the shore. There was a great spike of rusted metal sticking out into the river—I hauled myself up upon it and sat there, panting. I had saved my bow and two arrows and the knife I found in the Dead Place but that was all. My raft went whirling downstream toward the Bitter Water. I looked after it, and thought if it had trod me under, at least I would be safely dead. Nevertheless, when I had dried my bowstring and restrung it, I walked forward to the Place of the Gods.

It felt like ground underfoot; it did not burn me. It is not true what some of the tales say, that the ground there burns forever, for I have been there. Here and there were the marks and stains of the Great Burning, on the ruins, that is true. But they were old marks and old stains. It is not true either, what some of our priests say, that it is an island covered with fogs and enchantments. It is not. It is a great Dead Place—greater than any Dead Place we know. Everywhere in it there are god-roads, though most are cracked and broken. Everywhere there are the ruins of the high towers of the gods. **H**

How shall I tell what I saw? I went carefully, my strung bow in my hand, my skin ready for danger. There should have been the wailings of spirits and the shrieks of demons, but there were not. It was very silent and sunny where I had landed—the wind and the rain and the birds that drop seeds had done their work—the grass grew in the cracks of the broken stone. It is a fair island—no wonder the gods built there. If I had come there, a god, I also would have built.

G **Reading Focus** Visualizing Re-read the description of the god-roads. What do you think they might be?

H **Literary Focus** Plot and Setting What has changed the narrator's ideas about the Place of the Gods?

Vocabulary **customs** (KUHS tuhmz) *n.*: habits; traditions.

How shall I tell what I saw? The towers are not all broken—here and there one still stands, like a great tree in a forest, and the birds nest high. But the towers themselves look blind, for the gods are gone. I saw a fish-hawk, catching fish in the river. I saw a little dance of white butterflies over a great heap of broken stones and columns. I went there and looked about me—there was a carved stone with cut-letters, broken in half. I can read letters but I could not understand these. They said UBTREAS. There was also the shattered image of a man or a god. It had been made of white stone and he wore his hair tied back like a woman's. His name was ASHING, as I read on the cracked half of a stone. I thought it wise to pray to ASHING, though I do not know that god. **❶**

How shall I tell what I saw? There was no smell of man left, on stone or metal. Nor were there many trees in that wilderness of stone. There are many pigeons, nesting and dropping in the towers—the gods must have loved them, or, perhaps, they used them for sacrifices. There are wild cats that roam the god-roads, green-eyed, unafraid of man. At night they wail like demons but they are not demons. The wild dogs are more dangerous, for they hunt in a pack, but them I did not meet till later. Everywhere there are the carved stones, carved with magical numbers or words.

I went north—I did not try to hide myself. When a god or a demon saw me, then I would die, but meanwhile I was no longer afraid. My hunger for knowledge burned in me—there was so much that I could not understand. After a while, I knew that my belly was hungry. I could have hunted for my meat, but I did not hunt. It is known that the gods did not hunt as we do—they got their food from enchanted boxes and jars. Sometimes these are still found in the Dead Places—once, when I was a child and foolish, I opened such a jar and tasted it and found the food sweet. But my father found out and punished me for it strictly, for, often, that food is death. Now, though, I had long gone past what was forbidden, and I entered the likeliest towers, looking for the food of the gods. **❶**

I found it at last in the ruins of a great temple in the midcity. A mighty temple it must have been, for the roof was painted like the sky at night with its stars—that much I could see, though the colors were faint and dim. It went down into great caves and tunnels—perhaps they kept their slaves there. But when I started to climb down, I heard the squeaking of rats, so I did not go—rats are unclean, and there must have been many tribes of them, from the squeaking. But near there, I found food, in the heart of a ruin, behind a door that still opened. I ate only the fruits from the jars—they had a very sweet taste. There was drink, too, in bottles of glass—the drink of the gods was strong and made my head swim. After I had eaten and drunk, I slept on the top of a stone, my bow at my side.

> My hunger for knowledge burned in me—there was so much that I could not understand.

---

❶ Reading Focus Visualizing What does the narrator see in the Place of the Gods?

❶ Literary Focus Plot and Setting Why might eating from the "enchanted boxes and jars" lead to death?

When I woke, the sun was low. Looking down from where I lay, I saw a dog sitting on his haunches. His tongue was hanging out of his mouth; he looked as if he were laughing. He was a big dog, with a gray-brown coat, as big as a wolf. I sprang up and shouted at him but he did not move—he just sat there as if he were laughing. I did not like that. When I reached for a stone to throw, he moved swiftly out of the way of the stone. He was not afraid of me; he looked at me as if I were meat. No doubt I could have killed him with an arrow, but I did not know if there were others. Moreover, night was falling.

I looked about me—not far away there was a great, broken god-road, leading north. The towers were high enough, but not so high, and while many of the dead houses were wrecked, there were some that stood. I went toward this god-road, keeping to the heights of the ruins, while the dog followed. When I had reached the god-road, I saw that there were others behind him. If I had slept later, they would have come upon me asleep and torn out my throat. As it was, they were sure enough of me; they did not hurry. When I went into the dead house, they kept watch at the entrance—doubtless they thought they would have a fine hunt. But a dog cannot open a door and I knew, from the books, that the gods did not like to live on the ground but on high.

I had just found a door I could open when the dogs decided to rush. Ha! They were surprised when I shut the door in their faces—it was a good door, of strong metal. I could hear their foolish baying[3] beyond it but I did not stop to answer them. I was in darkness—I found stairs and climbed. There were many stairs, turning around till my head was dizzy. At the top was another door—I found the knob and opened it. I was in a long small chamber—on one side of it was a bronze door that could not be opened, for it had no handle. Perhaps there was a magic word to open it but I did not have the word. I turned to the door in the opposite side of the wall. The lock of it was broken and I opened it and went in. **Ⓚ**

Within, there was a place of great riches. The god who lived there must have been a powerful god. The first room was a small anteroom[4]—I waited there for some time, telling the spirits of the place that I came in peace and not as a robber. When it seemed to me that they had had time to hear me, I went on. Ah, what riches! Few, even, of the windows had been broken—it was all as it had been. The great windows that looked over the city had not been broken at all though they were dusty and streaked with many years. There were coverings on the floors, the colors not greatly faded, and the chairs were soft and deep. There were pictures upon the walls, very strange, very wonderful—I remember one of a bunch of flowers in a jar—if you came close to it, you could see nothing but bits of color, but if you stood away from it, the flowers might have been picked yesterday. It made my heart feel strange to look at this picture—and to look at the figure of a bird, in some hard clay, on a table and see it so like our birds. Everywhere there were books and writings, many in tongues that I could not read. The god who lived there must have been a wise god and full of knowledge. I felt I had right there, as I sought knowledge also.

---

3. **baying** (BAY ihng): long, deep howl or bark.

4. **anteroom** (AN tee room): a small room connected to a larger room.

Ⓚ **Reading Focus** **Visualizing** What kind of door might not have a handle?

Nevertheless, it was strange. There was a washing-place but no water—perhaps the gods washed in air. There was a cooking-place but no wood, and though there was a machine to cook food, there was no place to put fire in it. Nor were there candles or lamps—there were things that looked like lamps but they had neither oil nor wick. All these things were magic, but I touched them and lived—the magic had gone out of them. Let me tell one thing to show. In the washing-place, a thing said "Hot" but it was not hot to the touch—another thing said "Cold" but it was not cold. This must have been a strong magic but the magic was gone. I do not understand—they had ways—I wish that I knew. **L**

It was close and dry and dusty in their house of the gods. I have said the magic was gone but that is not true—it had gone from the magic things but it had not gone from the place. I felt the spirits about me, weighing upon me. Nor had I ever slept in a Dead Place before—and yet, tonight, I must sleep there. When I thought of it, my tongue felt dry in my throat, in spite of my wish for knowledge. Almost I would have gone down again and faced the dogs, but I did not.

I had not gone through all the rooms when the darkness fell. When it fell, I went back to the big room looking over the city and made fire. There was a place to make fire and a box with wood in it, though I do not think they cooked there. I wrapped myself in a floor-covering and slept in front of the fire—I was very tired.

Now I tell what is very strong magic. I woke in the midst of the night. When I woke, the fire had gone out and I was cold. It seemed to me that all around me there were whisperings and voices. I closed my eyes to shut them out. Some will say that I slept again, but I do not think that I slept. I could feel the spirits drawing my spirit out of my body as a fish is drawn on a line.

Why should I lie about it? I am a priest and the son of a priest. If there are spirits, as they say, in the small Dead Places near us, what spirits must there not be in that great Place of the Gods? And would not they wish to speak? After such long years? I know that I felt myself drawn as a fish is drawn on a line. I had stepped out of my body—I could see my body asleep in front of the cold fire, but it was not I. I was drawn to look out upon the city of the gods.

It should have been dark, for it was night, but it was not dark. Everywhere there were lights—lines of light—circles and blurs of light—ten thousand torches would not have been the same. The sky itself was alight—you could barely see the stars for the glow in the sky. I thought to myself, "This is strong magic," and trembled. There was a roaring in my ears like the rushing of rivers. Then my eyes grew used to the light and my ears to the sound. I knew that I was seeing the city as it had been when the gods were alive. **M**

That was a sight indeed—yes, that was a sight: I could not have seen it in the body—my body would have died. Everywhere went the gods, on foot and in chariots—there were gods beyond number and counting and their chariots blocked the streets. They had turned night to day for their pleasure—they did not sleep with the sun. The noise of their coming and going was the noise of many waters. It was magic what they could do—it was magic what they did.

I looked out of another window—the great vines of their bridges were mended and the

---

L **Reading Focus** Visualizing What details of the setting remind you of civilization today?

M **Literary Focus** Plot and Setting What vision of the setting does the narrator have?

god-roads went east and west. Restless, restless were the gods, and always in motion! They burrowed tunnels under rivers—they flew in the air. With unbelievable tools they did giant works—no part of the earth was safe from them, for, if they wished for a thing, they summoned it from the other side of the world. And always, as they labored and rested, as they feasted and made love, there was a drum in their ears—the pulse of the giant city, beating and beating like a man's heart.

Were they happy? What is happiness to the gods? They were great, they were mighty, they were wonderful and terrible. As I looked upon them and their magic, I felt like a child—but a little more, it seemed to me, and they would pull down the moon from the sky. I saw them with wisdom beyond wisdom and knowledge beyond knowledge. And yet not all they did was well done—even I could see that—and yet their wisdom could not but grow until all was peace.

Then I saw their fate come upon them and that was terrible past speech. It came upon them as they walked the streets of their city. I have been in the fights with the Forest People—I have seen men die. But this was not like that. When gods war with gods, they use weapons we do not know. It was fire falling out of the sky and a mist that poisoned. It was the time of the Great Burning and the Destruction. They ran about like ants in the streets of their city—poor gods, poor gods! Then the towers began to fall. A few escaped—yes, a few. The legends tell it. But, even after the city had become a Dead Place, for many years the poison was still in the ground. I

saw it happen, I saw the last of them die. It was darkness over the broken city and I wept.

All this, I saw. I saw it as I have told it, though not in the body. When I woke in the morning, I was hungry, but I did not think first of my hunger, for my heart was perplexed and confused. I knew the reason for the Dead Places but I did not see why it had happened.

Reading Focus Visualizing What details help you understand what happened to the gods?

Vocabulary perplexed (puhr PLEHKST) *adj.*: puzzled; confused.

It seemed to me it should not have happened, with all the magic they had. I went through the house looking for an answer. There was so much in the house I could not understand—and yet I am a priest and the son of a priest. It was like being on one side of the great river, at night, with no light to show the way.

Then I saw the dead god. He was sitting in his chair, by the window, in a room I had not entered before and, for the first moment, I thought that he was alive. Then I saw the skin on the back of his hand—it was like dry leather. The room was shut, hot and dry—no doubt that had kept him as he was. At first I was afraid to approach him—then the fear left me. He was sitting looking out over the city—he was dressed in the clothes of the gods. His age was neither young nor old—I could not tell his age. But there was wisdom in his face and great sadness. You could see that he would have not run away. He had sat at his window, watching his city die—then he himself had died. But it is better to lose one's life than one's spirit—and you could see from the face that his spirit had not been lost. I knew that, if I touched him, he would fall into dust—and yet, there was something unconquered in the face.

That is all of my story, for then I knew he was a man—I knew then that they had been men, neither gods nor demons. It is a great knowledge, hard to tell and believe. They were men—they went a dark road, but they were men. I had no fear after that—I had no fear going home, though twice I fought off the dogs and I was hunted for two days by the Forest People. When I saw my father again, I prayed and was purified. He touched my lips and my breast, he said, "You went away a boy. You come back a man and a priest." I said, "Father, they were men! I have been in the Place of the Gods and seen it! Now slay me, if it is the law—but still I know they were men."

He looked at me out of both eyes. He said, "The law is not always the same shape—you have done what you have done. I could not have done it my time, but you come after me. Tell!"

I told and he listened. After that, I wished to tell all the people but he showed me otherwise. He said, "Truth is a hard deer to hunt. If you eat too much truth at once, you may die of the truth. It was not idly that our fathers forbade the Dead Places." He was right—it is better the truth should come little by little. I have learned that, being a priest. Perhaps, in the old days, they ate knowledge too fast.

Nevertheless, we make a beginning. It is not for the metal alone we go to the Dead Places now—there are the books and the writings. They are hard to learn. And the magic tools are broken—but we can look at them and wonder. At least, we make a beginning. And, when I am chief priest we shall go beyond the great river. We shall go to the Place of the Gods—the place newyork—not one man but a company. We shall look for the images of the gods and find the god ASHING and the others—the gods Lincoln and Biltmore[5] and Moses[6]. But they were men who built the city, not gods or demons. They were men. I remember the dead man's face. They were men who were here before us. We must build again. ⓞ

---

5. **Biltmore:** New York City hotel.
6. **Moses:** Robert Moses (1888–1981), New York City public official who oversaw many large construction projects such as bridges and public buildings.

ⓞ **Literary Focus** Plot and Setting   Where is the Place of the Gods?

Applying Your Skills

RA.L.10.3 Distinguish how conflicts, parallel plots and subplots affect the pacing of action in literary text. **RP.10.1** Apply reading comprehension strategies, including making predictions, comparing and contrasting, recalling and summarizing and making inferences and drawing conclusions. *Also covered* **VO.10.3; WA.10.1.b**

By the Waters of Babylon

Respond and Think Critically

Reading Focus

Quick Check

1. Why is the river sacred to John's people? Why are they frightened of the Place of the Gods?

2. What does John's father think of John's dream? Why does he think John should take a journey?

Read with a Purpose

3. What does John discover on his journey? What happened to the Place of the Gods?

Reading Skills: Visualizing

4. How does visualizing the dead "god" in the Place of the Gods help you understand the conclusion that John draws about past events?

✅ Vocabulary Check

For each of the following Vocabulary words, choose the best synonym (word with a similar meaning).

5. **ignorant**
   a. wise   b. unaware   c. slow

6. **customs**
   a. roles   b. presents   c. habits

7. **perplexed**
   a. confused   b. enlightened   c. complicated

Literary Focus

Literary Analysis

8. **Interpret** Locate the following descriptions of the story's setting: the god-roads, the high towers of the gods, the statue of ASHING, the Great Burning, the caves and tunnels. What is John really seeing?

9. **Evaluate** What does John mean when he says the gods "ate knowledge too fast"? Do we eat knowledge too fast today? Explain.

10. **Extend** Benét wrote this story in the late 1930s, shortly before the outbreak of World War II and the invention of the atomic bomb. Are his warnings about humanity's power to destroy itself still relevant today? Why or why not?

Literary Skills: Plot and Setting Across Genres

11. **Analyze** "By the Waters of Babylon" is about the discovery, or re-discovery, of a ruined city. How does Benét use setting to create mood? How does the setting contribute to the story's plot?

Literary Skills Review: Conflict

12. **Analyze** A **conflict** is a struggle between opposing forces. In an **external conflict,** a character struggles against an outside force, such as another character, society, or something in nature. An **internal conflict** is a struggle within one character's mind. Describe the external and internal conflicts that John faces in this story.

Writing Focus

Think as a Reader/Writer

Use It in Your Writing Benét creates images of a city both alien and familiar. Write a description of a once unfamiliar place that is now a part of your everyday life, such as your school or a new neighborhood. Use descriptive words and phrases to show how your perception of the place has changed.

Coyote Kills the GIANT

Retold by **Richard Erdoes** and **Alfonso Ortiz**

Read with a Purpose

Read to learn how a Native American trickster saves the day.

Preparing to Read for this selection is on page 61.

Build Background

Tricksters are clever characters who may lie, play tricks, and get into trouble, but who also use their wits to triumph over their enemies. Sometimes they are creators who transform the world in some way. **Coyote** is a trickster who appears in many Native American tales. In the one you're about to read, he is a survivor—and a hero.

Coyote was walking one day when he met Old Woman. She greeted him and asked where he was headed.

"Just roaming around," said Coyote.

"You better stop going that way, or you'll meet a giant who kills everybody."

"Oh, giants don't frighten me," said Coyote (who had never met one). "I always kill them. I'll fight this one too, and make an end of him."

"He's bigger and closer than you think," said Old Woman.

"I don't care," said Coyote, deciding that a giant would be about as big as a bull moose and calculating that he could kill one easily.

So Coyote said good-bye to Old Woman and went ahead, whistling a tune. On his way he saw a large fallen branch that looked like a club. Picking it up, he said to himself, "I'll hit the giant over the head with this. It's big enough and heavy enough to kill him." He walked on and came to a huge cave right in the middle of the path. Whistling merrily, he went in. **Ⓐ**

Suddenly Coyote met a woman who was crawling along on the ground. "What's the matter?" he asked.

"I'm starving," she said, "and too weak to walk. What are you doing with that stick?"

"I'm going to kill the giant with it," said Coyote, and he asked if she knew where he was hiding.

Feeble as she was, the woman laughed. "You're already in the giant's belly."

"How can I be in his belly?" asked Coyote. "I haven't even met him."

"You probably thought it was a cave when you walked into his mouth," the woman said, and sighed. "It's easy to walk in, but nobody ever walks out. This giant is so big you can't take him in with your eyes. His belly fills a whole valley."

Coyote threw his stick away and kept on walking. What else could he do? Soon he came across some more people lying around half dead. "Are you sick?" he asked.

"No," they said, "just starving to death. We're trapped inside the giant."

Ⓐ **Literary Focus** Plot and Setting   Where is Coyote going? What is the purpose of his journey?

"You're foolish," said Coyote. "If we're really inside this giant, then the cave walls must be the inside of his stomach. We can just cut some meat and fat from him."

"We never thought of that," they said.

"You're not as smart as I am," said Coyote.

Coyote took his hunting knife and started cutting chunks out of the cave walls. As he had guessed, they were indeed the giant's fat and meat, and he used it to feed the starving people. He even went back and gave some meat to the woman he had met first. Then all the people imprisoned in the giant's belly started to feel stronger and happier, but not completely happy. "You've fed us," they said, "and thanks. But how are we going to get out of here?"

"Don't worry," said Coyote. "I'll kill the giant by stabbing him in the heart. Where is his heart? It must be around here someplace."

"Look at the volcano puffing and beating over there," someone said. "Maybe it's the heart."

"So it is, friend," said Coyote, and began to cut at this mountain.

Then the giant spoke up. "Is that you, Coyote? I've heard of you. Stop this stabbing and cutting and let me alone. You can leave through my mouth; I'll open it for you."

"I'll leave, but not quite yet," said Coyote, hacking at the heart. He told the others to get ready. "As soon as I have him in his death throes, there will be an earthquake. He'll open his jaw to take a last breath, and then his mouth will close forever. So be ready to run out fast!"

Coyote cut a deep hole in the giant's heart, and lava started to flow out. It was the giant's blood. The giant groaned, and the ground under the people's feet trembled. **B**

"Quick, now!" shouted Coyote. The giant's mouth opened and they all ran out. The last one was the wood tick. The giant's teeth were closing on him, but Coyote managed to pull him through at the last moment.

"Look at me," cried the wood tick, "I'm all flat!"

"It happened when I pulled you through," said Coyote. "You'll always be flat from now on. Be glad you're alive."

"I guess I'll get used to it," said the wood tick, and he did. **C**

B **Reading Focus** Visualizing How is the giant similar to a volcano?

C **Literary Focus** Plot and Setting What happens to the wood tick when he tries to escape?

Hanging Out (1986) by Gilbert Lujan. Collection of the Artist. Courtesy of Daniel Saxon Gallery.

Analyzing Visuals **Viewing and Interpreting** What does the animal in this image have in common with Coyote? Explain.

Applying Your Skills

RA.L.10.3 Distinguish how conflicts, parallel plots and subplots affect the pacing of action in literary text. **RA.L.10.5** Analyze how an author's choice of genre affects the expression of a theme or topic. *Also covered* **RP.10.1; WA.10.1.b**

Coyote Kills the Giant

Respond and Think Critically

Reading Focus

Quick Check

1. Why does Coyote plan to kill the giant? How does he feel when he learns that he's already inside the belly of the giant?

2. How does Coyote help the people he finds in the giant's belly?

Read with a Purpose

3. How does Coyote kill the giant? What else does he accomplish at the same time?

Reading Skills: Comparing Texts

4. As you read the selections, you compared various aspects of the texts. Fill in the rest of the chart now. Then, answer this question: How are the journeys in each story similar and how are they different?

Selection	Basic Situation	Conflict	Resolution
By the Waters of Babylon	John must go on a journey.		
Coyote Kills the Giant	Coyote seeks the giant		

My Answer:

Literary Focus

Literary Analysis

5. **Evaluate** What is the purpose of the brief mention of the wood tick at the end of the folk tale? Is this an effective ending? Why or why not?

6. **Extend** The giant's belly is an enormous cavern, and his heart is a fiery volcano. What other geological or natural features might make suitable body parts for the giant?

Literary Skills: Plot and Setting Across Genres

7. **Compare and Contrast** What purpose do John and Coyote have for going on their journeys?

8. **Compare and Contrast** What similarities and differences can you find between the settings of the two stories?

Literary Skills Review: Folk Tale

9. **Analyze** A **folk tale** is a traditional story passed down from generation to generation. Folk tales often explain beliefs or natural phenomenon. What belief or phenomenon does "Coyote Kills the Giant" explain?

Writing Focus

Think as a Reader/Writer

Use It in Your Writing Erdoes and Ortiz retell the tale of "Coyote Kills the Giant" without long descriptions. Rewrite one portion of the story, expanding the descriptions of the setting. Use descriptive words and phrases to bring the mood, atmosphere, and setting to life.

OH **RP.10.1** Apply reading comprehension strategies, including making predictions, comparing and contrasting, recalling and summarizing and making inferences and drawing conclusions. **WA.10.1.b** Write narratives that: use a range of strategies and literary devices including figurative language and specific narration; and *Also covered* **WA.10.4.c**

By the Waters of Babylon / Coyote Kills the Giant

Writing Focus

Write a Comparison-Contrast Essay

The selections you just read both feature characters on journeys. In what ways are these journeys similar? In what ways are they different? Write an essay in which you compare the journeys and their outcomes. Refer back to the charts you made as you read. Think about the following points:

- What is the purpose of John's journey? of Coyote's?
- What conflicts does each character face?
- How does the setting play a role in each story?
- How do the results of each journey differ? What does each character learn about himself and the world?

Evaluation Criteria for an Essay

An effective essay—

- begins with an introduction to the topic and presents a thesis statement
- develops each main idea in well-organized paragraphs
- provides ample support for main ideas
- cites examples from the texts
- uses transitions that smoothly and clearly connect ideas
- is free from errors in spelling, grammar, and punctuation

What Do You Think Now

How can a journey change someone both physically and emotionally?

CHOICES

As you respond to the Choices, use these **Academic Vocabulary** where appropriate: <u>aspects</u>, <u>credible</u>, <u>tension</u>, and <u>evaluation</u>.

REVIEW
Write a Summary

Timed └Writing The narrator of "By the Waters of Babylon" embarks on a journey of discovery. Write a summary of the story's plot, and explain what important discoveries the narrator makes on his journey.

CONNECT
Write a Folk Tale

Folk tales are traditional stories that have been passed down from generation to generation. The British writer Rudyard Kipling wrote a series of tales called *Just So Stories* to explain why animals are the way they are, for example, "How the Camel Got His Hump." Choose some natural phenomenon that is part of your life today, and create a folk tale explaining how it came to be.

EXTEND
Talk About Today's World

Group Discussion In "By the Waters of Babylon," the narrator sees buildings, houses, statues, and various other items belonging to an earlier civilization. What if someone from a future civilization uncovered some of our modern-day artifacts? What items would this person find? What would this person think about our society? Get together in a small group and discuss your ideas.

Learn It Online
Discover more using Internet links at:

go.hrw.com | L10-77 | **Go**

Analyzing Main Idea and Supporting Details

CONTENTS

What Do You Think

Are humans and animals all that different?

 QuickWrite

Think about how some animals seem to act as if they are human. Take notes on the animal behaviors you have observed.

Preparing to Read

RA.I.10.5 Analyze an author's implicit and explicit argument, perspective or viewpoint in text. *Also covered* **RA.I.10.4**

from **In the Shadow of Man / What Your Pet Is Thinking**

Reader/Writer
Notebook

Use your **RWN** to complete the activities for these selections.

Informational Text Focus

Main Idea and Supporting Details The **main idea** is the central idea expressed in a paragraph or in an entire essay or article. The main idea might be expressed in a topic sentence, or it might be implied, or hinted at. You might have to consider all of the details in the text and make an inference, or educated guess, about the writer's main idea. Good writers provide specific details to support their main idea. **Supporting details** might include examples, facts, anecdotes, quotations, or statistics.

Tips for Finding Main Idea and Supporting Details

- Read the selection title. Titles often suggest the main idea.
- Skim the introduction of the article or essay. Writers often state the main idea in their opening paragraphs. They may even give an overview of the details they will use to support it.
- Read the final paragraph of the article or essay to see if the writer has restated the main idea of the text.

Into Action Use a concept map like the one at right to help you identify the main idea and supporting details expressed in the selections that follow.

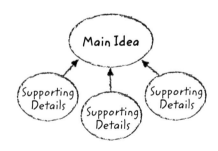

Vocabulary

from In the Shadow of Man

devoid (dih VOYD) *adj.:* completely missing; lacking. *One chimpanzee was devoid of shoulder hair.*

belligerent (buh LIHJ uhr uhnt) *adj.:* warlike; fond of fighting. *One of the chimpanzees was belligerent and often threatened Goodall.*

What Your Pet Is Thinking

abstractions (ab STRAK shuhnz) *n.:* ideas or concepts. *Scientists study animals to see if they can solve problems and form abstractions.*

empathy (EHM puh thee) *n.:* ability to feel another's emotions. *Some studies seem to indicate that animals feel empathy for others.*

altruistic (al troo IHS tihk) *adj.:* having an unselfish concern for others. *Scientists have observed animals that seem to display altruistic behavior.*

Writing Focus   Preparing for **Constructed Response**

As you read the selections, note key sentences in which the writers sum up major points and jot these down in your *Reader/Writer Notebook*. Look also for examples, facts, anecdotes, quotations, and statistics that support the main idea.

Language Coach

Derivations *Pathos* is a Greek word meaning "feeling." Which word on the list is derived from *pathos?* What other words can you name that also stem from *pathos?*

Learn It Online

Do pictures and animation help you learn? Try the *PowerNotes* lesson at:

go.hrw.com   L10-79   **Go**

from In the Shadow of Man

by **Jane Goodall**

Read with a Purpose
Read this selection to learn about the surprising discoveries Goodall makes as she observes chimpanzees.

Build Background
Jane Goodall is known for her detailed observations of chimpanzees in their natural environment. Between 1960 and 1975, Goodall observed chimpanzee behavior in the Gombe Stream Game Reserve in Tanzania. Her research corrected several misunderstandings about chimpanzees. As this selection opens, Goodall has established a camp in the Mlinda Valley in what is now the Gombe Stream National Park. She has climbed what is called the Peak above the valley in order to observe chimpanzees in their natural habitat.

As the weeks went by the chimpanzees became less and less afraid. Quite often when I was on one of my food-collecting expeditions I came across chimpanzees unexpectedly, and after a time I found that some of them would tolerate my presence provided they were in fairly thick forest and I sat still and did not try to move closer than sixty to eighty yards. And so, during my second month of watching from the Peak, when I saw a group settle down to feed I sometimes moved closer and was thus able to make more detailed observations. **A**

It was at this time that I began to recognize a number of different individuals. As soon as

I was sure of knowing a chimpanzee if I saw it again, I named it. Some scientists feel that animals should be labeled by numbers—that to name them is anthropomorphic[1]—but I have always been interested in the *differences* between individuals, and a name is not only more individual than a number but also far easier to remember. Most names were simply those which, for some reason or other, seemed to suit the individuals to whom I attached them. A few chimps were named because some facial expression or mannerism reminded me of human acquaintances. **B**

---

1. **anthropomorphic** (an thruh puh MAWR fihk): giving human qualities to nonhuman things.

A **Informational Focus** Main Idea and Supporting Details What information about chimpanzees is given in this paragraph?

B **Informational Focus** Main Idea and Supporting Details Why does Goodall name the chimps?

Chimpanzee catching ants on a tree with a stick. Masai Mara National Reserve, Kenya.

The easiest individual to recognize was old Mr. McGregor. The crown of his head, his neck, and his shoulders were almost entirely devoid of hair, but a slight frill remained around his head rather like a monk's tonsure.[2] He was an old male—perhaps between thirty and forty years of age (chimpanzees in captivity can live more than fifty years). During the early months of my acquaintance with him, Mr. McGregor was somewhat belligerent. If I accidentally came across him at close quarters he would threaten me with an upward and backward jerk of his head and a shaking of branches before climbing down and vanishing from my sight. He reminded me, for some reason, of Beatrix Potter's old gardener in *The Tale of Peter Rabbit*.

Ancient Flo with her deformed, bulbous nose and ragged ears was equally easy to recognize. Her youngest offspring at that time were two-year-old Fifi, who still rode everywhere on her mother's back, and her juvenile son, Figan, who was always to be seen wandering around with his mother and little sister. He was then about seven years old; it was approximately a year before he would attain puberty. Flo often traveled with another old mother, Olly. Olly's long face was also distinctive; the fluff of hair on the back of her head—though no other feature—reminded me of my aunt, Olwen. Olly, like Flo, was accompanied by two children, a daughter younger than Fifi, and an adolescent son about a year older than Figan.

Then there was William, who, I am certain, must have been Olly's blood brother. I never saw any special signs of friendship between

2. **tonsure** (TAHN shuhr): top of a man's head left bare by shaving. Certain orders of monks have the tonsure.

Vocabulary **devoid** (dih VOYD) *adj.:* completely missing; lacking. **belligerent** (buh LIHJ uhr uhnt) *adj.:* warlike; fond of fighting.

them, but their faces were amazingly alike. They both had long upper lips that wobbled when they suddenly turned their heads. William had the added distinction of several thin, deeply etched scar marks running down his upper lip from his nose.

Two of the other chimpanzees I knew well by sight at that time were David Graybeard and Goliath. Like David and Goliath in the Bible, these two individuals were closely associated in my mind because they were very often together. Goliath, even in those days of his prime, was not a giant, but he had a splendid physique and the springy movements of an athlete. He probably weighed about one hundred pounds. David Graybeard was less afraid of me from the start than were any of the other chimps. I was always pleased when I picked out his handsome face and well-marked silvery beard in a chimpanzee group, for with David to calm the others, I had a better chance of approaching to observe them more closely.

Before the end of my trial period in the field I made two really exciting discoveries—discoveries that made the previous months of frustration well worth while. And for both of them I had David Graybeard to thank. **C**

One day I arrived on the Peak and found a small group of chimps just below me in the upper branches of a thick tree. As I watched I saw that one of them was holding a pink-looking object from which he was from time to time pulling pieces with his teeth. There was a female and a youngster and they were both reaching out toward the male, their hands actually touching his mouth. Presently the female picked up a piece of the pink thing and put it to

her mouth: it was at this moment that I realized the chimps were eating meat.

After each bite of meat the male picked off some leaves with his lips and chewed them with the flesh. Often, when he had chewed for several minutes on this leafy wad, he spat out the remains into the waiting hands of the female. Suddenly he dropped a small piece of meat, and like a flash the youngster swung after it to the ground. Even as he reached to pick it up the undergrowth exploded and an adult bushpig charged toward him. Screaming, the juvenile leaped back into the tree. The pig remained in the open, snorting and moving backward and forward. Soon I made out the shapes of three small striped piglets. Obviously the chimps were eating a baby pig. The size was right and later, when I realized that the male was David Graybeard, I moved closer and saw that he was indeed eating piglet.

For three hours I watched the chimps feeding. David occasionally let the female bite pieces from the carcass and once he actually detached a small piece of flesh and placed it in her outstretched hand. When he finally climbed down there was still meat left on the carcass; he carried it away in one hand, followed by the others.

Of course I was not sure, then, that David Graybeard had caught the pig for himself, but even so, it was tremendously exciting to know that these chimpanzees actually ate meat. Previously scientists had believed that although these apes might occasionally supplement their diet with a few insects or small rodents and the like they were primarily vegetarians and fruit eaters. No one had suspected that they might hunt larger mammals. **D**

C **Informational Focus** Main Idea and Supporting Details What topic will Goodall discuss in the next paragraphs?

D **Informational Focus** Main Idea and Supporting Details What did Goodall learn about the chimps from this encounter? How does this discovery support her main idea?

It was within two weeks of this observation that I saw something that excited me even more. By then it was October and the short rains had begun. The blackened slopes were softened by feathery new grass shoots and in some places the ground was carpeted by a variety of flowers. The Chimpanzees' Spring, I called it. I had had a frustrating morning, tramping up and down three valleys with never a sign or sound of a chimpanzee. Hauling myself up the steep slope of Mlinda Valley I headed for the Peak, not only weary but soaking wet from crawling through dense undergrowth. Suddenly I stopped, for I saw a slight movement in the long grass about sixty yards away. Quickly focusing my binoculars I saw that it was a single chimpanzee, and just then he turned in my direction. I recognized David Graybeard.

Cautiously I moved around so that I could see what he was doing. He was squatting beside the red earth mound of a termite nest, and as I watched I saw him carefully push a long grass stem down into a hole in the mound. After a moment he withdrew it and picked something from the end with his mouth. I was too far away to make out what he was eating, but it was obvious that he was actually using a grass stem as a tool.

I knew that on two occasions casual observers in West Africa had seen chimpanzees using objects as tools: one had broken open palm-nut kernels by using a rock as a hammer, and a group of chimps had been observed pushing sticks into an underground bees' nest and licking off the honey. Somehow I had never dreamed of seeing anything so exciting myself.

For an hour David feasted at the termite mound and then he wandered slowly away. When I was sure he had gone I went over to examine the mound. I found a few crushed insects strewn about, and a swarm of worker termites sealing the entrances of the nest passages into which David had obviously been poking his stems. I picked up one of his discarded tools and carefully pushed it into a hole myself. Immediately I felt the pull of several

Analyzing Visuals Viewing and Interpreting
What does this photograph of Goodall and a baby chimpanzee show you that the text does not?

termites as they seized the grass, and when I pulled it out there were a number of worker termites and a few soldiers, with big red heads, clinging on with their mandibles.[3] There they remained, sticking out at right angles to the stem with their legs waving in the air.

Before I left I trampled down some of the tall dry grass and constructed a rough hide—just a few palm fronds leaned up against the low branch of a tree and tied together at the top. I planned to wait there the next day. But it was another week before I was able to watch a chimpanzee "fishing" for termites again. Twice chimps arrived, but each time they saw me and moved off immediately. Once a swarm of fertile winged termites—the princes and princesses, as they are called—flew off on their nuptial flight, their huge white wings fluttering frantically as they carried the insects higher and higher. Later I realized that it is at this time of year, during the short rains, when the worker termites extend the passages of the nest to the surface, preparing for these emigrations. Several such swarms emerge between October and January. It is principally during these months that the chimpanzees feed on termites.

On the eighth day of my watch David Graybeard arrived again, together with Goliath, and the pair worked there for two hours. I could see much better: I observed how they scratched open the sealed-over passage entrances with a thumb or forefinger. I watched how they bit ends off their tools when they became bent, or used the other end, or discarded them in favor of new ones. Goliath once moved at least fifteen yards from the heap to select a firm-looking piece of vine, and both males often picked three or four stems while they were collecting tools, and put the spares beside them on the ground until they wanted them.

Most exciting of all, on several occasions they picked small leafy twigs and prepared them for use by stripping off the leaves. This was the first recorded example of a wild animal not merely *using* an object as a tool, but actually modifying an object and thus showing the crude beginnings of tool*making*.   **E**

Previously man had been regarded as the only toolmaking animal. Indeed, one of the clauses commonly accepted in the definition of man was that he was a creature who "made tools to a regular and set pattern." The chimpanzees, obviously, had not made tools to any set pattern. Nevertheless, my early observations of their primitive toolmaking abilities convinced a number of scientists that it was necessary to redefine man in a more complex manner than before. Or else, as Louis Leakey put it, we should by definition have to accept the chimpanzee as Man.   **F**

I sent telegrams to Louis about both of my new observations—the meat-eating and the toolmaking—and he was of course wildly enthusiastic. In fact, I believe that the news was helpful to him in his efforts to find further financial support for my work. It was not long afterward when he wrote to tell me that the National Geographic Society in the United States had agreed to grant funds for another year's research.

---

3. **mandibles** (MAN duh buhlz): mouth parts that bite or hold food.

Read with a Purpose   What discoveries about chimps does Goodall make?

E **Informational Focus** Main Idea and Supporting Details What has Goodall learned about the chimps from this second encounter?

F **Informational Focus** Main Idea and Supporting Details What sentence states the main idea of this selection?

Applying Your Skills

RA.I.10.5 Analyze an author's implicit and explicit argument, perspective or viewpoint in text. **RA.I.10.4** Assess the adequacy, accuracy and appropriateness of an author's details, identifying persuasive techniques and examples of propaganda, bias and stereotyping. *Also covered* **VO.10.3**

from **In the Shadow of Man**

Practicing the Standards

Informational Text and Vocabulary

1. What is the **main idea** of the selection?

   A Studying chimpanzees is the best way to learn about human behavior.

   B Chimpanzees and humans share many of the same traits and behaviors.

   C Chimpanzees will approach humans once they learn to trust them.

   D All chimpanzees have unique personalities.

2. Which of the following *best* explains why Goodall named individual chimpanzees rather than assigning them numbers?

   A She believed that all living creatures should have names.

   B She was paying tribute to the friends and family members after whom she named the chimpanzees.

   C She found it easier to recall names than numbers.

   D She believed that other scientists were wrong to assign numbers to animals and decided to take a stand.

3. What **details** support the idea that the chimpanzees were making tools?

   A Goodall observed them selecting materials to use for tools.

   B Goodall observed them modifying an object for use as a tool.

   C Goodall observed them placing spare tools on the ground nearby.

   D all of the above

4. Why was Goodall surprised to observe the chimpanzees eating the pig?

   A Scientists had believed that chimps were vegetarians.

   B It had been thought that chimps ate only rodents.

   C Scientists had thought the chimps were not capable of catching a pig.

   D Chimpanzees and pigs were usually friendly.

5. *Devoid* means —

   A lacking something

   B accounted for

   C filled up

   D starting over

6. A *belligerent* person is —

   A uncertain

   B aggressive

   C kindhearted

   D self-centered

Writing Focus   **Constructed Response**

Create an outline that shows the main idea and supporting details in Goodall's text.

What <u>aspects</u> of chimpanzee behavior are similar to those of humans?

What Your Pet Is Thinking

by SHARON BEGLEY

from **The Wall Street Journal**

Read with a Purpose

As you read the following newspaper article, see if the writer presents a balanced account about what pets are thinking.

Preparing to Read for this selection is on page 79.

Build Background

This article refers to studies on animal behavior and contains references to certain specialized sciences. The article refers to these sciences:

primatology: study of primates—mammals that have flexible hands and feet, each with five digits

ecology: study of the relationship between living things and their environment

evolutionary biology: study of living organisms as they develop over time

As you read, be alert to definitions of other specialized sciences that are mentioned in the article.

From the day they brought her home, the D'Avellas' black-and-white mutt loathed ringing phones. At the first trill, Jay Dee would bolt from the room and howl until someone picked up. But within a few weeks, the D'Avellas began missing calls: When the phone rang, their friends later told them, someone would pick up and then the line would go dead.

One evening, Aida D'Avella solved the mystery. Sitting in the family room of her Newark, N.J., home, Ms. D'Avella got up as the phone rang, but the dog beat her to it. Jay Dee ran straight to the ringing phone, lifted the receiver off the hook in her jaws, replaced it and returned contentedly to her spot on the rug.

Just about every pet lover has a story about the astonishing intelligence of his cat, dog, bird, ferret or chinchilla. Ethologists, the scientists who study animal behavior, have amassed thousands of studies showing that animals can count, understand cause and effect, form abstractions, solve problems, use tools and even deceive. But lately scientists have

Vocabulary **abstractions** (ab STRAK shuhnz) *n.:* ideas or concepts.

African elephant carrying a tusk.

gone a step further: Researchers around the world are providing tantalizing evidence that animals not only learn and remember but that they may also have consciousness—in other words, they may be capable of thinking about their thoughts and knowing that they know. **(A)**

In the past few years, top journals have been publishing reports on self-awareness in dolphins and wild chimps whose different nut-cracking "technologies" constitute unique cultures. Others argue that rats have a sense of fun, mice show empathy for cage-mates and scrub jays are capable of "mental time travel" that enables them to remember where they stashed worms and seeds. . . .

(A) **Informational Focus** **Main Idea and Supporting Details** Which sentence in this paragraph states the main idea of the article?

Vocabulary **empathy** (EHM puh thee) *n.:* ability to feel another's emotions.

Some researchers say humans may be a bit too eager to attribute high-level mental functioning to animals, and end up inferring mental states that don't exist. Bonnie Beaver, professor of veterinary medicine at Texas A&M University and former president of the American Veterinary Medicine Association, says that when dogs act distressed in a boarding kennel, they're showing unfamiliarity with the surroundings, not resentment that their owner is vacationing in Bali. And if a dog looks guilty over leaving a mess on the rug, it is being submissive, she says, not showing a more complex emotion. "Most times," she says, "owners are reading things that are not there."

Not too long ago, scientists scoffed at the idea that animals could have consciousness. Philosophers haggle[1] endlessly about the meaning of the word, of course. But they generally agree that it isn't enough to solve problems, learn or remember—a semiconductor can do that—but to be aware of the contents of one's own mind. When it comes to animals, the question "was thought of as impossible to answer with objective observations," says Clive Wynne, an associate professor of psychology at the University of Florida, Gainesville. Now he sees an increase in such studies aimed at discovering what's going on inside animals' heads. . . . **B**

A key ingredient of consciousness is having a sense of self, a feeling that there's a "you" inside your brain. One sign of that is being able to imagine yourself in a different time and place. Some scientists have said that's why chimps in a forest pick up a stone so that they can crack a nut that they left far away, and why New Caledonian crows make hook-shaped devices to fish for bugs. **C**

But maybe, skeptics say, chimps and crows learned that a rock, or hook, equals lunch and just act reflexively. To try to rule this out, scientists at the Max Planck Institute for Evolutionary Anthropology in Leipzig, Germany, taught orangutans and bonobos, considered the great apes closest to humans, how to use tools to snare grapes that were otherwise out of reach. Then they gave the animals a chance to take the right tools into a "waiting room," where they were kept for times ranging from five minutes to overnight, before being led back to the room with the grapes. The clever move, of course, was to grab a tool before going to the waiting room.

All ten animals managed this at least sometimes, the researchers reported in May in the journal *Science*. Because the animals had to plan so far ahead, the scientists argue, the experiment showed an ability to anticipate needs. "It's hard to argue that these animals do not have consciousness," says primatologist Frans de Waal at Yerkes. **D**

Dissenters argue that any behavior that meets a basic need such as hunger shouldn't be ascribed to anything as lofty as consciousness. More and more, however, scientists are observing what they call altruistic behavior that has no evident purpose. Prof. de Waal once watched as a bonobo picked up a starling. The bonobo carried it outside its enclosure and set the bird on its feet. When it didn't fly away, the ape took it to higher ground, carefully unfolded its wings and tossed it into the air. Still having no luck, she stood guard over it and protected it from a young bonobo that was nearby.

Since such behavior doesn't help the bonobo to survive, it's unlikely to be genetically programmed, says Marc Bekoff, emeritus professor[2] of ecol-

---

1. **haggle** (HAG uhl): to argue or debate.

2. **emeritus** (ih MEHR uh tuhs) **professor:** retired professor.

B **Informational Focus** Main Idea and Supporting Details What contradictory idea has now been presented? What details support that position?

C **Informational Focus** Main Idea and Supporting Details What is the main idea of this paragraph?

D **Informational Focus** Main Idea and Supporting Details How do the details in these last two paragraphs support the main idea of the article?

Vocabulary **altruistic** (al troo IHS tihk) *adj.*: having an unselfish concern for others.

ogy and evolutionary biology at the University of Colorado, Boulder. If a person acted this way, "we would say this reflects planning, thought and caring," he adds. "When you see behaviors that are too flexible and variable to be preprogrammed, you have to consider whether they are the result of true consciousness." **E**

In June 2006, scientists reported new insights about compassion in African elephants. These animals often seem curious about the bodies of dead elephants, but no one knew whether they felt compassion for the dying or dead. A matriarch in the Samburu Reserve in northern Kenya, which researchers had named Eleanor, collapsed in October 2003. Grace, matriarch of a different family, walked over and used her tusks to lift Eleanor onto her feet, according to Iain Douglas-Hamilton of Save the Animals, Nairobi, and colleagues at the University of Oxford and the University of California, Berkeley, reporting in the journal *Applied Animal Behaviour Science.*

But Eleanor was too shaky to stand. Grace tried again, this time pushing Eleanor to walk, but Eleanor again fell. Grace appeared "very stressed," called loudly and often, and kept nudging and pushing Eleanor. Although she failed, Grace stayed with the dying elephant as night fell. Eleanor died the next day.

Grace's interest in an unrelated animal can't be explained by her genetic disposition to help a close relative, a behavior that's been well established. The scientists instead argue that the elephant was showing compassion. Mr. Douglas-Hamilton has also seen elephants guard and help unrelated elephants who have been hit by tranquilizer darts to let researchers tag the animals. Since standing by an animal that has been shot puts the other animals in harm's way, it's hard to argue self-interest. **F**

Critics say that consciousness is in the eye of besotted[3] observers, and animals are no more than stimulus-response machines. Florida's Prof. Wynne, for one, is skeptical that chimps know what they know. "To know one's own mental states does not necessarily imply conscious awareness," he says. "You can be unconsciously aware of what you know." Game-show contestants, for instance, sometimes press a buzzer to answer before they consciously know the answer—knowing unconsciously that they know.

Anyone whose dog has ever run to the front door, leash in its mouth, assumes that animals form intentions. But that might also reflect dumb learning: the dog figured out that leash equals walk. A computer could be rigged to learn the same cause-

3. **besotted** (bih SAHT ihd): acting foolish or silly about something.

E **Informational Focus** Main Idea and Supporting Details What idea is supported by these details?

F **Informational Focus** Main Idea and Supporting Details What position is supported by the account of the two elephants?

Analyzing Visuals   **Viewing and Interpreting** What incident in the text is illustrated by this photograph?

and-effect relationship. Some scientists also see intentionality when beavers plug holes in their dam, bowerbirds build baroque nests, ants cultivate fungus farms and plovers feign injury to lure predators away from their hatchlings. But many researchers give genes, not conscious intentions, the credit for these clever behaviors.

As for emotions, the conventional view has long been that while animals might seem to be sad, happy, curious or angry, these weren't true emotions: The creature didn't know that it felt any of these things. Daniel Povinelli of the University of Louisiana, who has done pioneering studies of whether chimps understand that people and other chimps have mental states, wonders whether chimps are aware of their emotions: "I don't think there is persuasive evidence of that." **Ⓖ**

The trouble is that all sorts of animals—from those in the African bush to those in your living room—keep acting as if they truly do have emotions remarkably like humans'. In 2006, Ya Ya, a panda in a Chinese zoo, accidentally crushed her newborn to death. She seemed inconsolable—wailing and frantically searching for the tiny body. The keeper said that when he called her name, she just looked up at him with tear-filled eyes before lowering her head again. The conventional view is that these were instinctive, reflexive reactions, and that Ya Ya didn't know she was sad. As the evidence for animal consciousness piles up, that view becomes harder to support.

Read with a Purpose Has this writer presented a balanced view on the question of animal consciousness? Do you find her conclusions <u>credible</u>? Explain.

Ⓖ **Informational Focus** **Main Idea and Supporting Details** What is the purpose of these last two paragraphs?

Applying Your Skills

OH **RA.I.10.5** Analyze an author's implicit and explicit argument, perspective or viewpoint in text. **RA.I.10.4** Assess the adequacy, accuracy and appropriateness of an author's details, identifying persuasive techniques and examples of propaganda, bias and stereotyping. *Also covered* **VO.10.3**

What Your Pet Is Thinking

Practicing the Standards

Informational Text and Vocabulary

1. What is the **main idea** of the article?

A Animals seem to have consciousness.

B Animals can learn complex tricks.

C Animals do not have instincts.

D Animals are intelligent.

2. The **supporting details** presented in this newspaper article are based on —

A research

B other newspaper articles

C private conversations

D the writer's opinions

3. Which of the following observations is a **supporting detail** for the author's main idea?

A Orangutans and bonobos use tools to reach food.

B African elephants show compassion to each other.

C A dog can learn to pick up the telephone.

D Geese fly south for the winter.

4. Critics of the author's **main idea** say that —

A animals are merely tricking their owners in order to get food

B scientists are being emotional

C computers could be rigged to get the same effects

D the results of the experiments were falsified

5. *Abstractions* are —

A concepts or ideas

B mechanics

C construction work

D fine art

6. A person with *empathy* can —

A be very cruel

B share the emotions of other people

C display a competitive streak

D work well with animals

7. An *altruistic* person is —

A gifted

B frightened

C unselfish

D dangerous

Writing Focus   Constructed Response

List three details that support the writer's main idea. Then, write down the detail you found most persuasive and explain why.

 What Do You Think Now?

How does the study of animal behavior challenge our ideas about what makes human beings unique? Explain.

Literary Skills Review

Plot and Setting   **Directions:** Read the following selection. Then, read and respond to the questions that follow.

Snow by **Julia Alvarez**

Our first year in New York we rented a small apartment with a Catholic school nearby, taught by the Sisters of Charity, hefty women in long black gowns and bonnets that made them look peculiar, like dolls in mourning. I liked them a lot, especially my grandmotherly fourth-grade teacher, Sister Zoe. I had a lovely name, she said, and she had me teach the whole class how to pronounce it. *Yo-lan-da.* As the only immigrant in my class, I was put in a special seat in the first row by the window, apart from the other children, so that Sister Zoe could tutor me without disturbing them. Slowly, she enunciated the new words I was to repeat: *laundromat, cornflakes, subway, snow.*

Soon I picked up enough English to understand holocaust[1] was in the air. Sister Zoe explained to a wide-eyed classroom what was happening in Cuba. Russian missiles were being assembled, trained supposedly on New York City. President Kennedy, looking worried too, was on the television at home, explaining we might have to go to war against the Communists. At school, we had air-raid drills: An ominous bell would go off and we'd file into the hall, fall to the floor, cover our heads with our coats, and imagine our hair falling out, the bones in our arms going soft. At home, Mami and my sisters and I said a rosary[2] for world peace. I heard new vocabulary: *nuclear bomb, radioactive fallout, bomb shelter.* Sister Zoe explained how it would happen. She drew a picture of a mushroom on the blackboard and dotted a flurry of chalk marks for the dusty fallout that would kill us all.

The months grew cold, November, December. It was dark when I got up in the morning, frosty when I followed my breath to school. One morning, as I sat at my desk daydreaming out the window, I saw dots in the air like the ones Sister Zoe had drawn—random at first, then lots and lots. I shrieked, "Bomb! Bomb!" Sister Zoe jerked around, her full black skirt ballooning as she hurried to my side. A few girls began to cry.

But then Sister Zoe's shocked look faded. "Why, Yolanda dear, that's snow!" She laughed. "Snow."

"Snow," I repeated. I looked out the window warily. All my life I had heard about the white crystals that fell out of American skies in the winter. From my desk I watched the fine powder dust the sidewalk and parked cars below. Each flake was different, Sister Zoe had said, like a person, irreplaceable and beautiful.

---

1. **holocaust** (HAHL uh kawst): great or total destruction of life.

2. **rosary** (ROH zuhr ee): in the Roman Catholic religion, a series of prayers counted off on a special set of beads.

1. You know the story's setting is the past because
   A. it is winter.
   B. the action takes place at a school.
   C. Sister Zoe is the teacher of the class.
   D. President Kennedy is on television.

2. Which of the following is an example of external conflict in the story?
   A. Russia's relationship with Cuba
   B. Tension between the U.S. and Cuba
   C. The children's fears about the bombings
   D. Sister Zoe's treatment of Yolanda

3. In the story's sequence of events, which event happens first?
   A. Yolanda sees snow for the first time.
   B. The class has an air-raid drill.
   C. Yolanda teaches the class to say her name.
   D. Sister Zoe explains what is happening in Cuba.

4. The climax of the story occurs when —
   A. Sister Zoe draws a picture of a mushroom
   B. air-raid drills are held at Yolanda's school
   C. a concerned President Kennedy is shown on television
   D. Yolanda screams when she sees the snow

5. Which word best captures the story's overall mood?
   A. lighthearted
   B. tense
   C. somber
   D. angry

Short Answer

6. Explain what happens in the story's resolution. Cite two details from the passage to support your explanation.

Extended Response

7. How does setting affect the plot in this story? If the story were to take place in another time, would the events still make sense? Write a brief description of the story's setting, and then identify the point in the story where the setting most directly affects the plot.

Informational Skills Review

Main Idea and Supporting Details   **Directions:** Read the following
selection. Then, read and respond to the questions that follow.

Wolf Speak by **Ruth A. Musgrave** for *National Geographic Kids*

If you want to understand wolf speak, you need to use your ears, eyes, and even your nose. Wolves talk to each other using their voices, body language, and, yes, body odor.

Wolves live in packs. Their survival depends on working as a team to find food, protect pack members, and raise pups. Being able to clearly read and express each wolf's rank is a matter of great importance.

Read My Lips and Ears and Shoulders

From head to tail, wolves express information through subtle and obvious body language. Facial expressions and how high a tail is held tell a wolf's confidence level or where it fits within the pack. The higher a wolf ranks, the higher it stands and holds its head, ears, and tail. The lower it ranks, the lower it drops everything, even flopping to the ground belly-side up. Wolves even puff up their fur or flatten it to express themselves.

From Growl to Howl

Yips, yaps, barks, and squeaks are all wolf sounds. Wolves usually use vocals when interacting with each other up close. Scientists have trouble eavesdropping on these shy animals, so little is known about wolves' private conversations. But they're sure vocalizations must be important. Even a three-week-old puppy can mimic almost all the adult sounds.

The howl is a wolf's long-distance call. In a forest, a howl might be heard six miles away. On the tundra it can be heard up to ten miles away. A wolf may howl to locate its pack. Or it may be announcing its availability to join or form a new pack. Packs howl together in a chorus to strengthen the team, warn other wolves away from their territory, or coordinate movements of pack members.

Body Language

When a wolf growls, others know it's angry, right? Not necessarily. They also need to see and smell the message to understand it completely.

For example, if the growling wolf's chest is on the ground, the rump is in the air, and its tail is wagging—possibly fanning good-to-neutral smells—it is inviting play. However, if that growling wolf is standing tall, has an open-mouthed snarl, a stare that could freeze water, and a tail held high—perhaps giving off scents indicating dominance—it's delivering a serious warning.

Talk to the Paw

With a sense of smell hundreds to millions of times better than humans', it's no wonder scent is a powerful and important part of wolf communication. Wolves intentionally leave their scent by marking trees and bushes with urine.

They also leave messages through scents left by scent glands in their feet and other body parts.

These odors aren't generally obvious to humans, but for wolves, sniffing tells all: the identity of an animal, its social status, whether it's an adult or immature animal, how healthy it is, what it's been eating, if it's ready to breed, and much more.

Why do wolves have such a complex communication system? "Pack members must live and work together to survive," explains wolf expert David Mech. "Like any good team, they rely on clear communication." As scientists continue learning how to understand wolf speak, they use their best tools—sniffing, spying, and eavesdropping.

1. What is the main idea of the article?
   A. Wolves communicate by howling and barking.
   B. Wolves' sense of smell is far better than ours.
   C. Wolves depend on a complicated system of communication.
   D. Wolves have expressive faces.

2. Look at the section entitled "Read My Lips and Ears and Shoulders." What is the main idea of this section?
   A. Wolves often talk with their tails.
   B. Wolves' body language reveals important information.
   C. Wolves show social rank by flopping to the ground.
   D. Wolves depend on their social structure for food and safety.

3. Which detail below would strengthen the author's position in the section entitled "Talk to the Paw"?
   A. An anecdote about a lost wolf finding its pack by smell
   B. A description of a wolf's typical body language around humans

C. A biological explanation of how a wolf can puff up its fur
D. An example of wolf pups that couldn't survive in the wild because they were born at a zoo

Short Answer
4. Explain how the author supports her main idea. Support your explanation with two details from the passage.

Extended Response
5. Think about the main ideas and supporting details presented in this article. Which are the most important? How do you know? Write a one-paragraph summary of the most important information in this article. Keep your paragraph short—no longer than five sentences.

Vocabulary Skills Review

Synonyms **Directions:** Choose the best synonym for the underlined word in each sentence.

1. In "The Leap," the <u>edifice</u> of the circus tent burns down, killing Harry Avalon.
   A. bottom
   B. structure
   C. poles
   D. appearance

2. He <u>complied</u> with his wife's request to move the ladder underneath the window of the burning house.
   A. refused
   B. got angry
   C. became nervous
   D. obeyed

3. The narrator of "The Leap" grew up in a small town, which she found <u>constricting</u>.
   A. exciting
   B. boring
   C. quaint
   D. limiting

4. In "Contents of the Dead Man's Pocket," Tom's hands tremble <u>imperceptibly</u> as he balances himself on the ledge.
   A. violently
   B. loudly
   C. invisibly
   D. softly

5. In "The Trip," Murad <u>pondered</u> the possible outcome of his escape attempt for months.
   A. thought about
   B. forgot about
   C. talked about
   D. fought with

6. The <u>prospect</u> of a life away from Morocco seemed promising to Murad.
   A. threat
   B. routine
   C. answer
   D. idea

7. One passenger threw up, causing a <u>putrid</u> odor to contaminate the boat.
   A. mild
   B. frightening
   C. rotten
   D. vivid

8. Coyote was <u>perplexed</u> by the starving people he found in the giant's belly.
   A. scared
   B. disgusted
   C. confused
   D. worried

9. In "By the Waters of Babylon," John is <u>ignorant</u> of the ways of the Forest People.

A. unaware

B. humble

C. insulted

D. disbelieving

10. John's people have numerous <u>customs</u> and rituals, such as singing and fasting.

A. clothes

B. meals

C. business

D. traditions

11. Rescuers had difficulty <u>extricating</u> Anna from the collapsed tent.

A. rescuing

B. untangling

C. catching

D. noticing

12. Balancing carefully, Anna took a <u>tentative</u> step on the tree branch.

A. flimsy

B. tight

C. hesitant

D. graceful

13. Tom's hands <u>rebounded</u> from the glass, nearly causing him to lose his balance.

A. retrieved

B. shattered

C. slashed

D. bounced

14. The window glass fogged slightly with Tom's <u>exhalation</u>.

A. breath

B. sweat

C. memory

D. effort

Academic Vocabulary

Directions: Choose the best synonym for the underlined Academic Vocabulary word in each sentence below.

15. An <u>evaluation</u> of Goodall's work showed that her conclusions were correct.

A. summary

B. judgment

C. opinion

D. assignment

16. The plot of "The Trip" is <u>credible</u> in part because of the details the author provides.

A. believable

B. beautiful

C. inspiring

D. doubtful

Read On

FICTION

About Time

Jack Finney's flair for fast-paced time-travel stories with a comic edge is beautifully realized in his short story collection *About Time*. In these tales you'll enter places where odd neighbors, magical coin collections, X-ray–vision eyeglasses, and disappearing dogs are your passports to the world of the past. Read these stories to see how time travel may not be as promising as it seems.

FICTION

Hope and Other Dangerous Pursuits

Thirty people, one raft. A dark, dangerous night. As a group of Moroccans flee to Spain in the middle of the night, four characters in Laila Lalami's book *Hope and Other Dangerous Pursuits* spend their journey reflecting on their lives and clinging to hope for the future. Struggling with poverty, dashed dreams, and crises of family and faith, these voyagers are willing to risk it all as they float across the Strait of Gibraltar toward freedom.

FICTION

Fahrenheit 451

The sky is full of smoke and ashes, but the cause isn't a wildfire or war. In Ray Bradbury's futuristic world, people are forbidden to read, and any books that are found are immediately burned by "firemen." Then one day a fireman named Guy Montag begins to question the wisdom of what he's doing. As he dares to enter the forbidden world of knowledge, he soon discovers a secret and beautiful world.

NONFICTION

Animals in Translation

Do animals see the same world we do? How do they really think and feel? In this fascinating book, a scientist who has lived with autism explores the world of the animal mind. Through her research, Temple Grandin shows that autistic people and animals experience their environments in similar ways—responding to details with a focus and passion that often approaches genius. *Animals in Translation* provides a unique viewpoint on animal behavior.

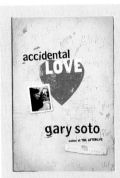

FICTION
Accidental Love

It all starts when Marisa picks up the wrong cell phone after a fight with Roberto, a boy who has gotten her girlfriend in trouble. Marisa is a *chola* and she isn't petite; she's a lot of girl and not ashamed of it. When she and Rene meet to exchange phones, she sees a skinny nerd who wears a calculator on his belt. He also loves chess and the science club. So why can't Marisa stay away from him? In this lighthearted novel of first love, Soto shows readers that opposites do attract.

NONFICTION
The Hot Zone

For a suspenseful and very true story get *The Hot Zone* by Richard Preston. This nonfiction thriller focuses on a deadly virus that almost escaped from a research laboratory in Reston, Virginia. Find out how this tropical threat was brought under control–barely. Even Stephen King was terrified: "The first chapter of *The Hot Zone* is one of the most horrifying things I've read in my whole life—and then it gets worse. That's what I keep marveling over: it keeps getting worse. What a remarkable piece of work."

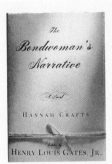

FICTION
The Bondwoman's Narrative

In his introduction to *The Bondwoman's Narrative*, Harvard scholar Henry Louis Gates, Jr., says it is "the first novel written by a female slave, and perhaps the first novel written by any black woman at all." A former slave herself, Hannah Crafts is the author of this autobiographical novel, telling of her escape from slavery. She is finally captured and sold to a new master whose wife will force her to marry. In desperation, Crafts comes up with the daring scheme to escape to the north disguised as a man.

FICTION
Fallen Angels

Richie Parry wants nothing more than to attend college and become a great writer someday. When his hopes for college are dashed, he makes a choice that will define the rest of his life: He signs up to fight in the Vietnam War. Walter Dean Myers's novel *Fallen Angels* is the gritty story of an African American private who finds himself in an atmosphere of violence, prejudice, and fear—yet somehow manages to form lasting friendships with some of the other soldiers he meets. Together they share the same dream—getting out alive.

Learn It Online
Explore novels—and find tips for choosing, reading, and studying works—with *NovelWise* at:

go.hrw.com   L10-99   Go

Character

INFORMATIONAL TEXT FOCUS

Synthesizing Sources: Drawing Conclusions

"For me it's always about complex characters who are somewhat unpredictable, going through some sort of a struggle."

—**Steve Buscemi**

What Do **You** Think **What makes us the way we are?**

The Family (La familia) (1987) by Rufino Tamayo. Oil on canvas (135 cm × 195 cm).

Learn It Online
To understand the role of characters in novels, visit *NovelWise* at:

go.hrw.com | L10-101 | **Go**

Literary Focus

by **Carol Jago**

What Makes a Character Believable?

Think of characters as the actors in a story. When characters are believable, they seem like actual people and we are able to identify with their conflicts and experiences. We care what happens to them. Writers use a variety of techniques to create characters. In this collection, you'll meet many kinds of characters. See how the writers have made them come alive.

Character Traits

Characters are defined by their **traits,** or special qualities. For example, a character might be selfish, brave, or outspoken. In "Two Kinds," the narrator has a common character trait: She thinks she is a failure.

> It was not the only disappointment my mother felt in me. In the years that followed, I failed her so many times, each time asserting my own will, my right to fall short of expectations.
>
> from "Two Kinds" by Amy Tan

Characterization

A writer reveals character in two ways. In **direct characterization,** a writer describes a character's traits. In the novel *The Kite Runner,* the narrator tells us directly that his friend Hassan is utterly honest.

> To this day, I find it hard to gaze directly at people like Hassan, people who mean every word they say.
>
> from *The Kite Runner* by Khaled Hosseini

In **indirect characterization,** the writer lets us see a character in action. We might also learn what the character looks like, hear what the character says, share the character's thoughts, and watch how other people respond to him or her. With all this evidence from indirect characterization, we infer what the character is like.

> He was pretending he was not in the war, pretending he had not watched Billy Boy Watkins die of a heart attack that afternoon. He was pretending he was a boy again.
>
> from "Where Have You Gone, Charming Billy?" by Tim O'Brien

"O.K., so I dig a hole and put the bone in the hole. But what's my motivation for burying it?"

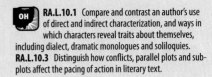
RA.L.10.1 Compare and contrast an author's use of direct and indirect characterization, and ways in which characters reveal traits about themselves, including dialect, dramatic monologues and soliloquies.
RA.L.10.3 Distinguish how conflicts, parallel plots and sub-plots affect the pacing of action in literary text.

Characters and Motivation

Like people, fictional characters have reasons for behaving the way they do. These reasons are called **motivations,** and they stem from a character's goals or desires. You can discover motivation by answering the question "What does this character want?"

In the story "Where Have You Gone, Charming Billy?" the main character is a soldier in Vietnam. He does not want to let his father know how frightened he was during the war.

> Then he would tell his father the story of Billy Boy Watkins. But he would never let on how frightened he had been. "Not so bad," he would say instead, making his father feel proud.
>
> from "Where Have You Gone, Charming Billy?" by Tim O'Brien

Types of Characters

The main character in the story—the one who drives the action—is the **protagonist.** The character who prevents the protagonist from getting what he or she wants is the **antagonist.**

Critics often use the following terms to refer to fictional characters:

Flat Character A **flat character** is a two-dimensional character with only one or two key personality traits: "Amy is exceptionally stubborn."

Round Character A **round character** has dimensions of a person from real life, with many traits and complexities.

Stock Character A **stock character** is one who fits our preconceived notions of a "type" (such as the mad scientist or the nutty professor).

Characters in Conflict

Often, what you want is at odds with what someone else wants. You might want to spend the afternoon playing your guitar, but your neighbor, who works nights, pounds on the door and yells for you to be quiet. **Conflict** is the struggle at the heart of every story and is closely tied to character motivation. To understand a conflict, start by examining what the characters want.

In "Two Kinds," Jing-mei's mother wants Jing-mei to be a child prodigy, but the constant pressure to succeed makes Jing-mei want to rebel.

> And after seeing my mother's disappointed face once again, something inside of me began to die. I hated the tests, the raised hopes and failed expectations. . . .
>
> I won't let her change me, I promised myself.
>
> from "Two Kinds" by Amy Tan

Your Turn Analyze Character

Think of a famous person. Write a paragraph describing him or her, and use at least three methods of indirect characterization. You might describe the person's appearance, actions, speech, or effect on others. Do not, however, include the person's name. Then, exchange your character description with a partner's. Do you recognize the person your partner has described? Why or why not? Based on your partner's response, would you make any changes to your own characterization?

Learn It Online
Do pictures help you learn? Try the *PowerNotes* version of this lesson on:

go.hrw.com | L10-103 | Go

Analyzing Visuals

How Can You Analyze Character in Paintings?

Some portraits are so realistic they seem like photographs. They show people and characters at one moment in time, often in the midst of an action or interaction. Other portraits are more abstract; the painters characterize their subjects with a unique blend of color, composition, and style. Learning to "read" paintings, like learning to analyze literature, can help you enter the worlds of these people and characters.

Analyzing Portraits

Use these guidelines to help you analyze paintings of people and characters:

1. Identify the subject of the painting. What is he or she doing?

2. Study the painting's composition. What do you see in the foreground? in the background? Which detail is most prominent?

3. Look for details that reveal character traits. What is the subject's appearance, facial expression, and body language? Which of these details is most striking?

4. Notice the painter's use of color and light. What meanings are associated with these colors? What mood do they create?

Look at the details of the painting to help you answer the questions on page 105.

RA.L.10.1 Compare and contrast an author's use of direct and indirect characterization, and ways in which characters reveal traits about themselves, including dialect, dramatic monologues and soliloquies.

1. Notice where the young man and the young woman are focusing their attention. What might they be feeling and thinking about?

2. The young man is prominently located in the foreground of the painting. What might this suggest about his relationship with the young woman?

3. What does the painter's use of color and light suggest about these **characters**?

4. How would you describe the young man and woman? What **character traits** does this painting convey?

Andrew and Missy (2006) by Billy Sullivan. Oil on linen (30" x 42"). Courtesy of the artist and Nicole Klagsbrun Gallery, New York.

Your Turn Write About Character

Look through this book, and choose a portrait that you find intriguing. Study the artwork, and write a brief description. Then, explain how the artist uses details, color, and composition to suggest character traits and interactions.

Reading Focus

by **Kylene Beers**

What Skills Can Help You Understand Characters?

Characters in literature can be as puzzling and complicated as the people we know in real life. Authors often make readers work to figure out what makes the characters in their stories tick. Making inferences, comparing and contrasting, and understanding historical context are three strategies that will help you understand the characters you meet.

Making Inferences About Characters

Every day, you make hundreds of **inferences** (intelligent guesses) based on current evidence and prior knowledge.

- **Current evidence** is the information that is in front of you right now.
- **Prior knowledge** is what you already know.

For example, you are going to a movie with a friend. She is twenty minutes late. The last time she was late, you missed the previews. You *infer* that the same thing will happen again.

You make inferences about characters the same way. A story might show you how they look, think, speak, and act. It might show you how other people respond to a character. You use these clues along with your prior knowledge about human nature to decide what kinds of people these characters are. In the excerpt below, you can see that the narrator finds the bright side even in a very bad situation.

> Night was falling, and we were stranded out there in the open.
>
> But at least it wasn't cold; that was a blessing. And at least we were not alone. For that, too, I felt grateful.
>
> from "Escape from Afghanistan" by Farah Ahmedi with Tamim Ansary

Making Inferences About Motivation

Learning to make inferences also comes in handy when you are trying to figure out *why* a character acts or speaks in certain ways. The underlying reason for a character's actions is called **motivation.** When you discover a character's motivation, you understand more about his or her personality. Writers rarely state a character's motivation directly. When you read, you must make inferences from the clues the writer plants.

Following is a list of questions you can ask yourself as you read the short stories in this collection:

- What does each character want?
- What does each character want to avoid?
- What conflicts do the characters face?
- What happens as a result of these conflicts— how do the characters change?

RP.10.1 Apply reading comprehension strategies, including making predictions, comparing and contrasting, recalling and summarizing and making inferences and drawing conclusions. **RP.10.2** Answer literal, inferential, evaluative and synthesizing questions to demonstrate comprehension of grade-appropriate print texts and electronic and visual media.

Comparing and Contrasting Characters

Writers often present us with characters whose traits, problems, or motivations are either very similar or very different. Often, these similarities and differences are sources of the conflict that propels the story forward. **Comparing and contrasting** the characters will deepen your understanding of each character's role in the conflict and lead you to a greater understanding of the story's larger truths.

In "The First Seven Years," the shoemaker Feld shows his misunderstanding of his assistant Sobel.

> He [Feld] had once asked him, Sobel, why you read so much? and the assistant could not answer him. Did you ever study in a college someplace? he had asked, but Sobel shook his head. He read, he said, to know. But to know what, the shoemaker demanded, and to know, why? Sobel never explained.
>
> from "The First Seven Years" by
> Bernard Malamud

The traits of the two characters can be shown on a chart.

Character	Character Traits
Feld	asks lots of questions, curious
Sobel	private, untalkative

Understanding Historical Context

What is happening in the world around you? **Historical context** consists of the social, political, and cultural forces of a story's time and place. As you work to understand characters' motivations, remember that people often behave a certain way because of their situation in a specific place and time.

Your Turn   Apply Reading Skills

In the passage that follows, Paul, a young U.S. soldier, is experiencing his first night in Vietnam. Knowing something about the historical context (the social, political, and cultural forces at the time of the story) is helpful:

- The Vietnam War involved terrifying guerrilla combat and surprise attacks.
- The jungle around Paul may be full of enemy fighters who will kill him if he makes a sound.
- As a U.S. soldier, he feels bound to a standard of courage and strength.

Now, read the passage and answer the questions that follow.

> "You're the new guy?"
>
> "Yes." He did not want to admit it, being new to the war.
>
> The soldier grunted and handed him a stick of gum. "Chew it quiet—OK? Don't blow no bubbles or nothing."
>
> from "Where Have You Gone,
> Charming Billy?" by Tim O'Brien

1. Why might Paul not want to admit that he's new?

2. Why does the other soldier not want Paul to blow bubbles?

3. What can you infer about the other soldier from his speech?

Now go to the Skills in Action: Reading Model

Learn It Online
Try the *PowerNotes* version of this lesson on:

go.hrw.com | L10-107 | **Go**

Build Background

This story is set at Mount Baker, which is located in the Cascade mountain range in Washington State. Powder is light, dry snow—the kind considered the best for skiing.

Reading Focus

Making Inferences We can infer from the narrator's description that his father is fun loving and somewhat irresponsible.

Literary Focus

Character The conflicts introduced here are external, between the narrator and his father and between the boy's father and mother. The boy wants to get home for Christmas Eve; the father wants to ski. He probably also wants to keep his son with him for as long as he can.

Read with a Purpose As you read "Powder," think about what motivates the narrator's father to act the way he does.

Powder

by **Tobias Wolff**

Just before Christmas my father took me skiing at Mount Baker. He'd had to fight for the privilege of my company, because my mother was still angry with him for sneaking me into a nightclub during our last visit, to see Thelonious Monk.[1]

He wouldn't give up. He promised, hand on heart, to take good care of me and have me home for dinner on Christmas Eve, and she relented. But as we were checking out of the lodge that morning it began to snow, and in this snow he observed some quality that made it necessary for us to get in one last run. We got in several last runs. He was indifferent to my fretting.[2] Snow whirled around us in bitter, blinding squalls, hissing like sand, and still we skied. As the lift bore us to the peak yet again, my father looked at his watch and said, "Criminey. This'll have to be a fast one."

By now I couldn't see the trail. There was no point in trying. I stuck to him like white on rice and did what he did and somehow made it to the bottom without sailing off a cliff. We returned our skis and my father put chains on the Austin-Healy[3] while I swayed from foot to foot, clapping my mittens and wishing I were home. I could see everything. The green tablecloth, the plates with the holly pattern, the red candles waiting to be lit.

---

1. **Thelonious Monk** (1917–1982): American jazz musician, famed as a pianist and composer; one of the creators of the bop style of jazz.
2. **fretting** (FREH tihng): worrying.
3. **Austin-Healy:** classic sports car of the 1960s.

Analyzing Visuals

Viewing and Interpreting
How does this image reflect the mood in the story?

We passed a diner on our way out. "You want some soup?" my father asked. I shook my head. "Buck up," he said. "I'll get you there. Right, doctor?"

I was supposed to say, "Right, doctor," but I didn't say anything.

A state trooper waved us down outside the resort. A pair of sawhorses were blocking the road. The trooper came up to our car and bent down to my father's window. His face was bleached by the cold. Snowflakes clung to his eyebrows and to the fur trim of his jacket and cap.

"Don't tell me," my father said.

The trooper told him. The road was closed. It might get cleared, it might not. Storm took everyone by surprise. So much, so fast. Hard to get people moving. Christmas Eve. What can you do?

My father said, "Look. We're talking about four, five inches. I've taken this car through worse than that."

The trooper straightened up, boots creaking. His face was out of sight but I could hear him. "The road is closed."

My father sat with both hands on the wheel, rubbing the wood with his thumbs. He looked at the barricade for a long time. He seemed to be trying to master the idea of it. Then he thanked the trooper, and with a weird, old-maidy show of caution turned the car around. "Your mother will never forgive me for this," he said.

"We should have left before," I said. "Doctor."

He didn't speak to me again until we were both in a booth at the diner, waiting for our burgers. "She won't forgive me," he said. "Do you understand? Never."

"I guess," I said, but no guesswork was required; she wouldn't forgive him.

Literary Focus

Character The narrator tells you how he was supposed to reply to his father. This interaction (or lack of one) tells you that the narrator is not happy with his father and does not want to go play his game.

Literary Focus

Character The narrator uses mostly indirect characterization to draw a picture of his father. He describes his father's speech, actions, and the effect that his father's actions have on him.

Reading Model

"I can't let that happen." He bent toward me. "I'll tell you what I want. I want us to be together again. Is that what you want?"

I wasn't sure, but I said, "Yes, sir."

He bumped my chin with his knuckles. "That's all I needed to hear."

When we finished eating he went to the pay phone in the back of the diner, then joined me in the booth again. I figured he'd called my mother, but he didn't give a report. He sipped at his coffee and stared out the window at the empty road. "Come on!" When the trooper's car went past, lights flashing, he got up and dropped some money on the check. "Okay. *Vámonos.*"[4]

Reading Focus

Making Inferences We can infer from the father's actions that he has been waiting for the trooper to leave the barricade. We can make a pretty good guess about what might happen next.

The wind had died. The snow was falling straight down, less of it now; lighter. We drove away from the resort, right up to the barricade. "Move it," my father told me. When I looked at him he said, "What are you waiting for?" I got out and dragged one of the sawhorses aside, then pushed it back after he drove through. When I got inside the car, he said, "Now you're an accomplice.[5] We go down together." He put the car in gear and looked at me. "Joke, doctor."

"Funny, doctor."

Down the first long stretch I watched the road behind us, to see if the trooper was on our tail. The barricade vanished. Then there was nothing but snow: snow on the road, snow kicking up from the chains, snow on the trees, snow in the sky; and our trail in the snow. I faced around and had a shock. The lie of the road behind us had been marked by our own tracks, but there were no tracks ahead of us. My father was breaking virgin snow between a line of tall trees. He was humming "Stars Fell on Alabama." I felt snow brush along the floorboards under my feet. To keep my hands from shaking I clamped them between my knees.

My father grunted in a thoughtful way and said, "Don't ever try this yourself."

"I won't."

"That's what you say now, but someday you'll get your license and then you'll think you can do anything. Only you won't be able to do this. You need, I don't know—a certain instinct."

"Maybe I have it."

---

4. *vámonos* (VAH moh nohs): Spanish for "let's go."
5. **accomplice** (uh KAHM plihs): partner in crime.

"You don't. You have your strong points, but not . . . you know. I only mention it because I don't want you to get the idea this is something just anybody can do. I'm a great driver. That's not a virtue, okay? It's just a fact, and one you should be aware of. Of course you have to give the old heap some credit, too—there aren't many cars I'd try this with. Listen!"

I listened. I heard the slap of the chains, the stiff, jerky rasp of the wipers, the purr of the engine. It really did purr. The car was almost new. My father couldn't afford it, and kept promising to sell it, but here it was.

I said, "Where do you think that policeman went to?"

"Are you warm enough?" He reached over and cranked up the blower. Then he turned off the wipers. We didn't need them. The clouds had brightened. A few sparse, feathery flakes drifted into our slipstream and were swept away. We left the trees and entered a broad field of snow that ran level for a while and then tilted sharply downward. Orange stakes had been planted at intervals in two parallel lines and my father ran a course between them, though they were far enough apart to leave considerable doubt in my mind as to where exactly the road lay. He was humming again, doing little scat riffs[6] around the melody.

"Okay then. What are my strong points?"

"Don't get me started," he said. "It'd take all day."

"Oh, right. Name one."

"Easy. You always think ahead."

True. I always thought ahead. I was a boy who kept his clothes on numbered hangers to ensure proper rotation. I bothered my teachers for homework assignments far ahead of their due dates so I could make up schedules. I thought ahead, and that was why I knew that there would be other troopers waiting for us at the end of our ride, if we got there. What I did not know was that my father would wheedle and plead his way past them—he didn't sing "O Tannenbaum"[7] but just about—and get me home for dinner, buying a little more time before my mother decided to make the split final. I knew we'd get caught; I was resigned to it. And maybe for this reason I stopped moping and began to enjoy myself.

---

6. **scat riffs:** short, improvised musical phrases in the style of scat, a kind of jazz singing.

7. **"O Tannenbaum":** title of a German Christmas carol, known in English as "O Christmas Tree."

Reading Focus

Making Inferences Notice how the father answers his son's question with another question. You can infer from this exchange that the father is avoiding answering his son's question.

Reading Focus

Comparing and Contrasting We learn from this passage that the narrator tries to avoid conflicts by thinking ahead. Furthermore, we learn that his father overcomes conflicts with charm and the ability to think quickly in difficult situations.

Why not? This was one for the books. Like being in a speedboat, only better. You can't go downhill in a boat. And it was all ours. And it kept coming, the laden trees, the unbroken surface of snow, the sudden white vistas. Here and there I saw hints of the road, ditches, fences, stakes, but not so many that I could have found my way. But then I didn't have to. My father in his forty-eighth year, rumpled, kind, bankrupt of honor, flushed with certainty. He was a great driver. All persuasion, no coercion.[8] Such subtlety at the wheel, such tactful pedalwork. I actually trusted him. And the best was yet to come— switchbacks and hairpins impossible to describe. Except maybe to say this: If you haven't driven fresh powder, you haven't driven.

8. **coercion** (koh UR shuhn): use of force.

Read with a Purpose Why did the narrator's father want to stay late at Mount Baker? What motivated him to drive on the roads even though they were closed?

Reading Focus

Making Inferences We can infer from the narrator's reaction here that trust is something he does not often feel when it comes to his father. Now that he does trust him, he is able to enjoy the ride.

MEET THE WRITER

Tobias Wolff (1945–   )

A Rootless Childhood

Tobias Wolff's parents divorced when he was young, and he spent much of his childhood traveling the country with his mother. Wolff was a teenager before he even met his older brother, Geoffrey, who had been living with his father since the divorce. Both boys grew up to become writers.

"A Sense of Who We Are"

Wolff is best known for his short stories, which have won numerous awards. He says, "There is a need in us for exactly what literature can give, which is a sense of who we are . . . a sense of the workings of what we used to call the soul."

Think About the Writer How might Wolff's childhood experiences have inspired this story?

Still from *This Boy's Life,* a film based on Tobias Wolff's book by the same name, starring Robert De Niro (left) and Leonardo DiCaprio.

OH **RA.L.10.1** Compare and contrast an author's use of direct and indirect characterization, and ways in which characters reveal traits about themselves, including dialect, dramatic monologues and soliloquies. *Also covered* **RA.L.10.3; RP.10.1; VO.10.6**

Into Action: Interview

Prepare to be interviewed as if you were the father or the son in "Powder." Before the interview, fill in a chart like the one below to clarify your traits, motivations, and conflicts.

	Son	Father
Character Traits	thinks ahead; orderly; wants to please his father	
Motivations		
Conflicts		

Work with another student who has analyzed the other character. Have your partner interview you as the character you have chosen. Then, interview your partner. Your interview should help you understand what motivates each character.

Talk About . . .

1. In groups of four, discuss the different ways in which the narrator and his father deal with conflict. Do most people try to avoid conflict or welcome it? Try to use each Academic Vocabulary word listed at the right at least once in your discussion.

Write About . . .

2. How would you describe the son's <u>attitude</u> toward his father?

3. What do the father's actions <u>reveal</u> about his character?

4. What new knowledge about his father and about himself does the narrator <u>acquire</u>?

5. What <u>traditions</u> might the father be handing down to his son, intentionally or not?

Writing Focus

Think as a Reader/Writer

In Collection 2, you'll learn more about how authors use characterization to make their characters come to life.

Academic Vocabulary

Talking and Writing About Short Stories
Academic Vocabulary is the language you use to write and talk about literature. Use these words to discuss the short stories you read in this collection. The words are underlined throughout the collection.

acquire (uh KWYR) *v.*: get or gain. *The main character in O'Brien's story will acquire new knowledge of himself and the war he is fighting.*

attitude (AT uh tood) *n.*: a state of mind or feeling about something. *She had a positive attitude toward work.*

reveal (rih VEEL) *v.*: make known; show. *The way a person acts in a crisis may reveal a lot about his or her character.*

tradition (truh DIHSH uhn) *n.*: handing down of beliefs, opinions, customs, and stories. *The tradition of passing down quilts from mother to daughter resulted in a beautiful family collection.*

Your Turn

Copy the words from the Academic Vocabulary list into your *Reader/Writer Notebook*. Try to use each word at least once as you read and discuss the stories in the following collection.

Everyday Use

by **Alice Walker**

Cotton Fields, Sunflowers, Blackbirds and Quilting Bees (1997) by Faith Ringgold. © Faith Ringgold, 1997.

at Do

ou

ink

How does our heritage
contribute to who we are?

 QuickWrite

List some of the many elements that can be p
heritage. Which elements do you think are n

Reader/Writer
Notebook

Use your **RWN** to complete the activities for this selection.

OH RA.L.10.1 Compare and contrast an author's use of direct and indirect characterization, and ways in which characters reveal traits about themselves, including dialect, dramatic monologues and soliloquies. **RP.10.1** Apply reading comprehension strategies, including making predictions, comparing and contrasting, recalling and summarizing and making inferences and drawing conclusions.

Literary Focus

Character Traits Like real people, characters in literature have **traits**—special qualities, features, beliefs, and quirks—that make them distinct and realistic. Often, a character's traits are <u>revealed</u> through his or her actions. A character's traits make him or her act in a way that affects the development of a story. In "Everyday Use," notice the character traits that make the story's three women different.

Reading Focus

Making Inferences About Characters An **inference** is an intelligent guess you make based on evidence. In a story, evidence includes details about how the characters look, what they say and do, and what other characters think about them. From this evidence, you can infer character traits that the author doesn't specifically describe.

Into Action As you read "Everyday Use," take note of what the characters say and do. Use a chart like this one to keep track of the clues.

Character	Details
Maggie	• homely and ashamed • looks at her sister with a mixture of envy and awe

Writing Focus

Think as a Reader/Writer

Find It in Your Reading We learn about characters from what they say to each other in the story's dialogue. As you read, pay attention to the dialogue between Mama and Dee. Write down in your *Reader/Writer Notebook* some of the dialogue that <u>reveals</u> character traits of each of them.

TechFocus As you read, create a list of events you would include in a video or film version of this selection.

Vocabulary

sidle (SY duhl) *v.:* move in a slow, sideways manner. *Maggie will sidle through the doorway as though she doesn't want to be seen.*

furtive (FUR tihv) *adj.:* secretive; trying not to be seen. *Dee likes to make a big entrance, but Maggie is furtive and shy.*

cowering (KOW uhr ihng) *v.* used as *adj.:* crouching or hiding in shame or fear. *The cowering Maggie was barely visible behind her mother.*

oppress (uh PREHS) *v.:* hold down unjustly; burden. *Dee believed society wanted to oppress her and her heritage.*

Language Coach

Antonyms and Synonyms An **antonym** is a word that has the opposite or nearly opposite meaning of another word. A synonym is a word with the same meaning as another word. Which of the Vocabulary words above is an antonym for *support*?

 Learn It Online
For a preview of this story, see the video introduction on:

go.hrw.com | L10-115 | **Go**

MEET THE WRITER

Learn It Online
Get more on the author's life at:
go.hrw.com L10-116 Go

Alice Walker
(1944–   )

Pulitzer
Prize
WINNER

National
Book Award
WINNER

Humble Beginnings

Alice Walker overcame impoverished beginnings and a potentially crippling accident to become a prominent writer. The youngest of eight children, she was born in the small town of Eatonton, Georgia. At eight years old, she was blinded in one eye by a shot from a BB gun. The resulting scar made her painfully shy and self-conscious, and she spent her time alone, reading and writing stories. With a scholarship for students with disabilities, she attended Spelman College, a college for African American women in Atlanta, Georgia, later transferring to Sarah Lawrence College in New York.

"The Cheapest Thing to Do"

Women have always played an important role in Walker's life. She grew up believing there was nothing her mother couldn't do. Empowerment of women is a major theme in Walker's writing. Her novel, *The Color Purple,* won the Pulitzer Prize for Fiction and has been made into a movie and musical. She has published fiction, poems, and essays, so it is surprising that she never intended to be a writer. "I remember wanting to be a scientist, wanting to be a pianist, wanting to be a painter. But all the while I was writing. We were really poor, and writing was about the cheapest thing to do."

Think About the Writer   How did Walker's early hardships influence her writing?

Build Background

This story takes place in the rural South in the 1960s, a time of rapid, sometimes violent change that affected people's values and ways of life. The civil rights movement brought national attention to the bitter struggle for racial equality. At the same time, U.S. society was depending more and more on industry and technology and less and less on agriculture. In "Everyday Use," these social changes shape the way the characters interact.

Preview the Selection

Mama, the narrator of the story, has worked on a farm much of her life.

Dee is Mama's older daughter, who moved away from the farm to get an education.

Maggie is the younger daughter, who still lives on the farm with Mama.

Read with a Purpose Read this story to understand a conflict between two ideas of a family's heritage.

Everyday Use

by **Alice Walker**

I will wait for her in the yard that Maggie and I made so clean and wavy yesterday afternoon. A yard like this is more comfortable than most people know. It is not just a yard. It is like an extended living room. When the hard clay is swept clean as a floor and the fine sand around the edges lined with tiny, irregular grooves, anyone can come and sit and look up into the elm tree and wait for the breezes that never come inside the house.

Maggie will be nervous until after her sister goes: She will stand hopelessly in corners, homely and ashamed of the burn scars down her arms and legs, eyeing her sister with a mixture of envy and awe. She thinks her sister has held life always in the palm of one hand, that "no" is a word the world never learned to say to her. **Ⓐ**

You've no doubt seen those TV shows where the child who has "made it" is confronted, as a surprise, by her own mother and father, tottering in weakly from backstage. (A pleasant surprise, of course: What would they do if parent and child came on the show only to curse out and insult each other?) On TV mother and child embrace and smile into each other's faces. Sometimes the mother and father weep; the child wraps them in her arms and leans across the table to tell how she would not have made it without their help. I have seen these programs.

Sometimes I dream a dream in which Dee and I are suddenly brought together on a TV program of this sort. Out of a dark and soft-seated limousine I am ushered into a bright room filled with many people. There I meet a smiling, gray, sporty man like Johnny Carson[1] who shakes my hand and tells me what a fine girl I have. Then we are on the stage, and Dee is embracing me with tears in her eyes. She pins on my dress a large orchid, even though she had told me once that she thinks orchids are tacky flowers. **Ⓑ**

In real life I am a large, big-boned woman with rough, man-working hands. In the winter

---

1. **Johnny Carson** (1925–2005): famous television personality and former host of *The Tonight Show*.

Ⓐ **Literary Focus** **Character Traits** What word could you use to describe one of Maggie's character traits revealed in this sentence?

Ⓑ **Reading Focus** **Making Inferences** Based on this passage, what can you infer about the narrator's relationship with Dee?

I wear flannel nightgowns to bed and overalls during the day. I can kill and clean a hog as mercilessly as a man. My fat keeps me hot in zero weather. I can work outside all day, breaking ice to get water for washing; I can eat pork liver cooked over the open fire minutes after it comes steaming from the hog. One winter I knocked a bull calf straight in the brain between the eyes with a sledgehammer and had the meat hung up to chill before nightfall. But of course all this does not show on television. I am the way my daughter would want me to be: a hundred pounds lighter, my skin like an uncooked barley pancake. My hair glistens in the hot bright lights. Johnny Carson has much to do to keep up with my quick and witty tongue.

But that is a mistake. I know even before I wake up. Who ever knew a Johnson with a quick tongue? Who can even imagine me looking a strange white man in the eye? It seems to me I have talked to them always with one foot raised in flight, with my head turned in whichever way is farthest from them. Dee, though. She would always look anyone in the eye. Hesitation was no part of her nature. **C**

"How do I look, Mama?" Maggie says, showing just enough of her thin body enveloped in pink skirt and red blouse for me to know she's there, almost hidden by the door.

"Come out into the yard," I say.

Have you ever seen a lame animal, perhaps a dog run over by some careless person rich enough to own a car, sidle up to someone who is ignorant enough to be kind to him? That is the way my Maggie walks. She has been like this, chin on chest, eyes on ground, feet in shuffle, ever since the fire that burned the other house to the ground.

Dee is lighter than Maggie, with nicer hair and a fuller figure. She's a woman now, though sometimes I forget. How long ago was it that the other house burned? Ten, twelve years? Sometimes I can still hear the flames and feel Maggie's arms sticking to me, her hair smoking and her dress falling off her in little black papery flakes. Her eyes seemed stretched open, blazed open by the flames reflected in them. And Dee. I see her standing off under the sweet gum tree she used to dig gum[2] out of, a look of concentration on her face as she watched the last dingy gray board of the house fall in toward the red-hot brick chimney. Why don't you do a dance around the ashes? I'd wanted to ask her. She had hated the house that much.

I used to think she hated Maggie, too. But that was before we raised the money, the church and me, to send her to Augusta to school. She used to read to us without pity, forcing words, lies, other folks' habits, whole lives upon us two, sitting trapped and ignorant underneath her voice. She washed us in a river of make-believe, burned us with a lot of knowledge we didn't necessarily need to know. Pressed us to her with the serious ways she read, to shove us away at just the moment, like dimwits, we seemed about to understand. **D**

Dee wanted nice things. A yellow organdy[3] dress to wear to her graduation from high school; black pumps to match a green suit she'd made from an old suit somebody gave me. She

---

2. **gum:** juice from certain trees; resin.
3. **organdy** (AWR guhn dee): a light, transparent fabric made from cotton.

C **Literary Focus** Character Traits What does this passage suggest about Dee's character?

Vocabulary **sidle** (SY duhl) *v.*: move in a slow, sideways manner.

D **Reading Focus** Making Inferences How does the narrator feel about Dee's reading to her and Maggie? Explain.

Viewing and Interpreting How are the setting and the characters in this painting similar to those in the story?

Quilts on the Line (1990) by Ana Bel Lee Washington.

was determined to stare down any disaster in her efforts. Her eyelids would not flicker for minutes at a time. Often I fought off the temptation to shake her. At sixteen she had a style of her own: and knew what style was.

I never had an education myself. After second grade the school closed down. Don't ask me why: In 1927 colored asked fewer questions than they do now. Sometimes Maggie reads to me. She stumbles along good-naturedly but can't see well. She knows she is not bright. Like good looks and money, quickness passed her by. She will marry John Thomas (who has mossy teeth in an earnest face), and then I'll be free to sit

here and I guess just sing church songs to myself. Although I never was a good singer. Never could carry a tune. I was always better at a man's job. I used to love to milk till I was hooked in the side in '49. Cows are soothing and slow and don't bother you, unless you try to milk them the wrong way. **E**

I have deliberately turned my back on the house. It is three rooms, just like the one that burned, except the roof is tin; they don't make shingle roofs anymore. There are no real windows, just some holes cut in the sides, like the portholes in a ship, but not round and not square, with rawhide holding the shutters up on

---

E **Reading Focus** **Making Inferences** How do you think the narrator (Mama) feels toward Maggie? What clues in the text help you make this inference?

the outside. This house is in a pasture, too, like the other one. No doubt when Dee sees it she will want to tear it down. She wrote me once that no matter where we "choose" to live, she will manage to come see us. But she will never bring her friends. Maggie and I thought about this and Maggie asked me, "Mama, when did Dee ever *have* any friends?" Ⓕ

She had a few. Furtive boys in pink shirts hanging about on washday after school. Nervous girls who never laughed. Impressed with her, they worshiped the well-turned phrase, the cute shape, the scalding humor that erupted like bubbles in lye.[4] She read to them.

When she was courting Jimmy T, she didn't have much time to pay to us but turned all her faultfinding power on him. He *flew* to marry a cheap city girl from a family of ignorant, flashy people. She hardly had time to recompose herself.

When she comes, I will meet—but there they are!

Maggie attempts to make a dash for the house, in her shuffling way, but I stay her with my hand. "Come back here," I say. And she stops and tries to dig a well in the sand with her toe.

It is hard to see them clearly through the strong sun. But even the first glimpse of leg out of the car tells me it is Dee. Her feet were always neat looking, as if God himself shaped them with a certain style. From the other side of the car comes a short, stocky man. Hair is all over his head a foot long and hanging from his chin like a kinky mule tail. I hear Maggie suck in her breath. "Uhnnnh" is what it sounds like. Like when you see the wriggling end of a snake just in front of

your foot on the road. "Uhnnnh."

Dee next. A dress down to the ground, in this hot weather. A dress so loud it hurts my eyes. There are yellows and oranges enough to throw back the light of the sun. I feel my whole face warming from the heat waves it throws out. Earrings gold, too, and hanging down to her shoulders. Bracelets dangling and making noises when she moves her arm up to shake the folds of the dress out of her armpits. The dress is loose and flows, and as she walks closer, I like it. I hear Maggie go "Uhnnnh" again. It is her sister's hair. It stands straight up like the wool on a sheep. It is black as night and around the edges are two long pigtails that rope about like small lizards disappearing behind her ears.

"Wa-su-zo-Tean-o!"[5] she says, coming on in that gliding way the dress makes her move. The short, stocky fellow with the hair to his navel is all grinning, and he follows up with "Asalamalakim,[6] my mother and sister!" He moves to hug Maggie but she falls back, right up against the back of my chair. I feel her trembling there, and when I look up I see the perspiration falling off her chin.

"Don't get up," says Dee. Since I am stout, it takes something of a push. You can see me trying to move a second or two before I make it. She turns, showing white heels through her sandals, and goes back to the car. Out she peeks next with a Polaroid. She stoops down quickly and lines up picture after picture of me sitting there in front of the house with Maggie cowering behind me. She never takes a shot without making sure the

---

4. **lye** (ly): a chemical once used to make soap.

5. **Wa-su-zo-Tean-o:** a greeting used by the Buganda people of Uganda that means "good morning."

6. **Asalamalakim** (ah suh lahm ah LAY kuhm): an Arabic greeting meaning "peace be with you."

Ⓕ **Literary Focus** Character Traits What does Maggie's comment suggest about Dee's character?

Vocabulary **furtive** (FUR tihv) *adj.*: secretive; trying not to be seen. **cowering** (KOW uhr ihng) *v.* used as *adj.*: crouching or hiding in shame or fear.

house is included. When a cow comes nibbling around in the edge of the yard, she snaps it and me and Maggie *and* the house. Then she puts the Polaroid in the back seat of the car and comes up and kisses me on the forehead.

Meanwhile, Asalamalakim is going through motions with Maggie's hand. Maggie's hand is as limp as a fish, and probably as cold, despite the sweat, and she keeps trying to pull it back. It looks like Asalamalakim wants to shake hands but wants to do it fancy. Or maybe he don't know how people shake hands. Anyhow, he soon gives up on Maggie. **G**

"Well," I say. "Dee."

"No, Mama," she says. "Not 'Dee,' Wangero Leewanika Kemanjo!"[7]

"What happened to 'Dee'?" I wanted to know.

"She's dead," Wangero said. "I couldn't bear it any longer, being named after the people who oppress me." **H**

"You know as well as me you was named after your aunt Dicie," I said. Dicie is my sister. She named Dee. We called her "Big Dee" after Dee was born.

"But who was *she* named after?" asked Wangero.

"I guess after Grandma Dee," I said.

"And who was she named after?" asked Wangero.

"Her mother," I said, and saw Wangero was getting tired. "That's about as far back as I can trace it," I said. Though, in fact, I probably could have carried it back beyond the Civil War through the branches.

"Well," said Asalamalakim, "there you are."

"Uhnnnh," I heard Maggie say.

"There I was not," I said, "before 'Dicie' cropped up in our family, so why should I try to trace it that far back?"

He just stood there grinning, looking down on me like somebody inspecting a Model A[8] car. Every once in a while he and Wangero sent eye signals over my head. **I**

"How do you pronounce this name?" I asked.

"You don't have to call me by it if you don't want to," said Wangero.

"Why shouldn't I?" I asked. "If that's what you want us to call you, we'll call you."

"I know it might sound awkward at first," said Wangero.

"I'll get used to it," I said. "Ream it out again."

Well, soon we got the name out of the way. Asalamalakim had a name twice as long and three times as hard. After I tripped over it two or three times, he told me to just call him Hakim-a-barber. I wanted to ask him was he a

> "What happened to 'Dee'?" I wanted to know. "She's dead," Wangero said.

---

7. **Wangero Leewanika Kemanjo:** names from a variety of groups in East Africa.

8. **Model A:** a type of car produced by Ford in 1903 and again in 1927.

G **Reading Focus** Making Inferences What can you infer about Dee's friend from this passage?

H **Literary Focus** Character Traits How is Dee's view of herself different from her mother's view?

Vocabulary **oppress** (uh PREHS) *v.*: hold down unjustly; burden.

I **Reading Focus** Making Inferences Why might Dee and her friend be acting this way?

barber, but I didn't really think he was, so I didn't ask.

"You must belong to those beef-cattle peoples down the road," I said. They said "Asalamalakim" when they met you, too, but they didn't shake hands. Always too busy: feeding the cattle, fixing the fences, putting up salt-lick shelters, throwing down hay. When the white folks poisoned some of the herd, the men stayed up all night with rifles in their hands. I walked a mile and a half just to see the sight.

Hakim-a-barber said, "I accept some of their doctrines, but farming and raising cattle is not my style." (They didn't tell me, and I didn't ask, whether Wangero—Dee—had really gone and married him.)

We sat down to eat and right away he said he didn't eat collards,[9] and pork was unclean. Wangero, though, went on through the chitlins[10] and corn bread, the greens, and everything else. She talked a blue streak over the sweet potatoes. Everything delighted her. Even the fact that we still used the benches her daddy made for the table when we couldn't afford to buy chairs. **J**

"Oh, Mama!" she cried. Then turned to Hakim-a-barber. "I never knew how lovely these benches are. You can feel the rump prints," she said, running her hands underneath her and along the bench. Then she gave a sigh, and her hand closed over Grandma Dee's butter dish. "That's it!" she said. "I knew there was something I wanted to ask you if I could have." She jumped up from the table and went over in the corner where the churn[11] stood, the milk in it clabber[12] by now. She looked at the churn and looked at it.

"This churn top is what I need," she said. "Didn't Uncle Buddy whittle it out of a tree you all used to have?"

"Yes," I said.

"Uh huh," she said happily. "And I want the dasher, too."

"Uncle Buddy whittle that, too?" asked the barber.

Dee (Wangero) looked up at me.

"Aunt Dee's first husband whittled the dash," said Maggie so low you almost couldn't hear her. "His name was Henry, but they called him Stash."

"Maggie's brain is like an elephant's," Wangero said, laughing. "I can use the churn top as a centerpiece for the alcove table," she said, sliding a plate over the churn, "and I'll think of something artistic to do with the dasher." **K**

When she finished wrapping the dasher, the handle stuck out. I took it for a moment in my hands. You didn't even have to look close to see where hands pushing the dasher up and down to make butter had left a kind of sink in the wood. In fact, there were a lot of small sinks; you could see where thumbs and fingers had sunk into the wood. It was beautiful light-yellow wood, from a tree that grew in the yard where Big Dee and Stash had lived.

After dinner Dee (Wangero) went to the trunk at the foot of my bed and started rifling through it. Maggie hung back in the kitchen over the dishpan. Out came Wangero with two quilts. They had been pieced by Grandma Dee, and then Big Dee and me had hung them on the quilt

---

9. **collards** (KAHL uhrdz): a vegetable related to the cabbage that has dark green, edible leaves.
10. **chitlins** (CHIHT lihnz): the large intestines of a pig, boiled or stewed.

---

11. **churn** (churn): a device used to make butter.
12. **clabber** (KLAB uhr): thickened or curdled milk that is used in making butter.

J Reading Focus **Making Inferences** What difference can you infer between Dee and Hakim-a-barber from this paragraph?

K Literary Focus **Character Traits** What is Dee suggesting when she compares Maggie's brain to an elephant's?

frames on the front porch and quilted them. One was in the Lone Star pattern. The other was Walk Around the Mountain. In both of them were scraps of dresses Grandma Dee had worn fifty and more years ago. Bits and pieces of Grandpa Jarrell's paisley shirts. And one teeny faded blue piece, about the size of a penny matchbox, that was from Great Grandpa Ezra's uniform that he wore in the Civil War.

"Mama," Wangero said sweet as a bird. "Can I have these old quilts?"

I heard something fall in the kitchen, and a minute later the kitchen door slammed.

"Why don't you take one or two of the others?" I asked. "These old things was just done by me and Big Dee from some tops your grandma pieced before she died."

"No," said Wangero. "I don't want those. They are stitched around the borders by machine."

"That'll make them last better," I said.

"That's not the point," said Wangero. "These are all pieces of dresses Grandma used to wear. She did all this stitching by hand. Imagine!" She held the quilts securely in her arms, stroking them.

"Some of the pieces, like those lavender ones, come from old clothes her mother handed down to her," I said, moving up to touch the quilts. Dee (Wangero) moved back just enough so that I couldn't reach the quilts. They already belonged to her.

"Imagine!" she breathed again, clutching them closely to her bosom.

"The truth is," I said, "I promised to give them quilts to Maggie, for when she marries John Thomas."

Ⓛ Literary Focus **Character Traits** Are you surprised by Dee's behavior? Why or why not?

CULTURE LINK

Quilting

Quilting is a form of needlework that has been practiced for centuries, usually by women. Quilts are made from scraps of fabric or old clothing. To make a quilt, a quilter sews pieces of fabric together and then onto a piece of batting, or stuffing. Traditional quilting patterns and techniques are passed on from generation to generation. Quilts are functional—they keep beds warm and serve as a way to reuse small scraps of fabric—and they are beautiful. Today, people cherish quilts not only for their history and usefulness but also for their artistic value.

Ask Yourself

Which character would you side with in the conflict over the quilts? Why?

She gasped like a bee had stung her.

"Maggie can't appreciate these quilts!" she said. "She'd probably be backward enough to put them to everyday use." **(M)**

"I reckon she would," I said. "God knows I been saving 'em for long enough with nobody using 'em. I hope she will!" I didn't want to bring up how I had offered Dee (Wangero) a quilt when she went away to college. Then she had told me they were old-fashioned, out of style.

"But they're *priceless!*" she was saying now, furiously; for she has a temper. "Maggie would put them on the bed and in five years they'd be in rags. Less than that!"

"She can always make some more," I said. "Maggie knows how to quilt."

Dee (Wangero) looked at me with hatred. "You just will not understand. The point is *these* quilts, these quilts!"

"Well," I said, stumped. "What would *you* do with them?"

"Hang them," she said. As if that was the only thing you *could* do with quilts.

Maggie by now was standing in the door. I could almost hear the sound her feet made as they scraped over each other.

"She can have them, Mama," she said, like somebody used to never winning anything or having anything reserved for her. "I can 'member Grandma Dee without the quilts." **(N)**

I looked at her hard. She had filled her bottom lip with checkerberry snuff, and it gave her face a kind of dopey, hangdog look. It was Grandma Dee and Big Dee who taught her how to quilt herself. She stood there with her scarred hands hidden in the folds of her skirt. She looked at her sister with something like fear, but she wasn't mad at her. This was Maggie's portion. This was the way she knew God to work.

When I looked at her like that, something hit me in the top of my head and ran down to the soles of my feet. Just like when I'm in church and the spirit of God touches me and I get happy and shout. I did something I never had done before: hugged Maggie to me, then dragged her on into the room, snatched the quilts out of Miss Wangero's hands, and dumped them into Maggie's lap. Maggie just sat there on my bed with her mouth open.

"Take one or two of the others," I said to Dee.

But she turned without a word and went out to Hakim-a-barber.

"You just don't understand," she said, as Maggie and I came out to the car.

"What don't I understand?" I wanted to know.

"Your heritage," she said. And then she turned to Maggie, kissed her, and said, "You ought to try to make something of yourself, too, Maggie. It's really a new day for us. But from the way you and Mama still live, you'd never know it." **(O)**

She put on some sunglasses that hid everything above the tip of her nose and her chin.

Maggie smiled, maybe at the sunglasses. But a real smile, not scared. After we watched the car dust settle, I asked Maggie to bring me a dip of snuff. And then the two of us sat there just enjoying, until it was time to go in the house and go to bed.

(M) **Reading Focus** Making Inferences What can you infer about Dee's intentions with the quilts?

(N) **Literary Focus** Character Traits What do Maggie's words reveal about her character?

(O) **Literary Focus** Character Traits Why does Dee think she is superior to her family?

Applying Your Skills

RA.L.10.1 Compare and contrast an author's use of direct and indirect characterization, and ways in which characters reveal traits about themselves, including dialect, dramatic monologues and soliloquies. *Also covered* **RA.L.10.3; RP.10.1**

Everyday Use

Respond and Think Critically

Reading Focus

Quick Check

1. According to Mama, how is Dee different from her and Maggie?

2. What different uses would Maggie and Dee have for the quilts?

3. What is the significance of the story's title?

Read with a Purpose

4. This story focuses on the idea of family heritage. What is the conflict between the two visions of that heritage? Why does Dee accuse Mama of not understanding her heritage?

Reading Skills: Making Inferences About Characters

5. Use the evidence you collected about the characters to make an inference. Add a column titled "Inference" onto your chart, and then fill in the column with one statement that sums up the character.

Character	Details	Inference
Maggie	• homely and ashamed • looks at her sister with a mixture of envy and awe	Maggie feels inferior to Dee and may be jealous of Dee's good looks.

Literary Focus

Literary Analysis

6. **Analyze** What can you conclude about each character (Maggie and Dee) based on her feelings toward the quilts?

7. **Infer** Dee has left behind her rural Southern life and reinvented herself. Why, then, does she want to have the churn and the quilts?

Literary Skills: Character Traits

8. **Describe** Name a few of Mama's character traits. Cite details from the text to support your answer.

Literary Skills Review: Conflict

9. **Explain** The driving force of any story is **conflict.** Explain the conflicts Mama faces in the story. How are these conflicts resolved?

Writing Focus

Think as a Reader/Writer

Use It in Your Writing Now that you are familiar with each character's voice, write a brief dialogue in which Maggie tells Dee the history of a quilt that both sisters want to have. What do the sisters' words reveal about their relationship? How do their differing opinions and beliefs show in what they say?

What Do You Think Now

What role do your heritage and family traditions play in your life today?

Applying Your Skills

Everyday Use

Vocabulary Development

Vocabulary Check

Match the Vocabulary words with their definitions.

1. **sidle**
2. **oppress**
3. **cowering**
4. **furtive**

  a. hiding in shame or fear
  b. secretive
  c. move slowly in a sideways manner
  d. hold down unjustly

Vocabulary Skills: Clarifying Word Meanings

As you read, you may come across words whose meanings you do not know for certain. The best way to learn what a word means is to look in a dictionary, but you may not always have a dictionary handy as you are reading. As an alternative, you can ask three questions to help you determine the word's meaning:

1. How is the word used?
2. What other words does it bring to mind?
3. What is the word's context?

To answer the first question, look at how the word is used in the sentence. Is it a noun, a verb, or an adjective?

Then, look carefully at the word and say it aloud. Pay attention to any similarities between it and other words you know. Those familiar words may give you a hint about the word's meaning.

Finally, look for context clues in the sentence or surrounding sentences that will help you determine the word's meaning.

Your Turn

Go back to the story, and select at least four words that are unfamiliar to you or whose meanings are not clear. Use those words to complete a chart like the one below.

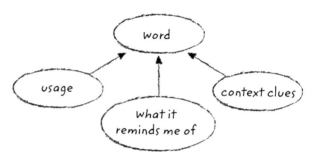

Language Coach

Antonyms and Synonyms Find a synonym or antonym (or both) for each Vocabulary word below. Use a thesaurus for help.

1. sidle
2. oppress
3. cowering
4. furtive

Academic Vocabulary

Talk About . . .
Do you think that one character (Mama or Dee) has more respect than the other for family traditions? Discuss your opinion with a partner. Use the underlined Academic Vocabulary word in your discussion.

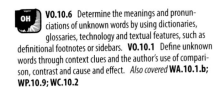
VO.10.6 Determine the meanings and pronunciations of unknown words by using dictionaries, glossaries, technology and textual features, such as definitional footnotes or sidebars. **VO.10.1** Define unknown words through context clues and the author's use of comparison, contrast and cause and effect. *Also covered* **WA.10.1.b; WP.10.9; WC.10.2**

Grammar Link

Dialogue

Dialogue plays an important role in stories. It helps you learn more about the characters and reveals aspects of their personalities. Dialogue also moves the plot forward. Remembering some grammar rules when writing dialogue is important.

First, the words of a speaker are set off from the rest of the text by **quotation marks.** Remember that quotation marks always come in pairs. One set marks the beginning of what a speaker says. The other set marks the end.

"Were Dee and Hakim married?" Charles asked.

Second, a comma usually comes before or after a **speaker tag.** A speaker tag is a phrase, such as "she said," that tells the reader who is talking.

Troy said, "I enjoy all of Alice Walker's stories."

If the speaker tag comes in the middle of the speaker's words, use two commas, one on each side of the tag.

"I enjoy all of Alice Walker's stories," said Helen, "but I like this one the best."

Finally, commas before a speaker tag, periods, and most other types of punctuation go inside the quotation marks.

Kelly asked, "Why did Dee want the quilts?"

"She thought they were art," said LaVonne, "but she shouldn't try to take them from her sister."

Your Turn

Rewrite the dialogue with correct punctuation.

1. Kevin asked Why is Maggie so shy?
2. Because she was scarred by the fire Kimberly answered.
3. I think replied Morgan Maggie was intimidated by her sister and that is why she acted shy.

CHOICES

As you respond to the Choices, use these **Academic Vocabulary** words as appropriate: acquire, attitude, reveal, and tradition.

REVIEW
Create a Storyboard

TechFocus Create a storyboard of the scenes you would include in a film version of "Everyday Use." Focus on the scenes that reveal the personality and traits of each character. How would you visually depict the characters? What dialogue would you include? Exchange storyboards with a partner, and give feedback about his or her choices and what changes you might make.

CONNECT
Explain Symbols of Heritage

Timed ⌐Writing The handmade quilts in this story hold special significance for Maggie, Dee, and Mama. The quilts are reminders of their heritage, of their culture, and of their family. Brainstorm some items in your home that have similar importance. Now, choose one item and write an essay explaining its significance to you.

EXTEND
Create a New Scene

Imagine what happens after Dee leaves her mother and sister. What would Dee say to Hakim-a-barber as they are driving away? How might she explain her mother's refusal to let her take the quilts? How would he respond? Write a dialogue between Dee and Hakim-a-barber that answers these questions.

Learn It Online
Expand your understanding of this story at:

go.hrw.com | L10-127 | **Go**

Where Have You Gone, Charming Billy?

by **Tim O'Brien**

What Do You? Think

How do life-threatening situations form who we are?

QuickTalk

In the Vietnam War, many young American men were sent overseas to fight in a war they knew little about. Get together in a small group, and talk about how you think those soldiers might have felt.

Reader/Writer Notebook

Use your **RWN** to complete the activities for this selection.

OH **RA.L.10.1** Compare and contrast an author's use of direct and indirect characterization, and ways in which characters reveal traits about themselves, including dialect, dramatic monologues and soliloquies.
RP.10.2 Answer literal, inferential, evaluative and synthesizing questions to demonstrate comprehension of grade-appropriate print texts and electronic and visual media.

Literary Focus

Characterization Authors <u>reveal</u> the personality of a **character** in several different ways—by telling the reader directly what the character is like, by describing how the character looks and dresses, by letting the character speak or act for himself or herself, or by showing us the character's thoughts and feelings.

Literary Perspectives Apply the literary perspective described on page 131 as you read this story.

Reading Focus

Understanding Historical Context "Where Have You Gone, Charming Billy?" re-creates a young U.S. soldier's fears on his first night in the field during the Vietnam War. To appreciate the details in the story, you need to understand its **historical context**—the social, cultural, and political issues of the time and place in which the story is set. There were no "front lines" in the war, and fighting took the form of unexpected guerrilla skirmishes. From moment to moment, the main character doesn't know what to expect—from his strange surroundings or from his own heart.

Into Action As you read, make a web diagram like the one on the right to keep track of details relating to the story's historical context.

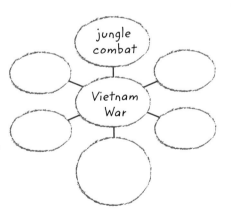

Vocabulary

stealth (stehlth) *n.*: secretiveness; sly behavior. *The soldiers moved with stealth toward the enemy camp.*

diffuse (dih FYOOS) *adj.*: spread out; unfocused. *Exhausted after the march, Mark felt a diffuse ache through his entire body.*

skirted (SKURT ihd) *v.*: passed along the border or side of something. *Watchful for traps, the men skirted the main path.*

inert (ihn URT) *adj.*: motionless; here, dead. *Paul stared at the inert body of the American soldier.*

valiantly (VAL yuhnt lee) *adv.*: bravely. *Though they were very frightened, the troops fought valiantly.*

Language Coach

Definitions The word *stealth* can be used as both a noun and an adjective. You may have heard the term *stealth bomber,* which refers to a plane that is undetectable by radar. Use a dictionary to find another definition for *diffuse* used as a verb.

Writing Focus

Think as a Reader/Writer

Find It in Your Reading As you read this selection, pay attention to the techniques that O'Brien uses to <u>reveal</u> and develop Paul's character over the course of the story. In your *Reader/Writer Notebook,* write down references to passages that give you particular insight into Paul's personality and motivations.

 Learn It Online
Hear a professional actor read this story. Visit the selection online at:

go.hrw.com L10-129   **Go**

Learn It Online
Learn more about the author at:
go.hrw.com L10-130 Go

Tim O'Brien
(1946–   )

National
Book Award
WINNER

The Power of the Heart

The Vietnam War made Tim O'Brien a writer. He was drafted into the U.S. Army immediately after graduating from Macalester College in St. Paul, Minnesota, in 1968. He then spent two years in Vietnam.

When he returned from Vietnam, O'Brien used his imagination to cope with memories of the war. Many of his stories are told from the point of view of a young soldier named Paul Berlin. These stories eventually grew into a novel, *Going After Cacciato*, which won the National Book Award in 1979.

"Security and Sanity"

The following is from O'Brien's personal account of the war, *If I Die in a Combat Zone, Box Me Up and Ship Me Home*:

"One of the most persistent and appalling thoughts which lumbers through your mind as you walk through Vietnam at night is the fear of getting lost, of becoming detached from the others, of spending the night alone in that frightening and haunted countryside. It was dark. We walked in a single file, perhaps three yards apart. . . . We veered off the road, through clumps of trees, through tangles of bamboo and grass, zigzagging through graveyards of dead Vietnamese. . . . The man to the front and the man to the rear were the only holds on security and sanity."

Think About the Writer — How might writing about the Vietnam War help O'Brien deal with his experiences there?

Build Background

The Vietnam War lasted from 1965 to 1973. It began because the United States was worried about the spread of Communism in Asia. (Communism is a form of government in which one party holds power and controls the economy.) After Vietnam won independence from France in 1954, a split occurred in Vietnam. The result was a Communist government in the north and a pro-Western government in the south. The United States sent troops to South Vietnam to help defend it against the north, but the North Vietnamese government eventually won the conflict.

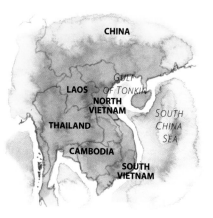

Preview the Selection

In "Where Have You Gone, Charming Billy?" you'll meet **Private First Class Paul Berlin,** a young soldier experiencing a baffling and terrifying new world.

The Vietnam Veterans Memorial, Washington D.C.

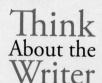

Where Have You Gone, Charming Billy?

by **Tim O'Brien**

The platoon of twenty-six soldiers moved slowly in the dark, single file, not talking. One by one, like sheep in a dream, they passed through the hedgerow, crossed quietly over a meadow, and came down to the rice paddy.[1] There they stopped. Their leader knelt down, motioning with his hand, and one by one the other soldiers squatted in the shadows, vanishing in the primitive stealth of warfare. For a long time they did not move. Except for the sounds of their breathing, the twenty-six men were very quiet: some of them excited by the adventure, some of them afraid, some of them exhausted from the long night march, some of them looking forward to reaching the sea, where they would be safe. At the rear of the column, Private First Class Paul Berlin lay quietly with his forehead resting on the black plastic stock of his rifle, his eyes closed. He was pretending he was not in the war, pretending he had not watched Billy Boy Watkins die of a heart attack that afternoon. He was pretending he was a boy again, camping with his father in the midnight summer along the Des Moines

River. In the dark, with his eyes pinched shut, he pretended. He pretended that when he opened his eyes, his father would be there by the campfire and they would talk softly about whatever came to mind and then roll into their sleeping bags, and that later they'd wake up and it would be morning and there would not be a war, and that Billy Boy Watkins had not died of a heart attack that afternoon. He pretended he was not a soldier. **A**

A **Literary Focus** Characterization What impression do you have of Paul after reading this passage?

Literary Perspectives

Analyzing Biographical Information Use the **biographical perspective** to see how the events and circumstances that shape an author's life often become the basis for much of his or her fiction. Knowing this biographical information can be useful when examining themes, historical context, and the creation of fictional characters within a piece of writing. In this story, we follow a frightened and nervous soldier during his first experiences in the Vietnam War. He has just seen a fellow soldier die from a heart attack. Tim O'Brien, the author, fought as an infantry soldier in Vietnam for two years, and most of his writing focuses on this war. As you read, be sure to notice the notes and questions in the text, which will guide you in using this perspective.

---

1. **rice paddy:** flooded field for growing rice.

Vocabulary **stealth** (stehlth) *n.:* secretiveness; sly behavior.

In the morning, when they reached the sea, it would be better. The hot afternoon would be over, he would bathe in the sea, and he would forget how frightened he had been on his first day at the war. The second day would not be so bad. He would learn.

There was a sound beside him, a movement, and then a breathed "Hey!"

He opened his eyes, shivering as if emerging from a deep nightmare.

"Hey!" a shadow whispered. "We're *moving*. Get up."

"Okay."

"You sleepin', or something?"

"No." He could not make out the soldier's face. With clumsy, concrete hands he clawed for his rifle, found it, found his helmet.

The soldier shadow grunted. "You got a lot to learn, buddy. I'd shoot you if I thought you was sleepin'. Let's go."

Private First Class Paul Berlin blinked.

Ahead of him, silhouetted against the sky, he saw the string of soldiers wading into the flat paddy, the black outline of their shoulders and packs and weapons. He was comfortable. He did not want to move. But he was afraid, for it was his first night at the war, so he hurried to catch up, stumbling once, scraping his knee, groping as though blind; his boots sank into the thick paddy water, and he smelled it all around him. He would tell his mother how it smelled: mud and algae and cattle manure and chlorophyll; decay, breeding mosquitoes and leeches as big as mice; the fecund[2] warmth of the paddy

2. **fecund** (FEE kuhnd): fertile; producing abundantly.

waters rising up to his cut knee. But he would not tell how frightened he had been. **B**

Once they reached the sea, things would be better. They would have their rear guarded by three thousand miles of ocean, and they would swim and dive into the breakers and hunt crayfish and smell the salt, and they would be safe.

He followed the shadow of the man in front of him. It was a clear night. Already the Southern Cross was out. And other stars he

---

B **Reading Focus** **Historical Context** How does this description of the setting help you understand the story's historical context?

Analyzing Visuals **Viewing and Interpreting** Do the details in the photograph match your idea of the story's Vietnam setting? Why or why not?

could not yet name—soon, he thought, he would learn their names. And puffy night clouds. There was not yet a moon. Wading through the paddy, his boots made sleepy, sloshing sounds, like a lullaby, and he tried not to think. Though he was afraid, he now knew that fear came in many degrees and types and peculiar categories, and he knew that his fear now was not so bad as it had been in the hot afternoon, when poor Billy Boy Watkins got killed by a heart attack. His fear now was diffuse and unformed: ghosts in the tree line, night-time fears of a child, a boogeyman in the closet that his father would open to show empty, saying, "See? Nothing there, champ. Now you can sleep." In the afternoon it had been worse: The fear had been bundled and tight and he'd been on his hands and knees, crawling like an insect, an ant escaping a giant's footsteps, and thinking nothing, brain flopping like wet cement in a

---

Vocabulary **diffuse** (dih FYOOS) *adj.:* spread out; unfocused.

mixer, not thinking at all, watching while Billy Boy Watkins died. **C**

Now, as he stepped out of the paddy onto a narrow dirt path, now the fear was mostly the fear of being so terribly afraid again.

He tried not to think.

There were tricks he'd learned to keep from thinking. Counting: He counted his steps, concentrating on the numbers, pretending that the steps were dollar bills and that each step through the night made him richer and richer, so that soon he would become a wealthy man, and he kept counting and considered the ways he might spend the money after the war and what he would do. He would look his father in the eye and shrug and say, "It was pretty bad at first, but I learned a lot and I got used to it." Then he would tell his father the story of Billy Boy Watkins. But he would never let on how frightened he had been. "Not so bad," he would say instead, making his father feel proud.

Songs, another trick to stop from thinking: *Where have you gone, Billy Boy, Billy Boy, oh, where have you gone, charming Billy? I have gone to seek a wife, she's the joy of my life, but she's a young thing and cannot leave her mother,* and other songs that he sang in his thoughts as he walked toward the sea. And when he reached the sea, he would dig a deep hole in the sand and he would sleep like the high clouds and he would not be afraid anymore.

The moon came out. Pale and shrunken to the size of a dime.

The helmet was heavy on his head. In the morning he would adjust the leather binding. He would clean his rifle, too. Even though he had been frightened to shoot it during the hot afternoon, he would carefully clean the breech and the muzzle and the ammunition so that next time he would be ready and not so afraid. In the morning, when they reached the sea, he would begin to make friends with some of the other soldiers. He would learn their names and laugh at their jokes. Then when the war was over, he would have war buddies, and he would write to them once in a while and exchange memories. **D**

Walking, sleeping in his walking, he felt better. He watched the moon come higher.

Once they skirted a sleeping village. The smells again—straw, cattle, mildew. The men were quiet. On the far side of the village, buried in the dark smells, a dog barked. The column stopped until the barking died away; then they marched fast away from the village, through a graveyard filled with conical-shaped burial mounds and tiny altars made of clay and stone. The graveyard had a perfumy smell. A nice place to spend the night, he thought. The mounds would make fine battlements,[3] and the smell was nice and the place was quiet. But they went on, passing through a hedgerow and across another paddy and east toward the sea.

He walked carefully. He remembered what he'd been taught: Stay off the center of the path, for that was where the land mines and booby traps were planted, where stupid and lazy soldiers like to walk. Stay alert, he'd been taught. Better alert than inert. Ag-ile, mo-bile, hos-tile. He wished he'd paid better attention to the

---

3. **battlements** (BAT uhl muhnts): fortifications from which to shoot.

C **Literary Focus** Characterization What can you tell about Paul from his thoughts?

D **Reading Focus** Historical Context Do the situations and feelings expressed here seem specifically related to this war, or are they general for all wars? Explain.

Vocabulary **skirted** (SKURT ihd) *v.:* passed along the border or side of something.
inert (ihn URT) *adj.:* motionless; here, dead.

training. He could not remember what they'd said about how to stop being afraid; they hadn't given any lessons in courage—not that he could remember—and they hadn't mentioned how Billy Boy Watkins would die of a heart attack, his face turning pale and the veins popping out. **E**

Private First Class Paul Berlin walked carefully.

Stretching ahead of him like dark beads on an invisible chain, the string of shadow soldiers whose names he did not yet know moved with the silence and slow grace of smoke. Now and again moonlight was reflected off a machine gun or a wristwatch. But mostly the soldiers were quiet and hidden and faraway-seeming in a peaceful night, strangers on a long street, and he felt quite separate from them, as if trailing behind like the caboose on a night train, pulled along by inertia, sleepwalking, an afterthought to the war.

So he walked carefully, counting his steps. When he had counted to 3,485, the column stopped.

One by one the soldiers knelt or squatted down.

The grass along the path was wet. Private First Class Paul Berlin lay back and turned his head so that he could lick at the dew with his eyes closed, another trick to forget the war. He might have slept. "I *wasn't* afraid," he was screaming or dreaming, facing his father's stern eyes. "I wasn't afraid," he was saying. When he opened his eyes, a soldier was sitting beside him, quietly chewing a stick of Doublemint gum.

"You sleepin' again?" the soldier whispered.

"No," said Private First Class Paul Berlin. "Hell, no."

The soldier grunted, chewing his gum. Then he twisted the cap off his canteen, took a swallow, and handed it through the dark.

"Take some," he whispered.

"Thanks."

"You're the new guy?"

"Yes." He did not want to admit it, being new to the war.

The soldier grunted and handed him a stick of gum. "Chew it quiet—OK? Don't blow no bubbles or nothing."

"Thanks. I won't." He could not make out the man's face in the shadows. **F**

They sat still and Private First Class Paul

E **Literary Perspectives** **Biographical Perspective** Do you think something like this might have really happened to the author? Why or why not?

F **Reading Focus** **Historical Context** Does this passage help put the story's setting or context in a new perspective? Explain.

Berlin chewed the gum until all the sugars were gone; then the soldier said, "Bad day today, buddy."

Private First Class Paul Berlin nodded wisely, but he did not speak.

"Don't think it's always so bad," the soldier whispered. "I don't wanna scare you. You'll get used to it soon enough. . . . They been fighting wars a long time, and you get used to it."

"Yeah."

"You will."

They were quiet awhile. And the night was quiet, no crickets or birds, and it was hard to imagine it was truly a war. He searched for the soldier's face but could not find it. It did not matter much. Even if he saw the fellow's face, he would not know the name; and even if he knew the name, it would not matter much. **G**

"Haven't got the time?" the soldier whispered.

"No."

"Rats. . . . Don't matter, really. Goes faster if you don't know the time, anyhow."

"Sure."

"What's your name, buddy?"

"Paul."

"Nice to meet ya," he said, and in the dark beside the path, they shook hands. "Mine's Toby. Everybody calls me Buffalo, though." The soldier's hand was strangely warm and soft. But it was a very big hand. "Sometimes they just call me Buff," he said.

And again they were quiet. They lay in the grass and waited. The moon was very high now and very bright, and they were waiting for cloud cover. The soldier suddenly snorted.

"What is it?"

"Nothin'," he said, but then he snorted again. "A bloody *heart attack*!" the soldier said. "Can't get over it—old Billy Boy croaking from a lousy heart attack. . . . A heart attack—can you believe it?" **H**

The idea of it made Private First Class Paul Berlin smile. He couldn't help it.

"Ever hear of such a thing?"

"Not till now," said Private First Class Paul Berlin, still smiling.

"Me neither," said the soldier in the dark. "Gawd, dying of a heart attack. Didn't know him, did you."

"No."

"Tough as nails."

"Yeah."

"And what happens? A heart attack. Can you imagine it?"

"Yes," said Private First Class Paul Berlin. He wanted to laugh. "I can imagine it." And he imagined it clearly. He giggled—he couldn't help it. He imagined Billy's father opening the telegram: SORRY TO INFORM YOU THAT YOUR SON BILLY BOY WAS YESTERDAY SCARED TO DEATH IN ACTION IN THE REPUBLIC OF VIETNAM, VALIANTLY SUCCUMBING[4] TO A HEART ATTACK SUFFERED WHILE UNDER ENORMOUS STRESS, AND IT IS WITH GREATEST SYMPATHY THAT . . . He giggled again. He rolled onto his belly and pressed his face into his arms. His body was shaking with giggles. **I**

The big soldier hissed at him to shut up, but he could not stop giggling and remembering the hot afternoon, and poor Billy Boy, and how

---

4. **succumbing** (suh KUHM ihng): here, dying from.

G Reading Focus Historical Context Why wouldn't it matter if Paul Berlin knew the other soldier's name?

H Literary Focus Characterization What do you learn about Buffalo from this dialogue?

I Reading Focus Historical Context Why does Paul Berlin giggle when imagining the telegram to Billy's father?

Vocabulary **valiantly** (VAL yuhnt lee) *adv.*: bravely.

Point Man by Sergeant James A. Fairfax. USMC Art Collection.

they'd been drinking Coca-Cola from bright-red aluminum cans, and how they'd started on the day's march, and how a little while later poor Billy Boy stepped on the mine, and how it made a tiny little sound—*poof*—and how Billy Boy stood there with his mouth wide open, looking down at where his foot had been blown off, and how finally Billy Boy sat down very casually, not saying a word, with his foot lying behind him, most of it still in the boot.

He giggled louder—he could not stop. He bit his arm, trying to stifle it, but remembering: "War's over, Billy," the men had said in consola-tion, but Billy Boy got scared and started crying and said he was about to die. "Nonsense," the medic said, Doc Peret, but Billy Boy kept bawling, tightening up, his face going pale and transparent and his veins popping out. Scared stiff. Even when Doc Peret stuck him with morphine, Billy Boy kept crying.

"Shut up!" the big soldier hissed, but Private First Class Paul Berlin could not stop. Giggling and remembering, he covered his mouth. His eyes stung, remembering how it was when Billy Boy died of fright.

"Shut up!"

But he could not stop giggling, the same way Billy Boy could not stop bawling that afternoon.

Afterward Doc Peret had explained: "You see, Billy Boy really died of a heart attack. He was scared he was gonna die—so scared he had himself a heart attack—and that's what really killed him. I seen it before."

So they wrapped Billy in a plastic poncho, his eyes still wide open and scared stiff, and they carried him over the meadow to a rice paddy, and then when the medevac helicopter[5] arrived, they carried him through the paddy and put him aboard, and the mortar rounds were falling everywhere, and the helicopter pulled up, and Billy Boy came tumbling out, falling slowly and then faster, and the paddy water sprayed up as if Billy Boy had just executed a long and dangerous dive, as if trying to escape Graves Registration, where he would be tagged and sent home under a flag, dead of a heart attack.

"Shut up!" the soldier hissed, but Paul Berlin could not stop giggling, remembering: scared to death.

Later they waded in after him, probing for Billy Boy with their rifle butts, elegantly and delicately probing for Billy Boy in the stinking paddy, singing—some of them—*Where have you gone, Billy Boy, Billy Boy, oh, where have you gone, charming Billy?* Then they found him. Green and covered with algae, his eyes still wide open and scared stiff, dead of a heart attack suffered while—

---

5. **medevac** (from *medical evacuation*) **helicopter:** helicopter used to evacuate wounded soldiers to hospitals and medical care.

"Shut up!" the soldier said loudly, shaking him.

But Private First Class Paul Berlin could not stop. The giggles were caught in his throat, drowning him in his own laughter: scared to death like Billy Boy.

Giggling, lying on his back, he saw the moon move, or the clouds moving across the moon. Wounded in action, dead of fright. A fine war story. He would tell it to his father, how Billy Boy had been scared to death, never letting on . . . He could not stop.

The soldier smothered him. He tried to fight back, but he was weak from the giggles.

The moon was under the clouds and the column was moving. The soldier helped him up. "You OK now, buddy?"

"Sure."

"What was so bloody funny?"

"Nothing."

"You can get killed, laughing that way."

"I know. I know that."

"You got to stay calm, buddy." The soldier handed him his rifle. "Half the battle, just staying calm. You'll get better at it," he said. "Come on, now."

He turned away and Private First Class Paul Berlin hurried after him. He was still shivering.

He would do better once he reached the sea, he thought, still smiling a little. A funny war story that he would tell to his father, how Billy Boy Watkins was scared to death. A good joke. But even when he smelled salt and heard the sea, he could not stop being afraid.

J **Literary Focus** Characterization What does Paul's hysterical reaction tell you about him?

K **Literary Focus** Characterization What does this exchange tell you about Buffalo?

Applying Your Skills

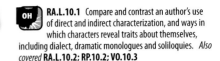**RA.L.10.1** Compare and contrast an author's use of direct and indirect characterization, and ways in which characters reveal traits about themselves, including dialect, dramatic monologues and soliloquies. *Also covered* **RA.L.10.2; RP.10.2; VO.10.3**

Where Have You Gone, Charming Billy?

Respond and Think Critically

Reading Focus

Quick Check

1. Summarize the story of Billy Boy's death for a partner. Tell *what* happened, to *whom* it happened, *where* it happened, *why* it happened, and *how* it happened.

Read with a Purpose

2. Does Paul's reaction to the events in the story surprise you at all? Explain.

Reading Skills: Analyzing Historical Context

3. Look back at the diagram you created as you read. Which details struck you the most? Why? What do these details tell you about the message the author is trying to communicate?

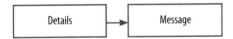

✓ Vocabulary Check

Answer *true* (T) or *false* (F) to each of the following statements. Then, briefly explain your answer.

4. A student's **diffuse** thinking will help him do well on exams.
5. An **inert** butterfly is easy to catch.
6. The **stealth** of a leopard will help it catch its prey.
7. A knight who fights **valiantly** should be ashamed.
8. If you **skirted** a baseball field, you would likely end up standing in its center.

Literary Focus

Literary Analysis

9. **Interpret** Besides reaching a place of relative safety or not having to be a soldier anymore, what would you say Paul wants most?

10. **Evaluate** How does Paul's <u>attitude</u> toward Billy Boy's death change over the course of the selection? What accounts for this change?

11. **Literary Perspectives** How does this story likely reflect O'Brien's <u>attitude</u> toward war?

Literary Skills: Characterization

12. **Evaluate** O'Brien develops characters by using dialogue, showing us character interactions, and telling us Paul Berlin's inner thoughts. Which technique did you find most effective? Why?

Literary Skills Review: Setting

13. **Analyze** The **setting** is the time and location in which a story takes place. How does setting contribute to this story's mood?

Writing Focus

Think as a Reader/Writer

Use It in Your Writing Choose a character in this story other than Paul Berlin. Then, using some of O'Brien's techniques of characterization, write a one-paragraph character sketch about this person.

What Do **You Think Now** What parts of the story did you find the most frightening or stressful? Did the situation Paul was in change him? Explain.

Preparing to Read

Two Kinds by **Amy Tan**

Courtesy of the artist and www.artscenechina.com

Contemplations by Hao Shiming (1977–). Chinese ink on silk (90 cm x 71 cm).

What Do You Think?

Can a negative experience ever be a good thing? How might it influence who we become?

 QuickWrite

Think about people who have had a positive influence on you. Then, think about people who have had an negative influence. Which influence had a bigger impact? Write about it.

Reader/Writer
Notebook

Use your **RWN** to complete the activities for this selection.

RA.L.10.1 Compare and contrast an author's use of direct and indirect characterization, and ways in which characters reveal traits about themselves, including dialect, dramatic monologues and soliloquies.
RP.10.1 Apply reading comprehension strategies, including making predictions, comparing and contrasting, recalling and summarizing and making inferences and drawing conclusions.

Literary Focus

Character Interactions and Motivation Actors studying their parts ask, "Why do I do this?" to discover their character's **motivation,** or the reasons for a behavior. Often, conflicts occur when characters are motivated to influence each other—in **character interactions** like the one between the mother and daughter in "Two Kinds."

Literary Perspectives Apply the literary perspective described on page 143 as you read this story.

Reading Focus

Making Inferences About Motivation

Authors rarely explain a character's motivation directly. Instead, they plant clues, and we must make inferences about what those clues mean. **Making an inference** means making a reasonable guess based on evidence and prior knowledge. To infer a character's motivation, pay attention to what the character thinks, says, and does. Then, make a guess based on those clues and what you already know about the story, the character, and human nature.

Into Action Make a chart like the one below for Jing-mei and her mother. Note the clues that help you infer each character's motivation.

Character	Clue	Motivation
Jing-mei	daydreams about becoming a prodigy	wants to be extraordinary, perfect; wants her parents to love her

Writing Focus

Think as a Reader/Writer

Find It in Your Reading Tan uses dialogue to show the conflict between her characters. Pay special attention to the dialect that the mother speaks—she is a Chinese immigrant. Note unique details of her speech in your *Reader/Writer Notebook*.

Learn It Online
For a preview of this story, see the video introduction on:

go.hrw.com | L10-141 | **Go**

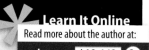
Learn It Online
Read more about the author at:
go.hrw.com **L10-142** **Go**

Amy Tan
(1952–   )

Self-Discovery

Amy Tan's mother wanted her to be a neurosurgeon and a concert pianist. Instead, Tan—who from a young age loved the library— found her own road to success by becoming a writer.

Tan's first novel, *The Joy Luck Club,* is a collection of related stories told by four mothers and four daughters. "When I wrote these stories, it was as much a discovery to me as to any reader reading them for the first time," Tan has said. "Things would surprise me. I would sit there laughing and I would say, 'Oh you're kidding!' It was like people telling me the stories, and I would write them down as fast as I could." Published in 1989 to rave reviews, *The Joy Luck Club* became an immediate bestseller.

The Power of Language

Tan says that she grew up with two Englishes—American English and Chinese English. Tan was born in Oakland, California, two and a half years after her parents fled China's Communist revolution and settled in the United States.

Here is what Tan says about being a writer between two cultures: "I am a writer. I am fascinated by language in daily life. I spend a great deal of my time thinking about the power of language—the way it can evoke an emotion, a visual image, a complex idea, or a simple truth. Language is the tool of my trade. And I use them all—all the Englishes I grew up with."

Think
About the
Writer
How do you think Tan's attitude toward writing has contributed to her success?

Build Background

The protagonist of "Two Kinds," Jing-mei, is an American girl born to Chinese parents. Like other children of immigrants, Chinese American children often have one foot in the world their parents left behind and one foot in the United States. The differences between the two cultures can cause a conflict between second-generation American children and their parents.

Preview the Selection

Much as Amy Tan's mother did, the mother in "Two Kinds" wants her daughter, **Jing-mei,** to be a concert pianist.

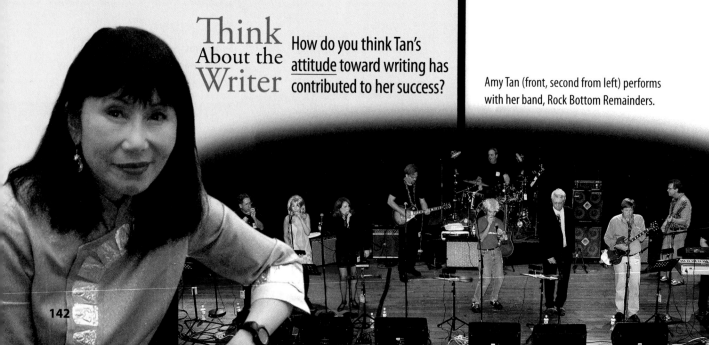

Amy Tan (front, second from left) performs with her band, Rock Bottom Remainders.

Read with a Purpose Read to discover how one girl rebels against her mother's high expectations.

Two Kinds

by **Amy Tan**

My mother believed you could be anything you wanted to be in America. You could open a restaurant. You could work for the government and get good retirement. You could buy a house with almost no money down. You could become rich. You could become instantly famous.

"Of course you can be prodigy, too," my mother told me when I was nine. "You can be best anything. What does Auntie Lindo know? Her daughter, she is only best tricky."

America was where all my mother's hopes lay. She had come here in 1949 after losing everything in China: her mother and father, her family home, her first husband, and two daughters, twin baby girls. But she never looked back with regret. There were so many ways for things to get better. **Ⓐ**

We didn't immediately pick the right kind of prodigy. At first my mother thought I could be a Chinese Shirley Temple.[1] We'd watch Shirley's old movies on TV as though they were training films. My mother would poke my arm and say, "*Ni kan*"—You watch. And I would see Shirley tapping her feet, or singing a sailor song, or pursing her lips into a very round O while saying, "Oh my goodness."

"*Ni kan*," said my mother as Shirley's eyes flooded with tears. "You already know how. Don't need talent for crying!"

Soon after my mother got this idea about Shirley Temple, she took me to a beauty training school in the Mission district and put me in the hands of a student who could barely hold the scissors without shaking. Instead of getting big fat curls, I emerged with an uneven mass of crinkly black fuzz. My mother dragged me off to the bathroom and tried to wet down my hair.

---

1. **Shirley Temple** (1928–   ): child movie star who was popular during the 1930s. Mothers all across the United States tried to set their daughters' hair to look like Shirley Temple's sausage curls.

Ⓐ Literary Focus Character What are the mother's reasons for wanting her daughter to excel?

Vocabulary **prodigy** (PRAHD uh jee) *n.*: child having extraordinary talent.

Literary Perspectives

Analyzing Credibility: Character Often, people behave in unbelievable ways—both in real life and in fiction. They say things that break the rules of polite social interaction. They survive extreme conditions. They accomplish amazing feats. Fiction often deals with these jaw-dropping, odds-defying moments. Part of the fiction writer's job is to present these moments in such a way that you can believe they *would* happen in the circumstances of the story. Think about which scenes in this selection seem unbelievable. As you read, be sure to notice the notes and questions in the text, which will guide you in using this perspective.

"You look like Negro Chinese," she lamented, as if I had done this on purpose.

The instructor of the beauty training school had to lop off these soggy clumps to make my hair even again. "Peter Pan is very popular these days," the instructor assured my mother. I now had hair the length of a boy's, with straight-across bangs that hung at a slant two inches above my eyebrows. I liked the haircut and it made me actually look forward to my future fame.

In fact, in the beginning, I was just as excited as my mother, maybe even more so. I pictured this prodigy part of me as many different images, trying each one on for size. I was a dainty ballerina girl standing by the curtains, waiting to hear the right music that would send me floating on my tiptoes. I was like the Christ child lifted out of the straw manger, crying with holy indignity. I was Cinderella stepping from her pumpkin carriage with sparkly cartoon music filling the air.

In all of my imaginings, I was filled with a sense that I would soon become *perfect*. My mother and father would adore me. I would be beyond reproach. I would never feel the need to sulk for anything. **Ⓑ**

But sometimes the prodigy in me became impatient. "If you don't hurry up and get me out of here, I'm disappearing for good," it warned. "And then you'll always be nothing."

Every night after dinner, my mother and I would sit at the Formica kitchen table. She would present new tests, taking her examples from stories of amazing children she had read in *Ripley's Believe It or Not,* or *Good Housekeeping, Reader's Digest,* and a dozen other magazines she kept in a pile in our bathroom. My mother got these magazines from people whose houses she cleaned. And since she cleaned many houses each week, we had a great assortment. She would look through them all, searching for stories about remarkable children.

The first night she brought out a story about a three-year-old boy who knew the capitals of all the states and even most of the European countries. A teacher was quoted as saying the little boy could also pronounce the names of the foreign cities correctly.

"What's the capital of Finland?" my mother asked me, looking at the magazine story.

All I knew was the capital of California, because Sacramento was the name of the street we lived on in Chinatown. "Nairobi!"[2] I guessed, saying the most foreign word I could think of. She checked to see if that was possibly one way to pronounce "Helsinki" before showing me the answer.

The tests got harder—multiplying numbers in my head, finding the queen of hearts in a deck of cards, trying to stand on my head without using my hands, predicting the daily temperatures in Los Angeles, New York, and London.

One night I had to look at a page from the Bible for three minutes and then report everything I could remember. "Now Jehoshaphat had riches and honor in abundance and . . . that's all I remember, Ma," I said. **Ⓒ**

And after seeing my mother's disappointed face once again, something inside of me began to die. I hated the tests, the raised hopes and failed expectations. Before going to bed that

---

2. **Nairobi** (ny ROH bee): capital of Kenya, a nation in Africa.

Ⓑ **Literary Focus** **Character** What motivates Jing-mei to try to become the prodigy her mother wants?

Ⓒ **Reading Focus** **Making Inferences** What examples from this passage show you that the narrator's mother is determined?

night, I looked in the mirror above the bathroom sink and when I saw only my face staring back—and that it would always be this ordinary face—I began to cry. Such a sad, ugly girl! I made high-pitched noises like a crazed animal, trying to scratch out the face in the mirror.

And then I saw what seemed to be the prodigy side of me—because I had never seen that face before. I looked at my reflection, blinking so I could see more clearly. The girl staring back at me was angry, powerful. This girl and I were the same. I had new thoughts, willful thoughts, or rather thoughts filled with lots of won'ts. I won't let her change me, I promised myself. I won't be what I'm not. **D**

So now, on nights when my mother presented her tests, I performed listlessly, my head propped on one arm. I pretended to be bored. And I was. I got so bored I started counting the bellows of the foghorns out on the bay while my mother drilled me in other areas. The sound was comforting and reminded me of the cow jumping over the moon. And the next day, I played a game with myself, seeing if my mother would give up on me before eight bellows. After a while I usually counted only one, maybe two bellows at most. At last she was beginning to give up hope.

Two or three months had gone by without any mention of my being a prodigy again. And then one day my mother was watching *The Ed Sullivan Show* on TV. The TV was old and the sound kept shorting out. Every time my mother got halfway up from the sofa to adjust the set,

> I won't let her change me, I promised myself. I won't be what I'm not.

the sound would go back on and Ed would be talking. As soon as she sat down, Ed would go silent again. She got up, the TV broke into loud piano music. She sat down. Silence. Up and down, back and forth, quiet and loud. It was like a stiff embraceless dance between her and the TV set. Finally she stood by the set with her hand on the sound dial.

She seemed entranced by the music, a little frenzied piano piece with this mesmerizing quality, sort of quick passages and then teasing, lilting ones before it returned to the quick, playful parts.

"*Ni kan*," my mother said, calling me over with hurried hand gestures. "Look here."

I could see why my mother was fascinated by the music. It was being pounded out by a little Chinese girl, about nine years old, with a Peter Pan haircut. The girl had the sauciness of a Shirley Temple. She was proudly modest like a proper Chinese child. And she also did this fancy sweep of a curtsy, so that the fluffy skirt of her white dress cascaded slowly to the floor like the petals of a large carnation. **E**

In spite of these warning signs, I wasn't worried. Our family had no piano and we couldn't afford to buy one, let alone reams of sheet music and piano lessons. So I could be generous in my comments when my mother bad-mouthed the little girl on TV.

"Play note right, but doesn't sound good! No singing sound," complained my mother.

D **Literary Focus** Character Why is the narrator angry and determined to resist her mother's expectations?

E **Literary Focus** Character How does the narrator's mother react to the child's performance?

Vocabulary **listlessly** (LIHST lihs lee) *adv.*: without energy or interest.
mesmerizing (MEHS muh ryz ihng) *v.* used as *adj.*: spellbinding; fascinating.

"What are you picking on her for?" I said carelessly. "She's pretty good. Maybe she's not the best, but she's trying hard." I knew almost immediately I would be sorry I said that.

"Just like you," she said. "Not the best. Because you not trying." She gave a little huff as she let go of the sound dial and sat down on the sofa.

The little Chinese girl sat down also to play an encore of "Anitra's Dance" by Grieg.[3] I remember the song, because later on I had to learn how to play it.

Three days after watching *The Ed Sullivan Show*, my mother told me what my schedule would be for piano lessons and piano practice. She had talked to Mr. Chong, who lived on the first floor of our apartment building. Mr. Chong was a retired piano teacher, and my mother had traded housecleaning services for weekly lessons and a piano for me to practice on every day, two hours a day, from four until six.

When my mother told me this, I felt as though I had been sent to hell. I whined and then kicked my foot a little when I couldn't stand it anymore.

"Why don't you like me the way I am? I'm *not* a genius! I can't play the piano. And even if I could, I wouldn't go on TV if you paid me a million dollars!" I cried.

My mother slapped me. "Who ask you be genius?" she shouted. "Only ask you be your best. For you sake. You think I want you be genius? Hnnh! What for! Who ask you!"

"So ungrateful," I heard her mutter in Chinese. "If she had as much talent as she has temper, she would be famous now."

Mr. Chong, whom I secretly nicknamed Old Chong, was very strange, always tapping his

fingers to the silent music of an invisible orchestra. He looked ancient in my eyes. He had lost most of the hair on top of his head and he wore thick glasses and had eyes that always looked tired and sleepy. But he must have been younger than I thought, since he lived with his mother and was not yet married.

I met Old Lady Chong once and that was enough. She had this peculiar smell like a baby that had done something in its pants. And

---

3. **Grieg** (greeg): Edvard Grieg (1843–1907), Norwegian composer. "Anitra's Dance" is from his *Peer Gynt Suite.*

Analyzing Visuals

Viewing and Interpreting
How does the attitude of the girl in this painting compare with Jing-mei's attitude in the story?

Daydreaming (2006) by Hao Shiming. Chinese ink on silk (103 x 76 cm). Courtesy of the artist and www.artscenechina.com.

Our lessons went like this. He would open the book and point to different things, explaining their purpose: "Key! Treble! Bass! No sharps or flats! So this is C major! Listen now and play after me!"

And then he would play the C scale a few times, a simple chord, and then, as if inspired by an old, unreachable itch, he gradually added more notes and running trills and a pounding bass until the music was really something quite grand.

I would play after him, the simple scale, the simple chord, and then I just played some nonsense that sounded like a cat running up and down on top of garbage cans. Old Chong smiled and applauded and then said, "Very good! But now you must learn to keep time!"

So that's how I discovered that Old Chong's eyes were too slow to keep up with the wrong notes I was playing. He went through the motions in half-time. To help me keep rhythm, he stood behind me, pushing down on my right shoulder for every beat. He balanced pennies on top of my wrists so I would keep them still as I slowly played scales and arpeggios.[5] He had me curve my hand around an apple and keep that shape when playing chords. He marched

her fingers felt like a dead person's, like an old peach I once found in the back of the refrigerator; the skin just slid off the meat when I picked it up.

I soon found out why Old Chong had retired from teaching piano. He was deaf. "Like Beethoven!" he shouted to me. "We're both listening only in our head!" And he would start to conduct his frantic silent sonatas.[4]

---

4. **sonatas** (suh NAH tuhz): musical compositions, usually for one or two instruments.

5. **arpeggios** (ahr PEHJ ee ohz): chords whose notes are played quickly one after another rather than at the same time.

stiffly to show me how to make each finger dance up and down, staccato,[6] like an obedient little soldier.

He taught me all these things, and that was how I also learned I could be lazy and get away with mistakes, lots of mistakes. If I hit the wrong notes because I hadn't practiced enough, I never corrected myself. I just kept playing in rhythm. And Old Chong kept conducting his own private reverie.[7]

So maybe I never really gave myself a fair chance. I did pick up the basics pretty quickly, and I might have become a good pianist at that young age. But I was so determined not to try, not to be anybody different, that I learned to play only the most earsplitting preludes, the most discordant hymns.   **F**

Over the next year, I practiced like this, dutifully in my own way. And then one day I heard my mother and her friend Lindo Jong both talking in a loud bragging tone of voice so others could hear. It was after church, and I was leaning against the brick wall, wearing a dress with stiff white petticoats. Auntie Lindo's daughter, Waverly, who was about my age, was standing farther down the wall, about five feet away. We had grown up together and shared all the closeness of two sisters squabbling over crayons and dolls. In other words, for the most part, we hated each other. I thought she was snotty. Waverly Jong had gained a certain amount of fame as "Chinatown's Littlest Chinese Chess Champion."

---

6. **staccato** (stuh KAHT oh): with clear-cut breaks between notes.
7. **reverie** (REHV uh ree): daydream.

F **Reading Focus** Making Inferences Why doesn't the narrator try to become a good pianist?

Vocabulary **discordant** (dihs KAWR duhnt) *adj.:* clashing; not harmonious.

"She bring home too many trophy," lamented Auntie Lindo that Sunday. "All day she play chess. All day I have no time do nothing but dust off her winnings." She threw a scolding look at Waverly, who pretended not to see her.

"You lucky you don't have this problem," said Auntie Lindo with a sigh to my mother.

And my mother squared her shoulders and bragged: "Our problem worser than yours. If we ask Jing-mei wash dish, she hear nothing but music. It's like you can't stop this natural talent."

And right then, I was determined to put a stop to her foolish pride.   **G**

A few weeks later, Old Chong and my mother conspired to have me play in a talent show which would be held in the church hall. By then, my parents had saved up enough to buy me a secondhand piano, a black Wurlitzer spinet with a scarred bench. It was the showpiece of our living room.

For the talent show, I was to play a piece called "Pleading Child" from Schumann's[8] *Scenes from Childhood*. It was a simple, moody piece that sounded more difficult than it was. I was supposed to memorize the whole thing, playing the repeat parts twice to make the piece sound longer. But I dawdled over it, playing a few bars and then cheating, looking up to see what notes followed. I never really listened to what I was playing. I daydreamed about being somewhere else, about being someone else.

The part I liked to practice best was the fancy curtsy: right foot out, touch the rose on

---

8. **Schumann's** (SHOO mahnz): Robert Schumann (1810–1856), German composer.

G **Reading Focus** Making Inferences Why does the narrator say her mother has "foolish pride"?

the carpet with a pointed foot, sweep to the side, left leg bends, look up and smile.

My parents invited all the couples from the Joy Luck Club[9] to witness my debut. Auntie Lindo and Uncle Tin were there. Waverly and her two older brothers had also come. The first two rows were filled with children both younger and older than I was. The littlest ones got to go first. They recited simple nursery rhymes, squawked out tunes on miniature violins, twirled Hula-Hoops, pranced in pink ballet tutus, and when they bowed or curtsied, the audience would sigh in unison, "Awww," and then clap enthusiastically.

When my turn came, I was very confident. I remember my childish excitement. It was as if I knew, without a doubt, that the prodigy side of me really did exist. I had no fear whatsoever, no nervousness. I remember thinking to myself, This is it! This is it! I looked out over the audience, at my mother's blank face, my father's yawn, Auntie Lindo's stiff-lipped smile, Waverly's sulky expression. I had on a white dress layered with sheets of lace, and a pink bow in my Peter Pan haircut. As I sat down I envisioned people jumping to their feet and Ed Sullivan rushing up to introduce me to everyone on TV. **H**

And I started to play. It was so beautiful. I was so caught up in how lovely I looked that at first I didn't worry how I would sound. So it was a surprise to me when I hit the first wrong note and I realized something didn't sound quite

> I heard a little boy whisper loudly to his mother, "That was awful."

right. And then I hit another, and another followed that. A chill started at the top of my head and began to trickle down. Yet I couldn't stop playing, as though my hands were bewitched. I kept thinking my fingers would adjust themselves back, like a train switching to the right track. I played this strange jumble through two repeats, the sour notes staying with me all the way to the end.

When I stood up, I discovered my legs were shaking. Maybe I had just been nervous and the audience, like Old Chong, had seen me go through the right motions and had not heard anything wrong at all. I swept my right foot out, went down on my knee, looked up and smiled. The room was quiet, except for Old Chong, who was beaming and shouting, "Bravo! Bravo! Well done!" But then I saw my mother's face, her stricken face. The audience clapped weakly, and as I walked back to my chair, with my whole face quivering as I tried not to cry, I heard a little boy whisper loudly to his mother, "That was awful," and the mother whispered back, "Well, she certainly tried."

And now I realized how many people were in the audience, the whole world it seemed. I was aware of eyes burning into my back. I felt the shame of my mother and father as they sat stiffly throughout the rest of the show.

We could have escaped during intermission. Pride and some strange sense of honor must have anchored my parents to their chairs. And so we watched it all: the eighteen-year-old boy with a fake mustache who did a magic show and juggled flaming hoops while riding a uni-

---

9. Joy Luck Club: social club to which Jing-mei's mother and three other Chinese mothers belong.

H **Reading Focus** Making Inferences What does Jing-mei's reaction here suggest about her willingness to make her mother's dream come true?

"Lots of talented kids," Auntie Lindo said vaguely, smiling broadly.

"That was somethin' else," said my father, and I wondered if he was referring to me in a humorous way, or whether he even remembered what I had done.

Waverly looked at me and shrugged her shoulders. "You aren't a genius like me," she said matter-of-factly. And if I hadn't felt so bad, I would have pulled her braids and punched her stomach.

But my mother's expression was what devastated me: a quiet, blank look that said she had lost everything. I felt the same way, and it seemed as if everybody were now coming up, like gawkers at the scene of an accident, to see what parts were actually missing. When we got on the bus to go home, my father was humming the busy-bee tune and my mother was silent. I kept thinking she wanted to wait until we got home before shouting at me. But when my father unlocked the door to our apartment, my mother walked in and then went to the back, into the bedroom. No accusations. No blame. And in a way, I felt disappointed. I had been waiting for her to start shouting, so I could shout back and cry and blame her for all my misery. **J**

I assumed my talent-show fiasco meant I never had to play the piano again. But two days later, after school, my mother came out of the kitchen and saw me watching TV.

cycle. The breasted girl with white makeup who sang from *Madama Butterfly*[10] and got honorable mention. And the eleven-year-old boy who won first prize playing a tricky violin song that sounded like a busy bee. **I**

After the show, the Hsus, the Jongs, and the St. Clairs from the Joy Luck Club came up to my mother and father.

---

10. *Madama Butterfly:* opera by the Italian composer Giacomo Puccini (1858–1924).

I **Literary Focus** Character Why does Jing-mei's family sit through the rest of the talent show?

J **Literary Focus** Character Jing-mei and her mother feel the same way here. Why do their shared feelings fail to bring them together?

Vocabulary **fiasco** (fee AS koh) *n.:* total failure.

"Four clock," she reminded me as if it were any other day. I was stunned, as though she were asking me to go through the talent-show torture again. I wedged myself more tightly in front of the TV.

"Turn off TV," she called from the kitchen five minutes later.

I didn't budge. And then I decided. I didn't have to do what my mother said anymore. I wasn't her slave. This wasn't China. I had listened to her before and look what happened. She was the stupid one.

She came out from the kitchen and stood in the arched entryway of the living room. "Four clock," she said once again, louder.

"I'm not going to play anymore," I said nonchalantly. "Why should I? I'm not a genius."

She walked over and stood in front of the TV. I saw her chest was heaving up and down in an angry way.

"No!" I said, and I now felt stronger, as if my true self had finally emerged. So this was what had been inside me all along.

"No! I won't!" I screamed.

She yanked me by the arm, pulled me off the floor, snapped off the TV. She was frighteningly strong, half pulling, half carrying me toward the piano as I kicked the throw rugs under my feet. She lifted me up and onto the hard bench. I was sobbing by now, looking at her bitterly. Her chest was heaving even more and her mouth was open, smiling crazily, as if she were pleased I was crying.

"You want me to be someone that I'm not!" I sobbed. "I'll never be the kind of daughter you want me to be!"

"Only two kinds of daughters," she shouted in Chinese. "Those who are obedient and those who follow their own mind! Only one kind of daughter can live in this house. Obedient daughter!" **K**

"Then I wish I wasn't your daughter. I wish you weren't my mother," I shouted. As I said these things, I got scared. It felt like worms and toads and slimy things crawling out of my chest, but it also felt good, as if this awful side of me had surfaced, at last.

"Too late change this," said my mother shrilly.

And I could sense her anger rising to its breaking point. I wanted to see it spill over. And that's when I remembered the babies she had lost in China, the ones we never talked about. "Then I wish I'd never been born!" I shouted. "I wish I were dead! Like them." **L**

It was as if I had said the magic words. Alakazam!—and her face went blank, her mouth closed, her arms went slack, and she backed out of the room, stunned, as if she were blowing away like a small brown leaf, thin, brittle, lifeless.

It was not the only disappointment my mother felt in me. In the years that followed, I failed her so many times, each time asserting my own will, my right to fall short of expectations. I didn't get straight A's. I didn't become class president. I didn't get into Stanford.[11] I dropped out of college.

For unlike my mother, I did not believe I could be anything I wanted to be. I could only be me.

---

11. **Stanford:** high-ranking university in Palo Alto, California.

K Literary Focus Character How do the opposing motives of mother and daughter drive the plot?

Vocabulary **nonchalantly** (NAHN shuh luhnt lee) *adv.*: without interest or concern; indifferently.

L Literary Perspectives Credibility Is it believable that Jing-mei would speak so cruelly to her mother? Explain.

And for all those years, we never talked about the disaster at the recital or my terrible accusations afterward at the piano bench. All that remained unchecked, like a betrayal that was now unspeakable. So I never found a way to ask her why she had hoped for something so large that failure was inevitable.

And even worse, I never asked her what frightened me the most: Why had she given up hope?

For after our struggle at the piano, she never mentioned my playing again. The lessons stopped. The lid to the piano was closed, shutting out the dust, my misery, and her dreams. **Ⓜ**

So she surprised me. A few years ago, she offered to give me the piano, for my thirtieth birthday. I had not played in all those years. I saw the offer as a sign of forgiveness, a tremendous burden removed.

"Are you sure?" I asked shyly. "I mean, won't you and Dad miss it?"

"No, this your piano," she said firmly. "Always your piano. You only one can play."

"Well, I probably can't play anymore," I said. "It's been years."

"You pick up fast," said my mother, as if she knew this was certain. "You have natural talent. You could been genius if you want to."

"No, I couldn't."

"You just not trying," said my mother. And she was neither angry nor sad. She said it as if to announce a fact that could never be disproved. "Take it," she said.

But I didn't at first. It was enough that she had offered it to me. And after that, every time I saw it in my parents' living room, standing in front of the bay windows, it made me feel proud, as if it were a shiny trophy I had won back. **Ⓝ**

Last week I sent a tuner over to my parents' apartment and had the piano reconditioned, for purely sentimental reasons. My mother had died a few months before, and I had been getting things in order for my father, a little bit at a time. I put the jewelry in special silk pouches. The sweaters she had knitted in yellow, pink, bright orange—all the colors I hated—I put those in mothproof boxes. I found some old Chinese silk dresses, the kind with little slits up the sides. I rubbed the old silk against my skin, then wrapped them in tissue and decided to take them home with me.

After I had the piano tuned, I opened the lid and touched the keys. It sounded even richer than I remembered. Really, it was a very good piano. Inside the bench were the same exercise notes with handwritten scales, the same secondhand music books with their covers held together with yellow tape.

I opened up the Schumann book to the dark little piece I had played at the recital. It was on the left-hand side of the page, "Pleading Child." It looked more difficult than I remembered. I played a few bars, surprised at how easily the notes came back to me.

And for the first time, or so it seemed, I noticed the piece on the right-hand side. It was called "Perfectly Contented." I tried to play this one as well. It had a lighter melody but the same flowing rhythm and turned out to be quite easy. "Pleading Child" was shorter but slower; "Perfectly Contented" was longer but faster. And after I played them both a few times, I realized they were two halves of the same song.

Ⓜ **Reading Focus** Making Inferences Why do you think the mother gives up hope?

Ⓝ **Literary Focus** Character Why does the mother give the piano to Jing-mei?

Applying Your Skills

OH **RA.L.10.1** Compare and contrast an author's use of direct and indirect characterization, and ways in which characters reveal traits about themselves, including dialect, dramatic monologues and soliloquies. *Also covered* **RP.10.1**

Two Kinds

Respond and Think Critically

Reading Focus

Quick Check

1. How does Jing-mei feel about her mother's plans for her?

2. Why does Jing-mei say hurtful things to her mother in their last struggle over piano lessons?

Read with a Purpose

3. How does Jing-mei rebel against her mother's high expectations?

Reading Skills: Making Inferences About Motivation

4. Examine the chart you created for Jing-mei and her mother. How are the characters' desires similar? How are they different?

Character	Clue	Motivation
Jing-mei	daydreams about becoming a prodigy	wants to be extraordinary, perfect; wants her parents to love her
Jing-mei's mother	pressures Jing-mei to be a prodigy	wants a better life for herself and her family

Literary Focus

Literary Analysis

5. **Infer** Jing-mei's mother says, "You already know how. Don't need talent for crying!" What does her comment <u>reveal</u> about Jing-mei?

6. **Explain** On page 145, Jing-mei is grateful that her mother is "beginning to give up hope." Yet later she is frightened by her mother's loss of hope. Explain Jing-mei's conflicting feelings.

7. **Connect** What do you think the title of the story means? How are the two Schumann pieces related to the story's title?

8. **Literary Perspectives** Did you find the characters of Jing-mei and her mother believable? Why or why not? Support your answer with details from the text.

9. **Analyze** Explain Jing-mei's revelation about the Schumann pieces at the end of this story. How does this relate to the story's title?

Literary Skills: Character Interactions and Motivation

10. **Explain** What is the mother's motivation for pushing Jing-mei to be a prodigy?

Literary Skills Review: Conflict

11. **Summarize** A story's **conflict,** or struggle, occurs when a character is motivated to fulfill a desire but is prevented from doing so. Identify the central conflict in "Two Kinds." Is it internal or external? What, or who, causes it, and why?

Writing Focus

Think as a Reader/Writer

Use It in Your Writing Write a letter from the adult Jing-mei that is addressed to her deceased mother. Explain the reasons behind her behavior as a girl and the conflicting feelings she had about her mother's goals for her.

What Do You Think Now

Do someone's high expectations of you ever make you want to give up, or do they make you try harder?

Applying Your Skills

Two Kinds

Vocabulary Development

Vocabulary Check

Choose the Vocabulary word that best answers each question.

prodigy
listlessly
mesmerizing
discordant
fiasco
nonchalantly

1. Which word with a suffix means to do something "without desire"?

2. Which adjective is most likely derived from the name of hypnotist Friedrich Anton Mesmer?

3. Which word has the synonyms *disaster, mess,* and *failure*?

4. Which noun might describe a talented child?

5. Which adverb might describe a casual or indifferent way of doing things?

6. Which word's root most likely comes from the French *corde,* meaning "the string of a musical instrument"?

Vocabulary Skills: Semantic Maps

When you face a list of unfamiliar words, **semantic maps** provide one way to decode them. The semantic map below uses context clues to define *fiasco.*

Your Turn

With a partner, create a semantic map, as shown in the example, for each Vocabulary word. Follow the steps below. Use a dictionary or thesaurus to help.

1. Write the Vocabulary word in the top box.

2. List at least one synonym and, when possible, one antonym.

3. Then, write a sentence in the lower box that clarifies the meaning of the Vocabulary word.

Language Coach

Synonyms Using a dictionary and a thesaurus will help you find synonyms with different shades of meaning. Look up each of the Vocabulary words in a dictionary and a thesaurus. Which of the synonyms listed is closest in meaning to the word as it is used in the story? Then, use these synonyms in example sentences describing the story's characters and main events.

Academic Vocabulary

Write About . . .
In the last four paragraphs of the story, what does the author <u>reveal</u> about Jing-mei's feelings toward her mother? Using the underlined Academic Vocabulary word, write a paragraph explaining your response.

Grammar Link

Main and Subordinate Clauses

A sentence is made up of one or more **clauses,** or groups of words that contain both a subject and a verb. Not all clauses are created equal. Some clauses, like adult people, are independent; that is, they can stand alone. An **independent clause,** also called a **main clause,** has a subject and a verb, and it expresses a complete thought.

MAIN CLAUSE: *I played a few bars.*

Other clauses are **dependent** or **subordinate;** that is, they cannot stand alone. A subordinate clause has a subject and a verb, but it does not express a complete thought. It must rely on a main clause to communicate a whole idea. A subordinate clause standing alone is one kind of **sentence fragment.** A sentence fragment does not express a complete thought.

SUBORDINATE CLAUSE: *Though I wasn't sure I'd remember the notes* (**sentence fragment**)

A sentence made up of a main clause and a subordinate clause is called a **complex sentence.**

COMPLEX SENTENCE: *I played a few bars, though I wasn't sure I'd remember the notes.*

Your Turn

Rewrite the following paragraph to correct sentence fragments and create complex sentences.

The plot would not have been believable. If Old Chong, the piano teacher, weren't completely deaf. Anyone can hear the wrong notes. If he or she only listens to Jing-mei's playing. When she starts playing before a hearing audience. Jing-mei realizes for the first time what she has done. She feels terrible. Because she has humiliated herself and her parents.

CHOICES

As you respond to the Choices, use these **Academic Vocabulary** words as appropriate: acquire, attitude, reveal, and tradition.

REVIEW
Create a Play
Group Activity With a small group, create a play based on a scene in "Two Kinds." Use dialogue from the story, focusing on character interaction, to create the script. If necessary, write new dialogue to help the audience better understand each character's motivation. Perform your scene for the class.

CONNECT
Give Relationship Advice
Timed └Writing Do you think Jing-mei's mother is right to push Jing-mei so hard, or do you agree with Jing-mei that her mother's pride is foolish? Do you think that Jing-mei is cruel to her mother? Pretend you are a relationship coach, and write a paragraph analyzing their relationship. Support your statements with details from the story.

EXTEND
Fill in the Blanks
The story "Two Kinds" begins when Jing-mei is a young girl and ends many years later, when she is an adult. But we never find out what happened to Jing-mei in between those periods. What career might she have chosen? Where might she live? In Jing-mei's first-person voice, write the middle of the story describing her life as an adult.

Learn It Online
There's more to this story than meets the eye. Expand your view at:

go.hrw.com   L10-155   **Go**

The First Seven Years

by **Bernard Malamud**

What makes us willing
to make sacrifices?

QuickWrite

What kind of sacrifice would you make to achieve
something important to you? Write a paragraph
about a situation in which a sacrifice might be
necessary.

The Shoemaker (1930) by Tadeusz Makowski
(1882–1932). Oil on canvas (100.5 cm x 81 cm).
Museum Narodowe Warsaw, Poland.

Reader/Writer
Notebook

Use your **RWN** to complete the activities for this selection.

OH **RA.L.10.1** Compare and contrast an author's use of direct and indirect characterization, and ways in which characters reveal traits about themselves, including dialect, dramatic monologues and soliloquies.
RP.10.1 Apply reading comprehension strategies, including making predictions, comparing and contrasting, recalling and summarizing and making inferences and drawing conclusions.

Literary Focus

Direct and Indirect Characterization Writers bring characters to life directly and indirectly. An author uses **direct characterization** when he or she tells specifically what a character is like, usually by describing the character's appearance or personality. When authors use **indirect characterization,** they <u>reveal</u> information about a character through the character's words, thoughts, or actions or through what other characters say about the character. Malamud uses both techniques in "The First Seven Years."

Reading Focus

Comparing and Contrasting Characters You can better understand characters by observing how they are similar to or different from other characters. Notice the characters' traits and the way characters act and interact in various situations.

Into Action Set up a chart like the one below to **compare and contrast** Feld and Sobel. As you read, make notes about each character's traits, circumstances, and motives.

Character	Feld	Sobel
Traits	practical	studious, hardworking
Circumstances	owner of shoe shop	
Motives		

Writing Focus

Think as a Reader/Writer

Find It in Your Reading Malamud creates characters who are very different from one another. Each character's personality becomes clearer as the story progresses. As you read, use your *Reader/Writer Notebook* to record examples of direct and indirect characterization that are particularly effective.

Vocabulary

obligation (ahb luh GAY shuhn) *n.:* duty. *Feld considered it an obligation to educate his daughter.*

temperamental (tehm puhr uh MEHN tuhl) *adj.:* moody; easily irritated. *Sobel's temperamental nature caused him to be easily offended.*

unscrupulous (uhn SKROO pyuh luhs) *adj.:* unprincipled; not concerned with right and wrong. *The man who replaced Sobel turned out to be unscrupulous and untrustworthy.*

discern (dih SURN) *v.:* recognize or distinguish. *Through the snow, the shoemaker could not discern who was coming toward him.*

wrath (rath) *n.:* great anger; rage. *Sobel reacted with wrath when his boss called him old and ugly.*

Language Coach

Related Words The word *temperamental* comes from the word *temper,* meaning "frame of mind or mood." If someone is grumpy, we can say he or she has a bad *temper.* Think of other words that have the word part *temper.* Are their meanings similar?

Learn It Online
Upgrade your vocabulary using Word Watch at:

go.hrw.com | L10-157 | **Go**

Bernard Malamud
(1914–1986)

National Book Award **WINNER**

Pulitzer Prize **WINNER**

A Born Storyteller

Bernard Malamud was lucky to have a vivid imagination when he was a child. Growing up poor in New York City—in an apartment with no books, no pictures, and no music—he needed to find some way to keep busy and entertain himself. He therefore turned to the fancies of his own mind and began to make up stories. He "told stories for praise," as he later put it, and took joy in captivating his audience.

From Teacher to Award-Winning Author

Malamud began publishing relatively late in his life, after teaching English for many years in the schools of his native New York City. He soon made up for lost time. When he was in his forties, he began writing stories with the goal of getting them published. He won a National Book Award in 1959 for a collection of short stories, *The Magic Barrel*. He won the same award as well as the Pulitzer Prize for his 1966 novel, *The Fixer*. Most of Malamud's stories center on characters who are somehow redeemed by love. He found it most fulfilling to write about ordinary people to whom readers could relate and about universal joys and sorrows.

Think About the Writer Why might Malamud have focused his writing on the joys and sorrows of ordinary people?

Build Background

This short story takes place in the United States not long after World War II. Most of the characters are Polish immigrants who came to the United States to escape from the Nazis, who occupied Poland during the war.

Preview the Selection

Feld is a Polish shoemaker focused on his daughter's future.

Max is a young college student dedicated to his education.

Sobel is Feld's middle-aged assistant, who works hard for little in return.

Miriam is Feld's daughter, who he wants to marry Max.

The First Seven Years

by **Bernard Malamud**

Feld, the Shoemaker, was annoyed that his helper, Sobel, was so insensitive to his reverie[1] that he wouldn't for a minute cease his fanatic pounding at the other bench. He gave him a look, but Sobel's bald head was bent over the last[2] as he worked and he didn't notice. The shoemaker shrugged and continued to peer through the partly frosted window at the near-sighted haze of falling February snow. Neither the shifting white blur outside, nor the sudden deep remembrance of the snowy Polish village where he had wasted his youth could turn his thoughts from Max the college boy, (a constant visitor in the mind since early that morning when Feld saw him trudging through the snowdrifts on his way to school) whom he so much respected because of the sacrifices he had made throughout the years—in winter or direst heat—to further his education. An old wish returned to haunt the shoemaker: that he had had a son instead of a daughter, but this blew away in the snow for Feld, if anything, was a practical man. Yet he could not help but contrast the diligence of the boy, who was a

---

1. **reverie** (REHV uhr ee): daydreaming.
2. **last** (last): wooden or metal model of a foot on which a shoemaker makes or repairs shoes.

peddler's son, with Miriam's unconcern for an education. True, she was always with a book in her hand, yet when the opportunity arose for a college education, she had said no she would rather find a job. He had begged her to go, pointing out how many fathers could not afford to send their children to college, but she said she wanted to be independent. As for education, what was it, she asked, but books, which Sobel, who diligently read the classics, would as usual advise her on. Her answer greatly grieved her father. **A**

A figure emerged from the snow and the door opened. At the counter the man withdrew from a wet paper bag a pair of battered shoes for repair. Who he was the shoemaker for a moment had no idea, then his heart trembled as he realized, before he had thoroughly discerned the face, that Max himself was standing there, embarrassedly explaining what he wanted done to his old shoes. Though Feld listened eagerly, he couldn't hear a word, for the opportunity that had burst upon him was deafening.

He couldn't exactly recall when the thought had occurred to him, because it was clear he had more than once considered suggesting to the boy that he go out with Miriam. But he

---

A **Literary Focus** Characterization What kind of characterization is used in the first half of this paragraph?

had not dared speak, for if Max said no, how would he face him again? Or suppose Miriam, who harped so often on independence, blew up in anger and shouted at him for his meddling? Still, the chance was too good to let by: all it meant was an introduction. They might long ago have become friends had they happened to meet somewhere, therefore was it not his duty—an obligation—to bring them together, nothing more, a harmless connivance[3] to replace an accidental encounter in the subway, let's say, or a mutual friend's introduction in the street? Just let him once see and talk to her and he would for sure be interested. As for Miriam, what possible harm for a working girl in an office, who met only loud-mouthed salesmen and illiterate shipping clerks, to make the acquaintance of a fine scholarly boy? Maybe he would awaken in her a desire to go to college; if not—the shoemaker's mind at last came to grips with the truth—let her marry an educated man and live a better life. **Ⓑ**

When Max finished describing what he wanted done to his shoes, Feld marked them, both with enormous holes in the soles which he pretended not to notice, with large white-chalk x's, and the rubber heels, thinned to the nails, he marked with o's, though it troubled him he might have mixed up the letters. Max inquired the price, and the shoemaker cleared his throat and asked the boy, above Sobel's insistent hammering, would he please step through the side door there into the hall. Though surprised, Max did as the shoemaker requested, and Feld went

in after him. For a minute they were both silent, because Sobel had stopped banging, and it seemed they understood neither was to say anything until the noise began again. When it did, loudly, the shoemaker quickly told Max why he had asked to talk to him.

"Ever since you went to high school," he said, in the dimly-lit hallway, "I watched you in the morning go to the subway to school, and I said always to myself, this is a fine boy that he wants so much an education."

"Thanks," Max said, nervously alert. He was tall and grotesquely thin, with sharply cut features, particularly a beak-like nose. He was wearing a loose, long slushy overcoat that hung down to his ankles, looking like a rug draped over his bony shoulders, and a soggy, old brown hat, as battered as the shoes he had brought in. **Ⓒ**

"I am a business man," the shoemaker abruptly said to conceal his embarrassment, "so I will explain you right away why I talk to you. I have a girl, my daughter Miriam—she is nineteen—a very nice girl and also so pretty that everybody looks on her when she passes by in the street. She is smart, always with a book, and I thought to myself that a boy like you, an educated boy—I thought maybe you will be interested sometime to meet a girl like this." He laughed a bit when he had finished and was tempted to say more but had the good sense not to.

Max stared down like a hawk. For an uncomfortable second he was silent, then he asked, "Did you say nineteen?"

"Yes."

"Would it be all right to inquire if you have a picture of her?"

---

3. **connivance** (kuh NY vuhns): an act of conspiring; secret agreement between two people for a dishonest purpose.

Ⓑ **Literary Focus** Characterization How does the author reveal more about Feld in this paragraph?

Ⓒ **Literary Focus** Characterization What impression this characterization of Max give you?

Vocabulary **obligation** (ahb luh GAY shuhn) n.: duty.

The Promenade (1917) by Marc Chagall (1887–1985). (67" x 64 ⅜").

Russian State Museum, St. Petersburg, Russia/ © 2008 Artists Rights Society (ARS), NY/ADAGP, Paris.

"Just a minute." The shoemaker went into the store and hastily returned with a snapshot that Max held up to the light.

"She's all right," he said.

Feld waited.

"And is she sensible—not the flighty kind?"

"She is very sensible."

After another short pause, Max said it was okay with him if he met her. **D**

"Here is my telephone," said the shoemaker, hurriedly handing him a slip of paper. "Call her up. She comes home from work six o'clock."

Max folded the paper and tucked it away into his worn leather wallet.

"About the shoes," he said. "How much did you say they will cost me?"

"Don't worry about the price."

"I just like to have an idea."

"A dollar—dollar fifty. A dollar fifty," the shoemaker said.

At once he felt bad, for he usually charged two twenty-five for this kind of job. Either he should have asked the regular price or done the work for nothing.

Later, as he entered the store, he was startled by a violent clanging and looked up to see Sobel pounding with all his might upon the naked last. It broke, the iron striking the floor and jumping with a thump against the wall, but before the enraged shoemaker could cry out,

D **Reading Focus** Comparing and Contrasting What similarities do you notice between Feld and Max in this conversation?

the assistant had torn his hat and coat from the hook and rushed out into the snow.

So Feld, who had looked forward to anticipating how it would go with his daughter and Max, instead had a great worry on his mind. Without his temperamental helper he was a lost man, especially since it was years now that he had carried the store alone. The shoemaker had for an age suffered from a heart condition that threatened collapse if he dared exert himself. Five years ago, after an attack, it had appeared as though he would have either to sacrifice his business upon the auction block and live on a pittance thereafter, or put himself at the mercy of some unscrupulous employee who would in the end probably ruin him. But just at the moment of his darkest despair, this Polish refugee, Sobel, appeared one night from the street and begged for work. He was a stocky man, poorly dressed, with a bald head that had once been blond, a severely plain face and soft blue eyes prone to tears over the sad books he read, a young man but old—no one would have guessed thirty. Though he confessed he knew nothing of shoemaking, he said he was apt and would work for a very little if Feld taught him the trade. Thinking that with, after all, a landsman,[4] he would have less to fear than from a complete stranger, Feld took him on and within six weeks the refugee rebuilt as good a shoe as he, and not long

> ## Feld frequently asked himself what keeps him here? Why does he stay?

thereafter expertly ran the business for the thoroughly relieved shoemaker. **E**

Feld could trust him with anything and did, frequently going home after an hour or two at the store, leaving all the money in the till, knowing Sobel would guard every cent of it. The amazing thing was that he demanded so little. His wants were few; in money he wasn't interested—in nothing but books, it seemed—which he one by one lent to Miriam, together with his profuse,[5] queer written comments, manufactured during his lonely rooming house evenings, thick pads of commentary which the shoemaker peered at and twitched his shoulders over as his daughter, from her fourteenth year, read page by sanctified[6] page, as if the word of God were inscribed on them. To protect Sobel, Feld himself had to see that he received more than he asked for. Yet his conscience bothered him for not insisting that the assistant accept a better wage than he was getting, though Feld had honestly told him he could earn a handsome salary if he worked elsewhere, or maybe opened a place of his own. But the assistant answered, somewhat ungraciously, that he was not interested in going elsewhere, and though Feld frequently asked himself what keeps him here? why does he stay? he finally answered it that the man, no doubt because of his terrible experiences as a refugee, was afraid of the world. **F**

---

4. **landsman:** a fellow Jew who comes from the same area in Eastern Europe.

5. **profuse** (pruh FYOOS): plentiful; given freely.
6. **sanctified** (SANGK tuh fyd): blessed.

E **Literary Focus** Characterization What is the author revealing about Sobel's character? How?

F **Reading Focus** Comparing and Contrasting How do Feld and Sobel seem to differ in their interactions with other people?

After the incident with the broken last, angered by Sobel's behavior, the shoemaker decided to let him stew for a week in the rooming house, although his own strength was taxed dangerously and the business suffered. However, after several sharp nagging warnings from both his wife and daughter, he went finally in search of Sobel, as he had once before, quite recently, when over some fancied slight—Feld had merely asked him not to give Miriam so many books to read because her eyes were strained and red—the assistant had left the place in a huff, an incident which, as usual, came to nothing for he had returned after the shoemaker had talked to him, and taken his seat at the bench. But this time, after Feld had plodded through the snow to Sobel's house—he had thought of sending Miriam but the idea became repugnant[7] to him—the burly landlady at the door informed him in a nasal voice that Sobel was not at home, and though Feld knew this was a nasty lie, for where had the refugee to go? still for some reason he was not completely sure of—it may have been the cold and his fatigue—he decided not to insist on seeing him. Instead he went home and hired a new helper.

Having settled the matter, though not entirely to his satisfaction, for he had much more to do than before, and so, for example, could no longer lie late in bed mornings because he had to get up to open the store for the new assistant, a speechless, dark man with an irritating rasp as he worked, whom he would not trust with the key as he had Sobel. Furthermore, this one, though able to do a fair repair job, knew nothing of grades of leather or prices, so Feld had to make his own purchases; and every night at closing time it was necessary to count the money in the till and lock up. However, he was not dissatisfied, for he lived much in his thoughts of Max and Miriam. The college boy had called her, and they had arranged a meeting for this coming Friday night. The shoemaker would personally have preferred Saturday, which he felt would make it a date of the first magnitude, but he learned Friday was Miriam's choice, so he said nothing. The day of the week did not matter. What mattered was the aftermath. Would they like each other and want to be friends? He sighed at all the time that would have to go by before he knew for sure. Often he was tempted to talk to Miriam about the boy, to ask whether she thought she would like his type—he had told her only that he considered Max a nice boy and had suggested he call her—but the one time he tried she snapped at him—justly—how should she know? **G**

At last Friday came. Feld was not feeling particularly well so he stayed in bed, and Mrs. Feld thought it better to remain in the bedroom with him when Max called. Miriam received the boy, and her parents could hear their voices, his throaty one, as they talked. Just before leaving, Miriam brought Max to the bedroom door and he stood there a minute, a tall, slightly hunched figure wearing a thick, droopy suit, and apparently at ease as he greeted the shoemaker and his wife, which was surely a good sign. And Miriam, although she had worked all day, looked fresh and pretty. She was a large-framed girl with a well-shaped body, and she had a fine open face and soft hair. They made, Feld thought, a first-class couple.

---

7. **repugnant** (rih PUHG nuhnt): distasteful; offensive.

G **Reading Focus** Comparing and Contrasting What are three ways that Sobel was a better worker than the new assistant?

Miriam returned after 11:30. Her mother was already asleep, but the shoemaker got out of bed and after locating his bathrobe went into the kitchen, where Miriam, to his surprise, sat at the table, reading.

"So where did you go?" Feld asked pleasantly.

"For a walk," she said, not looking up.

"I advised him," Feld said, clearing his throat, "he shouldn't spend so much money."

"I didn't care."

The shoemaker boiled up some water for tea and sat down at the table with a cupful and a thick slice of lemon.

"So how," he sighed after a sip, "did you enjoy?"

"It was all right."

He was silent. She must have sensed his disappointment, for she added, "You can't really tell much the first time."

"You will see him again?"

Turning a page, she said that Max had asked for another date.

"For when?"

"Saturday."

"So what did you say?"

"What did I say?" she asked, delaying for a moment—"I said yes."

Afterward she inquired about Sobel, and Feld, without exactly knowing why, said the assistant had got another job. Miriam said nothing more and began to read. The shoemaker's conscience did not trouble him; he was satisfied with the Saturday date.

During the week, by placing here and there a deft question, he managed to get from Miriam some information about Max. It surprised him to learn that the boy was not studying to be either a doctor or lawyer but was taking a business course leading to a degree in accountancy. Feld was a little disappointed because he thought of accountants as bookkeepers and would have preferred "a higher profession." However, it was not long before he had investigated the subject and discovered that Certified Public Accountants were highly respected people, so he was thoroughly content as Saturday approached. But because Saturday was a busy day, he was much in the store and therefore did not see Max when he came to call for Miriam. From his wife he learned there had been nothing especially revealing about their meeting. Max had rung the bell and Miriam had got her coat and left with him—nothing more. Feld did not probe, for his wife was not particularly observant. Instead, he waited up for Miriam with a newspaper on his lap, which he scarcely looked at so lost was he in thinking of the future. He awoke to find her in the room with him, tiredly removing her hat. Greeting her, he was suddenly inexplicably afraid to ask anything about the evening. But since she volunteered nothing he was at last forced to inquire how she had enjoyed herself. Miriam began something non-committal but apparently changed her mind, for she said after a minute, "I was bored." **H**

When Feld had sufficiently recovered from his anguished disappointment to ask why, she answered without hesitation, "Because he's nothing more than a materialist."

"What means this word?"

"He has no soul. He's only interested in things."

H **Literary Focus** **Characterization** What method of characterization is used in this paragraph?

Bible Stories

The title of this story is an **allusion,** or an indirect reference, to the Old Testament story of Jacob and Rachel, which is in the book of Genesis. In that story, Jacob works for Rachel's father, Laban, for seven years to win Rachel's hand in marriage. Laban treats Jacob like a son but opposes his marriage to Rachel. Ultimately, Laban demands another seven years of work, which Jacob performs out of love for Rachel.

Ask Yourself

By alluding to the story of Jacob and Rachel, what is Malamud suggesting about Sobel, Miriam, and Feld? What clues does the Bible reference offer about the theme of Malamud's story?

The Meeting of Jacob and Rachel (1853) by William Dyce (1806—1864). Oil on canvas (58 cm x 58 cm).

He considered her statement for a long time but then asked, "Will you see him again?"

"He didn't ask."

"Suppose he will ask you?"

"I won't see him."

He did not argue; however, as the days went by he hoped increasingly she would change her mind. He wished the boy would telephone, because he was sure there was more to him than Miriam, with her inexperienced eye, could discern. But Max didn't call. As a matter of fact he took a different route to school, no longer passing the shoemaker's store, and Feld was deeply hurt.

Then one afternoon Max came in and asked for his shoes. The shoemaker took them down from the shelf where he had placed them, apart from the other pairs. He had done the work himself and the soles and heels were well built and firm. The shoes had been highly polished and somehow looked better than new. Max's Adam's apple went up once when he saw them, and his eyes had little lights in them.

"How much?" he asked, without directly looking at the shoemaker. ❶

"Like I told you before," Feld answered sadly. "One dollar fifty cents."

Max handed him two crumpled bills and received in return a newly-minted silver half dollar.

He left. Miriam had not been mentioned. That night the shoemaker discovered that his new assistant had been all the while stealing from him, and he suffered a heart attack.

Though the attack was very mild, he lay in bed for three weeks. Miriam spoke of going for Sobel, but sick as he was Feld rose in wrath against the idea. Yet in his heart he knew there was no other way, and the first weary day back in the shop thoroughly convinced him, so that night after supper he dragged himself to Sobel's rooming house.

Vocabulary **discern** (dih SURN) *v.:* recognize or distinguish.
wrath (rath) *n.:* great anger; rage.

❶ **Literary Focus** Characterization Explain how Max's behavior supports Miriam's characterization of him.

He toiled up the stairs, though he knew it was bad for him, and at the top knocked at the door. Sobel opened it and the shoemaker entered. The room was a small, poor one, with a single window facing the street. It contained a narrow cot, a low table and several stacks of books piled haphazardly around on the floor along the wall, which made him think how queer Sobel was, to be uneducated and read so much. He had once asked him, Sobel, why you read so much? and the assistant could not answer him. Did you ever study in a college someplace? he had asked, but Sobel shook his head. He read, he said, to know. But to know what, the shoemaker demanded, and to know, why? Sobel never explained, which proved he read much because he was queer. **J**

Feld sat down to recover his breath. The assistant was resting on his bed with his heavy back to the wall. His shirt and trousers were clean, and his stubby fingers, away from the shoemaker's bench, were strangely pallid. His face was thin and pale, as if he had been shut in this room since the day he had bolted from the store.

"So when you will come back to work?" Feld asked him.

To his surprise, Sobel burst out, "Never."

Jumping up, he strode over to the window that looked out upon the miserable street. "Why should I come back?" he cried.

"I will raise your wages."

"Who cares for your wages!"

The shoemaker, knowing he didn't care, was at a loss what else to say.

"What do you want from me, Sobel?"

"Nothing."

"I always treated you like you was my son."

Sobel vehemently denied it. "So why you look for strange boys in the street they should go out with Miriam? Why you don't think of me?"

The shoemaker's hands and feet turned freezing cold. His voice became so hoarse he couldn't speak. At last he cleared his throat and croaked, "So what has my daughter got to do with a shoemaker thirty-five years old who works for me?"

"Why do you think I worked so long for you?" Sobel cried out. "For the stingy wages I sacrificed five years of my life so you could have to eat and drink and where to sleep?"

"Then for what?" shouted the shoemaker.

"For Miriam," he blurted— "for her."

The shoemaker, after a time, managed to say, "I pay wages in cash, Sobel," and lapsed into silence. Though he was seething with excitement, his mind was coldly clear, and he had to admit to himself he had sensed all along that Sobel felt this way. He had never so much as thought it consciously, but he had felt it and was afraid.

"Miriam knows?" he muttered hoarsely.

"She knows."

"You told her?"

"No."

"Then how does she know?"

"How does she know?" Sobel said, "because she knows. She knows who I am and what is in my heart."

Feld had a sudden insight. In some devious[8] way, with his books and commentary, Sobel had given Miriam to understand that he loved her. The shoemaker felt a terrible anger at him for his deceit.

---

8. **devious** (DEE vee uhs): roundabout; indirect. *Devious* can also mean "deceitful."

J **Reading Focus** Comparing and Contrasting How do Feld's and Sobel's ideas about reading and education differ?

Interior With a Young Girl Writing (1905) by Felix Edouard Vallotton.

"Sobel, you are crazy," he said bitterly. "She will never marry a man so old and ugly like you."

Sobel turned black with rage. He cursed the shoemaker, but then, though he trembled to hold it in, his eyes filled with tears and he broke into deep sobs. With his back to Feld, he stood at the window, fists clenched, and his shoulders shook with his choked sobbing.

Watching him, the shoemaker's anger diminished. His teeth were on edge with pity for the man, and his eyes grew moist. How strange and sad that a refugee, a grown man, bald and old with his miseries, who had by the skin of his teeth escaped Hitler's incinerators,[9] should fall in love, when he had got to America, with a girl less than half his age. Day after day, for five years he had sat at his bench, cutting and hammering away, waiting for the girl to become a woman, unable to ease his heart with speech, knowing no protest but desperation.

"Ugly I didn't mean," he said half aloud.

> "Sobel, you are crazy," he said bitterly. "She will never marry a man so old and ugly like you."

9. **Hitler's incinerators:** furnaces in which the Nazis burned the bodies of Jews and other people in the death camps during World War II.

Then he realized that what he had called ugly was not Sobel but Miriam's life if she married him. He felt for his daughter a strange and gripping sorrow, as if she were already Sobel's bride, the wife, after all, of a shoemaker, and had in her life no more than her mother had had. And all his dreams for her—why he had slaved and destroyed his heart with anxiety and labor—all these dreams of a better life were dead. **L**

The room was quiet. Sobel was standing by the window reading, and it was curious that when he read he looked young.

"She is only nineteen," Feld said brokenly. "This is too young yet to get married. Don't ask her for two years more, till she is twenty-one, then you can talk to her."

Sobel didn't answer. Feld rose and left. He went slowly down the stairs but once outside, though it was an icy night and the crisp falling snow whitened the street, he walked with a stronger stride.

But the next morning, when the shoemaker arrived, heavy-hearted, to open the store, he saw he needn't have come, for his assistant was already seated at the last, pounding leather for his love.

K **Literary Focus** Characterization What does Feld's reaction reveal about him?

L **Reading Focus** Comparing and Contrasting What can you conclude about Feld from this paragraph?

Applying Your Skills

RA.L.10.1 Compare and contrast an author's use of direct and indirect characterization, and ways in which characters reveal traits about themselves, including dialect, dramatic monologues and soliloquies. *Also covered* **RA.L.10.8; RP.10.1; VO.10.3; WA.10.1.b**

The First Seven Years

Respond and Think Critically

Reading Focus

Quick Check

1. How does Feld treat Sobel?

2. Why does Sobel quit working at the store? Why does he return?

Read with a Purpose

3. What do each of the main characters—Feld, Max, and Sobel—want in this story?

Reading Skills: Comparing and Contrasting Characters

4. Review the chart you started to compare characters. Then, answer this question: In what ways are Feld and Sobel alike and different? Think about their backgrounds, their present situations, and their relationships with others.

> Alike
>
> Different

✓ Vocabulary Check

Match each Vocabulary word with its definition.

5. **obligation**   a. moody
6. **temperamental**   b. rage
7. **unscrupulous**   c. distinguish
8. **discern**   d. duty
9. **wrath**   e. unprincipled

Literary Focus

Literary Analysis

10. **Summarize** List the reasons that Feld believes Sobel is a bad match for Miriam. Do you think his reasons are justified? Explain.

11. **Evaluate** At what point in the story did you realize that Sobel was in love with Miriam? What details suggested this fact?

Literary Skills: Characterization

12. **Analyze** Which of the author's techniques gave you the best idea of Feld's character: using direct characterization, describing his actions, or revealing his thoughts?

Literary Skills Review: Mood

13. **Describe** A work's atmosphere, or **mood,** is the overall feeling created in the work. How would you describe the mood of this story? Explain.

Writing Focus

Think as a Reader/Writer

Use It in Your Writing Review the examples of direct and indirect characterization you noted. Then, using both methods, write a paragraph about an interesting person you know.

 What Do You Think Now

What sacrifices does Sobel make? Why do you think he is willing to make these sacrifices?

Comparing Characters Across Genres

Kabul, Afghanistan.

CONTENTS

What Do **You** **Think?** How are we shaped by the time and place in which we live?

QuickTalk

Think about your life today. How might your life be different if you exchanged places with someone your age in another country? Discuss your ideas with a partner.

Preparing to Read

from The Kite Runner / Escape from Afghanistan

RA.L.10.1 Compare and contrast an author's use of direct and indirect characterization, and ways in which characters reveal traits about themselves, including dialect, dramatic monologues and soliloquies. *Also covered* **RP.10.2; RP.10.1**

Reader/Writer Notebook

Use your **RWN** to complete the activities for these selections.

Literary Focus

Characters in Conflict: Historical Context Often, to understand a character's conflict, you need to understand the historical context of a story or other narrative. **Historical context** refers to the time and place in which the story is set, including the social and cultural background, significant events occurring at the time, and even aspects of daily life. The conflicts that characters undergo are frequently a direct result of the historical context. Understanding the social norms and class structure that existed in Afghanistan at the time will help you understand the unspoken conflict between Amir and Hassan in *The Kite Runner*. Although Amir is Hassan's friend, he is also his servant and part of the Hazara ethnic minority in Afghanistan.

Reading Focus

Comparing and Contrasting Characters As you read, pay attention to each main character's background, present circumstances, and details about their culture, and their relationships with others. Record details about Amir and Ahmedi (from "Escape to Afghanistan") in a chart like this one.

Amir	Farah Ahmedi
is friend of the son of a servant (Hassan)	

Writing Focus

Think as a Reader/Writer

Find It in Your Reading Writers tend to *show* their readers—rather than *tell* them—what the characters experience. Writers often do so by using sensory language—words and phrases that enable you to see, hear, feel, taste, and smell just as the characters do. As you read the following selections, notice the sensory language the writers use and list examples in your *Reader/Writer Notebook*.

Vocabulary

from The Kite Runner

coveted (KUHV iht ehd) *v.* used as *adj.*: very much desired. *The fastest kite of the year was a coveted prize.*

abhor (ab HAWR) *v.*: strongly hate. *Afghans abhor rules that limit their lives.*

integrity (ihn TEHG ruh tee) *n.*: honesty or trustworthiness. *Because he was honest himself, Hassan believed in Amir's integrity.*

Escape from Afghanistan

gorges (GAWRJ ehz) *n.*: deep valleys with steep sides; ravines. *The trek through the rocky gorges was dangerous.*

clamor (KLAM uhr) *n.*: loud uproar. *The people at the gate to Pakistan created a clamor as they struggled to get through.*

chide (chyd) *v.*: scold mildly. *Ahmedi did not chide her mother for moving slowly.*

Language Coach

Word Origins The word *gorge* comes from an Old French word meaning "throat." Used as a verb, the word *gorges* means "swallows or eats greedily." How does the meaning of the noun *gorges* relate to this definition?

Learn It Online

Do pictures and animation help you learn? Try the *PowerNotes* lesson on:

go.hrw.com L10-171   Go

Khaled Hosseini
(1965–   )

Clash of Worlds

Khaled Hosseini was born in Afghanistan in 1965, before the country was controlled by first the Soviets and then the Taliban. At the time of the Soviet invasion in 1979, Hosseini's father was a diplomat assigned to the Afghan embassy in Paris. The family returned to Afghanistan in 1980 to find that the Soviets' bloody coup had drastically changed their homeland. Later the same year, the family received political asylum in the United States and moved to California.

Hosseini graduated from medical school in 1996. He practices medicine in addition to writing. He has spent most of his life in the United States, and like many Americans he is a fan of football and rock music. But Hosseini has never forgotten his heritage. Writing *The Kite Runner*, he wanted to make sure that the Afghanistan he remembered would never be forgotten.

> "I wanted to write about Afghanistan before the Soviet war because that is largely a forgotten period in modern Afghan history. . . . I wanted to remind people that Afghans had managed to live in peaceful anonymity for decades."

Farah Ahmedi
(1988–   )

Escape to a Better Future

When she was seven years old, Farah Ahmedi stepped on a land mine and lost a leg. By the time she was fourteen, she had lost her father, her sisters, and her home to civil unrest in her homeland of Afghanistan. Despite her losses, she maintains a positive attitude and focuses on helping other people. In the prologue of her book *The Story of My Life,* she writes, "Out of my losses have come tremendous gifts as well."

Think About the Writers

Why do you think it's important to read writers like Hosseini and Ahmedi who are from Afghanistan?

Preview the Selections

The following excerpt from *The Kite Runner* is about the unspoken competition between **Amir,** the son of a wealthy businessman, and Amir's loyal friend **Hassan,** the son of a servant in Amir's home.

"Escape from Afghanistan" revisits **Farah Ahmedi's** experiences as she and her ill mother flee war-torn Afghanistan.

from The Kite Runner

by **Khaled Hosseini**

Read with a Purpose
Read this novel excerpt to learn about the complex relationships the narrator, Amir, has with his friend Hassan and with his father, whom he calls Baba.

Build Background
The following excerpt from the novel *The Kite Runner* takes place in the 1970s, before the devastating destruction that civil war and the Soviet invasion imposed upon the people of Afghanistan. Kite fighting is a national pastime in Afghanistan and a favorite annual winter event for the narrator and his friend.

Winter.

Here is what I do on the first day of snowfall every year: I step out of the house early in the morning, still in my pajamas, hugging my arms against the chill. I find the driveway, my father's car, the walls, the trees, the rooftops, and the hills buried under a foot of snow. I smile. The sky is seamless and blue, the snow so white my eyes burn. I shovel a handful of the fresh snow into my mouth, listen to the muffled stillness broken only by the cawing of crows. I walk down the front steps, barefoot, and call for Hassan to come out and see.

Winter was every kid's favorite season in Kabul, at least those whose fathers could afford to buy a good iron stove. The reason was simple: They shut down school for the icy season. Winter to me was the end of long division and naming the capital of Bulgaria, and the start of three months of playing cards by the stove with Hassan, free Russian movies on Tuesday mornings at Cinema Park, sweet turnip *qurma* over rice for lunch after a morning of building snowmen.

And kites, of course. Flying kites. And running them.

For a few unfortunate kids, winter did not spell the end of the school year. There were the so-called voluntary winter courses. No kid I knew ever volunteered to go to these classes; parents, of course, did the volunteering for them. Fortunately for me, Baba was not one of them. I remember one kid, Ahmad, who lived across the street from us. His father was some kind of doctor, I think. Ahmad had epilepsy and always wore a wool vest and thick black-rimmed glasses—he was one of Assef's[1] regular victims. Every morning, I watched from my bedroom window as their Hazara[2] servant shoveled snow from the driveway, cleared the way for the black Opel. I made a point of watching Ahmad and his father get into the car, Ahmad in his wool vest and winter coat, his schoolbag filled with books and pencils. I waited until they pulled away, turned the corner, then I slipped back into bed in my flannel pajamas. I pulled the blanket to my chin and watched the snowcapped hills in the north

---

1. **Assef's:** referring to a local bully.
2. **Hazara:** one of several ethnic minority groups in Afghanistan, the Hazara are of Mongolian descent.

Analyzing Visuals

Viewing and Interpreting
What details in this photo-graph are similar to details in the story?

Boy with a kite in Kabul, Afghanistan.

through the window. Watched them until I drifted back to sleep.

Ⓐ

I loved wintertime in Kabul. I loved it for the soft pattering of snow against my window at night, for the way fresh snow crunched under my black rubber boots, for the warmth of the cast-iron stove as the wind screeched through the yards, the streets. But mostly because, as the trees froze and ice sheathed the roads, the chill between Baba and me thawed a little. And the reason for that was the kites. Baba and I lived in the same house, but in different spheres of existence. Kites were the one paper-thin slice of intersection between those spheres.

Every winter, districts in Kabul held a kite-fighting tournament. And if you were a boy living in Kabul, the day of the tournament was undeniably the highlight of the cold season. I never slept the night before the tournament. I'd roll from side to side, make shadow animals on

the wall, even sit on the balcony in the dark, a blanket wrapped around me. I felt like a soldier trying to sleep in the trenches the night before a major battle. And that wasn't so far off. In Kabul, fighting kites *was* a little like going to war.

As with any war, you had to ready your-self for battle. For a while, Hassan and I used to build our own kites. We saved our weekly allowances in the fall, dropped the money in a little porcelain horse Baba had brought one time from Herat. When the winds of winter began to blow and snow fell in chunks, we undid the snap under the horse's belly. We went to the bazaar[3] and bought bamboo, glue, string, and paper. We spent hours every day shaving bamboo for the center and cross spars, cut-ting the thin tissue paper which made for easy

3. **bazaar** (buh ZAHR): open-air market found espe-cially in the Middle East that has shops or stalls selling a variety of goods.

Ⓐ **Reading Focus** Compare and Contrast Why was winter better for some children in Kabul than others?

dipping and recovery. And then, of course, we had to make our own string, or *tar*. If the kite was the gun, then *tar,* the glass-coated cutting line, was the bullet in the chamber. We'd go out in the yard and feed up to five hundred feet of string through a mixture of ground glass and glue. We'd then hang the line between the trees, leave it to dry. The next day, we'd wind the battle-ready line around a wooden spool. By the time the snow melted and the rains of spring swept in, every boy in Kabul bore telltale horizontal gashes on his fingers from a whole winter of fighting kites. I remember how my classmates and I used to huddle, compare our battle scars on the first day of school. The cuts stung and didn't heal for a couple of weeks, but I didn't mind. They were reminders of a beloved season that had once again passed too quickly. Then the class captain would blow his whistle and we'd march in a single file to our classrooms, longing for winter already, greeted instead by the specter of yet another long school year. **B**

But it quickly became apparent that Hassan and I were better kite fighters than kite makers. Some flaw or other in our design always spelled its doom. So Baba started taking us to Saifo's to buy our kites. Saifo was a nearly blind old man who was a *moochi* by profession—a shoe repairman. But he was also the city's most famous kite maker, working out of a tiny hovel on Jadeh Maywand, the crowded street south of the muddy banks of the Kabul River. I remember you had to crouch to enter the prison cell–sized store, and then had to lift a trapdoor to creep down a set of wooden steps to the dank basement where Saifo stored his coveted kites. Baba would buy us each three identical kites and spools of glass string. If I changed my mind and asked for a bigger and fancier kite, Baba would buy it for me—but then he'd buy it for Hassan too. Sometimes I wished he wouldn't do that. Wished he'd let me be the favorite.

The kite-fighting tournament was an old winter tradition in Afghanistan. It started early in the morning on the day of the contest and didn't end until only the winning kite flew in the sky—I remember one year the tournament outlasted daylight. People gathered on sidewalks and roofs to cheer for their kids. The streets filled with kite fighters, jerking and tugging on their lines, squinting up to the sky, trying to gain position to cut the opponent's line. Every kite fighter had an assistant—in my case, Hassan—who held the spool and fed the line.

One time, a bratty Hindi[4] kid whose family had recently moved into the neighborhood told us that in his hometown, kite fighting had strict rules and regulations. "You have to play in a boxed area and you have to stand at a right angle to the wind," he said proudly. "And you can't use aluminum to make your glass string."

Hassan and I looked at each other. Cracked up. The Hindi kid would soon learn what the British learned earlier in the century, and what the Russians would eventually learn by the late 1980s: that Afghans are an independent people. Afghans cherish custom but abhor rules. And so it was with kite fighting. The rules were simple: No rules. Fly your kite. Cut the opponents. Good luck. **C**

---

4. **Hindi:** the official language of northern India; used here to refer to a person of Hindu descent.

B **Reading Focus** Compare and Contrast In what ways is kite fighting similar to war?

C **Literary Focus** Characters in Conflict Describe the conflicts revealed here.

Vocabulary **coveted** (KUHV iht ehd) *v.* used as *adj.*: very much desired.
abhor (ab HAWR) *v.*: strongly hate.

Except that wasn't all. The real fun began when a kite was cut. That was where the kite runners came in, those kids who chased the windblown kite drifting through the neighborhoods until it came spiraling down in a field, dropping in someone's yard, on a tree, or a rooftop. The chase got pretty fierce; hordes of kite runners swarmed the streets, shoved past each other like those people from Spain I'd read about once, the ones who ran from the bulls.[5] One year a neighborhood kid climbed a pine tree for a kite. A branch snapped under his weight and he fell thirty feet. Broke his back and never walked again. But he fell with the kite still in his hands. And when a kite runner had his hands on a kite, no one could take it from him. That wasn't a rule. That was custom.

For kite runners, the most coveted prize was the last fallen kite of a winter tournament. It was a trophy of honor, something to be displayed on a mantle for guests to admire. When the sky cleared of kites and only the final two remained, every kite runner readied himself for the chance to land this prize. He positioned himself at a spot that he thought would give him a head start. Tense muscles readied themselves to uncoil. Necks craned. Eyes crinkled. Fights broke out. And when the last kite was cut, all hell broke loose.   (D)

Over the years, I had seen a lot of guys run kites. But Hassan was by far the greatest kite runner I'd ever seen. It was downright eerie the way he always got to the spot the kite would

land *before* the kite did, as if he had some sort of inner compass.

I remember one overcast winter day, Hassan and I were running a kite. I was chasing him through neighborhoods, hopping gutters, weaving through narrow streets. I was a year older than him, but Hassan ran faster than I did, and I was falling behind.

"Hassan! Wait!" I yelled, my breathing hot and ragged.

He whirled around, motioned with his hand. "This way!" he called before dashing around another corner. I looked up, saw that the direction we were running was opposite to the one the kite was drifting.

"We're losing it! We're going the wrong way!" I cried out.

"Trust me!" I heard him call up ahead. I reached the corner and saw Hassan bolting along, his head down, not even looking at the sky, sweat soaking through the back of his shirt. I tripped over a rock and fell—I wasn't just slower than Hassan but clumsier too; I'd always envied his natural athleticism. When I staggered to my feet, I caught a glimpse of Hassan disappearing around another street corner. I hobbled after him, spikes of pain battering my scraped knees.

I saw we had ended up on a rutted dirt road near Isteqlal Middle School. There was a field on one side where lettuce grew in the summer, and a row of sour cherry trees on the other. I found Hassan sitting cross-legged at the foot of one of the trees, eating from a fistful of dried mulberries.

"What are we doing here?" I panted, my stomach roiling with nausea.

He smiled. "Sit with me, Amir agha."[6]

---

5. **those people . . . ran from the bulls:** Amir is referring to the running of the bulls that takes place during the Fiesta de San Fermin in Pamplona, Spain. In this yearly festival, participants run with selected bulls for half a mile through the town.

---

6. **agha:** Farsi for *sir.*

(D) **Literary Focus** Characters in Conflict   What does this event <u>reveal</u> about the Afghan people?

I dropped next to him, lay on a thin patch of snow, wheezing. "You're wasting our time. It was going the other way, didn't you see?"

Hassan popped a mulberry in his mouth. "It's coming," he said. I could hardly breathe and he didn't even sound tired.

"How do you know?" I said.

"I know."

"How can you *know*?"

He turned to me. A few sweat beads rolled from his bald scalp. "Would I ever lie to you, Amir agha?"

Suddenly I decided to toy with him a little. "I don't know. Would you?"

"I'd sooner eat dirt," he said with a look of indignation.

"Really? You'd do that?"

He threw me a puzzled look. "Do what?"

"Eat dirt if I told you to," I said. I knew I was being cruel, like when I'd taunt him if he didn't know some big word. But there was something fascinating—albeit in a sick way—about teasing Hassan. Kind of like when we used to play insect torture. Except now, he was the ant and I was holding the magnifying glass.

His eyes searched my face for a long time. We sat there, two boys under a sour cherry tree, suddenly looking, *really* looking, at each other. That's when it happened again: Hassan's face changed. Maybe not *changed,* not really, but suddenly I had the feeling I was looking at two faces, the one I knew, the one that was my first memory, and another, a second face, this one lurking just beneath the surface. I'd seen it happen before—it always shook me up a little. It just appeared, this other face, for a fraction of a moment, long enough to leave me with the unsettling feeling that maybe I'd seen it someplace before. Then Hassan blinked and it was just him again. Just Hassan.

"If you asked, I would," he finally said, looking right at me. I dropped my eyes. To this day, I find it hard to gaze directly at people like Hassan, people who mean every word they say.

"But I wonder," he added. "Would you ever ask me to do such a thing, Amir agha?" And, just like that, he had thrown at me his own little test. If I was going to toy with him and challenge his loyalty, then he'd toy with me, test my integrity.

I wished I hadn't started this conversation. I forced a smile. "Don't be stupid, Hassan. You know I wouldn't."

Hassan returned the smile. Except his didn't look forced. "I know," he said. And that's the thing about people who mean everything they say. They think everyone else does too. **E**

"Here it comes," Hassan said, pointing to the sky. He rose to his feet and walked a few paces to his left. I looked up, saw the kite plummeting toward us. I heard footfalls, shouts, an approaching melee of kite runners. But they were wasting their time. Because Hassan stood with his arms wide open, smiling, waiting for the kite. And may God—if He exists, that is—strike me blind if the kite didn't just drop into his outstretched arms.

E Literary Focus **Characters in Conflict** What does this conversation <u>reveal</u> about the relationship between Amir and Hassan?

Vocabulary **integrity** (ihn TEHG ruh tee) *n.*: honesty or trustworthiness.

Applying Your Skills

RA.L.10.1 Compare and contrast an author's use of direct and indirect characterization, and ways in which characters reveal traits about themselves, including dialect, dramatic monologues and soliloquies. *Also covered* **RP.10.2; RP.10.1; WA.10.1.b**

from The Kite Runner

Respond and Think Critically

Reading Focus

Quick Check

1. How do Amir and Hassan prepare for the kite tournament?

2. What does the kite runner do? What makes Hassan an excellent kite runner?

Read with a Purpose

3. What troubles Amir in his relationship with Hassan?

Reading Skills: Compare and Contrast Characters

4. Review the notes about Amir that you took while reading the story. What are Amir's main conflicts? Add them to the chart.

Amir	Farah Ahmedi
is friend of the son of a servant (Hassan)	
conflict: wants approval from Baba	

✓ Vocabulary Check

Match the Vocabulary word in the first column with its definition in the second column.

5. **coveted** a. honesty; trustworthiness
6. **integrity** b. hate; loathe
7. **abhor** c. very much desired

Literary Focus

Literary Analysis

8. **Analyze** Although Amir and Hassan are friends, they inhabit two separate worlds. How are the two boys alike? How are they different?

9. **Infer** Amir thinks he sees a change in Hassan's face as they test each other's loyalty. What do you think Hassan's change of expression might signify?

Literary Skills: Characters in Conflict

10. **Explain** How does Amir's conflict with Hassan reflect the historical context of the period? How might the story have been different if Hassan were not the son of Amir's servant?

Literary Skills Review: Narrator

11. **Analyze** A **narrator** is the person who tells a story, often from his or her own point of view. How might this novel excerpt have been told differently if Hassan were the narrator? How might he describe Amir?

Writing Focus

Think as a Reader/Writer

Use It in Your Writing Review the sensory details that you noted in your *Reader/Writer Notebook*. Then, write a paragraph describing a competition in which you have taken part or watched in person. Make sure to use sensory details and imagery that will enable your reader to see, hear, taste, smell, and feel this experience.

ESCAPE FROM AFGHANISTAN

by **Farah Ahmedi** with **Tamim Ansary**

Read with a Purpose

Read this memoir to learn how Ahmedi and her mother overcome enormous challenges to escape from Afghanistan.

Preparing to Read for this selection is on page 171.

Build Background

As a child in Afghanistan, Farah Ahmedi lost her leg when she stepped on a land mine. After recuperating in Germany, she returned to her homeland—now in the midst of a civil war. One day, a bomb landed on her home and instantly killed her father and sisters. Her brothers, fearing they would be drafted into the Taliban army, escaped to Pakistan. Left without male relatives in a male-dominated society, Farah and her mother decided they, too, must try to escape. The following selection is from Ahmedi's memoir *The Other Side of the Sky*.

One day we got a letter, hand-carried to us by some traveler. Alas, it was not from my brothers. It came from my mother's cousin in Quetta, a city on the Pakistan side of the Afghan border. We had lost track of her and did not even know she was there, but somehow, six months after my father's death, she had heard about the event and about our quandary.

Come to Quetta, she wrote. *Get across the border somehow, and then come directly to Quetta. Do not tarry in Peshawar. That is a Taliban stronghold, a Pashtun[1] city. You won't be welcome there. In fact, you will be in danger, for the Taliban come from that region, and they are prejudiced against Hazaras. Peshawar is a dangerous place for two Hazara women on their own. Do not even go into the city, if you*

can avoid it. Just come to Quetta. And she gave directions for finding her house once we got to her city. **A**

This cousin of my mother's had moved to Quetta some time ago. She had a settled life there. She had lost her husband, but she had a brother and two sons living in Turkmenistan.[2] Those men had gotten out of Afghanistan during the Communist era.[3] They had gone to Turkmenistan to study, and then, because the country had dissolved into civil war, they had simply stayed. They now worked in that former Soviet republic and sent bits of money from time to time; that's what my mother's cousin lived on.

---

1. **Pashtun:** the majority ethnic group in Afghanistan. The Taliban are Pashtun.

2. **Turkmenistan:** a country in central Asia that borders Afghanistan.

3. **Communist era:** In the late 1970s, for economic reasons, Afghanistan adopted a communistic government and aligned itself with the Soviet Union.

A **Literary Focus** Characters in Conflict What does the letter indicate about the conflict Ahmedi and her mother face?

Well, we talked it over with our neighbors and decided that we had to do it. We made inquiries and learned that we could pay a man to serve as our escort on the bus to Jalalabad.[4] That would get us out of Taliban-dominated Kabul. From Jalalabad to the border, we would be on our own. As for getting across the border, no one knew what that entailed. And as for making the journey from the border to Quetta, that was like asking how to get from one part of the moon to another part. No one could give us any advice on that subject. We would just have to figure things out when we got there.

By the time we left Afghanistan, the warm days had come. We wrapped the few possessions we would take along in little cloth bundles. We could not take much, for we would have to carry whatever we took, and while I could not handle much of a load, my poor mother was in even worse shape. The day my father died, her asthma took a turn for the worse. Now she was rasping with every breath, and exertion of any kind tightened up her air passages. We had no medicine for her condition. When it got bad, all she could do was rest, so the last thing we needed was extra baggage.

We made it to Jalalabad by bus. We could not have gotten there any other way. The stretch of road between Kabul and Jalalabad goes over some of the country's steepest mountains, cutting through two rugged gorges. The Kabul River pours through those gorges in a series of thundering cataracts, and the highway has been cut into nearly solid rock, folding back and forth, back and forth like a ribbon along the riverbank.

_____

4. **Jalalabad:** a city in Afghanistan near the Pakistani border.

Once the road descended out of those gorges, the weather changed. The temperature rose. Now we were in the Jalalabad valley, which was dotted with groves of orange trees and lemon trees. The bus let us off in a crowded bazaar. We were frightened to be there alone and frightened to have to ask for advice and directions, but we addressed our questions to women as much as possible or to family groups that included women. In this way we found out how to get to the "other" bus station.

This other bus station wasn't really a station. There was no building, no ticket booth, and no station agent—nothing like that. The so-called bus station looked like any other part of the bazaar: It was just a road lined on both sides with merchants' stalls. Along this strip of bazaar, however, men cruised back and forth in vans they owned, looking for people who wanted to go to the border. If you just stood at the curb, they pulled over and offered you a ride.

Before we got on, though, other people waiting there for rides advised us to get some plastic bags. We didn't know why, but we figured we had better do whatever other travelers were doing. They no doubt knew more than we did. Curiously enough, some of the stalls in that vicinity sold plastic bags as if this were a normal travel need.

Shortly after we took up our post by the side of the road, a van pulled over. Instantly, a crowd surged toward its door. People fought and threw elbows to get to the front so they could board. That's how it was at the "bus station." Only the most aggressive travelers got rides. Each van could carry ten or twelve people, if they squeezed; and they always squeezed. The drivers wanted to make as much money as they could. We were unable to get onto the first van.

_____

Vocabulary **gorges** (GAWRJ ehz) *n. pl.*: deep valleys with steep sides; ravines.

Afghan refugees.

We could not get on the next one, either. By the third one, however, I saw what we needed to do, and taking my mother by the arm, I shoved and pushed with the others until we made it to the door of the van. **B**

It wasn't all that far from Jalalabad to the border, but we were traveling in the heat of mid-afternoon. Dust boiled up around the car and got in through the windows. My mother began to wheeze and gasp. I worried that she might stop breathing right then and there, so I tried to shield her with my body, tried to keep the other passengers from pressing in on her so that she would have her own space to breathe out of. Meanwhile, the dust mingled with the sweat running down my face, turning to mud by the time it reached my chin.

At that moment I discovered what the plastic bags were for: One of the men in the backseat vomited loudly, barely getting his awful

stew into his bag. The nasty odor immediately pervaded the entire van. My nostrils puckered, and I felt my own vomit rising. I grabbed for my bag. Within minutes, all of us passengers were filling up our plastic bags. No, it wasn't far from Jalalabad to the border, just a couple of hours, but that ride felt like it would never end.

About half a mile from the border the van pulled over to the side of the road. "This is as far as we go," the driver said. "That's the border up ahead. You see those two buildings and the gate between them? That's it. If you can get through that gate, you're in Pakistan. About half a mile up the road on the other side, if you can get to the other side, you'll find other cars like this one offering rides to Peshawar."

Well, we got out and started trudging toward the border station. We were not alone. The whole stretch of road was filled with people hoping to get across the border that day—

B **Literary Focus** **Characters in Conflict** What are some of the conflicts Ahmedi and her mother have faced so far?

hundreds of families. I don't know how many. I wasn't counting. I didn't count. I was distracted by the scene I saw up ahead.

The gate to Pakistan was closed, and I could see that the Pakistani border guards were letting no one through. People were pushing and shoving and jostling up against that gate, and the guards were driving them back. As we got closer, the crowd thickened, and I could hear the roar and clamor at the gate. The Afghans were yelling something, and the Pakistanis were yelling back. My mother was clutching her side and gasping for breath, trying to keep up. I felt desperate to get through, because the sun was setting, and if we got stuck here, what were we going to do? Where would we stay? There was nothing here, no town, no hotel, no buildings, just the desert.

Yet we had no real chance of getting through. Big strong men were running up to the gate in vain. The guards had clubs, and they had carbines, too, which they turned around and used as weapons. Again and again, the crowd surged toward the gate and the guards drove them back with their sticks and clubs, swinging and beating until the crowd receded. And after that, for the next few minutes, on our side of the border, people milled about and muttered and stoked their own impatience and worked up their rage, until gradually the crowd gathered strength and surged against that gate again, only to be swept back.

We never even got close to the front. We got caught up in the thinning rear end of the crowd, and even so, we were part of each wave,

> We were all just ordinary folks caught in a bad situation, sharing the same fate.

pulled forward, driven back. It was hard for me to keep my footing, and my mother was clutching my arm now, just hanging on, just trying to stay close to me, because the worst thing would have been if we had gotten separated. Finally, I saw that it was no use. We were only risking injury. We drifted back, out of the crowd. In the thickening dusk we could hear the dull roar of people still trying to get past the border guards, but we receded into the desert, farther and farther back from the border gate.

Night was falling, and we were stranded out there in the open.

But at least it wasn't cold; that was a blessing. And at least we were not alone. For that, too, I felt grateful. Hundreds of us were hunkering out there on the desert floor, in the shadows of the high hills that marked the border. We were clotted into family groups. Some groups managed to get fires going, which added a feeling of cheer. They chatted quietly around their fires, and we could hear their voices. There was something companionable about it, really. We were all just ordinary folks caught in a bad situation, sharing the same fate. No one there meant anybody harm. **C**

Had I been alone, I would have felt frightened, but with that sea of families surrounding me, I felt safe, even if they were strangers. My mother and I had our little cloth bundles, in which we were each carrying some extra clothes, and we had our head scarves. We put those under our heads as pillows and slept under the stars. It wasn't bad. We did manage to catch some sleep.

Vocabulary   **clamor** (KLAM uhr) *n.:* loud uproar.

C **Reading Focus** **Compare and Contrast** How are Ahmedi and her mother similar to and different from the others?

Then dawn came, and we again had to make our way to the road and try to get across that border. What else could we do? We could not go back, nor could we stay in that wasteland indefinitely. We *had* to get through. But once again, the guards were keeping the gate closed, beating and hitting anyone who got close enough each time the crowd rushed.

On that second day, however, I learned that it was all a question of money. Someone told me about this, and then I watched closely and saw that it was true. Throughout the day, while some of the guards confronted the crowds, a few others lounged over to the side. People approached them quietly. Money changed hands, and the guards then let those people quietly through a small door to the side. Hundreds could have flowed through the main gate had it been opened, but only one or two could get through the side door at a time. The fact that the guards were taking bribes did us no good whatsoever. We did not have the money to pay them. What little we had we would need to get from Peshawar to Quetta. And so the second day passed. **Ⓓ**

At the end of that day we found ourselves camping near a friendly family. We struck up a conversation with them. The woman told us that her husband, Ghulam Ali, had gone to look for another way across the border. He was checking out a goat path that supposedly went over the mountains several miles northeast of the border station. If one could get to Pakistan safely by that route, he would come back for his family. "You can go with us," the woman said.

Later that night her husband showed up. "It works," he said. "Smugglers use that path, and they bribe the guards to leave it unguarded. Of course, we don't want to run into any smugglers, either, but if we go late at night, we should be fine."

His wife then told him our story, and Ghulam Ali took pity on us. "Yes, of course you can come with us," he said. "But you have had two hard days. You will need some rest before you attempt this mountain crossing. Spend tonight here and sleep well, knowing that you will have nothing to do tomorrow except lounge around, rest, and catch your breath. Tomorrow, do not throw yourself against those border guards again. Let your only work be the gathering of your strength. Then tomorrow night we will all go over the mountain together, with God's grace. I will show you the way. If God wills it, we will follow that smugglers' path to safety. You and your mother are in my care now."

So we spent the whole next day there. It was terribly warm and we had no water, but we walked a little way and found a mosque that refugees like us had built over the years, so that people waiting to get across the border would have a place to say their prayers. We got some water to drink at the mosque, and we said *namaz*[5] there too. Somehow we obtained a bit of bread as well. I can't remember how that turned up, but there it was, and we ate it. We sustained our strength. After sunset we lay down just as if we were going to spend another night. In fact, I did fall asleep for a while. Long after dark—or early the next morning, to be exact, before the sun came up—that man shook us awake. "It's time," he said.

---

5. *namaz:* required prayers in Islam.

Ⓓ **Literary Focus** **Characters in Conflict** What difficulties contribute to the conflicts Ahmedi and her mother are experiencing?

We got up and performed our ablutions[6] quickly in the darkness, with just sand, because that's allowed when you have no access to water. We said our prayers. Then Ghulam Ali began to march into the darkness with his family, and we trudged along silently behind them. After several miles the path began to climb, and my mother began to wheeze. Her asthma was pretty bad at this point, poor thing. No doubt, her anxiety made it worse, but in such circumstances how could she rid herself of anxiety? It was no use knowing that her difficulty was rooted in anxiety, just as it was no use knowing that we could have moved more quickly if we had possessed wings. Life is what it is. The path over that mountain was not actually very long, only a couple of miles. Steep as it was, we could have gotten over in little more than an hour if not for my mother. Because of her, we had to pause every few minutes, so our journey took many hours.

I myself hardly felt the exertion. I was walking quite well that day, quite athletically. I had that good prosthetic[7] leg from Germany. The foot was a little worn by then, but not enough to slow me down. Thinking back, I'm puzzled, actually. How did I scale that mountain so easily? How did I climb down the other side? These days I find it hard to clamber up two or

---

6. **ablutions** (ab LOO shuhnz): bathing or washing, especially as a ritual.

7. **prosthetic** (prahs THEHT ihk): referring to an artificial limb.

three flights of stairs, even. I don't know what made me so supple and strong that day, but I felt no hardship, no anxiety or fear, just concentration and intensity. Perhaps my mother's problems distracted me from my own. That might account for it. Perhaps desperation gave me energy and made me forget the rigor of the climb. Well, whatever the reason, I scrambled up like a goat. The family we were following had a girl only a bit younger than me, and she was moving slowly. Her family used my example to chide her. They kept saying, "Look at that girl. She's missing a leg, and yet she's going faster

than you. Why can't you keep up? Hurry now!"

That Ghulam Ali was certainly a good man, so patient with us and so compassionate. He had never seen us before, and yet when he met us, he said, "I will help you." That's the thing about life. You never know when and where you will encounter a spot of human decency. I have felt alone in this world at times; I have known long periods of being no one. But then, without warning, a person like Ghulam Ali just turns up and says, "I see you. I am on your side." Strangers have been kind to me when it mattered most. That sustains a person's hope and faith.

Anyway, climbing up that mountain on the Afghanistan side took some effort, but after we topped the crest, even my mother found the going down part fairly easy. We hardly stopped at all on the downward side. Going up took hours; coming down took minutes, or so it seemed.

As soon as we reached the bottom of the slope, Ghulam Ali told us we were now officially in Pakistan. We peered around. The landscape looked just the same here as it did back where we came from. And yet we were in Pakistan. We had escaped from Afghanistan. We started laughing. We couldn't stop. We tried to stop our mouths with our palms, and we could not do it. The laughter just insisted on bursting forth from us. Happiness filled our hearts. My mother's asthma disappeared without a trace for one whole hour. Yes, for one whole hour there, my mother could breathe. You might as well say we had been in prison for thirty years and had suddenly been released— that was the kind of joy we felt. **F**

E **Reading Focus** Compare and Contrast Why do you think Ahmedi is able to climb the mountain pass so easily?

Vocabulary **chide** (chyd) *v.*: scold mildly.

F **Reading Focus** Compare and Contrast What are Ahmedi's first impressions of Pakistan? How is it similar to Afghanistan?

Applying Your Skills

RA.L.10.1 Compare and contrast an author's use of direct and indirect characterization, and ways in which characters reveal traits about themselves, including dialect, dramatic monologues and soliloquies. *Also covered* **RP.10.2; RP.10.1; WP.10.9**

Escape from Afghanistan

Respond and Think Critically

Reading Focus

Quick Check

1. Why must Ahmedi and her mother escape from Afghanistan? Where are they planning to go?

2. What help do Ahmedi and her mother receive?

Read with a Purpose

3. Name three challenges the narrator and her mother experience on their journey. How do they overcome each of the challenges?

Reading Skills: Compare and Contrast Characters

4. Review the notes about Ahmedi that you took while reading the story. What are Ahmedi's main conflicts? Add them to the chart. Then, ask yourself how her conflicts are similar to and different from those of Amir.

Amir	Farah Ahmedi
is friend of the son of a servant (Hassan)	is trying to escape from Afghanistan with her mother
conflict: wants approval from Baba	conflict: doesn't know where to find the bus to Jalalabad

✓ Vocabulary Check

Match the Vocabulary word in the first column with its definition in the second column.

5. **gorges**   a. loud uproar
6. **clamor**   b. ravines
7. **chide**   c. to scold or find fault

Literary Focus

Literary Analysis

8. **Evaluate** Just before crossing the mountain, Ahmedi says, "Life is what it is." What do you think she means? Do you agree with her?

9. **Analyze** What character traits does Ahmedi display in this selection? Find details from the text that support your answers.

Literary Skills: Characters in Conflict

10. **Synthesize** What conflicts that Ahmedi faces result from the historical situation in Afghanistan at the time?

Literary Skills Review: Tone

11. **Describe** A writer's **tone** is his or her <u>attitude</u> toward a subject. How would you describe Ahmedi's tone in this portion of her memoir? Explain.

Writing Focus

Think as a Reader/Writer

Use It in Your Writing Review the sensory details from "Escape from Afghanistan" that you noted in your *Reader/Writer Notebook*. Think of stories and true-life accounts you have read about dangerous journeys. Then, write a brief summary of the journey. Use sensory details and imagery to describe the characters and settings.

RP.10.1 Apply reading comprehension strategies, including making predictions, comparing and contrasting, recalling and summarizing and making inferences and drawing conclusions. **WA.10.4.c** Write informational essays or reports, including research that: create an organizing structure appropriate to the purpose, audience and context.

from **The Kite Runner / Escape from Afghanistan**

Writing Focus

Write a Comparison-Contrast Essay

Compare and contrast the characters in the excerpt from *The Kite Runner* and "Escape from Afghanistan" in a brief essay. How are the characters similar? How are they different? Ask yourself the following questions when gathering ideas for your essay:

- How do the different genres contribute to the similarities and differences?
- What are the authors' attitudes toward their characters and toward the historical events in Afghanistan?
- What conflicts have the characters encountered, and how do they react to these conflicts?

Evaluation Criteria for an Essay

An effective essay

- begins with an introduction to the topic and presents a thesis statement
- develops each main idea in well-organized paragraphs
- provides ample support for main ideas
- cites examples from the texts
- uses transitions that smoothly and clearly connect your ideas
- is free from errors in spelling, grammar, and punctuation

What Do **You Think Now?** How does Afghanistan shape the main characters in these selections? Explain.

CHOICES

As you respond to the Choices, use the **Academic Vocabulary** words as appropriate: acquire, attitude, tradition, and reveal.

REVIEW
Compare Conflict

Timed ⌐Writing Reflect on other stories you've read or movies you've seen. Is the conflict in any of these driven by historical context? Write an essay describing this conflict and comparing and contrasting that conflict with the conflicts in *The Kite Runner* and "Escape from Afghanistan." Use details from the selections to support your ideas.

CONNECT
Research Afghanistan

The Kite Runner is set in a peaceful Afghanistan, before the Soviet invasion and the civil war. "Escape from Afghanistan" shows some negative effects of these conflicts. Using varied resources, research both of these conflicts. Answer the following questions: When did the conflicts begin? How long did they last? How did each conflict end? What effect did the conflicts have on Afghan society? Present your findings to the class.

EXTEND
Continue the Journey

At the end of "Escape from Afghanistan," Ahmedi and her mother successfully enter Pakistan. But this is only part of the journey. What other conflicts or hardships do they encounter? Read the rest of *The Other Side of the Sky,* and report the outcome of Ahmedi's journey to the class.

Synthesizing Sources: Drawing Conclusions

Dr. Martin Luther King, Jr., waves to supporters in Washington, D.C.

CONTENTS

What Do You Think

What makes some events or experiences more meaningful than others?

 QuickTalk

With a partner, take turns describing a significant experience in your life. What made it significant?

INTERVIEWS
Preparing to Read

MLK's Legacy / A Young Boy's Stand

Informational Text Focus

Synthesizing Sources: Drawing Conclusions When you research a subject, you need to look at different sources to get a balanced view. The following selections are **primary sources**—first-hand accounts that have not been interpreted or edited. Putting together and evaluating information from different sources is called **synthesizing** information. Synthesizing will help you **draw conclusions,** or make judgments about what you read.

Tips for Drawing Conclusions from Sources

- Look for the main ideas and supporting details in each source. Restate each idea in your own words.
- Determine the credibility of each source. Does the writer provide sufficient and relevant information to support the main ideas?
- Based on the information, what conclusions can you draw about the subject?

Into Action Use a graphic organizer such as the one below to identify main ideas in sources and draw conclusions as you read.

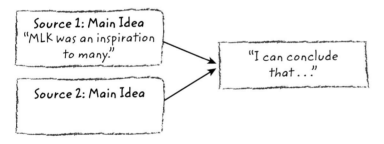

Source 1: Main Idea
"MLK was an inspiration to many."

Source 2: Main Idea

"I can conclude that..."

Writing Focus — Preparing for **Constructed Response**

When you synthesize sources in an essay or report, you should state the main ideas and relevant details in each piece. As you read the following selections, look for the main message in each and the details that support that message. List your findings in your *Reader/Writer Notebook.*

R.10.4 Evaluate and systematically organize important information, and select appropriate sources to support central ideas, concepts and themes.

Reader/Writer
Notebook

Use your **RWN** to complete the activities for these selections.

Vocabulary

MLK's Legacy

compassionate (kuhm PASH uh niht) *adj.*: sympathetic; willing to help others. *Congressman Lewis offered several examples of Dr. King's compassionate nature.*

discrimination (dihs krihm uh NAY shuhn) *n.*: prejudiced, unfair treatment. *Civil rights leaders tried to fight the discrimination against African Americans that was rampant at the time.*

undisputed (uhn dihs PYOO tihd) *adj.*: without doubt. *The importance of MLK's leadership during the civil rights movement is undisputed.*

A Young Boy's Stand

hostile (HAHS tuhl) *adj.*: very unfriendly. *Jerome found a hostile audience on the bus.*

Language Coach

Related Words Some of the words above have different forms. The adjective *hostile*, for example, is related to the noun *hostility*. How many related words can you find for the other words above? Use a dictionary to help you.

 Learn It Online

To read more sources like these, go to the Interactive Reading Workshops on:

go.hrw.com | L10-189 | **Go**

Preparing to Read **189**

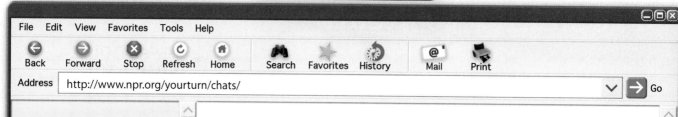

File   Edit   View   Favorites   Tools   Help

Back   Forward   Stop   Refresh   Home   Search   Favorites   History   Mail   Print

Address   http://www.npr.org/yourturn/chats/   Go

Read with a Purpose

As you read this interview, notice how Lewis uses his personal experiences to describe the contribution of Dr. Martin Luther King, Jr., to the civil rights movement.

Build Background

Until the late 1950s, schools, restaurants, and other public facilities in many Southern states were segregated. African Americans were even restricted from using certain public restrooms and drinking fountains. Dr. Martin Luther King, Jr., a Baptist minister from Montgomery, Alabama, organized a series of nonviolent protests throughout Southern communities and other states. In the following online interview, the host (and other participants) ask Congressman John Lewis to comment on the legacy of Dr. Martin Luther King, Jr.

MLK's Legacy: An Interview with Congressman John Lewis

by National Public Radio

Congressman John Lewis.

January 14, 1999

npr_host: At this point we'd like to welcome Congressman Lewis.

Congressman_John_Lewis: Good evening. It's great to be here.

npr_host: Can you tell us a bit about your firsthand experience with the civil rights movement?

Congressman_John_Lewis: I was born in Alabama, fifty miles from Montgomery, in southeast Alabama, in a little town of about thirteen thousand people just outside of Troy. When I would visit the cities of Montgomery or Birmingham, I saw the signs that said white men and white women; I saw the signs that said colored lady, colored men. In 1950 when I was ten years old, I tried to check a book out of the local library, I tried to get a library card, and I was told that the library was only for white people and not people of color. It had an unbelievable impact on me. I couldn't understand it. But in 1955 when I was fifteen years old, I heard about Martin Luther King Jr. and Rosa Parks.[1] And three years later I met MLK, and a year later I got involved in the civil rights movement.

Congressman_John_Lewis: Dr. King was one of the most inspiring human beings I ever met. He was such a warm, compassionate, and loving human being.

---

1. **Rosa Parks:** On December 1, 1955, Rosa Parks, an African American woman in Montgomery, Alabama, was arrested for refusing to give up her seat on a bus to a white person. The bus boycott staged in protest of Parks's arrest grew into a massive organized effort that was the first of many protests in the civil rights movement.

Vocabulary   **compassionate** (kuhm PASH uh niht) *adj.:* sympathetic; willing to help others.

RELATED
In 1965, King organized a march from Selma to Montgomery, Alabama, to protest unfair voting practices.

The first day of the Selma-to-Montgomery march. John Lewis and Martin Luther King both marched.

npr_host: How was Dr. King inspiring on a personal level, as much as in public?

Congressman_John_Lewis: MLK Jr. taught me how to say no to segregation, and I can hear him saying now . . . when you straighten up your back—no man can ride you. He said stand up straight and say no to racial discrimination. **A**

npr_host: You took very quick action. Tell us more, please.

Congressman_John_Lewis: As a young student I got involved in that, studying the philosophy and the discipline of nonviolence. And as students—young people, black and white, we would go downtown in Nashville, Atlanta, Birmingham, and other cities in the South . . . and we would sit down—we did what we called sit-ins at lunch counters. These places refused to serve black students. And we'd have white students and black students sitting together. And some of the places were like Woolworth stores, where you could go in and buy things, but you couldn't order a hamburger. And while [we were] sitting, sometimes people would come in and beat us, light cigarettes out in our hair, down our backs, throw us off the lunch counter stools, and sometimes kick us and leave us lying down on the floor. We got arrested. When I was growing up, I was told over and over again—don't get into trouble. So as students we were getting into trouble—but it was good trouble. **B**

> **A** **Informational Focus** Drawing Conclusions What do you think MLK meant by this advice to "straighten up your back"?
>
> **B** **Informational Focus** Drawing Conclusions What does Lewis mean when he says the trouble he got into "was good trouble"? Explain.
>
> **Vocabulary** **discrimination** (dihs krihm uh NAY shuhn) *n*.: prejudiced, unfair treatment.

krockett_2065101 asks: What is the one thing that you remember most about MLK?

Congressman_John_Lewis: Dr. King had a great sense of humor, and he loved a good meal. From time to time when we were traveling in the South, he would see some restaurant or a hole-in-the-wall place to eat, and he would say, we should stop—we should get something to eat; it may be our last chance; we should go on a full stomach.

Congressman_John_Lewis: But on one occasion, on—March 1965 we were walking along, marching, and it started to rain. I didn't have anything on my head. He had a little brown cap he was wearing. He took the cap off his head and gave it to me, and he said, "John, you should put this on—you've been hurt." A few days earlier I had been beaten by a group of state troopers, and I had a concussion. So he thought it was important that my head be protected. I'll never forget it; it was such an act of compassion and concern.

Musicman_21 asks: Was it intimidating meeting MLK?

Congressman_John_Lewis: Well, the first time I met him, I was only eighteen years old in 1958, and he had emerged for me as someone bigger than life. Two miles from where I grew up in Alabama, there was a white college—Troy State College—and I had applied to go there. I never heard anything from the school, so I wrote MLK a letter and told him about my desire to go to the school. He wrote me back and sent me a round-trip Greyhound bus ticket and invited me to come to Montgomery to meet with him. One Saturday, my father drove me to the Greyhound bus station; I traveled the fifty miles from my home. A young black lawyer met me at the bus station in Montgomery and drove me to the First Baptist Church—that was Rev. Abernathy . . . a friend of Dr. King and a leader in the local movement with Dr. King. We entered the office of the church, and MLK stood up from behind a desk, and he said something like, "Are you the boy from Troy? Are you John Lewis?" **C**

Congressman_John_Lewis: I was scared; I was nervous; I didn't know what I was going to say. And I said—Dr. King, I am John Robert Lewis. I gave my whole name; I didn't want there to be any mistake.

Congressman_John_Lewis: That was the beginning of our relationship. We became friends. We became brothers in a struggle. He was my leader. He was my hero.

DC_Vyf asks: Why did you decide to run for Congress?

Congressman_John_Lewis: When I would make trips to D.C. during the height of the civil rights movement . . . I had a chance to meet many members of Congress, and I had been involved in getting people to register (to vote), and I thought somehow and some way I could make a contribution by being involved in politics.

C **Informational Focus** **Drawing Conclusions** What conclusions can you draw about Dr. Martin Luther King, Jr., from this story told by John Lewis?

DC_Vyf asks: How does one keep struggling for social change in this environment? How does one keep [one's] spirits up?

Congressman_John_Lewis: You must never, ever give up. Let me give you an example. I just finished a book called *Walking with the Wind: A Memoir of the Movement;* it's published by Simon and Schuster. In the prologue of the book, I tell a story about when I was growing up, and I was only about seven or eight years old, but I remember like it was yesterday.

Congressman_John_Lewis: One Saturday afternoon a group of my sisters and brothers, along with some of my first cousins, about twelve or fifteen of us—young children were outside playing

Members of the Freedom Riders, including MLK and John Lewis.

in the yard, and a storm came up . . . an unbelievable storm occurred and the only adult around was my aunt who lived in this old house. A shotgun house—a house with a tin roof, small . . . The wind started blowing, the lightning started flashing, and we were all in the house. My aunt was terrified; she thought the house would blow away. So she suggested we should hold hands, and we were crying, all of us.

Congressman_John_Lewis: So when one side of the house appeared to be lifted from its foundation, we'd try and hold it down with our little bodies . . . and when the other corner of the house appeared to be lifting up, we'd walk over there . . . trying to hold it down. Thunder may roll, lightning may flash . . . but we may never leave the house. **Ⓓ**

Karq asks: How do you think MLK would fare in today's political arena?

Congressman_John_Lewis: Today, MLK would be the undisputed moral leader in America. If he were here today . . . he'd say we're majoring in minor things. He'd be very disappointed that we're wasting so much of our time, so much of our energy and resources on investigation rather than dealing with the basic needs of people.

Lovely_Ca_97 asks: If there is any advice you could give to our generation, what would it be?

Congressman_John_Lewis: This generation should study contemporary history: read the books, listen to the tapes, watch the video, study the early days of the civil rights movement and be inspired. They too can act.

Read with a Purpose   Which personal experiences with MLK had the greatest impact on Congressman Lewis?

Ⓓ **Informational Focus** Drawing Conclusions Why do you think Lewis tells this story?

Vocabulary **undisputed** (uhn dihs PYOO tihd) *adj.:* without doubt.

RELATED
In 1961, groups of civil rights activists set out to test the segregation law by riding public transportation throughout the South. They called themselves the Freedom Riders.

🌐 Internet

File   Edit   View   Favorites   Tools   Help

Back   Forward   Stop   Refresh   Home   Search   Favorites   History   Mail   Print

Address   http://www.storycorps.net   Go

Jerome Smith with his friend Carol Bebelle.

Read with a Purpose
As you read, take note of the effects of one incident on a person's life.

Build Background
In the 1950s and 1960s, many communities across the South enforced segregation of public transportation. Civil rights protests eventually led to greater civil liberties for African Americans and others across the nation.

StoryCorps was created in 2003 to record the oral history of ordinary people. Booths and recording studios around the country are available where people can interview friends and family members about their life experiences. These oral histories are then stored in the Library of Congress.

A Young Boy's Stand on a New Orleans Streetcar
StoryCorps

December 1, 2006

It was fifty-six years ago that Jerome Smith, then ten years old, removed the screen that acted as a barrier between white and black passengers on a New Orleans streetcar. "The streetcar became very hostile," Smith recalls.

The event took place five years before Rosa Parks energized the civil rights movement on December 1, 1955, when she refused to give up her bus seat to a white passenger in Montgomery, Alabama.

Smith says that as he sat in the white section of the streetcar in Louisiana, an older black woman from the rear of the car descended on him, hitting him so hard that "it felt like there was a bell ringing in my head."

The woman loudly said she'd teach the boy a lesson, telling him, "You should never do that, disrespect white people. You have no business trying to sit with them."

She forced Smith off the streetcar, and around the back of an auto store. But once they were behind the building, the woman's tone changed.

"Never, ever stop," the woman told Smith as she began to cry. "I'm proud of you," she said. "Don't you ever quit."   **A**

Smith, who went on to help found the New Orleans chapter of CORE, The Congress of Racial Equality, says it was that moment that made him who he is today.

"Even though I didn't know the words 'civil rights' then," Smith says, "that opened up the door."   **B**

Smith currently directs the Tambourine and Fan, a New Orleans organization that teaches young people about civil rights, leadership and political engagement.

> **A Informational Focus** Drawing Conclusions Why do you think the woman on the streetcar began to cry?
>
> **B Informational Focus** Drawing Conclusions Why might this event have been life changing for Smith?
>
> **Vocabulary** **hostile** (HAHS tuhl) *adj.*: very unfriendly.

Applying Your Skills

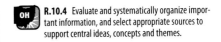

OH **R.10.4** Evaluate and systematically organize important information, and select appropriate sources to support central ideas, concepts and themes.

MLK's Legacy / A Young Boy's Stand

Practicing the Standards

Informational Text and Vocabulary

1. Which of the following statements is an accurate **conclusion** from the two interviews?

A Adolescent experiences affected the career choices of both Lewis and Smith.

B The fight for civil liberties was effortless.

C Minor protests had little impact on the civil rights movement.

D The teachings of Dr. Martin Luther King, Jr., affected Smith more than they did Lewis.

2. When Lewis says, "This generation should study ... the early days of the civil rights movement and be inspired," you can **conclude** that he believes —

A nothing in contemporary history is inspiring

B the fight for civil rights is not over

C it is important to learn about the past

D history has a tendency to repeat itself

3. Lewis's and Smith's willingness to be interviewed might lead you to the **conclusion** that they want to —

A gain approval for their work

B entertain listeners

C find volunteers

D explain how they were affected

4. An *undisputed* winner is —

A a sore loser

B the definite winner

C the winner of a tiebreaker

D the likely winner

5. A *compassionate* person is —

A jealous

B grateful

C supportive

D enraged

6. A *hostile* crowd might —

A make a peaceful protest

B be difficult to get through

C yell and scream

D present a convincing story

7. *Discrimination* results from —

A curiosity

B jealousy

C respect

D prejudice

Writing Focus Constructed Response

What do each of these two selections say about taking a stand? Review the notes you took on main ideas and supporting details, and then state the main idea of each in your own words.

What Do You Think Now? How do other people influence our beliefs and ideals? Explain, using examples from your own life or someone else's.

Literary Skills Review

Plot and Setting   **Directions:** Read the following selection. Then, read and respond to the questions that follow.

The Cookies by **Naomi Shihab Nye**

On Union Boulevard, St. Louis, in the 1950's, there were women in their eighties who lived with the shades drawn, who hid like bats in the caves they claimed for home. Neighbors of my grandmother, they could be faintly heard through a ceiling or wall. A drawer opening. The slow thump of a shoe. Who they were and whom they were mourning (someone had always just died) intrigued me. Me, the child who knew where the cookies waited in Grandma's kitchen closet. Who lined five varieties up on the table and bit from each one in succession, knowing my mother would never let me do this at home. Who sold Girl Scout cookies door-to-door in annual tradition, who sold fifty boxes, who won The Prize. My grandmother told me which doors to knock on. Whispered secretly, "She'll take three boxes—wait and see."

Hand-in-hand we climbed the dark stairs, knocked on the doors. I shivered, held Grandma tighter, remember still the smell which was curiously fragrant, a sweet soup of talcum powder, folded curtains, roses pressed in a book. Was that what years smelled like? The door would miraculously open and a withered face framed there would peer oddly at me as if I had come from another world. Maybe I had. "Come in," it would say, or "Yes?" and I would mumble something about cookies, feeling foolish, feeling like the one who places a can of beans next to an altar marked *For the Poor* and then has to stare at it—the beans next to the cross—all through the worship. Feeling I should have brought more, as if I shouldn't be selling something to these women, but giving them a gift, some new breath, assurance that there was still a child's world out there, green grass, scabby knees, a playground where you could stretch your legs higher than your head. There were still Easter eggs lodged in the mouths of drainpipes and sleds on frozen hills, that joyous scream of flying toward yourself in the snow. Squirrels storing nuts, kittens being born with eyes closed; there was still everything tiny, unformed, flung wide open into the air!

But how did you carry such an assurance? In those hallways, standing before those thin gray wisps of women, with Grandma slinking back and pushing me forward to go in alone, I didn't know. There was something here which also smelled like life. But it was a life I hadn't learned yet. I had never outlived anything I knew of, except one yellow cat. I had never saved a photograph. For me life was a bounce, an unending burst of pleasures. Vaguely I imagined what a life of recollection could be, as already I was haunted by a sense of my own lost baby years, golden rings I slipped on and off my heart. Would I be one of those women?

Their rooms were shrines of upholstery and lace. Silent radios standing under stacks of magazines. Did they work? Could I turn the knobs? Questions I wouldn't ask here. Windows with shades pulled low, so the light peeping through took on a changed quality, as if it were brighter or dimmer than I remembered. And portraits, photographs, on walls, on tables, faces strangely familiar, as if I were destined to know them. I asked no questions and the women never questioned me. Never asked where the money went, had the price gone up since last year, were there any additional flavors. They bought what they remembered—if it was peanut-butter last year, peanut-butter this year would be fine. They brought the coins from jars, from pocketbooks without handles, counted them carefully before me, while I stared at their thin crops of knotted hair. A Sunday brooch pinned loosely to the shoulder of an everyday dress. What were these women thinking of?

And the door would close softly behind me, transaction complete, the closing click like a drawer sliding back, a world slid quietly out of sight, and I was free to return to my own universe, to Grandma standing with arms folded in the courtyard, staring peacefully up at a bluejay or sprouting leaf. Suddenly I'd see Grandma in her dress of tiny flowers, curly gray permanent, tightly laced shoes, as one of *them*—but then she'd turn, laugh, "Did she buy?" and again belong to me.

Gray women in rooms with the shades drawn . . . weeks later the cookies would come. I would stack the boxes, make my delivery rounds to the sleeping doors. This time I would be businesslike, I would rap firmly. "Hello Ma'am, here are the cookies you ordered." And the face would peer up, uncertain . . . cookies? . . . as if for a moment we were floating in the space between us. What I did (carefully balancing boxes in both my arms, wondering who would eat the cookies—I was the only child ever seen in that building) or what she did (reaching out with floating hands to touch what she had bought) had little to do with who we were, had been, or ever would be.

---

1. What internal conflict does the narrator have when she knocks on the old women's doors?

   A. She is afraid to talk to strangers.

   B. She is angry with her grandmother.

   C. She worries about not selling the cookies.

   D. She feels foolish for not bringing something better.

2. What character trait does the narrator exhibit when she goes back to deliver the cookies?

   A. She is more businesslike.

   B. She is quiet and shy.

   C. She is more talkative.

   D. She is much more excited.

PREPARING FOR THE OHIO GRADUATION TEST

Literary Skills Review CONTINUED

RA.L.10.1 Compare and contrast an author's use of direct and indirect characterization, and ways in which characters reveal traits about themselves, including dialect, dramatic monologues and soliloquies.

3. According to the narrator, what character traits does Grandma have in common with the other women in the building?

   A. She decorates her home the same way.

   B. She wears similar clothing.

   C. She likes the same kinds of cookies.

   D. She is always mourning somebody.

4. The narrator's description of her grandmother's scent is an example of

   A. character motivation.

   B. indirect characterization.

   C. direct characterization.

   D. interaction between characters.

5. Why is the grandmother probably motivated to help the narrator sell cookies?

   A. She wants her to sell the most cookies.

   B. She wants her neighbors to meet her granddaughter.

   C. She wants to teach her to be generous.

   D. She wants to assure her granddaughter of her love.

6. Which of the following passages is an example of direct characterization of Grandma?

   A. "My grandmother told me which doors to knock on. Whispered secretly, 'She'll take three boxes—wait and see.'"

   B. "Suddenly I'd see Grandma in her dress of tiny flowers, curly gray permanent, tightly laced shoes, as one of *them*—but then she'd turn, laugh, 'Did she buy?' and again belong to me."

   C. "In those hallways, standing before those thin gray wisps of women, with Grandma slinking back and pushing me forward to go in alone, I didn't know."

   D. "Me, the child who knew where the cookies waited in Grandma's kitchen closet."

7. The characters in this selection embody contrasting qualities. The main contrast is between

   A. buyer and seller.

   B. rich and poor.

   C. age and youth.

   D. joy and pain.

Short Answer

8. This passage contains indirect characterization. Explain what indirect characterization is and provide one example from the passage.

Extended Response

9. In this selection, the narrator says that her grandmother's neighbors looked at her "as if I had come from another world." What are the two worlds described in the selection? How does each world affect each character—the narrator and her grandmother? Write two paragraphs, one about each world. Cite examples from the text.

Informational Skills Review

Context Clues   **Directions:** Use the context clues in the following passages to identify the meaning of the italicized Vocabulary words.

Interview with Alice Walker

from **A Communion of the Spirits** by **Roland L. Freeman**

I asked Alice to talk first about the tradition of quilting in her family.

Well, my mother was a quilter, and I remember many, many afternoons of my mother and the neighborhood women sitting on the porch around the quilting frame, quilting and talking, you know; getting up to stir something on the stove and coming back and sitting down.

The first quilt I worked on was the *In Love and Trouble* quilt. And I did that one when I was living in Mississippi. It was during a period when we were wearing African-inspired dresses. So all of the pieces are from dresses that I actually wore. This yellow and black fabric I bought when I was in Uganda, and I had a beautiful dress made of it that I wore and wore and wore and eventually I couldn't wear it anymore; partly I had worn it out and also I was pregnant, so it didn't fit, and I used that and I used the red and white and black, which was a long, floor-length dress that I had when I was pregnant with my daughter, Rebecca. . . . I took these things apart or I used scraps. I put them together in this quilt, because it just seemed perfect. Mississippi was full of political and social struggle, and regular quilts were all African American with emphasis on being here in the United States. But because of the African

consciousness that was being raised and the way that we were all wearing our hair in naturals and wearing all of these African dresses, I felt the need to blend these two traditions. So it's a quilt of great memory and importance to me. I use it a lot and that's why it's so worn.

I asked her if she had made a quilt for her daughter.

No. I'm sure that she will make her own quilt. I'll be happy to leave her these if they are not worn out, which they will probably be, but I hope that she will make quilts for her own grounding and her own connection to me and to her grandmother and to her great-grandmother. I've seen quilts that my grandmother made. They tended to be very serviceable, very heavy and really for warmth, and, well of course, beautiful. My daughter has a quilt that she travels with. It's just a beautiful simple quilt that she loves. I gave it to her because she just feels like you can't sleep under just any old thing. It's got to be something that is congenial with your dreams—your dream sense, your dreamtime. I'm trying to think of where I got it. I think that I just bought it somewhere. I believe it is from Texas.

I asked Alice what she'd like to say to people in general about quilting.

That they should learn to do it. That they should think less about collecting quilts and give more thought to making them. Because, really, that is the power. It may do all kinds of good things, too, to collect what others have made, but I think that it is essential that we know how to express, you know, our own sense of connection. And there is no better sense of understanding our own creation than to create, and so we should do that.

"Thinkin' on Marryin'"

from **The Quilters: Women and Domestic Art**
by **Patricia Cooper** and **Norma Bradley Allen**

Back when I was a girl, quilts was something that a family had to have. It takes a whole lot of cover to keep warm in one of them old open houses on the plains.

When a girl was thinkin' on marryin', and we all done a lot of that, she had to start thinkin' on gettin' her quilts pieced. The way I done mine was real nice, I think. Papa had laid up a beautiful arbor[1] with the brush he had cleared from the land. It was set up a ways back of the house. Well, I jest went out under that arbor, set up my frame, and went to quiltin' outdoors. Now some thought that was real funny, but I sure thought it was nice.

Mama gave me one real beautiful quilt, a Lone Star that she had done herself. I made three by myself that I don't reckon were much to look at, but I was awful proud of them then. And that's what I set out with when I married my sweetheart. Now that's a story. You won't believe it to look at me now, but I married me the finest-looking young man for three counties around when I was eighteen. And I didn't meet him at no dance neither. I don't reckon I would have stood a chance there. These big size tens were never so graceful. They're just good strong platforms for standin' on.

Anyways, what I was doin' was settin' there under that quiltin' arbor one spring afternoon, April fourteenth, just quiltin' and dreamin' a dream on ever' stitch and just plannin' who might share 'em with me.

And this deep, fine voice says, "Pardon me, ma'am, but I've been seein' you out here ever' day for weeks and I jest got up my nerve to come over and speak to you and see what you were workin' on with such care."

Lordy, girl, I married him and, as I recall it now, that was the longest speech he ever said at one time to this day.

---

1. **arbor** (AHR buhr): shady covering, usually made of plants.

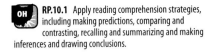

RP.10.1 Apply reading comprehension strategies, including making predictions, comparing and contrasting, recalling and summarizing and making inferences and drawing conclusions.

1. What can you conclude that the quilts represent to Walker?

   A. dreams

   B. love

   C. success

   D. connection

2. What conclusion can you draw about Walker's view of collecting quilts?

   A. Collecting quilts is just another way of being creative.

   B. Collecting quilts is a good way to express your sense of grounding.

   C. Collecting quilts is not as good as creating your own.

   D. Collecting quilts is good for people who do not know how to make them.

3. From both articles you can conclude that quilting is

   A. tedious.

   B. difficult.

   C. rewarding.

   D. expensive.

4. What can you conclude about women's lives in the community where the narrator of "Thinkin' on Marryin'" spent her childhood?

   A. Young women were not encouraged to marry.

   B. Women waited for men to initiate courtship.

   C. Women were not allowed out of the house to socialize.

   D. Young women rarely married before they were twenty.

5. Both writers mention the influence of older women. You can conclude that these writers

   A. are unsure about their own abilities.

   B. are eager to learn family traditions.

   C. prefer the quilts made by the older women.

   D. don't make equally beautiful quilts.

Short Answer

6. What can you conclude about Alice Walker's decision not to make a quilt for her daughter? Support your conclusion with a detail from the passage.

Extended Response

7. These selections describe two women's experiences with quilt making. What general conclusions can you draw about quilting from these sources? What specific conclusions can you draw about the writers' attitudes toward quilting? Write a one-paragraph essay explaining what you learned from both selections.

Vocabulary Skills Review

Plot and Setting   **Directions:** Read the following selection. Then, read and respond to the questions that follow.

1. In "Everyday Use," Dee's childhood friends included <u>furtive</u> boys who seemed to wish they could become invisible.

   In this passage, <u>furtive</u> means

   A. trying to get attention.

   B. trying to cause problems.

   C. trying to remain unnoticed.

   D. trying to impress.

2. Nervous and shy, Maggie was always <u>cowering</u> behind Mama's back in photographs.

   In this passage, <u>cowering</u> means

   A. huddling in fear.

   B. smiling broadly.

   C. making faces.

   D. shivering as if cold.

3. In "Two Kinds," Jing-mei's mother wanted her to be a <u>prodigy</u> like Waverly Jong, a talented chess player.

   In this passage, <u>prodigy</u> means

   A. daughter.

   B. young genius.

   C. musician.

   D. chess player.

4. Pretending to be bored, Jing-mei <u>listlessly</u> endured her mother's tests.

   In this passage, <u>listlessly</u> means

   A. without fear.

   B. without embarrassment.

   C. without talent.

   D. without energy.

5. Jing-mei played only <u>discordant</u> music, and Mr. Chong, who was deaf, had no idea how bad it sounded.

   In this passage, <u>discordant</u> means

   A. dissonant.

   B. melodious.

   C. popular.

   D. rhythmic.

6. Unlike the success Jing-mei had imagined, her debut as a pianist was an embarrassing <u>fiasco</u>.

   In this passage, <u>fiasco</u> means

   A. triumph.

   B. failure.

   C. surprise.

   D. pain.

7. In "Where Have You Gone, Charming Billy?" Paul Berlin thinks about the difference between the concrete fear he felt when Billy Boy Watkins died and the <u>diffuse</u>, unformed fear he feels as they march.

   In this passage, <u>diffuse</u> means

   A. strong.

   B. intense.

   C. indistinct.

   D. defined.

8. To remain unnoticed as they marched, they carefully skirted villages along the way.

   In this passage, skirted means

   A. walked through.

   B. walked around.

   C. walked into.

   D. walked away from.

9. In "The First Seven years," Feld thinks that he has an obligation to introduce Max to his daughter, Miriam; he believes he should do it.

   In this passage, obligation means

   A. duty.

   B. occupation.

   C. desire.

   D. request.

10. Feld believes that there is more to Max than Miriam can discern—Feld is able to see those things in Max that Miriam cannot.

    In this passage, discern means

    A. express.

    B. ignore.

    C. know.

    D. perceive.

11. In *The Kite Runner,* Saifo kites are the most famous and coveted kites in the city.

    In this passage, coveted means

    A. expensive.

    B. disappointing.

    C. desirable.

    D. unpleasant.

12. Some people abhor the winter, but Amir absolutely loves it.

    In this passage, abhor means

    A. adore.

    B. worry about.

    C. are amused by.

    D. detest.

13. Hassan is a character with integrity. He says what he means, he believes what he says, and he would never lie.

    In this passage, integrity means

    A. dishonesty.

    B. sincerity.

    C. hypocrisy.

    D. problems.

Academic Vocabulary

Directions: Use context clues in the passage to identify the meaning of the following Academic Vocabulary word.

14. In *The Kite Runner,* the boys saved their allowances so that they could acquire the bamboo, glue, string, and paper to build a kite.

    In this passage, acquire means

    A. construct.

    B. get.

    C. list.

    D. build.

Read On

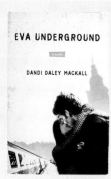

FICTION
Eva Underground

Senior year can be challenging enough, without losing a mother and suddenly being moved across the Atlantic. When Eva Lott finds herself uprooted by her father to participate in Poland's underground movement against communism, she struggles with loneliness and isolation in a country of strangers—until she meets Tomek, a handsome political activist. Dandi Daley Mackall writes about love, dreams, and the desire for freedom that keeps hope alive in the most barren of places.

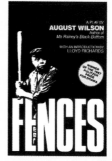

DRAMA
Fences

Can a father's desire to protect his child actually cause harm? In August Wilson's *Fences*, a father and his son have conflicting views about the boy's future. Having been excluded from baseball's Major Leagues because of his race, Troy Maxson finds it difficult to encourage his son's dreams of playing ball. Any reader who has struggled with the generation gap between parent and child will connect to the emotional depth of this Pulitzer Prize–winning play.

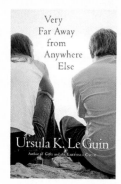

FICTION
Very Far Away from Anywhere Else

In this Ursula K. Le Guin tale, Owen and Natalie are young and gifted. They also feel isolated from their superficial peers. When these two high school seniors come together in friendship, Owen finally finds acceptance, and Natalie finds a way to connect to the world outside that of music. Together, the two of them learn to navigate the difficult journey of adulthood.

NONFICTION
A Summer Life

Growing up can be an awkward—and often hilarious—experience. In a series of entertaining essays on various topics, such as "The Shirt," "The Haircut," "The Drive-In Movies," and "The Computer Date," Gary Soto <u>reveals</u> what it was like to grow up in a Mexican American family in California's San Joaquin Valley. Anyone who has struggled through the experience of coming-of-age will find something to relate to in these vivid scenes and memories of a mischievous boy's life.

FICTION

The Sound of Waves

When Shinji first glimpsed Hatsue resting on the sand at twilight, he thought she was the most beautiful girl he had ever seen. What begins as an awkward friendship soon blossoms into a relationship of great tenderness and trust. Soon the young couple's families are doing everything to tear them apart—and Shinji must prove his worth at great risk to himself. Set in a small Japanese fishing village, Yukio Mishima's novel is one of the great love stories of the twentieth century.

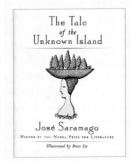

FICTION

The Tale of the Unknown Island

By the Nobel Prize-winning author José Saramago, this novel starts out as simply a fairy tale: Wanting to discover an unknown island, a man goes to the king's door and asks for a boat. A palace cleaning woman overhears his request and follows the man, since she has never seen an unknown island herself. Their journey becomes a moving allegory of love and discovery, loss and gain—all revealed in a timeless story packed with substance, humor, and truth.

FICTION

Washington Square

It's the mid-nineteenth-century, and Catherine Sloper lives with her father in New York City's fashionable Washington Square. Catherine, a plain, awkward, and soft-spoken young woman, is generally thought to be "unmarriageable." When a poor but handsome suitor courts her, her father tries to end the relationship, believing that the young man has eyes only for the family fortune. Should Catherine listen to her father or her heart? Henry James's work reveals a woman's inner strength in a way that you might not expect.

FICTION

The Living Is Easy

As a child, Cleo, the main character in Dorothy West's novel, realizes that men have it easy: All they do is work. But "it was women who did the lying awake, the planning, the sorrowing, the scheming to stretch a dollar." She leaves the South, moves to Boston, and marries Bart Judson, a black businessman who lets Cleo handle the money. The novel follows Cleo's strong-willed determination to become one of Boston's black elite and to prove to herself and to her extended family that money can buy happiness, even if it can't.

Learn It Online
Find tips for exploring novels with *NovelWise* at:

go.hrw.com | L10-205 | **Go**

Narrator and Voice

INFORMATIONAL TEXT FOCUS
Analyzing Audience and Purpose

"From a certain point onward there is no longer any turning back. That is the point that must be reached."

—**Franz Kafka**

What Do You Think

How do people react when they are in a situation they cannot change?

Negotiator (2003)
by Wes Hempel.
Oil on canvas (44cm × 52cm)
Courtesy of the artist.

 Learn It Online
Tell your story in a whole new way. Try digital story-telling—we'll show you how on:

go.hrw.com | L10-207 | **Go**

Literary Focus

by **Carol Jago**

What Do You Need to Know About Narrator and Voice?

Successful recording artists have distinctive voices. Something about their phrasing, accents, and word choice draws us in and makes us want to hear more. The same is true of compelling narrators, the people who tell stories from different points of view. Listening to narrators with interesting voices encourages us to read on.

First-Person Narrator

A **first-person narrator** is a character in the story. Like a friend telling you about an exciting experience, the first-person narrator uses the pronoun *I* to describe events he or she has experienced. What we know about the story is limited to what the first-person narrator knows, perceives, and describes. (Literary critics sometimes use the term **persona** to refer to this fictional first-person narrator.)

Sometimes, we must decide whether the narrator is reliable—that is, whether we can trust his or her version of events. Often, we must infer a truth that the narrator might not reveal directly.

In "Housepainting," the first-person narrator is Annie, a thirteen-year-old girl watching her older sister struggle with their parents' expectations.

> I was hacking at a milky dandelion root when I heard an engine idling. A small brown car, loaded down with boxes and luggage, turned laboriously into the driveway. Through the open window I heard a scrape as my father pushed aside his footrest. My mother's window shade snapped up and she peered outside, one hand on her tousled hair.
>
> from "Housepainting"
> by Lan Samantha Chang

Omniscient Narrator

Unlike the first-person narrator, the **omniscient narrator** knows *everything* that is going on in the story. (*Omniscient* means "all-knowing.") The omniscient narrator, who does not participate in the story's action, can tell us what every character thinks and feels. An omniscient narrator uses the third-person pronouns *he, she,* and *they.*

In the following excerpt from "The Storyteller," the omniscient narrator describes an interaction among some bored, noisy children, their aunt, and a bachelor who is sharing their train compartment.

> The frown on the bachelor's face was deepening to a scowl. He was a hard, unsympathetic man, the aunt decided in her mind. . . .
>
> "Come over here and listen to a story," said the aunt, when the bachelor had looked twice at her and once at the communication cord.
>
> The children moved listlessly toward the aunt's end of the carriage. Evidently her reputation as a storyteller did not rank high in their estimation.
>
> from "The Storyteller" by Saki

Third-Person-Limited Narrator

Between the two extremes of the omniscient and first-person points of view is the **third-person-limited narrator.** Like an omniscient narrator, a third-person-limited narrator tells the story using the third-person pronouns *he, she,* and *they.* However, the third-person-limited narrator focuses on the experiences of only one character. What we learn about the story is limited to what this character feels and perceives.

In the following passage from "Evacuation Order No. 19," the narrator presents an exchange between two characters. Because the narrator is third person, we do not actually see the events through either character's eyes. But because the narrator is third-person *limited,* the story focuses on the experience of only one character, Mrs. Hayashi. We have access to her thoughts, but not Joe's.

> He reached into his shirt pocket and gave her two caramel candies wrapped in gold foil. "For the children," he said. She slipped the caramels into her purse but left the money. She thanked him for the candy and walked out of the store.
>
> "That's a nice red dress," he called out after her.
>
> She turned around and squinted at him over the top of her glasses. "Thank you," she said. "Thank you, Joe." Then the door slammed behind her and she was alone on the sidewalk again and she realized that in all the years she had been going to Joe Lundy's store she had never once called him by his name until now.
>
> from "Evacuation Order No. 19"
> by Julie Otsuka

Voice

Even if you don't know the song, you can usually recognize the voice of your favorite singer. Just as no two people have exactly the same singing voice, no two writers have the same **voice,** or distinctive use of language. Factors that shape a writer's voice include **diction** (choice of words), **tone** (the writer's attitude toward the subject, the characters, or the audience), and sentence structure.

Your Turn Tell a Story

Read the following passage from "Housepainting." Then, rewrite it with an omniscient narrator. Do you learn anything new about the characters?

> "Hey, Annie, I got you something."
>
> She pulled a package wrapped in flowered paper from a shopping bag. She never came home without presents for everyone, and she never left without a bag full of goodies from home. . . .
>
> I looked at the package: a book. I stifled a groan. Frances never knew what I wanted.
>
> "Well, open it," my mother said.
>
> I tore off the paper. It was a thick volume about the history of medicine. This was supposed to be of great interest to me, because of a family notion that I would become a doctor, like Wei. I did not want to be a doctor.
>
> from "Housepainting"
> by Lan Samantha Chang

Learn It Online

Try the *PowerNotes* version of this lesson on:

go.hrw.com L10-209 **Go**

Analyzing Visuals

How Can You Recognize Point of View in Art?

Like a story's narrator, an artist portrays a subject from a particular standpoint, or point of view. One artist, for example, might portray a subject realistically, while another might intentionally distort it. An artist's "voice" is created through his or her unique use of colors, materials, and shapes.

1. What aspects of the guitar does Picasso emphasize by using rectangles and squares?

2. Picasso leaves out many intricate details of the guitar. What is the effect of leaving out these details?

3. Picasso's guitar is a sculpture made from cardboard and string. What overall effect does Picasso's **point of view** create?

Maquette for Guitar (1912) by Pablo Picasso (1881–1973).
The Museum of Modern Art, New York/
© 2009 Estate of Pablo Picasso/Artists Rights Society (ARS), NY.

1. What effect does Arcuri create through the use of color, light, and shadow?

2. Compared with Picasso's sculpture, how does Arcuri handle the intricate details of the guitar?

3. How would you describe Arcuri's **point of view** and its effect on the viewer?

After Hours by Frank Arcuri. Oil on linen (16" × 18"). Courtesy of the artist.

Analyzing Two Pieces of Art on the Same Subject

Use these guidelines to help you compare point of view in art:

1. Compare the works of art. How are they similar and different?
2. What does each artist emphasize or downplay about the subject?
3. How do the colors, shapes, and materials underscore the differences between the two works of art?
4. Consider both viewpoints. What does each artist's unique perspective tell you about the subject?

Your Turn   Write About Two Pieces of Art

Look through this book and find two pieces of art on the same subject. Study the artworks, and write a brief paragraph comparing and contrasting them. Focus on the artists' points of view and their use of colors, shapes, and lines.

Reading Focus

What Reading Skills Help You Analyze Point of View?

We all tell certain stories for certain reasons. For example, you might tell a group of friends about an embarrassing moment in order to entertain them, or to make them understand why the experience was significant for you. Authors tell their stories for different reasons, too. Sometimes you might have to ask questions as you read. By answering these questions, you can better understand both the author and the story.

Analyzing Writer's Purpose

When a writer sits down and begins writing, he or she has a **purpose**—a reason for writing. The purpose may be something as simple as sharing a feeling or experience, or something much more complex, such as persuading a reader of the importance of a certain subject. In fiction, writers rarely state their purposes directly.

A writer's purpose may be closely tied to the **voice** he or she uses to tell a story. The words a writer chooses are clues that can help you draw conclusions about his or her purpose.

In "Evacuation Order No. 19," Julie Otsuka describes a Japanese-American family's frightening, confusing experience as they are suddenly uprooted from their home.

> Tomorrow she and the children would be leaving. She did not know where they were going or how long they would be gone or who would look after the house while they were away. She knew only that tomorrow they had to go.
>
> from "Evacuation Order No. 19" by Julie Otsuka

Part of Otsuka's purpose in this passage is to make you experience the disorientation and fear of her main character. Knowing this, you can identify her larger purpose for writing the story.

Questioning

To learn more about a story's narrator, ask questions as you read. In some stories, for example, the narrator may be giving you a true account of events. In another story, however, the narrator may be withholding key information from you or distorting events in order to achieve a specific purpose.

As you read the stories in this collection, use a chart like the one below to keep track of your questions and the answers you find.

My Questions	Answers
Who is telling the story?	
Is the narrator a story character or is he or she outside the action?	
Is the narrator focusing on only one character or on many?	

212 Unit 1 • Collection 3

RA.I.10.1 Identify and understand organizational patterns and techniques, including repetition of ideas, syntax and word choice, that authors use to accomplish their purpose and reach their intended audience. **RP.10.1** Apply reading comprehension strategies, including making predictions, comparing and contrasting, recalling and summarizing and making inferences and drawing conclusions.

Drawing Conclusions

By interacting with a story, you are putting together information you've learned in order to **draw conclusions,** or come to some understanding about the story as a whole. Like people, stories are more interesting when they have a secret or two. You must learn to rely on your own perception of what is happening. In this collection, you will learn to draw conclusions about the narrators from their words and actions.

As you read these stories, keep track of the conclusions you draw. A good strategy is to find a key detail, make a connection to real life, and then draw a conclusion based on that information.

Use a chart like the one below to keep track of your conclusions. This example comes from the story "Housepainting" on page 233.

Event	My Connection	My Conclusion
The narrator's mother wants her to weed before her sister comes home.	Her mother wants the house to look good for her daughter.	

Your Turn   Apply Reading Skills

Read the following passage from "The Storyteller." What words offer clues about the author's purpose? What questions might you ask about the story's narrator? What conclusions about the narrator might you draw?

The occupants of the carriage were a small girl, and a smaller girl, and a small boy. An aunt belonging to the children occupied one corner seat, and the further corner seat on the opposite side was occupied by a bachelor who was a stranger to their party, but the small girls and the small boy emphatically occupied the compartment. Both the aunt and the children were conversational in a limited, persistent way, reminding one of the attentions of a housefly that refused to be discouraged. Most of the aunt's remarks seemed to begin with "Don't," and nearly all the children's remarks began with "Why?" The bachelor said nothing out loud.

from "The Storyteller" by Saki

Now go to the Skills in Action: Reading Model

"And what's the story behind the story?"

Learn It Online
Try the *PowerNotes* version of this lesson on:
go.hrw.com   L10-213   **Go**

Build Background

Pheasants are medium-to-large game birds that live in the grasslands of the United States and are often hunted for food. They are especially good at hiding, which makes it a challenge for hunters to find them.

Read with a Purpose   Read this short story to discover how a group of boys act in a local crisis.

What Happened During the Ice Storm

by **Jim Heynen**

One winter there was a freezing rain. "How beautiful!" people said when things outside started to shine with ice. But the freezing rain kept coming. Tree branches glistened like glass. Then broke like glass. Ice thickened on the windows until everything outside blurred. Farmers moved their livestock into the barns, and most animals were safe. But not the pheasants. Their eyes froze shut.

Some farmers went ice-skating down the gravel roads with clubs to harvest pheasants that sat helplessly in the roadside ditches. The boys went out into the freezing rain to find pheasants too. They saw dark spots along a fence. Pheasants, all right. Five or six of them. The boys slid their feet along slowly, trying not to break the ice that covered the snow. They slid up close to the pheasants. The pheasants pulled their heads down between their wings. They couldn't tell how easy it was to see them huddled there.

The boys stood still in the icy rain. Their breath came out in slow puffs of steam. The pheasants' breath came out in quick little white puffs. Some of them lifted their heads and turned them from side to side, but they were blindfolded with ice and didn't flush.[1] The boys had not brought clubs, or sacks, or anything but themselves. They stood over the pheasants, turning their own heads, looking at each other, each expecting the other to do something. To pounce on a pheasant, or to yell "Bang!" Things around them were shining and dripping with icy rain. The barbed-wire fence. The fence posts. The broken stems of grass. Even the grass seeds. The grass seeds looked like little yolks inside gelatin whites. And the pheasants looked like unborn birds glazed in egg white. Ice was hardening on the boys' caps and coats. Soon they would be covered with ice too.

Then one of the boys said, "Shh." He was taking off his coat, the thin layer of ice splintering in flakes as he pulled his arms from the sleeves. But the inside of the coat was dry and warm. He covered two of the crouching pheasants with his coat, rounding the back of it over them like a shell. The other boys did the same. They covered all the helpless pheasants. The small gray hens and the larger brown cocks. Now the boys felt the rain soaking through their shirts and freezing. They ran across the slippery fields, unsure of their footing, the ice clinging to their skin as they made their way toward the blurry lights of the house.

Read with a Purpose What is surprising about the boys' actions? Explain.

Cock Pheasant in Snow
by Bernd Poppelman.
Courtesy of Josef Mensing Gallery, Hamm-Rhynern, Germany.

Jim Heynen
(1940–   )

Farm Boy

Like the boys in "What Happened During the Ice Storm," Jim Heynen grew up on a farm in northwestern Iowa. He was a student in one of the last one-room schoolhouses in the state. In those days, local farm families would pool their money and then help one another with the big job of harvesting wheat and oats. As they worked, Heynen says, people had a lot of time to tell stories. Growing up with this oral tradition encouraged Heynen to become a storyteller himself: "When I am writing these stories, it's as if I am hearing the voice passed down to me through an oral tradition. A really good story that has been passed down orally glistens in a pure and simple language, yet sounds natural, sounds easy—as if anybody could have written or told it."

Writing to Irritate and Delight

Heynen writes brief, often comic short stories and poems that are appreciated for their unique voice and vivid imagery of rural life. Several of his stories are about "the boys"—a group of mischievous farm boys who have amusing adventures. When one interviewer asked why he writes, Heynen replied, "To delight people I admire and to irritate people I dislike. And often I do it to see if I can make something outside myself that is more pleasant and admirable than what I find inside myself."

Think About the Writer How might the story you have just read delight some people and irritate others?

RA.L.10.8 Analyze the author's use of point of view, mood and tone. *Also covered* RA.I.10.1; RP.10.1; VO.10.6

Into Action: Narrator and Voice

Voice is created by an author's word choice. Analyze the voice of this story's narrator by filling in the chart below. An example entry has been done for you.

Details from Text	Effect It Creates
But not the pheasants.	This fragment is clipped and terse.

Description of Voice:

_____

Talk About . . .

With a partner, discuss the story's events, the conclusions you drew as you read, and whether those conclusions proved to be accurate. Try to use each Academic Vocabulary word listed at the right in your discussion.

Write About . . .

Answer the following questions about "What Happened During the Ice Storm." Definitions for the underlined Academic Vocabulary words appear at the right.

1. How do the boys' ideas about the pheasants <u>correspond</u> to what they find?

2. What do the boys <u>perceive</u> when they go out into the rain?

3. What is the effect of the sensory details in the story? Why do you think the author <u>incorporated</u> so many of them?

4. Is the plot of this story <u>complex</u> or simple? Explain.

Writing Focus

Think as a Reader/Writer

In Collection 3, you'll encounter different narrators and voices. On the Preparing to Read pages you will explore ways in which the writers use techniques to create memorable stories. On the Applying Your Skills pages you will have a chance to practice those techniques in your own writing.

Academic Vocabulary for Collection 3

Talking and Writing About Short Stories

Academic Vocabulary is the language you use to write and talk about literature. Use these words to discuss the stories you read in this collection. The words are underlined throughout the collection.

complex (kahm PLEHKS) *adj.:* made up of many parts; complicated. *Although the story sounds simple, the plot is rather complex.*

correspond (kawr uh SPAHND) *v.:* agree or be in harmony; be similar. *Often a character's voice corresponds to his or her actions.*

perceive (puhr SEEV) *v.:* be aware of; sense; observe. *By paying attention to how a character deals with conflict, we can perceive more about his or her personality.*

incorporate (ihn KAWR puh rayt) *v.:* make something a part of something else. *Writers often incorporate details from their own background into their writing.*

Your Turn _____

Copy the Academic Vocabulary into your *Reader/Writer Notebook*. Use these words as you read and discuss the following stories.

The Storyteller

by **Saki**

The Dream Child (1990) by Graham Arnold. Oil painting.
Courtesy of the artist and Ruralist Fine Art Limited, United Kingdom.

What Do **You** **Think**

How can stories influence behavior or situations?

 QuickWrite

List several of your favorite stories or books from when you were younger. Why did they capture your interest? Write a paragraph explaining why these stories appealed to you.

Reader/Writer Notebook

Use your **RWN** to complete the activities for this selection.

OH **RA.L.10.8** Analyze the author's use of point of view, mood and tone. **RA.I.10.1** Identify and understand organizational patterns and techniques, including repetition of ideas, syntax and word choice, that authors use to accomplish their purpose and reach their intended audience.

Literary Focus

Omniscient Narrator An **omniscient narrator** is an all-knowing observer who can reveal the thoughts, feelings, and motives of every character in a story. In "The Storyteller," the omniscient narrator lets us in on the thoughts and attitudes of all the characters. As you read, think about how the comments by the narrator might lead us to perceive the writer's purpose.

Reading Focus

Identifying Writer's Purpose Humorous stories can seem like pure entertainment. However, the writers of these stories often have a more serious and complex purpose. Read "The Storyteller" closely, and look for key passages and loaded words that reveal the narrator's attitude toward the characters. Which characters does Saki poke fun at?

Into Action While you read, complete a chart like the one below to help you find clues that reveal the narrator's attitude.

Key Passage or Loaded Word	Narrator's Attitude
Most of the aunt's remarks begin with "Don't."	The aunt is not effective with children.
The aunt responds weakly.	

Writing Focus

Think as a Reader/Writer

Find It in Your Reading "The Storyteller" is a **satire**—a piece of writing that ridicules the shortcomings of people or institutions in an attempt to bring about change. Greed, injustice, cruelty, and stupidity are all targets of the satirist. As you read this story, try to figure out whom or what Saki is ridiculing. Record your findings in your *Reader/ Writer Notebook*.

TechFocus As you read the story, notice the different ideas the characters have about children. Think about how you would plan a survey about the best way to raise children in modern society.

Vocabulary

sultry (SUHL tree) *adj.:* hot and humid; sweltering. *The passengers were uncomfortable in the sultry train car.*

persistent (puhr SIHS tuhnt) *adj.:* continuing; stubborn. *The children were persistent with their many questions.*

resolute (REHZ uh loot) *adj.:* determined. *The young girl's resolute willpower was admirable.*

petulant (PEHCH uh luhnt) *adj.:* impatient; irritable; peevish. *The children grew petulant as their questions went unanswered.*

conviction (kuhn VIHK shuhn) *n.:* strong belief; certainty. *All of the children agreed with conviction that their aunt's story was horrible.*

Language Coach

Multiple-Meaning Words Some words have more than one meaning. You use context clues to figure out which meaning is intended in a text. Which word from the list above also refers to a guilty verdict in a court of law?

 Learn It Online
See a good reader in action, and practice your own skills, at:

go.hrw.com | L10-219 | **Go**

Learn It Online
Learn more about Saki's life at:
go.hrw.com L10-220 Go

Saki (H.H. Munro)
(1870–1916)

A Difficult Beginning

Saki is the pen name of Hector Hugh Munro, who was born in Burma, the son of a British military officer. His mother died before he was two, and he and his siblings were sent to England to live with their grandmother and two strict aunts. (We find bad-tempered aunts in several Saki stories, including "The Storyteller.")

A sickly child, Munro had little formal schooling until he was sent to a boarding school at age fourteen. "You can't expect a boy to be vicious till he's been to a good school," Munro wrote somewhat bitterly in one of his stories.

A Promising Career Cut Short

Early in his writing career Munro worked as a political satirist and a foreign correspondent for various newspapers. Eventually he found a wide audience for his humorous, satiric, and often cynical short stories.

Although Munro was forty-three when World War I began, he enlisted in the British army, eager for "the excitement of real warfare." He was killed on the front lines in France by a German sniper.

Think About the Writer How might Munro's childhood experiences have influenced the style of his writing?

Build Background

In "The Storyteller," the children and their aunt travel by train to a distant town. Railroad travel was common for long distances before cars and airplanes became standard. Passenger cars were divided into compartments, and passengers did not always have their choice of traveling companions.

Preview the Selection

On a hot day on an even hotter train, three fidgety children begin to annoy a bachelor, a single man, who happens to share their compartment. As the aunt attempts to quiet the children, the bachelor listens in.

Shwe Dagon, The Pilgrim's Rest, Burma (1900-1910) by Vincent Clarence Scott O'Connor. Photo.
© Royal Geographic Society, London, UK.

The Storyteller

by **Saki**

It was a hot afternoon, and the railway carriage was correspondingly sultry, and the next stop was at Templecombe, nearly an hour ahead. The occupants of the carriage were a small girl, and a smaller girl, and a small boy. An aunt belonging to the children occupied one corner seat, and the further corner seat on the opposite side was occupied by a bachelor who was a stranger to their party, but the small girls and the small boy emphatically occupied the compartment. Both the aunt and the children were conversational in a limited, persistent way, reminding one of the attentions of a housefly that refused to be discouraged. Most of the aunt's remarks seemed to begin with "Don't," and nearly all the children's remarks began with "Why?" The bachelor said nothing out loud. **Ⓐ**

"Don't, Cyril, don't," exclaimed the aunt, as the small boy began smacking the cushions of the seat, producing a cloud of dust at each blow. "Come and look out of the window," she added.

The child moved reluctantly to the window. "Why are those sheep being driven out of that field?" he asked.

"I expect they are being driven to another field where there is more grass," said the aunt weakly.

"But there is lots of grass in that field," protested the boy; "there's nothing else but grass there. Aunt, there's lots of grass in that field."

"Perhaps the grass in the other field is better," suggested the aunt fatuously.[1]

"Why is it better?" came the swift, inevitable question.

"Oh, look at those cows!" exclaimed the aunt. Nearly every field along the line had contained cows or bullocks, but she spoke as though she were drawing attention to a rarity.

"Why is the grass in the other field better?" persisted Cyril.

The frown on the bachelor's face was deepening to a scowl. He was a hard, unsympathetic man, the aunt decided in her mind. She was utterly unable to come to any satisfactory decision about the grass in the other field. **Ⓑ**

The smaller girl created a diversion by beginning to recite "On the Road to Mandalay."[2] She only knew the first line, but she put her limited knowledge to the fullest possible

---

1. **fatuously** (FACH oo uhs lee): foolishly.
2. **"On the Road to Mandalay"**: long poem by the English writer Rudyard Kipling (1865–1936). The first line is "By the old Moulmein Pagoda, lookin' eastward to the sea."

Ⓐ Reading Focus Identifying Writer's Purpose Why do you suppose Saki describes the aunt as "belonging" to the children?

Ⓑ Literary Focus Omniscient Narrator What details reveal that the narrator is omniscient?

Vocabulary **sultry** (SUHL tree) *adj.*: hot and humid; sweltering.
persistent (puhr SIHS tuhnt) *adj.*: continuing; stubborn.

The Long Journey (1923)
by Frederick Cayley Robinson
(1862–1927).

use. She repeated the line over and over again in a dreamy but **resolute** and very audible voice; it seemed to the bachelor as though someone had had a bet with her that she could not repeat the line aloud two thousand times without stopping. Whoever it was who had made the wager was likely to lose his bet.

"Come over here and listen to a story," said the aunt, when the bachelor had looked twice at her and once at the communication cord.[3] **C**

The children moved listlessly toward the aunt's end of the carriage. Evidently her reputa-

---

3. **communication cord:** on a train, a cord that can be pulled to call the conductor.

Vocabulary **resolute** (REHZ uh loot) *adj.:* determined.

C **Reading Focus** Identifying Writer's Purpose What is the writer's attitude toward these characters? How does the writer build tension in this scene?

finally saved from a mad bull by a number of rescuers who admired her moral character.

"Wouldn't they have saved her if she hadn't been good?" demanded the bigger of the small girls. It was exactly the question that the bachelor had wanted to ask.

"Well, yes," admitted the aunt lamely, "but I don't think they would have run quite so fast to her help if they had not liked her so much."

"It's the stupidest story I've ever heard," said the bigger of the small girls, with immense conviction.

"I didn't listen after the first bit, it was so stupid," said Cyril.

The smaller girl made no actual comment on the story, but she had long ago recommenced a murmured repetition of her favorite line.

"You don't seem to be a success as a storyteller," said the bachelor suddenly from his corner.

The aunt bristled in instant defense at this unexpected attack.

"It's a very difficult thing to tell stories that children can both understand and appreciate," she said stiffly.

"I don't agree with you," said the bachelor.

"Perhaps *you* would like to tell them a story," was the aunt's retort.

"Tell us a story," demanded the bigger of the small girls.

"Once upon a time," began the bachelor, "there was a little girl called Bertha, who was extraordinarily good."

The children's momentarily aroused interest began at once to flicker; all stories seemed dreadfully alike, no matter who told them.

"She did all that she was told, she was

tion as a storyteller did not rank high in their estimation.

In a low, confidential voice, interrupted at frequent intervals by loud, petulant questions from her listeners, she began an unenterprising and deplorably uninteresting story about a little girl who was good, and made friends with everyone on account of her goodness, and was

---

Vocabulary **petulant** (PEHCH uh luhnt) *adj.*: impatient; irritable; peevish.
conviction (kuhn VIHK shuhn) *n.*: strong belief; certainty.

Literary Focus Omniscient Narrator What opinion is the omniscient narrator offering in this passage?

always truthful, she kept her clothes clean, ate milk puddings as if they were jam tarts, learned her lessons perfectly, and was polite in her manners."

"Was she pretty?" asked the bigger of the small girls.

"Not as pretty as any of you," said the bachelor, "but she was horribly good."

There was a wave of reaction in favor of the story; the word horrible in connection with goodness was a novelty that commended itself. It seemed to introduce a ring of truth that was absent from the aunt's tales of infant life.

"She was so good," continued the bachelor, "that she won several medals for goodness, which she always wore, pinned onto her dress. There was a medal for obedience, another medal for punctuality, and a third for good behavior. They were large metal medals and they clicked against one another as she walked. No other child in the town where she lived had as many as three medals, so everybody knew that she must be an extra good child."

"Horribly good," quoted Cyril.

"Everybody talked about her goodness, and the Prince of the country got to hear about it, and he said that as she was so very good she might be allowed once a week to walk in his park, which was just outside the town. It was a beautiful park, and no children were ever allowed in it, so it was a great honor for Bertha to be allowed to go there."

"Were there any sheep in the park?" demanded Cyril.

"No," said the bachelor, "there were no sheep."

"Why weren't there any sheep?" came the inevitable question arising out of that answer.

The aunt permitted herself a smile, which might almost have been described as a grin.

"There were no sheep in the park," said the bachelor, "because the Prince's mother had once had a dream that her son would either be killed by a sheep or else by a clock falling on him. For that reason the Prince never kept a sheep in his park or a clock in his palace." **E**

The aunt suppressed a gasp of admiration.

"Was the Prince killed by a sheep or by a clock?" asked Cyril.

"He is still alive, so we can't tell whether the dream will come true," said the bachelor unconcernedly; "anyway, there were no sheep in the park, but there were lots of little pigs running all over the place."

"What color were they?"

"Black with white faces, white with black spots, black all over, gray with white patches, and some were white all over."

The storyteller paused to let a full idea of the park's treasures sink into the children's imaginations; then he resumed:

"Bertha was rather sorry to find that there were no flowers in the park. She had promised her aunts, with tears in her eyes, that she would not pick any of the kind Prince's flowers, and she had meant to keep her promise, so of course it made her feel silly to find that there were no flowers to pick."

"Why weren't there any flowers?"

"Because the pigs had eaten them all," said the bachelor promptly. "The gardeners had told the Prince that you couldn't have pigs and flowers, so he decided to have pigs and no flowers."

There was a murmur of approval at the excellence of the Prince's decision; so many people would have decided the other way. **F**

E **Literary Focus** Omniscient Narrator The bachelor is the omniscient narrator of the story he tells. What does his story reveal both about the story's characters *and* the story's listeners?

F **Reading Focus** Identifying Writer's Purpose Why is the park in the bachelor's story filled with pigs instead of flowers? How does this detail support Saki's purpose in telling his story?

"There were lots of other delightful things in the park. There were ponds with gold and blue and green fish in them, and trees with beautiful parrots that said clever things at a moment's notice, and hummingbirds that hummed all the popular tunes of the day. Bertha walked up and down and enjoyed herself immensely, and thought to herself: 'If I were not so extraordinarily good I should not have been allowed to come into this beautiful park and enjoy all that there is to be seen in it,' and her three medals clinked against one another as she walked and helped to remind her how very good she really was. Just then an enormous wolf came prowling into the park to see if it could catch a fat little pig for its supper."

"What color was it?" asked the children, amid an immediate quickening of interest.

"Mud-color all over, with a black tongue and pale gray eyes that gleamed with unspeakable ferocity. The first thing that it saw in the park was Bertha; her pinafore[4] was so spotlessly

4. **pinafore** (PIHN uh fawr): apronlike garment that young girls used to wear over their dresses.

LE LOUP

Brown Wolf in the Snow by R. Sula Neziere.

white and clean that it could be seen from a great distance. Bertha saw the wolf and saw that it was stealing toward her, and she began to wish that she had never been allowed to come into the park. She ran as hard as she could, and the wolf came after her with huge leaps and bounds. She managed to reach a shrubbery of myrtle bushes and she hid herself in one of the thickest of the bushes. The wolf came sniffing among the branches, its black tongue lolling out of its mouth and its pale gray eyes glaring with rage. Bertha was terribly frightened and thought to herself: 'If I had not been so extraordinarily good I should have been safe in the town at this moment.' However, the scent of the myrtle was so strong that the wolf could not sniff out where Bertha was hiding, and the bushes were so thick that he might have hunted about in them for a long time without catching sight of her, so he thought he might as well go off and catch a little pig instead. Bertha was trembling very much at having the wolf prowling and sniffing so near her, and as she trembled the medal for obedience clinked against the medals for good conduct and punctuality. The wolf was just moving away when he heard the sound of the medals clinking and stopped to listen; they clinked again in a bush quite near him. He dashed into the bush, his

She ran as hard as she could, and the wolf came after her with huge leaps and bounds.

pale gray eyes gleaming with ferocity and triumph, and dragged Bertha out and devoured her to the last morsel. All that was left of her were her shoes, bits of clothing, and the three medals for goodness." **G**

"Were any of the little pigs killed?"

"No, they all escaped."

"The story began badly," said the smaller of the small girls, "but it had a beautiful ending."

"It is the most beautiful story that I ever heard," said the bigger of the small girls, with immense decision.

"It is the *only* beautiful story I have ever heard," said Cyril.

A dissentient[5] opinion came from the aunt.

"A most improper story to tell young children! You have undermined the effect of years of careful teaching."

"At any rate," said the bachelor, collecting his belongings preparatory to leaving the carriage, "I kept them quiet for ten minutes, which was more than you were able to do."

"Unhappy woman!" he observed to himself as he walked down the platform of Templecombe station; "for the next six months or so those children will assail her in public with demands for an improper story!"

---

5. **dissentient** (dihs SEHN shuhnt): dissenting; disagreeing.

G **Reading Focus** Identifying Writer's Purpose In what way is Bertha's fate ironic, or contrary to our expectations?

(Above) *Fairy Child Crying* (1968) by Sir Peter Blake (1932–)
Watercolor (15.2 cm × 15.2 cm).
Courtesy of the artist and Ruralist Fine Art Limited, United Kingdom/
© 2009 Artists Rights Society (ARS), NY/DACS, London.

Applying Your Skills

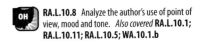
The Storyteller

Respond and Think Critically

Reading Focus

Quick Check

1. This is a **frame story,** in which one or more stories are told within another. Describe the exposition, or basic situation, that provides the frame for both the aunt's and the bachelor's stories.

2. What is the first "ring of truth" that the children perceive in the bachelor's story?

Read with a Purpose

3. What point does the bachelor make? How is it different from the point the aunt makes?

Reading Skills: Identifying Writer's Purpose

4. Add a row to your chart describing Saki's purpose for writing this story.

Key Passages or Loaded Words	Narrator's Attitude
The aunt's remarks begin with "Don't."	The aunt is not effective with children.

Author's Purpose for Writing:

_____

Literary Focus

Literary Analysis

5. **Interpret** The bachelor supplies both logic and information as he builds the setting for Bertha's downfall. Why do you think these surprises seem believable to the children?

6. **Draw Conclusions** What aspects of "The Storyteller" make it a satire? What is Saki poking fun at with this story? How does he use humor and exaggeration to make his point? Support your answers with examples from the story.

Literary Skills: Omniscient Narrator

7. **Contrast** How would the story be different if either the aunt or the bachelor, rather than the omniscient narrator, were telling it from the first-person point of view? What would be lost?

Literary Skills Review: Character Motivation

8. **Explain** A character's **motivation** is the reason behind the character's actions or behavior. What is the aunt's motivation for telling the children a story? the bachelor's motivation? At the end of the bachelor's story, how does the aunt react?

Writing Focus

Think as a Reader/Writer

Use It in Your Writing **Satire** generates laughter at the expense of others in the hopes of changing their behavior. Make a list of your "pet peeves," or behaviors that annoy you. Create a character who has one or more of these traits, and write a satirical paragraph poking fun at this character.

What Do You Think Now

Is goodness always rewarded? Whose version of life—the bachelor's or the aunt's—do you think is true to life? Why?

Applying Your Skills

The Storyteller

Vocabulary Development

Vocabulary Check

For each Vocabulary word, choose the **antonym,** or word with an opposite meaning.

1. **sultry**   a. casual
2. **persistent**   b. chilly
3. **petulant**   c. uncertainty
4. **conviction**   d. short-lived
5. **resolute**   e. indecisive

Vocabulary Skills: Using Context Clues

When you come across an unfamiliar word, look at the big picture, and use **context clues,** or the words and sentences surrounding the unfamiliar word. There are several types of clues. Sometimes the context will include a built-in definition or synonym, a restatement, an example, or an antonym.

Look at the sample sentences below, and see how the italicized context clues help you figure out the definition of the boldface words.

Built-in Definition
   The boy showed his dislike of the aunt's story with **conviction,** or *certainty*.

Restatement
   The **petulant** young child showed his *impatience*.

Example
   Both the aunt and the children were conversational in a limited, **persistent** way, *reminding one of the attentions of a housefly that refused to be discouraged*.

Antonym
   The train car was not *cool* or *comfortable*, but **sultry.**

Your Turn _____

Give the meaning of the italicized word, and identify **context clues** that helped you find the meaning.

1. She began a "*deplorably* uninteresting story about a little girl who was good."
2. The wolf "*devoured* her to the last morsel." All that was left were her shoes and medals.

Language Coach

Multiple-Meaning Words In which answer is the boldface word used the same way as in this quote from "The Storyteller"?

   "Evidently her reputation as a storyteller did not rank high in their **estimation.**"

a. The plumber provided an **estimation** of what the work would cost.

b. In my **estimation,** the performance was a little dull.

Academic Vocabulary

Talk About . . .
The bachelor <u>incorporates</u> details into his story that the children <u>perceive</u> as having "a ring of truth." Discuss this statement with a partner. Do you agree or disagree? Give reasons for your opinion.

OH **V0.10.1** Define unknown words through context clues and the author's use of comparison, contrast and cause and effect. **V0.10.6** Determine the meanings and pronunciations of unknown words by using dictionaries, glossaries, technology and textual features, such as definitional footnotes or sidebars. *Also covered* **WA.10.1.a; WP.10.15**

Grammar Link

Inverted Order: Verbs Before Subjects

In most sentences, verbs follow their <u>corresponding</u> subjects. In sentences with **inverted order,** the subject follows the verb. Identifying the subjects and verbs in these sentences can be challenging.

Questions generally use inverted order.
"Why **is it** better?" (subject = *it*)
"**Was she** pretty?" (subject = *she*)

Sentences that begin with the words *here* or *there* also use inverted order.
"There **were** no **sheep** in the park."
(subject = *sheep*)
"There **were lots** of other delightful things in the park." (subject = *lots*)

Clauses beginning with *here* or *there* use inverted order even in sentences that do not begin with *here* or *there*.
"I expect they are being driven to another field where there **is** more **grass**." (subject = *grass*)

Your Turn

Writing Applications Identify the subjects and verbs in the following sentences. Then rewrite the sentences according to the instructions, using inverted order.

1. You have heard of a writer named H. H. Munro. (Change into a question.)
2. The reason the name is not familiar is simple. (Change sentence to begin with *there*.)
3. The stories in this collection are wonderful. (Change to a question.)
4. An excellent example of Saki's style is here. (Change sentence to begin with *here*.)

CHOICES

As you respond to the Choices, use these **Academic Vocabulary** words as appropriate: <u>complex</u>, <u>correspond</u>, <u>incorporate</u>, <u>perceive</u>.

REVIEW
Explore Point of View

Timed ⌐Writing In "The Storyteller," both the aunt's and bachelor's stories are told from the omniscient point of view. Choose one of their stories, the aunt's or the bachelor's, and write an essay describing how that story would have been different if it had been told by a first-person narrator. Be sure to cite examples from the text.

CONNECT
Design a Survey

TechFocus With a partner, create a survey of ten questions about the best way to raise children in modern society. E-mail the survey, in PDF format, to teenagers and adults you know. Once you have gathered the results, <u>incorporate</u> them into an article for the school newspaper.

EXTEND
Write a Satire

In the telling of the bachelor's story, Saki used satire to make fun of unimaginative caregivers who sugarcoat fairy tales in order to teach lessons to children. Like Saki, write a short story that satirizes some aspect of society. For example, you may want to satirize people who are overly concerned with money, fashion, or fame.

Learn It Online
There's more to this story than meets the eye. Expand your view with these Internet links:

go.hrw.com | L10-229 | **Go**

HOUSEPAINTING

by **Lan Samantha Chang**

Houses (2005) by Jennifer Bartlett. Collection of Fred Jones Jr. Museum of Art, The University of Oklahoma.

What Do **You** **Think** How can someone else's decision affect your own life?

QuickWrite

Think about a movie you've seen or a book you've read in which one character's decision had an impact on another. Write a paragraph describing the decision and its consequences.

Reader/Writer Notebook

Use your **RWN** to complete the activities for this selection.

OH · **RA.L.10.8** Analyze the author's use of point of view, mood and tone. **RP.10.1** Apply reading comprehension strategies, including making predictions, comparing and contrasting, recalling and summarizing and making inferences and drawing conclusions.

Literary Focus

First-Person Narrator A **first-person narrator** is a character who tells the story. You can see the events of the story only through that character's eyes—you know only what that character knows. You also hear the distinct voice of that character, revealing his or her inner thoughts and feelings. As you read "Housepainting," notice how the first-person point of view influences how we <u>perceive</u> details and events.

Reading Focus

Questioning As you read a story, you might ask, "Why did the character react that way?" or, "Why is she upset?" Good writers, like Chang, sometimes invite questions by purposely leaving some things unanswered. Asking these questions—and then finding the answers—helps you experience a story.

Into Action While you read the story, take note of your questions. Use a chart like the one below to keep track of your questions.

My Questions	Answers
Why does the author begin the story with this family conversation?	

Writing Focus

Think as a Reader/Writer

Find It in Your Reading The first-person narrator of "Housepainting" is not part of the story's central conflict. However, the events in the story have profound implications for her future. Part of the tension in the story lies in the conflict between what she knows and what we, as readers, gradually realize. As you read, think about what the author chooses to tell us and what she leaves out. Take note of any symbols she uses and details she includes that might be important, and write them down in your *Reader/Writer Notebook*.

Vocabulary

extraneous (ehk STRAY nee uhs) *adj.*: external; not belonging. *Annie felt like an extraneous member of the family at times.*

transfixed (trans FIHKST) *v.* used as *adj.*: motionless. *Frances watched, transfixed, as Wei painted the house yellow.*

exasperated (ehg ZAS puh ray tihd) *v.* used as *adj.*: irritated; annoyed. *Annie's mother was exasperated by her daughter's mixed emotions.*

infuriated (ihn FYUR ee ay tihd) *v.*: made very angry. *Frances's behavior would have infuriated most men.*

contorted (kuhn TAWR tihd) *v.*: twisted out of shape. *Frances's face contorted with anger.*

Language Coach

Derivations By adding prefixes and suffixes to a base word, you create derivations. For example, the word *infuriated* is a derivation of the word *fury*. Use a dictionary to find derivations of the word *contort*.

Learn It Online
There's more to words than just definitions. Practice your vocabulary skills at:

 go.hrw.com L10-231 Go

Lan Samantha Chang
(1965–)

A Product of Two Cultures

Lan Samantha Chang grew up in the Midwest, but her parents were from China. They fled the country in 1949, when the Communists took control. Chang says that her curiosity about her parents' past has been one of the reasons she writes fiction. When she was growing up, her family was one of only three Chinese families in a town of about fifty thousand.

> "We were geographically isolated; months would go by when we did not have contact with Chinese or Chinese Americans outside of our immediate family. This meant that my sisters and I gained most of our knowledge of China and Chinese culture from our parents, and there were many things my parents did not, or would not, talk about."

From Medicine to Literature

Chang's parents wanted all their daughters to become doctors, and Chang did head for Yale, planning to become a dermatologist. However, she dropped medicine for East Asian studies. Then, in her second year of graduate school—to the dismay of her parents—Chang left the graduate program to study writing at the esteemed Writers' Workshop at the University of Iowa. In 2005, she was asked to head the Workshop— the first woman and the first Asian American to be so honored.

Think About the Writer How might Chang's childhood isolation from other Chinese families influence her writing?

Build Background

In "Housepainting," the narrator's mother makes a brief reference to her hardships as a young girl in China. Between 1945 and 1949, China was in the middle of a civil war. After the Communist Red Army devastated the Nationalists during the final year of fighting, the Communist Party seized control of the country. Millions of Nationalist supporters fled to Taiwan and to the United States.

Preview the Selection

Annie, the narrator, is a thirteen-year-old awaiting a visit from her older sister **Frances,** a college student. Along for the visit is Frances's boyfriend, **Wei,** whose plans may throw the family into turmoil.

Chang teaches a class at the University of Iowa Writers' Workshop.

HOUSEPAINTING

by **Lan Samantha Chang**

The day before my sister brought her boyfriend home, we had a family conference over fried rice and Campbell's chicken noodle.

"This is the problem," my mother said. "The thistles are overpowering our mailbox." She looked at my father. "Could you do something about them before Frances and Wei get here?"

My father grunted from behind his soup. He drank his Campbell's Chinese-style, with the bowl raised to his mouth. "Frances won't care about the thistles," he said. "She thinks only about coming home."

"But what about Wei?" my mother said. "This isn't his home. To him it's just a house that hasn't been painted in ten years. With weeds." She scowled. To her the weeds were a matter of honor. Although Wei had been dating my sister for four years and had visited us three times, he was technically a stranger and subject to the rules of "saving face."[1]

My father slurped. "Frances is a *xiaoxun*[2] daughter," he said. "She wants to see family, not our lawn. Wei is a good *xiaoxun* boy. He wants Frances to see her family; he doesn't care about the lawn."

---

1. **saving face:** preventing embarrassment; preserving one's dignity.
2. *xiaoxun* (SHOW shuhn).

Xiaoxun means "filial," or "dutiful to one's parents."

I was almost to the bottom of my bowl of rice when I noticed my parents were looking at me. "Oh," I said. "Okay, I'll do it." **(A)**

"Thank you, Annie," said my mother.

The next afternoon I went to work on the weeds. My father loved Wei and Frances, but he hated yard work. Whenever I read about Asian gardeners, I thought my father must have come over on a different boat.

It was a beautiful midwestern afternoon, sunny and dry, with small white clouds high up against a bright blue sky. I wore a pair of my father's old gloves to pull the thistles but kicked off my sandals, curled my toes around the hot reassuring dirt. Inside the house, my mother napped with the air conditioner humming in the window. My father sat in front of the television, rereading the Chinese newspaper from New York that my parents always snatched out of the mail as if they were receiving news of the emperor from a faraway province. I felt an invisible hand hovering over our shabby blue house, making sure everything stayed the same. **(B)**

I was hacking at a milky dandelion root when I heard an engine idling. A small brown car, loaded down with boxes and luggage, turned laboriously into the driveway. Through

---

(A) **Literary Focus** First-Person Narrator What do you learn about the narrator's family from this discussion?

(B) **Reading Focus** Questioning What questions do you have about the family based on the details the narrator provides?

Housepainting **233**

the open window I heard a scrape as my father pushed aside his footrest. My mother's window shade snapped up and she peered outside, one hand on her tousled hair. I rose to meet the car, conscious of my dirt-stained feet, sweaty glasses, and muddy gardening gloves. **(C)**

"Annie!" Frances shouted from the rolled-down window. She half-emerged from the car and shouted my name again.

"Wow," I said. "You guys are early. I thought you wouldn't get here until five o'clock."

"That was the plan," said Wei, "but your sister here was so excited about getting home that I begged off from call a few hours early." He grinned. He was always showing off about how well he knew my sister. But other than that he had very few defects, even to my critical thirteen-year-old mind. He was medium-sized and steady, with a broad, cheerful dark face and one gold-rimmed tooth.

My mother and father rushed out the front door and let it slam.

"Hi, Frances!" they said. "Hi, Wei!" I could tell my mother had stopped to comb her hair and put on lipstick.

We stood blinking foolishly in the sunlight as Wei and Frances got out of the car. My family does not hug. It is one of the few traditions that both my parents have preserved from China's pre-Revolutionary times.

Frances came and stood in front of my mother. "Let me look at you," my mother said. Her gaze ran over my sister in a way that made me feel knobby and extraneous.

Frances was as beautiful as ever. She did not look like she had been sitting in a car all day.

Her white shorts and her flowered shirt were fresh, and her long black hair rippled gently when she moved her head. People were always watching Frances, and Wei was no exception. Now he stared transfixed, waiting for her to turn to talk to him, but she did not.

Still facing my mother, Frances said, "Wei, could you get the stuff from the car?"

"I'll help you!" my father said. He walked around the back of the car and stood awkwardly aside to let Wei open the trunk. "So, how is medical school?" I heard him ask. They leaned into the trunk, their conversation muffled by the hood. I looked at their matching shorts, polo shirts, brown arms and sturdy legs. When Wei came to visit, my father always acted like a caged animal that has been let outside to play with another of its kind. **(D)**

Afterward, we sat in the kitchen and drank icy sweet green-bean porridge from rice bowls. Frances nudged me.

"Hey, Annie, I got you something."

She pulled a package wrapped in flowered paper from a shopping bag. She never came home without presents for everyone, and she never left without a bag full of goodies from home. It was as if she could maintain a strong enough sense of connection to us only by touching things that had actually belonged, or would soon belong, to us.

I looked at the package: a book. I stifled a groan. Frances never knew what I wanted.

"Well, open it," my mother said.

I tore off the paper. It was a thick volume about the history of medicine. This was

---

(C) **Literary Focus** **First-Person Narrator** What details does the narrator include here that clue you in to her character?

(D) **Reading Focus** **Questioning** Why do you think Annie's father acts this way?

Vocabulary **extraneous** (ehk STRAY nee uhs) *adj.*: external; not belonging.
transfixed (trans FIHKST) *v.* used as an *adj.*: motionless.

supposed to be of great interest to me, because of a family notion that I would become a doctor, like Wei. I did not want to be a doctor.  **E**

"This is great! Thanks, Frances," I said.

"Very nice," said my mother.

"Ma, I left your present in my room," Frances said. "Let's go get it." They left the kitchen. My father and Wei began a heated discussion about Wimbledon.[3] After a few minutes, I got bored and went to find my mother and Frances.

From the entrance to the hall I could see that the bedroom door was closed. I stopped walking and snuck up to the door on the balls of my feet. I crouched against the door to listen.

"I don't *know*, Mom," Frances was saying. She sounded close to tears.

"What is it that you don't know?" my mother asked her. When my mother got upset, her sentences became more formal and her Chinese accent more obvious. "Are you unsure that he really cares about you, or are you unsure about your feelings for him?"

"I know he cares about me," she said. She had answered my mother's question. There followed a pause in the conversation.

Then my mother said, "Well, I think he is a very nice boy. Daddy likes him very much."

"And of course that's the most important thing," said my sister, her anger startling me. I wrapped my arms around my knees.

"You know that is not true." My mother sounded exasperated. "Your father enjoys spending time with other men, that is all. There aren't very many Chinese men in this area for

him to talk to. He also likes Wei because he is capable of giving you the kind of life we have always wanted you to have. Is there something . . ." She paused. "What is wrong with him?"

Frances burst into a sob.

"There's nothing *wrong* with him. There's *nothing* wrong with him. It's just—oh, I just don't know—I don't know." She was almost shouting, as if my mother didn't understand English. "You and Dad don't think about me at *all!*"

I imagined my mother's face, thin and tight, frozen in the light from the window. "Don't speak to me that way," she said stiffly. "I am only trying to help you decide. You are very young. You have never lived through a war.[4] You don't know about the hardships of life as much as your father and I do."

---

3. **Wimbledon:** famous international tennis tournament held in the town of Wimbledon, in southeastern England.

4. **"You have never lived through a war":** The narrator's mother is referring to the civil war that took place in China in the 1940s.

E **Literary Focus** First-Person Narrator What information do you get from the first-person narrator that you would not have gotten if the story had been told by someone else?

Vocabulary **exasperated** (ehg ZAS puh ray tihd) *v.* used as *adj.:* irritated; annoyed.

"I'm *sorry*," my sister said, and sobbed even louder. I got up and snuck away down the hall. **F**

My parents often mentioned the war, especially when I complained about doing something I didn't want to do. If I couldn't get a ride to the swimming pool, my mother told me about when *she* was in seventh grade and had to walk to school every day past a lot of dead bodies. My mother was a brave seventh grader who knew how to shoot a gun and speak four dialects. But what did I know? I'd lived in the Midwest my whole life. I ate Sugar Pops and drank milk from a cow. To me, an exciting time meant going downtown to the movies without my parents. **G**

That night Wei and Frances and I went to a movie starring Kevin Costner and a blond woman whose name I don't remember. On the way to the theater the car was very quiet. When we arrived, I stood in line to get popcorn and then went into the dim, virtually empty theater to look for Wei and Frances. I saw them almost immediately. They were quarreling. Wei kept trying to take Frances's hand, and she kept snatching it away. As I approached, I heard him say, "Just tell me what you want from me. What do you want?"

"I don't know!" Frances said. I approached. She looked up. "Mmm—popcorn! Sit down, Annie. I have to go to the bathroom." Her look said: Don't you dare say a word.

I watched her hurry up the aisle. "What's wrong with her?"

Wei shook his head a minute, trying to dislodge an answer. "I don't know." My first time alone with him. We sat staring awkwardly at the empty screen. Then he turned to me as if struck by an important thought.

"Annie, what would *you* think if Francie and I got married?"

Despite what I had overheard between Frances and my mother, my stomach gave a little jump. I thought about what to say.

"That would be nice," I said.

"You think so?" Wei said eagerly. "Listen, can you tell her that? I've got to convince her. It's like she can't make up her own mind. Why do you think that is?"

"I don't know," I said. "I guess she hasn't had much practice." Although I'd never thought about it before, I knew that I was right. *Xiaoxun* meant that your parents made up your mind. I pictured Wei wrapped up in flowered paper, another gift my sister brought back and forth.

Wei sat sunk in his seat, a speculative look on his face. "Hmm," he said. "Hmm."

I began to feel uncomfortable, as if I were sitting next to a mad scientist. "I can't wait to see this movie," I said quickly. "Frances and I think Kevin Costner is cute." I stuffed a handful of popcorn into my mouth. While I was chewing, Frances finally came back and sat down between us.

"How about it, Frances?" Wei said. "Do you think Kevin Costner is cute?"

I looked at Wei's face and suddenly realized that he could not look more different from Kevin Costner. **H**

"Actually, Frances doesn't like him," I blurted out. "I just—"

At that moment the screen lit up, and despite myself, I gave an audible sigh of relief.

My father was waiting for us when we got

F **Reading Focus** Questioning Why do you think Frances reacts this way to her mother's statement?

G **Literary Focus** First-Person Narrator How do the narrator's comments provide you with insight into her character?

H **Reading Focus** Questioning What questions does this scene raise in your mind about Wei's future with Frances?

home, under the lamp with the Chinese newspaper, in his sagging easy chair. This habit of waiting had always infuriated Frances, who felt compelled by guilt to return at a reasonable hour.

Wei greeted my father cheerfully. "Hi, Mr. Wang. Waiting up for us?"

"Oh no," my father said, regarding Wei with pleasure.

"I'm glad you're still up," Wei said, with a look of heavy male significance. "I wanted to talk to you about something."

This time I had no desire to listen in on the conversation. I headed for the bathroom as fast as I could. Frances hurried behind me.

"Aren't you going to talk with them?" I said.

Frances grabbed the doorknob. "Just shut up," she said. She closed the door behind us, and we stood for a minute in the pink-tiled room under the glow of the ceiling light. Frances leaned against the counter and sighed. I sat down on the toilet seat.

"You know," she muttered, "I really do think Kevin Costner is cute."

"Me too," I said. I stared at the tiny speckle pattern on the floor tiles.

From the kitchen we heard a burble of laughter.

"Dad really likes Wei," I said.

Frances sighed. "It's not just Dad. Mom likes him too. She's just too diplomatic⁵ to show it. Dad is more obvious." She raised her eyebrows. "At least I know exactly where I stand with Dad."

Her words frightened me.

"I don't get it," I burst out in spite of myself. "Why did you go out with him for four years if you don't really like him?"   ⓘ

5. **diplomatic** (dihp luh MAT ihk): skilled in handling sensitive issues or people.

Frances ran her hand around a water faucet. "He reminded me of home," she said. "Why did you sign up for biology instead of art class?" She slid quickly off the counter. "Come on, kiddo, time to hit the sack."

The next morning I slept late. Around eleven I was awakened by a muffled bang near my bedroom window. My mind whirled like a pinwheel: What on earth—? I jumped out of bed and pushed up the bottom of the shade.

Two male legs, clad in shorts, stood on a ladder to the right of my window. Then Wei bent down, his smile startling me.

He was holding a paintbrush.

"What are you doing?" I almost shrieked.

"Just giving your father a little help with the house," he said.

I pulled the shade down, grabbed some clothes, and hurried out of my room to find my mother. As I passed Frances's room, I saw her sitting on her bed, fully dressed, with a completely blank expression on her face.

My mother was in the kitchen, cutting canned bamboo shoots into long thin strips.

"Where is Dad?"

"Don't shout, Annie," she said. "He went to the hardware store to match some more paint."

"Why is Wei painting the house?"

My mother lined up a handful of bamboo shoots and began cutting them into cubes. "He's just being helpful."

"Why is Dad letting him be so helpful?" I couldn't find the right question. Wei must have asked my father if he needed help with the house. Why had my father consented? Why was he accepting help from an outsider?   ⓙ

ⓘ **Literary Focus** First-Person Narrator Why is the narrator scared by Frances's attitude toward Wei?

ⓙ **Literary Focus** First-Person Narrator What do the narrator's comments reveal about her parents?

Vocabulary **infuriated** (ihn FYUR ee ay tihd) *v.*: made very angry.

Analyzing Visuals **Viewing and Interpreting** Does the girl in this image remind you of either Annie or Frances? Explain.

The Lily (2005) by Gu Zhinong.
Courtesy of the artist and Contemporary
Chinese Fine Art, Laguna Beach, CA.

My mother turned and looked at me. "Because Wei wanted to help, that's all. Why don't you go and wash up? You're thirteen years old; I shouldn't have to remind you to wash your face."

The next few days passed in a blur, marked only by the growing patch of fresh pale-yellow paint that grew to cover one side of our blue house and then the back. Wei worked steadily and cheerfully, with minimal help from my father. My mother went outside now and then to give him cold drinks and to comment on the evenness of his job, or something like that. Frances stayed in her room reading. I reported to her.

"Wei's finished with the back side and now he's starting on the garage," I said.

"Leave me alone," Frances said.

I went further into the room and stood in front of her until she looked up. "I said leave me *alone*, Annie! I'm warning you—"

"Well, why don't *you* say something about it?" I demanded. "Why didn't you tell him you didn't want him to do it?"

Her face contorted in something between anger and tears. "I can't tell him! He won't listen to me! He says he's just doing them a favor!" She bent over her book and flipped her hair angrily in front of her, shielding her face. "Go away!"

I left the room.

With things at home going so well, my parents left the next morning on a day trip to Chicago. Every now and then they made the four-hour drive to buy supplies—dried mushrooms, canned vegetables—from a Chinese grocery there. After they left, we ate breakfast, with Wei and I making awkward conversation because Frances wouldn't talk to us. Then Wei got up and went out to the front yard. From an open window I watched him pry the lid off a can of paint and stir with a wooden stick from the hardware store. Frances went out on the front porch and stood at the top of the steps looking down at him.

"You can stop now, Wei," I heard her say.

He glanced up, puzzled.

"You don't have to paint today. Mom and Dad aren't around to see what a dutiful boy you are."

Wei didn't have a short fuse.[6] He shook his head slowly and looked back down at what he was doing.

Frances tried again. "It makes me sick," she said, "to see you groveling[7] like this around my parents."

Wei didn't answer.

"What is it with you?" she sneered.

Finally his eyes flickered. "My painting the house," he said, "is something between me and your parents. If you don't like it, why don't you go pick a fight with them? And why did you wait until they left to pick a fight with me?" **K**

Frances's upper lip pulled back toward her nose. I thought she was sneering at him again, but when she turned back to the house, I realized she was crying. She looked horrible. She slammed the door, rushed past me, and ran into the garage, where she and Wei had parked the brown car. Then before Wei and I could stop her, she drove away down the street.

She came back in about an hour. I sat inside pretending to read a book, but Frances didn't

---

6. **short fuse:** quick temper.
7. **groveling** (GRAHV uhl ihng): behaving humbly in front of authority in a way that suggests a lack of self-respect.

Vocabulary   contorted (kuhn TAWR tihd) *v.*: twisted out of shape.

K **Reading Focus** Questioning Why do you think Wei is really painting the house?

reenter the house, so I figured she and Wei were talking out there. I was surprised when he came inside. "Where's Frances?" he said.

"I thought she was with you."

"Nope. Just finished the front. I'm about to put a second coat on the south side. Want to take a look?"

"Okay." I put down my book. We walked outside and around the house.

There stood Frances with her hair up in a painter's cap, busily putting blue back over Wei's work, painting fast, as high as she could reach. Two new cans stood in the grass. She had finished most of the side and had worked almost up to the corner.

Frances turned to look at us. There were splotches of blue paint on her hands and clothes.

"I liked it better the old way," she said. She glared at Wei, waiting for him to get angry, but he stood perfectly still. I felt cool sweat break out on my neck and forehead.

Finally Wei said, "If you wanted it blue again, you just had to tell me."

Frances threw her brush on the ground and burst into tears. She shouted at Wei, "I hate you! You too, Annie! I hate both of you! I hate everything!" She looked at the house. "I don't care what color it is, I just hate everything!"

I took a step backward, but Wei walked right up to her and put his hand on her shoulder. Frances hid her face in her hands and sobbed. They stood like that for a long time, Frances crying and mumbling under her breath, and then she began to repeat one sentence over and over. I leaned forward, straining to make it out.

"Mom and Dad are going to *kill* me." **L**

Wei looked relieved. "If we all start now, we can probably paint yellow over it before they get home," he said.

Two days later Wei finished the house. He and my father drove to the hardware store to buy white paint for the trim. I was sitting in the family room, listlessly leafing through a *Time* magazine, when Frances stopped in the door.

"Hey, Annie. Wanna go out and take a look?"

"Okay," I said, surprised by her sudden friendliness.

We walked out the front door, crossed the street, and stood facing the house. The street lamps had just turned on, and the house glowed gently in the twilight. Our raggedy lawn and messy garden were hidden in the shadows.

We stood for some time, and then Frances said, "I told Wei that I would marry him."

I looked at her. Her face was expressionless in the glow from the street lamp. Finally she turned and briefly met my eyes.

"It's not worth the trouble," she said. "Let's not talk about it anymore, okay?"

"Okay," I said. Without talking, we crossed the street and approached the house. It was a beautiful evening. My mother stood behind the kitchen window, washing the dishes. Frances walked smoothly at my side, her long hair flowing back in the dusk. I glanced up at the roof in a hopeful way, but the imaginary hand that had hovered over our home had disappeared. I blinked my eyes a couple of times and looked again, but it was gone. **M**

"Come on, Annie," my sister said, holding the door. "Hurry up, or the mosquitoes will get in."

I took a deep breath and went inside.

L Reading Focus **Questioning** The writer does not directly state what Annie, Wei, or Frances is feeling in this scene. How do you think each character feels?

M Literary Focus **First-Person Narrator** How has the narrator's attitude toward her family changed? Explain.

Applying Your Skills

RA.L.10.8 Analyze the author's use of point of view, mood and tone. **RP.10.1** Apply reading comprehension strategies, including making predictions, comparing and contrasting, recalling and summarizing and making inferences and drawing conclusions. *Also covered* **V0.10.3; WA.10.2**

Respond and Think Critically

Reading Focus

Quick Check

1. How does Frances feel about Wei? How is she influenced by her parents' expectations?
2. What is the story's main conflict? How does it get resolved?

Read with a Purpose

3. How is Annie affected by her sister's problems?

Reading Skills: Questioning

4. Refer to the questions you recorded as you read the story. Then, record your answers. Re-read the story to clear up any remaining questions.

My Questions	Answers
Why does the author begin the story with this family conversation?	to give the reader a feel for the family or to tell the reader that Frances is coming for a visit

✔ Vocabulary Check

Answer *true* or *false* to the following statements, and briefly explain your answers. Vocabulary words are boldface.

5. Something **extraneous** does not belong.
6. Someone who is **transfixed** is in constant motion.
7. If someone is **exasperated,** she is about to lose her patience.
8. If you **infuriated** someone, you made her happy.
9. Someone who **contorted** his face kept it still.

Literary Focus

Literary Analysis

10. **Infer** Why is Frances angry about Wei's painting the house?
11. **Infer** Why do you think Frances paints over the yellow and makes the house blue again?
12. **Evaluate** Were you surprised by Frances's decision to marry Wei? Explain.

Literary Skills: First-Person Narrator

13. **Interpret** Annie, the first-person narrator, is only thirteen years old and doesn't fully understand what is happening in her family. What lies beneath all of the actions and dialogue in the story?

Literary Skills Review: Mood

14. **Analyze** What is the **mood,** or emotional effect, of this story? How does the author's use of descriptive language establish the mood?

Writing Focus

Think as a Reader/Writer

Use It in Your Writing Refer to the symbols and details that you noted during your reading. Then, write a paragraph analyzing Chang's use of symbols and details. Did they help you understand the underlying meaning of the story? Explain.

What Do You Think Now? Why do you think Frances's decision has such a strong impact on Annie?

Evacuation Order No. 19

by **Julie Otsuka**

American Diary: April 21, 1942 (1997) by Roger Shimomura.
Collection of Esther Weissman. Courtesy of the artist and Greg Kucera Galleries, Seattle.

What Do You Think

How do people cope with hardships that require enormous changes in their lives?

🎧 QuickTalk

What events in history or in the present have forced people to change their lives completely? Discuss this question for a few minutes with a partner.

Reader/Writer Notebook

Use your **RWN** to complete the activities for this selection.

OH **RA.L.10.8** Analyze the author's use of point of view, mood and tone. **RP.10.1** Apply reading comprehension strategies, including making predictions, comparing and contrasting, recalling and summarizing and making inferences and drawing conclusions.

Literary Focus

Third-Person-Limited Narrator The **third-person-limited narrator,** who is not a character in the story, zooms in on the thoughts, actions, and feelings of only *one* character. In "Evacuation Order No. 19," we follow a woman named Mrs. Hayashi, who finds herself one day bewildered, alone, and alienated in a society she once trusted. The narrator allows us to share in Mrs. Hayashi's experiences, but we can only guess at what the other characters in the story are thinking and feeling.

Literary Perspectives Apply the literary perspective described on page 245 as you read the story.

Reading Focus

Drawing Conclusions When you put "two and two together" you are drawing conclusions, weighing the evidence to form an idea about something. As you read this story, draw conclusions about Mrs. Hayashi and her experiences.

Into Action Note key details in the story that hint at what is happening. List these details as you read, and write your conclusions about the meaning of the details.

Story Details	My Conclusions
After seeing signs in her town, Mrs. Hayashi begins packing.	The signs probably say that she has to evacuate.

Language Coach

Oral Fluency The word ending *–ed* is not usually pronounced as a separate syllable. Instead the sound /d/ or /t/ is added to the end of the base word. Which two words on the list above end with the /d/ sound? Which ends with the /t/ sound?

Writing Focus

Think as a Reader/Writer

Find It in Your Reading As you read the story, notice how the writer uses repeated sentence structures to emphasize certain ideas. "*It hung* in the window of Woolworth's. *It hung* by the entrance to the YMCA. *It was nailed* . . ." In your *Reader/Writer Notebook,* take note of the repeated structures you find.

Learn It Online
Find the *PowerNotes* introduction to this story on:

go.hrw.com   L10-243   **Go**

Julie Otsuka
(1962–)

The Character Took Up Residence in Her Head

Julie Otsuka was born and raised near Berkeley, California, where "Evacuation Order No. 19" is set. Her story takes place during World War II when Japanese Americans, including Otsuka's family, were forced to leave their homes and report to internment camps. Otsuka says this about the story:

> "I had no idea when I started writing 'Evacuation Order No. 19'—the first chapter of my novel—that it would turn into something larger. . . . But the character of the woman in the story simply took up residence, one day, in my head: I saw her standing alone on a street, reading the evacuation notice for the first time, and then I followed her home to see who she was, and what she might do after that."

They Didn't Talk About It

Otsuka's grandfather was arrested the day after the attack on Pearl Harbor. Later, other relatives were sent to the camps. Otsuka said in an interview, "Aside from those basic facts . . . the novel is entirely made up. The characters in the novel don't resemble anyone in my own family. And since my family didn't talk about the internment much, I had to recreate that time for myself."

Think About the Writer How do you think Otsuka's personal connection to these events might affect the way she tells her story?

Build Background

After Japanese forces bombed the American fleet in Pearl Harbor in Hawaii on December 7, 1941, the United States declared war on Japan. On February 19, 1942, President Roosevelt issued Executive Order 9066, authorizing the exclusion of people of Japanese descent from certain areas of the United States. By September 1942, more than 120,000 Japanese Americans had been sent to ten internment camps throughout the country. No charges were filed against these people, but they were still treated like criminals. Their personal liberties were taken away, and most of them also lost their homes, their jobs, and all their personal property.

Preview the Selection

This story follows **Mrs. Hayashi** as she prepares to leave her home in Berkeley, California, for an internment camp. Her young son and daughter will go with her; her husband, **Junior,** has already been taken to a camp.

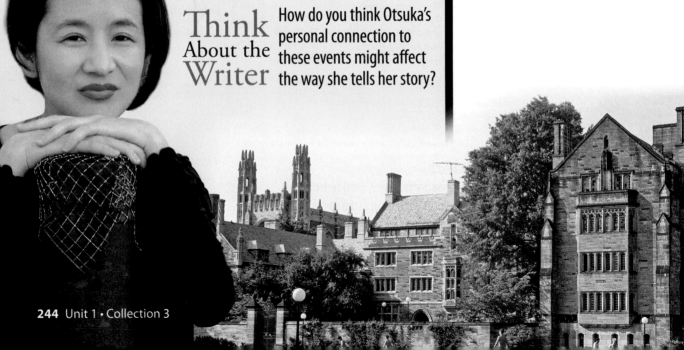

Evacuation Order No. 19

by **Julie Otsuka**

Overnight the sign had appeared. On billboards and trees and all of the bus stop benches. It hung in the window of Woolworth's. It hung by the entrance to the YMCA. It was nailed to the door of the municipal court and stapled, at eye level, to every other telephone pole along University Avenue. Mrs. Hayashi was returning a book to the library when she saw the sign in a post office window. It was a sunny day in Berkeley[1] in the spring of 1942 and she was wearing new glasses and could see everything clearly for the first time in weeks. She no longer had to squint but she squinted out of habit anyway. She read the sign from top to bottom and then, still squinting, she took out a pen and read the sign from top to bottom again. The print was small and dark. Some of it was tiny. She wrote down a few words on the back of a bank receipt, then turned around and went home and began to pack. **Ⓐ**

_____

1. **Berkeley:** city in California on the shore of San Francisco Bay.

_____

Ⓐ **Reading Focus** Drawing Conclusions   What do you think the sign says?

When the overdue notice from the library arrived in the mail nine days later she still had not finished packing. The children had just left for school and boxes and suitcases were scattered across the floor of the house. She tossed the envelope into the nearest suitcase and walked out the door.

Outside the sun was warm and the palm fronds were clacking idly against the side of the house. She pulled on her white silk gloves and began to walk east on Ashby. She crossed California Street and bought several bars of

Literary Perspectives

Analyzing Historical Context   The social, political, economic, and cultural characteristics of a particular time make up a story's historical context. In order to understand some stories, you have to know something about the historical time in which they are set. With this story, for example, you must understand what was happening to Japanese Americans in the United States during World War II. How was this particular historical period different from our own time? How was it similar? As you read, be sure to notice the questions in the text that guide you in thinking about the historical perspective.

Lux soap and a large jar of face cream at the Rumford Pharmacy. She passed the thrift shop and the boarded-up grocery but saw no one she knew on the sidewalk. At the newsstand on the corner of Grove she bought a copy of the *Berkeley Gazette*. She scanned the headlines quickly. The Burma Road had been severed and one of the Dionne quintuplets[2]—Yvonne—was still recovering from an ear operation. Sugar rationing would begin on Tuesday. She folded

---

2. **Burma Road . . . Dionne quintuplets:** The Burma Road, about 700 miles long, was completed in 1938 by the Chinese and was used to transport supplies during China's war with Japan. The Dionne quintuplets, born in 1934 in Canada, were the first quintuplets known to have survived infancy.

the paper in half but was careful not to let the ink darken her gloves.   **Ⓑ**

At Lundy's Hardware she stopped and looked at the display of victory garden shovels in the window. They were well-made shovels with sturdy metal handles and she thought, for a moment, of buying one—the price was right and she did not like to pass up a bargain. Then she remembered that she already had a shovel at home in the shed. In fact, she had two. She did not need a third. She smoothed down her dress and went into the store.

"Nice glasses," Joe Lundy said the moment she walked through the door.

"You think?" she asked. "I'm still not used to them yet." She picked up a hammer and

Vocabulary **severed** (SEHV uhrd) *v.:* cut; broke off. **rationing** (RASH uh nihng) *v. used as n.:* distribution in small amounts.

Ⓑ Literary Perspectives **Historical Context** What specific details give you a sense of the story's setting?

Homes of Japanese Americans in San Francisco (1942). Photo by Dorothea Lange.

gripped the handle firmly. "Do you have any-thing bigger?" she asked. Joe Lundy said that what she had in her hand was the biggest hammer he had. She put the hammer back on the rack.

"How's your roof holding out?" he asked.

"I think the shingles are rotting. It just sprung another leak."

"It's been a wet year."

Mrs. Hayashi nodded. "But we've had some nice days." She walked past the venetian blinds and the blackout shades[3] to the back of the store. She picked out two rolls of tape and a ball of twine and brought them back to the register. "Every time it rains I have to set out the bucket," she said. She put down two quarters on the counter.

"Nothing wrong with a bucket," said Joe Lundy. He pushed the quarters back toward her across the counter but he did not look at her. "You can pay me later," he said. Then he began to wipe the side of the register with a rag. There was a dark stain there that would not go away.

"I can pay you now," she said.

"Don't worry about it." He reached into his shirt pocket and gave her two caramel candies wrapped in gold foil. "For the children," he said. She slipped the caramels into her purse but left the money. She thanked him for the candy and walked out of the store.

"That's a nice red dress," he called out after her.

She turned around and squinted at him over the top of her glasses. "Thank you," she said. "Thank you, Joe." Then the door slammed

---

3. **blackout shades:** black shades drawn to hide house lights that might be targeted by enemy airplanes at night.

behind her and she was alone on the sidewalk again and she realized that in all the years she had been going to Joe Lundy's store she had never once called him by his name until now. Joe. It sounded strange to her. Wrong, almost. But she had said it. She had said it out loud. She wished she had said it earlier. **C**

She wiped her forehead with her handkerchief. The sun was bright and Mrs. Hayashi was not a woman who liked to sweat in public. She took off her glasses and crossed to the shady side of the street. At the corner of Shattuck she took the streetcar downtown. She got off in front of J. F. Hink's department store and rode the escalator to the third floor and asked the salesman if they had any duffel bags but they did not, they were all sold out. He had sold the last one a half hour ago. He suggested she try JCPenney but they were sold out of duffel bags there too. They were sold out of duffel bags all over town. **D**

When she got home she took off her red dress and put on her faded blue one—her housedress. She twisted her hair up into a bun and put on an old pair of comfortable shoes. She had to finish packing. She rolled up the Oriental rug in the living room. She took down the mirrors. She took down the curtains and shades. She carried the tiny bonsai tree out to the yard and set it down on the grass beneath the eaves where it would not get too much shade or too much sun but just the right amount of each. She brought the wind-up Victrola and the Westminster chime clock downstairs to the basement.

Upstairs, in the boy's room, she unpinned the One World One War map of the world from the wall and folded it neatly along the crease

---

C Literary Focus **Third-Person-Limited Narrator** What does the narrator tell us here about Mrs. Hayashi's feelings?

D Reading Focus **Drawing Conclusions** Why do you suppose all the duffel bags are sold out?

Evacuation Order No. 19 **247**

lines. She wrapped up his stamp collection, and the painted wooden Indian with the long head-dress he had won at the Sacramento State Fair. She pulled out his Joe Palooka comic books from under the bed. She emptied the drawers. Some of his clothes—the clothes he would need—she left out for him to put into his suitcase later. She placed his baseball glove on his pillow. The rest of his things she put into boxes and carried into the sunroom.

The door to the girl's room was closed. Above the doorknob was a note that had not been there the day before. It said, "Do Not Disturb." Mrs. Hayashi did not open the door. She went down the stairs and removed the pictures from the walls. There were only three: the painting of Princess Elizabeth that hung in the dining room, the picture of Jesus in the foyer, and, in the kitchen, a framed reproduction of Millet's *The Gleaners*.[4] She placed Jesus and the little princess together facedown in a box. She made sure to put Jesus on top. She took *The Gleaners* out of its frame and looked at the picture one last time. She wondered why she had let it hang in the kitchen for so long. It bothered her, the way those peasants were forever bent over above that endless field of wheat. "Look up!" she wanted to say to them. "Look up, look up!" *The Gleaners,* she decided, would have to go. She set the picture outside with the garbage. **E**

In the living room she emptied all the books from the shelves except Audubon's *Birds of America.* In the kitchen she emptied the cupboards. She set aside a few things for later

---

4. *The Gleaners:* famous painting by the French artist Jean Millet (1814–1875) showing three peasants bending over to gather kernels of wheat.

that evening. Everything else—the china, the silver, the set of ivory chopsticks her mother had sent to her fifteen years ago from Hawaii on her wedding day—she put into boxes. She taped the boxes shut with the tape she had bought from Lundy's Hardware Store and carried them one by one up the stairs to the sunroom. When she was done she locked the door with two padlocks and sat down on the landing with her dress pushed up above her knees and lit a cigarette. Tomorrow she and the children would be leaving. She did not know where they were going or how long they would be gone or who would look after the house while they were away. She knew only that tomorrow they had to go.

There were things they could take with them: bedding and linen, forks, spoons, plates, bowls, cups, clothes. These were the words she had written down on the back of the bank receipt. Pets were not allowed. That was what the sign had said.

It was late April. It was the fourth week of the fifth month of the war and Mrs. Hayashi, who did not always follow the rules, followed the rules. She gave the cat to the Greers next door. She caught the chicken that had been running wild in the yard since the fall and snapped its neck beneath the handle of a broomstick. She plucked out the feathers and set the carcass into a pan of cold water in the sink. **F**

By early afternoon Mrs. Hayashi's handkerchief was soaked. She was breathing hard and her nose was itching from the dust. Her back ached. She slipped off her shoes and massaged the bunions on her feet, then went into the kitchen and turned on the radio. Enrico Caruso was singing "La donna è mobile" again. His

---

E **Reading Focus** Drawing Conclusions Why do you think Mrs. Hayashi is bothered by *The Gleaners*?

F **Literary Focus** Third-Person-Limited Narrator What do these actions reveal about Mrs. Hayashi's character?

voice was full and sweet. She opened the refrigerator and took out a plate of rice balls stuffed with pickled plums. She ate them slowly as she listened to the tenor sing. The plums were dark and sour. They were just the way she liked them.

When the aria was over she turned off the radio and put two rice balls into a blue bowl. She cracked an egg over the bowl and added some salmon she had cooked the night before. She brought the bowl outside to the back porch and set it down on the steps. Her back was throbbing but she stood up straight and clapped her hands three times.

A small white dog came limping out of the trees.

"Eat up, White Dog," she said. White Dog was old and ailing but he knew how to eat. His head bobbed up and down above the bowl. She sat down beside him and watched. When the bowl was empty he looked up at her. One of his eyes was clouded over. She rubbed his stomach and his tail thumped against the wooden steps.

"Good dog," she said.

She stood up and walked across the yard and White Dog followed her. The tomato garden had gone to seed and the plum tree was heavy with rotting fruit. Weeds were everywhere. She had not mowed the grass for months. Junior usually did that. Junior was her husband. Junior's father was Isamu Hayashi, Senior, but Junior was just Junior. Once in a while he was Sam. Last December Junior had been arrested and sent to Missoula, Montana, on a train. In March he had been sent to Fort Sam Houston, Texas. Now he was living just north of the Mexican border in Lordsburg, New Mexico. Every few days he sent her a letter. Usually he told her about the weather. The

weather in Lordsburg was fine. On the back of every envelope was stamped "Alien Enemy Mail, Censored." **G**

Mrs. Hayashi sat down on a rock beneath the persimmon tree. White Dog lay at her feet and closed his eyes. "White Dog," she said, "look at me." White Dog raised his head. She was his mistress and he did whatever she asked. She put on her white silk gloves and took out a roll of twine. "Now just keep looking at me," she said. She tied White Dog to the tree. "You've been a good dog," she said. "You've been a good white dog."

Somewhere in the distance a telephone rang. White Dog barked. "Hush," she said. White Dog grew quiet. "Now roll over," she said. White Dog rolled over and looked up at her with his good eye. "Play dead," she said. White Dog turned his head to the side and closed his eyes. His paws went limp. Mrs. Hayashi picked up the large shovel that was leaning against the trunk of the tree. She lifted

---

G **Literary Perspectives** Historical Context What does this passage tell you about the government's attitude toward Japanese Americans during this period?

Vocabulary **censored** (SEHN suhrd) *v.*: examined for the purpose of removing anything objectionable.

it high in the air with both hands and brought the blade down swiftly on his head. White Dog's body shuddered twice and his hind legs kicked out into the air, as though he were trying to run. Then he grew still. A trickle of blood seeped out from the corner of his mouth. She untied him from the tree and let out a deep breath. The shovel had been the right choice. Better, she thought, than a hammer. **ⓗ**

Beneath the tree she began to dig a hole. The soil was hard on top but soft and loamy beneath the surface. It gave way easily. She plunged the shovel into the earth again and again until the hole was deep. She picked up White Dog and dropped him into the hole. His body was not heavy. It hit the earth with a quiet thud. She pulled off her gloves and looked at them. They were no longer white. She dropped them into the hole and picked up the shovel again. She filled up the hole. The sun was hot and the only place there was any shade was beneath the trees. Mrs. Hayashi was standing beneath the trees. She was forty-one and tired. The back of her dress was drenched with sweat. She brushed her hair out of her eyes and leaned against the tree. Everything looked the same as before except the earth was a little darker where the hole had been. Darker and wetter. She plucked two persimmons from a low hanging branch and went back inside the house.

When the children came home from school she reminded them that early the next morning they would be leaving. Tomorrow they were going on a trip. They could only bring with them what they could carry.

"I already know that," said the girl. She knew how to read signs on trees. She tossed her books onto the sofa and told Mrs. Hayashi that her teacher Mr. Rutherford had talked for an entire hour about prime numbers and coniferous trees.

"Do you know what a coniferous tree is?" the girl asked.

Mrs. Hayashi had to admit that she did not. "Tell me," she said, but the girl just shook her head no.

> Tomorrow they were going on a trip. They could only bring with them what they could carry.

"I'll tell you later," she said. She was ten years old and she knew what she liked. Boys and black licorice and Dorothy Lamour.[5] Her favorite song on the radio was "Don't Fence Me In." She adored her pet macaw.[6] She went to the bookshelf and took down *Birds of America*. She balanced the book on her head and walked slowly, her spine held erect, up the stairs to her room. **ⓘ**

A few seconds later there was a loud thump and the book came tumbling back down the stairs. The boy looked up at his mother. He was seven and a small, black fedora was tilted to one side of his head. "She has to stand up straighter," he said softly. He went to the foot of the stairs and stared at the book. It had landed

---

5. **Dorothy Lamour** (1914–1996): popular movie star of the late 1930s and 1940s. During World War II she helped sell government bonds.

6. **macaw** (muh KAW): exotic-looking parrot from South and Central America.

ⓗ Reading Focus Drawing Conclusions Why does Mrs. Hayashi kill the dog?

Vocabulary **drenched** (drehncht) *v.* used as *adj.*: soaked.

ⓘ Literary Focus Third-Person-Limited Narrator How does the narrator's description of what the girl says and does influence your impression of her?

face open to a picture of a small brown bird. A marsh wren. "You have to stand up straighter," he shouted.

"It's not that," came the girl's reply. "It's my head."

"What's wrong with your head?" shouted the boy.

"Too round. Too round on *top.*"

He closed the book and turned to his mother. "Where's White Dog?" he asked.

He went out to the porch and clapped his hands three times.

"White Dog!" he yelled. He clapped his hands again. "White Dog!" He called out several more times, then went back inside and stood beside Mrs. Hayashi in the kitchen. She was slicing persimmons. Her fingers were long and white and they knew how to hold a knife. "That dog just gets deafer every day," he said.

He sat down and turned the radio on and off, on and off, while Mrs. Hayashi arranged the persimmons on a plate. The Radio City Symphony was performing Tchaikovsky's *1812 Overture.* Cymbals were crashing. Cannons boomed. Mrs. Hayashi set the plate down in front of the boy. "Eat," she said. He reached for a persimmon just as the audience burst into applause. "Bravo," they shouted, "bravo, bravo!" The boy turned the dial to see if he could find *Speaking of Sports* but all he could find was the news and a Sammy Kaye serenade. He turned off the radio and took another persimmon from the plate.

"It's so hot in here," he said.

"Take off your hat then," said Mrs. Hayashi, but the boy refused. The hat was a present from Junior. It was big on him but he wore it every day. She poured him a glass of cold barley water and he drank it all in one gulp. **J**

The girl came into the kitchen and went to the macaw's cage by the stove. She leaned over and put her face close to the bars. "Tell me something," she said.

The bird fluffed his wings and danced from side to side on his perch. "Baaaak," he said.

"That's not what I wanted to hear," said the girl.

"Take off your hat," said the bird.

The girl sat down and Mrs. Hayashi gave her a glass of cold barley water and a long silver spoon. The girl licked the spoon and stared at her reflection. Her head was upside down. She dipped the spoon into the sugar bowl.

"Is there anything wrong with my face?" she asked.

"Why?" said Mrs. Hayashi.

"People were staring." **K**

"Come over here."

The girl stood up and walked over to her mother. "Let me look at you," said Mrs. Hayashi.

"You took down the mirrors," the girl said.

"I had to. I had to put them away."

"Tell me how I look."

Mrs. Hayashi ran her hands across the girl's face. "You look fine," she said. "You have a fine nose."

"What else?" asked the girl.

"You have a fine set of teeth."

"Teeth don't count."

"Teeth are essential."

Mrs. Hayashi rubbed the girl's shoulders. The girl leaned back against her mother's knees and closed her eyes. Mrs. Hayashi pressed her fingers deep into the girl's neck until she felt her begin to relax. "If there was something wrong with my face," the girl asked, "would you tell me?"

J Reading Focus **Drawing Conclusions** What can you conclude about the way the boy feels about his father?

K Literary Perspectives **Historical Context** Given what you know about the story's historical context, explain why people might be staring at the girl.

"Turn around."

The girl turned around.

"Now look at me."

She looked at her mother.

"You have the most beautiful face I have ever seen."

"You're just saying that."

"No, I mean it."

The boy turned on the radio. The weatherman was giving the forecast for the next day. He was predicting rain and cooler temperatures. "Sit down and drink your water," the boy said to his sister. "Don't forget to take your umbrella tomorrow," said the weatherman.

The girl sat down. She drank her barley water and began to tell Mrs. Hayashi all about coniferous trees. Most of them were evergreens but some were just shrubs. Not all of them had cones. Some of them, like the yew, only had seedpods.

"That's good to know," said Mrs. Hayashi. Then she stood up and told the girl it was time to practice the piano for Thursday's lesson.

"Do I have to?"

Mrs. Hayashi thought for a moment. "No," she said, "only if you want to."

"Tell me I have to."

"I can't."

The girl went out to the living room and sat down on the piano bench. "The metronome's[7] gone," she called out.

"Just count to yourself then," said Mrs. Hayashi.

---

7. **metronome's** (MEHT ruh nohmz): A metronome is a clockwork device that helps a player keep tempo on the piano.

Women unpacking during the time of Japanese internment.

". . . three, five, seven . . ." The girl put down her knife and paused. They were eating supper at the table. Outside it was dusk. The sky was dark purple and a breeze was blowing in off the bay. Hundreds of jays were twittering madly in the Greers' magnolia tree next door. A drop of rain fell on the ledge above the kitchen sink and Mrs. Hayashi stood up and closed the window.

"Eleven, thirteen," said the girl. She was practicing her prime numbers for Monday's test.

"Sixteen?" said the boy.

"No," said the girl. "Sixteen's got a square root."

"I forgot," said the boy. He picked up a drumstick and began to eat.

"You never knew," said the girl.

"Forty-one," said the boy. "Eighty-six." He wiped his mouth with a napkin. "Twelve," he added.

The girl looked at him. Then she turned to her mother. "There's something wrong with this chicken," she said. "It's too tough." She put down her fork. "I can't swallow another bite."

"Don't, then," said Mrs. Hayashi.

"I'll eat it," said the boy. He plucked a wing from his sister's plate and put it into his mouth. He ate the whole thing. Then he spit out the bones and asked Mrs. Hayashi where they were going the next day.

"I don't know," she said.

The girl stood up and left the table. She sat down at the piano and began to play a piece by Debussy from memory. "Golliwogg's Cakewalk." The melody was slow and simple. She had played it at a recital the summer before and her father had sat in the audience and clapped and clapped. She played the piece all the way through without missing a note. When she began to play it a second time the boy got up and went to his room and began to pack.

The first thing he put inside of his suitcase was his baseball glove. He slipped it into the large pocket with the red satin lining. The pocket bulged. He threw in his clothes and tried to close the lid but the suitcase was very full. He sat on top of it and the lid sank down slowly as the air hissed out. Suddenly he stood up again. The lid sprang open. There was something he had forgotten. He went to the closet in the hall and brought back his polka-dotted umbrella. He held it out at arm's length and shook his head sadly. The umbrella was too long. There was no way it would fit inside the suitcase. **L**

Mrs. Hayashi stood in the kitchen, washing her hands. The children had gone to bed and the house was quiet. The pipes were still hot from the day and the water from the faucet was warm. She could hear thunder in the distance—thunder and, from somewhere deep beneath the house, crickets. The crickets had come out early that year and she liked to fall asleep to their chirping. She looked out the window above the sink. The sky was still clear and she could see a full moon through the branches of the maple tree. The maple was a sapling with delicate leaves that turned bright red in the fall. Junior had planted it for her four summers ago. She turned off the tap and looked around for the dish towel but it was not there. She had already packed the towels. They were in the suitcase by the door in the hall.

She dried her hands on the front of her dress and went to the bird cage. She lifted off the green cloth and undid the wire clasp on the door. "Come on out," she said. The bird stepped cautiously onto her finger and looked at her.

L Literary Focus **Third-Person-Limited Narrator** Why do you think the narrator has focused on the boy's actions?

Young girl with her bags packed waiting to be interned. Photo by Dorothea Lange.

"It's only me," she said. He blinked. His eyes were black and bulbous. They had no center.

"Get over here," he said, "get over here now." He sounded just like Junior. If she closed her eyes she could easily imagine that Junior was right there in the room with her.

Mrs. Hayashi did not close her eyes. She knew exactly where Junior was. He was sleeping on a cot—a cot or maybe a bunk bed—some-where in a tent in Lordsburg where the weather was always fine. She pictured him lying there

with one arm flung across his eyes and she kissed the top of the bird's head.

"I am right here," she said. "I am right here, right now."

She gave him a sunflower seed and he cracked the shell open in his beak. "Get over here," he said again.

She opened the window and set the bird out on the ledge.

"You're all right," the bird said.

She stroked the underside of his chin and

he closed his eyes. "Silly bird," she whispered. She closed the window and locked it. Now the bird was outside on the other side of the glass. He tapped the pane three times with his claw and said something but she did not know what it was. She could not hear him anymore.

She rapped back.

"Go," she said. The bird flapped his wings and flew up into the maple tree. She grabbed the broom from behind the stove and went outside and shook the branches of the tree. A spray of water fell from the leaves. "Go," she shouted. "Get on out of here."

The bird spread his wings and flew off into the night. **Ⓜ**

She went back inside the kitchen and took out a bottle of plum wine from beneath the sink. Without the bird in the cage, the house felt empty. She sat down on the floor and put the bottle to her lips. She swallowed once and looked at the place on the wall where *The Gleaners* had hung. The white rectangle was glowing in the moonlight. She stood up and traced around its edges with her finger and began to laugh—quietly at first, but soon her shoulders were heaving and she was doubled over and gasping for breath. She put down the bottle and waited for the laughter to stop but it would not, it kept on coming until finally the tears were running down her cheeks. She picked up the bottle again and drank. The wine was dark and sweet. She had made it herself last fall. She took out her handkerchief and wiped her mouth. Her lips left a dark stain on the cloth. She put the cork back into the bottle and pushed it in as far as it would go. "La donna è mobile," she sang to herself as she went down the stairs to the basement. She hid the bottle behind the old rusted furnace where no one would ever find it. **Ⓝ**

In the middle of the night the boy crawled into her bed and asked her, over and over again, "What is that funny noise? What is that funny *noise*?"

Mrs. Hayashi smoothed down his black hair. "Rain," she whispered.

The boy understood. He fell asleep at once. Except for the sound of the rain the house was quiet. The crickets were no longer chirping and the thunder had come and gone. Mrs. Hayashi lay awake worrying about the leaky roof. Junior had meant to fix it but he never had. She got up and placed a tin bucket on the floor to catch the water. She felt better after she did that. She climbed back into bed beside the boy and pulled the blanket up around his shoulders. He was chewing in his sleep and she wondered if he was hungry. Then she remembered the candy in her purse. The caramels. She had forgotten about the caramels. What would Joe Lundy say? He would tell her she was wearing a nice red dress. He would tell her not to worry about it. She knew that. She closed her eyes. She would give the caramels to the children in the morning. That was what she would do. She whispered a silent prayer to herself and drifted off to sleep as the water dripped steadily into the bucket. The boy shrugged off the blanket and rolled up against the wall where it was cool.

In a few hours he and the girl and Mrs. Hayashi would report to the Civil Control Station at the First Congregational Church on Channing Way. They would pin their identifi-

---

Ⓜ **Reading Focus** **Drawing Conclusions** Considering what Mrs. Hayashi does to prepare for the journey, how long do you think she expects to be gone?

Ⓝ **Reading Focus** **Drawing Conclusions** Why do you suppose Mrs. Hayashi laughs? Why does she cry?

cation numbers to their collars and grab their suitcases and climb onto the bus. The bus would drive south on Shattuck and then turn west onto Ashby Avenue. Through the dusty pane of the window Mrs. Hayashi would see the newsstand on the corner of Grove. She would see the boarded-up grocery and the sign in front of it—a new sign, a sign she had not seen before—that said, "Thank you for your patronage. God be with you until we meet again." She would see the thrift shop and the Rumford Pharmacy. She would see her house with its gravel walkway and its small but reliable rosebush that had blossomed every May for the last ten years in a row. She would see Mrs. Greer next door watering her lawn but she would not wave to her. The bus would speed through a yellow light and turn left onto Route 80, then cross the Bay Bridge and take them away.

Three years and four months later they would return. It would be early autumn and the war would be over. The furniture in the house would be gone but the house would still be theirs. The sunroom would be empty. The stovepipe would be missing from the stove and there would be no motor inside the washing machine. In the mailbox there would be an overdue notice. Mrs. Hayashi would owe the library $61.25 in fines and her borrowing privileges would be temporarily suspended. The bonsai tree would be dead but the maple would be thriving. So would the persimmon tree. Six months later Junior would come home from New Mexico a tired and sick old man. Mrs. Hayashi would not recognize him at first but the girl would know who her father was the moment he stepped off the train. The following summer Junior would have a stroke and Mrs. Hayashi would go to work for the first time in her life. For five and sometimes six days a week she would clean other people's houses much better than she ever had her own. Her back would grow strong and the years would go by quickly. Junior would have two more strokes and then die. The children would grow up. The boy would become a lieutenant colonel in the army and the girl would become my mother. She would tell me many things but she would never speak of the war. The bottle of plum wine would continue to sit, unnoticed, gathering dust behind the furnace in the basement. It would grow darker and sweeter with every passing year. The leak in the roof has still, to this day, not been properly fixed. **P**

Boy surrounded by adults and suitcases on his way to a Japanese internment camp. Photo by Russell Lee.

Applying Your Skills

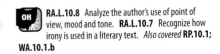 **RA.L.10.8** Analyze the author's use of point of view, mood and tone. **RA.L.10.7** Recognize how irony is used in a literary text. *Also covered* **RP.10.1; WA.10.1.b**

Evacuation Order No. 19

Respond and Think Critically

Reading Focus

Quick Check

1. List three of the errands that Mrs. Hayashi performs at the beginning of the story and explain the ultimate reason for each.

2. Name at least three things that the family has to give up when they move to the camp.

Read with a Purpose

3. How is Mrs. Hayashi's life different after she returns from the camp?

Reading Skills: Drawing Conclusions

4. Review your chart and place a check mark next to conclusions that proved correct. If any of your conclusions were incorrect, write down the correct interpretation of the passage.

Story Details	My Conclusions	Correct?
Mrs. Hayashi begins packing.	The sign probably says that she has to evacuate.	✓

Other Interpretations:

Literary Focus

Literary Analysis

5. **Analyze** What do Mrs. Hayashi's actions, words, and feelings tell you about her character? How does she change over the course of the story? Support your answer with details from the text.

6. **Literary Perspectives** Which of the story details <u>correspond</u> to the historical background provided on page 244?

7. **Interpret** The mother is identified only as "Mrs. Hayashi," and the son and daughter are never named. Why is this significant?

8. **Evaluate** Can Mrs. Hayashi be thought of as a hero? Cite specific details in your answer.

Literary Skills: Third-Person-Limited Narrator

9. **Evaluate** At the end of this story, the narrator, speaking as "I" for the first time, identifies herself as Mrs. Hayashi's granddaughter. How does this shift in point of view affect your response to the story? Are there details in the story that this narrator could not possibly have known? Explain.

Literary Skills Review: Irony

10. **Analyze** Recall that **irony** is a contrast between expectation and reality, between what we think is appropriate and what actually happens. Why is it ironic that the boy and the girl in the story have so many typical American interests?

Writing Focus

Think as a Reader/Writer

Use It in Your Writing Imitating Otsuka's style, write a description of a character's specific actions in a time of crisis, using repetition of sentence structures to help emphasize key ideas.

 What Do You Think Now

How does Mrs. Hayashi react to Evacuation Order No. 19? How might a different kind of person respond to the crisis?

Applying Your Skills

Evacuation Order No. 19

Vocabulary Development

Vocabulary Check

Fill in each blank with the correct Vocabulary word.

severed
rationing
censored
drenched

1. After the race, Tim's shirt was _____ with sweat.

2. A falling tree branch _____ the electrical line, cutting off our power.

3. The military _____ information about the top-secret mission.

4. The government sometimes imposes _____ to make sure all people get what they need.

Vocabulary Skills: Suffixes

A **suffix** is a letter or group of letters placed at the end of a word that changes its meaning or part of speech. In the word *slowly,* for example, adding the suffix *–ly* changes the word *slow* from an adjective to an adverb.

The chart below lists some common suffixes, their meanings, and examples of each.

Suffix	Meaning	Example
-ance, -ence	act, condition	radiance, excellence
-ism	act	criticism
-able	manner	negotiable
-ness	quality	goodness
-less	lacking	hopeless
-ful	full of	hopeful
-ion	action, condition	elation
-er, -or	doer	inheritor

Your Turn

1. What suffix would you use to turn the word *power* into a word that means "without power"?

2. What suffix would you use to name someone who hunts? who writes? who thinks?

3. Think of three nouns with the suffix *–ism*.

Language Coach

Oral Fluency In English, the letters *c* and *s* have different pronunciations depending on the letters that follow. The letter *c* can have a hard sound, such as in *candy,* or a soft sound, such as in *city*. A *c* is almost always soft when followed by *e, i,* or *y*.

The letter *s* can occasionally make a *sh* sound when followed by a *u,* as in the word *sure.* Most words that begin with *s,* like *supper* and *sun,* have regular *s* sounds. Practice pronouncing the following words:

censored	century	sugar
capital	cash	severed
calculate	coast	cymbal

Academic Vocabulary

Talk About ...
How do the photographs that accompany the selection <u>correspond</u> with the story's events? Does the use of photographs help you <u>perceive</u> the world the characters inhabit? Discuss your responses with a partner. Use the underlined Academic Vocabulary words in your discussion.

VO.10.5 Use knowledge of Greek, Latin and Anglo-Saxon roots, prefixes and suffixes to understand complex words and new subject-area vocabulary. **VO.10.6** Determine the meanings and pronunciations of unknown words by using dictionaries, glossaries, technology and textual features, such as definitional footnotes or sidebars. *Also covered* **WA.10.1.b; WP.10.15**

Grammar Link

Subject-Verb Agreement

Verbs must agree with their subjects in number. If a subject is singular, it takes a singular verb. Plural subjects take plural verbs.

> The **hat was** a present from Junior.

> The **pipes were** still hot from the day.

The number of a subject is not changed by a word or a phrase or clause that follows the subject.

> The **pictures** on the wall **were** taken down.

The indefinite pronouns *anybody, anyone, anything, each, either, everybody, everyone, everything, neither, nobody, no one, nothing, one, somebody,* and *something* are singular and take singular verbs.

> **Everybody was** aware of the sign.

Both, few, many, and *several* are plural and take plural verbs.

> **Few** on the street **were** upset.

All, any, more, most, none, and *some* are singular if they refer to singular nouns and plural if they refer to plural nouns.

> **Most** of them **were** evergreens.

> **Most** of the world **was** at war.

Your Turn

Which of the verbs in parentheses in the following sentences is correct? To answer, you will first have to identify the subject of the sentence.

1. Both the boy and girl (*is/are*) typical American kids.
2. This story describes the night the family (*prepares/prepare*) to leave home.
3. None of the people (*knows/know*) their destination.
4. Neither the girl nor the boy (*knows/know*) what happened to White Dog.

CHOICES

As you respond to the Choices, use the **Academic Vocabulary** words as appropriate: complex, correspond, perceive, incorporate.

REVIEW
Compare and Contrast

Timed └Writing The story's narrator has a significant impact on how we perceive the story's characters. In an essay describe the narrator's persona, and analyze the effect of the narrator on readers. Use details from the story to explain your ideas.

CONNECT
Write a Letter

Imagine you were friends with the Hayashis. Write a letter to them in which you express your thoughts on their situation. Also in your letter, give news from "home" and attempt to soothe and bolster your friends' spirits.

EXTEND
Explore Point of View

TechFocus In Otsuka's story, the narrator focuses on Mrs. Hayashi's experiences and her responses to the family's situation. What different experiences and reactions might another character have had in a similar situation? Write a version of a scene from the story from the point of view of another character, such as Mrs. Hayashi's son or daughter, or even Joe Lundy or Mrs. Greer. Then make a digital presentation of your scene.

Learn It Online

Find information about making digital presentations at:

go.hrw.com | L10-259 | **Go**

Author Study: Julia Alvarez

CONTENTS

What Do
You
Think What challenges face someone raised in two different cultures?

 QuickTalk

The United States is home to more people from different cultures than any other country in the world. With a partner, discuss the cultures with which you are familiar and explain how they operate within the larger American culture.

Preparing to Read

My First Free Summer / Exile /
All-American Girl

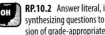 **RP.10.2** Answer literal, inferential, evaluative and synthesizing questions to demonstrate comprehension of grade-appropriate print texts and electronic and visual media. *Also covered* **RA.I.10.1**

Reader/Writer Notebook

Use your **RWN** to complete the activities for these selections.

Literary Focus

Literary Criticism: Biographical Approach Writers typically write about things they know and care about. Sometimes, this means writers write about their culture and other significant events in their lives. When you use a **biographical approach** to literary criticism, you use what you know about a writer's life to analyze and respond to a text. Knowing what a writer considers important may give you a clue to the **themes,** or central insights, of his or her work.

Reading Focus

Analyzing Works by One Author Reading several works by one author can give you a deeper understanding of the writer. Each work will add another layer to your appreciation. As you read the selections, look for the images, events, and ideas that appear more than once.

Into Action Use a chart like the one below to note ways in which Alvarez's work reflects her background.

Author's Life	"My First Free Summer"	"Exile"	"All-American Girl"
Culture	Alvarez's extended family is important to her.		
Historical Setting	The Dominican Republic is ruled by a dictator.		

Writing Focus

Think as a Reader/Writer

Find It in Your Reading Alvarez uses **imagery,** language that appeals to the five senses—sight, smell, hearing, taste, and touch—to describe the world around her. As you read the following selections, list in your *Reader/Writer Notebook* examples of the images that make an impression on you.

Vocabulary

My First Free Summer

repressive (rih PREHS ihv) *adj.:* exerting strict control over; brutal. *The country was controlled by a repressive dictator.*

extenuating (ehk STEHN yoo ay tihng) *v.* used as *adj.:* making something seem less severe by offering an excuse. *Her grandfather's donation was an extenuating circumstance that kept the narrator from being expelled from school.*

principles (PRIHN suh puhlz) *n.:* fundamental truths or beliefs. *Her mother believed in the American principles of freedom and a good education.*

replete (rih PLEET) *adj.:* full of; abundant. *She wanted a summer replete with trips to the beach and outings with her cousins.*

contradiction (kahn truh DIHK shuhn) *n.:* a statement that opposes or disagrees with someone or something; disagreement. *She would not accept contradiction—they were going whether they liked it or not.*

Language Coach

Homonyms A **homonym** is a word that sounds the same as another word but has a different spelling and meaning. *Principles* and *principals* are homonyms. Use a dictionary to find the meaning of *principals.*

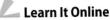 **Learn It Online**
Go beyond the definitions with Word Watch at:

| go.hrw.com | L10-261 | **Go** |

Julia Alvarez

(1950–   )

A Dominican Childhood

"I guess the first thing I should say is that I was *not* born in the Dominican Republic," writes Julia Alvarez on her Web site. Alvarez was born in New York City. When she was only three months old, her parents decided to return to their native Dominican Republic, which was suffering under the brutal dictatorship of Rafael Trujillo. There, her father got involved with the rebel underground, and eventually the family was forced to flee the country. Alvarez was ten when she and her family returned to New York City, where in a struggle to master the English language, she discovered books and the world of the imagination.

President Rafael Trujillo.

"Coming Home at Last"

In an essay about her return to New York, Alvarez wrote, "All my childhood I had dressed like an American, eaten American foods, and befriended American children. I had gone to an American school and spent most of the day speaking and reading English. At night, my prayers were full of blond hair and blue eyes and snow. . . . All my childhood I had longed for this moment of arrival. And here I was, an American girl, coming home at last."

Alvarez, age 10.

Although Alvarez had attended an American school in the Dominican Republic, as a new student in New York, she found she had to pay close attention to understand what others were saying. "I couldn't tell where one word ended and another began. . . . As a kid, I loved stories, hearing them, telling them. Since ours was an oral culture, stories were not written down. It took coming to this country for reading and writing to become allied in my mind with storytelling."

An Alvarez Time Line

1960 Alvarez and her family flee the Dominican Republic.

1975 Alvarez earns a master's degree in creative writing from Syracuse University; she begins a teaching career as a writer-in-residence for the Kentucky Arts Commission.

1950   **1960**   **1970**

1950 Alvarez is born in New York City. She and her parents move back to the Dominican Republic.

1971 Alvarez receives a bachelor's degree from Middlebury College.

The Song of Life

Today, Alvarez, who taught for a time at Middlebury College in Vermont and served later as its writer-in-residence, is most famous for her stories—some of which are collected in a prize-winning book titled *How the García Girls Lost Their Accents* (1991)—and for her poetry. She has also written novels, essays, and books for children. Alvarez and her husband, Bill Eichner, run a sustainable farm and literacy center in the Dominican Republic that she writes about in her children's book *A Cafecito Story*. She explains her interest in writing in different genres: "You go where your life takes you and the song comes out of that adventure."

Harvesting coffee at Fundacion Finca Alta Gracia Coffee Farm and Literacy Center in the Dominican Republic.

Key Elements of Alvarez's Writing

Sensory images and **figurative language** convey the flavor of the author's native culture and language.

Strong characterization helps readers understand and connect with characters.

Themes deal with the complex issues of cultural adaptation and cultural identity.

Spanish words interwoven seamlessly with English words help illustrate the writer's heritage.

A **playful, adventurous style** allows the writer to deal with difficult issues in lively, imaginative ways.

Think About the Writer How might Alvarez's experiences in New York City and the Dominican Republic have shaped her writing?

1987 Alvarez receives a National Endowment for the Arts grant for a poetry manuscript.

1991 Alvarez's first novel, *How the García Girls Lost Their Accents*, is published.

1992 The American Library Association chooses *How the García Girls Lost Their Accents* as a Notable Book.

1994 The American Library Association selects *In the Time of the Butterflies* as a Notable Book.

1998 Alvarez becomes a professor at Middlebury College.

2000 Latino.com names *In the Name of Salome* one of the top ten books of the year; *Latina* magazine names Alvarez Woman of the Year.

2002 The American Library Association selects *Before We Were Free* as the Best Book for Young Adults; Alvarez receives the Hispanic Heritage Award in Literature at the Kennedy Center, in Washington, D.C.

2006 Alvarez's sixth novel, *Saving the World*, is published.

2007 Alvarez publishes *Once upon a Quinceañera*, a nonfiction book about the Latino tradition that celebrates the birthdays of fifteen-year-old girls.

1980 | **1990** | **2000** | **2010**

My First Free SUMMER

by **Julia Alvarez**

Read with a Purpose
As you read "My First Free Summer," examine how the author, as a young girl, sees her definition of freedom change.

Build Background
Julia Alvarez spent a large part of her childhood in the Dominican Republic, where she lived with her extended family on her grandparents' property. At the time, the Dominican Republic was under the control of the dictator Rafael Trujillo. Alvarez and her sisters attended an American school called the Carol Morgan School, where they met the children of many American diplomats. When Trujillo's reign was threatened, many Americans and anti-Trujillo advocates fled the country.

I never had summer—I had summer school. First grade, summer school. Second grade, summer school. Thirdgradesummer schoolfourthgradesummerschool. In fifth grade, I vowed I would get interested in fractions, the presidents of the United States, Mesopotamia; I would learn my English.

That was the problem. English. My mother had decided to send her children to the American school so we could learn the language of the nation that would soon be liberating us. For thirty years, the Dominican Republic had endured a bloody and repressive dictatorship. From my father, who was involved in an underground plot, my mother knew that *los américanos* had promised to help bring democracy to the island.

"You have to learn your English!" Mami kept scolding me. **A**

"But why?" I'd ask. I didn't know about my father's activities. I didn't know the dictator was bad. All I knew was that my friends who were attending Dominican schools were often on holiday to honor the dictator's birthday, the dictator's saint day, the day the dictator became the dictator, the day the dictator's oldest son was born, and so on. They marched in parades and visited the palace and had their picture in the paper. **B**

Meanwhile, I had to learn about the pilgrims with their funny witch hats, about the 50 states and where they were on the map, about Dick and Jane and their tame little pets, Puff and Spot, about freedom and liberty and justice for all— while being imprisoned in a hot classroom with

---

A **Literary Focus** Biographical Approach Why does Alvarez's mother want her children to learn English?

Vocabulary **repressive** (rih PREHS ihv) *adj.*: exerting strict control over; brutal.

B **Literary Focus** Biographical Approach In what ways does the narrator already sense that she is something of an exile from Dominican culture?

a picture of a man wearing a silly wig hanging above the blackboard. And all of this learning I had to do in that impossibly difficult, rocks-in-your-mouth language of English! **C**

Somehow, I managed to scrape by. Every June, when my prospects looked iffy, Mami and I met with the principal. I squirmed in my seat while they arranged for my special summer lessons.

"She is going to work extra hard. Aren't you, young lady?" the principal would quiz me at the end of our session.

My mother's eye on me, I'd murmur, "Yeah."

"Yes, what?" Mami coached.

"Yes." I sighed. "Sir."

It's a wonder that I just wasn't thrown out, which was what I secretly hoped for. But there were extenuating circumstances, the grounds on which the American school stood had been donated by my grandfather. In fact, it had been my grandmother who had encouraged Carol Morgan to start her school. The bulk of the student body was made up of the sons and daughters of American diplomats and business people, but a few Dominicans—most of them friends or members of my family—were allowed to attend.

"You should be grateful!" Mami scolded on the way home from our meeting. "Not every girl is lucky enough to go to the Carol Morgan School!"

In fifth grade, I straightened out. "Yes, ma'am!" I learned to say brightly. "Yes, sir!" To wave my hand in sword-wielding swoops so I could get called on with the right answer. What

---

C **Reading Focus** **Analyzing Works by One Author** What does Alvarez's description of English suggest about how she felt about having to learn the language?

Vocabulary **extenuating** (ehk STEHN yoo ay tihng) *v.* used as *adj.:* making something seem less severe by offering an excuse.

The Dominican Republic

The Dominican Republic is a small nation on the island of Hispaniola in the Caribbean Sea. Dominican people have long experienced periods of civil and political unrest. The dictator Rafael Trujillo ruled the country mercilessly from 1930 to 1961, leading a corrupt and violent regime during which he murdered his opponents, censored media outlets, and appropriated wealth for himself and his family. Those who dared to speak out against him were in danger of being jailed or tortured by his secret police. Alvarez's father was involved with an underground plot to unseat Trujillo, thus risking his safety and the safety of his family.

Ask Yourself

Knowing this history of the Dominican Republic, why do you think Alvarez calls this essay "My First Free Summer"?

had changed me? Gratitude? A realization of my luckiness? No, sir! The thought of a fun summer? Yes, ma'am! I wanted to run with the pack of cousins and friends in the common yard that connected all our properties. To play on the trampoline and go off to la playa[1] and get brown as a berry. I wanted to be free. Maybe American principles had finally sunk in!

The summer of 1960 began in bliss: I did not have to go to summer school! *Attitude much improved. Her English progressing nicely. Attentive and cooperative in classroom.* I grinned as Mami read off the note that accompanied my report card of Bs. **D**

But the yard replete with cousins and friends that I had dreamed about all year was deserted. Family members were leaving for the United States, using whatever connections they could drum up. The plot had unraveled. Every day there were massive arrests. The United States had closed its embassy and was advising Americans to return home.

My own parents were terrified. Every night black Volkswagens blocked our driveway and stayed there until morning. "Secret police," my older sister whispered.

"Why are they secret if they're the police?" I asked.

Analyzing Visuals   **Viewing and Interpreting** How does this beach image compare to the narrator's ideas about summer fun at the beach?

La Pelota (1995) by John Valadez.

"Shut up!" my sister hissed. "Do you want to get us all killed?"

Day after day, I kicked a deflated beach ball around the empty yard, feeling as if I'd been tricked into good behavior by whomever God put in charge of the lives of 10-year-olds. I was bored. Even summer school would have been better than this! **E**

One day toward the end of the summer, my mother summoned my sisters and me. She wore

---

1. **la playa:** Spanish for "the beach."

D **Reading Focus** **Analyzing Works by One Author** Why does Alvarez's struggle with English play such a prominent role in her work?

E **Literary Focus** **Biographical Approach** At this point in the essay, Alvarez is still a young child. What are her main concerns in life?

Vocabulary   **principles** (PRIHN suh puhlz) *n.:* fundamental truths or beliefs.
replete (rih PLEET) *adj.:* full of; abundant.

that too-bright smile she sometimes pasted on her terrified face.

"Good news, girls! Our papers and tickets came! We're leaving for the United States!"

Our mouths dropped. We hadn't been told we were going on a trip anywhere, no less to some place so far away.

I was the first to speak up. "But why?"

My mother flashed me the same look she used to give me when I'd ask why I had to learn English.

I was about to tell her that I didn't want to go to the United States, where summer school had been invented and everyone spoke English. But my mother lifted a hand for silence. "We're leaving in a few hours. I want you all to go get ready! I'll be in to pack soon." The desperate look in her eyes did not allow for contradiction. We raced off, wondering how to fit the contents of our Dominican lives into four small suitcases.

Our flight was scheduled for that afternoon, but the airplane did not appear. The terminal filled with soldiers, wielding machine guns, checking papers, escorting passengers into a small interrogation room. Not everyone returned.

"It's a trap," I heard my mother whisper to my father.

This had happened before, a cat-and-mouse game the dictator liked to play. Pretend that he was letting someone go, and then at the last minute, their family and friends conveniently gathered together—wham! The secret police would haul the whole clan away.

Of course, I didn't know that this was what my parents were dreading. But as the hours ticked away, and afternoon turned into evening and evening into night and night into midnight with no plane in sight, a light came on in my head. If the light could be translated into words, instead, they would say: Freedom and liberty and justice for all . . .² I knew that ours was not a trip, but an escape. We had to get to the United States. **F**

The rest of that night is a blur. It is one, then two the next morning. A plane lands, lights flashing. We are walking on the runway, climbing up the stairs into the cabin. An American lady wearing a cap welcomes us. We sit down, ready to depart. But suddenly, soldiers come on board. They go seat by seat, looking at our faces. Finally, they leave, the door closes, and with a powerful roar, we lift off and I fall asleep.

Next morning, we are standing inside a large, echoing hall as a stern American official reviews our documents. What if he doesn't let us in? What if we have to go back? I am holding my breath. My parents' terror has become mine.

He checks our faces against the passport pictures. When he is done, he asks, "You girls ready for school?" I swear he is looking at me.

"Yes, sir!" I speak up.

The man laughs. He stamps our papers and hands them to my father. Then, wonderfully, a smile spreads across his face. "Welcome to the United States," he says, waving us in.

---

2. **Freedom and liberty and justice for all:** a loose reference to the Pledge of Allegiance, which ends "with liberty and justice for all."

Vocabulary **contradiction** (kahn truh DIHK shuhn) *n.:* a statement that opposes or disagrees with someone or something; disagreement.

F **Literary Focus** Biographical Approach How has Alvarez's attitude toward freedom changed?

EXILE

by **Julia Alvarez**

Read with a Purpose
Read to discover more about Alvarez's hurried move to the United States.

Preparing to Read for this selection is on page 261.

Build Background
Under Rafael Trujillo's dictatorship, all political parties and associations that opposed him were outlawed. He also ordered the massacre of thousands of Haitians and renamed Santo Domingo, the capital of the Dominican Republic, Ciudad Trujillo.

Ciudad Trujillo, New York City, 1960

The night we fled the country, Papi,
you told me we were going to the beach,
hurried me to get dressed along with the others,
while posted at a window, you looked out

5   at a curfew-darkened Ciudad Trujillo,
speaking in worried whispers to your brothers,
which car to take, who'd be willing to drive it,
what explanation to give should we be discovered . . .

On the way to the beach, you added, eyeing me.
10 The uncles fell in, chuckling phony chuckles,
What a good time she'll have learning to swim!
Back in my sisters' room Mami was packing

a hurried bag, allowing one toy apiece,
her red eyes belying her explanation:°
15 *a week at the beach so Papi can get some rest.*
She dressed us in our best dresses, party shoes. **A**

14. belying (bih LY ihng): misrepresenting; proving false.

A **Literary Focus** **Biographical Approach** What do you think the phrases in italics represent? Who is speaking?

Room on the Verge (1993) by Patssi Valdes. Courtesy of the artist.
Collection of Cheech and Patti Marin.

Something was off, I knew, but I was young
and didn't think adult things could go wrong.
So as we quietly filed out of the house

20   we wouldn't see again for another decade,

I let myself lie back in the deep waters,
my arms out like Jesus' on His cross,
and instead of sinking down as I'd always done,
magically, that night, I could stay up,

25   floating out, past the driveway, past the gates,
in the black Ford, Papi grim at the wheel,
winding through back roads, stroke by difficult stroke,
out on the highway, heading toward the coast.   **B**

B **Reading Focus** Analyzing Works by One Author   How does the comparison
in lines 21–28 reflect a major theme of Alvarez's writing?

Past the checkpoint, we raced towards the airport,
30   my sisters crying when we turned before
the family beach house, Mami consoling,
there was a better surprise in store for us!

She couldn't tell, though, until . . . until we were there.
But I had already swum ahead and guessed
35   some loss much larger than I understood,
more danger than the deep end of the pool.

At the dark, deserted airport we waited.
All night in a fitful sleep, I swam.
At dawn the plane arrived, and as we boarded,
40   Papi, you turned, your eyes scanned the horizon

as if you were trying to sight a distant swimmer,
your hand frantically waving her back in,
for you knew as we stepped inside the cabin
that a part of both of us had been set adrift.   **C**

45   Weeks later, wandering our new city, hand in hand,
you tried to explain the wonders: escalators
as moving belts; elevators: pulleys and ropes;
blond hair and blue eyes: a genetic code.

We stopped before a summery display window
50   at Macy's, *The World's Largest Department Store,*
to admire a family outfitted for the beach:
the handsome father, slim and sure of himself,

so unlike you, Papi, with your thick mustache,
your three-piece suit, your fedora hat,° your accent.
55   And by his side a girl who looked like Heidi
in my storybook waded in colored plastic.

54. fedora hat: a felt hat with a creased rim.

C Literary Focus **Biographical Approach** How do lines 34–44 reflect Alvarez's feelings about leaving her native country?

The Dream (2000) by Patssi Valdes. Collection of the artist.

Analyzing Visuals

Viewing and Interpreting What images from the poem can you find in this painting?

We stood awhile, marveling at America,
both of us trying hard to feel luckier
than we felt, both of us pointing out
60   the beach pails, the shovels, the sandcastles

no wave would ever topple, the red and blue boats.
And when we backed away, we saw our reflections
superimposed,° big-eyed, dressed too formally
with all due respect as visitors to this country. **D**

65   Or like, Papi, two swimmers looking down
at the quiet surface of our island waters,
seeing their faces right before plunging in,
eager, afraid, not yet sure of the outcome.

63. **superimposed:** put on top of something else.

D **Reading Focus** Analyzing Works by One Author How does the author's attitude toward her exile compare to her feelings at the end of "My First Free Summer"?

ALL-AMERICAN GIRL

by **Julia Alvarez**

Read with a Purpose
Read this poem to find the speaker's definition of "all-American."

Preparing to Read for this selection is on page 261.

Build Background
Alvarez uses both Spanish and English words to illustrate her adaptation to American life and culture. As Alvarez implies here, Spanish and other Romance languages are often thought of as showing more feeling or warmth than other languages. Spanish is called a Romance language because it developed from Latin, the language of the Roman Empire. By contrast, English developed from Anglo-Saxon, a language related to German.

I wanted stockings, makeup, store-bought clothes;
I wanted to look like an American girl;
to speak my English so you couldn't tell
I'd come from somewhere else. I locked myself
5   in the bathroom, trying to match my face
with words in my new language: *grimace, leer,*
disgust, disdain—feelings I had yet to feel
in English. (And would *tristeza* even feel
the same as *sadness* with its Saxon sound?
10 Would *pity* look as soulful as *piedad*?) Ⓐ

I didn't know if I could ever show
genuine feeling in a borrowed tongue.
If *cortesía*° would be misunderstood
as brown-nosing or cries of *alegría*°
15 translate as terror. So, mirror in hand,
I practiced foreign faces, Anglo grins,
repressing a native Latin fluency
for the cooler mask of English ironies.
I wanted the world and words to match again
20 as when I had lived solely in Spanish. Ⓑ

13. *cortesía:* Spanish for "courtesy."

14. *alegría:* Spanish for "cheerfulness" or "exhilaration."

Ⓐ **Reading Focus** **Analyzing Works by One Author** What conflict presented in this stanza is common in Alvarez's writing?

Ⓑ **Reading Focus** **Analyzing Works by One Author** How does Alvarez's native language influence her writing?

Analyzing Visuals

Viewing and Interpreting
Does the mood in this painting remind you of the mood in the poem? Why or why not?

Through the Looking Glass (2000) by Anne Belov. Collection of the artist.

But my face wouldn't obey—like a tide
it was pulled back by my lunatic heart
to its old habits of showing feelings.
Long after I'd lost my heavy accent,
25 my face showed I had come from somewhere else.
I couldn't keep the southern continent
out of the northern *vista*° of my eyes,
or cut my *cara*° off to spite my face.
I couldn't look like anybody else
30 but who I was: an all-American girl. Ⓒ

27. *vista:* Spanish for "sight" or "view."

28. *cara:* Spanish for "face."

Ⓒ **Literary Focus** Biographical Approach What does this poem reflect about Alvarez's struggles while growing up?

Applying Your Skills

OH **RP.10.2** Answer literal, inferential, evaluative and synthesizing questions to demonstrate comprehension of grade-appropriate print texts and electronic and visual media. **RA.L.10.11** Explain ways in which an author develops a point of view and style, and cite specific examples from the text. *Also covered* **RA.I.10.1; V0.10.3; WA.10.1.c**

My First Free Summer / Exile / All-American Girl

Respond and Think Critically

Reading Focus

Quick Check

1. Why does the narrator of "My First Free Summer" attend a special school?

2. In "Exile," why does the father lie to his family?

3. In "All-American Girl," how does the speaker feel about her two languages?

Read with a Purpose

4. How does Alvarez define "all-American"?

Reading Skills: Analyzing Works by One Author

5. As you read, you kept a chart noting how Julia Alvarez's work reflects her background. Using your chart, write a statement that summarizes how her background influences her writing.

✓ Vocabulary Check

Match each Vocabulary word on the left with its definition on the right.

6. **repressive**   a. beliefs
7. **extenuating**   b. full of
8. **principles**   c. disagreement
9. **replete**   d. justifying
10. **contradiction** e. controlling

Literary Focus

Literary Analysis

11. **Analyze** Whom is the speaker addressing in the poem "Exile"? How can you tell?

12. **Analyze** What internal conflict does the speaker in "All-American Girl" face?

Literary Skills: Biographical Approach

13. **Analyze** Why do you think the speaker in "All-American Girl" is unable to "keep the southern continent out of the northern *vista*" of her eyes? Is Alvarez still looking south? Explain.

14. **Extend** Though these selections are autobiographical, there is still a distinction between Alvarez the narrator and Alvarez the character. What separates the two? Why might Alvarez choose to maintain this separation?

Literary Skills Review: Extended Metaphor

15. **Analyze** A **metaphor** compares two unlike things. An **extended metaphor** develops the comparison over several lines or throughout an entire poem. Identify the extended metaphor in "Exile," citing examples from the text.

Writing Focus

Think as a Reader/Writer

Use It in Your Writing Think of an event or personal experience that has left a vivid impression on you. Write a brief narrative describing this event. Work to maintain a clear, consistent voice throughout your narrative. Pay attention to your word choice, sentence structure, and attitude and to how these aspects of your voice relate to the event you are describing.

What Do You Think Now

What has Alvarez gained by living in two cultures?

Preparing to Read

Antojos

RA.L.10.4 Interpret universal themes across different works by the same author or by different authors. **RA.L.10.8** Analyze the author's use of point of view, mood and tone. *Also covered* **RP.10.1**

Reader/Writer Notebook

Use your **RWN** to complete the activities for this selection.

Literary Focus

Theme and Narrator The **theme** of a story is the message about life that the story reveals. Themes are almost never directly stated; they are implied. Clues to a story's theme may be provided by the story's **narrator.** "Antojos" is told in the **third-person-limited point of view.** As the reader, you can <u>perceive</u> only one character's thoughts and feelings. As you read "Antojos," think about why the author would give you this inside look into the main character.

Reading Focus

Analyzing Themes Across Genres Different **genres,** or categories of writing, have different purposes. Writers choose a genre based on the point they want to make and how they want to make it. Nonfiction usually states a message directly; fiction, on the other hand, might imply the message. Fiction also allows writers to craft a story around a theme. When you **analyze themes across genres,** you think about the different ways in which writers can convey the same message with different genres.

Into Action As you read "Antojos," use a chart like the one at right to identify details about the characters and setting that are similar to the details in the other selections by Alvarez. What might these details reveal about a main theme in her writing?

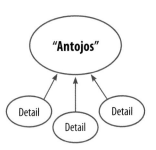

Vocabulary

lurching (LURCH ihng) *v.:* leaning or rolling suddenly to one side. *The car was lurching along the steep, uneven dirt road.*

devouring (dih VOWR ihng) *v.:* eating hungrily. *Yolanda was devouring the guavas she had just picked.*

collusion (kuh LOO zhuhn) *n.:* secret agreement. *Yolanda's family seemed to be working in collusion to shelter her.*

vigorously (VIHG uhr uhs lee) *adv.:* in a strong, active, forceful way. *The man shook the tire vigorously as he tried to remove it from the car.*

Language Coach

Suffixes A word part added to the end of a word to change its meaning is a **suffix.** Common suffixes include *–ion, –ous,* and *–ly.* Which of the above Vocabulary words has two suffixes?

Writing Focus

Think as a Reader/Writer

Find It in Your Reading As you read "Antojos," look for words, sentences, or figures of speech that help you envision the story's tropical setting. Write them down in your *Reader/Writer Notebook.*

Preparing to Read **275**

Antojos

by **Julia Alvarez**

Read with a Purpose
As you read, think about how the main character struggles with living in two cultures.

Build Background
The Dominican Republic, where this story takes place, is about twice the size of New Hampshire and is filled with rugged hills and valleys. The title of this story, "Antojos," is Spanish for "cravings."

For the first time since Yolanda had reached the hills, there was a shoulder on the left side of the narrow road. She pulled the car over out of a sense of homecoming: every other visit she had stayed with her family in the capital.

Once her own engine was off, she heard the sound of another motor, approaching, a pained roar as if the engine were falling apart. She made out an undertow of men's voices. Quickly, she got back into the car, locked the door, and pulled off the shoulder, hugging her right side of the road.

—Just in time too. A bus came lurching around the curve, obscuring her view with a belching of exhaust, the driver saluting or warning with a series of blasts on his horn. It was an old army bus, the official name brushed over with paint that didn't quite match the regulation gray. The passengers saw her only at the last moment, and all up and down her side of the bus, men poked out of the windows, hooting and yelling, waving purple party flags, holding out bottles and beckoning to her. She speeded up and left them behind, the small compact climbing easily up the snakey highway, its well-oiled hum a gratifying sound after the hullabaloo of the bus.

She tried the radio again, but all she could tune to was static even here on the summit hills. She would have to wait until she got to the coast to hear news of the hunger march in the capital. Her family had been worried that trouble would break out, for the march had been scheduled on the anniversary of the failed revolution nineteen years ago today. A huge turnout was expected. She bet that bus she had just passed had been delayed by breakdowns on its way to the capital. In fact, earlier on the road when she had first set out, Yolanda had passed buses and truckloads of men, drinking and shouting slogans. It crossed her mind that her family had finally agreed to loan her a car because they knew she'd be far safer on the north coast than in the capital city where revolutions always broke out. **Ⓐ**

Vocabulary **lurching** (LURCH ihng) *v.*: leaning or rolling suddenly to one side.

Ⓐ **Reading Focus** **Analyzing Themes Across Genres** The selection begins with a description of the setting. What elements of the setting introduce a conflict?

The hills began to plane out into a high plateau, the road widening. Left and right, roadside stands began appearing. Yolanda slowed down and kept an eye out for guavas,[1] supposedly in season this far north. Piled high on wooden stands were fruits she hadn't seen in so many years: pinkish-yellow mangoes, and tamarind pods oozing their rich sap, and small cashew fruits strung on a rope to keep them from bruising each other. There were little brown packets of roasted cashews and bars of milk fudge wrapped in waxed paper and tied with string, the color of which told what filling was inside the bar. Strips of meat, buzzing with flies, hung from the windows of butcher stalls. An occasional display of straw hats and baskets and hammocks told that tourists sometimes did pass by here. Looking at the stores spread before her, it was hard to believe the poverty the organizers of the march kept discussing on the radio. There seemed to be plenty here to eat—except for guavas.

In the capital, her aunts had plied her with what she most craved after so many years away. "Any little *antojo*, you must tell us!" They wanted to spoil her, so she'd stay on in her nativeland before she forgot where she had come from. "What exactly does it mean, *antojo*?" Yolanda asked. Her aunts were proven right: After so many years away, their niece was losing her Spanish. **(B)**

"An *antojo*—" The aunts exchanged quizzical looks. "How to put it? An *antojo* is like a craving

> There seemed to be plenty here to eat— except for guavas.

for something you have to eat."

A cousin blew out her cheeks. "Calories."

An *antojo*, one of the older aunts continued, was a very old Spanish word from before "your United States was thought of," she added tartly. In the countryside some *campesinos*[2] still used the word to mean possession by an island spirit demanding its due.

Her island spirit certainly was a patient soul, Yolanda joked. She hadn't had her favorite *antojo*, guavas, since her last trip seven years ago. Well, on this trip, her aunts promised, Yoyo could eat guavas to her heart's content. But when the gardener was summoned, he wasn't so sure. Guavas were no longer in season, at least not in the hotter lowlands of the south. Maybe up north, the chauffeur could pick her up some on his way back from some errand. Yolanda took this opportunity to inform her aunts of her plans: she could pick the guavas herself when she went up north in a few days.

—She was going up north? By herself? A woman alone on the road! "This is not the States." Her old aunts had tried to dissuade her. "Anything can happen." When Yolanda challenged them, "What?" they came up with boogeymen stories that made her feel as if she were talking to china dolls. Haitian hougans[3] and Communist kidnappers. "And Martians?" Yolanda wanted to tease them. They had led such sheltered lives, riding from one safe place to another in their air-conditioned cars. **(C)**

She had left the fruit stands behind her and was approaching a compound very much

---

1. **guavas** (GWAH vuhz): sweet tropical fruits shaped like pears that are yellow or red in color.
2. *campesinos* (kahm puh SEE nohs): Spanish word meaning "farmers."

---

3. **hougans**: priests in the voodoo religion, which originated in Africa but is popular in Haiti.

(B) Reading Focus Analyzing Themes Across Genres What might Yolanda's loss of Spanish symbolize?

(C) Literary Focus Theme and Narrator What do you learn about Yolanda and her family from this paragraph?

like her family's in the capital. The underbrush stopped abruptly at a high concrete wall, topped with broken bottle glass. Parked at the door was a chocolate brown Mercedes. Perhaps the owners had come up to their country home for the weekend to avoid the troubles in the capital?

Just beyond the estate, Yolanda came upon a small village—ALTAMIRA in rippling letters on the corrugated tin roof of the first little house. It was a little cluster of houses on either side of the road, a good place to stretch her feet before what she'd heard was a steep and slightly (her aunts had warned "very") dangerous descent to the coast. Yolanda pulled up at a cantina,[4] the thatched roof held up by several posts. Instead of a menu, there was a yellowing, grimy poster for Palmolive soap tacked on one of the posts with a picture of a blonde woman under a spraying shower, her head thrown back in seeming ecstasy, her mouth opened in a wordless cry. ("Palmolive"? Yolanda wondered.) Yolanda felt even thirstier and grimier looking at this lathered beauty after her hot day on the road.

An old woman emerged at last from a shack behind the cabaña,[5] buttoning up a torn housedress, and followed closely by a little boy, who kept ducking behind her whenever Yolanda smiled at him. Asking him his name just drove him further into the folds of the old woman's skirt.

"You must excuse him, Doña,"[6] she apologized. "He's not used to being among people." But Yolanda knew the old woman meant, not the people in the village, but the people with money who drove through Altamira to the beaches on the coast. "Your name," the old woman repeated, as if Yolanda hadn't asked him in Spanish. The little boy mumbled at the ground. "Speak up!" the old woman scolded, but her voice betrayed pride when she spoke up for him. "This little know-nothing is José Duarte Sanchez y Mella Garcia."

Yolanda laughed. Not only were those a lot of names for such a little boy, but they certainly were momentous: the surnames of the three liberators of the country![7]

"Can I serve the Doña in any way?" the old woman asked. Yolanda gave the tree line beyond the old woman's shack a glance. "You think you might have some guavas around?"

The old woman's face scrunched up. "Guavas?" she murmured and thought to herself a second. "Why, they're all around, Doña. But I can't say as I've seen any."

"With your permission—" José Duarte had joined a group of little boys who had come out of nowhere and were milling around the car, boasting how many automobiles they had ridden in. At Yolanda's mention of guavas, he sprung forward, pointing across the road towards the summit of the western hills. "I know where there's a whole grove of them." Behind him, his little companions nodded.

"Go on, then!" His grandmother stamped her foot as if she were scatting a little animal. "Get the Doña some."

A few boys dashed across the road and disappeared up a steep path on the hillside, but before José could follow, Yolanda called him back. She wanted to go along too. The little boy looked towards his grandmother, unsure of what to think. The old woman shook her head. The Doña would get hot, her nice clothes would get all dirty. José would get the Doña as many guavas as she was wanting.

"But they taste so much better when you've picked them yourself," Yolanda's voice had an

---

4. **cantina** (kan TEE nuh): a small bar or restaurant.

5. **cabaña** (kuh BAHN yuh): a small shelter; cabin.

6. **Doña** (DOH nyuh): Spanish word meaning "Madam."

---

7. **the three liberators of the country:** Juan Pablo Duarte (1813–1876), Francisco del Rosario Sánchez (1817–1861), and Matías Ramón Mella (1816–1864) freed the Dominican Republic from Haiti in 1844.

edge, for suddenly, it was as if the old woman had turned into the long arm of her family, keeping her away from seeing her country on her own.

The few boys who had stayed behind with José had congregated around the car. Each one claimed to be guarding it for the Doña. It occurred to Yolanda that there was a way to make this a treat all the way around. "What do you say we take the car?"

"*Si, Si, Si,*" the little boys screamed in a riot of excitement.

The old woman hushed them but agreed that was not a bad idea if the Doña insisted on going. There was a dirt road up ahead she could follow a ways and then cross over onto the road that was paved all the way to the coffee barns. The old woman pointed south in the direction of the big house. Many workers took that short cut to work.

They piled into the car, half a dozen little boys in the back, and José as co-pilot in the passenger seat beside Yolanda. They turned onto a bumpy road off the highway, which got bumpier and bumpier, and climbed up into wilder, more desolate country. Branches scraped the sides and pebbles pelted the underside of the car. Yolanda wanted to turn back, but there was no room to maneuver the car around. Finally, with a great snapping of twigs and thrashing of branches across the windshield, as if the countryside were loath to release them, the car burst forth onto smooth pavement and the light of day. On either side of the road were groves of guava trees. Among them, the boys who had gone ahead on foot were already pulling down branches and shaking loose a rain of guavas. The fruit was definitely in season.

For the next hour or so, Yolanda and her crew scavenged the grove, the best of the pick going into the beach basket Yolanda had gotten

Local Painting, Dominican Republic.

out of the trunk, with the exception of the ones she ate right on the spot, relishing the slightly bumpy feel of the skin in her hand, devouring the crunchy, sweet, white meat. The boys watched her, surprised by her odd hunger. **D**

Yolanda and José, partners, wandered far from the path that cut through the grove. Soon they were bent double to avoid getting entangled in the thick canopy of branches overhead. Each addition to the basket caused a spill from the stash already piled high above the brim. Finally, it was a case of abandoning the treasure in order to cart some of it home. With José hugging the basket to himself and Yolanda parting the wayward branches in front of them, they headed back towards the car.

When they finally cleared the thicket of guava branches, the sun was low on the western horizon. There was no sign of the other boys. "They must have gone to round up the goats," José observed.

D **Literary Focus** **Theme and Narrator** What does the reference to Yolanda's hunger as "odd" suggest about the story's theme?

Vocabulary **devouring** (dih VOWR ihng) *v.*: eating hungrily.

Yolanda glanced at her watch: it was past six o'clock. She'd never make the north coast by nightfall, but at least she could get off the dangerous mountain roads while it was still light. She hurried José back to the car, where they found a heap of guavas the other boys had left behind on the shoulder of the road. Enough guavas to appease even the greediest island spirit for life!

They packed the guavas in the trunk quickly and climbed in, but the car had not gone a foot before it lurched forward with a horrible hobble. Yolanda closed her eyes and laid her head down on the wheel, then glanced over at José. The way his eyes were searching the inside of the car for a clue as to what could have happened, she could tell he didn't know how to change a flat tire either.

It was no use regretting having brought the car up that bad stretch of road. The thing to do now was act quickly. Soon the sun would set and night would fall swiftly, no lingering dusk as in the States. She explained to José that they had a flat tire and had to hike back to town and send for help down the road to the big house. Whoever tended to the brown Mercedes would know how to change the tire on her car.

"With your permission," José offered meekly. He pointed down the paved road. "This goes directly to the big house." The Doña could just wait in the car and he would be back in no time with someone from the Miranda place.

She did not like the idea of staying behind in the car, but José could probably go and come back much quicker without her. "All right," she said to the boy. "I'll tell you what." She pointed to her watch. It was almost six thirty. "If you're back by the time this hand is over here, I'll give you"—she held up one finger—"a dollar." The boy's mouth fell open. In no time, he had shot out of his side of the car and was headed at a run toward the Miranda place. Yolanda climbed out as well and walked down a pace, until the boy had disappeared in one of the turnings of the road.

Suddenly, the countryside was so very quiet. She looked up at the purple sky. A breeze was blowing through the grove, rustling the leaves, so they whispered like voices, something indistinct. Here and there a light flickered on the hills, a *campesino* living out his solitary life. This was what she had been missing without really knowing that she was missing it all these years. She had never felt at home in the States, never, though she knew she was lucky to have a job, so she could afford her own life and not be run by her family. But independence didn't have to be exile. She could come home, home to places like these very hills, and live here on her own terms. **Ⓔ**

Heading back to the car, Yolanda stopped. She had heard footsteps in the grove. Could José be back already? Branches were being thrust aside, twigs snapped. Suddenly, a short, dark man, and then a slender, light-skin man emerged from a footpath on the opposite side of the grove from the one she and José had scavenged. They wore ragged work clothes stained with patches of sweat; their faces were drawn and tired. Yolanda's glance fell on the machetes that hung from their belts.

The men's faces snapped awake from their stupor at the sight of her. They looked beyond her at the car. "Yours?" the darker man spoke first. It struck her, even then, as an absurd question. Who else's would it be here in the middle of nowhere?

"Is there some problem?" the darker man spoke up again. The taller one was looking her

---

Ⓔ **Reading Focus** **Analyzing Themes Across Genres** What might the details in this passage reveal about the selection's theme?

up and down with interest. They were now both in front of her on the road, blocking her escape. Both—she had looked them up and down as well—were strong and quite capable of catching her if she made a run for the Mirandas'. Not that she could have moved, for her legs seemed suddenly to have been hammered into the ground beneath her. She thought of explaining that she was just out for a drive before dinner at the big house, so that these men would think someone knew where she was, someone would come looking for her if they tried to carry her off. But she found she could not speak. Her tongue felt as if it'd been stuffed in her mouth like a rag to keep her quiet.

The two men exchanged a look—it seemed to Yolanda of collusion. Then the shorter, darker one spoke up again, "Señorita, are you all right?" He peered at her. The darkness of his complexion in the growing darkness of the evening made it difficult to distinguish an expression. He was a short man, no taller than Yolanda, but he gave the impression of being quite large, for he was broad and solid, like something not yet completely carved out of a piece of wood. His companion was slim and tall and of a rich honey-brown color which matched his honey-brown eyes. Anywhere else, Yolanda would have found him extremely attractive, but here on a lonely road, with the sky growing darker by seconds, his good looks seemed dangerous, a lure to catch her off her guard.

"Can we help you?" the shorter man repeated.

The handsome one smiled knowingly. Two long, deep dimples appeared like gashes on either side of his mouth. "*Americana*," he said to the darker man in Spanish, pointing to the car. "She doesn't understand."

The darker man narrowed his eyes and studied Yolanda a moment. "*Americana*?" he asked her as if not quite sure what to make of her.

She had been too frightened to carry out any strategy, but now a road was opening before her. She laid her hand on her chest—she could feel her pounding heart—and nodded. Then, as if the admission itself loosened her tongue, she explained in English how it came that she was on a back road by herself, her craving for guavas, her never having learned to change a flat. The two men stared at her, uncomprehending, rendered docile by her gibberish. Strangely enough, it soothed her to hear herself speaking something they could not understand. She thought of something her teacher used to say to her when as a young immigrant girl she was learning English, "Language is power." It was her only defense now. **F**

> She had been too frightened to carry out any strategy, but now a road was opening before her.

Yolanda made the motions of pumping. The darker man looked at the other, who had shown better luck at understanding the foreign lady. But his companion shrugged, baffled as well. "I'll show you," Yolanda waved for them to follow her. And suddenly, as if after pulling and pulling at roots, she had finally managed to yank them free of the soil they had clung to, she found she could move her own feet forward to the car.

The small group stood staring at the sagging tire a moment, the two men kicking at it as if punishing it for having failed the Señorita. They squatted by the passenger's side, conversing in low tones. Yolanda led them to the rear of the car, where the men lifted the spare out of its

---

Vocabulary **collusion** (kuh LOO zhuhn) *n.*: secret agreement.

F **Reading Focus** Analyzing Themes Across Genres Why does Yolanda decide to speak English instead of Spanish?

Viewing and Interpreting What aspects of José's personality can you see in these boys?

sunken nest—then set to work, fitting the inter-locking pieces of the jack, unpacking the tools from the deeper hollows of the trunk. They laid their machetes down on the side of the road, out of the way. Yolanda turned on the headlights to help them see in the growing darkness. Above the small group, the sky was purple with twilight.

There was a problem with the jack. It squeaked and labored, but the car would not rise. The shorter man squirmed his way underneath and placed the mechanism deeper under the bowels of the car. There, he pumped vigorously, his friend bracing him by holding him down by the ankles. Slowly, the car rose until the wheel hung suspended. When the man came out from under the car, his hand was bloody where his knuckles had scraped against the pavement.

Yolanda pointed to the man's hand. She had been sure that if any blood were going to be spilled tonight, it would be hers. She offered him the towel she kept draped on her car seat to absorb her perspiration. But he waved it away and sucked his knuckles to make the bleeding stop.

Once the flat had been replaced with the spare, the two men lifted the deflated tire into the trunk and put away the tools. They handed Yolanda her keys. There was still no sign of José and the Mirandas. Yolanda was relieved. As she had waited, watching the two men hard at work, she had begun to dread the boy's return with help. The two men would realize she spoke Spanish. It was too late to admit that she had tricked them, to explain she had done so only because she had thought her survival was on the line. The least she could do now was to try and repay them, handsomely, for their trouble.

"I'd like to give you something," she began reaching for the purse she'd retrieved from the trunk. The English words sounded hollow on her tongue. She rolled up a couple of American bills and offered them to the men. The shorter man held up his hand. Yolanda could see where the

Vocabulary **vigorously** (VIHG uhr uhs lee) *adv.:* in a strong, active, forceful way.

282 Unit 1 • Collection 3

blood had dried dark streaks on his palm. "No, no, Señorita. *Nuestro plaçer.*" Our pleasure.

Yolanda turned to the taller one, who had struck her as more pliant than his sterner companion. "Please," she urged the bills on him. But he too looked down at the ground with the bashfulness she had observed in José of country people not wanting to offend. She felt the poverty of her response and stuffed the bills quickly in his pocket. **G**

The two men picked up their machetes and raised them to their shoulders like soldiers their guns. The tall man motioned towards the big house. "*Directo, directo,*" he enunciated the words carefully. Yolanda looked in the direction of his hand. In the faint light of what was left of day, she could barely make out the road ahead. It was as if the guava grove had overgrown into the road and woven its mat of branches so securely and tightly in all directions, she would not be able to escape.

But finally, she was off! While the two men waited a moment on the shoulder to see if the tire would hold, Yolanda drove a few yards, poking her head out the window before speeding up. "*Gracias!*" she called, and they waved, appreciatively, at the foreign lady making an effort in their native tongue. When she looked for them in her rear-view mirror, the two men had disappeared into the darkness of the guava grove. **H**

Just ahead, her lights described the figure of a small boy: José was walking alone, listlessly, as if he did not particularly want to get to where he was going.

Yolanda leaned over and opened the door for him. The small overhead light came on; she saw that the boy's face was streaked with tears.

"Why, what's wrong, José?"

The boy swallowed hard. "They would not come. They didn't believe me." He took little breaths between words to keep his tears at bay. He had lost his chance at a whole dollar. "And the guard, he said if I didn't stop telling stories, he was going to whip me."

"What did you tell him, José?"

"I told him you had broken your car and you needed help fixing it."

She should have gone along with José to the Mirandas.' Given all the trouble in the country, they would be suspicious of a boy coming to their door at nightfall with some story about a lady on a back road with a broken car. "Don't you worry, José," Yolanda patted the boy. She could feel the bony shoulder through the thin fabric of his worn shirt. "You can still have your dollar. You did your part."

But the shame of being suspected of lying seemed to have obscured any immediate pleasure he might feel in her offer. Yolanda tried to distract him by asking what he would buy with his money, what he most craved, thinking that on a subsequent trip, she might bring him his little *antojo.* But José Duarte Sanchez y Mella said nothing, except a bashful thank you when she let him off at the cantina with his promised dollar. In the glow of the headlights, Yolanda made out the figure of the old woman in the black square of her doorway, waving good-bye. Above the picnic table on a near post, the Palmolive woman's skin shone; her head was thrown back, her mouth opened as if she were calling someone over a great distance.

G **Literary Focus** Theme and Narrator Why does Yolanda feel "poverty" in her response?

H **Reading Focus** Analyzing Themes Across Genres Why does the narrator refer to Yolanda as the "foreign lady"?

Applying Your Skills

OH RA.L.10.4 Interpret universal themes across different works by the same author or by different authors. **RA.L.10.8** Analyze the auithor's use of point of view, mood and tone. **RA.L.10.9** Explain how authors use symbols to create broader meanings. *Also covered* RP.10.1; VO.10.3

Antojos

Respond and Think Critically

Reading Focus

Quick Check

1. In what way is Yolanda different from her aunts? How do they <u>perceive</u> their differences?
2. How does Yolanda interact with José and the two men?

Read with a Purpose

3. How does the search for the guavas reflect Yolanda's personal struggle?

Reading Skills: Analyzing Themes

4. While reading "Antojos," you kept notes about details that you have already encountered in the other selections by Alvarez. Look back at your diagram, and highlight the details that you think are important clues to the themes in Alvarez's work.

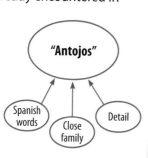

✔ Vocabulary Check

Answer *true* or *false* for each of the following statements, and briefly explain your answer.

5. Someone who is **lurching** is standing up straight.
6. Someone who is **devouring** something is very hungry.
7. If two people are in **collusion,** they have an agreement.
8. If someone shakes something **vigorously,** he or she is using a lot of force.

Literary Focus

Literary Analysis

9. **Draw Conclusions** Why does Alvarez prominently feature guavas in this story? What do they represent to Yolanda?
10. **Interpret** Why do you think Alvarez chose to title this story "Antojos," or "cravings"?

Literary Skills: Theme and Narrator

11. **Synthesize** Yolanda expects to feel intimacy when she returns to her native country. Instead, she feels disconnected. How does this experience relate to the theme of the story?
12. **Analyze** Why do you think Alvarez chose to use the third-person-limited point of view in this story? How might the story have been different had she chosen to write from a different point of view?

Literary Skills Review: Symbol

13. **Draw Conclusions** A **symbol** is a person, place, or thing that has meaning of its own but stands for something else as well. One image in this story is the Palmolive sign in Altamira. What do you think it symbolizes? Explain.

Writing Focus

Think as a Reader/Writer

Use It in Your Writing Think of a place that has shaped the way you look at the world. Write two paragraphs that describe this setting. As you write, think about figurative language, the pattern of your sentences, and the words you choose—in short, your style.

OH **RA.L.10.11** Explain ways in which an author develops a point of view and style, and cite specific examples from the text. **VO.10.6** Determine the meanings and pronunciations of unknown words by using dictionaries, glossaries, technology and textual features, such as definitional footnotes or sidebars. *Also covered* **WA.10.2**

Author Study: Julia Alvarez

Writing Focus

Write an Essay

Use It In Your Writing Alvarez's writing reflects her cultural background and is filled with references to her native language. Her fiction, nonfiction, and poetry all incorporate colorful images, dramatic sights and sounds, and vibrant emotions.

Write an essay in which you analyze Alvarez's style. Think about what type of narrator she uses in each genre and how the choice of narrator affects your response to the characters and settings. You might also consider how Alvarez uses the following to create such vivid details in these selections:

- figurative language, including metaphors
- sensory images
- word choice, including Spanish words
- sentence structure

Begin with an introductory paragraph in which you introduce your topic and general thoughts on it. In the body of your essay, state your ideas and support them by citing details from the texts. Finally, conclude your essay by explaining the effect of these devices on your reading. How does Alvarez's style contribute to her overall purpose? Proofread your final draft to correct errors in grammar, spelling, and punctuation.

What Do You Think Now

What struggles does someone face when trying to adjust to a new culture and language? What has to be left behind?

CHOICES

As you respond to the Choices, use the **Academic Vocabulary** words as appropriate: complex, correspond, perceive, and incorporate.

REVIEW
Analyze a Group of Works

Timed ∟Writing Now that you have read four works by Alvarez, make a list of the ways in which her personal experiences have informed the poems and short story you have read. Give examples from the biographical information provided, the essay, and the selections to support your ideas.

CONNECT
Analyze Universal Themes

Alvarez's work focuses on Latino culture and language, but it also contains universal themes about home and identity. Write an essay in which you analyze the themes in Alvarez's works. Begin by determining the theme in each piece. Then, explore how this theme changes from one selection to the next and, to conclude, write a statement of the works' universal theme.

EXTEND
Extend a Metaphor

Re-read the poem "Exile," and pay close attention to the way in which Alvarez develops the extended metaphor. Next, think of a subject that has special meaning for you. It could be a person, a hobby, an abstract idea such as loyalty, or another subject of your choosing. Think of something to which you can compare your subject and write a poem that contains an extended metaphor. Your metaphor should extend through at least three stanzas.

Analyzing Audience and Purpose

CONTENTS

What Do You Think? How do people from different cultures learn to live together?

QuickWrite

Think about the people you know in school or in your neighborhood who have diverse backgrounds and beliefs. Write a few sentences explaining how cultural differences can enrich a community.

Islam in America

RA.I.10.1 Identify and understand organizational patterns and techniques, including repetition of ideas, syntax and word choice, that authors use to accomplish their purpose and reach their intended audience.

Reader/Writer Notebook

Use your **RWN** to complete the activities for this selection.

Informational Text Focus

Analyzing Audience and Purpose Every writer begins with a **purpose**—a reason for writing a particular text. He or she may want to tell a story, provide information, make an argument for a change in thought or action, or express personal feelings. Of course, writers don't work in a vacuum; they intend to reach a specific audience. Writers often adopt a particular tone to help communicate ideas to their readers. **Tone,** which is a writer's attitude toward a topic, is conveyed through word choice. As you read, use the questions below to help you identify the writer's intended audience:

- What does the author assume readers know about the topic? Is the text written for people who know very little about the topic or for those who already have some knowledge?
- What is the tone of the text? That is, what attitude does the writer have toward the subject or toward the audience?
- Who would be interested in reading this text?

Into Action As you read, use a chart like the one below to answer questions about the intended audience.

What does the author assume about readers' knowledge?	
What is the author's attitude toward the subject?	
What is the author's attitude toward readers?	
Who would be interested in this topic?	

Vocabulary

affiliations (uh fihl ee AY shuhnz) *n.*: connections; relationships. *People form affiliations with religious, social, and cultural groups.*

integration (ihn tuh GRAY shuhn) *n.*: the process of combining or including. *The integration of diverse groups into one society can be a difficult process.*

misperceptions (mihs puhr SEHP shuhnz) *n.*: incorrect ideas or understandings. *Many people have misperceptions of Muslim beliefs and practices.*

prohibits (proh HIHB ihts) *v.*: forbids; prevents. *Some people believe that Islamic teaching prohibits dating.*

Language Coach

Suffixes A **suffix** is a word part added to the end of another word to change that word's meaning. Three of the words on the above list contain the suffix *–tion*, which, when added to a word, signifies a new state of being. Identify the base words of these words. How does their meaning change when the suffix *–tion* is added?

Writing Focus — Preparing for **Constructed Response**

In your *Reader/Writer Notebook,* note the information that Smith presents that a non-Muslim might not know. This information might include facts about Islam or different ways that Muslims practice their faith.

Learn It Online
Do pictures and animation help you learn? Try the *PowerNotes* lesson on:

go.hrw.com	L10-287	

ISLAM ⬡⬡⬡ IN ⬡⬡⬡ AMERICA

by Patricia Smith *from* **The New York Times Upfront**

Read with a Purpose
As you read, think about the ways that we, as a society, define what it means to be American.

Build Background
In 1965, President Lyndon B. Johnson signed an immigration bill that made it easier for people to immigrate to the United States based on their skills rather than their country of origin. This led to a surge in immigration from Middle Eastern countries. In his remarks at the signing of this immigration bill on October 3, 1965, Johnson said, "Our beautiful America was built by a nation of strangers . . . joining and blending in one mighty and irresistible tide."

Like most American teenagers, 17-year-old Sana Haq enjoys hanging out with her friends and going to the movies. She just got her driver's license, and she's stressing over college applications. But Sana, a high school senior from Norwood, N. J., is an observant Muslim, and that makes her different from most of her friends.

She prays five times a day, as Islam requires. She wears only modest clothing—no shorts, no bathing suits, nothing too snug. Going to the mall for a pair of jeans can turn into a week-long quest because most are too tight or low-cut to meet her definition of "decent." Ⓐ

Islam, she says, affects every aspect of her life. "If you ask me to describe myself in one word, that word would be Muslim," says Sana, who was born in the U.S. to Pakistani immigrants. "Not American, not Pakistani, not a teenager. Muslim. It's the most important thing to me."

Largely because of immigrant families like Sana's, Islam is one of the fastest growing religions in the U.S. Since the Census doesn't track religious affiliations, the number of American Muslims is hard to pin down, but estimates range from 1.5 million to 9 million.

Ⓐ **Informational Focus** Audience and Purpose Why does the author include basic information about Islam in the opening paragraphs?

Vocabulary **affiliations** (uh fihl ee AY shuhnz) *n.:* connections; relationships.

Whatever its size, the Muslim community in the U.S. is very diverse. According to a 2004 poll by Georgetown University and Zogby polling, South Asians (Indians, Pakistanis, Bangladeshis, etc.) are the largest group, followed by Arabs and African-Americans. (Starting in the 1960s, a significant number of blacks in the U.S. converted to Islam.) Thirty-six percent of American Muslims were born in the U.S.; the other 64 percent come from 80 different countries. . . . **B**

Trying to carve an American Muslim identity out of this diversity is one of the challenges facing young Muslims. "They are creating traditions and a culture that is particular to them and not imported from another majority-Muslim country," says Tayyibah Taylor, editor of *Azzizah*, a Muslim women's magazine published in Atlanta. "Something that blends their American way of thinking and their American way of living with Islamic guidelines."

B **Informational Focus** Audience and Purpose   What is the purpose of the statistical data in the article?

Contrast with Europe

As a group, American Muslims have a higher median income than Americans as a whole, and they vote in higher numbers. In addition, they are increasingly contributing to American culture, forming Muslim comedy groups, rap groups, Scout troops, magazines, and other media.

Their integration into American society and culture stands in contrast to Europe's Muslim communities, which have remained largely on the economic and political fringes. In November 2005 Muslims rioted in many French cities.

In parts of the U.S. with large Muslim populations, Islam mingles with American traditions. At Dearborn High School in Dearborn, Mich., about one third of the students—and the football team—are Muslim. Because Ramadan (the Muslim holy month that requires dawn-to-dusk fasting) coincided with football season this year, Muslim players had to wake up at 4:30 for a predawn breakfast; go through their classes without eating or drinking; and start most Friday night games before darkness allowed them to break their fasts.

"When you start your day off fasting and you get to football at the end of the day, that's the challenge," says Hassan Cheaib, a 17-year-old senior. "You know you've worked hard. You know you've been faithful . . . After fasting all day, you feel like a warrior."

Because some of Islam's social tenets—modesty and chastity, for example—are so different from American norms, they can present a challenge for young Muslims. For Sana, adherence to Islam means she doesn't date. "Dating means going out with someone and spending intimate time with them, and for me, that's not allowed," she explains. "But it's not that I don't talk to guys. I have guy friends."

Impact of 9/11

The terrorist attacks of Sept. 11, 2001, were a transformative moment for Muslims in America. On the one hand, there has been an increase in anti-Muslim feeling, discrimination, and hate crimes. On the other hand, many Muslims have responded by taking more interest in their religion and reaching out more to non-Muslims.

"September 11 exposed American Muslims for the first time to a large degree of hostility," says Ishan Bagby, a professor of Islamic Studies at the University of Kentucky. "So Muslims have come to the conclusion that isolation is a danger, because if people don't know you it's easy for them to accept the worst stereotypes."

According to one 2003 poll, 63 percent of Americans say they do not have a good understanding of Islam as a religion. Indeed, many young Muslims spend a lot of time correcting common misperceptions about Islam: that it condones terrorism (it doesn't); and that it denies women equal rights (it doesn't, though many majority-Muslim cultures and countries do). **C**

C **Informational Focus** Audience and Purpose Why do you think the author "corrects" these common misunderstandings?

Vocabulary **integration** (ihn tuh GRAY shuhn) *n.*: the process of combining or including.
misperceptions (mihs puhr SEHP shuhnz) *n.*: incorrect ideas or understandings.

Analyzing Visuals

Viewing and Interpreting
Explain why this photograph might be titled *Islam in America*.

Islamic Center of Greater Toledo, Ohio.

When Ibrahim Elshamy, 18, was growing up in Manchester, N. H., Islam was a regular part of his life. Every Friday he left school at lunch to attend services at a mosque. Now a freshman at Dartmouth College in Hanover, N. H., his religion remains important. Two days after his arrival on campus, he contacted the Muslim student group. And five times a day, he returns to his dorm room to say his prayers.

In college, Ibrahim has found for the first time a Muslim community in which he feels at home. The mosque he and his Egyptian father attended in Manchester attracted many Arab, Asian, and African immigrants. The problem with that, he says, was that people melded their cultural traditions with their practice of Islam. As an American-born Muslim, he found that frustrating.

"Here at Dartmouth, it was extremely refreshing," he says, "because I was finally around Muslims who were exactly like me in that respect."

Professor Bagby says many young Muslims want to distinguish between Islam's teachings and the cultural traditions often associated with Islam, particularly the role of women. Stressing that nothing in the Koran itself prohibits women's full participation (in religion or in life), American women are increasingly demanding not only equal participation but leadership roles in the mosque. "It's definitely rocking some boats," says Tayyibah Taylor of *Azzizah*.

"More American"

Samiyyah Ali, 17, grew up in Atlanta and describes herself as a practicing Muslim, rather than an observant one. She uses the principles of Islam to guide her but doesn't worry about following every last tenet. Like 20 percent of American Muslims, she is African-American. Her parents converted to Islam before she was born.

Other than her name, there's not much about Samiyyah that would tell a stranger she is Muslim. She's a senior at Westminster Academy, a coed private school where she's a cheerleader, on the varsity track and field team, in the dance club, and on the school newspaper staff. And she does date.

She views the Koran as something that should not be followed literally, much like other historical documents that should be understood in context. "A lot of stuff is still applicable—honor and respect is always applicable," says Samiyyah. "But other things that are cultural—even ideas about sex—need to be taken in context. Back then people got married when they were fourteen. Maybe because my family is a convert family, we're just not so orthodox." **D**

The Muslim community in America is currently undergoing a generational shift. Most American mosques were formed by first-generation immigrants, and as their American-born children take over, the norms are changing.

"Islam in America will feel a lot different in the next 40 years," Professor Bagby says. "It'll feel more American, that's for sure."

Read with a Purpose How do different cultural groups contribute to American society?

Vocabulary **prohibits** (proh HIHB ihts) *v.*: forbids; prevents.

D **Informational Focus** Audience and Purpose Why do you think the author incorporates comments from a less orthodox Muslim at this point in the article?

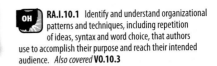

RA.I.10.1 Identify and understand organizational patterns and techniques, including repetition of ideas, syntax and word choice, that authors use to accomplish their purpose and reach their intended audience. *Also covered* **VO.10.3**

Islam in America

Practicing the Standards

Informational Text and Vocabulary

1. Who is the intended **audience** for this article?

A European Muslims

B American Muslims

C Non-Muslim Americans

D Non-Muslim Europeans

2. What is the author's **purpose** in this article?

A To inform

B To stir emotions

C To persuade

D To entertain

3. By quoting many sources, the author —

A provides a diversity of opinion and experience

B remains objective toward her subject

C shows that she doesn't understand the subject very well

D avoids expressing her own opinion

4. A person with *affiliations* —

A teaches moral lessons

B criticizes others

C practices a religion

D belongs to groups

5. *Integration* is the process of —

A connecting

B combining

C perceiving

D preventing

6. A *misperception* is —

A a confident manner

B a bad judgment

C a lack of integrity

D an incorrect view

7. When the law *prohibits* something, it —

A condones it

B forbids it

C ignores it

D legalizes it

Writing Focus   Constructed Response

What might a non-Muslim learn about Islam from this article? Make a list of three main ideas in the article. Then, give supporting details for each.

What Do You Think Now

How have many Muslims in the United States maintained their cultural identity? What challenges have they faced?

RA.L.10.5 Analyze how an author's choice of genre affects the expression of a theme or topic. *Also covered* **RA.I.10.1**

WEB ESSAY
Preparing to Read

We Are Each Other's Business

Informational Text Focus

Analyzing Audience and Purpose Authors of informational pieces often customize their information for a specific **audience** and **purpose.** For example, an author of an article on the rain forest will adjust the vocabulary and amount of technical information if the readers are children. If the same author is speaking to a group of scientists at a conference, the content, vocabulary, and length will be very different. In both situations the purpose is to inform, but the author makes adjustments for each audience.

Some informational topics have a wider public audience than others. Knowing this, the author may incorporate a broader range of examples—hoping to appeal to many readers.

Into Action Use the chart below to help you determine the author's purpose in "We Are Each Other's Business." For each category in the left-hand column, find an example from the text and place that in the right-hand column.

Information About the Author	Eboo Patel—American Muslim
Examples/anecdotes	
Direct statements by author	
Quotations	"We are each other's magnitude and bond."
Author's purpose	

Writing Focus Preparing for **Constructed Response**

As you read "We Are Each Other's Business," use your *Reader/Writer Notebook* to note ways in which Patel illustrates his ideas with references to art and literature. What point does he make about the Norman Rockwell illustration? How does he use a Gwendolyn Brooks poem to support his ideas?

Reader/Writer Notebook

Use your **RWN** to complete the activities for this selection.

Vocabulary

piety (PY uh tee) *n.:* religious devotion. *Patel believes that expressions of piety are not enough; belief must be demonstrated by a person's actions.*

bigotry (BIHG uh tree) *n.:* intolerance or prejudice. *Some students showed bigotry when they shouted anti-Semitic slurs in the hallway.*

complicity (kuhm PLIHS uh tee) *n.:* being an accomplice or partner in wrongdoing. *Patel's complicity in the actions of anti-Semitic students made him feel ashamed.*

Language Coach

Etymology The Latin word *complex* means "participant" or "associate." Which Vocabulary word, and what part of that word's definition, have the same origin? Use a dictionary to find the origin of the other words on the list.

 Learn It Online
Do pictures and animation help you learn? Try the *PowerNotes* lesson on:

go.hrw.com   L10-294   **Go**

File   Edit   View   Favorites   Tools   Help

| Back | Forward | Stop | Refresh | Home | Search | Favorites | History | Mail | Print |

Address   http://www.npr.org   ⌄   → Go

Read with a Purpose

Does pluralism mean we *tolerate* one another's differences, or *celebrate* them? Read to discover one person's answer to that question.

Build Background

Pluralism is defined as "a condition in which ethnic or other minority groups are able to maintain their identities in a society." In a pluralistic society, people retain their individual, cultural, or religious identities and still consider themselves part of the larger society—not in conflict with it.

This Web essay comes from a national media project called *This I Believe* in which National Public Radio (NPR) airs three-minute essays by individuals expressing their core values and beliefs. NPR also posts the essays on its Web site.

We Are Each Other's Business
by **Eboo Patel**

I am an American Muslim. I believe in pluralism. In the Holy Quran,[1] God tells us, "I created you into diverse nations and tribes that you may come to know one another." I believe America is humanity's best opportunity to make God's wish that we come to know one another a reality.   **A**

In my office hangs Norman Rockwell's illustration *Freedom of Worship*. A Muslim holding a Quran in his hands stands near a Catholic woman fingering her rosary. Other figures have their hands folded in prayer and their eyes filled with piety. They stand shoulder-to-shoulder facing the same direction, comfortable with the presence of one another and yet apart. It is a vivid depiction of a group living in peace with its diversity, yet not exploring it.

We live in a world where the forces that seek to divide us are strong. To overcome them, we must do more than simply stand next to one another in silence.   **B**

I attended high school in the western suburbs of Chicago. The group I ate lunch with included a Jew, a Mormon, a Hindu, a Catholic, and a Lutheran. We were all devout to a degree, but we almost never talked about religion. Somebody would announce at the table that they couldn't eat a certain kind of food, or any food at all, for a period of time. We all knew religion hovered behind this, but nobody ever offered any explanation deeper than "my mom said," and nobody ever asked for one.

---

1. **Holy Quran:** the main religious text of Islam (sometimes spelled *Koran*).

A **Informational Focus** Audience and Purpose What beliefs does the author express at the beginning of his essay? To whom might this essay appeal?

B **Informational Focus** Audience and Purpose What is the author encouraging his audience to do?

Vocabulary   **piety** (PY uh tee) *n.:* religious devotion.

A few years after we graduated, my Jewish friend from the lunchroom reminded me of an experience we both wish had never happened. A group of thugs in our high school had taken to scrawling anti-Semitic slurs on classroom desks and shouting them in the hallway.

I did not confront them. I did not comfort my Jewish friend. Instead I averted my eyes from their bigotry, and I avoided the eyes of my friend because I couldn't stand to face him.

Save Freedom of Worship (1943) by Norman Rockwell. Permission of the Norman Rockwell Family Agency.

My friend told me he feared coming to school those days, and he felt abandoned as he watched his close friends do nothing. Hearing him tell me of his suffering—and my complicity—is the single most humiliating experience of my life.

C

My friend needed more than my silent presence at the lunch table. I realize now that to believe in pluralism means I need the courage to act on it. Action is what separates a belief from an opinion. Beliefs are imprinted through actions.

In the words of the American poet Gwendolyn Brooks: "We are each other's business; we are each other's harvest; we are each other's magnitude and bond."

I cannot go back in time and take away the suffering of my Jewish friend, but through action I can prevent it from happening to others.

D

Read with a Purpose   How do you and the people you know tolerate or celebrate differences?

C **Informational Focus** Audience and Purpose Why does the author describe this humiliating experience?

D **Informational Focus** Audience and Purpose What action might the author be considering when he writes, "Through action I can prevent it from happening to others"?

Vocabulary **bigotry** (BIHG uh tree) *n.*: intolerance or prejudice.
complicity (kuhm PLIHS uh tee) *n.*: being an accomplice or partner in wrongdoing.

WEB ESSAY
Applying Your Skills

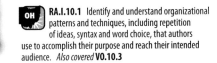

RA.I.10.1 Identify and understand organizational patterns and techniques, including repetition of ideas, syntax and word choice, that authors use to accomplish their purpose and reach their intended audience. *Also covered* **VO.10.3**

We Are Each Other's Business

Practicing the Standards

Informational Text and Vocabulary

1. What emotional response is the author trying to evoke in his audience?

   A Anger

   B Compassion

   C Trust

   D Fear

2. The author appeals to his readers' emotions by—

   A including facts and statistics

   B offering a variety of viewpoints

   C relating a personal story

   D presenting religious information

3. Which sentence *best* expresses the author's **purpose** for writing this essay?

   A "They stand shoulder-to-shoulder facing the same direction, comfortable with the presence of one another and yet apart."

   B "I realize now that to believe in pluralism means I need the courage to act on it."

   C "I am an American Muslim."

   D "We live in a world where the forces that seek to divide us are strong."

4. *Piety* refers to —

   A intolerance

   B communication

   C creative pursuits

   D religious devotion

5. A person who shows *bigotry* acts with —

   A prejudice

   B devotion

   C confidence

   D emotions

6. *Complicity* means the state of being —

   A religious

   B an accomplice

   C prejudiced

   D in charge of

Writing Focus   Constructed Response

Think about the title of this essay, "We Are Each Other's Business." How does this title illustrate Patel's idea of pluralism? Write a brief explanation using examples from the essay.

What Do You Think Now

Living in a diverse society can have rewards as well as challenges. In what ways can our diversity be beneficial?

Literary Skills Review

Narrator and Voice   **Directions:** Read the following selection. Then, read and respond to the questions that follow.

The Bear's Speech by **Julio Cortázar**
translated by **Paul Blackburn**

I'm the bear in the pipes of the house, I climb through the pipes in the hours of silence, the hot-water pipes, the radiator pipes, the air-conditioning ducts. I go through the pipes from apartment to apartment and I am the bear who goes through the pipes.

I think that they like me because it's my hair that keeps the conduits clean, I run unceasingly through the tubes and nothing pleases me more than slipping through the pipes, running from floor to floor. Once in a while I stick my paw out through a faucet and the girl on the third floor screams that she's scalded herself, or I growl at oven height on the second, and Wilhelmina the cook complains that the chimney is drawing badly. At night I go quietly and it's when I'm moving most quickly that I raise myself to the roof by the chimney to see if the moon is dancing up there, and I let myself slide down like the wind to the boilers in the cellar. And in summer I swim at night in the cistern, prickled all over with stars, I wash my face first with one paw then with the other, finally with both together, and that gives me a great joy.

Then I slide back down through the pipes of the house, growling happily, and the married couples stir in their beds and deplore the quality of the installation of the pipes. Some even put on the light and write a note to themselves to be sure to remember to complain when they see the superintendent. I look for the tap that's always running in some apartment and I stick my nose out and look into the darkness of rooms where those beings who cannot walk through the pipes live, and I'm always a little sorry for them, heavy beings, big ones, to hear how they snore and dream aloud and are so very much alone. When they wash their faces in the morning, I caress their cheeks and lick their noses and I leave, somewhat sure of having done some good.

1. Who is the narrator of this story?
   A. the superintendent of the building
   B. Wilhelmina the cook
   C. a girl living on the third floor
   D. a bear who travels through pipes

2. What type of narrator does this story have?
   A. first person
   B. second person
   C. third-person limited
   D. omniscient

3. How do the residents of the house interpret the bear's activities?
   A. They think the pipes are faulty.
   B. They know there is a bear in the pipes.
   C. They worry that the bear will hurt them.
   D. They think the pipes are well maintained.

4. Which of the following does not contribute to the author's voice?
   A. humor
   B. long sentences
   C. tone
   D. suspense

5. Why does the bear feel sorry for people?
   A. because their taps leak
   B. because they are not married
   C. because they have to write notes
   D. because they are alone

6. What does the bear not do in the story?
   A. keep the pipes clean
   B. growl
   C. look in on people
   D. talk to the people in the house

7. If the story were told by Wilhelmina, what kind of narrator would it have?
   A. first person
   B. second person
   C. third-person limited
   D. omniscient

Short Answer
8. Describe the author's tone. Cite two examples from the passage to support your description.

Extended Response
9. List five words you would normally use to describe a bear. Then, list five words you would use to describe the bear in this story. Write a paragraph explaining how and why your lists are different.

Informational Skills Review

Audience and Purpose **Directions:** Read the following selection. Then, read and respond to the questions that follow.

Larger Than Life by **Sebastian Junger**

The caption identified the man as Scott Fischer, leader of one of the disastrous expeditions on Everest in 1996, but no matter how long I stared at the photo, I couldn't tell if it was the Fischer I knew. This man had long hair and a three-week mountain beard; my Fischer had been a National Outdoor Leadership School (NOLS) instructor in the summer of 1976 and—at least in my memory—was clean-shaven and close-cropped. He was also just about everything a 14-year-old boy would want to be: strong, handsome, well liked, and outrageously confident. Not only did my old NOLS instructor bear no resemblance to the man in the photo, but it was inconceivable that the Scott Fischer I knew could have died on Everest. To me, he was simply too good at climbing—at everything—to die. I put the magazine back in the rack and walked away.

A year later I was on a flight from L.A. to New York, reading furiously through Jon Krakauer's account of the Everest tragedy, *Into Thin Air.* Fischer was from New Jersey, I read, and had worked for years as a guide and instructor. He took insane risks on climbs and should have died years ago. He left a string of broken hearts a mile long in his wake. I closed the book and looked out the airplane window. We were flying at roughly the height of Mount Everest. It was the same guy, all right, and he was dead.

My earliest memory of Scott is from a rest break on my first day at NOLS in Wyoming. We were struggling up the flanks of the Wind River Range under a cold rain, and I asked if it always rained like this out West. I'd never been past Ohio and just wanted to know whether this was what the rest of the trip would be like. Scott threw his head back and laughed. "No, it almost never rains in July," he said. "In fact I've never even seen it like this."

He was right; we spent the next 30 days drenched in western sun. There were 12 students in our group and three instructors, all first-rate climbers, but Scott was clearly the one to study. At 20, he wasn't that much older than the rest of us, but he gave the impression that he could do absolutely anything. One day, one of the three female students sprained her ankle and he took her pack, 60 pounds on top of the 80 he was already carrying. He walked all day with it, uphill, downhill, across streams, over scree, at a steady hammering pace that even the other instructors had trouble keeping up with. Most days he walked with large stones in his hands, which he lifted like barbells at each step. It was to keep himself in shape for climbing. The boys either admired him, as I did, or dismissed him as a show-off. The girls just stared. . . .

Scott was one of the few instructors who led back-to-back trips, and whatever pleasures awaited him in town, it was clear that

RA.I.10.1 Identify and understand organizational patterns and techniques, including repetition of ideas, syntax and word choice, that authors use to accomplish their purpose and reach their intended audience.

the mountains were his main priority. He intended to become the best climber in the world and had no problem saying so. At the end of a day of hiking, as people straggled into camp, Scott would find some obscenely difficult bouldering problem and work on it until dark. Every so often, if we were camped near some cliffs, I would look up to see Scott far above me, unroped, climbing some offset crack. He climbed slowly and deliberately and with tremendous strength. He climbed in a way that almost made you feel sorry for the rock. He climbed as if he couldn't fall.

He had fallen, of course—only once, according to him—and the story became legend in our small group. A few years earlier another climber had set up a faulty anchor, and Scott clipped in for a rappel without checking the rope. He stepped to the edge of the cliff, leaned back, and fell. He dropped 150 feet, rotating slowly, and landed in a sitting position in an angled snowbank. It was the only position he could have landed in and survived. He regained consciousness days later, in a hospital bed. He'd shattered his pelvis and broken numerous other bones, but he was alive. He had no memory of the climb, or the fall, or the evacuation. As far as Scott was concerned, one moment he was in the mountains, the next moment he was in bed.

I was the youngest in the group, and in some ways the trip was one long, homesick, forced march. But whenever I began to lose heart, there was always Scott to emulate. On hikes—when not lifting rocks—he would hook his thumbs under the shoulder straps of his pack, and I started doing that, too, because it made me feel like I could walk as fast as he did. On steep snow Scott had a slow, methodical way of kicking steps into the incline that made an ascent look easy, almost inviting; I copied it as best I could. He did little to conceal his impatience with the slower, clumsier students, and I desperately tried to set myself apart from them. "We split into three groups and hiked four and a half miles with packs, uphill to a new camp place on Twin Lakes," I wrote in my journal on July 25, 1976. "I was the leader [of my group] and personally I think I did real well, and so did Scott."

I was trying to impress him, but I was also trying to learn something that I could bring home with me. I was a hopelessly solitary kid, and I saw in Scott some kind of salvation from the insecurities that battered me back home. Practically everything he did, the way he climbed, the way he walked, even the way he stood oozed a blithe confidence, and for years I used it all as a model for what I wanted to be. It was an image mostly untarnished by reality and made uncomplicated by the passage of time. The only flaw that I acknowledged in him—a fearlessness so extreme that it seemed close to a death pact with the mountains—was too disconcerting to deal with. I just wrote it off as something I would understand when I got older.

"Scott is the lead instructor, he's blond, looks like Robert Redford except his nose is too big, and he's real strong," I wrote in my

Informational Skills Review

OH **RA.I.10.1** Identify and understand organizational patterns and techniques, including repetition of ideas, syntax and word choice, that authors use to accomplish their purpose and reach their intended audience.

CONTINUED

journal another day. "The only thing I don't like about him is that at times he isn't really concerned with your safety, like when we crossed the Popo Agie River. He lets things go unheeded."

The crossing of the Popo Agie, a chest-deep torrent that we encountered a week into our trip, was a debacle from the start. Scott went across first, setting up a grab-line from one bank to the other, and then the rest of us followed. Within half an hour one girl slipped and almost drowned under her pack, another girl was washed downstream and had to be saved by an instructor, and one of the boys dislocated his shoulder. It frightened everybody—instructors included—except Scott. If anything, he seemed puzzled that people could get in trouble in such a mundane way. Crossing a river? It didn't even register on his scale of challenges. At age 20 he seemed in a desperate hurry to get to his future, and accidents just slowed him down.

Our course lasted 30 days, and the last four were called "survival." We finished off our food, and the instructors had us split into three groups and prepared us to fend for ourselves on a long, famished trek out of the mountains. We had fishing poles and a rudimentary knowledge of wild plants to sustain us, but basically we just went hungry. Mark and Tom—the other two instructors—were to join us at the trailhead, but Scott was going back into the high peaks to meet another NOLS group. He said good-bye to us, shouldered his pack, and headed off up the trail. He had his thumbs hooked under his shoulder straps, as usual, and he never looked back around. I never saw him again.

1. What is the purpose of including the incident at Popo Agie in the selection?
   A. to emphasize Scott's disregard for safety
   B. to show readers that Scott wasn't a good leader
   C. to explain why Scott was not easily frightened
   D. to highlight Scott's survival expertise

2. To which audience might this selection most likely appeal?
   A. photographers
   B. mountain climbers
   C. science teachers
   D. members of sports teams

Short Answer

3. Describe the author's tone in the opening two paragraphs. Cite two examples from the passage to support your description.

Extended Response

4. The author chooses to open with the revelation that Scott Fischer is dead. Write a short paragraph describing the effect this has on the reader and how the effect would have been different if this fact were revealed at the end of the story instead.

Vocabulary Skills Review

OH V0.10.1 Define unknown words through context clues and the author's use of comparison, contrast and cause and effect.

Context Clues

Directions: Use context clues from the sentences to respond to each question.

1. In "Evacuation Order No. 19," Junior's letters to his wife are censored because he is considered an "enemy alien."

   In this sentence, censored means

   A. gratifying.

   B. available.

   C. applauded.

   D. restricted.

2. During the war, the government imposed rationing because there was a limited supply of some goods.

   In this sentence, rationing means

   A. abundance .

   B. limits on the amount each person can have.

   C. lower prices.

   D. feasting.

3. In "Housepainting," Annie's parents are exasperated by Frances's reluctance to marry.

   In this sentence, exasperated means

   A. scared.

   B. excited.

   C. annoyed.

   D. delighted .

4. Wei stares at Frances and seems to be transfixed by her beauty.

   In this sentence, transfixed means

   A. mesmerized.

   B. bored.

   C. aggravated.

   D. bothered.

5. Frances is infuriated when Wei begins to paint the house yellow, so she starts to paint it blue again.

   In this sentence, infuriated means

   A. sleepy.

   B. angered.

   C. hesitant.

   D. excited.

6. In "The Storyteller," the children's persistent questions begin to irritate the bachelor.

   In this sentence, persistent means

   A. pleasant.

   B. insightful.

   C. frequent.

   D. respectful.

Academic Vocabulary

Directions: Use context clues from the sentence to respond to the question.

7. It was a hot afternoon, so the air inside the train car was correspondingly humid.

   In this passage, correspondingly means

   A. refreshingly.

   B. comfortably.

   C. similarly.

   D. pleasingly.

Read On

FICTION
The Complete Saki

What do you do when you're fed up with society? You play practical jokes, of course! Reginald and Clovis are two rebellious young men who stir up plenty of mischief at the expense of their polite and pompous relatives and neighbors. These are just two of the outrageous characters that can be found in Saki's collected writings, *The Complete Saki,* which are full of satire, wit, dark humor, and surprise endings.

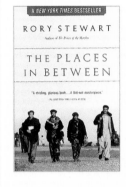

NONFICTION
The Places in Between

In January 2002, Rory Stewart walked across Aghanistan, surviving by his wits, his knowledge of Persian dialects and Muslim customs, and the kindness of strangers. By day he walked through moutains covered in snow, hamlets burned by the Taliban, and communities thriving amid the remains of medieval civilizations. By night, he slept on villagers' floors, shared their meals, and listened to their stories. *The Places in Between,* is a touching and surprising look at the encounters Stewart faced on his journey.

NONFICTION
Hiroshima

August 6, 1945. The United States dropped the first atomic bomb on Hiroshima, Japan, and more than half of the city's population perished. How did the rest survive? In 1946, John Hersey visited Hiroshima and interviewed people who suddenly had to face terror, confusion, illness, and isolation. The product of that visit is this detailed, compelling narrative that takes us into the minds of six people who relied on wits and luck to survive that terrible day.

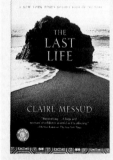

FICTION
The Last Life

Narrated by a fifteen-year-old girl with a ruthless regard for the truth, this beautifully told novel of lies and ghosts, love and honor, is set in colonial Algeria, the south of France, and New England. It is the tale of the LaBasse family, whose world begins to crumble when long-hidden shame emerges. In *The Last Life,* Claire Messud skillfully and inexorably describes how the stories we tell ourselves, and the lies to which we cling, can turn on us in a moment.

NONFICTION
Swimming to Antarctica

By the age of sixteen, Lynne Cox had broken all records for swimming the English Channel. Her daring sense of adventure led her to the Bering Strait, where she swam in thirty-eight-degree water in just a swimsuit, cap, and goggles. She also was the first to swim the Strait of Magellan, narrowly escaped sharks off the Cape of Good Hope, and was cheered across the Cook Strait by dolphins. *Swimming to Antarctica* chronicles her adventures.

FICTION
Watership Down

When land developers begin to dig up the English country-side, they have no idea that their labor means life or death for a band of talking rabbits. Led by brave Hazel, eleven of the rabbits set off on a dangerous journey battling illness, injuries, and evil animals in search of a new place to live. If you're in the mood for an action-packed fantasy, one that also serves as a rich allegorical tale of human beings and nature, then Richard Adams's book is for you.

FICTION
El Bronx Remembered

Growing up isn't easy in these bittersweet stories of Puerto Rican immigrants. Nicholasa Mohr shows us life's little ironies: the pet chicken in the kitchen that refuses to lay eggs; graduating with honors but having to wear your uncle's orange shoes to the ceremony; realizing that your friend looks better dead than when he was alive, and discovering once again that the perfect boyfriend is, as usual, imperfect.

NONFICTION
Barrio Boy

Ernesto Galarza, a teacher and political activist, is probably best known for his autobiography *Barrio Boy*. Galarza first describes his early boyhood in western Mexico, a beautiful rural setting rich in song, folklore, and customs. Then the Mexican Revolution begins, and Galarza's family flees to a very different place: a barrio in Sacramento, California. He tells the story of a family caught between their heritage and their adopted land.

Learn It Online
Master your knowledge with *NovelWise*:

go.hrw.com | L10-305 | Go

Symbolism and Irony

INFORMATIONAL TEXT FOCUS

Synthesizing Sources: Using Primary and Secondary Sources

"It is our choices that show what we truly are, far more than our abilities."

—**J. K. Rowling**

What Do You Think

What do our choices reveal about who we really are?

Detail from *Backgammon* (2002) by Jeffrey Gold. Courtesy of the artist and Forum Gallery, New York.

Literary Focus

by **Carol Jago**

How Do Symbolism and Irony Help Writers Tell Stories?

Good stories not only entertain us—they also give us insight into common human experiences. Like life itself, good stories contain surprises and uncertainties. They also hint at a deeper meaning below the surface of events. How do storytellers express the meaning behind ordinary things and events? How do they challenge our expectations?

Symbolism

Writers use **symbols** to invest objects, events, settings, animals, or people with deeper connections and associations. In a story a symbol can be a setting, character, object, name, or anything that has a literal meaning while also suggesting a deeper meaning. In "Through the Tunnel," Doris Lessing has created two settings: a crowded beach and a rocky bay. It is not long before we begin to suspect that the settings have more than a literal meaning.

> Going to the shore on the first morning of the vacation, the young English boy stopped at a turning of the path and looked down at a wild and rocky bay and then over to the crowded beach he knew so well from other years.
>
> from "Through the Tunnel"
> by Doris Lessing

Use a checklist like the one below to analyze possible symbols in a story.

Is _____ a symbol for something else?
✓ Is it an object? a character or an animal? an idea?
✓ Does it appear throughout the story?
✓ Could it stand for some idea or emotion beyond its literal meaning?

Allegory

An **allegory** is a type of story in which all the characters symbolize certain vices and virtues. Two examples of allegories are **fables,** which use animal characters to teach practical lessons, and **parables,** which use everyday situations to teach lessons about ethics or morality. Characters in an allegory might even have names that describe what they symbolize, such as Pilgrim or Ignorance.

Irony

We recognize **irony** when someone says one thing but means the opposite and when a situation or a person turns out to be the opposite of what we expect. If a story is totally predictable, it isn't true to life. Writers use irony to create uncertainty and sometimes even shock. There are three basic types of irony: verbal, situational, and dramatic.

Verbal Irony If you've ever said, "I'm just *thrilled* there's a test today," you were using verbal irony. **Verbal irony** occurs when someone *says* one thing but *means* the opposite, as in this passage from Shirley Jackson's story "The Possibility of Evil":

RA.L.10.7 Recognize how irony is used in a literary text. **RA.L.10.9** Explain how authors use symbols to create broader meanings.

> "I suppose you've got young Don all upset about the fact that his daughter is already six months old and hasn't yet begun to learn to dance?"
>
> from "The Possibility of Evil" by Shirley Jackson

Of course *no* six-month-old baby should be expected to dance! Here, Miss Strangeworth is using verbal irony to comment on an anxious mother's fretfulness. What she says and what she means are very different things.

Situational Irony **Situational irony** describes an occurrence that is not just surprising; it is the *opposite* of what we expected. The situation seems to mock human intentions and the confidence with which we plan our futures. In the following passage from "A Very Old Man with Enormous Wings," a couple examines a winged man who has fallen into their backyard:

> He was dressed like a ragpicker. There were only a few faded hairs left on his bald skull and very few teeth in his mouth, and his pitiful condition of a drenched great grandfather had taken away any sense of grandeur he might have had. His huge buzzard wings, dirty and half plucked, were forever entangled in the mud. They . . . called in a neighbor woman who knew everything about life and death. . . .
>   "He's an angel," she told them.
>
> from "A Very Old Man with Enormous Wings" by Gabriel García Márquez

We might expect the couple to think that the old man is a fraud, but we would not expect such a bedraggled, winged old man to be called an angel.

Dramatic Irony **Dramatic irony** occurs when we know something that a character in the story does not know. This type of irony, often found in plays and movies, creates anticipation and suspense as we wait for the character to learn what we already know to be the truth. In the following passage, "our man" is ignorant of what is about to happen:

> So our man relaxed with the others, some of whom would owe their lives to him.
>
> from "The Man in the Water" by Roger Rosenblatt

We know what the passengers do not know: Their plane is about to fall into the frozen Potomac River.

Your Turn   Analyze Symbolism and Irony

Put your knowledge of symbolism and irony to the test by completing the following activities:

1. Imagine that you are explaining irony to someone. Make up an example of each type of irony: verbal, situational, and dramatic. Ask a partner to evaluate your examples for clarity.

2. In a small group, discuss symbols you have seen in television programs and movies. Write down three symbols, and explain what they represent.

Learn It Online
Do pictures help you learn? Try the *PowerNotes* version of this lesson on:

go.hrw.com   L10-309   Go

Analyzing Visuals

How Do Artists Use Symbolism and Irony in Art?

You already know about symbols in literature. But how can you identify symbols in art? Some are obvious. For example, flags are often symbols of patriotism. Others are more subtle. In the painting to the right, you will explore the artist's use of symbols to create meaning. You will also examine the artist's **ironic** point of view.

Analyzing a Painting for Symbolism and Irony

This painting's title, *Three Sphinxes of Bikini,* will help you analyze its symbolic meaning. Bikini, part of an island chain in the Pacific Ocean, was the site of many experimental atomic explosions conducted by the United States between 1946 and 1958. A sphinx, which has a human head and a lion's body, is an ancient creature from Greek and Egyptian mythology. Generally, a sphinx represents wisdom. Use these guidelines to analyze paintings with symbols:

1. Identify the subject of the painting. Does the painting remind you of something or someone else? What new insight does it give you?

2. What symbols do you see in the painting?

3. Study the title of the painting. Does it surprise you? Why or why not?

4. In what way might placing the symbol(s) in a different context change the symbolic meaning?

> Look at the details of the painting to help you answer the questions on page 311.

  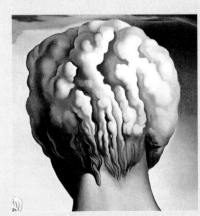

RA.L.10.7 Recognize how irony is used in a literary text. **RA.L.10.9** Explain how authors use symbols to create broader meanings.

1. Notice that the heads in the painting are turned away, so we cannot see their faces. If we could see them, what expressions do you think they might have?

2. What elements of nature can you find in the painting? What might these elements represent?

3. Given the historical and literary context of the painting, what do you think these three heads might **symbolize**?

4. What makes this combination of images particularly **ironic**? What has the artist gained by giving one image two **symbolic meanings**?

Three Sphinxes of Bikini by Salvador Dali. Courtesy of the Morohashi Museum, Fukushima, Japan/© 2009 Salvador Dali, Gala-Salvador Dali Foundation/Artists Rights Society (ARS), NY.

Your Turn Write About Symbolism

Find a painting in this book that contains one or more symbols. Write a paragraph explaining its symbolic meaning and consider whether the painting contains irony. Use details from the painting to support your interpretation.

Reading Focus

by **Kylene Beers**

What Skills Help You Understand Symbolism and Irony?

Have you ever read a sentence or paragraph and then realized you have no idea what it said? We read by scanning words on a page with our eyes, but if we don't process the words with our brains, we don't really understand what we read. Active reading means interacting with the text by asking questions and looking for the story's basic truths. Becoming a more active reader helps you recognize symbolism and irony.

Monitoring Your Reading

When you **monitor your reading,** you increase the possibility that you will understand something— about the world, about human nature, about the power of language—that you didn't understand before.

Two excellent ways to monitor your reading are to **ask questions** and to **re-read the text.** Read the following passage from Doris Lessing's "Through the Tunnel," and keep track of the questions that pop into your head:

> There was no one visible; under him, in the water, the dim shapes of the swimmers had disappeared. Then one and then another of the boys came up on the far side of the barrier of rock, and he understood that they had swum though some gap or hole in it.
>
> from "Through the Tunnel"
> by Doris Lessing

This passage might raise several questions: *Who is the boy in the story? How have the other swimmers disappeared? What is the gap or hole?*

Asking questions like these is a smart way to stay engaged with a text. A good story does not give up all its secrets at once, and you will think of many questions as you read. Use the following list as a guide:

- What's happened so far?
- What's going to happen next?
- What did that character mean when he or she said, "_____"?
- What is the setting, and how does it affect the story?
- What images or objects in the story might stand for something else?

In many stories everything seems perfectly clear the first time through. Other stories puzzle and tease us, leaving us with unanswered questions. These stories invite you to peel away their layers to get at the core meaning. Once you finish reading a story, you may want—or need—to **re-read** the text to find its deeper meanings and answers to any questions.

RP.10.3 Monitor own comprehension by adjusting speed to fit the purpose, or by skimming, scanning, reading on, looking back, note taking or summarizing what has been read so far in text. **RP.10.1** Apply reading comprehension strategies, including making predictions, comparing and contrasting, recalling and summarizing and making inferences and drawing conclusions. **RA.I.10.4** Assess the adequacy, accuracy and appropriateness of an author's details, identifying persuasive techniques and examples of propaganda, bias and stereotyping.

Analyzing Details

At its most basic level, analyzing means asking the questions *Why?* and *What does it mean?* As you re-read, you may be searching for answers to questions. You may also notice details that your eye skipped over during your first reading. Writers plant significant details as signposts or clues, but a reader often doesn't recognize the importance of these details until he or she has finished the story. One way to **analyze details** is to compare and contrast details from a story with knowledge you already possess.

This passage from "The Masque of the Red Death" describes a place that is probably unlike anywhere you have ever been. However, some of the details refer to things you probably *do* know about and recognize.

> The seventh apartment was closely shrouded in black velvet tapestries that hung all over the ceiling and down the walls . . . The [window] panes here were scarlet—a deep blood color [and] the effect of the firelight that streamed upon the dark hangings through the blood-tinted panes was ghastly in the extreme, and produced so wild a look upon the countenances of those who entered that there were few of the company bold enough to set foot within its precincts at all.
>
> from "The Masque of the Red Death" by Edgar Allan Poe

Even if you have never been in a place like this one, you know that "blood color" is a dark, thick red. Since you probably know how firelight looks when it flickers across surfaces, you already have a good picture of a room that you have never seen.

Making Generalizations

When you **make generalizations** about a story, you make broad statements based on details from the story. Making generalizations helps you find the basic truths of a story by using prior knowledge. As you read, try to associate details from the story with details from your own life.

Your Turn   Apply Reading Skills

Read the following passage from "The Possibility of Evil" by Shirley Jackson. Then, make a generalization about Miss Strangeworth, and support it with two specific details from the text.

> Martha Harper was not as young as she used to be, Miss Strangeworth thought. She probably could use a good, strong tonic.
>
> "Martha," she said, "you don't look well."
>
> "I'm perfectly all right," Mrs. Harper said shortly. She handed her money to Mr. Lewis, took her change and her sugar, and went out without speaking again. Looking after her, Miss Strangeworth shook her head slightly. Martha definitely did *not* look well.

Now go to the Skills in Action: Reading Model

Learn It Online
Try the *PowerNotes* version of this lesson on:

go.hrw.com   L10-313   **Go**

Build Background

Magic realism is a literary style that emerged in Latin America and has since been imitated by writers the world over. It combines incredible events with realistic details and relates them all in a matter-of-fact tone. The term *magic realism* was coined in 1949 by the Cuban writer Alejo Carpentier and describes a blurring of the lines that usually separate what seems real to the reader from what seems imagined or unreal. Carpentier believed that by incorporating magic, myth, imagination, and religion into literature, authors can expand our rigid concept of reality.

Reading Focus

Questioning After reading this passage, readers might ask, "What is the real reason the narrator and his sister have shut themselves off from the world?"

Read with a Purpose As you read, think about how the takeover in this story is different from what you might expect.

House Taken Over

by **Julio Cortázar**
translated by **Paul Blackburn**

We liked the house because, apart from its being old and spacious (in a day when old houses go down for a profitable auction of their construction materials), it kept the memories of great-grandparents, our paternal grandfather, our parents and the whole of childhood.

Irene and I got used to staying in the house by ourselves, which was crazy, eight people could have lived in that place and not have gotten in each other's way. We rose at seven in the morning and got the cleaning done, and about eleven I left Irene to finish off whatever rooms and went to the kitchen. We lunched at noon precisely; then there was nothing left to do but a few dirty plates. It was pleasant to take lunch and commune with the great hollow, silent house, and it was enough for us just to keep it clean. We ended up thinking, at times, that that was what had kept us from marrying. Irene turned down two suitors for no particular reason, and María Esther went and died on me before we could manage to get engaged. We were easing into our forties with the unvoiced concept that the quiet, simple marriage of sister and brother was the indispensable end to a line established in this house by our grandparents. We would die here someday, obscure and distant cousins would inherit the place, have it torn down, sell the bricks and get rich on the building plot; or more justly and better yet, we would topple it ourselves before it was too late.

The Window at the Country House
(1915) by Marc Chagall.

Tretyakov Gallery, Moscow, Russia/Artists Rights Society (ARS), NY/© 2008 ADAGP, Paris.

Analyzing Visuals   **Viewing and Interpreting**   What similar elements can you find in this painting and the story?

Irene never bothered anyone. Once the morning housework was finished, she spent the rest of the day on the sofa in her bedroom, knitting. I couldn't tell you why she knitted so much; I think women knit when they discover that it's a fat excuse to do nothing at all. But Irene was not like that, she always knitted necessities, sweaters for winter, socks for me, handy morning robes and bedjackets for herself. Sometimes she would do a jacket, then unravel it the next moment because there was something that didn't please her; it was pleasant to see a pile of tangled wool in her knitting basket fighting a losing battle for a few hours to retain its shape. Saturdays I went downtown to buy wool; Irene had faith in my good taste, was pleased with the

Literary Focus

Symbolism   Symbols are usually visual, and they usually reappear throughout a story. As you continue reading, you'll notice that the narrator keeps mentioning Irene's knitting. Here, the knitting symbolizes Irene's obsession with meaningless routine.

colors and never a skein[1] had to be returned. I took advantage of these trips to make the rounds of the bookstores, uselessly asking if they had anything new in French literature. Nothing worthwhile had arrived in Argentina since 1939.

But it's the house I want to talk about, the house and Irene, I'm not very important. I wonder what Irene would have done without her knitting. One can reread a book, but once a pullover is finished you can't do it over again, it's some kind of disgrace. One day I found that the drawer at the bottom of the chiffonier,[2] replete with mothballs, was filled with shawls, white, green, lilac. Stacked amid a great smell of camphor[3]—it was like a shop; I didn't have the nerve to ask her what she planned to do with them. We didn't have to earn our living, there was plenty coming in from the farms each month, even piling up. But Irene was only interested in the knitting and showed a wonderful dexterity, and for me the hours slipped away watching her, her hands like silver sea-urchins, needles flashing, and one or two knitting baskets on the floor, the balls of yarn jumping about. It was lovely.

How not to remember the layout of that house. The dining room, a living room with tapestries, the library and three large bedrooms in the section most recessed, the one that faced toward Rodríguez Peña.[4] Only a corridor with its massive oak door separated that part from the front wing, where there was a bath, the kitchen, our bedrooms and the hall. One entered the house through a vestibule[5] with enameled tiles, and a wrought-iron grated door opened onto the living room. You had to come in through the vestibule and open the gate to go into the living room; the doors to our bedrooms were on either side of this, and opposite it was the corridor leading to the back section; going down the passage, one swung open the oak door beyond which was the other part of the house; or just before the door, one could turn to the left and go down a narrower passageway which led to the kitchen and the bath. When the door was open, you became aware of the size of the house; when it was closed, you had the impression of an apartment, like the ones they build today, with barely enough room to move around in. Irene and I always lived in

---

1. **skein** (skayn): coiled length of thread or yarn.
2. **chiffonier** (shihf uh NIHR): high, narrow chest of drawers, with or without a mirror.
3. **camphor:** chemical used as an insect repellent.
4. **Rodríguez Peña:** street in Buenos Aires, Argentina.
5. **vestibule:** small entrance hall.

this part of the house and hardly ever went beyond the oak door except to do the cleaning. Incredible how much dust collected on the furniture. It may be Buenos Aires is a clean city, but she owes it to her population and nothing else. There's too much dust in the air, the slightest breeze and it's back on the marble console tops and in the diamond patterns of the tooled-leather desk set. It's a lot of work to get it off with a feather duster; the motes rise and hang in the air, and settle again a minute later on the pianos and the furniture.

I'll always have a clear memory of it because it happened so simply and without fuss. Irene was knitting in her bedroom, it was eight at night, and I suddenly decided to put the water up for *maté*.[6] I went down the corridor as far as the oak door, which was ajar, then turned into the hall toward the kitchen, when I heard something in the library or the dining room. The sound came through muted and indistinct, a chair being knocked over onto the carpet or the muffled buzzing of a conversation. At the same time or a second later, I heard it at the end of the passage which led from those two rooms toward the door. I hurled myself against the door before it was too late and shut it, leaned on it with the weight of my body; luckily, the key was on our side; moreover, I ran the great bolt into place, just to be safe.

I went down to the kitchen, heated the kettle, and when I got back with the tray of *maté*, I told Irene:

"I had to shut the door to the passage. They've taken over the back part."

She let her knitting fall and looked at me with her tired, serious eyes.

"You're sure?"

I nodded.

"In that case," she said, picking up her needles again, "we'll have to live on this side."

I sipped at the *maté* very carefully, but she took her time starting her work again. I remember it was a grey vest she was knitting. I liked that vest.

The first few days were painful, since we'd both left so many things in the part that had been taken over. My collection of French literature, for example, was still in the library. Irene had left several folios of stationery and a pair of slippers that she used a lot in the

---

6. *maté* (MAH tay): tealike beverage made from the dried leaves of a South American evergreen tree.

Reading Focus

Questioning The narrator refers ominously to "it," but we don't know what "it" is. A few sentences later the narrator says he hears "something." Readers might ask what "it" is and what that "something" could be.

Reading Focus

Questioning Who are "they"? The narrator and his sister seem unsurprised by "their" presence.

winter. I missed my briar pipe, and Irene, I think, regretted the loss of an ancient bottle of Hesperidin.[7] It happened repeatedly (but only in the first few days) that we would close some drawer or cabinet and look at one another sadly.

"It's not here."

One thing more among the many lost on the other side of the house.

But there were advantages, too. The cleaning was so much simplified that, even when we got up late, nine thirty for instance, by eleven we were sitting around with our arms folded. Irene got into the habit of coming to the kitchen with me to help get lunch. We thought about it and decided on this: while I prepared the lunch, Irene would cook up dishes that could be eaten cold in the evening. We were happy with the arrangement because it was always such a bother to have to leave our bedrooms in the evening and start to cook. Now we made do with the table in Irene's room and platters of cold supper.

Since it left her more time for knitting, Irene was content. I was a little lost without my books, but so as not to inflict myself on my sister, I set about reordering papa's stamp collection; that killed some time. We amused ourselves sufficiently, each with his own thing, almost always getting together in Irene's bedroom, which was the more comfortable. Every once in a while, Irene might say:

"Look at this pattern I just figured out, doesn't it look like clover?"

After a bit it was I, pushing a small square of paper in front of her

---

7. **Hesperidin** (hehs PEHR uh dihn): liquid made from the rinds of citrus fruits and used for various medicinal purposes.

Reading Focus

Making Generalizations After reading this passage, readers might make a generalization about the narrator and his sister: They are closed off from the world and adjust to a strange routine.

Analyzing Visuals Viewing and Interpreting Is this how you picture the house in the story? Explain.

The Empire of Lights (1954), by René Magritte, oil on canvas. Peggy Guggenheim Foundation, Venice, Italy/© 2009 C. Herscovici, London/ Artists Rights Society (ARS), NY.

so that she could see the excellence of some stamp or another from Eupen-et-Malmédy.[8] We were fine, and little by little we stopped thinking. You can live without thinking.

(Whenever Irene talked in her sleep, I woke up immediately and stayed awake. I never could get used to this voice from a statue or a parrot, a voice that came out of the dreams, not from a throat. Irene said that in my sleep I flailed about enormously and shook the blankets off. We had the living room between us, but at night you could hear everything in the house. We heard each other breathing, coughing, could even feel each other reaching for the light switch when, as happened frequently, neither of us could fall asleep.

Aside from our nocturnal rumblings, everything was quiet in the house. During the day there were the household sounds, the metallic click of knitting needles, the rustle of stamp-album pages turning. The oak door was massive, I think I said that. In the kitchen or the bath, which adjoined the part that was taken over, we managed to talk loudly, or Irene sang lullabies. In a kitchen there's always too much noise, the plates and glasses, for there to be interruptions from other sounds. We seldom allowed ourselves silence there, but when we went back to our rooms or to the living room, then the house grew quiet, half-lit, we ended by stepping around more slowly so as not to disturb one another. I think it was because of this that I woke up irremediably and at once when Irene began to talk in her sleep.)

Except for the consequences, it's nearly a matter of repeating the same scene over again. I was thirsty that night, and before we went to sleep, I told Irene that I was going to the kitchen for a glass of water. From the door of the bedroom (she was knitting) I heard the noise in the kitchen; if not the kitchen, then the bath, the passage off at that angle dulled the sound. Irene noticed how brusquely I had paused, and came up beside me without a word. We stood listening to the noises, growing more and more sure that they were on our side of the oak door, if not the kitchen then the bath, or in the hall itself at the turn, almost next to us.

We didn't wait to look at one another. I took Irene's arm and forced her to run with me to the wrought-iron door, not waiting to look back. You could hear the noises, still muffled but louder, just behind us. I slammed the grating and we stopped in the vestibule. Now there was nothing to be heard.

---

8. **Eupen-et-Malmédy** (uh PEHN ay MAHL may dee): district in eastern Belgium.

> ## Literary Focus
>
> **Irony** Irene sings lullabies, but there are no children in the house. Readers might wonder what this detail suggests about Irene's mental state.

"They've taken over our section," Irene said. The knitting had reeled off from her hands and the yarn ran back toward the door and disappeared under it. When she saw that the balls of yarn were on the other side, she dropped the knitting without looking at it.

"Did you have time to bring anything?" I asked hopelessly.

"No, nothing."

We had what we had on. I remembered fifteen thousand pesos in the wardrobe in my bedroom. Too late now. I still had my wrist watch on and saw that it was 11 P.M. I took Irene around the waist (I think she was crying) and that was how we went into the street. Before we left, I felt terrible; I locked the front door up tight and tossed the key down the sewer. It wouldn't do to have some poor devil decide to go in and rob the house, at that hour and with the house taken over.

Literary Focus

Irony Notice the irony in the narrator's concern about the house being robbed. Since he is leaving the house, why would he care?

Read with a Purpose What has actually been "taken over" here? Are the brother and sister really in danger?

MEET THE WRITER

Julio Cortázar
(1914–1984)

Scared Sick

When he was nine years old, the Argentine writer Julio Cortázar read a book of Edgar Allan Poe's stories. "The book scared me," he said, "and I was ill for three months because I believed in it." Cortázar remained a Poe fan throughout his lifetime. He translated several of Poe's works into Spanish.

Reality and Magic

Cortázar is often compared with fellow Latin American fiction writers Jorge Luis Borges and Gabriel García Márquez. Like Borges and García Márquez, Cortázar creates realistic characters and settings, only to surprise us with fantastic details. We also see in Cortázar's work his love of jazz; his stories are often filled with energy and a sense of improvisation.

Think About the Writer Cortázar was a great fan of Edgar Allan Poe. How is this story similar to Poe's horror stories?

OH **RA.L.10.9** Explain how authors use symbols to create broader meanings. **RA.L.10.7** Recognize how irony is used in a literary text. *Also covered* **RP.10.3; RP.10.1; RA.I.10.4; VO.10.6**

Into Action: Symbolism and Irony

"House Taken Over" is a mysterious story. Use a chart like the following to identify symbols and to explain what you think they represent. Then, write a statement explaining the function of irony in the story.

Symbol	Possible Meaning of Symbol
the house	sanity
the doors	

Talk About . . .

1. With a partner, discuss the questions you have about this strange story. Use specific details from the story in your discussion. Try to use each Academic Vocabulary word listed at the right in your discussion.

Write About . . .

Use the underlined Academic Vocabulary words in your answers to the following questions about "House Taken Over":

2. What meaning do you <u>derive</u> from the symbol of the doors?

3. What is unusual about the way the brother and sister <u>interact</u>?

4. How do the brother and sister <u>function</u> once they shut the back door?

5. What is <u>significant</u> about the items the brother and sister leave behind?

Writing Focus

Think as a Reader/Writer

In Collection 4, you'll read several stories that include symbolism and irony. The Writing Focus activities on the Preparing to Read pages will alert you to different elements of writer's craft. On the Applying Your Skills pages you will have a chance to practice using those techniques in your own writing.

Academic Vocabulary for Collection 4

Talking and Writing About Short Stories

Academic Vocabulary is the language you use to talk and write about literature. Use these words to discuss the stories you read in this collection. The words are underlined throughout the collection.

derive (dih RYV) *v.:* obtain from a source or origin. *Symbolism helps you derive meaning from a story.*

function (FUHNGK shuhn) *v.:* act in a specific manner; work. *The setting of the story functions on both literal and symbolic levels.*

interact (ihn tuhr AKT) *v.:* act upon each other. *We can tell a lot about characters by the way they interact with each other.*

significant (sihg NIHF uh kuhnt) *adj.:* meaningful; important. *The sister's knitting is a significant symbol in the story.*

Your Turn

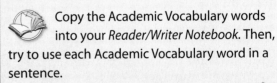 Copy the Academic Vocabulary words into your *Reader/Writer Notebook*. Then, try to use each Academic Vocabulary word in a sentence.

Through the
Tunnel by **Doris Lessing**

Emerald Coast by Bob Brown. Oil on canvas (66 cm × 76.2 cm).   Private collection.

What Do You Think?

Why do most young people feel, at one time or another, the need to prove their strength, endurance, or maturity?

QuickWrite

Think of a character in a book or a movie who faced a tough challenge. What physical and mental tests did he or she meet with? How did the character feel at the end of the ordeal? Write a brief summary of the character's experience.

Reader/Writer Notebook

OH **RA.L.10.9** Explain how authors use symbols to create broader meanings. **RP.10.3** Monitor own comprehension by adjusting speed to fit the purpose, or by skimming, scanning, reading on, looking back, note taking or summarizing what has been read so far in text. **RA.I.10.4** Assess the adequacy, accuracy and appropriateness of an author's details, identifying persuasive techniques and examples of propaganda, bias and stereotyping.

Use your **RWN** to complete the activities for this selection.

Literary Focus

Symbolism When reading a story, we often sense that its meaning goes deeper than what is happening on its surface. Writers often use symbols to suggest these deeper meanings. **Symbols** are people, places, things, or events that are what you expect them to be but that also stand for something else. As you read, think about the underwater tunnel in this story. Is it simply a tunnel, or does it also <u>function</u> as a symbol? What might the tunnel symbolize?

Reading Focus

Monitoring Your Reading When you **monitor your reading,** you do several things: You ask questions, you analyze <u>significant</u> details, you make generalizations, and you re-read the text. Using these skills helps you understand the deeper meanings of a story.

Into Action As you read "Through the Tunnel," monitor your reading with a chart like the one shown here. Write down details that you think are especially important. Then, write down questions that you have about the meaning of these details.

Details	Questions
Jerry keeps submerging to search for the hidden tunnel.	Why is he so determined to find the tunnel?

Writing Focus

Think as a Reader/Writer

Find It in Your Reading Symbols often carry powerful associations and emotional overtones. For Jerry, a young boy, the tunnel is not just a watery cave; it has a greater meaning as well. As you read "Through the Tunnel," note additional images and events that might have symbolic meaning for Jerry. In your *Reader/Writer Notebook,* jot down your ideas about what these symbols might represent. What words and phrases suggest that the story has a deeper meaning?

TechFocus As you read the story, think about how you might create a soundtrack to reflect the story's mood and tension.

Vocabulary

contrition (kuhn TRIHSH uhn) *n.:* regret or sense of guilt at having done wrong. *Jerry felt contrition when he thought of his mother alone on the beach.*

defiant (dih FY uhnt) *adj.:* challenging authority. *Jerry was defiant when he asked for the goggles.*

inquisitive (ihn KWIHZ uh tihv) *adj.:* questioning or curious. *His interest in the tunnel was more than inquisitive; it was almost an obsession.*

minute (my NOOT) *adj.:* tiny; very small. *With the goggles in place, Jerry was able to see many minute fish drifting through the water.*

incredulous (ihn KREHJ uh luhs) *adj.:* disbelieving; skeptical. *Jerry was incredulous when he realized he could hold his breath for two minutes.*

Language Coach

Word Origins The Latin word *quaerere* means "to seek." What Vocabulary word above has this origin? Check a dictionary to make sure you are correct. What other words can you think of that have the same origin?

 Learn It Online
See a good reader in action, and practice your own skills, at:

go.hrw.com   L10-323   **Go**

Doris Lessing
(1919–   )

Nobel Prize WINNER

Out of Africa

A difficult childhood gave Doris Lessing the tools to become one of the most admired writers of our day. Lessing was born in Persia (now Iran), where her British father worked in banking. When she was five, her father moved the family to a farm in Southern Rhodesia (now Zimbabwe). Life there was challenging, and the nearest neighbor was miles away. Lessing has also acknowledged the advantages of that life: Without any company, she enriched her mind by reading classic European and American literature.

An Instrument of Change

At age fourteen, Lessing quit school and went to work in Salisbury, the capital of Rhodesia. Salisbury had a white population of about ten thousand and a larger black population that, as Lessing was shocked to discover, "didn't count." She became involved in radical politics and was twice married and twice divorced. In 1949, with her two-year-old son and the manuscript of her first novel, *The Grass Is Singing,* she immigrated to England. The novel was one of the earliest treatments in fiction of Africa's racial problems. Lessing says she writes to inspire equality and to be "an instrument of change":

> "It is not merely a question of preventing evil, but of strengthening a vision of good which may defeat the evil."

Think About the Writer How might Lessing's perception of good and evil influence her writing?

Build Background

This story takes place at an unnamed seaside resort frequented by British tourists. This resort could be located on the Mediterranean Sea, perhaps along the coast of France or northern Africa.

Preview the Selection

Jerry, a young British boy, is on vacation with his mother. He is drawn to a "wild bay" and to a challenge that could mean the loss of his life.

Through the Tunnel

by **Doris Lessing**

Going to the shore on the first morning of the vacation, the young English boy stopped at a turning of the path and looked down at a wild and rocky bay and then over to the crowded beach he knew so well from other years. His mother walked on in front of him, carrying a bright striped bag in one hand. Her other arm, swinging loose, was very white in the sun. The boy watched that white naked arm and turned his eyes, which had a frown behind them, toward the bay and back again to his mother. When she felt he was not with her, she swung around. "Oh, there you are, Jerry!" she said. She looked impatient, then smiled. "Why, darling, would you rather not come with me? Would you rather—" She frowned, conscientiously worrying over what amusements he might secretly be longing for, which she had been too busy or too careless to imagine. He was very familiar with that anxious, apologetic smile. Contrition sent him running after her. And yet, as he ran, he looked back over his shoulder at the wild bay; and all morning, as he played on the safe beach, he was thinking of it. **A**

Next morning, when it was time for the routine of swimming and sunbathing, his mother said, "Are you tired of the usual beach, Jerry? Would you like to go somewhere else?"

"Oh, no!" he said quickly, smiling at her out of that unfailing impulse of contrition—a sort of chivalry.[1] Yet, walking down the path with her, he blurted out, "I'd like to go and have a look at those rocks down there."

She gave the idea her attention. It was a wild-looking place, and there was no one there, but she said, "Of course, Jerry. When you've had enough, come to the big beach. Or just go straight back to the villa, if you like." She walked away, that bare arm, now slightly reddened from yesterday's sun, swinging. And he almost ran after her again, feeling it unbearable that she should go by herself, but he did not.

She was thinking. Of course he's old enough to be safe without me. Have I been keeping him too close? He mustn't feel he ought to be with me. I must be careful.

---

1. **chivalry** (SHIHV uhl ree): here, an act of gentlemanly politeness.

A **Literary Focus** Symbolism In this story, setting and symbolism are closely related. What might the "safe beach" and the "wild bay" represent?

Vocabulary **contrition** (kuhn TRIHSH uhn) *n.:* regret or sense of guilt at having done wrong.

He was an only child, eleven years old. She was a widow. She was determined to be neither possessive nor lacking in devotion. She went worrying off to her beach. **B**

As for Jerry, once he saw that his mother had gained her beach, he began the steep descent to the bay. From where he was, high up among red-brown rocks, it was a scoop of moving bluish green fringed with white. As he went lower, he saw that it spread among small promontories and inlets of rough, sharp rock, and the crisping, lapping surface showed stains of purple and darker blue. Finally, as he ran sliding and scraping down the last few yards, he saw an edge of white surf and the shallow, luminous movement of water over white sand and, beyond that, a solid, heavy blue.

He ran straight into the water and began swimming. He was a good swimmer. He went out fast over the gleaming sand, over a middle region where rocks lay like discolored monsters under the surface, and then he was in the real sea—a warm sea where irregular cold currents from the deep water shocked his limbs. **C**

When he was so far out that he could look back not only on the little bay but past the promontory that was between it and the big beach, he floated on the buoyant surface and looked for his mother. There she was, a speck of yellow under an umbrella that looked like a slice of orange peel. He swam back to shore, relieved at being sure she was there, but all at once very lonely.

On the edge of a small cape that marked the side of the bay away from the promontory was a loose scatter of rocks. Above them, some boys were stripping off their clothes. They came running, naked, down to the rocks. The English boy swam toward them but kept his distance

Swimmer in Yellow (1990) by Gareth Lloyd Ball. Private Collection.

Analyzing Visuals

Viewing and Interpreting In what way might the distortion of the swimmer in this painting mirror Jerry's anxiety?

at a stone's throw. They were of that coast; all of them were burned smooth dark brown and speaking a language he did not understand. To be with them, of them, was a craving that filled his whole body. He swam a little closer; they turned and watched him with narrowed, alert dark eyes. Then one smiled and waved. It was enough. In a minute, he had swum in and was on the rocks beside them, smiling with a

---

B **Reading Focus** **Monitoring Your Reading** What questions do you have about the story so far?

C **Literary Focus** **Symbolism** What word in this paragraph suggests that the rocks might symbolize something?

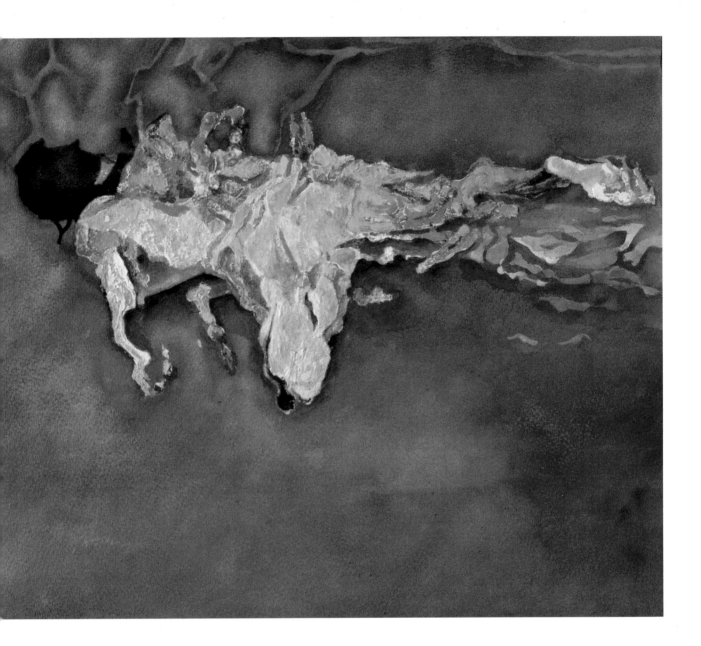

desperate, nervous supplication.[2] They shouted cheerful greetings at him; and then, as he preserved his nervous, uncomprehending smile, they understood that he was a foreigner strayed from his own beach, and they proceeded to forget him. But he was happy. He was with them.

They began diving again and again from a high point into a well of blue sea between rough, pointed rocks. After they had dived and come up, they swam around, hauled themselves up, and waited their turn to dive again. They were big boys—men, to Jerry. He dived, and they watched him; and when he swam around to take his place, they made way for him. He felt he was accepted and he dived again, carefully, proud of himself. **D**

---

2. **supplication** (suhp luh KAY shuhn): humble appeal or request.

D **Reading Focus** **Monitoring Your Reading** Which details in this passage tell you what Jerry wants?

Soon the biggest of the boys poised himself, shot down into the water, and did not come up. The others stood about, watching. Jerry, after waiting for the sleek brown head to appear, let out a yell of warning; they looked at him idly and turned their eyes back toward the water. After a long time, the boy came up on the other side of a big dark rock, letting the air out of his lungs in a sputtering gasp and a shout of triumph. Immediately the rest of them dived in. One moment, the morning seemed full of chattering boys; the next, the air and the surface of the water were empty. But through the heavy blue, dark shapes could be seen moving and groping.

Jerry dived, shot past the school of underwater swimmers, saw a black wall of rock looming at him, touched it, and bobbed up at once to the surface, where the wall was a low barrier he could see across. There was no one visible; under him, in the water, the dim shapes of the swimmers had disappeared. Then one and then another of the boys came up on the far side of the barrier of rock, and he understood that they had swum through some gap or hole in it. He plunged down again. He could see nothing through the stinging salt water but the blank rock. When he came up, the boys were all on the diving rock, preparing to attempt the feat again. And now, in a panic of failure, he yelled up, in English, "Look at me! Look!" and he began splashing and kicking in the water like a foolish dog. **E**

> They must all be drowning beneath him, in the watery caves of the rock!

They looked down gravely, frowning. He knew the frown. At moments of failure, when he clowned to claim his mother's attention, it was with just this grave, embarrassed inspection that she rewarded him. Through his hot shame, feeling the pleading grin on his face like a scar that he could never remove, he looked up at the group of big brown boys on the rock and shouted, *"Bonjour! Merci! Au revoir! Monsieur, monsieur!"*[3] while he hooked his fingers round his ears and waggled them.

Water surged into his mouth; he choked, sank, came up. The rock, lately weighted with boys, seemed to rear up out of the water as their weight was removed. They were flying down past him now, into the water; the air was full of falling bodies. Then the rock was empty in the hot sunlight. He counted one, two, three . . .

At fifty, he was terrified. They must all be drowning beneath him, in the watery caves of the rock! At a hundred, he stared around him at the empty hillside, wondering if he should yell for help. He counted faster, faster, to hurry them up, to bring them to the surface quickly, to drown them quickly—anything rather than the terror of counting on and on into the blue emptiness of the morning. And then, at a hundred and sixty, the water beyond the rock was

---

3. *Bonjour! Merci! Au revoir! Monsieur, monsieur!:* French for "Hello! Thank you! Goodbye! Mister, mister!"

E **Reading Focus** Monitoring Your Reading   Why does Jerry act foolishly?

full of boys blowing like brown whales. They swam back to the shore without a look at him.

He climbed back to the diving rock and sat down, feeling the hot roughness of it under his thighs. The boys were gathering up their bits of clothing and running off along the shore to another promontory. They were leaving to get away from him. He cried openly, fists in his eyes. There was no one to see him, and he cried himself out.

It seemed to him that a long time had passed, and he swam out to where he could see his mother. Yes, she was still there, a yellow spot under an orange umbrella. He swam back to the big rock, climbed up, and dived into the blue pool among the fanged and angry boulders. Down he went, until he touched the wall of rock again. But the salt was so painful in his eyes that he could not see. **F**

He came to the surface, swam to shore, and went back to the villa to wait for his mother. Soon she walked slowly up the path, swinging her striped bag, the flushed, naked arm dangling beside her. "I want some swimming goggles," he panted, defiant and beseeching.

She gave him a patient, inquisitive look as she said casually, "Well, of course, darling."

But now, now, now! He must have them this minute, and no other time. He nagged and pestered until she went with him to a shop. As soon as she had bought the goggles, he grabbed them from her hand as if she were going to claim them for herself, and was off, running down the steep path to the bay.

Jerry swam out to the big barrier rock, adjusted the goggles, and dived. The impact of the water broke the rubber-enclosed vacuum, and the goggles came loose. He understood that he must swim down to the base of the rock from the surface of the water. He fixed the goggles tight and firm, filled his lungs, and floated, face down, on the water. Now he could see. It was as if he had eyes of a different kind—fish eyes that showed everything clear and delicate and wavering in the bright water.

Under him, six or seven feet down, was a floor of perfectly clean, shining white sand, rippled firm and hard by the tides. Two grayish shapes steered there, like long, rounded pieces of wood or slate. They were fish. He saw them nose toward each other, poise motionless, make a dart forward, swerve off, and come around again. It was like a water dance. A few inches above them the water sparkled as if sequins were dropping through it. Fish again—myriads of minute fish, the length of his fingernail—were drifting through the water, and in a moment he could feel the innumerable tiny touches of them against his limbs. It was like swimming in flaked silver. The great rock the big boys had swum through rose sheer out of the white sand—black, tufted lightly with greenish weed. He could see no gap in it. He swam down to its base. **G**

Again and again he rose, took a big chestful of air, and went down. Again and again he groped over the surface of the rock, feeling it, almost hugging it in the desperate need to find

---

F **Literary Focus** Symbolism What words in this passage suggest that the rocks are symbols?

Vocabulary **defiant** (dih FY uhnt) *adj.*: challenging authority.
inquisitive (ihn KWIHZ uh tihv) *adj.*: questioning or curious.
minute (my NOOT) *adj.*: tiny; very small.

G **Reading Focus** Monitoring Your Reading Re-read this description. What details help you visualize this setting?

the entrance. And then, once, while he was clinging to the black wall, his knees came up and he shot his feet out forward and they met no obstacle. He had found the hole.

He gained the surface, clambered about the stones that littered the barrier rock until he found a big one, and with this in his arms, let himself down over the side of the rock. He dropped, with the weight, straight to the sandy floor. Clinging tight to the anchor of stone, he lay on his side and looked in under the dark shelf at the place where his feet had gone. He could see the hole. It was an irregular, dark gap; but he could not see deep into it. He let go of his anchor, clung with his hands to the edges of the hole, and tried to push himself in.

He got his head in, found his shoulders jammed, moved them in sidewise, and was inside as far as his waist. He could see nothing ahead. Something soft and clammy touched his mouth; he saw a dark frond[4] moving against the grayish rock, and panic filled him. He thought of octopuses, of clinging weed. He pushed himself out backward and caught a glimpse, as he retreated, of a harmless tentacle of seaweed drifting in the mouth of the tunnel. But it was enough. He reached the sunlight, swam to shore, and lay on the diving rock. He looked down into the blue well of water. He knew he must find his way through that cave, or hole, or tunnel, and out the other side. **Ⓗ**

---

4. **frond** (frahnd): large leaf or leaflike part of seaweed.

Ⓗ **Literary Focus** Symbolism Why do you think Jerry feels he must find his way through the tunnel? What could the tunnel represent?

Woman Reading (2002) by Mary Robertson. Courtesy of the artist and George Krevsky Gallery.

First, he thought, he must learn to control his breathing. He let himself down into the water with another big stone in his arms, so that he could lie effortlessly on the bottom of the sea. He counted. One, two, three. He counted steadily. He could hear the movement of blood in his chest. Fifty-one, fifty-two. . . . His chest was hurting. He let go of the rock and went up into the air. He saw that the sun was low. He rushed to the villa and found his mother at her supper. She said only, "Did you enjoy yourself?" and he said, "Yes."

All night the boy dreamed of the water-filled cave in the rock, and as soon as breakfast was over, he went to the bay.

That night, his nose bled badly. For hours he had been underwater, learning to hold his breath, and now he felt weak and dizzy. His mother said, "I shouldn't overdo things, darling, if I were you."

That day and the next, Jerry exercised his lungs as if everything, the whole of his life, all that he would become, depended upon it. Again his nose bled at night, and his mother insisted on his coming with her the next day. It was a torment to him to waste a day of his careful self-training, but he stayed with her on that other beach, which now seemed a place for small children, a place where his mother might lie safe in the sun. It was not his beach. **❶**

He did not ask for permission, on the following day, to go to his beach. He went, before his mother could consider the complicated rights and wrongs of the matter. A day's rest, he discovered, had improved his count by ten. The big boys had made the passage while he counted a hundred and sixty. He had been counting fast, in his fright. Probably now, if he tried, he could get through that long tunnel, but he was not going to try yet. A curious, most unchildlike persistence, a controlled impatience, made him wait. In the meantime, he lay underwater on the white sand, littered now by stones he had brought down from the upper air, and studied the entrance to the tunnel. He knew every jut and corner of it, as far as it was possible to see. It was as if he already felt its sharpness about his shoulders.

He sat by the clock in the villa, when his mother was not near, and checked his time. He was incredulous and then proud to find he could hold his breath without strain for two minutes. The words "two minutes," authorized by the clock, brought close the adventure that was so necessary to him. **❶**

In another four days, his mother said casually one morning, they must go home. On the day before they left, he would do it. He would do it if it killed him, he said defiantly to himself. But two days before they were to leave—a day of triumph when he increased his count by fifteen—his nose bled so badly that he turned dizzy and had to lie limply over the big rock like a bit of seaweed, watching the thick red blood flow onto the rock and trickle slowly down to the sea. He was frightened. Supposing

❶ Literary Focus **Symbolism** Why is the beach "not his beach"? What does this detail hint at concerning the symbolic meaning of the two beaches?

❶ Literary Focus **Symbolism** This passage describes Jerry's literal efforts to achieve his goal. How is he changing?

Vocabulary **incredulous** (ihn KREHJ uh luhs) *adj.:* disbelieving; skeptical.

he turned dizzy in the tunnel? Supposing he died there, trapped? Supposing—his head went around, in the hot sun, and he almost gave up. He thought he would return to the house and lie down, and next summer, perhaps, when he had another year's growth in him—then he would go through the hole.

But even after he had made the decision, or thought he had, he found himself sitting up on the rock and looking down into the water; and he knew that now, this moment, when his nose had only just stopped bleeding, when his head was still sore and throbbing—this was the moment when he would try. If he did not do it now, he never would. He was trembling with fear that he would not go; and he was trembling with horror at the long, long tunnel under the rock, under the sea. Even in the open sunlight, the barrier rock seemed very wide and very heavy; tons of rock pressed down on where he would go. If he died there, he would lie until one day—perhaps not before next year—those big boys would swim into it and find it blocked. **K**

He put on his goggles, fitted them tight, tested the vacuum. His hands were shaking. Then he chose the biggest stone he could carry and slipped over the edge of the rock until half of him was in the cool enclosing water and half in the hot sun. He looked up once at the empty sky, filled his lungs once, twice, and then sank fast to the bottom with the stone. He let it go and began to count. He took the edges of the hole in his hands and drew himself into it, wriggling his shoulders in sidewise as he remembered he must, kicking himself along with his feet.

Soon he was clear inside. He was in a small rock-bound hole filled with yellowish-gray water. The water was pushing him up against the roof. The roof was sharp and pained his back. He pulled himself along with his hands—fast, fast—and used his legs as levers. His head knocked against something; a sharp pain dizzied him. Fifty, fifty-one, fifty-two . . . He was without light, and the water seemed to press upon him with the weight of rock. Seventy-one, seventy-two . . . There was no strain on his lungs. He felt like an inflated balloon, his lungs were so light and easy, but his head was pulsing.

He was being continually pressed against the sharp roof, which felt slimy as well as sharp. Again he thought of octopuses, and wondered if the tunnel might be filled with weed that could tangle him. He gave himself a panicky, convulsive kick forward, ducked his head, and swam. His feet and hands moved freely, as if in open water. The hole must have widened out. He thought he must be swimming fast, and he was frightened of banging his head if the tunnel narrowed.

A hundred, a hundred and one . . . The water paled. Victory filled him. His lungs were beginning to hurt. A few more strokes and he would be out. He was counting wildly; he said a hundred and fifteen and then, a long time later, a hundred and fifteen again. The water was a clear jewel-green all around him. Then he saw, above his head, a crack running up through the rock. Sunlight was falling through it, showing the clean, dark rock of the tunnel, a single mussel[5] shell, and darkness ahead. **L**

---

5. **mussel** (MUHS uhl): shellfish, similar to a clam or an oyster, that attaches itself to rocks.

K **Literary Focus** Symbolism In what literal and symbolic ways is Jerry now entering an underworld?

L **Reading Focus** Monitoring Your Reading What questions do you have about what will happen next?

He was at the end of what he could do. He looked up at the crack as if it were filled with air and not water, as if he could put his mouth to it to draw in air. A hundred and fifteen, he heard himself say inside his head—but he had said that long ago. He must go on into the blackness ahead, or he would drown. His head was swelling, his lungs cracking. A hundred and fifteen, a hundred and fifteen, pounded through his head, and he feebly clutched at rocks in the dark, pulling himself forward, leaving the brief space of sunlit water behind. He felt he was dying. He was no longer quite conscious. He struggled on in the darkness between lapses into unconsciousness. An immense, swelling pain filled his head, and then the darkness cracked with an explosion of green light. His hands, groping forward, met nothing; and his feet, kicking back, propelled him out into the open sea.

He drifted to the surface, his face turned up to the air. He was gasping like a fish. He felt he would sink now and drown; he could not swim the few feet back to the rock. Then he was clutching it and pulling himself up onto it. He lay face down, gasping. He could see nothing but a red-veined, clotted dark. His eyes must have burst, he thought; they were full of blood. He tore off his goggles and a gout[6] of blood went into the sea. His nose was bleeding, and the blood had filled the goggles.

He scooped up handfuls of water from the cool, salty sea, to splash on his face, and did not know whether it was blood or salt water he tasted. After a time, his heart quieted, his eyes cleared, and he sat up. He could see the local boys diving and playing half a mile away. He did not want them. He wanted nothing but to get back home and lie down. **Ⓜ**

In a short while, Jerry swam to shore and climbed slowly up the path to the villa. He flung himself on his bed and slept, waking at the sound of feet on the path outside. His mother was coming back. He rushed to the bathroom, thinking she must not see his face with blood-stains, or tearstains, on it. He came out of the bathroom and met her as she walked into the

> He felt he would sink now and drown; he could not swim the few feet back to the rock.

villa, smiling, her eyes lighting up.

"Have a nice morning?" she asked, laying her hand on his warm brown shoulder a moment.

"Oh, yes, thank you," he said.

"You look a bit pale." And then, sharp and anxious, "How did you bang your head?"

"Oh, just banged it," he told her. **Ⓝ**

She looked at him closely. He was strained; his eyes were glazed-looking. She was worried. And then she said to herself, Oh, don't fuss! Nothing can happen. He can swim like a fish.

They sat down to lunch together.

"Mummy," he said, "I can stay underwater for two minutes—three minutes, at least." It came bursting out of him.

"Can you, darling?" she said. "Well, I shouldn't overdo it. I don't think you ought to swim anymore today."

She was ready for a battle of wills, but he gave in at once. It was no longer of the least importance to go to the bay.

---

6. **gout** (gowt): large glob.

Ⓜ **Reading Focus** Monitoring Your Reading Why is Jerry no longer interested in the local boys?

Ⓝ **Literary Focus** Symbolism Why does Jerry evade his mother's question about how he banged his head? What might Jerry's passage through the dangerous tunnel symbolize?

Applying Your Skills

OH **RA.L.10.9** Explain how authors use symbols to create broader meanings. **RA.L.10.8** Analyze the author's use of point of view, mood and tone. **RA.L.10.5** Analyze how an author's choice of genre affects the expression of a theme or topic. *Also covered* **RP.10.3; RP.10.1; RA.I.10.4; WA.10.4.d**

Through the Tunnel

Respond and Think Critically

Reading Focus

Quick Check

1. Why is it so important to Jerry to <u>interact</u> with the boys on the beach? What do they represent to him?

2. By the end of the story, how does Jerry's relationship with his mother change?

Read with a Purpose

3. Why does Jerry feel he has to risk his life and go through the dangerous tunnel? What breakthrough does he achieve by the story's end?

Reading Skills: Monitoring Your Reading

4. Re-read "Through the Tunnel" to find answers to the questions you wrote in your chart. Add a third column to the chart to record the answers to your questions.

Details	My Questions	My Answers
Jerry keeps submerging to search for the hidden tunnel.	Why is he so determined to find the tunnel?	Maybe it represents something he needs to do in order to become a grown-up.

Literary Focus

Literary Analysis

5. **Analyze** In a quest story the hero or heroine goes on a journey in search of something of great value. He or she endures hardships and danger and, as a result of the journey, undergoes an important change. How could Jerry's story be seen as a quest?

Literary Skills: Symbolism

6. **Interpret** What do you think these specific elements in the story symbolize?
   - The "wild bay"
   - The rocks
   - The "safe beach"
   - The tunnel
   - Jerry's passage through the tunnel

Literary Skills Review: Omniscient Narrator

7. **Contrast** "Through the Tunnel" is told from the point of view of an all-knowing, or **omniscient,** narrator. Although the narrator focuses mainly on Jerry, we also learn some of Jerry's mother's thoughts and feelings. How would the story be different if Jerry's mother were telling it?

Writing Focus

Think as a Reader/Writer

Use It in Your Writing Review your notes about the words and phrases that suggest symbolic meaning in the story. Then, think of a place that is important to you. What might that place symbolize? What words and phrases could you use to underscore that symbolic meaning? In your *Reader/Writer Notebook*, write a brief description of the place, but do not explicitly say what it represents.

 What Do You Think Now

What has Jerry proved by swimming through the tunnel? How might his life be different from this point forward?

Vocabulary Development

Vocabulary Check

Choose the Vocabulary word that best completes each of the following sentences.

| contrition |
| defiant |
| inquisitive |
| minute |
| incredulous |

1. Jerry felt _____ when he left his mother to go to the beach.
2. Thousands of _____ fish swam in the tunnel.
3. When Jerry saw the kids appear on the other side of the tunnel, he was _____.
4. Jerry's mother was curious about his activities and gave him an _____ look.
5. Because he didn't want to hurt his mother's feelings, Jerry felt a sense of _____ when he said he wanted to swim on the other beach.

Vocabulary Skills: Word Analogies

In an **analogy,** the words in one pair relate to each other in the same way as the words in a second pair. Many kinds of relationships are possible in an analogy.

- A pair of words can be **synonyms** (TIMID : MEEK) or **antonyms** (TIMID : BOLD).
- One word in a pair can describe a **characteristic** of the other word (KNIFE : SHARP).
- The words in a pair can each express a different **degree of intensity** (LIKE : LOVE).

Analogies are frequently written as follows:

HUGE : ELEPHANT :: minute : gnat

You would read this analogy this way: *"Huge is to elephant as minute is to gnat."*

To solve an analogy, first identify the relationship between the first pair of words. Then, express the analogy in sentence or question form. Finally, find the word that makes the relationship of the second pair of words the same as the first.

Your Turn

Choose the Vocabulary word that best completes each analogy below.

1. SADNESS : MOURNING :: _____ : regret
2. SECURE : SAFE :: _____ : curious
3. NEEDY : BEGGAR :: _____ : skeptic
4. BRILLIANT : SMART :: _____ : stubborn
5. BLACK : WHITE :: _____ : large

Language Coach

Word Origins Dictionaries give the origin, or etymology, of a word. Here is a word map for *defiant (defy):*

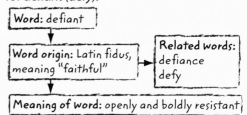

For each Vocabulary word, make a word map like the one for *defiant.*

Academic Vocabulary

Talk About . . .

In "Through the Tunnel," Jerry's <u>interactions</u> with his mother are brief, but they <u>function</u> as a way to give the reader information about what Jerry is thinking and feeling. Discuss with a partner what information is revealed in Jerry's final discussion with his mother, and why it is <u>significant</u>.

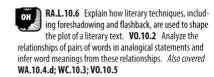

RA.L.10.6 Explain how literary techniques, including foreshadowing and flashback, are used to shape the plot of a literary text. **VO.10.2** Analyze the relationships of pairs of words in analogical statements and infer word meanings from these relationships. *Also covered* **WA.10.4.d; WC.10.3; VO.10.5**

Grammar Link

Participles

A **participle** is a verb form that can be used as an adjective to modify nouns and pronouns. Two examples are **running** *water* and **cleared** *land*. Present participles always end in –*ing,* and most past participles end in –*ed* or –*d.* Because they combine the action of verbs and the descriptive power of adjectives, participles create vivid pictures in few words.

> "He could see nothing through the <u>stinging</u> salt water but the blank rock."
> "It was like swimming in <u>flaked</u> silver."

A **participial phrase** consists of a participle and all of its complements and modifiers. The entire phrase is used as an adjective.

> "He was in a small rock-bound hole <u>filled with yellowish-gray water</u>."

Your Turn

Identify the participial phrases and the participles used as adjectives in the following sentences. Also identify the noun or pronoun each participle modifies.

1. Killer whales, long known and feared, are not nearly as vicious as many people think.

2. Perching patiently on a rocky outcropping, one researcher identified numerous whales gathered in Johnstone Strait, near Vancouver Island.

3. Cruising and playing in groups called pods, whales are highly social animals.

4. Nature can be cruel, recognizing neither kindness nor morality.

5. At the end of the summer, one whale, weakened by hunger, was left behind by its pod.

CHOICES

As you respond to the Choices, use these **Academic Vocabulary** words as appropriate: <u>derive</u>, <u>function</u>, <u>interact</u>, <u>significant</u>.

REVIEW
Analyze Symbolism
Timed LWriting "Through the Tunnel" is a memorable story. Write a brief essay describing Lessing's use of symbolism. Support your analysis by citing appropriate passages from the text.

CONNECT
Plan a Soundtrack
TechFocus As you read the story, you took notes about how you might develop a soundtrack to enhance its meaning. What kind of music and sound effects could you include? Would you use existing recordings or create your own music and sound effects? What equipment would you need? Develop a proposal for your soundtrack, and discuss it with a partner.

EXTEND
Investigate Initiation Rites
Research Activity An initiation rite marks a young person's transition into adulthood. There are many such rites in American society: confirmation, bar or bat mitzvah, *quinceañera,* graduation, and even the senior prom. Research an initiation rite from your own or another culture. What is involved? Is the rite different for girls than for boys? What is it supposed to accomplish? Share your findings with the class.

 Learn It Online
There's more to this story than meets the eye. Expand your view with these Internet links:

go.hrw.com | L10-337 | **Go**

The **Possibility** of **Evil**

by **Shirley Jackson**

Parkville, Main Street Missouri (1933) by Gale Stockwell (1907–1983).
Smithsonian American Art Museum, Washington, DC.

What Do You Think

Do our choices about how we present ourselves to the world conceal or reveal our personalities?

 QuickWrite

Write a brief description of someone who presents an outward appearance that is completely different from what is on the inside. Think of a character from film or television, or make up your own.

Reader/Writer
Notebook
Use your **RWN** to complete the activities for this selection.

OH **RA.L.10.7** Recognize how irony is used in a literary text. **RP.10.1** Apply reading comprehension strategies, including making predictions, comparing and contrasting, recalling and summarizing and making inferences and drawing conclusions.

Literary Focus

Irony In the broadest sense, **irony** is a clash between expectations and reality. Irony can take several forms. **Verbal irony** occurs when someone says one thing but means the opposite. **Situational irony** happens when a situation or a person turns out to be the opposite of what we expect. In **dramatic irony** the reader knows something important that some or all of the characters do not know. As you read "The Possibility of Evil," look for all three types of irony.

Literary Perspectives Apply the literary perspective described on page 341 as you read this story.

Reading Focus

Making Generalizations A **generalization** is a broad statement <u>derived</u> from many separate details. For example, when you identify a story's **theme**—the truth that the story reveals about human nature—you make a generalization. You take into account all the important details in the story and formulate a statement that reveals a broader truth.

Into Action Use a chart like the one below to note details of Miss Strangeworth's words and actions. As you read, think about what these details reveal about the dark side of human nature.

Story Details	What the Details Reveal
Miss Strangeworth knows everyone in town.	

Vocabulary

indulgently (ihn DUHL juhnt lee) *adv.:* in a very easygoing manner. *Miss Strangeworth knew how much the new parents loved their baby; she indulgently admired the way they fussed over the child.*

degraded (dih GRAYD ihd) *v.* used as *adj.:* wicked; morally corrupted. *Miss Strangeworth believed it was her duty to protect her town from degraded morals.*

reprehensible (rehp rih HEHN suh buhl) *adj.:* deserving of criticism. *She saw nothing reprehensible in her own actions.*

potential (puh TEHN shuhl) *adj.:* possible; unrealized; undeveloped. *Miss Strangeworth wanted to wipe out the Harris boy's potential badness before it started.*

Language Coach

Context Clues Sometimes, writers give clues about a word's meaning by placing a definition nearby. Look at this sentence: *It won't be possible to know the potential worth of the diamond before it is cut.* Which word or words tell you what *potential* means?

Writing Focus

Think as a Reader/Writer

Find It in Your Reading As you read "The Possibility of Evil," jot down in your *Reader/Writer Notebook* details that you find <u>significant</u> about Miss Strangeworth's character.

Learn It Online
There's more to words than just definitions. Get more information at:

go.hrw.com   L10-339   **Go**

Shirley Jackson
(1919–1965)

Both Sides of Human Nature

Shirley Jackson wrote two very different kinds of fiction. Some of her most famous stories are darkly pessimistic, portraying people as capable of nasty deeds. Other stories are comical, often based on the antics of her four lively children. The hilarious stories Jackson wrote about her family are collected in two books, *Life Among the Savages* (1953), which Jackson herself called a disrespectful memoir of her children, and *Raising Demons* (1957).

The most famous example of Jackson's darker fiction is a disturbing story called "The Lottery," which, when it was published in *The New Yorker* in 1948, provoked widespread public outrage. Jackson was surprised at this response. She commented, "It had simply never occurred to me that these millions and millions of people . . . would sit down and write me letters I was downright scared to open. . . . Even my mother scolded me."

At Least She Could Sit Down

Jackson once said that she spent half her life doing common tasks at home (the family lived in a big, rambling old house in Vermont) and tending to four rambunctious children. Despite the uproar, she still found time to write.

Think About the Writer According to her biography, what two sides of life did Jackson explore in her writing?

Build Background
This story takes place in a small town with generic street names such as Main Street. Sometimes, authors are purposely vague about the exact geographic location of the action so that the reader may believe that the events could be happening any-where—in this case, "Anytown, U.S.A."

Preview the Selection
In this story you will meet **Adela Strangeworth,** a seventy-one-year-old woman who has almost never left her hometown. She knows and seems to worry about everybody in town.

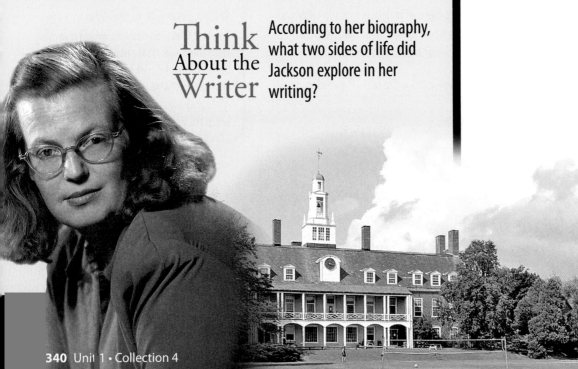

The Possibility of Evil

by **Shirley Jackson**

M iss Adela Strangeworth stepped daintily along Main Street on her way to the grocery. The sun was shining, the air was fresh and clear after the night's heavy rain, and everything in Miss Strangeworth's little town looked washed and bright. Miss Strangeworth took deep breaths, and thought that there was nothing in the world like a fragrant summer day. **(A)**

She knew everyone in town, of course; she was fond of telling strangers—tourists who sometimes passed through the town and stopped to admire Miss Strangeworth's roses—that she had never spent more than a day outside this town in all her long life. She was seventy-one, Miss Strangeworth told the tourists, with a pretty little dimple showing by her lip, and she sometimes found herself thinking that the town belonged to her. "My grandfather built the first house on Pleasant Street," she would say, opening her blue eyes wide with the wonder of it. "This house, right here. My family has lived here for better than a hundred years. My grandmother planted these roses, and my mother tended them, just as I do. I've watched my town grow; I can remember when Mr. Lewis, Senior, opened the grocery store, and the year the river flooded out the shanties on the

low road, and the excitement when some young folks wanted to move the park over to the space in front of where the new post office is today. They wanted to put up a statue of Ethan Allen"[1]—Miss Strangeworth would frown a little and sound stern—"but it should have been a statue of my grandfather. There wouldn't have

---

1. **Ethan Allen** (1738–1789): folk hero of Vermont who commanded the Green Mountain Boys during the American War of Independence.

Literary Perspectives

Analyzing Philosophical Context Everyone has a philosophy of life—a way of thinking about the world—that reflects his or her beliefs about what is true and most important. All literature reflects, in one way or another, the philosophy of its authors, who have underlying assumptions regarding the larger questions about life and its meaning. Analyzing literature from this perspective asks us to uncover and consider the philosophical arguments of an author when we read literary works. For example, an author may invent a character that represents his or her philosophy, or a narrator may comment on a story's characters and events in order to express a consciously held opinion or an underlying assumption about life and its meaning. As you read, use the notes and questions in the text to guide you in using this perspective.

(A) Reading Focus Making Generalizations From this brief introductory paragraph, what generalizations can you make about the setting of the story?

been a town here at all if it hadn't been for my grandfather and the lumber mill."

Miss Strangeworth never gave away any of her roses, although the tourists often asked her. The roses belonged on Pleasant Street, and it bothered Miss Strangeworth to think of people wanting to carry them away, to take them into strange towns and down strange streets. When the new minister came, and the ladies were gathering flowers to decorate the church, Miss Strangeworth sent over a great basket of gladioli; when she picked the roses at all, she set them in bowls and vases around the inside of the house her grandfather had built. **B**

Walking down Main Street on a summer morning, Miss Strangeworth had to stop every minute or so to say good morning to someone or to ask after someone's health. When she came into the grocery, half a dozen people turned away from the shelves and the counters to wave at her or call out good morning.

"And good morning to you, too, Mr. Lewis," Miss Strangeworth said at last. The Lewis family had been in the town almost as long as the Strangeworths; but the day young Lewis left high school and went to work in the grocery, Miss Strangeworth had stopped calling him Tommy and started calling him Mr. Lewis, and he had stopped calling her Addie and started calling her Miss Strangeworth. They had been in high school together, and had gone to picnics together, and to high school dances and basketball games; but now Mr. Lewis was behind the counter in the grocery, and Miss Strangeworth was living alone in the Strangeworth house on Pleasant Street. **C**

"Good morning," Mr. Lewis said, and added politely, "lovely day."

"It is a very nice day," Miss Strangeworth said as though she had only just decided that it would do after all. "I would like a chop, please, Mr. Lewis, a small, lean veal chop. Are those strawberries from Arthur Parker's garden? They're early this year."

"He brought them in this morning," Mr. Lewis said.

"I shall have a box," Miss Strangeworth said. Mr. Lewis looked worried, she thought, and for a minute she hesitated, but then she decided that he surely could not be worried over the strawberries. He looked very tired indeed. He was usually so chipper, Miss Strangeworth thought, and almost commented, but it was far too personal a subject to be introduced to Mr. Lewis, the grocer, so she only said, "And a can of cat food and, I think, a tomato."

Silently, Mr. Lewis assembled her order on the counter and waited. Miss Strangeworth looked at him curiously and then said, "It's Tuesday, Mr. Lewis. You forgot to remind me."

"Did I? Sorry."

"Imagine your forgetting that I always buy my tea on Tuesday," Miss Strangeworth said gently. "A quarter pound of tea, please, Mr. Lewis."

"Is that all, Miss Strangeworth?"

"Yes, thank you, Mr. Lewis. Such a lovely day, isn't it?"

"Lovely," Mr. Lewis said.

Miss Strangeworth moved slightly to make room for Mrs. Harper at the counter. "Morning, Adela," Mrs. Harper said, and Miss

---

B **Reading Focus** Making Generalizations What do the details in these last two paragraphs suggest about Miss Strangeworth?

C **Reading Focus** Making Generalizations What do these details suggest about the relationship between Miss Strangeworth and Mr. Lewis?

Analyzing Visuals **Viewing and Interpreting** How does this painting of a woman compare with the description of Miss Strangeworth in the story?

Aunt Lila (1943) by Dod Procter. Penlee House Gallery and Museum, Penzance, Cornwall, UK.

Strangeworth said, "Good morning, Martha."

"Lovely day," Mrs. Harper said, and Miss Strangeworth said, "Yes, lovely," and Mr. Lewis, under Mrs. Harper's glance, nodded.

"Ran out of sugar for my cake frosting," Mrs. Harper explained. Her hand shook slightly as she opened her pocketbook. Miss Strangeworth wondered, glancing at her quickly, if she had been taking proper care of herself. Martha Harper was not as young as she used to be, Miss Strangeworth thought. She probably could use a good, strong tonic.

"Martha," she said, "you don't look well."

"I'm perfectly all right," Mrs. Harper said shortly. She handed her money to Mr. Lewis, took her change and her sugar, and went out without speaking again. Looking after her, Miss Strangeworth shook her head slightly. Martha definitely did *not* look well.

D

Carrying her little bag of groceries, Miss Strangeworth came out of the store into the bright sunlight and stopped to smile down on the Crane baby. Don and Helen Crane were really the two most infatuated[2] young parents she had ever known, she thought indulgently, looking at the delicately embroidered baby cap and the lace-edged carriage cover.

"That little girl is going to grow up expecting luxury all her life," she said to Helen Crane.

Helen laughed. "That's the way we want her

> "A princess can be a lot of trouble sometimes," Miss Strangeworth said dryly. "How old is her highness now?"

to feel," she said. "Like a princess."

"A princess can be a lot of trouble sometimes," Miss Strangeworth said dryly. "How old is her highness now?"

"Six months next Tuesday," Helen Crane said, looking down with rapt wonder at her child. "I've been worrying, though, about her. Don't you think she ought to move around more? Try to sit up, for instance?"

"For plain and fancy worrying," Miss Strangeworth said, amused, "give me a new mother every time."

"She just seems—slow," Helen Crane said.

"Nonsense. All babies are different. Some of them develop much more quickly than others."

"That's what my mother says." Helen Crane laughed, looking a little bit ashamed.

"I suppose you've got young Don all upset about the fact that his daughter is already six months old and hasn't yet begun to learn to dance?"

"I haven't mentioned it to him. I suppose she's just so precious that I worry about her all the time."

"Well, apologize to her right now," Miss Strangeworth said. "*She* is probably worrying about why you keep jumping around all the time." Smiling to herself and shaking her old head, she went on down the sunny street, stopping once to ask little Billy Moore why he wasn't out riding in his daddy's shiny new car, and talking for a few minutes outside the library with Miss Chandler, the librarian, about the

---

2. **infatuated** (ihn FACH oo ayt ihd): carried away by foolish love or affection.

D **Literary Focus** Irony What is ironic about Mrs. Harper's statement? Is she "perfectly all right"?

Vocabulary **indulgently** (ihn DUHL juhnt lee) *adv.*: in a very easygoing manner.

new novels to be ordered, and paid for by the annual library appropriation.[3] Miss Chandler seemed absentminded and very much as though she was thinking about something else. Miss Strangeworth noticed that Miss Chandler had not taken much trouble with her hair that morning, and sighed. Miss Strangeworth hated sloppiness.

Many people seemed disturbed recently, Miss Strangeworth thought. Only yesterday the Stewarts' fifteen-year-old Linda had run crying down her own front walk and all the way to school, not caring who saw her. People around town thought she might have had a fight with the Harris boy, but they showed up together at the soda shop after school as usual, both of them looking grim and bleak. Trouble at home, people concluded, and sighed over the problems of trying to raise kids right these days. **E**

From halfway down the block Miss Strangeworth could catch the heavy accent of her roses, and she moved a little more quickly. The perfume of roses meant home, and home meant the Strangeworth House on Pleasant Street. Miss Strangeworth stopped at her own front gate, as she always did, and looked with deep pleasure at her house, with the red and pink and white roses massed along the narrow lawn, and the rambler going up along the porch; and the neat, the unbelievably trim lines of the house itself, with its slimness and its washed white look. Every window sparkled, every curtain hung stiff and straight, and even the stones of the front walk were swept and clear. People around town wondered how old

---

3. **appropriation** (uh proh pree AY shuhn): money set aside for special use.

Miss Strangeworth managed to keep the house looking the way it did, and there was a legend about a tourist once mistaking it for the local museum and going all through the place without finding out about his mistake. But the town was proud of Miss Strangeworth and her roses and her house. They had all grown together. Miss Strangeworth went up her front steps, unlocked her front door with her key, and went into the kitchen to put away her groceries. She debated having a cup of tea and then decided that it was too close to midday dinnertime; she would not have the appetite for her little chop if she had tea now. Instead she went into the light, lovely sitting room, which still glowed from the hands of her mother and her grandmother, who had covered the chairs with bright chintz and hung the curtains. All the furniture was spare and shining, and the round hooked rugs on the floor had been the work of Miss Strangeworth's grandmother and her mother. Miss Strangeworth had put a bowl of her red roses on the low table before the window, and the room was full of their scent. **F**

Miss Strangeworth went to the narrow desk in the corner, and unlocked it with her key. She never knew when she might feel like writing letters, so she kept her notepaper inside, and the desk locked. Miss Strangeworth's usual stationery was heavy and cream-colored, with "Strangeworth House" engraved across the top, but, when she felt like writing her other letters, Miss Strangeworth used a pad of various-colored paper, bought from the local newspaper shop. It was almost a town joke, that colored paper, layered in pink and green and blue and yellow; everyone in town bought it and used it for odd,

---

E **Reading Focus** Making Generalizations What details suggest that something is disturbing Helen Crane, Miss Chandler, and Linda Stewart?

F **Reading Focus** Making Generalizations What does the description of Miss Strangeworth's house suggest about her life?

informal notes and shopping lists. It was usual to remark, upon receiving a note written on a blue page, that so-and-so would be needing a new pad soon—here she was, down to the blue already. Everyone used the matching envelopes for tucking away recipes, or keeping odd little things in, or even to hold cookies in the school lunch boxes. Mr. Lewis sometimes gave them to the children for carrying home penny candy.

Although Miss Strangeworth's desk held a trimmed quill pen, which had belonged to her grandfather, and a gold-frost fountain pen, which had belonged to her father, Miss Strangeworth always used a dull stub of pencil when she wrote her letters, and she printed them in a childish block print. After thinking for a minute, although she had been phrasing the letter in the back of her mind all the way home, she wrote on a pink sheet: *Didn't you ever see an idiot child before? Some people just shouldn't have children, should they?* **G**

She was pleased with the letter. She was fond of doing things exactly right. When she made a mistake, as she sometimes did, or

---

G **Literary Focus** **Irony** Think back to Miss Strangeworth's earlier conversation with Helen Crane. How is this letter an example of verbal irony?

Long Shadows (2005) by Jennifer E. Young (1967–). Oil on canvas. 12" × 12". © Jennifer E. Young.

when the letters were not spaced nicely on the page, she had to take the discarded page to the kitchen stove and burn it at once. Miss Strangeworth never delayed when things had to be done.

After thinking for a minute, she decided that she would like to write another letter, perhaps to go to Mrs. Harper, to follow up the ones she had already mailed. She selected a green sheet this time and wrote quickly: *Have you found out yet what they were all laughing about after you left the bridge club on Thursday? Or is the wife really always the last one to know?*

Miss Strangeworth never concerned herself with facts; her letters all dealt with the more negotiable[4] stuff of suspicion. Mr. Lewis would never have imagined for a minute that his grandson might be lifting petty cash from the store register if he had not had one of Miss Strangeworth's letters. Miss Chandler, the librarian, and Linda Stewart's parents would have gone unsuspectingly ahead with their lives, never aware of possible evil lurking nearby, if Miss Strangeworth had not sent letters to open their eyes. Miss Strangeworth would have been genuinely shocked if there *had* been anything between Linda Stewart and the Harris boy, but, as long as evil existed unchecked in the world, it was Miss Strangeworth's duty to keep her town alert to it. It was far more sensible for Miss Chandler to wonder what Mr. Shelley's first wife had really died of than to take a chance on not knowing. There were so many wicked people

---

4. **negotiable** (nih GOH shuh buhl): here, referring to details that can be interpreted in several ways.

in the world and only one Strangeworth left in town. Besides, Miss Strangeworth liked writing her letters. Ⓗ

She addressed an envelope to Don Crane after a moment's thought, wondering curiously if he would show the letter to his wife, and using a pink envelope to match the pink paper. Then she addressed a second envelope, green, to Mrs. Harper. Then an idea came to her and she selected a blue sheet and wrote: *You never know about doctors. Remember they're only human and need money like the rest of us. Suppose the knife slipped accidentally. Would Doctor Burns get his fee and a little extra from that nephew of yours?*

She addressed the blue envelope to old Mrs. Foster, who was having an operation next month. She had thought of writing one more letter, to the head of the school board, asking how a chemistry teacher like Billy Moore's father could afford a new convertible, but all at once she was tired of writing letters. The three she had done would do for one day. She could write more tomorrow; it was not as though they all had to be done at once.

She had been writing her letters—sometimes two or three every day for a week, sometimes no more than one in a month—for the past year. She never got any answers, of course, because she never signed her name. If she had been asked, she would have said that her name, Adela Strangeworth, a name honored in the town for so many years, did not belong on such trash. The town where she lived had to be kept clean and sweet, but people everywhere were lustful and evil and degraded, and needed to be watched;

Ⓗ **Literary Perspectives** Philosophical Context Do you think the author believes that Miss Strangeworth's actions are necessary and important? Why or why not?

Vocabulary **degraded** (dih GRAYD ihd) *v.* used as *adj.*: wicked; morally corrupted.

the world was so large, and there was only one Strangeworth left in it. Miss Strangeworth sighed, locked her desk, and put the letters into her big, black leather pocketbook, to be mailed when she took her evening walk.

She broiled her little chop nicely, and had a sliced tomato and good cup of tea ready when she sat down to her midday dinner at the table in her dining room, which could be opened to seat twenty-two, with a second table, if necessary, in the hall. Sitting in the warm sunlight that came through the tall windows of the dining room, seeing her roses massed outside, handling the heavy, old silverware and the fine, translucent china, Miss Strangeworth was pleased; she would not have cared to be doing anything else. People must live graciously, after all, she thought, and

> This was, after all, her town, and these were her people; if one of them was in trouble, she ought to know about it.

sipped her tea. Afterward, when her plate and cup and saucer were washed and dried and put back onto the shelves where they belonged, and her silverware was back in the mahogany silver chest, Miss Strangeworth went up the graceful staircase and into her bedroom, which was the front room overlooking the roses, and had been her mother's and her grandmother's. Their Crown Derby dresser set[5] and furs had been kept here, their fans and silver-backed brushes and their own bowls of roses; Miss Strangeworth kept a bowl of white roses on the bed table. ❶

She drew the shades, took the rose-satin spread from the bed, slipped out of her dress and her shoes, and lay down tiredly. She knew that no doorbell or phone would ring; no one in town would dare to disturb Miss Strangeworth during her afternoon nap. She slept, deep in the rich smell of roses.

After her nap she worked in her garden for a little while, sparing herself because of the heat; then she went in to her supper. She ate asparagus from her own garden, with sweet-butter sauce, and a soft-boiled egg, and, while she had her supper, she listened to a late-evening news broadcast and then to a program of classical music on her small radio. After her dishes were done and her kitchen set in order, she took up her hat—Miss Strangeworth's hats were proverbial[6] in the town; people believed that she had inherited them from her mother and her grandmother—and, locking the front door of her house behind her, set off on her evening walk, pocketbook under her arm. She nodded to Linda Stewart's father, who was washing his car in the pleasantly cool evening. She thought that he looked troubled.

There was only one place in town where she could mail her letters, and that was the new post office, shiny with red brick and silver letters. Although Miss Strangeworth had never

---

5. **Crown Derby dresser set:** comb, brush, and mirror that are made of very fine china (called Crown Derby) and that are placed on a dresser or bureau.

6. **proverbial** (pruh VUR bee uhl): well known because often talked about.

---

❶ **Literary Focus** Irony In what way is Miss Strangeworth's thought that "people must live graciously" an example of situational irony?

given the matter any particular thought, she had always made a point of mailing her letters very secretly; it would, of course, not have been wise to let anyone see her mail them. Consequently, she timed her walk so she could reach the post office just as darkness was starting to dim the outlines of the trees and the shapes of people's faces, although no one could ever mistake Miss Strangeworth, with her dainty walk and her rustling skirts.

There was always a group of young people around the post office, the very youngest roller-skating upon its driveway, which went all the way around the building and was the only smooth road in town; and the slightly older ones already knowing how to gather in small groups and chatter and laugh and make great, excited plans for going across the street to the soda shop in a minute or two. Miss Strangeworth had never had any self-consciousness before the children. She did not feel that any of them were staring at her unduly[7] or longing to laugh at her; it would have been most reprehensible for their parents to permit their children to mock Miss Strangeworth of Pleasant Street. Most of the children stood back respectfully as Miss Strangeworth passed, silenced briefly in her presence, and some of the older children greeted her, saying soberly, "Hello, Miss Strangeworth."

Miss Strangeworth smiled at them and quickly went on. It had been a long time since she had known the name of every child in town. The mail slot was in the door of the post office.

The children stood away as Miss Strangeworth approached it, seemingly surprised that anyone should want to use the post office after it had been officially closed up for the night and turned over to the children. Miss Strangeworth stood by the door, opening her black pocketbook to take out the letters, and heard a voice which she knew at once to be Linda Stewart's. Poor little Linda was crying again, and Miss Strangeworth listened carefully. This was, after all, her town, and these were her people; if one of them was in trouble, she ought to know about it. **J**

"I can't tell you, Dave," Linda was saying— so she *was* talking to the Harris boy, as Miss Strangeworth had supposed—"I just *can't*. It's just *nasty*."

"But why won't your father let me come around anymore? What on earth did I do?"

"I can't tell you. I just wouldn't tell you for *any*thing. You've got to have a dirty dirty mind for things like that."

"But something's happened. You've been crying and crying, and your father is all upset. Why can't *I* know about it, too? Aren't I like one of the family?"

"Not anymore, Dave, not anymore. You're not to come near our house again; my father said so. He said he'd horsewhip you. That's all I can tell you: You're not to come near our house anymore."

"But I didn't *do* anything."

"Just the same, my father said . . ."

Miss Strangeworth sighed and turned away.

---

7. **unduly** (uhn DOO lee): improperly; excessively.

Vocabulary **reprehensible** (rehp rih HEHN suh buhl) *adj*.: deserving of criticism.

J Literary Focus **Irony** Given what we know about Miss Strangeworth, what is ironic about her view of the townspeople?

There was so much evil in people. Even in a charming little town like this one, there was still so much evil in people.

She slipped her letters into the slot, and two of them fell inside. The third caught on the edge and fell outside, onto the ground at Miss Strangeworth's feet. She did not notice it because she was wondering whether a letter to the Harris boy's father might not be of some service in wiping out this potential badness. Wearily Miss Strangeworth turned to go home to her quiet bed in her lovely house, and never heard the Harris boy calling to her to say that she had dropped something.

"Old lady Strangeworth's getting deaf," he said, looking after her and holding in his hand the letter he had picked up.

"Well, who cares?" Linda said. "Who cares anymore, anyway?"

"It's for Don Crane," the Harris boy said, "this letter. She dropped a letter addressed to Don Crane. Might as well take it on over. We pass his house anyway." He laughed. "Maybe it's got a check or something in it and he'd be just as glad to get it tonight instead of tomorrow."

"Catch old lady Strangeworth sending anybody a check," Linda said. "Throw it in the post office. Why do anyone a favor?" She sniffed. "Doesn't seem to me anybody around here cares about us," she said. "Why should we care about them?"

"I'll take it over, anyway," the Harris boy said. "Maybe it's good news for them. Maybe they need something happy tonight, too. Like us." **Ⓚ**

Sadly, holding hands, they wandered off down the dark street, the Harris boy carrying Miss Strangeworth's pink envelope in his hand.

Miss Strangeworth awakened the next morning with a feeling of intense happiness and, for a minute, wondered why, and then remembered that this morning three people would open her letters. Harsh, perhaps, at first, but wickedness was never easily banished, and a clean heart was a scoured heart. She washed her soft, old face and brushed her teeth, still sound in spite of her seventy-one years, and dressed herself carefully in her sweet, soft clothes and buttoned shoes. Then, going downstairs, reflecting that perhaps a little waffle would be agreeable for breakfast in the sunny dining room, she found the mail on the hall floor, and bent to pick it up. A bill, the morning paper, a letter in a green envelope that looked oddly familiar. Miss Strangeworth stood perfectly still for a minute, looking down at the green envelope with the penciled printing, and thought: It looks like one of my letters. Was one of my letters sent back? No, because no one would know where to send it. How did this get here?

Miss Strangeworth was a Strangeworth of Pleasant Street. Her hand did not shake as she opened the envelope and unfolded the sheet of green paper inside. She began to cry silently for the wickedness of the world when she read the words: *Look out at what used to be your roses.* **Ⓛ**

Ⓚ Literary Focus Irony In what way is the Harris boy's comment an example of dramatic irony?

Ⓛ Literary Perspectives Philosophical Context What underlying assumptions about human nature does the author reveal in these last two paragraphs?

Vocabulary **potential** (puh TEHN shuhl) *adj.*: possible; unrealized; undeveloped.

Applying Your Skills

RA.L.10.7 Recognize how irony is used in a literary text. RA.L.10.2 Analyze the features of setting and their importance in a literary text. *Also covered* RP.10.1; VO.10.3; WA.10.1.b

The Possibility of Evil

Respond and Think Critically

Reading Focus

Quick Check

1. How does Miss Strangeworth feel about her family background? her town? her roses?

2. Why does Miss Strangeworth send the letters? What effect do they have on their recipients?

Read with a Purpose

3. What does the title of the story mean? Where in the story is it explained?

Reading Skills: Making Generalizations

4. Add a row to your chart, and make generalizations about the story's theme based on the details you collected.

Story Details	What the Details Reveal
Miss Strangeworth knows everyone in town.	

Generalizations:

✓ Vocabulary Check

Answer the following questions about the boldface Vocabulary words. Be sure to explain your responses.

5. If a mother treats her child **indulgently,** is she being easygoing or strict?

6. Is *corrupt* a synonym or an antonym for the word **degraded**?

7. If an action is **reprehensible,** is it admirable or deserving of criticism?

8. If you say someone has a great deal of **potential,** are you complimenting or criticizing the person?

Literary Focus

Literary Analysis

9. **Identify** What details early in the story **foreshadow,** or hint at, Miss Strangeworth's secret?

10. **Speculate** What reasons can you propose for Miss Strangeworth's unexpected actions?

11. **Literary Perspectives** Draw conclusions about the author's views of society and of evil. On what do you base your conclusions?

Literary Skills: Irony

12. **Analyze** There are three types of irony in this story: situational, verbal, and dramatic. Give an example of each one.

13. **Analyze** In what way does the story's title reflect the ironies in the story itself?

Literary Skills Review: Setting

14. **Identify** Details in the **setting,** the time and place the story is set, contribute to the story's irony. Explain why those details are ironic.

Writing Focus

Think as a Reader/Writer

Use It in Your Writing Review your notes about the setting and Miss Strangeworth. In your *Reader/Writer Notebook,* describe another character whose inner life contrasts with his or her outer world.

 What Do You Think Now

Could someone like Miss Strangeworth really exist, or do you think her character is unbelievable? Explain.

A Very Old Man with Enormous Wings

by **Gabriel García Márquez**

What Do **You** Think? How do you respond when something unexpected happens?

QuickWrite

Think of an unusual or startling event that you witnessed. Write a paragraph about how you reacted, and speculate about whether you would react the same way if the event occurred again.

Man with One Wing (1992)
by Clifford Goodenough.
Courtesy the artist.

Reader/Writer Notebook

Use your **RWN** to complete the activities for this selection.

RA.L.10.7 Recognize how irony is used in a literary text. **RA.L.10.11** Explain ways in which an author develops a point of view and style, and cite specific examples from the text.

Literary Focus

Magic Realism and Irony **Magic realism** is characterized by elements of fantasy casually inserted into earthy, realistic settings. In this story, for example, an ordinary old man falls from the sky into a muddy courtyard—surprisingly, he has a pair of real wings. Magic realists often use irony to help us see the fantastic in reality and the reality in fantasy. **Irony** is the discrepancy between appearances and reality, or between what is expected or seems appropriate and what actually happens.

Literary Perspectives Apply the literary perspective described on page 355 as you read this story.

Reading Focus

Analyzing Details García Márquez includes many striking descriptive details to bring his settings and characters to life. Figurative language appealing to the senses of sight, hearing, touch, taste, and smell helps you better imagine and experience the world in the story.

Into Action As you read, use a chart like the one below to keep track of García Márquez's use of sensory details.

Details About Setting	Details About Old Man
smell of rotten shellfish	dressed like a ragpicker

Writing Focus

Think as a Reader/Writer

Find It in Your Reading García Márquez is a master of irony. As you read, think about the expectations he establishes, beginning with the story's title. How does he defy your expectations and surprise you? In your *Reader/Writer Notebook*, jot down the details that you find ironic.

TechFocus As you read the story, think about how you might use the Internet to report and comment on strange events that occur.

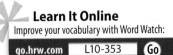

Learn It Online
Improve your vocabulary with Word Watch:

go.hrw.com   L10-353   **Go**

Gabriel García Márquez (1928–)

Nobel Prize WINNER

Tales of a Vivid Past

Gabriel García Márquez sets much of his fiction in the imaginary town of Macondo, which in many ways resembles the sleepy backwater town of Aracataca, Colombia, where he was born. Young Gabriel was raised by his maternal grandparents in a large old house crowded with relatives and relics of the family's past. His grandmother told him tales of ancestors, spirits, and ghosts; and his grandfather spoke continually of a past so vivid that it became as real to the young boy as the present.

A Blend of the Real and the Fantastic

In 1967, García Márquez became an international celebrity with the publication of his novel *One Hundred Years of Solitude*, a saga of seven generations of Macondo's founding family. In 1982, he won the Nobel Prize in literature for his fiction, "in which the fantastic and the realistic are combined in a richly composed world of imagination." García Márquez noted wryly, "It always amuses me that the biggest praise for my work comes for the imagination, while the truth is that there's not a single line in all my work that does not have a basis in reality."

"When you are young," says the author, "you write . . . almost like writing a poem. You write on impulses and inspiration. You have so much inspiration that you are not concerned with technique. You just see what comes out, without worrying much about what you are going to say and how."

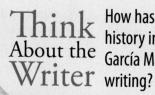

Think About the Writer How has his family's history influenced García Márquez's writing?

Build Background

This story was published with six other stories in a book called *The Incredible and Sad Story of Innocent Erendira and Her Heartless Grandmother*. In this story collection, García Márquez seems to be responding to the celebrity status he gained with his first novel. This story about the old man hints at his own discomfort with fame.

Preview the Selection

Pelayo and his wife, **Elisenda**, find an old man with wings lying in the mud in their courtyard. Because their baby is very ill, they assume he is an angel who has come to take the child away.

A banner reads *Aracataca Macondo, yes*. Some people from Aracataca, Colombia, where García Márquez was born, wanted to change the town's name to *Aracataca Macondo*. *Macondo* is the name of the fictitious town where *One Hundred Years of Solitude* is set.

A Very Old Man with Enormous Wings

by **Gabriel García Márquez**
translated by **Gregory Rabassa**

On the third day of rain they had killed so many crabs inside the house that Pelayo had to cross his drenched courtyard and throw them into the sea, because the newborn child had a temperature all night and they thought it was due to the stench. The world had been sad since Tuesday. Sea and sky were a single ash-gray thing, and the sands of the beach, which on March nights glimmered like powdered light, had become a stew of mud and rotten shellfish. The light was so weak at noon that when Pelayo was coming back to the house after throwing away the crabs, it was hard for him to see what it was that was moving and groaning in the rear of the courtyard. He had to go very close to see that it was an old man, a very old man, lying face down in the mud, who, in spite of his tremendous efforts, couldn't get up, impeded by his enormous wings. **Ⓐ**

Ⓐ **Reading Focus** Analyzing Details What details from this opening paragraph help you see, smell, and feel the setting?

Vocabulary **stench** (stehnch) *n.*: offensive smell.
impeded (ihm PEED ihd) *v.* used as *adj.*: obstructed; blocked, as by some obstacle.

Frightened by that nightmare, Pelayo ran to get Elisenda, his wife, who was putting compresses on the sick child, and he took her to the rear of the courtyard. They both looked at the fallen body with mute stupor.[1] He was dressed like a ragpicker. There were only a few faded

---

1. **stupor** (STOO puhr): dullness of the mind and senses.

Literary Perspectives

Analyzing Style This perspective builds on what you have learned about authors' techniques, such as figurative language, imagery, characterization, and other literary tools that writers use to help convey the mood, tone, and theme of a literary text. You probably have noticed that different authors use these techniques to create very recognizable styles. An author's style is like a kind of literary fingerprint. Ernest Hemingway, for example, uses short simple sentences in a journalistic style. Edgar Allan Poe uses more florid language and complex sentences that help create a sense of foreboding. When you analyze an author's style, consider sentence structure, vocabulary, and use of dialogue and recurring themes or topics. As you read, use the notes and questions in the text to guide you in using this perspective.

hairs left on his bald skull and very few teeth in his mouth, and his pitiful condition of a drenched great-grandfather had taken away any sense of grandeur he might have had. His huge buzzard wings, dirty and half plucked, were forever entangled in the mud. They looked at him so long and so closely that Pelayo and Elisenda very soon overcame their surprise and in the end found him familiar. Then they dared speak to him, and he answered in an incomprehensible dialect with a strong sailor's voice. That was how they skipped over the inconvenience of the wings and quite intelligently concluded that he was a lonely castaway from some foreign ship wrecked by the storm. And yet, they called in a neighbor woman who knew everything about life and death to see him, and all she needed was one look to show them their mistake. **B**

"He's an angel," she told them. "He must have been coming for the child, but the poor fellow is so old that the rain knocked him down."

On the following day everyone knew that a flesh-and-blood angel was held captive in Pelayo's house. Against the judgment of the wise neighbor woman, for whom angels in those times were the fugitive survivors of a celestial conspiracy,[2] they did not have the heart to club him to death. Pelayo watched over him all afternoon from the kitchen, armed with his bailiff's[3] club, and before going to bed, he dragged him out of the mud and locked him up with the hens in the wire chicken coop. In the middle of the night, when the rain stopped, Pelayo and Elisenda were still killing crabs. A short time afterward the child woke up without a fever and with a desire to eat. Then they felt magnanimous[4] and decided to put the angel on a raft

---

2. **celestial conspiracy:** According to the Book of Revelation in the Bible (12:7–9), Satan originally was an angel who led a rebellion in Heaven. As a result, he and his followers, called the fallen angels, were cast out of Heaven.
3. **bailiff's** (BAY lihfs): A bailiff is a minor local official.
4. **magnanimous** (mag NAN uh muhs): generous; noble.

B **Literary Perspectives** Analyzing Style García Márquez is known for his simple yet highly descriptive style. What picture does he paint for you in this paragraph?

356

Analyzing Visuals

Viewing and Interpreting How do the reactions of the children to the "stranger" in this photograph compare to the reactions of the villagers to the old man in the story?

with fresh water and provisions for three days and leave him to his fate on the high seas. But when they went out into the courtyard with the first light of dawn, they found the whole neighborhood in front of the chicken coop having fun with the angel, without the slightest reverence,[5] tossing him things to eat through the openings in the wire as if he weren't a supernatural creature but a circus animal. (C)

Father Gonzaga arrived before seven o'clock, alarmed at the strange news. By that time onlookers less frivolous than those at dawn had already arrived and they were making all kinds of conjectures[6] concerning the captive's future. The simplest among them thought that he should be named mayor of the world. Others of sterner mind felt that he should be promoted to the rank of five-star general in order to win all wars. Some visionaries hoped that he could be put to stud in order to implant on earth a race of winged wise men who could take charge of the universe. But Father Gonzaga, before becoming a priest, had been a robust woodcutter. Standing by the wire, he reviewed his catechism[7] in an instant and asked them to open the door so that he could take a close look at that pitiful man who looked more like a huge decrepit hen

among the fascinated chickens. He was lying in a corner drying his open wings in the sunlight among the fruit peels and breakfast leftovers that the early risers had thrown him. Alien to the impertinences[8] of the world, he only lifted his antiquarian[9] eyes and murmured something in his dialect when Father Gonzaga went into the chicken coop and said good morning to him in Latin. The parish priest had his first suspicion of an impostor when he saw that he did not understand the language of God or know how to greet His ministers. Then he noticed that seen close up, he was much too human: He had an unbearable smell of the outdoors, the back side of his wings was strewn with parasites and his main feathers had been mistreated by terrestrial[10] winds, and nothing about him measured up to the proud dignity of angels. Then he came out of the chicken coop and in a brief sermon warned the curious against the risks of being ingenuous.[11] He reminded them that the devil had the bad habit of making use of carnival tricks in order to confuse the unwary. He argued that if wings were not the essential element in determining the difference between a hawk and an airplane, they were even less so in the recognition of angels. Nevertheless, he promised

---

5. **reverence** (REHV uhr uhns): attitude or display of deep respect and awe.
6. **conjectures** (kuhn JEHK churz): guesses not completely supported by evidence.
7. **catechism** (KAT uh kihz uhm): book of religious principles, consisting of a series of questions and answers.

8. **impertinences** (ihm PUR tuh nuhns uhz): insults; disrespectful acts or remarks.
9. **antiquarian** (an tuh KWAIR ee uhn): ancient.
10. **terrestrial** (tuh REHS tree uhl): earthly.
11. **ingenuous** (ihn JEHN yoo uhs): too trusting; tending to believe too readily.

(C) **Literary Focus** Magic Realism and Irony Given that the old man is an angel, what is ironic, or inappropriate, about the way he is treated?

Vocabulary frivolous (FRIHV uh luhs) *adj.*: not properly serious; silly.

to write a letter to his bishop so that the latter would write to his primate[12] so that the latter would write to the Supreme Pontiff[13] in order to get the final verdict from the highest courts. **D**

His prudence fell on sterile hearts. The news of the captive angel spread with such rapidity that after a few hours the courtyard had the bustle of a marketplace, and they had to call in troops with fixed bayonets to disperse the mob that was about to knock the house down. Elisenda, her spine all twisted from sweeping up so much marketplace trash, then got the idea of fencing in the yard and charging five cents admission to see the angel.

The curious came from far away. A traveling carnival arrived with a flying acrobat, who buzzed over the crowd several times, but no one paid any attention to him because his wings were not those of an angel but, rather, those of a sidereal[14] bat. The most unfortunate invalids on earth came in search of health: a poor woman who since childhood had been counting her heartbeats and had run out of numbers; a Portuguese man who couldn't sleep because the noise of the stars disturbed him; a sleepwalker who got up at night to undo the things he had done while awake; and many others with less serious ailments. In the midst of that shipwreck disorder that made the earth tremble, Pelayo

and Elisenda were happy with fatigue, for in less than a week they had crammed their rooms with money and the line of pilgrims waiting their turn to enter still reached beyond the horizon. **E**

The angel was the only one who took no part in his own act. He spent his time trying to get comfortable in his borrowed nest, befuddled by the hellish heat of the oil lamps and sacramental candles that had been placed along the wire. At first they tried to make him eat some mothballs, which, according to the wisdom of the wise neighbor woman, were the food prescribed for angels. But he turned them down, just as he turned down the papal[15] lunches that the penitents[16] brought him, and they never found out whether it was because he was an angel or because he was an old man that in the end he ate nothing but eggplant mush. His only supernatural virtue seemed to be patience. Especially during the first days, when the hens pecked at him, searching for stellar parasites that proliferated in his wings, and the cripples pulled out feathers to touch their defective parts with, and even the most merciful threw stones at him, trying to get him to rise so they could see him standing. The only time they succeeded in arousing him was when they burned his side with an iron for branding

---

12. **primate:** here, an archbishop or highest-ranking bishop in a country or province.
13. **Supreme Pontiff:** pope, head of the Roman Catholic Church.
14. **sidereal** (sy DIHR ee uhl): relating to the stars or constellations.

15. **papal** (PAY puhl): here, fit for the pope.
16. **penitents** (PEHN uh tuhnts): people who repent their sins.

D **Literary Focus** Magic Realism and Irony According to the priest, why is the winged man not an angel?

E **Literary Perspectives** Analyzing Style How does García Márquez use sentence structure and word choice to create a striking description of the visitors?

Vocabulary **prudence** (PROO duhns) *n.:* good judgment; cautiousness.

Analyzing Visuals **Viewing and Interpreting** In what way do these images mirror the style of magic realism?

steers, for he had been motionless for so many hours that they thought he was dead. He awoke with a start, ranting in his hermetic[17] language and with tears in his eyes, and he flapped his wings a couple of times, which brought on a whirlwind of chicken dung and lunar dust and a gale of panic that did not seem to be of this world. Although many thought that his reaction had been one not of rage but of pain, from then on they were careful not to annoy him, because the majority understood that his passivity was not that of a hero taking his ease but that of a cataclysm[18] in repose.

Father Gonzaga held back the crowd's frivolity with formulas of maidservant inspiration while awaiting the arrival of a final judgment on the nature of the captive. But the mail from Rome showed no sense of urgency. They spent their time finding out if the prisoner had a navel, if his dialect had any connection with Aramaic,[19] how many times he could fit on the head of a pin, or whether he wasn't just a Norwegian with wings. Those meager letters might have come and gone until the end of time if a providential[20] event had not put an end to the priest's tribulations.[21] **F**

It so happened that during those days, among so many other carnival attractions, there arrived in town the traveling show of the woman who had been changed into a spider for having disobeyed her parents. The admission to see her was not only less than the admission to see the angel, but people were permitted to ask her all manner of questions about her absurd state and to examine her up and down so that no one would ever doubt the truth of her horror. She was a frightful tarantula the size of a ram and with the head of a sad maiden. What was most heart-rending, however, was not her outlandish shape but the sincere affliction[22] with which she recounted the details of her misfortune. While still practically a child, she had sneaked out of her parents' house to go to a dance, and while she was coming back through the woods after having danced all night without permission, a fearful thunderclap rent the sky in two and through the crack came the lightning bolt of brimstone that changed her into a spider. Her only nourishment came from the meatballs that charitable souls chose to toss into her mouth. A spectacle like that, full of so much human truth and with such a fearful lesson, was bound to defeat without even trying that of a haughty angel who scarcely deigned to look at mortals. Besides, the few miracles attributed to the angel showed a certain mental disorder, like the blind man who didn't recover his sight but grew three new teeth, or the paralytic who didn't get to walk but almost won the lottery, or the leper whose sores sprouted sunflowers.

---

17. **hermetic** (huhr MEHT ihk): difficult to understand; mysterious.

18. **cataclysm** (KAT uh klihz uhm): disaster; sudden, violent event.

19. **Aramaic:** ancient Middle Eastern language spoken by Jesus and his disciples.

20. **providential** (prahv uh DEHN shuhl): fortunate; like something caused by a divine act.

21. **tribulations** (trihb yuh LAY shuhnz): conditions of great unhappiness, such as those oppression causes.

---

22. **affliction** (uh FLIHK shuhn): suffering; distress.

F **Literary Focus** Magic Realism and Irony How are the priest's request and Rome's replies ironic?

Vocabulary **meager** (MEE guhr) *adj.*: scanty; not full or rich.

Those consolation miracles, which were more like mocking fun, had already ruined the angel's reputation when the woman who had been changed into a spider finally crushed him completely. That was how Father Gonzaga was cured forever of his insomnia and Pelayo's courtyard went back to being as empty as during the time it had rained for three days and crabs walked through the bedrooms. **G**

The owners of the house had no reason to lament. With the money they saved they built a two-story mansion with balconies and gardens and high netting so that crabs wouldn't get in during the winter, and with iron bars on the windows so that angels wouldn't get in. Pelayo also set up a rabbit warren close to town and gave up his job as bailiff for good, and Elisenda bought some satin pumps with high heels and many dresses of iridescent silk, the kind worn on Sunday by the most desirable women in those times. The chicken coop was the only thing that didn't receive any attention. If they washed it down with creolin and burned tears of myrrh[23] inside it every so often, it was not in homage to the angel but to drive away the dung-heap stench that still hung everywhere like a ghost and was turning the new house into an old one. At first, when the child learned to walk, they were careful that he not get too close to the chicken coop. But then they began to lose their fears and got used to the smell, and before the child got his second teeth, he'd gone inside the chicken coop to play, where the wires were falling apart. The angel was no less standoffish with him than with other mortals, but he tolerated the most ingenious infamies[24] with the patience of a dog who had no illusions. They both came down with chickenpox at the same time. The doctor who took care of the

---

23. **myrrh** (mur): sweet-smelling substance used in making perfume.
24. **infamies** (IHN fuh meez): disrespectful acts; insults.

G ⬛ **Literary Focus** **Magic Realism and Irony** What is humorously ironic about the angel's "miracles"?

child couldn't resist the temptation to listen to the angel's heart, and he found so much whistling in the heart and so many sounds in his kidneys that it seemed impossible for him to be alive. What surprised him most, however, was the logic of his wings. They seemed so natural on that completely human organism that he couldn't understand why other men didn't have them too.

When the child began school, it had been some time since the sun and rain had caused the collapse of the chicken coop. The angel went dragging himself about here and there like a stray dying man. They would drive him out of the bedroom with a broom and a moment later find him in the kitchen. He seemed to be in so many places at the same time that they grew to think that he'd been duplicated, that he was reproducing himself all through the house, and the exasperated and unhinged Elisenda shouted that it was awful living in that hell full of angels. He could scarcely eat and his antiquarian eyes had also become so foggy that he went about bumping into posts. All he had left were the bare cannulae[25] of his last feathers. Pelayo threw a blanket over him and extended him the charity of letting him sleep in the shed, and only then did they notice that he had a temperature at night and was delirious with the tongue twisters of an old Norwegian. That was one of the few times they became alarmed, for they thought he was going to die and not even the wise neighbor woman had been able to tell them what to do with dead angels. **(H)**

And yet he not only survived his worst winter but seemed improved with the first sunny days. He remained motionless for several days in the farthest corner of the courtyard, where no one would see him, and at the beginning of December some large, stiff feathers began to grow on his wings, the feathers of a scarecrow, which looked more like another misfortune of decrepitude.[26] But he must have known the reason for those changes, for he was quite careful that no one should notice them, that no one should hear the sea chanteys that he sometimes sang under the stars. One morning Elisenda was cutting some bunches of onions for lunch when a wind that seemed to come from the high seas blew into the kitchen. Then she went to the window and caught the angel in his first attempts at flight. They were so clumsy that his fingernails opened a furrow in the vegetable patch and he was on the point of knocking the shed down with the ungainly flapping that slipped on the light and couldn't get a grip on the air. But he did manage to gain altitude. Elisenda let out a sigh of relief, for herself and for him, when she saw him pass over the last houses, holding himself up in some way with the risky flapping of a senile vulture. She kept watching him even when she was through cutting the onions and she kept on watching until it was no longer possible for her to see him, because then he was no longer an annoyance in her life but an imaginary dot on the horizon of the sea. **(I)**

---

25. **cannulae** (KAN yoo ly): here, tubes that hold the feathers.

26. **decrepitude** (dih KREHP uh tood): feebleness; weakness usually due to old age.

(H) **Literary Focus** Magic Realism and Irony What is ironic about Pelayo and Elisenda's fear that the angel will die?

(I) **Literary Perspectives** Analyzing Style Vivid language is a key element of García Márquez' style. What are some particularly vivid phrases or word pictures in this passage?

Applying Your Skills

RA.L.10.7 Recognize how irony is used in a literary text. RA.L.10.11 Explain ways in which an author develops a point of view and style, and cite specific examples from the text. RA.L.10.2 Analyze the features of setting and their importance in a literary text. *Also covered* RA.I.10.1; WA.10.1.b

A Very Old Man with Enormous Wings

Respond and Think Critically

Reading Focus

Quick Check

1. What do Pelayo and Elisenda think the old man is? What does their neighbor think?

2. How does the winged man change the lives of Pelayo and Elisenda?

Read with a Purpose

3. How do the townspeople initially react to the old man? How does their attitude toward him change over time? Explain.

Reading Skills: Analyzing Details

4. While reading the story, you kept track of sensory details. Now, review your chart entries. Circle details that are grounded in realism; underline details that seem magical, or based in fantasy.

Details About Setting	Details About Old Man
smell of rotten shellfish	dressed like a ragpicker

Literary Focus

Literary Analysis

5. **Analyze** Explain how this story could be seen as revealing one of these themes:
   - We wish for miracles, but when they come, we cannot accept them.
   - People will destroy anything that they cannot understand or control.
   - People will try to make money from anything, even miracles.

6. **Literary Perspectives** What elements make García Márquez's style unique? What effect do these elements have on a reader that another author's style might not?

Literary Skills: Magic Realism and Irony

7. **Identify** Review the uses of irony in this story. List three uses of irony that you find most entertaining, or most shocking, and give reasons for your choice.

8. **Analyze** What details in this story illustrate the characteristics of magic realism—that is, what details in the story are fantastic? What details are commonplace and realistic?

Literary Skills Review: Setting

9. **Hypothesize** The time and place in which a story occurs is its **setting**. How would you characterize the setting of this story? Is it realistic? Why or why not?

Writing Focus

Think as a Reader/Writer

Use It in Your Writing In a paragraph or two, describe a fantastical situation that is totally different from anything that usually happens on earth. Include one ironic detail—something that is just the opposite of what usually happens.

What Do You Think Now

What does their <u>interaction</u> with the old man reveal about the villagers? How would you react in a similar situation? Explain.

Applying Your Skills

A Very Old Man with Enormous Wings

Vocabulary Development

Vocabulary Check

Match each Vocabulary word with its definition.

1. **impeded**   a. lacking fullness or richness
2. **meager**   b. very bad smell
3. **stench**   c. unimportant or silly
4. **prudence**   d. obstructed
5. **frivolous**   e. good judgment

Vocabulary Skills: Roots and Related Words

When you trace word origins, you find that many words come from common roots. A **root** is the part of a word that carries the word's core meaning. English has many words with Greek and Latin roots.

Knowing a word's root will help you understand the word's related forms. For example, *antique, antiquated, antiquarian,* and *antiquity* all have the same Latin root *antiquus,* which means "ancient" or "old."

Your Turn

Use a dictionary to find the roots for the following words from the selection:

temperature   **grandeur**   **reverence**
affliction   **lament**   **spectacle**

Place your findings for each word in a chart like the one below. Identify words <u>derived</u> from the roots.

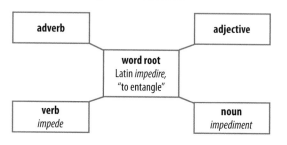

Language Coach

Suffixes Recognizing and knowing how to use individual suffixes can increase your vocabulary. The suffixes *–ence* and *–ance* function by turning verbs or adjectives into nouns. For example, the verb *revere* becomes *reverence.* Sometimes adding a suffix means you have to take away a letter at the end of a word or rearrange the letters slightly. For example, the adjective *prudent* becomes *prudence.*

For each of the words below, list its part of speech, and add a suffix to turn the word into a noun. Use a dictionary to make sure that you have spelled the words correctly.

1. confer
2. distant
3. differ
4. remember
5. perform
6. competent

Academic Vocabulary

Talk About . . .

During one <u>interaction</u> the townspeople try to brand the angel. What is the angel's reaction, and how is it <u>significant</u> to the story? Use Academic Vocabulary in your discussion.

Grammar Link

Sentence Length and Structure

Experienced writers use a variety of sentence types to make their writing interesting. A paragraph of short, simple sentences, for example, can seem choppy; one full of long, complex sentences can be confusing. As you read about the sentence types below, remember that an **independent clause** expresses a complete thought and can stand alone. A **subordinate clause** cannot stand alone.

A **simple sentence** has one independent clause.
> *His huge wings were entangled in the mud.*

A sentence with more than one independent clause is a **compound sentence.**
> *His wings were entangled, / and he could not get up.*

A **complex sentence** has one independent clause and at least one subordinate clause.
> *Because his huge wings were entangled, / he fell.*

A **compound-complex sentence** has two or more independent clauses and at least one subordinate clause.
> *As the rain fell, / his huge wings became entangled, / and he could not get up.*

Your Turn

Writing Applications Rewrite the following paragraph by combining the sentences in different ways.

> Pelayo ran to get Elisenda. She was his wife. She was putting compresses on the sick child. He took her to the rear of the courtyard. They both looked at the fallen body with mute stupor. He was dressed like a ragpicker. There were only a few faded hairs left on his bald skull. There were very few teeth in his mouth. His huge buzzard wings were dirty. They were half plucked.

CHOICES

As you respond to the Choices, use these **Academic Vocabulary** words as appropriate: derive, function, interact, and significant.

REVIEW
Analyze the Story
Timed └Writing García Márquez has said, "It always amuses me that the biggest praise for my work comes for the imagination, while the truth is that there's not a single line in all my work that does not have a basis in reality." Upon what underlying reality might this story be based? Write an essay explaining your answer. Provide details and quotes from the text to support your opinion.

CONNECT
Write a Letter
The townspeople don't understand the old man's language. What is going through the old man's mind as he patiently endures the chicken coop? Write a letter to Pelayo and Elisenda that the old man might have written before flying away. Include details about his home, why he strayed into the yard, how humanity looks from his perspective, and where he is heading now. Write in the first-person point of view.

EXTEND
Create a Special Report
TechFocus How might you use the Internet to tell the world about the old man's arrival? Sketch a design for a Web site, which could include interviews, photographs, streaming video, and a forum.

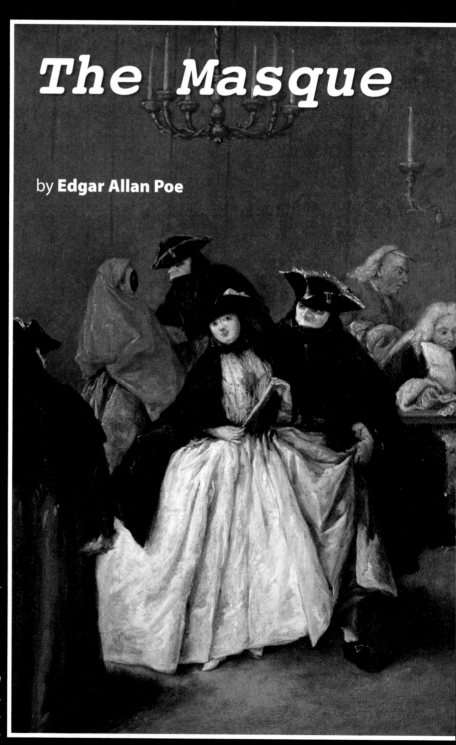

The Masque

by **Edgar Allan Poe**

What Do You? Think

What realities of life must all people face, no matter who they are?

🕑 QuickTalk

How do some people use money and power to try to avoid the upsetting realities of life— realities that we all must face? Discuss your responses to this question with a partner.

?Ed./the tearsheet provided for caption below- does not match our file.

please advise

Masked Ball in the Card Room (c. 1757–1760) by Pietro Longhi. Oil on canvas (62.5 cm × 51 cm). Accademia, Venice, Italy.

Reader/Writer Notebook

Use your **RWN** to complete the activities for this selection.

OH **RA.L.10.5** Analyze how an author's choice of genre affects the expression of a theme or topic. **RP.10.3** Monitor own comprehension by adjusting speed to fit the purpose, or by skimming, scanning, reading on, looking back, note taking or summarizing what has been read so far in text. **RP.10.1** Apply reading comprehension strategies, including making predictions, comparing and contrasting, recalling and summarizing and making inferences and drawing conclusions.

Literary Focus

Allegory An **allegory** is a narrative that is really a double story. One story takes place on the surface and is meant to be taken literally. In the other story, characters and places symbolize abstract ideas or states of being, such as love, freedom, evil, goodness, and heaven or hell. Often the characters and places in allegories have names that suggest what they stand for. In one famous allegory the main character is called Pilgrim. His name suggests that he represents all people as they travel through life.

Reading Focus

Monitoring Your Reading All good readers pause from time to time to ask themselves questions. If they are reading a story, they want to be sure they know who the characters are and what conflicts the characters are facing. Good readers also pause to visualize the story's settings and <u>significant</u> plot events. All of these strategies are part of **monitoring your reading.** If you do not monitor your reading, you may finish a story without a clear idea of what happened or what it meant.

Into Action While you read this story, monitor your understanding by writing down questions in a chart like the one below.

Page Number	My Questions
369	Why does the prince retreat to his abbey?

Vocabulary

profuse (pruh FYOOS) *adj.*: abundant; plentiful. *A symptom of the Red Death was profuse bleeding.*

emanating (EHM uh nayt ihng) *v.* used as *adj.*: coming forth; emerging, as from a source. *The light emanating from Prince Prospero's rooms did not come from candles.*

pervaded (puhr VAYD ihd) *v.*: spread throughout. *Laughter pervaded the room.*

propriety (pruh PRY uh tee) *n.*: quality of being appropriate or proper. *At least one of Prince Prospero's guests did not behave with propriety.*

tangible (TAN juh buhl) *adj.*: capable of being touched or felt. *The joy of the guests was so great that it was almost tangible.*

Language Coach

Antonyms Antonyms are words with opposite or nearly opposite meanings. Identify the Vocabulary word that is an antonym for the underlined word in this sentence: *As the party went on, many guests showed <u>abandon</u> as they threw off their cares.*

Writing Focus

Think as a Reader/Writer

Find It in Your Reading As you read, think about the elements in the story that seem to stand for something else. In your *Reader/Writer Notebook,* jot down details that suggest the deeper, allegorical nature of the story.

 Learn It Online
Hear a professional actor read this story. Visit the selection online at:

go.hrw.com | L10-367 | **Go**

Learn It Online
Get more on the author's life at:
go.hrw.com L10-368 **Go**

Edgar Allan Poe

(1809–1849)

Nightmare Worlds

Edgar Allan Poe invented the popular mystery and horror genres, but his dark nightmarish writings brought him little comfort or security during his own lifetime.

Poe's tragic personal history began when his father deserted his mother, a popular young actress. Poe was not yet three years old when his mother died in 1811 in a rooming house in Richmond, Virginia. The Allans, a wealthy, childless couple, took the boy in and gave him an education, expecting him to take over the family business. Poe, however, wanted to be a writer. He began an unsteady literary career, working for a number of periodicals in Baltimore and New York.

Depressing Endings

Always in search of a family, Poe moved in with his aunt, and in 1836, he married her thirteen-year-old daughter, Virginia Clemm. Poe managed somehow to keep his little household together, although his drinking often caused conflicts with other writers and critics. In 1845, he made his mark with "The Raven," a poem that he sold to a newspaper for about fifteen dollars and that became an instant hit.

In 1847, Virginia died of tuberculosis, and Poe's loneliness and drinking increased. Outside a tavern in Baltimore on October 3, 1849, Poe was found disoriented and suffering from exposure. Several days later, he died from causes still unknown.

Think About the Writer How do Poe's dark themes reflect the tragedies in his own life?

Build Background

The bubonic plague swept through Europe and Asia in the fourteenth century. The epidemic killed as much as two thirds of the population in some parts of Europe. Poe called the disease "the Red Death" because blood oozed from painful sores on the victims' bodies. The plague was more commonly called the Black Death because of the black spots that appeared on the victims' faces.

Preview the Selection

Prince Prospero, a fourteenth-century prince, throws a lavish costume party, or masque, in an abbey, where his guests have gone to escape the plague that is killing people around the country.

The Masque of the Red Death

by **Edgar Allan Poe**

The "Red Death" had long devastated the country. No pestilence[1] had ever been so fatal, or so hideous. Blood was its Avatar[2] and its seal—the redness and the horror of blood. There were sharp pains, and sudden dizziness, and then profuse bleeding at the pores, with dissolution.[3] The scarlet stains upon the body and especially upon the face of the victim were the pest ban which shut him out from the aid and from the sympathy of his fellow men. And the whole seizure, progress, and termination of the disease were the incidents of half an hour. **Ⓐ**

But the Prince Prospero was happy and dauntless and sagacious.[4] When his dominions were half depopulated, he summoned to his presence a thousand hale and lighthearted friends from among the knights and dames of his court, and with these retired to the deep seclusion of one of his castellated abbeys.[5] This was an extensive and magnificent structure, the creation of the prince's own eccentric yet august[6] taste. A strong and lofty wall girdled it in. This wall had gates of iron. The courtiers, having entered, brought furnaces and massy hammers and welded the bolts. They resolved to leave means neither of ingress or egress[7] to the sudden impulses of despair or of frenzy from within. The abbey was amply provisioned. With such precautions the courtiers might bid defiance to contagion. The external world could take care of itself. In the meantime it was folly to grieve, or to think. The prince had provided all the appliances of pleasure. There were buffoons, there were improvisatori,[8] there were ballet dancers, there were musicians, there was Beauty, there was wine. All these and security were within. Without was the "Red Death." **Ⓑ**

---

1. **pestilence** (PEHS tuh luhns): any infectious disease, especially one of epidemic proportions.
2. **Avatar** (av uh TAHR): embodiment; concrete expression of.
3. **dissolution** (dihs uh LOO shuhn): here, death.
4. **sagacious** (suh GAY shuhs): wise; showing sound judgment.
5. **castellated abbeys:** monasteries built with towers.
6. **august** (aw GUHST): grand; majestic; noble.
7. **ingress or egress:** entrance or exit.
8. **improvisatori:** poets who make up a verse on the spur of the moment.

Ⓐ Reading Focus Monitoring Your Reading What is the Red Death?

Ⓑ Reading Focus Monitoring Your Reading How does Prince Prospero try to keep the Red Death out of his abbey?

Vocabulary **profuse** (pruh FYOOS) *adj.*: abundant; plentiful.

It was toward the close of the fifth or sixth month of his seclusion, and while the pestilence raged most furiously abroad, that the Prince Prospero entertained his thousand friends at a masked ball of the most unusual magnificence. **C**

It was a voluptuous scene, that masquerade. But first let me tell of the rooms in which it was held. There were seven—an imperial suite. In many palaces, however, such suites form a long and straight vista, while the folding doors slide back nearly to the walls on either hand, so that the view of the whole extent is scarcely impeded. Here the case was very different; as might have been expected from the duke's love of the *bizarre.* The apartments were so irregularly disposed that the vision embraced but little more than one at a time. There was a sharp turn at every twenty or thirty yards, and at each turn a novel effect. To the right and left, in the middle of each wall, a tall and narrow Gothic window looked out upon a closed corridor which pursued the windings of the suite. These windows were of stained glass whose color varied in accordance with the prevailing hue of the decorations of the chamber into which it opened. That at the eastern extremity was hung, for example, in blue—and vividly blue were its windows. The second chamber was purple in its ornaments and tapestries, and here the panes were purple. The third was green throughout, and so were the casements. The fourth was furnished and lighted with orange—the fifth with white—the sixth with violet. The seventh apartment was closely shrouded in black velvet tapestries that hung all over the ceiling and down the walls, falling in heavy folds upon a carpet of the same material and hue. But in this chamber only, the color of the windows failed to correspond with the decorations. The panes here were scarlet—a deep blood color. Now in no one of the seven apartments was there any lamp or candelabrum, amid the profusion of golden ornaments that lay scattered to and fro or depended from the roof. There was no light of any kind emanating from lamp or candle within the suite of chambers. But in the corridors that followed the suite, there stood, opposite to each window, a heavy tripod, bearing a brazier of fire that projected its rays through the tinted glass and so glaringly illumined the room. And thus were produced a multitude of gaudy and fantastic appearances. But in the western or black chamber the effect of the firelight that streamed upon the dark hangings through the blood-tinted panes was ghastly in the extreme, and produced so wild a look upon the countenances of those who entered that there were few of the company bold enough to set foot within its precincts at all. **D**

It was in this apartment, also, that there stood against the western wall a gigantic clock of ebony. Its pendulum swung to and fro with a dull, heavy, monotonous clang; and when the minute hand made the circuit of the face, and the hour was to be stricken, there came from the brazen lungs of the clock a sound which was clear and loud and deep and exceedingly musical, but of so peculiar a note and emphasis that, at each lapse of an hour, the musicians of the orchestra were constrained to pause, momentarily, in their performance, to hearken to the sound; and thus the waltzers perforce ceased their evolutions; and there was a brief

---

C **Literary Focus** **Allegory** Allegories often feature characters whose names hint at another meaning. What might Prince Prospero's name suggest about what he represents?

D **Literary Focus** **Allegory** What might the last room represent?

Vocabulary **emanating** (EHM uh nayt ihng) *v.* used as *adj.:* coming forth; emerging, as from a source.

disconcert[9] of the whole gay company; and, while the chimes of the clock yet rang, it was observed that the giddiest grew pale, and the more aged and sedate[10] passed their hands over their brows as if in confused reverie or meditation. But when the echoes had fully ceased, a light laughter at once pervaded the assembly; the musicians looked at each other and smiled as if at their own nervousness and folly, and made whispering vows, each to the other, that the next chiming of the clock should produce in them no similar emotion; and then, after the lapse of sixty minutes (which embrace three thousand and six hundred seconds of the Time that flies), there came yet another chiming of the clock, and then were the same disconcert and tremulousness[11] and meditation as before. **E**

But, in spite of these things, it was a gay and magnificent revel. The tastes of the duke were peculiar. He had a fine eye for colors and effects. He disregarded the *decora*[12] of mere fashion. His plans were bold and fiery, and his conceptions glowed with barbaric lustre. There are some who would have thought him mad. His followers felt that he was not. It was necessary to hear and see and touch him to be *sure* that he was not. **F**

---

9. **disconcert** (dihs kuhn SURT): disturb; upset.
10. **sedate** (sih DAYT): calm; composed; serious.

11. **tremulousness** (TREHM yuh luhs nehs): trembling; fearfulness.
12. *decora*: Latin for "accepted standards of good taste."

E **Literary Focus** Allegory What does the guests' response to the chiming of the clock suggest about what it might represent?

Vocabulary **pervaded** (puhr VAYD ihd) *v.*: spread throughout.

F **Reading Focus** Monitoring Your Reading Why might Prince Prospero be perceived as mad?

He had directed, in great part, the moveable embellishments of the seven chambers, upon occasion of this great *fête;*[13] and it was his own guiding taste which had given character to the masqueraders. Be sure they were grotesque. There were much glare and glitter and piquancy[14] and phantasm[15]—much of what has been since seen in *Hernani.*[16] There were arabesque[17] figures with unsuited limbs and appointments. There were delirious fancies such as the madman fashions. There was much of the beautiful, much of the wanton, much of the *bizarre,* something of the terrible, and not a little of that which might have excited disgust. To and fro in the seven chambers there stalked, in fact, a multitude of dreams. And these—the

dreams—writhed in and about, taking hue from the rooms, and causing the wild music of the orchestra to seem as the echo of their steps. And, anon,[18] there strikes the ebony clock which stands in the hall of the velvet. And then, for a moment, all is still, and all is silent save the voice of the clock. The dreams are stiff-frozen as they stand. But the echoes of the chime die away—they have endured but an instant—and a light, half-subdued laughter floats after them as they depart. And now again the music swells, and the dreams live, and writhe to and fro more merrily than ever, taking hue from the many-tinted windows through which stream the rays from the tripods. But to the chamber which lies most westwardly of the seven, there are now none of the maskers who venture; for the night is waning away; and there flows a ruddier light through the blood-colored panes; and the blackness of the sable drapery appalls; and to him whose foot falls upon the sable carpet, there comes

---

13. *fête:* French for "party" or "celebration."
14. **piquancy** (PEE kuhn see): quality of being pleasantly exciting.
15. **phantasm** (FAN taz uhm): illusion.
16. *Hernani:* romantic tragedy by the French writer Victor Hugo, first performed in 1830. It is set in a magnificent Spanish court.
17. **arabesque** (ar uh BEHSK): fantastic; elaborate.

---

18. **anon** (uh NAHN): soon.

from the near clock of ebony a muffled peal more solemnly emphatic than any which reaches *their* ears who indulge in the more remote gaieties of the other apartments. **G**

But these other apartments were densely crowded, and in them beat feverishly the heart of life. And the revel went whirlingly on, until at length there commenced the sounding of midnight upon the clock. And then the music ceased, as I have told; and the evolutions of the waltzers were quieted; and there was an uneasy cessation[19] of all things as before. But now there were twelve strokes to be sounded by the bell of the clock; and thus it happened, perhaps, that more of thought crept, with more of time, into the meditations of the thoughtful among those who revelled. And thus, too, it happened, perhaps, that before the last echoes of the last chime had utterly sunk into silence, there were many individuals in the crowd who had found leisure to become aware of the presence of a masked figure which had arrested the attention of no single individual before. And the rumor of this new presence having spread itself whisperingly around, there arose at length from the whole company a buzz, or murmur, expressive of disapprobation[20] and surprise—then, finally, of terror, of horror, and of disgust.

In an assembly of phantasms such as I have painted, it may well be supposed that no ordinary appearance could have excited such sensation. In truth the masquerade license of the night was nearly unlimited; but the figure in question had out-Heroded Herod,[21] and gone beyond the bounds of even the prince's indefinite decorum. There are chords in the hearts of the most reckless which cannot be touched without emotion. Even with the utterly lost, to whom life and death are equally jests, there are matters of which no jest can be made. The whole company, indeed, seemed now deeply to feel that in the costume and bearing of the stranger neither wit nor propriety existed. The figure was tall and gaunt, and shrouded from head to foot in the habiliments[22] of the grave. The mask which concealed the visage was made so nearly to resemble the countenance of a stiffened corpse that the closest scrutiny must have had difficulty in detecting the cheat. And yet all this might have been endured, if not approved, by the mad revelers around. But the mummer[23] had gone so far as to assume the type of the Red Death. His vesture[24] was dabbled in *blood*—and his broad brow, with all the features of the face, was besprinkled with the scarlet horror. **H**

When the eyes of Prince Prospero fell upon this spectral image (which with a slow and solemn movement, as if more fully to sustain its *role*, stalked to and fro among the waltzers), he was seen to be convulsed, in the first moment with a strong shudder either of

---

19. **cessation** (seh SAY shuhn): ceasing; stopping.
20. **disapprobation** (dihs ap ruh BAY shuhn): disapproval.

21. **out-Heroded Herod:** Herod was the Biblical king who had Hebrew baby boys slaughtered in an attempt to kill the infant Jesus. To "out-Herod Herod" is to be worse than the worst tyrant.
22. **habiliments** (huh BIHL uh muhnts): articles of clothing.
23. **mummer** (MUHM uhr): person who wears a mask or disguise, especially for performance.
24. **vesture** (VEHS chuhr): garments.

G **Literary Focus** Allegory Who or what could the masqueraders represent?

H **Reading Focus** Monitoring Your Reading Re-read the description of the masked guest. What do you think his costume is?

Vocabulary **propriety** (pruh PRY uh tee) *n.*: quality of being appropriate or proper.

terror or distaste; but, in the next, his brow reddened with rage.

"Who dares?" he demanded hoarsely of the courtiers who stood near him—"who dares insult us with this blasphemous mockery? Seize him and unmask him—that we may know whom we have to hang at sunrise, from the battlements!" **❶**

It was in the eastern or blue chamber in which stood the Prince Prospero as he uttered these words. They rang throughout the seven rooms loudly and clearly—for the prince was a bold and robust man, and the music had become hushed at the waving of his hand.

It was in the blue room where stood the prince, with a group of pale courtiers by his side. At first, as he spoke, there was a slight rushing movement of this group in the direction of the intruder, who at the moment was also near at hand, and now, with deliberate and stately step, made closer approach to the speaker. But from a certain nameless awe with which the mad assumptions of the mummer had inspired the whole party, there were found none who put forth hand to seize him; so that, unimpeded, he passed within a yard of the prince's person; and, while the vast assembly, as if with one impulse, shrank from the centers of the rooms to the walls, he made his way uninterruptedly, but with the same solemn and measured step which had distinguished him from the first, through the blue chamber to the purple—through the purple to the green— through the green to the orange—through this again to the white—and even thence to the violet, ere a decided movement had been made to arrest him. It was then, however, that the Prince Prospero, maddening with rage and the shame of his own momentary cowardice, rushed hurriedly through the six chambers, while none followed him on account of a deadly terror that had seized upon all. He bore aloft a drawn dagger, and had approached, in rapid impetuosity, to within three or four feet of the retreating figure, when the latter, having attained the extremity of the velvet apartment, turned suddenly and confronted his pursuer. There was a sharp cry—and the dagger dropped gleaming upon the sable carpet, upon which, instantly afterwards, fell prostrate in death the Prince Prospero. Then, summoning the wild courage of despair, a throng of the revelers at once threw themselves into the black apartment, and, seizing the mummer, whose tall figure stood erect and motionless within the shadow of the ebony clock, gasped in unutterable horror at finding the grave cerements[25] and corpselike mask which they handled with so violent a rudeness, untenanted by any tangible form. **❿**

And now was acknowledged the presence of the Red Death. He had come like a thief in the night. And one by one dropped the revelers in the blood-bedewed halls of their revel, and died each in the despairing posture of his fall. And the life of the ebony clock went out with that of the last of the gay. And the flames of the tripods expired. And Darkness and Decay and the Red Death held illimitable dominion[26] over all. **Ⓚ**

---

25. **grave cerements** (SIHR muhnts): garments a body is wrapped in for burial.

26. **dominion** (duh MIHN yuhn): control; rule.

---

❶ Reading Focus **Monitoring Your Reading** What questions do you have about the guest at this point?

❿ Reading Focus **Monitoring Your Reading** What has Prince Prospero's death revealed about the unwanted guest?

Ⓚ Literary Focus **Allegory** What does the fate of the revelers represent on a symbolic level?

Vocabulary **tangible** (TAN juh buhl) *adj.*: capable of being touched or felt.

Applying Your Skills

OH **RA.L.10.5** Analyze how an author's choice of genre affects the expression of a theme or topic. **RA.L.10.3** Distinguish how conflicts, parallel plots and subplots affect the pacing of action in literary text. *Also covered* RP.10.3; RP.10.1; VO.10.3; WA.10.1.c

The Masque of the Red Death

Respond and Think Critically

Reading Focus

Quick Check

1. Describe the seven rooms of the prince's suite. Why do the guests avoid the seventh room?

2. What is so shocking about the guest who appears at midnight?

Read with a Purpose

3. What is Poe suggesting about the limits of human power to escape death and fate?

Reading Skills: Monitoring Your Reading

4. Now that you have finished the story, add a new column to your chart, and complete it by answering your questions.

Page Number	My Questions	Answers
369	Why does the prince retreat to his abbey?	He wants to escape death.

✓ Vocabulary Check

Answer *true* or *false* to the following statements, and briefly explain your answers. Vocabulary words are boldface.

5. If the figure had been **tangible,** the guests would have been able to touch him.

6. If light was **emanating** from the rooms, they were dark.

7. **Profuse** bleeding is very minimal and scanty.

8. If the guest had **propriety,** he would dress in a suitable way.

9. If laughter has **pervaded** a room, the laughter has spread throughout the room.

Literary Focus

Literary Analysis

10. **Analyze** Re-read the long paragraph on pages 372–373 describing the masquerade. What details in this description suggest madness?

11. **Infer** Why do the revelers become quiet every time the clock chimes?

Literary Skills: Allegory

12. **Summarize** Sum up the story beneath the surface story. In your summary, explain what the story's characters, events, places, and colors represent. What do you think this story might be saying about our passage through life to death?

Literary Skills Review: Climax

13. **Explain** The **climax** of a story is the moment of greatest suspense and emotion, when you know how the main conflict is resolved. What happens at the climax of this story?

Writing Focus

Think as a Reader/Writer

Use It in Your Writing Write the outline of an allegory of your own about a group of people who retreat to a place they think is secure from danger. Give your characters and your setting significant names that suggest what they represent.

What Do **You Think Now** Could Prince Prospero and his guests have escaped death? Or could they merely postpone it?

Comparing Themes Across Texts

CONTENTS

What Do You Think

How do you balance the will to survive with the urge to help others?

 QuickWrite

Think about a story or movie in which a character has to choose between saving himself or herself and saving others. In a short paragraph, describe the situation and its outcome.

Preparing to Read

The Seventh Man / The Man in the Water

 Reader/Writer Notebook

Use your **RWN** to complete the activities for these selections.

Literary Focus

Irony and Symbols **Irony** is often used to reveal surprising quirks and contradictions of human behavior. Irony might be **verbal** (saying one thing but meaning another), **situational** (a discrepancy between what is expected and what happens), or **dramatic** (the reader knows a character's fate before the character knows it). In some texts, **symbols** help communicate irony—revealing meaning to you but not to the characters. As you read, think about how the symbol of water <u>signifies</u> the underlying irony in each work. Also consider how the use of irony and symbol helps convey a work's theme.

Reading Focus

Finding Themes The **theme** of a literary work is the work's central insight or message about life. You can find the theme by analyzing details and evidence in the text.

Into Action As you read each selection, pay special attention to irony—what does the irony in each text reveal about human nature? Keep a list like the one below, noting key details that suggest what the theme might be.

Details from "The Seventh Man"	Details from "The Man in the Water"
The wave "just barely missed me . . . it swallowed everything that mattered most to me."	

Writing Focus

Think as a Reader/Writer

Find It in Your Reading Both Murakami and Rosenblatt use figurative language to describe extraordinary events. As you read, write down examples of this figurative language in your *Reader/Writer Notebook*.

Vocabulary

The Seventh Man

momentum (moh MEHN tuhm) *n.:* force with which something moves. *As the wind picked up, the storm gathered momentum.*

ominous (AHM uh nuhs) *adj.:* unfavorable; threatening. *Although it was not raining, the dark clouds looked ominous.*

sentiment (SEHN tuh muhnt) *n.:* tender feeling. *The man was filled with sentiment when he rediscovered his old friend's artwork from long ago.*

The Man in the Water

chaotic (kay AHT ihk) *adj.:* very confused; completely disordered. *Rescuers struggled to find survivors in the chaotic scene.*

implacable (ihm PLAK uh buhl) *adj.:* relentless; not affected by attempts at change. *The man was struggling against an implacable enemy.*

Language Coach

Oral Fluency The letter cluster *ch* can be pronounced one of two ways—a soft *ch*, as in *chair*, or a hard *k*, as in *chasm*. How do you pronounce *chaotic*? What other words begin with a *ch* that is pronounced like a hard *k*?

 Learn It Online
There's more to words than just definitions. Get the whole story on:

go.hrw.com | L10-377 | **Go**

Haruki Murakami
(1949–   )

A New Voice for Japan

As a boy, Haruki Murakami preferred reading American paperbacks to studying traditional Japanese literature. He went on to become a novelist and short-story writer known for unique and whimsical works that break away from typical Japanese forms. He is among the leaders of a new generation of Japanese writers who have left behind the generally favored realistic style. Murakami combines mystery, comedy, and fantasy in his work, while keeping his messages practical, profound, and believable.

"Everything passes. Nobody gets anything for keeps. And that's how we've got to live."

Roger Rosenblatt
(1940–   )

Searching for the Good and the Mysterious

Much like Murakami, Roger Rosenblatt explores the mysteries of humanity, but in nonfiction. Rosenblatt taught literature and writing at Harvard before turning to journalism, and he has written for such publications as *Time* and the *Washington Post*. He has also written or coauthored numerous books, including *Witness: The World Since Hiroshima* and *Rules for Aging*. Many of his books reflect Rosenblatt's search for the redeeming aspects of human nature. Rosenblatt says that an element of mystery is what characterizes his best essays and short stories. He hopes, he says, "not to solve a particular mystery but to feel it more deeply. . . . Certain stories people do not want to understand. The mystery makes them feel closer to one another than would any solution."

Think About the Writers What might draw two writers with such different backgrounds to such similar themes?

Preview the Selections

In "The Seventh Man" the narrator listens to an unnamed man tell of a horrific typhoon that tore through the man's village when he was just a child. The storm put him and his best friend, **K,** in life-threatening danger.

"The Man in the Water" tells the true heroic tale of one anonymous man who saves the lives of several people after a terrifying plane crash in Washington, D.C.

The Seventh Man

by **Haruki Murakami,** translated by **Jay Rubin**

Read with a Purpose
Read the following story to see how a traumatic event from his childhood stays with the main character forever.

Build Background
The central event in the following story is caused by a typhoon—a violent tropical storm similar to a hurricane. Sometimes during a typhoon, a storm surge, or sudden rise in sea level, can reach twenty feet above normal.

A huge wave nearly swept me away," said the seventh man, almost whispering. "It happened one September afternoon when I was ten years old."

The man was the last one to tell his story that night. The hands of the clock had moved past ten. The small group that huddled in a circle could hear the wind tearing through the darkness outside, heading west. It shook the trees, set the windows to rattling, and moved past the house with one final whistle.

"It was the biggest wave I had ever seen in my life," he said. "A strange wave. An absolute giant."

He paused.

"It just barely missed me, but in my place it swallowed everything that mattered most to me and swept it off to another world. I took years to find it again and to recover from the experience—precious years that can never be replaced."

The seventh man appeared to be in his mid-fifties. He was a thin man, tall, with a mustache, and next to his right eye he had a short but deep-looking scar that could have been made by the stab of a small blade. Stiff, bristly patches of white marked his short hair. His face had the look you see on people when they can't quite find the words they need. In his case, though, the expression seemed to have been there from long before, as though it were part of him. The man wore a simple blue shirt under a gray tweed coat, and every now and then he would bring his hand to his collar. None of those assembled there knew his name or what he did for a living.

He cleared his throat, and for a moment or two his words were lost in silence. The others waited for him to go on.

"In my case, it was a wave," he said. "There's no way for me to tell, of course, what it will be for each of you. But in my case it just happened to take the form of a gigantic wave. It presented itself to me all of a sudden one day, without warning, in the shape of a giant wave. And it was devastating. Ⓐ

I grew up in a seaside town in S— Prefecture.[1] It was such a small town, I doubt

---

1. **prefecture** (PREE fehk chuhr): country's subdivision that is the territory of a particular *prefect*, or government official.

Ⓐ **Literary Focus Symbols** What clues in this passage suggest that the wave might symbolize something significant to the seventh man?

Melancholy by Edvard Munch. National Gallery, Oslo, Norway/© 2009 The Munch Museum/ The Munch-Ellingson Group/Artists Rights Society (ARS), NY.

that any of you would recognize the name if I were to mention it. My father was the local doctor, and so I had a rather comfortable childhood. Ever since I could remember, my best friend was a boy I'll call K. His house was close to ours, and he was a grade behind me in school. We were like brothers, walking to and from school together, and always playing together when we got home. We never once fought during our long friendship. I did have a brother, six years older, but what with the age difference and differences in our personalities, we were never very close. My real brotherly affection went to my friend K.

K was a frail, skinny little thing, with a pale complexion and a face almost pretty enough to be a girl's. He had some kind of speech impediment,[2] though, which might have made him seem retarded to anyone who didn't know him. And because he was so frail, I always played his

protector, whether at school or at home. I was kind of big and athletic, and the other kids all looked up to me. But the main reason I enjoyed spending time with K was that he was such a sweet, pure-hearted boy. He was not the least bit retarded, but because of his impediment, he didn't do too well at school. In most subjects, he could barely keep up. In art class, though, he was great. Just give him a pencil or paints and he would make pictures that were so full of life that even the teacher was amazed. He won prizes in one contest after another, and I'm sure he would have become a famous painter if he had continued with his art into adulthood. He liked to do seascapes. He'd go out to the shore for hours, painting. I would often sit beside him, watching the swift, precise movements of his brush, wondering how, in a few seconds, he could possibly create such lively shapes and colors where, until then, there had been only blank white paper. I realize now that it was a matter of pure talent. **B**

---

2. **impediment** (ihm PEHD uh muhnt): difficulty or obstruction.

B Reading Focus **Finding Themes** Like the seventh man, K has difficulty speaking. What insight about the nature of their relationship might this similarity suggest?

One year, in September, a huge typhoon hit our area. The radio said it was going to be the worst in ten years. The schools were closed, and all the shops in town lowered their shutters in preparation for the storm. Starting early in the morning, my father and brother went around the house nailing shut all the storm doors, while my mother spent the day in the kitchen cooking emergency provisions. We filled bottles and canteens with water, and packed our most important possessions in rucksacks for possible evacuation. To the adults, typhoons were an annoyance and a threat they had to face almost annually, but to the kids, removed as we were from such practical concerns, it was just a great big circus, a wonderful source of excitement. **C**

Just after noon the color of the sky began to change all of a sudden. There was something strange and unreal about it. I stayed outside on the porch, watching the sky, until the wind began to howl and the rain began to beat against the house with a weird dry sound, like handfuls of sand. Then we closed the last storm door and gathered together in one room of the darkened house, listening to the radio. This particular storm did not have a great deal of rain, it said, but the winds were doing a lot of damage, blowing roofs off houses and capsizing[3] ships. Many people had been killed or injured by flying debris. Over and over again, they warned people against leaving their homes. Every once in a while, the house would creak and shudder as if a huge hand were shaking it, and sometimes there would be a great crash of some heavy-sounding object against a storm door. My father guessed that these were tiles blowing off the neighbors' houses. For lunch we ate the rice and omelets my mother had cooked, listening to the radio and waiting for the typhoon to blow past.

But the typhoon gave no sign of blowing past. The radio said it had lost **momentum** almost as soon as it came ashore at S— Prefecture, and now it was moving northeast at the pace of a slow runner. The wind kept up its savage howling as it tried to uproot everything that stood on land and carry it to the far ends of the earth.

Perhaps an hour had gone by with the wind at its worst like this when a hush fell over everything. All of a sudden it was so quiet, we could hear a bird crying in the distance. My father opened the storm door a crack and looked outside. The wind had stopped, and the rain had ceased to fall. Thick, gray clouds edged across the sky, and patches of blue showed here and there. The trees in the yard were still dripping their heavy burden of rainwater.

"We're in the eye of the storm," my father told me. "It'll stay quiet like this for a while, maybe fifteen, twenty minutes, kind of like an intermission. Then the wind'll come back the way it was before."

I asked him if I could go outside. He said I could walk around a little if I didn't go far. "But I want you to come right back here at the first sign of wind."

I went out and started to explore. It was hard to believe that a wild storm had been blowing there until a few minutes before. I looked up at the sky: I felt the storm's great "eye" up there, fixing its cold stare on all of us

---

3. capsizing (KAP syz ihng): overturning.

C **Literary Focus** **Irony** What is ironic about the difference between how the children and the adults view the oncoming typhoon?

Vocabulary **momentum** (moh MEHN tuhm) *n.*: force with which something moves.

below. No such "eye" existed, of course: we were just in that momentary quiet spot at the center of the pool of whirling air. **Ⓓ**

While the grown-ups checked for damage to the house, I went down to the beach. The road was littered with broken tree branches, some of them thick pine boughs that would have been too heavy for an adult to lift alone. There were shattered roof tiles everywhere, cars with cracked windshields, and even a doghouse that had tumbled into the middle of the street. A big hand might have swung down from the sky and flattened everything in its path.

K saw me walking down the road and came outside.

"Where are you going?" he asked.

"Just down to look at the beach," I said.

Without a word, he came along with me. He had a little white dog that followed after us.

"The minute we get any wind, though, we're going straight back home," I said, and K gave me a silent nod.

The shore was a two-hundred-yard walk from my house. It was lined with a concrete breakwater—a big dike that stood as high as I was tall in those days. We had to climb a short stairway to reach the water's edge. This was where we came to play almost every day, so there was no part of it we didn't know well. In the eye of the typhoon, though, it all looked different: the color of the sky and of the sea, the sound of the waves, the smell of the tide, the whole expanse of the shore. We sat atop the breakwater for a time, taking in the view without a word to each other. We were supposedly in the middle of a great typhoon, and yet the waves were strangely hushed. And the point where they washed against the beach was

much farther away than usual, even at low tide. The white sand stretched out before us as far as we could see. The whole, huge space felt like a room without furniture, except for the band of flotsam[4] that lined the beach.

We stepped down to the other side of the breakwater and walked along the broad beach, examining the things that had come to rest there. Plastic toys, sandals, chunks of wood that had probably once been parts of furniture, pieces of clothing, unusual bottles, broken crates with foreign writing on them, and other, less recognizable items: it was like a big candy store. The storm must have carried these things from very far away. Whenever something unusual caught our attention, we would pick it up and look at it every which way, and when we were done, K's dog would come over and give it a good sniff.

We couldn't have been doing this more than five minutes when I realized that the waves had come up right next to me. Without any sound or other warning, the sea had suddenly stretched its long, smooth tongue out to where I stood on the beach. I had never seen anything like it before. Child though I was, I had grown up on the shore and knew how frightening the ocean could be—the savagery with which it could strike unannounced. And so I had taken care to keep well back from the water-line. In spite of that, the waves had slid up to within inches of where I stood. And then, just as soundlessly, the water drew back—and stayed back. The waves that had approached me were as unthreatening as waves can be—a gentle washing of the sandy beach. But something ominous about them—something like the

---

4. **flotsam** (FLAHT suhm): wreckage from a ship that has been washed ashore.

Ⓓ **Reading Focus** **Finding Themes** The seventh man says he felt the eye of the storm looking down on him. What might this image suggest about this story's theme?

Vocabulary **ominous** (AHM uh nuhs) *adj.*: unfavorable; threatening.

touch of a reptile's skin—had sent a chill down my spine. My fear was totally groundless—and totally real. I knew instinctively that they were alive. The waves were alive. They knew I was here and they were planning to grab me. I felt as if some huge man-eating beast were lying somewhere on a grassy plain, dreaming of the moment it would pounce and tear me to pieces with its sharp teeth. I had to run away. **E**

"I'm getting out of here!" I yelled to K. He was maybe ten yards down the beach, squatting with his back to me, and looking at something. I was sure I had yelled loud enough, but my voice did not seem to have reached him. He might have been so absorbed in whatever it was he had found that my call made no impression on him. K was like that. He would get involved with things to the point of forgetting everything else.

Or possibly I had not yelled as loudly as I thought. I do recall that my voice sounded strange to me, as though it belonged to someone else.

Then I heard a deep rumbling sound. It seemed to shake the earth. Actually, before I heard the rumble I heard another sound, a weird gurgling as though a lot of water was surging up through a hole in the ground. It continued for a while, then stopped, after which I heard the strange rumbling. Even that was not enough to make K look up. He was still squatting, looking down at something at his feet, in deep concentration. He probably did not hear the rumbling. How he could have missed such an earthshaking sound, I don't know. This may seem odd, but it might have been a sound that only I could hear—some special kind of sound.

> The waves were alive. They knew I was here and they were planning to grab me.

Not even K's dog seemed to notice it, and you know how sensitive dogs are to sound.

I told myself to run over to K, grab hold of him, and get out of there. It was the only thing to do. I *knew* that the wave was coming, and K didn't know. As clearly as I knew what I ought to be doing, I found myself running the other way—running full speed toward the dike, alone. What made me do this, I'm sure, was fear, a fear so overpowering it took my voice away and set my legs to running on their own. I ran stumbling along the soft sand beach to the breakwater, where I turned and shouted to K. **F**

"Hurry, K! Get out of there! The wave is coming!" This time my voice worked fine. The rumbling had stopped, I realized, and now, finally, K heard my shouting and looked up. But it was too late. A wave like a huge snake with its head held high, poised to strike, was racing toward the shore. I had never seen anything like it in my life. It had to be as tall as a three-story building. Soundlessly (in my memory, at least, the image is soundless), it rose up behind K to block out the sky. K looked at me for a few seconds, uncomprehending. Then, as if sensing something, he turned toward the wave. He tried to run, but now there was no time to run. In the next instant, the wave had swallowed him. It hit him full on, like a locomotive at full speed.

The wave crashed onto the beach, shattering into a million leaping waves that flew through the air and plunged over the dike where I stood. I was able to dodge its impact by ducking behind the breakwater. The spray wet my clothes, nothing more. I scrambled back up onto the wall and

---

E **Literary Focus** Symbols The seventh man compares the sea to a tongue and to a man-eating beast. Why do you think the author chose these symbols?

F **Reading Focus** Finding Themes Here, the seventh man tells us what he was thinking and what he failed to do. How might this information relate to a theme of the story?

scanned the shore. By then the wave had turned and, with a wild cry, it was rushing back out to sea. It looked like part of a gigantic rug that had been yanked by someone at the other end of the earth. Nowhere on the shore could I find any trace of K, or of his dog. There was only the empty beach. The receding wave had now pulled so much water out from the shore it seemed to expose the entire ocean bottom. I stood alone on the breakwater, frozen in place.

The silence came over everything again—a desperate silence, as though sound itself had been ripped from the earth. The wave had swallowed K and disappeared into the far distance. I stood there, wondering what to do. Should I go down to the beach? K might be down there somewhere, buried in the sand . . . . But I decided not to leave the dike. I knew from experience that big waves often came in twos and threes.

I'm not sure how much time went by—maybe ten or twenty seconds of eerie emptiness—when, just as I had guessed, the next wave came. Another gigantic roar shook the beach, and again, after the sound had faded, another huge wave raised its head to strike. It towered before me, blocking out the sky, like a deadly cliff. This time, though, I didn't run. I stood rooted to the seawall, entranced, waiting for it to attack. What good would it do to run, I thought, now that K had been taken? Or perhaps I simply froze, overcome with fear. I can't be sure what it was that kept me standing there.

The second wave was just as big as the first—maybe even bigger. From far above my head it began to fall, losing its shape, like a brick wall slowly crumbling. It was so huge that it no longer looked like a real wave. It seemed to be some other thing, something from another, far-off world, that just happened to assume the shape of a wave. I readied myself for the moment the darkness would take me. I didn't even close my eyes. I remember hearing my heart pound with incredible clarity.

The moment the wave came before me, however, it stopped. All at once it seemed to run out of energy, to lose its forward motion and simply hover there, in space, crumbling in stillness. And in its crest, inside its cruel, transparent tongue, what I saw was K. **G**

Some of you may find this impossible to believe, and if so, I don't blame you. I myself have trouble accepting it even now. I can't explain what I saw any better than you can, but I know it was no illusion, no hallucination. I am telling you as honestly as I can what happened at that moment—what really happened. In the tip of the wave, as if enclosed in some kind of transparent capsule, floated K's body, reclining on its side. But that is not all. K was looking straight at me, smiling. There, right in front of me, close enough so that I could have reached out and touched him, was my friend, my friend K who, only moments before, had been swallowed by the wave. And he was smiling at me. Not with an ordinary smile—it was a big, wide-open grin that literally stretched from ear to ear. His cold, frozen eyes were locked on mine. He was no longer the K I knew. And his right arm was stretched out in my direction, as if he were trying to grab my hand and pull me into that other world where he was now. A little closer, and his hand would have caught mine. But, having missed, K then smiled at me one more time, his grin wider than ever.

I seem to have lost consciousness at that point. The next thing I knew, I was in bed in my father's clinic. As soon as I awoke, the nurse went to call my father, who came running. He took my pulse, studied my pupils, and put his

---

G **Literary Focus** Irony What ironic twist occurs in this passage?

hand on my forehead. I tried to move my arm, but I couldn't lift it. I was burning with fever, and my mind was clouded. I had been wrestling with a high fever for some time, apparently. "You've been asleep for three days," my father said to me. A neighbor who had seen the whole thing had picked me up and carried me home. They had not been able to find K. I wanted to say something to my father. I *had* to say something to him. But my numb and swollen tongue could not form words. I felt as if some kind of creature had taken up residence in my mouth. My father asked me to tell him my name, but before I could remember what it was, I lost consciousness again, sinking into darkness.

Altogether, I stayed in bed for a week on a liquid diet. I vomited several times, and had bouts of delirium.[5] My father told me afterward I was so bad that he had been afraid that I might suffer permanent neurological[6] damage from the shock and high fever. One way or another, though, I managed to recover—physically, at least. But my life would never be the same again. **Ⓗ**

They never found K's body. They never found his dog, either. Usually when someone drowned in that area, the body would wash up a few days later on the shore of a small inlet

---

5. **delirium** (dih LIHR ee uhm): temporary disorientation associated with fevers.
6. **neurological** (nur uh LAHJ uh kuhl): brain related.

Ⓗ **Reading Focus** **Finding Themes** The seventh man's life will never be the same. What does this episode suggest about the events and actions that shape us?

Under the Wave off Kanagawa from the series Thirty-Six Views of Mount Fuji by Hokusai.

Analyzing Visuals   **Viewing and Interpreting** What details in this image remind you of the wave in the story?

to the east. K's body never did. The big waves probably carried it far out to sea—too far for it to reach the shore. It must have sunk to the ocean bottom to be eaten by the fish. The search went on for a very long time, thanks to the cooperation of the local fishermen, but eventually it petered out. Without a body, there was never any funeral. Half-crazed, K's parents would wander up and down the beach every day, or they would shut themselves up at home, chanting sutras.[7]

As great a blow as this had been for them, though, K's parents never chided[8] me for having taken their son down to the shore in the midst of a typhoon. They knew how I had always loved and protected K as if he had been my own little brother. My parents, too, made a point of never mentioning the incident in my presence. But I knew the truth. I knew that I could have saved K if I had tried. I probably could have run over and dragged him out of the reach of the wave. It would have been close, but as I went over the timing of the events in memory, it always seemed to me that I could have made it. As I said before, though, overcome with fear, I abandoned him there and saved only myself. It pained me all the more that K's parents failed to blame me and that everyone else was so careful never to say anything to me about what had happened. It took me a long time to recover from the emotional shock. I stayed away from school for weeks. I hardly ate a thing, and spent each day in bed, staring at the ceiling.

> Overcome with fear, I abandoned him there and saved only myself.

K was always there, lying in the wave tip, grinning at me, his hand out-stretched, beckoning. I couldn't get that searing image out of my mind. And when I managed to sleep, it was there in my dreams—except that, in my dreams, K would hop out of his capsule in the wave and grab my wrist to drag me back inside with him.

And then there was another dream I had. I'm swimming in the ocean. It's a beautiful summer afternoon, and I'm doing an easy breaststroke far from shore. The sun is beating down on my back, and the water feels good. Then, all of a sudden, someone grabs my right leg. I feel an ice-cold grip on my ankle. It's strong, too strong to shake off. I'm being dragged down under the surface. I see K's face there. He has the same huge grin, split from ear to ear, his eyes locked on mine. I try to scream, but my voice will not come. I swallow water, and my lungs start to fill.

I wake up in the darkness, screaming, breathless, drenched in sweat. ❶

At the end of the year, I pleaded with my parents to let me move to another town. I couldn't go on living in sight of the beach where K had been swept away, and my nightmares wouldn't stop. If I didn't get out of there, I'd go crazy. My parents understood and made arrangements for me to live elsewhere. I moved to Nagano Prefecture in January to live with my father's family in a mountain village near Komoro. I finished elementary school in Nagano and stayed on through junior and senior high school there. I never went home, even for holidays. My parents came to visit me now and then.

---

7. **sutras** (SOO truhz): Buddhist rules expressing truth or wisdom.
8. **chided** (CHYD ihd): scolded.

---

❶ **Literary Focus** **Symbols** What might these dreams about K signify to the seventh man?

I live in Nagano to this day. I graduated from a college of engineering in the city of Nagano and went to work for a precision tool-maker in the area. I still work for them. I live like anybody else. As you can see, there's nothing unusual about me. I'm not very sociable, but I have a few friends I go mountain climbing with. Once I got away from my hometown, I stopped having nightmares all the time. They remained a part of my life, though. They would come to me now and then, like bill collectors at the door. It happened whenever I was on the verge of forgetting. And it was always the same dream, down to the smallest detail. I would, wake up screaming, my sheets soaked with sweat.

This is probably why I never married. I didn't want to wake someone sleeping next to me with my screams in the middle of the night. I've been in love with several women over the years, but I never spent a night with any of them. The terror was in my bones. It was something I could never share with another person.

I stayed away from my hometown for over forty years. I never went near that seashore—or any other. I was afraid that, if I did, my dream might happen in reality. I had always enjoyed swimming, but after that day I never even went to a pool. I wouldn't go near deep rivers or lakes. I avoided boats and wouldn't take a plane to go abroad. Despite all these precautions, I couldn't get rid of the image of myself drowning. Like K's cold hand, this dark premonition[9] caught hold of my mind and refused to let go.

Then, last spring, I finally revisited the beach where K had been taken by the wave.

My father had died of cancer the year before, and my brother had sold the old house. In going through the storage shed, he had found a cardboard carton crammed with childhood things of mine, which he sent to me in Nagano. Most of it was useless junk, but there was one bundle of pictures that K had painted and given to me. My parents had probably put them away for me as a keepsake of K, but the pictures did nothing but reawaken the old terror. They made me feel as if K's spirit would spring back to life from them, and so I quickly returned them to their paper wrapping, intending to throw them away. I couldn't make myself do it, though. After several days of indecision, I opened the bundle again and forced myself to take a long, hard look at K's watercolors.

Most of them were landscapes, pictures of the familiar stretch of ocean and sand beach and pine woods and the town, and all done with that special clarity and coloration I knew so well from K's hand. They were still amazingly vivid despite the years, and had been executed with even greater skill than I recalled. As I leafed through the bundle, I found myself steeped in warm memories. The deep feelings of the boy K were there in his pictures—the way his eyes were opened on the world. The things we did together, the places we went together began to come back to me with great intensity. And I realized that his eyes were my eyes, that I myself had looked upon the world back then with the same lively, unclouded vision as the boy who had walked by my side.

I made a habit after that of studying one of K's pictures at my desk each day when I got home from work. I could sit there for hours with one painting. In each I found another of those soft landscapes of childhood that I had shut out of my memory for so long. I had a

---

9. premonition (prehm uh NIHSH uhn): foreshadowing or warning of what is to come.

Drowning Man II (1983) by Richard Brosman. Courtesy of the artist and the National Gallery of Australia.

sense, whenever I looked at one of K's works, that something was permeating[10] my very flesh.

Perhaps a week had gone by like this when the thought suddenly struck me one evening: I might have been making a terrible mistake all those years. As he lay there in the tip of the wave, surely, K had not been looking at me with hatred or resentment; he had not been trying to take me away with him. And that terrible grin he had fixed me with: that, too, could have been an accident of angle or light and shadow, not a conscious act on K's part. He had probably already lost consciousness, or perhaps he had been giving me a gentle smile of eternal parting. The intense look of hatred I had thought I saw

---

10. **permeating** (PUR mee ayt ihng): penetrating; spreading through.

on his face had been nothing but a reflection of the profound terror that had taken control of me for the moment.

The more I studied K's watercolor that evening, the greater the conviction with which I began to believe these new thoughts of mine. For no matter how long I continued to look at the picture, I could find nothing in it but a boy's gentle, innocent spirit.

I went on sitting at my desk for a very long time. There was nothing else I could do. The sun went down, and the pale darkness of evening began to envelop the room. Then came the deep silence of night, which seemed to go on forever. At last, the scales tipped, and dark gave way to dawn. The new day's sun tinged the sky with pink, and the birds awoke to sing.

It was then I knew I must go back.

I threw a few things in a bag, called the company to say I would not be in, and boarded a train for my old hometown.

I did not find the same quiet little seaside town that I remembered. An industrial city had sprung up nearby during the rapid development of the sixties, bringing great changes to the landscape. The one little gift shop by the station had grown into a mall, and the town's only movie theater had been turned into a supermarket. My house was no longer there. It had been demolished some months before, leaving only a scrape on the earth. The trees in the yard had all been cut down, and patches of weeds dotted the black stretch of ground. K's old house had disappeared as well, having been replaced by a concrete parking lot full of commuters' cars and vans. Not that I was overcome by sentiment. The town had ceased to be mine long before.

I walked down to the shore and climbed the steps of the breakwater. On the other side, as always, the ocean stretched off into the distance, unobstructed, huge, the horizon a single straight line. The shoreline, too, looked the same as it had before: the long beach, the lapping waves, people strolling at the water's edge. The time was after four o'clock, and the soft sun of late afternoon embraced everything below as it began its long, almost meditative, descent to the west. I lowered my bag to the sand and sat down next to it in silent appreciation of the gentle seascape. Looking at this scene, it was impossible to imagine that a great typhoon had once raged here, that a massive wave had swallowed my best friend in all the world. There was almost no one left now, surely, who remembered those terrible events. It began to seem as if the whole thing were an illusion that I had dreamed up in vivid detail.

And then I realized that the deep darkness inside me had vanished. Suddenly. As suddenly as it had come. I raised myself from the sand and, without bothering either to take off my shoes or roll up my cuffs, walked into the surf to let the waves lap at my ankles. Almost in reconciliation, it seemed, the same waves that had washed up on the beach when I was a boy were now fondly washing my feet, soaking black my shoes and pant cuffs. There would be one slow-moving wave, then a long pause, and then another wave would come and go. The people passing by gave me odd looks, but I didn't care. I had found my way back again, at last.

I looked up at the sky. A few gray cotton chunks of cloud hung there, motionless. They seemed to be there for me, though I'm not sure why I felt that way. I remembered having looked up at the sky like this in search of the "eye" of the typhoon. And then, inside me, the axis of time gave one great heave. Forty long years collapsed like a dilapidated house, mixing old time and new time together in a single swirling mass. All sounds faded, and the light around me shuddered. I lost my balance and fell into the waves. My heart throbbed at the back of my throat, and my arms and legs lost all sensation. I lay that way for a long time, face in the water, unable to stand. But I was not afraid. No, not at all. There was no longer anything for me to fear. Those days were gone. **(K)**

I stopped having my terrible nightmares. I no longer wake up screaming in the middle of the night. And I am trying now to start life over again. No, I know it's probably too late to start again. I may not have much time left to live. But even if it comes too late, I am grateful that, in the end, I was able to attain a kind of salvation, to effect some sort of recovery. Yes, grateful: I could have come to the end of my life unsaved, still screaming in the dark, afraid.

The seventh man fell silent and turned his gaze upon each of the others. No one spoke or moved or even seemed to breathe. All were waiting for the rest of his story. Outside, the wind had fallen, and nothing stirred. The seventh man brought his hand to his collar once again, as if in search of words.

"They tell us that the only thing we have to fear is fear itself, but I don't believe that," he said. Then, a moment later, he added: "Oh, the fear is there, all right. It comes to us in many different forms, at different times, and overwhelms us. But the most frightening thing we can do at such times is to turn our backs on it, to close our eyes. For then we take the most precious thing inside us and surrender it to something else. In my case, that something was the wave." **(L)**

(K) Literary Focus Symbols How does the water <u>function</u> as a symbol in this passage? Has water's meaning changed from the beginning of the story? Explain.

(L) Reading Focus Finding Themes The seventh man has finished his story. What message does he have for his listeners?

Applying Your Skills

RA.L.10.9 Explain how authors use symbols to create broader meanings. RA.L.10.7 Recognize how irony is used in a literary text. RA.L.10.4 Interpret universal themes across different works by the same author or by different authors. *Also covered* VO.10.3; WA.10.1.b

The Seventh Man

Respond and Think Critically

Reading Focus

Quick Check

1. How does K die? How does the seventh man react to his death?

2. Why does the seventh man say he has attained "a kind of salvation"? From what has he been saved?

Read with a Purpose

3. Why does K's death have such a lasting affect on the seventh man? How has it changed him?

Reading Skills: Finding Themes

4. While reading, you kept track of details that gave you insight into the story's theme. Now, add a row, and write a theme statement for "The Seventh Man."

Details from "The Seventh Man"	Details from "The Man in the Water"
The wave "just barely missed me . . . it swallowed everything that mattered most to me."	
Theme Statement: Survival can be a hollow victory if you lose the things that make life worth living.	

✔ Vocabulary Check

Match the Vocabulary word in the first column with its definition in the second column.

5. **momentum**   a. tender feeling

6. **ominous**   b. force; motion

7. **sentiment**   c. unfavorable; threatening

Literary Focus

Literary Analysis

8. **Make Judgments** Do you think the seventh man is to blame for K's death? Explain your answer with details from the text.

9. **Analyze** What is the theme of "The Seventh Man"? How do irony and symbolism help reveal this theme?

Literary Skills: Irony and Symbols

10. **Interpret** Water is a significant symbol throughout this story. What does it represent?

Literary Skills Review: Frame Story

11. **Evaluate** A **frame story** is a story that contains one or more additional stories. The seventh man tells his story to a group of people during a storm. Why do you think the author chose this form of storytelling? What does framing the story accomplish?

Writing Focus

Think as a Reader/Writer

Use It in Your Writing As you read, you noted examples of Murakami's use of figurative language in your *Reader/Writer Notebook*. Now, write a one-paragraph description of an ordinary object, using figurative language to bring your writing to life.

 What Do You Think Now In what ways does the seventh man's near-death experience affect his life? How might his life have been different if he had saved K?

THE MAN IN THE WATER

by **Roger Rosenblatt**

Read with a Purpose
Read to discover one man's extraordinary response to a life-threatening disaster.

Preparing to Read for this essay is on page 377.

Build Background
The disaster described in this essay occurred on January 13, 1982. Washington, D.C., was blanketed in wet snow flurries when Air Florida Flight 90 took off from Washington National Airport (now Reagan National Airport). Just after takeoff the plane hit the Fourteenth Street Bridge, crushed five cars, tipped over a truck, and then crashed into the Potomac River. Seventy-eight people died, including four motorists. Of the seventy-nine people aboard the plane, only five survived—four passengers and one flight attendant. The probable cause of the accident was ice on the plane's wings.

As disasters go, this one was terrible but not unique, certainly not among the worst on the roster of U.S. air crashes. There was the unusual element of the bridge, of course, and the fact that the plane clipped it at a moment of high traffic, one routine thus intersecting another and disrupting both. Then, too, there was the location of the event. Washington, the city of form and regulations, turned chaotic, deregulated, by a blast of real winter and a single slap of metal on metal. The jets from Washington National Airport that normally swoop around the presidential monuments like famished gulls were, for the moment, emblemized[1] by the one that fell; so there was that detail. And there was the aesthetic clash[2] as well—blue-and-green Air Florida, the name a flying garden, sunk down among gray chunks in a black river. All that was worth noticing, to be sure. Still, there was nothing very special in any of it, except death, which, while always special, does not necessarily bring millions to tears or to attention. Why, then, the shock here?

Perhaps because the nation saw in this disaster something more than a mechanical failure. Perhaps because people saw in it no failure at all, but rather something successful about their makeup. Here, after all, were two forms of nature in collision: the elements and human character. Last Wednesday, the elements, indifferent as ever, brought down Flight 90. And on that same afternoon, human nature—groping and flailing in mysteries of its own—rose to the occasion. **A**

Of the four acknowledged heroes of the event, three are able to account for their behavior. Donald Usher and Eugene Windsor, a park-police helicopter team, risked their lives every

---

1. **emblemized** (EHM bluh myzd): represented; symbolized.
2. **aesthetic** (ehs THEHT ihk) **clash:** unpleasant visual contrast.

Vocabulary **chaotic** (kay AHT ihk) *adj.:* very confused; completely disordered.

A **Literary Focus** **Irony** The author says that people saw "something successful" in this crash. How is this statement ironic?

Analyzing Visuals

Viewing and Interpreting
What details are shown in this photograph that are not revealed in the essay?

One of the passengers of the Air Florida jetliner being pulled to shore by a U.S. Park Police helicopter. Another passenger at lower left clings to the ice, waiting to be rescued.

time they dipped the skids[3] into the water to pick up survivors. On television, side by side in bright blue jumpsuits, they described their courage as all in the line of duty. Lenny Skutnik, a 28-year-old employee of the Congressional Budget Office, said: "It's something I never thought I would do"—referring to his jumping into the water to drag an injured woman to shore. Skutnik added that "somebody had to go in the water," delivering every hero's line that is no less admirable for its repetitions. In fact, nobody had to go into the water. That

---

3. **skids:** long, narrow pieces used in place of wheels for aircraft landing gear.

somebody actually did so is part of the reason this particular tragedy sticks in the mind.

But the person most responsible for the emotional impact of the disaster is the one known at first simply as "the man in the water." (Balding, probably in his 50s, an extravagant moustache.) He was seen clinging with five other survivors to the tail section of the airplane. This man was described by Usher and Windsor as appearing alert and in control. Every time they lowered a lifeline and flotation ring to him, he passed it on to another of the passengers. "In a mass casualty, you'll find people like him," said Windsor. "But I've never seen one with that commitment." When the helicopter came back for him, the man had gone under. His selflessness was one reason the story held national attention; his anonymity[4] another. The fact that he went unidentified invested him with a universal character. For a while he was Everyman, and thus proof (as if one needed it) that no man is ordinary. **Ⓑ**

Still, he could never have imagined such a capacity in himself. Only minutes before his character was tested, he was sitting in the ordinary plane among the ordinary passengers, dutifully listening to the stewardess telling him to fasten his seat belt and saying something about the "No Smoking" sign. So our man relaxed with the others, some of whom would owe their lives to him. Perhaps he started to read, or to doze, or to regret some harsh remark made in the office that morning. Then suddenly he knew that the trip would not be ordinary. Like every other person on that flight, he was desperate to live, which makes his final act so stunning.

For at some moment in the water he must have realized that he would not live if he continued to hand over the rope and ring to others. He *had* to know it, no matter how gradual the effect of the cold. In his judgment he had no choice. When the helicopter took off with what was to be the last survivor, he watched everything in the world move away from him, and he deliberately let it happen.

Yet there was something else about our man that kept our thoughts on him, and which keeps our thoughts on him still. He was *there,* in the essential, classic circumstance. Man in nature. The man in the water. For its part, nature cared

nothing about the five passengers. Our man, on the other hand, cared totally. So the timeless battle commenced in the Potomac. For as long as that man could last, they went at each other, nature and man; the one making no distinctions of good and evil, acting on no principles, offering no lifelines; the other acting wholly on distinctions, principles, and, one supposes, on faith. **Ⓒ**

Since it was he who lost the fight, we ought to come again to the conclusion that people are powerless in the world. In reality, we believe the reverse, and it takes the act of the man in the water to remind us of our true feelings in this matter. It is not to say that everyone would have acted as he did, or as Usher, Windsor, and Skutnik. Yet whatever moved these men to challenge death on behalf of their fellows is not peculiar to them. Everyone feels the possibility in himself. That is the abiding wonder of the story. That is why we would not let go of it. If the man in the water gave a lifeline to the people gasping for survival, he was likewise giving a lifeline to those who observed him.

The odd thing is that we do not even really believe that the man in the water lost his fight. "Everything in Nature contains all the powers of Nature," said Emerson. Exactly. So the man in the water had his own natural powers. He could not make ice storms, or freeze the water until it froze the blood. But he could hand life over to a stranger, and that is a power of nature too. The man in the water pitted himself against an implacable, impersonal enemy; he fought it with charity; and he held it to a standoff. He was the best we can do. **Ⓓ**

---

4. anonymity (an uh NIHM uh tee): unknown identity.

Ⓑ **Reading Focus** **Finding Themes** What theme can you derive from the details in this paragraph?

Ⓒ **Reading Focus** **Finding Themes** What might this conflict between the man and nature suggest about the theme of this essay?

Ⓓ **Literary Focus** **Irony** What is ironic about this description of the man as a powerful force of nature?

Vocabulary **implacable** (ihm PLAK uh buhl) *adj.:* relentless; not affected by attempts at change.

Applying Your Skills

RA.L.10.9 Explain how authors use symbols to create broader meanings. **RA.L.10.7** Recognize how irony is used in a literary text. **RA.L.10.4** Interpret universal themes across different works by the same author or by different authors. *Also covered* **RA.L.10.5; RA.I.10.5; VO.10.3; WA.10.4.d**

The Man in the Water

Respond and Think Critically

Reading Focus

Quick Check

1. Briefly describe the disaster at the center of this essay. Besides the man in the water, who are the other three heroes? What does each hero do?

2. According to Rosenblatt, why did people see the disaster as "more than a mechanical failure"?

Read with a Purpose

3. Why does the man in the water receive more attention than the other heroes? In what ways were his actions extraordinary?

Reading Skills: Finding Themes

4. While reading, you kept track of details that gave you insight into the selections' themes. Write a theme statement for "The Man in the Water." Then, describe how the selections' themes are similar and different.

Details from "The Seventh Man"	Details from "The Man in the Water"
The wave "just barely missed me . . . it swallowed everything that mattered most to me."	
Theme Statement: Survival can be a hollow victory if you lose the things that make life worth living.	Theme Statement:

✓ Vocabulary Check

Write whether each statement is *true* or *false*. If it false, explain why. Vocabulary words are boldface.

5. The **implacable** enemies were easily defeated.

6. **Chaotic** conditions are neat and well ordered.

Literary Focus

Literary Analysis

7. **Evaluate** The final two paragraphs of the essay make specific points about human nature. Explain in your own words what Rosenblatt is saying. Then, give your opinion of his ideas.

8. **Compare** According to Rosenblatt, the man in the water exemplifies, or illustrates, the conflict between human beings and nature. What quality do nature and the man have in common?

Literary Skills: Irony and Symbols

9. **Infer** Find three examples of situational irony in this essay, and explain the irony of each.

Literary Skills Review: Main Idea

10. **Analyze** Often, the theme of an essay is closely tied to its **main idea,** or the central thought. What is the main idea in this essay? Which passages illustrate this idea most effectively?

Writing Focus

Think as a Reader/Writer

Use It in Your Writing Review the notes in your *Reader/Writer Notebook*. Then, think about a recent event you witnessed at school or in your community. Write an article about the event, using figurative language to make the writing more descriptive.

 What Do You Think Now

The man in the water sacrifices himself to save others. What lesson might the survivors of the crash have learned?

RA.L.10.4 Interpret universal themes across different works by the same author or by different authors. **RA.L.10.5** Analyze how an author's choice of genre affects the expression of a theme or topic. **WA.10.4.c** Write informational essays or reports, including research that: create an organizing structure appropriate to the purpose, audience and context; *Also covered* **WP.10.6**

The Seventh Man / The Man in the Water

Writing Focus

Write a Comparison-Contrast Essay

In an essay, compare and contrast the themes of "The Seventh Man" and "The Man in the Water." Before you begin writing, consider these points:

- What do the themes of each selection have in common? How are they different?
- How are the themes in each selection conveyed?
- How does the genre of a selection affect the way the author presents his or her theme?

Introduction In your introduction, mention the authors and titles of the two selections, and state your **thesis**—your overall idea about the two works.

Body The body of your essay should fully explore the works' similarities and differences. Look for details and examples from the text to support your claims. The **point-by-point method** is a good way of organizing the details in the body of essay. When using this method, you present the elements one by one. For example, you might first discuss the relationship between irony and theme in "The Seventh Man" and then discuss the same relationship in "The Man in the Water."

Conclusion Finally, write a conclusion to sum up your main points. Proofread your finished essay to correct errors in grammar, spelling, and punctuation.

What Do You Think Now?

Do all people possess the capacity to act as heroes, or are most people inclined to save themselves first? Explain.

CHOICES

As you respond to the Choices, use these **Academic Vocabulary** words as appropriate: <u>derive</u>, <u>function</u>, <u>interact</u>, and <u>significant</u>.

REVIEW
Write a Story

Think about the symbols in "The Seventh Man" and "The Man in the Water" as well as the conflict of humanity versus nature in both selections. Then, write a short story involving a character who battles nature. Use one or more symbols in your own writing. Once you have finished your story, read it aloud to the class.

CONNECT
Explain a Position

Timed ㄴWriting Both selections feature people in terrifying situations. One defies fear but pays with his life; the other succumbs to his fear and lives. It is perhaps easy to deem these characters either brave or cowardly, but is it fair to judge them by the same standard? Write a brief essay in response to this question, citing details from the selections as well as from your own experience.

EXTEND
Research a Disaster

In "The Seventh Man," K dies in a storm surge, a giant wave associated with a typhoon. A similar phenomenon is the tsunami, a wave caused by an underwater earthquake. In December 2004, a massive tsunami struck Southeast Asia, causing widespread devastation. Research this disaster by looking for photographs and eyewitness accounts. Then, share your findings with the class.

Primary and Secondary Sources

Titanic.

CONTENTS

What Do You Think

What choices led to so few people's surviving the sinking of the *Titanic*?

QuickWrite

The sinking of the *Titanic* is a famous disaster. Versions of the story have appeared in songs and movies—some accurate, some fictional. Write a few sentences stating what you know—or think you know—about this event.

Preparing to Read

R.M.S. Titanic / A Fireman's Story / From a Lifeboat

 R.10.4 Evaluate and systematically organize important information, and select appropriate sources to support central ideas, concepts and themes. *Also covered* **R.10.2; RA.I.10.5**

Reader/Writer Notebook

Use your **RWN** to complete the activities for these selections.

Informational Text Focus

Primary and Secondary Sources The materials you find when researching historical information can be classified into two categories:

- A **primary source** is original material that has not been interpreted by other writers. Examples of primary sources are autobiographies, letters, oral histories, and eyewitness accounts.

- A **secondary source** is based on other sources. Information from these sources is interpreted, summarized, or retold by another writer. Examples of secondary sources are encyclopedias, many newspaper and magazine articles, biographies, and textbooks.

A primary source has the advantage of being a firsthand account of an event. In "A Fireman's Story" and "From a Lifeboat," you learn about the sinking of the *Titanic* from people who were actually there. The disadvantage of a primary source is that it includes only one person's perspective. It may be very **subjective,** based on emotion or opinion. Thus, it can be unreliable.

A secondary source, such as "R.M.S. Titanic," often covers a topic more broadly. However, this broader coverage does not necessarily mean that the source is **objective,** or factual. Authors often include their opinions and feelings on the topic.

Into Action As you read these selections, note objective and subjective language in a chart like the one below.

Objective Details	Subjective Details
"Westbound steamers report bergs growlers and field ice."	"Out of the dark she came, a vast, dim, white, monstrous shape."

Vocabulary

R.M.S. Titanic

ascertain (as uhr TAYN) *v.:* find out with certainty; determine. *The captain needed to ascertain if the ship had indeed hit an iceberg.*

corroborated (kuh RAHB uh rayt ihd) *v.:* supported; upheld the truth of. *Several accounts corroborated the report that the lifeboats were not filled.*

perfunctory (puhr FUHNGK tuhr ee) *adj.:* done with little care or thought; indifferent. *The efforts to gather more people into the lifeboats were perfunctory at best.*

pertinent (PUR tuh nuhnt) *adj.:* having some association with the subject. *Baldwin tried to select only pertinent information from the dozens of accounts.*

Language Coach

Context Clues Sometimes writers provide clues about a word's meaning by placing a definition nearby. Look at this sentence: *Baldwin had to decide which details were pertinent to his report; many details were irrelevant, or less important, than others.* Which words tell you what *pertinent* means?

Writing Focus   Preparing for **Constructed Response**

As you read the following selections, you may notice differences among the accounts of the *Titanic's* sinking. Some of the details may conflict. Note these differences in your *Reader/Writer Notebook*.

 Learn It Online
To read more articles like these, go to the interactive Reading Workshops on:

go.hrw.com   L10-397   **Go**

R.M.S. Titanic

by **Hanson W. Baldwin**

Read with a Purpose
Read to discover how a writer synthesizes factual reports from many sources into a single narrative about a terrible tragedy.

Build Background
This 1934 article describes the sinking of the *Titanic,* which had occurred in 1912. Hanson W. Baldwin conducted extensive research, reviewing ship's logs, interviews, and other records. Since the publication of the article, more information has been found—a 1986 underwater exploration of the wreck did not find the three-hundred-foot slash in the ship that Baldwin describes. Instead, divers saw buckled seams and separated plates in the ship's hull. This damage, rather than a large gash, is probably what caused the ship to sink.

· · · · · · · · · · · · · [I] · · · · · · · · · · · · ·

The White Star liner *Titanic,* largest ship the world had ever known, sailed from Southampton on her maiden voyage to New York on April 10, 1912. The paint on her strakes[1] was fair and bright; she was fresh from Harland and Wolff's Belfast yards, strong in the strength of her forty-six thousand tons of steel, bent, hammered, shaped, and riveted through the three years of her slow birth.

There was little fuss and fanfare at her sailing; her sister ship, the *Olympic*—slightly smaller than the *Titanic*—had been in service for some months and to her had gone the thunder of the cheers.

But the *Titanic* needed no whistling steamers or shouting crowds to call attention to her superlative qualities. Her bulk dwarfed the ships near her as longshoremen singled up her mooring lines and cast off the turns of heavy rope from the dock bollards.[2] She was not only the largest ship afloat, but was believed to be the safest. Carlisle, her builder, had given her double bottoms and had divided her hull into sixteen watertight compartments, which made her, men thought, unsinkable. She had been built to be and had been described as a gigantic lifeboat. Her designers' dreams of a triple-screw[3] giant, a luxurious, floating hotel, which could speed to New York at twenty-three knots, had been carefully translated from blueprints and mold loft lines at the Belfast yards into a living reality. Ⓐ

The *Titanic*'s sailing from Southampton, though quiet, was not wholly uneventful. As the liner moved slowly toward the end of her dock that April day, the surge of her passing sucked

---

1. **strakes** (strayks): single lines of metal plating extending the whole length of a ship.

2. **bollards** (BAHL uhrdz): strong posts on a pier or wharf for holding a ship's mooring ropes.

3. **triple-screw:** three propellered.

Ⓐ **Informational Focus** Primary and Secondary **Sources** What facts are presented in these opening paragraphs?

Reading room on upper promenade of the *Titanic* (c. 1910).

away from the quay[4] the steamer *New York*, moored just to seaward of the *Titanic*'s berth. There were sharp cracks as the manila mooring lines of the *New York* parted under the strain. The frayed ropes writhed and whistled through the air and snapped down among the waving crowd on the pier; the *New York* swung toward the *Titanic*'s bow, was checked and dragged back to the dock barely in time to avert a collision. Seamen muttered, thought it an ominous start. **B**

Past Spithead and the Isle of Wight the *Titanic* steamed. She called at Cherbourg at dusk and then laid her course for Queenstown. At 1:30 P.M. on Thursday, April 11, she stood out of Queenstown harbor, screaming gulls soaring in her wake, with 2,201 persons—men, women, and children—aboard.

Occupying the Empire bedrooms and Georgian suites of the first-class accommodations were many well-known men and women—Colonel John Jacob Astor and his young bride; Major Archibald Butt, military aide to President Taft, and his friend Frank D. Millet, the painter; John B. Thayer, vice president of the Pennsylvania Railroad, and Charles M. Hays, president of the Grand Trunk Railway of Canada; W. T. Stead, the English journalist; Jacques Futrelle, French novelist; H. B. Harris, theatrical manager, and Mrs. Harris; Mr. and Mrs. Isidor Straus; and J. Bruce Ismay, chairman and managing director of the White Star Line.

Down in the plain wooden cabins of the steerage class were 706 immigrants to the land of promise, and trimly stowed in the great holds was a cargo valued at $420,000: oak beams, sponges, wine, calabashes,[5] and an odd miscellany of the common and the rare.

The *Titanic* took her departure on Fastnet Light[6] and, heading into the night, laid her course for New York. She was due at quarantine[7] the following Wednesday morning.

---

4. **quay** (kee): dock.

5. **calabashes** (KAL uh bash uhz): large smoking pipes made from the necks of gourds.

6. **Fastnet Light:** lighthouse at the southwestern tip of Ireland. After the Fastnet Light there is only open sea until the coast of North America.

7. **quarantine** (KWAWR uhn teen): place where a ship is held in port after arrival to determine whether its passengers and cargo are free of communicable diseases. *Quarantine* can also be used to refer to the length of time a ship is held.

B **Informational Focus** Primary and Secondary Sources What is significant about these details?

Sunday dawned fair and clear. The *Titanic* steamed smoothly toward the west, faint streamers of brownish smoke trailing from her funnels. The purser held services in the saloon in the morning; on the steerage deck aft[8] the immigrants were playing games and a Scotsman was puffing "The Campbells Are Coming" on his bagpipes in the midst of the uproar.

At 9:00 A.M. a message from the steamer *Caronia* sputtered into the wireless shack:

> Captain, *Titanic*—Westbound steamers report bergs growlers and field ice 42 degrees N. from 49 degrees to 51 degrees W. 12th April.
>
> Compliments—Barr.

It was cold in the afternoon; the sun was brilliant, but the *Titanic*, her screws turning over at seventy-five revolutions per minute, was approaching the Banks.[9]

In the Marconi cabin[10] Second Operator Harold Bride, earphones clamped on his head, was figuring accounts; he did not stop to answer when he heard *MWL*, Continental Morse for the nearby Leyland liner, *Californian*, calling the *Titanic*. The *Californian* had some message about three icebergs; he didn't bother then to take it down. About 1:42 P.M. the rasping spark of those days spoke again across the water. It was the *Baltic*, calling the *Titanic*, warning her of ice on the steamer track. Bride took the message down and sent it up to the bridge.[11] The officer-of-the-deck glanced at it; sent it to the bearded master of the *Titanic*, Captain E. C. Smith,[12] a veteran of the White Star service. It was lunchtime then; the captain, walking along the promenade deck, saw Mr. Ismay, stopped, and handed him the message without comment. Ismay read it, stuffed it in his pocket, told two ladies about the icebergs, and resumed his walk. Later, about 7:15 P.M., the captain requested the return of the message in order to post it in the chart room for the information of officers. **C**

Dinner that night in the Jacobean dining room was gay. It was bitter on deck, but the night was calm and fine; the sky was moonless but studded with stars twinkling coldly in the clear air.

After dinner some of the second-class passengers gathered in the saloon, where the Reverend Mr. Carter conducted a "hymn sing-song." It was almost ten o'clock and the stewards were waiting with biscuits and coffee as the group sang:

> O, hear us when we cry to Thee
> For those in peril on the sea. **D**

On the bridge Second Officer Lightoller—short, stocky, efficient—was relieved at ten o'clock by First Officer Murdoch. Lightoller had talked with other officers about the proximity of ice; at least five wireless ice warnings had reached the ship; lookouts had been cautioned to be alert; captains and officers expected to reach the field at any time after 9:30 P.M. At

---

8. **aft:** in the rear of a ship.
9. **Banks:** Grand Banks, shallow waters near the southeast coast of Newfoundland.
10. **Marconi cabin:** room where messages were received and sent by radio.

11. **bridge:** raised structure on a ship. The ship is controlled from the bridge.
12. Smith's initials were actually E. J., not E. C.

C **Informational Focus** Primary and Secondary Sources
From what types of primary sources might Baldwin have <u>derived</u> the information in this paragraph?

D **Informational Focus** Primary and Secondary Sources
Why do you think Baldwin chose to include some of the lyrics from this hymn?

twenty-two knots, its speed unslackened, the *Titanic* plowed on through the night.

Lightoller left the darkened bridge to his relief and turned in. Captain Smith went to his cabin. The steerage was long since quiet; in the first and second cabins lights were going out; voices were growing still; people were asleep. Murdoch paced back and forth on the bridge, peering out over the dark water, glancing now and then at the compass in front of Quartermaster Hichens at the wheel.

In the crow's-nest, lookout Frederick Fleet and his partner, Leigh, gazed down at the water, still and unruffled in the dim, starlit darkness. Behind and below them the ship, a white shadow with here and there a last winking light; ahead of them a dark and silent and cold ocean. **E**

There was a sudden clang. "Dong-dong. Dong-dong. Dong-dong. Dong!" The metal clapper of the great ship's bell struck out 11:30. Mindful of the warnings, Fleet strained his eyes, searching the darkness for the dreaded ice. But there were only the stars and the sea.

In the wireless room, where Phillips, first operator, had relieved Bride, the buzz of the *Californian*'s set again crackled into the earphones:

Californian: "Say, old man, we are stuck here, surrounded by ice."

Titanic: "Shut up, shut up; keep out. I am talking to Cape Race; you are jamming my signals."

Then, a few minutes later—about 11:40 . . .

> Hichens strained at the wheel; the bow swung slowly to port. The monster was almost upon them now.

· · · · · · · · · · · · [II] · · · · · · · · · · · ·

Out of the dark she came, a vast, dim, white, monstrous shape, directly in the *Titanic*'s path. For a moment Fleet doubted his eyes. But she was a deadly reality, this ghastly *thing*. Frantically, Fleet struck three bells—*something dead ahead*. He snatched the telephone and called the bridge:

"Iceberg! Right ahead!"

The first officer heard but did not stop to acknowledge the message.

"Hard-a-starboard!"

Hichens strained at the wheel; the bow swung slowly to port. The monster was almost upon them now.

Murdoch leaped to the engine-room telegraph. Bells clanged. Far below in the engine room those bells struck the first warning. Danger! The indicators on the dial faces swung round to "Stop!" Then "Full speed astern!" Frantically the engineers turned great valve wheels; answered the bridge bells . . .

There was a slight shock, a brief scraping, a small list to port. Shell ice—slabs and chunks of it—fell on the foredeck. Slowly the *Titanic* stopped.

Captain Smith hurried out of his cabin.

"What has the ship struck?"

Murdoch answered, "An iceberg, sir. I hard-a-starboarded and reversed the engines, and I was going to hard-a-port around it, but she was too close. I could not do any more. I have

---

E **Informational Focus** **Primary and Secondary Sources**
Why does the author include the names of minor crew members here? What effect does it have on you?

(left to right) Cover of White Star Line's advertisement for *Titanic;* the *Titanic's* captain, E. J. Smith; *The Illustrated London News,* headline: "ICEBERG."

closed the watertight doors."

Fourth Officer Boxhall, other officers, the carpenter, came to the bridge. The captain sent Boxhall and the carpenter below to ascertain the damage.

A few lights switched on in the first and second cabins; sleepy passengers peered through porthole glass; some casually asked the stewards:

"Why have we stopped?"

"I don't know, sir, but I don't suppose it is anything much."

In the smoking room a quorum[13] of gamblers and their prey were still sitting round a poker table; the usual crowd of kibitzers[14] looked on. They had felt the slight jar of the collision and had seen an eighty-foot ice mountain glide by the smoking-room windows, but the night was calm and clear, the *Titanic* was "unsinkable"; they hadn't bothered to go on deck.

But far below, in the warren of passages on the starboard side forward, in the forward holds and boiler rooms, men could see that the *Titanic's* hurt was mortal. In No. 6 boiler room, where the red glow from the furnaces lighted up the naked, sweaty chests of coal-blackened firemen, water was pouring through a great gash about two feet above the floor plates. This was no slow leak; the ship was open to the sea; in ten minutes there were eight feet of water in No. 6. Long before then the stokers had raked the flaming fires out of the furnaces and had scrambled through the watertight doors in No. 5 or had climbed up the long steel ladders to safety. When Boxhall looked at the mailroom in No. 3 hold, twenty-four feet above the keel, the mailbags were already floating about in the slushing water. In No. 5 boiler room a stream of water spurted into an empty bunker. All six compartments forward of No. 4 were open to

13. **quorum** (KWAWR uhm): number of people required for a particular activity—in this case, for a game.
14. **kibitzers** (KIHB iht suhrz): talkative onlookers who often give unwanted advice.

Vocabulary   **ascertain** (as uhr TAYN) *v.:* find out with certainty; determine.

F **Informational Focus** Primary and Secondary Sources
With matter-of-fact exposition, Baldwin takes us step by step along the starboard side of the ship, describing the damage. What words indicate his change to a more subjective tone at the end of this passage?

the sea; in ten seconds the iceberg's jagged claw had ripped a three-hundred-foot slash in the bottom of the great *Titanic*.

Reports came to the bridge; Ismay in dressing gown ran out on deck in the cold, still, starlit night, climbed up the bridge ladder.

"What has happened?"

Captain Smith: "We have struck ice."

"Do you think she is seriously damaged?"

Captain Smith: "I'm afraid she is."

Ismay went below and passed Chief Engineer William Bell, fresh from an inspection of the damaged compartments. Bell corroborated the captain's statement; hurried back down the glistening steel ladders to his duty. Man after man followed him—Thomas Andrews, one of the ship's designers, Archie Frost, the builder's chief engineer, and his twenty assistants—men who had no posts of duty in the engine room but whose traditions called them there.

On deck, in corridor and stateroom, life flowed again. Men, women, and children awoke and questioned; orders were given to uncover the lifeboats; water rose into the firemen's quarters; half-dressed stokers streamed up on deck. But the passengers—most of them—did not know that the *Titanic* was sinking. The shock of the collision had been so slight that some were not awakened by it; the *Titanic* was so huge that she must be unsinkable; the night was too calm, too beautiful, to think of death at sea. Ⓖ

Captain Smith half ran to the door of the radio shack. Bride, partly dressed, eyes dulled with sleep, was standing behind Phillips, waiting.

"Send the call for assistance."

The blue spark danced: "CQD—CQD—CQD—CQ—"[15]

Miles away Marconi men heard. Cape Race heard it, and the steamships *La Provence* and *Mt. Temple*.

The sea was surging into the *Titanic*'s hold. At 12:20 the water burst into the seamen's quarters through a collapsed fore-and-aft wooden bulkhead. Pumps strained in the engine rooms—men and machinery making a futile fight against the sea. Steadily the water rose.

The boats were swung out—slowly, for the deckhands were late in reaching their stations; there had been no boat drill, and many of the crew did not know to what boats they were assigned. Orders were shouted; the safety valves had lifted, and steam was blowing off in a great rushing roar. In the chart house Fourth Officer Boxhall bent above a chart, working rapidly with pencil and dividers.

12:25 A.M. Boxhall's position is sent out to a fleet of vessels: "Come at once; we have struck a berg."

To the Cunarder *Carpathia* (Arthur Henry Rostron, Master, New York to Liverpool, fifty-eight miles away): "It's a CQD, old man. Position 41–46N.; 50–14 W."

The blue spark dancing: "Sinking; cannot hear for noise of steam."

12:30 A.M. The word is passed: "Women and children in the boats." Stewards finish waking their passengers below; life preservers are tied on; some men smile at the precaution. "The *Titanic* is unsinkable." The *Mt. Temple* starts for the *Titanic*; the *Carpathia*, with a double watch

---

15. **CQD:** call by radio operators, inviting others to communicate with them.

Vocabulary **corroborated** (kuh RAHB uh rayt ihd) *v.:* supported; upheld the truth of.

in her stokeholds, radios, "Coming hard." The CQD changes the course of many ships—but not of one; the operator of the *Californian,* nearby, has just put down his earphones and turned in.

The CQD flashes over land and sea from Cape Race to New York; newspaper city rooms leap to life and presses whir.

On the *Titanic,* water creeps over the bulkhead between Nos. 5 and 6 firerooms. She is going down by the head; the engineers—fighting a losing battle—are forced back foot by foot by the rising water. Down the promenade deck, Happy Jock Hume, the bandsman, runs with his instrument.

12:45 A.M. Murdoch, in charge on the starboard side, eyes tragic, but calm and cool, orders boat No. 7 lowered. The women hang back; they want no boat ride on an ice-strewn sea; the *Titanic* is unsinkable. The men encourage them, explain that this is just a precautionary measure: "We'll see you again at breakfast." There is little confusion; passengers stream slowly to the boat deck. In the steerage the immigrants chatter excitedly.

A sudden sharp hiss—a streaked flare against the night; Boxhall sends a rocket toward the sky. It explodes, and a parachute of white stars lights up the icy sea. "God! Rockets!" The band plays ragtime.

No. 8 is lowered, and No. 5. Ismay, still in dressing gown, calls for women and children, handles lines, stumbles in the way of an officer, is told to "get the hell out of here." Third Officer Pitman takes charge of No. 5; as he swings into the boat, Murdoch grasps his hand. "Goodbye and good luck, old man."

No. 6 goes over the side. There are only twenty-eight people in a lifeboat with a capacity of sixty-five.

A light stabs from the bridge; Boxhall is calling in Morse flashes, again and again, to a strange ship stopped in the ice jam five to ten miles away. Another rocket drops its shower of sparks above the ice-strewn sea and the dying ship.

1:00 A.M. Slowly the water creeps higher; the fore ports of the *Titanic* are dipping into the sea. Rope squeaks through blocks; lifeboats drop jerkily seaward. Through the shouting on the decks comes the sound of the band playing ragtime.

The "Millionaires' Special" leaves the ship—boat No. 1, with a capacity of forty people, carries only Sir Cosmo and Lady Duff Gordon and ten others. Aft, the frightened immigrants mill and jostle and rush for a boat. An officer's fist flies out; three shots are fired in the air, and the panic is quelled. . . . Four Chinese sneak unseen into a boat and hide in the bottom. **Ⓗ**

1:20 A.M. Water is coming into No. 4 boiler room. Stokers slice and shovel as water laps about their ankles—steam for the dynamos, steam for the dancing spark! As the water rises, great ash hoes rake the flaming coals from the furnaces. Safety valves pop; the stokers retreat aft, and the watertight doors clang shut behind them.

The rockets fling their splendor toward the stars. The boats are more heavily loaded now, for the passengers know the *Titanic* is sinking. Women cling and sob. The great screws aft are rising clear of the sea. Half-filled boats are ordered to come alongside the cargo ports and take on more passengers, but the ports are never opened—and the boats are never filled. Others pull for the steamer's light miles away but never reach it; the lights disappear; the unknown ship steams off.

Ⓗ **Informational Focus** Primary and Secondary Sources
Do the details in these two paragraphs likely come from one primary source or more than one? Explain.

The water rises and the band plays ragtime.

1:30 A.M. Lightoller is getting the port boats off; Murdoch, the starboard. As one boat is lowered into the sea, a boat officer fires his gun along the ship's side to stop a rush from the lower decks. A woman tries to take her Great Dane into a boat with her; she is refused and steps out of the boat to die with her dog. Millet's "little smile which played on his lips all through the voyage" plays no more; his lips are grim, but he waves goodbye and brings wraps for the women.

Benjamin Guggenheim, in evening clothes, smiles and says, "We've dressed up in our best and are prepared to go down like gentlemen."

1:40 A.M. Boat 14 is clear, and then 13, 16, 15, and C. The lights still shine, but the *Baltic* hears the blue spark say, "Engine room getting flooded."

The *Olympia* signals, "Am lighting up all possible boilers as fast as can."

Major Butt helps women into the last boats and waves goodbye to them. Mrs. Straus puts her foot on the gunwale of a lifeboat; then she draws back and goes to her husband: "We have been together many years; where you go, I will go." Colonel John Jacob Astor puts his young wife in a lifeboat, steps back, taps cigarette on fingernail: "Goodbye, dearie; I'll join you later."

1:45 A.M. The foredeck is under water; the fo'c'sle[16] head almost awash; the great stern is lifted high toward the bright stars; and still the band plays. Mr. and Mrs. Harris approach a lifeboat arm in arm.

Officer: "Ladies first, please."

Harris bows, smiles, steps back: "Of course, certainly; ladies first."

---

16. **fo'c'sle** (FOHK suhl): forecastle, front upper deck of a ship.

(clockwise from top left) Lookout Frederick Fleet; First Operator Jack Phillips; Molly Brown (nicknamed "unsinkable" by the Associated Press) helped row a lifeboat and nurse survivors; Colonel John Jacob Astor, wealthy hotel owner, went down with the *Titanic*.

Boxhall fires the last rocket, then leaves in charge of boat No. 2.

2:00 A.M. She is dying now; her bow goes deeper, her stern higher. But there must be steam. Below in the stokeholds the sweaty firemen keep steam up for the flaring lights and the dancing spark. The glowing coals slide and tumble over the slanted grate bars; the sea pounds behind that yielding bulkhead. But the spark dances on. ➊

The *Asian* hears Phillips try the new signal—SOS.

Boat No. 4 has left now; boat D leaves ten minutes later. Jacques Futrelle clasps his wife:

➊ **Informational Focus** Primary and Secondary Sources
How could you rewrite this paragraph more objectively?

"For God's sake, go! It's your last chance; go!" Madame Futrelle is half forced into the boat. It clears the side.

There are about 660 people in the boats and 1,500 still on the sinking *Titanic.*

On top of the officers' quarters, men work frantically to get the two collapsibles stowed there over the side. Water is over the forward part of A deck now; it surges up the companionways toward the boat deck. In the radio shack, Bride has slipped a coat and life jacket about Phillips as the first operator sits hunched over his key, sending—still sending—"41–46 N.; 50–14 W. CQD—CQD—SOS—SOS—"

The captain's tired white face appears at the radio-room door. "Men, you have done your full duty. You can do no more. Now, it's every man for himself." The captain disappears—back to his sinking bridge, where Painter, his personal steward, stands quietly waiting for orders. The spark dances on. Bride turns his back and goes into the inner cabin. As he does so, a stoker, grimed with coal, mad with fear, steals into the shack and reaches for the life jacket on Phillips's back. Bride wheels about and brains him with a wrench.

2:10 A.M. Below decks the steam is still holding, though the pressure is falling—rapidly. In the gymnasium on the boat deck, the athletic instructor watches quietly as two gentlemen ride the bicycles and another swings casually at the punching bag. Mail clerks stagger up the boat-deck stairways, dragging soaked mail sacks. The spark still dances. The band still plays—but not ragtime:

> Nearer my God to Thee.
> Nearer to Thee . . .

> Men swim away from the sinking ship; others drop from the stern.

A few men take up the refrain; others kneel on the slanting decks to pray. Many run and scramble aft, where hundreds are clinging above the silent screws on the great uptilted stern. The spark still dances and the lights still flare; the engineers are on the job. The hymn comes to its close. Bandmaster Hartley, Yorkshireman violinist, taps his bow against a bulkhead, calls for "Autumn" as the water curls about his feet, and the eight musicians brace themselves against the ship's slant. People are leaping from the decks into the nearby water—the icy water. A woman cries, "Oh, save me, save me!" A man answers, "Good lady, save yourself. Only God can save you now." The band plays "Autumn":

> God of Mercy and Compassion!
> Look with pity on my pain . . .

The water creeps over the bridge where the *Titanic*'s master stands; heavily he steps out to meet it.

2:17 A.M. "CQ—" The *Virginian* hears a ragged, blurred CQ, then an abrupt stop. The blue spark dances no more. The lights flicker out; the engineers have lost their battle.

2:18 A.M. Men run about blackened decks; leap into the night; are swept into the sea by the curling wave that licks up the *Titanic*'s length. Lightoller does not leave the ship; the ship leaves him; there are hundreds like him, but only a few who live to tell of it. The funnels still swim above the water, but the ship is climbing to the perpendicular; the bridge is under and most of the foremast; the great stern rises like a squat leviathan.[17] Men swim away from the sinking ship; others drop from the stern.

---

17. leviathan (luh VY uh thuhn): Biblical sea monster, perhaps a whale.

The band plays in the darkness, the water lapping upward:

> Hold me up in mighty waters,
> Keep my eyes on things above,
> Righteousness, divine atonement,
> Peace and everlas . . .

The forward funnel snaps and crashes into the sea; its steel tons hammer out of existence swimmers struggling in the freezing water. Streams of sparks, of smoke and steam, burst from the after funnels. The ship upends to 50—to 60 degrees.

Down in the black abyss of the stokeholds, of the engine rooms, where the dynamos have whirred at long last to a stop, the stokers and the engineers are reeling against the hot metal, the rising water clutching at their knees. The boilers, the engine cylinders, rip from their bed plates; crash through bulkheads; rumble—steel against steel.

The *Titanic* stands on end, poised briefly for the plunge. Slowly she slides to her grave—slowly at first, and then more quickly—quickly—quickly.

2:20 A.M. The greatest ship in the world has sunk. From the calm, dark waters, where the floating lifeboats move, there goes up, in the white wake of her passing, "one long continuous moan." **J**

· · · · · · · · · · · · · [III] · · · · · · · · · · · ·

The boats that the *Titanic* had launched pulled safely away from the slight suction of the sinking ship, pulled away from the screams that came from the lips of the freezing men and women in the water. The boats were poorly manned and badly equipped, and they had been unevenly loaded. Some carried so few seamen that women bent to the oars. Mrs. Astor tugged at an oar handle; the Countess of Rothes took a tiller. Shivering stokers in sweaty, coal-blackened singlets and light trousers steered in some boats; stewards in white coats rowed in others. Ismay was in the last boat that left the ship from the starboard side; with Mr. Carter of Philadelphia and two seamen he tugged at the oars. In one of the lifeboats an Italian with a broken wrist—disguised in a woman's shawl and hat—huddled on the floorboards, ashamed now that fear had left him. In another rode the only baggage saved from the *Titanic*—the carryall of Samuel L. Goldenberg, one of the rescued passengers.

There were only a few boats that were heavily loaded; most of those that were half empty made but perfunctory efforts to pick up the moaning swimmers, their officers and crew fearing they would endanger the living if they pulled back into the midst of the dying. Some boats beat off the freezing victims; fear-crazed men and women struck with oars at the heads of swimmers. One woman drove her fist into the face of a half-dead man as he tried feebly to climb over the gunwale. Two other women helped him in and staunched the flow of blood from the ring cuts on his face.

One of the collapsible boats, which had floated off the top of the officers' quarters when the *Titanic* sank, was an icy haven for thirty or forty men. The boat had capsized as the ship sank; men swam to it, clung to it, climbed upon its slippery bottom, stood knee-deep in water in the freezing air. Chunks of ice swirled about their legs; their soaked clothing clutched their bodies in icy folds. Colonel Archibald Gracie was cast up there, Gracie who had leaped from

---

J **Informational Focus** Primary and Secondary Sources
Which details from this section seem to be based on fact, and which seem to be based on emotion or opinion?

Vocabulary **perfunctory** (puhr FUHNGK tuhr ee) *adj.:* done with little care or thought; indifferent.

the stern as the *Titanic* sank; young Thayer who had seen his father die; Lightoller who had twice been sucked down with the ship and twice blown to the surface by a belch of air; Bride, the second operator, and Phillips, the first. There were many stokers, half naked; it was a shivering company. They stood there in the icy sea, under the far stars, and sang and prayed—the Lord's Prayer. After a while a lifeboat came and picked them off, but Phillips was dead then or died soon afterward in the boat.

Only a few of the boats had lights; only one—No. 2—had a light that was of any use to the *Carpathia*, twisting through the ice field to the rescue. Other ships were "coming hard" too; one, the *Californian*, was still dead to opportunity.

The blue sparks still danced, but not the *Titanic*'s. *La Provence* to *Celtic*: "Nobody has heard the *Titanic* for about two hours." **Ⓚ**

It was 2:40 when the *Carpathia* first sighted the green light from No. 2 boat; it was 4:10 when she picked up the first boat and learned that the *Titanic* had foundered.[18] The last of the moaning cries had just died away then.

Captain Rostron took the survivors aboard, boatload by boatload. He was ready for them, but only a small minority of them required much medical attention. Bride's feet were twisted and frozen; others were suffering from exposure; one died, and seven were dead when taken from the boats, and were buried at sea.

It was then that the fleet of racing ships learned they were too late; the *Parisian* heard

the weak signals of *MPA*, the *Carpathia*, report the death of the *Titanic*. It was then—or soon afterward, when her radio operator put on his earphones—that the *Californian*, the ship that had been within sight as the *Titanic* was sinking, first learned of the disaster.

And it was then, in all its white-green majesty, that the *Titanic*'s survivors saw the iceberg, tinted with the sunrise, floating idly, pack ice jammed about its base, other bergs heaving slowly nearby on the blue breast of the sea.

· · · · · · · · · · · · [**IV**] · · · · · · · · · · · · ·

But it was not until later that the world knew, for wireless then was not what wireless is today, and garbled messages had nourished a hope that all of the *Titanic*'s company were safe. Not until Monday evening, when P.A.S. Franklin, vice president of the International Mercantile Marine Company, received relayed messages in New York that left little hope, did the full extent of the disaster begin to be known. Partial and garbled lists of the survivors; rumors of heroism and cowardice; stories spun out of newspaper imagination, based on a few bare facts and many false reports, misled the world, terrified and frightened it. It was not until Thursday night, when the *Carpathia* steamed into the North River, that the full truth was pieced together.

Flashlights flared on the black river when the *Carpathia* stood up to her dock. Tugs nosed about her, shunted her toward Pier 54. Thirty thousand people jammed the streets; ambulances and stretchers stood on the pier; coroners and physicians waited.

---

18. **foundered** (FOWN duhrd): filled with water, so that it sank; generally, collapsed; failed.

Ⓚ **Informational Focus** Primary and Secondary Sources
The image of the dancing blue spark is used throughout this account of the *Titanic*'s sinking. What do you think it symbolizes?

In midstream the Cunarder dropped over the *Titanic's* lifeboats; then she headed toward the dock. Beneath the customs letters on the pier stood relatives of the 711 survivors, relatives of the missing—hoping against hope. The *Carpathia* cast her lines ashore; stevedores[19] looped them over bollards. The dense throngs stood quiet as the first survivor stepped down the gangway. The woman half staggered—led by customs guards—beneath her letter. A "low wailing" moan came from the crowd; fell, grew in volume, and dropped again.

Thus ended the maiden voyage of the *Titanic.* The lifeboats brought to New York by the *Carpathia,* a few deck chairs and gratings awash in the ice field off the Grand Bank eight hundred miles from shore, were all that was left of the world's greatest ship.

· · · · · · · · · · · · · [V] · · · · · · · · · · · · ·

The aftermath of weeping and regret, of recriminations[20] and investigations, dragged on for weeks. Charges and countercharges were hurled about; the White Star Line was bitterly criticized; Ismay was denounced on the floor

---

19. **stevedores** (STEE vuh dawrz): persons who load and unload ships.

20. **recriminations** (rih krihm uh NAY shuhnz): accusations against an accuser; countercharges.

Analyzing Visuals **Viewing and Interpreting** Does this accompanying image affect the emotional impact of the text? Explain. Illustration of *Titanic* sinking in front of lifeboats.

of the Senate as a coward but was defended by those who had been with him on the sinking *Titanic* and by the Board of Trade investigation in England.

It was not until weeks later, when the hastily convened Senate investigation in the United States and the Board of Trade report in England had been completed, that the whole story was told. The Senate investigating committee, under the chairmanship of Senator Smith, who was attacked in both the American and the British press as a "backwoods politician," brought out numerous pertinent facts, though its proceedings verged at times on the farcical.[21] Senator Smith was ridiculed for his lack of knowledge of the sea when he asked witnesses, "Of what is an iceberg composed?" and "Did any of the passengers take refuge in the watertight compartments?" The senator seemed particularly interested in the marital status of Fleet, the lookout, who was saved. Fleet, puzzled, growled aside, "Wot questions they're arskin' me!"

The report of Lord Mersey, wreck commissioner in the British Board of Trade's investigation, was tersely damning.

The *Titanic* had carried boats enough for 1,178 persons, only one third of her capacity. Her sixteen boats and four collapsibles had saved but 711 persons; 400 people had needlessly lost their lives. The boats had been but partly loaded; officers in charge of launching them had been afraid the falls[22] would break or the boats buckle under their rated loads; boat crews had been slow in reaching their stations; launching arrangements were confused because no boat drill had been held; passengers were loaded into the boats haphazardly because no boat assignments had been made. **L**

But that was not all. Lord Mersey found that sufficient warnings of ice on the steamer track had reached the *Titanic*, that her speed of twenty-two knots was "excessive under the circumstances," that "in view of the high speed at which the vessel was running it is not considered that the lookout was sufficient," and that her master made "a very grievous mistake"—but should not be blamed for negligence. Captain Rostron of the *Carpathia* was highly praised. "He did the very best that could be done." The *Californian* was damned. The testimony of her master, officers, and crew showed that she was not, at the most, more than nineteen miles away from the sinking *Titanic* and probably no more than five to ten miles distant. She had seen the *Titanic*'s lights; she had seen the rockets; she had not received the CQD calls because her radio operator was asleep. She had attempted to get in communication with the ship she had sighted by flashing a light, but vainly.

"The night was clear," reported Lord Mersey, "and the sea was smooth. When she first saw the rockets, the *Californian* could have pushed through the ice to the open water without any serious risk and so have come to the assistance of the *Titanic*. Had she done so she might have saved many if not all of the lives that were lost.

"She made no attempt."

---

21. **farcical** (FAHR suh kuhl): absurd; ridiculous; like a farce (an exaggerated comedy).
22. **falls:** chains used for hoisting.

L **Informational Focus** Primary and Secondary Sources Is the information in this paragraph objective or subjective? Explain.

Read with a Purpose What information about the disaster did you find most surprising or tragic?

Vocabulary **pertinent** (PUR tuh nuhnt) *adj.*: having some association with the subject.

A Fireman's Story

by Harry Senior

I was in my bunk when I felt a bump. One man said, "Hello. She has been struck." I went on deck and saw a great pile of ice on the well deck before the forecastle, but we all thought the ship would last some time, and we went back to our bunks. Then one of the firemen came running down and yelled, "All muster for the lifeboats." I ran on deck, and the captain said, "All firemen keep down on the well deck. If a man comes up, I'll shoot him."

Then I saw the first lifeboat lowered. Thirteen people were on board, eleven men and two women. Three were millionaires, and one was Ismay [J. Bruce Ismay, managing director of the White Star Line; a survivor]. **Ⓐ**

Then I ran up onto the hurricane deck and helped to throw one of the collapsible boats onto the lower deck. I saw an Italian woman holding two babies. I took one of them and made the woman jump overboard with the baby, while I did the same with the other. When I came to the surface, the baby in my arms was dead. I saw the woman strike out in good style, but a boiler burst on the Titanic and started a big wave. When the woman saw that wave, she gave up. Then, as the child was dead, I let it sink too.

I swam around for about half an hour, and was swimming on my back when the Titanic went down. I tried to get aboard a boat, but some chap hit me over the head with an oar. There were too many in her. I got around to the other side and climbed in. **Ⓑ**

J. Bruce Ismay, director of the White Star Line.

Read with a Purpose

As you read, notice the contrast between Senior's matter-of-fact style and the emotional events he reports.

Preparing to Read for this eyewitness account is on page 397.

Build Background

The lifeboats of the "unsinkable" *Titanic* carried fewer than one third of the approximately 2,200 people aboard; 1,517 people died. These two selections are the eyewitness accounts of two survivors.

Read with a Purpose Describe the contrast between what is being reported and the manner in which Senior reports it.

Ⓐ **Informational Focus** Primary Sources What details in this paragraph conflict with Baldwin's report?

Ⓑ **Informational Focus** Primary Sources Note that this writer uses many short sentences in his account. How is this style different from Baldwin's?

Rescuing *Titanic* Survivors.

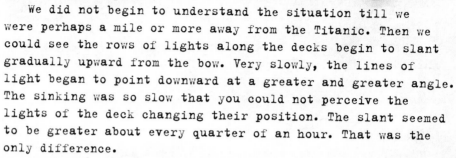

From a Lifeboat

by Mrs. D. H. Bishop

We did not begin to understand the situation till we were perhaps a mile or more away from the Titanic. Then we could see the rows of lights along the decks begin to slant gradually upward from the bow. Very slowly, the lines of light began to point downward at a greater and greater angle. The sinking was so slow that you could not perceive the lights of the deck changing their position. The slant seemed to be greater about every quarter of an hour. That was the only difference.

In a couple of hours, though, she began to go down more rapidly. Then the fearful sight began. The people in the ship were just beginning to realize how great their danger was. When the forward part of the ship dropped suddenly at a faster rate, so that the upward slope became marked, there was a sudden rush of passengers on all the decks toward the stern. It was like a wave. We could see the great black mass of people in the steerage sweeping to the rear part of the boat and breaking through into the upper decks. At the distance of about a mile, we could distinguish everything through the night, which was perfectly clear. We could make out the increasing excitement on board the boat as the people, rushing to and fro, caused the deck lights to disappear and reappear as they passed in front of them.

This panic went on, it seemed, for an hour. Then suddenly the ship seemed to shoot up out of the water and stand there perpendicularly. It seemed to us that it stood upright in the water for four full minutes.

Then it began to slide gently downward. Its speed increased as it went down headfirst, so that the stern shot down with a rush.

The lights continued to burn till it sank. We could see the people packed densely in the stern till it was gone. . . . .

As the ship sank, we could hear the screaming a mile away. Gradually it became fainter and fainter and died away. Some of the lifeboats that had room for more might have gone to their rescue, but it would have meant that those who were in the water would have swarmed aboard and sunk them. **Ⓐ**

Read with a Purpose What overall impression of the disaster does this account convey?

Read with a Purpose
Read this moment-by-moment account of the sinking of the *Titanic* to learn one survivor's impression of the disaster.

Preparing to Read for this eyewitness account is on page 397.

Ruth Becker and her brother Richard survived in separate lifeboats.

Ⓐ **Informational Focus** **Primary and Secondary Sources** Is Bishop's last statement an objective or subjective comment on the event? Explain.

Applying Your Skills

R.10.4 Evaluate and systematically organize important information, and select appropriate sources to support central ideas, concepts and themes. **R.10.3** Determine the accuracy of sources and the credibility of the author by analyzing the sources' validity. *Also covered* **RA.I.10.5; WA.10.4.d**

R.M.S. Titanic / A Fireman's Story / From a Lifeboat

Practicing the Standards

Informational Text and Vocabulary

1. Baldwin includes all the following **sources** *except* —
   A transcripts of radio messages
   B letters
   C dialogue
   D minute-by-minute details

2. All the **sources** agree that —
   A the band continued to play until the ship sank
   B the lifeboats were not all full
   C you could hear screaming from a mile away
   D J. Bruce Ismay survived the disaster

3. Which of the following is a **secondary source**?
   A A speech given by the captain
   B An interview with J. Bruce Ismay
   C A magazine article about the *Titanic*
   D A letter from a survivor

4. Which sentence states an **objective** fact?
   A "The water rises and the band plays ragtime."
   B "The night was too calm, too beautiful, to think of death at sea."
   C "It was like a wave."
   D "The greatest ship in the world has sunk."

5. To *ascertain* the facts, you should —
   A make sure they are correct
   B interpret them differently
   C explain them to someone else
   D replace them with opinions

6. If evidence *corroborated* your recollection, it —
   A supported your recollection
   B refuted your recollection
   C confused your recollection
   D opposed your recollection

7. *Pertinent* information is —
   A true
   B relevant
   C confusing
   D biased

8. If you make a *perfunctory* inspection, you are —
   A careless
   B thorough
   C fast
   D wrong

Writing Focus Constructed Response

As you read, you noted differences among the accounts of the *Titanic*'s sinking. Write a one-page summary of "R.M.S. Titanic," including Baldwin's most significant facts. Then, include details from the other accounts that refute or vary from his conclusions.

What Do You Think Now

Why did some people survive the *Titanic* disaster, whereas others did not? How might more people have been saved?

Symbolism and Irony   **Directions:** Read the following short story. Then, read and respond to the questions that follow.

The Princess and the Tin Box

by **James Thurber**

Once upon a time, in a far country, there lived a King whose daughter was the prettiest princess in the world. Her eyes were like the cornflower, her hair was sweeter than the hyacinth, and her throat made the swan look dusty.

From the time she was a year old, the Princess had been showered with presents. Her nursery looked like Cartier's window. Her toys were all made of gold or platinum or diamonds or emeralds. She was not permitted to have wooden blocks or china dolls or rubber dogs or linen books, because such materials were considered cheap for the daughter of a king.

When she was seven, she was allowed to attend the wedding of her brother and throw real pearls at the bride instead of rice. Only the nightingale, with his lyre of gold, was permitted to sing for the Princess. The common blackbird, with his boxwood flute, was kept out of the palace grounds. She walked in silver-and-samite slippers to a sapphire-and-topaz bathroom and slept in an ivory bed inlaid with rubies.

On the day the Princess was eighteen, the King sent a royal ambassador to the courts of five neighboring kingdoms to announce that he would give his daughter's hand in marriage to the prince who brought her the gift she liked the most.

The first prince to arrive at the palace rode a swift white stallion and laid at the feet of the Princess an enormous apple made of solid gold which he had taken from a dragon who had guarded it for a thousand years. It was placed on a long ebony table set up to hold the gifts of the Princess's suitors. The second prince, who came on a gray charger, brought her a nightingale made of a thousand diamonds, and it was placed beside the golden apple. The third prince, riding on a black horse, carried a great jewel box made of platinum and sapphires, and it was placed next to the diamond nightingale. The fourth prince, astride a fiery yellow horse, gave the Princess a gigantic heart made of rubies and pierced by an emerald arrow. It was placed next to the platinum-and-sapphire jewel box.

Now the fifth prince was the strongest and handsomest of all the five suitors, but he was the son of a poor king whose realm had been overrun by mice and locusts and wizards and mining engineers so that there was nothing much of value left in it. He came plodding up to the palace of the Princess on a plow horse, and he brought her a small tin box filled with mica and feldspar and hornblende which he had picked up on the way.

The other princes roared with disdainful laughter when they saw the tawdry gift the fifth prince had brought to the Princess. But she examined it with great interest and squealed with delight, for all her life she had been glutted with precious stones and priceless metals, but she had never seen tin before or mica or feldspar or hornblende. The tin box was placed next to the ruby heart pierced with an emerald arrow.

"Now," the King said to his daughter, "you must select the gift you like best and marry the prince that brought it."

The Princess smiled and walked up to the table and picked up the present she liked the most. It was the platinum-and-sapphire jewel box, the gift from the third prince.

"The way I figure it," she said, "is this. It is a very large and expensive box, and when we are married, I will meet many admirers who will want to give me precious gems with which to fill it to the top. Therefore, it is the most valuable of all the gifts my suitors have brought me, and I like it the best."

The Princess married the third prince that very day in the midst of great merriment and high revelry. More than a hundred thousand pearls were thrown at her and she loved it.

Moral: All those who thought that the Princess was going to select the tin box filled with worthless stones instead of the other gifts will kindly stay after class and write one hundred times on the blackboard, "I would rather have a hunk of aluminum silicate than a diamond necklace."

PREPARING FOR THE OHIO GRADUATION TEST

Literary Skills Review CONTINUED

OH **RA.L.10.9** Explain how authors use symbols to create broader meanings. **RA.L.10.7** Recognize how irony is used in a literary text.

1. How are the gifts of the first four princes similar?

   A. They are made from precious materials.

   B. They are more valuable than anything the Princess has ever been given before.

   C. They are useful objects.

   D. They please the King more than they please the Princess.

2. What does the fifth prince's horse symbolize?

   A. his enthusiasm

   B. his intelligence

   C. his poverty

   D. his strength

3. The Princess's choice at the end of the story is an example of

   A. verbal irony.

   B. situational irony.

   C. poetic irony.

   D. dramatic irony.

4. What is the most likely reason to expect the Princess to accept the gift of the fifth prince?

   A. The fifth prince is the strongest and most handsome.

   B. Most fairy tales include morals praising the value of originality over monetary value.

   C. Her father liked the fifth prince the best.

   D. She feels sorry for the fifth prince because he is poor.

5. Why is the moral of this story ironic?

   A. The reader expects the author to criticize the fifth prince for giving the Princess a tin box.

   B. The reader expects the author to find fault with the Princess's values.

   C. The reader expects the author to praise the King for thinking of his daughter's happiness.

   D. The reader expects the author to express admiration for the third prince's clever gift.

6. The symbols of the horses and gifts in this parable enhance the story's irony because they

   A. are elements commonly found in fairy tales.

   B. emphasize the contrast between the fifth prince and the others.

   C. make the tin box seem valuable.

   D. show that the princes traveled a long way to see the Princess.

Short Answer

7. Describe the tone of this fable. Cite a detail from the fable to support your description.

Extended Response

8. Think about the outcome of this story. What did you expect the Princess to do? Were you surprised by her actions? Identify two details that led you to expect a different outcome.

Informational Skills Review

Primary and Secondary Sources **Directions:** Read the following magazine article and journal entry about Hurricane Katrina. Then, read and respond to the questions that follow.

Mission Katrina by **Sean Price**

Like many natives of Louisiana, Jessica Guidroz grew up with a ho-hum attitude about hurricanes. The big storms routinely blew in from the Gulf of Mexico, dumped some rain, knocked over some trees, and then moved on. "I've pretty much lived here in the New Orleans area my whole life, and I had never evacuated for a hurricane," she said.

But Guidroz is telling a different story now: On Monday, August 29, 2005, Hurricane Katrina bore down on parts of Louisiana, Mississippi, and Alabama. Guidroz was a 26-year-old petty officer in the U.S. Coast Guard. As part of the Coast Guard's New Orleans search and rescue team, she was ordered northward to Baton Rouge to wait out the violent weather. Returning to New Orleans soon after the storm, her team found that about 80 percent of the city was under water. Training and experience could not fully prepare the officers—or civilians involved—for something on that scale. "None of us had ever seen anything like that," she said.

The Job Ahead

Guidroz became one of some 1,200 Coast Guard personnel who fanned out to help people caught in the rising flood waters. They were part of a much larger army of rescue workers that included thousands of police, firefighters, military personnel, people from private groups like the Red Cross, and workers from dozens of state and federal agencies. The scope of their job was staggering. Katrina cut a swath of destruction roughly equal to the size of Great Britain. The storm and its aftermath directly affected at least 1.5 million people. "You can see images on TV," says Coast Guard Lt. Commander Shannon Gilreath, "but until you flew over and saw the extent of it, it's hard to get your mind around just how large an area we're talking about."

Damage Control

Guidroz said the stench covering New Orleans was overpowering. The storm killed more than 1,800 people and thousands of animals. The water blanketing the city quickly filled up with sewage, gasoline from cars, and garbage.

"Just imagine walking into a room and the smell hits you and makes you instantly nauseous," Guidroz said. "That's the smell you experienced." And yet, after a few hours, people got used to even that odor. "Your adrenaline's going, you've got a job to do, and it's, like, sensory overload," she said. For 19 days, Guidroz's team worked from sunup to sundown, helping survivors escape from New Orleans. At first, she patrolled the city in a small boat, knocking on rooftops to find trapped people. Later she helped ferry more than 2,000 people stranded near the University of New Orleans area to sites where they could be evacuated. That job alone took seven days.

During that time, the evacuees received little food or water. They had almost no way to wash or clean up while waiting in the humid New Orleans heat. Media images of people stranded under similar conditions at the Superdome and New Orleans convention center outraged many Americans. The Federal Emergency Management Agency is charged with spearheading government response to disasters. But the process seemed to move in slow motion in the wake of the storm, and the agency drew heavy criticism.

Guidroz says that her nearly three weeks of rescue work in post-Katrina New Orleans have marked her. She wrestles with memories of people who died, of children living in filth, and of sick people frantic for food or medicine. Yet she is glad that she and her Coast Guard team members were able to help so many people.

"Emotionally, the entire thing was hard," she said. "But stuff like that brings you even closer together."

from Katrina Came Calling
by **Josh Neufeld**

Shortly after Hurricane Katrina struck the Gulf Coast, the cartoonist and author Josh Neufeld signed up with the Red Cross and served for three weeks as a volunteer in Biloxi/Gulfport, Mississippi. This excerpt is from his online journal "Katrina Came Calling."

Gulfport, MS—October 27, 11:34 P.M.
We're part of the five-ERV[1] contingent which serves Long Beach, a working-class community adjacent to Gulfport. It's on the other side of the tracks (literally) from the devastation on the beachfront, but still suffered a lot of destruction. There wasn't much flooding, but many homes are badly damaged, with fallen trees, crushed porches, holes in roofs, etc. Some homes are abandoned, some have been condemned by the authorities, and many people are living in FEMA trailers or tents—often in their own front yards. . . .

I usually serve meals for the lunch run and do the window for dinner (or "supper," as they

---

1. **ERV:** emergency response vehicle.

call it here). I put out a lot of energy when I sit at the window, chatting with folks, asking after older family members, bantering with the kids, and generally being friendly, and I've found that I just can't handle expending that much adrenaline all day. The upside is that I've become a regular on this route, and everybody knows me, even asking about me on my day off, but the downside is that I sometimes feel afraid of letting people down, of not being as emotionally present and friendly as they've become accustomed to. . . .

These neighborhoods have no infrastructure left, few convenience stores, no restaurants. Not to mention that many people are now out of work, or spending all their money trying to rebuild their property, or waiting for their Section 8 homes to be repaired. The last thing many of them have time to do is worry about where their next meal is coming from.

October 31, 6:38 A.M.

As the weeks have gone by since Katrina hit, people (at least in our area of Long Beach) have been starting to get their lives back in order. Electrical, gas, water, and phone lines are being re-established, and folks are getting their appliances working again. As that starts to happen, they need us less and less.

We still serve just as many meals—if not more—but it's turning into convenience feeding rather than the life-or-death kind. Convenience feeding is something the Red Cross is willing to do for awhile, but we don't want folks to get accustomed to it, as they need to regain their autonomy and ability to take care of themselves.

We can tell our route is becoming majority convenience feeding in a number of ways. One is that the kids are starting to demand bags of snacks and skipping the meals. This means their parents are feeding them dinner and the kids are looking to the ERV for free goodies. The other way we can tell is that the last couple of days people have been asking us how much longer we're going to be coming around. They know they're eating on borrowed time.

There are still a number of special cases, like the folks at "tent city," a scrap of lawn in front of a torn-up house with about five tents pitched about. Those folks are in desperate straits, with lots of kids, and many mouths to feed. And there's Alma Felton, the 86-year-old invalid who's all alone at lunchtimes (her daughter gets her meals for her at suppertime); or 85-year-old Mr. Williams; or Mr. & Mrs. Wally, who were promised meals-on-wheels by FEMA but never got any. . . . But other than those individuals, I'd say about 90% of our route is convenience feeding at this point.

Something happened yesterday night that cemented this in my mind. Ann, one of the three "old ladies" at the end of the street, came out with a little gift: a delicious loaf of garlic bread and some homemade gumbo. . . . But

PREPARING FOR THE OHIO GRADUATION TEST

Informational Skills Review

R.10.4 Evaluate and systematically organize important information, and select appropriate sources to support central ideas, concepts and themes. R.10.2 Identify appropriate sources and gather relevant information from multiple sources. *Also covered* RA.I.10.5

CONTINUED

when your clients are giving *you* food instead of taking it from the ERV, that's a sign the neighborhood's coming back.

If that's true, my three weeks in the area have come at a remarkable time. When I got here the neighborhood was wiped out, people were desperate for free home-cooked meals, and as grateful as you could be. Three weeks later, services are being restored, people are moving back into the neighborhood, and they look to us for goodies rather than the necessities. Altogether, it's like a microcosm of the essential services the Red Cross provides, helping a community recover from a disaster, and I've been privileged to be a part of it.

1. Which of the following sentences is the most objective?

   A. "But other than those individuals, I'd say about 90% of our route is convenience feeding at this point."

   B. "As part of the Coast Guard's New Orleans search and rescue team, she was ordered northward to Baton Rouge to wait out the violent weather."

   C. "If that's true, my three weeks in the area have come at a remarkable time."

   D. "'Just imagine walking into a room and the smell hits you and makes you instantly nauseous,' Guidroz said."

2. Which source might Sean Price have used to write "Mission Katrina"?

   A. "Katrina Came Calling"

   B. an encyclopedia article about Katrina

   C. an interview with Jessica Guidroz

   D. a newspaper article about the Red Cross

3. Which of the following sentences expresses an opinion?

   A. "On Monday, August 29, 2005, Hurricane Katrina bore down on parts of Louisiana, Mississippi, and Alabama."

   B. "The last thing many of them have time to do is worry about where their next meal is coming from."

   C. "Some homes are abandoned, some have been condemned by the authorities, and many people are living in FEMA trailers or tents—often in their own front yards."

   D. "The Federal Emergency Management Agency is charged with spearheading government response to disasters."

Short Answer

4. Explain what kind of source the article about Jessica Guidroz is. Cite a detail from the article to support your explanation

Extended Response

5. In your opinion, which article gave you greater insight into the experience of providing assistance in the aftermath of Katrina? Explain, using details from the selections to support your response.

Vocabulary Skills Review

V0.10.2. Analyze the relationships of pairs of words in analogical statements (e.g., synonyms and antonyms, connotation and denotation) and infer word meanings from these relationships. *Also covered* **V0.10.1**

Synonyms

Directions: Choose the best synonym for the underlined word in each sentence.

1. Jerry feels <u>contrition</u> at first when he thinks his mother feels abandoned.

   A. anxiety

   B. anger

   C. regret

   D. sympathy

2. When he asks for swimming goggles, his mother gives him an <u>inquisitive</u> look.

   A. startled

   B. concerned

   C. frightened

   D. curious

3. Miss Strangeworth saw <u>potential</u> evil in most of the town's residents.

   A. harmful

   B. powerful

   C. possible

   D. little

4. She thought the relationship between Linda Stewart and the Harris boy was <u>reprehensible</u>.

   A. sophisticated

   B. unacceptable

   C. innocent

   D. unusual

5. One symptom of the Red Death was <u>profuse</u> bleeding.

   A. painful

   B. abundant

   C. scarce

   D. complete

6. The stranger's appearance at the ball showed a complete lack of <u>propriety</u>.

   A. humor

   B. preparation

   C. honor

   D. decency

7. The masked figure had no <u>tangible</u> form.

   A. touchable

   B. recognizable

   C. colorful

   D. remarkable

8. The townspeople did not show <u>prudence</u> before approaching the strange creature.

   A. affection

   B. respect

   C. stupidity

   D. caution

Academic Vocabulary

Directions: Choose the *best* synonym for the underlined Academic Vocabulary word.

9. Josh Neufeld and the other volunteers were able to <u>derive</u> satisfaction from helping people after Hurricane Katrina.

   A. spread

   B. share

   C. obtain

   D. reject

Read On

NONFICTION

The Perfect Storm

What began as a routine sword-fishing expedition became a nightmare for six young fishermen from Gloucester, Massachusetts. A freakish combination of three weather systems resulted in "the perfect storm"—a monstrous tempest with one-hundred-foot waves that overpowered the *Andrea Gail's* crew on one fateful night in October. This riveting true story by Sebastian Junger boasts many heroes: the fishermen, the search-and-rescue crews, and the courageous families of the men who vanished at sea.

FICTION

The Joy Luck Club

Once a week the members of the Joy Luck Club, four mothers of four daughters, meet to eat, play mah-jongg, and share the joys and struggles of their lives as Chinese Americans. In this moving novel, sixteen interwoven stories show the complexities of parent-child relationships, marriage, careers, and the challenge of balancing loyalties between two cultures. Amy Tan's novel *The Joy Luck Club* portrays the pain and humor that are present in all families struggling to find joy in their lives.

FICTION

Jesse

In his first young-adult novel, Gary Soto paints a moving portrait of seventeen-year-old Jesse, who has left his parents' home to live with his older brother. These Mexican American brothers hope junior college will help them escape the tedium of physical labor. Their struggles are both humorous and true to life as the brothers come to terms with what is possible for each of them in an imperfect world.

NONFICTION

Babylon's Ark

In this wrenching and inspirational account, the South African conservationist Lawrence Anthony describes his struggle to save the animals in the Baghdad Zoo after the U.S.-led invasion of Iraq in 2003. Many of the animals had been killed during the invasion, and the remainder were starving and in filthy cages. Anthony spearheaded efforts to feed these abandoned animals, with the help of keepers from the Kuwait Zoo as well as American soldiers. *Babylon's Ark* is the story of one man's amazing quest.

DRAMA

Twelve Angry Men

This Reginald Rose play takes place in a jury room, where twelve men try to decide if an accused teenager is guilty of murdering his father. As the play opens and the jurors talk among themselves, it seems that all the evidence is stacked against the teen. There are eyewitnesses, a unique murder weapon, and a motive. But one juror is unsure and votes "not guilty." As the jurors argue, review the evidence, and try to keep their emotions from interfering with reason, the suspense over the final verdict becomes almost unbearable.

FICTION

The Third Man

Rollo Martins comes to war-torn Vienna at the request of his friend Harry Lime, only to discover that Lime has been run over by a car and is being buried in the local cemetery. At the cemetery, Martins meets a Scotland Yard agent, who tells him that Lime was a criminal. Martins refuses to believe this and begins investigating Lime's death. Before long, it is clear that the facts don't add up and that nothing is the way it seems to be. Graham Greene's short novel is the source for the famous movie *The Third Man,* starring Orson Welles.

FICTION

Interpreter of Maladies

Jhumpa Lahiri won the 2000 Pulitzer Prize for fiction for *Intepreter of Maladies,* her first collection of short stories. Her characters are often Indian Americans or Indian immigrants dealing with the contrasts between American and Indian culture. Lahiri also explores the difficulties that married couples can have communicating, asserting independence, and gaining mutual respect, especially when their marriages have been arranged and they barely know each other.

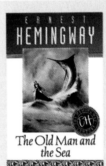

FICTION

The Old Man and the Sea

Ernest Hemingway earned his fame from his spare, powerful writing style and his ability to make words come alive on the page. His novella *The Old Man and the Sea* showcases Hemingway's finest talents. It is the story of Santiago, an aging Cuban fisherman who glimpses an irresistible catch from his boat: a magnificent marlin that bobs to the surface of the Gulf Stream. Amazingly, the great fish takes the hook into its mouth—and then swims for its life. A classic conflict of human versus nature ensues.

Learn It Online

Explore other novels—and find tips for choosing, reading, and studying works—at:

go.hrw.com | L10-423 | Go

Writing Workshop

Autobiographical Narrative

Write with a Purpose

Write an autobiographical narrative about a significant experience. Your **purpose** for writing is to entertain your audience and to explain the significance of the experience. Your **audience** is your classmates and others who can relate to your experience.

A Good Autobiographical Narrative

- conveys a single experience, or related experiences, using the key elements of storytelling: plot, character, and setting
- includes important background information
- uses specific details
- includes dialogue and actions or both to reveal personalities
- conveys the writer's feelings and thoughts
- shows the significance of the experience

See page 432 for complete rubric.

Think as a Reader/Writer
In this unit, you've seen how fiction writers create compelling short stories. Elements of short stories are also present in a strong **autobiographical narrative,** the true story of a personal experience. Before you write your own autobiographical narrative, read this excerpt from Jane Goodall's autobiographical book *In the Shadow of Man:*

Hauling myself up the steep slope of Mlinda Valley I headed for the Peak, not only weary but soaking wet from crawling through dense undergrowth. Suddenly I stopped, for I saw a slight movement in the long grass about sixty yards away. Quickly focusing my binoculars I saw that it was a single chimpanzee, and just then he turned in my direction. I recognized David Graybeard. . . .

On the eighth day of my watch David Graybeard arrived again, together with Goliath, and the pair worked there for two hours. I could see much better: I observed how they scratched open the sealed-over passage entrances with a thumb or forefinger. I watched how they bit ends off their tools when they became bent, or used the other end, or discarded them in favor of new ones. Goliath once moved at least fifteen yards from the heap to select a firm-looking piece of vine, and both males often picked three or four stems while they were collecting tools. . . .

Most exciting of all, on several occasions they picked small leafy twigs and prepared them for use by stripping off the leaves. This was the first recorded example of a wild animal not merely *using* an object as a tool, but actually modifying an object and thus showing the crude beginnings of toolmaking.

← Goodall uses **details** to describe the **setting** and an obstacle, the steep slope she must climb.

← **Details** give readers a vivid picture of the **characters**, the chimpanzees.

← Goodall conveys her feelings and the **significance** of her experience.

Reader/Writer Notebook

Use your **RWN** to complete the activities for this workshop.

Think About the Professional Model

With a partner, discuss the following questions about the model:

1. How does Goodall create a vivid setting?

2. What other elements of short stories are present in Goodall's narrative?

WA.10.1.c Write narratives that: include an organized, well-developed structure. **WP.10.3** Establish and develop a clear thesis statement for informational writing or a clear plan or outline for narrative writing. **WP.10.8** Use paragraph form in writing, including topic sentences that arrange paragraphs in a logical sequence, using effective transitions and closing sentences and maintaining coherence across the whole through the use of parallel structures.

Prewriting

Choose an Experience

Most people have had at least one memorable experience that they want to share with others. Start planning your autobiographical narrative by listing three significant experiences you have had. For each one, write what happened, who participated, and why the event was significant. After completing your list, consider which experience is most important to you and which is the clearest in your memory. Think about which experience you might like to share with others. Then, choose one experience as the topic of your narrative.

Gather Details About Events, Characters, and Setting

Details are essential to your narrative because they make events vivid for readers and bring your experience to life. Rather than telling what happened ("I had a hard, wet journey up the mountain"), use details to show what happened as Goodall does: "Hauling myself up the steep slope of Mlinda Valley I headed for the Peak, not only weary but soaking wet from crawling through dense undergrowth." One way to gather details is to use a word web like the one below by a student writer for each important person, place, event, or other element of your experience.

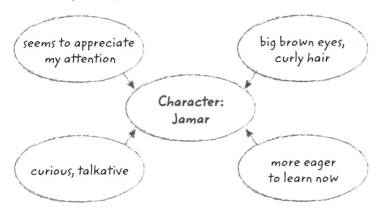

Think About Purpose and Audience

A basic principle of good writing requires you to keep considerations—**purpose** and **audience**—in mind as you write, no matter what you're writing. Your purpose is to describe an experience that had a significant effect on your life. Make sure you provide readers with the background information they will need to understand the significance of your experience fully. You might introduce yourself as you were before the experience in order to provide a hint about the effect the event had on you.

Autobiographical Narrative

Determine Significance

What made your experience **significant** to you? Did it teach you something, change your opinion about a topic, or affect the way you see yourself? Write a sentence that expresses thoughts or ideas you had before the experience. Then, write a sentence that describes how those thoughts or ideas changed after the experience. Keep the sentences in mind as you decide what to include in your narrative and what to leave out.

Before: I wasn't sure about tutoring.　　*After:* I learned so much from Jamar.

Organize Your Ideas

A writer draws readers into a narrative by making the characters and setting come alive. Consider the following suggestions as you plan each part of your essay:

* In the introduction, capture your reader's interest. Introduce your **characters** and the **setting.** Give any background information readers will need to understand your narrative. Finally, hint at the reason your experience is **significant.**

* In the body, tell the story of your experience. Be sure the **order of events** is clear. Include **factual and sensory details.** Include a **conflict,** or some obstacle or problem you faced.

* In the conclusion, discuss the **significance** of your experience. What did it mean to you?

Use a graphic organizer like the one below to plan your autobiographical narrative.

Autobiographical Narrative Action Plan

Characters	Me, Jamar
Setting	Taylor Elementary library
Conflict or Obstacles	Jamar not showing up, me not wanting to go
Introduction	Describe Jamar, and tell where I meet him. Give background information about how I help him.
Body	Give details about the experience. Tell about a specific experience with Jamar and how I relate to him. Tell about the difficulties of tutoring him.
Conclusion	Tell about what helping him meant to me and what I learned from tutoring him.

Your Turn

Organize Your Ideas After you determine the significance of the experience, organize your ideas by making an **autobiographical narrative action plan.** Share your plan with a partner, and ask for suggestions about additional details you might add when you start writing.

Drafting

Draft Your Narrative

Use the framework at right and your action plan to guide you as you write a first draft of your autobiographical narrative.

Use First-Person Point of View

Because an autobiography is the author's own story, it is written from the **first-person point of view.** Use the first-person pronouns *I, me,* and *we* in your narrative. Be sure that you tell the story from your perspective—what you saw and felt.

Order the Events

Chronological order, telling events in the order in which they happened, is often easiest for readers to follow. You may also find as you begin writing that a **flashback** would work well. For example, the narrative might start at the end and then "flash back" to the earlier events that led up to that point. Use **transitional words and phrases,** such as *at first, then, next,* or *last week,* to help your readers understand the order of events.

> **Structure of Autobiographical Narrative**
>
> **Introduction**
> - Start with an interesting opener.
> - Provide necessary background information.
> - Hint at the significance of the experience.
>
> **Body**
> - Organize events so that they are easy to follow.
> - Include details about people, places, thoughts, and feelings.
> - Use figurative language and precise action verbs.
>
> **Conclusion**
> - Reflect on what the experience meant to you.
> - End with a direct statement of the significance of the experience.

◉ Writing Tip

When you use your **first-person point of view**, you can't foretell the thoughts and feelings of characters other than yourself, the narrator; you wouldn't know these. Instead, you might tell what others said or how their facial expressions suggested their thoughts or feelings.

Grammar Link Using Transitional Words and Phrases

An autobiographical narrative includes elements of plot, with actions occurring over time and in various places. To help your readers follow the order and progress of events, use transitional phrases to show that time has progressed and that places may have changed. These words and phrases answer the questions *how, when,* and *where.* In the examples below from *In the Shadow of Man,* Jane Goodall uses transitional phrases to assist the reader.

"**Suddenly** I stopped, for I saw a slight movement in the long grass. . . ."

"**On the eighth day of my watch** David Graybeard arrived again. . . ."

"**Most exciting of all,** on several occasions they picked small leafy twigs. . . ."

Your Turn _____

Write Your Draft Following your autobiographical narrative action plan, write a draft of your story. Keep in mind the **first-person point of view** and the **order** in which you will tell specific events from your experience. Use transitional words and phrases to help readers keep track of the order in which the events take place.

Autobiographical Narrative

Peer Review

Trade essays with a classmate. Answer each question in this chart, and make suggestions for improvement. Be sure to write notes for your partner, and refer to them as you discuss your tips for revision.

Evaluating and Revising

Read the questions in the left-hand column of the chart, and then use the tips in the middle column to help you make revisions to your essay. The right-hand column suggests techniques you can use to revise your draft.

Autobiographical Narrative: Guidelines for Content and Organization

Evaluation Questions	Tips	Revision Techniques
1. Does the introduction capture the reader's interest?	**Put a star** next to the sentences in the introduction that get the reader's attention.	**Replace** the opening sentence, or **rearrange** details to engage the reader.
2. Does your narrative include essential background information?	**Put parentheses** around sentences that give background information.	**Add** needed background information. **Delete** unnecessary background details.
3. Is your narrative about a single experience or related experiences?	**Put an X** next to any event not related to this experience.	**Cut** events you have marked with an X.
4. Is the order of events clear?	**Number** the events in your narrative to reflect their actual chronological order.	**Rearrange** events, or **add** transitions to make the sequence of events clear.
5. Does your narrative include factual and sensory details?	**Highlight** factual and sensory details.	**Add** necessary factual and sensory details, or **elaborate** on existing details.
6. Does your conclusion directly state the significance of the experience?	**Double-underline** sentences in the conclusion that state the significance of the experience.	**Add** sentences that tell why the experience was important to you.
7. Is the language clear and vivid?	**Circle** verbs, adjectives, and adverbs. Are there more accurate or lively alternatives?	**Replace** unclear or uninteresting verbs and modifiers with precise, vivid ones.

Student Draft

Lessons from Jamar

by Ivylyn Paul, Quincy Senior High School

His name is Jamar, a skinny ten-year-old kid with big brown eyes, a sweet smile, and wild, curly hair. I walk over to Taylor Elementary to see him every day when I am finished with my classes. We work on fifth grade math for twenty to twenty-five minutes. It's only a few minutes of my day, and then I leave. I am Jamar's tutor, but in a way, he is also my teacher.

At first, Miss Hernandez would call a lot to say Jamar wouldn't be there—he was sick or in trouble and had detention. Jamar was often distracted and grumpy, and we wouldn't get very much accomplished. On days when it rained, while I was walking to his school, I would actually think about not going. But as the year has progressed, my relationship with Jamar has changed. He is often happy to see me; when he's had a good day at school, he wants to tell me about it. Once, when we finished early, he showed me the pet lizards in his classroom and how to feed them. Sometimes he smiles and doesn't want our session to end.

> ← Ivylyn begins by introducing the **major character, background information** about the **experience,** and the **setting.**
>
> ← Ivylyn tells about the experience in **chronological order** and relates some of the **conflicts,** or obstacles she encounters.
>
> ← Notice that this sentence is vague, and does not vividly describe what the sessions are like. Ivylyn can improve her description by adding **details** that help readers understand why Jamar doesn't want the sessions to end.

MINI-LESSON ▶ **How to Add Details to Show, Not Tell**

Replace vague statements with more specific details to help your reader "see" and "feel" the experience. Ivylyn tells her readers that Jamar doesn't want the sessions to end. She made the following revision to help her readers imagine what a session was like:

Ivylyn's Draft of Paragraph 2

> Sometimes he smiles and doesn't want our session to end.

Ivylyn's Revision—Add a Paragraph

> . . . lizards in his classroom and how to feed them. ~~Sometimes he smiles and doesn't want our session to end.~~
>
> *Sometimes he doesn't want our session to end. He looks up at me with that crooked, shy smile as we sit side by side at a small wooden table in the library. He'll pull a math paper from his tattered, old backpack and quietly ask me to do just one more problem. The red marks on the paper and the plea in his eyes say it all. Grabbing my pencil, I start explaining the problem. Jamar scoots his chair closer to mine, his sigh the afternoon's music.*

Your Turn _____

Add Details Read your draft, and then ask yourself the questions below to determine if you need to revise for specificity. Make any necessary changes.

- Does each sentence help my readers imagine my experience?
- Which details would make my narrative more vivid and accessible to my readers?

Student Draft *continues*

Sometimes instead of my asking all the questions, Jamar asks me about my school or something about my life. That's how I knew we were really developing a relationship beyond tutoring. One day, when Jamar was learning about geography in class, he asked me if I had ever been to London. As I told him about seeing the guards at Buckingham Palace, his eyes grew bright with curiosity. I remember being his age, I began to learn that the world is bigger than the classroom, too.

The rewards of tutoring Jamar are not the monetary rewards that the world tells me to achieve. I have learned the value of responsibility. I like feeling that someone depends on me—that I'm responsible for something—and knowing that I will show up every day.

Note how Ivylyn includes a **specific detail,** recounting a day when Jamar asked her a question, as she reflects on the similarities between her childhood and Jamar's.

The **conclusion** of the autobiographical narrative focuses on what the experience of tutoring has meant to Ivylyn. Note that although her ideas are closely related, the logical flow between them could be stronger.

MINI-LESSON ▶ How to Create Coherence

Your writing should be **coherent,** or flow logically from one subject to another. To create coherence, you may need to add transitions to show how your ideas connect to one another. You will want to be sure that the major ideas are linked from beginning to end as you write your conclusion. Think about linking ideas coherently to move smoothly from describing your experience to relating your reflections on your experience.

Ivylyn inserted the following sentences into her conclusion to make the final paragraph stronger and more coherent. She deletes weaker phrasing to make a connection to the first half of the narrative when she remembers that Jamar was often absent. She links the idea of "monetary rewards" with her personal satisfaction and growth in tutoring Jamar. In doing so, she makes the significance of the experience clearer and more connected to the narrative as a whole.

Ivylyn's Revision of Paragraph 5

The rewards of tutoring Jamar are not the monetary rewards that the world tells me to achieve. *I am not paid a penny to come each day, but the experience rewards me in other ways.* I have learned the value of responsibility. I like knowing that someone depends on me—~~that I'm responsible for something—and knowing that I will show up every day~~*that I am responsible for another person. Someone else can depend on me. Of course, we do make progress in Jamar's math work, but just being there is important enough for both of us.*

Your Turn _____

Create Coherence Read your draft, and use the questions below to revise your work if necessary to create a more logical flow:

- Does each sentence flow logically from one idea to another?
- What transitional words, phrases, or sentences could I add to make my ideas flow more logically?

Proofreading and Publishing

Proofreading

Proofread your work by looking for errors in grammar, punctuation, and word usage. Read your essay aloud slowly, and examine each word and punctuation mark carefully.

Then, form groups, and make each group member responsible for finding a specific type of error: grammar, punctuation, or word usage. Pass your narrative around the group until it has been checked for each type of error.

Grammar Link **Avoiding Run-on Sentences and Comma Splices**

Be careful to avoid run-on sentences, two independent clauses punctuated as one sentence, and comma splices, two independent clauses incorrectly separated by a comma. Ivylyn used a comma splice in the following sentence but corrected it by replacing the comma with a period, making two complete sentences. Complete clauses that are related can also be joined by a semicolon or a colon.

I remember being his age. I began to learn that the world is bigger than the classroom, too.

Reference Note   To learn more about run-on sentences, see the Language Handbook.

Publishing

Now it is time to share your experience with others. Here are a few suggestions for presenting your work to others:

- Take turns reading your narratives aloud in a group.
- Turn your narrative into a paper or digital scrapbook. Add special lettering, photographs, drawings, or mementos.
- Submit your essay to an online literary magazine.
- Post your work on your class, school, or personal Web page.

Reflect on the Process

Thinking about how you wrote your autobiographical narrative will help you with other writing you do. In your *Reader/Writer Notebook,* briefly respond to these questions:

1. What techniques helped you choose details that best described your characters and setting?

2. What have you learned from this workshop that might help you with other types of writing?

Proofreading Tip

Using the right verb tense will help your reader understand the sequence of events in your narrative. Ask a partner to help you catch errors in verb tense. Have the partner read the narrative to make sure you consistently use past tense to refer to events in the past and shift to present tense only to describe present circumstances or feelings.

Submission Ideas

- school newspaper
- online literary magazine
- your personal Web page
- class or school Web page
- paper or digital scrapbook
- digital narrative

Your Turn _____

Proofread and Publish   As you proofread, look for independent clauses that are punctuated incorrectly, making run-on sentences or comma splices. When you are satisfied that your work is free from errors, share it with others.

Scoring Rubric

Use one of the following rubrics to evaluate your autobiographical narrative from the Writing Workshop or from the activity on the next page. Your teacher will tell you which rubric to use.

6-Point Scale

Score 6 *Demonstrates advanced success*
- focuses consistently on narrating a single incident
- shows effective narrative sequence throughout, with smooth transitions
- offers a thoughtful, creative approach to the narration
- develops the story thoroughly, using precise and vivid descriptive and narrative details
- exhibits mature control of written language

Score 5 *Demonstrates proficient success*
- focuses on narrating a single incident
- shows effective narrative sequence, with transitions
- offers a thoughtful approach to the narration
- develops the story competently, using descriptive and narrative details
- exhibits sufficient control of written language

Score 4 *Demonstrates competent success*
- focuses on narrating a single incident, with minor distractions
- shows effective narrative sequence, with minor lapses
- offers a mostly thoughtful approach to the narration
- develops the story adequately, with some descriptive and narrative details
- exhibits general control of written language

Score 3 *Demonstrates limited success*
- includes some loosely related material that distracts from the writer's narrative focus
- shows some organization, with noticeable flaws in the narrative flow
- offers a routine, predictable approach to the narration
- develops the story with uneven use of descriptive and narrative detail
- exhibits limited control of written language

Score 2 *Demonstrates basic success*
- includes loosely related material that seriously distracts from the writer's narrative focus
- shows minimal organization, with major gaps in the narrative flow
- offers a narrative that merely skims the surface
- develops the story with inadequate descriptive and narrative detail
- exhibits significant problems with control of written language

Score 1 *Demonstrates emerging effort*
- shows little awareness of the topic and the narrative purpose
- lacks organization
- offers an unclear and confusing narrative
- develops the story with little or no detail
- exhibits major problems with control of written language

4-Point Scale

Score 4 *Demonstrates advanced success*
- focuses consistently on narrating a single incident
- shows effective narrative sequence throughout, with smooth transitions
- offers a thoughtful, creative approach to the narration
- develops the story thoroughly, using precise and vivid descriptive and narrative details
- exhibits mature control of written language

Score 3 *Demonstrates competent success*
- focuses on narrating a single incident, with minor distractions
- shows effective narrative sequence, with minor lapses
- offers a mostly thoughtful approach to the narration
- develops the story adequately, with some descriptive and narrative details
- exhibits general control of written language

Score 2 *Demonstrates limited success*
- includes some loosely related material that distracts from the writer's narrative focus
- shows some organization, with noticeable flaws in the narrative flow
- offers a routine, predictable approach to the narration
- develops the story with uneven use of descriptive and narrative detail
- exhibits limited control of written language

Score 1 *Demonstrates emerging effort*
- shows little awareness of the topic and the narrative purpose
- lacks organization
- offers an unclear and confusing narrative
- develops the story with little or no detail
- exhibits major problems with control of written language

Autobiographical Narrative

When responding to a prompt about a personal experience, use what you have learned from your reading, from writing your own autobiographical narrative, and from studying the rubric on page 432. Use the steps below to develop a response to the following prompt:

Writing Prompt

How would you define *friendship*? Write an autobiographical narrative about an experience that you believe demonstrates what it means to be a good friend.

Study the Prompt

Begin by reading the prompt carefully. Circle or underline key words: *friendship, demonstrates, good friend.* Re-read the prompt to see if there is additional information that can help you.

The prompt asks you to tell a story from your life that demonstrates good friendship. Organize your response around a **specific experience,** and provide sufficient **background information** to give your reader context. Be sure also to relate your thoughts and feelings about the experience.

Your response should be based on your own experience. Do not write a story you have simply read or heard about. Unless you were personally involved, the story you tell will not be autobiographical. **Tip:** Spend about five minutes studying the prompt.

Plan Your Response

Make a list of positive experiences you have had with friends. Then, using a chart like the one below, record *how* the action demonstrated good friendship and *why* it was **significant** to you.

Experience	How It Demonstrated Good Friendship	Why It Is Significant

Choose an experience from your list that clearly demonstrates good friendship. Then, answer these questions about your chosen experience:

- What background information do my readers need to understand the experience?
- How can I *show* readers, rather than *tell* them, about my experience?
- How will I reveal my thoughts and feelings?
- How will I show a clear connection between the experience and what it means to be a friend?

Tip: Spend about ten minutes planning your response.

Respond to the Prompt

Use your thoughts and notes to begin writing. Remember to include **specific details** so your readers can "see" your experience. Include enough **background information** to give your readers the context they need. **Tip:** Spend about twenty minutes writing your autobiographical narrative.

Improve Your Response

Revising Go back to the key aspects of the prompt. Is your response about your own experience? Have you explained what friendship means to you? Do **sensory details** and **narrative actions** help convey the story? If not, add these elements.

Proofreading Edit your response to correct errors in grammar, spelling, punctuation, and capitalization. Make sure that your edits are neat and legible.

Checking Your Final Copy Before you turn in your response, read it once more to catch errors you may have missed. **Tip:** Save ten minutes to improve your response.

Presenting an Oral Narrative

Speak with a Purpose

Adapt your written narrative into an oral narrative. Practice delivering it to a friend. Then, present your story to the class.

Think as a Reader/Writer

Would you rather read a story or listen to a story? Chances are, even if you love to read, you enjoy hearing a well-told tale. An interesting oral story has many of the same elements of a well-written story: an entertaining and clear story line; appealing, realistic characters; and vivid words and images. However, there are differences between writing a narrative and telling one.

Writing a Story	Telling a Story Aloud
Writers might include long, complex paragraphs because readers can take their time with a story. Readers can re-read parts and stop frequently to ask questions.	Oral storytellers' tales must be well-paced with clear plots and details because listeners have only one chance to hear the details.
Writers can use elegant words and long, complex sentences.	Oral storytellers need to use conversational language and relatively simple sentences.
Writers must rely on word choice and sentence structure to convey emotion.	Oral storytellers can use their voices, faces, and body language to engage the audience.

Adapt Your Narrative

Make It Lively

How can you turn your written autobiographical narrative into an oral narrative? Start by making sure that your story is easy to follow. Include all the important details, but keep to the point. Most importantly, make your presentation lively and entertaining. Here are some steps to help you adapt your narrative for an oral presentation:

1. Read through your story to remind yourself of your central idea—the dominant impression or the significance of your experience.

2. Cross out events or points that are not essential to your central idea. Highlight the essential ideas or events.

3. To organize your ideas, make a chart showing the sequence of events. (See the one at left for Julia Alvarez's "My First Free Summer.")

4. Look over your written story for sensory details. In "My First Free Summer," when Julia Alvarez says, "I kicked a deflated beach ball around the empty yard," we can feel the deflated ball and see the yard. Keep descriptive details such as these in your oral presentation.

Reader/Writer Notebook

Use your **RWN** to complete the activities in this workshop.

C.10.9 Deliver formal and informal descriptive presentations that convey relevant information and descriptive details. **C.10.8.c** Deliver informational presentations that: include an effective introduction and conclusion and use a consistent organizational structure; **C.10.6** Adjust volume, phrasing, enunciation, voice modulation and inflection to stress important ideas and impact audience response.

5. Find places where you have described the actions, gestures, and feelings of your characters. For example, we know what kind of person Alvarez is when she tells us that in class she waved her hand "in sword-wielding swoops." We feel her fear when she tells us, "'Shut up!' my sister hissed. 'Do you want to get us all killed?'" Keep as many of these details as you can in your oral presentation.

6. On a card, write the opening sentence to your story. You might be able to use the first sentence from your written story—or you might find you need to spice up your opening to get your listeners' attention.

7. Transfer each major point to a card, including important or intriguing details. Keep these notes short and precise: In summer I played with a "deflated beach ball"; during class I waved my hand with "sword-wielding swoops."

8. On the last card, write a strong concluding statement—one that summarizes the dominant impression or relays the story's significance. You may want to memorize this statement so that you can deliver it with confidence.

Deliver Your Narrative

Emphasize the Details

The sensory details of your writing bring it to life for your readers. When giving a presentation, you can use your voice, facial expressions, and gestures to convey the details, especially those about character, feeling, and action.

- Practice your speech so that you only glance at your note cards to remind you of the sequence and important points.
- Using your cards, tell your story to an imaginary audience or a partner. Memorize portions of your story so you can make eye contact with the audience as much as possible.
- Memorize your opening and closing sentences.
- Practice varying the tone, pitch, and pace of your voice to show emotion.
- Present your oral narrative to the class. Be confident, make eye contact, and invite your classmates into the world of your story.

A Good Oral Presentation

- has an engaging introduction
- invites the audience's sympathy
- surprises the audience
- makes the audience curious
- organizes ideas clearly so listeners can easily follow along
- includes elements of good storytelling, such as plot, character, and setting
- engages the audience with a dynamic and expressive performance

○ Speaking Tip

The tone and pitch of your voice as well as your speaking pace can enhance your story. A slow, quiet voice builds suspense. A stage whisper draws the audience in. A quickened pace signals rising action or the climax of your story.

Learn It Online
For ideas, see the *Digital Storytelling* site at:

go.hrw.com   L10-435   **Go**

Writing Skills Review

Autobiographical Narrative   **Directions:** Read the following paragraph from a student's autobiographical narrative. Then, answer the questions below it.

(1) I remember the day we moved into our first house. (2) It was at least 100 degrees out. (3) We must have looked at a thousand houses before deciding. (4) Dad and some of his friends were carrying boxes from the moving truck into the house. (5) My sister Brooke and I wanted to help, but Mom kept yelling at us to stay out of the way. (6) She didn't seem to understand that those boxes held our whole lives up until that point. (7) Seashell collections, art projects we made in kindergarten, photos of our cat Mandy who died a year ago. (8) We finally gave up, though, and went upstairs to our new bedrooms in the big house (at least it seemed big to us, moving from a one-bedroom apartment). (9) We had picked out our rooms—our own rooms—the day before. (10) My room was small and had flowered wallpaper and cream-colored carpet. (11) Brooke had the big room next to mine. (12) That first day, waiting for our boxes, we discovered that, even though we had separate rooms, we could talk to each other through the heating vents. (13) We never told Mom and Dad, but we whispered to each other through the vents every night for months.

1. Which sentence could be added at the end to explain the significance of the heating vents to the girls?

   A. Moving into a new house is always very exciting.

   B. It helped us feel less lonely in our new, strange rooms.

   C. It took us three weeks to unpack all of our boxes.

   D. Mom and Dad would get mad if we stayed up after "lights out."

2. Which sentence could be deleted to make the narrative more focused?

   A. sentence 3

   B. sentence 4

   C. sentence 8

   D. sentence 12

3. To add sensory details to the narrative, which revision of sentence 4 would be the best choice?

   A. Dad and three or four of his best friends were carrying boxes from the moving truck into the house.

   B. Dad and his friends Blake, Jeff, and Dave were carrying boxes from the moving truck into the house.

   C. Dad and some of his friends were carrying boxes from the moving truck into the house, and I wished I was big enough to help them.

   D. Dad and some of his friends were carrying boxes from the moving truck into the house, with sweat dripping off their foreheads into their eyes.

WP.10.12 Add and delete information and details to better elaborate on stated central idea and more effectively accomplish purpose. *Also covered:* **WP.10.9; WP.10.13**

4. What factual information would help you better understand the narrative?

    A. the age of the narrator

    B. the price of the house

    C. the location of the house

    D. the clothing each character is wearing

5. Which revision of sentence 7 is correct?

    A. Seashell collections; art projects we made in kindergarten; photos of our cat Mandy who died a year ago.

    B. Seashell collections, and art projects we made in kindergarten, and photos of our cat Mandy, who died a year ago.

    C. It was seashell collections, art projects, and photos of our cat Mandy.

    D. They held seashell collections, art projects we made in kindergarten, and photos of our cat Mandy, who died a year ago.

6. Which sentence reveals important background information?

    A. sentence 1

    B. sentence 5

    C. sentence 8

    D. sentence 12

7. Which precise, vivid verb could replace the verb went in sentence 8?

    A. progressed

    B. trudged

    C. ran

    D. receded

8. Where in the narrative could the writer add dialogue that would reveal the children's personalities?

    A. after sentence 1

    B. after sentence 2

    C. after sentence 10

    D. after sentence 12

9. Which sentence reveals the narrator's inner thoughts and feelings?

    A. sentence 2

    B. sentence 4

    C. sentence 6

    D. sentence 10

10. Which sentence summarizes the narrator's feelings about moving to a larger home?

    A. You never really get used to living in a larger home.

    B. Moving to a larger home is scary and exciting at the same time.

    C. I wish we had stayed in our apartment.

    D. I was glad to get my own room, because my sister and I never really got along.

UNIT 2

Nonfiction
Writers on Writing

Azadeh Moaveni on Nonfiction Azadeh Moaveni is an Iranian American journalist and writer whose work explores the complex lives of people in Iran and the Middle East. Her memoir *Lipstick Jihad* is the story of her life growing up "Iranian in America and American in Iran."

"The term *nonfiction* sounds as dry as toast and until I was twenty, I refused to read the genre altogether. Nonfiction carried the whiff of the classroom, and in the library of my imagination, it was non-entertaining. That attitude stuck until the day I read *Shah of Shahs* by Ryszard Kapuscinski—an account of the 1979 Iranian Revolution, an upheaval that transported most of my Iranian family to the United States. The book conveyed historical information, but it kept me up all night, my skin tingling with excitement, for it was as spellbinding as any novel. Told in fragments, each one as luminous and atmospheric as a photograph, the book chronicles the revolution as a series of moments. We do not learn that it began on a particular day of a particular year, but at precisely the moment when a policeman threatens a man in a crowd, who for the first time in his life doesn't budge.

The best works of nonfiction entertain in order to instruct. But compared to novels or poetry, nonfiction is tricky to define. Most dictionaries describe it as prose that deals with 'facts and reality.' This slim label must somehow fit everything that we consider nonfiction today: literary journalism, biography, memoir, criticism, commentary, history, travel writing, political treatise, meditation, personal essay. Because it is meant to be sculpted out of reality rather than a writer's imagination, we expect nonfiction to contain Truth. In practice, though, the borders are more blurry.

I understood the shared ground between nonfiction and novels best when I began writing a memoir. In trying to flesh out my characters, build dramatic suspense, compose my narrative with elegance, I saw that my storytelling required as much imagination as it did recollection. I was writing about people, and while I could record their words and behavior, I could only construe their thoughts. The purpose of books based on 'facts and reality' is the same as literature—to help us make sense of the world, to pull it close to examine its flaws, then hold it away to better marvel at its beauty.

Nonfiction also gives us the raw material for a shared conversation. I traveled to Iraq as a journalist shortly after the fall of Saddam Hussein, and wrote a long article about how the growing violence in Baghdad was causing families to keep their young girls out of school. My story made its way around the world, and contributed to the debate about the Iraq war. This, perhaps, is the unique, crucial function of nonfiction. It helps us make sense of the larger than life events that define our age, to get behind the headlines and recognize the humanity we share with people in distant lands. I still keep a dog-eared copy of *Shah of Shahs* by my bedside, for it inspired me to become a journalist and a writer, to spin lyrical tales out of reality and make the world a more fathomable place. "

Think as a Writer

Azadeh Moaveni says one purpose of nonfiction is to "make sense of the larger than life events that define our age." Has any piece of nonfiction had this impact on you? Explain.

Form and Style

INFORMATIONAL TEXT FOCUS
Generating Research Questions

"Life is either a daring adventure
or nothing. To keep our faces
toward change and behave like
free spirits in the presence of
fate is strength undefeatable."

—**Helen Keller**

What Do
You
Think
What gives an event meaning in
our lives?

Learn It Online
Check out *WordSharp* at:

go.hrw.com | L10-441 | **Go**

Literary Focus

by **Carol Jago**

How Do You Recognize Form and Style?

When you describe friends as stylish, you probably mean they have a distinctive way of dressing or wearing their hair, or they have a certain swagger to their walk. We admire style even when we hesitate to imitate it ourselves. Good writers develop a style all their own. You can sometimes recognize their work even without their signature.

Forms of Nonfiction

Nonfiction comes in many **forms**—biographies, autobiographies, memoirs, essays, and news articles, to name just a few. What unites these forms is that they all involve real, rather than imaginary, subjects.

Biography When you read Doris Kearns Goodwin's *Team of Rivals*, you're reading a **biography**—an account of a person's life written by someone else. Like most biographers, Goodwin relies on primary and secondary sources to write about her subject's life.

Autobiography An **autobiography** is a writer's account of his or her own life. This work usually describes a writer's life chronologically, from childhood to adulthood.

Memoir A **memoir** is a type of autobiography that usually focuses on a significant event or period in a writer's life.

Personal Essay Another, shorter type of autobiographical writing is the **personal essay,** which focuses on a subject of particular interest to the writer. The following excerpt describes the author's difficulty with her multicultural identity.

> When I was growing up in Rhode Island in the 1970s I felt neither Indian nor American. Like many immigrant offspring I felt intense pressure to be two things, loyal to the old world and fluent in the new, approved of on either side of the hyphen.
>
> from "My Two Lives"
> by Jhumpa Lahiri

Journalism In a newspaper or magazine article, the writer, or **journalist,** presents facts, statistics, and statements by other people in a straightforward manner. In some works, such as the magazine article "Into Thin Air," the journalist is a participant in the events. This chart will help you classify nonfiction:

Biography	Autobiography, Memoir	Journalism
the story of someone else's life	the story of the writer's life	an informative report, sometimes involving the writer
uses third-person point of view (he, she, they)	uses first-person point of view (I, we)	uses first-person or third-person point of view
based on facts	based on experience	based on both facts and experience

RA.I.10.1 Identify and understand organizational patterns and techniques, including repetition of ideas, syntax and word choice, that authors use to accomplish their purpose and reach their intended audience. **RA.L.10.11** Explain ways in which an author develops a point of view and style, and cite specific examples from the text.

Style

If you read two biographies of Abraham Lincoln and find one boring and the other compelling, how do you explain your reaction? You could be responding to the authors' different styles. An author's **style** is the way he or she uses language.

Diction A major component of style is **diction**—the way a writer uses words. If you write a scientific paper, will you discuss a *busted leg* or a *fractured femur*? If you write a story for young children, will you call the hero *pertinacious* or simply *stubborn*? In general, long words with Latin roots (like *pertinacious*) tend to sound formal and intellectual. Contractions (like *I've* and *didn't*) and slang are conversational and less formal.

Doris Kearns Goodwin's biography of Lincoln uses both formal and informal vocabulary, active verbs, and quotations from primary sources.

> When Stanton and Welles arrived at the crammed room in the Petersen boardinghouse, they found that Lincoln had been placed diagonally across a bed to accommodate his long frame. Stripped of his shirt, "his large arms," Welles noted, "were of a size which one would scarce have expected from his spare appearance."
>
> from *Team of Rivals*
> by Doris Kearns Goodwin

Figurative Language Style also involves the use of **figurative language**—imaginative comparisons between seemingly unlike things. Some common figures of speech are **metaphor** (Gordon Parks calling his camera a weapon) and **personification** (Barbara Kingsolver referring to water lilies as "praying hands"). Such comparisons reveal the author's way of seeing the world.

Sentence Structure Sentence patterns create rhythm and pace. Short, simple sentences can create suspense or excitement. Long, complex sentences might slow your reading. In this excerpt, the long sentence mirrors the characters' slow progress up the mountain.

> Plainly exhausted, Doug mumbled something from behind his oxygen mask that I didn't catch, shook my hand weakly, and continued plodding upward.
>
> from "Into Thin Air"
> by Jon Krakauer

Tone An author's attitude toward a subject or character is **tone.** In Frank McCourt's "Typhoid Fever," we can hear the narrator's ten-year-old voice vividly because the author's diction and sentence structure mimic a child's voice. The tone is tender—one of an adult poking gentle fun at the boy he once was.

Mood The overall feeling or atmosphere an author creates is called **mood.** Mood is often created by the story's setting. In "Typhoid Fever," the hospital setting creates a gloomy mood.

Your Turn Analyze Style

Describe the style of this brief passage from "High Tide in Tucson" by Barbara Kingsolver.

"That is how I became goddess of a small universe of my own creation—more or less by accident. My subjects owe me their very lives. Blithely they ignore me."

Learn It Online
Try the *PowerNotes* version of this lesson on:
go.hrw.com L10-443 **Go**

Analyzing Visuals

How Do Artists Convey Style?

Just as some writers write in different genres, artists create paintings in different forms (for example, landscape, still life, and portrait). However, within a particular form, artists make individual choices about color, shapes, brush strokes, and the use of light and shadow. These choices help to infuse the work of art with an artist's particular style.

Analyzing the Style of a Painting

Use these guidelines to help you analyze works of art.

1. What is the painting about? Is there action, or is it a still scene?
2. Consider the manner in which the painting's subject is presented. Is the subject depicted in a realistic or nonrealistic way?
3. Identify the artist's technique. How does the artist use color, texture, and shapes to show the subject matter?
4. What mood is created by the artist's use of light and shadow?
5. How is the painting different from other paintings of similar subjects?

Look at the details below to help you answer the questions on page 445.

Details of *American Interior.*

1. What is the subject of this painting? Is the subject depicted realistically or imaginatively? Explain.

2. What are the predominant—most extensive or prevailing—colors in the artwork? What effect do the color choices create?

3. What **mood** has the artist created through the use of light and shadow?

4. What adjectives would you choose to describe the **style** of this still-life painting?

American Interior (1934) by Charles Sheeler.   Yale University Art Gallery.

Your Turn   Write About an Artist's Style

Flip through this book, and find a painting or photo that appeals to you. Study the work, and write a brief description of the style, explaining how the artist uses colors, shapes, texture, lines, and light to convey the artwork's style.

Reading Focus

by **Kylene Beers**

What Skills Help You Understand Form and Style?

Why does one person want to read an adventure novel and another want to read a true account of an adventure? Just as we have different purposes for reading fiction and nonfiction, authors have different purposes for what they write. They choose particular forms and use a particular style to communicate their ideas. You will see how identifying an author's purpose and perspective, evaluating word choice, and identifying cause and effect can help you understand nonfiction.

Identifying an Author's Purpose

Three common **purposes** for writing are to inform, to persuade, and to entertain. Writers may write with more than one purpose. In his memoir, Gordon Parks describes his personal awakening as a photographer in the context of a much larger social awakening. Parks's purpose is to inform his readers by showing how he learned a tough lesson.

> Using my camera effectively against intolerance was not so easy as I had assumed it would be. One evening, when Stryker and I were in the office alone, I confessed this to him. "Then at least you have learned the most important lesson," he said.
>
> from "A Choice of Weapons"
> by Gordon Parks

To help you determine an author's purpose, ask yourself the following questions:

- What is the author trying to say?
- Am I being introduced to a new concept or point of view?
- What effect does reading this have on me?

Evaluating Word Choice

Skillful writers choose words that evoke emotions or lead us to certain conclusions. Evaluating **word choice** means judging how and why a writer's words relate to his or her **purpose,** or reason for writing.

In her essay "High Tide in Tucson," Barbara Kingsolver speaks directly to the reader with the pronoun *you*. This word helps her create an intimate tone, appropriate to her message of hope.

> Everywhere you look, joyful noise is clanging to drown out quiet desperation. The choice is draw the blinds and shut it all out, or believe.
>
> from "High Tide in Tucson"
> by Barbara Kingsolver

The words and phrases an author uses are part of his or her style. As you read, ask yourself these questions to help you evaluate an author's word choice:

- What words or phrases catch your attention?
- Does the author present a familiar message in a new or different way?
- How does the author's tone affect his or her purpose for writing?

OH **RA.I.10.1** Identify and understand organizational patterns and techniques, including repetition of ideas, syntax and word choice, that authors use to accomplish their purpose and reach their intended audience. **RA.I.10.5** Analyze an author's implicit and explicit argument, perspective or viewpoint in text.

Identifying Cause and Effect

Everything happens for a reason—a **cause.** Identifying causes and **effects,** or results, can be of particular use when reading true accounts of an event. In order to help readers recognize causes and their effects, writers use words and phrases like *because, since, then, so,* and *as a result.*

In his article about climbing Mount Everest, Jon Krakauer describes part of his harrowing descent from the mountain.

> As I began my descent, I was indeed anxious, but my concern had little to do with the weather. A check of the gauge on my oxygen tank had revealed that it was almost empty. I needed to get down, fast.
>
> from "Into Thin Air" by Jon Krakauer

In this passage, Krakauer explains why he is in serious danger (the cause) and how he has to take an even more dangerous action in order to survive (the effect).

Identifying a Writer's Perspective

A writer's **perspective** is his or her stance or viewpoint about a situation. As you read, think about who the writer is and what kind of position he or she takes toward his or her subject. Is the writer critical or opinionated, curious or passionate, objective or indifferent? Knowing a writer's perspective can help you understand and evaluate a text.

Your Turn Apply Reading Skills

Read the following passage from Azadeh Moaveni's memoir, *Lipstick Jihad,* about her first trip to Iran as a child. In your *Reader/Writer Notebook,* jot down words that help you determine her purpose. Then, write a few sentences identifying her purpose and evaluating how her word choice helped you determine that.

> It was so cool and quiet up in the *toot* (mulberry) tree that I never wanted to come down. I didn't have to; the orchard was so dense that I could scramble from the limb of one tree to another, plucking the plump, red berries as I went along. The sweet juice made my fingers stick together, but I couldn't stop climbing. The trees stretched out as far as I could see, a glorious forest of mulberries, ripe for my picking. I loved mulberries, but until that summer in Tehran, I had only tasted them dried, from little plastic packets sold in the Iranian grocery store in San Jose. Riveted by the abundance, and the squishy texture of the berry in its fresh form—a whole new delight—I had spent the better part of the afternoon perched in the shady canopy of the orchard. "Azadeh jan, I am going to count to *three,* and you had better come down," came Maman's glaring voice from somewhere far below. I gave in, but only because of the preliminary pangs of the hideous stomachache to come.

Now go to the Skills in Action: Reading Model

Learn It Online
Try the *PowerNotes* version of this lesson on:
go.hrw.com | L10-447 | **Go**

Build Background

The author's parents are from Calcutta, India, the capital of the Indian state of West Bengal. At home, the author and her parents follow Bengali traditions.

Read with a Purpose Read this personal essay to discover how the author copes with two conflicting aspects of her identity.

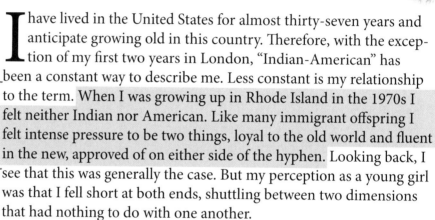

My Two Lives

by **Jhumpa Lahiri**

I have lived in the United States for almost thirty-seven years and anticipate growing old in this country. Therefore, with the exception of my first two years in London, "Indian-American" has been a constant way to describe me. Less constant is my relationship to the term. When I was growing up in Rhode Island in the 1970s I felt neither Indian nor American. Like many immigrant offspring I felt intense pressure to be two things, loyal to the old world and fluent in the new, approved of on either side of the hyphen. Looking back, I see that this was generally the case. But my perception as a young girl was that I fell short at both ends, shuttling between two dimensions that had nothing to do with one another.

At home I followed the customs of my parents, speaking Bengali and eating rice and dal[1] with my fingers. These ordinary facts seemed part of a secret, utterly alien way of life, and I took pains to hide them from my American friends. For my parents, home was not our house in Rhode Island but Calcutta, where they were raised. I was aware that the things they lived for—the Nazrul[2] songs they listened to on the reel-to-reel,[3] the family they missed, the clothes my mother wore that were not available in any store in any mall—were at once as precious and as worthless as an outmoded currency.

I also entered a world my parents had little knowledge or control of: school, books, music, television, things that seeped in and became a fundamental aspect of who I am. I spoke English without an accent, comprehending the language in a way my parents still do not. And yet there was evidence that I was not entirely American. In addition to my distinguishing name and looks, I did not attend Sunday school, did not know how to ice-skate, and disappeared to India for months

---

1. **dal:** an Indian dish made of lentils or peas and spices.
2. **Nazrul:** Kazi Nazrul Islam (1898–1976), Bengali musician and poet who combined northern Indian classical music with Bengali folk tunes.
3. **reel-to-reel:** a type of audiotape player, which preceded cassette tape players.

Reading Focus

Identifying Author's Purpose This passage and the title of the essay establish Lahiri's purpose, which is to inform readers about her struggle to find an identity in the United States without losing touch with her Bengali heritage.

Literary Focus

Style Notice the words Lahiri chooses to describe her Bengali lifestyle at home. Words and phrases like *secret*, *utterly alien*, and *took pains* convey the sense of isolation Lahiri felt as a child.

Literary Focus

Form The focus on Lahiri's own experiences and the pronouns *I* and *my* tell you that this is a personal essay.

at a time. Many of these friends proudly called themselves Irish-American or Italian-American. But they were several generations removed from the frequently humiliating process of immigration, so that the ethnic roots they claimed had descended underground whereas mine were still tangled and green. According to my parents I was not American, nor would I ever be no matter how hard I tried. I felt doomed by their pronouncement, misunderstood and gradually defiant. In spite of the first lessons of arithmetic, one plus one did not equal two but zero, my conflicting selves always canceling each other out.

When I first started writing I was not conscious that my subject was the Indian-American experience. What drew me to my craft was the desire to force the two worlds I occupied to mingle on the page as I was not brave enough, or mature enough, to allow in life. My first book was published in 1999, and around then, on the cusp of a new century, the term "Indian-American" has become part of this country's vocabulary. I've heard it so often that these days, if asked about my background, I use the term myself, pleasantly surprised that I do not have to explain further. What a difference from my early life, when there was no such way to describe me, when the most I could do was to clumsily and ineffectually explain.

As I approach middle age, one plus one equals two, both in my work and in my daily existence. The traditions on either side of the hyphen dwell in me like siblings, still occasionally sparring, one outshining the other depending on the day. But like siblings they are intimately familiar with one another, forgiving and intertwined. When my husband and I were married five years ago in Calcutta we invited friends who had never been to India, and they came full of enthusiasm for a place I avoided talking about in my childhood, fearful of what people might say. Around non-Indian friends, I no longer feel compelled to hide the fact that I speak another language. I speak Bengali to my children, even though I lack the proficiency to teach them to read or write the language. As a child I sought perfection and so denied myself the claim to any identity. As an adult I accept that a bicultural upbringing is a rich but imperfect thing.

While I am American by virtue of the fact that I was raised in this country, I am Indian thanks to the efforts of two individuals. I feel Indian not because of the time I've spent in India or because of my genetic composition but rather because of my parents' steadfast presence in my life. They live three hours from my home; I speak to them daily and see them about once a month. Everything will change once they die. They will take certain things with them—conversations in another tongue, and perceptions about the difficulties of being

Literary Focus

Style The author uses formal diction and sentence structure. These stylistic choices create a tone of distance and isolation that reflects the author's sense of detachment from both her American and her Indian identities.

Reading Focus

Evaluating Word Choice
Lahiri's use of the word *siblings* reinforces a new sense of harmony between the two parts of her identity. This shift signals a turning point in the essay, as does the use of earlier phrases ("one plus one" and "either side of the hyphen") in a new context.

Reading Focus

Identifying Cause and Effect In this passage, Lahiri describes what will happen (effect) when her parents die (cause).

Literary Focus

Style In the concluding paragraph, Lahiri's diction and sentence structure mirror the resolution of the central problem in this essay. She recognizes the equal weight of conflicting concepts: departure and arrival; richness and poverty; fiction and life; Indian and American.

foreign. Without them, the back-and-forth life my family leads, both literally and figuratively, will at last approach stillness. An anchor will drop, and a line of connection will be severed.

I have always believed that I lack the authority my parents bring to being Indian. But as long as they live they protect me from feeling like an impostor. Their passing will mark not only the loss of the people who created me but the loss of a singular way of life, a singular struggle. The immigrant's journey, no matter how ultimately rewarding, is founded on departure and deprivation, but it secures for the subsequent generation a sense of arrival and advantage. I can see a day coming when my American side, lacking the counterpoint India has until now maintained, begins to gain ascendancy and weight. It is in fiction that I will continue to interpret the term "Indian-American," calculating that shifting equation, whatever answers it may yield.

Read with a Purpose By the end of the essay, how have the author's feelings about her identity changed?

MEET THE WRITER

Jhumpa Lahiri (1967–)

Pulitzer Prize WINNER

Stories of Calcutta

As a child, Jhumpa Lahiri traveled with her family to Calcutta and often stayed there for months at a time: "These trips, to a vast, unruly, fascinating city so different from the small New England town where I was raised, shaped my perceptions of the world and of people from a very early age. I learned there was another side, a different version to everything." Lahiri's first book, a collection of short stories called *Interpreter of Maladies* (2000), won the Pulitzer Prize in Fiction. In 2003, she published her first novel, *The Namesake*, which was turned into a film in 2007.

Think About the Writer
Which influences Lahiri more in her writing: Calcutta or New England? Explain.

Lahiri with husband, Albarto Vourvoulias, in traditional Bengali wedding outfits.

Wrap Up

OH **RA.L.10.11** Explain ways in which an author develops a point of view and style, and cite specific examples from the text. **RA.L.10.5** Analyze how an author's choice of genre affects the expression of a theme or topic. *Also covered* **VO.10.6**

Into Action: Elements of Style

In "My Two Lives," Lahiri uses unique diction, sentence structure, and tone. Another aspect of her style is the use of figurative language. Find examples of these elements of style in her essay, and note them in a chart like the one below.

Element of Style	Example from the Essay
Diction	"I felt intense pressure to be two things, loyal to the old world and fluent in the new."
Sentence Structure	
Tone	
Figurative Language	

Talk About . . .

In groups of three, analyze Lahiri's style and the way she develops the subject of her essay—the divided self. Try to use each Academic Vocabulary word at the right at least once in your discussion.

Write About . . .

Answer the following questions about "My Two Lives." Academic Vocabulary words are underlined below and defined at the right.

1. What was a major component of Lahiri's growing identity as an American?

2. How were the experiences of Lahiri's parents and other immigrants different from those of subsequent generations?

3. In what ways is Lahiri's experience equivalent to that of other children of immigrants?

4. Is the use of figurative language an effective technique in this essay? Explain.

Writing Focus

Think as a Reader/Writer

In Collection 5, you will encounter authors who make biography, autobiography, memoir, and journalism as exciting as fiction. You'll see how these authors use elements of style. Then, you'll use these elements to make your own nonfiction come to life.

Academic Vocabulary for Collection 5

Talking and Writing About Nonfiction
Academic Vocabulary is the language you use to write and talk about literature. Use these words to discuss the selections you read in this collection. These words are underlined throughout the collection.

component (kuhm POH nuhnt) *n.*: necessary or essential part; element. *Diction is one component of style.*

subsequent (SUHB suh kwuhnt) *adj.*: coming next; following. *In subsequent paragraphs, Lahiri describes how her feelings changed over the years.*

equivalent (ih KWIHV uh luhnt) *adj.*: equal in value, strength, or force. *Synonyms have equivalent meanings but sometimes different connotations.*

technique (tehk NEEK) *n.*: method used to accomplish something. *Andy Harris uses a dangerous technique to reach Camp Four: He slides down the ice bulge on his behind.*

Your Turn

Work with a partner to write another sentence for each Academic Vocabulary word, using the definitions given above.

from
Team of Rivals

by **Doris Kearns Goodwin**

What Do **You** Think?

What makes an event historically important, and how do we come to understand its lasting significance?

QuickTalk

With a partner, brainstorm a list of historical events that seem particularly important to you. How did you learn about these events (from a teacher? a textbook? a TV show?), and what techniques were used to convey their importance?

Portrait of Abraham Lincoln, four days before his assassination.

Reader/Writer Notebook

Use your **RWN** to complete the activities for this selection.

OH **RA.L.10.11** Explain ways in which an author develops a point of view and style, and cite specific examples from the text. **RA.I.10.1** Identify and understand organizational patterns and techniques, including repetition of ideas, syntax and word choice, that authors use to accomplish their purpose and reach their intended audience.

Literary Focus

Style in Biography **Style** refers to the particular way a writer uses language. An author's **diction** (word choice), sentence structure, use of figurative language and imagery, and **tone** (attitude) all contribute to creating his or her style. Writing a **biography,** the true story of someone's life, requires the use of facts and quotations, which gives some biographies a formal style. Goodwin, however, uses the storytelling techniques of fiction to present factual information in this biography. As you read, think about the characteristics of her style.

Reading Focus

Analyzing Cause and Effect History consists of a series of cause-and-effect relationships, many of which become clear only when we look back at events. One action or decision—a **cause**—can start a chain reaction in which the **effects** cause other events to occur, and so on. As you read, analyzing cause-and-effect relationships can enhance your understanding of events and the reasons that an author includes certain facts.

Into Action As you read, fill in a cause-and-effect chart. Record causes in the boxes on the left and their effects in the corresponding boxes on the right. You can list more than one effect in each box.

Cause	Effect
Lincoln plans to attend theater.	
Booth decides to assassinate him that night.	

Writing Focus

Think as a Reader/Writer

Find It in Your Reading Goodwin intersperses quotations throughout her biography. As you read, note examples of passages that include quotations and record these in your *Reader/Writer Notebook*. Think about how this use of quoted material adds interest to the narrative.

Vocabulary

tyrant (TY ruhnt) *n.:* harsh, unjust ruler. *John Wilkes Booth considered Lincoln a tyrant who tried to crush the South.*

exalted (ehg ZAWL tihd) *v.:* held in high regard; glorified. *General Grant, because he admired Lincoln, exalted him.*

deflected (dih FLEHKT ihd) *v.:* turned aside. *During the attack, the assassin's knife was deflected.*

vitality (vy TAL uh tee) *n.:* physical strength; energy for life. *Despite Lincoln's vitality, he did not survive the gunshot wound.*

magnanimous (mag NAN uh muhs) *adj.:* honorable; noble; generous and forgiving. *According to General Grant, Lincoln was a magnanimous man.*

Language Coach

Word Origins The Latin word *flectere* means "to bend." Words that derive from *flectere* include *reflect* and *flexible*. Which word on the Vocabulary list above also comes from *flectere*? What other words can you think of that derive from *flectere*? Be sure to check your answers in a dictionary.

Learn It Online
Use Word Watch to master new terms.

go.hrw.com L10-453 **Go**

Doris Kearns Goodwin
(1943–   )

Pulitzer Prize WINNER

Twin Loves

Growing up in Brooklyn during the 1950s, Doris Kearns Goodwin had two loves: baseball and history. She shared her love for history with her mother and her love for baseball with her father, which she wrote about in her memoir *Wait till Next Year* (1997). Her passion for history led her to earn a doctorate degree in government from Harvard University.

Goodwin has written biographies of several presidents, including Lyndon B. Johnson and John F. Kennedy. For *No Ordinary Time,* a study of President Franklin Delano Roosevelt and his wife, Eleanor, Goodwin received the Pulitzer Prize.

"Unequalled Power"

Goodwin's book *Team of Rivals* (2005) is another important study of a historical figure. In the introduction, she writes, "After living with the subject of Abraham Lincoln for a decade . . . reading what he himself wrote and what hundreds of others have written about him, following the arc of his ambition, and assessing the inevitable mixture of human foibles and strengths that made up his temperament, after watching him deal with the terrible deprivations of his childhood, the deaths of his children, and the horror that engulfed the entire nation, I find that after nearly two centuries, the uniquely American story of Abraham Lincoln has unequalled power to captivate the imagination and to inspire emotion."

Think About the Writer

How have Goodwin's childhood passions played a role in her life as a writer?

Build Background

The events in this action-packed biography begin on the night of April 14, 1865. Only days before, Robert E. Lee's surrender to Ulysses S. Grant had ended the Civil War. The war began when eleven states of the largely agricultural South seceded from an increasingly urban and industrial North. Decades-old tensions over slavery, trade, and social inequality exploded into violence. The bloody conflict claimed more American lives than any other war, before or since. Though the North eventually prevailed, the nation remained bitterly divided after the war.

Preview the Selection

Abraham Lincoln, the sixteenth president of the United States, served from 1861 to 1865. He was president during the Civil War and was elected to a second term before he was assassinated by **John Wilkes Booth,** an actor who was a fierce supporter of slavery and the South.

As this selection opens, Abraham and **Mary Lincoln** are on their way to Ford's Theatre. At the same time, Booth was meeting with three men to plot a triple assassination.

White House Fellows Doris Kearns (Goodwin), Betsy Levin, and Barbara Currier meet with President Johnson in the Oval Office, White House, Washington, D.C.

Who's Who in
Team *of* Rivals

On April 14, 1865, John Wilkes Booth shot President Lincoln in Ford's Theatre in Washington, D.C. Here are the key people who played a role in the events described in this excerpt from Goodwin's biography of Lincoln.

William H. Seward: The secretary of state in Lincoln's administration, Seward survived the assassination plot and served in this role under President Andrew Johnson.

Andrew Johnson: Lincoln's vice president. Johnson became president after Lincoln was assassinated.

Lewis Powell: Powell served in the Confederate army during the Civil War but was captured by the Union army after being wounded in the Battle of Gettysburg. He was hanged for his role in the assassination plot.

David Herold: Herold's role in the plot to assassinate Seward was to wait outside Seward's home with Powell's horse so that Powell could flee on horseback. Herold subsequently escaped with Booth to a farm in Virginia, where he surrendered once the two men were discovered. He was hanged for his participation in the assassination plot.

George Atzerodt: A German immigrant, he was hanged for his role in the assassination plot.

The Seward Family: At the Seward home on the night of the assassination plot were Seward's wife, Frances; the Sewards' son Augustus (Gus); their son Frederick (Fred) and his wife, Anna; and the Sewards' daughter, Fanny. The Sewards' son William (Will) and his wife, Jenny, were not at home.

Edwin Stanton: secretary of war in the Lincoln administration.

George Robinson: soldier posted at Seward's home while Seward was recuperating from a carriage accident.

Emerick Hansell: State Department messenger.

Dr. Verdi: doctor who, at Seward's home, treated the five people wounded by Powell.

Mary Todd Lincoln: wife of President Lincoln, whom she married in 1842.

Clara Harris; Henry Rathbone: Engaged to be married, Harris and Rathbone had been invited by President and Mrs. Lincoln to accompany them to Ford's Theatre on the night that Lincoln was assassinated.

Charles Leale; Charles Sabin Taft: doctors who were the first to attend to Lincoln after he was shot. Taft's half sister, Julia, was friendly with the Lincoln family.

Joseph Sterling; J. G. Johnson: Sterling, a clerk in the War Department, and Johnson were roommates.

Gideon Welles: secretary of the navy in the Lincoln administration.

Salmon Portland Chase: chief justice appointed to the Supreme Court by Lincoln.

Robert Todd Lincoln: oldest of the Lincolns' four sons and the only one of their children to survive into adulthood.

John Hay: assistant private secretary to Lincoln.

Thomas Pendel: guard and chief doorkeeper at the White House. He frequently took care of Lincoln's son Tad, who called him "Tom Pen."

Thomas (Tad) Lincoln: youngest of the Lincolns' four sons.

Ulysses S. Grant: commander in chief of the Union army during the Civil War. He later served as the eighteenth president of the United States.

John A. Dix: major general in the Union army during the Civil War.

from Team of Rivals

by **Doris Kearns Goodwin**

As the Lincolns rode to Ford's Theatre on 10th Street, John Wilkes Booth and three conspirators[1] were a block away at the Herndon House. Booth had devised a plan that called for the simultaneous assassinations of President Lincoln, Secretary of State Seward, and Vice President Johnson. Having learned that morning of Lincoln's plan to attend the theater, he had decided that this night would provide their best opportunity. The powerfully built Lewis Powell, accompanied by David Herold, was assigned to kill Seward at his Lafayette Square home. Meanwhile, the carriage maker George Atzerodt was to shoot the vice president in his suite at the Kirkwood Hotel. Booth, whose familiarity with the stagehands would ensure access, would assassinate the president.

Just as Brutus had been honored for slaying the tyrant Julius Caesar,[2] Booth believed he would be exalted for killing an even "greater tyrant." Assassinating Lincoln would not be enough. "Booth knew," his biographer observes, "that in the end, the Brutus conspiracy was foiled by Marc Antony, whose famous oration made outlaws of the assassins and a martyr of Caesar."[3] William Henry Seward, Lincoln's Mark Antony, must not live. Finally, to throw the entire North into disarray,[4] the vice president must die as well. The triple assassinations were set for 10:15 P.M.

Still bedridden, Seward had enjoyed his best day since his nearly fatal carriage accident nine days earlier. Fanny Seward noted in her diary that he had slept well the previous night and had taken "solid food for the first time." In the afternoon, he had "listened with a look of pleasure to the narrative of the events of the

---

1. **conspirators** (kuhn SPIHR uh tuhrz): people who take part in a criminal plot.
2. **Brutus . . . Julius Caesar:** Julius Caesar (100?–44 B.C.) was a Roman general and dictator. He was killed by a team of assassins—which included Brutus (85?–42 B.C.), a general and statesman—who believed that Caesar was too power hungry to be allowed to rule.

3. **the Brutus conspiracy . . . martyr of Caesar:** At Caesar's funeral, Marc Antony (83?–30 B.C.), a Roman general and politician, delivered a speech that cast Caesar as a martyr—a person killed because of his or her beliefs. The enraged mob turned against the assassins, who ultimately fled Rome.
4. **disarray** (dihs uh RAY): disorder; confusion.

Vocabulary   **tyrant** (TY ruhnt) *n.*: harsh, unjust ruler.
exalted (ehg ZAWL tihd) *v.*: held in high regard; glorified.

Cabinet meeting," which Fred, as assistant secretary, had attended in his father's stead. Later in the afternoon, he had listened to Fanny's reading of "Enoch Arden" and remarked on how much he enjoyed it.

The three-story house was full of people. The entire family, except Will and Jenny, were there—Frances, Augustus, Fred, Anna, and Fanny. In addition to the half-dozen household servants and the State Department messenger rooming on the third floor, two soldiers had been assigned by Stanton to stay with Seward. In the early evening, Edwin Stanton had stopped by to check on his friend and colleague. He stayed for a while, chatting with other visitors until martial music in the air reminded him that War Department employees had planned on serenading him that night at his home six blocks away. **Ⓐ**

After all the guests left, "the quiet arrangements for the night" began. To ensure that Seward was never left alone, the family members had taken turns sitting by his bed. That night Fanny was scheduled to stay with him until 11 P.M., when her brother Gus would relieve her. George Robinson, one of the soldiers whom Stanton had detailed to the household, was standing by. Shortly after 10 P.M., Fanny noticed that her father was falling asleep. She closed the pages of the *Legends of Charlemagne,* turned down the gas lamps, and took a seat on the opposite side of the bed.

Fred Seward later wrote that "there seemed nothing unusual in the occurrence, when a tall, well dressed, but unknown man presented himself" at the door. Powell told the servant who answered the bell that he had some medicine for Mr. Seward and had been instructed by his physician to deliver it in person. "I told him he could not go up," the servant later testified, "that if he would give me the medicine, I would tell Mr. Seward how to take it." Powell was so insistent that the boy stepped aside. When he reached the landing, Fred Seward stopped him. "My father is asleep; give me the medicine and the directions; I will take them to him." Powell argued that he must deliver it in person, but Fred refused. **Ⓑ**

At this point, Fred recalled, the intruder "stood apparently irresolute." He began to head down the stairs, then "suddenly turning again, he sprang up and forward, having drawn a Navy revolver, which he levelled, with a muttered oath, at my head, and pulled the trigger." This was the last memory Fred would have of that night. The pistol misfired, but Powell brought it down so savagely that Fred's skull was crushed in two places, exposing his brain and rendering him unconscious.

Hearing the disturbance, Private Robinson ran to the door from Seward's bedside. The moment the door was opened, Powell rushed inside, brandishing his now broken pistol in one hand and a large knife in the other. He slashed Robinson in the forehead with his knife, knocking him "partially down," and headed toward Seward. Fanny ran beside Powell, begging him not to kill her father. When Seward heard the word "kill," he awakened, affording him "one glimpse of the assassin's face bending over" before the large bowie knife plunged into his neck and face, severing his cheek so badly that "the flap hung loose on his neck." Oddly, he would later recall that his only impressions

---

Ⓐ **Reading Focus** Cause and Effect How might the fact that Seward's house was full of people affect Powell's assassination attempt?

Ⓑ **Literary Focus** Style Why might Goodwin have included direct quotations from Fred Seward and the servant in this passage?

John Wilkes Booth

John Wilkes Booth, born May 10, 1838, came from a family of actors and was himself fairly popular as an actor during the Civil War. During the war years, he sympathized with the South and supported the continuation of slavery, directly opposing President Lincoln's policies. In 1864, Booth started recruiting like-minded individuals to join him in kidnapping Lincoln. When that plan seemed destined to fail, he switched tactics and decided to assassinate Lincoln instead. Booth, after he shot Lincoln in Ford's Theatre, escaped to a farm in Virginia, where he was found after a two-week search. Booth, who died on April 26, 1865, either shot himself to avoid surrender or was shot by a soldier.

Ask Yourself

How might Booth's experience as an actor have helped him convince others to join his plot?

John Wilkes Booth.

were what a fine-looking man Powell was and "what handsome cloth that overcoat is made of." **C**

Fanny's screams brought her brother Gus into the room as Powell advanced again upon Seward, who had been knocked to the floor by the force of the blows. Gus and the injured Robinson managed to pull Powell away, but not before he struck Robinson again and slashed Gus on the forehead and the right hand. When Gus ran for his pistol, Powell bolted down the stairs, stabbing Emerick Hansell, the young State Department messenger, in the back before he bolted out the door and fled through the city streets. **D**

The clamor had roused the entire household. Anna sent the servant to fetch Dr. Verdi, while Private Robinson, though bleeding from his head and shoulders, lifted Seward onto the bed and instructed Fanny about "staunching[5] the blood with clothes & water." Still fearing that another assassin might be hiding in the house, Frances and Anna checked the attic while Fanny searched the rooms on the parlor floor.

Dr. Verdi would never forget his first sight of Seward that night. "He looked like an exsanguinated[6] corpse. In approaching him my feet went deep in blood. Blood was streaming from an extensive gash in his swollen cheek; the cheek was now laid open." So "frightful" was the

---

5. **staunching** (stawnch ihng): stopping or decreasing the flow of something. Also spelled *stanching*.
6. **exsanguinated** (ehks SANG gwuh nayt ihd): drained of blood.

C **Literary Focus** Style Why do you think Goodwin chose to include Seward's impression of Powell here?

D **Literary Focus** Style What effect does Goodwin create by using a series of action verbs in this paragraph?

wound and "so great was the loss of blood" that Verdi assumed the jugular vein must have been cut. Miraculously, it was not. Further examination revealed that the knife had been deflected by the metal contraption holding Seward's broken jaw in place. In bizarre fashion, the carriage accident had saved his life. **E**

"I had hardly sponged his face from the bloody stains and replaced the flap," Verdi recalled, "when Mrs. Seward, with an intense look, called me to her. 'Come and see Frederick,' said she." Not understanding, he followed Frances to the next room, where he "found Frederick bleeding profusely from the head." Fred's appearance was so "ghastly" and his wounds so large that Verdi feared he would not live, but with the application of "cold water pledgets,"[7] he was able to stanch the bleeding temporarily.

Once Fred was stabilized, Frances drew Dr. Verdi into another room on the same floor. "For Heaven's sake, Mrs. Seward," asked the befuddled doctor, "what does all this mean?" Verdi found Gus lying on the bed with stab wounds on his hand and forehead, but assured Frances that he would recover. Frances barely had time to absorb these words of comfort before entreating Dr. Verdi to see Private Robinson. "I ceased wondering," Verdi recalled, "my mind became as if paralyzed; mechanically I followed her and examined Mr. Robinson. He had four or five cuts on his shoulders."

> "And all this," Verdi thought, "the work of one man—yes, of one man!"

---

7. **pledgets** (PLEHJ ihts): small pads used on wounds.

"Any more?" Verdi asked, though not imagining the carnage could go on. "Yes," Frances answered, "one more." She led him to Mr. Hansell, "piteously groaning on the bed." Stripping off the young man's clothes, Verdi "found a deep gash just above the small of the back, near the spine."

"And all this," Verdi thought, "the work of one man—yes, of one man!" **F**

In preparing for the attack on the vice president, George Atzerodt had taken a room at the Kirkwood Hotel, where Johnson was staying. At 10:15, he was supposed to ring the bell of Suite 68, enter the room by force, find his target, and murder him. When first informed that the original plan to kidnap the president had shifted to a triple assassination, he had balked. "I won't do it," he had insisted. "I enlisted to abduct the President of the United States, not to kill." He had eventually agreed to help, but fifteen minutes before the appointed moment, seated at the bar of the Kirkwood House, he changed his mind, left the hotel, and never returned. **G**

John Wilkes Booth had left little to chance in his plot to kill the president. Though already well acquainted with the layout of Ford's Theatre, Booth had attended a dress rehearsal the day before to better rehearse his scheme for shooting Lincoln in the state box and then escaping into the alley beside the theater. That morning he had again visited the theater to collect his mail, chatting amiably in the front lobby

---

E **Reading Focus** Cause and Effect What happens to Powell's knife when he stabs Seward?

F **Literary Focus** Style How does the inclusion of Verdi's thoughts affect your impression of Powell's attacks?

G **Reading Focus** Cause and Effect Why do you think Atzerodt decided to drop out of the assassination plot at the last moment?

Vocabulary **deflected** (dih FLEHKT ihd) v.: turned aside.

with the theater owner's brother, Harry Ford. Booth had already taken his place inside the theater when the Lincolns arrived.

The play had started as the presidential party entered the flag-draped box in the dress circle. The notes of "Hail to the Chief" brought the audience to their feet, applauding wildly and craning to see the president. Lincoln responded "with a smile and bow" before taking his seat in a comfortable armchair at the center of the box, with Mary by his side. Clara Harris was seated at the opposite end of the box, while Henry Rathbone occupied a small sofa on her left. Observing the president and first lady, one theatergoer noticed that she "rested her hand on his knee much of the time, and often called his attention to some humorous situation on the stage." Mary herself later recalled that as she snuggled ever closer to her husband, she had whispered, "What will Miss Harris think of my hanging on to you so?" He had looked at her and smiled. "She won't think any thing about it." **Ⓗ**

During the performance, the White House footman delivered a message to the president. At about twelve minutes after ten, the impeccably dressed John Wilkes Booth presented his calling card to the footman and gained admittance to the box. Once inside, he raised his pistol, pointed it at the back of the president's head, and fired.

As Lincoln slumped forward, Henry Rathbone attempted to grab the intruder. Booth pulled out his knife, slashed Rathbone in the chest, and managed to leap from the box onto the stage fifteen feet below. "As he jumped," one eyewitness recalled, "one of the spurs on his riding-boots caught in the folds of the flag draped over the front, and caused him to fall partly on his hands and knees as he struck the stage." Another onlooker observed that "he was suffering great pain," but, "making a desperate effort, he struggled up." Raising "his shining dagger in the air, which reflected the light as though it had been a diamond," he shouted the now historic words of the Virginia state motto—"Sic semper tyrannis" (Thus always to tyrants)—and ran from the stage.

Until the screams broke forth from the president's box, many in the audience thought the dramatic moment was part of the play. Then they saw Mary Lincoln frantically waving. "They have shot the President!" she cried. "They have shot the President!" Charles Leale, a young doctor seated near the presidential box, was the first to respond. "When I reached the President," he recalled, "he was almost dead, his eyes were closed." Unable at first to locate the wound, he stripped away Lincoln's coat and collar. Examining the base of the skull, he discovered "the perfectly smooth opening made by the ball." Using his finger "as a probe" to remove "the coagula[8] which was firmly matted with the hair," he released the flow of blood, relieving somewhat the pressure on Lincoln's brain. Another doctor, Charles Sabin Taft, Julia Taft's half brother, soon arrived, and the decision was made to remove the president from the crowded box to a room in the Petersen boardinghouse across the street. **Ⓘ**

By this time, people had massed in the

---

8. **coagula** (koh AG yuh luh): clots.

Ⓗ **Literary Focus** **Style** Explain how the inclusion of these intimate details about the Lincolns is a good example of Goodwin's use of the techniques of fiction.

Ⓘ **Reading Focus** **Cause and Effect** What factors led to the success of Booth's plot to assassinate Lincoln, including Booth's escape?

John Wilkes Booth shoots President Abraham Lincoln as he watches a play at Ford's Theatre in Washington, D.C., 1865.

street. The word began to spread that assassins had attacked not only Lincoln but Seward as well. Joseph Sterling, a young clerk in the War Department, rushed to inform Stanton of the calamity. On his way, he encountered his roommate, J. G. Johnson, who joined him on the terrible errand. "When Johnson and I reached Stanton's residence," Sterling recalled, "I was breathless," so when Stanton's son Edwin Jr. opened the door, Johnson was the one to speak. "We have come," Johnson said, "to tell your father that President Lincoln has been shot."

Young Stanton hurried to his father, who had been undressing for bed. When the war secretary came to the door, Sterling recalled, "he fairly shouted at me in his heavy tones: 'Mr. Sterling what news is this you bring?'" Sterling told him that both Lincoln and Seward had been assassinated. Desperately hoping this news was mere rumor, Stanton remained calm and skeptical. "Oh, that can't be so," he said, "that can't be so!" But when another clerk arrived at the door to describe the attack on Seward, Stanton had his carriage brought around at once, and against the appeals of his wife, who feared that he, too, might be a target, he headed for Seward's house at Lafayette Square.

The news reached Gideon Welles almost simultaneously. He had already gone to bed when his wife reported someone at the door. "I arose at once," Welles recorded in his diary, "and raised a window, when my messenger, James called to me that Mr. Lincoln the President had been shot," and that Seward and his son had been assassinated. Welles thought the story "very incoherent and improbable," but the messenger assured him that he had already been to Seward's house to check its veracity before coming to see his boss. Also ignoring his wife's protests, Welles dressed and set forth in the foggy night for the Seward house on the other side of the square. **J**

Upon reaching Seward's house, Welles and Stanton were shocked at what they found. Blood was everywhere—on "the white wood work of the entry," on the stairs, on the dresses of the women, on the floor of the bedroom. Seward's bed, Welles recalled, "was saturated with blood. The Secretary was lying on his back, the upper part of his head covered by a cloth, which extended down over his eyes." Welles questioned Dr. Verdi in a whisper, but Stanton was unable to mute his stentorian voice until the doctor asked for quiet. After looking in on Fred's unconscious form, the two men walked together down the stairs. In the lower hall, they exchanged what information they had regarding the president. Welles thought they should go to the White House, but Stanton believed Lincoln was still at the theater. Army quartermaster general Meigs, who had just come to the door, implored them not to go to 10th Street, where thousands of people had gathered. When they insisted, he decided to join them.

Twelve blocks away, in his home at Sixth and E streets, Chief Justice Chase had already retired for the night. Earlier that afternoon, he had taken a carriage ride with Nettie, intending to stop at the White House to remonstrate[9] with Lincoln over his too lenient approach to Reconstruction[10] and his failure to demand universal suffrage.[11] At the last minute, "uncertain how [Lincoln] would take it," Chase had decided to wait until the following day.

He was fast asleep when a servant knocked on his bedroom door. There was a gentleman downstairs, the servant said, who claimed "the President had been shot." The caller was a Treasury employee who had actually witnessed the shooting "by a man who leaped from the box upon the stage & escaped by the rear."

> Blood was everywhere— on "the white wood work of the entry," on the stairs, on the dresses of the women, on the floor of the bedroom.

9. **remonstrate** (rih MAHN strayt): present an argument against something.
10. **Reconstruction:** period after the Civil War during which the eleven Southern states that had seceded from the Union were readmitted to it.
11. **suffrage** (SUHF rihj): right to vote.

J **Literary Focus** **Style** What details does Goodwin include that show you how people reacted to the assassination?

Chase hoped "he might be mistaken," but in short order, three more callers arrived. Each "confirmed what I had been told & added that Secretary Seward had also been assassinated, and that guards were being placed around the houses of all the prominent officials, under the apprehension that the plot had a wide range. My first impulse was to rise immediately & go to the President . . . but reflecting that I could not possibly be of any service and should probably be in the way of those who could, I resolved to wait for morning & further intelligence. In a little while the guard came—for it was supposed that I was one of the destined victims—and their heavy tramp-tramp was heard under my window all night. . . . It was a night of horrors."

When Stanton and Welles arrived at the crammed room in the Petersen boardinghouse, they found that Lincoln had been placed diagonally across a bed to accommodate his long frame. Stripped of his shirt, "his large arms," Welles noted, "were of a size which one would scarce have expected from his spare appearance." His devastating wound, the doctors reported with awe, "would have killed most men instantly, or in a very few minutes. But Mr. Lincoln had so *much vitality*" that he continued to struggle against the inevitable end.

Mary spent most of the endless night weeping in an adjoining parlor, where several women friends tried vainly to comfort her. "About once an hour," Welles noted, she "would repair to the bedside of her dying husband and with lamentation[12] and tears remain until overcome by emotion." She could only rotely repeat the question "Why didn't he shoot me? Why didn't he shoot me?" Though everyone in

Exterior view of William Petersen's boardinghouse, in Washington, D.C., during the 1900s.

12. **lamentation** (lam uhn TAY shuhn): loud crying.

Ⓚ Literary Focus Style What is important about the details Goodwin includes in this description of Lincoln?

Vocabulary **vitality** (vy TAL uh tee) *n.*: physical strength; energy for life.

the room knew the president was dying, Mary was not told, out of fear that she would collapse. Whenever she came into the room, Dr. Taft recalled, "clean napkins were laid over the crimson stains on the pillow."

Early on, Mary sent a messenger for Robert, who had remained at home that night in the company of John Hay. He had already turned in when the White House doorkeeper came to his room. "Something happened to the President," Thomas Pendel told Robert, "you had better go down to the theater and see what it is." Robert asked Pendel to get Hay. Reaching Hay's room, Pendel told him, "Captain Lincoln wants to see you at once. The President has been shot." Pendel recalled that when Hay heard the news, "he turned deathly pale, the color entirely leaving his cheeks." The two young men jumped in a carriage, picking up Senator Sumner along the way.

Mary was torn over whether to summon Tad, but was apparently persuaded that the emotional boy would be devastated if he saw his father's condition. Tad and his tutor had gone that night to Grover's Theatre to see *Aladdin*. The theater had been decorated with patriotic emblems, and a poem commemorating Fort Sumter's recapture was read aloud between the acts. An eyewitness recalled that the audience was "enjoying the spectacle of Aladdin" when the theater manager came forward, "as pale as a ghost." A look of "mortal agony" contorted his face as he announced to the stunned audience that the president had been shot at Ford's Theatre. In the midst of the pandemonium[13] that followed, Tad was seen running "like a young deer, shrieking in agony." **L**

_____
13. **pandemonium** (pan duh MOH nee uhm): uproar; noisy disorder.

"Poor little Tad," Pendel recalled, returned to the White House in tears. "O Tom Pen! Tom Pen!" Tad wailed. "They have killed Papa dead. They've killed Papa dead!" Pendel carried the little boy into Lincoln's bedroom. Turning down the bedcovers, he helped Tad undress and finally got him to lie down. "I covered him up and laid down beside him, put my arm around him, and talked to him until he fell into a sound sleep."

By midnight the entire cabinet, with the exception of Seward, had gathered in the small room at the Petersen boardinghouse. An eyewitness noted that Robert Lincoln "bore himself with great firmness, and constantly endeavored to assuage the grief of his mother by telling her to put her trust in God." Despite his brave attempts to console others, he was sometimes "entirely overcome" and "would retire into the hall and give vent to most heartrending lamentations." Almost no one was able to contain his grief that night, for as one witness observed, "there was not a soul present that did not love the president."

To Edwin Stanton fell the onerous task of alerting the generals, taking the testimony of witnesses at the theater, and orchestrating the search for the assassins. "While evidently swayed by the great shock which held us all under its paralyzing influence," Colonel A. F. Rockwell noted, "he was not only master of himself but unmistakably the dominating power over all. Indeed, the members of the cabinet, much as children might to their father, instinctively deferred to him in all things."

Throughout the night, Stanton dictated numerous dispatches, which were carried to the War Department telegraph office by a relay team of messengers positioned nearby. "Each

_____

L **Reading Focus** Cause and Effect Why did Mary not tell Tad that Lincoln had been shot?

messenger," Stanton's secretary recalled, "after handing a dispatch to the next, would run back to his post to wait for the next." The first telegram went to General Grant, requesting his immediate presence in Washington. "The President was assassinated at Ford's Theater at 10.30 to-night and cannot live. . . . Secretary Seward and his son Frederick were also assassinated at their residence and are in a dangerous condition." The dispatch reached Grant in the Bloodgood Hotel, where he was taking supper. He "dropped his head," Horace Porter recalled, "and sat in perfect silence." Noticing that he had turned "very pale," Julia Grant guessed that bad news had arrived and asked him to read the telegram aloud. "First prepare yourself for the most painful and startling news that could be received," he warned. As he made plans to

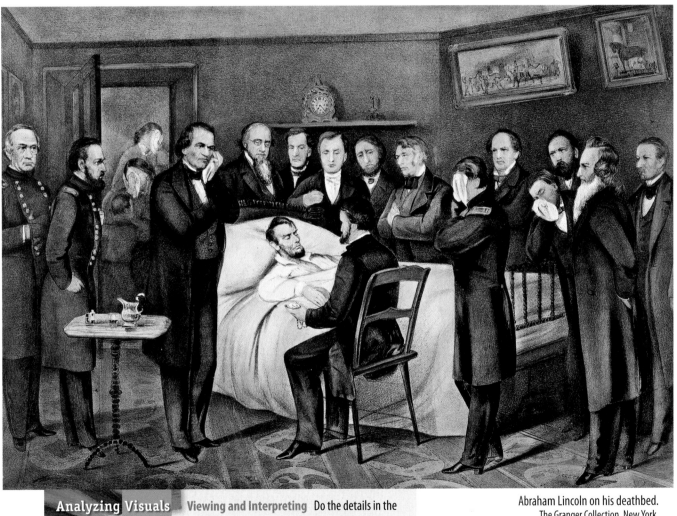

Analyzing Visuals   **Viewing and Interpreting**   Do the details in the painting mirror the details in the text? Explain.

Abraham Lincoln on his deathbed.
The Granger Collection, New York.

Lewis Powell, also known as Lewis Payne (1844–1865).
The Granger Collection, New York.

return to Washington, he told Julia that the tidings filled him "with the gloomiest apprehension. The President was inclined to be kind and magnanimous, and his death at this time is an irreparable loss to the South, which now needs so much both his tenderness and magnanimity."

At 1 A.M., Stanton telegraphed the chief of police in New York, telling him to "send here immediately three or four of your best detectives." Half an hour later, he notified General Dix, "The wound is mortal. The President has been insensible ever since it was inflicted, and is now dying." Three hours later, he updated Dix: "The President continues insensible and is sinking." Early eyewitness accounts, Stanton revealed, suggested "that two assassins were engaged in the horrible crime, Wilkes Booth being the one that shot the President."

Shortly after dawn, Mary entered the room for the last time. "The death-struggle had begun," Welles recorded. "As she entered the chamber and saw how the beloved features were distorted, she fell fainting to the floor." Restoratives[14] were given, and Mary was assisted back to the sofa in the parlor, never again to see her husband alive.

No sooner had "the town clocks struck seven," one observer recalled, than "the character of the President's breathing changed. It became faint and low. At intervals it altogether ceased, until we thought him dead. And then it would be again resumed." Lincoln's nine-hour struggle had reached its final moments. "Let us pray," Reverend Phineas D. Gurley said, and everyone present knelt.

At 7:22 A.M., April 15, 1865, Abraham Lincoln was pronounced dead. Stanton's concise tribute from his deathbed still echoes. "Now he belongs to the ages."[15]

---

14. **restoratives** (rih STAWR uh tihvz): medicines or other substances used to bring back health or consciousness.
15. Other sources quote Stanton as saying, "Now he belongs to the angels."

M Reading Focus Cause and Effect According to Grant, how would the South have benefited from Lincoln's generosity?

N Literary Focus Style How does Goodwin create suspense in her description of Lincoln's final hours?

Vocabulary **magnanimous** (mag NAN uh muhs) *adj.*: honorable; noble; generous and forgiving.

Applying Your Skills

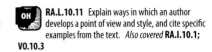**RA.L.10.11** Explain ways in which an author develops a point of view and style, and cite specific examples from the text. *Also covered* **RA.I.10.1; VO.10.3**

from **Team of Rivals**

Respond and Think Critically

Reading Focus

Quick Check

1. Why did Booth plot to assassinate Lincoln, Seward, and Johnson? How successful was he?

2. What were the key events on the night of April 14, 1865?

Read with a Purpose

3. How did Powell and Booth each carry out his part of the plot? Why were eyewitnesses as well as other people so shocked by their actions?

Reading Skills: Analyzing Cause and Effect

4. Go back to the cause-and-effect chart that you made. Imagine that in place of one of the causes you recorded, someone had taken a different action or made a different decision. How might the corresponding effects of this cause, as well as the course of events described in the selection as a whole, have changed?

✔ Vocabulary Check

Match each Vocabulary word in the column on the left with its definition in the column on the right.

5. **tyrant**   a. physical strength
6. **exalted**   b. harsh ruler
7. **deflected**   c. honorable
8. **vitality**   d. glorified
9. **magnanimous**   e. turned aside

Literary Focus

Literary Analysis

10. **Evaluate** Why do you think Goodwin relies heavily on quoted material that indicates what people said on the night Lincoln died? Do you think the use of quotations adds to or detracts from the account? Explain.

11. **Analyze** How would you characterize Lincoln and his effect on those around him? Use details from the selection to support your response.

Literary Skills: Style in Biography

12. **Evaluate** Describe Goodwin's overall style in this biography. Do you think it is effective? Why or why not?

Literary Skills Review: Description

13. **Analyze** Which descriptions in this excerpt have the most emotional impact? Explain.

Writing Focus

Think as a Reader/Writer

Use It in Your Writing Choose one of the passages you noted in your *Reader/Writer Notebook* and rewrite it, replacing the quoted material with paraphrased content. Share your rewrite with a classmate, and discuss how the impact of the two versions is different.

What Do You Think Now How does Goodwin show that Lincoln's assassination was a national tragedy?

from

A Choice of Weapons

by **Gordon Parks**

What Do
You
Think

How can our perspective contribute to the meaning of an event?

QuickTalk

With a partner, discuss what you know about the civil rights movement. What issues were people concerned about at that time? Which events and people had a significant impact on society? What else would you like to learn about this important period in history?

Department Store, Birmingham, Alabama, 1956, by Gordon Parks. Photograph. Silver dye bleach print 16 ¼ in. × 16 in.

Courtesy of the Corcoran Gallery of Art, Washington, DC. The Gordon Parks Foundation. ©Gordon Parks.

Reader/Writer
Notebook

Use your **RWN** to complete the activities for
this selection.

RA.L.10.8 Analyze the author's use of point of view, mood and tone. **RA.L.10.5** Analyze how an author's choice of genre affects the expression of a theme or topic. **RA.I.10.1** Identify and understand organizational patterns and techniques, including repetition of ideas, syntax and word choice, that authors use to accomplish their purpose and reach their intended audience.

Literary Focus

Memoir and Mood A **memoir** is a type of autobiography that
focuses on a specific time or historical event rather than on the writer's life as a whole. A memoir can provide an unusual perspective on a
particular set of events by letting the reader share the insights of the
writer. A good memoir evokes a powerful **mood,** or feeling, to connect the reader to the writer's experiences. In "A Choice of Weapons,"
a tense mood brings out the drama and meaning of Gordon Parks's
struggle against discrimination.

Literary Perspectives Apply the literary perspective described on
page 471 as you read this excerpt from Parks's memoir.

Reading Focus

Identifying an Author's Purpose Writers have different **purposes,** or reasons for writing. One purpose of a memoir is to share an
experience that has had an impact on the writer's life. In "A Choice of
Weapons," Parks shares how an experience shaped his beliefs about
society, art, and feelings of moral responsibility. Other purposes for
writing include entertaining the reader and persuading the reader.

Into Action As you read, create a
chart with examples from the text
showing the different purposes
Parks may have had when writing.
At what point is he trying to entertain you or persuade you rather than
provide you with information?

Purpose	Detail from Text
to inform	
to persuade	
to entertain	

Writing Focus

Think as a Reader/Writer

Find It in Your Reading Parks responds to real-life events with
an **interior monologue**—the thoughts he has but does not voice as
events unfold around him. As you read, look for places where Parks
reveals his thoughts without interrupting the main action. Write
down examples in your *Reader/Writer Notebook.*

Language Coach

Suffixes A **suffix** is a word part that when
added to the end of a word, changes that
word's meaning. You can change some
Vocabulary words into nouns by adding the
suffixes *–tion* or *–sion* to the base word. For
example, *eroded* becomes *erosion*. Add suffixes to create the noun forms of *exasperate*
and *exploited*. Check the correct spelling in a
dictionary.

Learn It Online
There's more to words than just definitions. Get the
whole story on:

go.hrw.com | L10-469 | **Go**

Gordon Parks
(1912–2006)

Success Against the Odds

Gordon Parks faced extreme challenges from the moment he entered this world. His heart was not beating, and doctors believed he was dead. A quick-thinking doctor dunked him in ice water to jump-start his heart.

Parks's path to recognition was not easy. He grew up in a poor family in Kansas. At fifteen, orphaned by his mother's death, he went to live with a sister in Minnesota. He eventually dropped out of high school and supported himself through odd jobs.

A Master of Many Trades

At the age of twenty-six, Parks bought his first camera for the cost of a month's worth of meals. As he became proficient as a photographer, he began to document the civil rights movement and the struggles of poor and oppressed people in the United States and abroad.

In 1963, Parks began writing fiction. Later, he released several autobiographical works as well. Much of his writing deals with the experiences of African Americans and their struggles against prejudice. Parks also directed films, including an adaptation of his book *The Learning Tree* in 1969. In addition to having been a filmmaker, writer, and photographer, Parks was a talented painter, choreographer, and composer. "At first I wasn't sure that I had the talent," he said, "but I did know I had a fear of failure, and that fear compelled me to fight off anything that might abet it."

Think About the Writer How did Parks's many skills give him an advantage in expressing his views and opinions?

Build Background

This memoir is set in Washington, D.C., during World War II. In addition to dealing with the war, the United States was just coming out of the Great Depression, a period of economic crisis lasting from 1929 until 1939. The photography skills Parks developed at this time served him well. His photography later played an important role in the civil rights movement.

Preview the Selection

In this memoir, **Gordon Parks** presents himself as a confident young man, bursting with talent and eager to make an impression in the world. He has come to Washington, D.C., to work in the photography department of the Farm Security Administration. His boss, **Roy Stryker,** has different ideas about what Parks needs to learn.

Gordon Parks (center) poses with close to one hundred prominent black photographers in 2002 on his ninetieth birthday in Harlem.

from

A Choice of Weapons

by **Gordon Parks**

I came to Washington, excited and eager, on a clear cold day in January. I had been singled out for an unusual blessing. I felt a notch above normal things, bursting with a new strength that would be unleashed upon this historic place. The White House, the Capitol and all the great buildings wherein great men had helped shape the destinies of the world—I would borrow from their tradition, feel their presence, touch their stone. I would walk under trees and on paths where Presidents had once walked. My mind hurried the taxi along to the place where I was to stay. It hastened my unpacking and raced ahead of the streetcar that carried me to the red brick building at Fourteenth and Independence avenues where I would meet Stryker and the photographers of the Farm Security Administration.[1] And I walked confidently down the corridor, following the arrows to my destination, sensing history all around me, feeling knowledge behind every door I passed. I was so uplifted that the plainness of the office I finally entered dumbfounded me. The barnlike room with the plain furniture and bulky file cabinets was as ordinary as any other office I had seen but even more so. No photographs were on the walls and there were no photographers around; ordinary dust clung to the windows and the air was no different from that I had breathed back in Kansas. I stood waiting, a little disappointed,

---

1. **Farm Security Administration:** a division of the Department of Agriculture in the 1930s. Its job was to document rural America in photographs.

Literary Perspectives

Analyzing Political Context The word *political* refers to the way that different people or groups have or use power within a system. Often, literary texts reflect political ideas in the way that they portray social beliefs and practices. When you apply this literary perspective, consider the social and historical context of the work. Ask yourself these questions:

- When do the events occur, and how do the different groups of people interact?
- Does the work reinforce social stereotypes or undermine them?
- What beliefs do the people hold? Does the author seem to agree or disagree with those beliefs?
- What do you think the author would like to change about a political situation?

As you read this selection, use the Literary Perspectives questions in the text to guide you in applying this perspective.

Gordon Parks at *Life* magazine.

sons running toward their shack through the dust storm.

"Arthur? This is Roy."

I'm here, I thought; at last I'm here.

As he talked I observed the chubby face topped with a mane of white hair, the blinking piercingly curious eyes, enlarged under thick bifocal lenses. There was something boyish, something fatherly, something tyrannical, something kind and good about him. He did not seem like anyone I had ever known before.

They talked for about ten minutes. "That was Rothstein." Stryker said, hanging up. "He had bad luck with one of his cameras." The way he said this pulled me in as if I were already accepted; as if I had been there for years. The indoctrination[3] had begun. "Now tell me about yourself and your plans," he said with a trace of playfulness in his voice. I spent a lot of time telling him perhaps more than he bargained for. After I had finished, he asked me bluntly, "What do you know about Washington?" **B**

"Nothing much," I admitted.

"Did you bring your cameras with you?"

"Yes, they're right here in this bag." I took out my battered Speed Graphic and a Rolleiflex and proudly placed them on his desk.

He looked at them approvingly and then asked me for the bag I had taken them from. He then took all my equipment and locked it in a closet behind him. "You won't be needing those for a few days," he said flatly. He lit a cigarette and leaned back in his chair and continued, "I have some very specific things I would like you to do this week. And I would like you to follow

wondering what I had really expected. I didn't know, I finally realized. **A**

A tall blonde girl who said her name was Charlotte came forward and greeted me. "Mr. Stryker will be with you in a minute," she said. She had just gotten the words out when he bounced out and extended his hand. "Welcome to Washington. I'm Roy," were his first words. "Come into the office and let's get acquainted." I will like this man, I thought.

He motioned me to a chair opposite his desk but before he could say anything his telephone rang. "It's Arthur Rothstein[2] phoning from Montana," Charlotte called from the outer office. The name flashed my thoughts back to the night on the dining car when I first saw it beneath the picture of the farmer and his two

---

2. **Arthur Rothstein:** photographer known for his pictures of migrant workers and of the Dust Bowl, the area that suffered extreme erosion during the droughts of the 1930s.

3. **indoctrination** (ihn dahk truh NAY shuhn): the teaching of a set of ideas or beliefs.

A **Literary Focus** Memoir and Mood What vivid words or phrases contribute to the mood of this opening paragraph?

B **Literary Focus** Memoir and Mood What mood is evoked by this description of Parks's first meeting with Roy Stryker?

my instructions faithfully. Walk around the city. Get to know it. Buy yourself a few things—you have money, I suppose."

"Yes, sir."

"Go to a picture show, the department stores, eat in the restaurants and drugstores. Get to know this place." I thought his orders were a bit trivial, but they were easy enough to follow. "Let me know how you've made out in a couple of days," he said after he had walked me to the door.

"I will," I promised casually. And he smiled oddly as I left.

I walked toward the business section and stopped at a drugstore for breakfast. When I sat down at the counter the white waiter looked at me as though I were crazy. "Get off of that stool," he said angrily. "Don't you know colored people can't eat in here? Go round to the back door if you want something." Everyone in the place was staring at me now. I retreated, too stunned to answer him as I walked out the door.   **C**

I found an open hot dog stand. Maybe this place would serve me. I approached the counter warily. "Two hot dogs, please."

"To take out?" the boy in the white uniform snapped.

"Yes, to take out," I snapped back. And I walked down the street, gulping down the sandwiches.

I went to a theater.

"What do you want?"

"A ticket."

"Colored people can't go in here. You should know that."

I remained silent, observing the ticket seller with more surprise than anything else. She looked at me as though I were insane. What is this, I wondered. Was Stryker playing some sort of joke on me? Was this all planned to exasperate me? Such discrimination here in Washington, D.C., the nation's capital? It was hard to believe.   **D**

Strangely, I hadn't lost my temper. The experience was turning into a weird game, and I would play it out—follow Roy's instructions to the hilt. I would try a department store now; and I chose the most imposing one in sight, Julius Garfinckel. Its name had confronted me many times in full-page advertisements in fashion magazines. Its owners must have been filled with national pride—their ads were always identified with some sacred Washington monument. Julius Garfinckel. Julius Rosenwald.[4] I lumped them with the names of Harvey Goldstein,[5] and Peter Pollack[6]—Jews who had helped shift the course of my life. I pulled myself together and entered the big store, with nothing particular in mind. The men's hats

---

4. **Julius Rosenwald:** former president and chairman of the board at Sears, Roebuck and Co. He also created the Julius Rosenwald Fellowship, given to African Americans to obtain graduate and professional education. Parks won this fellowship in 1941; it allowed him to work for the FSA.

5. **Harvey Goldstein:** photographer and friend of Parks who taught him about photography.

6. **Peter Pollack** (1909–1978): photographer who published the book *The Picture History of Photography* in 1958.

C **Reading Focus** **Author's Purpose** What might this exchange suggest about one purpose of this memoir?

D **Literary Perspectives** **Political Context** What political issue is at stake here?

Vocabulary **trivial** (TRIHV ee uhl) *adj.:* unimportant; not significant.
exasperate (ehg ZAS puh rayt) *v.:* greatly irritate or disturb.

were on my right so I arbitrarily chose that department. The salesman appeared a little on edge but he sold me a hat. Then leaving I saw an advertisement for camel's-hair coats on an upper floor. I had wanted one since the early days at the Minnesota Club. It was possible now. The elevator operator's face brought back memories of the doorman at the Park Central Hotel on that first desperate morning in New York.

"Can I help you?" His question was shadowed with arrogance.

"Yes. Men's coats, please." He hesitated for a moment, then closed the door and we went up.

The game had temporarily ended on the first floor as far as I was concerned. The purchase of the hat had relieved my doubts about discrimination here; the coat was the goal now. The floor was bare of customers. Only four salesmen stood eying me as I stepped from the elevator. None of them offered assistance so I looked at them and asked to be shown a camel's-hair coat.

No one moved. "They're to your left," someone volunteered.

I walked to my left. There were the coats I wanted, several racks of them. But no one attempted to show them to me.

"Could I get some help here?" I asked.

One man sauntered over. "What can I do for you?"

"I asked you for a camel's-hair coat."

"Those aren't your size."

"Then where are my size?"

"Probably around to your right."

"Probably around to my right?" The game was on again. "Then show them to me."

"That's not my department."

"Then whose department is it?"

"Come to think of it, I'm sure we don't have your size in stock."

"But you don't even know my size."

"I'm sorry. We just don't have your size."

"Well, I'll just wait here until you get one my size." Anger was at last beginning to take over. There was a white couch in the middle of the floor. I walked over and sprawled out leisurely on it, took a newspaper from my pocket and pretended to read. My blackness stretched across the white couch commanded attention. The manager arrived, posthaste,[7] a generous smile upon his face. My ruse[8] had succeeded, I thought.

"I'm the manager of this department. What can I do for you?"

"Oh, am I to have the honor of being waited on by the manager? How nice," I said, smiling with equal graciousness.   **E**

"Well, you see, there's a war on. And we're very short of help. General Marshall[9] was in here yesterday and *he* had to wait for a salesman. Now please understand that—"

"But I'm not General Marshall and there's no one here but four salesmen, you and me. But I'll wait here until they're not so busy. I'll wait right here." He sat down in a chair beside me and we talked for a half hour—about weather, war, food, Washington, and even camel's-hair coats. But I was never shown one. Finally, after

---

7. **posthaste** (pohst HAYST): rapidly.
8. **ruse** (rooz): a trick or scheme to mislead others.
9. **General Marshall** (1880–1959): George C. Marshall, general of the army and U.S. Army chief of staff during World War II.

E **Literary Focus** Memoir and Mood What attitudes do Parks and the manager display in this dialogue?

Analyzing Visuals **Viewing and Interpreting** From what you've read about Parks in the memoir, why do you think he might have chosen this scene to photograph?

Ella Watson (from Parks's famous photo, *American Gothic,* page 479) with three grandchildren and adopted daughter.

he ran out of conversation, he left. I continued to sit there under the gaze of the four puzzled salesmen and the few customers who came to the floor. At last the comfort of the couch made me sleepy; and by now the whole thing had become ridiculous. I wouldn't have accepted a coat if they had given me the entire rack. Suddenly I thought of my camera, of Stryker. I got up and hurried out of the store and to his office. He was out to lunch when I got back. But

I waited outside his door until he returned. **F**

"I didn't expect you back so soon," he said. "I thought you'd be out seeing the town for a couple of days."

"I've seen enough of it in one morning," I replied sullenly. "I want my cameras."

"What do you intend to do with them?"

"I want to show the rest of the world what your great city of Washington, D.C., is really like. I want—"

F **Reading Focus** **Author's Purpose** How does Parks's sudden thought relate to the memoir's purpose?

"Okay. Okay." The hint of that smile was on his face again. And now I was beginning to understand it. "Come into my office and tell me all about it," he said. He listened patiently. He was sympathetic; but he didn't return my equipment.

"Young man," he finally began, "you're going to face some very hard facts down here. Whatever else it may be, this is a Southern city. Whether you ignore it or tolerate it is up to you. I purposely sent you out this morning so that you can see just what you're up against." He paused for a minute to let this sink in. Then he continued. "You're going to find all kinds of people in Washington and a good cross-section of the types are right here in this building. You'll have to prove yourself to them, especially the lab people. They are damned good technicians—but they are all Southerners. I can't predict what their attitudes will be toward you and I warn you I'm not going to try to influence them one way or the other. It's completely up to you. I do think they will respect good craftsmanship. Once you get over that hurdle I honestly believe you will be accepted as another photographer—not just as a Negro photographer. There is a certain amount of resentment against even the white photographers until they prove themselves. Remember, these people slave in hot darkrooms while they think about the photographers enjoying all the glamour and getting all the glory. Most of them would like to be on the other end." **G**

We were walking about the building now, and as he introduced me to different people his words took on meaning. Some smiled and extended their hands in welcome. Others, espe-cially those in the laboratory, kept working and acknowledged me with cold nods, making their disdain obvious. Any triumph over them would have to be well earned, I told myself. Stryker closed the door when we were back in his office. "Go home," he advised, "and put it on paper."

"Put what on paper?" I asked, puzzled.

"Your plan for fighting these things you say you just went through. Think it out construc-tively. It won't be easy. You can't take a picture of a white salesman, waiter or ticket seller and just say they are prejudiced. That isn't enough. You've got to verbalize the experience first, then find logical ways to express it in pictures. The right words too are important; they should underscore your photographs. Think in terms of images and words. They can be mighty pow-erful when they are fitted together properly." **H**

I went home that evening and wrote. I wrote of just about every injustice that I had ever experienced. Kansas, Minnesota, Chicago, New York and Washington were all forged together in the heat of the blast.

Images and words images and words images and words—I fell asleep trying to arrange an acceptable marriage of them.

Stryker read what I had written with a troubled face. I watched his eyes move over the lines, his brows furrow from time to time. When he had finished we both sat quietly for a few minutes. "You've had quite a time," he finally said, "but you have to simplify all this material. It would take many years and all the photographers on the staff to fulfill what you have put down here. Come outside; I want to show you something." He took me over to the file and opened a drawer marked "Dorothea

G **Literary Perspectives** Political Context What political realities is Parks beginning to understand?

H **Reading Focus** Author's Purpose Why do you think Parks chose to include these words by Stryker?

Lange."[10] "Spend the rest of the day going through this set of pictures. Each day take on another drawer. And go back and write more specifically about your visual approach to things."

For several weeks I went through hundreds of photographs by Lange, Russell Lee, Jack Delano, Carl Mydans, John Vachon, Arthur Rothstein, Ben Shahn, Walker Evans, John Collier and others. The disaster of the thirties was at my fingertips: the gutted cotton fields, the eroded farmland, the crumbling South, the unending lines of dispossessed migrants,[11] the pitiful shacks, the shameful city ghettos, the breadlines and bonus marchers, the gaunt faces of men, women and children caught up in the tragedy; the horrifying spectacles of sky blackened with locusts, and swirling dust and towns flooded with muddy rivers. There were some no doubt who laid these tragedies to God. But research accompanying these stark photographs accused man himself—especially the lords of the land. In their greed and passion for wealth, they had gutted the earth for cotton; overworked the farms; exploited the tenant farmers and sharecroppers who, broken, took to the highways with their families in search of work. They owned the ghettos as well as the impoverished souls who inhabited them. No, the indictment[12] was against man, not God; the proof

was there in those ordinary steel files. It was a raw slice of contemporary America—clear, hideous and beautifully detailed in images and words. I began to get the point.

For some time now I had passed the cafeteria in the building without entering. It was not that they wouldn't serve me, because I saw other Negroes eating there. It was the sight of them huddled in the rear that turned me from the door. I knew that I would eventually eat there—but never in the back. Since I was more or less Stryker's responsibility I didn't want to saddle him with any more problems. The

Self-portrait by Gordon Parks (1948). Photograph.

---

10. **Dorothea Lange:** well-known documentary photographer, famous for her photos of the Great Depression.
11. **dispossessed migrants:** people who have lost their homes and who travel around looking for work.
12. **indictment** (ihn DYT muhnt): formal accusation of wrongdoing.

Vocabulary **eroded** (ih ROHD ihd) *v.* used as *adj.*: worn away. **exploited** (ehk SPLOYT ihd) *v.*: used selfishly for one's own advantage.

agency was already under fire from certain politicians who opposed Roosevelt's New Deal policies.[13] Nevertheless, I knew that when the time came I would not take a seat in the rear. **❶**

The test came on the day I met John Vachon. He was the first of the photographers I got to know. He too was from Minnesota and we became friends right away. When he invited me to eat with him that afternoon I was at last deprived of any alibi; so I accepted his invitation. The face of the cafeteria manager turned as red as his hair when we sat down together, but he said nothing. He had decided to lay the problem in Stryker's lap, I found out later that day. But his complaint was met with stern rebuff. "There is no rule that says he has to eat in the rear," Stryker said icily. Then when I entered several days later, the manager openly suggested that I take one of the tables in the rear. But I refused even to answer him. He never bothered me again but I began to collect stares from some of the Negro patrons. One gray-haired, light-skinned Negro gentleman approached me in the corridor one day. "Young man," he said, "you're going to cause trouble for all of us."

"Why?" I asked politely.

"Eating out of your place in the cafeteria. I've eaten in there for nearly twenty years, right back there in the rear, and you should do the same."

"Then I'm very sorry for you, sir," I answered, "but I won't ever eat back there."

"What's the matter? Are you any better than the rest of us Negroes?"

"No, sir. It's just that I don't feel that the whites are any better than me. I won't let them make a place for me." **❿**

He looked at me for a moment. Hopelessness was in his eyes. "I just don't understand you young Negroes any more," he said and walked off shaking his head. And I was honestly sad for this old man. But I could no more understand him than he could me; we were centuries apart. And there came a time, that same year, when he ate there in the rear alone. One day someone told me that he had died. And I thought about him during the rest of that week: he was part of the old order that was passing on, and I didn't know how to feel about his death. **Ⓚ**

Using my camera effectively against intolerance was not so easy as I had assumed it would be. One evening, when Stryker and I were in the office alone, I confessed this to him. "Then at least you have learned the most important lesson," he said. He thought for a moment, got up and looked down the corridor, then called me to his side. There was a Negro charwoman[14] mopping the floor. "Go have a talk with her before you go home this evening. See what she has to say about life and things. You might find her interesting."

This was a strange suggestion, but after he had gone I went through the empty

---

13. **New Deal policies:** domestic program created by President Franklin D. Roosevelt to pull the country out of the Depression. It lifted many Americans out of economic hardship.

14. **charwoman:** cleaning woman.

---

❶ Literary Focus Memoir and Mood Does the description of the cafeteria situation create a mood similar to that of an earlier scene? Explain.

❿ Reading Focus Author's Purpose How is Parks's purpose in writing this memoir similar to his purpose in integrating the cafeteria?

Ⓚ Literary Perspectives Political Context Parks and the old man have different responses to the issue of racial inequality. Contrast their perspectives.

Analyzing Visuals **Viewing and Interpreting** This photograph is titled *American Gothic,* after a famous painting by Grant Wood of the same name. Wood's painting depicts a farmer, who is holding a pitchfork, and his unmarried daughter in front of a farmhouse, and it came to represent the rural values of the American Midwest. From what you have learned about Parks so far, why do you think he chose to use the same title for his photograph?

American Gothic (Ella Watson, a government charwoman in Washington, D.C., standing in front of an American flag) by Gordon Parks. Photograph.

building searching for her. I found her in a notary public's office and introduced myself. She was a tall spindly woman with sharp features. Her hair was swept back from graying temples; a sharp intelligence shone in the eyes behind the steel-rimmed glasses. We started off awkwardly, neither of us knowing my reason for starting the conversation. At first it was a meaningless exchange of words. Then, as if a dam had broken within her, she began to spill out her life story. It was a pitiful one. She had struggled alone after her mother had died and her father had been killed by a lynch mob.[15] She had gone through high school, married and become pregnant. Her husband was accidentally shot to death two days before the daughter was born. By the time the daughter was eighteen she had given birth to two illegitimate children, dying two weeks after the second child's birth. What's more, the first child had been stricken with paralysis a year before its mother died. Now this woman was bringing up these grandchildren on a salary hardly suitable for one person. **(L)**

"Who takes care of them while you are at work?" I asked after a long silence.

> "This woman has done you a great service. I hope you understand this." I did understand.

"Different neighbors," she said, her heavily veined hands tightening about the mop handle.

"Can I photograph you?" The question had come out of an elaboration of thoughts. I was escaping the humiliation of not being able to help.

"I don't mind," she said.

My first photograph of her was unsubtle. I overdid it and posed her, Grant Wood[16] style, before the American flag, a broom in one hand, a mop in the other, staring straight into the camera. Stryker took one look at it the next day and fell speechless. **(M)**

"Well, how do you like it?" I asked eagerly.

He just smiled and shook his head. "Well?" I insisted.

"Keep working with her. Let's see what happens," he finally replied. I followed her for nearly a month—into her home, her church and wherever she went. "You're learning," Stryker admitted when I laid the photographs out before him late one evening. "You're showing you can involve yourself in other people. This woman has done you a great service. I hope you understand this." I did understand. **(N)**

---

15. **lynch mob:** a crowd that puts someone to death, usually by hanging, without a lawful trial.

16. **Grant Wood** (1891–1942): American artist known for his paintings of the Midwest.

(L) Literary Focus Memoir and Mood Which words best describe the mood evoked by the charwoman's story?

(M) Literary Perspectives Political Context What political statement or message might Parks be making here?

(N) Reading Focus Author's Purpose What purpose of the memoir does the final paragraph clarify?

Applying Your Skills

 **RA.L.10.8** Analyze the author's use of point of view, mood and tone. **RA.L.10.7** Recognize how irony is used in a literary text. *Also covered* **RA.I.10.1; VO.10.3; WA.10.1.b**

from **A Choice of Weapons**

Respond and Think Critically

Reading Focus

Quick Check

1. Once Parks becomes familiar with Washington, D.C., what are his goals?
2. Briefly summarize what life was like for African Americans in Washington, D.C., in the 1940s.

Read with a Purpose

3. What surprises Parks most about Washington, D.C.? What is the biggest challenge he faces?

Reading Skills: Identifying an Author's Purpose

4. Review the chart you completed as you read the selection. Then, write a few sentences describing how Parks accomplishes all three purposes listed on the chart.

Purpose	Detail from Text
to inform	
to persuade	
to entertain	

✔ Vocabulary Check

Decide whether each of the following statements is *true* or *false,* and briefly explain your answer.

5. A **trivial** detail is very important.
6. To **exasperate** is to irritate or disturb.
7. Something that is **eroded** is worn away.
8. If you **exploited** friends, you used them.

Literary Focus

Literary Analysis

9. **Evaluate** What are two techniques Parks uses to fight the racism he encounters? Explain how successful he is in each case.
10. **Literary Perspectives** What does Parks's response to the treatment he receives in Washington, D.C., reveal about his beliefs?

Literary Skills: Memoir and Mood

11. **Analyze** In the memoir, Parks describes his response to discrimination. How do his responses affect the mood of the memoir?

Literary Skills Review: Irony

12. **Identify** Recall that **irony** is a contrast between what is expected and what actually happens. Find an example of irony in "A Choice of Weapons." Explain what makes the situation ironic.

Writing Focus

Think as a Reader/Writer

Use It in Your Writing As you read, you noted examples of Parks's interior monologue. Now, think of a story or film and write a two- or three-paragraph memoir about an event from a character's point of view. Work the character's interior monologue into your description.

 What Do **You Think Now** Think about the title of the memoir. How can a camera be used as a weapon?

Typhoid Fever
by **Frank McCourt**

What Do **You** **Think**

Are our strongest memories formed by happy or sad events? Why do you think that is so?

 QuickWrite

What do you remember from your childhood that was important, unusual, or funny? Write a few sentences about an early memory from the perspective of your childhood self.

Reader/Writer Notebook

Use your **RWN** to complete the activities for this selection.

OH **RA.L.10.8** Analyze the author's use of point of view, mood and tone. **RA.I.10.1** Identify and understand organizational patterns and techniques, including repetition of ideas, syntax and word choice, that authors use to accomplish their purpose and reach their intended audience.

Literary Focus

Style: Diction, Tone, and Voice Writers distinguish themselves by their particular use of language, or **style.** Style includes

- a writer's **diction** (the words he or she chooses)
- the complexity or simplicity of the writer's **sentence structure** (how the writer puts words together)
- the **tone** (or attitude) the writer takes toward his or her subject
- **voice** (a writer's distinct use of language)

In his memoirs, Frank McCourt creates a unique voice to tell his painful story of growing up poor in Ireland. Read a passage aloud, and you'll hear McCourt's strong, true voice spring to life.

Reading Focus

Evaluating Word Choice In "Typhoid Fever," McCourt's words highlight the differences between characters. Some speak formally, and others speak in colloquial, informal language. Some characters seem to say what they mean; others don't. Examining McCourt's word choice will give you insight into his attitude toward these characters.

Into Action: As you read "Typhoid Fever," use a chart like the one below to record examples of word choice for each character's speech.

Character	Examples of Word Choice
Patricia Madigan	"You won't be able to stop marching and saluting."

Writing Focus

Think as a Reader/Writer

Find It in Your Reading Some of McCourt's words may be unfamiliar because they are from a **dialect,** or variation of English. For example, McCourt refers to his mother as "Mam." As you read, note these words and their meanings in your *Reader/Writer Notebook*.

TechFocus As you read, think about how each of the characters might describe himself or herself. How could you create a video about these characters? What <u>components</u> would it include?

Vocabulary

internal (ihn TUR nuhl) *adj.:* on the inside. *Many diseases affect internal organs.*

relapse (REE laps) *n.:* process of slipping back into a former state. *The nurse thinks that singing and talking might lead to Frankie's relapse.*

induced (ihn DOOST) *v.* used as *adj.:* persuaded; led on. *Induced by Frankie, Seamus learned the rest of "The Highwayman."*

potent (POH tuhnt) *adj.:* powerful. *The potent words of Shakespeare and Alfred Noyes help Frankie find humor and beauty in an otherwise dismal place.*

clamoring (KLAM uhr ihng) *v.* used as *adj.:* crying out; demanding. *Frankie imagined a group of sick children clamoring for his chocolate bar.*

Language Coach

Denotations/Connotations The dictionary definition of a word is the word's **denotation.** A word's **connotation** is the feeling or association attached to it. Think about the connotations of these Vocabulary words. Answer these questions in your *Reader/Writer Notebook:*

- Would extremely hungry people be *asking* or *clamoring* for food? Why?
- Would the most effective medicine be *potent* or *strong*? Why?

Learn It Online

For a preview of this autobiography, see the video introduction on:

go.hrw.com   L10-483

Frank McCourt
(1930–   )

Pulitzer Prize WINNER

Across the Ocean and Back

Frank McCourt was born in Brooklyn, New York, to poor Irish immigrants. When he was four, his family, hoping to escape their poverty, moved to Ireland. Unfortunately, they found themselves in even worse conditions than those they had fled. McCourt's father eventually abandoned his family, and they were left to struggle on their own.

At age nineteen, McCourt returned to New York City, where he went to school and later joined the army. Eventually, he began teaching writing to high school students. He finally published his first book, *Angela's Ashes,* when he was sixty-six. The book dominated the bestseller lists, won the Pulitzer Prize and the National Book Critics Circle Award, and was made into a movie.

"We Were Street Kids"

A sequel, *'Tis* (1999), recounts McCourt's life as a young man in New York City, where he held a variety of jobs—from housekeeping at a hotel to acting to unloading meat trucks.

When he asked how he found such humor in his poverty-stricken childhood, McCourt replied: "When you have nothing—no TV, no radio, no music—you have only the language. So you use it. We were street kids—we saw the absurdity and laughed at it. And we were fools; we were always dreaming. Bacon and eggs—we dreamed of that."

Think About the Writer

Why do you think McCourt waited until he was sixty-six to write about his childhood?

Build Background

Angela's Ashes is Frank McCourt's gritty, moving memoir of growing up in Limerick, Ireland, in the 1930s and 1940s. McCourt's family lived in a filthy, overcrowded slum, and bacterial diseases such as typhoid fever and diphtheria were common.

Because both diseases spread easily, people with these illnesses are quarantined. In Ireland they were isolated in "fever hospitals." Most of these hospitals were run by the Catholic Church and staffed by nuns. McCourt caught typhoid fever at age ten and was sent to a fever hospital.

Preview the Selection

This section of McCourt's autobiography introduces you to **Frankie,** Frank McCourt as a ten-year-old with typhoid fever. Frankie is staying in a fever hospital. There, he befriends **Patricia Madigan,** a thirteen-year-old girl who is in the room next to his, and **Seamus,** one of the hospital staff members.

Children on Atlantic Avenue in Bedford Stuyvesant, Brooklyn, New York, 1939.

Typhoid Fever

from Angela's Ashes

by **Frank McCourt**

The room next to me is empty till one morning a girl's voice says, Yoo hoo, who's there?

I'm not sure if she's talking to me or someone in the room beyond.

Yoo hoo, boy with the typhoid, are you awake?

I am.

Are you better?

I am.

Well, why are you here?

I don't know. I'm still in the bed. They stick needles in me and give me medicine.

What do you look like?

I wonder, What kind of a question is that? I don't know what to tell her. **Ⓐ**

Yoo hoo, are you there, typhoid boy?

I am.

What's your name?

Frank.

That's a good name. My name is Patricia Madigan. How old are you?

Ten.

Oh. She sounds disappointed.

But I'll be eleven in August, next month.

Well, that's better than ten. I'll be fourteen in September. Do you want to know why I'm in the Fever Hospital?

I do.

I have diphtheria and something else.

What's something else?

They don't know. They think I have a disease from foreign parts because my father used to be in Africa. I nearly died. Are you going to tell me what you look like?

I have black hair.

You and millions.

I have brown eyes with bits of green that's called hazel.

You and thousands.

I have stitches on the back of my right hand and my two feet where they put in the soldier's blood.

Oh, did they?

They did.

You won't be able to stop marching and saluting.

There's a swish of habit and click of beads and then Sister Rita's voice. Now, now, what's this? There's to be no talking between two rooms

---

Ⓐ **Literary Focus** **Style** What impression of the narrator do you get from these first few lines? Explain.

especially when it's a boy and a girl. Do you hear me, Patricia?

I do, Sister.

Do you hear me, Francis?

I do, Sister.

You could be giving thanks for your two remarkable recoveries. You could be saying the rosary.[1] You could be reading *The Little Messenger of the Sacred Heart*[2] that's beside your beds. Don't let me come back and find you talking.

She comes into my room and wags her finger at me. Especially you, Francis, after thousands of boys prayed for you at the Confraternity.[3] Give thanks, Francis, give thanks. **B**

She leaves and there's silence for awhile. Then Patricia whispers, Give thanks, Francis, give thanks, and say your rosary, Francis, and I laugh so hard a nurse runs in to see if I'm all right. She's a very stern nurse from the County Kerry and she frightens me. What's this, Francis? Laughing? What is there to laugh about? Are you and that Madigan girl talking? I'll report you to Sister Rita. There's to be no laughing for you could be doing serious damage to your internal apparatus.

She plods out and Patricia whispers again in a heavy Kerry accent, No laughing, Francis, you could be doin' serious damage to your internal apparatus. Say your rosary, Francis, and pray for your internal apparatus.

Mam visits me on Thursdays. I'd like to see my father, too, but I'm out of danger, crisis time is over, and I'm allowed only one visitor. Besides, she says, he's back at work at Rank's Flour Mills and please God this job will last a while with the war on and the English desperate for flour. She brings me a chocolate bar and that proves Dad is working. She could never afford it on the dole.[4] He sends me notes. He tells me my brothers are all praying for me, that I should be a good boy, obey the doctors, the nuns, the nurses, and don't forget to say my prayers. He's sure St. Jude pulled me through the crisis because he's the patron saint of desperate cases and I was indeed a desperate case.

Patricia says she has two books by her bed. One is a poetry book and that's the one she loves. The other is a short history of England and do I want it? She gives it to Seamus, the man who mops the floors every day, and he brings it to me. He says, I'm not supposed to be bringing anything from a dipteria[5] room to a typhoid room with all the germs flying around and hiding between the pages and if you ever catch dipteria on top of the typhoid they'll know and I'll lose my good job and be out on the street singing patriotic songs with a tin cup in my hand, which I could easily do because there isn't a song ever written about Ireland's sufferings I don't know and a few songs about the joy of whiskey too. **C**

Oh, yes, he knows Roddy McCorley. He'll sing it for me right enough but he's barely into the first verse when the Kerry nurse rushes in.

---

1. **rosary** (ROH zuhr ee): set of prayers that Roman Catholics recite while holding a string of beads.
2. *The Little Messenger of the Sacred Heart:* religious publication for children.
3. **Confraternity:** here, a religious organization made up of nonclergy, or laypersons.

---

4. **dole** (dohl): government payment to unemployed people; also, money or food given to those in need.
5. **dipteria**: dialect for *diphtheria*.

B **Reading Focus** Evaluating Word Choice In what way do repetition and word choice reveal Sister Rita's character?

C **Literary Focus** Style Seamus is a colorful character. How are his diction and dialect different from those of the others? What attitude does McCourt seem to have toward him? Explain.

Vocabulary **internal** (ihn TUR nuhl) *adj.:* on the inside.

What's this, Seamus? Singing? Of all the people in this hospital you should know the rules against singing. I have a good mind to report you to Sister Rita.

Ah, don't do that, nurse.

Very well, Seamus. I'll let it go this one time. You know the singing could lead to a relapse in these patients.

When she leaves he whispers he'll teach me a few songs because singing is good for passing the time when you're by yourself in a typhoid room. He says Patricia is a lovely girl the way she often gives him sweets from the parcel her mother sends every fortnight.[6] He stops mopping the floor and calls to Patricia in the next room, I was telling Frankie you're a lovely girl, Patricia, and she says, You're a lovely man, Seamus. He smiles because he's an old man of forty and he never had children but the ones he can talk to here in the Fever Hospital. He says, Here's the book, Frankie. Isn't it a great pity you have to be reading all about England after all they did to us, that there isn't a history of Ireland to be had in this hospital.

The book tells me all about King Alfred and William the Conqueror and all the kings and queens down to Edward, who had to wait forever for his mother, Victoria, to die before he could be king. The book has the first bit of Shakespeare I ever read.

> I do believe, *induced by potent*
>   *circumstances,*
> That thou art mine enemy.

---

6. **fortnight:** chiefly British for "two weeks."

Vocabulary **relapse** (REE laps) *n.*: process of slipping back into a former state.
induced (ihn DOOST) *v.* used as *adj.*: persuaded; led on.
potent (POH tuhnt) *adj.*: powerful.

Diphtheria and Typhoid

Dr. Bela Schick administering diphtheria test at Mt. Sinai Hospital, January 25, 1925, New York.

Diphtheria and typhoid are severe and often deadly infections. The diphtheria bacterium infects the nose and throat and is spread through coughing and sneezing. The illness is so contagious that doctors place infected people in quarantine (isolation from non-infected people). Common symptoms of diphtheria include fever, fatigue, chills, and a sore throat. In serious cases the infection can attack the heart and nerves, leading to heart inflammation and paralysis, and ultimately death.

Unlike diphtheria, typhoid fever is caused by contaminated food or water, and it is not contagious. It is, however, life threatening and kills thousands of people every year. The most common symptom of typhoid is a persistent, high fever; untreated, it wastes the entire body. Today, immunizations are available for both diseases.

Ask Yourself

How does knowledge about these illnesses give you further insight into how Patricia and Frankie interact?

The history writer says this is what Catherine, who is a wife of Henry the Eighth, says to Cardinal Wolsey, who is trying to have her head cut off. I don't know what it means and I don't care because it's Shakespeare and it's like having jewels in my mouth when I say the words. If I had a whole book of Shakespeare they could keep me in the hospital for a year.

Patricia says she doesn't know what induced means or potent circumstances and she doesn't care about Shakespeare, she has her poetry book and she reads to me from beyond the wall a poem about an owl and a pussycat that went to sea in a green boat with honey and money and

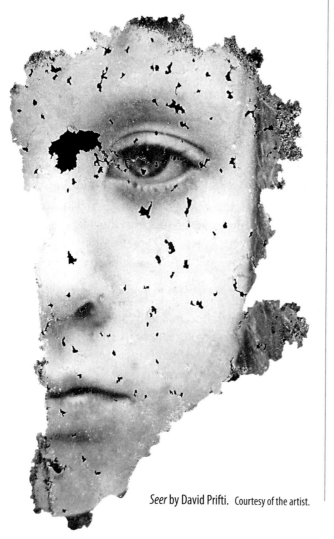

Seer by David Prifti. Courtesy of the artist.

it makes no sense and when I say that Patricia gets huffy and says that's the last poem she'll ever read to me. She says I'm always reciting the lines from Shakespeare and they make no sense either. Seamus stops mopping again and tells us we shouldn't be fighting over poetry because we'll have enough to fight about when we grow up and get married. Patricia says she's sorry and I'm sorry too so she reads me part of another poem[7] which I have to remember so I can say it back to her early in the morning or late at night when there are no nuns or nurses about,

The wind was a torrent of darkness among the
*   gusty trees,*
The moon was a ghostly galleon tossed upon
*   cloudy seas,*
The road was a ribbon of moonlight over the
*   purple moor,*
And the highwayman came riding—
*   Riding—riding—*
The highwayman came riding, up to the old inn
*   door.*

He'd a French cocked-hat on his forehead, a
*   bunch of lace at his chin,*
A coat of the claret velvet, and breeches of brown
*   doeskin,*
They fitted with never a wrinkle. His boots were
*   up to the thigh.*
And he rode with a jeweled twinkle,
*   His pistol butts a-twinkle,*
His rapier hilt a-twinkle, under the jeweled sky. **D**

---

7. **reads . . . poem:** The reference is to "The Highwayman" by the British poet Alfred Noyes (1880–1958). The poem is based on a true story about a highwayman who fell in love with an innkeeper's daughter in eighteenth-century England. Highwaymen, who robbed wealthy stagecoach passengers, were at that time popular romantic figures.

D **Literary Focus** **Style** How is the style of the poem different from the style of the story?

Every day I can't wait for the doctors and nurses to leave me alone so I can learn a new verse from Patricia and find out what's happening to the highwayman and the landlord's red-lipped daughter. I love the poem because it's exciting and almost as good as my two lines of Shakespeare. The redcoats are after the highwayman because they know he told her, I'll come to thee by moonlight, though hell should bar the way.

I'd love to do that myself, come by moonlight for Patricia in the next room not giving a hoot though hell should bar the way. She's ready to read the last few verses when in comes the nurse from Kerry shouting at her, shouting at me, I told ye there was to be no talking between rooms. Diphtheria is never allowed to talk to typhoid and visa versa. I warned ye. And she calls out, Seamus, take this one. Take the by. Sister Rita said one more word out of him and upstairs with him. We gave ye a warning to stop the blathering but ye wouldn't. Take the by, Seamus, take him.

Ah, now, nurse, sure isn't he harmless. 'Tis only a bit o' poetry.

Take that by, Seamus, take him at once.

He bends over me and whispers, Ah, I'm sorry, Frankie. Here's your English history book. He slips the book under my shirt and lifts me from the bed. He whispers that I'm a feather. I try to see Patricia when we pass through her room but all I can make out is a blur of dark head on a pillow.

Sister Rita stops us in the hall to tell me I'm a great disappointment to her, that she expected me to be a good boy after what God had done for me, after all the prayers said by hundreds of boys at the Confraternity, after all the care from the nuns and nurses of the Fever Hospital, after the way they let my mother and father in to see me, a thing rarely allowed, and this is how I repaid them lying in the bed reciting silly poetry back and forth with Patricia Madigan knowing very well there was a ban on all talk between typhoid and diphtheria. She says I'll have plenty of time to reflect on my sins in the big ward upstairs and I should beg God's forgiveness for my disobedience reciting a pagan[8] English poem about a thief on a horse and a maiden with red lips who commits a terrible sin when I could have been praying or reading the life of a saint. She made it her business to read that poem so she did and I'd be well advised to tell the priest in confession. **E**

The Kerry nurse follows us upstairs gasping and holding on to the banister. She tells me I better not get the notion she'll be running up to this part of the world every time I have a little pain or a twinge.

There are twenty beds in the ward, all white, all empty. The nurse tells Seamus put me at the far end of the ward against the wall to make sure I don't talk to anyone who might be passing the door, which is very unlikely since there isn't another soul on this whole floor. She tells Seamus this was the fever ward during the Great Famine[9] long ago and only God knows how many died here brought in too late for anything but a wash before they were buried and there are stories of cries and moans in the far reaches of the night. She says 'twould break your heart to think of what the English did to us, that if they

---

8. **pagan** (PAY guhn): here, non-Christian.
9. **Great Famine:** refers to a terrible famine in Ireland from 1845 to 1849, when failed potato crops resulted in the starvation and death of about one million people.

E **Literary Focus** Style How is the author's attitude toward Sister Rita revealed in this passage?

didn't put the blight[10] on the potato they didn't do much to take it off. No pity. No feeling at all for the people that died in this very ward, children suffering and dying here while the English feasted on roast beef and guzzled the best of wine in their big houses, little children with their mouths all green from trying to eat the grass in the fields beyond, God bless us and save us and guard us from future famines.

Seamus says 'twas a terrible thing indeed and he wouldn't want to be walking these halls in the dark with all the little green mouths gaping at him. The nurse takes my temperature, 'Tis up a bit, have a good sleep for yourself now that you're away from the chatter with Patricia Madigan below who will never know a gray hair.

She shakes her head at Seamus and he gives her a sad shake back.

Nurses and nuns never think you know what they're talking about. If you're ten going on eleven you're supposed to be simple like my uncle Pat Sheehan who was dropped on his head. You can't ask questions. You can't show you understand what the nurse said about Patricia Madigan, that she's going to die, and you can't show you want to cry over this girl who taught you a lovely poem which the nun says is bad. **F**

The nurse tells Seamus she has to go and he's to sweep the lint from under my bed and mop up a bit around the ward. Seamus tells me she's a right oul' witch for running to Sister Rita and complaining about the poem going between the two rooms, that you can't catch a disease from a poem unless it's love ha ha and that's not bloody likely when you're what? ten going on eleven? He never heard the likes of it,

a little fella shifted upstairs for saying a poem and he has a good mind to go to the *Limerick Leader* and tell them print the whole thing except he has this job and he'd lose it if ever Sister Rita found out. Anyway, Frankie, you'll be outa here one of these fine days and you can read all the poetry you want though I don't know about Patricia below, I don't know about Patricia, God help us.

He knows about Patricia in two days because she got out of the bed to go to the lavatory when she was supposed to use a bedpan and collapsed and died in the lavatory. Seamus is mopping the floor and there are tears on his cheeks and he's saying, 'Tis a dirty rotten thing to die in a lavatory when you're lovely in yourself. She told me she was sorry she had you reciting that poem and getting you shifted from the room, Frankie. She said 'twas all her fault. **G**

It wasn't, Seamus.

I know and didn't I tell her that.

Patricia is gone and I'll never know what happened to the highwayman and Bess, the landlord's daughter. I ask Seamus but he doesn't know any poetry at all especially English poetry. He knew an Irish poem once but it was about fairies and had no sign of a highwayman in it. Still he'll ask the men in his local pub where there's always someone reciting something and he'll bring it back to me. Won't I be busy meanwhile reading my short history of England and finding out all about their perfidy.[11] That's what Seamus says, perfidy, and I don't know what it means and he doesn't know what it means but if it's something the English do it must be terrible.

---

10. **blight** (blyt): kind of plant disease.

---

11. **perfidy** (PUHR fuh dee): treachery; betrayal.

F **Literary Focus** Style In this passage, McCourt channels the frustrations of his youth. What words does he repeat, and what effect does that repetition have on you?

G **Reading Focus** Evaluating Word Choice What words and phrases create a vivid portrait of Seamus in the last two paragraphs?

He comes three times a week to mop the floor and the nurse is there every morning to take my temperature and pulse. The doctor listens to my chest with the thing hanging from his neck. They all say, And how's our little soldier today? A girl with a blue dress brings meals three times a day and never talks to me. Seamus says she's not right in the head so don't say a word to her.

The July days are long and I fear the dark. There are only two ceiling lights in the ward and they're switched off when the tea tray is taken away and the nurse gives me pills. The nurse tells me go to sleep but I can't because I see people in the nineteen beds in the ward all dying and green around their mouths where they tried to eat grass and moaning for soup Protestant soup any soup and I cover my face with the pillow hoping they won't come and stand around the bed clawing at me and howling for bits of the chocolate bar my mother brought last week. **Ⓗ**

No, she didn't bring it. She had to send it in because I can't have any more visitors. Sister Rita tells me a visit to the Fever Hospital is a privilege and after my bad behavior with Patricia Madigan and that poem I can't have the privilege anymore. She says I'll be going home in a few weeks and my job is to concentrate on getting better and learn to walk again after being in bed for six weeks and I can get out of bed tomorrow after breakfast. I don't know why she says I have to learn how to walk when I've been walking since I

Ⓗ Literary Focus Style In this paragraph, part of Frankie's narrative forms one long sentence with thoughts connected by the word *and*. Why do you think McCourt chose to do this?

Analyzing Visuals Viewing and Interpreting Find a passage in the story that matches the mood of the sculpture. Explain your choice.

Amanda Pox by David Prifti.
Courtesy of the artist.

was a baby but when the nurse stands me by the side of the bed I fall to the floor and the nurse laughs, See, you're a baby again.

I practice walking from bed to bed back and forth back and forth. I don't want to be a baby. I don't want to be in this empty ward with no Patricia and no highwayman and no red-lipped landlord's daughter. I don't want the ghosts of children with green mouths pointing bony fingers at me and clamoring for bits of my chocolate bar.

Seamus says a man in his pub knew all the verses of the highwayman poem and it has a very sad end. Would I like him to say it because he never learned how to read and he had to carry the poem in his head? He stands in the middle of the ward leaning on his mop and recites,

> I don't want the ghosts of children with green mouths pointing bony fingers at me and clamoring for bits of my chocolate bar.

Tlot-tlot, *in the frosty silence!* Tlot-tlot, *in the echoing night!*
Nearer he came and nearer! Her face was like a light!
Her eyes grew wide for a moment; she drew one last deep breath,
Then her fingers moved in the moonlight,
Her musket shattered the moonlight,
Shattered her breast in the moonlight and warned him—with her death.

He hears the shot and escapes but when he learns at dawn how Bess died he goes into a rage and returns for revenge only to be shot down by the redcoats.

> *Blood-red were his spurs in the golden noon;*
> *wine-red was his velvet coat,*
> *When they shot him down on the highway,*
> *Down like a dog on the highway,*
> *And he lay in his blood on the highway, with a bunch of lace at his throat.*

Seamus wipes his sleeve across his face and sniffles. He says, There was no call at all to shift you up here away from Patricia when you didn't even know what happened to the highwayman and Bess. 'Tis a very sad story and when I said it to my wife she wouldn't stop crying the whole night till we went to bed. She said there was no call for them redcoats to shoot that highwayman, they are responsible for half the troubles of the world and they never had any pity on the Irish, either. Now if you want to know any more poems, Frankie, tell me and I'll get them from the pub and bring 'em back in my head.

Vocabulary **clamoring** (KLAM uhr ihng) *v.* used as *adj.:* crying out; demanding.

Applying Your Skills

OH **RA.L.10.8** Analyze the author's use of point of view, mood and tone. *Also covered* **RA.L.10.15.** **RA.I.10.1; WA.10.4.d**

Typhoid Fever

Respond and Think Critically

Reading Focus

Quick Check

1. Why are Frankie and Patricia in the hospital? How do they become friends?

2. Why is Frankie moved to another floor?

Read with a Purpose

3. How does Frankie acquire his love of poetry?

Reading Skills: Evaluating Word Choice

4. Add another column to your word choice chart. In this column, identify McCourt's **tone,** or attitude, toward each character.

Character	Example	Tone
Patricia Madigan	"You won't be able to stop marching and saluting."	informal and casual; shows Patricia as sharp witted, friendly, and fearless
Seamus		

Literary Focus

Literary Analysis

5. **Analyze** The nurse from Kerry asks, "What is there to laugh about?" What *is* there to laugh about in this story? What role can humor play in a sad story?

6. **Evaluate** According to Seamus, there is a similarity between what has happened to the highwayman and what has happened to Frankie. What is it? Do you agree with Seamus's conclusion? Why or why not?

Literary Skills: Style

7. **Analyze** Using details from the story, write a few sentences analyzing the tone of the memoir. How does the author's tone help create McCourt's voice?

8. **Analyze** Describe how the author's use of diction and sentence structure contributes to the style of the work.

Literary Skills Review: Indirect Characterization

9. **Evaluate** In **direct characterization** the author states what a character is like. Using **indirect characterization,** an author can describe a character's speech, appearance, thoughts, feelings, and actions. The author can also show what other people think of the character. How does McCourt use indirect characterization to describe Seamus? Cite examples from the text.

Writing Focus

Think as a Reader/Writer

Use It in Your Writing As you read, you noted examples of dialect in the autobiography in your *Reader/Writer Notebook*. Write a brief essay explaining how dialect brings McCourt's characters to life.

 What Do You Think Now? How will Frankie remember Patricia Madigan—with sadness, happiness, or a mixture of the two? Explain.

Applying Your Skills

Typhoid Fever

Vocabulary Development

Vocabulary Check

Match each Vocabulary word with its definition.

1. **relapse**
2. **clamoring**
3. **induced**
4. **potent**
5. **internal**

a. crying out; demanding
b. persuaded
c. on the inside
d. process of slipping back into a former state
e. powerful

Vocabulary Skills: Antonyms

An **antonym** is a word that means the opposite (or nearly the opposite) of another word. Words can have many antonyms. For example, one antonym of *excited* is *calm*. Another antonym is *bored*. You can use a thesaurus to find antonyms as well as **synonyms**—words that have similar meanings.

Your Turn

Choose the best antonym for each word in capital letters. Remember that an **antonym** is a word with the opposite meaning of another word.

1. INDUCED: (a) persuaded (b) attempted (c) discouraged
2. POTENT: (a) impossible (b) weak (c) strong
3. CLAMORING: (a) creating (b) whispering (c) opening
4. RELAPSE: (a) deterioration (b) improvement (c) forgetfulness
5. INTERNAL: (a) central (b) interior (c) external

Language Coach

Denotations/Connotations Choose four words (not Vocabulary words) from the selection that have strong connotations. In your *Reader/Writer Notebook,* write the denotation and connotation of each word.

Academic Vocabulary

Talk About . . .

Dialogue is a major <u>component</u> of this excerpt. McCourt's unusual <u>technique</u> of using dialogue with no punctuation marks helps the characters become the center of the story. If McCourt had written a newspaper article instead of an autobiography with dialogue, would the story have a similar effect? Why or why not? Discuss your ideas with a partner, using the underlined Academic Vocabulary words in your discussion.

Learn It Online
Sharpen your word skills with *WordSharp*:

go.hrw.com   L10-494   **Go**

Grammar Link

Usage and Style: Creating Voice

To help create the distinctive voice of his memoir, McCourt draws on **informal** or **nonstandard usage** to replace some **standard usage**—grammatically correct and appropriate language. He does so to help you sense that you are overhearing someone's thoughts. He also wants to represent realistic **dialect,** the characteristic way people talk in different regions (in this case, Ireland). To appreciate the effect, read these passages aloud.

1. "Patricia says she doesn't know what induced means or potent circumstances and she doesn't care about Shakespeare, she has her poetry book and she reads to me from beyond the wall a poem about an owl and a pussycat that went to sea in a green boat with honey and money and it makes no sense and when I say that Patricia gets huffy and says that's the last poem she'll ever read to me."

2. "We gave ye a warning to stop the blathering but ye wouldn't. Take the by, Seamus, take him.
    Ah, now, nurse, sure isn't he harmless. 'Tis only a bit o' poetry."

Your Turn

Writing Applications Suppose you are an editor in the publishing house that has accepted McCourt's manuscript. Your job is to "clean up" his writing, to "correct" it so that it will conform to standard English usage. Revise the above passages by correcting spelling and punctuating sentences for clarity. Then, compare your edited manuscripts in class. What has happened to McCourt's voice? Are the passages still compelling? Discuss.

VO.10.3 Infer the literal and figurative meaning of words and phrases and discuss the function of figurative language, including metaphors, similes, idioms and puns. *Also covered* **VO.10.6; WA.10.1.c; WA.10.2; WA.10.4.d; WP.10.15**

CHOICES

As you respond to the Choices, use these **Academic Vocabulary** words as appropriate: component, subsequent, equivalent, and technique.

REVIEW
Write a Newspaper Article

Imagine that you are a reporter from a local paper and that you are writing a feature about conditions at the fever hospital. Then, use some of the details in "Typhoid Fever" to plan interviews with the hospital staff, patients, and visitors. Finally, write the opening paragraphs of your newspaper article. Be sure to include different points of view.

CONNECT
Contrast Characters

Timed ⌛Writing Seamus and Sister Rita have very different ideas about what is important. Write a brief essay in which you contrast these characters. Begin by identifying two comments and/or actions by each character that you think reflects his or her values and beliefs.

EXTEND
Create a Video Portrait

⚡TechFocus McCourt has created vivid portraits of Patricia Madigan, Frankie, and Seamus. Now, think about creating a digital narrative to flesh out these characters even more. With a partner, plan to film a video in which you describe one of these characters. Use a storyboard to plan your video, and create a script. You can tell your story from the first-person point of view of one of the characters or provide a third-person narrative.

Learn It Online
Find instruction on digital storytelling and a storyboard template on:

go.hrw.com   L10-495   **Go**

from High Tide in Tucson

by **Barbara Kingsolver**

Fish Magic (1925) by Paul Klee. Oil and watercolor on canvas on panel (30 ⅜" × 38 ⅜"). The Louise and Walter Annenberg Collection. Philadelphia Museum of Art/©2009 Artists Rights Society (ARS), NY/VG Bild-Kunst, Bonn.

What Do You Think

What role does nature play in our lives? How can nature surprise us?

QuickWrite

Think of an experience you had with nature or something you observed in nature. Maybe you were camping, or hiking, or simply going for a walk. Did anything surprise you? Write a paragraph or two describing the experience.

Reader/Writer
Notebook

Use your **RWN** to complete the activities for this selection.

OH **RA.L.10.11** Explain ways in which an author develops a point of view and style, and cite specific examples from the text. **RA.I.10.1** Identify and understand organizational patterns and techniques, including repetition of ideas, syntax and word choice, that authors use to accomplish their purpose and reach their intended audience.

Literary Focus

Style In literary works, **style** refers to the particular way writers use language to express their feelings and ideas. Style is largely created through **diction,** or word choice, as well as sentence structure. Diction has a powerful effect on creating **tone** (the writer's attitude toward the subject or audience). Another aspect of style is a writer's use of **figurative language** (expressions and comparisons such as metaphors and similes). Style can be described as plain, ornate, formal, ironic, conversational, sentimental, and so on. In "High Tide in Tucson," Barbara Kingsolver creates a deeply personal style.

Reading Focus

Analyzing Author's Purpose Is the author writing to entertain you, persuade you, or inform you? How does the author want you to feel? When you ask questions like these, you are analyzing an author's **purpose,** his or her reason for writing. Observing an author's style is one way to gain insight into his or her purpose. For example, when Kingsolver describes a pond as "a small blue eye in the blistered face of desert," she may be implying that the pond gives her a new way of seeing. Her purpose may be to share this way of seeing with you.

Into Action Notice Kingsolver's style—her distinctive diction, sentence structure, and use of figurative language—in "High Tide in Tucson." As you read the essay, note examples of her style. Think about how the author's purpose may relate to her style.

Diction (Word Choice)	"absurd optimism"
Figurative Language	
Sentence Structure	

Writing Focus

Think as a Reader/Writer

Find It in Your Reading Kingsolver's style is personal and intimate. Find instances in the essay in which she describes her feelings and reactions. Note these in your *Reader/Writer Notebook*.

Vocabulary

absurd (ab SURD) *adj.:* plainly not logical, true, or sensible. *My friend thought my idea of building a pond in the desert was absurd.*

spontaneous (spahn TAY nee uhs) *adj.:* taking place without external cause or help. *Kingsolver was surprised by the spontaneous appearance of so many living things at the pond.*

vain (vayn) *adj.:* having too much pride in one's looks. *The mourning doves, gazing at their reflections in the pond, seemed vain.*

engulfing (ehn GUHLF ihng) *v.:* swallowing up by surrounding completely. *The frog snapped up the beetle, engulfing the insect in its mouth.*

adjacent (uh JAY suhnt) *adj.:* neighboring; next to each other. *Perched on adjacent rocks, the birds could have opened their wings and touched each other.*

Language Coach

Homonyms The word *vain* is a **homonym,** a word that is pronounced in the same way as another word—in this case, *vein*. Use a dictionary as you read to find the meaning of this word, and look for other words in your reading that might be homonyms.

 Learn It Online
There's more to words than just definitions. Get the whole story on:

go.hrw.com | L10-497 | **Go**

Barbara Kingsolver
(1955–   )

A Life in Motion

Barbara Kingsolver grew up in eastern Kentucky, but she knew she would make her life elsewhere. Of her birthplace, she says, "The options were limited—grow up to be a farmer or a farmer's wife."

After graduating with a degree in biology from DePauw University in Indiana, she lived and worked in Greece, France, and England. Then, upon returning to the United States, she settled in Tucson, Arizona, where she lived for twenty-five years. Kingsolver now lives with her family on a farm in southwestern Virginia.

Connected to Nature

Kingsolver has always had a strong interest in nature. She lists among her childhood influences the family vegetable garden, the fields and woods near her home, and her parents' tolerance of nature study (and intolerance of television). Environmental activism is a continuing part of Kingsolver's life; her nonfiction book *Animal, Vegetable, Miracle* tells the story of her family's yearlong effort to acquire as much of their food as possible from local sources and their own farm.

Kingsolver has written short stories, essays, poems, and several bestselling novels, in which she expresses her specific concerns for the world—for both people and nature. Explaining her commitment to doing good in the world, she says, "It's what you do that makes your soul, not the other way around."

Think About the Writer — How did Kingsolver's upbringing influence the direction she took in her life and her writing?

Build Background

In this essay, the author describes a pond she created in her backyard in Tucson, Arizona. To understand the extraordinary nature of this pond, it is important to realize that Tucson has a dry desert climate with an average annual rainfall of about twelve inches. A permanent pond in such conditions is a rarity.

Preview the Selection

The narrator and author, **Barbara Kingsolver,** reflects on what she has learned about life in the unlikeliest of places.

Read with a Purpose Read this essay to discover what Barbara Kingsolver learns from observing nature.

from High Tide in Tucson

by **Barbara Kingsolver**

After two days of gentle winter rains, the small pond behind my house is lapping at its banks, content as a well-fed kitten. This pond is a relative miracle. Several years ago I talked a man I knew who was handy with a bulldozer into damming up the narrow wash[1] behind my house. This was not a creek by any stretch of imagination—even so thirsty an imagination as mine. It was only a little strait where, two or three times a year when the rain kept up for more than a day, water would run past in a hurry on its way to flood the road and drown out the odd passing Buick. All the rest of the time this little valley lay empty, a toasted rock patch pierced with cactus.

I cleared out the brush and, with what my bulldozer friend viewed as absurd optimism, directed the proceedings. After making a little hollow, we waterproofed the bottom and lined the sides with rocks, and then I could only stand by to see what would happen. When the rains came my pond filled. Its level rises and falls some, but for years now it has remained steadfastly *pond,* a small blue eye in the blistered face of desert. **A**

That part was only hydrology[2] and luck, no miracle. But this part is: within hours of its creation, my pond teemed with life. Backswimmers, whirligig beetles, and boatmen darted down through the watery strata.[3]

---

1. **wash** (wahsh): bed of a stream that flows only for part of the year; this word is mainly used in the western United States.

2. **hydrology** (hy DRAHL uh jee): scientific study of the properties of water and its effects.

3. **strata** (STRAY tuh): layers (plural of *stratum*).

A **Reading Focus** **Author's Purpose** What does Kingsolver's description of the pond as a "relative miracle" suggest about her purpose for writing the essay?

Vocabulary **absurd** (ab SURD) *adj.:* plainly not logical, true, or sensible.

Water striders dimpled the surface. Tadpoles and water beetles rootled the furry bottom. Dragonflies hovered and delicately dipped their tails, laying eggs. Eggs hatched into creeping armadas of larvae.[4] I can't imagine where all these creatures came from. There is no other permanent water for many miles around. How did they know? What jungle drums told them to come here? Surely there are not, as a matter of course, aquatic creatures dragging themselves by their elbows across the barren desert *just in case?* **Ⓑ**

I'm tempted to believe in spontaneous generation.[5] Rushes have sprung up around the edges of my pond, coyotes and javelinas[6] come down to drink and unabashedly wallow, nighthawks and little brown bats swoop down at night to snap insects out of the air. Mourning doves, smooth as cool gray stones, coo at their own reflections. Families of Gambel's quail come each and every spring morning, all lined up puffed and bustling with their seventeen children, Papa Quail in proud lead with his ridiculous black topknot feather boinging out ahead of him. Water lilies open their flowers at sunup and fold them, prim as praying hands, at dusk. A sleek male Cooper's hawk and a female great horned owl roost in the trees with their constant predators' eyes on dim-witted quail and vain dove, silently taking turns with the night and day shifts.

For several years that Cooper's hawk was the steadiest male presence in my life. I've stood alone in his shadow through many changes of season. I've been shattered and reassembled a few times over, and there have been long days when I felt my heart was simply somewhere else—possibly on ice, in one of those igloo coolers that show up in the news as they are carried importantly onto helicopters. "So what?" life asked, and went on whirling recklessly around me. Always, every minute, something is eating or being eaten, laying eggs, burrowing in mud, blooming, splitting its seams, dividing itself in two. What a messy marvel, fecundity.[7] **Ⓒ**

That is how I became goddess of a small universe of my own creation—more or less by accident. My subjects owe me their very lives. Blithely they ignore me. I stand on the banks, wide-eyed, receiving gifts in every season. In May the palo verde trees lean into their reflections, so heavy with blossoms the desert looks thick and deep with golden hoarfrost.[8] In November the purple water lilies are struck numb with the first frost, continuing to try to open their final flowers in slow motion for the rest of the winter. Once, in August, I saw

---

4. **armadas** (ahr MAH duhz) **of larvae** (LAHR vee): large groups of immature insects.
5. **spontaneous generation:** the supposed development of living organisms from nonliving matter.
6. **javelinas** (hah vuh LEE nuhz): wild animals related to pigs.

7. **fecundity** (fih KUHN duh tee): fertility; the ability to produce life in large quantities.
8. **hoarfrost** (HAWR frawst): ice crystals that form on a surface when dew freezes.

Ⓑ **Literary Focus** Style What figurative language does Kingsolver use to personify the pond animals in this passage?

Ⓒ **Reading Focus** Author's Purpose What might the Cooper's hawk represent?

Vocabulary **spontaneous** (spahn TAY nee uhs) *adj.:* taking place without external cause or help.
vain (vayn) *adj.:* having too much pride in one's looks.

a tussle in the reeds that turned out to be two bull snakes making a meal of the same frog. Their dinner screeched piteously while the snakes' heads inched slowly closer together, each of them engulfing a drumstick, until there they were at last, nose to scaly nose. I watched with my knuckles in my mouth, anxious to see whether they would rip the frog in two like a pair of pants. As it turned out, they were nowhere near this civilized. They lunged and thrashed, their long bodies scrawling whole cursive alphabets into the rushes, until one of the snakes suddenly let go and curved away. **D**

Last May, I saw a dragonfly as long as my hand—longer than an average-sized songbird. She circled and circled, flexing her body, trying to decide if my little lake was worthy of her precious eggs. She was almost absurdly color-

---

D **Literary Focus** Style What types of figurative language does Kingsolver use in this passage?

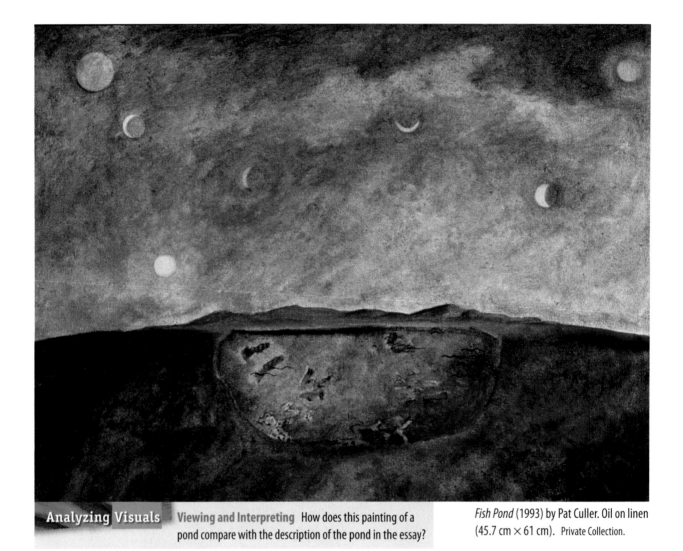

Fish Pond (1993) by Pat Culler. Oil on linen (45.7 cm × 61 cm). Private Collection.

ful, sporting a bright green thorax and blue abdomen. Eventually she lit on the tip of the horsetail plant that sends long slender spikes up out of the water. She was joined on the tips of five adjacent stalks by five other dragonflies, all different: an orange-bodied one with orange wings, a yellow one, a blue-green one, one with a red head and purple tail, and a miniature one in zippy metallic blue. A dragon-fly bouquet. Be still, and the world is bound to turn herself inside out to entertain you. Everywhere you

look, joyful noise is clanging to drown out quiet desperation. The choice is draw the blinds and shut it all out, or believe.

What to believe in, exactly, may never turn out to be half as important as the daring act of belief. A willingness to participate in sunlight, and the color red. An agreement to enter into a conspiracy with life, on behalf of both frog and snake, the predator and the prey, in order to come away changed. **E**

Vocabulary **adjacent** (uh JAY suhnt) *adj.:* neighboring; next to each other.

E **Literary Focus** Style What effect do the incomplete sentences in this paragraph have on you?

Applying Your Skills

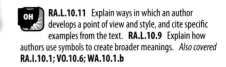

RA.L.10.11 Explain ways in which an author develops a point of view and style, and cite specific examples from the text. **RA.L.10.9** Explain how authors use symbols to create broader meanings. *Also covered* **RA.I.10.1; VO.10.6; WA.10.1.b**

from **High Tide in Tucson**

Respond and Think Critically

Reading Focus

Quick Check

1. Why is Kingsolver amazed by the appearance of the various animals at her pond?

Read with a Purpose

2. What does Kingsolver learn about herself and about life from observing the pond?

Reading Skills: Analyzing Author's Purpose

3. As you read, you noted examples of Kingsolver's diction, use of figurative language, and sentence structure. Now, add a row to your chart and explain what these elements of style reveal about her purpose. Does she have more than one purpose for writing?

Diction (Word Choice)	"absurd optimism"
Figurative Language	
Sentence Structure	

Author's Purpose:

✓ Vocabulary Check

Choose the best synonym for each word.

4. **absurd**
   a. hopeful   b. logical   c. foolish

5. **engulfing**
   a. holding tight   b. sailing   c. surrounding

6. **adjacent**
   a. between   b. next to   c. above

7. **vain**
   a. strong   b. conceited   c. bashful

8. **spontaneous**
   a. cautious   b. quiet   c. automatic

Literary Focus

Literary Analysis

9. **Evaluate** In the final paragraph, Kingsolver says that the *act* of believing may be more important than *what* you believe. Do the details in the essay support this conclusion? Explain.

Literary Skills: Style

10. **Explain** Authors' styles often support the messages they want to convey. Choose a passage from the essay, and write three or four sentences explaining how Kingsolver's style choices—diction, figurative language, and sentence structure—help convey her message.

Literary Skills Review: Symbolism

11. **Analyze** A **symbol** is a person, animal, place, thing, or idea that stands for something beyond itself. What does the pond symbolize for Kingsolver? Explain.

Writing Focus

Think as a Reader/Writer

Use It in Your Writing Write a paragraph about a favorite place. Like Kingsolver, choose words, figures of speech, and sentence structures that reflect your feelings. For example, you might use short, rapid sentences to describe the quick pace of a city street.

What Do **You Think Now** How does nature sometimes overcome our expectations? How did nature inspire Kingsolver?

Preparing to Read

from Into Thin Air

by **Jon Krakauer**

Ropes left by previous Mount Everest expeditions. This photograph came from Scott Fischer's last roll of film, removed from his body after the storm on May 10,1996, which killed nine climbers.

What Do You Think?

Why do you think some people are drawn to risk and adventure?

 QuickTalk

With a classmate, discuss an adventure you might like to have. Where would you go? What challenges might you encounter?

Reader/Writer Notebook

Use your **RWN** to complete the activities for this selection.

RA.L.10.11 Explain ways in which an author develops a point of view and style, and cite specific examples from the text. **RA.I.10.1** Identify and understand organizational patterns and techniques, including repetition of ideas, syntax and word choice, that authors use to accomplish their purpose and reach their intended audience.

Literary Focus

Style The way an author puts words together—**sentence structure**—is one aspect of his or her **style.** A writer may use mostly long, elaborate sentences or simple, direct ones. A complicated thought might require a complicated sentence. By contrast, an action-filled passage might have many short, quick sentences. Another aspect of a writer's style is **mood,** or the atmosphere a writer creates. For example, the mood could be joyful, gloomy, or humorous. As you read "Into Thin Air," pay attention to how the mood changes.

Reading Focus

Identifying Cause and Effect A **cause** is the reason *why* something happens. An **effect** is the *result* of something that has happened. A single effect may have several causes, and a single cause may lead to many effects. Everything that happens in this tragic story is connected by a complex pattern of causes and effects.

Into Action As you read, look for the causes that lead to the disasters on Mount Everest. Look for the effects of certain decisions made by the climbers, and note them on a chart like this one.

```
  Cause  ┐
         ├──▶  Effect
  Cause  ┘
```

Writing Focus

Think as a Reader/Writer

Find It in Your Reading Krakauer creates **suspense**—the anxiety we feel about the upcoming events in a story—by occasionally referring to dangerous events to come. For example, he mentions a "blanket of clouds" that grows more and more threatening. As you read "Into Thin Air," note these references in your *Reader/Writer Notebook*.

TechFocus While reading "Into Thin Air," consider what aspects of the author's experience would make a good slide show. Which details would be easier to understand with visuals?

Vocabulary

deteriorate (dih TIHR ee uh rayt) *v.*: get worse. *Storm clouds blew in, and the weather started to deteriorate rapidly.*

benign (bih NYN) *adj.*: not dangerous. *The clouds appeared benign, but the storm was on its way.*

crucial (KROO shuhl) *adj.*: very important. *Extra oxygen is crucial for people climbing Mount Everest.*

jeopardize (JEHP uhr dyz) *v.*: put in danger or at risk. *Some decisions may jeopardize other people's safety.*

tenuous (TEHN yoo uhs) *adj.*: thin or slight; weak; fragile. *The climbers' oxygen-deprived brains had a tenuous grip on reality.*

Language Coach

Context Clues Sometimes writers give clues about a word's meaning by placing a definition nearby. This technique is especially helpful for understanding technical vocabulary. Look at these sentences: *Climbers depend on crampons. Without these spiked plates attached to the bottoms of their shoes, climbers would be in constant danger of slipping.* Which words tell you what *crampons* means?

Learn It Online

Check out the *PowerNotes* introduction to this story on:

 go.hrw.com L10-505   **Go**

Jon Krakauer
(1954–   )

Journalist and Climber

Some children idolize baseball players or movie stars. Jon Krakauer's heroes were mountain climbers. At the age of eight, Krakauer made his first climb, and after college he became a "climbing bum." During the 1980s, he began writing articles on outdoor subjects.

In 1996, *Outside* magazine asked Krakauer to write about Mount Everest. When he joined the Everest trek, he had already won critical and public acclaim for his book *Into the Wild,* an insightful report on an idealistic young loner whose dream of living deep in the Alaskan wilderness cost him his life. Krakauer was an experienced climber at the time of the journey, but he had never been above 17,200 feet. He later said, "If you don't understand Everest and appreciate its mystique, you're never going to understand this tragedy and why it's quite likely to be repeated."

Hot Story, Cold Mountain

After the disaster, Krakauer conducted dozens of interviews with other survivors. His article, completed five weeks after his return from Nepal, was published in September 1996. Krakauer still felt such a need to get the experience off his chest that he soon expanded the article into a book, *Into Thin Air,* which was an immediate bestseller. Despite that success, Krakauer has suffered grief and guilt over the disaster on Mount Everest. He has said, "I'm never climbing it again, never. . . . I wish I hadn't gone this time."

Build Background

The first recorded conquest of Mount Everest was achieved by Edmund Hillary of New Zealand and Tenzing Norgay of Nepal in 1953. Since then, more than 1,300 climbers have reached the summit, but about 170 have lost their lives. In May 1996, *Outside* magazine financed Jon Krakauer's climb, which he undertook as a client of a commercial expedition. The day he reached the summit of Mount Everest, eight other climbers died on the mountain.

Everest expeditions ascend the mountain in stages. From Base Camp, at 17,600 feet, they make short trips up and down to acclimatize, or get used to higher elevations. This process may last several weeks before the final climb to the top, which is also done in stages. Krakauer's group made camp at 19,500 feet, 21,300 feet, 24,000 feet, and 26,000 feet. The area above 25,000 feet is known as the Death Zone. Here the air is so lacking in oxygen that it is almost impossible for climbers to make rational decisions. Everest's summit is covered in icy, packed snow and the extreme cold makes it impossible for animals, or even plants, to live there. Krakauer's report covers seventy-two hours of the mountain's worst tragedy to date.

Think About the Writer — What challenges might a journalist face who writes about an event in which he or she is also a participant?

Mount Everest, the highest mountain on earth.

Everest Summit
29,035 feet

The Hillary Step

The Balcony
27,600 feet

The South Summit
28,710 feet

Camp Four
26,000 feet

South Col

To Camp Three

CHINA

The Himalayas

TIBET
Mt. Everest

NEPAL
KATMANDU

INDIA

(Below) Members of Jon Krakauer's expedition team, led by Rob Hall. Rob Hall is in the front row, third from the left. Next to him, fourth from the left, is Andy Harris, and Jon Krakauer is sitting next to him. Beck Weathers is standing in the second row, third from the left.

from Into Thin Air

by **Jon Krakauer**

Straddling the top of the world, one foot in Tibet and the other in Nepal, I cleared the ice from my oxygen mask, hunched a shoulder against the wind, and stared absently at the vast sweep of earth below. I understood on some dim, detached level that it was a spectacular sight. I'd been fantasizing about this moment, and the release of emotion that would accompany it, for many months. But now that I was finally here, standing on the summit of Mount Everest, I just couldn't summon the energy to care.

It was the afternoon of May 10. I hadn't slept in 57 hours. The only food I'd been able to force down over the preceding three days was a bowl of Ramen soup and a handful of peanut M&M's. Weeks of violent coughing had left me with two separated ribs, making it excruciatingly painful to breathe. Twenty-nine thousand twenty-eight feet[1] up in the troposphere,[2] there was so little oxygen reaching my brain that my mental capacity was that of a slow child. Under the circumstances, I was incapable of feeling much of anything except cold and tired. **Ⓐ**

I'd arrived on the summit a few minutes after Anatoli Boukreev,[3] a Russian guide with an American expedition, and just ahead of Andy Harris, a guide with the New Zealand–based commercial team that I was a part of and someone with whom I'd grown to be friends during the last six weeks. I snapped four quick photos of Harris and Boukreev striking summit poses, and then turned and started down. My watch read 1:17 P.M. All told, I'd spent less than five minutes on the roof of the world.

After a few steps, I paused to take another photo, this one looking down the Southeast Ridge, the route we had ascended. Training my lens on a pair of climbers approaching the summit, I saw something that until that moment had escaped my attention. To the south, where the sky had been perfectly clear just an hour earlier, a blanket of clouds now hid Pumori, Ama Dablam, and the other lesser peaks surrounding Everest. **Ⓑ**

---

1. **Twenty-nine thousand . . . feet:** In 1999, after this article was written, scientists using sophisticated equipment determined the elevation of Everest to be 29,035 feet, not 29,028 feet, as previously believed.

2. **troposphere** (TROH puh sfihr): portion of the atmosphere directly below the stratosphere (extends from six to eight miles above the earth's surface).

3. **Anatoli Boukreev:** Boukreev was killed in an avalanche about a year and a half later, on December 25, 1997, while climbing Annapurna in the Himalayas.

Ⓐ Reading Focus Cause and Effect Why doesn't Krakauer feel excited when he reaches the top of the mountain?

Ⓑ Literary Focus Style How does the word *escaped* add to the mood of the story?

Days later—after six bodies had been found, after a search for two others had been abandoned, after surgeons had amputated the gangrenous[4] right hand of my teammate Beck Weathers—people would ask why, if the weather had begun to deteriorate, had climbers on the upper mountain not heeded the signs? Why did veteran Himalayan guides keep moving upward, leading a gaggle of amateurs, each of whom had paid as much as $65,000 to be ushered safely up Everest, into an apparent death trap?

Nobody can speak for the leaders of the two guided groups involved, for both men are now dead. But I can attest that nothing I saw early on the afternoon of May 10 suggested that a murderous storm was about to bear down on us. To my oxygen-depleted mind, the clouds drifting up the grand valley of ice known as the Western Cwm looked innocuous, wispy, insubstantial. Gleaming in the brilliant midday sun, they appeared no different from the harmless puffs of convection condensation that rose from the valley almost daily. As I began my descent, I was indeed anxious, but my concern had little to do with the weather. A check of the gauge on my oxygen tank had revealed that it was almost empty. I needed to get down, fast. **C**

The uppermost shank of the Southeast Ridge is a slender, heavily corniced fin[5] of rock and wind-scoured snow that snakes for a quarter-mile toward a secondary pinnacle known as the South Summit. Negotiating the serrated[6] ridge presents few great technical hurdles, but the route is dreadfully exposed. After 15 minutes of cautious shuffling over a 7,000-foot abyss,[7] I arrived at the notorious Hillary Step, a pronounced notch in the ridge named after Sir Edmund Hillary, the first Westerner to climb the mountain, and a spot that does require a fair amount of technical maneuvering. As I clipped into a fixed rope and prepared to rappel[8] over the lip, I was greeted by an alarming sight.

Thirty feet below, some 20 people were queued up[9] at the base of the Step, and three climbers were hauling themselves up the rope that I was attempting to descend. I had no choice but to unclip from the line and step aside.

The traffic jam comprised climbers from three separate expeditions: the team I belonged to, a group of paying clients under the leadership of the celebrated New Zealand guide Rob Hall; another guided party headed by American Scott Fischer; and a nonguided team from Taiwan. Moving at the snail's pace that is the norm above 8,000 meters, the throng labored up the Hillary Step one by one, while I nervously bided my time.

Harris, who left the summit shortly after I did, soon pulled up behind me. Wanting to conserve whatever oxygen remained in my tank, I asked him to reach inside my backpack and turn off the valve on my regulator, which he did. For the next ten minutes I felt surprisingly good. My head cleared. I actually seemed less tired than with the gas turned on. Then, abruptly, I felt

---

4. **gangrenous** (GANG gruh nuhs): characterized by tissue decay resulting from a lack of blood supply.
5. **corniced** (KAWR nihst) **fin:** ridge with an overhanging mass of snow or ice deposited by the wind.
6. **serrated** (SEHR ayt ihd): notched like a saw.

7. **abyss** (uh BIHS): deep crack or opening in the earth's surface.
8. **rappel** (rah PEHL): descend a mountain by means of a double rope arranged around the climber's body so that he or she can control the slide downward.
9. **queued** (kyood) **up:** lined up.

Vocabulary **deteriorate** (dih TIHR ee uh rayt) *v.:* get worse.

C **Literary Focus** Style In this paragraph, the last sentence is shorter than the other sentences. What effect does this style have on the mood?

like I was suffocating. My vision dimmed and my head began to spin. I was on the brink of losing consciousness.

Instead of turning my oxygen off, Harris, in his hypoxically[10] impaired state, had mistakenly cranked the valve open to full flow, draining the tank. I'd just squandered the last of my gas going nowhere. There was another tank waiting for me at the South Summit, 250 feet below, but to get there I would have to descend the most exposed terrain on the entire route without benefit of supplemental oxygen. **(D)**

But first I had to wait for the crowd to thin. I removed my now useless mask, planted my ice ax into the mountain's frozen hide, and hunkered on the ridge crest. As I exchanged banal[11] congratulations with the climbers filing past, inwardly I was frantic: "Hurry it up, hurry it up!" I silently pleaded. "While you guys are messing around here, I'm losing brain cells by the millions!"

Most of the passing crowd belonged to Fischer's group, but near the back of the parade two of my teammates eventually appeared: Hall and Yasuko Namba. Girlish and reserved, the 47-year-old Namba was 40 minutes away from becoming the oldest woman to climb Everest and the second Japanese woman to reach the highest point on each continent, the so-called Seven Summits.

Later still, Doug Hansen—another member of our expedition, a postal worker from Seattle who had become my closest friend on

the mountain—arrived atop the Step. "It's in the bag!" I yelled over the wind, trying to sound more upbeat than I felt. Plainly exhausted, Doug mumbled something from behind his oxygen mask that I didn't catch, shook my hand weakly, and continued plodding upward. **(E)**

The last climber up the rope was Fischer, whom I knew casually from Seattle, where we both lived. His strength and drive were legendary—in 1994 he'd climbed Everest without using bottled oxygen—so I was surprised at how slowly he was moving and how hammered he looked when he pulled his mask aside to say hello. "Bruuuuuuce!" he wheezed with forced cheer, employing his trademark, fratboyish greeting. When I asked how he was doing, Fischer insisted he was feeling fine: "Just dragging a little today for some reason. No big deal." With the Hillary Step finally clear, I clipped into the strand of orange rope, swung quickly around Fischer as he slumped over his ice ax, and rappelled over the edge.

It was after 2:30 when I made it down to the South Summit. By now tendrils of mist were wrapping across the top of 27,890-foot Lhotse and lapping at Everest's summit pyramid. No longer did the weather look so benign. I grabbed a fresh oxygen cylinder, jammed it onto my regulator, and hurried down into the gathering cloud.

Four hundred vertical feet above, where the summit was still washed in bright sunlight under an immaculate cobalt sky, my compadres[12] were dallying, memorializing their arrival at the apex of the planet with photos and high-fives—and

---

10. **hypoxically** (hy PAHK sih kuhl lee): characterized by hypoxia, a condition resulting from a decrease in the oxygen reaching body tissues. Hypoxia is a common condition at very high altitudes.
11. **banal**: everyday; commonplace.

---

12. **compadres** (kuhm PAH drayz): close friends; in this case, fellow members of the climbing team.

(D) Reading Focus Cause and Effect What happened to Krakauer's remaining oxygen?

(E) Literary Focus Style Krakauer often uses dashes to set off added information in his sentences. What effect does the use of dashes create?

Vocabulary **benign** (bih NYN) *adj.*: not dangerous.

High Altitude

High-altitude mountaineering places the human body under severe stress. One of the most common problems is altitude sickness, also called mountain sickness. The symptoms of altitude sickness include headache, nausea, breathlessness, and exhaustion. In acute cases it can turn into a life-threatening condition when fluid floods the lungs or the brain.

The sickness is caused by the low atmospheric pressures and reduced oxygen found at high elevations. It can occur at any point above eight thousand feet. The higher the altitude is, the lower is the amount of oxygen in the air. The air at twenty-five thousand feet has two-thirds less oxygen than the air at sea level. Climbers of Mount Everest try to lessen the effects of altitude sickness by acclimating themselves slowly to atmospheric conditions. Often they spend several weeks at Mount Everest Base Camp before moving on to higher elevations.

Ask Yourself

How does altitude sickness play a role in this true story?

Climber using oxygen mask while on Lhotse (mountain near Mount Everest), Nepal.

using up precious ticks of the clock. None of them imagined that a horrible ordeal was drawing nigh. None of them suspected that by the end of that long day, every minute would matter. . . .

At 3 P.M., within minutes of leaving the South Summit, I descended into clouds ahead of the others. Snow started to fall. In the flat, diminishing light, it became hard to tell where the mountain ended and where the sky began. It would have been very easy to blunder off the edge of the ridge and never be heard from again. The lower I went, the worse the weather became.

When I reached the Balcony again, about 4 P.M., I encountered Beck Weathers standing alone, shivering violently. Years earlier, Weathers had undergone radial keratotomy to correct his vision. A side effect, which he discovered on Everest and consequently hid from Hall, was that in the low barometric pressure at high altitude, his eyesight failed. Nearly blind when he'd left Camp Four in the middle of the night but hopeful that his vision would improve at daybreak, he stuck close to the person in front of him and kept climbing. **F**

Upon reaching the Southeast Ridge shortly after sunrise, Weathers had confessed to Hall that he was having trouble seeing, at which point Hall declared, "Sorry, pal, you're going down. I'll

F **Reading Focus** **Cause and Effect** What effect could Weathers's attempt to conceal his eye problem have on the other members of the expedition?

send one of the Sherpas[13] with you." Weathers countered that his vision was likely to improve as soon as the sun crept higher in the sky; Hall said he'd give Weathers 30 minutes to find out—after that, he'd have to wait there at 27,500 feet for Hall and the rest of the group to come back down. Hall didn't want Weathers descending alone. "I'm dead serious about this," Hall admonished his client. "Promise me that you'll sit right here until I return."

"I crossed my heart and hoped to die," Weathers recalls now, "and promised I wouldn't go anywhere." Shortly after noon, Hutchison, Taske, and Kasischke[14] passed by with their Sherpa escorts, but Weathers elected not to accompany them. "The weather was still good," he explains, "and I saw no reason to break my promise to Rob."

By the time I encountered Weathers, however, conditions were turning ugly. "Come down with me," I implored, "I'll get you down, no problem." He was nearly convinced, until I made the mistake of mentioning that Groom was on his way down, too. In a day of many mistakes, this would turn out to be a crucial one. "Thanks anyway," Weathers said. "I'll just wait for Mike. He's got a rope; he'll be able to short-rope[15] me." Secretly relieved, I hurried toward the South Col, 1,500 feet below. **Ⓖ**

These lower slopes proved to be the most difficult part of the descent. Six inches of powder snow blanketed outcroppings of loose shale. Climbing down them demanded unceasing concentration, an all but impossible feat in my current state. By 5:30, however, I was finally within 200 vertical feet of Camp Four, and only one obstacle stood between me and safety: a steep bulge of rock-hard ice that I'd have to descend without a rope. But the weather had deteriorated into a full-scale blizzard. Snow pellets born on 70-mph winds stung my face; any exposed skin was instantly frozen. The tents, no more than 200 horizontal yards away, were only intermittently visible through the whiteout. There was zero margin for error. Worried about making a critical blunder, I sat down to marshal my energy.

Suddenly, Harris[16] appeared out of the gloom and sat beside me. At this point there was no mistaking that he was in appalling shape. His cheeks were coated with an armor of frost, one eye was frozen shut, and his speech was slurred. He was frantic to reach the tents. After briefly discussing the best way to negotiate the ice, Harris started scooting down on his butt, facing forward. "Andy," I yelled after him, "it's crazy to try it like that!" He yelled something back, but the words were carried off by the screaming wind. A second later he lost his purchase[17] and was rocketing down on his back.

Two hundred feet below, I could make out Harris's motionless form. I was sure he'd broken at least a leg, maybe his neck. But then he stood up, waved that he was OK, and started stumbling toward camp, which was for the moment in plain sight, 150 yards beyond.

---

13. **Sherpas** (SHUR puhz): members of a Tibetan people living on the southern slopes of the Himalayas. As experienced mountain climbers, Sherpas are often hired to act as guides or provide support for mountaineering expeditions.

14. **Hutchison, Taske, and Kasischke:** three clients on Rob Hall's team.

15. **short-rope:** assist a weak or injured climber by hauling him or her.

16. **Harris:** After writing this article, Krakauer discovered through conversations with Martin Adams (a client on Scott Fischer's team) that the person he thought was Harris was, in fact, Martin Adams.

17. **purchase:** firm hold.

Ⓖ Reading Focus Cause and Effect In what way does Weathers's promise to Hall influence Krakauer's <u>subsequent</u> decision?

Vocabulary **crucial** (KROO shuhl) *adj.:* very important.

I could see three or four people shining lights outside the tents. I watched Harris walk across the flats to the edge of camp, a distance he covered in less than ten minutes. When the clouds closed in a moment later, cutting off my view, he was within 30 yards of the tents. I didn't see him again after that, but I was certain that he'd reached the security of camp, where Sherpas would be waiting with hot tea. Sitting out in the storm, with the ice bulge still standing between me and the tents, I felt a pang of envy. I was angry that my guide hadn't waited for me.

Twenty minutes later I was in camp. I fell into my tent with my crampons still on, zipped the door tight, and sprawled across the frost-covered floor. I was drained, more exhausted than I'd ever been in my life. But I was safe. Andy was safe. The others would be coming into camp soon. We'd done it. We'd climbed Mount Everest. **H**

> Sitting out in the storm, with the ice bulge still standing between me and the tents, I felt a pang of envy.

It would be many hours before I learned that everyone had in fact not made it back to camp— that one teammate was already dead and that 23 other men and women were caught in a desperate struggle for their lives. . . .

Meanwhile, Hall and Hansen were still on the frightfully exposed summit ridge, engaged in a grim struggle of their own. The 46-year-old Hansen, whom Hall had turned back just below this spot exactly a year ago, had been determined to bag the summit this time around. "I want to get this thing done and out of my life," he'd told me a couple of days earlier. "I don't want to have to come back here."

Indeed Hansen had reached the top this time, though not until after 3 P.M., well after Hall's predetermined turnaround time. Given Hall's conservative, systematic nature, many people wonder why he didn't turn Hansen around when it became obvious that he was running late. It's not far-fetched to speculate that because Hall had talked Hansen into coming back to Everest this year, it would have been especially hard for him to deny Hansen the summit a second time—especially when all of Fischer's clients were still marching blithely toward the top.

"It's very difficult to turn someone around high on the mountain," cautions Guy Cotter, a New Zealand guide who summited Everest with Hall in 1992 and was guiding the peak for him in 1995 when Hansen made his first attempt. "If a client sees that the summit is close and they're dead set on getting there, they're going to laugh in your face and keep going up."

In any case, for whatever reason, Hall did not turn Hansen around. Instead, after reaching the summit at 2:10 P.M., Hall waited for more than an hour for Hansen to arrive and then headed down with him. Soon after they began their descent, just below the top, Hansen apparently ran out of oxygen and collapsed. "Pretty much the same thing happened to Doug in '95," says Ed Viesturs, an American who guided the peak for Hall that year. "He was fine during the ascent, but as soon as he started down he lost it mentally and physically. He turned into a real zombie, like he'd used everything up." **I**

At 4:31 P.M., Hall radioed Base Camp to say that he and Hansen were above the Hillary Step

---

H **Literary Focus** Style Read this paragraph aloud. How would you describe its rhythm and pace?

I **Reading Focus** Cause and Effect Why does Krakauer think Hall led Hansen to the top after the turnaround time?

Rob Hall, leader of Krakauer's expedition team.

and urgently needed oxygen. Two full bottles were waiting for them at the South Summit; if Hall had known this he could have retrieved the gas fairly quickly and then climbed back up to give Hansen a fresh tank. But Harris, in the throes of his oxygen-starved dementia,[18] overheard the 4:31 radio call while descending the Southeast Ridge and broke in to tell Hall that all the bottles at the South Summit were empty. So Hall stayed with Hansen and tried to bring the

helpless client down without oxygen, but could get him no farther than the top of the Hillary Step.

Cotter, a very close friend of both Hall and Harris, happened to be a few miles from Everest Base Camp at the time, guiding an expedition on Pumori. Overhearing the radio conversations between Hall and Base Camp, he called Hall at 5:36 and again at 5:57, urging his mate to leave Hansen and come down alone. . . . Hall, however, wouldn't consider going down without Hansen.

There was no further word from Hall until the middle of the night. At 2:46 A.M. on May 11, Cotter woke up to hear a long, broken transmission, probably unintended: Hall was wearing a remote microphone clipped to the shoulder strap of his backpack, which was occasionally keyed on by mistake. In this instance, says Cotter, "I suspect Rob didn't even know he was transmitting. I could hear someone yelling—it might have been Rob, but I couldn't be sure because the wind was so loud in the background. He was saying something like 'Keep moving! Keep going!' presumably to Doug, urging him on."

If that was indeed the case, it meant that in the wee hours of the morning Hall and Hansen were still struggling from the Hillary Step toward the South Summit, taking more than 12 hours to traverse a stretch of ridge typically covered by descending climbers in half an hour. **J**

Hall's next call to Base Camp was at 4:43 A.M. He'd finally reached the South Summit but was unable to descend farther, and in a series of transmissions over the next two hours he sounded confused and irrational. "Harold[19] was with me last night," Hall insisted, when in fact Harris had reached the South Col at sunset. "But he doesn't seem to be with me now. He was very weak."

18. **dementia** (dih MEHN shuh): mental impairment.

19. **Harold:** Andy Harris's nickname.

J Literary Focus Style Notice that this paragraph is only one sentence long. What effect does this change in style have on the reader?

Mackenzie[20] asked him how Hansen was doing. "Doug," Hall replied, "is gone." That was all he said, and it was the last mention he ever made of Hansen.

On May 23, when Breashears and Viesturs, of the IMAX team,[21] reached the summit, they found no sign of Hansen's body but they did find an ice ax planted about 50 feet below the Hillary Step, along a highly exposed section of ridge where the fixed ropes came to an end. It is quite possible that Hall managed to get Hansen down the ropes to this point, only to have him lose his footing and fall 7,000 feet down the sheer Southwest Face, leaving his ice ax jammed into the ridge crest where he slipped.

During the radio calls to Base Camp early on May 11, Hall revealed that something was wrong with his legs, that he was no longer able to walk and was shaking uncontrollably. This was very disturbing news to the people down below, but it was amazing that Hall was even alive after spending a night without shelter or oxygen at 28,700 feet in hurricane-force wind and minus-100-degree windchill.

At 5 A.M., Base Camp patched through a call on the satellite telephone to Jan Arnold, Hall's wife, seven months pregnant with their first child in Christchurch, New Zealand. Arnold, a respected physician, had summited Everest with Hall in 1993 and entertained no illusions about the gravity of her husband's predicament. "My heart really sank when I heard his voice," she recalls. "He was slurring his words markedly. He sounded like Major Tom[22] or something, like he was just floating away. I'd been up there; I knew what it could be like in bad weather. Rob and I had talked about the impossibility of being rescued from the summit ridge. As he himself had put it, 'You might as well be on the moon.'"

By that time, Hall had located two full oxygen bottles, and after struggling for four hours trying to de-ice his mask, around 8:30 A.M. he finally started breathing the life-sustaining gas. Several times he announced that he was preparing to descend, only to change his mind and remain at the South Summit. The day had started out sunny and clear, but the wind remained fierce, and by late morning the upper mountain was wrapped with thick clouds. Climbers at Camp Two reported that the wind over the summit sounded like a squadron of 747s, even from 8,000 feet below. . . .

Throughout that day, Hall's friends begged him to make an effort to descend from the South Summit under his own power. At 3:20 P.M., after one such transmission from Cotter, Hall began to sound annoyed. "Look," he said, "if I thought I could manage the knots on the fixed ropes with me frostbitten hands, I would have gone down six hours ago, pal. Just send a couple of the boys up with a big thermos of something hot—then I'll be fine."

At 6:20 P.M., Hall was patched through a second time to Arnold in Christchurch. "Hi, my sweetheart," he said in a slow, painfully distorted voice. "I hope you're tucked up in a nice warm bed. How are you doing?"

"I can't tell you how much I'm thinking about you!" Arnold replied. "You sound so much better than I expected. . . . Are you warm, my darling?"

"In the context of the altitude, the setting, I'm reasonably comfortable," Hall answered, doing his best not to alarm her.

"How are your feet?"

"I haven't taken me boots off to check, but I think I may have a bit of frostbite."

---

20. **Mackenzie:** Dr. Caroline Mackenzie was Base Camp doctor for Rob Hall's team.

21. **IMAX team:** another team of climbers, who were shooting a $5.5-million, giant-screen movie about Mount Everest. The movie was released in 1998.

22. **Major Tom:** reference to the David Bowie song "Space Oddity," which is about an astronaut, Major Tom, who is lost and floating in space.

"I'm looking forward to making you completely better when you come home," said Arnold. "I just know you're going to be rescued. Don't feel that you're alone. I'm sending all my positive energy your way!" Before signing off, Hall told his wife, "I love you. Sleep well, my sweetheart. Please don't worry too much." **K**

These would be the last words anyone would

K **Literary Focus** Style How does Hall's conversation with his wife influence the mood of the narrative?

hear him utter. Attempts to make radio contact with Hall later that night and the next day went unanswered. Twelve days later, when Breashears and Viesturs climbed over the South Summit on their way to the top, they found Hall lying on his right side in a shallow ice-hollow, his upper body buried beneath a drift of snow. **L**

Early on the morning of May 11, when I returned to Camp Four, Hutchison, standing in for Groom, who was unconscious in his tent, organized a team of four Sherpas to locate the bodies of our teammates Weathers and Namba. The Sherpa search party, headed by Lhakpa Chhiri, departed ahead of Hutchison, who was so exhausted and befuddled that he forgot to put his boots on and left camp in his light, smooth-soled liners. Only when Lhakpa Chhiri pointed out the blunder did Hutchison return for his boots. Following Boukreev's directions, the

L **Reading Focus** Cause and Effect What are some causes of Hall's death?

Analyzing Visuals

Viewing and Interpreting
How does the mood of this photograph compare to the mood of the article?

On May 10, 1996, eighteen climbers await their turn at Hillary Step, under an hour from Mount Everest's summit.

Sherpas had no trouble locating the two bodies at the edge of the Kangshung Face.

The first body turned out to be Namba, but Hutchison couldn't tell who it was until he knelt in the howling wind and chipped a three-inch-thick carapace of ice from her face. To his shock, he discovered that she was still breathing. Both her gloves were gone, and her bare hands appeared to be frozen solid. Her eyes were dilated.[23] The skin on her face was the color of porcelain. "It was terrible," Hutchison recalls. "I was overwhelmed. She was very near death. I didn't know what to do."

He turned his attention to Weathers, who lay 20 feet away. His face was also caked with a thick armor of frost. Balls of ice the size of grapes were matted to his hair and eyelids. After cleaning the frozen detritus[24] from his face, Hutchison discovered that he, too, was still alive: "Beck was mumbling something, I think, but I couldn't tell what he was trying to say. His right glove was missing and he had terrible frostbite. He was as close to death as a person can be and still breathing."

Badly shaken, Hutchison went over to the Sherpas and asked Lhakpa Chhiri's advice. Lhakpa Chhiri, an Everest veteran respected by Sherpas and sahibs[25] alike for his mountain savvy, urged Hutchison to leave Weathers and Namba where they lay. Even if they survived long enough to be dragged back to Camp Four, they would certainly die before they could be carried down to Base Camp, and attempting a rescue would needlessly jeopardize the lives of the other climbers on the Col, most of whom were going to have enough trouble getting themselves down safely.

Hutchison decided that Chhiri was right. There was only one choice, however difficult: Let nature take its inevitable course with Weathers and Namba, and save the group's resources for those who could actually be helped. It was a classic act of triage.[26] When Hutchison returned to camp at 8:30 A.M. and told the rest of us of his decision, nobody doubted that it was the correct thing to do. **Ⓜ**

Later that day a rescue team headed by two of Everest's most experienced guides, Pete Athans and Todd Burleson, who were on the mountain with their own clients, arrived at Camp Four. Burleson was standing outside the tents about 4:30 P.M. when he noticed someone lurching slowly toward camp. The person's bare right hand, naked to the wind and horribly frostbitten, was outstretched in a weird, frozen salute. Whoever it was reminded Athans of a mummy in a low-budget horror film. The mummy turned out to be none other than Beck Weathers, somehow risen from the dead.

A couple of hours earlier, a light must have gone on in the reptilian core of Weathers' comatose[27] brain, and he regained consciousness. "Initially I thought I was in a dream," he recalls. "Then I saw how badly frozen my right hand was, and that helped bring me around to reality.

---

23. **dilated:** made wider; here, referring to the pupil of the eye.
24. **detritus** (dih TRY tuhs): debris.
25. **sahibs** (SAH ihbz): term used by Sherpas to refer to the paying members of the expeditions.

26. **triage** (tree AHZH): assigning of priorities of medical care based on chances for survival.
27. **comatose** (KOHM uh tohs): deeply unconscious due to injury or disease.

Ⓜ Reading Focus Cause and Effect Why does Hutchison decide to leave Weathers and Namba where they lie?

Vocabulary **jeopardize** (JEHP uhr dyz) v.: put in danger or at risk.

Finally I woke up enough to recognize that the cavalry[28] wasn't coming so I better do something about it myself." **N**

Although Weathers was blind in his right eye and able to focus his left eye within a radius of only three or four feet, he started walking into the teeth of the wind, deducing correctly that camp lay in that direction. If he'd been wrong he would have stumbled immediately down the Kangshung Face, the edge of which was a few yards in the opposite direction. Ninety minutes later he encountered "some unnaturally smooth, bluish-looking rocks," which turned out to be the tents of Camp Four.

The next morning, May 12, Athans, Burleson, and climbers from the IMAX team short-roped Weathers down to Camp Two. On the morning of May 13, in a hazardous helicopter rescue, Weathers and Gau[29] were evacuated from the top of the icefall by Lieutenant Colonel Madan Khatri Chhetri of the Nepalese army. A month later, a team of Dallas surgeons would amputate Weathers' dead right hand just below the wrist and use skin grafts to reconstruct his left hand.

After helping to load Weathers and Gau into the rescue chopper, I sat in the snow for a long while, staring at my boots, trying to get some grip, however **tenuous**, on what had happened over the preceding 72 hours. Then, nervous as a cat, I headed down into the icefall for one last trip through the maze of decaying seracs.[30]

I'd always known, in the abstract, that climbing mountains was a dangerous pursuit. But until I climbed in the Himalayas this spring, I'd never actually seen death at close range. And there was so much of it: Including three members of an Indo-Tibetan team who died on the north side just below the summit in the same May 10 storm

> I'd always known,
> in the abstract, that
> climbing mountains was
> a dangerous pursuit.

and an Austrian killed some days later, 11 men and women lost their lives on Everest in May 1996, a tie with 1982 for the worst single-season death toll in the peak's history. . . .[31]

Climbing mountains will never be a safe, predictable, rule-bound enterprise. It is an activity that idealizes risk-taking; its most celebrated figures have always been those who stuck their necks out the farthest and managed to get away with it. Climbers, as a species, are simply not distinguished by an excess of common sense. And that holds especially true for Everest climbers: When presented with a chance to reach the planet's highest summit, people are surprisingly quick to abandon prudence altogether. "Eventually," warns Tom Hornbein, 33 years after his ascent of the West Ridge, "what happened on Everest this season is certain to happen again." **O**

---

28. **cavalry** (KAV uhl ree): soldiers on horseback or motorized transport; an allusion to the idea that troops were not coming to the rescue.

29. **Gau:** "Makalu" Gau Ming-Ho, leader of the Taiwanese National Expedition, another team climbing on Everest.

---

30. **seracs** (say RAKS): pointed masses of ice.

31. **death toll . . . history:** It was actually the worst death toll on record. After Krakauer wrote this article, a twelfth death was discovered.

N **Reading Focus** Cause and Effect How did Weathers save his own life?

O **Literary Focus** Style How do these last two paragraphs differ from the rest of the article?

Vocabulary **tenuous** (TEHN yoo uhs) *adj.:* thin or slight; weak; fragile.

Applying Your Skills

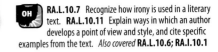
from Into Thin Air

Respond and Think Critically

Reading Focus

Quick Check

1. Make a list of the main events in this article. Identify the events during which Krakauer or other climbers were in serious danger.

Read with a Purpose

2. What risks did Krakauer and the other climbers take? What is their general attitude toward risk?

Reading Skills: Analyzing Cause and Effect

3. Review your cause-and-effect chart. Then, consider which event might have been most easily prevented. Which events caused the most serious or disastrous results?

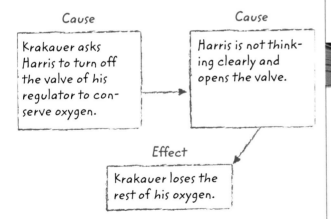

Cause

Krakauer asks Harris to turn off the valve of his regulator to conserve oxygen.

Cause

Harris is not thinking clearly and opens the valve.

Effect

Krakauer loses the rest of his oxygen.

Literary Focus

Literary Analysis

4. **Interpret** In a 1996 interview, Krakauer said, "We should think of Everest not as a mountain, but as the geologic embodiment of a myth." What do you think he meant?

Literary Skills: Style

5. **Evaluate** At what points in the article does Krakauer use shorter sentences? What effect does this style have on the reader? Explain your answer.

6. **Explain** How does Krakauer shift moods throughout the article? List some of the emotions he describes. How does his participation in the events he describes affect the mood of his narrative? Explain.

Literary Skills Review: Situational Irony

7. **Identify** This article contains many examples of **situational irony**—occasions when the opposite of what you expect to happen occurs. Identify two examples of situational irony. Explain both what you expected to happen and what does happen in the narrative.

Writing Focus

Think as a Reader/Writer

Use It in Your Writing Krakauer begins this article at the point when he reaches the top of Everest; then he reveals the nature of the tragedy that occurred. How does this technique of **flashback,** a shift to an earlier event, contribute to the narrative's suspense? Pick an event from today's news that interests you. Then, write a brief report of the event by using a journalistic style similar to Krakauer's.

What Do **You Think Now** What does Krakauer say about why mountain climbers take such risks? Do his conclusions apply to other risk takers as well? Explain.

Applying Your Skills

from **Into Thin Air**

Vocabulary Development

Vocabulary Check

Match each Vocabulary word with its synonym.

1. **benign**   a. decline
2. **crucial**   b. weak
3. **deteriorate** c. harmless
4. **tenuous**   d. endanger
5. **jeopardize** e. essential

Vocabulary Skills: Analogies

An **analogy** consists of two pairs of words. The words in the first pair relate to each other in the same way as the words in the second pair. For example, HOT : COLD and *tall : short* have the same relationship: Both pairs are **antonyms,** or opposites. Words can have many different kinds of relationships.
Examples:

Synonyms—FATIGUED : TIRED
Antonyms—FATIGUED : ENERGETIC
One word describes the other word—
FLOWER : FRAGRANT
One word is part of the other—KEYS : PIANO

Your Turn

Identify the relationship between the words in the first pair and choose the Vocabulary word that makes the second word pair have the same relationship as the first.

| benign |
| crucial |
| deteriorate |
| tenuous |
| jeopardize |

1. MISLEAD : DECEIVE :: _____ : endanger
2. TRIVIAL : MINOR :: _____ : important
3. WEAKEN : STRENGTHEN :: _____ : improve
4. STRONG : POWERFUL :: _____ : weak
5. MINOR : MAJOR :: _____ : harmful

Language Coach

Context Clues Almost every kind of work has its own **jargon,** or technical vocabulary. If you encounter one of these unfamiliar terms, you can figure out its meaning by looking at **context clues**—the other words in the sentence and the sentences around it. Find three examples in the selection of technical vocabulary and jargon related to mountain climbing. Use context to guess their meaning. Then, look in a dictionary to check your guesses.

Academic Vocabulary

Talk About . . .

In a small group, discuss the sequence of events in the article. What event begins the narrative? How does each subsequent event build on the rest to create suspense? What other techniques does Krakauer use to build suspense? Use the underlined Academic Vocabulary words in your discussion.

Learn It Online
Increase your word skills with *WordSharp*:

go.hrw.com   L10-520   Go

RA.L.10.8 Analyze the author's use of point of view, mood and tone. **VO.10.2** Analyze the relationships of pairs of words in analogical statements and infer word meanings from these relationships. *Also covered* **VO.10.6; WP.10.8; WA.10.5.a**

Grammar Link

Transitional Words and Phrases

Transitional words and phrases serve as signposts to help readers follow your thoughts. Transitions help you combine short, choppy sentences to form sentences that flow together. When you write, choose appropriate transitions to connect related ideas.

- **To compare:** *also, similarly, too, and, in addition*
- **To contrast:** *but, however, in contrast, even though*
- **To show cause and effect:** *for, so, as a result, because*
- **To give an example:** *for instance, for example, in fact, in other words*

Jon Krakauer has had real adventures; *for example,* he climbed Mount Everest. He expected a great experience, *but* he endured a disaster.

Your Turn

Use transitional words and phrases to show relationships between the following sentence pairs.

1. Krakauer was almost out of oxygen. He started the climb down.
2. He was relieved to be heading back to the camp. He got caught in a snowstorm.
3. The snow on Everest is not like snow you've seen. It hits you in the face at 70 miles per hour.
4. Krakauer struggled down through the snow. Other climbers were still going up.

Writing Applications Choose a piece of your own writing to enrich with transitional words and phrases. Identify related sentence pairs that are not connected by transitional words or phrases. Add transitions, using correct punctuation.

CHOICES

As you respond to the Choices, use these **Academic Vocabulary** words as appropriate: <u>component</u>, <u>subsequent</u>, <u>equivalent</u>, and <u>technique</u>.

REVIEW
Map Mood

Write a paragraph describing the ways in which the mood shifts as events unfold in the excerpt from "Into Thin Air." How and why do you think the author chose to create the different moods that he did? Use details from the text to illustrate your points.

CONNECT
Write a Persuasive Essay

Timed ⌐**Writing** Write a brief essay responding to one of these questions: (1) Is mountain climbing a foolhardy risk or a worthwhile adventure? (2) Should people pursuing dangerous sports have to pass a test or be licensed? Base your views on evidence as well as your opinions or experiences.

EXTEND
Plan a Slide Show

TechFocus With a small group, plan a slide show highlighting the key details and events in the article. Review the article, and decide which parts of the account could best be represented with photographs, diagrams, or other visuals. Decide how you will make your slides once you have gathered the images.

Learn It Online
Create multimedia presentations. Visit *MediaScope* at:
go.hrw.com | L10-521 | Go

Comparing Themes Across Genres

CONTENTS

A firefighter uses a thermal imaging device to look for signs of life on September 12, 2001.

What Do You Think

In the event of a disaster, would most people risk their lives to save a stranger?

 QuickWrite

Think of true stories you have heard about people who, facing danger and death, save the lives of strangers. Why do some people risk their own lives to save others? Why do some people look out for themselves first? Write down your thoughts.

Preparing to Read

from **102 Minutes/And of Clay Are We Created**

RA.L.10.5 Analyze how an author's choice of genre affects the expression of a theme or topic. *Also covered* **RA.I.10.1**

Literary Focus

Themes Across Genres Writers throughout history have explored universal themes in a variety of **genres,** or types of literature. As you read the following selections, note how the writers explore similar subjects and express similar ideas in two different genres—nonfiction and fiction. Writers express their insights about these subjects through **themes** in fiction and through **main ideas** in nonfiction.

Reading Focus

Analyzing an Author's Purpose When writing, authors may have one or more **purposes** in mind—to inform, persuade, entertain, or move their readers. Their purposes affect the choices they make about content, style, and the genre they choose.

Into Action As you read, use a chart like this one to note details from the texts. Then note what each detail suggests about the authors' purposes.

	Details	Purpose
102 Minutes		
And of Clay . . .		

Writing Focus

Think as a Reader/Writer

Find It in Your Reading As you read, look for **imagery** (language that appeals to our senses) that you find powerful. Record these images in your *Reader/Writer Notebook.*

TechFocus As you read, think about how technology can be used to give personal experiences universal meaning.

Reader/Writer Notebook

Use your **RWN** to complete the activities for these selections.

Vocabulary

***from* 102 Minutes**

extricate (EHKS truh kayt) *v.:* set free; release. *Crews worked for hours to extricate the men buried under the rubble.*

And of Clay Are We Created

tenacity (tih NAS uh tee) *n.:* stubborn persistence and determination. *Rolf Carlé showed tenacity during the rescue attempt.*

equanimity (ee kwuh NIHM uh tee) *n.:* calmness; composure. *Trapped in the mud, Azucena displayed equanimity.*

fortitude (FAWR tuh tood) *n.:* strength to endure pain or danger. *The girl's fortitude helped her endure the ordeal.*

resignation (rehz ihg NAY shuhn) *n.:* passive acceptance; submission. *Determined to save Azucena, Rolf showed no signs of resignation.*

Language Coach

Multiple-Meaning Words Many words in the English language have more than one meaning. *Resignation,* for example, means both "passive acceptance" and "the giving up of a job or a position." Write two sentences, and use a different meaning of *resignation* in each.

 Learn It Online
There's more to words than just definitions. Get the whole story on:

go.hrw.com   L10-523   **Go**

Learn It Online
Learn more about Isabel Allende at:
go.hrw.com L10-524 Go

Jim Dwyer
(1957–   )

Kevin Flynn
(1956–   )

Pulitzer Prize WINNER

City Boys

Jim Dwyer, a native New Yorker and the son of Irish immigrants, currently writes for *The New York Times*. In 1995, as a reporter for *Newsday*, he was awarded a Pulitzer Prize for Commentary for his compassionate writing about New York City.

Kevin Flynn is also an award-winning reporter. Like Dwyer, he is from New York City and works for *The New York Times*. Flynn was serving as police bureau chief for the *Times* on September 11, 2001.

Isabel Allende
(1942–   )

"Story Hunter"

Isabel Allende (ah YEHN deh) describes herself as a "good listener and a story hunter" who reads newspapers in search of story ideas. Allende was born in Peru, but she grew up in Chile. She eventually became a journalist. Soon after her uncle, Salvador Allende, the president of Chile, was killed in 1973, Isabel and her husband and children fled to Venezuela. They lived there in exile for thirteen years before moving to the United States.

Allende earned some acclaim for the columns she wrote in Chile. However, the poet Pablo Neruda told her, "You are a horrible journalist. But—you are a wonderful storyteller! You have the imagination of a great writer." Allende was nearly forty years old before she began to fully explore her gifts as a fiction writer. Of her writing she says, "When you accept as a writer that fiction is lying, then you become free; you can do anything."

Think About the Writers

What might fiction writers and journalists have in common? How might they be different?

Preview the Selections

In the following excerpt from *102 Minutes*, police officers **Will Jimeno** and **John McLoughlin** are trapped under rubble during the 2001 terrorist attack on the World Trade Center in New York City. **David Karnes**, a former Marine, and **Chuck Sereika**, a former emergency medical worker, come to their rescue.

In the short story "And of Clay Are We Created," **Azucena**, a thirteen-year-old girl trapped in a mudslide, struggles to survive while **Rolf Carlé**, a TV news reporter, attempts to rescue her.

from 102 Minutes:
The Untold Story of the Fight to Survive Inside the Twin Towers
by **Jim Dwyer** and **Kevin Flynn**

Read with a Purpose
Read this gripping account to discover how two men were rescued from the rubble after the Twin Towers collapsed in New York City on September 11, 2001.

Build Background
On September 11, 2001, terrorists hijacked four airplanes and crashed two of them into the Twin Towers of the World Trade Center in New York City. Set on fire, both towers eventually collapsed, trapping many people—including firefighters, police officers, medical workers, and office workers—in the rubble. The site of the devastation came to be known as Ground Zero. After the tragedy, reporters Jim Dwyer and Kevin Flynn interviewed rescuers and survivors of the World Trade Center attack and studied oral histories, e-mails, telephone messages, and radio transmissions. Their book, *102 Minutes: The Untold Story of the Fight to Survive Inside the Twin Towers,* is a moving account of what happened from the time the first plane struck until the collapse of the second tower. The following excerpt describes the terrifying situation of two members of the Port Authority Police Department that day.

11:00 A.M. GROUND ZERO

Will Jimeno found himself buried but alive, pinned below the burning ground at the center of the trade center plaza. A load of concrete had fallen onto his lap, and a cinder-block wall rested on one of his feet. The oxygen tank strapped to his back also was wedged into rubble, fixing him in a semblance of a seated position, bent at a forty-five-degree angle. Of the four other Port Authority police officers who had been running with him through the concourse, pushing a cart full of rescue gear, only one, Sgt. John McLoughlin, was still alive. Two members of their group had been killed immediately by the collapse of the south tower. A third officer, Dominick Pezzulo, had managed to free himself and was picking at the rubble around Jimeno when the collapse of the north tower killed him.

Now Jimeno was slumped in the hole, talking occasionally with McLoughlin, who was even deeper in the heap than Jimeno. The two men had no view of each other.

"Can you see sky?" McLoughlin asked.

"No sky, but light," Jimeno replied.

The sergeant worked his radio. No one answered. McLoughlin, who over the years had led elevator rescues at the trade center and rappelled[1] into the blind shafts, told Jimeno that the rescue operations would have to pull back

---

1. **rappelled** (ra PEHLD): descended a wall or shaft by using a rope to make a series of short drops.

for a day, until the scene was stable. They were on their own. **Ⓐ**

All across the northeastern United States, people were essentially on their own, stepping into the first minutes of a new epoch[2] without the protections of an old world order whose institutions and functions seemed to have turned instantly decrepit.[3] So a consideration of the events of September 11, 2001, could begin at any one of numerous spots across the globe, at almost any moment over the preceding four decades: the end of the Cold War;[4] the collapse of the Soviet Union;[5] any hour of any year in the unfinished history of the Middle East; in the often empty and petty exercise of authority in the capital of the world's only superpower; at the boiling, nihilistic[6] springs of religious fundamentalism[7] that not only have endured but have thrived as forces in opposition to globalism, capitalism, modernism.

Those historic currents, and others, merged and crashed on the morning of September 11 at the two towers of the World Trade Center, and at the Pentagon, and in a field in Pennsylvania. The particulars of the era that had just passed— the expectations of protection, the habits of defense, the sense of safety—seemed to have fossilized[8] from one breath to the next. What happened in New York City that morning was replicated through all the arms of government, differing only in details, duration, and cost. **Ⓑ**

An hour or so after the collapse, Will Jimeno, buried beneath the plaza, heard a voice coming through the same hole where the light was entering. The voice wanted to know if a particular person was down in the hole. Jimeno could not quite make out the name, but he was delighted by the sound of another human voice.

"No, but Jimeno and McLoughlin, PAPD, are down here," he yelled.

The voice did not answer, but moved off, and they heard no more from him.

Balls of fire tumbled into their tiny space, a gust of wind or a draft steering them away, the fire spending itself before it could find another morsel of fuel. Jimeno, thirty-three years old, felt that death was near. His wife, Allison, and their four-year-old daughter, Bianca, would be sad, but proud, he thought. The Jimenos' second child was due at the end of November. So he prayed. **Ⓒ**

Please, God, let me see my little unborn child.

---

2. **epoch** (EHP uhk): particular period of history.

3. **decrepit** (dih KREHP iht): broken down; weakened.

4. **Cold War:** state of hostility and rivalry between the United States and the Soviet Union, as well as their allies, which began after World War II and ended by 1991.

5. **collapse of the Soviet Union:** The Soviet Union, established in 1922, was dissolved in 1991 after the republics that made up the union achieved independence.

6. **nihilistic** (ny uh LIHS tihk): characterized by a destructive, violent rejection of established beliefs.

7. **religious fundamentalism:** religious movement that promotes the strict following of religious principles.

8. **fossilized** (FAHS uh lyzd): here, become out-of-date.

Ⓐ Literary Focus Themes Across Genres Jimeno and McLoughlin are "on their own." What theme do you think the authors might explore in this article?

Ⓑ Reading Focus Analyzing Author's Purpose In the last two paragraphs, why do you think the authors decided to interrupt their account to reflect on the historic currents in the last four decades?

Ⓒ Reading Focus Analyzing Author's Purpose Why do you think the authors include Jimeno's thoughts about his family? How do these details affect you?

Trade Center workers flee as firefighters rush up the stairs.

Jimeno tried to make a bargain. He might die, but surely there was a way he could do something for this child.

Somehow in the future, he prayed, let me touch this baby.

Then shots rang out.

The fireballs had apparently heated up the gun of the late Dominick Pezzulo. The rounds pinged off pipes and concrete, erratic and unpredictable, until the last of the ammunition was gone.

With his one free arm, Jimeno reached his gun belt for something to dig with. He had graduated from the Port Authority Police Academy in January and was issued the standard police tools, but he already owned his own handcuffs—a pair made by Smith & Wesson, bought when he was a security guard in a store, arresting shoplifters. He scraped at the rubble with them, but the cuffs slipped out of his hands, and he could not find them again.

No one had heard from Chuck Sereika, and by midmorning, the messages had piled up on his telephone answering machine and in his e-mail. Can't believe it. Hope you're okay. Our hearts are with you.

Sereika woke up. He had slept through everything, not a whisper of trouble in his apartment in midtown Manhattan. The e-mails told him something awful had happened, then news on his computer spelled it out, and as he blinked into the new world, he heard the messages on his answering machine. His sister had called.

"I love you," she said. "I know you're down there helping."

Actually, he had been moping. In his closet, he found a paramedic[9] sweatshirt and a badge he had not used for years. He had lost his paramedic license, let it lapse after he squandered too many days and nights carousing. He had gone into rehab programs, slipped, then climbed back on the wagon. He had fought his way back to sobriety, but the paramedic work was behind him. He still had the sweatshirt, though, and no one had taken the badge away. Maybe he could do some splints and bandages. He walked outside. Midtown Manhattan was teeming with people, a stream of humanity trooping in the middle of avenues, the subways shut down and scarcely a bus to be seen. The only way to move was on foot, and by the tens of thousands, people were walking north, or over to the river for ferries, or into Penn Station for a commuter train that would take them east to Long Island or west to New Jersey. **D**

Sereika walked a few blocks from his apartment to St. Luke's-Roosevelt Hospital Center. Then he hitched rides on ambulances going downtown.

---

9. **paramedic** (PAR uh mehd ihk): of or relating to a person trained to provide emergency medical care.

D **Literary Focus** **Themes Across Genres** In what way does Sereika's past make him an unlikely hero?

Seven World Trade Center—a forty-seven-story building—collapsed at 5:20 that afternoon. The firefighters had decided to let the fire there burn itself out. There was no one inside. Against all that had happened, the loss of even such an enormous building seemed like a footnote.

David Karnes had arrived downtown not long after its collapse, and as far as he could see, the searches were confined entirely to the periphery of the complex, picking through the rubble at the edges for signs of life. Other structures were now burning—the low-rise building at 4 World Trade Center was shooting flames—and all hands were staying clear of the ruins of the two towers and the plaza between them.

Karnes had started the morning in a business suit, working as an accountant for Deloitte and Touche in Wilton, Connecticut. After the attacks, he drove from Connecticut to Long Island and went to a storage facility where he kept his Marine kit. His utility trousers and jacket were freshly pressed, though his commitment had ended months earlier. Trim as a whip, he slipped into them, drove to a barber, and ordered a high and tight haircut. He stopped at his church and asked for prayers with the pastor, then with the top down on his new convertible, drove straight for lower Manhattan.

He found the rescue workers in shock, depressed, doing little by way of organized searches. Karnes spotted another Marine, a man named Sergeant Thomas, no first name.

"Come on, Sergeant," Karnes said. "Let's take a walk."

Not another soul was around them. They swept across the broken ground, yelling, "United States Marines. If you can hear us, yell or tap."

No one answered. They moved forward, deeper into the rubble. The fires roared at 4 World Trade Center. They plowed across the jagged, fierce ground. **Ⓔ**

Lost in thought, waiting for release, Will Jimeno listened to the trade center complex ripping itself apart. He had gotten tired of shouting at phantoms. He asked McLoughlin to put out a radio message that Officer Jimeno wanted his newborn baby to be named Olivia. The sergeant was in excruciating pain, his legs crushed. There was nothing to do, Jimeno thought, except wait until they sent out rescue parties in the morning. If they lived that long.

Then came the voice.

"United States Marines. If you can hear us, yell or tap."

What? That was a person.

Jimeno shouted with every bit of strength he had.

"Right here! Jimeno and McLoughlin, PAPD! Here!"

"Keep yelling," Karnes said.

It took a few minutes, but Karnes found the hole.

"Don't leave," Jimeno pleaded.

"I'm not going anywhere," Karnes said. **Ⓕ**

Karnes pulled out his cell phone and dialed 911, but the call did not go through. He tried again, without success. How could he get help, without leaving Jimeno and McLoughlin? Maybe the problem was with phone lines downtown, and he could find an electronic bridge via someone outside the city. He dialed his sister in a suburb of Pittsburgh and got through. She called the local police. They

---

Ⓔ **Literary Focus** Themes Across Genres What does Karnes's decision to put on his uniform and join the rescue efforts suggest about him?

Ⓕ **Reading Focus** Analyzing Author's Purpose How do you think Jimeno and McLoughlin are feeling at this point? Why do you think the authors avoid stating the men's feelings directly?

were able to reach the New York police. The message had traveled 300 miles from the pile to Pennsylvania, then 300 miles back to police headquarters, but the NYPD finally learned that a few blocks away, two cops were buried in the middle of the pile, and a United States Marine was standing by to direct the rescuers.

Chuck Sereika had been wandering the edge of that pile as evening approached, when he heard people yelling that someone had been found in the center of the place. Sereika set out, walking part of the way with a firefighter. They could see the flames roaring from the remains of 4 World Trade Center, an eight-story building. The firefighter peeled away. By himself, Sereika stumbled and climbed, until he found Dave Karnes standing alone. From the surface, he could see nothing of Will Jimeno, but he could hear him. Sereika squeezed his way into a crevice, inching his way down the rubble, finally spotting Jimeno's hand.

"Hey," Sereika said.

"Don't leave me," Jimeno said.

Sereika felt for a pulse. A good, strong distal pulse,[10] a basic in emergency care.

"Don't leave me," Jimeno said.

"We're not going to leave you," Sereika said. He pawed at the rubble and found Jimeno's gun, which he passed up to Karnes. Then he sent word for oxygen and an intravenous setup.[11] Two emergency service police officers,

---

10. **distal pulse:** *Distal* means "away from the center of the body." Here, *distal pulse* refers to the pulse in the wrist.

11. **intravenous setup:** equipment used to administer medicine or other substances directly into a vein.

Analyzing Visuals **Viewing and Interpreting** What does this photograph reveal about the challenges facing the rescuers?

A firefighter searches for survivors in the rubble of the Twin Towers.

529

Scott Strauss and Paddy McGee, soon arrived, and Sereika handed rocks and rubble back to them. A fireman, Tom Ascher, arrived with a hose to fight off the flames. They could hear McLoughlin calling out for help. **G**

We will get there, they promised.

The basics of trauma care are simple: provide fluids and oxygen. Simple—except that in the hole at the trade center, they could not take the next step in the classic formula: "load and go." First they had to extricate Jimeno, a highly delicate proposition.

Sereika could hear 4 World Trade Center groaning to its bones. To shift large pieces off Jimeno risked starting a new slide. There was room in the hole only for one person at a time, and Sereika was basically on top of him. It was not unlike working under the dashboard of a car, except the engine was on fire and the car was speeding and about to crash. The space was filled with smoke. Strauss and McGee were carefully moving the rubble, engineering on the fly, so that they could shift loads without bringing more debris down on themselves or on Jimeno and McLoughlin. Tools were passed from the street along a line of helpers. A hand-held air chisel. Shears. When the Hurst jaws of life[12] tool arrived, the officers wanted to use it to lift one particularly heavy section, but they could not quite get solid footing on the rubble. Sereika, the lapsed paramedic, immediately sized up the problem and shimmed rubble into place for the machine to rest on.

The work inched forward, treacherous and hot and slow.

After four hours, at 11 P.M., Will Jimeno was freed. They loaded him into a basket, slid him up the path to the surface. That left only John McLoughlin, deeper still, but none of the group in and around the hole could go on. They called down a fresh team that would work until the morning before they finally pulled him out, not long before the last survivor from stairway B, Genelle Guzman, would also be reached.

Aboveground, the men who had gone into the hole with Will Jimeno found they could barely walk. Smoke reeked from the hair on their heads, soot packed every pore on their skin. Sereika stumbled up from the crevice in time to see Jimeno in his basket being passed along police officers and firefighters who had set up a line, scores of people deep, across the jagged, broken ground.

He could not keep up with his patient. He could just about get himself to the sidewalk. He had worked for hours alongside the other men, first names only, and Sereika was employed by no official agency, no government body. Once they left the hole, the men lost track of each other. Just as people had come to work by themselves hours earlier, at the start of the day—an entire age ago—now Chuck Sereika was starting for home on his own. His old paramedic shirt torn, he plodded north in the late-summer night, alone, scuffling down streets blanketed by the dust that had been the World Trade Center. **H**

---

12. **Hurst jaws of life:** tool used to remove victims from collapsed concrete and steel structures.

G **Literary Focus** Themes Across Genres Jimeno worries that his rescuers might leave him, but his rescuers insist that they will stay. What main idea about the victims and rescuers do the authors suggest by focusing on these events?

H **Literary Focus** Themes Across Genres What ideas about heroism do the authors suggest by emphasizing that Sereika is "on his own" at the end of the selection?

Vocabulary **extricate** (EHKS truh kayt) v.: set free; release.

Applying Your Skills

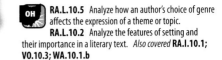

RA.L.10.5 Analyze how an author's choice of genre affects the expression of a theme or topic.
RA.L.10.2 Analyze the features of setting and their importance in a literary text. *Also covered* **RA.I.10.1; VO.10.3; WA.10.1.b**

from 102 Minutes

Respond and Think Critically

Reading Focus

Quick Check

1. Why couldn't Jimeno and McLoughlin free themselves from the rubble?

2. How did Sereika and Karnes play an essential role in the rescue of Jimeno?

Read with a Purpose

3. How were Jimeno and McLoughlin rescued? What obstacles did the rescuers face?

Reading Skills: Analyzing an Author's Purpose

4. Review the chart you created. Based on the details you noted, what do you think is the authors' overall purpose in writing this work?

	Details	Purpose
102 Minutes	3 of 5 officers killed	to show role of luck in Jimeno's rescue
And of Clay . . .		

✓ Vocabulary Check

Tell whether the following statement is true (T) or false (F). Then, use the word correctly in a sentence.

5. It is best to fly a kite in an open area to avoid having to **extricate** it from the branches of trees.

Literary Focus

Literary Analysis

6. **Analyze** Consider the sequence of events in the selection, and note how the authors tell about Jimeno, Sereika, and Karnes in alternating passages. How does this structure create suspense?

Literary Skills: Themes Across Genres

7. **Compare** Explain how Karnes and Sereika are similar and different. What main idea about heroes is suggested by these similarities and differences?

8. **Analyze** Throughout the selection, the authors emphasize that people are strangers and that they are alone. However, they also point out that the rescue depended on the efforts of many people. What main idea is suggested by these two points?

Literary Skills Review: Setting and Mood

9. **Describe** Which details of the **setting** (place and time) do the authors emphasize in this selection? Explain the **mood,** or feeling, evoked by these details.

Writing Focus

Think as a Reader/Writer

Use It in Your Writing Write a brief description of a dramatic event in your community. In order to make the event vivid for your readers, use imagery to show what you and others saw, heard, felt, smelled, or tasted.

AND OF CLAY ARE WE CREATED

by **Isabel Allende**

translated by **Margaret Sayers Peden**

Read with a Purpose
Read this story to explore how a journalist is affected by the plight of a girl trapped by a mudslide.

Preparing to Read for this selection is on page 523.

Build Background
On November 13, 1985, the long-dormant Nevado del Ruiz volcano erupted in the country of Colombia in South America. Molten rock and hot gases melted the volcano's thick ice cap and sent deadly mudslides down its slopes. More than 23,000 people died in the disaster—most of them in the town of Armero. Omayra Sánchez, a thirteen-year-old girl trapped in the mud, became the focus of much media attention. Allende uses these facts as the basis for this work of fiction. In her story, the trapped girl is named Azucena, and the man who attempts to rescue her is journalist Rolf Carlé.

They discovered the girl's head protruding from the mudpit, eyes wide open, calling soundlessly. She had a First Communion name, Azucena.[1] Lily. In that vast cemetery where the odor of death was already attracting vultures from far away, and where the weeping of orphans and wails of the injured filled the air, the little girl obstinately clinging to life became the symbol of the tragedy. The television cameras transmitted so often the unbearable image of the head budding like a black squash from the clay that there was no one who did not recognize her and know her name. And every time we saw her on the screen, right behind her was Rolf Carlé,[2] who had gone there on assignment, never suspecting that he would find a fragment of his past, lost thirty years before.

First a subterranean[3] sob rocked the cotton fields, curling them like waves of foam.

Geologists had set up their seismographs[4] weeks before and knew that the mountain had awakened again. For some time they had predicted that the heat of the eruption could detach the eternal ice from the slopes of the volcano, but no one heeded their warnings; they sounded like the tales of frightened old women. The towns in the valley went about their daily life, deaf to the moaning of the earth, until that fateful Wednesday night in November when a prolonged roar announced the end of the world, and walls of snow broke loose, rolling in an avalanche of clay, stones, and water that descended on the villages and buried them beneath unfathomable meters of telluric[5] vomit. As soon as the survivors emerged from the paralysis of that first awful terror, they could see that houses, plazas, churches, white cotton plantations, dark coffee forests, cattle pastures—all had disappeared. Much later, after soldiers and volunteers had arrived to rescue the

---

1. **Azucena** (ah soo SAY nah): Spanish for "lily."
2. **Rolf Carlé** (RAWLF kahr LAY).
3. **subterranean** (suhb tuh RAY nee uhn): underground.

4. **seismographs** (SYZ muh grafs): instruments that measure and record earthquakes and other tremors.
5. **telluric** (teh LUR ihk): of or from the earth.

living and try to assess the magnitude of the cataclysm,[6] it was calculated that beneath the mud lay more than twenty thousand human beings and an indefinite number of animals putrefying in a viscous soup.[7] Forests and rivers had also been swept away, and there was nothing to be seen but an immense desert of mire.[8] **(A)**

When the station called before dawn, Rolf Carlé and I were together. I crawled out of bed, dazed with sleep, and went to prepare coffee while he hurriedly dressed. He stuffed his gear in the green canvas backpack he always carried, and we said goodbye, as we had so many times before. I had no presentiments. I sat in the kitchen, sipping my coffee and planning the long hours without him, sure that he would be back the next day.

He was one of the first to reach the scene, because while other reporters were fighting their way to the edges of that morass[9] in jeeps, bicycles, or on foot, each getting there however he could, Rolf Carlé had the advantage of the television helicopter, which flew him over the avalanche. We watched on our screens the footage captured by his assistant's camera, in which he was up to his knees in muck, a microphone in his hand, in the midst of a bedlam[10] of lost

children, wounded survivors, corpses, and devastation. The story came to us in his calm voice. For years he had been a familiar figure in newscasts, reporting live at the scene of battles and catastrophes with awesome tenacity. Nothing could stop him, and I was always amazed at his equanimity in the face of danger and suffering; it seemed as if nothing could shake his fortitude or deter his curiosity. Fear seemed never to touch him, although he had confessed to me that he was not a courageous man, far from it. I believe that the lens of the camera had a strange effect on him; it was as if it transported him to a different time from which he could watch events without actually participating in them. When I knew him better, I came to realize that this fictive distance seemed to protect him from his own emotions. **(B)**

Rolf Carlé was in on the story of Azucena from the beginning. He filmed the volunteers who discovered her, and the first persons who tried to reach her; his camera zoomed in on the girl, her dark face, her large desolate eyes, the plastered-down tangle of her hair. The mud was like quicksand around her, and anyone attempting to reach her was in danger of sinking. They threw a rope to her that she made no effort to grasp until they shouted to her to catch it; then she pulled a hand from the mire and tried to move, but immediately sank a little deeper. Rolf threw down his knapsack and the rest of his equipment and waded into the quagmire, commenting for his assistant's microphone that it was cold and that one could begin to smell the stench of corpses.

---

6. **cataclysm** (KAT uh klihz uhm): disaster; great upheaval causing sudden, violent changes.
7. **putrefying in a viscous soup:** rotting in a thick mixture.
8. **mire** (myr): deep mud.
9. **morass** (muh RAS): bog; swamp.
10. **bedlam** (BEHD luhm): place or situation filled with noise and confusion.

(A) Reading Focus Analyzing Author's Purpose Why do you think Allende begins the story with a description of Azucena instead of with the details of the volcanic eruption?

(B) Literary Focus Themes Across Genres What qualities in Allende's description of Rolf Carlé are similar to those of the rescuers in the excerpt from *102 Minutes*?

Vocabulary **tenacity** (tih NAS uh tee) *n.:* stubborn persistence and determination.
equanimity (ee kwuh NIHM uh tee) *n.:* calmness; composure.
fortitude (FAWR tuh tood) *n.:* strength to endure pain or danger.

"What's your name?" he asked the girl, and she told him her flower name. "Don't move, Azucena," Rolf Carlé directed, and kept talking to her, without a thought for what he was saying, just to distract her, while slowly he worked his way forward in mud up to his waist. The air around him seemed as murky as the mud.

It was impossible to reach her from the approach he was attempting, so he retreated and circled around where there seemed to be firmer footing. When finally he was close enough, he took the rope and tied it beneath her arms, so they could pull her out. He smiled at her with that smile that crinkles his eyes and makes him look like a little boy; he told her that everything was fine, that he was here with her now, that soon they would have her out. He signaled the others to pull, but as soon as the cord tensed, the girl screamed. They tried again, and her shoulders and arms appeared, but they could move her no farther; she was trapped. Someone suggested that her legs might be caught in the collapsed walls of her house, but she said it was not just rubble, that she was also held by the bodies of her brothers and sisters clinging to her legs.

"Don't worry, we'll get you out of here," Rolf promised. Despite the quality of the transmission, I could hear his voice break, and I loved him more than ever. Azucena looked at him, but said nothing.

During those first hours Rolf Carlé exhausted all the resources of his ingenuity to rescue her. He struggled with poles and ropes, but every tug was an intolerable torture for the imprisoned girl. It occurred to him to use one of the poles as a lever but got no result and had to abandon the idea. He talked a couple of soldiers into working with him for a while, but they had to leave because so many other victims were calling for help. The girl could not move, she barely could breathe, but she did not seem desperate, as if an ancestral resignation allowed her to accept her fate. The reporter, on the other hand, was determined to snatch her from death. Someone brought him a tire, which he placed beneath her arms like a life buoy, and then laid a plank near the hole to hold his weight and allow him to stay closer to her. As it was impossible to remove the rubble blindly, he tried once or twice to dive toward her feet, but emerged frustrated, covered with mud, and spitting gravel. He concluded that he would have to have a pump to drain the water, and radioed a request for one, but received in return a message that there was no available transport

---

C **Literary Focus** Themes Across Genres In the last four paragraphs, the journalist has taken on the role of a rescuer. Which details suggest that he is forging a bond with the girl?

Vocabulary **resignation** (rehz ihg NAY shuhn) *n.*: passive acceptance; submission.

and it could not be sent until the next morning.

"We can't wait that long!" Rolf Carlé shouted, but in the pandemonium[11] no one stopped to commiserate. Many more hours would go by before he accepted that time had stagnated and reality had been irreparably distorted.

A military doctor came to examine the girl, and observed that her heart was functioning well and that if she did not get too cold she could survive the night.

"Hang on, Azucena, we'll have the pump tomorrow," Rolf Carlé tried to console her.

"Don't leave me alone," she begged.

"No, of course I won't leave you." **D**

Someone brought him coffee, and he helped the girl drink it, sip by sip. The warm liquid revived her and she began telling him about her small life, about her family and her school, about how things were in that little bit of world before the volcano had erupted. She was thirteen, and she had never been outside her village. Rolf Carlé, buoyed by a premature optimism, was convinced that everything would end well: the pump would arrive, they would drain the water, move the rubble, and Azucena would be transported by helicopter to a hospital where she would recover rapidly and where he could visit her and bring her gifts. He thought, She's already too old for dolls, and I don't know what would please her; maybe a dress. I don't know much about women, he concluded, amused, reflecting that although he had known many women in his lifetime, none had taught him these details. To pass the hours he began to tell Azucena about his travels and adventures as a newshound, and when he exhausted his memory, he called upon

imagination, inventing things he thought might entertain her. From time to time she dozed, but he kept talking in the darkness, to assure her that he was still there and to overcome the menace of uncertainty.

That was a long night.

Many miles away, I watched Rolf Carlé and the girl on a television screen. I could not bear the wait at home, so I went to National Television, where I often spent entire nights with Rolf editing programs. There, I was near his world, and I could at least get a feeling of what he lived through during those three decisive days. I called all the important people in the city, senators, commanders of the armed forces, the North American ambassador, and the president of National Petroleum, begging them for a pump to remove the silt, but obtained only vague promises. I began to ask for urgent help on radio and television, to see if there wasn't *someone* who could help us. Between calls I would run to the newsroom to monitor the satellite transmissions that periodically brought new details of the catastrophe. While reporters selected scenes with most impact for the news report, I searched for footage that featured Azucena's mud pit. The screen reduced the disaster to a single plane and accentuated the tremendous distance that separated me from Rolf Carlé; nonetheless, I was there with him. The child's every suffering hurt me as it did him; I felt his frustration, his impotence. Faced with the impossibility of communicating with him, the fantastic idea came to me that if I tried, I could reach him by force of mind and in that way give him encouragement. I concentrated until I was dizzy—a frenzied and

11. **pandemonium** (pan duh MOH nee uhm): wild disorder; great confusion.

D **Reading Focus** **Analyzing Author's Purpose** The story consists mostly of narration. Why do you think Allende chooses to use dialogue here?

futile activity. At times I would be overcome with compassion and burst out crying; at other times, I was so drained I felt as if I were staring through a telescope at the light of a star dead for a million years. **E**

I watched that hell on the first morning broadcast, cadavers of people and animals awash in the current of new rivers formed overnight from the melted snow. Above the mud rose the tops of trees and the bell towers of a church where several people had taken refuge and were patiently awaiting rescue teams. Hundreds of soldiers and volunteers from the Civil Defense were clawing through rubble searching for survivors, while long rows of ragged specters awaited their turn for a cup of hot broth. Radio networks announced that their phones were jammed with calls from families offering shelter to orphaned children. Drinking water was in scarce supply, along with gasoline and food. Doctors, resigned to amputating arms and legs without anesthesia, pled that at least they be sent serum and painkillers and antibiotics; most of the roads, however, were impassable, and worse were the bureaucratic obstacles that stood in the way. To top it all, the clay contaminated by decomposing bodies threatened the living with an outbreak of epidemics. **F**

Azucena was shivering inside the tire that held her above the surface. Immobility and tension had greatly weakened her, but she was conscious and could still be heard when a microphone was held out to her. Her tone was humble, as if apologizing for all the fuss. Rolf Carlé had a growth of beard, and dark circles beneath his eyes; he looked near exhaustion. Even from that enormous distance I could sense the quality of his weariness, so different from the fatigue of other adventures. He had completely forgot-

ten the camera; he could not look at the girl through a lens any longer. The pictures we were receiving were not his assistant's but those of other reporters who had appropriated Azucena, bestowing on her the pathetic responsibility of embodying the horror of what had happened in that place. With the first light Rolf tried again to dislodge the obstacles that held the girl in her tomb, but he had only his hands to work with; he did not dare use a tool for fear of injuring her. He fed Azucena a cup of the cornmeal mush and bananas the Army was distributing, but she immediately vomited it up. A doctor stated that she had a fever, but added that there was little he could do: Antibiotics were being reserved for cases of gangrene.[12] A priest also passed by and blessed her, hanging a medal of the Virgin around her neck. By evening a gentle, persistent drizzle began to fall.

"The sky is weeping," Azucena murmured, and she, too, began to cry.

"Don't be afraid," Rolf begged. "You have to keep your strength up and be calm. Everything will be fine. I'm with you, and I'll get you out somehow."

Reporters returned to photograph Azucena and ask her the same questions, which she no longer tried to answer. In the meanwhile, more television and movie teams arrived with spools of cable, tapes, film, videos, precision lenses, recorders, sound consoles, lights, reflecting screens, auxiliary motors, cartons of supplies, electricians, sound technicians, and cameramen: Azucena's face was beamed to millions of screens around the world. And all the while Rolf Carlé kept pleading for a pump. The improved

---

12. **gangrene** (GANG green): death or decay of flesh, usually caused by disease.

E Reading Focus **Analyzing Author's Purpose** The narrator is emotionally involved in the events of this story. Why do you think Allende chose to use this first-person narrator to tell the story?

F Reading Focus **Analyzing Author's Purpose** What do you think Allende wants the reader to feel about the tragedy?

technical facilities bore results, and National Television began receiving sharper pictures and clearer sound; the distance seemed suddenly compressed, and I had the horrible sensation that Azucena and Rolf were by my side, separated from me by impenetrable glass. I was able to follow events hour by hour; I knew everything my love did to wrest the girl from her prison and help her endure her suffering; I overheard fragments of what they said to one another and could guess the rest; I was present when she taught Rolf to pray, and when he distracted her with the stories I had told him in a thousand and one nights beneath the white mosquito netting of our bed. **G**

When darkness came on the second day, Rolf tried to sing Azucena to sleep with old Austrian folk songs he had learned from his mother, but she was far beyond sleep. They spent most of the night talking, each in a stupor of exhaustion and hunger, and shaking with cold. That night, imperceptibly, the unyielding floodgates that had contained Rolf Carlé's past for so many years began to open, and the torrent of all that had lain hidden in the deepest and most secret layers of memory poured out, leveling before it the obstacles that had blocked his consciousness for so long. He could not tell it all to Azucena; she perhaps did not know there was a world beyond the sea or time previous to her own; she was not capable of imagining Europe in the years of the war. So he could not tell her of defeat, nor of the afternoon the Russians had

led them to the concentration camp to bury prisoners dead from starvation. Why should he describe to her how the naked bodies piled like a mountain of firewood resembled fragile china? How could he tell this dying child about ovens and gallows? Nor did he mention the night that he had seen his mother naked, shod in stiletto-heeled red boots, sobbing with humiliation. There was much he did not tell, but in those hours he relived for the first time all the things his mind had tried to erase. Azucena had surrendered her fear to him and so, without wishing it, had obliged Rolf to confront his own. There, beside that hellhole of mud, it was impossible for Rolf to flee from himself any longer, and the visceral[13] terror he had lived as a boy suddenly invaded him.

He reverted to the years when he was the age of Azucena, and younger, and, like her, found himself trapped in a pit without escape, buried in life, his head barely above ground; he saw before his eyes the boots and legs of his father, who had removed his belt and was whipping it in the air with the never-forgotten hiss of a viper coiled to strike. Sorrow flooded through him, intact and precise, as if it had lain always in his mind, waiting. He was once again in the armoire[14] where his father locked him to punish him for imagined misbehavior, there where for eternal

Sorrow flooded through him, intact and precise.

13. **visceral** (VIHS uhr uhl): intuitive or emotional rather than intellectual.
14. **armoire** (ahr MWAHR): large cupboard for holding clothes.

G **Literary Focus** **Themes Across Genres** What do the details in this paragraph suggest about the ways in which Rolf is both able and unable to help Azucena?

(Above) *Shadow of a Magnitude* (1999) by David Prifti. Sculpture.
Courtesy of the artist.

hours he had crouched with his eyes closed, not to see the darkness, with his hands over his ears, to shut out the beating of his heart, trembling, huddled like a cornered animal. Wandering in the mist of his memories he found his sister Katharina, a sweet, retarded child who spent her life hiding, with the hope that her father would forget the disgrace of her having been born. With Katharina, Rolf crawled beneath the dining room table, and with her hid there under the long white tablecloth, two children forever embraced, alert to footsteps and voices. Katharina's scent melded with his own sweat, with aromas of cooking, garlic, soup, freshly baked bread, and the unexpected odor of putrescent[15] clay. His sister's hand in his, her frightened breathing, her silk hair against his cheek, the candid gaze of her eyes. Katharina . . . Katharina materialized before him, floating on the air like a flag, clothed in the white tablecloth, now a winding sheet, and at last he could weep for her death and for the guilt of having abandoned her. He understood then that all his exploits as a reporter, the feats that had won him such recognition and fame, were merely an attempt to keep his most ancient fears at bay, a stratagem[16] for taking refuge behind a lens to test whether reality was more tolerable from that perspective. He took excessive risks as an exercise of courage, training by day to conquer the monsters that tormented him by night. But he had come face to face with the moment of truth; he could not continue to escape his past. He

> She had not come to dry his tears, but to tell him to pick up a shovel.

was Azucena; he was buried in the clayey mud; his terror was not the distant emotion of an almost forgotten childhood, it was a claw sunk in his throat. In the flush of his tears he saw his mother, dressed in black and clutching her imitation-crocodile pocketbook to her bosom, just as he had last seen her on the dock when she had come to put him on the boat to South America. She had not come to dry his tears, but to tell him to pick up a shovel: the war was over and now they must bury the dead. **(H)**

"Don't cry. I don't hurt anymore. I'm fine," Azucena said when dawn came.

"I'm not crying for you," Rolf Carlé smiled. "I'm crying for myself. I hurt all over."

The third day in the valley of the cataclysm began with a pale light filtering through storm clouds. The President of the Republic visited the area in his tailored safari jacket to confirm that this was the worst catastrophe of the century; the country was in mourning; sister nations had offered aid; he had ordered a state of siege; the Armed Forces would be merciless, anyone caught stealing or committing other offenses would be shot on sight. He added that it was impossible to remove all the corpses or count the thousands who had disappeared; the entire valley would be declared holy ground, and bishops would come to celebrate a solemn mass for the souls of the victims. He went to the Army field tents to offer relief in the form of vague promises to crowds of the rescued, then to the improvised hospital to offer a word of encouragement to doctors and nurses worn down from so many

---

15. **putrescent** (pyoo TREHS uhnt): rotting.
16. **stratagem** (STRAT uh juhm): plan or scheme for achieving some goal.

(H) Literary Focus **Themes Across Genres** How is Carlé's interaction with Azucena changing him? In what way do the parallels between the two characters hint at a theme in the story?

hours of tribulations.[17] Then he asked to be taken to see Azucena, the little girl the whole world had seen. He waved to her with a limp statesman's hand, and microphones recorded his emotional voice and paternal tone as he told her that her courage had served as an example to the nation. Rolf Carlé interrupted to ask for a pump, and the President assured him that he personally would attend to the matter. I caught a glimpse of Rolf for a few seconds kneeling beside the mud pit. On the evening news broadcast, he was still in the same position; and I, glued to the screen like a fortuneteller to her crystal ball, could tell that something fundamental had changed in him. I knew somehow that during the night his defenses had crumbled and he had given in to grief; finally he was vulnerable. The girl had touched a part of him that he himself had no access to, a part he had never shared with me. Rolf had wanted to console her, but it was Azucena who had given him consolation. **❶**

I recognized the precise moment at which Rolf gave up the fight and surrendered to the torture of watching the girl die. I was with them, three days and two nights, spying on them from the other side of life. I was there when she told him that in all her thirteen years no boy had ever loved her and that it was a pity to leave this world without knowing love. Rolf assured her that he loved her more than he could ever love anyone, more than he loved his mother, more than his sister, more than all the women who had slept in his arms, more than he loved me, his life companion, who would have given anything to be trapped in that well in her place, who would have exchanged her

life for Azucena's, and I watched as he leaned down to kiss her poor forehead, consumed by a sweet, sad emotion he could not name. I felt how in that instant both were saved from despair, how they were freed from the clay, how they rose above the vultures and helicopters, how together they flew above the vast swamp of corruption and laments. How, finally, they were able to accept death. Rolf Carlé prayed in silence that she would die quickly, because such pain cannot be borne.

By then I had obtained a pump and was in touch with a general who had agreed to ship it the next morning on a military cargo plane. But on the night of that third day, beneath the unblinking focus of quartz lamps and the lens of a hundred cameras, Azucena gave up, her eyes locked with those of the friend who had sustained her to the end. Rolf Carlé removed the life buoy, closed her eyelids, held her to his chest for a few moments, and then let her go. She sank slowly, a flower in the mud.

You are back with me, but you are not the same man. I often accompany you to the station and we watch the videos of Azucena again; you study them intently, looking for something you could have done to save her, something you did not think of in time. Or maybe you study them to see yourself as if in a mirror, naked. Your cameras lie forgotten in a closet; you do not write or sing; you sit long hours before the window, staring at the mountains. Beside you, I wait for you to complete the voyage into yourself, for the old wounds to heal. I know that when you return from your nightmares, we shall again walk hand in hand, as before. **❶**

---

17. **tribulations** (trihb yuh LAY shuhnz): miseries; sufferings.

---

❶ Reading Focus Analyzing Author's Purpose Why do you think Allende includes this scene in which the president visits the area?

❶ Reading Focus Analyzing Author's Purpose In this final paragraph, the narrator speaks directly to Carlé. What effect does Allende achieve by ending the story with such an intimate moment?

Applying Your Skills

RA.L.10.5 Analyze how an author's choice of genre affects the expression of a theme or topic. **RA.L.10.11** Explain ways in which an author develops a point of view and style, and cite specific examples from the text. **RA.L.10.9** Explain how authors use symbols to create broader meanings. *Also covered* **RA.I.10.1; VO.10.3; WA.10.1.b**

And of Clay Are We Created

Respond and Think Critically

Reading Focus

Quick Check

1. What emotions and qualities does Azucena display in the face of her tragic situation?
2. How does Rolf Carlé try to help Azucena?

Read with a Purpose

3. What does Carlé realize on the second night of the rescue attempt? How does he change as a result?

Reading Skills: Analyzing an Author's Purpose

4. Review your chart. What do you think is Allende's overall purpose in writing this story? How is it similar to that of Dwyer and Flynn?

	Details	Purpose
102 Minutes	3 of 5 officers killed	to show role of luck in Jimeno's rescue
And of Clay . . .	Rolf will find part of his past.	to arouse reader's curiosity

✔ Vocabulary Check

Tell whether each statement is true (T) or false (F).

5. Someone with **tenacity** does not give up easily.
6. A person who displays **equanimity** in the face of trouble will be nervous and upset.
7. Heroes typically show **fortitude** when they take great risks in order to save the lives of others.
8. If people protest against a judge's decision, they show **resignation.**

Literary Focus

Literary Analysis

9. **Analyze** Explain how the narrator is both "separated" from Carlé and "there with him" as events unfold in the story. How would you describe the narrator's feelings for him?

10. **Evaluate** In what ways are the media in the story both powerful and powerless? Do you think Allende is critical of the media? Explain.

Literary Skills: Themes Across Genres

11. **Synthesize** The story's title contains an **allusion,** or familiar reference, to passages from the Bible in which people are viewed as being shaped from clay. A number of world religions and myths also refer to people as being created from earth (or clay or dust) and being returned to earth. Why might Allende have titled the story "And of Clay Are We Created"? What universal theme is suggested by this title?

Literary Skills Review: Symbolism

12. **Analyze** Azucena serves as a **symbol** (a person or an object or event that stands both for itself and for something else). What does Azucena symbolize in the story?

Writing Focus

Think as a Reader/Writer

Use It in Your Writing Imagine that after the failed rescue attempt, Rolf Carlé recorded his experiences in a journal. Write one journal entry from his point of view in which you use imagery to help convey his reactions.

Wrap Up

RA.L.10.5 Analyze how an author's choice of genre affects the expression of a theme or topic. **RA.I.10.1** Identify and understand organizational patterns and techniques, including repetition of ideas, syntax and word choice, that authors use to accomplish their purpose and reach their intended audience. *Also covered* **VO.10.6; WA.10.4.c; WA.10.1.b; C.10.8.b**

from 102 Minutes / And of Clay Are We Created

Writing Focus

Write a Comparison-Contrast Essay

Topic Throughout time, people from many cultures have shared stories about heroism. Write an essay in which you compare and contrast Chuck Sereika and Rolf Carlé in the excerpt from *102 Minutes* and in "And of Clay Are We Created." Answer the following questions in your essay: Do you think each man is a hero? What theme or main idea about heroism does each author express? In your essay, consider the following points:

- the nature of the disaster and the situation of the victims in each work
- the actions and attitudes of Sereika and Carlé as well as their pasts
- the fates of the victims

Organization You can organize the ideas in your comparison-contrast essay in one of two ways:

- **Block Method:** Using this method, you will organize your essay by subject. First, present all your ideas about *102 Minutes*. Then, present all your ideas about "And of Clay Are We Created."
- **Point-by-Point Method:** Using this method, you will organize your essay by related ideas. Discuss your first idea as it relates to each selection. Then, discuss subsequent ideas as they relate to each selection.

What Do **You** **Think** **Now**

What do these two selections reveal about how some people respond to the suffering of others?

CHOICES

As you respond to the Choices, use these **Academic Vocabulary** words as appropriate: component, subsequent, equivalent, and technique.

REVIEW

Compare Genres

With a partner, brainstorm a list of other works in a variety of genres, such as myths, graphic novels, and movies, which focus on fictional or real heroes. How do the heroes and themes or main ideas in these works compare with those in *102 Minutes* and "And of Clay Are We Created"? Create a chart to identify the universal themes in these genres.

CONNECT

Write a Critical Review

Timed ⏱**Writing** Consider the events described in *102 Minutes* and "And of Clay Are We Created," the themes or main ideas and the genres of each selection, and the authors' writing styles. What techniques do the authors use? Which selection did you find more powerful? Why? Write a critical review expressing your opinion. Be sure to support your opinion with details from the works.

EXTEND

Deliver an Oral Presentation

TechFocus Use the Internet to research a recent natural disaster, and then consider these questions: Are certain aspects of the disaster covered in multiple sources? Do certain images appear repeatedly? Does Internet coverage make aspects of the disaster seem universal? Is coverage on the Internet equivalent to print and television coverage? Deliver an oral presentation to share your analysis.

Generating Research Questions

Woman at memorial for World Trade Center victims.

 In the face of a national tragedy, how do we account for our mistakes?

 QuickTalk

With a partner, discuss what you know about 9/11. What problems did rescue workers and first responders face in New York and at the Pentagon? How were rescue efforts hindered?

GRAPHIC ADAPTATION
Preparing to Read

from The 9/11 Report

R.10.1 Compose open-ended questions for research, assigned or personal interest, and modify questions as necessary during inquiry and investigation to narrow the focus or extend the investigation.

Reader/Writer Notebook

Use your **RWN** to complete the activities for this selection.

Informational Text Focus

Generating Research Questions Doing research involves asking questions and searching for answers. You can start by identifying a subject and determining what you already know about it. Then, ask questions on topics you want to know more about. By creating answerable questions, you will have a guide to your research.

Tips for Generating Good Questions

Stay focused. Don't write a long list of questions covering everything you could possibly ask about a broad, general subject. Stick to a narrowed topic. Try to identify the **main idea** of your topic in order to keep your questions focused.

Do what reporters do. Research questions that can be answered with *yes* or *no* will get you nowhere. When reporters investigate a story, their questions begin with *who, what, where, when, why,* and *how.* Asking these *5W-How?* **questions** will lead you to specific information.

Be realistic. Ask questions that you think you can answer with the resources available to you.

Into Action Before you begin, create a **KWL chart** to help you focus your research. In the **K** column, list what you already know about the topic. In the **W** column, list the questions you have—what you want to learn. You'll fill out the **L** column once you've done the research, telling what you've learned.

K—Know	W—Want to Learn	L—Learned

Vocabulary

unprecedented (uhn PREHS uh dehn tihd) *adj.:* never done before; new. *The severity of the attacks was unprecedented on American soil.*

integrated (IHN tuh gray tihd) *v.* used as *adj.:* made up of elements that work together; combined. *The response teams needed an integrated communications system.*

Language Coach

Prefixes A **prefix** is a group of letters added to the beginning of another word or word root that changes that word's meaning. For example, the prefix *un–* means "not." Based on this information, what do you think *precedented* means? List at least five other words that begin with the prefix *un–*.

Writing Focus Preparing for **Constructed Response**

Use the tips for generating research questions to come up with an appropriate research question for the following selection.

Learn It Online
To read more articles like this, go to the interactive Reading Workshops on:

go.hrw.com L10-543

Build Background

On September 11, 2001, terrorists hijacked four planes from eastern U.S. airports: Two planes were piloted into the World Trade Center in New York City, one plane crashed into the Pentagon in Washington, D.C., and one plane crashed in an open field in Pennsylvania after the passengers apparently took control. Both of the World Trade Center towers collapsed, causing 2,750 deaths. At the Pentagon, 184 people were killed, and 40 people were killed in Pennsylvania.

In December 2002, President George W. Bush established a 9/11 Commission—also called the National Commission on Terrorist Attacks Upon the United States—to create a full report of the circumstances around the 9/11 attacks, to investigate whether these attacks could have been prevented, and to recommend actions to try to ensure that attacks like these would not happen again. The 9/11 Commission published its findings in a report released in July 2004.

ABOUT THE 9/11 REPORT

From Text to Graphics

In 2006, fellow cartoonists Ernie Colón and Sid Jacobson decided to adapt *The 9/11 Report* into a graphic form.

"Our desire to adapt *The 9/11 Report* arose from the desire to render the complex accessible. After both of us struggled with the verbal labyrinth of the original report, we decided there must be a better way. Then it occurred to us . . . that visually adapting the information in the report—comics, the graphic medium—was the better way. We could tell the story graphically to make it more easily understood. . . . What was more, we could make it more informative, more available, and, to be frank, more likely to be read in its entirety."

Tips for Reading Graphic Texts

When reading graphic texts, it's important to look at the images and read the accompanying text. Here are some tips for reading graphic texts:

- Read the panels as you would a printed page. Read from left to right and from the top of the page to the bottom.
- Read one panel at a time. First, read the text in the panel. Then, study the illustration.
- Look carefully at the faces of the characters. Think about what their facial expressions or body language tells you.
- Ask yourself, "What do the pictures add to the text?"

Terms to Know

Knowing the meanings of these abbreviations will help you understand the text.

FDNY: Fire Department of New York
WTC: World Trade Center
NYPD: New York Police Department
PAPD: Port Authority Police Department

The following excerpt from *The 9/11 Report* is from Chapter 9: "Heroism and Horror."

from THE 9/11 REPORT

A Graphic Adaptation
by Sid Jacobson and Ernie Colón

Based on the Final Report of the National Commission
on Terrorist Attacks Upon the United States

SEPTEMBER 11, 2001, WAS A DAY OF UNPRECEDENTED SHOCK AND SUFFERING IN THE HISTORY OF THE UNITED STATES. THE NATION WAS UNPREPARED. HOW DID THIS HAPPEN, AND HOW CAN WE AVOID SUCH TRAGEDY AGAIN? TEN COMMISSIONERS WERE GIVEN A SWEEPING MANDATE TO FIND ANSWERS AND OFFER RECOMMENDATIONS. ON JULY 22, 2004, THEY ISSUED THEIR REPORT...

A

With a foreword by the Chair and
Vice Chair of the 9/11 Commission,
Thomas H. Kean and Lee H. Hamilton

A **Informational Focus** **Research Questions** What questions were posed by the ten commissioners who made up the 9/11 Commission?

Vocabulary **unprecedented** (uhn PREHS uh dehn tihd) *adj.:* never done before; new.

Emergency Response at the Pentagon

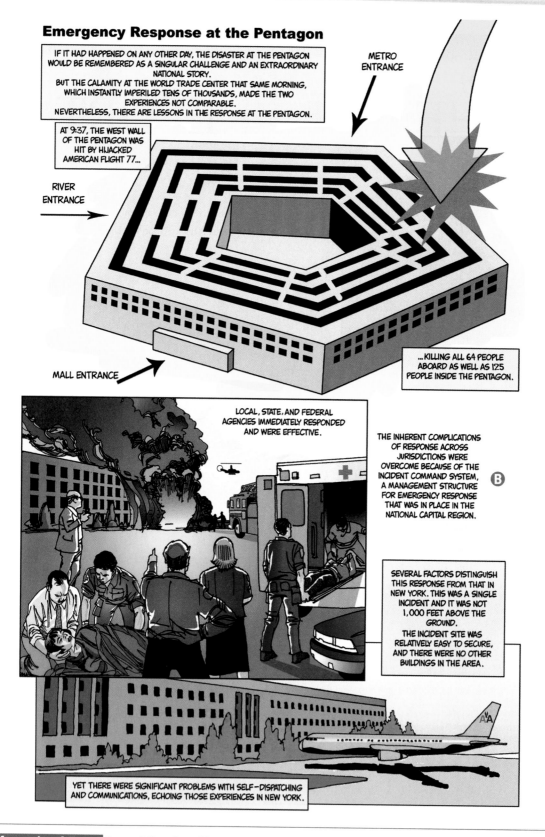

IF IT HAD HAPPENED ON ANY OTHER DAY, THE DISASTER AT THE PENTAGON WOULD BE REMEMBERED AS A SINGULAR CHALLENGE AND AN EXTRAORDINARY NATIONAL STORY.
BUT THE CALAMITY AT THE WORLD TRADE CENTER THAT SAME MORNING, WHICH INSTANTLY IMPERILED TENS OF THOUSANDS, MADE THE TWO EXPERIENCES NOT COMPARABLE.
NEVERTHELESS, THERE ARE LESSONS IN THE RESPONSE AT THE PENTAGON.

METRO ENTRANCE

AT 9:37, THE WEST WALL OF THE PENTAGON WAS HIT BY HIJACKED AMERICAN FLIGHT 77...

RIVER ENTRANCE

...KILLING ALL 64 PEOPLE ABOARD AS WELL AS 125 PEOPLE INSIDE THE PENTAGON.

MALL ENTRANCE

LOCAL, STATE, AND FEDERAL AGENCIES IMMEDIATELY RESPONDED AND WERE EFFECTIVE.

THE INHERENT COMPLICATIONS OF RESPONSE ACROSS JURISDICTIONS WERE OVERCOME BECAUSE OF THE INCIDENT COMMAND SYSTEM, A MANAGEMENT STRUCTURE FOR EMERGENCY RESPONSE THAT WAS IN PLACE IN THE NATIONAL CAPITAL REGION. **B**

SEVERAL FACTORS DISTINGUISH THIS RESPONSE FROM THAT IN NEW YORK. THIS WAS A SINGLE INCIDENT AND IT WAS NOT 1,000 FEET ABOVE THE GROUND.
THE INCIDENT SITE WAS RELATIVELY EASY TO SECURE, AND THERE WERE NO OTHER BUILDINGS IN THE AREA.

YET THERE WERE SIGNIFICANT PROBLEMS WITH SELF-DISPATCHING AND COMMUNICATIONS, ECHOING THOSE EXPERIENCES IN NEW YORK.

B **Informational Focus** Research Questions Where might you look to find more information about the Incident Command System?

Analysis

IN NEW YORK, THE FDNY, NYPD, THE PORT AUTHORITY, WTC EMPLOYEES, AND THE WTC OCCUPANTS THEMSELVES DID THEIR BEST TO COPE WITH AN UNIMAGINABLE CATASTROPHE FOR WHICH THEY WERE UNPREPARED IN TERMS OF TRAINING AND MIND-SET.

IT HAS BEEN ESTIMATED THAT BETWEEN 16,400 AND 18,800 CIVILIANS WERE IN THE WTC AS OF 8:46 ON SEPTEMBER 11. AT MOST, 2,152 INDIVIDUALS DIED AT THE WTC COMPLEX WHO WERE NOT RESCUE WORKERS OR ON THE TWO PLANES.

OUT OF THIS NUMBER, 1,942 WERE AT OR ABOVE THE IMPACT ZONES. THIS DATA STRONGLY SUPPORTS THAT THE EVACUATION WAS A SUCCESS FOR CIVILIANS BELOW THE IMPACT.

THE EVACUATION WAS AIDED BY CHANGES MADE BY THE PORT AUTHORITY IN RESPONSE TO THE 1993 BOMBING, REDUCING EVACUATION TIME FROM MORE THAN FOUR HOURS TO UNDER AN HOUR ON SEPTEMBER 11.

WE'VE GOT TO GET OUT OF HERE!

THE "FIRST" RESPONDERS ON 9/11 WERE PRIVATE-SECTOR CIVILIANS. BECAUSE 85% OF OUR NATION'S INFRASTRUCTURE IS CONTROLLED BY THE PRIVATE SECTOR, CIVILIANS ARE LIKELY TO BE THE FIRST RESPONDERS IN ANY FUTURE CATASTROPHE. THEREFORE, THE COMMISSION MAKES THE FOLLOWING CONCLUSIONS.

THE CIVILIANS AT OR ABOVE THE IMPACT ZONE HAD THE SMALLEST HOPE OF SURVIVAL. THEIR ONLY HOPE WAS A SWIFT AIR RESCUE, BUT THIS WAS IMPOSSIBLE.

WTC 2
WTC 1

78TH 84TH FLOORS
94TH 98TH FLOORS

THE WTC LACKED ANY PLAN FOR EVACUATION OF THE UPPER FLOORS IN THE EVENT ALL STAIRWELLS WERE IMPASSABLE.

NO DECISION HAS BEEN CRITIZED MORE THAN THAT OF BUILDING PERSONNEL NOT TO EVACUATE THE SOUTH TOWER AFTER THE NORTH WAS HIT.

LESS UNDERSTANDABLE TO THE COMMISSION WAS THE INSTRUCTION TO SOME CIVILIANS WHO HAD REACHED THE LOBBY TO RETURN TO THEIR OFFICES!

C

NYPD 911 OPERATORS AND FDNY DISPATCH WERE NOT ADEQUATELY INTEGRATED AND GAVE OUT WRONG DIRECTIONS.

ONE LESSON IS THE NEED TO INTEGRATE THEM INTO THE RESPONSE SYSTEM AND INVOLVE THEM IN PROVIDING UP-TO-DATE ASSISTANCE AND INFORMATION.

SORRY, THIS IS RESERVED FOR FIRE TRUCKS ONLY.

LADDER 2 FIRE

INDIVIDUALS SHOULD KNOW THE EXACT LOCATION OF EVERY STAIRWELL AND HAVE ACCESS AT ALL TIMES TO FLASHLIGHTS.

THOUGH MAYOR GIULIANI'S EMERGENCY DIRECTIVE OF JULY 2001 WAS FOLLOWED TO SOME DEGREE ...

...IT IS CLEAR THAT THE RESPONSE LACKED THE KIND OF INTEGRATED COMMUNICATION AND UNIFIED COMMAND CONTEMPLATED IN THE DIRECTIVE.

C **Informational Focus** Research Questions What questions do you have about the instruction given by building personnel?

Vocabulary **integrated** (IHN tuh gray tihd) *v.* used as *adj.*: made up of elements that work together; combined.

D Informational Focus **Research Questions** What questions do you have about the plan adopted in May 2004? Where could you go to find more information?

Read with a Purpose What problems existed in the emergency responses to the terrorist attacks?

GRAPHIC ADAPTATION
Applying Your Skills

VO.10.3 Infer the literal and figurative meaning of words and phrases and discuss the function of figurative language, including metaphors, similes, idioms and puns. *Also covered* **R.10.1**

from The 9/11 Report

Practicing the Standards

Informational Text and Vocabulary

1. Which of the following research questions is *not* related to the issues in this selection?

   A Who were the hijackers involved in the 9/11 attacks?

   B How has communication between agencies improved since *The 9/11 Report?*

   C Why was the Pentagon site easier to secure than the WTC site?

   D What factors contributed to the chaos at the rescue sites of the Pentagon and WTC?

2. What questions are *not* answered in this excerpt?

   A How many people were killed as a result of the crash into the Pentagon?

   B Who had the lowest chance of survival at the WTC?

   C Who were the first responders at the WTC?

   D What was wrong with the radios used by the Port Authority Police Department?

3. Which statement *best* sums up the **main idea** of this selection?

   A The first responders at the WTC were primarily civilians.

   B The NYPD was the most successful department involved at the WTC.

   C Both civilians and emergency personnel need to be better prepared for terrorist attacks in the future.

   D There were fewer communication problems at the Pentagon than at the WTC.

4. Which of the following questions is unanswerable, even with further research?

   A What efforts have been made to change the emergency response plans?

   B How has the FDNY resolved its dispatching problems?

   C When will terrorists attack the United States again?

   D Why did the 9/11 Commission find the 2004 Emergency Response Plan insufficient?

5. An *unprecedented* event is one that —

   A happens all the time

   B will never happen

   C has never happened before

   D will happen in the future

6. An *integrated* effort is —

   A doomed

   B combined

   C influential

   D isolated

Writing Focus   Constructed Response

Develop two research questions about this excerpt from *The 9/11 Report*. Make sure your questions are focused and answerable.

What Do You Think Now

Do you think the report from the 9/11 Commission helped identify problems with the response systems? Explain.

Literary Skills Review

Form and Style **Directions:** Read the following selection. Then, read and respond to the questions that follow.

Mint Snowball by **Naomi Shihab Nye**

My great-grandfather on my mother's side ran a drugstore in a small town in central Illinois. He sold pills and rubbing alcohol from behind the big cash register and creamy ice cream from the soda fountain. My mother remembers the counter's long polished sweep, its shining face. She twirled on the stools. Dreamy fans. Wide summer afternoons. Clink of nickels in anybody's hand. He sold milkshakes, cherry cokes, old-fashioned sandwiches. What did an old-fashioned sandwich look like? Dark wooden shelves. Silver spigots on chocolate dispensers.

My great-grandfather had one specialty: a Mint Snowball which he invented. Some people drove all the way in from Decatur just to taste it. First he stirred fresh mint leaves with sugar and secret ingredients in a small pot on the stove for a very long time. He concocted a flamboyant elixir of mint. Its scent clung to his fingers even after he washed his hands. Then he shaved ice into tiny particles and served it mounted in a glass dish. Permeated with mint syrup. Scoops of rich vanilla ice cream to each side. My mother took a bite of minty ice and ice cream mixed together. The Mint Snowball tasted like winter. She closed her eyes to see the Swiss village my great-grandfather's parents came from. Snow frosting the roofs. Glistening, dangling spokes of ice.

Before my great-grandfather died, he sold the recipe for the mint syrup to someone in town for one hundred dollars. This hurt my grandfather's feelings. My grandfather thought he should have inherited it to carry on the tradition. As far as the family knew, the person who bought the recipe never used it. At least not in public. My mother had watched my grandfather make the syrup so often she thought she could replicate it. But what did he have in those little unmarked bottles? She experimented. Once she came close. She wrote down what she did. Now she has lost the paper.

Perhaps the clue to my entire personality connects to the lost Mint Snowball. I have always felt out-of-step with my environment, disjointed in the modern world. The crisp flush of cities makes me weep. Strip centers, Poodle grooming and take-out Thai. I am angry over lost department stores, wistful for something I have never tasted or seen.

Although I know how to do everything one needs to know—change airplanes, find my exit off the interstate, charge gas, send a fax—there is something missing. Perhaps the stoop of my great-grandfather over the pan, the slow patient swish of his spoon. The spin of my mother on the high stool with her whole life in front of her, something fine and fragrant still to happen. When I breathe a handful of mint, even pathetic sprigs from my sunbaked Texas earth, I close my eyes. Little chips of ice on the tongue, their cool slide down. Can we follow the long river of the word "refreshment" back to its spring? Is there another land for me? Can I find any lasting solace in the color green?

1. Which of the following statements <u>best</u> describes the form of this selection?

   A. It covers the writer's life chronologically, from childhood to adulthood.

   B. It presents facts and ideas in a straightforward manner.

   C. It focuses on a subject relevant to the writer's life.

   D. It relies on both primary and secondary sources.

2. Which of the following is an example of figurative language?

   A. "Can we follow the long river of the word 'refreshment' back to its spring?"

   B. "My great-grandfather had one specialty: a Mint Snowball which he invented."

   C. "My mother had watched my grandfather make the syrup so often she thought she could replicate it."

   D. "Scoops of rich vanilla ice cream to each side."

3. Which of the following choices <u>best</u> describes the diction of "Mint Snowball"?

   A. formal

   B. simple

   C. conversational

   D. old-fashioned

4. Which of the following passages contributes <u>most</u> to the mood of this selection?

   A. "My great-grandfather on my mother's side ran a drugstore in a small town in central Illinois."

   B. "Some people drove all the way in from Decatur just to taste it."

   C. "As far as the family knew, the person who bought the recipe never used it."

   D. "The spin of my mother on the high stool with her whole life in front of her, something fine and fragrant still to happen."

Short Answer

5. Explain how you would classify this selection. Cite a detail from the passage to support your explanation.

Extended Response

6. Consider the following passage: "My mother remembers the counter's long polished sweep, its shining face. She twirled on the stools. Dreamy fans. Wide summer afternoons. Clink of nickels in anybody's hand." Examine the structure of the sentences in this passage. Then, write a paragraph in which you describe Nye's style in this essay.

Informational Skills Review

Generating Research Questions   **Directions:** Read the following selection. Then, read and respond to the questions that follow.

9/11 Dogs Seemed to Escape Illnesses by **Amy Westfeldt**

NEW YORK — They dug in the toxic World Trade Center dust for survivors, and later for the dead. Their feet were burned by white-hot debris. But unlike thousands of others who toiled at ground zero after Sept. 11, these rescue workers aren't sick.

Scientists have spent years studying the health of search-and-rescue dogs that nosed through the debris at ground zero, and to their surprise, they have found no sign of major illness in the animals.

They are trying to figure out why this is so.

"They didn't have any airway protection, they didn't have any skin protection. They were sort of in the worst of it," said Cynthia Otto, a veterinarian at the University of Pennsylvania, where researchers launched a study of 97 dogs five years ago.

Although many ground zero dogs have died — some of rare cancers — researchers say many have lived beyond the average life span for dogs and are not getting any sicker than average.

Owners of the dogs dispute the findings, saying there is a definite link between the toxic air and their pets' health.

Otto has tracked dogs that spent an average of 10 days after the 2001 terrorist attacks at either the trade center site, the landfill in New York where most of the debris was taken, or the heavily damaged Pentagon.

As of last month, she said, 30 percent of the dogs deployed after Sept. 11 had died, compared with 22 percent of those in a comparison group of dogs who were not pressed into service. The difference was not considered statistically significant, Otto said.

But she added: "We have to keep looking."

A separate study, to be published soon by a doctor at New York's Animal Medical Center, focused on about two dozen New York police dogs and comes to similar conclusions.

The results have baffled doctors. A study released last month found that 70 percent of the people who worked at ground zero suffer severe respiratory problems; scientists thought that the dogs might have similar health problems.

The dogs' owners and scientists have many theories why dogs aren't showing the same level of illness as people. Their noses are longer, possibly serving as a filter to protect their lungs from toxic dust and other debris, they say. The dogs were at the site an average of several days, while many people who report lung disease and cancer spent months cleaning up after the attacks.

The research isn't persuasive to many owners of dogs that died after working at the trade center site.

Joaquin Guerrero, a police officer in Saginaw, Mich., took two dogs, Felony and Rookie, to ground zero for 10 days after the attacks. While Felony remains healthy, Rookie died at age 9 in 2004 of cancer of the mouth. Guerrero believes his death was caused by exposure to ground zero.

"If the people are getting it, you know dogs are showing signs of it," Guerrero said.

Scott Shields' golden retriever, Bear, located the body of a fire chief and many other victims at ground zero. The 11-year-old dog died a year after the attacks of several types of cancer.

"He had never been sick a day in his life" before going to the site, where he sustained a wound to his back from steel debris, Shields said.

Shields, who heads a search-and-rescue dog foundation named after Bear, said Bear "died from bad government" and the toxic air at ground zero. He said that studies under way should have included every dog that worked at the site, and that the Penn study is flawed because it tries to compare dogs that worked at the Pentagon as well as in New York.

Otto said that some of the dogs that worked at the sites could not be found and other dogs' owners were not willing to subject their pets to annual blood tests and X-rays.

Mary Flood, whose 11 ½-year-old black Labrador, Jake, is completely healthy five years after working at ground zero, said that dogs' much shorter life span may also make it harder to track long-term illness.

"Maybe there's not enough time to develop these things before they're no longer with us," she said.

---

1. Which of the following questions about current studies is most easily answered?

   A. What are the authors of the studies trying to find out?

   B. What do most scientists think about the conclusions of the Penn study?

   C. What additional studies are being conducted?

   D. Was Scott Shields interviewed for the study?

2. Mary Flood's comment that "there's not enough time" refers to

   A. time to make a vaccine to prevent cancer in dogs.

   B. time to make the dogs better rescuers.

   C. time to find all the dogs that worked at WTC.

   D. time to make conclusive research since dogs have shorter life spans than humans.

3. Which of the following research questions is not related to the issues in this article?

A. What is the normal life expectancy of rescue dogs?

B. Is there a difference between the number of rescue dogs who died after working at the Pentagon and the number of those who died after working at the WTC?

C. Why are human rescue workers dying?

D. Why have more rescue dogs not been affected by the toxic debris?

4. A question about the number of human rescuers and rescue dogs at ground zero would probably be

A. easily answerable.

B. difficult to answer.

C. irrelevant to the issue.

D. more important than other questions.

5. All of the following explanations are presented in this article except that

A. the noses of dogs act as a protective filter from the harmful debris.

B. the rescue dogs at the WTC were more susceptible to harmful debris than those at the Pentagon.

C. the dogs spent less time than humans in the debris.

D. some rescue dogs have died from rare cancers.

6. If you were researching the effect of toxic debris on rescue dogs, which question would provide the most relevant information?

A. How many rescue dogs were dispatched at both sites, the landfill in New York and the Pentagon?

B. What breeds of rescue dogs were used?

C. Did the rescue dogs show any sign of illness after working in the debris?

D. What is the major cause of death in rescue dogs?

Short Answer

7. What evidence does Otto provide to conclude that rescue dogs from 9/11 remain unharmed? Cite a quote from the passage to support your answer, and give the paragraph number of the quote.

Extended Response

8. People have different opinions about how the rescue dogs were affected by their work at ground zero. List three of these opinions.

Vocabulary Skills Review

V0.10.1 Define unknown words through context clues and the author's use of comparison, contrast and cause and effect. *Also covered:* **V0.10.2**

Synonyms **Directions:** Choose the synonym (the word with the same or nearly the same meaning) for the underlined word in each sentence.

1. At first, Parks thinks Mr. Stryker's instructions to eat, shop, and go to the movie theater are trivial, but later he sees their significance.
   A. mystifying
   B. unimportant
   C. difficult
   D. easy

2. In "Into Thin Air," oxygen tanks are crucial for the climbers' survival.
   A. useful
   B. essential
   C. unnecessary
   D. optional

3. In "Team of Rivals," the messenger's incoherent story seems so terrible and unlikely that Gideon Welles doesn't believe him.
   A. confusing
   B. horrible
   C. unbelievable
   D. familiar

4. In "Typhoid Fever," Frankie induced Seamus to find the words to the rest of the poem "The Highwayman."
   A. required
   B. forced
   C. expected
   D. persuaded

5. In "And of Clay Are We Created," Rolf Carlé works with tenacity to free Azucena.
   A. persistence
   B. anger
   C. hesitation
   D. hope

6. The mountain climbers in "Into Thin Air" think the clouds visible from Mt. Everest are benign.
   A. distant
   B. harmless
   C. beautiful
   D. delicate

Academic Vocabulary

Directions: Choose the best synonym for each boldfaced Academic Vocabulary word.

7. Subsequent reports shed light on the controversy.
   A. previous
   B. style
   C. following
   D. immediate

8. An essay's main idea is equivalent to a story's theme.
   A. opposite
   B. close to
   C. almost
   D. equal to

Read On

FICTION

Tales of the Unexpected

Facing the unexpected can be very challenging—and in the case of Roald Dahl's stories, quite hilarious. In this collection of Dahl's best tales, characters find themselves in entertainingly horrible situations, from a wife's revenge on an annoying husband to a "royal jelly" that has a startling effect on the baby who consumes it. All of these dark stories promise plenty of laughter and unforgettable surprises.

FICTION

A Haunted House and Other Stories

Did you know that in addition to her famous novels *Mrs. Dalloway* and *To the Lighthouse*, Virginia Woolf wrote short stories? Collected here by her husband are eighteen of her short works, originally published in 1944. Read a few of these short stories to see why Woolf is considered one of the major literary figures of the twentieth century.

FICTION

Karoo Boy

Imagine losing a twin brother in a freak accident and then having to move to a small town away from everything you know. Douglas, who lived in South Africa during the turbulent 1970s, learns to face these lonely obstacles by befriending a beautiful girl and an old garage worker who help him navigate his realities and dreams. Troy Blacklaws's novel offers a moving portrait of coming-of-age, of the South African landscape, and of the challenge of defeating racism in daily life.

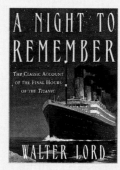

NONFICTION

A Night to Remember

What happened just before the *Titanic* collided with an iceberg? How did the survivors make it through the freezing night after watching their ship go down? Four decades after the event, Walter Lord interviewed hundreds of the *Titanic*'s passengers to create a gripping narrative of how the tragic events unfolded on that night in April 1912. Considered the finest book about the *Titanic* disaster, *A Night to Remember* is filled with deeply personal accounts of those who survived as well as tributes to those who didn't.

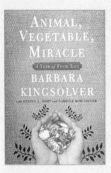

NONFICTION

Animal, Vegetable, Miracle

After years in the dry land of Arizona, where she made her home, Barbara Kingsolver moved with her family to a farm in southern Appalachia. There, she and her family took on the challenge of spending a year eating only locally grown food. Written as a diary narrative, Kingsolver's book reflects on the food they grew and the local organic growers on whom they came to rely. Join the family as they work out the kinks of farm life and thrive on the joy of producing their own harvest.

NONFICTION

A Star Is Found

This is the book for anyone who's ever wondered what Julia Roberts wore to the audition that won her her first major role, or anyone who's walked out of a movie saying, "That was the wrong actor for that role." Here is a first-of-its-kind look at how actors are chosen and careers are born. Two of the top casting directors in the business, who cast everyone from the Harry Potter kids to the new James Bond, offer an insider's tour of their craft. Along the way, we get to hear behind-the-scenes stories about dozens of actors, from Tom Cruise to Winona Ryder.

NONFICTION

Dust Tracks on a Road

Zora Neale Hurston's autobiography describes her upbringing in the all-African American town of Eatonville, Florida, where her father was mayor. Hurston describes her early fascination with folk tales and myths that would have a major influence on her later in life. She graduated from Barnard College and pursued a career as a folklorist. She became famous for collecting oral tales from men and women at sawmills, juke joints, and turpentine camps on Florida backroads.

NONFICTION

Warped Passages

At last! A book on current research in physics that even students of literature can understand. Lisa Randall, a theoretical physicist at Harvard, describes how physicists are searching for hidden dimensions to enable them to finally explain fundamental aspects of matter and energy. Each chapter of *Warped Passages* begins with a humorous story that identifies the key concept and ends with a helpful "What to Remember" section.

Persuasion

INFORMATIONAL TEXT FOCUS
Analyzing Arguments

"I can't believe the news today.
I can't close my eyes and make it go away."

—**Bono**

What Do
You
Think   What do we believe in, and why?

November, 2002
J. Crook.
te collection.

Literary Focus

by **Carol Jago**

What Is Persuasion?

Some people seem to know exactly the right thing to say in order to get what they want. They are skilled in the art of persuasion. Politicians understand that persuasion is the key to swaying voters and influencing public opinion. Writers use persuasion to convince others to change their ideas or to act in a specific way. Learning to analyze their techniques will help you evaluate the quality of their arguments.

Elements of Persuasion

When writers try to **persuade** you, they are trying to convince you to believe or to act in a certain way. You are most likely to agree with writers whose ideas seem credible and whose evidence seems valid. The structure and tone of an author's argument can also influence how you react.

Writer's Intent

In persuasive writing, the writer's **intent** is to convince you to think or act a certain way. Sometimes the writer's goal is to change the way you think, but a writer may also be calling you to action, and asking you to go out and *do* something. The writer communicates his or her intent objectively or subjectively. An **objective** approach uses provable facts. A **subjective** approach focuses on a writer's experiences, feelings, and opinions. Sometimes a writer uses both approaches.

Credibility and Evidence

Before you respond to a persuasive text, evaluate the writer's **credibility,** or believability. Credibility depends on a writer's qualifications as well as the quality of the evidence presented. A writer's qualifications might include expert status or work experience in the field about which he or she is writing.

Evidence Would you believe someone who tried to convince you by saying, "Because I say so"? Probably not. You must evaluate the person's argument carefully. To do so, make sure it is supported with enough **evidence,** or proof. An **appeal to logic** uses facts, statistics, and examples to speak to a reader's reason and common sense. **Emotional appeals** speak to a reader's emotions, such as fear, sympathy, or anger. An appeal to emotion may include **loaded words** (words with strong **connotations,** or associations) and **anecdotes** (stories or personal accounts of an event). Of course, a g[o]od argument appeals both to logic and to emot[ion]. "Free Minds and Hearts at Work," for exampl[e], Robinson describes the fight against pre[judice] well as his own feelings and experienc[e].

As you read, use a chart like the [one shown to] analyze the credibility of an argum[ent].

- Is the author's intent clear?
- Is the author qualified t[o write] about this subject?
- Is the author unfair[ly] prejudiced regardi[ng]
- Does the autho[r use subjective] or objective ev[idence]

OH **RA.I.10.4** Assess the adequacy, accuracy and appropriateness of an author's details, identifying persuasive techniques and examples of propaganda, bias and stereotyping. **RA.I.10.5** Analyze an author's implicit and explicit argument, perspective or viewpoint in text. **RA.I.10.6** Identify appeals to authority, reason and emotion.

Structure and Tone

Structure A good writer organizes an argument carefully and logically. An argument might be organized by cause and effect, problem and solution, chronological order, or question and answer. Readers generally remember the most about the beginning and end of a piece. Therefore, many writers structure an argument so that it moves from the least important idea to the most important idea, or from a general idea to a specific call to action.

Dr. Martin Luther King, Jr., begins his speech to the First Montgomery Improvement Association with general ideas and ends with a specific call to action.

> We are here in a general sense because first and foremost we are American citizens, and we are determined to apply our citizenship to the fullness of its meaning.
>
> from "There Comes a Time When People Get Tired" by Dr. Martin Luther King, Jr.

Tone A writer's **tone** reflects his or her attitude toward the subject or audience and is closely related to intent. In persuasive writing, for example, the writer's tone might be serious, sincere, concerned, or amused. In *Silent Spring*, Rachel Carson creates a serious tone with formal sentence structure and word choice.

> The countryside was, in fact, famous for the abundance and variety of its bird life, and when the flood of migrants was pouring through in spring and fall people traveled from great distances to observe them.
>
> from *Silent Spring* by Rachel Carson

In contrast, Judith Stone's lighthearted language gives her essay a tone that is informal, yet sincere.

> What a treat it was not to strike terror into the hearts of other living things! I could spend hours regarding rubbery black marine iguanas sunning in sloppy, chummy piles like discarded dime-store dinosaurs; instead of bolting, they simply grinned and dozed.
>
> from "Kiss and Tell" by Judith Stone

Identifying the tone of a text can help you evaluate the credibility of an argument. For example, if a writer uses a highly emotional tone for an argument that is meant to be objective, the argument might lack evidence and credibility.

Your Turn Analyze Persuasion

Read the following excerpt, and answer the questions below. Discuss your answers with a partner.

> For those of you who are black and are tempted to be filled with hatred and distrust at the injustice of such an act, against all white people, I can only say that I feel in my own heart the same kind of feeling. I had a member of my family killed, but he was killed by a white man.
>
> from "Eulogy for Martin Luther King, Jr.," by Robert F. Kennedy

1. What is the speaker's intent?

2. What is the tone of this passage?

3. Is the author appealing to logic or emotion, or both? Explain.

Learn It Online
Try the *PowerNotes* version of this lesson on:

go.hrw.com   L10-561   **Go**

Analyzing Visuals

How Do Artists Use Persuasion?

Writers persuade by using words that appeal to our logic and emotions. Artists may also use words to persuade—by combining words with striking images. Advertisements frequently feature a combination of persuasive words and images. Artwork that intends to send a message to its viewer must capitalize on a limited number of powerful words as well as clear, meaningful images to get its point across.

Analyzing Persuasion in Artwork

Use these guidelines to help you analyze persuasion in art:

1. Does the artwork include words? What is the artwork trying to persuade you to do?

2. What images does the artist include? What do the images tell you?

3. What elements of the artwork appeal to you? Does the art appeal to logic or to your emotions?

4. How does the combination of images and words work together to present a unified persuasive message?

Study the details of the advertisement to help you answer the questions on page 563.

No mosquitos!
SPONSORED BY THE VILLAGE OF SEA CLIFF

JUST ONE LONG STEP

Promotional poster displayed at the 1939 World's Fair in New York.

1. What is the subject of this advertisement? What is the advertisement trying to persuade people to do?

2. Which words in the advertisement are persuasive? How might they influence viewers?

3. What impact do the words *Just One Long Step* and the man striding over the water create? Is this an **appeal to emotion** or to **logic?** Explain.

4. What does the sponsor information tell you about the purpose of this advertisement?

Your Turn Write About Persuasion in Art

Think about a popular print advertisement you've seen lately. Then, answer these questions:

1. What do you notice first about the image? What is its subject?

2. Does the artist use both words and images to persuade, or only one or the other?

3. What is the artist trying to persuade you to do or think? Are you persuaded? Why or why not?

Reading Focus

by **Kylene Beers**

How Do You Evaluate Persuasive Arguments?

You've probably been warned, "Don't believe everything that you hear!" This is good advice. Because persuasive writers know how to appeal to your emotions and beliefs, you must read closely to decide whether their arguments are sound. When you read a persuasive work, don't blindly accept its argument. Be an active reader, and pay attention to the ways that the writer is trying to shape your opinions.

Summarizing

To evaluate an argument, you first have to understand exactly what an author is saying. **Summarizing** helps you break an argument down to its key elements. Once you determine the main ideas of a piece, you can form a summary. How would you summarize this excerpt from a speech by Dr. Martin Luther King, Jr.?

> We believe in the Christian religion. We believe in the teachings of Jesus. The only weapon that we have in our hands this evening is the weapon of protest. That's all.
>
> from "There Comes a Time When People Get Tired" by Dr. Martin Luther King, Jr.

A summary of this passage might read, "Dr. Martin Luther King, Jr., encourages his audience to use their faith as a weapon of protest."

To create an effective summary, begin by looking at the structure of the writing. Break the work into smaller parts. For longer works, you might first summarize each paragraph, page, section, or chapter. Then, use your own words to state the main ideas.

Questioning

Questioning When you **ask questions** about your reading, you create connections, form opinions, and deepen your understanding of a text. Asking questions can also help you determine whether an argument is sound.

As you read a text, you might ask, "What does the author mean here?" or "Do I agree with this claim?" You might also ask about a writer's purpose. When reading Robert F. Kennedy's "Eulogy to Martin Luther King, Jr.," you might wonder why he focuses here on the nation rather than on Dr. King.

> In this difficult day, in this difficult time for the United States, it is perhaps well to ask what kind of a nation we are and what direction we want to move in.
>
> from "Eulogy for Martin Luther King, Jr." by Robert F. Kennedy

Sometimes you may need to consult an outside source, such as an encyclopedia, to answer your questions. In this instance, you have to know about the historical context to answer the question. Often, however, you find answers in the text itself, either by reading on or by re-reading.

OH **RP.10.1** Apply reading comprehension strategies, including making predictions, comparing and contrasting, recalling and summarizing and making inferences and drawing conclusions. **RA.I.10.5** Analyze an author's implicit and explicit argument, perspective or viewpoint in text.

Drawing Conclusions

Perhaps the most important step in evaluating is drawing conclusions. **Drawing conclusions** about an argument is like completing a math problem:

| author's claim and evidence | + | your knowledge and experience | = | your conclusion |

You consider an author's claim and evidence, add your own knowledge and experience, and then come to an informed judgment, or conclusion, about the argument.

Questioning and drawing conclusions work hand in hand. For example, as you read the beginning of Rachel Carson's book *Silent Spring,* you might question why the author added the subtitle *A Fable for Tomorrow* and why she chose to begin her book in the following way:

> There was once a town in the heart of America where all life seemed to live in harmony with its surroundings.
>
> from *Silent Spring* by Rachel Carson

The book does not contain a direct answer to your questions. To answer them, you must draw conclusions based on the evidence Carson provides and your knowledge that fables are stories with lessons.

In her essay "Kiss and Tell," environmentalist Judith Stone argues that people care more about the environment when they travel to see animals in their natural habitats. Stone presents evidence from her own experiences and states her conclusions directly. To draw your own conclusions, you must examine her evidence and decide whether or not you agree.

Your Turn Apply Reading Skills

Read the following letter to a newspaper editor. Then, complete the activities below.

Dear Editor,

A large segment of our society has become coarse and uncivil. Good manners are almost extinct.

I remember a time when people acted like ladies and gentlemen. They spoke clearly and politely, and they were helpful to each other, doing small favors without expectation of a reward. Today, vulgarities are spewed from television, movies, music, and everyday conversation. When was the last time you saw anyone—male or female—hold open a door for another person? We certainly are living in an uncivil society.

Let's all mind our manners and make the world a better place!

Ruth Schmidt
Dixon, Illinois

1. In a small group, discuss these questions:
   - What does Schmidt want?
   - Which of her points do you agree with? Which points do you disagree with? Why?

2. Write a brief evaluation of Schmidt's argument. How would you improve it?

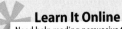
Now go to the Skills in Action: Reading Model

Learn It Online
Need help reading persuasive texts? Check out the interactive Reading Workshops on:

| go.hrw.com | L10-565 | **Go** |

Build Background

Until the 1940s, major-league baseball was segregated, or divided racially, like most of American society. Then, in 1945, the general manager of the Brooklyn Dodgers, Branch Rickey, signed an African American player named Jackie Robinson. Robinson had to tolerate racial taunts and threats from fans and fellow players for several years after he began playing for the Dodgers. Slowly, other managers—in baseball and other sports—began signing African American players. In 1952, Robinson read "Free Minds and Hearts at Work" as part of a radio program called *This I Believe.*

Literary Focus

Structure Robinson gets your attention by opening the paragraph with a question. The use of the word *first* signals that he is starting to lay out the points of his argument.

Read with a Purpose Read the following essay to learn how one man's beliefs not only shaped his life but also helped move society forward.

Free Minds and Hearts at Work

by **Jackie Robinson**

At the beginning of the World Series of 1947, I experienced a completely new emotion, when the National Anthem was played. This time, I thought, it is being played for me, as much as for anyone else. This is organized major league baseball, and I am standing here with all the others; and everything that takes place includes me.

About a year later, I went to Atlanta, Georgia, to play in an exhibition game. On the field, for the first time in Atlanta, there were Negroes and whites. Other Negroes, besides me. And I thought: What I have always believed has come to be.

And what is it that I have always believed? First, that imperfections are human. But that wherever human beings were given room to breathe and time to think, those imperfections would disappear, no matter how slowly. I do not believe that we have found or even approached perfection. That is not necessarily in the scheme of human events. Handicaps, stumbling blocks, prejudices—all of these are imperfect. Yet, they have to be reckoned with because they are in the scheme of human events.

Whatever obstacles I found made me fight all the harder. But it would have been impossible for me to fight at all, except that I was sustained by the personal and deep-rooted belief that my fight had a chance. It had a chance because it took place in a free society. Not once was I forced to face and fight an immovable object. Not once was the situation so cast-iron rigid that I had no chance at all. Free minds and human hearts were at work all around me; and so there was the probability of improvement. I look at my children now, and know that I must still prepare them to meet obstacles and prejudices.

Jackie Robinson safe on a double steal, May 18, 1952.

But I can tell them, too, that they will never face some of these prejudices because other people have gone before them. And to myself I can say that, because progress is unalterable, many of today's dogmas[1] will have vanished by the time they grow into adults. I can say to my children: There is a chance for you. No guarantee, but a chance.

And this chance has come to be, because there is nothing static with free people. There is no Middle Ages logic so strong that it can stop the human tide from flowing forward. I do not believe that every person, in every walk of life, can succeed in spite of any handicap. That would be perfection. But I do believe—and with every fiber in me—that what I was able to attain came to be because we put behind us (no matter how slowly) the dogmas of the past: to discover the truth of today; and perhaps find the greatness of tomorrow.

I believe in the human race. I believe in the warm heart. I believe in man's integrity. I believe in the goodness of a free society. And I believe that the society can remain good only as long as we are willing to fight for it—and to fight against whatever imperfections may exist.

My fight was against the barriers that kept Negroes out of baseball. This was the area where I found imperfection, and where I was best able to fight. And I fought because I knew it was not doomed to

---

1. **dogmas:** principles or beliefs.

be a losing fight. It couldn't be a losing fight—not when it took place in a free society.

And in the largest sense, I believe that what I did was done for me—that it was my faith in God that sustained me in my fight. And that what was done for me must and will be done for others.

Summarizing We might summarize Robinson's argument in the following way: Prejudice is one of humanity's many imperfections. In a free society like ours, we can change and improve. This belief is supported by human progress throughout history.

Read with a Purpose How did Robinson's commitment to his beliefs inspire change in American society?

MEET THE WRITER

Jackie Robinson
(1919–1972)

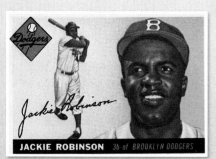

A Brooklyn Dodgers 1955 baseball card. The Granger Collection, New York.

Calm Under Pressure

Brooklyn Dodgers general manager Branch Rickey considered many African American baseball players for his team before choosing Jack Roosevelt Robinson, the man who would integrate major-league baseball. Rickey saw a gifted athlete who had excelled in baseball, football, basketball, and track while attending the University of California in Los Angeles. He saw a man who had stood up for civil rights in the army during World War II. He saw a man who remained calm under pressure. Robinson, because he felt a duty to do so, took on the role Rickey offered. "A life is not important except in the impact it has on other lives," he said.

Number 42

Robinson played for the Dodgers from 1947 until 1956 and helped them reach the World Series six times, with a series victory in 1955. He was an excellent second baseman, a star batter, and one of the best base stealers ever. He also spoke out against racism wherever he encountered it. To mark Robinson's contributions to baseball and to American society, major-league baseball retired his number, 42, in 1997, which means that no major-league player will wear it again.

Think About the Writer

What obstacles might Jackie Robinson battle if he were a young man today?

OH **RA.I.10.4** Assess the adequacy, accuracy and appropriateness of an author's details, identifying persuasive techniques and examples of propaganda, bias and stereotyping. *Also covered* **RP.10.1; RA.I.10.5; VO.10.6**

Into Action: Persuasion

Jackie Robinson's powerful essay includes a variety of persuasive techniques. With a partner, fill in a chart like the one below with details from Robinson's essay. Then, evaluate how well you feel Robinson presents his argument.

	Details from Essay
Author's Purpose	
Logical Appeals	
Emotional Appeals	
Tone	
Evaluation of Argument:	

Talk About . . .

1. In groups of three, discuss the strengths and weaknesses of Jackie Robinson's argument. Try to use each Academic Vocabulary word listed at the right in your discussion.

Write About . . .

Answer the following questions about Robinson's essay and Meet the Writer.

2. What did signing Jackie Robinson demonstrate to American society?

3. What does Robinson challenge his readers to do?

4. In what way was Robinson's talent evident to Branch Rickey, the manager of the Dodgers?

5. In a debate, what additional proof might Jackie Robinson give to support his arguments?

Writing Focus

Think as a Reader/Writer

The selections in Collection 6 are by turn funny, somber, insightful, sad, and provocative. The writers develop credible arguments by using logical structure, strong evidence, and a persuasive tone. In the collection's Writing Focus activities, you will practice using these persuasive techniques.

Academic Vocabulary for Collection 6

Talking and Writing About Persuasion

Academic Vocabulary is the language you use to write and talk about literature. Use these words to discuss the selections you read in this collection. The words in the collection are underlined.

challenge (CHAL uhnj) *v.:* call to a contest or fight; dare. *Branch Rickey was the first general manager to challenge discrimination in major-league baseball.*

debate (dih BAYT) *n.:* discussion of opposing arguments. *Jackie Robinson contributed to the national debate on race.*

demonstrate (DEHM uhn strayt) *v.:* show or prove by using evidence. *Branch Rickey believed that he should demonstrate his beliefs and not keep them hidden.*

evident (EHV uh duhnt) *adj.:* easy to understand; obvious. *It's evident that Jackie Robinson was a great athlete.*

Your Turn

Copy the Academic Vocabulary words into your *Reader/Writer Notebook*. As you read the selections, notice the use of persuasive techniques. Which of the authors are most successful? Why? Use the Academic Vocabulary words when answering these questions.

There Comes a Time When People Get Tired
by **Dr. Martin Luther King, Jr.**

Eulogy for Martin Luther King, Jr.
by **Robert F. Kennedy**

The Selma-to-Montgomery Civil Rights March, 1965. Courtesy of the Estate of James Karales

What Do
You
~~Think~~

How do our beliefs as a nation today compare to

 QuickWrite

List some of the beliefs that are most important to you. How would you react if they were threatened? What action could you take to preserve your right to

 **Reader/Writer Notebook**

Use your **RWN** to complete the activities for these selections.

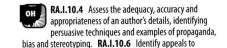 **RA.I.10.4** Assess the adequacy, accuracy and appropriateness of an author's details, identifying persuasive techniques and examples of propaganda, bias and stereotyping. **RA.I.10.6** Identify appeals to authority, reason and emotion. **RP.10.1** Apply reading comprehension strategies, including making predictions, comparing and contrasting, recalling and summarizing and making inferences and drawing conclusions.

Literary Focus

Persuasion: Appeals to Emotion Writers of persuasive texts sometimes appeal to your **emotions,** or feelings, rather than to logic. For example, a writer might want you to feel sympathy for a victim or outrage over an injustice. Writers may use emotional appeals in an attempt to override reason or to address issues that cannot be resolved by logic alone. **Loaded words** (words with **connotations,** or strong emotional associations) and **anecdotes** (brief stories) are two kinds of emotional appeals. As you read the selections that follow, look for the emotional appeals in each speech.

Literary Perspectives Apply the literary perspective described on page 577 as you read "Eulogy for Martin Luther King, Jr."

Reading Focus

Summarizing When you read a speech, a useful way to keep track of the writer's argument is to summarize its most important ideas. To **summarize,** find the main ideas the speaker mentions. Then, try to condense—that is, simplify—the main ideas into a statement of the writer's argument.

Into Action As you read, look closely at the ideas presented in each author's argument. For each speech, write down the main ideas in a chart like this one. Then, summarize each writer's message.

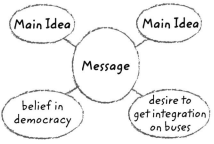

Writing Focus

Think as a Reader/Writer

Find It in Your Reading Both of the following writers strengthen their emotional appeals by using **figurative language,** imaginative comparisons between unlike things. As you read, jot down some examples of this figurative language in your *Reader/Writer Notebook.*

Vocabulary

There Comes a Time When People Get Tired

integrity (ihn TEHG ruh tee) *n.:* honesty and sincerity. *The protesters were not troublemakers but people of integrity who believed in their cause.*

advocating (AD vuh kayt ihng) *v.:* recommending; speaking in favor of. *Dr. Martin Luther King, Jr., was advocating nonviolent forms of protest.*

utopian (yoo TOH pee uhn) *adj.:* extremely idealistic but impractical. *His utopian plans would never have worked in the real world.*

coercion (koh UHR shuhn) *n.:* use of force or forceful persuasion. *Sometimes a little coercion is necessary to change unfair laws.*

Language Coach

Word Origins Learning a word's origin can help you remember its meaning. We owe the word *utopian* to Sir Thomas More, an English lawyer, who wrote a book called *Utopia* in 1516. A utopia is an ideal world—one that's impossibly perfect. More created the name of his imaginary island by combining the Greek *ou* (not) and *topos* (place). Use a dictionary to look up the origins of these other commonly used words: *sandwich, frankfurter,* and *boycott.*

 Learn It Online
There's more to words than just definitions. Get the whole story on:

go.hrw.com   L10-571   **Go**

Dr. Martin Luther King, Jr.
(1929–1968)

An American Hero

Dr. Martin Luther King, Jr., is one of the most influential figures in American history. Born in Atlanta, Georgia, King was the son of a Baptist preacher. He eventually decided that he also wanted to become a preacher and received a doctorate in theology in 1955.

King's impact on American society is immeasurable. His leadership during the civil rights movement led to the Civil Rights Act of 1964. This act outlawed discrimination based on race, color, religion, or gender and made segregation illegal. In 1964, at the age of thirty-five, King was awarded the Nobel Peace Prize for advocating nonviolent protest. Four years later, he was assassinated by a sniper in Memphis, Tennessee.

Robert F. Kennedy
(1925–1968)

Politician and Advocate

In an era of violent demonstrations, an unpopular war, and radical social change, Robert F. Kennedy offered a compassionate vision of social and economic equality. Serving as the attorney general during the presidency of his brother John F. Kennedy, he acted boldly to ensure that African Americans would not be deprived of equal rights. When the University of Mississippi admitted its first African American student, Kennedy sent U.S. marshals to ensure that the student would be allowed to attend class.

Kennedy carried the fight for racial equality over to his presidential campaign in 1968. However, he was assassinated in June of that same year, just two months after King was killed.

Think About the Writers

Why do you think King and Kennedy, who came from very different backgrounds, fought for the same issues?

Preview the Selections

The 1960s were tumultuous years. As more and more people joined the cause of the civil rights movement and demonstrations against the war in Vietnam, they met resistance and, often, violence.

Dr. Martin Luther King, Jr., delivered this speech, "There Comes a Time When People Get Tired," on December 5, 1955, to the First Montgomery Improvement Association Mass Meeting at Holt Street Baptist Church in Montgomery, Alabama.

Robert F. Kennedy delivered this eulogy for Dr. Martin Luther King, Jr., in Indianapolis, Indiana, several hours after King's assassination.

There Comes a Time When People Get Tired

by **Dr. Martin Luther King, Jr.**

Read with a Purpose
Read to discover how an American leader uses powerful language and emotional appeals to inspire his audience to action.

Build Background
In response to the arrest of Rosa Parks, who refused to give her seat on the bus to a white person, a group of activists formed the Montgomery Improvement Association and chose King as their leader. Thousands of residents boycotted the city's buses for more than a year by refusing to ride until the rules had changed. In 1965, the Supreme Court ruled that Montgomery's buses had to be integrated.

My friends, we are certainly very happy to see each of you out this evening. We are here this evening for serious business. We are here in a general sense because first and foremost we are American citizens, and we are determined to apply our citizenship to the fullness of its meaning. We are here also because of our love for democracy, because of our deep-seated belief that democracy transformed from thin paper to thick action is the greatest form of government on earth.

But we are here in a specific sense because of the bus situation in Montgomery.[1] We are here because we are determined to get the situation corrected. This situation is not at all new. The problem has existed over endless years. For many years now, Negroes in Montgomery and so many other areas have been inflicted with the paralysis of crippling fear on buses in our community. On so many occasions, Negroes have been intimidated and humiliated and oppressed because of the sheer fact that they were Negroes. I don't have time this evening to go into the history of these numerous cases. Many of them now are lost in the thick fog of oblivion, but at least one stands before us now with glaring dimensions. **(A)**

Just the other day, just last Thursday to be exact, one of the finest citizens in Montgomery—not one of the finest Negro citizens, but one of the finest citizens in Montgomery—was taken from a bus and carried to jail and arrested because she refused to get up to give her seat to a white person. Now the press would have us believe that she refused to leave a reserved section for Negroes, but I want you to know this evening that there is no reserved section. The law has never been clarified at that point. Now I think I speak with legal

---

1. **bus situation in Montgomery:** reference to the Montgomery bus boycott, which began after the arrest of Rosa Parks on December 1, 1955.

(A) Literary Focus Persuasion What loaded words can you find in the first two paragraphs?

Dr. Martin Luther King, Jr., standing in front of a bus at the end of the Montgomery bus boycott, December 26, 1956.

authority—not that I have any legal authority, but I think I speak with legal authority behind me—that the law, the ordinance, the city ordinance has never been totally clarified. **Ⓑ**

Mrs. Rosa Parks is a fine person. And, since it had to happen, I'm happy that it happened to a person like Mrs. Parks, for nobody can doubt the boundless outreach of her integrity. Nobody can doubt the height of her character, nobody can doubt the depth of her Christian

commitment and devotion to the teachings of Jesus. And I'm happy, since it had to happen, it happened to a person that nobody can call a disturbing factor in the community. Mrs. Parks is a fine Christian person, unassuming, and yet there is integrity and character there. And just because she refused to get up, she was arrested.

And you know, my friends, there comes a time when people get tired of being trampled over by the iron feet of oppression. There comes a time, my friends, when people get tired of being plunged across the abyss of humiliation, where they experience the bleakness of nagging despair. There comes a time when people get tired of being pushed out of the glittering sunlight of life's July and left standing amid the piercing chill of an alpine November. There comes a time. **Ⓒ**

We are here, we are here this evening because we are tired now. And I want to say that we are not here advocating violence. We have never done that. I want it to be known throughout Montgomery and throughout this nation that we are Christian people. We believe in the Christian religion. We believe in the teachings of Jesus. The only weapon that we have in our hands this evening is the weapon of protest. That's all.

And certainly, certainly, this is the glory of America, with all of its faults. This is the glory of our democracy. If we were incarcerated behind the iron curtains of a Communistic[2] nation, we couldn't do this. If we were dropped

---

2. **Communistic:** Under Communism, a government suppresses political opposition and limits individual freedoms.

Ⓑ Reading Focus Summarizing In one sentence, summarize the problems with the Montgomery bus system that King describes.

Ⓒ Literary Focus Persuasion What vivid words and phrases here add to the paragraph's emotional impact?

Vocabulary **integrity** (ihn TEHG ruh tee) *n.*: honesty and sincerity.
advocating (AD vuh kayt ihng) *v.*: recommending; speaking in favor of.

in the dungeon of a totalitarian regime,[3] we couldn't do this. But the great glory of American democracy is the right to protest for right. My friends, don't let anybody make us feel that we are to be compared in our actions with the Ku Klux Klan or with the White Citizens Council.[4] There will be no crosses burned at any bus stops in Montgomery. There will be no white persons pulled out of their homes and taken out on some distant road and lynched for not cooperating. There will be nobody among us who will stand up and defy the Constitution of this nation. We only assemble here because of our desire to see right exist. My friends, I want it to be known that we're going to work with grim and bold determination to gain justice on the buses in this city.

And we are not wrong; we are not wrong in what we are doing. If we are wrong, the Supreme Court of this nation is wrong. If we are wrong, the Constitution of the United States is wrong. If we are wrong, God Almighty is wrong. If we are wrong, Jesus of Nazareth was merely a utopian dreamer that never came down to Earth. If we are wrong, justice is a lie, love has no meaning. And we are determined here in Montgomery to work and fight until justice runs down like water, and righteousness like a mighty stream. **Ⓓ**

I want to say that in all of our actions, we must stick together. Unity is the great need of the hour, and if we are united we can get many of the things that we not only desire but

which we justly deserve. And don't let anybody frighten you. We are not afraid of what we are doing because we are doing it within the law. There is never a time in our American democracy that we must ever think we are wrong when we protest. We reserve that right. When labor all over this nation came to see that it would be trampled over by capitalistic power, it was nothing wrong with labor getting together and organizing and protesting for its rights. We, the disinherited of this land, we who have been oppressed so long, are tired of going through the long night of captivity. And now we are reaching out for the daybreak of freedom and justice and equality.

May I say to you, my friends, as I come to a close, and just giving some idea of why we are assembled here, that we must keep—and I want to stress this, in all of our doings, in all of our deliberations here this evening and all of the week and while, whatever we do, we must keep God in the forefront. Let us be Christian in all of our actions. But I want to tell you this evening that it is not enough for us to talk about love, love is one of the pivotal points of the Christian faith. There is another side called justice. And justice is really love in calculation. Justice is love correcting that which revolts against love.

The Almighty God himself is not only, not the God just standing out saying through Hosea,[5] "I love you, Israel." He's also the God that stands up before the nations and said: "Be still and know that I'm God, that if you don't obey me I will break the backbone of your power and slap you out of the orbits of

---

3. **totalitarian regime:** a government that suppresses all opposition by force.
4. **Ku Klux Klan . . . White Citizens Council:** white supremacist groups who have often used terrorism and violence against African Americans and other minorities.

---

5. **Hosea:** Hebrew prophet who lived during the eighth century B.C.

Ⓓ **Literary Focus** **Persuasion** How might King's repetition of key phrases appeal to his audience's emotions?

Vocabulary **utopian** (yoo TOH pee uhn) *adj.*: extremely idealistic but impractical.

Protesters during the third month of the Montgomery bus boycott, February 1956.

your international and national relationships." Standing beside love is always justice, and we are only using the tools of justice. Not only are we using the tools of persuasion, but we've come to see that we've got to use the tools of coercion. Not only is this thing a process of education, but it is also a process of legislation. **E**

And as we stand and sit here this evening and as we prepare ourselves for what lies ahead, let us go out with the grim and bold determination that we are going to stick together. We are going to work together. Right here in Montgomery, when the history books are written in the future, somebody will have to say, "There lived a race of people, a *black* people, 'fleecy locks and black complexion,' a people who had the moral courage to stand up for their rights. And thereby they injected a new meaning into the veins of history and of civilization." And we're going to do that. God grant that we will do it before it is too late. As we proceed with our program, let us think of these things. **F**

E **Reading Focus** Summarizing Summarize what King says about justice.

F **Literary Focus** Persuasion How does King's vision of the future make a fitting ending for his speech?

Vocabulary **coercion** (koh UHR shuhn) *n.*: use of force or forceful persuasion.

Eulogy for Martin Luther King, Jr.

by **Robert F. Kennedy**

Read with a Purpose

As you read this eulogy, pay attention to how the speaker uses powerful language to stir the emotions of his audience.

Preparing to Read for this selection is on page 571.

Build Background

Robert F. Kennedy, a senator from New York, was in Indiana campaigning for the 1968 presidential election when Dr. Martin Luther King, Jr., was assassinated. Both Kennedy and King fought for racial equality and opposed the Vietnam War.

I have bad news for you, for all of our fellow citizens, and people who love peace all over the world, and that is that Martin Luther King was shot and killed tonight.

Martin Luther King dedicated his life to love and to justice for his fellow human beings, and he died because of that effort.

In this difficult day, in this difficult time for the United States, it is perhaps well to ask what kind of a nation we are and what direction we want to move in. For those of you who are black—considering the evidence there evidently is that there were white people who were responsible—you can be filled with bitterness, with hatred, and a desire for revenge. We can move in that direction as a country, in great polarization—black people amongst black, white people amongst white, filled with hatred toward one another.

Or we can make an effort, as Martin Luther King did, to understand and to comprehend, and to replace that violence, that stain of bloodshed that has spread across our land, with an effort to understand with compassion and love.

For those of you who are black and are tempted to be filled with hatred and distrust at the injustice of such an act, against all white people, I can only say that I feel in my own heart the same kind of feeling. I had a member of my family killed, but he was killed by a white man. But we have to make an effort in the United States, we have to make an effort to understand, to go beyond these rather difficult times. **Ⓐ**

Literary Perspectives

Analyzing Biographical Context The biographical perspective asks readers to consider their knowledge of the author as they read and interpret literary texts. Because authors typically write about things they care deeply about and know well, the events and circumstances of their lives are often reflected in the works they create. Robert F. Kennedy was the brother of John F. Kennedy, the popular president of the United States who was assassinated in 1963. Kennedy served as attorney general in his brother's administration and later, in 1968, launched his own campaign for the presidency. Robert Kennedy was a passionate supporter of the civil rights movement and Dr. Martin Luther King, Jr. As you read, use the notes and questions in the text to guide you in using this perspective.

Ⓐ Literary Perspectives **Biographical Context** Why do you think Robert Kennedy refers to the assassination of his brother here?

Coretta Scott King and Robert F. Kennedy.

My favorite poet was Aeschylus.[1] He wrote: "In our sleep, pain which cannot forget falls drop by drop upon the heart until, in our own despair, against our will, comes wisdom through the awful grace of God."

What we need in the United States is not division; what we need in the United States is not hatred; what we need in the United States is not violence or lawlessness; but love and wisdom, and compassion toward one another, and a feeling of justice toward those who still suffer within our country, whether they be white or they be black.

So I shall ask you tonight to return home, to say a prayer for the family of Martin Luther King, that's true, but more importantly to say a prayer for our own country, which all of us

1. **Aeschylus** (EHS kuh luhs): a Greek playwright who lived during the sixth century B.C.

love—a prayer for understanding and that compassion of which I spoke.

We can do well in this country. We will have difficult times; we've had difficult times in the past; we will have difficult times in the future. It is not the end of violence; it is not the end of lawlessness; it is not the end of disorder.

But the vast majority of white people and the vast majority of black people in this country want to live together, want to improve the quality of our life, and want justice for all human beings who abide in our land.

Let us dedicate ourselves to what the Greeks wrote so many years ago: to tame the savageness of man and make gentle the life of this world.

Let us dedicate ourselves to that, and say a prayer for our country and for our people.

B **Literary Focus** **Persuasion** Kennedy chooses to discuss feelings here rather than facts. How does the discussion of emotions make the paragraph more persuasive?

C **Reading Focus** **Summarizing** In your own words, sum up the main ideas of Kennedy's speech.

Applying Your Skills

OH **RA.I.10.4** Assess the adequacy, accuracy and appropriateness of an author's details, identifying persuasive techniques and examples of propaganda, bias and stereotyping. **RA.I.10.6** Identify appeals to authority, reason and emotion. *Also covered* **RA.L.10.8; RP.10.1; WA.10.5.a**

There Comes a Time . . . / Eulogy for Martin Luther King, Jr.

Respond and Think Critically

Reading Focus

Quick Check

1. How does King hope to change the Montgomery bus situation?

2. In what ways does Kennedy hope Americans will imitate Dr. Martin Luther King, Jr.?

Read with a Purpose

3. How do King and Kennedy want to inspire the American people to act? Point out one goal that the speeches have in common and one way the speeches differ in purpose.

Reading Skills: Summarizing

4. While you read these selections, you kept track of the main ideas presented in each. Now, use those main ideas to write a brief summary of each selection.

Selection	My Summary
"There Comes a Time . . ."	
"Eulogy for Martin Luther King, Jr."	

Literary Focus

Literary Analysis

5. **Analyze** How does Kennedy portray the relationship between white and black people in his speech? What common ideals does he hope will draw them together?

6. **Make Judgments** Which speech do you find more persuasive? Why?

7. **Literary Perspectives** What historical events and issues form the backdrop of Kennedy's speech? What emotional appeals spring directly from Kennedy's personal experience with tragedy?

Literary Skills: Persuasion

8. **Evaluate** King and Kennedy both appeal to their listeners' emotions with loaded words and anecdotes. Write down two examples from each speech. What emotions do they stir? How do these appeals affect each speech?

Literary Skills Review: Tone

9. **Analyze** Tone is the writer's attitude toward his or her subject and audience. Tone is communicated through a writer's word choice, imagery, and details. What is King's tone in his speech? What is Kennedy's tone? Find details in the text to support your responses.

Writing Focus

Think as a Reader/Writer

Use It in Your Writing Consider an issue about which you feel strongly, preferably a situation that you would like to change. Write a persuasive paragraph in which you explain your point of view and try to inspire others to agree with you. Include figurative language as well as loaded words and anecdotes to persuade your audience.

 What Do You Think Now

In what ways have thinkers and activists such as King and Kennedy had an impact on how we regard ourselves as a nation?

Applying Your Skills

There Comes a Time . . . / Eulogy for Martin Luther King, Jr.

Vocabulary Development

Vocabulary Check

Identify each of the following statements as true (T) or false (F), and explain why.

1. A person of **integrity** is expected to act in an honest, professional manner.
2. A protester **advocating** a specific course of action is acting out against it.
3. A **utopian** society is one that is full of chaos.
4. Appeals to emotion are a form of **coercion.**

Language Coach

Word Origins Use a dictionary to find the word history, including the language of origin, for the Vocabulary words in the selections you have just read.

Academic Vocabulary

Talk About . . .

With a partner, discuss the main ideas of the speeches you have just read. How does King's speech <u>challenge</u> the injustice of discrimination? How does Kennedy's speech <u>demonstrate</u> his admiration for King? Use the underlined Academic Vocabulary words in your discussion.

Vocabulary Skills: Denotation and Connotation

Certain words have emotional overtones, or **connotations,** that go beyond their literal meanings, or **denotations.** Consider the difference between the two words in each of the following pairs:

young / immature	assertive / pushy
frugal / stingy	proud / smug

In each pair, the first word has more positive connotations than the second word. We are more likely to use the first word to describe ourselves and the second word to describe someone else. The British philosopher Bertrand Russell once gave a classic example of the different connotations of words: "I am firm. You are obstinate. He is a pig-headed fool."

Your Turn

Read the following passages, and write down what you think is the strongest word or phrase in each. Describe what the word or phrase suggests to you.

1. And you know, my friends, there comes a time when people get tired of being trampled over by the iron feet of oppression. There comes a time, my friends, when people get tired of being plunged across the abyss of humiliation, where they experience the bleakness of nagging despair.

   > from "There Comes a Time When People Get Tired" by Dr. Martin Luther King, Jr.

2. Or we can make an effort, as Martin Luther King did, to understand and to comprehend, and to replace that violence, that stain of bloodshed that has spread across our land, with an effort to understand with compassion and love.

   > from "Eulogy for Martin Luther King, Jr." by Robert F. Kennedy

Grammar Link

Parallel Structure

When ideas in a sentence have equal importance, express them in the same grammatical form. For example, balance a noun with a noun, or a phrase with the same type of phrase. This balance is called **parallel structure.**

> **NOT PARALLEL:** I like reading, writing, and to draw.
> **PARALLEL:** I like reading, writing, and drawing.
>
> **NOT PARALLEL:** Some of these stories are funny, entertaining, and teach me a lot.
> **PARALLEL:** Some of these stories are funny, entertaining, and educational.

In addition, ideas linked with **correlative conjunctions** (*both . . . and, either . . . or, neither . . . nor,* and *not only . . . but also*) must be parallel in structure.

> **NOT PARALLEL:** He not only was engaging people's minds but also touched their emotions.
> **PARALLEL:** He not only engaged people's minds but also touched their emotions.

Your Turn

Writing Applications Rewrite the following sentences using parallel structure.

1. Dr. Martin Luther King, Jr., was a preacher and to lead the civil rights movement.
2. He firmly believed that to segregate was unjust and equality for African Americans was a right.
3. He also believed that achieving his goals was as important as to act nonviolently.
4. He led peaceful protests and winning the Nobel Peace Prize.
5. King was neither a politician or was he a business leader, but he changed the United States forever.

CHOICES

As you respond to the Choices, use the **Academic Vocabulary** words as appropriate: <u>challenge</u>, <u>debate</u>, <u>demonstrate</u>, and <u>evident</u>.

REVIEW
Analyze Context

Timed LWriting Both Dr. Martin Luther King, Jr., and Robert F. Kennedy make strong persuasive appeals to their audiences. Write a brief essay in which you identify each speaker's audience and the circumstances under which each speech was made. How does the length of each speech reflect the time and place in which it was given?

CONNECT
Analyze a Speech

Find another speech by a current political leader. Then, write a brief analysis of the person's speech. Pay attention to any appeals to emotion or logic, and evaluate which parts of the speech you find most effective and why. If possible, play a recording of the speech for the rest of the class and then share your analysis.

EXTEND
Make a Time Line

Partner Activity With a partner, review what you know about the life, work, and goals of Dr. Martin Luther King, Jr. Make a list of his accomplishments. Then, use your list as a foundation to conduct research and discover more about his life and work. When you and your partner have finished your research, create a time line of King's life and his work for the civil rights movement.

Preparing to Read

from SILENT SPRING by **Rachel Carson**
Kiss and Tell by **Judith Stone**

Catena Aurea II (1996–1997) by Don Eddy. Acrylic on birch panels.
Courtesy of the artist and Nancy Hoffman Gallery, New York.

What Do You Think?

Do you believe people should do more to protect the environment? Explain.

QuickTalk

What effects do people have on the environment? Discuss both positive and negative effects with a small group of your classmates.

Reader/Writer
Notebook

Use your **RWN** to complete the activities for these selections.

OH **RA.I.10.5** Analyze an author's implicit and explicit argument, perspective or viewpoint in text.
RP.10.1 Apply reading comprehension strategies, including making predictions, comparing and contrasting, recalling and summarizing and making inferences and drawing conclusions.

Literary Focus

Argument: Structure and Tone An **argument** is a series of statements designed to convince you of something. When you analyze an argument, look at its **structure**—the organization of its main ideas. For example, a writer might start with the least important idea and then work toward the most important idea, or the reverse. Identifying the **tone,** or the writer's attitude toward the subject or audience, is also important. For example, if the writer's intent is to move you to act, he or she might use a serious, sincere, or concerned tone.

Reading Focus

Questioning and Drawing Conclusions To help you analyze an argument, you should **ask questions** as you read. Question the writer's intent, the main points and support, and your own reactions. For example, as you read "Kiss and Tell," you might wonder, "How could an interaction with an animal make the author want to save the planet?" Questioning also helps you **draw conclusions,** or formulate your own ideas, about the author's argument.

Into Action Use a chart like the one below to list your questions as you read the following selections.

Selection	My Questions
Silent Spring	What happened to the town?
Kiss and Tell	

Writing Focus

Think as a Reader/Writer

Find It in Your Reading Both Carson and Stone use specific details to illustrate their arguments. For example, instead of saying "Human pollution threatens biodiversity," Carson describes the "laurel, viburnum and alder, great ferns and wildflowers" that die off. As you read, look for details that support the writers' points. In your *Reader/Writer Notebook,* write the details you find most effective.

Vocabulary

from Silent Spring

prosperous (PRAHS puhr uhs) *adj.:* thriving; doing well. *The prosperous farms had an abundant harvest each year.*

blight (blyt) *n.:* disease that causes plants to wither and die. *The blight killed off most of the plants.*

Kiss and Tell

haphazard (hap HAZ uhrd) *adj.:* lacking direction; unplanned. *With only haphazard efforts, reform will not happen quickly.*

benevolent (buh NEHV uh luhnt) *adj.:* kind; generous toward others. *A kiss from a baby sea lion inspired Stone's benevolent view of nature.*

Language Coach

Prefixes A **prefix** is a word part added to the front of a word that changes the word's meaning. The prefix *bene–* comes from the Latin root *bene,* meaning "well." Can you think of any other words that use the prefix *bene–*? Try to list at least three. Consult a dictionary if you need help.

 Learn It Online
Build your understanding of terms with Word Watch:

| go.hrw.com | L10-583 | Go |

Rachel Carson
(1907–1964)

National Book Award WINNER

Never Silenced

Rachel Carson had two great inspirations: her mother, who loved reading and nature; and nature itself. Growing up in the country, Carson was "happiest with wild birds and creatures as companions." Her love of words led her to pursue writing in college. Then, after a class that reawakened her awe of nature's wonders, she switched her focus to zoology and marine biology. In 1951, she wrote *The Sea Around Us,* which won the National Book Award and was a national bestseller.

Gentle but fiercely determined to protect the natural world she so loved, Carson spoke out strongly in *Silent Spring* (1962) about the dangers of pesticides. Harshly criticized by the chemical companies and denounced as "hysterical," Carson stood firm on her science. In time, her work led to government policies protecting the environment from pesticides.

Judith Stone
(1950–   )

Learning and Growing

Judith Stone admits that she was once "a scientific illiterate." She jokes that she began to explore scientific subjects "partly because I felt uncomfortable living among natural and technological phenomena I found puzzling and unpredictable, and partly because someone paid me to do it." Her humor column for *Discover* magazine, "Light Elements," won a 1989 National Headliner Award. She is a contributing editor to *O, the Oprah Magazine,* and was formerly an editor at *Mirabella, McCall's,* and *Science Digest.*

Think About the Writers

What current environmental issue do you think would most concern Carson and Stone now?

Preview the Selections

Silent Spring begins with a fablelike passage set in a storybook American town. The town is not as perfect as it appears, however. Mysterious illnesses begin to sicken its animals, plants, and people. This grim scenario is a sobering look at potential threats to our environment.

In Judith Stone's essay "Kiss and Tell," she describes an eye-opening experience that forever changed the way she interacts with the world.

from SILENT SPRING

A Fable for Tomorrow

by **Rachel Carson**

Read with a Purpose
Read this selection to learn about one writer's vision of the threats to our environment.

Build Background

Rachel Carson's landmark book *Silent Spring* jump-started the modern environmental movement. The book examined the devastation caused by DDT, a chemical used as an insecticide. DDT was created in the late 1800s, but its effectiveness against mosquitoes and other insects was not discovered until 1939 by Paul Hermann Müller, who received a Nobel Prize for this discovery. DDT was widely used in the United States and in other parts of the world until Carson's book brought attention to its toxic effects on some species of birds and fish. By 1973, the United States had banned its use, as most of the world eventually did.

There was once a town in the heart of America where all life seemed to live in harmony with its surroundings. The town lay in the midst of a checkerboard of prosperous farms, with fields of grain and hillsides of orchards where, in spring, white clouds of bloom drifted above the green fields. In autumn, oak and maple and birch set up a blaze of color that flamed and flickered across a backdrop of pines. Then foxes barked in the hills and deer silently crossed the fields, half hidden in the mists of the fall mornings.

Along the roads, laurel, viburnum and alder,[1] great ferns and wildflowers delighted the traveler's eye through much of the year. Even in winter the roadsides were places of beauty, where countless birds came to feed on the berries and on the seed heads of the dried weeds rising above the snow. The countryside was, in fact, famous for the abundance and variety of its bird life, and when the flood of migrants[2] was pouring through in spring and fall people traveled from great distances to observe them. Others came to fish the streams, which flowed clear and cold out of the hills and contained shady pools where trout lay. So it had been from the days many years ago when the first settlers raised their houses, sank their wells, and built their barns. **Ⓐ**

Then a strange blight crept over the area and everything began to change. Some evil spell had settled on the community: mysterious maladies[3] swept the flocks of chickens; the cattle and sheep sickened and died. Everywhere was a shadow

---

1. **laurel, viburnum and alder:** species of shrubs and trees.

2. **migrants** (MY gruhnts): living creatures that roam or migrate; in this case, birds.

3. **maladies** (MAL uh deez): diseases; health disorders.

Vocabulary **prosperous** (PRAHS puhr uhs) *adj.*: thriving; doing well.
blight (blyt) *n.*: disease that causes plants to wither and die.

Ⓐ Literary Focus Argument How would you describe the tone of this opening paragraph?

Tree in Fog (2004) by Scott Prior. Oil on panel (10" × 9 ½"). Courtesy of the artist and Nancy Hoffman Gallery, New York.

of death. The farmers spoke of much illness among their families. In the town the doctors had become more and more puzzled by new kinds of sickness appearing among their patients. There had been several sudden and unexplained deaths, not only among adults but even among children, who would be stricken suddenly while at play and die within a few hours. **B**

There was a strange stillness. The birds, for example—where had they gone? Many people spoke of them, puzzled and disturbed. The feeding stations in the backyards were deserted. The few birds seen anywhere were moribund;[4] they trembled violently and could not fly. It was a spring without voices. On the mornings that had once throbbed with the dawn chorus of robins, catbirds, doves, jays, wrens, and scores of other bird voices there was now no sound; only silence lay over the fields and woods and marsh.

On the farms the hens brooded,[5] but no chicks hatched. The farmers complained that they were unable to raise any pigs—the litters were small and the young survived only a few days. The apple trees were coming into bloom but no bees droned among the blossoms, so there was no pollination and there would be no fruit.

The roadsides, once so attractive, were now lined with browned and withered vegetation as though swept by fire. These, too, were silent, deserted by all living things. Even the streams were now lifeless. Anglers[6] no longer visited them, for all the fish had died.

In the gutters under the eaves and between the shingles of the roofs, a white granular[7] powder still showed a few patches; some weeks before it had fallen like snow upon the roofs and the lawns, the fields and streams.

No witchcraft, no enemy action had silenced the rebirth of new life in this stricken world. The people had done it themselves.

This town does not actually exist, but it might easily have a thousand counterparts in America or elsewhere in the world. I know of no community that has experienced all the misfortunes I describe. Yet every one of these disasters has actually happened somewhere, and many real communities have already suffered a substantial number of them. A grim specter[8] has crept upon us almost unnoticed, and this imagined tragedy may easily become a stark reality we all shall know. **C**

---

4. **moribund** (MAWR uh buhnd): about to die.

---

5. **brooded** (BROOD ihd): sat on eggs to hatch them.
6. **anglers:** people who fish with a hook and a line.
7. **granular** (GRAN yuh luhr): made of small grains or particles.
8. **specter** (SPEHK tuhr): something that causes fear; literally, a ghost or phantom.

B **Reading Focus** Questioning What questions do you have about these changes in the town?

C **Literary Focus** Argument What is Carson's tone in this last paragraph? How does the tone reflect the main idea she reveals here?

Kiss and Tell

by Judith Stone

Read with a Purpose
Read this selection to understand why one woman becomes passionate about the environment.

Preparing to Read for this selection is on page 583.

Build Background
Inspired by an encounter with a baby sea lion on the remote Galapagos Islands, Stone wrote this essay to describe her awakening to environmentalism. This essay was originally published in the book *The Nature of Nature*, a collection of essays about the environment.

Until an infant sea lion kissed my foot, I had no real plan for saving the planet. But that ticklish reinitiation into the animal kingdom gave me notions. They didn't sort themselves out, though, until some time after the encounter on a serene beach in the far Galapagos, the chain of fifteen large and six small volcanic islands slung along the world's waist six hundred miles west of Ecuador.

Here, astonishingly, wild creatures—some of the rarest and most richly varied—don't flee humankind, despite a long history of betrayal to the brink of extinction. In the mere three decades since this place has been covered by the laws protecting paradises, all seems to have been forgiven. **(A)**

What a treat it was not to strike terror into the hearts of other living things! I could spend hours regarding rubbery black marine iguanas sunning in sloppy, chummy piles like discarded dime-store dinosaurs; instead of bolting, they simply grinned and dozed. A six-hundred-pound tortoise, who may well have lived a century and a half, regally extended his leathery neck for me to stroke. And, most thrilling of all, that curious month-old sea lion told me with a whisper of whiskers that I wasn't the enemy. **(B)**

Madly anthropomorphizing[1] on the strand, I regarded the pup's probing as a smooch and an invitation. Swimming with its sleek clan, I attempted to mimic their dipping and looping; they looked back as if to say, "You poor, pale, porky fish! Can't you manage any tricks?" I had never frolicked with wild things before, unless a New York City subway ride counts. It was almost more bliss than I could bear.

Back in the city, I recalled at odd moments the pup's huge eyes, its goofy, touching cry—a cross between a lamb's bleat and a car alarm. At the grocery store, offered a choice between a paper bag and a plastic one, I would try to calculate the ultimate benefits of each to sea lion and company. Haunted by the vision of a tiny, tender nose sliced by some discarded can tumbled from an overstuffed rogue[2] garbage barge,

---

1. **anthropomorphizing** (an thruh puh MAWR fyz ihng): giving animals human qualities.
2. **rogue** (rohg): without authorization.

(A) Literary Focus Argument What is the tone of this introductory section?

(B) Literary Focus Argument How does Stone structure her argument in this paragraph?

I got tough with my landlord, who is haphazard about recycling, despite city ordinances. I hate such confrontations. But the pup made me do it.

I wasted less. I made donations to organizations dedicated to saving our seas. After looking at photographs of small creatures suffocated in oil, I eschewed[3] a certain gasoline credit card, in spite of the inconvenience. I didn't do nearly enough, of course, but I was becoming a less lazy and more careful citizen of Earth. A princess was being transformed; that kiss had awakened sleeping duty. **C**

The more I traveled, the more I had to think about besides the pup. A moist, fern-fringed forest at the top of California, for example, and the feel of a particular seventeen-hundred-year-old redwood already ancient when Marco Polo met Kublai Khan[4] on his travels. Or the mouth of a cave in India's Thar Desert, where, at the final moment of sunset, a thousand swallows swooped through the new dark, grazing my hair, to shelter for the night.

There were people, too: Azucena, a ten-year-old coffee picker I met while touring a collective[5] in the cool mountains of Nicaragua; Kho Tan, an inspired guide through the ancient Burmese capital of Pagan, by the shore of the Irrawaddy; he'd led us among the town's two thousand temples shaped like bells and beehives and corncobs, and worried that his "unhandsome" salary wouldn't pay for the arthritis treatment his father needed; Solveig, who grows plums and cherries in the Norwegian village of Lofthus, on the Sorfjord; Costas, a fisherman on the tiny Greek island of Kastellorizon, who chatted with me while he mended his nets, holding the yellow strands with his toes as he wove. **D**

Because of these people and places, I can no longer ignore certain stories in the newspaper, damn it: A tanker sinks off Greece. Costas's catch! Acid rain from the factories of North America and Western Europe is showing up in the streams and soil of the Norwegian mountains. Solveig's plums! The repressive military regime cracks down again in Myanmar.[6] Can Kho Tan survive? Congress is stalling on an aid package to Nicaragua. Will Azucena ever have the chance to go to school? Believe me, I want to turn the page and get to the Bloomingdale's ads. But all these people and trees and fish I've met have been nagging at me, changing the way I read and shop and donate and vote.

Travel isn't just broadening, I've realized, but burdening, too. I now carry these lives and places with me. But I'm grateful for the ballast;[7] it's keeping me from tipping into total complacency. Call it benevolent narcissism:[8] Once I've been to a place, I care more about it. I'm grateful to the pup for the reconnection; I should have kissed *its* feet. And I hope to keep doing better, thanks

---

3. **eschewed** (ehs CHOOD): deliberately avoided.

4. **Marco Polo met Kublai Khan:** In the thirteenth century, Marco Polo (1254–1324), a trader and explorer from Venice, traveled to China and met Kublai Khan (1215–1294), a famous emperor of the Mongol dynasty.

5. **collective** (kuh LEHK tihv): farm owned and operated by a group of workers who share the profits equally.

6. **Myanmar:** largest mainland country in Southeast Asia; previously called Burma.

7. **ballast** (BAL uhst): something that stabilizes.

8. **narcissism** (NAHR sih sihz uhm): excessive admiration of one's self.

C **Reading Focus** Drawing Conclusions How has Stone's encounter with the sea lion pup changed her?

D **Reading Focus** Questioning Why does Stone mention all these people?

Vocabulary **haphazard** (hap HAZ uhrd) *adj.*: lacking direction; unplanned.
benevolent (buh NEHV uh luhnt) *adj.*: kind; generous toward others.

to the Greek (and Norwegian and Burmese and Nicaraguan) chorus in my head. **E**

And what if, I recently mused, people with power to do more were similarly affected? What if the folks with the whole world in their hands carried the whole world in their heads and hearts? I'm thinking especially of the corrupt and the careless, the shortsighted and the self-serving, the architects of human disasters and the violators of the wild.

So here's my plan: I want to sentence these people—the profligate,[9] the polluters—to . . . travel. In far, wild places.

Would those anxious to drill for oil in the Arctic National Wildlife Refuge be quite so interested once they'd waltzed with wolves there? Could the head of a waste-disposal company so readily approve a plan to dump lethal toxic sludge in an African village after playing tag with its children? If he'd spent a few weeks in a rain forest, with the wet, silvery web of life filigreed[10] on his face, would former United States Secretary of the Interior Manuel Lujan have been so quick to ask in 1990, "Do we have to save *every* subspecies?" **F**

It's easy to ignore or hate or hurt an abstraction, not so easy when a person or a place is specific and real to you. My scheme would make the world more specific, real, intimate.

Though I highly recommend it, these ecologically backward types I'm talking about needn't submit to a sea lion's kiss; I realize enforced bussing is highly controversial. There

---

9. **profligate** (PRAHF luh giht): referring to a group of people lacking morals.
10. **filigreed** (FIHL uh greed): decorated with a delicate lacelike design or material.

E **Reading Focus** Drawing Conclusions What conclusions does Stone draw about travel?

F **Literary Focus** Argument What does Stone propose as punishment for the polluters?

Environmentalism

Environmentalism is a social movement that encourages people to protect the natural environment from harmful effects of human lifestyles. These effects include pollution, the destruction of forests, and the extinction of animal species. Environmentalists work to educate the public about threats to the environment. They also <u>challenge</u> world leaders to take political steps to preserve and improve the quality of the environment. Not everyone agrees with methods recommended by environmentalists, but most people do agree that reducing pollution, keeping our water supply clean, and finding a balance between economic growth and environmental protection are important.

Ask Yourself

What are Stone's concerns about the environment, as mentioned in her essay?

Destroyed Earth by John Lund.

are only a couple of rules: They must break bread with people in the places where those people live, and they must look them in the eye. The regions they roam must be remote, lovely, and in peril.

"Oh, we get it," you're saying, winking broadly and nudging one another in the ribs. "If the CEO of Exxon had frolicked with an otter in Alaska's Prince William Sound,[11] he'd have been so concerned with the critter's welfare that he'd have insisted that more care be taken in overseeing the company's shipping subsidiary,[12] thus avoiding a mishap that caused several billion dollars' worth of damage, the deaths of tens of thousands of animals, and damage to shoreline

---

11. **Alaska's Prince William Sound:** In 1989, an Exxon tanker crashed into the reef here, and as a result, oil was released into the water. The accident caused major environmental destruction.
12. **subsidiary** (suhb SIHD ee ehr ee): a company owned in large part by another company.

and tidal zones that will persist well into the new millennium?" Yup. That's what I'm saying. **G**

As a young naturalist, Charles Darwin was inspired by the variety of wildlife in the Galapagos Islands to formulate his theory of evolution by natural selection. He found thirteen species of finch, identical except for tiny differences precisely suiting them to the islands on which they lived. Birds living among flowers had long slender beaks for sipping nectar; those surrounded by seeds instead of blossoms had thick, tough beaks that worked as nutcrackers. Darwin reasoned that the animals changed over time, passing on characteristics that helped them successfully adapt to their surroundings.

The Galapagos has inspired me to formulate the Sea Lion Theory of Global Salvation: Send the right people on an adventure vacation, and fast! As soon as possible, our species needs to evolve beaks capable of sipping this planet's nectar before its sweetness is forever lost. **H**

G **Literary Focus** Argument How would you describe the author's tone here?

H **Reading Focus** Questioning What questions do you have at the end of Stone's essay?

Applying Your Skills

RA.I.10.5 Analyze an author's implicit and explicit argument, perspective or viewpoint in text.
RA.L.10.8 Analyze the author's use of point of view, mood and tone. *Also covered* **RP.10.1; VO.10.3**

from Silent Spring / Kiss and Tell

Respond and Think Critically

Reading Focus

Quick Check

1. What changes occur in the town in Carson's essay? Why do they occur?

2. How does Stone begin to care about the environment?

Read with a Purpose

3. What do Carson and Stone each hope to accomplish with their concern for the environment?

Reading Skills: Questioning and Drawing Conclusions

4. As you read, you listed your questions about each selection. Now, complete the chart by answering your questions.

Selection	My Questions	My Answers
Silent Spring	What happened to the town?	
Kiss and Tell	Why is the sea lion important?	

✔ Vocabulary Check

Match each Vocabulary word with its definition.

5. **blight**   a. unplanned
6. **prosperous**   b. kind
7. **benevolent**   c. disease
8. **haphazard**   d. abundant

Literary Focus

Literary Analysis

9. **Interpret** Who or what is the "grim specter" described in Carson's essay?

10. **Analyze** What does the author of "Kiss and Tell" suggest we do with the "people with power"? Do you agree with her? Why or why not?

Literary Skills: Argument

11. **Compare and Contrast** Carson and Stone make similar points in different ways. Compare and contrast the tone of their arguments.

12. **Evaluate** Which selection did you find more persuasive? Why?

Literary Skills Review: Point of View

13. **Evaluate** **Point of view** refers to the vantage point of the narrator. Carson uses a third-person narrator and Stone uses first-person narration to share her experiences. Which narrator do you find more effective? Why?

Writing Focus

Think as a Reader/Writer

Use It in Your Writing Think of a topic about which you feel strongly. List specific details that would illustrate its importance. Then, write a persuasive paragraph about the topic, including details.

What Do You Think Now?

What steps should people take to protect the environment? What can you, as an individual, do?

Comparing Viewpoints: Pro and Con

CONTENTS

 What Do You Think? What do you believe our relationships with our pets can tell us about ourselves?

 QuickWrite
List the ways in which relationships between people are similar to and different from the relationships between people and their pets. What lessons might we learn from our pets about how we should interact with other people?

Preparing to Read

from **Cesar's Way / Pack of Lies**

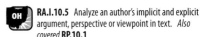

RA.I.10.5 Analyze an author's implicit and explicit argument, perspective or viewpoint in text. *Also covered* **RP.10.1**

Reader/Writer Notebook

Use your **RWN** to complete the activities for these selections.

Literary Focus

Arguments: Pro and Con In arguments, authors present a claim, or an opinion about a topic or an issue. They might use **logical appeals**—reasons backed up by evidence (facts, statistics, examples, and experts' opinions)—to support their claim. They may also use **emotional appeals,** such as loaded words and anecdotes, and adopt a particular **tone** (or attitude) to sway a reader's feelings. As you read these selections, determine which argument is more **credible,** or believable.

TechFocus While reading the selections, imagine how the authors might speak to each other about these issues. How might you create a videotaped record of their conversation?

Reading Focus

Questioning When you read persuasive texts, ask questions to help you pinpoint the strengths and weaknesses of the arguments.

Into Action As you read each selection, record your questions in a chart like the one below. Then, record any answers you find to your questions as you continue reading.

from Cesar's Way

Questions	Answers
Is there proof that dogs have a "pack instinct"?	

Writing Focus

Think as a Reader/Writer

Find It in Your Reading A writer's subject, purpose, and audience all influence his or her **diction,** or word choice. As you read the selections, consider how you would describe the authors' diction. Note examples of their word choice in your *Reader/Writer Notebook.*

Vocabulary

from Cesar's Way

primal (PRY muhl) *adj.:* first in importance; essential. *A dog's primal instinct is to belong to a pack.*

submissive (suhb MIHS ihv) *adj.:* obedient; under another's control. *Unlike leaders of packs, followers are submissive.*

Pack of Lies

intimidation (ihn tihm uh DAY shuhn) *n.:* inspiring fear; using threats or fear to influence behavior. *Some trainers use intimidation instead of rewards.*

punitive (PYOO nuh tihv) *adj.:* punishing; seeking to punish. *Frightening a dog is a punitive form of training.*

aggression (uh GREHSH uhn) *n.:* habit of attacking; unfriendly, destructive behavior. *Aggression can cause a dog to harm a person or another dog.*

Language Coach

Prefixes The prefix *sub–* comes from the Latin word for "under." Which Vocabulary word uses this prefix? What other words can you think of that use this prefix? Use a dictionary if you need help.

 Learn It Online
There's more to words than just definitions. Get the whole story on:

go.hrw.com L10-593 **Go**

Cesar Millan
(1969–   )

El Perrero—the Dogman

As a young child in Mexico, Cesar Millan loved observing the working dogs at his grandfather's farm. Millan calls these dogs, which lived in informal packs, his "true teachers in the art and science of canine psychology." When he was twenty-one, Millan came to the United States "with no money in [his] pocket and the dream and ambition to become the best dog trainer in the world." He began his career as a dog groomer and ultimately became a dog behavior specialist. He founded the Dog Psychology Center in Los Angeles, California, in 1997, and began hosting the television series *The Dog Whisperer* in 2004.

Mark Derr
(1950–   )

A Dog's Life

Mark Derr was born in Baltimore, Maryland, and raised in central Florida. When talking about his life, Derr says that he has "never been without a dog." For his book *Dog's Best Friend* (1997), he interviewed numerous dog experts, including veterinarians, researchers, dog trainers, and people who work with guide dogs, hunting dogs, sled dogs, and even Frisbee dogs. The purpose of the recommendations he makes in the book, Derr states, is to "improve the lot of dogs and our relationship with them." In addition to his two books and other writings about dogs, Derr reports on science and has published books about the environment and about Davy Crockett.

Think About the Writers

What do these biographies suggest about the similarities and differences between the authors?

from Cesar's Way

by **Cesar Millan**

Read with a Purpose
Read this selection to explore the author's views about leaders and followers in the human and animal worlds.

Build Background
TV personality Cesar Millan's dog-training methods have won him many fans. In his bestselling 2006 book, *Cesar's Way: The Natural, Everyday Guide to Understanding and Correcting Common Dog Problems,* Millan outlines his dog-training philosophy and shows how people can solve their dogs' behavior problems. This selection is an excerpt from the chapter titled "Power of the Pack."

A dog's pack is his life force. The pack instinct is his primal instinct. His status in the pack is his self, his identity. The pack is all important to a dog because if anything threatens the pack's harmony, it threatens each individual dog's harmony. If something threatens the pack's survival, it threatens the very survival of every dog in it. The need to keep the pack stable and running smoothly is a powerful motivating force in every dog—even in a pampered poodle that has never met another dog or left the confines of your backyard. Why? It's deeply ingrained in his brain. Evolution and Mother Nature took care of that.

It's vital for you to understand that your dog views all his interactions with other dogs, with you, and even with other animals in your household in the "pack" context. Humans—in fact, all primates—are pack animals, too.

In fact, dog packs are really not so different from the human equivalent of packs. We call our packs families. Clubs. Football teams. Churches. Corporations. Governments. Sure, we think of our social groups as infinitely more complicated than dogs' groups, but are they really all that different? When you break it down, the basics are the same: every one of the "packs" I've mentioned has a hierarchy,[1] or it doesn't work. There is a father or mother, a chairman, a quarterback, a minister, a CEO, a president. Then there are varying levels of status for the people under him or her. That's how a pack of canines[2] works, too. **Ⓐ**

---

1. **hierarchy** (HY uh rahr kee): structure in which the members of a group are ranked based on ability or status.
2. **canines** (KAY nynz): members of the family of mammals that includes dogs, wolves, and foxes.

Vocabulary **primal** (PRY muhl) *adj.:* first in importance; essential.

Ⓐ **Literary Focus** Argument How does Millan engage his audience members and speak to their concerns and feelings in these first paragraphs?

Cesar Millan (*right*) meets with a client and her dog.

The concept of pack and pack leader is directly related to the way in which dogs interact with us when we bring them into our homes.

The Natural Pack

If you study a wolf pack in the wild, you'll observe a natural rhythm to its days and nights. First, the animals in the pack walk, sometimes up to ten hours a day, to find food and water. Then they eat. If they kill a deer, the pack leader gets the biggest piece, but everyone cooperates in sharing the rest. They'll eat until the entire deer is gone—not just because they don't have

Saran Wrap in the wild, but because they don't know when there's going to be another deer again. What they eat today may have to hold them for a long time. That's where the expression "wolfing down" food comes from, and you'll see it in your own dog's behavior much of the time. Wolves don't necessarily eat just when they're hungry; they eat when the food is there. Their bodies are designed to conserve. It's the root of your own dog's often seemingly insatiable appetite.

Only after wolves and wild dogs have finished their daily work do they play. That's when they celebrate. And in nature, they usually go to sleep exhausted. Not once, while watching the dogs on my grandfather's farm, did I ever see a sleeping dog having nightmares, the way domestic dogs in America do. Their ears would twitch, their eyes would move, but there was no whimpering or whining or moaning. They were so completely worn out from their day's work and play that they slept peacefully, every night.

Every pack has its rituals. These include traveling, working for food and water, eating, playing, resting, and mating. Most important, the pack always has a pack leader. The rest of the animals are followers. Within the pack, the animals fall into their own order of status, usually determined by that animal's inborn energy level. The leader determines—and enforces—the rules and boundaries by which the members will live. **Ⓑ**

A puppy's first pack leader is his mother. From birth, puppies learn how to be cooperative members of a pack-oriented society. At about three or four months, after they're weaned, they fall into the regular pack structure, and take their cues from the pack leader, not their mother. In packs of wolves and wild dogs, the leader is often a male, because the hormone[3] testosterone—present in male puppies from the time they are very small—seems to be a cue to dominance[4] behaviors.

Though hormones are part of what makes a pack leader, energy plays an even greater role. When humans live in households with more than one dog, the dominant dog can be either male or female. The gender doesn't matter, only the inborn energy level, and who establishes dominance. In many packs, there is an "alpha couple," a male and female pair who seem to run things between them.

In the wild, pack leaders are born, not made. They don't take classes to become leaders; they don't fill out applications and go on interviews. Leaders develop early and they show their dominant qualities quite young. It's that all-important energy we discussed earlier that separates the pack leader from the follower. A pack leader must be born with high or very high energy. The energy must also be dominant energy, as well as calm-assertive[5] energy. Medium- and low-energy dogs do not make natural pack leaders. Most dogs—like most humans—are born to be followers, not leaders. Being a pack leader isn't only about dominance, it's also about responsibility. Think about our own species, and the percentage of people who would like to have the power and perks of the president, or the money and goodies of a Bill Gates.[6] Then tell those people that the trade-off is that they will have to work around the clock, 24-7, almost never see their families, and rarely take weekends off. Tell them they'll be financially responsible for thousands of people, or responsible for the national security of hundreds of millions of people. How many people

---

3. **hormone** (HAWR mohn): substance produced by the body that affects an organ or other tissues.
4. **dominance:** most powerful; having the most control.

5. **calm-assertive** (uh SUR tihv): Millan uses this term to mean relaxed but confident and in control.
6. **Bill Gates:** cofounder of the giant computer company Microsoft and one of the wealthiest people in the world.

Ⓑ **Reading Focus** **Questioning** Why might you question the truth of the statements in this paragraph?

would choose those leadership roles after being presented with such daunting realities? I believe most people would choose comfortable but simpler lives over great power and wealth—if they truly understood the work and sacrifice that leadership costs.

Similarly, in a dog's world, the pack leader has the responsibility for the survival of all the pack members. The leader leads the pack to food and water. He decides when to hunt; decides who eats, how much, and when; decides when to rest and when to sleep and when to play. The leader sets all the regulations and structures that the other pack members must live by. A pack leader has to have total confidence and know what he's doing. And just as in the human world, most dogs are born to follow rather than do all the work it takes to maintain the position of pack leader. Life is easier and less stressful for them when they live within the rules, boundaries, and limitations that the pack leader has set for them. . . . **C**

To Lead or to Follow?

To dogs, there are only two positions in a relationship: leader and follower. Dominant and submissive. It's either black or white. There is no in-between in their world. When a dog lives with a human, in order for the human to be able to control the dog's behavior, she must make the commitment to take on the role of pack leader, 100 percent of the time. It's that simple. . . .

A dog will usually accept a human as its pack leader if that human projects the correct calm-assertive energy, sets solid rules, boundaries, and limitations, and acts responsibly in the cause of the pack's survival. This doesn't mean that we can't still be uniquely *human* pack leaders. Just as dogs shouldn't have to give up what's unique about them to live with us, we shouldn't have to give up what's so special about being human. We are, for instance, the only pack leaders who are going to love the dogs in the way we humans define love. Their canine pack leader will not buy them squeaky toys or throw birthday parties for them. Their canine pack leader won't directly reward their good behavior. He won't turn around and say, "Gee, guys, thanks for following me ten miles." It's expected that they do that! A mother dog won't say, "You know, you pups have behaved so well today. Let's go to the beach!" In their natural world, the reward is in the process. (That's a concept we humans could sometimes do well to remember.) For a dog there's a reward in simply fitting in with the pack and helping to ensure its survival. Cooperation automatically results in the primal rewards of food, water, play, and sleep. Rewarding our dogs with treats and the things that they love is one way we can bond with them and reinforce good behavior. But if we don't project strong leadership energy before we give rewards, we're never going to have a truly functional "pack." **D**

Who's Top Dog in Your House?

Once my clients start to grasp the concept of the pack and the pack leader, they usually ask me, "How can I tell who's the pack leader in my house?" The answer is very simple: who controls the dynamics of your relationship?

C **Reading Focus** **Questioning** How might one know that dogs feel less stress when their lives are governed by rules?

D **Literary Focus** **Argument** What might be Millan's purpose in emphasizing that dog owners can "be uniquely *human* pack leaders"?

Vocabulary **submissive** (suhb MIHS ihv) *adj.:* obedient; under another's control.

There are dozens and dozens of different ways in which your dog will tell you, loud and clear, who's the dominant one between the two of you. If he jumps on you when you come home from work in the evening, he's not just happy to see you. He is the pack leader. If you open the door to go for a walk and he exits ahead of you, it's not just because he loves his walks so much. He is the pack leader. If he barks at you and then you feed him, it's not "cute." He is the pack leader. If you are sleeping and he wakes you up at five in the morning pawing you to say "Let me out; I gotta pee," then he's showing you even before the sun comes up who's running the house. Whenever he makes you do anything, he is the pack leader. Simple as that.

Most of the time dogs are the pack leaders of the human world because the human will say, "Isn't that adorable? He's trying to tell me something." There it is, that old *Lassie* syndrome again, "What's that, Lassie? Gramps fell down the well?"[7] Yes, in this case, human, your dog is trying to tell you something—he's trying to remind you that he is the leader and you are his follower. **E**

So, when you wake up on your own terms, you are the pack leader. When you open the door on your own terms, you are the pack leader. When you exit the house ahead of your dog, you are the pack leader. When you are the one who makes the decisions in the household,

Cesar Millan has said that dog owners in America give their dogs too much affection; dogs need "exercise, discipline . . . and *then* affection."

then you are the pack leader. And I'm not talking about 80 percent of the time. I'm talking about 100 percent of the time. If you give only 80 percent leadership, your dog will give you 80 percent following. And the other 20 percent of the time he will run the show. If you give your dog any opportunity for him to lead you, he will take it.

---

7. *Lassie* **syndrome . . . the well:** In a much-loved TV show that aired from 1954 until the early 1970s, Lassie, a collie dog, helped rescue people. The character originally appeared in a 1938 short story, and over the years she has been the subject of books, movies, and a second TV series.

E **Reading Focus** **Questioning** Do you think there are ever times when dogs might have important needs to communicate to us?

Leading Is a Full-time Job

Dogs need leadership, from the day they're born to the day they die. They instinctively need to know what their position is in regard to us. Usually owners have a position for their dogs in their hearts but not in their "packs." That's when the dogs take over. They take advantage of a human who loves them but offers no leadership. Dogs don't reason. They don't think, "Gee, it's so great that this person loves me. It makes me feel so good, I'll never attack another dog again." You can't say to a dog like you'd say to a child, "Unless you behave, you're not going to the dog park tomorrow." A dog can't make that connection. Any show of leadership you give dogs must be given at the moment of the behavior that needs correction.

In your household, anybody can be a pack leader. In fact, it is vital that all the humans in the house be the dog's pack leader—from the smallest infant to the oldest adult. Male or female. Everybody must get with the program.

Analyzing Visuals

Viewing and Interpreting
In what way is it <u>evident</u> in this photograph that Millan is the pack leader?

According to Millan, "A 45-minute power walk every morning" is the best thing you can do for your dog.

I go to many households where the dog respects one person, but runs roughshod over the rest of the family. This can be another recipe for disaster. In my family, I am the dogs' pack leader, but so are my wife and two sons. Andre and Calvin can walk through my pack dogs at the Dog Psychology Center without the dogs so much as blinking an eye. The boys learned pack leadership from watching me, but all children can be taught how to assert leadership with animals. **Ⓕ**

Pack leadership doesn't hinge on size or weight or gender or age. Jada Pinkett Smith weighs maybe 110 pounds soaking wet, but she was able to handle four Rottweilers at once even better than her husband was. Will Smith[8] was good with the dogs and they respected him, but Jada really put in the time and energy needed to be a strong pack leader. She's gone with me to the beach and the mountains, where I take the pack out for off-leash walks.

---

8. **Jada Pinkett Smith . . . Will Smith:** well-known actors who are married to each other.

Leading a dog on a walk—as evidenced by the dogs who live with the homeless—is the best way to establish pack leadership. It's a primal activity that creates and cements those pack leader–follower bonds. As simple as it sounds, it's one of the keys to creating stability in the mind of your dog.

In dogs that are trained for specific jobs, the pack leader doesn't even need to be out in front. In Siberian husky dogsled teams, though the human pack leader is at the back of the sled, it's she who is running the sled. Dogs who live with handicapped people—people in wheelchairs, the blind, people with special needs—often have to take the physical lead in some situations. But the person they are helping is always the one in control. It's a beautiful thing to watch a service dog who lives with a handicapped person. Often, the two seem to have a kind of supernatural connection between them—a sixth sense. They are so in tune with each other that the dog can often sense what that person needs before being given a command. That's the kind of bond dogs in packs have with one another. Their communication is unspoken, and it comes from the security they have within the pack structure. **Ⓖ**

With the proper calm-assertive energy, pack leadership, and discipline, you, too, can have this sort of deep connection with your dog. In order to accomplish this, however, it's important to be aware of the things you may be inadvertently doing that are contributing to your dog's problems.

Ⓕ Literary Focus Argument Is citing his personal experiences an effective way for Millan to support his point in this paragraph? Why or why not?

Ⓖ Literary Focus Argument How do the examples in this paragraph add complexity to Millan's argument?

Applying Your Skills

RA.I.10.5 Analyze an author's implicit and explicit argument, perspective or viewpoint in text. **RP.10.1** Apply reading comprehension strategies, including making predictions, comparing and contrasting, recalling and summarizing and making inferences and drawing conclusions. *Also covered* **VO.10.3; WA.10.5.a**

from Cesar's Way

Respond and Think Critically

Reading Focus

Quick Check

1. According to Millan, what purpose does a pack serve for wolves and wild dogs?

2. How does Millan think dogs often exert control over their owners? Why do many people fail to control the behavior of their dogs?

Read with a Purpose

3. Explain the ways in which Millan believes wolves, dogs, and people all take on similar roles as leaders and followers. Do you agree with his points about human society? Why or why not?

Reading Skills: Questioning

4. Review the chart you filled in as you read this selection. Then, add a third column titled "More Information Needed." Place a check mark in this column for any unanswered questions. What is the significance of your unanswered questions? Do they signal that Millan has made you curious to learn more about the subject, or do they point to weaknesses in his argument?

✓ Vocabulary Check

Explain why each statement is true (T) or false (F).

5. A **primal** instinct is one that an animal learns when it is domesticated.

6. A **submissive** child is one who rebels against rules.

Literary Focus

Literary Analysis

7. **Interpret** Discussing the rewards dogs receive for good behavior in nature, Millan says, "The reward is in the process." What does this statement mean? Explain whether you agree with him that people would "do well to remember" this concept.

8. **Interpet** Who is Millan's audience? How does he try to win over his audience members by addressing their needs and concerns?

Literary Skills: Argument

9. **Evaluate** What type of logical and emotional appeals does Millan present to support his claim? Do you find his argument convincing? Why or why not?

Literary Skills Review: Text Structures

10. **Evaluate** Writers of nonfiction often use subheadings to set off sections of their texts. What purpose does each subheading in this selection serve? Explain whether you think the subheadings are effective.

Writing Focus

Think as a Reader/Writer

Use It in Your Writing Write a persuasive paragraph in which you make an argument about the best way to improve relationships between animals and humans. Choose your words carefully to ensure that your diction suits your subject, purpose, and audience.

Pack of LIES

by **Mark Derr** from *The New York Times*

Read with a Purpose
Read this article to discover why the author thinks Cesar Millan's dog-training methods are harmful.

Preparing to Read for this selection is on page 593.

Build Background
In this op-ed article, Mark Derr, the author of two books about dogs, takes aim at Cesar Millan and his popular dog-training methods.

With a compelling personal story as the illegal immigrant made good because of his uncanny[1] ability to understand dogs, Cesar Millan has taken the world of canine behavior—or rather misbehavior—by storm. He has the top-rated program, "Dog Whisperer," on the National Geographic Channel, a best-selling book and a devoted following, and he has been the subject of several glowing magazine articles.

He is even preparing to release his own "Illusion" collar and leash set, named for his wife and designed to better allow people to walk their dogs the "Cesar way"—at close heel, under strict control.

Essentially, National Geographic and Cesar Millan have cleverly repackaged and promoted a simplistic view of the dog's social structure and constructed around it a one-size-fits-all, cookie-cutter approach to dog training. In Mr. Millan's world, dog behavioral problems result from a failure of the human to be the "pack leader," to dominate the dog (a wolf by any other name) completely. **(A)**

While Mr. Millan rejects hitting and yelling at dogs during training, his confrontational methods include physical and psychological intimidation, like finger jabs, choke collars, extended sessions on a treadmill and what is called flooding, or overwhelming the animal with the thing it fears. Compared with some training devices still in use—whips and cattle prods, for example—these are mild, but combined with a lack of positive reinforcement[2] or rewards, they place Mr. Millan firmly in a long tradition of punitive dog trainers.

Mr. Millan brings his pastiche[3] of animal

---

1. **uncanny** (uhn KAN ee): so remarkable as to seem unnatural or not normal.

2. **positive reinforcement:** rewards designed to encourage good behavior.
3. **pastiche** (pas TEESH): here, confused mixture.

(A) Reading Focus Questioning Does Derr's description of Millan's approach to dog training raise any questions in your mind about your own response to Millan's argument?

Vocabulary **intimidation** (ihn tihm uh DAY shuhn) *n.*: inspiring fear; using threats or fear to influence behavior.
punitive (PYOO nuh tihv) *adj.*: punishing; seeking to punish.

behaviorism and pop psychology into millions of homes a week. He's a charming, one-man wrecking ball directed at 40 years of progress in understanding and shaping dog behavior and in developing nonpunitive, reward-based training programs, which have led to seeing each dog as an individual, to understand what motivates it, what frightens it and what its talents and limitations are. Building on strengths and working around and through weaknesses, these trainers and specialists in animal behavior often work wonders with their dogs, but it takes time.

Mr. Millan supposedly delivers fast results. His mantra[4] is "exercise, discipline, affection," where discipline means "rules, boundaries, limitations." Rewards are absent and praise scarce, presumably because they will upset the state of

calm submission Mr. Millan wants in his dogs. Corrections abound as animals are forced to submit or face their fear, even if doing so panics them. **Ⓑ**

Mr. Millan builds his philosophy from a simplistic conception of the dog's "natural" pack, controlled by a dominant alpha animal (usually male). In his scheme, that leader is the human, which leads to the conclusion that all behavior problems in dogs derive from the failure of the owner or owners to dominate. (Conveniently, by this logic, if Mr. Millan's intervention doesn't produce lasting results, it is the owner's fault.) . . .

The notion of the "alpha pack leader" dominating all other pack members is derived from studies of captive packs of unrelated wolves and thus bears no relationship to the social structure of natural packs, according to L. David Mech, one of the world's leading wolf experts.

---

4. **mantra** (MAN truh): word or phrase repeated over and over, as in a prayer or a request for guidance.

Ⓑ **Reading Focus** **Questioning** What questions do you have about the role that affection plays in Millan's training methods?

In the wild, the alpha wolves are merely the breeding pair, and the pack is generally comprised of their juvenile offspring and pups.

"The typical wolf pack," Dr. Mech wrote in The Canadian Journal of Zoology in 1999, "is a family, with the adult parents guiding the activities of a group in a division-of-labor system." In a natural wolf pack, "dominance contests with other wolves are rare, if they exist at all," he writes. **C**

That's a far cry from the dominance model that Mr. Millan attributes to the innate need of dogs by way of wolves.

Unlike their wolf forebears,[5] dogs exist in human society. They have been selectively bred for 15,000 or more years to live with people. Studies have shown that almost from birth they are attentive to people, and that most are eager to please, given proper instruction and encouragement.

But sometimes the relationship goes very wrong, and it is time to call on a professional.

Aggression is perhaps the most significant of the behavioral problems that may afflict more than 20 percent of the nation's 65 million dogs, because it can lead to injury and death. Mr. Millan often treats aggression by forcing the dog to exercise extensively on a treadmill, by asserting his authority over the dog by rolling it on its back in the "alpha rollover," and through other forms of intimidation, including exposure to his pack of dogs.

Forcefully rolling a big dog on its back was once recommended as a way to establish dominance, but it is now recognized as a good way to get bitten. People are advised not to try it. In fact, many animal behaviorists believe that in the long run meeting aggression with aggression breeds more aggression.

More important, aggression often has underlying medical causes that might not be readily apparent—hip dysplasia[6] or some other hidden physical ailment that causes the dog to bite out of pain; hereditary forms of sudden rage that require a medical history and genealogy to diagnose; inadequate blood flow to the brain or a congenital brain malformation that produces aggression and can only be uncovered through a medical examination. Veterinary behaviorists, having found that many aggressive dogs suffer from low levels of serotonin,[7] have had success in treating such dogs with fluoxetine (the drug better known as Prozac).

Properly treating aggression, phobias, anxiety and fears from the start can literally save time and money. Mr. Millan's quick fix might make for good television and might even produce lasting results in some cases. But it flies in the face of what professional animal behaviorists—either trained and certified veterinarians or ethologists[8]—have learned about normal and abnormal behavior in dogs. **D**

---

5. **forebears** (FAWR bairz): ancestors.

6. **hip dysplasia:** disease affecting the hip joint, common among certain dog breeds.

7. **serotonin** (sihr oh TOH nuhn): chemical produced by the body that affects the brain and other organs.

8. **ethologists** (ih THAHL uh jihsts): scientists who study animal behavior.

C **Literary Focus** **Argument** How does the inclusion of this quotation affect the credibility of Derr's argument?

D **Literary Focus** **Argument** How does Derr challenge Millan's credibility in this paragraph?

Vocabulary **aggression** (uh GREHSH uhn) *n.:* habit of attacking; unfriendly, destructive behavior.

Applying Your Skills

RA.I.10.5 Analyze an author's implicit and explicit argument, perspective or viewpoint in text. **RP.10.1** Apply reading comprehension strategies, including making predictions, comparing and contrasting, recalling and summarizing and making inferences and drawing conclusions. *Also covered* **VO.10.3; WA.10.5.a**

Pack of Lies

Respond and Think Critically

Reading Focus

Quick Check

1. Why does Derr think that rewards-based training programs are effective?
2. How does Derr describe the differences between wolves and dogs?
3. According to Derr, what are some possible causes of misbehavior in dogs?

Read with a Purpose

4. Which of Millan's dog-training methods does Derr criticize? Why? What does Derr see as the potential negative effects of Millan's methods?

Reading Skills: Questioning

5. Add a third column titled "More Information Needed" to your "Pack of Lies" chart. For any questions that you were unable to answer, place a check mark in this column. Then, review your charts. Are there questions that you now realize you should have asked as you read the selections? What have you learned about being a critical reader from reading these selections?

✔ Vocabulary Check

Match each Vocabulary word in the column on the left with its definition in the column on the right.

6. **intimidation**   a. habit of attacking
7. **punitive**   b. inspiring fear
8. **aggression**   c. punishing

Literary Focus

Literary Analysis

9. **Infer** According to Derr's statements, how have the media and Millan himself promoted his dog-training methods? What is Derr's attitude toward these promotional efforts? Support your response with evidence from the article.

10. **Evaluate** What tone does Derr adopt when discussing Millan's philosophy and methods? Do you think Derr's tone supports or detracts from his purpose in the article? Explain.

Literary Skills: Argument

11. **Identify** What is Derr's claim in this article? Explain the flaws he sees in Millan's philosophy.

12. **Evaluate** What types of logical and emotional appeals does Derr present to undermine Millan's credibility? Explain whether you think Derr's argument is convincing.

Literary Skills Review: Title

13. **Analyze** The title of a work can serve several purposes. Explain the **pun,** or play on multiple-meaning words, in the title "Pack of Lies." What purposes does Derr achieve by using this title?

Writing Focus

Think as a Reader/Writer

Use It in Your Writing Choose a controversial issue—perhaps relating to your own life, your school, or the world. Write a paragraph in which you present the main argument of each side of the issue, and then conclude by stating your opinion. Use diction that suits your subject, purpose, and audience.

Wrap Up

from **Cesar's Way / Pack of Lies**

OH | **RP.10.1** Apply reading comprehension strategies, including making predictions, comparing and contrasting, recalling and summarizing and making inferences and drawing conclusions. **WA.10.4.c** Write informational essays or reports, including research that: create an organizing structure appropriate to the purpose, audience and context;

Writing Focus

Write a Comparison-Contrast Essay

Topic Now that you have read the excerpt from *Cesar's Way* and "Pack of Lies," who do you think is right, Cesar Millan or Mark Derr? Write an essay in which you compare and contrast their arguments and explain whose argument you find more credible. In your essay, consider the following items:

- each author's claim
- the authors' use of logical appeals to support their claims
- the authors' use of emotional appeals
- each author's tone

Structure An organized, well-developed essay should include these elements:

- an **introduction** containing a precise **thesis statement** expressing your opinion of the credibility of Millan's and Derr's arguments
- **body paragraphs** in which you compare and contrast the authors' arguments and support your analysis with examples, quotations, and details from the texts
- a **conclusion** in which you sum up your main points and perhaps present a closing insight or reflection

What Do You Think Now?

In what way might Millan's or Derr's ideas about dogs help people change their behavior toward each other?

CHOICES

As you respond to the Choices, use these **Academic Vocabulary** words as appropriate: challenge, debate, demonstrate, and evident.

REVIEW

Create a Video

TechFocus Plan to videotape an imagined conversation between Cesar Millan and Mark Derr. Write your script based on details in the selections, but also improvise some dialogue based on what you have learned about the writers. Ask your classmates to help you with acting and filming.

CONNECT

Write a Persuasive Essay

Timed Writing Write a brief essay in which you state your opinion about leadership. Consider these questions: Do you think leaders are "born," not "made"? What qualities or characteristics make someone a leader? Remember to use logical appeals to create a strong argument and to use emotional appeals to help win over your readers.

EXTEND

Debate Pro and Con Viewpoints

In groups of five, hold a debate with your classmates about the best way to train dogs. One student will serve as the moderator, and two students each will present Cesar Millan's and Mark Derr's positions. In preparing to defend your positions in the debate, remember to anticipate your opponents' arguments.

Analyzing an Argument

CONTENTS

What Do **You** Think

Do you believe that violent video games lead to destructive behavior? Explain.

 QuickTalk

With a small group of your classmates, discuss your opinions about video games. How can video games be beneficial? How can they be harmful? What effects do they have on teenagers?

Preparing to Read

Target Real Violence, Not Video Games / Harmless Fun?

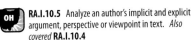 **RA.I.10.5** Analyze an author's implicit and explicit argument, perspective or viewpoint in text. *Also covered* **RA.I.10.4**

Reader/Writer Notebook

Use your **RWN** to complete the activities for these selections.

Informational Text Focus

Analyzing Arguments: Generalizations and Faulty Reasoning Persuasive writers try to convince you to think or act in a certain way. Sometimes a writer's argument contains **fallacies,** or mistakes in logical thinking. Here are some types of **faulty reasoning:**

- A **hasty generalization** is a broad, general statement or conclusion that is made on the basis of only one or two observations. Some **generalizations** (such as "All adult human beings walk upright") are valid (true), but a hasty generalization is a **fallacy.**

- **False cause and effect** occurs when one event is said to cause another event because the two events happened in sequence. ("As soon as I started jogging, my grades improved.")

- **Name-calling** uses labels to attack a person who holds an opposing view, instead of giving reasons or evidence to attack the view itself. ("Computer geeks are out of touch with the real world.")

- **Either-or fallacy** assumes that there are only two possible choices or solutions (usually extremes), even though there may be many. ("I have to get a driver's license, or I'll lose all my friends.")

- **Stereotyping** gives all members of a group the same, usually undesirable, characteristics. A stereotype assumes that everyone in that group is alike. ("Teenagers are very self-centered.")

Into Action As you read, look for examples of faulty reasoning. Use a graphic organizer like this one to record the examples you find.

Example of Faulty Reasoning	Type of Faulty Reasoning
"contrived laboratory experiments that purport to . . ."	name-calling—makes fun of the social scientists

Vocabulary

Target Real Violence . . .

saturated (SACH uh rayt ihd) *adj.:* filled completely. *The public has been saturated with varying opinions about video games.*

contrived (kuhn TRYVD) *adj.:* planned; manipulated. *The conclusions of the experiments were contrived to have a specific outcome.*

Harmless Fun?

obliterate (uh BLIHT uh rayt) *v.:* destroy; wipe out. *Some characters use violence to obliterate their enemies.*

Language Coach

Derivations The word *obliterated* comes from the Latin prefix *ob–* and *littera,* meaning "letter." The prefix *ob–* means "against," "toward," "on," "out," or "before." Think of three words that use the prefix *ob–* and use a dictionary to find out their derivations.

Writing Focus Preparing for **Constructed Response**

As you read, keep track of the strengths and weaknesses of these two selections in your *Reader/Writer Notebook.*

 Learn It Online
For more articles like this, go to the interactive Reading Workshops on:

go.hrw.com | L10-609 | **Go**

Target Real Violence, Not Video Games

by **Robert D. Richards** and **Clay Calvert**

Read with a Purpose
Read this editorial to learn about some specific issues in the debate about whether violent video games can lead to violent behavior.

Build Background
The debate over the effects of video-game violence has been a hot-button issue since the early 1990s. Some people say that playing violent video games leads to an increase in violent behavior, while others say there is no connection between video games and real life. Several scientific studies support each side of the argument.

We live in a society saturated with real-life violence—violence that is difficult to legislate away. So it is sadly not surprising when legislators attack fictional and fantasy images of violence portrayed in media products instead of dealing with actual crime.

In 2005, Illinois Gov. Rod Blagojevich signed into law a bill that limits the sale of graphically violent video games to minors. Specifically, it is now illegal for anyone in the state to sell or rent a "violent" video game to anyone under the age of 18.

At first blush, measures such as the one signed by the governor appear to protect the state's children—admittedly a noble effort.

Games like "Grand Theft Auto: San Andreas" clearly are offensive and any reasonable parent would not let his or her child play the game.

But the new Illinois law and a similar federal measure proposed by Sen. Hillary Rodham Clinton of New York amount to little more than flawed attempts by lawmakers to create a false sense of protection and security at the expense of the constitutional rights of the creators, manufacturers, and users of video games for entertainment purposes—and ultimately at the expense of the state's taxpayers. **Ⓐ**

What is even more troubling is that legislators have enacted this measure despite clear precedent that such bills violate settled constitutional law.

Ⓐ **Informational Focus** Faulty Reasoning What kind of faulty reasoning do the authors use in this paragraph?

Vocabulary **saturated** (SACH uh rayt ihd) *adj.*: filled completely.

In fact, every law restricting violent video games has met with the same fate: a federal court striking it down as unconstitutional.

As Judge Richard Posner of the Seventh Circuit United States Court of Appeals in Chicago—the federal appellate court covering Illinois—made clear in a case striking down an Indianapolis ordinance restricting minors' access to video games, the interactive nature of games does not make them any less deserving of First Amendment protection than other forms of media such as books and movies.

Writing in American Amusement Machine Association v. Kendrick, Judge Posner observed that "[a]ll literature (here broadly defined to include movies, television and other photo-graphic media and popular as well as highbrow[1] literature) is interactive; the better it is, the more interactive."

Legislators fully recognize they would face certain peril if they tried to ban books, movies, or TV programs, so instead they take on a new technology and try to convince their constituents that graphic depictions of violence in an interactive format somehow make it more harmful to minors.

The flaw in that reasoning is that no one has ever been able to prove through independent research that video games are harmful to children or to show that they cause violence. **B**

---

1. **highbrow:** intellectual.

B **Informational Focus** **Faulty Reasoning** What form of faulty reasoning are the authors critiquing in these two paragraphs?

Four gamers compete against one another.

There have been some contrived laboratory experiments that purport to show a correlation between viewing video games and increased aggression in some people, but aggression is not the same thing as violence, and correlation does not equal causation.[2]

In order for any law to restrict the First Amendment rights of citizens in this country, by barring certain content, the government must demonstrate a compelling interest. Provable harm to children would probably satisfy that burden, but no such evidence exists, and that's one reason measures like the one signed by Governor Blagojevich fail when challenged in court.

Gang members don't commit drive-by shootings simply because they played a video game, nor do school kids shoot others simply because they played a video game.

The factors influencing such violent acts are far more complex than that. Hundreds of thousands of kids who play video games, the vast majority of which do not portray violence, will never assault, attack, or otherwise harm anyone.

Federal courts in St. Louis and in the state of Washington have adopted Judge Posner's reasoning in striking down similar laws in those jurisdictions.

Blagojevich and the Illinois legislature share the responsibility for enacting measures that violate the Constitution, but the citizens of Illinois will share the expense of defending these invalid measures as inevitable court challenges move forward.

---

2. **correlation . . . causation:** Because two things are related to each other or occur simultaneously does not mean that one thing causes the other.

C **Informational Focus** Faulty Reasoning What is the false cause-and-effect relationship suggested in this paragraph?

Vocabulary **contrived** (kuhn TRYVD) *adj.*: planned; manipulated.

Harmless Fun?

from Weekly Reader

Read with a Purpose
Read this article to discover another writer's opinion of video games.

Build Background
Mortal Kombat was first released for arcades in 1992 and for home game consoles in 1993. The game's violence outraged both parents and politicians. As a result, the Entertainment Software Ratings Board (ESRB) was created in 1994. The ESRB rates interactive entertainment software (video games) by their age appropriateness. For example, almost all of Mortal Kombat's sequels are rated "Mature," which means that no one under seventeen can purchase them.

Say what you want, but in Mortal Kombat: Armageddon, the latest version of the wildly popular Mortal Kombat video game, the character Taven's signature move is known as the "Ring of Hatred." That's when he pounds the ground with his fist, creating a shockwave of fire. If he executes it just right, he will obliterate his opponent, leaving small bits of flesh, blood and internal organs splattered across the screen.

And Taven is one of the good guys.

You can see from this example that in the world of violent video games, players can channel their aggressions and take on virtual foes, with instant and typically graphic results. Die-hard video game addicts will tell you it is all harmless fun—at worst, a way to let off steam. But don't be so sure. **A**

In 1996, M. E. Ballard and J. R. Weist reported in the *Journal of Applied Social Psychology* that playing these kinds of games actually increased blood pressure in some players. Studies by P. J. Lynch in 1994 found that in aggressive children these games increased the flow of adrenaline.[1] These two studies prove that video games cause aggression. **B**

---

1. **adrenaline** (uh DREHN uh lihn): a hormone secreted by the brain and the adrenal glands that speeds up the heartbeat and increases energy.

A **Informational Focus** Generalizations The writer makes a generalization in this paragraph. Explain why this is a hasty generalization.

B **Informational Focus** Faulty Reasoning What do the studies by Ballard and Weist and Lynch prove?

Vocabulary **obliterate** (uh BLIHT uh rayt) *v.*: destroy; wipe out.

Can it be true, as profit-hungry game manufacturers claim, that virtual fights act as a substitute for actual fights? Are they a way to give a player his or her "adrenaline fix" harmlessly? Not necessarily. Researchers Craig A. Anderson, PhD, of Iowa State University, and Karen E. Dill, PhD, of Lenoir-Rhyne College, gathered 210 college students and had them play either a violent or a non-violent video game. Afterward, they had each student "punish" an opponent with a loud blast of noise. The students who played the violent game blasted the noise for a longer period of time than those who played the non-violent one. In addition, Anderson and Dill examined the video game habits of another 227 college students who had

exhibited actual aggressiveness. Anderson and Dill concluded, in the American Psychological Association's *Journal of Personality and Social Psychology,* that violent video games prime the brain for aggressive thoughts. In the longer term, they found, violent video games get players used to using violent means to solve their problems. **C**

"The player learns and practices new aggression-related scripts that can become more and more accessible for use when real-life conflict situations arise," said Anderson.

Who is most exposed to and damaged by these terrifying scripts? Children are. A study by the Kaiser Family Foundation found 83 percent of children between ages 8 and 18 have a video game console in their homes, and 40 percent had a console in their bedroom. And while the government began in 2000 to crack down on the marketing of violent video games to children, results are not so great. A 2007 investigation by the Federal Trade Commission found that out of 20 games with a rating of "M" (for Mature), 16 were advertised on Web sites popular among children. This must mean that young children are playing and learning from these hideous games without adult supervision.

Most grown-ups and young adults can distinguish between real violence and the virtual kind. They know where to draw the line. But what about those who don't? Children are still learning the boundaries of good behavior, and the do's and don'ts of problem solving. They are the real-life victims of video game manufacturers.

I'm not saying that violent video games are the root of all aggression in the world. But I don't see any evidence that the blood-soaked citizens of the screen world are doing anything to make the real world a better place.

C **Informational Focus** Generalizations How many students took part in these studies? Were there enough on which to base a generalization?

RA.I.10.5 Analyze an author's implicit and explicit argument, perspective or viewpoint in text. **RA. I.10.4** Assess the adequacy, accuracy and appropriateness of an author's details, identifying persuasive techniques and examples of propaganda, bias and stereotyping.

Target Real Violence, Not Video Games / Harmless Fun?

Practicing the Standards

Informational Text and Vocabulary

1. Which of the following is a **generalization**?

   A "Games like Grand Theft Auto: San Andreas are clearly offensive and any reasonable parent would not let his or her child play the game."

   B "And Taven is one of the good guys."

   C "Afterward, they had each student 'punish' an opponent with a loud blast of noise."

   D "That's when he pounds the ground with his fist, creating a shockwave of fire."

2. Which of the following *best* summarizes Richards and Calvert's main argument?

   A Video games teach important skills.

   B Legislators should stop trying to limit sales of video games and focus on real crime instead.

   C Video games do not cause people to act violently toward one another.

   D Studies showing video games cause violence are correct.

3. Which type of faulty reasoning is illustrated in the following: "I'm not saying that violent video games are the root of all aggression in the world. But I don't see any evidence that the blood-soaked citizens of the screen world are doing anything to make the real world a better place."

   A Name-calling

   B False cause and effect

   C Either-or fallacy

   D Stereotyping

4. A *contrived* outcome is —

   A focused

   B planned

   C simplistic

   D expensive

5. Something that is *saturated* is —

   A destroyed

   B empty

   C sweet

   D filled up

6. To *obliterate* means to—

   A forget

   B destroy

   C rebuild

   D cover up

Writing Focus — Constructed Response

Summarize the arguments in these articles in one or two sentences. Using the list you created while reading each selection, explain which editorial you found more persuasive, and why.

What Do You Think Now?

Do you believe that violent video games increase the level of violence in our society? Explain.

Literary Skills Review

Persuasion **Directions:** Read the following selection. Then, read and respond to the questions that follow.

Jackie Changed Face of Sports

by **Larry Schwartz**

It's not often that the essence of a man, especially a complicated man, can be summed up in one sentence. But then again, there haven't been many people like Jackie Robinson.

"A life is not important," he said, "except in the impact it has on other lives."

By that standard, few people—and no athlete—in the 20th century has impacted more lives. Robinson lit the torch and passed it on to several generations of African American athletes. While the Brooklyn Dodgers infielder didn't make a nation color blind, he at least made it more color friendly.

And he accomplished this feat by going against his natural instincts. He was an aggressive man, outraged at injustice, and quick to stand up for his rights. He had the guts to say no when ordered to the back of the bus in the army, and was court-martialed for his courage. His instinct wasn't to turn the other cheek, but to face problems head on. He was more prone to fighting back than holding back.

That's what Robinson had to do when Dodgers president Branch Rickey selected him to become the first African American to play in the majors in the 20th century. Rickey wanted a man who could restrain himself from responding to the ugliness of the racial hatred that was certain to come.

A shorthand version of their fateful conversation in August 1945:

Rickey: "I know you're a good ball player. What I don't know is whether you have the guts."

Robinson: "Mr. Rickey, are you looking for a Negro who is afraid to fight back?"

Rickey, exploding: "Robinson, I'm looking for a ballplayer with guts enough not to fight back."

This unwritten pact between two men would change the course of a country. Baseball might only be a game, but in the area of black and white, it often is a leader. Robinson's debut for the Dodgers in 1947 came a year before President Harry Truman desegregated the military and seven years before the Supreme Court ruled segregation in public schools was unconstitutional.

Rickey was dead-on about racism. As *Sports Illustrated*'s Bill Nack wrote: "Robinson was the target of racial epithets and flying cleats, of hate letters and death threats, of pitchers throwing at his head and legs, and catchers spitting on his shoes."

Robinson learned how to exercise self-control—to answer insults, violence and injustice with silence. A model of unselfish team play, he earned the respect of his teammates and, eventually, the opposition.

The six-foot, 195-pound Robinson was the Rookie of the Year and two years later he was MVP (Most Valuable Player). His lifetime average was .311[1] and he was voted into the Baseball Hall of Fame in his first year of eligibility.

Pigeon-toed and muscular, it was No. 42's aggressiveness on the basepaths that thrilled fans. It wasn't so much his two stolen-base titles or his 197 thefts. It was the way he was a disruptive force, dancing off the base, drawing every eye in the stadium, making the pitcher crazy, instilling the Dodgers with the spirit that would help them win six pennants in his ten seasons.

"Robinson could hit and bunt and steal and run," Roger Kahn wrote in *The Boys of Summer*. "He had intimidation skills, and he burned with a dark fire. He wanted passionately to win. He bore the burden of a pioneer and the weight made him stronger. If one can be certain of anything in baseball, it is that we shall not look upon his like again."

***

After a decade with Brooklyn, he was traded to the New York Giants in December 1956. A month later, the 37-year-old Robinson announced his retirement in   magazine.

_____

1. **lifetime average was .311:** ratio of base hits to number of times at bat. Robinson made a base hit a little more than three out of ten times he went to bat.

He became a vice president for Chock Full o' Nuts[2] before going into other businesses and politics. But his body, which had served him so well as an athlete, gave out early. Diabetes and heart disease weakened him and he was almost blind in middle age. On October 24, 1972, he died of a heart attack at 53.

In 1997, baseball dedicated the season to Robinson on the fiftieth anniversary of his debut.

How should we remember this grandson of a slave and son of a sharecropper? Maybe by what he told a white New Orleans sportswriter: "We ask for nothing special. We ask only to be permitted to live as you live, and as our nation's Constitution provides."

With such simple and justifiable demands, it's no wonder the man had such an impact on so many lives.

_____

2. **Chock Full o' Nuts:** company specializing in coffee.

Literary Skills Review CONTINUED

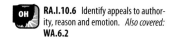

RA.I.10.6 Identify appeals to authority, reason and emotion. *Also covered:*
WA.6.2

1. Larry Schwartz wants to convince readers that Jackie Robinson did which of the following items?

   A. He changed America.

   B. He changed sports.

   C. He changed baseball.

   D. All of the above are correct.

2. Which of the following best describes Schwartz's portrayal of Robinson?

   A. fast and agressive, but weak and unhealthy

   B. competitive and self-unassuming, but poor and bankrupt

   C. proud and fiery, but disciplined and fair

   D. smart and confident, but self-indulgent and arrogant

3. Which statement about Robinson appeals to the emotions of readers?

   A. ". . . Dodgers president Branch Rickey selected him to become the first African American to play in the majors. . . ."

   B. "He had the guts to say no when ordered to the back of the bus in the army, and was court-martialed for his courage."

   C. "Robinson's debut for the Dodgers came a year before President Harry Truman desegregated the military and seven years before the Supreme Court ruled segregation in public schools was unconstitutional."

   D. "He became a vice president for Chock Full o' Nuts before going into other businesses and politics."

4. Which of the following statements about Robinson appeals to logic?

   A. "He was an aggressive man, outraged at injustice, and quick to stand up for his rights."

   B. "'Robinson was the target of racial epithets and flying cleats, of hate letters and death threats, of pitchers throwing at his head and legs, and catchers spitting on his shoes.'"

   C. "'He had intimidation skills, and he burned with a dark fire. He wanted passionately to win.'"

   D. "It was the way he was a disruptive force, dancing off the base, drawing every eye in the stadium, making the pitcher crazy, instilling the Dodgers with the spirit that would help them win six pennants in his ten seasons."

Short Answer

5. What evidence shows that Robinson was able to overcome opposition to his being a ballplayer? Cite three examples form the passage to support your answer.

Extended Response

6. Robinson said, "A life is not important except in the impact it has on other lives." Write a paragraph showing how Robinson demonstrated this, using three examples from the article "Jackie Changed Face of Sports."

Informational Skills Review

RA.I.10.5 Analyze an author's implicit and explicit argument, perspective or viewpoint in text.

Analyzing an Argument

Directions: Read the following two responses from an online forum. Then, respond to the questions that follow.

Online Opinions *from* The Life Press

Curfews

Let us hear from you in our online forum. Submission maximum is 500 words. Include name, address, and daytime phone number for verification.

Too Late

Many U.S. locales already require that teens be off the streets by 10 P.M. or 11 P.M. on weekdays. The hours vary by location, as does the level of law enforcement behind them, but the idea is the same: To maximize safety and minimize problems, it makes sense to limit the hours in which young people are allowed to roam. The public safety issues we have seen in major cities have led to the need for similar measures here as well.

While some may view these restrictions as negative, they are, in fact, benevolent. The fact is, there are hot spots where young people gather—and court trouble. There are parents who do not function as strong guides for their children. It takes just one night for the situation to ignite into something awful.

Curfews are a means of intervention, preventing teens from acting in criminal ways or from falling victim to criminals. They cut down on opportunities for young gang member wannabees to get in over their heads. The number of curfews has been rising steadily, according to the U.S. Council of Mayors, because a good idea catches on.

Those who oppose curfews tout an individual's rights to public freedoms. But that argument is naive. No freedom granted by the U.S. Constitution is entirely free of limits.

Recent research shows the brain does not fully mature until a person reaches his or her mid-twenties. And we don't need statistics to know that kids get in trouble. Adults do, too! The saving grace is that kids, until they reach the age of adulthood, can be saved from themselves.

Michael Mott
Ratchet, California

The Right to Be Out at Night

The basic concept of a curfew is that young people cannot be trusted to conduct themselves correctly after a certain time of night. But like the magic pumpkin in "Cinderella," this is a fairy tale.

People say that curfews protect teens from crime. But the issues involved are larger than that. In U.S. courts, many curfews have been challenged successfully because everyone has First Amendment rights, which allow for freedom of speech and public gatherings.

With a curfew in effect, teens are put under house arrest. There might be exceptions made if you are going to and from work or church or something else on a short list of sanctioned activities. But what if you just want to walk the dog at 11:30 P.M.—because you were studying and couldn't get it done earlier? Most kids who are out late are just getting from one place to another.

If we adopt a curfew, we are allowing the 5 percent who act up to control the lives of the other 95 percent. How are teens supposed to learn responsibility if they are not given it? Why must we live under restrictions when what is really needed is better crime prevention, education, and law enforcement?

Police officials will tell you that curfews reduce trouble on the streets. But studies have failed to prove that curfews are effective against crime. Crime may go down in some places; but it goes up in others.

The real reason for teen curfews is money. It's the same old story. After a new county curfew went into effect in the Detroit area, sales at a large mall there went up. Why? The older people were uncomfortable shopping around so many teens, and when the teens disappeared, the older people came back. But is money any reason to usurp rights? Whose rights will vanish next?

George Oh
Ratchet, California

1. Which of the following sentences is the first writer's opinion statement, or claim?
   A. "Many U.S. locales already require that teens be off the streets by 10 P.M. or 11 P.M. on weekdays."
   B. "To maximize safety and minimize problems, it makes sense to limit the hours in which young people are allowed to roam."
   C. "The fact is, there are hot spots where young people gather—and court trouble."
   D. "There are parents who do not function as strong guides for their children."

2. What is the first writer's intent?
   A. to persuade you that curfews can help parents be better guides for their sons and daughters
   B. to argue that an individual's rights to public freedoms are not important
   C. to evaluate the reasons why curfews don't work
   D. to persuade us that curfews help young people stay out of trouble

RA.I.10.5 Analyze an author's implicit and explicit argument, perspective or viewpoint in text. *Also covered:* RA.I.10.4

3. What does the writer of the second online response claim?

  A. concepts of trust and responsibility are learned best from one's parents

  B. teenagers cannot be trusted to behave correctly at night

  C. the idea that "young people cannot be trusted" is a false notion

  D. teenagers learn about trust when given fewer restrictions

4. What generalization does the second writer make about most teenagers who are out late?

  A. They are causing trouble with other kids.

  B. They are working evening jobs.

  C. They belong to gangs.

  D. They are just getting from one place to another.

5. What evidence does the second writer use to support the idea that curfews are ineffective?

  A. "Studies have failed to prove that curfews are effective against crime."

  B. "Most kids who are out late are just getting from one place to another."

  C. "Curfews have been challenged successfully because everyone has First Amendment rights."

  D. "The real reason for teen curfews is money."

6. Which of the following ideas from the second writer presents faulty reasoning?

  A. Curfews are established so money can be made by businesses, such as shopping malls.

  B. Curfews take away people's individual rights.

  C. Curfews, education, and the enforcement of laws are good ways to prevent crime.

  D. Curfews teach teenagers irresponsibility.

7. Which of the following statements is supported by evidence?

  A. "The number of curfews has been rising steadily, according to the U.S. Council of Mayors."

  B. "And we don't need statistics to know that kids get in trouble."

  C. "But studies have failed to prove that curfews are effective against crime."

  D. "The real reason for teen curfews is money."

Short Answer

8. What evidence does the first writer use to support his opinion? Cite two examples from his response to support your answer, and give the paragraph number in which the example appears.

Extended Response

9. Write a statement summarizing the main points of each argument. Explain which argument is more convincing, and why.

Vocabulary Skills Review

Multiple-Meaning Words   **Directions:** Read each quotation. Then, choose the sentence in which the underlined word has the same meaning as in the quotation.

1. "Can it be true, as profit-hungry game manufacturers claim, that virtual fights <u>act</u> as a substitute for actual fights?"

    A. The performer could dance and sing, but could not act very well.

    B. When interviewing for a job, remember to act in a professional manner.

    C. The heroic act of the firefighter earned him a commendation.

    D. Thalia will perform her juggling *act* next.

2. "It's easy to ignore or hate an abstraction, not so easy when a person or a <u>place</u> is specific and real to you."

    A. The place where the wedding was held was beautifully decorated.

    B. Laura, please place the bag of fruit on the table.

    C. As boss, it was her place to speak to the employee about lateness.

    D. After coming in third place, Alan accepted the medal.

3. "Children are <u>still</u> learning the boundaries of good behavior, and the do's and don'ts of problem solving."

    A. The day had been hectic, but the still air and quiet night made Chris feel calmer.

    B. You should take a still photo instead of filming the entire event.

    C. I am still finishing the science project and don't think it will be done in time.

    D. She tried to still the child by whispering softly into his ear.

4. "A six-hundred-<u>pound</u> tortoise, who may well have lived a century and a half, regally extended his leathery neck for me to stroke."

    A. Carefully pound the nail in with the hammer.

    B. Knock, don't pound, on the door!

    C. He can pound out a nice tune on the piano.

    D. Carmen purchased one pound of chicken for the stew she was planning to make for dinner.

5. "Though hormones are <u>part</u> of what makes a pack leader, energy plays an even greater role."

    A. You will have to part with some of your belongings to make room for mine.

    B. Every part of this essay needs more work before I hand it in.

    C. I asked the stylist to part my hair down the middle instead of on the side.

    D. Which part will you perform in the school play?

6. "Only after wolves and wild dogs have finished their daily work do they <u>play</u>."

    A. Francis will play the piano in the school band.

    B. The baby loves to play with his favorite rattle.

    C. She was the lead actress in a play based on the life of a famous artist.

    D. He is practicing his pitch and hopes to play for the school baseball team next year.

7. "Forcefully rolling a big dog on its <u>back</u> was once recommended as a way to establish dominance, but is now recognized as a good way to get bitten."

   A. The puppy came back when I called its name.

   B. Please take a seat near the back of the room.

   C. Keisha will testify and back up Gloria's story.

   D. Mom hurt her back while lifting the couch.

8. "Leaders develop early and they <u>show</u> their dominant qualities quite young."

   A. Ajay hoped his nervousness didn't show when he made his presentation.

   B. I'll need to leave by noon in order to watch my favorite television show.

   C. The usher will show you to your assigned seats when you hand him your tickets.

   D. She made a show of herself by yelling across the room.

9. "Everyone's a player, no one is paid, and all the entry fees go directly into the prize <u>pool</u>."

   A. The town will establish a supply pool to aid the victims of the flood.

   B. The water in the pool was too cold, so Julie didn't swim.

   C. Rain ran down the gutters and formed a pool near the foundation of the house.

   D. She explained the rules of pool to him while he set the balls on the table.

10. "That's when he pounds the <u>ground</u> with his fist, creating a shockwave of fire."

    A. She ground the spices into a fine powder before adding them to the soup.

    B. Roberto was unsure of his facts, so his argument was on shaky ground.

    C. Ants travel along the ground, unaware of the larger world around them.

    D. Louis ground out the work quickly yet accurately.

Academic Vocabulary

Directions: Choose the best synonym for each Academic Vocabulary word below.

11. <u>evident</u>
    A. hidden
    B. apparent
    C. hopeful
    D. proof

12. <u>demonstrate</u>
    A. explain
    B. prepare
    C. refuse
    D. direct

Read On

FICTION

The House on Mango Street

Sandra Cisneros captures the essence of childhood memories one vivid image at a time. Told through the point of view of Esperanza, a child growing up in poverty in Chicago, *The House on Mango Street* reveals the beauties and <u>challenges</u> of coming of age. Each of the book's vignettes, or literary sketches, brings to life a detail—a cloud, a car thief, or a cold rice sandwich—that shapes the life of a young girl dreaming of a better future.

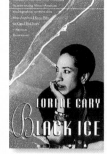

NONFICTION

Black Ice

How does it feel to be suddenly thrust into an unfamiliar setting? What is the price of success? In her autobiography, *Black Ice,* Lorene Cary recounts her experiences of being moved from an African American neighborhood in Philadelphia to an elite, formerly all-white prep school in New Hampshire. With gutsy honesty, Cary questions how to become a part of school life without sacrificing her identity, heritage, and values.

FICTION

Persuasion

More than seven years ago, Anne Elliot, the heroine of Jane Austen's novel, was in love with naval officer Frederick Wentworth. However, her godmother persuaded her not to marry him because he had no fortune. No other prospects have appeared, and Anne seems destined to remain unmarried. When Wentworth returns to the area, Anne's hopes rise, only to be thwarted when it appears that Wentworth is seeing another young woman. In *Persuasion,* appearance is one thing and reality another, so we are kept guessing about Anne's fate until the very end.

NONFICTION

Never Cry Wolf

For most people, living near a den of wolves is not an appealing prospect. Scientist Farley Mowat had no choice. The government's Wildlife Service sent him to northern Canada to investigate the wolves' killing of the endangered arctic caribou. Mowat found something he had never expected—sympathy for the noble wolf families—and a companionship with the local Inuit people. *Never Cry Wolf* is the true story of a life-changing experience.

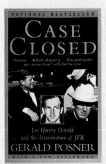

NONFICTION
Case Closed

Case Closed is Gerald Posner's step-by-step analysis of the assassination of President John F. Kennedy in 1963. Conspiracy buffs have always believed that there was more than one assassin and that there has been a government cover-up. Posner methodically strips away all the rumors, half-baked theories, and wild assertions. He provides new details about Oswald's life, new ballistic evidence, and computer enhancement of the film showing Kennedy being shot. This book is just as suspenseful as a good detective novel.

NONFICTION
An Ocean of Air

We spend our lives surrounded by air, hardly even noticing it. Air is the most miraculous substance on earth, responsible for our food, our weather, our water, and our ability to hear. In fact, we live at the bottom of an ocean of air. In her exuberant book, *An Ocean of Air*, gifted science writer Gabrielle Walker peels back the layers of our atmosphere with the stories of the people who uncovered its secrets.

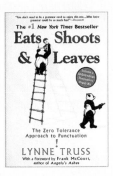

NONFICTION
Eats, Shoots & Leaves

Lynne Truss has done the impossible. She has written a bestseller about punctuation. Her book is a funny and persuasive pitch on the vital need to use correct punctuation in our daily communications. The title comes from a joke about a panda who walks into a cafe, orders a sandwich, eats it, and then draws a gun and fires a shot. As he exits the cafe, the panda is asked, "Why did you do that?" He replies, "I'm a panda; look it up!" and produces a wildlife book with a badly punctuated entry: "Panda—mammal; eats, shoots and leaves."

NONFICTION
The Writing Life: Writers on How They Think and Work

How do writers do it? Is writing in the morning better than writing at night? Where do writers get their inspiration? How do they cope with critics? Why should writers read? More than fifty writers in this collection of brief essays ponder and discuss these questions. The writers include Ray Bradbury, Ntozake Shange, Anita Desai, Julia Alvarez, Carl Sagan, Tracy Kidder, and Michael Chabon.

Writing Workshop

Persuasive Essay

Write with a Purpose

Write a persuasive essay on an issue about which you have a strong opinion. Your **purpose** for writing is to persuade others to agree with your position and action. Your **audience** will be individuals interested in this topic.

A Good Persuasive Essay

- presents your position on an important issue
- provides reasons and evidence to support the position
- uses emotional, logical, and ethical appeals
- addresses counterarguments, or "the other side" of the issue
- convinces readers to agree, take a stand, or take an action on the issue or topic

See page 634 for complete rubric.

Think as a Reader/Writer
In this collection, you've read persuasive texts on a variety of topics. Now, it's time to write your own **persuasive essay.** Before you begin, read this excerpt from a "Pack of Lies" by Mark Derr (page 603).

Essentially, National Geographic and Cesar Millan have cleverly repackaged and promoted a simplistic view of the dog's social structure and constructed around it a one-size-fits-all, cookie-cutter approach to dog training. In Mr. Millan's world, dog behavioral problems result from a failure of the human to be the "pack leader," to dominate the dog (a wolf by any other name) completely.

← Derr begins with his **opinion statement** and uses **emotional language** to show his attitude toward the subject.

While Mr. Millan rejects hitting and yelling at dogs during training, his confrontational methods include physical and psychological intimidation, like finger jabs, choke collars, extended sessions on the treadmill and what is called flooding, or overwhelming the animal with the thing it fears. . . .

← Derr **considers the opposing viewpoint,** making his own argument more balanced.

Rewards are absent and praise scarce, presumably because they will upset the state of calm submission Mr. Millan wants in his dogs. Corrections abound as animals are forced to submit or face their fear, even if doing so panics them.

← These descriptions **appeal to the reader's emotions.**

Mr. Millan builds his philosophy from a simplistic conception of the dog's "natural" pack, controlled by a dominant alpha animal (usually male). In his scheme, that leader is the human, which leads to the conclusion that all behavior problems in dogs derive from the failure of the owner or owners to dominate.

← Derr **appeals to logic** by examining Millan's philosophy.

Reader/Writer Notebook

Use your **RWN** to complete the activities for this workshop.

Think About the Professional Model

With a partner, discuss the following questions about the model:

1. What argument does Derr make about Millan's method? What emotional language reveals his attitude toward Millan's method?

2. Why do you think Derr uses description to appeal to emotion?

WA.10.5.a Write persuasive compositions that: support arguments with detailed evidence; WC.10.2 Use correct capitalization and punctuation.

Prewriting

Choose an Issue

An **issue** is a topic about which people have opposing opinions. For example, there are many different ways to train a dog. In the model, Derr offers his opinion about one training method. You will likely be a more successful persuasive writer if you choose an issue that matters to you.

Ask yourself the following questions to choose an issue:

- Will others have opposing opinions about this issue?
- Does this topic go beyond matters of personal taste or preference? (Why red is the best color, for example, is not a suitable issue. Color preferences cannot be argued.)

Write an Opinion, or Thesis, Statement

Once you've chosen an issue, make your position, or opinion, on the issue clear. Write an **opinion statement** that names the issue and states your position on it. Here is one student's opinion statement:

> position   issue
> Schools should allow fast food restaurants to offer menu items in the school cafeteria.

Gather Reasons and Evidence

The **reasons** you use to back up your opinion statement will communicate your perspective and show why you think your opinion is correct. **Evidence** will support these reasons. Evidence may be **facts** (information that can be proven true, such as statistics or the results of scientific studies); **examples** of specific ideas or situations; **expert opinions** (statements made by people who are experts on your issue), or **anecdotes** (brief, personal stories that support a point).

> **Opinion statement:** Schools should allow fast food restaurants to offer menu items in the school cafeteria.

Reasons	Evidence
Kids would have more choices about what to eat.	1) Now, kids can choose only bland cafeteria dishes or salad. 2) Students eat better when they have more choices.

Idea Starters

- issues that concern your friends or family
- current events discussed in newspapers or on online news sites or television
- items discussed by the student council or the board of education or at your local city council meetings

Your Turn _____

Get Started Making notes in your **RWN,** choose an issue, and write an opinion statement. Considering your purpose and audience, note the reasons for your opinion, and gather supporting evidence. Use a chart like the one on this page to organize your evidence.

Learn It Online
See how one writer met all the assignment criteria at:

go.hrw.com | L10-627 | Go

Think About Audience and Purpose

As you plan your essay, keep in mind that your **purpose** for writing is to convince others to share your opinion or to take a recommended course of action. Your **audience** is people who either disagree with you or have not yet formed an opinion. Be prepared to address any objections or **counterarguments** that readers may propose.

Persuasive Essay Action Plan

Here's one writer's persuasive essay action plan. Use this model to help you create your own plan.

Paragraph 1: Introduction

A. **Background Information:** *Fast food gives students more choices and a healthy and appealing menu and makes extra money for the school.*

B. **Opinion Statement:** *Schools should allow fast food restaurants to offer menu items in the school cafeteria.*

Paragraphs 2–4: Body

A. **Reason:** *Fast food will give students more choices and boost morale.*
   1. *Evidence: The current food is bland.*
   2. *Evidence: Students surveyed say they will eat better if they have better choices.*

B. **Reason:** *Fast food is no less healthful than cafeteria food.*
   1. *Evidence: Cafeteria food is not healthful and includes salt and fat.*
   2. *Evidence: Fast food is now prepared without trans fat.*

C. **Reason:** *Schools will profit.*
   1. *Evidence: Students pay a lot of money each year for food.*
   2. *Evidence: Restaurants will pay the school to serve their food.*

Paragraph 5: Conclusion

A. **Summary:** *Fast food restaurants give students many choices without negatively affecting students' health.*

B. **Call to Action:** *Allow fast food restaurants to serve food at our school cafeteria.*

Your Turn _____

Organize Your Ideas Now that you've gathered your evidence, write a **persuasive essay action plan.** Share your plan with a partner, and ask for feedback about your reasons and evidence.

Drafting

Organize and Draft Your Essay

Use the Persuasive Essay Action Plan on page 628 to organize your essay. Consider arranging your reasons in order of importance. Then, elaborate on each reason by including evidence.

Appeal to Your Audience

The **rhetorical devices** of logical appeals, emotional appeals, and ethical appeals are effective persuasive techniques. Try to include all three as you draft your essay.

- **Logical appeals** speak to your readers' minds. These appeals rely on your audience's ability to be reasonable and to use common sense. They include facts, logical arguments, and expert opinions.

- **Emotional appeals,** such as loaded language and appropriate anecdotes, speak to your readers' emotions, such as empathy, fear, and hope, to name a few.

- **Ethical appeals** speak to your readers' ethics, or moral values. These appeals rely on commonly accepted beliefs or values. For example, most people accept honesty and fairness as worthy values. A writer may use an ethical appeal to establish his or her credibility, or trustworthiness.

Writers often use several examples in a series to make their appeals more convincing. Note how to punctuate words, phrases, and clauses in a series.

Framework for a Persuasive Essay

Introduction
- Grab your readers' attention by asking a question, relating an anecdote, or presenting a startling statistic.
- Give background information to help readers understand the issue.
- Give an opinion statement that clearly states your position on the issue.

Body
- Give reasons that support your opinion statement.
- Provide evidence for each reason.
- Address possible counterarguments.

Conclusion
- Restate, but do not repeat, your opinion.
- Summarize the reasons for your opinion.
- If appropriate, include a call to action that tells readers what they can do to help change a situation.

● Writing Tip

Depending on your topic, you may want to include more than one type of **appeal.** For example, in the model essay, Derr appeals to both his readers' emotions and logic. Look for ways to include logical and emotional appeals so that you speak to your readers' minds as well as their hearts.

Grammar Link **Punctuating Words, Phrases, and Clauses in a Series**

Writers often list three or more items to support their position more convincingly. Use commas to separate items in a series, including single words, phrases, and clauses. When the last two items in a series are joined by *and, or,* or *nor,* the comma before the conjunction is sometimes omitted when the comma is not needed to make the meaning of the sentence clear. Notice how Mark Derr uses commas to punctuate the series in this sentence from "Pack of Lies."

"... his confrontational methods include physical and psychological intimidation, like finger jabs, choke collars, extended sessions on the treadmill and what is called flooding, or overwhelming the animal with the thing it fears."

Your Turn _____

Write Your Draft Following your Persuasive Essay Action Plan and the Writer's Framework, write a draft of your essay. Use emotional, logical, and ethical appeals. Use appropriate punctuation for items in a series.

Peer Review

Exchange essays with a classmate. Use the chart to the right, and remember to offer suggestions politely and constructively.

- Point out arguments that are clear and well supported as well as ideas that need clarifying.
- Look for reasons that need to be supported.
- Ask questions to help your peer think of additional counterarguments that may need to be addressed.

Evaluating and Revising

Read the questions in the left-hand column of the chart. Use the tips in the middle column to help you revise your essay. The right-hand column suggests techniques you can use to revise your draft.

Persuasive Essay: Guidelines for Content and Organization

Evaluation Questions	Tips	Revision Techniques
1. **Does the introduction grab the reader's attention and present a clear opinion statement?**	**Put a check mark** by sentences that get the reader interested. **Underline** the opinion statement.	**Add** an interesting opening statement. **Add** an opinion statement that clearly states your position on the issue.
2. **Does your introduction include background information on the issue?**	**Put a star** by sentences that give background information on the issue.	**Add** background information.
3. **Does the body include at least three reasons to support your position? Do the reasons contain logical, emotional, and ethical appeals?**	**Highlight** each reason. **Draw a box** around the part that indicates a logical, emotional, or ethical appeal.	**Add** reasons that appeal to readers' logic, emotions, or ethics. **Elaborate** to include missing types of appeals.
4. **Are the reasons organized effectively?**	**Number** reasons in the order of their importance. If the order seems illogical or ineffective, revise.	**Rearrange** the reasons by putting the most important reason first or last.
5. **Is each reason supported by at least two pieces of relevant evidence?**	**Circle** each piece of evidence (facts, examples, and so on). **Draw an arrow** from each item to the reason it supports.	**Add** evidence to support your reasons. **Rearrange** evidence so that each piece is in the paragraph containing the reason it supports.
6. **Does the conclusion restate your opinion on the issue? Does it include a call to action?**	**Underline** the restatement of the writer's opinion. **Put a check mark** next to the call to action.	**Add** a restatement of your opinion on the issue. **Add** a call to action.

Read this student's draft; note the comments on its strengths and suggestions for how it could be improved.

Expand Our Food Choices

by Elizabeth Naglak, Searcy High School

How does the idea of eating real fast food at school sound? This is a brilliant idea because it gives students a variety of choices, a healthy and appealing menu, and an experience to enjoy. The school also acquires another way to earn money. Schools should allow fast food restaurants to serve lunch in their cafeterias.

Ordinarily, students have the regular plate lunch or a salad every day. After a couple of months, these choices get old and unappetizing. "Kids get bored easily with the options we provide," noted cafeteria manager Ingrid Stone. If fast food restaurants appear in cafeterias, student will be eager for lunch. They will no longer have to eat the same foods on a daily basis. If students are offered a variety of choices, their morale is bound to increase. No students will skip lunch because they don't like the cafeteria food. Better-fed students are more productive and positive.

← Elizabeth introduces the **issue** and draws in the reader by asking a question and then gives her **opinion about the issue.**

← Elizabeth develops the first **reason** and provides **evidence** to support it.

← Elizabeth uses cause-effect reasoning.

MINI-LESSON **How to Use Emotional Language**

You can make your persuasive argument more powerful by including emotionally charged language. Note how Elizabeth's revision appeals to her readers through words and phrases such as "line up like sheep," "cold metal rails," and "bland, tasteless food" that appeal to the emotions. By adding emotional language, Elizabeth created a more vivid picture of the bland food available in the cafeteria.

Elizabeth's Revision of Paragraph Two

~~Ordinarily, students have the regular plate lunch or a salad every day.~~
~~After a couple of months, these choices get old and unappetizing.~~
Every day—day in, day out—students line up like sheep, pushing trays along the cold metal rails, facing an assembly line of bland, tasteless food as beige in color as their attitude about eating in the school cafeteria.

Your Turn _____

Add Details Read your draft, and then ask yourself:

- Does each sentence support my opinion statement?
- Do I use descriptive language to appeal to my readers' emotions?

Student Draft *continues*

This paragraph addresses the **counterargument** and proves it wrong with **facts** and **opinion**.

→   On the other hand, many critics of fast food chains say that the food they serve is bad for students' health. The real truth is that cafeteria food is not the most healthful food. Now students have choices of cookies, cake, brownies, various kinds of ice cream, fat-soaked meat, and side orders lacking vitamins and soaked in grease. It's not healthful for students to go hungry because they hate cafeteria food either. Many fast food companies are now preparing their food with zero trans fat. Although some critics believe that fast food is very unwholesome, it is obvious that it is no worse for teens than any other type of school-served food.

Elizabeth introduces her **strongest reason** in the final paragraph before the conclusion.

→   Finally, lunch is an important source of revenue for a school. Students who buy their lunch from the cafeteria bring hundreds of dollars into the school each year. On average, a student spends approximately $2.00 a day in the cafeteria. When this is multiplied by one thousand students, the profit is astronomical.

The **conclusion** summarizes the writer's reasons and includes a **call to action.**

→   Fast food restaurants in schools give students a plethora of choices without negatively affecting their health. School funds will grow. Everyone will benefit. Our school board should contact local fast food restaurants and ask them to provide school lunch options for our high school.

MINI-LESSON ▸ Adding Evidence to Support an Argument

When you present an argument, you should include enough evidence to support effectively all your reasons. In her fourth paragraph, Elizabeth needed to add information about how fast food restaurants would add revenue to the school.

Elizabeth's Revision of Paragraph Four

When this is multiplied by one thousand students, the profit is astronomical. ∧*Schools will earn more than twice as much money if they install fast food restaurants. Hungry students will buy more food, and the restaurants will pay a fee to operate in the school. School revenue will soar by adding simple alternatives to the cafeteria.*

Your Turn _____

Create Coherence Read your draft, and then ask yourself:

- Do I provide sufficient evidence to support my reasons?
- What additional evidence might help convince my readers to support my point of view?

Proofreading and Publishing

Proofreading

Don't ruin the impact of your well-crafted words by letting little mistakes show up in your final draft. If you find it hard to inspect your own paper for these mistakes, trade papers with a partner, and examine each other's work closely. Read your partner's essay at least twice. The first time you read it, focus on content and organization. Next, focus on style. Has your partner used the active voice? If your partner quoted any experts, are the quotations accurate and clear? Is the possessive formed correctly?

Grammar Link Show Possession Correctly

An apostrophe and the letter *s* are used to indicate ownership or close relationship, for example, *Terry's dog, parents' concerns,* or *children's games*. First determine if the word showing ownership is singular (one) or plural (more than one). Then, use the following simple rules to form the possessive correctly:

- A singular word forms the possessive by adding an apostrophe and an *s*. In the preceding example, the word *Terry* is singular—it refers to one person. The possessive form is **Terry's.**
- A plural word ending in *s* forms the possessive by adding only an apostrophe. In the preceding example, the word *parents* (more than one parent) ends in *s*. The possessive form is **parents'.**
- Some plural words do not end in *s,* such as the word *children*. In this case, the possessive is formed by adding an apostrophe and an *s*: **children's.**

Elizabeth uses many possessives in her draft and found the error below as she proofread.

Incorrect: On the other hand, critics of fast food chains say that the food they serve is bad for **students health.** (She refers to more than one student.)

Correct: students' health (added an apostrophe to indicate possession)

Publishing

Now it is time to share your experience. Here are a few suggestions for presenting your work to others:

- Take turns reading your narrative aloud in a group.
- Turn your narrative into a paper or digital scrapbook. Add special lettering, photographs, drawings, or mementos.

Reflect on the Process In your *Reader/Writer Notebook,* write a short response to these questions:

1. What techniques did you find most effective in presenting your opinion?
2. What have you learned from this workshop that might help you with other types of writing?

⬤ Proofreading Tip

Take a break before you proofread your essay. If you go right from revising to proofreading, you might be tired and overly familiar with your words. As a result, you could miss some obvious errors. After a short break, your brain will be clear and ready to catch mistakes.

Submission Ideas

- school newspaper
- online magazine related to your topic
- your personal Web page
- class or school Web page
- digital or paper scrapbook
- digital narrative

Your Turn _____

Proofread and Publish As you are proofreading, read carefully to make sure that each apostrophe you've included either shows possession or indicates a contraction. Add apostrophes when needed. If you are uncertain about the placement of an apostrophe, ask a peer or your teacher, or consult a reference book, such as the Language Handbook.

Scoring Rubric

Use one of the following rubrics to evaluate your persuasive essay from the Writing Workshop or from the activity on the next page. Your teacher will tell you which rubric to use.

6-Point Scale

Score 6 *Demonstrates advanced success*
- focuses consistently on a clear and reasonable position
- shows effective organization throughout, with smooth transitions
- offers thoughtful, creative ideas and reasons
- supports a position thoroughly, using convincing, fully elaborated reasons and evidence
- exhibits mature control of written language

Score 5 *Demonstrates proficient success*
- focuses on a clear and reasonable position
- shows effective organization, with transitions
- offers thoughtful ideas and reasons
- supports a position competently, using convincing reasons and evidence
- exhibits sufficient control of written language

Score 4 *Demonstrates competent success*
- focuses on a reasonable position, with minor distractions
- shows effective organization, with minor lapses
- offers mostly thoughtful ideas and reasons
- elaborates reasons and evidence with a mixture of the general and the specific
- exhibits general control of written language

Score 3 *Demonstrates limited success*
- includes some loosely related ideas that distract from the writer's position
- shows some organization, with noticeable gaps in the logical flow of ideas
- offers routine, predictable ideas and reasons
- supports ideas with uneven reasoning and elaboration
- exhibits limited control of written language

Score 2 *Demonstrates basic success*
- includes loosely related ideas that seriously distract from the writer's persuasive purpose
- shows minimal organization, with major gaps in the logical flow of ideas
- offers ideas and reasons that merely skim the surface
- supports ideas with inadequate reasoning and elaboration
- exhibits significant problems with control of written language

Score 1 *Demonstrates emerging effort*
- shows little awareness of the topic and purpose for writing
- lacks organization
- offers unclear and confusing ideas
- demonstrates minimal persuasive reasoning or elaboration
- exhibits major problems with control of written language

4-Point Scale

Score 4 *Demonstrates advanced success*
- focuses consistently on a clear and reasonable position
- shows effective organization throughout, with smooth transitions
- offers thoughtful, creative ideas and reasons
- supports a position thoroughly, using convincing, fully elaborated reasons and evidence
- exhibits mature control of written language

Score 3 *Demonstrates competent success*
- focuses on a reasonable position, with minor distractions
- shows effective organization, with minor lapses
- offers mostly thoughtful ideas and reasons
- elaborates reasons and evidence with a mixture of the general and the specific
- exhibits general control of written language

Score 2 *Demonstrates limited success*
- includes some loosely related ideas that distract from the writer's position
- shows some organization, with noticeable gaps in the logical flow of ideas
- offers routine, predictable ideas and reasons
- supports ideas with uneven reasoning and elaboration
- exhibits limited control of written language

Score 1 *Demonstrates emerging effort*
- shows little awareness of the topic and purpose for writing
- lacks organization
- offers unclear and confusing ideas
- demonstrates minimal persuasive reasoning or elaboration
- exhibits major problems with control of written language

Preparing for Timed ⏲ Writing

Persuasive Essay

When responding to a prompt asking you to write a persuasive essay, use what you have learned from your reading, from writing a persuasive essay on an issue of your choice, and from studying the rubric on the opposite page. Use the steps below to develop a response to the following prompt:

Writing Prompt

In response to unruly behavior by groups of teens, a local mall is considering instituting a policy requiring all persons under age sixteen to be accompanied by an adult when entering the mall. Write a persuasive essay stating your opinion about this proposal, and support it with reasons and evidence. Your audience is the mall owners.

Study the Prompt

Begin by reading the prompt carefully. Circle or underline key words: *policy, persons under age sixteen, accompanied by an adult, persuasive essay, audience, mall owners*. Reread the prompt to see if there is additional information that can help you.
Tip: Spend about five minutes studying the prompt.

Plan Your Response

The prompt asks you to write an essay convincing the mall owners to agree with your opinion about the policy. Decide how you feel about the policy. Do you believe it is fair? Will it prevent unruly behavior? Consider these questions, and then write your opinion statement.

Now, think of two to three reasons to support your opinion statement. Then, brainstorm evidence that will support your reasons. Answer these questions:

- What information do I have about this issue?
- What opinions can I include?
- How can I use appeals to emotion, reason, and ethics to convince my readers?

- How will I use emotional language to get my readers' attention?
- What reasons will most appeal to this audience? (For example, financial considerations will affect the mall owners' decision. How could you use this fact to appeal to the owners?)
Tip: Spend about ten minutes planning your response.

Respond to the Prompt

Use your answers to the questions and your outline to start writing your essay. Remember to include details that will appeal to your readers, the mall owners, and to conclude with a call to action.
Tip: Spend about twenty minutes writing your persuasive essay.

Improve Your Response

Revising Go back to the key aspects of the prompt. Does your essay include an opinion statement about the proposed policy? Will your reasons be convincing to mall owners? Have you included supporting evidence? If not, add these elements.

Proofreading Take a few minutes to edit your response to correct errors in grammar, spelling, punctuation, and capitalization. Make sure that your edits are neat and that the paper is legible.

Checking Your Final Copy Before you turn in your response, read it one more time to catch any errors you may have missed. Your essay will be more convincing if readers don't have to plow through errors to read it. **Tip:** Save five or ten minutes to improve your response.

Presenting an Argument

Speak with a Purpose

Adapt your persuasive essay into an oral presentation. Practice your argument and deliver it to an audience.

Think as a Reader/Writer

Do you remember the last persuasive speech you heard? Activists, politicians, and other professionals take great care to craft arguments that will convince audiences to agree with them. Good arguments can be made for or against almost any issue if the reasoning and evidence are strong, well-organized, and presented effectively. When delivering your argument, you can use body language and vocal inflections to emphasize your points. By adapting your persuasive essay into an oral presentation, you will increase the chance of swaying your audience.

Adapt Your Persuasive Essay

Make a Statement

Your purpose in presenting an argument is, first, to explain an issue and, second, to convince an audience that your position on the matter is correct. You must show the audience evidence that supports your view. You want the audience to feel the same way you do. These suggestions will help you present your argument:

- Rewrite your thesis statement to make your opinion clear. (The thesis of a persuasive speech is an assertion—a statement that identifies the issue and expresses your opinion about it.)

- The introduction to an effective persuasive speech is dramatic. Consider using a thought-provoking quotation, an illustrative anecdote, or a reference to an authority on the subject.

- The body of your persuasive speech supports your assertion using evidence. Choose the most effective reasons based on your audience. For example, an audience of classmates might respond favorably to emotional appeals while an audience of city council members might respond best to logical appeals.

- Begin with an attention-grabbing statement, and deliver your thesis. Then, present your argument with evidence that shows why your opinion is right. Arrange the reasons in order of importance, presenting the strongest reason last. End your speech with a call to action.

- Read your essay aloud and time yourself. Simplify your explanations and delete irrelevant information. A sentence that works on paper might be too complicated for a speech. Simplicity can help your audience grasp your ideas.

A Good Persuasive Argument

- connects the lives of listeners to the issue at hand
- includes reliable, varied evidence
- concludes with a restatement of the speaker's position
- motivates listeners to take action based on the speaker's argument

Reader/Writer Notebook

Use your **RWN** to complete the activities for this workshop.

Be sure that all evidence—facts, statistics, specific instances, and testimony—meets the standards in the following chart:

Evidence should have . . .	That means . . .
credibility	Evidence should come from a source recognized as an objective (rather than biased) authority on the subject.
validity	Evidence should have a clear connection to your argument. Valid evidence in favor of one viewpoint should not be interpreted to support the opposite side of the issue.
relevance	Evidence should have a close, logical relationship to the argument it supports. Relevant information should also be recent enough to relate directly to the issue being addressed.

Deliver Your Argument

Prepare to Practice

Fill in a chart, like the one below, to organize the main parts of your presentation. While practicing, use only these brief notes to help you remember the points you will present.

Speak Up, Speak Out

Practice your argument repeatedly. To help you gain confidence, rehearse your argument in front of a few friends. Practice speaking loudly, slowly, and expressively enough to make your arguments clear even to listeners in the back of the room. Also, use your voice as a persuasive tool by emphasizing specific points in your argument. Because this is a formal presentation, avoid slang, colloquialisms, and contractions.

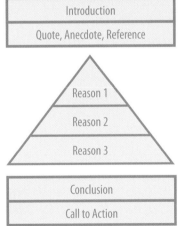

Introduction
Quote, Anecdote, Reference
Reason 1
Reason 2
Reason 3
Conclusion
Call to Action

Ask for a Response

After your presentation, ask for feedback. Have your classmates answer questions such as, "What concerns or counterarguments did you have that I did not address?" or "What was especially effective in my delivery?" Evaluate the responses so that you can make adjustments the next time you deliver a speech.

Speaking Tip

Pay attention to your body language. Appropriate gestures can strengthen your persuasiveness.

Learn It Online

See how pictures, music, and animation can make your argument more compelling at:

go.hrw.com | L10-637 | **Go**

Writing Skills Review

Persuasive Essay **Directions:** Read the following paragraph from a student's persuasive essay. Then, answer the questions that follow.

(1) Every day, children are bombarded with violent behavior on television, and parents need to take action to protect their children. (2) With each passing year, the amount of violence on television increases dramatically. (3) During their early years, children and young adults are forming their social, physical, and thinking abilities. (4) This growth can be affected by many factors, including television. (5) Watching violent television has negative effects on children's health. (6) However, parental monitoring of television programs is not enough. (7) Not only should parents remove televisions from the reach of vulnerable children, but they should also explain to children that they are only allowed to watch television with an adult. (8) Many studies have been done concluding that very young children cannot tell the difference between the fantasy world of staged television and reality.

1. Which of the following sentences would add an ethical appeal?
   A. The more children watch violence, the more aggressive they get.
   B. It is our responsibility to protect our children from things that can harm them.
   C. Ten percent of the violent behavior in American society can be attributed to television.
   D. It is disheartening to see parents use television as babysitters.

2. Which of the following sentences should be deleted to improve the organization of the argument?
   A. sentence 1
   B. sentence 3
   C. sentence 5
   D. sentence 8

3. Which sentence could be added as evidence to support the claim that there is too much violence on television?
   A. A recent study shows that 85 percent of cable television programming contains violence.
   B. Most violent programming comes on late at night.
   C. Think about the violence in the television shows you watch.
   D. Many parents do not watch television with their children.

4. How might the writer address the bias of some readers who think parental monitoring is a reasonable solution?
   A. by telling them that their opinion will be discussed in detail at a later time
   B. by ignoring their opinion
   C. by providing evidence that only 38 percent of parents monitor their children
   D. by restating his or her position

5. Which sentence adds an emotional appeal?

   A. Children should read books.

   B. Many television shows contain violence.

   C. Parents should supervise children.

   D. Children often mimic what they see on television—with harmful results.

6. Which of the following *best* states the writer's position?

   A. The amount of television violence rises each year.

   B. Violent episodes are shown on many channels.

   C. Parents should not allow children to watch television unsupervised.

   D. Children should not watch prime-time shows.

7. Which of the following words from the passage is a loaded word?

   A. children

   B. monitoring

   C. programs

   D. vulnerable

8. In this passage, what is the writer's tone?

   A. lighthearted and playful

   B. angry and sarcastic

   C. serious and concerned

   D. indifferent and uninterested

9. Which counterargument should the writer address in this essay?

   A. It is impossible to always monitor a child's television habits.

   B. Watching television can be educational.

   C. Viewing violence has little to no effect on children.

   D. Parental monitoring is the perfect solution.

10. Which of these sentences is a call to action?

   A. sentence 2

   B. sentence 6

   C. sentence 7

   D. sentence 8

11. Which of the following sentences would add a logical appeal?

   A. My friend Lamont does not like violent television shows.

   B. If violence on television is increasing, parental involvement in monitoring children's watching habits should also increase.

   C. A typical child in the United States watches twenty-eight hours of television weekly.

   D. Parents, please do not let your children watch television!

12. Which of the following would be the most convincing fact to add?

   A. a fact from a 1962 study on television's effect on children

   B. a fact from a 2005 study on the effects of parental monitoring

   C. a fact about how reading helps children learn

   D. a fact from a book written by a TV actor

UNIT 3

Poetry
Writers on Writing

Jennifer Chang on Poetry Jennifer Chang is a new voice on the American poetry scene. Her poem "Obedience, or The Lying Tale" was featured in *Best New Poets 2005,* and her first book, *The History of Anonymity,* was published in 2008.

Sometimes I write a poem when I am least inspired. When I sat down to write "Obedience, or The Lying Tale," I didn't have a word or image in my head. I was living in San Francisco, in a tiny apartment in which one room played triple-duty as bedroom, office, and living room. Normally this didn't bother me, but the week before I had returned from a month-long writer's retreat in Vermont. I had had a house to myself, three desks, two rocking chairs, a screened porch with a sweetly squeaky door, a long hallway that seemed to exist for no other purpose than to stretch the floor farther. Every day I wrote from morning to night, moving from desk to desk, poem to poem. My nearest neighbors were the trees, and this forest belonged to me alone. Or so I imagined. To return to my tiny apartment was to lose my exquisite dream of space and solitude. I looked around my room in San Francisco, not sure if that moment I was sitting on an office or living room chair. I felt cramped and a little sad, and I felt as empty as the page before me.

We've all experienced it. When doing what you really like becomes the last thing you want to do. You can leave or you can sit there and try. I tried. Lamely at first. I jotted down words I sort of liked and hadn't used before: *demon, curtsy, hurricane.* Then

I started to play with music. This is what usually gets me going: I hear sounds before I understand meanings. *the raccoons ransack a rabbit's unmasked hole.* I repeat because I like echo, and I like messing up repetition by varying a phrase or sentence each time I use it. I didn't know what I was doing. I really didn't. But soon I started to hear it: *I will . . . I will . . . I will . . .* I will cope with my tiny apartment, I thought. I will call my sister on her birthday. I will say thank you whenever I should. I will write this poem.

When I finished drafting the poem that day, I didn't have the poem you see now. It still needed lots of work. (Sometimes I think it still does!) The poem sprawled all over the page, one fat stanza. I liked certain phrases and not others. Every time I returned to it, I wanted to throw it away, like that first feeling I had—how easy to just leave. But the pleasure I have in writing is from the process. I like fussing. I like changing my mind, my words. I like thinking about how a different line break plays a different music or why a colon means more than a comma. I get lost in this process, but I also always find something of value in it: an image that clarifies a feeling, a smooth sentence, and, now and then, a bit of inspiration.

Think as a Writer

Jennifer Chang says she likes the process of writing poetry. Is there anything you do that gives you satisfaction from the process of doing it? Explain.

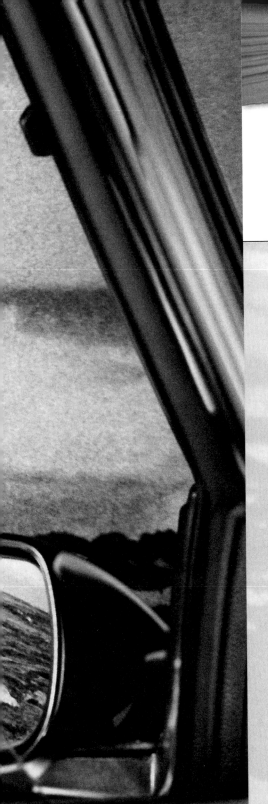

Poetry

"Ink runs from the corners of my mouth.
There is no happiness like mine.
I have been eating poetry."

—**Mark Strand**

What Do
You
Think How do we use our imagination
to transform our world?

Untitled from the Marea Baja series,
La Habana-Austin (2001–2003) by
Eduardo Munoz. Courtesy of the artist
and Sicardi Gallery, Texas.

Learn It Online
Explore poetry with the video *Perceptions* on:
go.hrw.com   L10-643   **Go**

Literary Focus

by **Carol Jago**

How Does Poetry Make Itself Heard?

Long before people communicated through writing, they uttered compelling combinations of words having the sounds of poetry. Yet after thousands of years, no one has produced a single definition of poetry. Imagery and form, figurative language, and sound devices are the means by which poetry makes itself heard.

Imagery and Form

Imagery An **image** is a representation of anything we can see, hear, taste, touch, or smell. A painter or a sculptor might create an image of an apple so true to life that we want to pick it up and eat it. A poet, using only words, can appeal to us in the same way. The language that appeals to our five senses and creates images in our minds is called **imagery.** In this example, evocative imagery creates the sensations of a nighttime thunderstorm.

> The lightning moved on, brilliant light alternating with pitch blackness, flashing white, then pink, then violet, the mountains and pines always springing back in the same place, their hugeness filling us with awe.
>
> from "A Storm in the Mountains"
> by Aleksandr Solzhenitsyn

Poetic Form Sometimes, when talking with a friend, you may need many words to express yourself. At other times, you need only a few. The way you speak may vary, too, depending on the situation. Similarly, poets can use various forms to express their thoughts and emotions. Here are some poetic forms included in this collection.

Lyric Poem A **lyric poem** expresses a speaker's emotions or thoughts—usually a single strong emotion. Most lyric poems are short and musical, such as "I Am Offering This Poem" by Jimmy Santiago Baca.

Free Verse Poetry that does not have a regular meter or rhyme scheme is called **free verse.** Poets writing in free verse follow the natural rhythms of ordinary speech. Naomi Shihab Nye's "The Flying Cat" is a free-verse poem.

Tanka **Tanka** is a Japanese poetic form with five unrhymed lines and exactly thirty-one syllables: five in lines 1 and 3 and seven in lines 2, 4, and 5. Tanka usually evoke a strong feeling with a single image.

Sonnet A **sonnet** is a fourteen-line lyric poem with a very specific structure. Like William Shakespeare's "Shall I Compare Thee to a Summer's Day?" most sonnets are written in **iambic pentameter** (see page 838) and have a regular **rhyme scheme.**

Ballad A **ballad** is a song that uses steady rhythm, strong rhymes, and repetition to tell a story. As you read "Bonny Barbara Allan," listen for the refrain that repeats with slight changes.

Ode A traditional **ode** is a long, lyric poem about a serious subject that is written in a dignified style. Pablo Neruda uses this form to celebrate an unusual subject in "Ode to My Socks."

Elegy An **elegy** is a solemn and formal lyric poem that mourns the loss of someone or something. Read "The Legend" to find out how an elegy can mourn the loss of more than one thing.

Figures of Speech

Is your friend as smart as a whip? Does he or she swim like a fish? A **figure of speech** is language in which one thing (in the examples above, your friend) is described in terms of another (a whip and a fish). Figures of speech are never literally true, but they suggest a powerful truth to our imaginations.

Simile A **simile** is a figure of speech that uses a connective word such as *like, as, than,* or *resembles* to compare things that seem to have little or nothing in common. Using a literal comparison, we might say, "His face was as red as his father's." If we use a simile, the image becomes more striking and imaginative: "His face was as red as a ripe tomato," or "His face was like a stop sign."

Similes are part of every poet's equipment. In a good simile, the comparison is unexpected but entirely reasonable. In this example, the speaker uses a simile to describe his father's death.

> Then he lay down
> to sleep like a snow-covered road
> winding through pines older than him,
> without any travelers, and lonely for no one.
>> from "Eating Together"
>> by Li-Young Lee

Metaphor A **metaphor** is another kind of comparison between unlike things. The comparison instantly reveals some reasonable connection. A metaphor is a more forceful comparison than a simile because no connective word is used. A **direct metaphor** says that something is something else. Rather than saying, "He lay down to sleep like a snow-covered road," we would say, "Lying down to sleep, he was a snow-covered road."

Metaphors are basic to everyday conversation because they allow us to speak in a kind of imaginative shorthand. Many of the metaphors we use in conversation are **implied:** "the long arm of the law," "this neck of the woods," "the foot of the mountain." All of these metaphors suggest comparisons between parts of the body and things quite different from the body. Even single words can contain implied metaphors: "She *barked* her command" compares a manner of speaking to the sound a dog makes.

Metaphors in poetry can be startling. In Rita Dove's poem "Grape Sherbet," the speaker uses a metaphor to characterize one family member who will not, or cannot, try the dessert.

> The diabetic grandmother
> stares from the porch,
> a torch
> of pure refusal.
>> from "Grape Sherbet"
>> by Rita Dove

Personification When we attribute human qualities to a nonhuman thing or to an abstract idea, we are using **personification.** We call some computers "user-friendly," for example, or say that "misery loves company." In "Shall I Compare Thee to a Summer's Day?" William Shakespeare personifies the sun by comparing it to "the eye of heaven."

Literary Focus

Sounds of Poetry

Poetry is a musical kind of speech. Like music, poetry is based on **rhythm**—that is, on the alternation of stressed and unstressed sounds that make the voice rise and fall.

Meter Poets have a choice in the kind of rhythm they can use. They can use **meter**—a strict rhythmic pattern of stressed and unstressed syllables in each line, or they can write in **free verse**—a loose kind of rhythm that sounds more like natural speech than like formal poetry.

The emphasis given to a word or a syllable is called a **stress** or an accent. In metrical poetry (poetry that has a meter), stressed and unstressed syllables are arranged in a regular pattern, as in the opening lines of one of William Shakespeare's most famous sonnets.

> Shall I compare thee to a summer's day?
>
> Thou art more lovely and more temperate.
>
> from "Shall I Compare Thee to a Summer's Day?" by William Shakespeare

The mark ′ indicates a stressed syllable. The mark ‿ indicates an unstressed syllable. Indicating the stresses this way is called **scanning** the poem.

In metrical poetry, variation is important. Without any variation, meter becomes mechanical and monotonous. With an occasional change, the poet can draw attention to key words in the poem. In the first line of Shakespeare's sonnet, the speaker breaks the rhythm to stress *thee,* drawing attention to the object of his devotion.

A line of metrical poetry is made up of metrical units called **feet.** A foot is a unit consisting of at least one stressed syllable and usually one or more unstressed syllables.

Here are the five most common metrical feet used by poets in English. Each example is followed by a single word that matches each pattern.

iamb (insist)

trochee (double)

anapest (understand)

dactyl (excellent)

spondee (fourteen)

(For more about these feet, see Meter in the Handbook of Literary Terms.)

Free Verse Early in the twentieth century, some American and English poets decided that they would concentrate on a new kind of poetry. Calling themselves **imagists,** they declared that imagery alone—without any elaborate metrics or stanza patterns—could carry the full emotional message of a poem. They called their poetry **free verse** because it was free from the old metric rules.

Robert Frost, who disliked free verse, said that writing without the metric rules was "like playing tennis with the net down." What he meant was that the net on the tennis court is like meter in poetry—the essential part of the game, which players must both respect and overcome. Nevertheless, more and more poets write in free-verse cadences that follow "curves of thought" or "shapes of speech."

All Kinds of Rhyme

Rhyme **Rhyme** is the repetition of the accented vowel sound and any sounds in words close

RA.L.10.11 Explain ways in which an author develops a point of view and style, and cite specific examples from the text. **RA.L.10.5** Analyze how an author's choice of genre affects the expression of a theme or topic. **RA.L.10.10** Describe the effect of using sound devices in literary texts.

together: *time* and *dime* and *history* and *mystery.* In poetry, rhymes may occur at the ends of lines—**end rhyme**—or within a line—**internal rhyme.** A perfect rhyme, like *verge* and *merge,* is an **exact rhyme.** When sounds are similar but not exact, as in *mystery* and *mastery,* the rhyme is an **approximate rhyme.** Some other names for approximate rhyme are **half rhyme, slant rhyme,** and **imperfect rhyme.**

Alliteration and Onomatopoeia

Alliteration The repetition of consonant sounds in words that appear close together is called **alliteration.** Strictly speaking, alliteration occurs at the beginnings of words or on accented syllables. The first two lines of "Sea Fever" by John Masefield include alliteration. Say these lines out loud to hear the effect of the repeated *s* and *st* sounds. Do the lines evoke the sound of waves hitting the beach?

> I mu_st_ go down to the _s_eas again, to the lonely _s_ea and the _s_ky,
> And all I a_sk_ is a tall ship and a _st_ar to _st_eer her by;
>
> from "Sea Fever" by John Masefield

"Well, you've brought me down to the sea again, to the lonely sea and sky. Now will you take me back to Vegas?"

Onomatopoeia The use of words that sound like what they mean (*snap, crackle*) is **onomatopoeia.** In its most basic form, onomatopoeia is a single word (*gurgle, bang, rattle, boom, hiss, buzz*) that echoes a natural or mechanical sound. For poets, onomatopoeia is a way of using words to convey both meaning and musicality.

Your Turn Analyze Poetry

Read this poem, and then complete the activities that follow.

Lost

Desolate and lone
All night long on the lake
Where fog trails and mist creeps,
The whistle of a boat
Calls and cries unendingly,
Like some lost child
In tears and trouble
Hunting the harbor's breast
And the harbor's eyes.

by Carl Sandburg

1. Find two examples of alliteration in the poem.
2. What is personified in the poem? What is it compared to?
3. What type of poem is this? Explain.

Learn It Online
Try the *PowerNotes* version of this lesson at:
go.hrw.com   L10-647   **Go**

Analyzing Visuals

How Do Artists Use Style to Create Effects?

Artists and writers use certain tools in their trade. Poets use imagery, figures of speech, meter, and rhyme to create certain effects. Artists use imagery as well, but they also use elements of style—such as line, color, shape, texture, and repetition—to create desired effects.

Analyzing Elements of Style in Art

Use these guidelines to help you analyze style in art:

1. Look for stylistic elements. Which do you notice first: visible lines, bold colors, recognizable shapes, or some other element?

2. Study the surface. Is it rough, smooth, soft, or hard? What might its texture indicate about the artist's approach to the subject?

3. Think about color. Does the artist use bright, pastel, or neutral colors? Do the colors help convey an overall message? If so, what is it?

4. Are there any repeating patterns in the artwork? If so, why do you think the artist decided to include them?

Look at the details of the artwork to help you answer the questions on page 649.

OH **RA.L.10.11** Explain ways in which an author develops a point of view and style, and cite specific examples from the text.

1. What elements of style are predominant in this artwork?

2. What effect does the artist's use of two contrasting colors (orange and blue) have?

3. This artwork includes lines that are not blended or hidden. How does this style affect the texture of the painting?

4. Why do you think the artist repeats the patterns in the background? What effect do you think the artist is trying to achieve?

Dragon motif on a dish (c. 1723–1735). China.

Your Turn   Write About Style in Art

Scan the book for another artwork with several stylistic elements. Then, write a brief description of the artwork's style. Explain how the artist uses the tools of line, color, shape, texture, or repetition to convey the overall message.

Reading Focus

by **Kylene Beers**

What Skills Help You Understand and Enjoy Poetry?

What type of poetry do you like? Do you like poems that rhyme? that tell a story? that make you laugh? Learning to read poetry well—looking closely at structure, images, and word choices—will help you enjoy the variety of poems in this collection. The strategies here will help you understand meaning and better appreciate the writers' craft.

Reading a Poem

Poetry can seem complicated at first, but it doesn't have to be difficult. Here are some tips you can use when you read a poem:

- Find punctuation showing where sentences and complete thoughts begin and end.
- If the words in a poem seem to be out of order, look for the subject, verb, and object of each sentence. In your mind, rearrange the order of the words to make sense of the poem.
- **Paraphrase** (restate in your own words) lines or stanzas. You can use a chart like the one below.

Line or Stanza	My Paraphrase

Reading Aloud

The sound of a poem is important to its meaning. You can appreciate the sounds and rhythms of poetry better when you hear a poem or read it aloud. When you read aloud, read slowly and clearly. Stop when punctuation indicates a pause. Read the poem several times. Each time you read a poem aloud, you'll understand and enjoy it more.

Visualizing

When you read a poem, your imagination translates the words into images. This process, which is called **visualizing,** makes poetry and other literature come alive. As you read a poem, pay attention to its descriptive words and phrases. Ask yourself which words and phrases appeal to the senses of sight, hearing, touch, taste, and smell. Then, relate the sensations in the poem to your own experiences.

A concept map like the one below can help you analyze a poet's use of sensory details. Write the image in the central oval. Then, write details from the poem that help you visualize the image and idea.

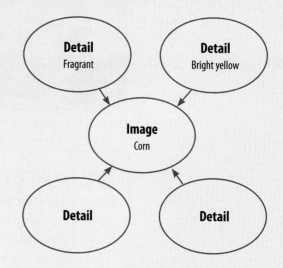

OH **RP.10.1** Apply reading comprehension strategies, including making predictions, comparing and contrasting, recalling and summarizing and making inferences and drawing conclusions. **RA.I.10.1** Identify and understand organizational patterns and techniques, including repetition of ideas, syntax and word choice, that authors use to accomplish their purpose and reach their intended audience.

Analyzing Word Choice and Syntax

A poet carefully chooses every word in order to create a precise impression. Often, a poet uses just a few words to convey different feelings and images.

Words have different shades of meaning. The **denotation** of a word is its literal, dictionary definition. The **connotations** of a word are all the meanings, associations, or emotions that have come to be attached to that word. For example, the words *thin* and *bony* have similar meanings but different connotations. The first is fairly neutral, but the second is somewhat negative.

As you read the poems in this collection, use a chart like the following to identify the connotations of key words.

Word	Denotation	Connotations

In addition to analyzing a poet's word choice, you can also examine the poem's **syntax,** or word order and grammar. Some poems include inverted, or reversed, word order. Instead of saying, "The day was long," a poet might emphasize the adjective by writing, "Long was the day." Analyzing word choice and syntax can reveal several things about what a poet wishes to convey. For example, is the word order inverted to fit the meter or to emphasize particular ideas? Is the grammar formal, or does the poet use a conversational style? Asking questions such as these as you read can reveal the poet's message and attitude toward the subject.

Your Turn Analyze Poetry

Read this poem aloud with a partner. Then, fill out a paraphrase chart, a concept map, or a connotations chart for the poem.

Moons

There are moons like continents,
diminishing to a white stone
softly smoking
in a fog-bound ocean.

5   Equinoctial° moons,
immense rainbarrels spilling
their yellow water.

Moons like eyes turned inward,
hard and bulging
10 on the blue cheek of eternity.

And moons half-broken,
eaten by eagle shadows . . .

But the moon of the poet
is soiled and scratched, its seas
15 are flowing with dust.

And other moons are rising,
swollen like boils—

in their bloodshot depths
the warfare of planets
20 silently drips and festers.
             by John Haines

5. equinoctial (ee kwuh NAHK shuhl): of the spring and fall equinoxes, when day and night are of equal length.

Now go to the Skills in Action: Reading Model

Learn It Online
Do pictures help you learn? Try the *PowerNotes* version of this lesson on:

go.hrw.com   L10–651   **Go**

Build Background

During the 1960s and 1970s, hundreds of thousands of people left Cuba for the United States and other countries. The Soviet Union had installed nuclear missile bases in Cuba in 1962, and many families fled their homes in fear of nuclear war. Shortages of food and fuel also made people leave the country. Virgil Suárez's family left Cuba at this time, but as Suárez describes in this poem, one uncle decided to stay behind in his home country.

Read with a Purpose As you read "The Stayer," think about what compels people to leave, or refuse to leave, their homes.

THE STAYER

by **Virgil Suárez**

> Simply, my uncle Chicho stayed
>   back in Cuba, against the family's
> advice, because everyone left
>
>   and he chose to stay, and this act
> 5   of staying marked him as "crazy"
>   with most of the men, and he stayed
>
> there in a shack behind my aunt's
>   clapboard house, sat in the dark
> of most days in the middle
>
> 10   of the packed-dirt floor and nodded
> at the insistence of light, the way
>   it darted through holes in the tin
>
> roof where the rain drummed
>   like the gallop of spooked horses.
> 15   This is where he was born, he chanted
>
>   under his breath to no one, why should
> he leave, live in perpetual longing
>   within exile? He learned long ago

Literary Focus

Imagery The description of the uncle sitting on a dirt floor and nodding sleepily at light darting through the roof creates contrasting images of light and dark, sleep and wakefulness, sanity and insanity.

Literary Focus

Alliteration The repetition of the *l* sound in *leave, live, longing, learned,* and *long* suggests a feeling of both sorrow and calm.

to count the passing of time
20   in how motes° danced in the shaft
of white light, the *chicharras*° echoed

their trill against the emptiness
of life, against the wake of resistance
in this place he knew as a child,

25   as a man, *un hombre,* bend against the idea
of leaving his country, call him *loco.*°
What nobody counted on was that answers

Literary Focus

Personification The comparison of the motes—insignificant specks of dust—to beautiful dancers is startling, suggesting that even the most ordinary things can be beautiful.

---

20. motes: specks of dust.
21. *chicharras:* cicadas, insects that create loud buzzing noises.
26. *loco:* crazy.

come on to those who sit in the
quiet of their own countries, tranquil
30   in the penumbra,° intent on hearing the song

of a *tomegüín°* as it calls for a mate
to come nest in the shrubs out there,
while in here, he witnesses how light

fills the emptiness with the meaning of stay.

---

30. penumbra: half-shadow.

31. *tomegüín:* a small bird that is native to Cuba.

Read with a Purpose Why did the speaker's family leave their home? Why did the uncle choose to stay?

MEET THE WRITER

Virgil Suárez (1962–   )

A Collector of Characters

By the time Virgil Suárez was twelve years old, his family had moved across the ocean twice—first from Cuba to Spain and then from Spain to the United States. These childhood experiences continue to influence the predominant themes of Suárez's works—family ties, immigration, and exile.

Never relying on research, Suárez draws upon his own memories of people and places for his work. He credits his family for providing him with a cast of characters and claims that he is lucky to be around such an interesting array of people.

"My Life Informs My Writing"

Suárez has won numerous awards, including Best American Poetry. His works include four novels, eight collections of poetry, and one collection of short fiction. Suárez notes, "I write about my life, and my life informs my writing."

Think About the Writer How do Suárez's life experiences and family background inform his writing?

SKILLS IN ACTION
Wrap Up

OH **RA.L.10.11** Explain ways in which an author develops a point of view and style, and cite specific examples from the text. **RA.L.10.10** Describe the effect of using sound devices in literary texts. *Also covered* **RA.L.10.5; RP.10.1; RA.I.10.1; VO.10.6**

Into Action: Identify Elements of Poetry

Use a chart to help you identify some of the elements of poetry in "The Stayer." In the right-hand column, list examples of each element.

Metaphor	
Simile	
Personification	
Meter	
Rhyme	
Alliteration	
Onomatopoeia	

When you have completed the chart, pair up with another student who has completed a similar chart. Have you identified the same elements in the poem?

Talk About . . .

1. With a partner, take turns reading "The Stayer" aloud. Discuss the effect of the poem's form and sound devices, such as meter, onomatopoeia, and alliteration. Try to use each Academic Vocabulary word listed at the right at least once in your discussion.

Write About . . .

Answer the following questions about "The Stayer."

2. How do the poem's images complement the speaker's feelings toward his uncle?

3. Where in the poem does the speaker's word choice evoke sympathy for his uncle?

4. How does the speaker transform the meaning of *crazy* into something else?

5. What is the literal meaning of the phrase *the meaning of stay*?

Writing Focus

Think as a Reader/Writer

Find It in Your Reading The poems in Collection 7, in all their varied forms, are packed full of imagery, figurative language, rhythm, and rhyme. On the Applying Your Skills pages, you will have a chance to apply these elements to your own writing so that you can give readers a clear picture of your thoughts and emotions.

Academic Vocabulary for Collection 7

Talking and Writing About Poetry Academic Vocabulary is the language you use to write and talk about literature. Use these words to discuss the poetry you read in this collection. The words are underlined throughout the collection.

transform (trans FAWRM) *v.:* change. *A poem can transform ordinary objects into unusual images.*

literal (LIHT uhr uhl) *adj.:* interpreting words the usual way. *A literal interpretation of a metaphor may not always make sense.*

evoke (ih VOHK) *v.:* bring out; call forth. *For some people, the uncle's condition in the poem may evoke sadness.*

complement (KAHM pluh mehnt) *v.:* complete; fulfill a lack of any kind. *The poem's title complements its theme.*

Your Turn

Copy the words from the Academic Vocabulary list into your *Reader/Writer Notebook.* Use each word at least once as you read and discuss the poems in this collection.

Imagery and Form

CONTENTS

La Mano del Desierto by Mario Irarrazabal. Sculpture. Installed in 1992 along the Pan-American highway near Antofagasta, Chile.

 **What Do You Think** How do images convey emotion and mood?

 QuickWrite
Pick an object in the classroom. Then, write a description of the object without naming it. Use words and phrases that create a visual image of the object.

Preparing to Read

Same Song

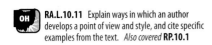
RA.L.10.11 Explain ways in which an author develops a point of view and style, and cite specific examples from the text. *Also covered* **RP.10.1**

Reader/Writer Notebook
Use your **RWN** to complete the activities for this selection.

Literary Focus

Imagery Language that appeals to the senses is called **imagery.** An image helps you use your imagination to re-create a person, a scene, or an object. When you hear the words *red wheelbarrow,* for example, you form a picture of this object in your mind's eye.

Allusion In this poem, the speaker makes an **allusion,** or indirect reference, to a classic fairy tale. If you recognize the allusion, be aware of the image it instantly forms in your mind. Allusions may refer to literature, history, myth, religion, politics, sports, science, or the arts.

Language Coach

Word Roots Mora names three muscles in her poem: *pectorals,* the chest muscles; *biceps,* the muscle at the front of the upper arm; and *triceps,* the muscle at the back of the upper arm. All three words have Latin roots. *Pectoral* comes from the Latin word for chest, *pectus.* *Bi–* means "two," and *tri–* means "three." *Biceps* literally means "two-headed muscle," because the muscle joins to the bone in two places. What can you guess about the triceps muscle?

Reading Focus

Visualizing Poetry often contains images with startling details. You may have never noticed a certain angle of light or the echo of a door slamming. Your ability to **visualize**—to see in your mind—what you are reading makes your reading more compelling. Take the time to visualize the images and to experience the smells, sounds, tastes, and textures in a poem.

Into Action As you read, use a chart like the one below to keep track of the images in "Same Song." Note both the images and the sense or senses they appeal to.

Image	Sense
"squeezes into faded jeans"	touch, sight

Writing Focus

Think as a Reader/Writer

Find It in Your Reading Mora uses a number of active verbs in her poem. As you read, jot down in your *Reader/Writer Notebook* the verbs Mora uses to describe the young people's actions. Consider what each teenager is trying to accomplish. Can you visualize their actions?

Learn It Online
See a good reader in action, and practice your own skills at:

go.hrw.com   L10-657   **Go**

Learn It Online
Get more on the author's life at:
go.hrw.com L10-658 Go

Pat Mora
(1942–)

"Am I Lucky!"

If Pat Mora has her way, every child will celebrate *Día de los niños/ Día de los libros* (Children's Day/Book Day). This annual celebration of language and literacy is held on April 30. Mora wants to bring all children the power and pleasure of what she calls "bookjoy."

"I was born in El Paso, Texas, and grew up in a bilingual home where books were an important part of my life. I can speak and write in both English and Spanish—am I lucky! I've always enjoyed reading all kinds of books and now I get to write them too—to sit and play with words on my computer."

Words That Fly

After receiving her master's degree from the University of Texas in El Paso, Mora taught in public schools and college. Her poetry has been collected in several volumes, including *Chants* (1984) and *Borders* (1986). Mora has written many children's books and also *House of Houses* (1997), a memoir about her Mexican American ancestors.

She has a clear idea of how writing should work:

> "We want those words to fly right off the page into the reader's heart."

Think About the Writer

How might Mora's command of two languages enrich her writing?

Build Background

Pat Mora wrote about her own daughter and son in "Same Song." She says she enjoys writing about family members, "like my aunt who danced on her ninetieth birthday, and my mother who wanted to be a rainbow tulip when she was in grade school."

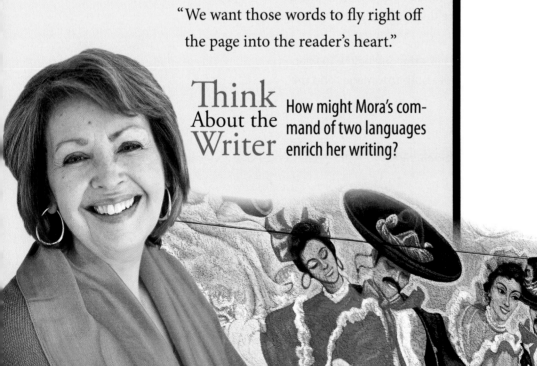

Same Song

by **Pat Mora**

While my sixteen-year-old son sleeps,
my twelve-year-old daughter
stumbles into the bathroom at six a.m.
plugs in the curling iron
5 squeezes into faded jeans
curls her hair carefully
strokes Aztec Blue shadow on her eyelids
smooths Frosted Mauve blusher on her cheeks
outlines her mouth in Neon Pink
10 peers into the mirror, mirror on the wall
frowns at her face, her eyes, her skin,
not fair.   **A**

At night this daughter
stumbles off to bed at nine
15 eyes half-shut while my son
jogs a mile in the cold dark
then lifts weights in the garage
curls and bench presses
expanding biceps, triceps, pectorals,
20 one-handed push-ups, one hundred sit-ups
peers into that mirror, mirror and frowns too.   **B**

for Libby

A **Literary Focus** Allusion To what fairy tale does Mora allude?

B **Reading Focus** Visualizing How does Mora help you visualize the son's workout?

Applying Your Skills

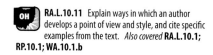

RA.L.10.11 Explain ways in which an author develops a point of view and style, and cite specific examples from the text. *Also covered* **RA.L.10.1; RP.10.1; WA.10.1.b**

Same Song

Respond and Think Critically

Reading Focus

Read with a Purpose

1. How do the son and daughter in this poem feel about the way they look? What specific words or phrases give you clues about their feelings?

Reading Skills: Visualizing

2. Return to the chart you used to track the imagery in the poem. Add a third column to analyze the images you have selected. Write down what each image illustrates about the characters or their actions.

Image	Sense	Illustrates
"squeezes into faded jeans"	touch, sight	Girl wants to appear trendy.

Literary Focus

Literary Analysis

3. **Infer** What do you think is the significance of the poem's title?

4. **Interpret** How do you interpret the word *fair* in line 12? What other meaning could it have?

5. **Analyze** What images does Mora use to help you visualize the daughter? What is the most striking image that illustrates the son's activities?

6. **Analyze** What **theme,** or message, do you think this poem conveys? Is the message relevant only to young people, or is it relevant to everyone? Explain.

Literary Skills: Imagery

7. **Interpret** What image do the allusions in lines 10–12 and 21 bring to mind? Does it have a positive or negative **connotation** (the associations and emotions evoked by the word)? Explain.

Literary Skills: Allusion

8. **Analyze** The speaker alludes to a well-known fairy tale. How do the girl and boy in this poem compare to the wicked queen in "Snow White"?

Literary Skills Review: Characterization

9. **Analyze** **Characterization** is the way an author reveals a character's personality. How would you characterize the girl and boy in this poem? How do these characters complement each other? Cite details from the poem.

Writing Focus

Think as a Reader/Writer

Use It in Your Writing Write a poem in which you characterize a friend, a family member, or a famous person through his or her habits or actions. Use vivid imagery to bring your subject to life. Add specific details and proper nouns that illustrate what your subject is like and what he or she does.

Think about your daily routine. What images would you use to describe a typical day in your life?

Eating Together / Grape Sherbet

RA.L.10.8 Analyze the author's use of point of view, mood and tone. **RA.I.10.4** Assess the adequacy, accuracy and appropriateness of an author's details, identifying persuasive techniques and examples of propaganda, bias and stereotyping.

Reader/Writer Notebook

Use your **RWN** to complete the activities for these selections.

Literary Focus

Speaker, Tone, and Voice The **speaker** in a poem is the voice that talks directly to you. It's a mistake to think that the writer and the speaker are always the same person. Sometimes the speaker is clearly the poet. Other times, the speaker is almost anyone (or anything) else—a fictional character, an animal, or even an object.

The choice of a speaker affects the poem's **tone,** the attitude the writer has toward his or her subject or audience. The speaker's tone and style of speaking create the speaker's **voice.**

Reading Focus

Analyzing Details Memories of family events often center on the sharing of food, especially comfort foods that <u>evoke</u> a sense of home. Both "Eating Together" and "Grape Sherbet" focus on images of family members gathering for a meal. The details of setting (place and time) and specific foods are intertwined with each speaker's memory of family members. Paying attention to these details will help you understand and appreciate the emotional content of the poems.

Into Action As you read each poem, make a chart like the one below to keep track of specific details and images in the poems.

	"Eating Together"	"Grape Sherbet"
Setting	before lunch; weeks after Father died	
Foods		
Family members		

Writing Focus

Think as a Reader/Writer

Find It in Your Reading As you read, look for images that appeal strongly to your senses of sight, smell, taste, touch, or hearing. Note these words and phrases in your *Reader/Writer Notebook*.

Vocabulary

Eating Together

deftly (DEHFT lee) *adv.:* quickly and skillfully. *She handled the utensil deftly.*

Grape Sherbet

dollop (DAHL uhp) *n.:* a small serving. *Each child received a dollop of mashed potatoes.*

diabetic (dy uh BEHT ihk) *adj.:* having diabetes, a disease in which the body is unable to properly process sugar. *Her diabetic grandmother could not eat the grape sherbet.*

Language Coach

Suffixes A **suffix** is a word part added to the end of a word or root. Often, adding a suffix changes the word's part of speech. Adding the suffix *–ic,* for example, turns a noun into an adjective. The noun *diabetes* plus *–ic* becomes the adjective *diabetic.* Use the suffix *–ic* to turn these nouns into adjectives: *athlete, poetry, allergy, geography,* and *drama.* You may have to add or drop letters.

 Learn It Online
Hear a professional actor read these poems. Visit the selections online at:

go.hrw.com   L10-661   **Go**

Learn It Online

Learn more about these authors at:

go.hrw.com L10-662 Go

Li-Young Lee
(1957–   )

A Stillness Like a "Deep Liberty"

Li-Young Lee was born in Jakarta, Indonesia, of Chinese parents who were political refugees. He was six years old when his family arrived in the United States. Lee grew up in a small town in Pennsylvania, where his father was the Presbyterian minister.

"On Sundays," he says, "if we weren't making rounds, we were at home observing silence. At least twice a week, our family kept a whole afternoon of quiet, neither speaking nor whispering, my father, my mother, my sister, three brothers, and I keeping everything to ourselves in the one house of three floors of square rooms and identical doors. It was clarifying, the quiet, and our stillness felt like a deep liberty. It was one more detail of my life with my father which made me feel strange in a world which found my family strange, with our accented speech and permanent bewilderment at meatloaf."

Rita Dove
(1952–   )

Pulitzer Prize WINNER

"Do the Best You Can in Whatever You Do"

Rita Dove, an avid reader, remembers that when she was growing up in Akron, Ohio, there was a feeling in the household "that the only ticket you have to a happy life is to do the best you can in whatever you do. And the one place we were allowed to go practically any time was the library, but we had to read all the books that we got. . . ." Rita Dove is the youngest person and the first African American to serve as poet laureate of the United States (1993–1995). She is a professor at the University of Virginia.

Think About the Writers

How did their parents' values prepare Lee and Dove to be writers?

Build Background

Each of the following poems focuses on a specific food-related image. "Eating Together" describes a family meal of steamed fish, and "Grape Sherbet" focuses on a Memorial Day treat. As you read, think about what each food represents to the poet.

Eating Together

by **Li-Young Lee**

In the steamer is the trout
seasoned with slivers of ginger,
two sprigs of green onion, and sesame oil.
We shall eat it with rice for lunch, **Ⓐ**
5 brothers, sister, my mother who will
taste the sweetest meat of the head,
holding it between her fingers
deftly, the way my father did **Ⓑ**
weeks ago. Then he lay down
10 to sleep like a snow-covered road
winding through pines older than him,
without any travelers, and lonely for no one.

Ⓐ Reading Focus **Analyzing Details** What details in the first four lines create a visual image for you?

Ⓑ Literary Focus **Speaker and Tone** What is the speaker's tone, or attitude, in his description of the way his mother holds the fish?

Vocabulary **deftly** (DEHFT lee) *adv.:* quickly and skillfully.

Hutong by Lincoln Seligman. Private collection.

Grape Sherbet

by **Rita Dove**

The day? Memorial.
After the grill
Dad appears with his masterpiece—
swirled snow, gelled light.
5 We cheer. The recipe's
a secret and he fights
a smile, his cap turned up
so the bib resembles a duck.

That morning we galloped
10 through the grassed-over mounds
and named each stone
for a lost milk tooth. Each dollop
of sherbet, later,
is a miracle,
15 like salt on a melon that makes it sweeter.  **Ⓐ**

Everyone agrees—it's wonderful!
It's just how we imagined lavender
would taste. The diabetic grandmother
stares from the porch,
20 a torch
of pure refusal.

We thought no one was lying
there under our feet,
we thought it
25 was a joke. I've been trying
to remember the taste,
but it doesn't exist.
Now I see why
you bothered,
30 father. **Ⓑ**

Cone (2005) by Donald Baechler. Collage and mixed media on canvas. Courtesy the artist and Studio d'Arte Raffaelli, Rome/© 2009 Donald Baechler/ Artists Rights Society (ARS), NY.

Ⓐ **Reading Focus** **Analyzing Details** What details in this stanza are clues to the speaker's age at the time of this memory?

Ⓑ **Literary Focus** **Speaker and Voice** At what point does the speaker's voice change from the voice of the child to the voice of an adult?

Vocabulary **dollop** (DAHL uhp) *n.:* a small serving.
diabetic (dy uh BEHT ihk) *adj.:* having diabetes, a disease in which the body is unable to properly process sugar.

OH **RA.L.10.8** Analyze the author's use of point of view, mood and tone. **RA.L.10.11** Explain ways in which an author develops a point of view and style, and cite specific examples from the text. *Also covered* **RA.I.10.4; VO.10.3; WA.10.1.b**

Eating Together / Grape Sherbet

Respond and Think Critically

Reading Focus

Read with a Purpose

1. Food is an important part of both poems, even though they focus, in the end, on different topics. What feelings do the poets associate with these memories of food and eating?

Reading Skills: Analyzing Details

2. As you read the poems, you used a chart to keep track of details. Now, add another row to your chart. In this row, write a statement explaining how these details <u>evoke</u> emotion.

	"Eating Together"	"Grape Sherbet"
Setting	before lunch; weeks after Father died	
Foods		
Family members		
Statement		

✓ Vocabulary Check

Match each word to its definition.

3. **deftly**   a. having diabetes
4. **dollop**   b. skillfully
5. **diabetic**   c. small serving

Literary Focus

Literary Analysis

6. **Interpret** In "Eating Together," what image does the speaker use to describe the father's death? What **mood** does this image <u>evoke</u>?

7. **Interpret** What do you think the speaker of "Grape Sherbet" means by "We thought no one was lying / there under our feet, / we thought it / was a joke"? What is the "joke"?

Literary Skills: Speaker, Tone, and Voice

8. **Identify** What is each poem's tone—the feeling or attitude the speaker takes toward the events being described? For each poem, identify the details that suggest that tone.

9. **Analyze** In "Grape Sherbet," the speaker is an adult recalling her childhood memories. How has she changed over time?

10. **Analyze** Note that "Grape Sherbet" begins as if the speaker is responding to a question. How does this establish the speaker's voice?

Literary Skills Review: Metaphor

11. **Analyze** A **metaphor** is a figure of speech that compares two unlike things without using a word of comparison. Explain the metaphor Dove uses to describe the grandmother (lines 18–21). What is she refusing?

Writing Focus

Think as a Reader/Writer

Use It in Your Writing Recollect a family meal or celebration. Then, write a poem that uses specific images to suggest your feelings about the event.

What Do **You** **Think** **Now** How do Lee and Dove <u>transform</u> the memory of everyday details into powerful images?

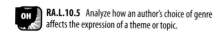

POETRY
Preparing to Read

The Legend / A Storm in the Mountains

RA.L.10.5 Analyze how an author's choice of genre affects the expression of a theme or topic.

Literary Focus

Elegy An **elegy** is a poem of mourning. Most elegies mark a particular person's death, but some elegies extend their subject to reflect on life, death, and the fleeting nature of beauty. Elegies are typically melancholy in tone. "The Legend" is one example of this kind of elegy.

Prose Poems A **prose poem** looks like an ordinary prose passage, yet it uses the elements of poetry—especially powerful imagery and figurative language. As with other poems, a prose poem allows us to enter the speaker's world and make our own meaning of it.

Literary Perspectives Apply the literary perspective described on page 669 as you read "The Legend."

Reading Focus

Reading a Poem To understand a poem, read it several times. First, notice its form and try to get a general idea of the poem's topic and mood. Then, analyze the poem's imagery, figurative language, and other elements. Read the poem aloud, listening to its sound effects.

Into Action Read each poem at least three times. As you read, use a chart like the one below to keep track of what you notice during each reading and what each element reveals about the poem's meaning.

"The Legend"	What I Notice	What It Means
First reading	Poem is an elegy.	Poem deals with death.
Second reading	"last flash of sunset"	symbol for death
Third reading		

Writing Focus

Think as a Reader/Writer

Find It in Your Reading The following poems describe events. What makes these events poetic? As you read, jot down unusual or striking details in your *Reader/Writer Notebook*.

Reader/Writer
Notebook

Use your **RWN** to complete the activities for these selections.

Vocabulary

A Storm in the Mountains

searing (SIHR ihng) *v.* used as *adj.:* burning; scorching. *The searing forks of lightning split the sky.*

ceaseless (SEES lihs) *adj.:* going all the time; never stopping. *The ceaseless roar of the falls made it impossible for us to talk.*

serpentine (SUR puhn teen) *adj.:* twisted or winding; like a snake. *Rainwater flowed down the hill in a serpentine stream.*

insignificant (ihn sihg NIHF uh kuhnt) *adj.:* having little importance or influence. *We felt insignificant next to the grandeur of the mountains.*

primal (PRY muhl) *adj.:* of early times; primitive. *Deep in the wilderness, we were in a primal world, untouched by civilization.*

Language Coach

Affixes Two of the Vocabulary words contain **affixes** (word parts added to the beginning or end of a word or root) with a negative meaning. The suffix *–less* means "without," as in *motionless* and *careless*. The prefixes *in–, un–,* and *non–* all mean "not." For each of these affixes, list three more examples.

 Learn It Online

Hear a professional actor read these two poems. Visit the selections online at:

go.hrw.com | L10-666 | Go

Garrett Hongo
(1951–)

For His Father

Garrett Hongo was born in Volcano, Hawaii, and grew up in Hawaii and Los Angeles. After graduating with honors from Pomona College, he toured Japan for a year and then returned to the United States to write and teach poetry. Hongo says that he writes his poems for his father, who "was a great example to me of a man who refused to hate or, being different himself, to be afraid of difference. . . . I want my poems to be equal to his heart."

Aleksandr Solzhenitsyn (1918–)

Nobel Prize WINNER

Russia's Nobel Laureate

Aleksandr Solzhenitsyn (sohl zhuh NEET sihn) catapulted to fame with his first novel, *One Day in the Life of Ivan Denisovich,* which details the daily life of a political prisoner. Solzhenitsyn wrote from firsthand knowledge. In 1945, he was arrested for criticizing the Soviet leader Joseph Stalin and sentenced to eight years in prison and labor camps plus an additional three years in exile. After his release, he taught mathematics and physics and continued writing. He was exiled from Russia in 1974 after publishing *The Gulag Archipelago.* Solzhenitsyn moved to Vermont and continued to publish novels about the Communist regime. In 1994, with the Communist regime no longer in power, Solzhenitsyn and his wife returned to their homeland.

When he accepted the Nobel Prize in Literature in 1970, Solzhenitsyn said, "The sole substitute for an experience which we have not ourselves lived through is art and literature."

Think About the Writers

Both writers draw from real life in their poetry. What makes a realistic description poetic?

Build Background

"The Legend" was inspired by a real-life event. One night, Garrett Hongo saw a TV news story about an Asian man who had been killed in an act of street violence. Much later, Hongo claims, this poem "just appeared." In lines 44–46 of "The Legend," Hongo alludes to an ancient Hawaiian legend about the Weaver Maid and the Herd Boy, who are responsible for making the stars turn and keeping them in place. The Weaver Maid is separated from her true love, the Herd Boy, by the entire expanse of the sky. One night a year, the universe takes pity on the lovers and builds a bridge across the heavens, allowing them to meet.

The Legend by **Garrett Hongo**

In Chicago, it is snowing softly
and a man has just done his wash for the week.
He steps into the twilight of early evening,
carrying a wrinkled shopping bag
5 full of neatly folded clothes,
and, for a moment, enjoys
the feel of warm laundry and crinkled paper,
flannellike against his gloveless hands.
There's a Rembrandt° glow on his face,
10 a triangle of orange in the hollow of his cheek
as a last flash of sunset
blazes the storefronts and lit windows of the street.
He is Asian, Thai or Vietnamese,

9. Rembrandt: Dutch painter (1606–1669) who was famous for his dramatic use of color and of light and shadow.

Ⓐ Literary Perspectives Analyzing Style To what senses does the imagery in this stanza appeal?

and very skinny, dressed as one of the poor
15 in rumpled suit pants and a plaid mackinaw,
dingy and too large.
He negotiates the slick of ice
on the sidewalk by his car,
opens the Fairlane's back door,
20 leans to place the laundry in,
and turns, for an instant,
toward the flurry of footsteps
and cries of pedestrians
as a boy—that's all he was—
25 backs from the corner package store
shooting a pistol, firing it,
once, at the dumbfounded man
who falls forward,
grabbing at his chest. **B**

30 A few sounds escape from his mouth,
a babbling no one understands
as people surround him
bewildered at his speech.
The noises he makes are nothing to them.
35 The boy has gone, lost
in the light array of foot traffic
dappling the snow with fresh prints.
Tonight, I read about Descartes'
grand courage to doubt everything
40 except his own miraculous existence°
and I feel so distinct
from the wounded man lying on the concrete
I am ashamed.

Let the night sky cover him as he dies.
45 Let the weaver girl cross the bridge of heaven
and take up his cold hands. **C**

IN MEMORY OF JAY KASHIWAMURA

B **Literary Focus** Elegy Is the tone in this stanza what you would
expect to find in an elegy? Explain.

C **Literary Perspectives** Analyzing Style How are the final three
lines different from the rest of the poem?

Literary Perspectives

Analyzing Style An author's style, or the way
he or she uses language, is like a literary fingerprint. Writers use figurative language, imagery,
word choice, and syntax (word order) to create
their distinctive styles. For example, Garrett
Hongo's writing intertwines Asian legends and
modern events. Hongo has said that this poem
"is a parable about mercy and fulfillment, the
response of the universe to the needs of the
human heart. The poem is the story of the
Weaver Girl and the Herd Boy, told in inner-city,
contemporary terms." As you read, think about
this poem from a stylistic perspective and consider what is distinctive about Hongo's use of
language. How do his word choices and images
present the poem's events in a distinctive way?
How does Hongo use these events to express a
theme? As you read, be sure to notice the notes
and questions in the text, which will guide you
in using this perspective.

38–40. Descartes' . . . existence:
René Descartes (1596–1650), a
French philosopher and math-
ematician, attempted to explain
the universe by using reason
alone. In his search for truth, he
discarded all traditional ideas
and doubted everything. The one
thing he could not doubt was the
fact that he was doubting, which
led him to conclude, "I think;
therefore I am."

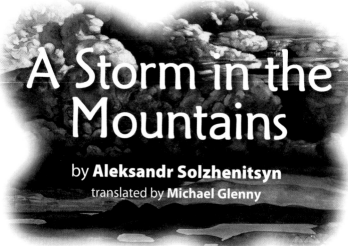

A Storm in the Mountains

by **Aleksandr Solzhenitsyn**

translated by **Michael Glenny**

Skyscape (detail) (1912) by Nikolai Konstantinovich Rerikh. Tretyahov Gallery, Moscow/Girdudon.

I t caught us one pitch-black night at the foot of the pass. We crawled out of our tents and ran for shelter as it came towards us over the ridge.

Everything was black—no peaks, no valleys, no horizon to be seen, only the searing flashes of lightning separating darkness from light, and the gigantic peaks of Belaya-Kaya and Djuguturlyuchat[1] looming up out of the night. The huge black pine trees around us seemed as high as the mountains themselves. For a split second we felt ourselves on terra firma;[2] then once more everything would be plunged into darkness and chaos.

The lightning moved on, brilliant light alternating with pitch blackness, flashing white,

then pink, then violet, the mountains and pines always springing back in the same place, their hugeness filling us with awe; yet when they disappeared we could not believe that they had ever existed.

The voice of the thunder filled the gorge, drowning the ceaseless roar of the rivers. Like the arrows of Sabaoth,[3] the lightning flashes rained down on the peaks, then split up into serpentine streams as though bursting into spray against the rock face, or striking and then shattering like a living thing. **A**

As for us, we forgot to be afraid of the lightning, the thunder, and the downpour, just as a droplet in the ocean has no fear of a hurricane. Insignificant yet grateful, we became part of this world—a primal world in creation before our eyes.

---

1. **Belaya-Kaya and Djuguturlyuchat:** two mountains in Russia.

2. **terra firma:** Latin expression meaning "solid ground."

---

3. **Sabaoth:** biblical term meaning "armies."

A **Literary Focus** Prose Poem What elements of poetry can you find in this paragraph?

Applying Your Skills

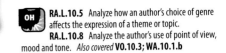
RA.L.10.5 Analyze how an author's choice of genre affects the expression of a theme or topic. **RA.L.10.8** Analyze the author's use of point of view, mood and tone. *Also covered* **VO.10.3; WA.10.1.b**

The Legend / A Storm in the Mountains

Respond and Think Critically

Reading Focus

Read with a Purpose

1. What details in "The Legend" do you think Hongo might have gotten from a news report? What details do you think he invented?

2. How does imagery help you share Solzhenitsyn's experience?

Reading Skills: Reading a Poem

3. Look at the charts you made as you read. With a partner, discuss what you learned from each reading. What might you have missed with only one reading?

✓ Vocabulary Check

Are the following statements true or false? Explain.

4. A **ceaseless** shriek lasts only a moment.
5. If something is **insignificant,** it is unimportant.
6. Something **primal** is modern.
7. A **serpentine** road goes straight ahead.
8. A hot grill is **searing** to the touch.

Literary Focus

Literary Analysis

9. **Compare** Which poem did you find more moving? Does this have more to do with the subject matter, the fact that the imagery is more vivid, or both? Explain.

10. **Literary Perspectives** What aspects of personal style does Hongo add to his poem?

Literary Skills: Prose Poem

11. **Evaluate** What makes "A Storm in the Mountains" a prose poem rather than a news report or some other kind of writing? Cite details to explain.

Literary Skills: Elegy

12. **Analyze** An elegy often celebrates the subject's life while also mourning the subject's death. Hongo does not follow this tradition. What does Hongo mourn? Use details from the poem to support your answer.

Literary Skills Review: Tone

13. **Analyze** Tone is a writer's attitude toward the subject, a character, or the reader. Explain each poet's attitude toward the events he describes, listing words and details that help create each poem's tone.

Writing Focus

Think as a Reader/Writer

Use It in Your Writing Think about a dramatic event that you have witnessed or that you have seen or read about in the news. List all of the details you can remember about the event. Who was involved? Where did it happen? What was the weather like? Then, write a prose poem about the event. Include vivid details that will make the reader feel like an eyewitness to the event.

What Do You Think Now

How can a common event, such as a thunderstorm, <u>transform</u> someone's view of the world?

Ode to My Socks

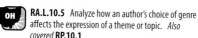
RA.L.10.5 Analyze how an author's choice of genre affects the expression of a theme or topic. *Also covered* **RP.10.1**

Reader/Writer
Notebook
Use your **RWN** to complete the activities for this selection.

Literary Focus

Ode A traditional **ode** is a long **lyric poem** (a poem that expresses a speaker's thoughts and emotions) that considers a serious subject and that is written in a dignified style. In ancient Greece and Rome, odes were recited or sung in public, often to celebrate a triumph in the Olympic Games. "Ode to My Socks" is from a collection of odes that Chilean poet Pablo Neruda wrote about everyday objects. As you read this ode, reflect on why Neruda might use a form associated with honor and nobility to celebrate an ordinary pair of socks.

Vocabulary

immense (ih MEHNS) *adj.:* very big; huge. *The speaker uses a comparison to suggest that his feet look immense.*

decrepit (dih KREHP iht) *adj.:* old and worn out. *The speaker's soft new socks are not decrepit.*

remorse (rih MAWRS) *n.:* deep regret for doing wrong. *The speaker imagines the remorse that explorers might feel for eating a rare animal.*

Reading Focus

Visualizing In "Ode to My Socks," the speaker compares his new socks and his feet to many other things, such as rabbits, fish, and blackbirds. At first, some of the comparisons may strike you as strange, even jarring. However, **visualizing,** or picturing in your mind, the things that are compared will help you infer the qualities shared by these items.

Into Action As you read, use a two-column chart to record the comparisons the speaker makes in the poem as well as the qualities shared by the items being compared.

Comparisons	Shared Qualities
1. two socks and rabbits (lines 6–7)	1. softness, fluffiness, silkiness
2.	2.

Language Coach

Prefixes A **prefix** is a word part added to the beginning of a word or a root word to form a new word. The word *immense* derives from the Latin prefix *in–*, meaning "not," and *mensus*, a form of the Latin word *metiri*, meaning "to measure." The origin of *immense* thus indicates that the word means "cannot be measured"—or "huge." What other words can you think of that contain the prefix *in–* or *im–*, meaning "not"? (Keep in mind that these prefixes can have other meanings as well.)

Writing Focus

Think as a Reader/Writer

Find It in Your Reading Neruda uses **imagery,** or language that appeals to our senses, to build his comparisons. As you read, record in your *Reader/Writer Notebook* examples of images and the senses to which they appeal. Is each image unfamiliar, unusual, or familiar? How does that quality affect your reaction to it?

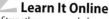
Learn It Online
Strengthen your vocabulary with Word Watch:

go.hrw.com | L10-672 | **Go**

Learn more about Neruda's life and work at:

go.hrw.com   L10-673   **Go**

Pablo Neruda
(1904–1973)

Nobel Prize WINNER

Youthful Ambition

Pablo Neruda, the most important Latin American poet of the twentieth century, was born in Chile and baptized Neftalí Ricardo Reyes Basoalto. When he was a teenager, he changed his name to avoid embarrassing his father, who frowned on his literary ambitions. Neruda wrote his first poems when he was very young, and by the time he was fifteen, several of his poems had been published.

Poet and Activist

Neruda served as a diplomat in Asia, Spain, France, and Mexico, all the while publishing prize-winning volumes of poetry. A lifelong political activist, he also wrote and spoke eloquently in support of Chile's Indians and workers struggling in poverty. Neruda was elected to Chile's senate, but a speech he gave that was highly critical of Chile's repressive government led to an order for his arrest. In 1949, Neruda fled Chile for three years until the order for his arrest was dropped.

In 1971, Neruda was awarded the Nobel Prize in Literature "for a poetry that with the action of an elemental force brings alive a continent's destiny and dreams." In his acceptance speech, he wrote, "I have always maintained that the writer's task has nothing to do with mystery or magic, and that the poet's, at least, must be a personal effort for the benefit of all. The closest thing to poetry is a loaf of bread or a ceramic dish or a piece of wood lovingly carved, even if by clumsy hands."

Think About the Writer

Why might Neruda have considered an item such as a loaf of bread to be "the closest thing to poetry"?

Pablo Neruda

"Yo llegué al cobre, a Chuquicamata.
Era tarde en las cordilleras.
El aire era como una copa fría,
de seca transparencia."

1904 12 JULIO 2004

Central Unitaria de trab

Ode to My Socks

by **Pablo Neruda**
translated by **Robert Bly**

Maru Mori brought me
a pair
of socks
which she knitted herself
5   with her sheepherder's hands,
two socks as soft
as rabbits.
I slipped my feet
into them
10 as though into
two
cases
knitted
with threads of
15 twilight
and goatskin.
Violent socks,
my feet were
two fish made
20 of wool,
two long sharks
sea-blue, shot
through
by one golden thread,
25 two immense blackbirds,
two cannons: Ⓐ
my feet

Ⓐ **Reading Focus** Visualizing What qualities might the socks share with sharks, blackbirds, and cannons?

Vocabulary **immense** (ih MEHNS) *adj.:* very big; huge.

were honored
in this way
30 by
these
heavenly
socks.
They were
35 so handsome
for the first time
my feet seemed to me
unacceptable
like two decrepit
40 firemen, firemen
unworthy
of that woven
fire,
of those glowing
45 socks.

Nevertheless
I resisted
the sharp temptation
to save them somewhere
50 as schoolboys
keep
fireflies,
as learned men
collect
55 sacred texts,
I resisted
the mad impulse

to put them
into a golden
60 cage
and each day give them
birdseed
and pieces of pink melon.
Like explorers
65 in the jungle who hand
over the very rare
green deer
to the spit°
and eat it
70 with remorse,
I stretched out
my feet
and pulled on
the magnificent
75 socks
and then my shoes. **B**

The moral
of my ode is this:
beauty is twice
80 beauty
and what is good is doubly
good
when it is a matter of two socks
made of wool
85 in winter.

_____

68. spit: thin rod or stick on which meat is roasted.

Vocabulary **decrepit** (dih KREHP iht) *adj.:* old and worn out.
remorse (rih MAWRS) *n.:* deep regret for doing wrong.

B **Literary Focus** Ode In this stanza, how does the speaker make the socks seem like objects of great worth?

Applying Your Skills

RA.L.10.5 Analyze how an author's choice of genre affects the expression of a theme or topic.
RA.L.10.8 Analyze the author's use of point of view, mood and tone. *Also covered* **RP.10.1; VO.10.3; WA.10.1.b**

Ode to My Socks

Respond and Think Critically

Reading Focus

Read with a Purpose

1. Use details from the poem to explain how the speaker feels about the socks. How does the fact that the socks are a handmade gift and are meant to be worn in winter contribute to your understanding of the significance of the socks?

Reading Skills: Visualizing

2. Choose three comparisons you recorded in the chart you filled in as you read. Then, for each comparison, write one or two sentences explaining what the comparison suggests about the socks.

✔ Vocabulary Check

For each Vocabulary word, choose the letter of the correct definition.

3. **immense**
   a. many   **b.** huge   **c.** loud

4. **decrepit**
   a. careless   **b.** slow   **c.** worn out

5. **remorse**
   a. regret   **b.** excitement **c.** release

Literary Focus

Literary Analysis

6. **Analyze** Explain the speaker's conflict and its resolution, which is described in the second stanza of the poem. What does the comparison in lines 64–76 suggest about the speaker's feelings concerning this resolution?

7. **Analyze** This poem's short lines, a number of which contain a single word, are an important aspect of the poem's style. Re-read lines 46–63. Why might Neruda have chosen to break up these lines in such a way? Do you see any patterns in these lines? If so, what is the effect?

Literary Skills: Ode

8. **Interpret** Explain the moral presented in the last stanza of the poem. What point is the speaker making about beauty and goodness?

9. **Interpret** Do you think Neruda wants this ode to be taken seriously, or is he writing a parody of an ode? (A **parody** is a humorous imitation of a serious work of literature, art, or music.) Cite details from the poem to support your opinion.

Literary Skills Review: Diction

10. **Evaluate** Look carefully at Neruda's **diction,** or word choice, in this poem. Do any words or phrases seem particularly suited to the style of a traditional ode? Do any seem more typical of everyday speech?

Writing Focus

Think as a Reader/Writer

Use It in Your Writing Write an ode to an object you see every day. Start by observing the object closely and making some notes about how it looks, what it resembles, and how it makes you feel.

What Do **You Think Now**

Why do certain objects become important or invaluable to us? How can they transform our view of the world?

POETRY
Preparing to Read

The Summer I Was Sixteen /
Obedience, or The Lying Tale

Literary Focus

Theme and Imagery The **theme** of a literary work is its central idea, or insight, about life. Poets rarely reveal the theme of a poem directly. Instead, through the meanings and emotions suggested by their **imagery,** or language that appeals to the senses, poets indirectly convey the larger meaning of a work. The following poems present different views of girls. As you read, examine each poem's imagery carefully. Then, consider what theme you think each poet expresses.

Reading Focus

Reading Aloud In a poem, a speaker's **voice** is created through his or her use of language and **tone,** or attitude. By reading a poem aloud, you will gain a fuller appreciation of a speaker's voice, thereby enhancing your understanding of the poem as a whole.

Into Action Read each poem silently at first, and use a chart like the one below to record notes about the speaker's voice. Then, read the poem aloud, and record any additional observations you have about her voice.

Voice in "The Summer I Was Sixteen"	Voice in "Obedience, or The Lying Tale"
Reading silently: voice of an adult looking back	Reading silently: voice of girl speaking directly to her mother
Reading aloud:	Reading aloud:

Writing Focus

Think as a Reader/Writer

Find It in Your Reading Both poets use words and phrases in an unusual manner to create striking images in their poems. As you read, record examples of these images in your *Reader/Writer Notebook*. Do you think these images are effective? Why or why not?

 RA.L.10.11 Explain ways in which an author develops a point of view and style, and cite specific examples from the text. **RA.L.10.4** Interpret universal themes across different works by the same author or by different authors. *Also covered* **RP.10.1**

 **Reader/Writer Notebook**

Use your **RWN** to complete the activities for these selections.

Vocabulary

The Summer I Was Sixteen

mirage (muh RAHZH) *n.:* illusion; something that appears to be real but does not truly exist. *At the pool, the girls seemed to see a mirage.*

sated (SAYT ihd) *v.* used as *adj.:* fully satisfied. *The girls felt sated after eating cotton candy.*

furtive (FUR tihv) *adj.:* secret; done in a sneaky manner. *The trees provided cover for their furtive actions.*

Obedience, or The Lying Tale

misgivings (mihs GIHV ihngz) *n.:* feelings of doubt or dread. *The speaker experiences misgivings about taking action.*

withered (WIHTH uhrd) *v.* used as *adj.:* wrinkled and shrunken. *The old ferryman looked withered.*

Language Coach

Related Meanings The words *sated* and *satiated,* which have similar meanings, should not be confused with *saturated,* which means "unable to hold more" or "wet through and through." Which word should be used to describe the ground after a rainstorm: *sated* or *saturated*?

 Learn It Online

There's more to words than just definitions. Get the whole story on:

go.hrw.com   L10-677   Go

Geraldine Connolly
(1947–   )

Images from the Past

The voices of a child and an adult echo throughout Geraldine Connolly's poetry. Born in Greensburg, Pennsylvania, Connolly has chronicled the story of her youth and her family in her poems. She writes about her boarding-school days, her struggles with her mother, her grandparents' migration from Poland to the United States, and her grandfather's experiences as a coal miner. An award-winning poet, Connolly has published two collections of poems. "The Summer I Was Sixteen" was selected by former U.S. poet laureate Billy Collins to be included in Poetry 180, a project devoted to encouraging students to read or hear a poem on each school day.

Jennifer Chang
(1976–   )

A New Voice

A rising voice in the American poetry scene, Jennifer Chang had her work published in *Best New Poets 2005*. Discussing the drafting of "Obedience, or The Lying Tale," Chang said, "I did very little planning or plotting during its development. I was mostly following the sound of the words." Chang's work has appeared in journals and anthologies, and her first collection, *The History of Anonymity*, was published in 2008. The winner of several fellowships, she is working toward her doctorate in English at the University of Virginia. She also serves as Communications Director at Kundiman, a nonprofit organization that supports emerging Asian American poets.

Think About the Writers

Whose poems would you suggest including in Poetry 180? Support your choices.

Build Background

"Obedience, or The Lying Tale" is filled with rich imagery drawn from Jennifer Chang's imagination as well as fairy tales from the Grimm brothers. You might recognize the wolf that appears in the poem from tales such as "Little Red Riding Hood." The "three gold hairs" and the gnawing mouse are allusions, or references, to the tale "The Devil with the Three Golden Hairs," and the title of the poem and the first and last lines are allusions to a story called "The Lying Tale."

Chang also alludes to Greek and Roman mythology—to the old ferryman Charon, who transports the dead across the river Styx in the Underworld and on to Elysium, the paradise where heroes are sent when they die.

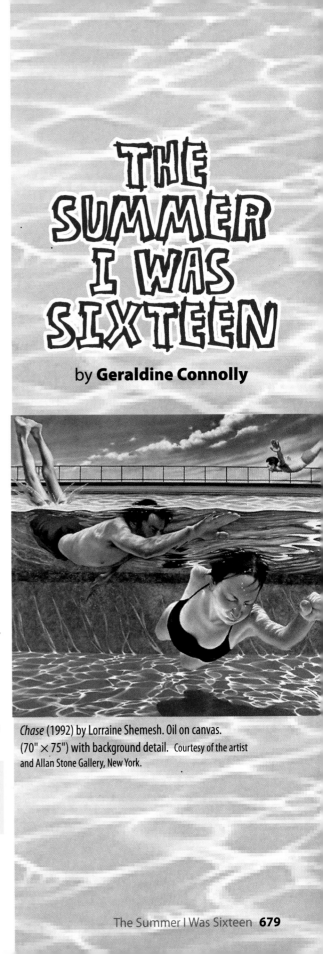

THE SUMMER I WAS SIXTEEN

by **Geraldine Connolly**

The turquoise pool rose up to meet us,
its slide a silver afterthought down which
we plunged, screaming, into a mirage of bubbles.
We did not exist beyond the gaze of a boy.   **Ⓐ**

5   Shaking water off our limbs, we lifted
up from ladder rungs across the fern-cool
lip of rim. Afternoon. Oiled and sated,
we sunbathed, rose and paraded the concrete,   **Ⓑ**

danced to the low beat of "Duke of Earl."
10 Past cherry colas, hot-dogs, Dreamsicles,
we came to the counter where bees staggered
into root beer cups and drowned. We gobbled

cotton candy torches, sweet as furtive kisses,
shared on benches beneath summer shadows.
15 Cherry. Elm. Sycamore. We spread our chenille
blankets across grass, pressed radios to our ears,

mouthing the old words, then loosened
thin bikini straps and rubbed baby oil with iodine
across sunburned shoulders, tossing a glance
20 through the chain link at an improbable world.

Ⓐ Literary Focus Theme and Imagery How do the speaker and her friends perceive their identity and the world, as suggested by the poem's fourth line?

Ⓑ Reading Focus Reading Aloud What does the speaker's use of the word *paraded* suggest about her attitude toward her teenage self, and how does the word contribute to her voice?

Vocabulary mirage (muh RAHZH) *n.*: illusion; something that appears to be real but does not truly exist.
sated (SAYT ihd) *v.* used as *adj.*: fully satisfied.
furtive (FUR tihv) *adj.*: secret; done in a sneaky manner.

Chase (1992) by Lorraine Shemesh. Oil on canvas.
(70" × 75") with background detail. Courtesy of the artist and Allan Stone Gallery, New York.

Obedience, or The Lying Tale

by **Jennifer Chang**

I will do everything you tell me, Mother.
I will charm three gold hairs
from the demon's head.
I will choke the mouse that gnaws
5   an apple tree's roots and keep its skin
for a glove. To the wolf, I will be
pretty and kind, and curtsy
his crossing of my path.

A **Reading Focus** **Reading Aloud**   How would you describe the speaker's tone in the first stanza?

Torso #6 by Robert Inman. Acrylic on paper (44" × 34").

The forest, vocal
10 even in its somber tread, rages.
A slope ends in a pit of foxes
drunk on rotten brambles of berries,
and the raccoons ransack°
a rabbit's unmasked hole.
15 What do they find but a winter's heap
of droppings? A stolen nest, the cracked shell

of another creature's child.
I imagine this is the rabbit way,
and I will not stray, Mother,
20 into the forest's thick,
where the trees meet the dark,
though I have known misgivings
of light as a hot hand that flickers
against my neck. The path ends

25 at a river I must cross. I will wait
for the ferryman
to motion me through. Into the waves,
he etches° with his oar
a new story: a silent girl runs away,
30 a silent girl is never safe.   **B**
I will take his oar in my hand. I will learn
the boat's rocking and bring myself back

and forth. To be good
is the hurricane of caution.
35 I will know indecision's rowing,
the water I lap into my lap
as he shakes his withered head.
Behind me is the forest. Before me
the field, a loose run of grass. I stay
40 in the river, Mother, I study escape.

13. ransack (RAN sak): search for goods to steal; rob.

28. etches (EHCH ihz): cuts into the surface of something in order to create a picture or pattern.

B **Literary Focus** Theme and Imagery Why does the speaker describe the story etched by the ferryman as a "new" story?

Vocabulary **misgivings** (mihs GIHV ihngz) *n.*: feelings of doubt or dread.
withered (WIHTH uhrd) *v.* used as *adj.*: wrinkled and shrunken.

Applying Your Skills

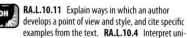
RA.L.10.11 Explain ways in which an author develops a point of view and style, and cite specific examples from the text. RA.L.10.4 Interpret universal themes across different works by the same author or by different authors. Also covered RA.L.10.8; RP.10.1; VO.10.3; WA.10.1.b

The Summer I Was Sixteen / Obedience, or The Lying Tale

Respond and Think Critically

Reading Focus

Read with a Purpose

1. What do the images in "The Summer I Was Sixteen" suggest about the speaker's experiences? To what senses do the images appeal?

2. Why do you think Chang titled her poem "Obedience, or The Lying Tale"? Explain who is lying to whom and about what she is lying.

Reading Skills: Reading Aloud

3. Review the chart you filled in as you read each poem. With a partner, take turns reading each poem aloud. Try to bring the speaker's voice to life. Do you and your partner read the poem differently? How does understanding voice help you appreciate the meaning of the poem?

✓ Vocabulary Check

Choose the word in parentheses that best completes each sentence.

4. Having **misgivings** can cause (*joy, uncertainty*).
5. A **withered** person is probably (*old, young*).
6. A **mirage** is likely to be (*imaginary, scary*).
7. When people are **sated,** they are (*satisfied, angry*).
8. A **furtive** action is carried out (*confidently, secretly*).

Literary Focus

Literary Analysis

9. **Interpret** Explain what the image of "the chain link" in the last line of Connolly's poem suggests. What is the "improbable world"?

10. **Synthesize** In the last stanza of Chang's poem, the speaker contemplates two options—the forest behind her and the field before her—as she "stud[ies] escape." What does she want to escape? What might these options represent, and what might she be seeking?

Literary Skills: Theme and Imagery

11. **Interpret** What do you think is the theme of Chang's poem? How does the imagery from children's tales help convey this theme?

12. **Interpret** What theme about the experiences of a teenage girl does Connolly express in her poem? Which images <u>evoke</u> this theme?

Literary Skills Review: Mood

13. **Compare and Contrast** Compare the **moods,** or the overall feelings and atmosphere, that Chang's and Connolly's poems <u>evoke</u>. What words help create these moods?

Writing Focus

Think as a Reader/Writer

Use It in Your Writing Choose a setting that would appeal to teenagers, and write a paragraph describing activities that take place in that setting. Use words in creative ways to produce fresh images.

What Do **You Think Now**

How do the speakers view the world at large? How do they view their own personal worlds?

POETRY
Preparing to Read

I Am Offering This Poem / Three Japanese Tanka

RA.L.10.5 Analyze how an author's choice of genre affects the expression of a theme or topic.

Reader/Writer Notebook

Use your **RWN** to complete the activities for these selections.

Literary Focus

Lyric Poetry A **lyric poem** expresses the thoughts and feelings of a speaker. Lyric poetry owes its name to the ancient Greeks, who used the word *lyrikos* to refer to brief poems they sang to the accompaniment of the lyre, a stringed instrument. Today most lyrics are short, and they are still musical. (You might know that the word *lyrics* also refers to the words of a song.) Unlike narrative poetry, which tells a story, lyric poetry uses language to suggest, rather than directly state, strong emotions.

Tanka The **tanka,** a Japanese poetic form, dates back to the seventh century and is written according to strict rules. In Japanese, tanka always have five unrhymed lines and a total of exactly thirty-one syllables. Lines 1 and 3 have five syllables each. Lines 2, 4, and 5 have seven syllables each. (The English translations do not always follow this strict syllable count.) A tanka contains a single image that <u>evokes</u> a strong feeling.

Language Coach

Multiple-Meaning Words Many English words have more than one meaning. The word *line,* for example, can mean "a group of people standing in a row" or "a group of words in a poem." Two multiple-meaning words in the following poems are *stalk* and *safe.* Write a pair of sentences for each word. Be sure that the meaning differs in each sentence. Use a dictionary if necessary.

Writing Focus

Think as a Reader/Writer

Find It in Your Reading In both "I Am Offering This Poem" and the three Japanese tanka, the poets use imagery to convey the depth of their speakers' feelings. As you read these poems, record in your *Reader/Writer Notebook* examples of the poets' imagery and the emotions each image <u>evokes</u> by appealing to the senses.

"Take a haiku, Miss Lee . . . ."

Learn It Online
Hear a professional actor read these poems. Visit the selections online at:

| go.hrw.com | L10-683 | **Go** |

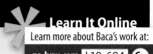

Learn It Online
Learn more about Baca's work at:
go.hrw.com L10-684 Go

Jimmy Santiago Baca (1952–   )

A Declaration of Life

Born in New Mexico of Mexican American and Apache ancestry, Jimmy Baca was abandoned by his parents when he was two years old. Baca's grandmother took care of him until, at the age of five, he was sent to an orphanage. When he was eleven, he ran away, living on the streets until, at the age of eighteen, he landed in prison for possessing drugs. In prison, feeling sure he was going to die, Baca notes, "I had to tell somebody that I was here." He taught himself to read and write and began writing poetry. Then, taking "a wild chance," he sent some poems to a magazine, which published them. Baca went on to become a highly acclaimed, award-winning poet.

Ono Komachi
(834–?)

A Leading Lady and Poet

Little is known about Ono Komachi's life. She may have been the daughter of a ninth-century Japanese lord and may have served at the imperial court. She was supposedly one of the most beautiful women of her time. Komachi was one of the great figures in an age when women dominated Japanese society and literature. In her hundred or so poems that survive, she illuminates the subject of love through her understanding of Buddhist ideas about the fleeting nature of existence.

The Poetess Ono Komachi (c. 1820) by Totoya Hokkei (1790–1850). Surimono print (20 cm × 17 cm). Spencer Museum of Art, the University of Kansas, the William Bridges Thayer Memorial.

Think About the Writers

What does the biographical information above suggest about the poets' views of life?

Build Background

The **tanka** may be the most beloved form of Japanese poetry. Invented more than a thousand years ago, tanka are still being composed by Japanese poets. Even today, the emperor of Japan holds an annual tanka-writing competition to celebrate the New Year.

I Am Offering This Poem

by **Jimmy Santiago Baca**

I am offering this poem to you,
since I have nothing else to give.
Keep it like a warm coat
when winter comes to cover you,
5   or like a pair of thick socks
the cold cannot bite through,   **Ⓐ**

      I love you,

I have nothing else to give you,
so it is a pot full of yellow corn
10   to warm your belly in winter,
it is a scarf for your head, to wear
over your hair, to tie up around your face,

      I love you,

Keep it, treasure this as you would
15   if you were lost, needing direction,
in the wilderness life becomes when mature;
and in the corner of your drawer,
tucked away like a cabin or hogan°
in dense trees, come knocking,
20   and I will answer, give you directions,
and let you warm yourself by this fire,
rest by this fire, and make you feel safe,

      I love you,

It's all I have to give,
25   and all anyone needs to live,
and to go on living inside,
when the world outside
no longer cares if you live or die;   **Ⓑ**
remember,

30   I love you.

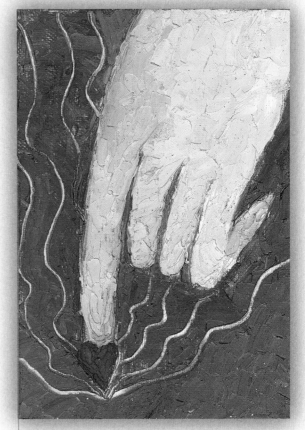

Hand and Heart by Jami Jennings.

18. hogan (HOH gahn): traditional Navajo structure made of earth and logs.

Ⓐ **Literary Focus** Lyric Poetry   What emotions are suggested by the images and comparisons in the first stanza?

Ⓑ **Literary Focus** Lyric Poetry   What do you think the speaker means when he says that his poem will help his beloved "go on living inside" when the outside world no longer cares?

Three Japanese Tanka

by **Ono Komachi**

translated by **Jane Hirshfield** with **Mariko Aratani**

1

*Sent anonymously to a man who had passed in front of
    the screens of my room*
Should the world of love
end in darkness,
without our glimpsing
that cloud-gap
where the moon's light fills the sky?

2

Sent to a man who seemed to have changed his mind
Since my heart placed me
on board your drifting ship,
not one day has passed
that I haven't been drenched
in cold waves.   Ⓐ

3

*Sent in a letter attached to a rice stalk with an empty
    seed husk*
How sad that I hope
to see you even now,
after my life has emptied itself
like this stalk of grain
into the autumn wind.   Ⓑ

Ⓐ **Literary Focus** Tanka What is the central image of this tanka?

Ⓑ **Literary Focus** Tanka In what ways does the English translation of
this tanka conform to the strict rules of the tanka form?

Murasaki Shikibu by Gakutei Harunobu, Japanese (active c. 1813–1868). Full color, ink, and gold on paper (15 ¹/₁₆" × 23 ³/₈").
Freer Gallery of Art, Smithsonian Institution, Washington, D.C. Gift of Charles Lang Freer.

Poetry in the Golden Age of Japan

In the imperial court of Heian-era Japan (794–1185), poetry had both private and public functions. In private, poetry was the accepted language of love. A gentleman showed his interest in a lady of the court by sending her an admiring five-line poem (a tanka). If the poem she wrote in reply was encouraging, he paid her a visit. Their exchange of poems continued throughout their relationship, and each new message had to be original and intriguing.

Lovers also valued skillful calligraphy, exquisite paper, and a tasteful presentation. To <u>complement</u> their poems, the lovers covered tinted bamboo paper with scattered designs and tiny flecks of gold and silver foil. The final creation, carefully sealed with a twig or spray of flowers, was often lovely enough to decorate a folding screen.

Although it could be as romantic and beautiful as private poetry, public poetry was presented and evaluated very differently. At popular poetry contests (*uta-awase*), competitors grouped themselves into two teams, Right and Left. A judge gave the teams a topic, such as "spring" or "names of things," and awarded a point to the side that created and recited the more pleasing composition. The team that had the most points after several rounds won. The government Office of Poetry preserved exceptional spoken poems in written anthologies.

Ask Yourself

If you were sending Baca's poem to someone today, how would you decorate and present it in order to reflect its mood?

Applying Your Skills

OH **RA.L.10.5** Analyze how an author's choice of genre affects the expression of a theme or topic. **WA.10.1.b** Write narratives that: use a range of strategies and literary devices including figurative language and specific narration.

I Am Offering This Poem / Three Japanese Tanka

Respond and Think Critically

Reading Focus

Read with a Purpose

1. **How** would you sum up the attitude toward love expressed in "I Am Offering This Poem"? How does this attitude compare with the attitudes expressed in the three tanka?

Literary Focus

Literary Analysis

2. **Analyze** Throughout Baca's poem, what figures of speech does the speaker use to suggest what the speaker's love can do for the person being addressed?

3. **Analyze** In lines 3–12 of Baca's poem, to what kinds of things does the speaker compare his love? Why might he have chosen these particular types of items?

4. **Interpret** In your own words, state the question the speaker poses in Komachi's first tanka. What might the contrast between darkness and light represent in the poem?

5. **Interpret** In Komachi's second tanka, to what might the "drifting ship" refer? Do you think the line that introduces the tanka by explaining to whom it was sent is necessary for understanding this **metaphor,** or comparison? Explain.

6. **Infer** What may have happened between the speaker and her beloved, based on Komachi's third tanka? What do the **simile** (a comparison using a connecting word such as *like* or *as*) and the imagery suggest about the speaker's life?

Literary Skills: Lyric Poetry and Tanka

7. **Analyze** When we talk of "love poems," we usually think of romantic love. Could Baca's lyric poem be addressed to a child? to a good friend? to a parent? to anyone else? Explain your response.

8. **Evaluate** The tanka were written many centuries ago, whereas "I Am Offering This Poem" was written by a contemporary poet. Do the sentiments expressed in the tanka seem any less contemporary than those expressed in Baca's lyric poem? Do the sentiments in the tanka still apply to people's feelings and experiences? Explain.

Literary Skills Review: Refrain

9. **Analyze** A **refrain** is a repeated word, phrase, line, or group of lines in a literary work or song. What line serves as the main refrain in "I Am Offering This Poem"? What purposes does Baca achieve by using this refrain?

Writing Focus

Think as a Reader/Writer

Use It in Your Writing Choose a subject that you feel strongly about, and then express this feeling in the form of a tanka. Remember to focus on a single image to suggest this emotion. Try to follow the rules of the tanka form as closely as you can.

What Do You Think Now

How can love <u>transform</u> a person's view of the world? How can poetry express that view?

POETRY
Preparing to Read

Shall I Compare Thee to a Summer's Day?

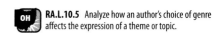 **RA.L.10.5** Analyze how an author's choice of genre affects the expression of a theme or topic.

 **Reader/Writer Notebook**

Use your **RWN** to complete the activities for this selection.

Literary Focus

Sonnet The poetic form favored (although not invented) by William Shakespeare is the **English sonnet** (also called the **Shakespearean sonnet** because he perfected the form). Its fourteen lines are divided into three **quatrains** (rhyming four-line stanzas) and a concluding **couplet** (a pair of rhyming lines). Each quatrain makes a point or gives an example, and the couplet sums up the whole poem. As you read this sonnet, note how the speaker expresses passionate feelings within the strictness of this form—not an easy task.

Reading Focus

Reading a Poem To help unlock a poem's meaning, look for punctuation that tells where sentences—and complete thoughts—begin and end. Rearrange inverted sentences, phrases, and words in your mind by placing subjects, verbs, and complements in the traditional order. Finally, **paraphrase,** or restate in your own words, each line of the poem to ensure that you understand it.

Into Action As you read this sonnet, use a chart to record your paraphrasing of the lines, placing words in their usual order.

Quatrain 1	I shall compare you to a summer day.
Quatrain 2	
Quatrain 3	
Couplet	

Vocabulary

temperate (TEHM puhr iht) *adj.*: not too hot or too cold; mild; moderate in behavior; self-restrained. *The speaker says his love's personality is more temperate than summer weather.*

complexion (kuhm PLEHK shuhn) *n.*: appearance of the skin, especially the face. *The speaker observes that time can dim a person's beautiful complexion.*

Language Coach

Antonyms The word *temperate* should not be confused with its antonym *temperamental*. (An **antonym** is a word with an opposite meaning.) *Temperamental* means "extremely sensitive," "easily upset," or "moody." Which word would best apply to a child who has trouble getting along with others? a child who is well behaved?

Writing Focus

Think as a Reader/Writer

Find It in Your Reading **Personification** is the use of human characteristics to describe objects or ideas. In your *Reader/Writer Notebook,* write down examples of personification you find in the poem.

 **Learn It Online**
Hear a professional actor read this poem. Visit the selection online at:

go.hrw.com   L10-690   **Go**

Read with a Purpose Read this sonnet to discover how the speaker praises his beloved.

Shall I Compare Thee to a Summer's Day?

by **William Shakespeare**

Shall I compare thee to a summer's day?
Thou art more lovely and more temperate.
Rough winds do shake the darling buds of May,
And summer's lease° hath all too short a date.

5 Sometime too hot the eye of heaven shines,
And often is his gold complexion dimmed;
And every fair from fair sometime declines,
By chance, or nature's changing course, untrimmed;°
But thy eternal summer shall not fade,

10 Nor lose possession of that fair thou ow'st,°
Nor shall Death brag thou wand'rest in his shade,
When in eternal lines to time thou grow'st:
    So long as men can breathe or eyes can see,
    So long lives this, and this gives life to thee.

4. lease (lees): allotted time.

8. untrimmed: without trimmings (decorations).

10. thou ow'st: you own.

Ⓐ Reading Focus Reading a Poem How would you rearrange the words in line 5 to place them in a more usual order?

Ⓑ Literary Focus Sonnet In line 14, what does *this* refer to? Explain the meaning of the couplet.

Vocabulary **temperate** (TEHM puhr iht) *adj.*: not too hot or too cold; mild; moderate in behavior; self-restrained.
complexion (kuhm PLEHK shuhn) *n.*: appearance of the skin, especially the face.

Detail from *Springtime* (1956) by Hovannes Zardarian.
Tretyakov Gallery, Moscow, Russia.

Applying Your Skills

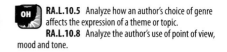
RA.L.10.5 Analyze how an author's choice of genre affects the expression of a theme or topic.
RA.L.10.8 Analyze the author's use of point of view, mood and tone.

Shall I Compare Thee to a Summer's Day?

Respond and Think Critically

Reading Focus

Read with a Purpose

1. How does the speaker answer the question he poses in the opening of the sonnet? Explain what he praises about his beloved and why he rejects the literal comparison between his beloved and the summer day.

Reading Skills: Reading a Poem

2. Compare your paraphrase of the poem with a partner's. How similar are your paraphrases? What are the reasons for any major differences? Add a row labeled "Evaluation" to the bottom of your chart, and note what you learned from this activity.

Quatrain 1	I shall compare you to a summer day.
Quatrain 2	
Quatrain 3	
Couplet	
Evaluation	

Literary Focus

Literary Analysis

3. **Interpret** Explain the metaphor and personification in lines 5–6. Why is the "eye of heaven" neither constant nor reliable?

4. **Analyze** According to lines 7–8, what can happen to any kind of beauty?

Literary Skills: Sonnet

5. **Interpret** Would you say that this sonnet is a love poem, or is it really about something else? Explain your interpretation.

6. **Extend** Explain whether the speaker's bold assertion in the couplet has proved true. In what ways can art immortalize someone? Provide examples to support your response.

7. **Evaluate** What might be the potential benefits and drawbacks of using the sonnet form to express feelings and ideas? Explain which aspects of the form you think Shakespeare uses to the greatest effect in this sonnet.

Literary Skills Review: Tone

8. **Analyze** Tone is a writer's or speaker's attitude toward his or her subject. What is the tone of this sonnet? What is the speaker's attitude toward his beloved, his poetry, and himself?

Writing Focus

Think as a Reader/Writer

Use It in Your Writing If you were the speaker's beloved, how would you react to this sonnet? Would you be flattered? irritated? confused? Respond to the speaker. Write the response in the form of a letter or, for a real challenge, a sonnet. Use personification to help you express your feelings and ideas.

 What Do You Think Now

What role do you think art has in the world today?

IMAGERY AND FORM
Wrap Up

OH **RA.L.10.5** Analyze how an author's choice of genre affects the expression of a theme or topic. **VO.10.4** Analyze the ways that historical events influenced the English language. *Also covered* **VO.10.6; WA.10.2; C.10.9**

Vocabulary Development

Vocabulary Check

Tell whether each sentence is true or false.

1. It frequently snows in **temperate** climates.
2. People put sunblock on their faces so that the sun does not damage their **complexions.**

Vocabulary Skills: Archaic Language

Shakespeare's plays are sometimes set in the present or in the recent past. In a contemporary movie version of *Hamlet,* for example, the prince works in a high-tech firm and intones his "To be or not to be" soliloquy (speech to himself) in a video store.

The English language has been through many changes and is changing still. New words and meanings are added, while others drift out of use. For example, in Shakespeare's day, the pronouns *thee* and *thou,* along with *thy* and *thine,* were used to address people with whom the speaker was familiar or intimate (wife, husband, close friend). *You, your,* and *yours* were used with people who were not intimate friends or who were the speaker's superiors (parents, bosses, kings). Shakespeare also used the verb endings *–st* and *–th* (as in *didst* and *goeth*), which are no longer used today. Today these words are archaic (except for *you* and *your,* of course). An **archaic** word is one that is no longer used.

Your Turn

What happens when you bring Shakespeare's language up to date? Find the archaic words in this sonnet, and replace each one with its modern equivalent. Then, read the sonnet aloud—first with the archaic words and then with the modern ones. Does the "translation" work?

CHOICES

As you respond to the Choices, use these **Academic Vocabulary** words as appropriate: transform, literal, evoke, and complement.

REVIEW
Compare and Contrast

Both tanka and sonnets have strict rules about their form. Think about the subject matter, form, and imagery of the tanka and the sonnet you have just read. Then, prepare a brief report comparing the imagery with the form in each poem. Can you draw any conclusions about the way imagery and form complement each other?

CONNECT
Prepare an Anthology

Group Project With a small group, find at least two examples each of prose poems, elegies, odes, tanka, and sonnets. Try to find examples from different eras and places on a wide variety of subjects. Then, create an anthology of these poems and make them available to your classmates.

EXTEND
Create Oral Histories

TechFocus Re-read "Eating Together" and "Grape Sherbet," two poems that deal with memory and family traditions. Then, interview someone you know—a relative, a friend, or a member of your community—about his or her own memories. Record or videotape this interview to create an oral history. Finally, write and record an introduction in which you offer your insights about the interview. With your interviewee's permission, share the oral history with your classmates.

Figures of Speech

CONTENTS

Plantoir (2000) by Claes Oldenburg and Coosje van Bruggen. Stainless steel, aluminum, reinforced plastic, painted with polyurethane enamel.
Photograph © 2002 The Metropolitan Museum.

What Do You Think

How can a poet <u>transform</u> an ordinary object into something extraordinary?

QuickWrite

Think of something that's familiar to you—perhaps a gadget, a place, or a feeling. How might you describe it to someone who is unfamiliar with it? Write a simple comparison.

Preparing to Read

Heart! We will forget him! /
The Moon was but a Chin of Gold

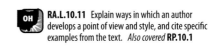 **RA.L.10.11** Explain ways in which an author develops a point of view and style, and cite specific examples from the text. *Also covered* **RP.10.1**

 **Reader/Writer Notebook**

Use your **RWN** to complete the activities for these selections.

Literary Focus

Personification and Metaphor A **metaphor** is a figure of speech in which two unlike things are compared without a connective word such as *like*, *as*, *than*, or *resembles*. **Personification** is a kind of metaphor in which a nonhuman thing or quality is talked about as if it were human. In "Heart! We will forget him!" the speaker addresses her heart as if it were a person who could listen, act, and feel. In "The Moon was but a Chin of Gold," the speaker compares the Moon to a beautiful woman.

Reading Focus

Visualizing Many figures of speech present visual images. To appreciate the power of these images, **visualize** them, or see them in your mind's eye. Focus on each image by closing your eyes and imagining what the speaker is describing.

Into Action For each image in "Heart! We will forget him!" and "The Moon was but a Chin of Gold," write what you see in your mind's eye.

"The Moon was but a Chin of Gold"

Images	What I See
"turns Her perfect Face / Upon the World below"	a full Moon

Writing Focus

Think as a Reader/Writer

Find It in Your Reading Emily Dickinson is known for her unusual punctuation and capitalization. She frequently uses dashes to insert pauses in unusual places and capitalizes words to give them emphasis. As you read her poems, notice these irregularities. Write a couple of these "irregular" lines in your *Reader/Writer Notebook*, and then "correct" them. Which version do you prefer? Why?

Vocabulary

The Moon was but a Chin of Gold

amplest (AM plehst) *adj.*: most abundant; fullest. *The hill outside town offers the amplest view of the night sky.*

hewn (hyoon) *v.* used as *adj.*: shaped by cutting or chiseling. *We examined precious stones hewn into various shapes.*

confer (kuhn FUR) *v.*: bestow or give. *The Moon confers its light upon the world.*

firmament (FUR muh muhnt) *n.*: the sky. *The stars and Moon appear in the wide firmament.*

Language Coach

Multiple-Meaning Words The word *confer* has more than one meaning. As used in "The Moon was but a Chin of Gold," it means "to give." You may have heard it used another way. What does it mean in this sentence? *You may want to confer with your teammates before you make your final decision.*

 **Learn It Online**
Take an in-depth look at terms using Word Watch at:

go.hrw.com L10-695 **Go**

Learn It Online
Learn more about Dickinson's life and work at:
go.hrw.com   L10-696   **Go**

Emily Dickinson

(1830–1886)

Shy Genius

Shy, reclusive Emily Dickinson rarely left Amherst, Massachusetts, her birthplace. There, she lived unknown as a poet except to her family and a few friends. She produced almost eighteen hundred exquisite short poems that are now regarded as one of the great expressions of American genius.

Dickinson was the bright, eldest daughter of a well-to-do religious family; her father was a lawyer. As a girl at boarding school, she seemed high spirited and happy. Then she became a young woman, and something occurred (a love that was not or could not be requited, biographers speculate). At age thirty-one, she simply withdrew from the world. She dressed all in white, refused to leave her home or meet strangers, and devoted her life to her family—and to writing poetry.

The Granger Collection, New York.

Letters to the World

Of her poetry, Dickinson wrote, "This is my letter to the World / That never wrote to Me. . . ." She wrote her poems on little pieces of paper, tied them in neat packets, and occasionally gave them to relatives as valentines or birthday greetings. Other times, she attached them to gifts of cookies or pies. In 1862, she sent four poems to the editor of the *Atlantic Monthly*. Only seven of her poems were published (anonymously) during her lifetime. When she died at age fifty-six, she had no idea that one day she would be honored as one of America's greatest poets.

In one of her many letters, Dickinson shared her definition of poetry:

"If I read a book [and] it makes my whole body so cold no fire ever can warm me I know that is poetry. If I feel physically as if the top of my head were taken off, I know that is poetry. These are the only ways I know it."

Think About the Writer

What might inspire a poet like Emily Dickinson, who lived a restricted life?

Heart! We will forget him!

by **Emily Dickinson**

Heart! We will forget him!
You and I— tonight!
You may forget the warmth he gave—
I will forget the light!

When you have done, pray tell me
That I may straight° begin!
Haste! lest while you're lagging
I remember him!

---

6. straight: immediately.

A **Literary Focus** **Personification** Why do you think the speaker treats her heart as a being separate from herself?

Blue Silhouette by Gerit Greve (c. 1951–1975).

Read with a Purpose Read this poem to appreciate Dickinson's description of the Moon as a woman.

The Moon was but a Chin of Gold

by **Emily Dickinson**

The Moon was but a Chin of Gold
A Night or two ago—
And now she turns Her perfect Face
Upon the World below—   **Ⓐ**

5   Her Forehead is of Amplest Blonde—
Her Cheek—a Beryl° hewn—
Her Eye unto the Summer Dew
The likest I have known—

Her Lips of Amber never part—
10   But what must be the smile
Upon Her Friend she could confer
Were such Her Silver Will—

And what a privilege to be
But the remotest Star—
15   For Certainty She takes Her Way
Beside Your Palace Door—

Her Bonnet is the Firmament—
The Universe—Her Shoe—
The Stars—the Trinkets at Her Belt—
20   Her Dimities°—of Blue—   **Ⓑ**

---

6. beryl: mineral that usually occurs in crystals of blue, green, pink, or yellow.

20. dimities: dresses made of dimity, a sheer, cool, cotton material.

Insomnia (2001) by John Hrehov. Courtesy of the artist and Denise Bibro Fine Art, New York.

Ⓐ Reading Focus Visualizing What shapes do you visualize for the Moon's "Chin of Gold" and "perfect Face"?

Ⓑ Literary Focus Personification What human qualities does the speaker give to the Moon?

Vocabulary amplest (AM plehst) *adj.:* most abundant; fullest.
hewn (hyoon) *v.* used as *adj.:* shaped by cutting or chiseling.
confer (kuhn FUR) *v.:* bestow or give.
firmament (FUR muh muhnt) *n.:* the sky.

Applying Your Skills

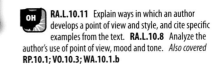

RA.L.10.11 Explain ways in which an author develops a point of view and style, and cite specific examples from the text. **RA.L.10.8** Analyze the author's use of point of view, mood and tone. *Also covered* **RP.10.1; VO.10.3; WA.10.1.b**

Heart! We will forget him! / The Moon was but a Chin of Gold

Respond and Think Critically

Reading Focus

Read with a Purpose

1. What different aspects of the beloved will the speaker forget in "Heart! We will forget him!"? What does the speaker's mind need the heart to do?

2. How does the speaker of "The Moon was but a Chin of Gold" envision the woman in the Moon? What is the speaker's attitude toward the Moon?

Reading Skills: Visualizing

3. Review your visualizations of the images from Dickinson's poems. In a few sentences, describe in your own words how visualizing the figures of speech helped you to understand and appreciate the poems.

✓ Vocabulary Check

Match each Vocabulary word to its synonym.

4. **amplest**   a. cut
5. **hewn**   b. sky
6. **confer**   c. fullest
7. **firmament**   d. grant or give

Literary Focus

Literary Analysis

8. **Infer** Who is the speaker of "Heart! We will forget him!"? What reveals the speaker's identity?

9. **Analyze** In "Heart! We will forget him!" which part of the speaker must begin the process of forgetting: her mind or heart? How do you know?

10. **Interpret** Paraphrase lines 3–4 of "Heart! We will forget him!" What does the speaker mean by "warmth" and "light"?

Literary Skills: Personification and Metaphor

11. **Analyze** How does personification in "Heart! We will forget him!" strengthen the poem's emotional impact?

12. **Describe** In "The Moon was but a Chin of Gold," what series of metaphors does Dickinson use to describe the Moon?

Literary Skills Review: Mood

13. **Analyze** **Mood** is the feeling and atmosphere that works of literature <u>evoke</u>. What is the mood of both "Heart! We will forget him!" and "The Moon was but a Chin of Gold"? How do specific words contribute to the mood of each poem?

Writing Focus

Think as a Reader/Writer

Use It in Your Writing In "Heart! We will forget him!" the speaker is trying to forget a person—presumably a person with whom she is in love. Imagine you are this unnamed character, and write a farewell poem to the speaker. Imitate Dickinson's style, capitalizing words for emphasis and inserting dashes for pauses within and at the ends of lines.

What Do You Think Now? How does Dickinson's imaginative use of language help readers see ordinary objects in extraordinary ways?

POETRY
Preparing to Read

since feeling is first

RA.L.10.11 Explain ways in which an author develops a point of view and style, and cite specific examples from the text. *Also covered* **RA.I.10.1**

Reader/Writer
Notebook

Use your **RWN** to complete the activities for this selection.

Literary Focus

Metaphor Like a simile, a **metaphor** is a surprising comparison between two unlike things. A metaphor is more direct than a simile—it usually states or implies that something *is* something else. In this poem, two lovers cannot bear to think of their love ending or of death separating them. Here the poet sings of love and puts down death, using two metaphors that only a writer would think of.

Reading Focus

Analyzing Word Choice Poets carefully consider their words because even synonyms can differ in subtle ways that affect meaning. For example, *large* and *gigantic* have similar meanings, but *gigantic* (related to *giant*) is more specific than *large*. A poet chooses a certain word for its associations, which enrich the meaning of the metaphor. Analyzing the poet's choice of words increases your understanding of the comparison and of the poem.

Into Action While you read this poem, pay attention to key words and their associations. Write the words and their associations in a chart.

Words	Associations
"fool"	silly, giggling

Writing Focus

Think as a Reader/Writer

Find It in Your Reading Experienced writers can be creative about applying the rules of grammar, punctuation, and capitalization. Notice examples of Cummings's creative punctuation and his unique interpretation of grammar rules in this poem. Record these examples in your *Reader/Writer Notebook*. Ask yourself, "Why might Cummings have broken rules of punctuation and grammar in a poem that actually uses punctuation and grammar as metaphors?"

Vocabulary

syntax (SIHN taks) *n.:* sentence structure; relationship of words in a sentence. *E. E. Cummings's syntax in the poem is unusual.*

gesture (JEHS chuhr) *n.:* a movement, usually by part of the body; an action. *The flutter of eyelids is an example of a gesture.*

parenthesis (puh REHN thuh sihs) *n.:* a curved line used in pairs to set off words or phrases, usually comments or explanations, in a sentence. *Although the poet uses the word* parenthesis, *the poem does not actually include a parenthesis.*

Language Coach

Plurals and Pronunciation The more common use of the word *parenthesis* is its plural form, *parentheses*, referring to the pair of curved lines used to set off information in a sentence. Although most plurals are formed by adding *–s* or *–es* to words, a few other words ending in *–sis* form their plurals by changing the final *–is* to *–es* (pronounced /ees/). According to these rules, what are the plural forms of *crisis, horse, glass, analysis,* and *school*?

Learn It Online
There's more to words than just definitions. Get the whole story at:

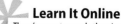go.hrw.com L10-700 Go

Learn more about Cummings at:
go.hrw.com L10-701 Go

E. E. Cummings (1894–1962)

"I Flourished Like the Wicked"

Edward Estlin Cummings grew up "only a butterfly's glide" from Harvard University in Cambridge, Massachusetts, and attended four Cambridge schools: "the first, private . . . where (in addition to learning nothing) I burst into tears and nosebleeds—the other three, public; where I flourished like the wicked and learned what the wicked learn, and where almost nobody cared about somebody else."

"Nobody Else Can Be Alive for You"

After graduating from Harvard, Cummings joined a U.S. ambulance corps in France during World War I. A French censor decided that one of Cummings's odd-looking letters home was suspicious. Cummings was arrested as a spy and held for three months in a prison camp, an experience he wrote about in his novel *The Enormous Room* (1922).

In his poetry, Cummings liked to use lowercase letters, space his words erratically across the page, and punctuate in his own style. Despite those oddities, his themes are familiar: the joy, wonder, and mystery of life and the miracle of individual identity. He once advised young poets to be themselves:

"Remember one thing only: that it's you—nobody else—who determines your destiny and decides your fate. Nobody else can be alive for you; nor can you be alive for anybody else."

Think About the Writer

What do Cummings's comments about his school experiences suggest about him as a writer?

since feeling is first

by **E. E. Cummings**

since feeling is first
who pays any attention
to the syntax of things
will never wholly kiss you;

5   wholly to be a fool
while Spring is in the world

my blood approves,
and kisses are a better fate
than wisdom
10   lady i swear by all flowers. Don't cry
—the best gesture of my brain is less than
your eyelids' flutter which says

we are for each other:then
laugh,leaning back in my arms
15   for life's not a paragraph   Ⓐ

And death i think is no parenthesis   Ⓑ

Ⓐ **Literary Focus** Metaphor Think about the features of a paragraph. Why might the speaker say life is not a paragraph?

Ⓑ **Reading Focus** Analyzing Word Choice *Parenthesis* can have three meanings: (1) a punctuation mark, (2) a word, phrase, or clause that adds an explanation or comment to a complete sentence, and (3) an interruption. Which meaning best fits the context of this poem? Why?

Vocabulary **syntax** (SIHN taks) *n.:* sentence structure; relationship of words in a sentence.
gesture (JEHS chuhr) *n.:* a movement, usually by part of the body; an action.
parenthesis (puh REHN thuh sihs) *n.:* a curved line used in pairs to set off words or phrases, usually comments or explanations, in a sentence.

Lovers (1929) by Marc Chagall. Oil on canvas (55" × 38"). © Tel Aviv Museum of Art.
Gift of Mr. Oscar Fischer, Tel Aviv, 1940/© 2008 Artists Rights Society (ARS), NY, ADAGP, Paris.

Analyzing Visuals

Viewing and Interpreting
In what way is the mood evoked by this painting reflected in the poem?

Applying Your Skills

RA.L.10.11 Explain ways in which an author develops a point of view and style, and cite specific examples from the text. RA.L.10.9 Explain how authors use symbols to create broader meanings. *Also covered* RA.I.10.1; VO.10.3; WA.10.1.b

since feeling is first

Respond and Think Critically

Reading Focus

Read with a Purpose

1. To whom does the speaker address this poem? How do you know?

Reading Skills: Analyzing Word Choice

2. Review your completed chart containing associations to words in the poem. In a third column, explain the effect created by these words and associations.

Word	Associations	Effect
"fool"	silly, giggling	

✔ Vocabulary Check

Choose the Vocabulary word that best completes each sentence.

3. To set off words, you need more than one (**parenthesis, simile**) in a sentence.
4. His smile was a friendly (**reminder, gesture**).
5. "Check your (**syntax, document**) before you turn in your sentences," the teacher reminded us.

Literary Focus

Literary Analysis

6. **Analyze** Notice the opposites Cummings uses. A person "who pays any attention to the syntax of things" (lines 2–3) is contrasted with someone who is "wholly . . . a fool" (line 5). What opposites does Cummings pose to wisdom (line 9), the brain (line 11), and life (line 15)? In each case, which opposite does the speaker choose?

7. **Interpret** How does the speaker contrast thinking and feeling?

8. **Infer** Why does Cummings mention spring in the poem and not the other seasons?

Literary Skills: Metaphor

9. **Explain** Cummings expresses his feelings about love and death in two metaphors. What are they, and what is being compared in these metaphors?

Literary Skills Review: Symbol

10. **Analyze** A **symbol** is a person, place, thing, or event that literally stands for itself and also for something beyond itself. In this poem, the speaker says his "blood approves" of spring and love. What might his blood symbolize?

Writing Focus

Think as a Reader/Writer

Use It in Your Writing In this poem, Cummings manipulates punctuation and capitalization to affect rhythm and tone and to comment on the importance (or unimportance) of syntax and rules in comparison to love and life. Write a brief poem, perhaps only a few lines, about a feeling, thought, or experience. Experiment with capitalization, punctuation, and spacing, and break grammar rules if you wish. How do these choices affect your poem's meaning?

What Do **You Think Now** How can a poet's playful use of language enable you to see the world differently? Explain.

POETRY
Preparing to Read

Simile / The Taxi

 RA.L.10.11 Explain ways in which an author develops a point of view and style, and cite specific examples from the text. *Also covered* **RA.I.10.1**

 **Reader/Writer Notebook**

Use your **RWN** to complete the activities for these selections.

Literary Focus

Simile A **simile** is a figure of speech that compares two unlike things by using a connecting word such as *like, as, than,* or *resembles.* Some similes, such as *as quiet as a mouse, like peas in a pod,* and *as busy as a bee,* are so overused they have become clichés. Rather than fall back on clichés, poets invent imaginative similes that no one has thought of yet. An **extended simile** continues the comparison for several lines or even throughout an entire poem.

Reading Focus

Analyzing Word Choice Skilled writers make every word count. Writers choose a word both for its **denotation**—the literal, or dictionary meaning, and its **connotation**—the associations and emotions attached to the word. For example, the words *large* and *bulky* have similar meanings, but *bulky* implies that something is not only big but also heavy, unwieldy, or clumsy.

Into Action As you read each poem, use concept maps to record key words and their connotations. In the center oval, write an important word from the poem. In the surrounding ovals, write some of the word's connotations.

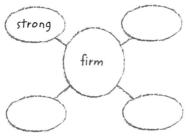

Writing Focus

Think as a Reader/Writer

Find It in Your Reading Each of the poems you are about to read centers on a question. Write or summarize the questions in your *Reader/Writer Notebook.* Then, write your answers to the following questions: What is the relationship between the poems' questions and the poems' themes? Why might the poets have chosen to use questions rather than statements?

Vocabulary

Simile

latent (LAY tuhnt) *adj.:* present but not active; concealed. *Though it stood still, the deer had a latent ability to run at a moment's notice.*

The Taxi

slackened (SLAK uhnd) *v.* used as *adj.:* made looser. *Drumheads should be tight when played; a slackened drum makes an odd sound.*

jutted (JUHT ihd) *v.* used as *adj.:* sticking out. *Everything seems harsh and sharp, from the jutted elbows of the passersby to the intense light of the lamps.*

Language Coach

Antonyms An **antonym** is a word that means the opposite of another word. Identify the antonyms of the Vocabulary words in the following sentences.

• I was walking my dog on a *slackened* leash, but when he ran after a squirrel, the leash became taut.

• In profile, one man had a chin that receded, while the other had one that *jutted.*

 Learn It Online
There's more to words than just definitions. Get the whole story on:

go.hrw.com | L10-705 | **Go**

N. Scott Momaday
(1934–   )

Pulitzer
Prize
WINNER

Heritage

N. Scott Momaday grew up hearing his father, a Kiowa storyteller, tell stories about the Kiowa people. As he grew older, he began writing these stories down so they would not be lost. Schooling was a problem at Jemez, New Mexico, where Momaday grew up, because there were no high schools nearby. He recalls his mother's influence: "I wanted, needed, to conceive of what my destiny might be, and my mother allowed me to believe that it might be worthwhile."

Momaday received his bachelor's degree from the University of New Mexico and his doctorate in English from Stanford University. He has created novels, memoirs, poems, and paintings that draw upon his Native American heritage.

Amy Lowell
(1874–1925)

Pulitzer
Prize
WINNER

A Self-Made Poet

Born to a wealthy and prominent Boston family, Amy Lowell was not shy about speaking up, even as a young girl. As a student, she was "totally indifferent to classroom decorum. Noisy, opinionated, and spoiled, she terrorized the other students and spoke back to her teachers." Because her family would not send her to college, Lowell took her higher education into her own hands, reading her way through her father's seven-thousand-volume library.

Lowell was very critical of her first poem, but later said, "[I] made myself a poet." After her death, Lowell was awarded the Pulitzer Prize in Poetry for her collection *What's O'clock* in 1926.

Think
About the
Writers
How might these poets' independent spirits influence their poetry?

Build Background

Early in her career, Amy Lowell discovered **imagism,** a movement in poetry that emphasized the use of clear, precise language to convey visual images. Although present in all of Lowell's poetry, imagism is especially evident in this poem, which was published as part of the collection titled *Sword Blades and Poppy Seeds* in 1914.

Simile

by **N. Scott Momaday**

What did we say to each other
that now we are as the deer   **Ⓐ**
who walk in single file
with heads high
with ears forward
with eyes watchful
with hooves always placed on firm ground
in whose limbs there is latent flight   **Ⓑ**

Ⓐ **Literary Focus** Simile   What has happened that causes the speaker to compare himself and his loved one with deer?

Ⓑ **Reading Focus** Analyzing Word Choice   What effect does the poet create by repeating the word *with* at the beginning of several lines?

Vocabulary   **latent** (LAY tuhnt) *adj.:* present but not active; concealed.

The Deer Wedding (1959) by Ivan Generalic. Private collection.

The Taxi

by **Amy Lowell**

Melancholy of Turin (1915) by Giorgio de Chirico.
Private collection/© 2009 Artists Rights Society (ARS), NY/SIAE, Rome.

When I go away from you
The world beats dead
Like a slackened drum. **A**
I call out for you against the jutted stars
5   And shout into the ridges of the wind.
Streets coming fast,
One after the other,
Wedge you away from me,
And the lamps of the city prick my eyes
10   So that I can no longer see your face.
Why should I leave you,
To wound myself upon the sharp edges of the night? **B**

A **Literary Focus** Simile What two things does the writer compare in this line? What mood does this simile evoke?

B **Reading Focus** Analyzing Word Choice Which words in this poem carry negative connotations?

Vocabulary **slackened** (SLAK uhnd) *v.* used as *adj.*: made looser.
jutted (JUHT ihd) *v.* used as *adj.*: sticking out.

Applying Your Skills

OH RA.L.10.11 Explain ways in which an author develops a point of view and style, and cite specific examples from the text. RA.L.10.8 Analyze the author's use of point of view, mood and tone. *Also covered* RA.I.10.1; VO.10.3; WA.10.1.b

Simile / The Taxi

Respond and Think Critically

Reading Focus

Read with a Purpose

1. What images does each poet use to describe the feeling of separation from a loved one?

Reading Skills: Analyzing Word Choice

2. Review the concept maps you created for each poem. Choose one key word. Then, think of another word with the same denotation but different connotations. Make a concept map for the new word. If you were to replace the original word in the poem with this word, how would the meaning change? Would the replacement word be effective? Explain.

rigid — unforgiving
hard
cold

✓ Vocabulary Check

Write true (T) or false (F) for each of the following sentences, and write a sentence explaining your answer.

3. If something is **latent,** it is easily seen.
4. A **slackened** rope is pulled tight.
5. Someone could trip over a **jutted** rock.

Literary Focus

Literary Analysis

6. **Compare and Contrast** What type of separation is described in each poem: physical, emotional, or both? What are some similarities and differences in the poets' descriptions of the feeling of separation?

7. **Evaluate** Explain whether the image of the deer in "Simile" is an effective simile for this particular situation. Is the image of "the sharp edges of the night" in "The Taxi" effective? Explain.

Literary Skills: Simile

8. **Extend** Momaday and Lowell use markedly different similes to capture the feeling of separation. What other similes might you use to describe this state or emotion?

Literary Skills Review: Mood

9. **Describe Mood** is the emotional effect or atmosphere of a work of literature. Describe the mood of each of these poems. What moods do the different types of separation evoke?

Writing Focus

Think as a Reader/Writer

Use It in Your Writing Review the questions in "Simile" and "The Taxi." Think of a question about yourself or another person. You should not be able to answer the question easily. Use the question as the theme for a short poem in **free verse** (without a set meter or form). Once you have your question, think about similes you can use to answer the question. Include the question and the similes in your poem.

What Do You Think Now? What can similes and other examples of figurative language convey that more literal descriptions cannot? Explain.

Preparing to Read

miss rosie / this morning

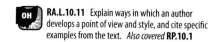

RA.L.10.11 Explain ways in which an author develops a point of view and style, and cite specific examples from the text. *Also covered* **RP.10.1**

Reader/Writer Notebook

Use your **RWN** to complete the activities for these selections.

Literary Focus

Idiom and Metaphor An **idiom** is an expression that cannot be understood as a mere <u>literal</u> definition of its words. For example, the literal meaning of *to fall in love* is absurd. The expression actually means that the experience of love is so overwhelming that it *feels like* losing your footing, plunging into a pool, or falling into a trap.

In the same way, many idioms contain implied **metaphors,** or comparisons between unlike things. When the speaker in "this morning" compares herself to a black bell, she is implying a comparison between the speaker and something that makes a beautiful sound.

> **Language Coach**
>
> **Root Words** In "this morning," Lucille Clifton uses the word *survive* three times. *Survive* includes the root *–viv–*, which means "to live." What other words do you know that have this root? Do they have related meanings? Explain.

Reading Focus

Reading Aloud In poems with little or no punctuation, reading aloud can help you get a sense of where ideas begin and end. Reading aloud can also help you understand idioms and metaphors.

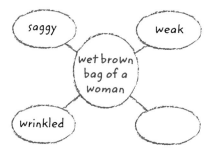

Into Action Slowly read aloud the following poems, listening for idioms and metaphors. Use a concept map like the one above to list feelings and images you associate with each figure of speech or idiom.

Writing Focus

Think as a Reader/Writer

Find It in Your Reading As you read these poems, notice how figures of speech give you a clear picture of each subject. List examples in your *Reader/Writer Notebook*.

Learn It Online
Hear a professional actor read these poems. Visit the selections online at:

go.hrw.com | L10-710 | **Go**

Lucille Clifton
(1936–   )

National
Book Award
WINNER

Perpetuation and Celebration

As a young adult, Lucille Clifton discovered that "one could write and take it seriously and have it matter." She has been writing fiction and poetry that matter ever since. One of Clifton's best-known works is *Generations* (1976), a poetic memoir composed of portraits of five generations of her family. The memoir begins with her great-great-grandmother, who was brought from Africa to New Orleans and sold into slavery. Like all of Clifton's work, *Generations* is honest but rarely bitter. As one critic observed, her purpose is perpetuation and celebration, not judgment.

An Ongoing Story

Clifton says that family stories are part of what makes us who we are. She remembers hearing her family's stories when she was growing up. "My father told those stories to me over and over. That made them seem important. . . . I think there is a matter of preserving the past for the future's sake. I think if we see our lives as an ongoing story, it's important to include all the ingredients of it and not have it in little compartments. . . . I've always wondered the hows and the whys to things. Why is this like this? What has gone into making us who we are? . . . What is destroying us? What will keep us warm?"

Think
About the
Writer

Why are family stories and connections important to Clifton?

Preview the Selections

The poem "miss rosie" is a descriptive portrait of the **Georgia Rose,** who has seen better days.

The speaker of "this morning" is a student at Eastern High School.

In both of these poems, pay attention to the repeated words and phrases, which will help you analyze the speaker's attitude.

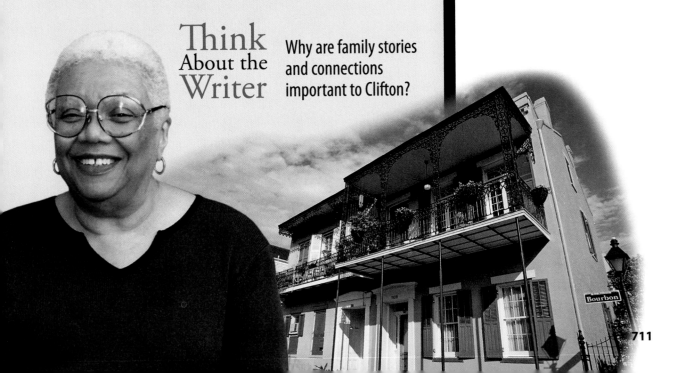

miss rosie

by **Lucille Clifton**

when i watch you
wrapped up like garbage
sitting, surrounded by the smell
of too old potato peels
5   or
when i watch you
in your old man's shoes
with the little toe cut out
sitting, waiting for your mind
10 like next week's grocery   Ⓐ
i say
when i watch you
you wet brown bag of a woman
who used to be the best looking gal in georgia
15 used to be called the Georgia Rose
i stand up
through your destruction
i stand up   Ⓑ

Ⓐ **Literary Focus** **Idiom and Metaphor** What is the significance of comparing Miss Rosie's mind to "next week's grocery"?

Ⓑ **Reading Focus** **Reading Aloud** Without periods and commas to guide you, how do you know where to pause as you read the poem aloud?

Detail from *Mirage* (1993)
by Catherine Howe.
Oil on canvas.
Collection Alan P. Power,
Venice, California.

this morning

by **Lucille Clifton**

this morning
this morning
    i met myself
coming in

5 a bright
jungle girl
shining
quick as a snake
a tall
10 tree girl a
me girl
    i met myself
this morning
coming in **Ⓐ**

15 and all day
i have been
a black bell
ringing
i survive
20   survive
survive **Ⓑ**

May Flowers from the series *May Days Long Forgotten* by Carrie Mae Weems.

Ⓐ Literary Focus Metaphor   What images do the metaphors in this stanza create?

Ⓑ Reading Focus Reading Aloud   What is the effect of the repetition when you read the poem aloud?

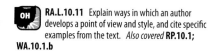

RA.L.10.11 Explain ways in which an author develops a point of view and style, and cite specific examples from the text. *Also covered* **RP.10.1; WA.10.1.b**

miss rosie / this morning

Respond and Think Critically

Reading Focus

Read with a Purpose

1. How has Miss Rosie changed over time? Why do you think the speaker does not say what changed Miss Rosie?

2. What words suggest that the speaker in "this morning" sees herself as unique?

Reading Skills: Reading Aloud

3. Look back at the concept maps you made as you read. For each idiom or metaphor, write a sentence stating its figurative meaning. Read the expression aloud. How do the feelings or associations tied to each expression make the expression's meaning richer?

saggy · weak · wet brown bag of a woman · wrinkled

Literary Focus

Literary Analysis

4. **Evaluate** Which figure of speech in "miss rosie" do you think is the most powerful? Explain.

5. **Analyze** Identify three examples of sensory imagery from "miss rosie," such as words describing touch or smell. In what way do these images shape your vision of Miss Rosie?

6. **Interpret** What might the speaker mean by "this morning / I met myself / coming in"?

7. **Compare and Contrast** Each of these poems paints a portrait of a person at a different stage of life. How are these people different from each other? What do they have in common?

Literary Skills: Idiom and Metaphor

8. **Interpret** The idiom "i stand up," used twice, gives the most important clue to how the writer wants us to feel about Miss Rosie. What does standing up in the face of Miss Rosie's decline mean? Why might the speaker be moved to "stand up" for Miss Rosie?

9. **Analyze** How does each metaphor in "this morning" <u>complement</u> the others?

Literary Skills Review: Simile

10. **Explain** A **simile** is a figure of speech that compares two *unlike* things by using a connective word such as *like, as, than,* or *resembles.* What similes do you find in these poems? What images do these similes create?

Writing Focus

Think as a Reader/Writer

Use It in Your Writing In very few words, Clifton gives us clear pictures of Miss Rosie and the speaker of "this morning." Write a brief paragraph or poem using figures of speech to describe someone you know.

What Do You Think Now

How does Clifton <u>transform</u> the subjects of "miss rosie" and "this morning" into something larger than themselves?

FIGURES OF SPEECH
Wrap Up

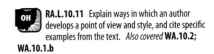

RA.L.10.11 Explain ways in which an author develops a point of view and style, and cite specific examples from the text. *Also covered* **WA.10.2; WA.10.1.b**

Vocabulary Development

Vocabulary Skills: Idioms

Remember that idioms, like other figures of speech, are not true in a <u>literal</u> sense. They are quite common, and you probably use them every day. "Raining cats and dogs," "to have the upper hand," and "under the weather" are examples. If you do not understand the meaning of an idiom, pay attention to the context in which it is used. If you overhear an expression with which you are not familiar, ask the speaker about it. To learn more about idioms, complete the following activities.

Your Turn

1. Re-read "miss rosie" and "this morning," and note all of the expressions you would classify as idioms. With a partner, discuss what emotions and images the idioms <u>evoke</u>.

2. Ask your family, your neighbors, or students in your school to list their favorite idioms in English or in other languages. With a small group of classmates, compile your surveys into a dictionary of idioms to share with the class.

Language Coach

Root Word The word root *–viv–* can mean "to live" or "life." Match the following words with their meanings.

1. **survive**   a. bring back to life; restore
2. **vivid**   b. lively; animated; full of energy
3. **revive**   c. continue to live
4. **vivacious** d. full of life; strong and clear

CHOICES

As you respond to the Choices, use these **Academic Vocabulary** words as appropriate: <u>transform</u>, <u>literal</u>, <u>evoke</u>, and <u>complement</u>.

REVIEW
Compare Poems

Timed ⏳ **Writing** In an essay, compare and contrast the use of figurative language by Dickinson, Lowell, and Clifton. Before you begin writing, identify metaphors, similes, and examples of personification in the poems. What do these figures of speech describe: people, feelings, or things?

CONNECT
Write a Description

Several of these poems are inspired by what the poets have seen and experienced. Think of something memorable that you have witnessed or experienced. Write a poem or descriptive paragraph about that event. Use figurative language in your description.

EXTEND
Research an Individual

TechFocus In "miss rosie," Lucille Clifton describes the <u>transformation</u> of Miss Rosie from "the Georgia Rose" to a "wet brown bag of a woman." Think of a public figure or a person from history —perhaps even someone you know—who experienced a drastic change during his or her lifetime. Use the Internet to do research on this person's life. What do we learn about ourselves by learning how other people change? On your school's Web site, post a brief summary of what you have learned.

 Learn It Online
There's more to these poems than meets the eye. Expand your view at:

go.hrw.com | L10-715 | **Go**

Sounds of Poetry

CONTENTS

STOMP performing their unique brand of theater, created by musicians using everyday objects in nontraditional ways.

 How do sounds inspire us?

 QuickTalk
Get together with a partner and talk about different sounds that you hear every day. What sounds do you find pleasant or painful? Why?

POETRY
Preparing to Read

Sea Fever

Reader/Writer Notebook

Use your **RWN** to complete the activities for this selection.

Literary Focus

Meter and Rhyme **Meter** is a generally regular pattern of stressed and unstressed syllables in poetry. Meter is measured in units called **feet.** A foot usually consists of one stressed syllable and one or more unstressed syllables.

Rhyme is probably the one feature most people identify with poetry, especially rhyme at the ends of lines in a poem. (Of course, many poems, especially modern ones, do not rhyme.) Rhyme is the repetition of vowel sounds and all sounds following them in words that are close together in a poem. *Glasses* and *masses* rhyme, as do *potato* and *tomato*. Usually, rhymes create a particular pattern in a poem, which is called a **rhyme scheme.**

Vocabulary

vagrant (VAY gruhnt) *adj.*: moving from place to place with no obvious means of support. *Many gypsies live a vagrant existence, never settling in one place for very long.*

whetted (HWEHT ihd) *adj.*: sharpened. *A whetted knife cuts more easily than a dull one does.*

Reading Focus

Reading Aloud Poetry is meant to be read aloud. Meter, one element of the music of poetry, sets the rhythm for reading. With a partner or a small group, take turns reading "Sea Fever" aloud. Pay attention to how the rhymes contribute to the overall sound and musicality of the poem. Where do you feel the rolling rhythm of the sea or hear the slap of the waves?

Into Action Before you read, write down the first few lines of the poem. Then, as you read, scan the poem by indicating the syllables that are stressed with / ′ / and the unstressed syllables with / ˘ /. Also, underline any repeated sounds. See below for an example.

I must go down to the seas again, to the lonely sea and the sky.

Language Coach

Multiple-Meaning Words Many words have more than one meaning. Sometimes you come across a familiar word, but the word does not make sense with the rest of the sentence. In "Sea Fever," for example, the word *breaking* (line 4) means "starting," not "falling to pieces." What do the words *running* (line 5) and *yarn* (line 11) mean in the poem? Use a dictionary to look up the words.

Writing Focus

Think as a Reader/Writer

Find It in Your Reading Poets often use repetition to emphasize an important idea. As you read the poem, write in your *Reader/Writer Notebook* the words and phrases that Masefield chooses to repeat.

 Learn It Online
There's more to words than just definitions. Get the whole story on:

go.hrw.com L10-717 **Go**

John Masefield
(1878–1967)

Sailor-Poet

John Masefield was born in England and orphaned by the time he was thirteen. As boys could do in those days, he left school, joined the merchant navy, and shipped around the world for several years. On a trip to New York, he jumped ship and lived for a time homeless in the city. He began to write poetry after coming across a collection of Chaucer's *Canterbury Tales* in a New York bookstore.

Masefield is best remembered today for poems inspired by the years he spent as a seaman, first on windjammers in the last days of the sailing ships and then on tramp steamers and ocean liners. No one has better <u>evoked</u> the sense of freedom and adventure, the taste of salt and spray associated with sailing "before the mast," or the pride that marked the crews of even the rustiest and dingiest of freighters.

For more than thirty years, Masefield served as Britain's poet laureate. Of his passion for sailing ships, the poet said:

"They were the only youth I had, and the only beauty I knew in my youth, and now that I am old, not many greater beauties seem to be in the world."

Think About the Writer

Why do you think John Masefield felt so passionately about sailing ships and about the sea?

Build Background

Although supertankers and cruise ships are much taller than sailing ships, the term *tall ship* is still used to describe a sailing vessel with high masts. For millions of sailors and nonsailors alike, the image of a tall ship triggers dreams of romance, freedom, and adventure, just as it did for Masefield.

"The wheel's kick" in line 3 is a reference to what can happen when a sudden shift in the wind or tide causes a ship's steering wheel to "kick over"—to spin out of control until the person at the helm can grab it and put the ship back on course. *Trick* is a sailing term for a round-trip voyage. Years ago, a "long trick" might have involved a voyage from England to China and back, a trip that could last for more than a year.

Sea Fever
by John Masefield

I must go down to the seas again, to the lonely sea and the sky,
And all I ask is a tall ship and a star to steer her by;
And the wheel's kick and the wind's song and the white sail's shaking,
And a gray mist on the sea's face and a gray dawn breaking.

5 I must go down to the seas again, for the call of the running tide
Is a wild call and a clear call that may not be denied;
And all I ask is a windy day with the white clouds flying,
And the flung spray and blown spume,° and the sea gulls crying.

I must go down to the seas again, to the vagrant gypsy life,
10 To the gull's way and the whale's way where the wind's like a whetted
      knife;
And all I ask is a merry yarn from a laughing fellow-rover.
And a quiet sleep and a sweet dream when the long trick's over. **Ⓐ**

8. **spume** (spyoom):
foam or froth on a
liquid, as on the sea.

Ⓐ Literary Focus Meter and Rhyme What is the rhyme scheme of these lines?

Vocabulary vagrant (VAY gruhnt) *adj.:* moving from place to place with no obvious
means of support.
whetted (HWEHT ihd) *adj.:* sharpened.

Applying Your Skills

RA.L.10.10 Describe the effect of using sound devices in literary texts. **RA.L.10.11** Explain ways in which an author develops a point of view and style, and cite specific examples from the text. *Also covered* **RP.10.1; VO.10.6; WA.10.1.b**

Sea Fever

Respond and Think Critically

Reading Focus

Read with a Purpose

1. What feelings does the speaker associate with sailing on the ocean? What kind of life does he yearn for?

Reading Skills: Reading Aloud

2. Look back at the lines you scanned from "Sea Fever." Discuss the meter with your partner or group. How would you describe it? Is it fast or slow, regular or irregular? Which line from the poem do you think best captures the movement of the ocean?

✓ Vocabulary Check

For each of the following Vocabulary words, pick the best synonym (word with a similar meaning).

3. **vagrant**
   a. hungry   **b.** wandering   **c.** lost

4. **whetted**
   a. flooded   **b.** sharpened   **c.** delivered

Literary Focus

Literary Analysis

5. **Infer** Think about expressions that use the term *fever* metaphorically, such as *spring fever* or *gold-rush fever*. What exactly is "sea fever"?

6. **Evaluate** Masefield wrote this poem to share his love of and excitement about the sea. After reading the poem, do you understand the appeal of sailing the seas as the speaker describes the experience? What appealed to you or failed to appeal to you?

7. **Analyze** What specific images in the poem help you see, hear, and even feel the life the speaker longs for?

Literary Skills: Meter and Rhyme

8. **Analyze** Read the poem aloud again. How does the meter reinforce the feeling of the wheel's kick and the roll of the sea?

9. **Identify** Masefield uses alliteration throughout the poem to create his sea song. Where is alliteration especially strong?

Literary Skills Review: Figurative Language

10. **Identify** **Figurative language** is based on some kind of comparison that is not literally true. A **metaphor** is a direct comparison, and a **simile** is a comparison using *like* or *as*. Find one metaphor and one simile in the poem. What feeling does each figure of speech evoke?

Writing Focus

Think as a Reader/Writer

Use It in Your Writing Masefield uses repetition to stress how strongly he feels "sea fever." Write a poem in which you describe a place you long to go back to, a person you wish you could see, or a goal you absolutely must accomplish. Try to use rhyme and meter to emphasize the mood, musicality, and sound of your poem.

What Do You Think Now?

What sounds of the sea served as inspiration for Masefield?

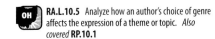

OH **RA.L.10.5** Analyze how an author's choice of genre affects the expression of a theme or topic. *Also covered* **RP.10.1**

Reader/Writer Notebook

Use your **RWN** to complete the activities for these selections.

Literary Focus

Ballad A **ballad** is a song or songlike poem that tells a story. Most ballads use simple language and two of the oldest elements of poetry: a strong meter and a **refrain** (whole lines or stanzas repeated at regular intervals). Traditional **folk ballads,** like "Bonny Barbara Allan," have been passed down orally from generation to generation. **Literary ballads**, such as "Ballad of the Landlord," are written by a known author and imitate folk ballads. Ballads are written to be sung; "Bonny Barbara Allan" is like a folk song, while "Ballad of the Landlord" is like an old blues song.

Literary Perspectives Apply the literary perspective described on page 724 as you read "Ballad of the Landlord."

Reading Focus

Reading a Poem Aloud Read "Bonny Barbara Allan" and "Ballad of the Landlord" in choral readings. Determine how many speakers the ballads have and which lines can be recited by a chorus. Experiment with the volume, pitch, and tone of your voice to express the speakers' feelings.

	Lines	Reading Aloud
Barbara Allan	1–7	Chorus speaks: stanza 2 sounds foreboding.
	8	Barbara— stern, cold voice
Landlord		

Into Action As you read, make a chart for reading the lines aloud. Note where to pause and how to vary the speakers' voices.

Writing Focus

Think as a Reader/Writer

Find It in Your Reading As you read, find expressions that reflect the **diction,** or word choice, of a young man in the 1600s and an African American in the 1930s. Note them in your *Reader/Writer Notebook.*

Vocabulary

Bonny Barbara Allan

courted (KAWRT ihd) *v.:* dated; wooed. *William courted Barbara Allan because he loved her.*

slighted (SLYT ihd) *v.:* paid too little attention to. *William slighted Barbara Allan when he forgot to mention her name.*

Language Coach

Denotation/Connotation Many words have a positive or negative emotional association (**connotation**) in addition to their literal, or dictionary, definition (**denotation**). For example, in "Bonny Barbara Allan," the literal meaning of *lapped* (line 51) is "wrapped around." *Lapped* also has a positive connotation of something that is loving and tender. Look through both poems and identify three words with positive or negative connotations. Explain each word's emotional associations.

Learn It Online
Hear a professional actor read these poems. Visit the selections online at:

| go.hrw.com | L10-721 | Go |

Bonny Barbara Allan

by **Anonymous**

Oh, in the merry month of May,
When all things were a-blooming,
Sweet William came from the Western states
And courted Barbara Allan.

5 But he took sick, and very sick
And he sent for Barbara Allan,
And all she said when she got there,
"Young man, you are a-dying."

"Oh yes, I'm sick, and I'm very sick,
10 And I think that death's upon me;
But one sweet kiss from Barbara's lips
Will save me from my dying." **Ⓐ**

"But don't you remember the other day
You were down in town a-drinking?
15 You drank your health to the ladies all around,
And slighted Barbara Allan."

"Oh yes, I remember the other day
I was down in town a-drinking;
I drank my health to the ladies all 'round.
20 But my love to Barbara Allan."

Lovers in a Garden (c. 1487–1495). Painting from a French illuminated manuscript. British Library, London.

Ⓐ Reading Focus **Reading Aloud** How should William sound as he speaks these lines?

Vocabulary **courted** (KAWRT ihd) *v.:* dated; wooed.
slighted (SLYT ihd) *v.:* paid too little attention to.

He turned his face to the wall;
She turned her back upon him;
The very last word she heard him say,
"Hardhearted Barbara Allan."

25   As she passed on through London Town,
She heard some bells a-ringing,
And every bell, it seemed to say,
"Hardhearted Barbara Allan."   **Ⓑ**

She then passed on to the country road,
30   And heard some birds a-singing;
And every bird, it seemed to say,
"Hardhearted Barbara Allan."

She hadn't got more than a mile from town
When she saw his corpse a-coming;
35   "O bring him here, and ease him down,
And let me look upon him.

"Oh, take him away! Oh, take him away!
For I am sick and dying!
His death-cold features say to me,
40   'Hardhearted Barbara Allan.'

"O Father, O Father, go dig my grave,
And dig it long and narrow;
Sweet William died for me today;
I'll die for him tomorrow."

45   They buried them both in the old graveyard,
All side and side each other.
A red, red rose grew out of his grave,
And a green briar out of hers.

They grew and grew so very high
50   That they could grow no higher;
They lapped, they tied in a truelove knot—
The rose ran 'round the briar.

Ⓑ **Literary Focus** Ballad   What is the refrain in this ballad? How does the repetition make you feel about Barbara Allan?

BALLAD OF THE LANDLORD

by **Langston Hughes**

Landlord, landlord,
My roof has sprung a leak.
Don't you 'member I told you about it
Way last week?

5   Landlord, landlord,
These steps is broken down.
When you come up yourself
It's a wonder you don't fall down. **Ⓐ**

Ten Bucks you say I owe you?
10   Ten Bucks you say is due?
Well, that's Ten Bucks more'n I'll pay you
Till you fix this house up new.

What? You gonna get eviction orders?
You gonna cut off my heat?
15   You gonna take my furniture and
Throw it in the street?

Um-huh! You talking high and mighty.
Talk on—till you get through.
You ain't gonna be able to say a word
20   If I land my fist on you.

Literary Perspectives

Analyzing Historical Context   When you analyze the historical context of a poem, you need to consider what was happening during the time period in which the author was writing. Hughes wrote "Ballad of the Landlord" during the 1930s. During this time, many African Americans migrated from the rural South to big cities in the North in search of work, a movement that came to be known as the Great Migration. This poem describes the anger and frustration African American tenants experienced in trying to get their landlords, many of whom were white, to make basic repairs to their apartments. As you read, use the notes and questions in the text to guide you in using this perspective.

Ⓐ Literary Focus Ballad   What characteristics of the ballad form can you find in these first stanzas?

They Live in Fire Traps by Jacob Lawrence. Gouache over graphite on paper.

Worcester Art Museum, Massachusetts/© 2009 The Jacob and Gwendolyn Lawrence Foundation, Seattle/Artists Rights Society (ARS), NY.

Police! Police!
Come and get this man!
He's trying to ruin the government
And overturn the Lord!

25   Copper's° whistle!
       Patrol bell!
       Arrest!

       Precinct Station.
       Iron cell.
30   Headlines in press:

       MAN THREATENS LANDLORD
       TENANT HELD NO BAIL
       JUDGE GIVES NEGRO 90 DAYS IN COUNTY JAIL **Ⓑ**

25. copper (KAHP uhr): police officer.

Ⓑ **Literary Perspectives** **Analyzing Historical Context** Which stanza clues you in to the time period of this poem?

Analyzing Visuals **Viewing and Interpreting** What details in this painting remind you of the first speaker in the poem?

Man with Dog (1999) by Willie Birch. RBC Dan Rauscher Art Collection. Courtesy Luise Ross Gallery, New York.

Applying Your Skills

RA.L.10.5 Analyze how an author's choice of genre affects the expression of a theme or topic.
RA.L.10.2 Analyze the features of setting and their importance in a literary text. *Also covered* RP.10.1; VO.10.3; WA.10.1.b

Bonny Barbara Allan / Ballad of the Landlord

Respond and Think Critically

Reading Focus

Read with a Purpose

1. Why do you think "Bonny Barbara Allan" has remained popular throughout the ages?
2. What conflict does Hughes describe in "Ballad of the Landlord"?

Reading Skills: Reading Aloud

3. Review the table you created as you read the ballads. Then, add a column on the right to identify the overall mood of the poems.

	Lines	Reading Aloud	Mood of Poem
"Barbara Allan"	1–7	Chorus speaks: stanza 2 sounds foreboding.	
	8	Barbara—stern, cold voice	
"Landlord"			

✓ Vocabulary Check

Choose the Vocabulary word that best completes each sentence.

      courted   **slighted**

4. The young man _____ the actress for months, bringing her flowers and writing her ballads.
5. Time and time again, he _____ her, reading or looking around the room while she talked.

Literary Focus

Literary Analysis

6. **Infer** Ballads don't always tell the whole story. What details are left out of "Bonny Barbara Allan"?
7. **Analyze** In "Ballad of the Landlord," who is speaking? What nontraditional devices does Hughes use to tell the story?
8. **Literary Perspectives** How does knowing the historical context of "Ballad of the Landlord" help you understand the poem?

Literary Skills: Ballad

9. **Evaluate** Which ballad do you think does a better job of expressing emotions? Which has the stronger effect on you? Support your answer with details from the poems.

Literary Skills Review: Setting and Mood

10. Describe the **setting** (time and place) of "Ballad of the Landlord." How does the poem's setting complement its mood?

Writing Focus

Think as a Reader/Writer

Use It in Your Writing The diction in both poems contributes to their tone and mood. Choose one ballad and rewrite it, using today's language.

 What Do You Think Now

What sounds and rhythms did you hear when you read these ballads aloud? What effect did they have on you?

Preparing to Read

The Flying Cat / Today

RA.L.10.5 Analyze how an author's choice of genre affects the expression of a theme or topic.
RA.L.10.11 Explain ways in which an author develops a point of view and style, and cite specific examples from the text. *Also covered* **RA.I.10.1**

Reader/Writer Notebook

Use your **RWN** to complete the activities for these selections.

Literary Focus

Free Verse Like many contemporary poets, Naomi Shihab Nye and Billy Collins write in **free verse.** This kind of poetry does not use a regular meter or rhyme scheme but instead attempts to imitate the natural rhythms of speech. The poems you are about to read have a distinct rhythm, created by a mix of long and short sentences and run-on lines (lines that do not end with punctuation). The repetition of words or grammatical structures also adds to the rhythm of each poem.

Reading Focus

Analyzing Word Choice A poet chooses words carefully for their sound, their meaning, and their **connotations** (the feelings or associations attached to a word). For example, in "The Flying Cat," Nye writes, "Sometimes you get an answer, / sometimes a click." Why do you think she chooses the word *click* instead of *dial tone*?

Into Action As you read each poem, create a chart like the one below. Write the words and phrases that suggest strong images or feelings in the left column, and describe the images and connotations associated with the words in the right column.

"The Flying Cat"

Word/Phrase	Image/Connotation
explode	a cat exploding / violent, horrific act

Vocabulary

The Flying Cat

droll (drohl) *adj.:* odd; wryly amusing.
From her droll expression, I knew that she thought my questions were ridiculous.

Today

intermittent (ihn tuhr MIHT uhnt) *adj.:* stopping and starting again. *The intermittent cloudiness did not spoil our picnic.*

Language Coach

Synonyms and Antonyms A **synonym** is a word with the same or nearly the same meaning as another word, and an **antonym** is a word with an opposite meaning. Synonyms for the word *intermittent* include *occasional* and *periodic.* One antonym is *constant.* As you read the following poems, use a dictionary to identify the synonyms and antonyms of at least three additional words. Keep in mind that not every word with a synonym has an antonym.

Writing Focus

Think as a Reader/Writer

Find It in Your Reading The speaker in each poem expresses strong emotions. Find the words that show how each speaker feels. Write the title of each poem in your *Reader/Writer Notebook* and list words or phrases that clearly suggest the speaker's feelings.

 Learn It Online
There's more to words than just definitions. Get the whole story on:

go.hrw.com | L10-728 | **Go**

Naomi Shihab Nye
(1952–   )

Moments We All Share

Naomi Shihab Nye writes poems, stories, essays, and songs. In her first two collections of poetry, *Different Ways to Pray* (1980) and *Hugging the Jukebox* (1982), Nye focuses on the experiences people from different cultures share. In *Yellow Glove* (1986), several poems deal with small, everyday objects—a recurring focus of her work.

> "Since I was a small child, I've felt that little inanimate things were very wise, that they had their own kind of wisdom, something to teach me if I would only pay the right kind of attention to them."

Billy Collins
(1941–   )

The Joy of the Everyday

Billy Collins is a bestselling poet whose free and flexible verse style is often witty and funny. His collections include *Sailing Alone Around the Room* (2001); *Picnic, Lightning* (1998); and *The Art of Drowning* (1995). In 2001 and 2002, Collins served consecutive terms as the U.S. Poet Laureate.

Think About the Writers

Both poets write about everyday objects and common experiences. Why do such subjects make poetry especially appealing?

Preview the Selections

In "The Flying Cat," the speaker addresses an unusual concern—what will happen to her cat in an airplane's baggage compartment. In "Today," the speaker describes a perfect spring day.

The Flying Cat

by **Naomi Shihab Nye**

Never, in all your career of worrying, did you imagine
what worries could occur concerning the flying cat.
You are traveling to a distant city.
The cat must travel in a small box with holes.

5   Will the baggage compartment be pressurized?
     Will a soldier's footlocker fall on the cat during take-off?
     Will the cat freeze?

You ask these questions one by one, in different voices
over the phone. Sometimes you get an answer,
10 sometimes a click.
Now it's affecting everything you do.
At dinner you feel nauseous, like you're swallowing **A**
at twenty thousand feet.
In dreams you wave fish-heads, but the cat has grown propellers,
15 the cat is spinning out of sight!

     Will he faint when the plane lands?
     Is the baggage compartment soundproofed?
     Will the cat go deaf? **B**

A **Reading Focus** Analyzing Word Choice Why does Nye use the word *nauseous* here? What is its effect?

B **Literary Focus** Free Verse Why does Nye indent this stanza and the second stanza?

Woman Riding Cat over City at Night by Jocelyne Santos.

"Ma'am, if the cabin weren't pressurized, your cat would explode."
20   And spoken in a droll impersonal tone, as if
the explosion of cats were another statistic!

Hugging the cat before departure, you realize again
the private language of pain. He purrs. He trusts you.
He knows little of planets or satellites,
25   black holes in space or the weightless rise of fear.

Vocabulary **droll** (drohl) *adj.*: odd; wryly amusing.

Today by **Billy Collins**

If ever there were a spring day so perfect,
so uplifted by a warm intermittent breeze

that it made you want to throw
open all the windows in the house

5   and unlatch the door to the canary's cage,
indeed, rip the little door from its jamb,

a day when the cool brick paths
and the garden bursting with peonies

seemed so etched in sunlight
10   that you felt like taking

a hammer to the glass paperweight
on the living room end table,

releasing the inhabitants
from their snow-covered cottage

15   so they could walk out,
holding hands and squinting

into this larger dome of blue and white,
well, today is just that kind of day.

Dreaming of Cherry Blossom (2004) by Liz Wright. Oil on canvas.
Private Collection.

Ⓐ **Reading Focus** Analyzing Word Choice Why do you think Collins chooses to use the word *squinting* here?

Vocabulary **intermittent** (ihn tuhr MIHT uhnt) *adj.:* stopping and starting again.

Applying Your Skills

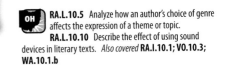

RA.L.10.5 Analyze how an author's choice of genre affects the expression of a theme or topic. RA.L.10.10 Describe the effect of using sound devices in literary texts. *Also covered* RA.I.10.1; VO.10.3; WA.10.1.b

The Flying Cat / Today

Respond and Think Critically

Reading Focus

Read with a Purpose

1. What insights does each poem give you into the poet's way of thinking about his or her subject?

Reading Skills: Analyzing Word Choice

2. Review the charts you created as you read and add a column to explain how word choice contributes to the overall feeling of each poem.

Poem	Word/ Phrase	Image/ Connotation	Overall Feeling
"The Flying Cat"	explode	a cat exploding/ violent, horrific act	

✓ Vocabulary Check

Choose the Vocabulary word that best completes each sentence.

droll   intermittent

3. The radio was so loud that she could not hear the _____ chirping of the birds.

4. He spoke in a _____, entertaining tone.

Literary Focus

Literary Analysis

5. **Interpret** Explain what you think the speaker in "The Flying Cat" means by "the private language of pain" (line 23).

6. **Interpret** How does the last stanza of "The Flying Cat" extend the poem's meaning?

7. **Infer** How does the image of breaking the paperweight contrast with other images in "Today"?

8. **Analyze** Study the **syntax** (grammatical structures) and length of "Today." How might you divide the poem into meaningful sections?

Literary Skills: Free Verse

9. **Analyze** Although "The Flying Cat" is written without rhyme or meter, it is organized with care. What examples of **parallelism** (words, phrases, or sentences with a similar grammatical structure) can you find in the poem?

10. **Evaluate** In "Today," what is the effect of the run-on lines within and between the couplets? What rhythm do they create?

Literary Skills Review: Alliteration

11. **Identify** One sound device poets often use is **alliteration**—the repetition of consonant sounds in words that are close together. Note examples of alliteration you find in each poem.

Writing Focus

Think as a Reader/Writer

Use It in Your Writing Review the words you jotted down as you read that convey strong emotion. Then, write a free-verse poem from the point of view of an airborne cat. Carefully choose words to convey your feelings about the flight. You might describe how you feel about your owner, what happens during the trip, and how you feel when you arrive at your destination.

Preparing to Read

Ex-Basketball Player / In the Well

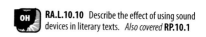 

RA.L.10.10 Describe the effect of using sound devices in literary texts. *Also covered* **RP.10.1**

Literary Focus

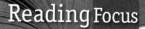

Sound Effects Some poems sound like free verse but are written within a tight structure. The basic beat of Updike's poem, for example, is **iambic pentameter**—five **iambs** (an unstressed syllable followed by a stressed syllable) to a line. This **meter** is closest to the rhythm of everyday English speech. You'll find many other sound effects in these poems: **end rhymes** (rhymes at the end of lines), **internal rhymes** (rhymes within lines), **assonance** (the repetition of vowel sounds within a line), and **alliteration** (the repetition of the same or similar consonant sounds in words that are close together).

Reading Focus

Reading Aloud When you read a poem aloud, it's tempting to pause at the end of each line—but don't. Read naturally, pausing at punctuation marks. Get together with a classmate. Take turns reading the poems aloud while your partner follows along in the text.

Into Action For each poem, create a chart like the one below. Compare the structure of the poem as it appears on the page and the sound of the poem as you read it aloud.

"Ex-Basketball Player"

Structure on the Page	Sound Effect
six lines per stanza	smooth-flowing rhythm

Writing Focus

Think as a Reader/Writer

Find It in Your Reading Both poems tell a story. In your *Reader/ Writer Notebook*, write a one- or two-sentence summary of each poem's narrative.

Reader/Writer Notebook
Use your **RWN** to complete the activities for these selections.

Language Coach

Synonyms Learning a **synonym**—a word that has the same or similar meaning as another word—is a good way to remember the meaning of a new word. For example, *tied* is a synonym of *cinched*. When you find an unfamiliar word, look it up in a dictionary or thesaurus. Then, check the definition for a synonym or think of one on your own. Find synonyms for these three words in Updike's poem: *bucketed* (line 15), *phosphates* (line 27), and *tiers* (line 29).

 Learn It Online
There's more to words than just definitions. Get the whole story on:

go.hrw.com   L10-734   **Go**

John Updike
(1932–)

Pulitzer
Prize
WINNER

An "Occasional" Poet

John Updike was born in the small town of Shillington, Pennsylvania. A year after he graduated from Harvard University, he got a job on the staff of the *New Yorker* magazine, which has published much of his writing ever since.

Although he has won fame for his novels and short stories, Updike is also a poet of great wit and craft. He is particularly drawn to "occasional" poetry—pieces inspired by odd or funny incidents reported in the newspapers or observed in the American landscape of housing developments, gas stations, and supermarkets. Despite his humorous approach, Updike is a sharp social observer and a moralist.

Andrew Hudgins
(1952–)

A Wandering Life

As the son of a career Air Force officer, Andrew Hudgins spent his childhood moving from one military base to another. Although he has lived all over the United States and overseas, Hudgins (who was born in Killeen, Texas) considers himself a Southerner. His writing often <u>evokes</u> images and speech patterns of the Deep South. Hudgins currently teaches at Ohio State University. In 2004, Hudgins participated in Operation Homecoming, an initiative by the National Endowment for the Arts in which distinguished writers visited military bases and offered writing workshops to returning troops and their families.

Think About the Writers

Poets are keen observers of the world around them. How do the poets' different backgrounds influence their choice of subjects?

Preview the Selections

In "Ex-Basketball Player," Updike explores the fate of a former high school athlete. In "In the Well," the speaker relates a frightening childhood incident.

Ex-Basketball Player by **John Updike**

Pearl Avenue runs past the high-school lot,
Bends with the trolley tracks, and stops, cut off
Before it has a chance to go two blocks,
At Colonel McComsky Plaza. Berth's Garage
5 Is on the corner facing west, and there,
Most days, you'll find Flick Webb, who helps Berth out. **Ⓐ**

Flick stands tall among the idiot pumps—
Five on a side, the old bubble-head style,
Their rubber elbows hanging loose and low.
10 One's nostrils are two S's, and his eyes
An E and O. And one is squat, without
A head at all—more of a football type.

Once Flick played for the high-school team, the Wizards.
He was good: in fact, the best. In '46
15 He bucketed three hundred ninety points,
A county record still. The ball loved Flick.
I saw him rack up thirty-eight or forty
In one home game. His hands were like wild birds.

He never learned a trade, he just sells gas,
20 Checks oil, and changes flats. Once in a while,
As a gag, he dribbles an inner tube,
But most of us remember anyway.
His hands are fine and nervous on the lug wrench.
It makes no difference to the lug wrench, though.

25 Off work, he hangs around Mae's luncheonette.
Grease-gray and kind of coiled, he plays pinball,
Smokes thin cigars, and nurses lemon phosphates.
Flick seldom says a word to Mae, just nods
Beyond her face toward bright applauding tiers
30 Of Necco Wafers, Nibs, and Juju Beads. **Ⓑ**

Ⓐ **Literary Focus** **Sound Effects** What is the basic meter of the first stanza?

Ⓑ **Reading Focus** **Reading Aloud** Read this stanza aloud, pausing and stopping for the punctuation. What is the speaker describing?

In the Well

by **Andrew Hudgins**

My father cinched the rope,
a noose around my waist,
and lowered me into
the darkness. I could taste  **A**

5 my fear. It tasted first
of dark, then earth, then rot.
I swung and struck my head
and at that moment got

another then: then blood,
10 which spiked my mouth with iron.
Hand over hand, my father
dropped me from then to then:

then water. Then wet fur,
which I hugged to my chest.
15 I shouted. Daddy hauled
the wet rope. I gagged, and pressed

my neighbor's missing dog
against me. I held its death
and rose up to my father.
20 Then light. Then hands. Then breath. **B**

A **Reading Focus** **Reading Aloud** What is the rhyme scheme in the first stanza?

B **Literary Focus** **Sound Effects** How is the last line different from the rest of the poem? What is its effect?

Applying Your Skills

RA.L.10.10 Describe the effect of using sound devices in literary texts. **RA.L.10.11** Explain ways in which an author develops a point of view and style, and cite specific examples from the text. *Also covered* **RP.10.1; WA.10.1.b**

Ex-Basketball Player / In the Well

Respond and Think Critically

Reading Focus

Read with a Purpose

1. Contrast Flick's present life, as described in "Ex-Basketball Player," with the life he led in high school.

2. What experience does the speaker in "In the Well" describe?

Reading Skills: Reading Aloud

3. Review the charts you created comparing the structure and sound effects of each poem. Add a third column to the charts, and identify the overall effect of hearing each poem read aloud.

"Ex-Basketball Player"

Structure on the Page	Sound Effect	Overall Effect
Six lines per stanza	Smooth-flowing rhythm	descriptive sketches; each stanza adds info to story of Flick

Literary Focus

Literary Analysis

4. **Interpret** In the last stanza of "Ex-Basketball Player," what is the candy compared to, and who sees it that way? What do you think this suggests about Flick's fantasies or dreams?

5. **Connect** What words and phrases in "In the Well" help you to relate to the speaker's sense of fear?

6. **Infer** Think about the final rhyming words of "In the Well": *death/breath*. Why do you think the poet chose these words for the final rhyme?

Literary Skills: Sound Effects

7. **Identify** In "Ex-Basketball Player," what different kinds of sound effects did you identify? Re-read especially for internal rhyme and alliteration.

8. **Evaluate** How does the repetition of certain phrases in "In the Well" mimic the lowering of the boy in the poem?

Literary Skills Review: Metaphor

9. **Identify** A **metaphor** is a direct comparison between two unlike things. Choose a metaphor from one of the poems. What is being compared? How does the metaphor transform an object into a symbol?

Writing Focus

Think as a Reader/Writer

Use It in Your Writing Think of an experience you have had that can be summed up briefly. First, write a one- or two-sentence summary. Then, write a poem to evoke feelings through vivid images and figures of speech. When you have finished, read your poem aloud and listen to its sound effects.

What Do You Think Now

Describe the feeling or mood suggested in each poem. Which sound effects help to evoke each mood?

POETRY
Preparing to Read

We Real Cool

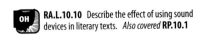

RA.L.10.10 Describe the effect of using sound devices in literary texts. *Also covered* **RP.10.1**

Reader/Writer Notebook

Use your **RWN** to complete the activities for this selection.

Literary Focus

Sound Effects Do you know the tongue twisters "Peter Piper picked a peck of pickled peppers" and "She sells seashells by the seashore"? Both contain examples of **alliteration**—the repetition of the same or similar consonant sounds at the beginning (usually) of words that are close together. By carefully choosing and arranging everyday English words, poets make music with the sounds of words. The literary devices of rhyme, rhythm, repetition, alliteration, and **onomatopoeia**—the use of a word, such as *buzz*, whose sound imitates or suggests its meaning—provide the sound effects.

Language Coach

Dialect A **dialect** is a way of speaking that is characteristic of a certain geographical area or a certain group of people. Everyone speaks a dialect of some kind, sometimes using special pronunciation, vocabulary, and grammar. Some dialects are closer to standard English than others. (Standard English is the dialect used in formal writing and spoken by TV and radio announcers.) When you read "We Real Cool," you will hear an example of a dialect spoken by some African American residents of Chicago in the 1960s. Look for other uses of dialect and informal English as you read the poem.

Reading Focus

Reading Aloud Read "We Real Cool" aloud, and listen carefully for the sound effects Brooks creates. Consider how the sounds contribute to the overall meaning and effect of the poem.

Into Action Fill in the chart below with examples of sound effects in "We Real Cool." Write phrases from the poem and then identify the type of sound effect.

Phrase	Sound Effect
1. lurk late	1. alliteration
2.	2.
3.	3.

Writing Focus

Think as a Reader/Writer

Find It in Your Reading Sometimes poets use words in unusual ways. For instance, a poet may use a noun or adjective as a verb, or a verb as a noun. Look for words that Brooks uses in unusual ways, and consider what effect this device creates. Write the words in your *Reader/Writer Notebook*, along with notes on their meaning.

Learn It Online
Listen to this poem online at:

go.hrw.com   L10-739   **Go**

Learn It Online
Learn more about Brooks at:
go.hrw.com L10-740 Go

Gwendolyn Brooks
(1917–2000)

Pulitzer Prize WINNER

A Chicago Poet

Though born in Topeka, Kansas, Gwendolyn Brooks was associated with Chicago for most of her life, especially with the city's large African American population. Skilled in writing many different kinds of poetry, Brooks wrote with both formal elegance and an ear for the natural speech rhythms of the people of Chicago's South Side. In an interview, Brooks gave the following answers to questions about her work:

Q. Why do you write poetry?
Brooks. I like the concentration, the crush; I like working with language, as others like working with paints and clay or notes.

Q. Has much of your poetry a racial element?
Brooks. Yes. It is organic, not imposed. It is my privilege to state "Negroes" not as curios but as people.

Q. What is your poet's premise [basic principle]?
Brooks. "Vivify [give life to] the contemporary fact," said Whitman. I like to vivify the *universal* fact, when it occurs to me. But the universal wears contemporary clothing very well.

Think About the Writer
What do you think Brooks means by "the universal wears contemporary clothing very well"?

The Granger Collection, New York.

Build Background

In 1966, the Broadside Press of Detroit, Michigan, published "We Real Cool" on a poster, also called a broadside, which is reproduced on the following page.

In an interview in 1970, Brooks said about reading her poem "We Real Cool" aloud: "The 'We'—you're supposed to stop after the 'We' and think about their [the pool players'] validity, and of course there's no way for you to tell whether it should be said softly or not, I suppose, but I say it rather softly because I want to represent their basic uncertainty, which they don't bother to question every day of course."

Read with a Purpose

Pay attention to the poem's sound effects as you read it aloud.

WE REAL COOL
BY GWENDOLYN BROOKS
The Pool Players
Seven at the Golden Shovel

WE REAL COOL. WE
LEFT SCHOOL. WE

LURK LATE. WE

STRIKE STRAIGHT. WE

SING SIN. WE
THIN GIN. WE

JAZZ JUNE. WE
DIE SOON.

Designed by Cledie Taylor
"We Real Cool" from Selected Poems by Gwendolyn Brooks
Copyright © 1959 by Gwendolyn Brooks Blakely
Reprinted by permission of the author and Harper & Row, Publishers
BROADSIDE No. 6. December 1966
BROADSIDE PRESS, 12651 OLD MILL PLACE, DETROIT, MICHIGAN 48238

Ⓐ

Ⓐ **Literary Focus** Sound Effects What sounds do you hear in these lines?

Applying Your Skills

RA.L.10.10 Describe the effect of using sound devices in literary texts. **RA.L.10.8** Analyze the author's use of point of view, mood and tone. *Also covered* **RP.10.1; WA.10.1.b**

We Real Cool

Respond and Think Critically

Reading Focus

Read with a Purpose

1. How are the poem's sound effects revealed as you read it aloud?

Reading Skills: Reading Aloud

2. Review the chart you created for "We Real Cool." Add a third column to write the meaning for each phrase you listed. Then, read the poem aloud again. This time replace Brooks's phrase with the meaning you listed. Which word choice adds more to the poem?

Phrase	Sound Effect	Meaning
lurk late	alliteration	Hang out after curfew

Literary Focus

Literary Analysis

3. **Connect** Brooks wrote "We Real Cool" in 1960. Do you think the poem is outdated, or does it still apply to life today? Explain, referring to details in the poem.

4. **Analyze** What purpose do the two lines immediately below the title serve? What **connotations,** or associations, do the words *shovel* and *golden* have?

5. **Interpret** What do you think is the poem's **theme,** or message?

6. **Analyze** The poem's **meter,** or pattern of stressed and unstressed syllables, is extremely unusual. Scan the poem. What meter does Brooks use to pound out the message?

7. **Infer** Why do you think the poem ends with "We / die soon"?

Literary Skills: Sound Effects

8. **Analyze** Describe the poem's unusual use of rhyme. Where are the rhyming words located?

9. **Identify** Where does Brooks use alliteration? When you read the poem aloud, how does the unusual repetition create meaning?

Literary Skills Review: Tone

10. **Analyze** How would you describe the poem's overall **tone**—the speaker's attitude toward the subject? What words would you use to describe the speaker's tone?

Writing Focus

Think as a Reader/Writer

Use It in Your Writing Write a poem in imitation of "We Real Cool." You could open with Brooks's title, or create one of your own. You might choose to build your poem on a series of statements that begin "I am . . ." or "We are . . ." Decide who will be the speaker (or speakers) of your poem and use today's language.

What Do **You Think Now** How do the sound effects in "We Real Cool" help carry the poem's theme? Explain.

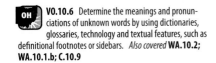

VO.10.6 Determine the meanings and pronunciations of unknown words by using dictionaries, glossaries, technology and textual features, such as definitional footnotes or sidebars. *Also covered* **WA.10.2; WA.10.1.b; C.10.9**

Vocabulary Development

Vocabulary Skills: Understanding Jargon

Jargon is the specialized vocabulary used by people doing particular jobs or sharing particular interests. Doctors have jargon, as do athletes, actors, computer users, and sailors. Every kind of job, sport, and hobby has its own jargon for equipment and techniques.

The word map below analyzes the word *dunk*, basketball jargon from John Updike's poem "Ex-Basketball Player."

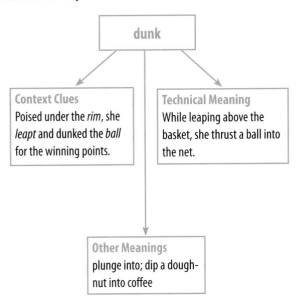

dunk

Context Clues
Poised under the *rim*, she *leapt* and dunked the *ball* for the winning points.

Technical Meaning
While leaping above the basket, she thrust a ball into the net.

Other Meanings
plunge into; dip a doughnut into coffee

Your Turn

Create a word map like the one above for each of the following technical terms, or jargon, from the poems in this section:

1. *pressurized* from "The Flying Cat"
2. *etched* from "Today"
3. *dribbles* from "Ex-Basketball Player"

CHOICES

As you respond to the Choices, use the **Academic Vocabulary** words as appropriate: <u>transform</u>, <u>literal</u>, <u>evoke</u>, and <u>complement</u>.

REVIEW
Compare Sound Effects

Timed └Writing Choose two poems from this section and read them aloud. Then, think about how they are alike and different, paying special attention to the sound effects produced by rhyme, rhythm, repetition, alliteration, and onomatopoeia. Write a brief essay comparing and contrasting these sound effects.

CONNECT
Present an Oral Interpretation

Group Activity With a small group, prepare and present an oral interpretation of "We Real Cool." Decide if you will use a single voice or several voices. Will you incorporate music that <u>evokes</u> the mood of the poem, and if so, what piece will you choose? Be sure to prepare a script indicating where speakers will vary their tone. Have your audience evaluate the performance.

EXTEND
Write a Musical Poem

Write a free-verse poem that imitates a specific kind of music or sound. (Before you begin to write, look back at the various sound effects of the poems in this section.) In your poem, include sensory details, figurative language, and sound effects to express your message.

Author Study: Robert Frost

CONTENTS

The poet Robert Frost delivering a lecture in 1942.

 What role do you think poetry plays in our lives?

 **QuickWrite**
Think of poems you have read and enjoyed. Why do poets write? Why do people read poetry? Jot down your thoughts.

Preparing to Read

After Apple-Picking / Mowing / Stopping by Woods on a Snowy Evening

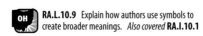
RA.L.10.9 Explain how authors use symbols to create broader meanings. *Also covered* **RA.I.10.1**

Literary Focus

Symbolic Meaning Snow is snow and apples are apples. In the hands of a poet, however, ordinary things can have **symbolic meanings**—that is, they stand for things other than themselves and suggest deeper layers of meaning. To determine if a poem has symbolic meaning, be alert to clues the poet plants—repetition, emphasis, word associations, and images.

Reading Focus

Analyzing Works by One Author To explore the characteristic features of a poet's style, first **compare** and **contrast** several poems. In your comparison, consider the poet's word choice, imagery, and use of sound devices (such as rhyme).

Into Action As you read the following poems, record your observations about Frost's style in a chart like the one below.

	Word Choice	Imagery	Sound Devices
"After Apple-Picking"			
"Mowing"	everyday language		
"Stopping by Woods …"			

Writing Focus

Think as a Reader/Writer

Find it in Your Reading Poets rely on words' **connotations**, or the associations and feelings they evoke, to appeal to the reader's emotions. As you read, identify words with strong positive or negative connotations. Record these words and their connotations in your *Reader/Writer Notebook*.

Reader/Writer Notebook

Use your **RWN** to complete the activities for these selections.

Vocabulary

After Apple-Picking

drowsing (DROWZ ihng) *v.:* falling half asleep; dozing. *Tired from his labor, the speaker is drowsing.*

cherish (CHEHR ihsh) *v.:* treat with love and tenderness. *At first the speaker views the apples as something to cherish.*

Mowing

earnest (UR nihst) *adj.:* serious and sincere. *The work is carried out in an earnest manner, not a playful one.*

Language Coach

Connotations As they write, poets consider the connotations of words. The word *earnest* has a positive connotation. The word *solemn,* however, has a negative connotation, even though the dictionary definitions of the two words are similar. Look at the other words on the Vocabulary list. What connotations do these words have? What related words might have negative connotations?

Learn It Online
There's more to words than just definitions. Get the whole story on:

go.hrw.com | L10-745 | **Go**

Robert Frost
(1874–1963)

Pulitzer Prize WINNER

City Roots

Although Robert Frost is universally regarded as the voice of rural New England and the farming life, he once declared, "I'm not a farmer, that's no pose of mine." Many critics have pointed out that Frost was a poet of contradictions who led a life of contradictions.

Frost did live on a farm in Derry, New Hampshire, from 1900 until 1909. However, he was city-bred. Born in San Francisco, California, in 1874, he lived there until the age of eleven, when his father died. His father wished to be buried in New England, and so Frost, his mother, and his younger sister traveled to New England—and stayed.

A Transatlantic Hit

Studying at Lawrence High School in Lawrence, Massachusetts, Frost gained a reputation as a poet and fell in love with Elinor Miriam White. They were co-valedictorians of their graduating class, and they married three years later in 1895. Although Frost received more than forty honorary degrees in the course of his life, he never completed his college education.

Frost earned a living as a mill worker, a reporter, a teacher, and a farmer, all while writing poetry. His first poem to be published professionally, "My Butterfly: An Elegy," appeared in a newspaper in 1894. Afterwards, Frost struggled to get more of his work published. In 1912, he and Elinor decided to move to England, which Frost viewed as a "place to be poor and to write poems." He went to England with "a loose-leaf heap" of poetry and published two collections—*A Boy's Will* (1913) and *North of Boston* (1914)—while he was there. The books were immediate successes on both sides of the Atlantic, and Frost went home to New England in 1915, finally able to make his living as a poet.

Public Success, Private Sorrow

Frost went on to become America's most beloved and honored poet of the twentieth century. He was the only poet ever to receive four Pulitzer Prizes. Frost was

A Frost Time Line

1885 After the death of his father, Frost moves to New England with his mother and sister.

1900 Frost and his family live on a farm in Derry, New Hampshire, until 1909.

1915 Moving back to the U.S., Frost makes his permanent home in New England.

1870	1880	1890	1900	1910

1874 Frost is born on March 26, in San Francisco, California.

1892 Frost graduates from high school as a co-valedictorian with Elinor Miriam White, whom he will marry in 1895.

1894 Frost's first poem published professionally, "My Butterfly: An Elegy," appears in *The Independent,* a New York paper.

1912 Frost and his family move to England, where he publishes his first two collections of poetry and gains acclaim as a poet.

also awarded a Congressional Gold Medal. In 1961 he became the first inaugural poet, reciting his poem "The Gift Outright" at President John F. Kennedy's inauguration. Frost taught and lectured widely and was affiliated on and off with Amherst College in Amherst, Massachusetts, for more than forty years.

Although Frost experienced professional success, his personal life was filled with sorrow, and he suffered from depression and anxiety. He was rocked by grief after the death of Elinor in 1938 and by the deaths of four of his six children. A fifth child suffered from mental illness, as did Frost's sister.

A Realist's Imagination

Frost was committed to exploring truth in his poems. He once said of poets, "We write of things we see and we write in accents we hear. Thus we gather both our material and our technique with the imagination from life." Frost expressed his ideas in the colloquial language and rhythms he heard in the everyday talk around him. His vivid imagery was grounded in the study he made of nature during his regular walks through woods and fields.

Frost's rendering of the world is made complex by the layers of meaning embedded in his poems. "All thought," Frost once stated, "is a feat of association." His poetry is filled with symbolic and meta-phoric meanings as well as irony, contradictions, and ambiguity. "One thing I care about," Frost explained, ". . . is taking poetry as the first form of understanding. If poetry isn't understanding all, the whole world, then it isn't worth anything. "

Think About the Writer

Which events in Frost's life might have influenced his poetry?

Key Elements of Frost's Writing

Precise, economical **imagery** creates a vivid sense of place, particularly the New England landscape. The voices of common people are captured through the use of **everyday language** and the **natural rhythms** of speech.

Meter and **rhyme** give his work a **lyrical** quality. Complex meanings are suggested by **symbols, metaphors, irony, contradictions**, and **ambiguity.**

Themes often focus on labor and the rural life, nature, individualism, journeys, decisions, and life's dark truths.

1924 Frost wins his first of four Pulitzer Prizes in poetry for his collection *New Hampshire: A Poem with Notes and Grace Notes.*

1949 Frost is appointed the Simpson Lecturer in Literature at Amherst College, a position he will hold until his death.

1962 Frost publishes *In the Clearing,* his eleventh and final collection of poetry.

1920   **1930**   **1940**   **1950**   **1960**

1947 *A Masque of Mercy,* the tenth collection of poems Frost produced between 1913 and 1947, is published.

1961 Frost recites his poem "The Gift Outright" at President John F. Kennedy's inauguration.

1963 Frost dies on January 29, in Boston, Massachusetts, at the age of eighty-eight.

After Apple-Picking

by **Robert Frost**

> ### Read with a Purpose
> As you read the poems, think about the importance of setting and how it relates to meaning.

My long two-pointed ladder's sticking through a tree
Toward heaven still,
And there's a barrel that I didn't fill
Beside it, and there may be two or three
5   Apples I didn't pick upon some bough.   **Ⓐ**
But I am done with apple-picking now.
Essence of winter sleep is on the night,
The scent of apples: I am drowsing off.
I cannot rub the strangeness from my sight
10 I got from looking through a pane of glass
I skimmed this morning from the drinking trough
And held against the world of hoary° grass.
It melted, and I let it fall and break.
But I was well
15 Upon my way to sleep before it fell,
And I could tell
What form my dreaming was about to take.
Magnified apples appear and disappear,
Stem end and blossom end,
20 And every fleck of russet° showing clear.
My instep arch not only keeps the ache,
It keeps the pressure of a ladder-round.
I feel the ladder sway as the boughs bend.
And I keep hearing from the cellar bin
25 The rumbling sound

12. hoary (HAWR ee): covered with hoarfrost, white crystals of ice. *Hoary* also means "very old; ancient."

20. russet (RUHS iht): yellowish or reddish brown.

Ⓐ **Literary Focus** **Symbolic Meaning** What might the unfilled barrel and the apples remaining on the tree represent?

Vocabulary **drowsing** (DROWZ ihng) *v.*: falling half asleep; dozing.

Of load on load of apples coming in. **B**
For I have had too much
Of apple-picking: I am overtired
Of the great harvest I myself desired.
30 There were ten thousand fruit to touch,
Cherish in hand, lift down, and not let fall.
For all
That struck the earth,
No matter if not bruised or spiked with stubble,
35 Went surely to the cider-apple heap
As of no worth.
One can see what will trouble
This sleep of mine, whatever sleep it is.
Were he not gone,
40 The woodchuck could say whether it's like his
Long sleep, as I describe its coming on,
Or just some human sleep.

B **Reading Focus** Analyzing Works by One Author   How does Frost use imagery
in lines 18–26 to suggest what is on the speaker's mind?

Vocabulary   **cherish** (CHEHR ihsh) *v.*: treat with love and tenderness.

The Mowers by Helen Allingham (1848–1926). Watercolor. John Spink Fine Watercolours, London, UK.

Mowing

by **Robert Frost**

There was never a sound beside the wood but one,
And that was my long scythe° whispering to the ground.
What was it it whispered? I knew not well myself;
Perhaps it was something about the heat of the sun,
5 Something, perhaps, about the lack of sound—
And that was why it whispered and did not speak. **Ⓐ**
It was no dream of the gift of idle hours,
Or easy gold at the hand of fay° or elf:
Anything more than the truth would have seemed too weak
10 To the earnest love that laid the swale° in rows,
Not without feeble-pointed spikes of flowers
(Pale orchises), and scared a bright green snake.
The fact is the sweetest dream that labour knows.
My long scythe whispered and left the hay to make.

2. scythe (syth): tool with a long blade set on a long handle, used for cutting grass or grain.

8. fay (fay): fairy.

10. swale (swayl): low piece of land.

Ⓐ **Reading Focus** **Analyzing Works by One Author** Describe the sound of the first six lines and the sound devices Frost uses to create this sound.

Vocabulary **earnest** (UR nihst) *adj.:* serious and sincere.

Stopping by Woods on a Snowy Evening

by **Robert Frost**

Whose woods these are I think I know.
His house is in the village, though;
He will not see me stopping here
To watch his woods fill up with snow.

5   My little horse must think it queer
To stop without a farmhouse near
Between the woods and frozen lake
The darkest evening of the year. **A**

He gives his harness bells a shake
10 To ask if there is some mistake.
The only other sound's the sweep
Of easy wind and downy flake.

The woods are lovely, dark, and deep,
But I have promises to keep,
15 And miles to go before I sleep,
And miles to go before I sleep.

A **Literary Focus** Symbolic Meaning What are the literal and symbolic meanings of the phrase "the darkest evening of the year"?

Applying Your Skills

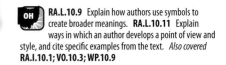

RA.L.10.9 Explain how authors use symbols to create broader meanings. **RA.L.10.11** Explain ways in which an author develops a point of view and style, and cite specific examples from the text. *Also covered* **RA.I.10.1; VO.10.3; WP.10.9**

After Apple-Picking / Mowing / Stopping by Woods on a Snowy Evening

Respond and Think Critically

Reading Focus

Read with a Purpose

1. Describe the settings in these three poems. Where and when does each one take place? What similarities and differences do you note from one setting to the next?

Reading Skills: Analyzing Works by One Author

2. Review the chart you filled in as you read. Then, add a row to the bottom of the chart. Record your conclusions about Frost's style based on your reading of these poems and what you have learned about the poet's beliefs.

✓ Vocabulary Check

Tell whether each statement is true (T) or false (F).

3. If you are **drowsing,** you are feeling energetic.
4. When you **cherish** something, you dislike it.
5. An **earnest** person approaches tasks seriously.

Literary Focus

Literary Analysis

6. **Interpret** In "After Apple-Picking," why might the speaker shift between the present and the past and not provide details in chronological order? In particular, why might he describe his dream in the present tense (lines 18–26), given that it has not yet occurred?

7. **Analyze** How do the attitudes of the horse and the speaker differ in "Stopping by Woods on a Snowy Evening"?

8. **Analyze** A poem's **theme** is an insight into life that the poet wants to convey. Try to express what you think is the theme of each poem.

Literary Skills: Symbolic Meaning

9. **Interpret** On a symbolic level, what do you think is "the great harvest" (line 29) that the speaker in "After Apple-Picking" once valued?

10. **Interpret** Note how many times the word *sleep* occurs in "After Apple-Picking." What kind of sleep do you think the speaker is talking about?

11. **Analyze** Explain what the woods in "Stopping by Woods on a Snowy Evening" might symbolize to the traveler. What has the speaker said no to in passing them by? What has he said yes to by continuing his passage?

12. **Interpret** What is literally happening in "Mowing"? What might mowing symbolize to the speaker?

Literary Skills Review: Personification

13. **Analyze** Identify the **personification,** the attribution of human qualities to nonhuman things, in all three poems. What purpose does it serve?

Writing Focus

Think as a Reader/Writer

Use it in Your Writing Write a poem in which you depict a setting you know well. Choose your words carefully. Consider how the words' connotations affect the emotional impact and meaning of your poem.

Preparing to Read

In Praise of Robert Frost

RA.L.10.11 Explain ways in which an author develops a point of view and style, and cite specific examples from the text. *Also covered* **RA.I.10.1**

 **Reader/Writer Notebook**

Use your **RWN** to complete the activities for this selection.

Literary Focus

Style Like poets, speakers pay great attention to the sound and rhythm of their words. Often they use **repetition** of words or phrases to create rhythm and to emphasize points. To form balanced sentences, they employ **parallel structure**—the use of the same grammatical form, such as two nouns, adjectives, or phrases to express related ideas or ideas of equal weight. Speakers also rely on **alliteration,** the repetition of initial consonant sounds in words that are close together. As you read this speech, consider how President Kennedy's style helps make his ideas strong and memorable.

Reading Focus

Analyzing an Author's Purpose Authors can have more than one purpose in mind when writing. When you analyze a speech's purpose, consider not only the main ideas, but also the speaker's identity, audience, and the occasion on which the speech is being delivered.

Into Action As you read, fill in a chart like the one below to help you determine the purposes of this speech. Add rows as needed.

Subject	Main Idea	Purposes
Robert Frost		
art and artist		

Writing Focus

Think as a Reader/Writer

Find It in Your Reading Writers use quotations to support their points or to enliven their writing. As you read the speech, note in your *Reader/Writer Notebook* the quotations Kennedy uses.

Vocabulary

indispensable (ihn dihs PEHN suh buhl) *adj.:* absolutely necessary; essential. *Kennedy declares that artists play an indispensable role in the nation.*

disinterested (dihs IHN tuhr uhs tihd) *adj.:* fair; lacking bias. *Disinterested critics can help strengthen a country.*

fortified (FAWR tuh fyd) *v.:* strengthened. *A country is fortified by the contributions of its heroes.*

disdains (dihs DAYNZ) *v.:* views something as lacking value or merit. *A country that disdains poetry does not understand how art can enrich a nation.*

skeptical (SKEHP tuh kuhl) *adj.:* doubting; questioning. *Kennedy describes the fate of a nation that is skeptical of the value of art.*

Language Coach

Prefixes Although the **prefixes** (word parts added to beginnings of words) *dis*– and *un*– both mean "not," the words *disinterested* and *uninterested* have different meanings. *Disinterested* means "fair; lacking bias," and *uninterested* means "lacking curiosity about something; not interested." Which word would you use to describe a child who is bored? Which would you use to describe a respected umpire?

 Learn It Online
Use Word Watch to research your vocabulary at:

go.hrw.com   L10-753   **Go**

IN PRAISE OF ROBERT FROST

by **John F. Kennedy**

Read with a Purpose

Read this speech to explore why President John F. Kennedy viewed Robert Frost as a hero.

Build Background

In October 1963, President John F. Kennedy delivered this tribute to Robert Frost at the groundbreaking ceremony for the Robert Frost Library at Amherst College. Quotations from the speech are inscribed on the walls of the John F. Kennedy Center for the Performing Arts in Washington, D.C.

This day, devoted to the memory of Robert Frost, offers an opportunity for reflection which is prized by politicians as well as by others and even by poets. For Robert Frost was one of the granite figures of our time in America. He was supremely two things— an artist and an American.

A nation reveals itself not only by the men it produces but also by the men it honors, the men it remembers.

In America our heroes have customarily run to men of large accomplishments. But today this college and country honors a man whose contribution was not to our size but to our spirit; not to our political beliefs but to our insight; not to our self-esteem but to our self-comprehension. **Ⓐ**

In honoring Robert Frost, we therefore can pay honor to the deepest sources of our national strength. That strength takes many forms, and the most obvious forms are not always the most significant.

The men who create power make an indispensable contribution to the nation's greatness. But the men who question power make a contribution just as indispensable, especially when that questioning is disinterested.

Ⓐ Literary Focus Style Identify the parallel structure in this paragraph, and explain how it contributes to the sound of the sentence.

Vocabulary **indispensable** (ihn dihs PEHN suh buhl) *adj.*: absolutely necessary; essential.
disinterested (dihs IHN tuhr uhs tihd) *adj.*: fair; lacking bias.

For they determine whether we use power or power uses us. Our national strength matters; but the spirit which informs and controls our strength matters just as much. This was the special significance of Robert Frost.

He brought an unsparing instinct for reality to bear on the platitudes and pieties[1] of society. His sense of the human tragedy fortified him against self-deception and easy consolation.

"I have been," he wrote, "one acquainted with the night."[2]

And because he knew the midnight as well as the high noon, because he understood the ordeal as well as the triumph of the human spirit, he gave his age strength with which to overcome despair.

At bottom he held a deep faith in the spirit of man. And it's hardly an accident that Robert Frost coupled poetry and power. For he saw poetry as the means of saving power from itself.

President John F. Kennedy and his wife, Jacqueline Kennedy, chat with Robert Frost in 1962.

When power leads man toward arrogance, poetry reminds him of his limitations. When power narrows the arrears[3] of man's concern, poetry reminds him of the richness and diversity of his existence. When power corrupts, poetry cleanses.

For art establishes the basic human truths which must serve as the touchstones[4] of our judgment. The artist, however faithful to his personal

---

1. **platitudes** (PLAT uh toodz) **and pieties** (PY uh teez): commonplace statements and sacred beliefs.
2. **"I have been . . . one acquainted with the night"**: first and last lines of Frost's poem titled "Acquainted with the Night."
3. **arrears** (uh RIHRZ): unfulfilled obligations.
4. **touchstones** (TUHCH stohnz): means used to test the value or excellence of something.

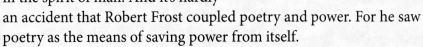

Vocabulary **fortified** (FAWR tuh fyd) *v.:* strengthened.

vision of reality, becomes the last champion of the individual mind and sensibility against an intrusive society and an officious state.

The great artist is thus a solitary figure. He has, as Frost said, "a lover's quarrel with the world."[5] In pursuing his perceptions of reality, he must often sail against the currents of his time. This is not a popular role. **B**

If Robert Frost was much honored during his lifetime, it was because a good many preferred to ignore his darker truths.

Yet in retrospect we see how the artist's fidelity has strengthened the fiber of our national life. If sometimes our great artists have been the most critical of our society, it is because their sensitivity and their concern for justice, which must motivate any true artist, makes him aware that our nation falls short of its highest potential.

I see little of more importance to the future of our country and our civilization than full recognition of the place of the artist. If art is to nourish the roots of our culture, society must set the artist free to follow his vision wherever it takes him.

We must never forget that art is not a form of propaganda; it is a form of truth. And as Mr. MacLeish[6] once remarked of poets, "there is nothing worse for our trade than to be in style."

In free society, art is not a weapon and it does not belong to the sphere of polemics[7] and ideology.[8] Artists are not engineers of the soul.

It may be different elsewhere. But democratic society—in it—the highest duty of the writer, the composer, the artist is to remain true to himself and to let the chips fall where they may.

In serving his vision of the truth, the artist best serves his nation. And the nation which disdains the mission of art invites the fate of Robert Frost's hired man—"the fate of having nothing to look backward to with pride and nothing to look forward to with hope."[9]

I look forward to a great future for America—a future in which our

---

5. **"a lover's . . . world":** from the last line of Frost's poem "The Lesson for Today."

6. **Mr. MacLeish:** Archibald Macleish (1892–1982), an American poet.

7. **polemics** (puh LEHM ihks): art or practice of debate.

8. **ideology** (y dee AHL uh jee): beliefs that form the foundation of a political, economic, or social system.

9. **hired man—"the fate . . . with hope":** reference to Frost's poem "The Death of the Hired Man."

B Reading Focus Analyzing an Author's Purpose In the last two paragraphs, how has Kennedy's focus changed?

Vocabulary **disdains** (dihs DAYNZ) *v.:* views something as lacking value or merit.

country will match its military strength with our moral restraint, its wealth with our wisdom, its power with our purpose.

I look forward to an America which will not be afraid of grace and beauty, which will protect the beauty of our national environment, which will preserve the great old American houses and squares and parks of our national past and which will build handsome and balanced cities for our future.

I look forward to an America which will reward achievement in the arts as we reward achievement in business or statecraft.[10]

I look forward to an America which will steadily raise the standards of artistic accomplishment and which will steadily enlarge cultural opportunities for all of our citizens.

And I look forward to an America which commands respect throughout the world not only for its strength but for its civilization as well.

And I look forward to a world which will be safe not only for democracy and diversity but also for personal distinction. **C**

Robert Frost was often skeptical about projects for human improvement. Yet I do not think he would disdain this hope.

As he wrote during the uncertain days of the Second War:

Take human nature altogether since time began . . .
And it must be a little more in favor of man,
Say a fraction of one percent at the very least . . .
Our hold on the planet wouldn't have so increased.[11]

Because of Mr. Frost's life and work, because of the life and work of this college, our hold on this planet has increased.

[signature]
January 20th/1961

---

10. **statecraft** (STAYT kraft): art of leadership in government affairs.
11. These lines are from Frost's poem "Our Hold on the Planet."

C **Literary Focus** Style Why might Kennedy have repeated the phrase "I look forward" in the last six paragraphs?

Vocabulary **skeptical** (SKEHP tuh kuhl) *adj.*: doubting; questioning.

Applying Your Skills

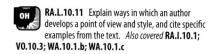 **RA.L.10.11** Explain ways in which an author develops a point of view and style, and cite specific examples from the text. *Also covered* **RA.I.10.1; V0.10.3; WA.10.1.b; WA.10.1.c**

In Praise of Robert Frost

Respond and Think Critically

Reading Focus

Quick Check

1. According to Kennedy, how do people "who question power" contribute to a nation?
2. Why does an artist become "a solitary figure"?
3. What are some of the things that Kennedy imagines for America's future?

Read with a Purpose

4. What contributions does Kennedy believe Frost has made to the country? Has Kennedy convinced you that Frost should be viewed in a heroic light? Why or why not?

Reading Skills: Analyzing an Author's Purpose

5. Review the chart you filled in. Then, explain the speech's purposes. Do you think Kennedy's primary purpose is to praise Frost? How does Kennedy's position as president affect your understanding of his purposes?

✓ Vocabulary Check

Match each word on the left with its definition.

6. **indispensable**   a. strengthened
7. **disinterested**   b. essential
8. **fortified**   c. doubting
9. **disdains**   d. fair
10. **skeptical**   e. views as lacking value

Literary Focus

Literary Analysis

11. **Analyze** Explain Kennedy's statement that "in serving his vision of the truth, the artist best serves his nation." In what way does Kennedy believe a country can benefit from its artists?

12. **Connect** How has reading this speech expanded your understanding of Robert Frost? What have you learned about the man, his poetry, or his importance to America?

Literary Skills: Style

13. **Analyze** Find examples of repetition, parallel structure, and alliteration in the speech. Then, read sections of the speech aloud to a partner and discuss the effects created by these elements of Kennedy's style.

Literary Skills Review: Implied Metaphor

14. **Interpret** An **implied metaphor** is a subtle comparison between two unlike things. What is the meaning of the implied metaphor in Kennedy's statement that Frost "knew the midnight as well as the high noon"?

Writing Focus

Think as a Reader/Writer

Use It in Your Writing Write a brief speech in praise of someone you admire, either a real person or a fictional character in a story or movie. Use quotations to help make your speech effective.

Author Study: Robert Frost

WA.10.2 Write responses to literature that organize an insightful interpretation around several clear ideas, premises or images and support judgments with specific references to the original text, to other texts, authors and to prior knowledge. **WA.10.4.d** Write informational essays or reports, including research that: support the main ideas with facts, details, examples and explanations from sources.

Writing Focus

Write a Response to Literature

In his speech "In Praise of Robert Frost," John F. Kennedy states that Frost contributed to the country's "spirit," "insight," and "self-comprehension." Compare two of the three poems you have read in light of Kennedy's statement. Do you think the poems provide insight into the human condition and help us understand ourselves? In your essay, consider the following items:

- the poems' symbolic meanings and themes
- how Frost's style helps him convey meaning
- the ways in which the knowledge you have gained about Frost helps illuminate the poems

Writing Tips Keep the following tips in mind:

- In your **introduction,** be sure to include a specific **thesis statement** that expresses the key point you will prove in your essay.
- In the **body,** cite details and quote lines from the poems to support your points.
- To present a strong **conclusion,** include a closing insight or reflection instead of only summarizing your main points.

What Do
You Think Now?

What do these selections suggest about the personal and public significance of poetry?

CHOICES

As you respond to the Choices, use the **Academic Vocabulary** words as appropriate: transform, literal, evoke, and complement.

REVIEW
Describe a Character

Timed └Writing Who is the traveler in "Stopping by Woods on a Snowy Evening"? Write a brief character sketch describing this traveler, elaborating on details to bring the character to life. Is the speaker a man or a woman? Do you think the speaker is married or single? old or young? Is the speaker happy, or sad? Cite details from the poem while composing your sketch.

CONNECT
Create a PowerPoint Presentation

TechFocus In his speech "In Praise of Robert Frost," Kennedy discusses how great artists serve society by being critical of its shortcomings. Think of an artist you admire—in the fields of music, film, literature, or visual arts—who has made such a contribution to society. Create a PowerPoint presentation to show how the artist has used art to serve his or her "vision of the truth."

EXTEND
Analyze a Poem

Read Frost's poems "Acquainted with the Night," "The Death of the Hired Man," and "Our Hold on the Planet," which Kennedy refers to in his speech. Then, choose one of the poems, and write a short essay in which you analyze the ways it complements what you have learned about Frost and his work. Consider the poem's meaning and style as well as Frost's attitudes and life experiences.

Literary Skills Review

Elements of Poetry   Directions: Read the following poem. Then, read and respond to the questions that follow.

The Writer by **Richard Wilbur**

In her room at the prow of the house
Where light breaks, and the windows
    are tossed with linden,
My daughter is writing a story.

5 I pause in the stairwell, hearing
From her shut door a commotion of
    typewriter-keys
Like a chain hauled over a gunwale.

Young as she is, the stuff
Of her life is a great cargo, and some of
    it heavy:
I wish her a lucky passage.

10 But now it is she who pauses,
As if to reject my thought and its easy
    figure.
A stillness greatens, in which

The whole house seems to be thinking,
And then she is at it again with a
    bunched clamor
15 Of strokes, and again is silent.

I remember the dazed starling
Which was trapped in that very room,
    two years ago;
How we stole in, lifted a sash

And retreated, not to affright it;
And how for a helpless hour, through
20   the crack of the door,
We watched the sleek, wild, dark

And iridescent creature
Batter against the brilliance, drop like a
    glove
To the hard floor, or the desk-top,

25 And wait then, humped and bloody,
For the wits to try it again; and how our
    spirits
Rose when, suddenly sure,

It lifted off from a chair-back,
Beating a smooth course for the right
    window
30 And clearing the sill of the world.

It is always a matter, my darling,
Of life or death, as I had forgotten. I
    wish
What I wished you before, but harder.

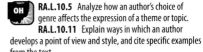
RA.L.10.5 Analyze how an author's choice of genre affects the expression of a theme or topic.
RA.L.10.11 Explain ways in which an author develops a point of view and style, and cite specific examples from the text.

1. "The Writer" can best be classified as
   A. a literary ballad.
   B. an ode.
   C. a free-verse poem.
   D. a sonnet.

2. Line 2 contains an example of
   A. internal rhyme.
   B. end rhyme.
   C. alliteration.
   D. iambic pentameter.

3. In the first three stanzas, the speaker compares the poem's setting to a
   A. good story.
   B. happy life.
   C. rescued bird.
   D. wish.

4. "Lucky passage" (line 9) is a metaphor for a
   A. good story.
   B. happy life.
   C. rescued bird.
   D. wish.

5. What figure of speech does the poet use in the phrase, "The whole house seems to be thinking"?
   A. simile
   B. metaphor
   C. implied metaphor
   D. personification

6. The poem makes a significant shift in stanza 6 when the speaker
   A. moves from the present to the future.
   B. describes a remembered event.
   C. introduces the first figure of speech.
   D. expresses his feelings about his daughter.

7. How does the poet use the image of the trapped starling?
   A. He compares it to his daughter's struggle.
   B. He suggests that we are all hopelessly trapped.
   C. It is an image of struggle and loss.
   D. It shows the relationship of writers to nature.

8. The "easy figure" in line 11 refers to the
   A. speaker's daughter.
   B. story the daughter is writing.
   C. figures of speech in the first three stanzas.
   D. dazed starling in stanza 6.

Short Answer
9. The poem contains an example of a simile. Cite the example and its line number. Explain how you know the example is a simile.

Extended Response
10. Re-read the last stanza of the poem. Then, write a paragraph explaining how this last stanza sums up the theme, or central idea, of the poem.

Vocabulary Skills Review

Multiple-Meaning Words **Directions:** Choose the answer that gives the meaning of the underlined word as it is used in the sentence.

1. The speaker in "Same Song" by Pat Mora describes her son, who "curls and <u>bench presses</u>" in the garage.

   <u>Bench presses</u> in this phrase means
   A. pushes against a heavy weight.
   B. extracts juice from.
   C. urges or requests with great force.
   D. forces someone to do something.

2. In "Eating Together," Li-Young Lee writes about "the trout / <u>seasoned</u> with slivers of ginger."

   In this context, <u>seasoned</u> means
   A. accustomed.
   B. made less harsh.
   C. experienced.
   D. with spices added.

3. The words <u>pitch-black</u> in the phrase "one <u>pitch-black</u> night" in "A Storm in the Mountains" refer to
   A. the angle, or degree, of a sloping surface.
   B. a rising and falling movement.
   C. the highness or lowness of a sound.
   D. extreme darkness.

4. In "The Legend," Garrett Hongo describes "a triangle of orange in the <u>hollow</u> of his cheek."

   In this line, <u>hollow</u> means
   A. a valley.
   B. a sunken place.
   C. something that is worthless or empty.
   D. hunger.

5. Hongo writes in "The Legend" that the unnamed man "<u>negotiates</u> the slick of ice on the sidewalk by his car."

   <u>Negotiates</u> here means
   A. attempts to settle a dispute.
   B. makes arrangements.
   C. manages to cross.
   D. transfers or sells.

6. In "Ode to My Socks," Pablo Neruda writes, "I resisted / the <u>sharp</u> temptation / to save them somewhere."

   What does <u>sharp</u> mean here?
   A. shrewd
   B. suitable for cutting
   C. harsh
   D. intense

7. Neruda's final stanza begins, "The <u>moral</u> / of my ode is this: / beauty is twice / beauty."

   <u>Moral</u> in this context means
   A. the difference between right and wrong.
   B. the lesson of a story or event.
   C. the ending of a long, serious poem.
   D. a measure or standard of behavior.

8. What is the meaning of <u>fair</u> in this line from "Shall I Compare Thee to a Summer's Day?": "And every <u>fair</u> from <u>fair</u> sometimes declines"?
   A. beauty
   B. sunny, clear weather
   C. festival or carnival
   D. honesty

9. Emily Dickinson writes these lines in "Heart! We will forget him": "When you have done, pray tell me / That I may straight begin."

In these lines, straight means

A. without curves.

B. honestly and sincerely.

C. right away.

D. standing upright.

10. In "Simile," Momaday writes, "the deer / who walk in single file."

What does file mean here?

A. a place to store papers

B. a line of persons or animals, one at a time

C. a tool for smoothing or grinding down metal

D. a collection of data on a computer

11. In "The Taxi," Amy Lowell writes, "Streets coming fast, / One after the other, / Wedge you away from me."

In this context, wedge means

A. to secure firmly in place.

B. to crowd together.

C. to split apart.

D. to introduce a change in a routine.

12. Flick Webb is the ex-basketball player in John Updike's poem. Consider the following line: "As a gag, he dribbles an inner tube."

What does gag mean in this context?

A. something put on or in the mouth to silence a person

B. a joke

C. an order to stop free speech

D. something that makes a person choke

13. When Updike writes in "Ex-Basketball Player" that Flick "never learned a trade," the word trade means

A. an exchange of goods or services.

B. the customers in a business.

C. a bargain.

D. any kind of skilled work.

14. In "We Real Cool" by Gwendolyn Brooks, the word cool in the title means

A. excellent.

B. slightly odd.

C. actual.

D. unfriendly.

Academic Vocabulary

Directions: Choose the answer that gives the meaning of the underlined Academic Vocabulary word.

15. A metaphor can transform an object into a symbol.

A. undo

B. translate

C. arrange

D. change

16. Poets evoke images in their works.

A. think

B. call forth

C. repair

D. undo

Read On

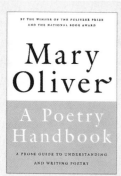

NONFICTION

A Poetry Handbook

From Pulitzer Prize–winning poet Mary Oliver comes *A Poetry Handbook: A Prose Guide to Understanding and Writing Poetry*. With passion, wit, and good common sense, Oliver describes the basic elements of poetry—meter and rhyme, form and diction, sound and sense. In her own words, Oliver explains her reasons for writing this handbook: "For poems are not words, after all, but fires for the cold, ropes let down to the lost, something as necessary as bread in the pockets of the hungry."

POETRY

Thomas and Beulah

Rita Dove won the Pulitzer Prize in poetry for *Thomas and Beulah,* a collection of poems based on the lives of her maternal grandparents. The poems are arranged chronologically in two separate sections that trace each grandparent's life from youth to marriage to old age and death. Instead of simply relating a step-by-step sequence of events, Dove dazzles the reader with vivid images that convey traumatic, joyous, and frustrating moments of memory. This is a book that you should read slowly to savor every emotion that the images evoke.

POETRY

Selected Poems

Pablo Neruda is regarded as one of the greatest poets of the twentieth century. His poems tackle a range of universal themes, including love, peace, war, and the beauty of the natural world. For a sampling of his best works, read *Selected Poems,* a bilingual edition that allows you to read his poetry in English translation and Neruda's native Spanish. These soulful, impassioned, and humane works may change the way you view poetry and life.

POETRY

Learning by Heart: Contemporary American Poetry About School

In this collection of 135 poems by contemporary poets, you will read about mean teachers, students who think they know more than their teachers (and students who do know more), and teachers who try to protect their students. You will also read poems about bullies, field trips, sports, classes that never seem to end, and even one about taking tests.

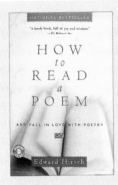

NONFICTION
How to Read a Poem

In this exploration of poetry and feeling, Edward Hirsch reminds us that even the greatest poems are incomplete without readers. His goal in *How to Read a Poem* is to make us better, more perceptive readers. He explains why poetry matters and shows us how to open up our imaginations so that the meaning of a poem can make a difference. Hirsch includes poems from around the world and analyzes the figures of speech, imagery, and poetic devices poets use to help us experience a poem.

POETRY
Cool Salsa

This collection of poems edited by Lori Carlson provides bilingual poems on growing up Latino in the United States. With contributions by poets such as Sandra Cisneros, Martín Espada, Gary Soto, and Pat Mora, *Cool Salsa* brings you the voices of young Latino America—teenagers struggling with their identity and looking to make themselves heard. The collection is divided into thematic sections that follow these poets as they travel from school days to their homeland and past memories and into the promising future.

NOVEL
Bronx Masquerade

After Mr. Ward's English class has spent a month reading poetry from the Harlem Renaissance, he assigns them an essay. One black student decides to write a poem instead, and Mr. Ward asks him to read it to the class. This is the start of Open Mike Fridays when students can read their poems aloud. In Nikki Grimes's *Bronx Masquerade,* students express their feelings about personal topics such as insensitive boyfriends, jealousy, problems with self-esteem, the power of love to heal, and pride of ethnic roots.

POETRY
Platero and I

"We understand each other. I let him go wherever he wishes and always he takes me where it is I wish to go." Such is the narrator's description of his faithful donkey, who brings a kind of enchantment to his small Spanish village. Juan Ramón Jiménez, winner of the 1956 Nobel Prize in literature, creates a tribute to friendship and the imagination through the deceptively simple autobiographical prose poems in *Platero and I.*

Writing Workshop

Response to Poetry

Write with a Purpose

Write a response to poetry that includes a clear thesis reflecting your analysis of a poem. Your **purpose** for writing is to provide insight into the craft and content of the poem. Your **audience** is others who have read the selection or who are interested in poetry.

A Good Response to Poetry

- provides necessary background information on a poem or poet
- includes a focused analysis and thesis
- identifies the speaker and his or her role in the poem
- analyzes the use of language
- examines the literal and the figurative meanings in the poem as they contribute to theme
- provides evidence from the text to support the analysis

See page 774 for complete rubric.

Reader/Writer Notebook

Use your **RWN** to complete the activities for this workshop.

Think as a Reader/Writer

In this collection, you've read many poems by many different writers. Now it is time to analyze a poem and write a **response to literature**—an in-depth examination of a piece of literature or poem. Read what Hortense J. Spillers says in an excerpt from "Gwendolyn the Terrible: Propositions on Eleven Poems," a response to the Gwendolyn Brooks poem "We Real Cool" (page 741).

> "We Real Cool," illustrates the wealth of implication that the poet can achieve in a very spare poem. . . . The simplicity of the poem is stark to the point of elaborateness. Less than lean, it is virtually coded. Made up entirely of monosyllables and end-stops, the poem is no non-sense at all. Gathered in eight units of three-beat lines, it does not necessarily invite inflection, but its persistent bump on "we" suggests waltz time to my ear. If the reader chooses to render the poem that way, she runs out of breath, or trips her tongue, but it seems that such "breathlessness" is exactly required of dudes hastening toward their death. Deliberately subverting the romance of sociological pathos, Brooks presents the pool players—"seven in the golden shovel"—in their own words and time. They make no excuse for themselves and apparently invite no one else to do so. The poem is their situation as *they* see it. In eight (could be nonstop) lines, here is their total destiny. Perhaps comic geniuses, they could well drink to this poem, making it a drinking/revelry song.

← Spillers's **thesis** is about the deceptive simplicity of the poem.

← She comments on how the sounds of the poem reflect its subject matter.

← Spillers uses examples from the poem to support her ideas.

Think About the Professional Model

With a partner, discuss the following questions about the model.

1. How does Spillers support the thesis statement?

2. What is the overall tone of the model? Did the author enjoy "We Real Cool"? Why do you think so?

OH **WA.10.2** Write responses to literature that organize an insightful interpretation around several clear ideas, premises or images and support judgments with specific references to the original text, to other texts, authors and to prior knowledge. **WP.10.3** Establish and develop a clear thesis statement for informational writing or a clear plan or outline for narrative writing.

Prewriting

Choose and Respond to a Poem

Before you delve into the deeper meanings of a poem, begin by responding personally to the poems you are considering as the subject of your analysis. Read or re-read each poem you are considering, asking yourself the questions listed below. Then, choose one poem for your analysis:

- How do I feel about this poem, including its speaker and characters?
- Do I have a clear understanding of the poem's theme, or statement about life?

Analyze the Poem

When you write a response to a poem, you will examine its elements in order to create a comprehensive literary analysis. Poets use different literary elements to achieve the effect they desire. As you read your poem, answer each of the following questions about the literary elements:

- **Title** Look at the title. What does the title reveal about the subject or theme of the poem? What conflicts, tensions, or comparisons are suggested?
- **Rhyme Scheme / Rhythm** What is the poem's rhyme scheme and meter? Read the poem aloud to hear the language and rhythm. How do the rhythm and rhyme contribute to the poem's tone and meaning?
- **Speaker** Who is the speaker in the poem? What does the speaker's **point of view** have to do with what is happening in the poem?
- **Tone** What is the poet's attitude toward the subject of the poem? How does the language, or **diction,** reveal the tone?
- **Figurative Language** How does the figurative language complement the meaning of the poem?
- **Diction** What deliberate and unique word choices contribute to the effect created by the poem?
- **Theme** What is the poet observing about life through the poem's theme? Remember to state the theme as a sentence rather than a phrase.

Think About Audience and Purpose

As you think about your poetry analysis, keep your **purpose** and **audience** in mind. Your purpose is to respond to the author's use of literary elements that shape the poem's meaning and to enhance your audience's understanding of the poem.

Idea Starters
- a favorite poem from this collection
- a poem from a favorite writer
- a poem about a subject you enjoy
- a poem that evokes strong feelings

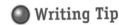 Writing Tip

Choose a poem that is complex enough for analysis but not so long that you cannot explain it in detail. A poem about 10–25 lines in length is a good choice. Also, when considering a poem, read it aloud so you catch subtleties and deeper meanings through the sound of the language.

Your Turn _____

Get Started Choose a poem to respond to. Then, making notes in your **RWN,** identify all the elements in your literary analysis and how they work together.

Learn It Online
An interactive graphic organizer can help you generate your response to literature. Try one at:

go.hrw.com | L10-767 | **Go**

Writing Tip

Which literary elements will serve as the focus, or subject, of your paper? Because poetic elements work closely together to create a memorable poem, it might be difficult to separate elements, such as imagery and figurative language, diction and tone, or speaker and point of view. Take a moment to evaluate what you will focus on in your analysis.

Create Your Thesis Statement

Review your analysis of the poem and determine which literary elements work most effectively in the poem. For example, in the professional model on page 766, Spillers asserts that the simplicity of "We Real Cool" is controlled by monosyllables and three-beat lines which replicate the pool players' dialogue. Spillers is focusing on the parts that combine to make up the whole.

In the same way, your analysis will reveal how the parts of your chosen poem work together to create a memorable effect. From the analysis, you will develop a **thesis statement,** an observation or assertion about the poem that you will support with evidence from the poem. Use the following steps to develop a thesis statement for your analysis.

- **Review your notes.** Look at the notes you took as you read your poem. What about your initial reaction strikes you?
- **Review your analysis.** Examine your answers to the literary analysis questions. Which literary elements are the most powerful in the poem?
- **Determine the poem's theme or observation about life.** Decide how the literary elements are related to the poem's theme.
- **Form your thesis statement by merging the literary elements with the theme.** Write a thesis statement that includes the relationship between the literary elements and the poem's theme.

One student analyzed John Masefield's "Sea Fever" and decided to focus on how the nautical images and conversational rhythm of the verse convey the longing of an old sailor. He put these ideas together in his **thesis statement.**

Analysis: *nautical images; speaker is sailor; conversational rhythm*

Sample Thesis: *Through conversational rhythm and nautical images, the poem reflects "sea fever"—a longing for the sea that characterizes all sailors.*

The student adds his interpretation, that the speaker represents all sailors, to strengthen the thesis statement.

Support Your Analysis

Support your thesis with **key points, details** from the poem, and **elaboration** about *how* the details support the key points:

Techniques for Determining Support	
Key Points	• Ask questions about the thesis. • Identify the important literary elements that support the thesis.
Supporting Details	• Paraphrase by restating a line in your own words. • Summarize the main points by condensing them. • Quote exact words from the poem.
Elaboration	• Explain how the details support the key points.

Your Turn _____

Create Your Thesis Statement and Support Now it is time to determine your thesis and its support. Follow the steps for creating your **thesis.** Then, read through the poem finding **supporting details** for your thesis, noting how you will apply each: paraphrased, summarized, or quoted.

Drafting

Follow the Writer's Framework

After you have decided how you will support your thesis, begin your first draft. Organize your key points in an order that makes sense for the analysis. You can list your key points by order of importance or according to the way in which the poem develops. Use the **framework** to the right for developing your paper.

Use the Literary Present Tense

When you write about literature, you should use the **literary present tense** to discuss the literary elements in the work. Instead of saying "the poet **described**," say "the poet **describes**." The samples in the Grammar Link below use the literary present.

Framework of Response to a Poem

Introduction
- Open your introductory paragraph with a captivating comment, observation, or question related to the poem.
- Provide necessary or interesting background information about the poem or the author.
- Include a thesis statement that explains how the literary elements work together to communicate the poem's theme.
- Include the author and title of the poem.

Body
- State your first key point with support and elaboration.
- Develop a separate paragraph for each of your other key points, using effective transitions between each one.
- Elaborate by explaining how each detail connects to each key point.

Conclusion
- Restate your thesis using different words.
- Leave your readers with an intriguing thought.

● Writing Tip

Referring to the framework and your notes, write a draft of your response. Be sure to order your key points logically and properly punctuate any supporting quotations.

Grammar Link Using Quotations Correctly

In your paper, you will include evidence from the poem as support for your points. This means you will directly quote lines from the poem. Be sure to follow the rules about punctuating direct quotations from poetry.

- Use quotation marks at the beginning and the end of material quoted directly from a poem.

    Masefield engages the reader's five senses when he describes "the flung spray," the blown spume," and the sea gulls crying."

- To indicate the end of a line in a poem, use a slash (/).

    The author writes, ". . .for the call of the running tide/Is a wild call and a clear call . . ." and gives the sea a voice.

- Retain the exact capitalization and punctuation of the poem in your quotation.

    He repeats "And all I ask" to great effect.

Your Turn

Organize and Draft Your Response to the Poem Before you write your draft, organize your analysis by writing each key point with supporting details and elaboration in the correct order. Then, refer to the framework you developed as you draft your analysis.

Peer Review

Work with a partner to discuss the questions at the right to evaluate your draft analysis of a poem. Use the revision techniques in the third column to improve your draft.

Evaluating and Revising

Read the questions in the left column of the chart and then use the tips in the middle column to help you make revisions to your response. The right column suggests techniques you can use to revise your draft.

Literary Analysis: Guidelines for Content and Organization

Evaluation Question	Tips	Revision Technique
1. Does the opening capture the reader's attention?	**Underline** the sentences that grab the reader. If no sentences are underlined, revise.	**Add** an observation, quote, question, or background information to your analysis.
2. Does the thesis statement connect the literary elements and the poem's theme?	**Put parentheses** around the thesis statement. Then **put brackets** around the literary elements and the theme.	**Rewrite** your thesis to show the connection between the elements and the theme.
3. Is the poem's speaker identified?	**Put a star next to** the references to the poem's speaker.	**Add** or clarify references to the speaker in the poem.
4. Does text evidence from the poem support each key point? Is sufficient elaboration provided for each point in the analysis?	**Put an *A*** next to the sentence that states the key point in each paragraph. **Put a *B*** next to text evidence details, and **put a *C*** next to elaboration on the details. If any letter is missing in a paragraph, revise.	**Add** one or more sentences that quote, summarize, or paraphrase text evidence to support your points. **Elaborate** by explaining how the details connect to the paragraph's key point.
5. Are smooth, effective transitions used between paragraphs?	**Circle** transitions used between paragraphs or key points.	If one paragraph leads abruptly into another, **add** a transitional word or phrase, or a direct reference between the key points.
6. Does the conclusion restate the thesis using different words? Does it leave readers with something to consider?	**Highlight** the restatement of the thesis. **Underline** the new thought. If either part is missing, revise.	**Add** a restatement of the thesis. **Add** a thought that applies the thesis to something the reader can relate to.

Read this student's draft with comments on its structure and suggestions for how it could be made even stronger.

Sea Fever
by Robert Scott, Twin Oaks High School

John Masefield was orphaned at thirteen, then joined the merchant marines, sailing around the world many times. Masefield is best known for his poems about the sea born from these experiences. "Sea Fever" is filled with nautical terms and images that reflect Masefield's years as a seaman. But the poem is more than personal nostalgia. Through conversational rhythm and nautical images, the poem reflects a longing for the sea that character-izes all sailors—sailors who share a "sea fever."

The repetition of the line, "I must go down to the seas again" and the many references to sea-going experiences such as "wheel's kick" and "white sail's shaking" identify the nautical background. He also states that this sea fever "may not be denied" because it is the only way of life he knows.

← Robert introduces Masefield with background information that relates to the poem.

← He identifies the **literary elements** he will focus on—nautical images and rhythm.

← Robert quotes from the poem to support the point about its natural meter.

MINI-LESSON ▸ How to Identify the Speaker in a Poem

Identifying the speaker in a poem is important for a complete and effective analysis. The speaker has characteristics just like a character in a play or story. You can identify the point of view and the speaker's characteristics from what he or she says and does. By including a statement about the nature of the speaker, the writer provides key information about the poem as a whole. Robert's revision makes the identity and role of the speaker clearer.

Robert's Draft of Paragraph Two:

The repetition of the line, "I must go down to the seas again" and the many references to sea-going experiences such as "wheel's kick" and "white sail's shaking" identify the nautical environment. He also states that this sea fever "may not be denied " because it is the only way of life he knows.

Robert's Revision of Paragraph Two:

The poem's speaker is obviously a seasoned sailor.∧The repetition of the line "I must go down to the seas again" at the beginning of each stanza and the many references to sea-going experiences such as the "wheel's kick" and the "white sail's shaking" identify his nautical background∧*and a life on the sea.* ~~He~~∧*The old sailor* also states that this sea fever "may not be denied" because it is the only way of life he knows∧*, making the old sailor's voice even more unmistakable.*

Your Turn _____

Identify the Speaker Read your draft and then ask yourself:

- Who is the speaker in the poem?
- Have I identified the speaker?
- Have I used text evidence to support his or her identity and importance?

Student Draft *continues*

Details from the poem support Robert's assertion. He **elaborates** and discusses these details.

Many of the poem's images are related to the natural environment associated with the sea: the wind, clouds, dawn, tide, spray, and sea gulls—even a "whale's way." However, these images are not threatening or dangerous. In fact, the aging seaman associates his life on the sea and his final quest with a "vagrant gypsy life," a "long trick," and a "merry yarn from a laughing fellow-rover." All of these images are as fun and rollicking as a grand adventure with friends.

Robert describes how two **key elements**—the **meter** and the **rhyme scheme**—contribute to the tone.

The iambic pentameter of the poem imitates natural speech, adding to the conversational tone and rhythm of the poem. The rhyme scheme of AA, BB adds to the light-hearted search for adventure that the sailor desires one last time. The rhyming couplets such as "running tide" and "may not be denied" emphasize the inevitable conclusion that his life will end happily at sea.

The **conclusion** ends the analysis with a comment on the poem's final line.

"Sea Fever" captures the voice of an experienced seaman who looks forward to what may be his last voyage—and even death—if it is on the sea: a final "quiet sleep and a sweet dream."

MINI-LESSON ▶ How to Create an Effective Conclusion

In this last paragraph, Robert emphasizes the depth of yearning the sailor has for the sea, but he does not restate his thesis in different words. An effective concluding paragraph essentially wraps up the thoughts discussed throughout the response and leaves the reader with a new perspective.

Robert's Draft of Paragraph Five:

"Sea Fever" captures the voice of an experienced seaman who looks forward to what may be his last voyage—and even death—if it is on the sea: a final "quiet sleep and a sweet dream."

Your Turn _____

Create an Effective Conclusion

- Re-read your final paragraph. Where is your summary and restatement of your thesis?
- What, if any, concluding ideas can you add to leave the reader with an intriguing thought?
- Revise your conclusion to make it more effective.

Robert's Revision of Paragraph Five:

The poem continues to its conclusion with the light-hearted tone and images of a benign sea that feels like home to the speaker. To read John Masefield's "Sea Fever" ~~captures the voice of~~ is to travel as if on a voyage of memory with a sailor whose passionate longing for the sea is undying. This ~~an~~ experienced seaman ~~who~~ looks forward to what may be his last voyage—and even death—if it is on the sea: a final "quiet sleep and a sweet dream."

WA.10.2 Write responses to literature that organize an insightful interpretation around several clear ideas, premises or images and support judgments with specific references to the original text, to other texts, authors and to prior knowledge.

Proofreading and Publishing

Proofreading

Now that you have evaluated and revised your response to the poem, it is time to produce a final copy for publishing. Proofread your paper—correcting any misspellings, punctuation errors, and problems in sentence structure.

● **Proofreading Tip**

Read your response aloud to a partner and have him or her take note of any awkward-sounding sentences or incomplete thoughts. Revise and re-read your paper aloud again.

> ### Grammar Link Using Colons
>
> The colon is a punctuation mark you may not use frequently, but it is helpful for listing images and other poetic devices. A colon means "note what follows." Use a colon before a list of items, especially after expressions such as *the following* or *as follows*. Often when analyzing literature, a writer will use a colon before a list of words or elements found in the poem. Robert uses a list of images in his third paragraph, and a colon to keep the list clean.
>
> Many of the poem's images are related to the natural environment associated with the sea:
>
> the wind, clouds, dawn, tide, spray, and sea gulls—even a "whale's way."

Publishing

Readers gain new insight into people's experiences through a response to poetry. Here are some ways to share your response with a wider audience:

- Submit your response to the school paper.
- Submit your response to a Web site that deals with your poem or author.
- Submit your analysis to a school or community literary magazine.
- Create a "coffee house" event to be held in the school library or other gathering place. You and your fellow students can read your chosen poems and your papers and can discuss the poems with other students.

Reflect on the Process In your *Reader/Writer Notebook*, write responses to the following questions:

1. How did your understanding of the poem change as you wrote your response?
2. What was the most important revision you made to your final draft? How did this revision improve the presentation of your response?
3. How has writing a response to poetry affected your understanding and appreciation of poetry?

Your Turn _____

Proofread and Publish As you **proofread** your draft, look for any places where you are listing words, phrases, or ideas. Revise by using colons appropriately. Make a final copy of your response and share it with an audience.

Scoring Rubric

You can use one of the rubrics below to evaluate your response to a poem from the Writing Workshop or the activity on the next page. Your teacher will tell you to use either the four-point or the six-point rubric.

6-Point Scale

Score 6 *Demonstrates advanced success*
- focuses consistently on a clear thesis
- shows effective organization throughout, with smooth transitions
- offers thoughtful, creative ideas
- develops ideas thoroughly, using examples, details, and fully-elaborated explanation
- exhibits mature control of written language

Score 5 *Demonstrates proficient success*
- focuses on a clear thesis
- shows effective organization, with transitions
- offers thoughtful ideas
- develops ideas competently, using examples, details, and well-elaborated explanation
- exhibits sufficient control of written language

Score 4 *Demonstrates competent success*
- focuses on a clear thesis, with minor distractions
- shows effective organization, with minor lapses
- offers mostly thoughtful ideas
- develops ideas adequately, a mixture of general and specific elaboration
- exhibits general control of written language

Score 3 *Demonstrates limited success*
- includes some loosely related ideas that distract from the writer's focus
- shows some organization, with noticeable gaps in the logical flow of ideas
- offers routine, predictable ideas
- develops ideas with uneven elaboration
- exhibits limited control of written language

Score 2 *Demonstrates basic success*
- includes loosely related ideas that seriously distract from the writer's focus
- shows minimal organization, with major gaps in the logical flow of ideas
- offers ideas that merely skim the surface
- develops ideas with inadequate elaboration
- exhibits significant problems with control of written language

Score 1 *Demonstrates emerging effort*
- shows little awareness of the topic and purpose for writing
- lacks organization
- offers unclear and confusing ideas
- develops ideas in only a minimal way, if at all
- exhibits major problems with control of written language

4-Point Scale

Score 4 *Demonstrates advanced success*
- focuses consistently on a clear thesis
- shows effective organization throughout, with smooth transitions
- offers thoughtful, creative ideas
- develops ideas thoroughly, using examples, details, and fully-elaborated explanation
- exhibits mature control of written language

Score 3 *Demonstrates competent success*
- focuses on a clear thesis, with minor distractions
- shows effective organization, with minor lapses
- offers mostly thoughtful ideas
- develops ideas adequately, a mixture of general and specific elaboration
- exhibits general control of written language

Score 2 *Demonstrates limited success*
- includes some loosely related ideas that distract from the writer's focus
- shows some organization, with noticeable gaps in the logical flow of ideas
- offers routine, predictable ideas
- develops ideas with uneven elaboration
- exhibits limited control of written language

Score 1 *Demonstrates emerging effort*
- shows little awareness of the topic and purpose for writing
- lacks organization
- offers unclear and confusing ideas
- develops ideas in only a minimal way, if at all
- exhibits major problems with control of written language

Response to a Poem

When responding to a prompt, use what you have learned from reading, writing your response to poetry, and studying the rubric on page 774. Use the steps below to develop a response to the following prompt.

OH **WA.10.2** Write responses to literature that organize an insightful interpretation around several clear ideas, premises or images and support judgments with specific references to the original text, to other texts, authors and to prior knowledge. *Also covered* **WP.10.3**

Writing Prompt

An exhausted apple-picker is the speaker in Robert Frost's poem "After Apple-Picking" (page 748).

> I am drowsing off . . . And I could tell
> What form my dreaming was about to take.
> Magnified apples appear and disappear,
> Stem end and blossom end,
> And every fleck of russet showing clear.

Write an essay responding to this image in Frost's poem. Use details from the poem to support your response.

Study the Prompt

Begin by reading the prompt carefully. Your purpose is to write a response to literature for this excerpt from a poem. Your goal is to provide a clear and detailed explanation of the image and the meaning it suggests. Note and underline the details of the image in the lines from Frost's poem. Ask yourself what ideas this image suggests.

Tip: Spend about five minutes studying the prompt.

Plan Your Response

Jot down the answer to the questions below. Your answers will become the key points of your analysis.

- What impression is formed in your mind by the details of the image?
- What might this image symbolize?

Then, as you prepare to write, ask yourself these questions to refine your response:

- What specific words or phrases in the excerpt from the poem are most important?
- How does the image point to a possible theme in the poem?

Tip: Spend about ten minutes planning your response.

Respond to the Prompt

Begin your response to the poem by writing an introductory pragraph that identifies the title and author of the poem, the main image in the poem, and what you think it represents. Then, in a thesis statement, provide a possible theme of the poem. In the body of your essay, support your points about the poem's imagery and theme by including specific words and phrases from the text.

Tip: Spend about twenty minutes writing your response to poetry.

Improve Your Response

Revising Go back to the key aspects of the prompt. Did you offer details of the image? Did you explain what the image has to do with the theme?

Proofreading Once you have made any necessary revisions to the content and organization in your essay, proofread to correct errors in grammar, spelling, punctuation, and capitalization. Make sure all of your edits are neat and that your paper is legible.

Checking Your Final Copy Before you turn your paper in, read it one more time to catch any errors you may have missed. You'll be glad you took one more look to present your best writing.

Tip: Save ten minutes to improve your paper.

Presenting a Response to Literature

Speak with a Purpose

Adapt your response to a poem into an oral response to a poem, and present it to the class. In your oral response you will demonstrate your grasp of the poem's meaning and the writer's techniques.

Think as a Reader/Writer When you wrote your response to a literary selection, you analyzed a poem and explained how it conveyed a thematic idea. Now, you will adapt your work into an oral presentation to discuss how the literary elements in the poem create meaning for the reader. Your presentation will show your audience that you have a firm grasp of the literary elements and theme of the poem you are analyzing.

Adapt Your Response to Literature

Parts of Your Presentation	Techniques for a Dramatic Interpretation
Introduction Identify • title • author • theme • element of text and stylistic device	Gain the attention of the audience with a • quotation from the literary selection that will arouse curiosity and interest • personal observation or anecdote from your own experience that is related to the meaning of the text • reference to a familiar source or famous person that will convey the ideas of the text
Body • Your judgment about the meaning of the text • References to the text, including quotations, paraphrases, and summaries • Explanations of the nuances, complexities, and ambiguities that you find in the text, relating to the theme • Elaboration of the details that support your ideas	• State emphatically what meaning the author has communicated about a thematic topic. • Focus on details from the text, showing how these details convey the author's meaning. • Use transitional words and phrases to direct the listeners' attention back to how the details of the text are related to the work's meaning or thematic idea. You can say, *Initially, Frost brings the distorted quality of dreams to the readers' attention with the image of . . . Next, he shocks us with . . .* • Read quotations from the text with expression, using gestures and inflection to stress ideas. • Make sure that you give meaning to each text reference by pointing out the events that surround it. • Relate each point and detail to your interpretation, showing how the text has created this meaningful effect.
Conclusion • Summarize your main idea, and explain the impact the text had on you.	• Use powerful language to restate your interpretation of the text. • Share your appreciation for the effect that the text has had on you.

Reader/Writer Notebook

Use your **RWN** to complete the activities for this workshop.

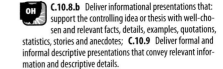

C.10.8.b Deliver informational presentations that: support the controlling idea or thesis with well-chosen and relevant facts, details, examples, quotations, statistics, stories and anecdotes; **C.10.9** Deliver formal and informal descriptive presentations that convey relevant information and descriptive details.

Deliver Your Response to Literature

Prepare Your Notes

- Use concise notes to guide your presentation. Write down the key words and phrases to remind yourself of your main points and the details needed to elaborate on your ideas.
- Print the transitional words that you will use to move from one thought to the next.
- Underline key words or phrases so that you can use your voice to add emphasis.
- The only notes that you will write out in full are the direct quotations from the literature that you are using.

Practice Your Dramatic Delivery

Although your speech is not memorized or fully written out, you can rehearse what you have planned. Think of yourself as an actor who is holding the interest of an audience with a dramatic explanation.

- Practice using your voice to emphasize your points. You can vary your inflection to draw your listeners' attention. Express emotion to create a mood that will reinforce the meaning or effect created by the text.
- Experiment with and select gestures that you can use to make your audience aware of the meanings that you are explaining. For example, you might put your hand over your eyes to show how a character is unwilling to face an unpleasant reality.
- Think of ways of presenting sections of the text that were problematic for you. Engage the audience by sharing what you thought and felt as you went through the process of unraveling the meaning of these passages. You could read the same line with two different tones and point out the ambiguity that you notice.
- Remember to make eye contact with individuals in the audience.

> ## A Good Oral Presentation
> - begins with a dramatic introduction that grabs the listeners' attention
> - includes the title, the author, and the literary element or stylistic device that pertains to the selection's themes
> - uses references from the text to support main points
> - includes details from the selection that support your interpretation
> - guides listeners through the presentation with transitional words and phrases
> - ends by restating thematic ideas and expressing appreciation for the effect the author has achieved

 Speaking Tip

By listing the key words and phrases of your presentation vertically, you will be able to move your finger down the list and keep your place. This way, you can look up from your notes and make eye contact with your audience.

Learn It Online
For ideas about gesture and facial expression, see *MediaScope* TV commercials at:

`go.hrw.com` `L10-777`   **Go**

Writing Skills Review

Response to a Poem **Directions:** Read the following paragraph from a student's response to a poem. Then, answer the questions that follow.

(1) Robert Frost's poem "After Apple-Picking" uses the metaphor of sleep to merge the worlds of wakefulness and dream, creativity and death. (2) In mostly rhymed iambic pentameter, the poem's uneven cadence keeps the reader alert even though the speaker refers to "sleep" and being "overtired" throughout the poem. (3) In poetry, sleep is typically a metaphor for death, which seems to lurk at both the beginning and the end of the poem. (4) The beginning of the poem has the speaker's ladder pointing "Toward heaven still," and the reference to the sleep of the woodchuck is the sleep of winter. (5) As spring is to youth and rebirth, winter is to death. (6) The speaker seems to hover near a dream state, on the verge of sleep, as he "cannot rub the strangeness from . . . sight," and he knows the form his "dreaming was about to take," as if not quite asleep. (7) He sees "Magnified apples appear and disappear," as if being taunted in some manner. But what of the "great harvest" he "desired"? (8) As fruit is an easy metaphor for creativity, the speaker had "ten thousand fruit to touch," and those that hit the ground were tossed into the pile for making cider. (9) In the end, the speaker's life's work—poetry?—becomes synonymous with picked fruit and his "sleep" not necessarily death, but hibernation.

1. Why is the description of the poem's form— iambic pentameter—important?

   A. It is the main theme.

   B. It is crucial for understanding the poem.

   C. It creates a tension with the theme.

   D. It is not useful.

2. Which sentence is the thesis statement?

   A. sentence 1

   B. sentence 2

   C. sentence 4

   D. sentence 9

3. Which literary elements does the essay address?

   A. rhyme scheme

   B. imagery

   C. rhyme scheme and point of view

   D. point of view

4. How does the student's response explain the meaning of the poem's figurative language?

   A. The figurative meaning is ironic.

   B. The figurative meaning of death or hibernation is prominent.

   C. The figurative meaning is the theme of being tired.

   D. The analysis does not address figurative meaning.

OH   **WA.10.2**   Write responses to literature that organize
an insightful interpretation around several clear
ideas, premises or images and support judgments
with specific references to the original text, to other texts,
authors and to prior knowledge. *Also covered:* **WP.10.13;
WP.10.6; WP.10.3**

5. Which of the following revisions would strengthen the student's analysis of the figurative language in the poem?

   A. Robert Frost's poem "After Apple-Picking" uses the metaphor of sleep to merge wakefulness and dreams with the figurative worlds of creativity and death.

   B. The beginning of the poem has the speaker's ladder pointing "Toward heaven still," and the figurative reference to the sleep of the woodchuck is the sleep of winter.

   C. He sees "Magnified apples appear and disappear," as if being taunted in some figurative manner. But what of the "great harvest" he "desired"?

   D. In the end, the speaker's life's work— poetry?—becomes synonymous with picked fruit and his figurative "sleep" not necessarily death, but hibernation.

6. Which sentence best recaps the thesis?

   A. Robert Frost's dreams merge the exhausting work of apple-picking and the poet's state of confusion.

   B. In the end, Frost's poem captures the frustrated life of the poet, who sees little worth in his artistic efforts.

   C. Through the curious world of dreams, Robert Frost unites a tired state of wakefulness with the temptation to rest and leave work or creativity behind.

   D. Robert Frost retires to a life of dreaming or writing poetry—as he feels he is no longer capable of work.

7. At the beginning of which sentence could the writer have added a transition, or connecting word, to make a smoother transition?

   A. sentence 1

   B. sentence 2

   C. sentence 3

   D. sentence 4

8. Which sentence would be a logical closing thought for the student's response?

   A. The speaker considers himself one with nature.

   B. Is his art in decline, or is it merely taking a respite?

   C. Fruit serves as a metaphor for creativity.

   D. He goes off to make cider.

9. Which idea requires more elaboration in the student's response?

   A. sleep as a metaphor for death

   B. the dream state imagery

   C. apples as a metaphor for creativity

   D. the use of tiredness as a theme

Drama
Writers on Writing

Carl Hancock Rux on Drama

Carl Hancock Rux is an award-winning playwright, actor, writer, and musician. Rux got his start doing spoken-word performances and gradually moved toward drama and music. His works explore themes of identity and race and are often inspired by historical events.

"Growing up in the New York City foster care system, the only concept I had of family was what I learned from social workers, judges and legal guardians—which is to say I knew nothing at all about family. The details of my biological history lived in a tightly guarded castle of case records: Like most children, I had no true understanding of race or gender politics, or the economic disempowerment that informed our East Harlem world. Increasingly I looked for stories that would provide me with answers. Comic book superheroes gave me a heroic sense of overcoming great obstacles; novels provided me with characters drawn similarly to my own, and poetry echoed my inner thoughts and gave me a telescope into the souls of others—but none of these came close to telling the tale I was the protagonist of. I wanted to experience something that seemed as magical, as elusive, as my own life—a tale that encompassed my personal landscape and at the same time, transcended it. Somewhere, there was a parallel universe of urbanity, familial wars, and a boy's lifelong quest to resolve his place in the world.

What came to me, in the hands of my fifth-grade schoolteacher, Mrs. Bougdanos, were the plays of Euripides. We read the plays out loud, each of us taking turns playing a different character; the son Hippolytus who appeals to his father Theseus to not lose trust in him. The self-righteousness of Pentheus and the woeful sorrow of his mother Agave, both cast under the spell of Dionysus. I rolled the sentences of these characters around in my mouth. I was enacting conversations that belonged to other people from another time, and yet something about these conversations pertained to me, *personally.*

Later, when my teacher introduced us to Eugene O'Neill's *Long Day's Journey into Night* and Arthur Miller's *Death of a Salesman,* I was able to speak the language of a father's blighted hope, against his son's objectives. In Lorraine Hansberry's *Raisin in the Sun,* I glimpsed dreams fraying against the harsh realities of race and poverty—and in all of it, there was hope. Reading plays (and later, writing them) allowed me to step into the shoes of other characters, and walk around my own neighborhood. My neighborhood became the ancient ruins of Greece; the abyss O'Neill's characters looked out into as they took their long day's journey into night. All the world was made up of gods and monsters, and everyone's struggle was the same as mine—to not give in to the frustration of the mystery or the foul air of discontent that (sometimes) hangs over human existence. All of life is a myth, I realized, neatly tucking away the details of our personal histories. If I can keep the conversations going, everything will be answered in its own time. "

Think as a Writer

Carl Hancock Rux found great inspiration in the works of other playwrights. Whose writing has inspired you?

Elements of Drama

INFORMATIONAL TEXT FOCUS
Analyzing an Argument

"There's something about the theater which makes my fingertips tingle."

—Wole Soyinka

What Do
You
Think

How do we know what choice to make—when it is not clear which choice is the right one?

Detail from *Fun Fair* (1979) by Boris Khomenko (1930–). Oil on canvas.

Learn It Online
For help reading Shakespeare's *The Tragedy of Julius Caesar*, check out *NovelWise*:

go.hrw.com   L10-783   **Go**

Literary Focus

What Are the Elements of Drama?

Do you enjoy live stage performances? Actors find a thrill in bringing a character to life before an audience. People have been acting in and watching dramatic performances for centuries. Many people—actors, directors, and experts in costumes, scenery, lighting, and makeup—help to bring the words of a playwright to life on the stage.

Origins of Drama

A **drama** is a story that is enacted in real space and time by live actors for a live audience. The earliest plays on record date to the fifth century B.C., when ancient Greeks held festivals to honor Dionysus, the god of wine and fertility. Playwrights competed for top honors at these festivals. Later, in medieval England, dramas celebrating religious themes became a popular form of entertainment. Western drama as we know it today developed from these early forms.

Forms of Drama

There are two main forms of classical drama: tragedy and comedy. A **tragedy** is a play ending in sorrow or regret. A **comedy** ends happily.

Tragedy Most tragedies revolve around a **tragic hero**—a noble figure who is admirable in many ways, but has a **tragic flaw,** a personal failing such as pride or jealousy. In classic Greek dramas, this flaw results in a choice that ultimately dooms the hero to a tragic end, usually death. Tragedies often pit human limitations against the larger forces of destiny—an almighty power or an indifferent universe.

Foil The **foil** is a character who is used to contrast another character, usually the tragic hero. Some foils highlight the contrast by showing opposite virtue.

Comedy A **comedy** also deals with human flaws but focuses on the lighter side. Comedic choices result in confusion and humor and lead to an expected, if exaggerated, outcome. In the following excerpt from Anton Chekhov's *The Brute,* Mr. Smirnov, in comic rage, denounces all women to a widow, Mrs. Popov. Only minutes later, he falls hopelessly in love with her.

> **Smirnov.** Appearances, I admit, can be deceptive. In appearance, a woman may be all poetry and romance, goddess and angel, muslin and fluff. To look at her exterior is to be transported to heaven. But I have looked at her interior, Mrs. Popov, and what did I find there—in her very soul? A crocodile. (*He has gripped the back of the chair so firmly that it snaps.*) And, what is more revolting, . . . a crocodile that thinks itself queen of the realm of love! Whereas, in sober fact, dear madam, if a woman can love anything except a lap dog, you can hang me by the feet on that nail.
>
> from *The Brute* by Anton Chekhov

RA.L.10.5 Analyze how an author's choice of genre affects the expression of a theme or topic. **RA.L.10.1** Compare and contrast an author's use of direct and indirect characterization, and ways in which characters reveal traits about themselves, including dialect, dramatic monologues and soliloquies.

Dramatic Structure

Although both short stories and dramas focus on the actions of made-up characters, there are major differences between the two genres. Short stories are written in prose, told by a narrator who describes the characters and action. A play, on the other hand, consists mostly of characters' words and actions.

Characters in Conflict Like all stories, plays involve characters who take action to resolve a problem, or **conflict.** Conflicts place the main character, or **protagonist,** in a difficult situation.

As the character in a play takes steps to resolve the conflict—to get what he or she wants—**complications** arise. These are obstacles that stand in the way of the character's attempt to achieve a goal. Eventually the events of the play build to a **climax,** an event that determines how the conflict will be resolved. The **resolution** of the play follows, as the conflict is resolved and the play comes to an end. A tragedy inevitably results in sorrow, disappointment, or death. A comedy ends on a lighter note, often with a wedding or other joyous occasion.

Forms of Conflict An **external conflict** exists between a character and an outside source—for example, other characters, nature, or circumstances beyond his or her control. Dramas often feature an **antagonist,** a main character who is in opposition to the protagonist. The antagonist creates problems for the protagonist in a variety of ways. The conflict in a comedy usually hinges on a problem of the heart, such as a thwarted courtship or a romantic misunderstanding. The conflict is resolved happily in a comedy, but there are always complications along the way.

Another form of conflict is **internal,** a struggle within a character torn between conflicting desires. For example, in William Shakespeare's *The Tragedy of Julius Caesar,* Brutus wants to be loyal to Caesar, but he also wants to do what is best for Rome.

> **Brutus.**
> It must be by his death; and for my part,
> I know no personal cause to spurn at him,
> But for the general. He would be crowned.
> How that might change his nature, there's
>   the question.
> It is the bright day that brings forth the
>   adder,
> And that craves wary walking. Crown him
>   that,
> And then I grant we put a sting in him
> That at his will he may do danger with.
> Th' abuse of greatness is when it disjoins
> Remorse from power; and, to speak truth of
>   Caesar,
> I have not known when his affections swayed
> More than his reason.
>
> from *The Tragedy of Julius Caesar*
> by William Shakespeare

Literary Focus

Setting the Stage

Drama involves much more than the written words on a page. Plays are meant to be performed. Theater artists—actors, directors, designers, lighting technicians, and stage crews—help the playwright's vision come alive on stage for an audience. Even the most basic performance involves a stage, costumes, lighting, and a set. These help the actors become the characters with whom the audience connects.

The **stages** on which actors perform can vary greatly. In Shakespeare's day, stages extended out into the audience, with audiences standing or sitting on three sides or watching from above in a balcony. Many stages today are set back from the audience, separated from them by a curtain. Other stages are set out in the middle of the audience, "in the round." With this design, audience members surround the stage on all sides.

Scene Design Sets, lights, costumes, and props help transform a bare stage into ancient Rome, a battlefield, or an abandoned farmhouse. Often a playwright will set the stage with directions at the beginning of a play, as in this excerpt.

> **Scene:** *The kitchen in the now abandoned farmhouse of John Wright, a gloomy kitchen, and left without having been put in order— unwashed pans under the sink, a loaf of bread outside the breadbox, a dish towel on the table—other signs of incompleted work.*
>
> from *Trifles* by Susan Glaspell

Scene design includes **lighting,** which can help establish a mood, and costumes. As with other design elements, costumes may be simple or elaborate. **Props** (short for properties) are portable items that actors carry or handle onstage in order to further the plot in the play.

Many people besides the actors are involved in bringing a production to life. The director oversees the production. Behind the scenes, stagehands design and create the sets, move equipment, open and close curtains, run the lighting and sound effects, and ensure that all runs smoothly.

Everyone in the production speaks a common language geared toward production. For example, "stage left" is to the actors' left, and "stage right" is to their right. "Downstage" is toward the audience, and "upstage" is away from them.

Dramatic Elements

Once the physical elements are in place for a production, the actors perform, using a variety of techniques to convey ideas and emotions to the audience.

Stage Directions Playwrights often include **stage directions,** notes on how actors should move and deliver the lines. In the following excerpt from Anton Chekhov's *The Brute,* stage directions describe how an actor should deliver a particular line.

> **Luka** *(upset).* There's someone asking for you, ma'am. Says he must—
>
> **Mrs. Popov.** I suppose you told him that since my husband's death I see no one?
>
> **Luka.** Yes, ma'am. I did, ma'am. But he wouldn't listen, ma'am. He says it's urgent.
>
> **Mrs. Popov** *(shrilly).* I see no one!!
>
> from *The Brute* by Anton Chekhov

RA.L.10.5 Analyze how an author's choice of genre affects the expression of a theme or topic.
RA.L.10.1 Compare and contrast an author's use of direct and indirect characterization, and ways in which characters reveal traits about themselves, including dialect, dramatic monologues and soliloquies.

Characters Onstage

The conversations of characters onstage are called **dialogue.** Dialogue and action move the play forward. Actors reveal characters' emotions, thoughts, and intentions through their voices, tone, actions, and body language. Certain dramatic techniques can help convey emotion and build tension in a play. The playwright often includes suggestions for these in the script.

Soliloquy A **monologue** is a speech delivered by one character to another character onstage. A **soliloquy,** on the other hand, is spoken by a character alone onstage, to himself or herself or directly to the audience. Soliloquies often express a character's deepest feelings and may signal an important change in the character's thinking. The following excerpt is from a soliloquy in *The Tragedy of Julius Caesar,* in which Cassius wonders aloud whether Brutus will join the conspiracy to kill Caesar.

> **Cassius.**
> Well, Brutus, thou art noble; yet I see
> Thy honorable may be wrough
> From that it is disposed; therefore it is meet
> That noble minds keep ever with their likes;
> For who so firm that cannot be seduced?
> Caesar doth bear me hard, but he loves Brutus.
> If I were Brutus now and he were Cassius,
> He should not humor me. . . .
>
> from *The Tragedy of Julius Caesar*
> by William Shakespeare

Asides Occasionally a character, especially in Shakespeare's plays, may also comment on the action in a play, using an **aside.** Asides are spoken to the audience or to one character, but other characters onstage do not hear what is said. In this aside from *Julius Caesar,* Trebonius lets the audience know that he has dark plans in store for Caesar.

> **Caesar.**
> . . . what, Trebonius,
>   I have an hour's talk in store for you;
>   Remember that you call on me today;
> Be near me, that I may remember you.
> **Trebonius.**
> Caesar, I will *(aside)* and so near will I be, that
> your best friends shall wish I had been further.
>
> from *The Tragedy of Julius Caesar*
> by William Shakespeare

Your Turn Analyze Drama

1. Name at least two differences between comedy and tragedy.

2. How might "fatal flaws" affect a character's ability to make wise or informed choices?

3. Think of a movie. Who is the protagonist? Who is the antagonist? What is the conflict, and how is it resolved?

4. Consider all of the theater jobs involved in putting on a play. Which do you think you would like to have? Why?

Learn It Online
Do pictures help you learn? Try the *PowerNotes* version of this lesson on:

go.hrw.com   L10-787   Go

Analyzing Visuals

How Do Different Directors Interpret the Same Character?

If you've ever read a book and then seen a movie version of it, you've seen how wildly someone else's interpretations can differ from your own. The same thing happens with plays. The script remains the same, but different directors add their own ideas and interpretations.

Analyzing Two Interpretations of the Same Character

Use these guidelines to help you:

1. Read the play or a summary of it. How do you envision the character based on information in the play?

2. How are the appearances of the characters the same or different?

3. What character traits does each director decide to heighten or downplay? Why?

4. Consider both directors' perspectives. What does each director's unique perspective tell you about the character?

5. Look at the character as a whole. How do the two interpretations add to your understanding of the character and the play?

1. Shylock, the **character** in this photograph, is a wealthy merchant. What details in the character's costume help you understand this?

2. Shylock forbids his daughter to marry and demands harsh payment for a loan. What emotion is suggested by his facial expression here?

3. Notice the background and modern dress in this photo. Why do you think a director might choose to present an old play in a modern **setting**?

The Merchant of Venice by William Shakespeare. Darko Tresnjak (director), F. Murray Abraham (Shylock). Theatre for a New Audience—NYC/Royal Shakespeare Company Swan Theatre, Stratford-upon-Avon, England. Part of "The Complete Works" Festival—4/06–3/07.

1. What emotion does the actor in this photograph seem to express? Explain.

2. Compare the two Shylocks. How are they different? In what ways are they similar?

3. What does the background in the photo indicate about the play's **setting**? Does it seem to be set in modern times or long ago?

The Merchant of Venice by William Shakespeare. Rebecca Gatward (director), John McEnery (Shylock) Shakespeare's Globe, London, England.

Your Turn   Write About a Character

Think about a movie version of a book you've read. Choose one of the main characters. How did you visualize this character when reading the book? Compare and contrast your vision of the character with that of the director.

Reading Focus

by **Kylene Beers**

What Skills Will Help You Analyze Drama?

When you read a play, you are actually reading a script. Pay attention to everything: stage directions, introductory notes, background information, comments about settings and scenes, and dialogue. Remember that the play was meant to be performed, not read.

Making Predictions

When you read a compelling story or watch an engrossing movie, you may be on the edge of your seat wanting to know what will happen next. Will the characters make good choices? Will they get what they want? How will the story end? Chances are you've tried to answer questions like these before reaching the end of a novel or movie. This process is called **making predictions.** Predicting while you are reading keeps you alert and involved in the action. Information and details in the play provide clues to what will happen. When you notice these clues and think about what they mean in the story, you are predicting.

Anton Chekhov, one of the playwrights featured in this collection, once said, "If a gun is hanging on the wall in the first act, it must fire in the last." What did he mean by this? If a playwright mentions a specific set element, such as a gun hanging on the wall, then readers (and directors and actors) know that it must play some part in the story. Everything included in a script or screenplay is there for a reason. As you read a play, record your predictions in a chart like the one below.

Clue	What It Might Mean	My Prediction

Making Inferences

Another productive strategy for reading drama is making inferences about characters, their motives, and their conflicts. When you **make an inference,** you use logic and reason to come to a conclusion about something not directly stated within the text. Making inferences depends on what you know about the character and the situation in which the character acts this way. As you read, pay attention to the way characters act and talk as well as to what they say. Read any stage directions provided by the playwright. Notice any differences between what the characters say and the way they are acting— and what this might mean. All of this information enables you to make logical and constructive inferences about the play.

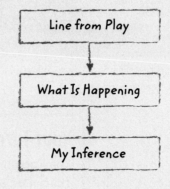

OH **RP.10.1** Apply reading comprehension strategies, including making predictions, comparing and contrasting, recalling and summarizing and making inferences and drawing conclusions.

Visualizing

Have you ever read a book that was made into a movie? Did the actors in the movie look and sound the way you had envisioned them in your mind? Did the sets in the movie match what you had pictured? While you were reading, you were **visualizing**—that is, you were seeing characters and actions in your mind's eye. Chances are that what you imagined and what a movie director imagined were different in some ways because visualizing is an individual process.

Drama is a visual art form. It is meant to be seen. When you read a play, visualize it being performed. Apply your visual skills to the specific information the playwright gives us, such as suggestions on set design, costumes, props, and lighting to create the desired mood, atmosphere, and overall feel of a play. Remember, however, the playwright does not tell us everything. The director visualizes what is unstated and guides the actors to produce that vision. Read a play as a director does, imagining the scenes, the characters, and the action.

Paraphrasing

Imagine you've just seen a great movie and you are about to describe it to your friends. What do you say? You try to retell the story in your own words. **Paraphrasing** is a similar process. When you paraphrase, you restate someone else's words or ideas in your own words—while giving credit to the original author. Paraphrasing is a good way to clarify your understanding of what you read. You might paraphrase a character's speech, a scene from a play, or the whole play.

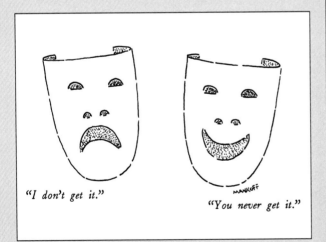

"I don't get it."

"You never get it."

Your Turn Apply Reading Skills

Read the following excerpt from *The Brute,* where Mrs. Popov is speaking to Smirnov. Visualize the scene as a director. Then, answer the questions.

> **Mrs. Popov.** Oh, nothing, you can go. Well, no, just a minute. No, you can go. Go! I detest you! But, just a moment. *(Throws the gun on the table.)* My fingers have gone to sleep holding that horrid thing. *(She is tearing her handkerchief to shreds.)* And what are you standing around for? Get out of here!
>
> from *The Brute* by Anton Chekhov

1. Paraphrase Mrs. Popov's speech.
2. Based on her words and actions, what can you infer about Mrs. Popov?
3. What might you predict about the action or character based on this speech?

Now go to the Skills in Action: Reading Model

Learn It Online
Try the *PowerNotes* version of this lesson on:

Build Background

On the Waterfront is a classic 1954 movie that won eight Academy Awards, including Best Screenplay. Legendary film star Marlon Brando won Best Actor for his portrayal of Terry Malloy, a boxer who takes on a corrupt union run by Johnny Friendly. The union, which represents the dock workers on the waterfront, is involved in illegal activities. Terry's older brother, Charley, is an attorney for this union.

The following excerpt opens with Charley trying to bribe Terry to take a job on the docks as head loader—and to keep his mouth shut. They are in a taxicab.

Reading Focus

Making Inferences Charley does not explicitly state what he means. The reader has to infer that he is asking Terry to overlook corruption.

Literary Focus

Conflict The stage direction and Terry's dialogue indicate Terry's conflict: He struggles between wanting to please his brother and wanting to do the right thing.

Read with a Purpose As you read this excerpt from a screenplay, follow Terry's struggles as he comes to the hardest decision of his life.

from On the Waterfront

by **Budd Schulberg**

Charley. There's a slot for a boss loader on the new pier we're opening up.

Terry (*interested*). Boss loader!

Charley. Ten cents a hundred pounds on everything that moves in and out. And you don't have to lift a finger. It'll be three-four hundred a week just for openers.

Terry. And for all that dough I don't do nothin'?

Charley. Absolutely nothing. You do nothing and you say nothing. You understand, don't you, kid?

Terry (*struggling with an unfamiliar problem of conscience and loyalties*). Yeah—yeah—I guess I do—but there's a lot more to this whole thing than I thought, Charley.

Charley. You don't mean you're thinking of testifying against—(*turns a thumb in toward himself*)

Terry. I don't know—I don't know! I tell you I ain't made up my mind yet. That's what I wanted to talk to you about.

Charley (*patiently, as to a stubborn child*). Listen, Terry, these piers we handle through the local—you know what they're worth to us?

Terry. I know. I know.

Charley. Well, then, you know Cousin Johnny isn't going to jeopardize a setup like that for one rubber-lipped—

Marlon Brando in *On the Waterfront*, c. 1954.

Analyzing Visuals **Viewing and Interpreting** How does this photograph of an actor playing the role of Terry compare to what you visualized while reading the text?

Terry *(simultaneous)* Don't say that!
Charley *(continuing)* —ex-tanker[1] who's walking on his heels—?
Terry. Don't say that!
Charley. What the heck!!!
Terry. I could have been better!
Charley. Listen, that isn't the point.
Terry. I could have been better!
Charley. The point is—there isn't much time, kid.

[*There is a painful pause, as they appraise each other.*]

Terry *(desperately)* I tell you, Charley, I haven't made up my mind!
Charley. Make up your mind, kid, I beg you, before we get to four thirty-seven River . . .
Terry *(stunned)* Four thirty-seven—that isn't where Gerry G . . .?

[CHARLEY *nods solemnly.* TERRY *grows more agitated.*]

---

1. **ex-tanker:** a tanker is a term for a boxer who intentionally loses a fight.

Reading Focus

Visualizing Visualize the two men looking at each other. How might actors convey this "painful pause"?

Terry. Charley . . . you wouldn't take me to Gerry G. . .?

[CHARLEY *continues looking at him. He does not deny it. They stare at each other for a moment. Then suddenly* TERRY *starts out of the cab.* CHARLEY *pulls a pistol.* TERRY *is motionless, now, looking at* CHARLEY.]

Charley. Take the boss loading, kid. For God's sake. I don't want to hurt you.
Terry *(hushed, gently guiding the gun down toward Charley's lap)* Charley . . . Charley . . . Wow. . . .
Charley *(genuinely).* I wish I didn't have to do this, Terry.

[TERRY *eyes him, beaten.* CHARLEY *leans back and looks at* TERRY *strangely.* TERRY *raises his hands above his head, somewhat in the manner of a prizefighter mitting the crowd. The image nicks* CHARLEY'S *memory.*]

Reading Focus

Making Predictions The stage directions may lead you to predict that the following dialogue will be about Terry's career as a boxer.

Terry *(an accusing sigh).* Wow. . . .
Charley *(gently).* What do you weigh these days, slugger?
Terry *(shrugs).* —eighty-seven, eighty-eight. What's it to you?
Charley *(nostalgically).* Gee, when you tipped one seventy-five you were beautiful. You should've been another Billy Conn. That skunk I got to manage you brought you along too fast.
Terry. It wasn't him! *(years of abuse crying out in him).* It was you, Charley. You and Johnny. Like the night the two of youse come in the dressing room and says, 'Kid, this ain't your night, we're going for the price on Wilson.' It ain't my night. I'd of taken Wilson apart that night! I was ready—remember the early rounds throwing them combinations. So what happens—This bum Wilson he gets the title shot—outdoors in the ball park!—and what do I get —a couple of bucks and a one-way ticket to Palookaville.[2] *(more and more aroused as he relives it)* It was you, Charley. You was my brother. You should of looked out for me. Instead of making me take them dives for the short-end money.

Literary Focus

Tragedy In these lines, Terry reveals his anguish and betrayal. Terry's tragic flaw is his love for and loyalty to his brother, which ultimately brings about his downfall.

Charley *(defensively).* I always had a bet down for you. You saw some money.
Terry *(agonized).* See! You don't understand!
Charley. I tried to keep you in good with Johnny.

---

2. **Palookaville:** slang for a place where second-rate fighters live.

Terry. You don't understand! I could've been a contender. I could've had class and been somebody. Real class. Instead of a bum, let's face it, which is what I am. It was you, Charley.

[CHARLEY *takes a long, fond look at* TERRY. *Then he glances quickly out the window. From* CHARLEY'S *angle. A gloomy light reflects the street numbers—433—435—*]

Terry. It was you, Charley . . .
Charley (*turning back to Terry, his tone suddenly changed*). Okay—I'll tell him I couldn't bring you in. Ten to one they won't believe it, but—go ahead, blow. Jump out, quick, and keep going . . . and God help you from here on in.

By letting Terry off the hook, Charley has signed his own death warrant. Sometime later a voice calls to Terry outside of his apartment to come down if he wants to see Charley. Terry and his girfriend, Edie, go down looking for Charley.

Same voice in fog. Wanna see Charley? He's over here.

Terry (*as they hurry forward*). Hey, Charley . . .

[*The headlights of a car suddenly illuminate* CHARLEY *against the wall.* CHARLEY *is leaning against the lamp post, in a very casual attitude, looking as dapper as usual.* TERRY *and* EDIE *run to him. The car drives off.*]

Terry. Looking for me, Charley?

[CHARLEY *seems to study them silently.* TERRY *nudges him.*]

Terry. Hey, Charley.

[CHARLEY *slides down the wall and crumples to the ground. Dead.* EDIE *screams.* TERRY *drops beside the body.*]

Terry. He's dead. He's dead. Those scummy, good-for-nuthin' butchers. . . .

Budd Schulberg
(1914–   )

Movie poster for *On the Waterfront*. An Elia Kazan Production with Marlon Brando, Eva Marie Saint, Karl Maiden, Lee J. Cobb, Sam Spiegel.

Hollywood Prince

Among the people he came to know well, Budd Schulberg counted the writers Sinclair Lewis, F. Scott Fitzgerald, and John Steinbeck. How did this ambitious writer get his start? Budd Schulberg was born in New York City in 1914, but he grew up in Hollywood. His father B. P. Schulberg, a powerful Hollywood figure, worked as a general manager for Paramount Studios, a well-known movie studio. His mother, Adela Schulberg, encouraged her son's interest in writing and poetry. By the age of seventeen, he was writing stories about movie stars as a publicist for Paramount. A few years later he became a screenwriter, and by age twenty-seven, Schulberg was a best-selling novelist.

"Art for People's Sake"

Some of Schulberg's work focused on political and social issues, such as those portrayed in *On the Waterfront*. Growing up in Hollywood, he saw how entertainment and stories could become meaningful by showing characters dealing with these issues. In 1972, he stated, "I believe in art, but I don't believe in art for art's sake . . . I believe in art for people's sake." In other words, art can be entertaining while also showing characters dealing with people rising to power. Not surprisingly, some of Schulberg's characters work in Hollywood. His first and best-known novel, *What Makes Sammy Run?* (1941) is about an office boy who becomes the head of a film studio. Schulberg was also a fan of boxing, and the sport made its way into his fiction. He wrote many nonfiction pieces, including a book on the famous boxer Muhammad Ali. In 1981, Schulberg published an autobiography, *Moving Pictures: Memories of a Hollywood Prince.*

Think About the Writer

Do you think that growing up in Hollywood put pressure on Schulberg to be successful? Why or why not?

OH **RA.L.10.5** Analyze how an author's choice of genre affects the expression of a theme or topic. **VO.10.6** Determine the meanings and pronunciations of unknown words by using dictionaries, glossaries, technology and textual features, such as definitional footnotes or sidebars.

Into Action

On the Waterfront is a screenplay—a particular kind of drama written for film. Imagine that you are adapting the screenplay for a live performance on a stage. How would you set the scene for the excerpt you just read? Use a chart like the one below to write notes on set design, lighting, costumes, and props.

Set Design	Lighting	Costumes	Props

Talk About . . .

1. In groups, discuss the dramatic elements in the excerpt from *On the Waterfront.* Try to use each Academic Vocabulary word listed at the right at least once in your discussion.

Write About . . .

2. What actions and dialogue from the excerpt highlight Terry and Charley's relationship?

3. What criteria does Terry use to make his decision? Are his values like his brother's? Explain.

4. What is the predominant tone, or feeling, in this excerpt?

5. What actor today would you choose to play the principal role of Terry? Explain your choice.

Academic Vocabulary for Collection 8

Talking and Writing About Drama

Academic Vocabulary is the language you use to write and talk about literature. Use these words to discuss the dramatic works you read in this collection. The words are underlined throughout the collection.

highlight (HY lyt) *v.*: make a subject or idea stand out so people will pay attention. *An antagonist sometimes serves to highlight the qualities of the protagonist.*

predominant (pree DAHM uh nuhnt) *adj.*: more powerful, common, or noticeable than others. *Amusement is the predominant response to comedy.*

principal (PRIHN suh puhl) *adj.*: most important. *Conflict is a principal element in drama.*

criteria (kry TIHR ee uh) *n.*: rules or standards for making a judgment; test. *Reviewers have many criteria about what makes a good play.*

Your Turn

Copy the words from the Academic Vocabulary list into your *Reader/Writer Notebook.* You may already be familiar with some of them. Use them as you read and discuss the plays in this collection.

Writing Focus

Think as a Reader/Writer

Notice how Schulberg's directions, punctuation, and spelling help actors present their lines with the right tone. As you read through Collection 8, keep track of the methods you think are effective in your *Reader/ Writer Notebook.* You can use these as models when you write your own dramatic scenes.

TRIFLES

by **Susan Glaspell**

Brandywine Valley (1940) by Andrew Wyeth (1917–). Watercolor (21 $\frac{7}{8}$" × 30 $\frac{1}{16}$"). ©Andrew Wyeth. The Armand Hammer Collection, Image ©2005 Courtesy of the Board of Trustees, National Gallery of Art, Washington.

What Do You Think

What events have the most impact on the choices we make? How do we choose when all options seem bleak?

QuickWrite

One of life's most painful experiences is being betrayed by someone you love. Think about relationships you've read about or seen on television. When does a relationship change from one of love to one of betrayal? Write a few notes on your thoughts.

Reader/Writer Notebook

Use your **RWN** to complete the activities for this selection.

OH **RA.L.10.5** Analyze how an author's choice of genre affects the expression of a theme or topic. **RA.L.10.7** Recognize how irony is used in a literary text. **RP.10.1** Apply reading comprehension strategies, including making predictions, comparing and contrasting, recalling and summarizing and making inferences and drawing conclusions.

Literary Focus

Dramatic Irony In plays revolving around a mystery, writers often use **dramatic irony**—situating events so the audience or reader knows something that a character or several characters do not. Sometimes events are downplayed, even though the audience knows that there is a deeper meaning to those events, or a character may make a casual comment that the audience knows is more important than it sounds. Dramatic irony helps build tension in a play, as the audience starts to wonder when the characters will figure out what's really going on.

Literary Perspectives Apply the literary perspective described on page 801 as you read this play.

Reading Focus

Making Inferences Although good actors are able to express what the characters are thinking and feeling, when you read a play you must make **inferences** based on clues provided in the stage directions and dialogue.

Into Action As you read *Trifles*, look for clues that will help you gain a deeper understanding of the characters and their reasons for making choices. What hints does the playwright provide to explain each character's choices? Use a chart to make notes about possible clues.

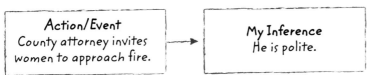

Action/Event
County attorney invites
women to approach fire.

→

My Inference
He is polite.

Writing Focus

Think as a Reader/Writer

Find It in Your Reading Glaspell uses casual language and **idioms**—or figurative expressions—to give the reader clues about the characters. As you read, note examples of this type of language in your *Reader/Writer Notebook*.

Vocabulary

abashed (uh BASHT) *adj.*: embarrassed and confused. *She was abashed after stating the obvious.*

reproach (rih PROHCH) *v.*: blame; express disapproval. *Do not reproach yourself—you tried your best.*

superstitious (soo puhr STIHSH uhs) *adj.*: having an irrational fear of the unknown, the mysterious, or the imaginary. *He was superstitious about black cats.*

facetiously (fuh SEE shuhs lee) *adv.*: in a joking way. *He addressed the ladies facetiously, making light of their concerns.*

Language Coach

Connotations Denotation is the exact meaning of a word, the one you would find in a dictionary. Connotation refers to a suggested meaning of a word. The title of this play, *Trifles*, means "small, unimportant things." After you read this play, you'll come to understand a connotation of *trifles*, the author's suggested meaning. As you read, look for other words in the play that have connotations that are different from their dictionary meanings.

Learn It Online
There's more to words than just definitions. Get the whole story on:

go.hrw.com | L10-799 | **Go**

Susan Glaspell
(1882–1948)

Pulitzer Prize WINNER

An Early Feminist

A novelist and playwright, Susan Glaspell brought interesting characters to life on the American stage and in her fiction. Her work centered on women and their places in society, often focusing on primary relationships in women's lives. Born in Davenport, Iowa, in 1882, Glaspell worked as a reporter for several years before moving to Greenwich Village, then the heart of an artists' community in New York City.

The Provincetown Players

Along with her husband, George Cram Cook, Glaspell founded the Provincetown Players, a theater group that performed one-act plays in Provincetown, Massachusetts, and later in New York. The group produced some of the first experimental theater in America, including early works by Eugene O'Neill and *Trifles*, which was produced in 1916. Set during a cold winter in the Midwest, *Trifles* focused on women and the men who did not understand them.

Glaspell won the Pulitzer Prize in 1931 for the play *Alison's House* about a family that discovers a woman's unpublished poems after she dies. Following *Alison's House*, Glaspell focused on fiction. She died in Provincetown in 1948.

Think About the Writer How might Glaspell's own experiences have affected her writings?

Build Background

Trifles is based on a real-life murder that Glaspell covered while working as a reporter for the *Des Moines Daily News*. A year after the play was produced, Glaspell rewrote it as a short story called "A Jury of Her Peers." Both the play and the story continue to highlight moral and ethical questions about the status of women today.

Preview the Selection

The principal—or main—character in this play is **Mrs. Wright,** although she is never seen on stage. As the play opens, the county attorney, the sheriff, the sheriff's wife, and a local couple **(the Hales)** visit the Wrights' home. The men search for evidence from the murder of **John Wright,** Mrs. Wright's husband. The women are there to collect items to take to Mrs. Wright, who is in jail under suspicion for the murder.

Wharf Theatre in Provincetown, MA. Site of the first plays produced by Provincetown Players, 1915–1916. Granger Collection, New York.

Read with a Purpose As you read this play, notice how the characters uncover the seemingly innocent everyday details that build up to a stunning tragedy.

TRIFLES

by **Susan Glaspell**

Characters in the Play

George Henderson, county attorney
Henry Peters, sheriff

Lewis Hale, a neighboring farmer
Mrs. Peters
Mrs. Hale

Scene: *The kitchen in the now abandoned farm-house of* JOHN WRIGHT, *a gloomy kitchen, and left without having been put in order—unwashed pans under the sink, a loaf of bread outside the breadbox, a dish towel on the table—other signs of incompleted work. At the rear the outer door opens and the* SHERIFF *comes in followed by the* COUNTY ATTORNEY *and* HALE. *The* SHERIFF *and* HALE *are men in middle life, the* COUNTY ATTORNEY *is a young man; all are much bundled up and go at once to the stove. They are followed by two women—the sheriff's wife first; she is a slight wiry woman, a thin nervous face.* MRS. HALE *is larger and would ordinarily be called more comfortable looking, but she is disturbed now and looks fearfully about as she enters. The women have come in slowly, and stand close together near the door.* **Ⓐ**

County Attorney (*rubbing his hands*). This feels good. Come up to the fire, ladies.
Mrs. Peters (*after taking a step forward*). I'm not—cold.

Sheriff (*unbuttoning his overcoat and stepping away from the stove as if to mark the beginning of official business*). Now, Mr. Hale, before we move things about, you explain to Mr. Henderson just what you saw when you came here yesterday morning.

Literary Perspectives

Analyzing Philosophical Context Have you ever watched a movie with a friend and, when you compared impressions afterward, discovered that your reactions were so different it almost seemed as though you saw two different films? Your impressions of the movie may have been colored by your different philosophies, or ways of viewing the world. Your differing philosophies may have caused you to focus on different aspects of the movie or form different opinions. Often a play or other piece of literature will reflect the author's philosophy. Susan Glaspell was known as a feminist. She was concerned about social issues that affect women and about women's position in society. As you read *Trifles*, pay attention to clues that will help you understand Susan Glaspell's philosophy.

Ⓐ **Reading Focus** Making Inferences What might the "incompleted work" in the house say about the people who live there?

County Attorney. By the way, has anything been moved? Are things just as you left them yesterday?

Sheriff (*looking about*). It's just the same. When it dropped below zero last night I thought I'd better send Frank out this morning to make a fire for us—no use getting pneumonia with a big case on, but I told him not to touch anything except the stove—and you know Frank.

County Attorney. Somebody should have been left here yesterday.

Sheriff. Oh—yesterday. When I had to send Frank to Morris Center for that man who went crazy—I want you to know I had my hands full yesterday. I knew you could get back from Omaha by today and as long as I went over everything here myself—

County Attorney. Well, Mr. Hale, tell just what happened when you came here yesterday morning.

Hale. Harry and I had started to town with a load of potatoes. We came along the road from my place and as I got here I said, "I'm going to see if I can't get John Wright to go in with me on a party telephone."[1] I spoke to Wright about it once before and he put me off, saying folks talked too much anyway, and all he asked was peace and quiet—I guess you know about how much he talked himself; but I thought maybe if I went to the house and talked about it before his wife, though I said to Harry that I didn't know as what his wife wanted made much difference to John—

County Attorney. Let's talk about that later, Mr. Hale. I do want to talk about that, but tell now just what happened when you got to the house.

Hale. I didn't hear or see anything; I knocked at the door, and still it was all quiet inside. I knew they must be up, it was past eight o' clock. So I knocked again, and I thought I heard somebody say, "Come in." I wasn't sure, I'm not sure yet, but I opened the door—this door (*indicating the door by which the two women are still standing*) and there in that rocker—(*pointing to it*) sat Mrs. Wright.

[*They all look at the rocker.*]

County Attorney. What—was she doing?

Hale. She was rockin' back and forth. She had her apron in her hand and was kind of—pleating[2] it.

County Attorney. And how did she—look?

Hale. Well, she looked queer.[3]

County Attorney. How do you mean—queer?

Hale. Well, as if she didn't know what she was going to do next. And kind of done up.

County Attorney. How did she seem to feel about your coming?

Hale. Why, I don't think she minded—one way or other. She didn't pay much attention. I said, "How do, Mrs. Wright it's cold, ain't it?" And she said, "Is it?"—and went on kind of pleating at her apron. Well, I was surprised; she didn't ask me to come up to the stove, or to set down, but just sat there, not even looking at me, so I said, "I want to see John." And then she—laughed. I guess you would call it a laugh. I thought of Harry and the team outside, so I said a little sharp: "Can't I see John?" "No," she says, kind o' dull like. "Ain't he home?" says I. "Yes," says she, "he's home." "Then why can't I see him?" I asked her, out of patience. "'Cause he's dead," says she. "*Dead*?" says I. She just nodded her head, not getting a bit excited, but rockin' back and forth. "Why—where is he?" says I, not knowing what to say. She just pointed upstairs—like that (*himself pointing to the room above*) I got up, with the idea of going up there. I walked from there to here—then I says, "Why,

---

1. **party telephone:** (no longer in use) telephone line shared with at least one other person; cheaper than a private line, a party line connected two or more users to the same phone number.

2. **pleating** (PLEET hing): arranging into folds.

3. **queer** (kweer): not usual or normal; strange; odd; peculiar.

Analyzing Visuals **Viewing and Interpreting** How do the details in the painting relate to the events in the play?

The Rocking Chair by Alberto Morocco. Private Collection, ©Agnew's, London, United Kingdom.

what did he die of?" "He died of a rope round his neck," says she, and just went on pleatin' at her apron. Well, I went out and called Harry. I thought I might—need help. We went upstairs and there he was lyin'. **Ⓑ**

County Attorney. I think I'd rather have you go into that upstairs, where you can point it all out. Just go on now with the rest of the story.

Hale. Well, my first thought was to get that rope off. It looked . . . *(stops, his face twitches)* . . . but Harry, he went up to him, and he said, "No, he's dead all right, and we'd better not touch anything." So we went back down stairs. She was still sitting that same way. "Has anybody been notified?" I asked. "No," says she unconcerned. "Who did this, Mrs. Wright?" said Harry. He said it business-like—and she stopped pleatin' of her apron. "I don't know," she says. "You don't *know*?" says Harry. "No," says she. "Weren't you sleepin' in the bed with him?" says Harry. "Yes," says she, "but I was on the inside." "Somebody slipped a rope round his neck and strangled him and you didn't wake up?" says Harry. "I didn't wake up," she said after him. We must 'a looked as if we didn't see how that could be, for after a minute she said, "I sleep sound." Harry was going to ask her more questions but I said maybe we ought to let her tell her story first to the coroner, or the sheriff, so Harry went fast as he could to Rivers' place, where there's a telephone.

County Attorney. And what did Mrs. Wright do when she knew that you had gone for the coroner?

Hale. She moved from that chair to this one over here *(pointing to a small chair in the corner)* and just sat there with her hands held together

> "Somebody slipped a rope round his neck and strangled him and you didn't wake up?"

and looking down. I got a feeling that I ought to make some conversation, so I said I had come in to see if John wanted to put in a telephone, and at that she started to laugh, and then she stopped and looked at me—scared. *(The* COUNTY ATTORNEY, *who has had his notebook out, makes a note.)* I dunno, maybe it wasn't scared. I wouldn't like to say it was. Soon Harry got back, and then Dr. Lloyd came, and you, Mr. Peters, and so I guess that's all I know that you don't. **Ⓒ**

County Attorney *(looking around)*. I guess we'll go upstairs first—and then out to the barn and around there. *(to the* SHERIFF*)* You're convinced that there was nothing important here—nothing that would point to any motive.

Sheriff. Nothing here but kitchen things.

[*The* COUNTY ATTORNEY, *after again looking around the kitchen, opens the door of a cupboard closet. He gets up on a chair and looks on a shelf. Pulls his hand away, sticky.*]

County Attorney. Here's a nice mess.

[*The women draw nearer.*]

Mrs. Peters *(to the other woman)*. Oh, her fruit; it did freeze. *(to the* COUNTY ATTORNEY*)* She worried about that when it turned so cold. She said the fire'd go out and her jars would break.

Sheriff. Well, can you beat the women! Held for murder and worryin' about her preserves.

County Attorney. I guess before we're through she may have something more serious than preserves to worry about.

Ⓑ **Literary Focus** **Dramatic Irony** What does Hale's description of Mrs. Wright suggest about her state of mind?

Ⓒ **Reading Focus** **Making Inferences** What does Hale's version of the events suggest he thinks about Mrs. Wright?

Hale. Well, women are used to worrying over trifles.[4] **D**

[*The two women move a little closer together.*]

County Attorney (*with the gallantry of a young politician*). And yet, for all their worries, what would we do without the ladies? (*The women do not unbend. He goes to the sink, takes a dipperful of water from the pail and pouring it into a basin, washes his hands. Starts to wipe them on the roller towel, turns it for a cleaner place.*) Dirty towels! (*kicks his foot against the pans under the sink*) Not much of a housekeeper, would you say, ladies?

Mrs. Hale (*stiffly*). There's a great deal of work to be done on a farm.

County Attorney. To be sure. And yet (*with a little bow to her*) I know there are some Dickson county farmhouses which do not have such roller towels.

[*He gives it a pull to expose its full length again.*]

Mrs. Hale. Those towels get dirty awful quick. Men's hands aren't always as clean as they might be.

County Attorney. Ah, loyal to your sex, I see. But you and Mrs. Wright were neighbors. I suppose you were friends, too.

Mrs. Hale (*shaking her head*). I've not seen much of her of late years. I've not been in this house—it's more than a year.

County Attorney. And why was that? You didn't like her?

Mrs. Hale. I liked her all well enough. Farmers' wives have their hands full, Mr. Henderson. And then—

---

4. **trifles** (TRY fuhlz): things that are of little value or small importance

County Attorney. Yes—?

Mrs. Hale (*looking about*). It never seemed a very cheerful place.

County Attorney. No—it's not cheerful. I shouldn't say she had the homemaking instinct.

Mrs. Hale. Well, I don't know as Wright had, either. **E**

County Attorney. You mean that they didn't get on very well?

Mrs. Hale. No, I don't mean anything. But I don't think a place'd be any cheerfuller for John Wright's being in it. **F**

County Attorney. I'd like to talk more of that a little later. I want to get the lay of things upstairs now.

[*He goes to the left, where three steps lead to a stair door.*]

Sheriff. I suppose anything Mrs. Peters does'll be all right. She was to take in some clothes for her, you know, and a few little things. We left in such a hurry yesterday.

County Attorney. Yes, but I would like to see what you take, Mrs. Peters, and keep an eye out for anything that might be of use to us.

Mrs. Peters. Yes, Mr. Henderson.

[*The women listen to the men's steps on the stairs, then look about the kitchen.*]

Mrs. Hale. I'd hate to have men coming into my kitchen, snooping around and criticizing.

[*She arranges the pans under sink which the COUNTY ATTORNEY had shoved out of place.*]

D **Literary Perspectives** Analyzing Philosophical Context What does this exchange tell you about the men's attitude toward women and their work?

E **Literary Focus** Dramatic Irony What does Mrs. Hale understand about the Wrights that the sheriff does not?

F **Reading Focus** Making Inferences What can you infer about John Wright from this comment by Mrs. Hale?

Mrs. Peters. Of course it's no more than their duty.

Mrs. Hale. Duty's all right, but I guess that deputy sheriff that came out to make the fire might have got a little of this on. *(gives the roller towel a pull)* Wish I'd thought of that sooner. Seems mean to talk about her for not having things slicked up when she had to come away in such a hurry.

Mrs. Peters *(who has gone to a small table in the left rear corner of the room, and lifted one end of a towel that covers a pan).* She had bread set.

[*Stands still.*]

Mrs. Hale *(eyes fixed on a loaf of bread beside the breadbox, which is on a low shelf at the other side of the room. Moves slowly toward it).* She was going to put this in there. *(Picks up loaf, then abruptly drops it. In a manner of returning to familiar things.)* It's a shame about her fruit. I wonder if it's all gone. *(Gets up on the chair and looks.)* I think there's some here that's all right, Mrs. Peters. Yes—here; *(holding it toward the window)* this is cherries, too. *(looking again)* I declare I believe that's the only one. *(Gets down, bottle in her hand. Goes to the sink and wipes it off on the outside.)* She'll feel awful bad after all her hard work in the hot weather. I remember the afternoon I put up my cherries last summer.

[*She puts the bottle on the big kitchen table, center of the room. With a sigh, is about to sit down in the rocking chair. Before she is seated realizes what chair it is; with a slow look at it, steps back. The chair which she has touched rocks back and forth.*] **G**

Analyzing Visuals **Viewing and Interpreting** Which character from the play might this painting illustrate? Explain.

Woman with Duck (1996) by Reg Cartwright, oil on board. Private Collection.

Mrs. Peters. Well, I must get those things from the front room closet. *(She goes to the door at the right, but after looking into the other room, steps back.)* You coming with me, Mrs. Hale? You could help me carry them.

[*They go in the other room; reappear,* MRS. PETERS *carrying a dress and skirt,* MRS. HALE *following with a pair of shoes.*]

Mrs. Peters. My, it's cold in there.

[*She puts the clothes on the big table, and hurries to the stove.*]

G Reading Focus **Making Inferences** Re-read these stage directions. Why does Mrs. Hale step back from the chair?

Mrs. Hale (*examining her skirt*). Wright was close. I think maybe that's why she kept so much to herself. She didn't even belong to the Ladies Aid. I suppose she felt she couldn't do her part, and then you don't enjoy things when you feel shabby. She used to wear pretty clothes and be lively, when she was Minnie Foster, one of the town girls singing in the choir. But that—oh, that was thirty years ago. This all you was to take in?

Mrs. Peters. She said she wanted an apron. Funny thing to want, for there isn't much to get you dirty in jail, goodness knows. But I suppose just to make her feel more natural. She said they was in the top drawer in this cupboard. Yes, here. And then her little shawl that always hung behind the door. (*opens stair door and looks*) Yes, here it is.

[*Quickly shuts door leading upstairs.*]

Mrs. Hale (*abruptly moving toward her*). Mrs. Peters?

Mrs. Peters. Yes, Mrs. Hale?

Mrs. Hale. Do you think she did it?

Mrs. Peters (*in a frightened voice*). Oh, I don't know.

Mrs. Hale. Well, I don't think she did. Asking for an apron and her little shawl. Worrying about her fruit.

Mrs. Peters (*Starts to speak, glances up, where footsteps are heard in the room above. In a low voice*). Mr. Peters says it looks bad for her. Mr. Henderson is awful sarcastic in a speech and he'll make fun of her sayin' she didn't wake up.

Mrs. Hale. Well, I guess John Wright didn't wake when they was slipping that rope under his neck.

Mrs. Peters. No, it's strange. It must have been done awful crafty and still. They say it was such a—funny way to kill a man, rigging it all up like that.

Mrs. Hale. That's just what Mr. Hale said. There was a gun in the house. He says that's what he can't understand.

Mrs. Peters. Mr. Henderson said coming out that what was needed for the case was a motive; something to show anger, or—sudden feeling.

Mrs. Hale (*who is standing by the table*). Well, I don't see any signs of anger around here. (*She puts her hand on the dish towel which lies on the table, stands looking down at table, one half of which is clean, the other half messy.*) It's wiped to here. (*Makes a move as if to finish work, then turns and looks at loaf of bread outside the breadbox. Drops towel. In that voice of coming back to familiar things.*) Wonder how they are finding things upstairs. I hope she had it a little more red-up[5] up there. You know, it seems kind of *sneaking.* Locking her up in town and then coming out here and trying to get her own house to turn against her!

Mrs. Peters. But Mrs. Hale, the law is the law.

Mrs. Hale. I s'pose 'tis. (*unbuttoning her coat*) Better loosen up your things, Mrs. Peters. You won't feel them when you go out.

[MRS. PETERS *takes off her fur tippet,[6] goes to hang it on hook at back of room, stands looking at the under part of the small corner table.*]

Mrs. Peters. She was piecing a quilt.

[*She brings the large sewing basket and they look at the bright pieces.*]

Mrs. Hale. It's log cabin pattern. Pretty, isn't it? I wonder if she was goin' to quilt it or just knot it?[7]

---

5. **red-up:** orderly; tidied up.
6. **tippet** (TIHP iht): scarf.
7. **quilt it or just knot it:** referring to two ways to finish a quilt. Quilting refers to using many small stitches to hold the layers of fabric together. To knot a quilt is simply to tie knots through the layers to hold them together. Quilting is much more labor intensive than knotting is.

[*Footsteps have been heard coming down the stairs. The* SHERIFF *enters followed by* HALE *and the* COUNTY ATTORNEY.]

Sheriff. They wonder if she was going to quilt it or just knot it!

[*The men laugh, the women look* abashed.]

County Attorney (*rubbing his hands over the stove*). Frank's fire didn't do much up there, did it? Well, let's go out to the barn and get that cleared up.

[*The men go outside.*]

Mrs. Hale (*resentfully*). I don't know as there's anything so strange, our takin' up our time with little things while we're waiting for them to get the evidence. (*She sits down at the big table smoothing out a block with decision.*) I don't see as it's anything to laugh about.   **Ⓗ**
Mrs. Peters (*apologetically*). Of course they've got awful important things on their minds.

[*Pulls up a chair and joins* MRS. HALE *at the table.*]

Mrs. Hale (*examining another block*). Mrs. Peters, look at this one. Here, this is the one she was working on, and look at the sewing! All the rest of it has been so nice and even. And look at this! It's all over the place! Why, it looks as if she didn't know what she was about!

[*After she has said this they look at each other, then start to glance back at the door. After an instant* MRS. HALE *has pulled at a knot and ripped the sewing.*]

Mrs. Peters. Oh, what are you doing, Mrs. Hale?
Mrs. Hale (*mildly*). Just pulling out a stitch or two that's not sewed very good. (*threading a needle*) Bad sewing always made me fidgety.
Mrs. Peters (*nervously*). I don't think we ought to touch things.
Mrs. Hale. I'll just finish up this end. (*suddenly stopping and leaning forward*) Mrs. Peters?
Mrs. Peters. Yes, Mrs. Hale?
Mrs. Hale. What do you suppose she was so nervous about?
Mrs. Peters. Oh—I don't know. I don't know as she was nervous. I sometimes sew awful queer when I'm just tired. (MRS. HALE *starts to say something, looks at* MRS. PETERS, *then goes on sewing.*) Well, I must get these things wrapped up. They may be through sooner than we think. (*putting apron and other things together*) I wonder where I can find a piece of paper, and string.   **Ⓘ**

Mrs. Hale. In that cupboard, maybe.
Mrs. Peters (*looking in cupboard*). Why, here's a birdcage. (*holds it up*) Did she have a bird, Mrs. Hale?
Mrs. Hale. Why, I don't know whether she did or not—I've not been here for so long. There was a man around last year selling canaries cheap, but I don't know as she took one; maybe she did. She used to sing real pretty herself.
Mrs. Peters (*glancing around*). Seems funny to think of a bird here. But she must have had one, or why would she have a cage? I wonder what happened to it.
Mrs. Hale. I s'pose maybe the cat got it.

Ⓗ **Reading Focus** Making Inferences Why does Mrs. Hale speak these lines resentfully?

Ⓘ **Reading Focus** Making Inferences Why is Mrs. Hale fixing Mrs. Wright's sloppy stitches?

Vocabulary **abashed:** (uh BASHT) *adj.*: embarrassed and confused.

Mrs. Peters. No, she didn't have a cat. She's got that feeling some people have about cats—being afraid of them. My cat got in her room and she was real upset and asked me to take it out.

Mrs. Hale. My sister Bessie was like that. Queer, ain't it?

Mrs. Peters (examining the cage). Why, look at this door. It's broke. One hinge is pulled apart.

Mrs. Hale (looking too). Looks as if someone must have been rough with it.

Mrs. Peters. Why, yes. **J**

[She brings the cage forward and puts it on the table.]

Mrs. Hale. I wish if they're going to find any evidence they'd be about it. I don't like this place.

Mrs. Peters. But I'm awful glad you came with me, Mrs. Hale. It would be lonesome for me sitting here alone.

Mrs. Hale. It would, wouldn't it? (dropping her sewing) But I tell you what I do wish, Mrs. Peters. I wish I had come over sometimes when she was here. I— (looking around the room) —wish I had.

Mrs. Peters. But of course you were awful busy, Mrs. Hale—your house and your children.

Mrs. Hale. I could've come. I stayed away because it weren't cheerful—and that's why I ought to have come. I—I've never liked this place. Maybe because it's down in a hollow and you don't see the road. I dunno what it is, but it's a lonesome place and always was. I wish I had come over to see Minnie Foster sometimes. I can see now— (shakes her head)

Mrs. Peters. Well, you mustn't reproach yourself, Mrs. Hale. Somehow we just don't see how it is with other folks until—something comes up.

Mrs. Hale. Not having children makes less

work—but it makes a quiet house, and Wright out to work all day, and no company when he did come in. Did you know John Wright, Mrs. Peters?

Mrs. Peters. Not to know him; I've seen him in town. They say he was a good man.

Mrs. Hale. Yes—good; he didn't drink, and kept his word as well as most, I guess, and paid his debts. But he was a hard man, Mrs. Peters. Just to pass the time of day with him—(shivers) Like a raw wind that gets to the bone. (pauses, her eye falling on the cage) I should think she would 'a wanted a bird. But what do you suppose went with it?

Mrs. Peters. I don't know, unless it got sick and died.

[She reaches over and swings the broken door, swings it again. Both women watch it.]

Mrs. Hale. You weren't raised round here, were you? (MRS. PETERS shakes her head.) You didn't know—her?

Mrs. Peters. Not till they brought her yesterday.

Mrs. Hale. She—come to think of it, she was kind of like a bird herself—real sweet and pretty, but kind of timid and—fluttery. How—she—did—change. (silence; then as if struck by a happy thought and relieved to get back to everyday things) Tell you what, Mrs. Peters, why don't you take the quilt in with you? It might take up her mind. **K**

Mrs. Peters. Why, I think that's a real nice idea, Mrs. Hale. There couldn't possibly be any objection to it, could there? Now, just what would I take? I wonder if her patches are in here—and her things.

J Reading Focus **Making Inferences** Why might it be significant that the birdcage "looks as if someone must have been rough with it"?

K Reading Focus **Making Inferences** What might you infer from the comparison between Mrs. Wright and a bird?

Vocabulary reproach: (rih PROHCH) v.: blame; express disapproval.

[*They look in the sewing basket.*]

Mrs. Hale. Here's some red. I expect this has got sewing things in it. *(Brings out a fancy box.)* What a pretty box. Looks like something somebody would give you. Maybe her scissors are in here. *(Opens box. Suddenly puts her hand to her nose.)* Why—(MRS. PETERS *bends nearer, then turns her face away.)* There's something wrapped up in this piece of silk.
Mrs. Peters. Why, this isn't her scissors.
Mrs. Hale *(lifting the silk).* Oh, Mrs. Peters—it's—

[MRS. PETERS *bends closer.*]

Mrs. Peters. It's the bird.
Mrs. Hale *(jumping up).* But, Mrs. Peters—look at it! Its neck! Look at its neck! It's all—other side *to.*
Mrs. Peters. Somebody—wrung—its—neck.

[*Their eyes meet. A look of growing comprehension, of horror. Steps are heard outside.* MRS. HALE *slips box under quilt pieces, and sinks into her chair. Enter* SHERIFF *and* COUNTY ATTORNEY. MRS. PETERS *rises.*] **Ⓛ**

County Attorney *(as one turning from serious things to little pleasantries).* Well, ladies, have you decided whether she was going to quilt it or knot it?
Mrs. Peters. We think she was going to—knot it. **Ⓜ**
County Attorney. Well, that's interesting, I'm sure. *(seeing the birdcage)* Has the bird flown?
Mrs. Hale *(putting more quilt pieces over the box).* We think the—cat got it.
County Attorney *(preoccupied).* Is there a cat?

[MRS. HALE *glances in a quick covert way at* MRS. PETERS.]

Mrs. Peters. Well, not *now.* They're superstitious, you know. They leave.
County Attorney *(to* SHERIFF PETERS, *continuing an interrupted conversation).* No sign at all of anyone having come from the outside. Their own rope. Now let's go up again and go over it piece by piece. *(They start upstairs.)* It would have to have been someone who knew just the—

[MRS. PETERS *sits down. The two women sit there not looking at one another, but as if peering into something and at the same time holding back. When they talk now it is in the manner of feeling their way over strange ground, as if afraid of what they are saying, but as if they can not help saying it.*]

Mrs. Hale. She liked the bird. She was going to bury it in that pretty box.
Mrs. Peters *(in a whisper).* When I was a girl—my kitten—there was a boy took a hatchet, and before my eyes—and before I could get there—*(covers her face an instant)* If they hadn't held me back I would have—*(catches herself, looks upstairs where steps are heard, falters weakly)*—hurt him.
Mrs. Hale *(with a slow look around her).* I wonder how it would seem never to have had any children around. *(pause)* No, Wright wouldn't like the bird—a thing that sang. She used to sing. He killed that, too.
Mrs. Peters *(moving uneasily).* We don't know who killed the bird.
Mrs. Hale. I knew John Wright.

Ⓛ **Reading Focus** **Making Inferences** What does the direction "A look of growing comprehension, of horror" signify?

Ⓜ **Literary Focus** **Dramatic Irony** What is ironic about Mrs. Wright's quilting technique?

Vocabulary **superstitious** (soo puhr STIHSH uhs) *adj.:* having an irrational fear of the unknown, the mysterious, or the imaginary.

Mrs. Peters. It was an awful thing was done in this house that night, Mrs. Hale. Killing a man while he slept, slipping a rope around his neck that choked the life out of him.

Mrs. Hale. His neck. Choked the life out of him.

[*Her hand goes out and rests on the birdcage.*]

Mrs. Peters *(with rising voice)*. We don't know who killed him. We don't *know*.

Mrs. Hale *(her own feeling not interrupted)*. If there'd been years and years of nothing, then a bird to sing to you, it would be awful—still, after the bird was still.

Mrs. Peters *(something within her speaking)*. I know what stillness is. When we homesteaded in Dakota, and my first baby died—after he was two years old, and me with no other then—

Mrs. Hale *(moving)*. How soon do you suppose they'll be through, looking for the evidence?

Mrs. Peters. I know what stillness is. *(pulling herself back)* The law has got to punish crime, Mrs. Hale.

Mrs. Hale *(not as if answering that)*. I wish you'd seen Minnie Foster when she wore a white dress with blue ribbons and stood up there in the choir and sang. *(a look around the room)* Oh, I *wish* I'd come over here once in a while! That was a crime! That was a crime! Who's going to punish that?

Mrs. Peters *(looking upstairs)*. We mustn't—take on.

Mrs. Hale. I might have known she needed help! I know how things can be—for women. I tell you, it's queer, Mrs. Peters. We live close together and we live far apart. We all go through the same things—it's all just a different kind of the same thing. *(brushes her eyes; noticing the bottle of fruit, reaches out for it)* If I was you, I wouldn't tell her her fruit was gone. Tell her it *ain't*. Tell her it's all right. Take this in to prove it to her. She—she may never know whether it was broke or not.

Mrs. Peters *(Takes the bottle, looks about for something to wrap it in; takes petticoat from the clothes brought from the other room, very nervously begins winding this around the bottle.*)

N **Reading Focus** **Making Inferences** How do the women connect "stillness" to the crime?

In false voice.) My, it's a good thing the men couldn't hear us. Wouldn't they just laugh! Getting all stirred up over a little thing like a—dead canary. As if that could have anything to do with—with—wouldn't they *laugh*!

[*The men are heard coming down stairs.*]

Mrs. Hale (*under her breath*). Maybe they would—maybe they wouldn't.
County Attorney. No, Peters, it's all perfectly clear except a reason for doing it. But you know juries when it comes to women. If there was some definite thing. Something to show—something to make a story about—a thing that would connect up with this strange way of doing it— **O**

[*The women's eyes meet for an instant. Enter* HALE *from outer door.*]

Hale. Well, I've got the team around. Pretty cold out there.
County Attorney. I'm going to stay here a while by myself. (*to the* SHERIFF) You can send Frank out for me, can't you? I want to go over everything. I'm not satisfied that we can't do better.
Sheriff. Do you want to see what Mrs. Peters is going to take in?

[*The* COUNTY ATTORNEY *goes to the table, picks up the apron, laughs.*]

County Attorney. Oh, I guess they're not very dangerous things the ladies have picked out.

(*Moves a few things about, disturbing the quilt pieces which cover the box. Steps back.*) No, Mrs. Peters doesn't need supervising. For that matter, a sheriff's wife is married to the law. Ever think of it that way, Mrs. Peters? **P**
Mrs. Peters. Not—just that way.
Sheriff (*chuckling*). Married to the law. (*moves toward the other room*) I just want you to come in here a minute, George. We ought to take a look at these windows.
County Attorney (*scoffingly*). Oh, windows!
Sheriff. We'll be right out, Mr. Hale.

[HALE *goes outside. The* SHERIFF *follows the* COUNTY ATTORNEY *into the other room. Then* MRS. HALE *rises, hands tight together, looking intensely at* MRS. PETERS, *whose eyes make a slow turn, finally meeting* MRS. HALE'S. *A moment* MRS. HALE *holds her, then her own eyes point the way to where the box is concealed. Suddenly* MRS. PETERS *throws back quilt pieces and tries to put the box in the bag she is wearing. It is too big. She opens box, starts to take bird out, cannot touch it, goes to pieces, stands there helpless. Sound of a knob turning in the other room.* MRS. HALE *snatches the box and puts it in the pocket of her big coat. Enter* COUNTY ATTORNEY *and* SHERIFF.]

County Attorney (*facetiously*). Well, Henry, at least we found out that she was not going to quilt it. She was going to—what is it you call it, ladies?
Mrs. Hale (*her hand against her pocket*). We call it—knot it, Mr. Henderson. **Q**

O Literary Focus **Dramatic Irony** What does the audience know that the county attorney does not?

P Reading Focus **Making Inferences** What is the county attorney implying when he asks Mrs. Peters this question?

Q Literary Perspectives **Analyzing Philosophical Context** How do you think the playwright views the women?

Vocabulary **facetiously** (fuh SEE shuhs lee) *adv.:* in a joking way.

Applying Your Skills

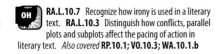 **RA.L.10.7** Recognize how irony is used in a literary text. **RA.L.10.3** Distinguish how conflicts, parallel plots and subplots affect the pacing of action in literary text. *Also covered* **RP.10.1; VO.10.3; WA.10.1.b**

Trifles

Respond and Think Critically

Reading Focus

Quick Check

1. Briefly summarize the reasons the characters have come to the Wrights' home, and describe what they find there.

Read with a Purpose

2. Which trifles—innocent everyday details—add up to murder in this play?

Reading Skills: Making Inferences

3. Review the chart you created. Add a box to your chart, and write a statement summing up each principal—or main—character.

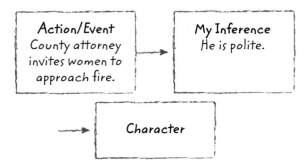

✓ Vocabulary Check

Match each Vocabulary word with the word or phrase that has a similar meaning.

4. **abashed**   a. irrational fear of the unknown
5. **reproach**   b. jokingly
6. **superstitious** c. embarrassed
7. **facetiously** d. disapproval

Literary Focus

Literary Analysis

8. **Draw Conclusions** At one point, Mrs. Hale laments that she had not visited Mrs. Wright often. Why does she call this a "crime"?

9. **Analyze** What is Mr. Hale's opinion of Mrs. Wright? Use examples from the text.

10. **Literary Perspectives** What does the author seem to say about relationships between men and women? What message is she sending?

Literary Skills: Dramatic Irony

11. **Analyze** Cite three examples of dramatic irony in the play and explain the importance of each.

Literary Skills Review: Setting and Plot

12. **Describe** What is the setting of the play? How does it frame the events of the play?

Writing Focus

Think as a Reader/Writer

Use It in Your Writing Review your *Reader/Writer Notebook* notes on casual language and **idioms.** Then, write an imaginary dialogue between two characters that suggests what will happen to Mrs. Wright. Try to write the dialogue so a classmate can identify the characters from the language.

 What Do You Think Now? Why do you think Mrs. Wright chose to kill her husband? What options did she have?

THE BRUTE
A JOKE IN ONE ACT

by **Anton Chekhov**

What Do You Think?

How do we know when we've mis-judged someone?

QuickTalk

Two people meet and dislike each other instantly. Eventually, however, they find themselves attracted to each other. Can you think of any other movies or TV shows where opposites attract? With a partner, discuss whether you think opposites attract in real life.

The photographs throughout the play are from the Expression Theater Ensemble's 2002 production of *The Brute*.

Reader/Writer Notebook

Use your **RWN** to complete the activities for this selection.

OH **RA.L.10.5** Analyze how an author's choice of genre affects the expression of a theme or topic. **RP.10.1** Apply reading comprehension strategies, including making predictions, comparing and contrasting, recalling and summarizing and making inferences and drawing conclusions.

Literary Focus

Comedy and Farce A **comedy** is a story that ends happily—often with a joyful celebration. In a typical comedy, the **plot** may take many surprising and hilarious twists to accomplish an ending where the power of love overcomes all obstacles.

A **farce** is a type of comedy in which exaggerated and often stereotyped characters are involved in ridiculous situations. The humor in farce is based on crude physical actions, or slapstick, and clowning. Characters may slip on banana peels, walk into doors, or disguise themselves in the clothes of the opposite sex. Today farce is often the basic ingredient in TV sitcoms.

Reading Focus

Making Predictions Chekhov's play spotlights two wildly antagonistic "battling lovers," Mrs. Popov and Mr. Grigory S. Smirnov. We know the two are going to end up together eventually. The question that keeps us in suspense is "*When* and *how* is that going to happen?" We make predictions about what will happen based on the characters' actions and dialogue.

Into Action As you read the play, note the places where you make predictions about the characters and their future. After you read, you can check to see how accurate your predictions were.

Character	What happens/What's said?	What I predict
Mrs. Popov	Says her life is over	She will change her mind.

Writing Focus

Think as a Reader/Writer

Find It in Your Reading In *The Brute,* Chekhov uses exaggeration to make the audience laugh. In your *Reader/Writer Notebook*, jot down examples of exaggerations that you find especially amusing.

Vocabulary

indisposed (ihn dihs POHZD) *adj.:* slightly ill. *She was indisposed with a fever.*

emancipation (ih man suh PAY shuhn) *n.:* liberation, the act of setting free. *The emancipation of women ushered in long-overdue rights and freedoms.*

insinuate (ihn SIHN yoo ayt) *v.:* suggest. *She will insinuate that he is being rude.*

impudence (IHM pyuh duhns) *n.:* quality of being disrespectful. *His impudence toward Mrs. Popov was almost unbearable.*

impunity (im PYOO nih tee) *n.:* freedom from punishment. *He sought impunity for his actions.*

Language Coach

Easily Confused Words At one point in the play, Smirnov says that he will "make a note to that effect." The noun *effect* is often confused with the verb *affect*. An *effect* is the result of something. *His rude behavior had an effect on her.* *Affect,* a verb, means "to have an effect on" or "to influence." *She was affected by his rude behavior.* Give examples of two other easily confused words.

 Learn It Online
There's more to words than just definitions. Get the whole story on:

go.hrw.com   L10-815   **Go**

Learn It Online
Get more on the author's life at:
go.hrw.com L10-816 Go

Anton Chekhov
(1860–1904)

"Slice-of-Life" Playwright

Anton Chekhov is one of two playwrights who have most influenced modern drama. (The other is the Norwegian writer Henrik Ibsen.) Chekhov's major plays are often called "slices of life." Rather than focusing on plot, they are more concerned with psychological insights, with the slow ebb and flow of moods, and with subtly shifting relationships.

Chekhov was born in a small seaport in southern Russia, the son of an unsuccessful shopkeeper. His family was poor and dependent on young Anton's financial support, which he earned by churning out short stories and sketches for humor magazines. At the same time, he was studying medicine at the University of Moscow. Chekhov graduated and became a doctor but did not practice medicine for long. Instead, he wrote hundreds of short stories and five major plays over the course of his short life.

Getting to the Brain

In one of his many letters, Chekhov advised Maxim Gorky, another famous Russian writer, that a sentence should "get its meaning through to the brain immediately, which is what good writing must do, and fast."

In his last years Chekhov, terminally ill with tuberculosis, wrote five full-length plays. These masterpieces are still performed today in theaters all over the world.

Think About the Writer Considering Chekhov's background, what kinds of plays would you expect him to have written?

Preview the Selection

The Brute is a play in which all the action takes place in one act—a single setting in a short span of time. The play centers on **Mrs. Popov,** a grieving widow. She employs **Luka,** who helps her around the house. **Mr. Smirnov,** a gentleman farmer and a business acquaintance of her late husband, also plays a central role. The characters will discover whether Mrs. Popov is capable of overcoming her grief.

A scene from the 1940 production of Anton Chekhov's classic play *Three Sisters* performed by the Moscow State Theater.

THE BRUTE
A JOKE IN ONE ACT

by **Anton Chekhov**
translated by **Eric Bentley**

Characters

Mrs. Popov, widow and landowner, small, with dimpled cheeks

Mr. Grigory S. Smirnov, gentleman farmer, middle-aged

Luka, Mrs. Popov's footman, an old man

Gardener

Coachman

Hired Men

The drawing room of a country house. MRS. POPOV *in deep mourning, is staring hard at a photograph.* LUKA *is with her.*

Luka. It's not right, ma'am, you're killing yourself. The cook has gone off with the maid to pick berries. The cat's having a high old time in the yard catching birds. Every living thing is happy. But you stay moping here in the house like it was a convent,[1] taking no pleasure in nothing. I mean it, ma'am! It must be a full year since you set foot out of doors.

Mrs. Popov. I must never set foot out of doors again, Luka. Never! I have nothing to set foot out of doors *for.* My life is done. *He* is in his grave. I have buried myself alive in this house. We are *both* in our graves. Ⓐ

Luka. You're off again, ma'am. I just won't listen to you no more. Mr. Popov is dead, but what can we do about that? It's God's doing. God's will be done. You've cried over him, you've done your share of mourning, haven't you? There's a limit to everything. You can't go on weeping and wailing forever. My old lady died, for that matter, and I wept and wailed over her a whole month long. Well, that was it. I couldn't weep and wail all my life, she just wasn't worth it. (*He sighs.*) As for the neighbors, you've forgotten all about them, ma'am. You don't visit them and you don't let them visit you. You and I are like a pair of

---

1. **convent** (KAHN vehnt): a community of nuns.

Ⓐ **Literary Focus** Comedy and Farce Clearly, Mrs. Popov is not dead. What does she mean by saying "We are *both* in our graves"?

spiders—excuse the expression, ma'am—here we are in this house like a pair of spiders, we never see the light of day. And it isn't like there was no nice people around either. The whole county's swarming with 'em. There's a regiment quartered at Riblov, and the officers are so good-looking! The girls can't take their eyes off them.—There's a ball at the camp every Friday.—The military band plays most every day of the week.—What do you say, ma'am? You're young, you're pretty, you could enjoy yourself! Ten years from now you may want to strut and show your feathers to the officers, and it'll be too late.

Mrs. Popov (*firmly*). You must never bring this subject up again, Luka. Since Popov died, life has been an empty dream to me, you know that. *You* may think I am alive. Poor ignorant Luka! You are wrong. I am dead. I'm in my grave. Never more shall I see the light of day, never strip from my body this . . . raiment[2] of death! Are you listening, Luka? Let his ghost learn how I love him! Yes, *I* know, and *you* know, he was often unfair to me, he was cruel to me, and he was unfaithful to me. What of it? *I* shall be faithful to *him*, that's all. I will show him how *I* can love. Hereafter, in a better world than this, he will welcome me back, the same loyal girl I always was— **Ⓑ**

Luka. Instead of carrying on this way, ma'am, you should go out in the garden and take a bit of a walk, ma'am. Or why not harness Toby and take a drive? Call on a couple of the neighbors, ma'am?

Mrs. Popov (*breaking down*). Oh, Luka!

Luka. Yes, ma'am? What have I said, ma'am? Oh dear!

---

2. **raiment** (RAY muhnt): clothing.

Mrs. Popov. Toby! You said Toby! He adored that horse. When he drove me out to the Korchagins and the Vlasovs, it was always with Toby! He was a wonderful driver, do you remember, Luka? So graceful! So strong! I can see him now, pulling at those reins with all his might and main! Toby! Luka, tell them to give Toby an extra portion of oats today.

Luka. Yes, ma'am.

[*A bell rings.*]

Mrs. Popov. Who is that? Tell them I'm not home.

Luka. Very good, ma'am. (*Exit.*)

Mrs. Popov (*gazing again at the photograph*). You shall see, my Popov, how a wife can love and forgive. Till death do us part. Longer than that. Till death reunite us forever! (*Suddenly a titter breaks through her tears.*) Aren't you ashamed of yourself, Popov? Here's your little wife, being good, being faithful, so faithful she's locked up here waiting for her own funeral, while you— doesn't it make you ashamed, you naughty boy? You were terrible, you know. You were unfaithful, and you made those awful scenes about it, you stormed out and left me alone for weeks— **Ⓒ**

[*Enter* LUKA.]

Luka (*upset*). There's someone asking for you, ma'am. Says he must—

Mrs. Popov. I suppose you told him that since my husband's death I see no one?

Luka. Yes, ma'am. I did, ma'am. But he wouldn't listen, ma'am. He says it's urgent.

Ⓑ **Literary Focus** Comedy and Farce Something that is absurd is so different from the truth that it is funny. What is absurd about Mrs. Popov's statements?

Ⓒ **Reading Focus** Making Predictions Will Mrs. Popov's unpleasant memories have an unintended effect? What might happen?

Mrs. Popov *(shrilly).* I see no one!!

Luka. He won't take no for an answer, ma'am. He just curses and swears and comes in anyway. He's a perfect monster, ma'am. He's in the dining room right now.

Mrs. Popov. In the dining room, is he? I'll give him his comeuppance. Bring him in here this minute. *(Exit LUKA. Suddenly sad again)* Why do they do this to me? Why? Insulting my grief, intruding on my solitude? *(She sighs.)* I'm afraid I'll have to enter a convent. I will, I *must* enter a convent.

[*Enter* MR. SMIRNOV *and* LUKA.]

Smirnov *(to LUKA).* Dolt! Idiot! You talk too much! *(Seeing* MRS. POVOV. *With dignity)* May I have the honor of introducing myself, madam? Grigory S. Smirnov, landowner and lieutenant of artillery, retired. Forgive me, madam, if I disturb your peace and quiet, but my business is both urgent and weighty.

Mrs. Popov *(declining to offer him her hand).* What is it you wish, sir?

Smirnov. At the time of his death, your late husband—with whom I had the honor to be acquainted, ma'am—was in my debt to the tune of twelve hundred rubles. I have two notes to prove it. Tomorrow, ma'am, I must pay the interest on a bank loan. I have therefore no alternative, ma'am, but to ask you to pay me the money today.

Mrs. Popov. Twelve hundred rubles? But what did my husband owe it to you for?

Smirnov. He used to buy his oats from me, madam.

Mrs. Popov *(to Luka, with a sigh).* Remember what I said, Luka: Tell them to give Toby an extra portion of oats today! *(Exit Luka.)* My dear Mr.—what was that name again?

Smirnov. Smirnov, ma'am.

Mrs. Popov. My dear Mr. Smirnov, if Mr. Popov

owed you money, you shall be paid—to the last ruble, to the last kopeck. But today—you must excuse me, Mr.—what was it?

Smirnov. Smirnov, ma'am.

Mrs. Popov. Today, Mr. Smirnov, I have no ready cash in the house. *(SMIRNOV starts to speak.)* Tomorrow, Mr. Smirnov, no, the day after tomorrow, all will be well. My steward[3] will be back from town. I shall see that he pays what is owing. Today, no. In any case, today is exactly seven months from Mr. Popov's death. On such a day you will understand that I am in no mood to think of money.

Smirnov. Madam, if you don't pay up now, you can carry me out feet foremost. They'll seize my estate.

Mrs. Popov. You can have your money. *(He starts to thank her.)* Tomorrow. *(He again starts to speak.)* That is: the day after tomorrow.

---

3. steward (STOO uhrd): person in charge of running an estate.

Smirnov. I don't need the money the day after tomorrow. I need it today.

Mrs. Popov. I'm sorry, Mr.—

Smirnov (shouting). Smirnov!

Mrs. Popov (sweetly). Yes, of course. But you can't have it today.

Smirnov. But I can't wait for it any longer!

Mrs. Popov. Be sensible, Mr. Smirnov. How can I pay you if I don't have it?

Smirnov. You don't have it?

Mrs. Popov. I don't have it.

Smirnov. Sure?

Mrs. Popov. Positive.

Smirnov. Very well. I'll make a note to that effect. (Shrugging) And then they want me to keep cool. I meet the tax commissioner on the street, and he says, "Why are you always in such a bad humor, Smirnov?" Bad humor! How can I help it, in God's name? I need money, I need it desperately. Take yesterday: I leave home at the crack of dawn; I call on all my debtors. Not a one of them pays up. Footsore and weary, I creep at midnight into some little dive and try to snatch a few winks of sleep on the floor by the vodka barrel. Then today, I come here, fifty miles from home, saying to myself, "At last, at last, I can be sure of something," and you're not in the mood! You give me a mood! How the devil can I help getting all worked up? **D**

Mrs. Popov. I thought I'd made it clear, Mr. Smirnov, that you'll get your money the minute my steward is back from town?

Smirnov. What the hell do I care about your steward? Pardon the expression, ma'am. But it was you I came to see.

Mrs. Popov. What language! What a tone to take to a lady! I refuse to hear another word. (Quickly, exit.)

Smirnov. Not in the mood, huh? "Exactly seven months since Popov's death," huh? How about me? (Shouting after her) Is there this interest to pay, or isn't there? I'm asking you a question: Is there this interest to pay, or isn't there? So your husband died, and you're not in the mood, and your steward's gone off someplace, and so forth and so on, but what can *I* do about all that, huh? What do *you* think I should do? Take a running jump and shove my head through the wall? Take off in a balloon? You don't know my *other* debtors. I call on Gruzdeff. Not at home. I look for Yaroshevitch. He's hiding out. I find Kooritsin. He kicks up a row, and I have to throw him through the window. I work my way right down the list. Not a kopeck. Then I come to you, and damn it, if you'll pardon the expression, you're not in the mood! (Quietly, as he realizes he's talking to air)

> I'm in a rage! I'm in a positively towering rage! Every nerve in my body is trembling at forty to the dozen!

I've spoiled them all, that's what; I've let them play me for a sucker. Well, I'll show them. I'll show this one. I'll stay right here till she pays up. Ugh! (He shudders with rage.) I'm in a rage! I'm in a positively towering rage! Every nerve in my body is trembling at forty to the dozen! I can't breathe, I feel ill, I think I'm going to faint, hey, you there!

[Enter Luka.]

Luka. Yes, sir? Is there anything you wish, sir?

Smirnov. Water! Water!! No, make it vodka. (Exit Luka.) Consider the logic of it. A fellow

---

D **Reading Focus** **Making Predictions** Do you think Mr. Smirnov will be paid back by the end of the play?

creature is desperately in need of cash, so desperately in need that he has to seriously contemplate hanging himself, and this woman, this mere chit of a girl, won't pay up, and why not? Because, forsooth, she isn't in the mood! Oh, the logic of women! Come to that, I never have liked them, I could do without the whole sex. Talk to a woman? I'd rather sit on a barrel of dynamite, the very thought gives me gooseflesh. Women! Creatures of poetry and romance! Just to see one in the distance gets me mad. My legs start twitching with rage. I feel like yelling for help. **E**

[*Enter* LUKA, *handing* SMIRNOV *a glass of water.*]

Luka. Mrs. Popov is indisposed, sir. She is seeing no one.
Smirnov. Get out. (*Exit* LUKA.) Indisposed, is she? Seeing no one, huh? Well, she can see me or not, but I'll be here, I'll be right here till she pays up. If you're sick for a week, I'll be here for a week. If you're sick for a year, I'll be here for a year. You won't get around *me* with your widow's weeds[4] and your schoolgirl dimples. I know all about dimples. (*Shouting through the window*) Semyon, let the horses out of those shafts, we're not leaving, we're staying, and tell them to give the horses some oats, yes, oats, you fool, what do you think? (*Walking away from the window*) What a mess, what an unholy mess! I didn't sleep last night, the heat is terrific today, not a one of 'em has paid up, and here's this—this skirt in mourning that's not in the mood! My head aches, where's that— (*He drinks from the glass.*) Water, ugh! You there!

---

4. **widow's weeds:** black clothing worn by a widow to mourn a husband's death.

[*Enter* LUKA.]

Luka. Yes, sir. You wish for something, sir?
Smirnov. Where's that confounded vodka I asked for? (*Exit* LUKA. SMIRNOV *sits and looks himself over.*) Oof! A fine figure of a man *I* am! Unwashed, uncombed, unshaven, straw on my vest, dust all over me. The little woman must've taken me for a highwayman. (*Yawns*) I suppose it wouldn't be considered polite to barge into a drawing room in this state, but who cares? I'm not a visitor, I'm a creditor—most unwelcome of guests, second only to Death. **F**

[*Enter* LUKA.]

Luka (*handing him the vodka*). If I may say so, sir, you take too many liberties, sir.
Smirnov. What?!
Luka. Oh, nothing, sir, nothing.
Smirnov. Who do you think you're talking to? Shut your mouth!
Luka (*aside*). There's an evil spirit abroad. The devil must have sent him. Oh! (*Exit* LUKA.)
Smirnov. What a rage I'm in! I'll grind the whole world to powder. Oh, I feel ill again. You there!

[*Enter* MRS. POPOV.]

Mrs. Popov (*looking at the floor*). In the solitude of my rural retreat, Mr. Smirnov, I've long since grown unaccustomed to the sound of the human voice. Above all, I cannot bear shouting. I must beg you not to break the silence.
Smirnov. Very well. Pay me my money and I'll go.
Mrs. Popov. I told you before, and I tell you again, Mr. Smirnov: I have no cash; you'll have

E **Literary Focus** Comedy and Farce Identify the examples of exaggeration in this soliloquy, a speech that expresses a character's inner feelings.

Vocabulary **indisposed** (ihn dihs POHZD) *adj.*: slightly ill.

F **Reading Focus** Making Predictions What does this short soliloquy reveal about Smirnov? What do you predict will happen to Smirnov?

to wait till the day after tomorrow. Can I express myself more plainly?

Smirnov. And *I* told *you* before, and *I* tell *you* again, that I need the money today, that the day after tomorrow is too late, and that if you don't pay, and pay now, I'll have to hang myself in the morning!

Mrs. Popov. But I have no cash. This is quite a puzzle.

Smirnov. You won't pay, huh?

Mrs. Popov. I *can't* pay, Mr. Smirnov.

Smirnov. In that case, I'm going to sit here and wait. *(Sits down)* You'll pay up the day after tomorrow? Very good. Till the day after tomor-row, here I sit. *(Pause. He jumps up.)* Now look, do I have to pay that interest tomorrow, or don't I? Or do you think I'm joking?

Mrs. Popov. I must ask you not to raise your voice, Mr. Smirnov. This is not a stable.

Smirnov. Who said it was? Do I have to pay the interest tomorrow or not?

Mrs. Popov. Mr. Smirnov, do you know how to behave in the presence of a lady?

Smirnov. No, madam, I do not know how to behave in the presence of a lady.

Mrs. Popov. Just what I thought. I look at you, and I say: ugh! I hear you talk, and I say to myself: "That man doesn't know how to talk to a lady."

Smirnov. You'd like me to come simpering[5] to you in French, I suppose. "*Enchanté, madame! Merci beaucoup* for not paying zee money, *madame! Pardonnez-moi* if I 'ave disturbed you, *madame*! How *charmante* you look in mourning, *madame*!" Ⓖ

Mrs. Popov. Now you're being silly, Mr. Smirnov.

Smirnov *(mimicking).* "Now you're being silly, Mr. Smirnov." "You don't know how to talk to a lady, Mr. Smirnov." Look here, Mrs. Popov, I've known more women than you've known kitty cats. I've fought three duels on their account. I've jilted twelve and been jilted by nine others. Oh, yes, Mrs. Popov, I've played the fool in my time, whispered sweet nothings, bowed and scraped and endeavored to please. Don't tell me I don't know what it is to love, to pine away with longing, to have the blues, to melt like butter, to be weak as water. I was full of tender emotion. I was carried away with passion. I squandered half my fortune on the sex. I chattered about women's emancipation. But there's an end to everything, dear madam. Burning eyes, dark eyelashes, ripe, red lips, dimpled cheeks, heaving bosoms, soft whisperings, the moon above, the lake below—I don't give a rap for that sort of nonsense any more, Mrs. Popov. I've found out about women. Present company excepted, they're liars. Their behavior is mere playacting; their conversation is sheer gossip. Yes, dear lady, women, young or old, are false, petty, vain, cruel, malicious, unreasonable. As for intelligence, any sparrow could give them points. Appearances, I admit, can be deceptive. In appearance, a woman may be all poetry and romance, goddess and angel, muslin[6] and fluff. To look at her exterior is to be transported to heaven. But I have looked at her interior, Mrs. Popov, and what did I find there—in her very soul? A crocodile. *(He has gripped the back of the chair so firmly that it snaps.)* And, what is more revolting, a crocodile with an illusion, crocodile that imagines tender sentiments are its own special province, a crocodile that thinks itself queen of the realm of love! Whereas, in sober fact, dear madam, if a woman can love anything except a lap dog, you can hang me by the feet on that nail. For a man, love is suffering, love is sacrifice. A woman just swishes her train around and tightens her grip on your nose. Now, you're a woman, aren't you, Mrs. Popov? You must be an expert on some of this. Tell me, quite frankly, did you ever know a woman to be—faithful, for instance? Or even sincere? Only old hags, huh? Though some women are old hags from birth. But as for the others? You're right: A faithful woman is a freak of nature—like a cat with horns.

Mrs. Popov. Who *is* faithful, then? Who *have* you cast for the faithful lover? Not man?

Smirnov. Right first time, Mrs. Popov: man.

Mrs. Popov *(going off into a peal of bitter laughter).* Man! Man is faithful! That's a new one! *(Fiercely)* What right do you have to say this, Mr. Smirnov? Men faithful? Let me tell you something. Of all the men I have ever known, my late husband Popov was the best. I loved him, and there are women who know how to love, Mr. Smirnov. I gave him my youth, my happiness,

---

Ⓖ **Literary Focus** Comedy and Farce In Chekhov's time, French was considered the language of refinement and good manners. What is exaggerated in Smirnov's use of it here? What tone of voice do you imagine Smirnov using?

Vocabulary **emancipation** (ih man suh PAY shuhn) *n.*: liberation; the act of setting free.

my life, my fortune. I worshipped the ground he trod on—and what happened? The best of men was unfaithful to me, Mr. Smirnov. Not once in a while. All the time. After he died, I found his desk drawer full of love letters. While he was alive, he was always going away for the weekend. He squandered my money. He flirted with other women before my very eyes. But, in spite of all, Mr. Smirnov, I was faithful. Unto death. And beyond. I am *still* faithful, Mr. Smirnov! Buried alive in this house, I shall wear mourning till the day I, too, am called to my eternal rest.

Smirnov (*laughing scornfully*). Expect me to believe that? As if I couldn't see through all this hocus-pocus. Buried alive! Till you're called to your eternal rest! Till when? Till some little poet—or some little subaltern[7] with his first moustache—comes riding by and asks: "Can that be the house of the mysterious Tamara, who for love of her late husband has buried herself alive, vowing to see no man?" Ha!   **H**

Mrs. Popov (*flaring up*). How dare you? How dare you insinuate—?

Smirnov. You may have buried yourself alive, Mrs. Popov, but you haven't forgotten to powder your nose.

Mrs. Popov (*incoherent*). How dare you? How—?

Smirnov. Who's raising his voice now? Just because I call a spade a spade. Because I shoot straight from the shoulder. Well, don't shout at me, I'm not your steward.

Mrs. Popov. I'm not shouting, you're shouting! Oh, leave me alone!

Smirnov. Pay me the money, and I will.

_____
7. **subaltern** (suh BAWL tuhrn): a person of low rank.

Mrs. Popov. You'll get no money out of me!

Smirnov. Oh, so that's it!

Mrs. Popov. Not a ruble, not a kopeck. Get out! Leave me alone!

Smirnov. Not being your husband, I must ask you not to make scenes with me. (*He sits.*) I don't like scenes.

Mrs. Popov (*choking with rage*). You're sitting down?   **I**

Smirnov. Correct, I'm sitting down.

Mrs. Popov. I asked you to leave!

Smirnov. Then give me the money. (*Aside*) Oh, what a rage I'm in, what a rage!

Mrs. Popov. The impudence of the man! I won't talk to you a moment longer. Get out. (*Pause*) Are you going?

Smirnov. No.

Mrs. Popov. No?!

Smirnov. No.

Mrs. Popov. On your head be it. Luka! (*Enter* LUKA.) Show the gentleman out, Luka.

Luka (*approaching*). I'm afraid, sir, I'll have to ask you, um, to leave, sir, now, um—

Smirnov (*jumping up*). Shut your mouth, you old idiot! Who do you think you're talking to? I'll make mincemeat of you.

Luka (*clutching his heart*). Mercy on us! Holy saints above! (*He falls into an armchair.*) I'm taken sick! I can't breathe!

Mrs. Popov. Then where's Dasha? Dasha! Dasha! Come here at once! (*She rings.*)

Luka. They gone picking berries, ma'am, I'm alone here—Water, water, I'm taken sick!

Mrs. Popov (*to* SMIRNOV). Get out, you!

Smirnov. Can't you even be polite with me, Mrs. Popov?

_____

H **Literary Focus** Comedy and Farce How does Smirnov make fun of Mrs. Popov here?

I **Reading Focus** Making Predictions Do you think Smirnov will leave without his money?

Vocabulary **insinuate** (ihn SIHN yoo ayt) *v.*: suggest.
impudence (IHM pyuh duhns) *n.*: quality of being disrespectful.

Mrs. Popov *(clenching her fists and stamping her feet)*. With you? You're a wild animal, you were never housebroken!

Smirnov. What? What did you say?

Mrs. Popov. I said you were a wild animal, you were never housebroken.

Smirnov *(advancing upon her)*. And what right do you have to talk to me like that?

Mrs. Popov. Like what?

Smirnov. You have insulted me, madam.

Mrs. Popov. What of it? Do you think I'm scared of you?

Smirnov. So you think you can get away with it because you're a woman. A creature of poetry and romance, huh? Well, it doesn't go down with me. I hereby challenge you to a duel.

Luka. Mercy on us! Holy saints alive! Water!

Smirnov. I propose we shoot it out.

Mrs. Popov. Trying to scare me again? Just because you have big fists and a voice like a bull? You're a brute.

Smirnov. No one insults Grigory S. Smirnov with impunity! And I don't care if you are a female.

Mrs. Popov *(trying to outshout him)*. Brute, brute, brute!

Smirnov. The sexes are equal, are they? Fine: Then it's just prejudice to expect men alone to pay for insults. I hereby challenge—

Mrs. Popov *(screaming)*. All right! You want to shoot it out? All right! Let's shoot it out!

Smirnov. And let it be here and now!

Mrs. Popov. Here and now! All right! I'll have Popov's pistols here in one minute! *(Walks away, then turns)* Putting one of Popov's bullets through your silly head will be a pleasure! *Au revoir. (Exit.)*

Smirnov. I'll bring her down like a duck, a sitting duck. I'm not one of your little poets, I'm no little subaltern with his first moustache. No, sir, there's no weaker sex where I'm concerned!

Luka. Sir! Master! *(He goes down on his knees.)* Take pity on a poor old man, and do me a favor: Go away. It was bad enough before, you nearly scared me to death. But a duel—!

Smirnov *(ignoring him)*. A duel! That's equality of the sexes for you! That's women's emancipation! Just as a matter of principle I'll bring her down like a duck. But what a woman! "Putting one of Popov's bullets through your silly head . . ."

J **Literary Focus** Comedy and Farce How do you visualize Luka's actions and tone of voice during this scene?

K **Literary Focus** Comedy and Farce What is farcical about Mrs. Popov's reaction now?

Vocabulary **impunity** (im PYOO nih tee) *n.:* freedom from punishment.

Her cheeks were flushed, her eyes were gleaming! And, by Heaven, she's accepted the challenge! I never knew a woman like this before!

Luka. Sir! Master! Please go away! I'll always pray for you!

Smirnov (*again ignoring him*). What a woman! Phew!! *She's* no sourpuss; *she's* no crybaby. She's fire-and-brimstone.[8] She's a human cannonball. What a shame I have to kill her!

Luka (*weeping*). Please, kind sir, please, go away!

Smirnov (*as before*). I like her, isn't that funny? With those dimples and all? I like her. I'm even prepared to consider letting her off that debt. And where's my rage? It's gone. I never knew a woman like this before. **Ⓛ**

[*Enter* MRS. POPOV *with pistols.*]

Mrs. Popov (*boldly*). Pistols, Mr. Smirnov! (*Matter of fact*) But before we start, you'd better show me how it's done, I'm not too familiar with these things. In fact I never gave a pistol a second look.

Luka. Lord, have mercy on us, I must go hunt up the gardener and the coachman. Why has this catastrophe fallen upon us, O Lord? (*Exit.*)

Smirnov (*examining the pistols*). Well, it's like this. There are several makes: One is the Mortimer, with capsules, especially constructed for dueling. What you have here are Smith and Wesson triple-action revolvers, with extractor, first-rate job, worth ninety rubles at the very least. You hold it this way. (*Aside*) My Lord, what eyes she has! They're setting me on fire.

---

8. **fire-and-brimstone:** in this context, spirited and extremely lively. This expression often refers to eternal punishment in hell or describes fiery religious sermons.

Mrs. Popov. This way?

Smirnov. Yes, that's right. You cock the trigger, take aim like this, head up, arm out like this. Then you just press with this finger here, and it's all over. The main thing is, keep cool, take slow aim, and don't let your arm jump. **Ⓜ**

Mrs. Popov. I see. And if it's inconvenient to do the job here, we can go out in the garden.

Smirnov. Very good. Of course, I should warn you: I'll be firing in the air.

Mrs. Popov. What? This is the end. Why?

Smirnov. Oh, well—because—for private reasons.

Mrs. Popov. Scared, huh? (*She laughs heartily.*) Now don't you try to get out of it, Mr. Smirnov. My blood is up. I won't be happy till I've drilled a hole through that skull of yours. Follow me. What's the matter? Scared?

Smirnov. That's right. I'm scared.

Mrs. Popov. Oh, come on, what's the matter with you?

Smirnov. Well, um, Mrs. Popov, I um, I like you.

Mrs. Popov (*laughing bitterly*). Good Lord! He likes me, does he? The gall[9] of the man. (*Showing him the door*) You may leave, Mr. Smirnov.

Smirnov (*Quietly puts the gun down, takes his hat, and walks to the door. Then he stops, and the pair look at each other without a word. Then, approaching gingerly*). Listen, Mrs. Popov. Are you still mad at me? I'm in the devil of a temper myself, of course. But then, you see—what I mean is—it's this way—the fact is—(*roaring*) Well, is it my fault if I like you? (*Clutches the back of a chair. It breaks.*) What fragile furniture you have here! I like you. Know what I mean? I could fall in love with you.

---

9. **gall** (gawl): nerve; rude boldness.

Ⓛ **Reading Focus** **Making Predictions** How will Smirnov proceed when Mrs. Popov returns with dueling pistols?

Ⓜ **Literary Focus** **Comedy and Farce** What is both humorous and ironic about this scene?

Analyzing Visuals   **Viewing and Interpreting**   How can you tell that this scene is a turning point in the play?

Mrs. Popov. I hate you. Get out!

Smirnov. What a woman! I never saw anything like it. Oh, I'm lost, I'm done for, I'm a mouse in a trap.

Mrs. Popov. Leave this house, or I shoot!

Smirnov. Shoot away! What bliss to die of a shot that was fired by that little velvet hand! To die gazing into those enchanting eyes. I'm out of my mind. I know: You must decide at once. Think for one second, then decide. Because if I leave now, I'll never be back. Decide! I'm a pretty decent chap. Landed gentleman, I should say. Ten thousand a year. Good stable. Throw a kopeck up in the air, and I'll put a bullet through it. Will you marry me?

Mrs. Popov *(indignant, brandishing*[10] *the gun).* We'll shoot it out! Get going! Take your pistol!

Smirnov. I'm out of my mind. I don't understand anything any more. *(Shouting)* You there! That vodka!

Mrs. Popov. No excuses! No delays! We'll shoot it out!

Smirnov. I'm out of my mind. I'm falling in love. I *have* fallen in love. *(He takes her hand vigorously; she squeals.)* I love you. *(He goes down on his knees.)* I love you as I've never loved before. I jilted twelve and was jilted by nine others. But I didn't love a one of them as I love you. I'm full of tender emotion. I'm melting like butter. I'm weak as water. I'm on my knees like a fool, and I offer you my hand. It's a shame; it's a disgrace. I haven't been in love in five years. I took a vow against it. And now, all of a sudden, to be swept off my feet, it's a scandal. I offer you my hand, dear lady. Will

> I'm out of my mind.
> I'm falling in love. I
> *have* fallen in love.

you or won't you? You won't? Then don't! *(He rises and walks toward the door.)*

Mrs. Popov. I didn't say anything.

Smirnov *(stopping).* What?

Mrs. Popov. Oh nothing, you can go. Well, no, just a minute. No, you can go. Go! I detest you! But, just a moment. Oh, if you knew how furious I feel! *(Throws the gun on the table)* My fingers have gone to sleep holding that horrid thing. *(She is tearing her handkerchief to shreds.)* And what are you standing around for? Get out of here!

Smirnov. Goodbye.

Mrs. Popov. Go, go, go! *(Shouting)* Where are you going? Wait a minute! No, no, it's all right, just go. I'm fighting mad. Don't come near me, don't come near me!

Smirnov *(who is coming near her).* I'm pretty disgusted with myself—falling in love like a kid, going down on my knees like some moon-gazing whippersnapper, the very thought gives me gooseflesh. *(Rudely)* I love you. But it doesn't make sense. Tomorrow, I have to pay that interest, and we've already started mowing. *(He puts his arm about her waist.)* I shall never forgive myself for this.

Mrs. Popov. Take your hands off me, I hate you! Let's shoot it out!

[*A long kiss. Enter* LUKA *with an axe, the* GAR-DENER *with a rake, the* COACHMAN *with a pitch-fork, hired men with sticks.*]

Luka *(seeing the kiss).* Mercy on us! Holy saints above!

Mrs. Popov *(dropping her eyes).* Luka, tell them in the stable that Toby is *not* to have any oats today. Ⓝ

---

10. **brandishing** (BRAN dihsh ing): waving something around in a challenging way.

Ⓝ **Literary Focus** Comedy and Farce What is the significance of Mrs. Popov's comment here?

Applying Your Skills

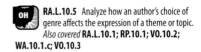 **RA.L.10.5** Analyze how an author's choice of genre affects the expression of a theme or topic.
Also covered **RA.L.10.1; RP.10.1; VO.10.2; WA.10.1.c; VO.10.3**

The Brute

Respond and Think Critically

Reading Focus

Quick Check

1. At the beginning of the play, what does each character want? By the end of the play, how has each character changed?

2. Explain the play's title. Who or what is the brute in the play?

Read with a Purpose

3. Do you find Chekhov's plot to be credible, or believable? Explain why or why not.

Reading Skills: Making Predictions

4. Review your chart to check your predictions. Were they accurate?

Character	What happens/ What's said?	What I predict	Was I right?
Mrs. Popov	Says her life is over	She will change her mind.	Yes

✓ Vocabulary Check

Choose the best Vocabulary word from the following list to complete each analogy below: **indisposed, emancipation, insinuate, impudence,** and **impunity.**

5. ACCEPTANCE : REJECTION :: _____ : ENSLAVEMENT

6. CALM : CHAOTIC :: _____ : RESPECT

7. JOYOUS : HAPPY :: ILL : _____

8. DEFY : RESIST :: SUGGEST : _____

9. VICTORY : DEFEAT :: PUNISHMENT : _____

Literary Focus

Literary Analysis

10. **Interpret** Why does Smirnov begin to change his mind about Mrs. Popov? At what climactic moment in the play do we know she has changed her mind too?

Literary Skills: Comedy and Farce

11. **Analyze** In tragedy, breaking a vow often leads to misery, but in this play, it leads to happiness. Explain how breaking vows leads to a happy ending for the main characters.

Literary Skills Review: Characterization

12. **Compare and Contrast** In this play, do opposites attract? Compare and contrast Mrs. Popov's and Mr. Smirnov's principal **character traits,** or aspects of their personalities. How does Chekhov establish these traits?

Writing Focus

Think as a Reader/Writer

Use It in Your Writing Imagine a situation in which you must overcome an obstacle to achieve a goal. Then, write a short monologue expressing your feelings in hugely exaggerated terms. For inspiration, refer to examples from *The Brute* that you recorded in your *Reader/Writer Notebook.*

 What can humor show us about the choices we make in life?

Preparing to Read

The Tragedy *of* Julius Caesar

by **William Shakespeare**

The performance photographs illustrating this play are from the 2006 Royal Shakespeare Company's production of *Julius Caesar*

What Do You Think?

What is more important—ambition or honor?

 QuickTalk

Think about this statement: "Power corrupts and absolute power corrupts absolutely." Do you know of any political figures who abuse their power? In a group, discuss how power can lead to corruption.

An **Introduction** to **Julius Caesar**

by **Robert Anderson**

The Play: A Betrayal of Trust

In a time of chaos, a great leader rises to power by promising to restore order. He rewards the loyal followers who have helped him. Soon he grows so powerful and arrogant that even his followers no longer trust him and conspire to kill him. In the hands of William Shakespeare, this true story from history became a great tragic drama, *The Tragedy of Julius Caesar*.

The Real Julius Caesar

Gaius Julius Caesar (c.100–44 B.C.) was a powerful general and a member of the Senate. He rose to political power by calling for reform of the Roman government. After centuries of rule by aristocrats, the Senate had become weak and corrupt. In 60 B.C. Caesar formed a three-man government, called the first triumvirate. The two other members of the triumvirate were Pompey, a strong general, and Crassus, one of the richest men in Rome. Caesar and Pompey were friends, and Pompey was married to Caesar's daughter.

Eager for still more power and realizing that he could achieve it only with conquests and money, Caesar left Rome for what has been called the Gallic Wars. (Like other Roman leaders, Caesar used the soldiers under his command as his private army.) For eight years

Caesar and his armies roamed Europe, subjugating France, Belgium, and parts of Holland, Germany, and Switzerland. Caesar amassed huge sums of money, which he sent back to Rome to gain favor among the people.

Caesar's daughter died in 54 B.C., and the relationship between Caesar and Pompey

Brutus by Michelangelo Buonarroti (1475–1564).
Marble. Museo Nazionale del Bargello, Florence, Italy.

The Death of Caesar by Vincenzo Camuccini (1773–1844). Oil on canvas. Private Collection.

became strained. After Crassus died in 53 B.C., civil war broke out between Caesar and Pompey. In 49 B.C. Pompey, jealous of Caesar's growing power and favor among the people, gave his support to the Senate, which was also wary of Caesar's ambitions.

Caesar considered himself a defender of the people, but his critics said that he gained the people's support with bribes and handouts. His enemies said that he deprived the Romans of their liberty.

Caesar refused the Senate's order to give up his command and return to Rome as a private citizen. Instead, in 48 B.C. he marched his army on Rome, took control, and had himself declared sole dictator of Rome. Then, he defeated Pompey in Greece and chased him to Egypt. There Pompey was murdered before Caesar could capture him. Caesar lingered in Egypt, bewitched by the twenty-two-year-old Cleopatra. After securing the throne of Egypt for Cleopatra, Caesar went to Spain, where he defeated an army led by Pompey's sons.

The Unconquerable God

When he returned to Rome, Caesar was invincible. He was declared dictator for ten years and saw to it that his supporters, including Brutus, became senators. Caesar made some of the reforms he had promised, but he also seized more power. His desire for power grew so obsessive that he had a statue of himself, bearing the inscription "To the Unconquerable God," erected in the temple of Quirinus. The common people loved Caesar, and he was declared dictator for life.

To a number of Romans, however, Caesar's ambition was deplorable. The last Roman king had been overthrown 450 years before, when the Romans set up a republican government. The idea of another king ruling the "free Romans" was unthinkable. As Caesar's arrogance and power became unbearable to certain senators, they made plans to assassinate him on March 15, 44 B.C. Shakespeare's play opens a month before the murder.

The First Roman Emperor

After the assassination, the main conspirators fled from Rome. Three of Caesar's closest followers, Antonius, Lepidus, and Octavius, formed a new government, the second triumvirate. The three dictators pursued and defeated Caesar's assassins, but then turned on each other in a long civil war. The eventual winner was Octavius, who was Caesar's great-nephew and heir. Octavius became Augustus Caesar, the first of the Roman emperors.

Gold coin ('De Quelen Aureus') showing Marcus Antonius (Mark Antony) (82–30 BCE).

William Shakespeare's Life: A Biographical Sketch

by **Robert Anderson**

Who was William Shakespeare, and what was he really like? More material has been written about Shakespeare and his works than about any other writer, yet we know little about the life of this great playwright and poet. What we do know comes mainly from public records.

Early Years in Stratford

We know that he was baptized on April 26, 1564, in Stratford-on-Avon, a town about one hundred miles northwest of London. William was one of eight children. His parents were John Shakespeare, a prosperous merchant and an important man in the town, and Mary Arden, the daughter of a local landowner.

William went to the local grammar school, which was very different from today's grammar schools. In those days it was rare for students to move on to a university. The Stratford grammar school provided the boys of Stratford (no girls went to school) with all their formal education. What they learned in this school was Latin—Latin grammar and Latin literature, including the schoolboys' favorite: Ovid's amorous retellings of the Greek and Roman myths.

In 1582, Shakespeare married Anne Hathaway, who was eight years older than he was, and in 1583, their first child, Susanna, was born. In 1585, Anne gave birth to twins, Hamnet and Judith. Then, from 1585 until 1592, Shakespeare's life is a mystery.

Illustration for the cover of *Finding Out, Shakespeare's World* by Janet and Anne Johnstone. Published by Purnell and Sons Ltd., Go London, 1964.

A Life in the Theater

Most scholars believe that Shakespeare went to London to seek his fortune the year after the twins were born. We know that by 1592 he had become an actor and a playwright, because in that year a rival playwright, Robert Green, scathingly warned other playwrights about the actor who had become writer, calling Shakespeare "an upstart crow."

In 1594, Shakespeare became a charter, or original, member of a theater company called the Lord Chamberlain's Men. We know from a Swiss traveler's letter that this group first performed *Julius Caesar* in 1599, the same year in which their new theater, the Globe, opened for business. In 1603, the Lord Chamberlain's Men became the King's Men. (Their patron was none other than King James himself.) Shakespeare acted and wrote for this company until he retired to Stratford in 1612. By that time he had written thirty-seven plays—comedies, histories, tragedies, and romances—including his tragic masterpieces *Hamlet, Othello, King Lear*, and *Macbeth*. He was also a great poet, famous for his sonnet series.

An Enduring Legacy

As a shareholder in the King's Men, Shakespeare had received part of the profits of every performance. He earned enough to buy a large house for his family in Stratford, to acquire land, and even to purchase a coat of arms—a sign that he had become a gentleman. Shakespeare died in Stratford on April 23, 1616, at the age of fifty-two. He was buried in the Holy Trinity Church at Stratford, where his grave can still be seen today.

After his death, his fellow writers and company members collected his plays and prepared them for publication. The first printed edition of Shakespeare's works, known as the First Folio, appeared in 1623. Its preface includes a poem entitled "To the Memory of My Beloved, the Author, Mr. William Shakespeare, and What He Hath Left Us" by Ben Jonson, an important Elizabethan playwright and poet. Jonson calls Shakespeare "Soul of the age! The applause! delight! and wonder of our stage!" and claims, "He was not of an age, but for all time!"

History has proved Ben Jonson right. William Shakespeare's plays have been translated into most languages and, more than four hundred years after they were written, are still being performed around the world.

William Shakespeare (1564–1616) represented at age 34, by Louis Coblizt. Copy after an anonymous English painting at the Royal Collections at Hampton Court. 1847. Chateaux de Versailles et de Trianon, Versailles, France.

The Elizabethan Stage

by **Robert Anderson**

You are in the audience of a spectacular theatrical performance, but you feel as if you are part of the action on stage. You could be a theatergoer in the early 1600s, or you could be attending a performance tonight. Today's modern theaters have a lot in common with the theater in Shakespeare's time. Like the Elizabethan stage, our arena stages and thrust stages are open and place the audience near the actors. The Elizabethan stage, however, would have seemed strange to American theatergoers of sixty or seventy years ago, who were accustomed to an enclosed stage with a velvet curtain that separated the audience from the actors.

As with Shakespeare's life, we have only sketchy information about the early English theater. Some of the details that we do have were gleaned from the structure of Shakespeare's plays. Shakespeare wrote his plays for his own theater company, the King's Men. He created parts with specific players in mind and crafted scenes that would work well in the spaces where the company performed.

It appears that wandering acting companies set up their stages—mere platforms—wherever they could find space, often in the courtyard of an inn. Many audience members, or "groundlings," stood around three sides of the stage. Those who paid extra money sat in chairs on the balconies surrounding the inn yard. Even the King's Men, one of the few companies with a permanent building, performed frequently in other spaces, such as royal palaces.

The Sets: Mostly Imagination

Because theater was mobile, the sets were minimal. In the opening scene of *Julius Caesar,* for example, a few statues set the scene on a street. In later scenes, a rustic bench indicates a garden, and a few steps tell us that we are in front of a large public building.

Shakespeare trusted his audience's imagination. He knew that he did not need elaborate sets to re-create a battle scene, a bedroom, or the Roman Forum. Without sets to move on and offstage, Shakespeare could change scenes with the fluidity we see in movies.

Although Shakespeare didn't use realistic settings, his kings and other characters were splendidly costumed. His staging called for flags, banners, musicians, and sound effects. There was no lighting equipment since plays were staged outdoors in the afternoon.

The Actors: All Males

In Shakespeare's time all actors were males. (Not until 1660 did women play in professional theaters.) Boys recruited from the choir schools were trained professionally to play the female roles. It was not too difficult to create the illusion that they were women. Shakespeare's plays were performed in contemporary Elizabethan costumes, and women's clothing was concealing, with long, full skirts flowing from narrow waists. Women also wore elaborate wigs and powdered their faces heavily.

Costume designs for Shakespeare's play *Henry VIII* (19th century).

Playwrights had to write scenes that would catch the attention of the audience—3,000 restless people who were also eating, drinking, and talking. Many actors used their bodies as much as their voices, with flamboyant gestures that we would consider overacting today. Actors had to continually move so that spectators on all three sides could catch their expressions and hear their voices. They usually had multiple roles and many costume changes during a single play.

Elaborate Costumes

Costumes were far more important than sets. Regardless of the era in which the action was taking place, the actors performed in contemporary Elizabethan costumes. Clothing helped the audience distinguish the characters at a distance and provided clues to the characters' social rank. The costumes of royal characters added to the rich spectacle that the audience wanted to see. Banners and flags added more pageantry.

The Globe—The "Wooden O"

The first permanent playhouse in England, known simply as The Theater, opened in 1576. Its owner was James Burbage, who later founded Shakespeare's company. In 1599, the company dismantled their building timber by timber and rowed the pieces across the Thames River. They reconstructed the building and named it the Globe.

In *Henry V*, Shakespeare calls the Globe "this wooden O." It consisted of an open space, perhaps sixty-five feet in diameter, surrounded by a more or less circular building thirty feet high with three tiers of balconies containing seats. The stage, which was forty feet by thirty feet, projected into the open space. It was five feet off the ground and had a trapdoor that was used for burials, surprise entrances, and mysterious exits. At the rear, there was a small curtained inner stage flanked by two entrances, with an upper stage above it, which was used for balcony scenes.

Julius Caesar was probably one of the first plays performed at the Globe. A visitor from Switzerland wrote the following account of a performance in September 1599:

"I went with my companions over the water, and . . . saw the tragedy of the first emperor Julius with at least fifteen characters very well acted. At the end of the comedy they danced according to their custom with extreme elegance."

Shakespeare's audience expected comic episodes, songs, and dances, even in a serious play. They came to the Globe for entertainment, and Shakespeare and his fellow players made sure they left happy.

Clockwise from left: Cate Blanchett as Queen Elizabeth I (2007); costume design for *Julius Caesar* from "La Mort de Pompee" (1906); Globe Theatre, London, UK.

How to Read
Shakespeare

Feel the Beat

As with all of Shakespeare's plays, *Julius Caesar* is written in blank verse. **Blank verse** mimics the natural rhythms of English speech. Blank verse is unrhymed **iambic pentameter**, which means that each line of the play's poetry is built on five iambs. An **iamb** consists of an unstressed syllable followed by a stressed syllable, as in the word *prepare*. Read the following lines aloud to feel the beat, or rhythm. The syllables marked with a (') should be stressed. Strike the beats with your fingers:

> The evil that men do lives after them,

> The good is oft interrèd with their bones.

A play written in this pattern would have a singsong effect. Like today's hip-hop artists, Shakespeare kept the rhythm interesting by adding pauses and sometimes reversing the stressed and unstressed syllables. Actors will also stress words differently depending on how they interpret their meaning. You will probably find variations when reading these lines aloud.

> This was the noblest Roman of them all.
> All the conspirators save only he
> Did that they did in envy of great Caesar.

Not all of Shakespeare's characters speak in blank verse. In *Julius Caesar,* you will notice that the commoners speak in ordinary prose.

MR. WILLIAM
SHAKESPEARES
COMEDIES,
HISTORIES, and
TRAGEDIES.
Publiſhed according to the True Originall Copies.

LONDON
Printed by Iſaac Iaggard, and Ed. Blount. 1623.

"Comedies, Histories and Tragedies" by William Shakespeare. First folio edition, 1623. The Granger Collection, New York.

Follow the Punctuation

Follow the punctuation marks, and resist the temptation to stop at the end of every line. In the first passage on this page, the lines are **end-stopped,** which means they end with a punctuation mark. In reading this passage, you pause at the end of the first line and come to a full stop at the end of the second line. In the next passage, you make a full stop at the end of the first line but not at the end of the second line. The second line has no punctuation: it is a **run-on** line. To determine the meaning, you must continue to the next line.

Archaic Words

In *Julius Caesar*, one character is a sooth-sayer. In Shakespeare's day the word *sooth* meant "truth." Today we would call such a person a fortuneteller or a psychic. At right are some other words from the play that are now **archaic,** or no longer in use.

ague: flu or fever

an: if

betimes: from time to time

fleering: flattering

hie: hurry

knave: servant, or person of humble birth

prithee: pray thee (beg you)

smatch: small amount

Words with Different Meanings

The most troublesome words in Shakespeare's plays are those that are still in use but now have different meanings. When Flavius calls the cobbler "thou naughty knave," the word *naughty* here means "worthless," so the sense of Flavius's line is different from what you might have thought. Below are other familiar words that had different meanings in Shakespeare's day.

closet: small room, often a private study

exhalations: meteors

gentle: noble

ghastly: ghostly

humor: temper or disposition

indifferently: impartially

just: true

sad: serious

saucy: presumptuous

soft: slowly; "wait a minute"

wit: intelligence

Act It Out!

Don't forget that this play was created for an audience—people just like the ones who flock to movies or rock concerts today. To get a feel for the play, plan to perform as much of it as possible.

You might begin with the first scene—a brief street scene in which a group of workers encounter two military officers. Here are two suggestions for an **oral interpretation:**

1. In small groups, assign a part to each group member.
2. For this first scene, you could do choral read-ings. Again, break into groups. Then, split your group into two smaller groups. Let one small group read the commoners' lines and the other small group read the speeches of the tribunes.

As you read the scene, don't worry about the poetry or the way the archaic words are pronounced. Instead, read the lines in the scene as if they were prose.

After your reading, discuss with the group what happens in the scene and how you feel about it. Who are these people? What is going on?

Now, give a **dramatic performance** of the scene. Assign the roles of actors, director, and audience. How will you set the scene? What are the characters doing as they speak? What props will you need?

The beginnings and endings of plays are important in Shakespeare. What did you learn from performing this opening scene?

DRAMA
Preparing to Read

The Tragedy of Julius Caesar

RA.L.10.6 Explain how literary techniques, including foreshadowing and flashback, are used to shape the plot of a literary text. **RA.L.10.5** Analyze how an author's choice of genre affects the expression of a theme or topic. *Also covered:* **RP.10.1**

Reader/Writer Notebook

Use your **RWN** to complete the activities for this selection.

Literary Focus

Tragedy A **tragedy** is a narrative that depicts serious events and ends unhappily for the main character, whose downfall is caused by his or her **tragic flaw** (a defect in character or judgment). In *The Tragedy of Julius Caesar,* the title character and those who plot against him have tragic flaws that fuel the <u>principal</u> events of the plot.

Reading Focus

Reading a Play Reading a play involves reading the lines and also reading *between* the lines. Based on a character's speeches and actions, you **make inferences** about what each character is *really* thinking and feeling. **Reading a play aloud** gives you a better understanding of characters' relationships. **Paraphrase** (restate information in your own words) to help you understand difficult passages.

Into Action Use a chart like the one below to track how characters feel about Caesar and how their loyalties shift. Note the words that show their attitudes.

Act and Scene	Character	For Caesar	Against Caesar
Act I, Scene 1	Cobbler and other commoners	"make holiday to . . . rejoice in his triumph"	

Language Coach

Shakespeare's Language Shakespeare's dialogue is mostly written in poetry—and was not meant to mimic everyday speech. The major characters in *The Tragedy of Julius Caesar* speak in verse, because Shakespeare felt that verse, with its intricate use of metaphors and imagery, could more profoundly express the feelings of his characters.

As you read *The Tragedy of Julius Caesar,* you will explore

- archaic meanings that are different from the meanings of words still used today
- archaic meanings of words that are no longer in use
- Shakespeare's use of puns
- ways to paraphrase inverted phrases
- origins of names from the play

Elements of Drama notes and questions appear throughout the play to aid your understanding of key elements of drama.

Staging the Play notes and questions are provided to help you envision the action of the play.

Writing Focus

Think as a Reader/Writer

Find It in Your Reading As you read, make notes in your *Reader/Writer Notebook* to help you follow the events in the play.

TechFocus Imagine you will be filming a scene from the play. As you read, think about where you would place the cameras, whether you would use close-ups, and how you would direct the actors.

 Learn It Online
Check out the *PowerNotes* introduction to this play on:

go.hrw.com L10-840 **Go**

Characters

Julius Caesar
Octavius Caesar
Marcus Antonius } triumvirate (three officials who share power) after
M. Aemilius Lepidus } the death of Julius Caesar

Cicero
Publius } senators
Popilius Lena

Marcus Brutus
Cassius
Casca
Trebonius
Ligarius } conspirators against Julius Caesar
Decius Brutus
Metellus Cimber
Cinna

Flavius
Marullus } tribunes (officials appointed to uphold law and order)

Artemidorus of Cnidos, a teacher of rhetoric
A Soothsayer
Cinna, a poet
Another poet

Lucilius
Titinius
Messala } friends of Brutus and Cassius
Young Cato
Volumnius

Varro
Clitus
Claudius
Strato } servants of Brutus
Lucius
Dardanius

Pindarus, servant of Cassius
Calphurnia, wife of Caesar
Portia, wife to Brutus
Senators, Citizens, Guards, Attendants, etc.

Scene: During most of the play, at Rome; later, near Sardis and near Philippi.

Note: The text of this play is taken in its entirety from *Signet Classic Shakespeare.* The editors of *Signet Classic Shakespeare* have refrained from making abundant changes in the text, but they have added line numbers and act and scene divisions, as well as indications of locale at the beginning of scenes.

Act I

Casca (left) and Cicero (right).
All of the performance photographs illustrating this play
are from the 2006 Royal Shakespeare Company production

Read with a Purpose As you read this first act, try to identify the motives of the people who oppose and support Julius Caesar.

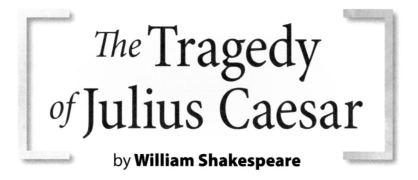

The Tragedy *of* Julius Caesar

by **William Shakespeare**

Act I

Scene 1. *Rome. A street.*

Enter FLAVIUS, MARULLUS, *and certain* COMMONERS *over the stage.*

Flavius.
Hence! Home, you idle creatures, get you home!
Is this a holiday? What, know you not,
Being mechanical,° you ought not walk
Upon a laboring day without the sign
5   Of your profession?° Speak, what trade art thou?
Carpenter. Why, sir, a carpenter.
Marullus.
Where is thy leather apron and thy rule?
What dost thou with thy best apparel on?
You, sir, what trade are you?
10 **Cobbler.** Truly, sir, in respect of° a fine workman, I am but,
as you would say, a cobbler.°
Marullus. But what trade art thou? Answer me directly.
Cobbler. A trade, sir, that, I hope, I may use with a safe con-
science, which is indeed, sir, a mender of bad soles.
Flavius.
15   What trade, thou knave? Thou naughty° knave, what
trade?
Cobbler. Nay, I beseech you, sir, be not out with me: yet, if
you be out, sir, I can mend you.

Marullus.

What mean'st thou by that? Mend me, thou saucy fellow?

Cobbler. Why, sir, cobble you.

Flavius.

20   Thou art a cobbler, art thou?

Cobbler. Truly, sir, all that I live by is with the awl:° I meddle with no tradesman's matters, nor women's matters; but withal,° I am indeed, sir, a surgeon to old shoes: when they are in great danger, I recover them. As proper men as

25   ever trod upon neat's leather° have gone upon my handiwork.   **Ⓐ**

Flavius.

But wherefore art not in thy shop today?

Why dost thou lead these men about the streets?

21. awl: a sharp, pointed tool for making holes in leather.

23. withal: nevertheless.

25. neat's leather: leather from cattle.

Ⓐ Literary Focus **Tragedy** Shakespeare often inserted puns and other comic "bits" into his tragedies. Why might he begin his tragedy on a comic note?

Commoners celebrate Caesar's victory.

Cobbler. Truly, sir, to wear out their shoes, to get myself

30   into more work. But indeed, sir, we make holiday to see

     Caesar and to rejoice in his triumph.°

Marullus.

     Wherefore rejoice? What conquest brings he home?

     What tributaries° follow him to Rome,

     To grace in captive bonds his chariot wheels?

35   You blocks, you stones, you worse than senseless things!

     O you hard hearts, you cruel men of Rome,

     Knew you not Pompey?° Many a time and oft

     Have you climbed up to walls and battlements,

     To tow'rs and windows, yea, to chimney tops,

40   Your infants in your arms, and there have sat

     The livelong day, with patient expectation,

     To see great Pompey pass the streets of Rome.

     And when you saw his chariot but appear,

     Have you not made an universal shout,

45   That Tiber trembled underneath her banks

     To hear the replication° of your sounds

     Made in her concave shores?°

     And do you now put on your best attire?

     And do you now cull out a holiday?

50   And do you now strew flowers in his way

     That comes in triumph over Pompey's blood?

     Be gone!

     Run to your houses, fall upon your knees,

     Pray to the gods to intermit° the plague

55   That needs must light on this ingratitude. **B**

Flavius.

     Go, go, good countrymen, and, for this fault,

     Assemble all the poor men of your sort;

     Draw them to Tiber banks and weep your tears

     Into the channel, till the lowest stream

60   Do kiss the most exalted shores of all.

[Exeunt all the COMMONERS.*]*

     See, whe'r their basest mettle° be not moved;

     They vanish tongue-tied in their guiltiness.

31. triumph: In Roman times, a triumph was an official parade to honor a military hero.

33. tributaries: captives.

? **Elements of Drama**
35. *This* **monologue,** *or long speech, reminds the audience of events that took place before the play's action begins. Who has conquered so far, and who has been defeated?*
37. Pompey: Roman politician and general defeated by Caesar in a civil war (49–48 B.C.).

46. replication: echo; copy.
47. concave shores: carved-out banks of the river.

54. intermit: hold back.

? **Staging the Play**
56–60. *Stage direction. Pay attention to the crowd's movements. What mood has taken over these commoners as they exit?*

61. basest mettle: a pun on "base metal." *Base* also meant lowborn, and *mettle* meant essential character.

B **Reading Focus** **Making Inferences** From this long speech, what can you infer about Marullus's attitude toward Pompey and toward Julius Caesar?

Go you down that way towards the Capitol;
This way will I. Disrobe the images,°
65   If you do find them decked with ceremonies.
Marullus.
    May we do so?
    You know it is the feast of Lupercal.°
Flavius.
    It is no matter; let no images
    Be hung with Caesar's trophies. I'll about
70   And drive away the vulgar° from the streets;
    So do you too, where you perceive them thick.
    These growing feathers plucked from Caesar's wing
    Will make him fly an ordinary pitch,°
    Who else would soar above the view of men
75   And keep us all in servile fearfulness.   **C**   [*Exeunt.*]

64. images: statues.

67. Lupercal: ancient fertility festival celebrated on February 15. In the ceremony, men raced around the Lupercal cave, where according to legend, Romulus and Remus, Rome's founders, were raised by wolves.

70. vulgar: common people.

73. pitch: height.

Scene 2. *A public place.*

Enter CAESAR, ANTONY (*dressed for the race*), CALPHURNIA,
    PORTIA, DECIUS, CICERO, BRUTUS, CASSIUS, CASCA, *a*
    SOOTHSAYER; *after them,* MARULLUS *and* FLAVIUS.

Caesar.
    Calphurnia!
Casca.   Peace, ho! Caesar speaks.
Caesar.   Calphurnia!
Calphurnia. Here, my lord.
Caesar.
    Stand you directly in Antonius' way
    When he doth run his course. Antonius!
5   **Antony.** Caesar, my lord?
Caesar.
    Forget not in your speed, Antonius,
    To touch Calphurnia; for our elders say
    The barren, touchèd in this holy chase,
    Shake off their sterile curse.°

Staging the Play
    Stage direction. A flourish of trumpets announces the approach of Caesar and his party. What costumes would highlight *the fact that these characters are from the upper classes?*

9. sterile curse: at the Lupercal festival, runners raced around the hill with whips. Romans believed women who stood in the path of the runners would become fertile.

C **Literary Focus** Tragedy This passage calls to mind the eagles that were symbols of a Roman army's power. What flaw in Caesar does the passage explain?

> These growing feathers plucked from Caesar's wing
> Will make him fly an ordinary pitch,
> Who else would soar above the view of men
> And keep us all in servile fearfulness.

Antony.   I shall remember:
10   When Caesar says "Do this," it is performed.
Caesar.
     Set on, and leave no ceremony out.
Soothsayer. Caesar!
Caesar. Ha! Who calls?
Casca.
     Bid every noise be still; peace yet again!
Caesar.
15   Who is it in the press° that calls on me?
     I hear a tongue, shriller than all the music,
     Cry "Caesar." Speak; Caesar is turned to hear.
Soothsayer.
     Beware the ides of March.°
Caesar.   What man is that?
Brutus.
     A soothsayer bids you beware the ides of March.
Caesar.
20   Set him before me; let me see his face.
Cassius.
     Fellow, come from the throng; look upon Caesar.
Caesar.
     What say'st thou to me now? Speak once again.
Soothsayer.
     Beware the ides of March.
Caesar.
     He is a dreamer, let us leave him. Pass.

             [*Sennet.° Exeunt all except* BRUTUS *and* CASSIUS.]

10. *What does this line tell you about Antony?*

Staging the Play
12. *Where do you think the soothsayer should appear? What should he sound like?*

15. press: crowd.

18. ides of March: March 15.

Stage direction. **Sennet:** a flourish or fanfare of trumpets.

Cassius.

25   Will you go see the order of the course? Ⓐ

Brutus. Not I.

Cassius. I pray you do.

Brutus.

    I am not gamesome: I do lack some part

    Of that quick spirit that is in Antony.

30   Let me not hinder, Cassius, your desires;

    I'll leave you.

Cassius.

    Brutus, I do observe you now of late;

    I have not from your eyes that gentleness

    And show of love as I was wont to have;

35   You bear too stubborn and too strange a hand°

    Over your friend that loves you.

Brutus.   Cassius,

    Be not deceived: if I have veiled my look,

    I turn the trouble of my countenance

    Merely upon myself. Vexèd I am

40   Of late with passions of some difference,°

    Conceptions only proper to myself,

    Which give some soil,° perhaps, to my behaviors;

    But let not therefore my good friends be grieved

    (Among which number, Cassius, be you one)

45   Nor construe° any further my neglect

    Than that poor Brutus, with himself at war,

    Forgets the shows of love to other men.

Cassius.

    Then, Brutus, I have much mistook your passion,°

    By means whereof this breast of mine hath buried

50   Thoughts of great value, worthy cogitations.°

    Tell me, good Brutus, can you see your face?

Brutus.

    No, Cassius; for the eye sees not itself

    But by reflection, by some other things.

Cassius.

    'Tis just:°

55   And it is very much lamented, Brutus,

35. You . . . hand: Cassius is comparing Brutus's treatment of him to the way a trainer handles a horse.

40. passions of some difference: conflicting feelings.

42. give some soil: stain or mar.

45. construe: interpret.

[?] 47. *How does Brutus explain his behavior?*

48. passion: feeling.

50. cogitations: reflections.

54. just: true.

Ⓐ **Literary Focus** Tragedy The main action of the play—the assassination plot—begins now with Cassius's casual question. Do you expect a change of mood or tone? Explain.

Analyzing Visuals **Viewing and Interpreting** How does each actor's body language add to what is being conveyed in the text during this scene?

Caesar (left) arrives in Rome with Calphurnia (right) and Cassius (behind).

That you have no such mirrors as will turn
Your hidden worthiness into your eye,
That you might see your shadow.° I have heard
Where many of the best respect° in Rome
60 (Except immortal Caesar), speaking of Brutus,
And groaning underneath this age's yoke,
Have wished that noble Brutus had his eyes.

Brutus.

Into what dangers would you lead me, Cassius,
That you would have me seek into myself
65 For that which is not in me? **B**

Cassius.

Therefore, good Brutus, be prepared to hear;
And since you know you cannot see yourself
So well as by reflection, I, your glass°
Will modestly discover to yourself
70 That of yourself which you yet know not of.
And be not jealous on° me, gentle Brutus:
Were I a common laughter,° or did use
To stale with ordinary oaths my love
To every new protester,° if you know
75 That I do fawn on men and hug them hard,
And after scandal them;° or if you know
That I profess myself in banqueting
To all the rout,° then hold me dangerous. **C**

[*Flourish and shout.*]

Brutus.

What means this shouting? I do fear the people
Choose Caesar for their king.
80 **Cassius.**   Ay, do you fear it?
Then must I think you would not have it so.

Brutus.

I would not, Cassius, yet I love him well.
But wherefore do you hold me here so long?
What is it that you would impart to me?

58. **shadow:** reflection (of what others think of him).

59. **respect:** reputation.

? Staging the Play
60. *How would Cassius make the remark in parentheses?*

68. **glass:** mirror.

71. **jealous on:** suspicious of.
72. **common laughter:** object of mockery.

74. In other words, if he swore to love everyone who came along.

76. **scandal them:** ruin them by gossip.

78. **rout:** common people; the mob.

? Staging the Play
79. *Offstage we hear a flourish (a brief piece of elaborate trumpet music) and the roar of the crowd. How would Brutus and Cassius react?*

B Literary Focus **Tragedy** What conflict does this question suggest?

C Reading Focus **Paraphrasing** What, in sum, is Cassius telling Brutus in this speech?

85   If it be aught toward the general good,
       Set honor in one eye and death i' th' other,
       And I will look on both indifferently;°   **87. indifferently:** impartially;
       For let the gods so speed me, as I love   fairly.
       The name of honor more than I fear death.   **D**

       Cassius.

90   I know that virtue to be in you, Brutus,
       As well as I do know your outward favor.°   **91. outward favor:** appearance.
       Well, honor is the subject of my story.
       I cannot tell what you and other men
       Think of this life, but for my single self,
95   I had as lief° not be, as live to be   **95. as lief** (leef): just as soon.
       In awe of such a thing as I myself.
       I was born free as Caesar; so were you: **Elements of Drama**
       We both have fed as well, and we can both   **97.** *This is a long and*
       Endure the winter's cold as well as he: *important* **monologue.** *What is*
                                                      Cassius's predominant *complaint*
100   For once, upon a raw and gusty day,   *about Caesar?*
       The troubled Tiber chafing with° her shores, **101. chafing with:** raging
       Caesar said to me "Dar'st thou, Cassius, now   against.
       Leap in with me into this angry flood,
       And swim to yonder point?" Upon the word,
105   Accout'red as I was, I plungèd in
       And bade him follow: so indeed he did.
       The torrent roared, and we did buffet it
       With lusty sinews, throwing it aside
       And stemming it with hearts of controversy.° **109. hearts of controversy:**
110   But ere we could arrive the point proposed,   hearts full of aggressive feelings,
       Caesar cried "Help me, Cassius, or I sink!"   or fighting spirit.
       I, as Aeneas,° our great ancestor,   **112. Aeneus** (ih NEE uhs): leg-
       Did from the flames of Troy upon his shoulder endary forefather of the Roman
       The old Anchises bear, so from the waves of Tiber people who, in Virgil's *Aeneid*,
115   Did I the tired Caesar. And this man   fled the burning city of Troy car-
       Is now become a god, and Cassius is   rying his aging father on his back.
       A wretched creature, and must bend his body
       If Caesar carelessly but nod on him.   **Staging the Play**
       He had a fever when he was in Spain,   **118.** *How should Cassius*
120   And when the fit was on him, I did mark   *say this last sentence?*
       How he did shake; 'tis true, this god did shake. **Staging the Play**
       His coward lips did from their color fly,   **121.** *What word should be*
                                                      stressed here in order to highlight
                                                      the point?

D **Literary Focus** **Tragedy** Is Brutus expressing noble sentiments here, or is he
being foolishly idealistic? How would you deliver this speech?

> Men at some time are masters of their fates:
> The fault, dear Brutus, is not in our stars,
> But in ourselves, that we are underlings.

And that same eye whose bend doth awe the world
Did lose his luster; I did hear him groan;
125 Ay, and that tongue of his, that bade the Romans
Mark him and write his speeches in their books,
Alas, it cried, "Give me some drink, Titinius,"
As a sick girl. Ye gods! It doth amaze me,
A man of such a feeble temper should
130 So get the start of the majestic world,
And bear the palm° alone. **E**

[*Shout. Flourish.*]

Brutus.
Another general shout?
I do believe that these applauses are
For some new honors that are heaped on Caesar.

Cassius.
135 Why, man, he doth bestride the narrow world
Like a Colossus,° and we petty men
Walk under his huge legs and peep about
To find ourselves dishonorable graves.
Men at some time are masters of their fates:
140 The fault, dear Brutus, is not in our stars,°
But in ourselves, that we are underlings. **F**
Brutus and Caesar: what should be in that "Caesar"?
Why should that name be sounded more than yours?
Write them together, yours is as fair a name;
145 Sound them, it doth become the mouth as well;
Weigh them, it is as heavy; conjure with 'em,

131. bear the palm: hold a palm branch, an award given to a victorious general.

? Elements of Drama
131. *What is Cassius's **motive** for telling Brutus these anecdotes about Caesar?*

136. Colossus: a gigantic statue of the sun god Helios that once straddled the entrance to the harbor at Rhodes, an island in the Aegean Sea. The statue was so huge that ships passed under its legs.

140. stars: It was common belief at the time that one's life was governed by the stars, or constellation, one was born under.

? Staging the Play
142. *There is often a pause here, after the Colossus metaphor. How would Cassius say the names Brutus and Caesar?*

E **Reading Focus** Reading Aloud How should Cassius's voice and tone change during this monologue?

F **Literary Focus** Tragedy How do these famous lines express the essence of the tragic drama?

"Brutus" will start a spirit as soon as "Caesar."
Now, in the names of all the gods at once,
Upon what meat doth this our Caesar feed,
150 That he is grown so great? Age, thou art shamed!
Rome, thou hast lost the breed of noble bloods!
When went there by an age, since the great flood,°
But it was famed with more than with one man?
When could they say (till now) that talked of Rome,
155 That her wide walks encompassed but one man?
Now is it Rome indeed, and room° enough,
When there is in it but one only man.
O, you and I have heard our fathers say,
There was a Brutus once that would have brooked°
160 Th' eternal devil to keep his state in Rome
As easily as a king.°

Brutus.
That you do love me, I am nothing jealous;
What you would work me to, I have some aim;°
How I have thought of this, and of these times,
165 I shall recount hereafter. For this present,
I would not so (with love I might entreat you)
Be any further moved. What you have said
I will consider; what you have to say
I will with patience hear, and find a time
170 Both meet° to hear and answer such high things.
Till then, my noble friend, chew upon this:
Brutus had rather be a villager
Than to repute himself a son of Rome
Under these hard conditions as this time
Is like to lay upon us. **G**

175 **Cassius.**   I am glad
That my weak words have struck but thus much show
Of fire from Brutus.

[*Enter* CAESAR *and his* TRAIN.]

Brutus.
The games are done, and Caesar is returning.

152. the great flood: in Greek mythology, a flood sent by Zeus to drown all the wicked people on earth.

156. Rome ... room: a pun; both words were pronounced "room" in Shakespeare's day.

159. brooked: put up with.

161. This refers to an ancestor of Brutus who, in the sixth century B.C., helped to expel the last king from Rome and set up the republic.

163. aim: idea.

170. meet: appropriate.

? **Staging the Play**
Stage direction. *Cassius and Brutus move downstage to allow Caesar and his train of followers to pass across the back of the stage. The audience sees both acting areas. How would Cassius and Brutus convey secrecy?*

G **Literary Focus** **Tragedy** A character foil is a character who serves as a contrast to another character so that each one stands out vividly. How is Cassius a foil to Brutus?

Cassius.

180

As they pass by, pluck Casca by the sleeve,
And he will (after his sour fashion) tell you
What hath proceeded worthy note today.

Brutus.

I will do so. But look you, Cassius,
The angry spot doth glow on Caesar's brow,

185

And all the rest look like a chidden° train:
Calphurnia's cheek is pale, and Cicero°
Looks with such ferret° and such fiery eyes
As we have seen him in the Capitol,
Being crossed in conference by some senators.

Cassius.

Casca will tell us what the matter is.

190 **Caesar.** Antonius.

Antony. Caesar?

Caesar.

Let me have men about me that are fat,
Sleek-headed men, and such as sleep a-nights.
Yond Cassius has a lean and hungry look;

195

He thinks too much: such men are dangerous.

Antony.

Fear him not, Caesar, he's not dangerous;
He is a noble Roman, and well given.°

Caesar.

Would he were fatter! But I fear him not.
Yet if my name were liable to fear,

200

I do not know the man I should avoid
So soon as that spare Cassius. He reads much,
He is a great observer, and he looks
Quite through the deeds of men.° He loves no plays,
As thou dost, Antony; he hears no music;

205

Seldom he smiles, and smiles in such a sort°
As if he mocked himself, and scorned his spirit
That could be moved to smile at anything.
Such men as he be never at heart's ease
Whiles they behold a greater than themselves,

210

And therefore are they very dangerous.
I rather tell thee what is to be feared
Than what I fear; for always I am Caesar.

184. chidden: corrected.

185. Cicero: a great orator who supported the Republic.

186. ferret: weasel-like animal, usually considered crafty.

? **Staging the Play**
190. *Cassius and Brutus move away, and we focus on Caesar. What attitudes should Caesar's body language convey?*

197. well given: well disposed to support Caesar.

203. In other words, he looks through what men do to search out their feelings and motives.

205. sort: manner.

Come on my right hand, for this ear is deaf,
And tell me truly what thou think'st of him.

[*Sennet. Exeunt* CAESAR *and his* TRAIN.]

Casca.

215   You pulled me by the cloak; would you speak with me?

Brutus.

Ay, Casca; tell us what hath chanced today,
That Caesar looks so sad.°

217. **sad:** serious.

Casca.

Why, you were with him, were you not?

Brutus.

I should not then ask Casca what had chanced.

220 **Casca.** Why, there was a crown offered him; and being
offered him, he put it by° with the back of his hand, thus;
and then the people fell a-shouting.

221. **put it by:** pushed it aside.

H **Literary Focus** **Tragedy** Caesar prides himself on how well he judges the character of others. What flaws does this speech reveal?

(Left to right) Cassius, Caesar, and Brutus.

Brutus. What was the second noise for?

Casca. Why, for that too.

Cassius.

225   They shouted thrice; what was the last cry for?

Casca. Why, for that too.

Brutus. Was the crown offered him thrice?

Casca. Ay, marry,° was't, and he put it by thrice, every time
        gentler than other; and at every putting-by mine honest
230   neighbors shouted.

Cassius.

        Who offered him the crown?

Casca. Why, Antony.

Brutus.

        Tell us the manner of it, gentle Casca.

Casca. I can as well be hanged as tell the manner of it: it was
235   mere foolery; I did not mark it. I saw Mark Antony offer
        him a crown—yet 'twas not a crown neither, 'twas one of
        these coronets°—and, as I told you, he put it by once; but
        for all that, to my thinking, he would fain° have had it.
        Then he offered it to him again; then he put it by
240   again; but to my thinking, he was very loath to lay his fin-
        gers off it. And then he offered it the third time. He put it
        the third time by; and still as he refused it, the rabblement
        hooted, and clapped their chopt° hands, and threw up
        their sweaty nightcaps,° and uttered such a deal
245   of stinking breath because Caesar refused the crown, that
        it had, almost, choked Caesar; for he swounded° and fell
        down at it. And for mine own part, I durst not laugh, for
        fear of opening my lips and receiving the bad air.

Cassius.

        But, soft,° I pray you; what, did Caesar swound?

250 **Casca.** He fell down in the market place, and foamed at
        mouth, and was speechless.

Brutus.

        'Tis very like he hath the falling-sickness.°

Cassius.

        No, Caesar hath it not; but you, and I,
        And honest Casca, we have the falling-sickness.

228. marry: mild oath meaning "by the Virgin Mary."

? Staging the Play
233. *How would Brutus and Cassius respond to the news about the crown?*

237. coronets: small crowns.
238. fain: happily.

243. chopt: chapped.
244. nightcaps: Casca is mockingly referring to the hats of the workingmen.
246. swounded: swooned; fainted.

249. soft: wait a minute.

252. falling-sickness: old term for the disease we now call epilepsy, which is marked by seizures and momentary loss of consciousness.

? 254. *What do you think Cassius means here?*

---

❶ Reading Focus Reading Aloud How does Casca's comic speech reveal upper-class attitudes? How would you deliver the speech?

> Three or four wenches, where I stood, cried
> "Alas, good soul!" and forgave him with all their hearts;
> but there's no heed to be taken of them.

255 **Casca.** I know not what you mean by that, but I am sure
Caesar fell down. If the tag-rag people° did not clap him
and hiss him, according as he pleased and displeased them,
as they use to do the players in the theater, I am no true
man.

Brutus.
What said he when he came unto himself?

260 **Casca.** Marry, before he fell down, when he perceived the
common herd was glad he refused the crown, he plucked
me ope° his doublet° and offered them his throat to cut.
An° I had been a man of any occupation,° if I would not
have taken him at a word, I would I might go to hell
265 among the rogues. And so he fell. When he came to himself again, he said, if he had done or said anything amiss,
he desired their worships to think it was his infirmity.
Three or four wenches,° where I stood, cried
"Alas, good soul!" and forgave him with all their hearts;
270 but there's no heed to be taken of them; if Caesar had
stabbed their mothers, they would have done no less.

Brutus.
And after that, he came thus sad away?

Casca. Ay.

Cassius.
Did Cicero say anything?

275 **Casca.** Ay, he spoke Greek.

Cassius. To what effect?

Casca. Nay, an I tell you that, I'll ne' er look you i' th' face
again. But those that understood him smiled at one
another and shook their heads; but for mine own part,

256. tag-rag people: contemptuous reference to the commoners in the crowd.

262. plucked me ope: plucked open. **doublet:** close-fitting jacket.
263. An: if. **man of any occupation:** working man.

268. wenches: girls or young women.

? **271.** *Casca gets very sarcastic here. What does he think of Caesar?*

280   it was Greek to me. I could tell you more news too:
      Marullus and Flavius, for pulling scarfs off Caesar's images,
      are put to silence.° Fare you well. There was more foolery
      yet, if I could remember it.   **J**

      Cassius. Will you sup with me tonight, Casca?

285   **Casca.** No, I am promised forth.°

      Cassius. Will you dine with me tomorrow?

      Casca. Ay, if I be alive, and your mind hold, and your dinner
         worth the eating.

      Cassius. Good; I will expect you.

290   **Casca.** Do so. Farewell, both.   [*Exit.*]

      Brutus.
         What a blunt fellow is this grown to be!
         He was quick mettle° when he went to school.

      Cassius.
         So is he now in execution
         Of any bold or noble enterprise,
295   However he puts on this tardy form.°
         This rudeness° is a sauce to his good wit,°
         Which gives men stomach to disgest° his words
         With better appetite.

      Brutus.
         And so it is. For this time I will leave you.
300   Tomorrow, if you please to speak with me,
         I will come home to you; or if you will,
         Come home to me, and I will wait for you.

      Cassius.
         I will do so. Till then, think of the world.°

                                          [*Exit* BRUTUS.]

         Well, Brutus, thou art noble; yet I see
305   Thy honorable mettle may be wrought
         From that it is disposed;° therefore it is meet
         That noble minds keep ever with their likes;
         For who so firm that cannot be seduced?
         Caesar doth bear me hard,° but he loves Brutus.
310   If I were Brutus now and he were Cassius,
         He should not humor° me. I will this night,

282. put to silence: silenced.

282. *Why are Marullus and Flavius silenced? What does this tell you about Caesar?*

285. forth: abroad; elsewhere.

292. quick mettle: lively of disposition.

295. tardy form: sluggish appearance.
296. rudeness: rough manner.
wit: intelligence.
297. disgest: digest.

303. the world: the state of affairs in Rome.

Elements of Drama
304. *Cassius delivers a soliloquy—a speech in which a character (who is usually alone onstage) expresses aloud thoughts and feelings that the audience overhears. How does Cassius feel about Brutus?*

306. In other words, he may be persuaded against his better nature to join the conspirators.

309. doth bear me hard: has a grudge against me.

311. humor: influence by flattery.

J **Literary Focus** **Tragedy** Casca's account is another episode of comic relief.
What serious events does he describe as "foolery"?

In several hands,° in at his windows throw,
As if they came from several citizens,
Writings, all tending to the great opinion
315 That Rome holds of his name; wherein obscurely
Caesar's ambition shall be glancèd at.° **Ⓚ**
And after this, let Caesar seat him sure;°
For we will shake him, or worse days endure.   [*Exit.*]

312. **hands:** varieties of handwriting.

316. **glancèd at:** touched on.
317. **seat him sure:** make his position secure.

Scene 3. *A street.*

Thunder and lightning. Enter from opposite sides CASCA *and*
    CICERO.

Cicero.
    Good even, Casca; brought you Caesar home?
    Why are you breathless? And why stare you so?
Casca.
    Are not you moved, when all the sway of earth°
    Shakes like a thing unfirm? O Cicero,
5   I have seen tempests, when the scolding winds
    Have rived° the knotty oaks, and I have seen
    Th' ambitious ocean swell and rage and foam,
    To be exalted with the threat'ning clouds;
    But never till tonight, never till now,
10 Did I go through a tempest dropping fire.
    Either there is a civil strife in heaven,
    Or else the world, too saucy° with the gods,
    Incenses them to send destruction.   **Ⓐ**
Cicero.
    Why, saw you anything more wonderful?
Casca.
15 A common slave—you know him well by sight—
    Held up his left hand, which did flame and burn
    Like twenty torches joined, and yet his hand,
    Not sensible of° fire, remained unscorched.
    Besides—I ha' not since put up my sword—
20 Against° the Capitol I met a lion,

? **Staging the Play**
    Stage direction. In Shakespeare's day, rattling a thin sheet of metal made thunder, and a mirror flashing in the sun created lightning. How might the actors themselves suggest stormy weather?

3. **all the sway of earth:** all the principles that govern earth.

6. **rived** (ryvd): split.

12. **saucy:** disrespectful; presumptuous.

? **Elements of Drama**
    13. *How is Casca different here from the way he was **characterized** earlier?*

18. **not sensible of:** not sensitive to.

20. **Against:** opposite or near.

Ⓚ **Reading Focus** Paraphrasing What tactic does Cassius plan to use in order to persuade Brutus?

Ⓐ **Literary Focus** Tragedy What is the penalty when people grow disrespectful of the gods?

Who glazed° upon me and went surly by
Without annoying me. And there were drawn
Upon a heap a hundred ghastly° women,
Transformèd with their fear, who swore they saw
25 Men, all in fire, walk up and down the streets.
And yesterday the bird of night° did sit
Even at noonday upon the market place,
Hooting and shrieking. When these prodigies°
Do so conjointly meet, let not men say,
30 "These are their reasons, they are natural,"
For I believe they are portentous° things
Unto the climate° that they point upon. **B**

21. **glazed:** stared.

23. **ghastly:** ghostly; pale.

26. **bird of night:** owl (believed to be a bad omen).
28. **prodigies:** extraordinary events.

31. **portentous** (pawr TEHN tuhs): ominous.
32. **climate:** region or place.

B Literary Focus Tragedy Shakespeare often uses disorder in nature to suggest a nation's disorder. What does Casca think about the night's strange events?

Caesar holds the laurel wreath.

Cicero.

Indeed, it is a strange-disposèd time:
But men may construe things after their fashion,
35   Clean from the purpose° of the things themselves.
Comes Caesar to the Capitol tomorrow?

Casca.

He doth; for he did bid Antonius
Send word to you he would be there tomorrow.

Cicero.

Good night then, Casca; this disturbèd sky
Is not to walk in.

40   **Casca.**   Farewell, Cicero.   [*Exit* CICERO.]

[*Enter* CASSIUS.]

Cassius.

Who's there?

Casca.   A Roman.

Cassius.   Casca, by your voice.

Casca.

Your ear is good. Cassius, what night is this?

Cassius.

A very pleasing night to honest men.

Casca.

Who ever knew the heavens menace so?

Cassius.

45   Those that have known the earth so full of faults.
For my part, I have walked about the streets,
Submitting me unto the perilous night,
And thus unbracèd,° Casca, as you see,
Have bared my bosom to the thunder-stone,
50   And when the cross° blue lightning seemed to open
The breast of heaven, I did present myself
Even in the aim and very flash of it. **C**

Casca.

But wherefore did you so much tempt the heavens?
It is the part° of men to fear and tremble
55   When the most mighty gods by tokens° send
Such dreadful heralds to astonish us.

35. Clean from the purpose: contrary to the real meaning.

? **43.** *Why would Cassius respond this way to the disordered night?*

48. unbracèd: with his jacket unfastened.

50. cross: jagged.

54. part: role.
55. tokens: signs.

C **Reading Focus** **Making Inferences** How does Cassius's response to the storm reflect his opinion of himself?

Cassius.

You are dull, Casca, and those sparks of life
That should be in a Roman you do want,°
Or else you use not. You look pale, and gaze,
60   And put on fear, and cast yourself in wonder,
To see the strange impatience of the heavens;
But if you would consider the true cause
Why all these fires, why all these gliding ghosts,
Why birds and beasts from quality and kind,°
65   Why old men, fools, and children calculate,°
Why all these things change from their ordinance,°
Their natures and preformèd faculties,°
To monstrous quality,° why, you shall find
That heaven hath infused them with these spirits°
70   To make them instruments of fear and warning
Unto some monstrous state.
Now could I, Casca, name to thee a man
Most like this dreadful night,
That thunders, lightens, opens graves, and roars
75   As doth the lion in the Capitol;
A man no mightier than thyself, or me,
In personal action, yet prodigious° grown
And fearful, as these strange eruptions are.   **D**

Casca.

'Tis Caesar that you mean, is it not, Cassius?

Cassius.

80   Let it be who it is; for Romans now
Have thews° and limbs like to their ancestors;
But, woe the while!° Our fathers' minds are dead,
And we are governed with our mothers' spirits;
Our yoke and sufferance° show us womanish.

Casca.

85   Indeed, they say the senators tomorrow
Mean to establish Caesar as a king;
And he shall wear his crown by sea and land,
In every place save here in Italy.

Cassius.

I know where I will wear this dagger then;
90   Cassius from bondage will deliver Cassius.
Therein,° ye gods, you make the weak most strong;

---

58. want: lack.

64. from quality and kind: act against their natures.

65. calculate: prophesy; try to predict the future.

66. ordinance: natural behavior.

67. preformèd faculties: natural qualities.

68. monstrous quality: unnatural condition.

69. spirits: supernatural powers.

? Staging the Play
72. *How might Cassius's tone of voice change here?*

77. prodigious: monstrous.

81. thews (thyooz): sinews or muscles.

82. woe the while: too bad for our times.

84. Our yoke and sufferance: our burden and our meek acceptance of it.

? Staging the Play
89–100. *Cassius's response to this news is usually played as one of anger. What is he probably holding in his hand?*

91. Therein: in other words, in the act of suicide.

D Reading Focus Paraphrasing How does Cassius explain the same omens Casca has seen?

Roman Beliefs

At the time of Julius Caesar, just about everyone believed in magic and omens. The Romans examined everyday occurrences for warnings of good and evil. They believed solar eclipses, lightning, and bad dreams were warnings from the gods. The owl was considered a bad omen. Once when an owl flew into Rome's Capitol, the Romans scrubbed the building with water and sulfur to drive out the owl's supposed evil influences.

Animals were killed and offered as sacrifices to the gods. Then, their entrails were examined by a *haruspex* (hah RUHS pehks), a soothsayer who specialized in foretelling events by studying the animals' internal organs. An animal sacrifice, followed by a reading of the omens, was part of any major public decision.

Ask Yourself **Do superstitions continue to influence how people think and behave today?**

Detail of initiation into the Cult of Dionysus. Fresco from Villa of Mysteries, Pompeii, Italy.

> Therein, ye gods, you tyrants do defeat.
> Nor stony tower, nor walls of beaten brass,
> Nor airless dungeon, nor strong links of iron,
> Can be retentive to° the strength of spirit;
> But life, being weary of these worldly bars,
> Never lacks power to dismiss itself.
> If I know this, know all the world besides,
> That part of tyranny that I do bear
> I can shake off at pleasure.   **E**   [*Thunder still.°*]
>
> **Casca.**   So can I;
> So every bondman° in his own hand bears
> The power to cancel his captivity.
> **Cassius.**
> And why should Caesar be a tyrant then?
> Poor man, I know he would not be a wolf
> But that he sees the Romans are but sheep;   **F**

95

100

105

95. be retentive to: restrain.

100. still: continues.

101. bondman: slave; loyal disciple.

E **Reading Focus** **Reading Aloud** Cassius threatens to commit suicide if Caesar becomes king. How and where might his tone of voice change?

F **Literary Focus** **Tragedy** What does Caesar's power say about the state of Roman society as a whole?

He were no lion, were not Romans hinds.°
Those that with haste will make a mighty fire
Begin it with weak straws. What trash is Rome,
What rubbish and what offal,° when it serves
110 For the base matter to illuminate
So vile a thing as Caesar! But, O grief,
Where hast thou led me? I, perhaps, speak this
Before a willing bondman; then I know
My answer must be made.° But I am armed,
115 And dangers are to me indifferent.

Casca.

You speak to Casca, and to such a man
That is no fleering° tell-tale. Hold, my hand.
Be factious° for redress of all these griefs,
And I will set this foot of mine as far
As who goes farthest.   [*They clasp hands.*]
120 **Cassius.**   There's a bargain made.
Now know you, Casca, I have moved already
Some certain of the noblest-minded Romans
To undergo with me an enterprise
Of honorable dangerous consequence;
125 And I do know, by this° they stay for me
In Pompey's porch,° for now, this fearful night,
There is no stir or walking in the streets,
And the complexion of the element°
In favor's like° the work we have in hand,
130 Most bloody, fiery, and most terrible.

[*Enter* CINNA.]

Casca.

Stand close° awhile, for here comes one in haste.

Cassius.

'Tis Cinna; I do know him by his gait;
He is a friend. Cinna, where haste you so?

Cinna.

To find out you. Who's that? Metellus Cimber?

Cassius.

135 No, it is Casca, one incorporate
To° our attempts. Am I not stayed for,° Cinna?

106. hinds: female deer. (The word also means "peasants" and "servants.")

109. offal: garbage; especially the parts of a butchered animal that are considered inedible or rotten.

114. My answer must be made: I must later answer for my words.

Elements of Drama
115. *Does Cassius seriously mean that Casca is a willing slave of Caesar's? Explain Cassius's* **motivation** *in saying this.*

117. fleering: flattering.
118. Be factious: Go ahead and organize a faction, or group, opposed to Caesar.

125. by this: by this time.
126. Pompey's porch: the entrance to a theater built by Pompey.
128. complexion of the element: appearance of the sky.
129. In favor's like: in appearance is like.

Elements of Drama
130. *At what point does this conversation between Cassius and Casca shift?*

131. close: hidden.

135–136. incorporate to: bound up with. **stayed for:** waited for.

Cinna.

I am glad on't. What a fearful night is this!
There's two or three of us have seen strange sights.

Cassius.

Am I not stayed for? Tell me.

Cinna. Yes, you are.

140   O Cassius, if you could
But win the noble Brutus to our party—

Cassius.

Be you content. Good Cinna, take this paper,
And look you lay it in the praetor's chair,°
Where Brutus may but find it; and throw this
145   In at his window; set this up with wax
Upon old Brutus' statue.° All this done,
Repair° to Pompey's porch, where you shall find us.
Is Decius° Brutus and Trebonius there?

Cinna.

All but Metellus Cimber, and he's gone
150   To seek you at your house. Well, I will hie,°
And so bestow these papers as you bade me.

Cassius.

That done, repair to Pompey's Theater.

[*Exit* CINNA.]

Come, Casca, you and I will yet ere day
See Brutus at his house; three parts of him
155   Is ours already, and the man entire
Upon the next encounter yields him ours.

Casca.

O, he sits high in all the people's hearts;
And that which would appear offense in us,
His countenance,° like richest alchemy,°
160   Will change to virtue and to worthiness.

Cassius.

Him, and his worth, and our great need of him,
You have right well conceited.° Let us go,
For it is after midnight, and ere day
We will awake him and be sure of him.

[*Exeunt.*]

---

143. praetor's (PRAY tuhrz)
chair: chief magistrate's chair;
Brutus's chair.

146. old Brutus' statue: statue of
Brutus's heroic ancestor.

147. Repair: go.

148. Decius: Decimus, a relative
of Brutus.

150. hie: hurry.

159. countenance: approval.
alchemy: "science" that tried to
change ordinary metal into gold.

162. conceited: Cassius is punning here. The word means both
"understood" and "described in
an elaborate metaphor" (called a
conceit).

Applying Your Skills

The Tragedy of Julius Caesar, Act I

Respond and Think Critically

Reading Focus

Quick Check

1. Why are the workers celebrating in Scene 1? Why does Marullus scold them?

2. What warning does the soothsayer give in Scene 2?

3. What happens when Caesar is offered the crown?

4. At the end of Scene 3, what happens to move along the conspiracy against Caesar?

Read with a Purpose

5. Brutus loves Rome and believes in the republic. Would he be betraying his ideals by aligning himself with Cassius? Why or why not?

Reading Skills: Reading a Play

6. Review the chart you began on page 840. Then, add a fifth column entitled "Motivation." In this column, write your ideas about the characters' principal reasons for thinking and acting as they do.

Literary Focus

Literary Analysis

7. **Compare and Contrast** A character **foil** is a character who serves as a contrast to another character. In what ways is Cassius a foil to Brutus in this act?

8. **Analyze** What is your impression of Cassius, the **protagonist,** or main character, who drives the action in Act I? By the act's end, what steps has he taken toward his goal?

9. **Interpret** Describe your impressions of Caesar's **character,** based on his speeches and actions and on what other characters say about him.

10. **Analyze** Shakespeare uses nature to mirror the disorder in human lives. What details in Scene 3 evoke a sense of danger and terror?

Literary Skills: Tragedy

11. **Analyze** How would you describe the tragedy's conflict as it is established in Act I?

Literary Skills Review: Character

12. **Evaluate** How would you evaluate the character of Brutus? Is he strong, weak, or something in between?

Writing Focus

Think as a Reader/Writer

Use It in Your Writing Review the speeches and events that you noted in your *Reader/Writer Notebook.* Choose a minor character. Write a dialogue between this character and a character of your invention, such as a friend. In your dialogue, have Shakespeare's character report on key events in Act I.

What Do You Think Now? If there is ever an honorable motive for betraying someone's trust, what might that motive be?

Vocabulary Development

Multiple Meanings: Recognizing Puns

Some people call puns juvenile humor, but Shakespeare's audiences enjoyed them, as do many people today. A **pun,** also called a play on words, is a word or phrase that means two different things at the same time. (Here's an old pun: What is black and white and read all over? Answer: a newspaper.)

In the first scene of *Julius Caesar,* when the cobbler says he is a cobbler, he plays on two meanings of the word. In Shakespeare's day the word could mean either "shoemaker" or "bungler." When he calls himself "a mender of bad soles," the cobbler also puns on the meaning of *soles. Soles* refers to parts of shoes but also sounds exactly like *souls.*

Some puns are based on two meanings of a word (*cobbler*). Others involve **homophones,** words that sound alike but have different meanings (*soles/souls*).

Here are two of Shakespeare's puns in Act I:

"All that I live by is with the awl. . . ." (Scene 1, line 21)

"I am . . . a surgeon to old shoes: when they are in great danger, I recover them." (Scene 1, lines 23–24)

Shakespeare used puns to add **comic relief**— moments of levity to occasionally lighten the tragic mood—to tragedies such as *Julius Caesar.* Moments of comic relief give the audience a little breather between the scenes of intense emotion in the play.

Your Turn

You could map the puns used by the cobbler and show the jokes like this:

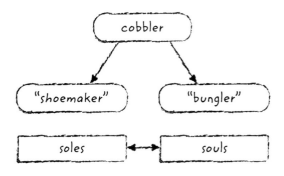

1. Make maps that explain the puns on *awl* and *recover* in the lines in the left column.

2. Use two of the words below (or words of your choice) to create original puns. Do a pun map of each one.

break   flour   son

Academic Vocabulary

Write About . . .

In a brief outline, list the principal characters in the first Act of *Julius Caesar.* Then, choose a line from the play that you think highlights each character's motivation and explain why. Share your responses with a partner.

Act II

Brutus and Portia.

Read with a Purpose Pay attention to the internal struggles of the characters as they contemplate the act of betrayal.

Act II

Scene 1. *Rome.*

Enter BRUTUS *in his orchard.*

Brutus.
What, Lucius, ho!
I cannot, by the progress of the stars,
Give guess how near to day. Lucius, I say!
I would it were my fault to sleep so soundly.
5   When, Lucius, when? Awake, I say! What, Lucius!

[*Enter* LUCIUS.]

Lucius. Called you, my lord?
Brutus.
Get me a taper° in my study, Lucius.
When it is lighted, come and call me here.
Lucius. I will, my lord.

[*Exit.*]

Brutus.
10   It must be by his death; and for my part, Ⓐ
I know no personal cause to spurn at° him,
But for the general.° He would be crowned.
How that might change his nature, there's the question.
It is the bright day that brings forth the adder,
15   And that craves° wary walking. Crown him that,
And then I grant we put a sting in him
That at his will he may do danger with.
Th' abuse of greatness is when it disjoins
Remorse° from power; and, to speak truth of Caesar,
20   I have not known when his affections swayed°

Staging the Play
1. *Stage direction.* We are in Brutus's luxurious private garden. On the right and left are the doorways of an impressive residence. What sounds and other special effects would show that the time is very late at night?

7. **taper:** candle.

11. **spurn at:** rebel against.
12. **the general:** the general good.

15. **craves:** demands.

19. **Remorse:** compassion.
20. **affections swayed:** emotions ruled.

Ⓐ **Reading Focus** **Reading a Play** What is the main idea of this soliloquy—of what is Brutus trying to convince himself?

More than his reason. But 'tis a common proof°
That lowliness° is young ambition's ladder,
Whereto the climber upward turns his face;
But when he once attains the upmost round,
25   He then unto the ladder turns his back,
Looks in the clouds, scorning the base degrees°
By which he did ascend. So Caesar may;
Then lest he may, prevent.° And, since the quarrel°
Will bear no color° for the thing he is,
30   Fashion it thus:° that what he is, augmented,
Would run to these and these extremities;
And therefore think him as a serpent's egg
Which hatched, would as his kind grow mischievous,
And kill him in the shell.   **Ⓑ**

[*Enter* LUCIUS.]

Lucius.
35   The taper burneth in your closet,° sir.
Searching the window for a flint, I found
This paper thus sealed up, and I am sure
It did not lie there when I went to bed.

[*Gives him the letter.*]

Brutus.
Get you to bed again; it is not day.
40   Is not tomorrow, boy, the ides of March?
Lucius. I know not, sir.
Brutus.
Look in the calendar and bring me word.
Lucius. I will, sir.   [*Exit.*]
Brutus.
The exhalations° whizzing in the air
45   Give so much light that I may read by them.

[*Opens the letter and reads.*]

"Brutus, thou sleep'st; awake, and see thyself.
Shall Rome, &c.° Speak, strike, redress.°
Brutus, thou sleep'st; awake."

21. common proof: matter of common experience.
22. lowliness: humility.

26. base degrees: low rungs of the ladder; also low offices and lower classes of people.
28. prevent: We must prevent it. **quarrel:** argument.
29. bear no color: bear no weight.
30. Fashion it thus: state the case this way.

? Elements of Drama
35. *The servant's words remind the audience of the action at the end of Act I. Who planted the paper Lucius is holding?*
35. closet: study.

44. exhalations: meteors.
? Staging the Play
46. *Stage direction. How might Brutus move and look as he reads the letter?*

47. &c.: et cetera. **redress:** correct a wrong.

Ⓑ **Literary Focus** Tragedy What extended metaphor does Brutus use to describe how Caesar may act if he is crowned king?

Analyzing Visuals **Viewing and Interpreting** What emotion does Brutus show as he speaks his soliloquy?

Such instigations have been often dropped
50   Where I have took them up.
"Shall Rome, &c." Thus must I piece it out:
Shall Rome stand under one man's awe? What, Rome?
My ancestors did from the streets of Rome
The Tarquin° drive, when he was called a king.
55   "Speak, strike, redress." Am I entreated
To speak and strike? O Rome, I make thee promise,
If the redress will follow, thou receivest
Thy full petition at the hand of Brutus!   **C**

[*Enter* LUCIUS.]

Lucius.

Sir, March is wasted fifteen days.

[*Knock within.*]

Brutus.

60   'Tis good. Go to the gate; somebody knocks.

[*Exit* LUCIUS.]

Since Cassius first did whet me against Caesar,
I have not slept.
Between the acting of a dreadful thing
And the first motion, all the interim is
65   Like a phantasma,° or a hideous dream.
The genius and the mortal instruments°
Are then in council, and the state of a man,
Like to a little kingdom, suffers then
The nature of an insurrection.   **D**

[*Enter* LUCIUS.]

Lucius.

70   Sir, 'tis your brother° Cassius at the door,
Who doth desire to see you.

54. Tarquin: Tarquinis Superbus, the last king of Rome.

? Staging the Play
58. *What action might Brutus engage in as he reads this message? What is his tone of voice at the end?*

65. phantasma: hallucination.
66. The genius and the mortal instruments: the mind (genius) and the emotions and physical powers of the body.

70. brother: brother-in-law. Cassius is married to Brutus's sister.

C **Reading Focus** Reading a Play   In Act I, Cassius played on Brutus's pride. How does this letter reinforce Cassius's arguments?

D **Reading Focus** Paraphrasing   In your own words, express Brutus's thoughts in lines 61–69.

Brutus.   Is he alone?

Lucius.

    No, sir, there are moe° with him.

Brutus.   Do you know them?

Lucius.

    No, sir; their hats are plucked about their ears,

    And half their faces buried in their cloaks,

75   That by no means I may discover them

    By any mark of favor.°

Brutus.   Let 'em enter.   [*Exit* LUCIUS.]

    They are the faction. O conspiracy,

    Sham'st thou to show thy dang'rous brow by night,

    When evils are most free? O, then by day

80   Where wilt thou find a cavern dark enough

    To mask thy monstrous visage? Seek none, conspiracy;

    Hide it in smiles and affability:

    For if thou path, thy native semblance on,°

    Not Erebus° itself were dim enough

85   To hide thee from prevention.

[*Enter the conspirators,* CASSIUS, CASCA, DECIUS, CINNA,
    METELLUS CIMBER, *and* TREBONIUS.]

Cassius.

    I think we are too bold upon° your rest.

    Good morrow, Brutus; do we trouble you?

Brutus.

    I have been up this hour, awake all night.

    Know I these men that come along with you?

Cassius.

90   Yes, every man of them; and no man here

    But honors you; and every one doth wish

    You had but that opinion of yourself

    Which every noble Roman bears of you.

    This is Trebonius.

Brutus.   He is welcome hither.

Cassius.

    This, Decius Brutus.

95 **Brutus.**   He is welcome too.

Cassius.

    This, Casca; this, Cinna; and this, Metellus Cimber.

---

72. moe: more.

76. favor: appearance.

83. In other words, if you walk (path) in your true way.

84. Erebus (EHR uh buhs): in Greek mythology, the dark region of the underworld.

? Staging the Play
Stage direction. From what is said of the conspirators, how would you imagine they are dressed?

86. bold upon: intrusive.

Brutus.
>They are all welcome.
>What watchful cares° do interpose themselves
>Betwixt your eyes and night?
100 **Cassius.** Shall I entreat a word?

[*They whisper.*]

Decius.
>Here lies the east; doth not the day break here?
Casca. No.
Cinna.
>O, pardon, sir, it doth; and yon gray lines
>That fret° the clouds are messengers of day.
Casca.
105 >You shall confess that you are both deceived.
>Here, as I point my sword, the sun arises,

98. **watchful cares:** cares that keep you awake.

? **Staging the Play**
Stage direction. *How would you place the actors onstage as Brutus and Cassius huddle and the others talk?*

104. **fret:** interlace.

Brutus and Caius Legarius (left).

Which is a great way growing on° the south,
Weighing the youthful season of the year.
Some two months hence, up higher toward the north
110 He first presents his fire; and the high east
Stands as the Capitol, directly here.

Brutus.
Give me your hands all over, one by one.

Cassius.
And let us swear our resolution.

Brutus.
No, not an oath. If not the face of men,°
115 The sufferance° of our souls, the time's abuse°—
If these be motives weak, break off betimes,°
And every man hence to his idle bed.   **E**
So let high-sighted tyranny range on
Till each man drop by lottery. But if these
120 (As I am sure they do) bear fire enough
To kindle cowards and to steel with valor
The melting spirits of women, then, countrymen,
What need we any spur but our own cause
To prick° us to redress? What other bond
125 Than secret Romans that have spoke the word,
And will not palter?° And what other oath
Than honesty to honesty engaged
That this shall be, or we will fall for it?
Swear priests and cowards and men cautelous,°
130 Old feeble carrions° and such suffering souls
That welcome wrongs; unto bad causes swear
Such creatures as men doubt; but do not stain
The even virtue of our enterprise,
Nor th' insuppressive mettle of our spirits,
135 To think that or our cause or our performance
Did need an oath; when every drop of blood
That every Roman bears, and nobly bears,
Is guilty of a several bastardy°
If he do break the smallest particle
140 Of any promise that hath passed from him.   **F**

---

107. growing on: tending toward.

114. If not the face of men: Our honest faces ought to be enough.
115. sufferance: endurance.
time's abuse: abuses of the times.
116. betimes: at once.

124. prick: urge.

126. palter: deceive.

129. cautelous: deceitful.
130. carrions: people so old or sick they are almost dead and rotting.

138. of a several bastardy: of several acts that are not truly "Roman."

E Reading Focus Making Inferences Why does Brutus draw back from swearing an oath? What do you infer from his reluctance?

F Literary Focus Tragedy What high ideals does Brutus use to justify the murder they are planning?

> If he love Caesar, all that he can do
> Is to himself—take thought and die for Caesar.
> And that were much he should, for he is given
> To sports, to wildness, and much company.

Cassius.
　But what of Cicero? Shall we sound him?
　I think he will stand very strong with us.

Casca.
　Let us not leave him out.

Cinna.　　　　　　　　No, by no means.

Metellus.
　O, let us have him, for his silver hairs
145　Will purchase us a good opinion,
　And buy men's voices to commend our deeds.
　It shall be said his judgment ruled our hands;
　Our youths and wildness shall no whit appear,
　But all be buried in his gravity.° **G**

Brutus.
150　O, name him not! Let us not break with him,°
　For he will never follow anything
　That other men begin.

Cassius.　　　　　　Then leave him out.

Casca.
　Indeed, he is not fit.

Decius.
　Shall no man else be touched but only Caesar?

Cassius.
155　Decius, well urged. I think it is not meet
　Mark Antony, so well beloved of Caesar,
　Should outlive Caesar; we shall find of° him
　A shrewd contriver;° and you know, his means,
　If he improve° them, may well stretch so far

---

149. gravity: seriousness and stability.

150. break with him: break our news to him; reveal our plan.

? Elements of Drama
152. *Why does Brutus decide not to ask Cicero to join them?*

153. *What kind of person does Casca seem to be?*

157. of: in.

158. shrewd contriver: dangerous schemer.

159. improve: make good use of.

G **Reading Focus** **Making Inferences** What can you infer from this passage about the ages of the conspirators?

160

As to annoy° us all; which to prevent,
Let Antony and Caesar fall together.

Brutus.

Our course will seem too bloody, Caius Cassius,
To cut the head off and then hack the limbs,
Like wrath in death and envy° afterwards;

165

For Antony is but a limb of Caesar.
Let's be sacrificers, but not butchers, Caius.
We all stand up against the spirit of Caesar,
And in the spirit of men there is no blood.
O, that we then could come by Caesar's spirit,

170

And not dismember Caesar! But, alas,
Caesar must bleed for it. And, gentle friends,
Let's kill him boldly, but not wrathfully;
Let's carve him as a dish fit for the gods,
Not hew him as a carcass fit for hounds.

175

And let our hearts, as subtle masters do,
Stir up their servants° to an act of rage,
And after seem to chide 'em. This shall make
Our purpose necessary, and not envious;
Which so appearing to the common eyes,

180

We shall be called purgers,° not murderers.
And for Mark Antony, think not of him;
For he can do no more than Caesar's arm
When Caesar's head is off. **Ⓗ**

Cassius.   Yet I fear him;
For in the ingrafted° love he bears to Caesar—

Brutus.

185

Alas, good Cassius, do not think of him.
If he love Caesar, all that he can do
Is to himself—take thought° and die for Caesar.
And that were much he should,° for he is given
To sports, to wildness, and much company.

Trebonius.

190

There is no fear in him;° let him not die,
For he will live and laugh at this hereafter.

[*Clock strikes.*]

---

160. annoy: harm.

❓ Elements of Drama
162. *Brutus contradicts Cassius for the second time. How is Cassius a* **foil** *for Brutus?*
164. envy: malice.

❓ Staging the Play
169–170. *How should Brutus act as he speaks this sentence?*

176. servants: hands or emotions.

180. purgers: healers.

184. ingrafted: firmly rooted.

187. take thought: take to thinking too much and become depressed.
188. In other words, that is too much to expect of him.
190. no fear in him: nothing to fear from him.

❓ Elements of Drama
191. *What do Brutus, Cassius, and Trebonius think of Mark Antony?*

Ⓗ Reading Focus **Paraphrasing** Restate in your own words Brutus's argument against killing Mark Antony.

Brutus.

Peace! Count the clock.

Cassius.   The clock hath stricken three.

Trebonius.

'Tis time to part.

Cassius.   But it is doubtful yet

Whether Caesar will come forth today or no;

195 For he is superstitious grown of late,

Quite from the main° opinion he held once

Of fantasy, of dreams, and ceremonies.°

It may be these apparent prodigies,°

The unaccustomed terror of this night,

200 And the persuasion of his augurers°

May hold him from the Capitol today.

Decius.

Never fear that. If he be so resolved,

I can o'ersway him; for he loves to hear

That unicorns may be betrayed with trees,

205 And bears with glasses, elephants with holes,

Lions with toils, and men with flatterers;

But when I tell him he hates flatterers,

He says he does, being then most flatterèd.

Let me work;

210 For I can give his humor° the true bent,

And I will bring him to the Capitol.   ❶

Cassius.

Nay, we will all of us be there to fetch him.

Brutus.

By the eighth hour; is that the uttermost?°

Cinna.

Be that the uttermost, and fail not then.

Metellus.

215 Caius Ligarius doth bear Caesar hard,

Who rated° him for speaking well of Pompey.

I wonder none of you have thought of him.

Brutus.

Now, good Metellus, go along by him.°

He loves me well, and I have given him reasons;

220 Send him but hither, and I'll fashion him.

196. main: strong.

197. ceremonies: rituals for predicting the future, usually by examining the entrails of sacrificed animals.

198. prodigies: disasters.

200. augurers (AW gyuhr urhz): those who foretell the future.

210. humor: mood.

213. uttermost: latest.

216. rated: berated; scolded.

218. him: his house.

---

❶ **Literary Focus** **Tragedy** According to Decius, what kind of man is Caesar? What is Decius planning to do?

Cassius.

    The morning comes upon 's; we'll leave you, Brutus.

    And, friends, disperse yourselves; but all remember

    What you have said, and show yourselves true Romans.

Brutus.

    Good gentlemen, look fresh and merrily.

225   Let not our looks put on° our purposes,

    But bear it as our Roman actors do,

    With untired spirits and formal constancy.°

    And so good morrow to you every one.

[Exeunt all except BRUTUS.]

    Boy! Lucius! Fast asleep? It is no matter;

230   Enjoy the honey-heavy dew of slumber.

    Thou hast no figures nor no fantasies°

    Which busy care draws in the brains of men;

    Therefore thou sleep'st so sound. **Ⓙ**

[Enter PORTIA.]

Portia.   Brutus, my lord.

Brutus.

    Portia, what mean you? Wherefore rise you now?

235   It is not for your health thus to commit

    Your weak condition to the raw cold morning.

Portia.

    Nor for yours neither. Y'have ungently, Brutus,

    Stole from my bed; and yesternight at supper

    You suddenly arose and walked about,

240   Musing and sighing, with your arms across;°

    And when I asked you what the matter was,

    You stared upon me with ungentle looks.

    I urged you further; then you scratched your head,

    And too impatiently stamped with your foot.

245   Yet I insisted, yet you answered not,

    But with an angry wafter° of your hand

    Gave sign for me to leave you. So I did,

    Fearing to strengthen that impatience

    Which seemed too much enkindled, and withal°

? Staging the Play

221. *How would you use lighting here to suggest the time?*

225. put on: display.

227. formal constancy: consistent good conduct.

231. figures . . . fantasies: figments of the imagination.

240. arms across: arms crossed, a sign of melancholy or depression in Shakespeare's day.

246. wafter: wave.

249. withal: also.

Ⓙ Reading Focus **Reading Aloud** Compare how Brutus addresses the conspirators to how he addresses his sleeping servant. How would you read lines 230–233?

Portia implores Brutus to tell her what is wrong.

<table>
<tr><td>

250

</td><td>

Hoping it was but an effect of humor,°
Which sometime hath his hour with every man.
It will not let you eat, nor talk, nor sleep,
And could it work so much upon your shape
As it hath much prevailed on your condition,

</td><td>

250. humor: moodiness.

</td></tr>
</table>

250   Hoping it was but an effect of humor,°
Which sometime hath his hour with every man.
It will not let you eat, nor talk, nor sleep,
And could it work so much upon your shape
As it hath much prevailed on your condition,
255   I should not know you Brutus. Dear my lord,
Make me acquainted with your cause of grief. **Ⓚ**

Brutus.
I am not well in health, and that is all.

Portia.
Brutus is wise and, were he not in health,
He would embrace the means to come by it.

Brutus.
260   Why, so I do. Good Portia, go to bed.

Portia.
Is Brutus sick, and is it physical°
To walk unbracèd° and suck up the humors°

250. humor: moodiness.

261. physical: healthy.
262. unbracèd: with his jacket open. **humors:** Here the word means "dampness (of the air)."

Ⓚ **Reading Focus** **Making Inferences** What can you infer about Portia's character from this passage?

Of the dank morning? What, is Brutus sick,
And will he steal out of his wholesome bed,
265 To dare the vile contagion of the night,
And tempt the rheumy and unpurgèd air°
To add unto his sickness? No, my Brutus;
You have some sick offense within your mind,
Which by the right and virtue of my place
270 I ought to know of; and upon my knees
I charm° you, by my once commended beauty,
By all your vows of love, and that great vow
Which did incorporate and make us one,
That you unfold to me, your self, your half,
275 Why you are heavy,° and what men tonight
Have had resort to you; for here have been
Some six or seven, who did hide their faces
Even from darkness.

Brutus.   Kneel not, gentle Portia.

Portia.
I should not need, if you were gentle Brutus.
280 Within the bond of marriage, tell me, Brutus,
Is it excepted° I should know no secrets
That appertain to you? Am I your self
But, as it were, in sort or limitation,
To keep with you at meals, comfort your bed,
285 And talk to you sometimes? Dwell I but in the suburbs
Of your good pleasure? If it be no more,
Portia is Brutus' harlot, not his wife.

Brutus.
You are my true and honorable wife,
As dear to me as are the ruddy drops
290 That visit my sad heart.

Portia.
If this were true, then should I know this secret.
I grant I am a woman; but withal
A woman that Lord Brutus took to wife.
I grant I am a woman; but withal
295 A woman well reputed, Cato's° daughter.
Think you I am no stronger than my sex,

266. unpurgèd air: The night was thought to be unhealthy, since the air was not purified (purged) by the sun.

271. charm: beg.

275. heavy: heavy-hearted, or depressed.

[?] Staging the Play
278. *What is Brutus doing here?*

281. excepted: made an exception.

295. Cato's: Cato was a highly respected leader who supported Pompey against Caesar. He killed himself to avoid living under the rule of a tyrant.

Being so fathered and so husbanded?
Tell me your counsels, I will not disclose 'em.
I have made strong proof of my constancy,
300   Giving myself a voluntary wound
Here in the thigh; can I bear that with patience,
And not my husband's secrets?

Brutus.   O ye gods,
Render me worthy of this noble wife! Ⓛ

[*Knock.*]

Hark, hark! One knocks. Portia, go in a while,
305   And by and by thy bosom shall partake
The secrets of my heart.
All my engagements I will construe to thee,
All the charactery of my sad brows.°
Leave me with haste.   [*Exit* PORTIA.]

[*Enter* LUCIUS *and* CAIUS LIGARUS.]

                 Lucius, who's that knocks?

Lucius.
310   Here is a sick man that would speak with you.

Brutus.
Caius Ligarius, that Metellus spake of.
Boy, stand aside. Caius Ligarius! How?

Ligarius.
Vouchsafe° good morrow from a feeble tongue.

Brutus.
O, what a time have you chose out, brave Caius,
315   To wear a kerchief!° Would you were not sick!

Ligarius.
I am not sick, if Brutus have in hand
Any exploit worthy the name of honor.

Brutus.
Such an exploit have I in hand, Ligarius,
Had you a healthful ear to hear of it.

Ligarius.
320   By all the gods that Romans bow before,
I here discard my sickness! Soul of Rome,

Staging the Play
300. *What does Portia suddenly do to prove her strength of character? How do you think Brutus should respond?*

308. In other words, the meaning of the worry lines written on his forehead.

313. Vouchsafe: please accept.

315. kerchief: scarf that shows he is sick.

Ⓛ **Literary Focus** Tragedy How does Portia show herself to be a good wife to Brutus? How does Brutus respond to her?

> Giving myself a voluntary wound
> Here in the thigh; can I bear
> that with patience,
> And not my husband's secrets?

Brave son, derived from honorable loins,
Thou, like an exorcist, hast conjured up
My mortifièd° spirit. Now bid me run,
325 And I will strive with things impossible,
Yea, get the better of them. What's to do?

Brutus.
A piece of work that will make sick men whole.

Ligarius.
But are not some whole that we must make sick?

Brutus.
That must we also. What it is, my Caius,
330 I shall unfold to thee, as we are going
To whom° it must be done.

Ligarius.   Set on° your foot,
And with a heart new-fired I follow you,
To do I know not what; but it sufficeth
That Brutus leads me on.   [*Thunder.*]

Brutus.   Follow me, then.   Ⓜ   [*Exeunt.*]

324. **mortifièd:** deadened.

331. **To whom:** to the house of whom.

331. **Set on:** set off on.

? 334. *Where are Brutus and Ligarius going?*

Scene 2. *Caesar's house.*

Thunder and lightning. Enter JULIUS CAESAR *in his nightgown.*

Caesar.
Nor heaven nor earth have been at peace tonight:
Thrice hath Calphurnia in her sleep cried out,
"Help, ho! They murder Caesar!" Who's within?

[*Enter a* SERVANT.]

? **Staging the Play**
Stage direction. Thunder is a kind of actor in Shakespeare's plays. Would you have the thunder sound alone or serve as background noise for the speeches?

Ⓜ **Reading Focus** **Reading Aloud** With a partner, read aloud the final speeches (lines 329–334) in this scene. How would Brutus and Ligarius read their lines?

Servant. My lord?

Caesar.

5   Go bid the priests do present° sacrifice,

    And bring me their opinions of success.°

Servant. I will, my lord.   [*Exit.*]

[*Enter* CALPHURNIA.]

Calphurnia.

    What mean you, Caesar? Think you to walk forth?

    You shall not stir out of your house today.   **Ⓐ**

Caesar.

10   Caesar shall forth. The things that threatened me

    Ne'er looked but on my back; when they shall see

    The face of Caesar, they are vanishèd.

Calphurnia.

    Caesar, I never stood on ceremonies,°

    Yet now they fright me. There is one within,

15   Besides the things that we have heard and seen,

    Recounts most horrid sights seen by the watch.°

    A lioness hath whelpèd° in the streets,

    And graves have yawned, and yielded up their dead;

    Fierce fiery warriors fought upon the clouds

20   In ranks and squadrons and right form of war,

    Which drizzled blood upon the Capitol;

    The noise of battle hurtled in the air,

    Horses did neigh and dying men did groan,

    And ghosts did shriek and squeal about the streets.

25   O Caesar, these things are beyond all use,°

    And I do fear them.

Caesar.   What can be avoided

    Whose end is purposed by the mighty gods?

    Yet Caesar shall go forth; for these predictions

    Are to° the world in general as to Caesar.

Calphurnia.

30   When beggars die, there are no comets seen;

    The heavens themselves blaze forth the death of princes. **Ⓑ**

---

5. present (PREHZ ehnt): immediate.

6. opinions of success: opinions about the course of events.

13. ceremonies: again, a reference to the priestly rituals that were supposed to reveal omens.

16. watch: watchman.

17. whelpèd: given birth.

25. beyond all use: beyond what we are used to.

❓ Staging the Play
26. *How would you direct Calphurnia to act while she is giving this speech?*

29. Are to: apply to.

Ⓐ Reading Focus **Reading a Play** This scene between Caesar and Calphurnia echoes the dialogue in Scene 1 between Brutus and Portia. The couples serve as foils for each other. Which couple seems happier, more suited to each other?

Ⓑ Reading Focus **Paraphrasing** In your own words, explain what Calphurnia means in lines 30–31.

Caesar.

Cowards die many times before their deaths;
The valiant never taste of death but once.
Of all the wonders that I yet have heard,
It seems to me most strange that men should fear,
Seeing that death, a necessary end,
Will come when it will come.   C

35

[*Enter a* SERVANT.]

What say the augurers?

Servant.

They would not have you to stir forth today.
Plucking the entrails of an offering forth,
They could not find a heart within the beast.

40

Caesar.

The gods do this in shame of cowardice:
Caesar should be a beast without a heart

Staging the Play
37. *The duty of the augurers was to tell from certain signs whether some action was favored by the gods. What is Caesar's mood as he hears of the augury this morning?*

C **Literary Focus** Tragedy What heroic qualities does Caesar reveal in this famous speech?

Caesar and servant (left).

If he should stay at home today for fear.
No, Caesar shall not. Danger knows full well

45   That Caesar is more dangerous than he.
We are two lions littered in one day,
And I the elder and more terrible.
And Caesar shall go forth.

Calphurnia.   Alas, my lord,
Your wisdom is consumed in confidence.   **Ⓓ**

50   Do not go forth today. Call it my fear
That keeps you in the house and not your own.
We'll send Mark Antony to the Senate House,
And he shall say you are not well today.
Let me, upon my knee, prevail in this.

Caesar.

55   Mark Antony shall say I am not well,
And for thy humor,° I will stay at home.

[*Enter* DECIUS.]

Here's Decius Brutus, he shall tell them so.

Decius.
Caesar, all hail! Good morrow, worthy Caesar;
I come to fetch you to the Senate House.

Caesar.

60   And you are come in very happy° time
To bear my greeting to the senators,
And tell them that I will not come today.
Cannot, is false; and that I dare not, falser:
I will not come today. Tell them so, Decius.

Calphurnia.
Say he is sick.

65 **Caesar.**   Shall Caesar send a lie?
Have I in conquest stretched mine arm so far
To be afeard to tell graybeards the truth?
Decius, go tell them Caesar will not come.

Decius.
Most mighty Caesar, let me know some cause,

70   Lest I be laughed at when I tell them so.

? Staging the Play
48. *Caesar could end this speech with arrogance, dignity, or even humor. How do you interpret his tone?*

56. humor: mood.
? Elements of Drama
56. *Here is a sudden change. Why has Caesar yielded to Calphurnia?*

60. happy: lucky.

? Staging the Play
65. *What do you think Caesar's tone of voice should be as he delivers this line?*

Ⓓ Literary Focus Tragedy Calphurnia puts her finger on Caesar's tragic flaw. What is Caesar's big mistake?

> Danger knows full well
> That Caesar is more dangerous than he.
> We are two lions littered in one day,
> And I the elder and more terrible.
> And Caesar shall go forth.

Caesar.
The cause is in my will: I will not come.
That is enough to satisfy the Senate.
But for your private satisfaction,
Because I love you, I will let you know.
75 Calphurnia here, my wife, stays° me at home. **E**
She dreamt tonight she saw my statue,°
Which, like a fountain with an hundred spouts,
Did run pure blood, and many lusty Romans
Came smiling and did bathe their hands in it.
80 And these does she apply for° warnings and portents
And evils imminent, and on her knee
Hath begged that I will stay at home today.

Decius.
This dream is all amiss interpreted;
It was a vision fair and fortunate:
85 Your statue spouting blood in many pipes,
In which so many smiling Romans bathed,
Signifies that from you great Rome shall suck
Reviving blood, and that great men shall press
For tinctures, stains, relics, and cognizance.°
90 This by Calphurnia's dream is signified.

Caesar.
And this way have you well expounded it.

Decius.
I have, when you have heard what I can say;
And know it now, the Senate have concluded

75. **stays:** keeps.
76. **statue:** pronounced here in three syllables (STATCH oo uh) for the sake of the meter.

80. **apply for:** explain as.

? **Elements of Drama**
83. *We know what Decius's purpose is, but Caesar does not. How should Decius explain the dream? Is he confident, fawning, nervous, or concerned?*

89. **cognizance:** identifying emblems worn by a nobleman's followers.

? **Staging the Play**
91. *A pause should be taken here. Caesar's fate is about to be sealed. Does he seem afraid, relieved, or amused?*

E **Reading Focus** **Making Inferences** Caesar uses his wife's fears as an excuse. What can you infer about Caesar's fears?

To give this day a crown to mighty Caesar.

95   If you shall send them word you will not come,
     Their minds may change. Besides, it were a mock
     Apt to be rendered, for someone to say
     "Break up the Senate till another time,
     When Caesar's wife shall meet with better dreams."
100 If Caesar hide himself, shall they not whisper
     "Lo, Caesar is afraid"?
     Pardon me, Caesar, for my dear dear love
     To your proceeding° bids me tell you this,
     And reason to my love is liable.°

Caesar.
105 How foolish do your fears seem now, Calphurnia!
     I am ashamèd I did yield to them.
     Give me my robe, for I will go.   **F**

[*Enter* BRUTUS, LIGARIUS, METELLUS CIMBER, CASCA, TREBO-
     NIUS, CINNA, *and* PUBLIUS.]

     And look where Publius is come to fetch me.
Publius.
     Good morrow, Caesar.
Caesar.   Welcome, Publius.
110 What, Brutus, are you stirred so early too?
     Good morrow, Casca. Caius Ligarius,
     Caesar was ne'er so much your enemy°
     As that same ague° which hath made you lean.
     What is't o'clock?
Brutus.   Caesar, 'tis strucken eight.
Caesar.
115 I thank you for your pains and courtesy.

[*Enter* ANTONY.]

     See! Antony, that revels long a-nights,
     Is notwithstanding up. Good morrow, Antony.
Antony.
     So to most noble Caesar.

103. **proceeding:** advancement.
104. **liable:** subordinate.

? **Staging the Play**
109. *What mood would the conspirators be in as they approach Caesar?*

112. **enemy:** Ligarius had supported Pompey in the civil war
and recently been pardoned.
113. **ague** (AY gyoo): fever.

? **Staging the Play**
117. *How can the actors playing Antony and Caesar establish the fact that a deep friendship exists between them?*

F **Literary Focus** **Tragedy** What makes Caesar suddenly change his mind? How
do you think Calphurnia will react?

Caesar.   Bid them prepare within.
I am to blame to be thus waited for.
120 Now, Cinna; now, Metellus; what, Trebonius,
I have an hour's talk in store for you;
Remember that you call on me today;
Be near me, that I may remember you.

Trebonius.
Caesar, I will (*aside*) and so near will I be,
125 That your best friends shall wish I had been further.

Caesar.
Good friends, go in and taste some wine with me,
And we (like friends) will straightway go together.

Brutus (*aside*).
That every like is not the same,° O Caesar,
The heart of Brutus earns° to think upon.   **G**   [*Exeunt.*]

? Staging the Play
124. An **aside** is a speech addressed to one other character or the audience, but out of hearing of the others on stage. How would this aside be spoken?

128. In other words, that those who appear to be friends are not really friends at all.
129. earns: grieves.

Scene 3. *A street near the Capitol, close to Brutus' house.*

Enter ARTEMIDORUS *reading a paper.*

Artemidorus. "Caesar, beware of Brutus; take heed of
Cassius; come not near Casca; have an eye to Cinna; trust
not Trebonius; mark well Metellus Cimber; Decius Brutus
loves thee not; thou hast wronged Caius Ligarius. There is
5 but one mind in all these men, and it is bent against Caesar.
If thou beest not immortal, look about you: security gives
way to conspiracy.° The mighty gods defend thee!   **A**
                    Thy lover,° Artemidorus."
Here will I stand till Caesar pass along,
10 And as a suitor° will I give him this.
My heart laments that virtue cannot live
Out of the teeth of emulation.°
If thou read this, O Caesar, thou mayest live;
If not, the Fates with traitors do contrive.   [*Exit.*]

7. In other words, a feeling of security gives the conspirators their opportunity.
8. lover: one who loves you; friend.
10. suitor: one who seeks a favor.
12. Out of the teeth of emulation: beyond the reach of envy.

G Literary Focus Tragedy Brutus grieves that those who appear friendly are not friends at all. Do you think he is having second thoughts? Why or why not?

A Reading Focus Reading a Play Artemidorus reminds the audience of the plot that is in motion. What is he going to do that might influence the outcome of events?

Scene 4. *Another part of the street.*

Enter PORTIA *and* LUCIUS.

Portia.
    I prithee, boy, run to the Senate House;
    Stay not to answer me, but get thee gone.
    Why dost thou stay?
Lucius.   To know my errand, madam.
Portia.
    I would have had thee there and here again
5   Ere I can tell thee what thou shouldst do there.
    O constancy,° be strong upon my side;
    Set a huge mountain 'tween my heart and tongue!
    I have a man's mind, but a woman's might.
    How hard it is for women to keep counsel!°
    Art thou here yet?
10 **Lucius.**   Madam, what should I do?
    Run to the Capitol, and nothing else?
    And so return to you, and nothing else?
Portia.
    Yes, bring me word, boy, if thy lord look well,
    For he went sickly forth; and take good note
15   What Caesar doth, what suitors press to him.
    Hark, boy, what noise is that?
Lucius.
    I hear none, madam.
Portia.   Prithee, listen well.
    I hear a bustling rumor° like a fray,°
    And the wind brings it from the Capitol.   Ⓐ
Lucius.
20   Sooth,° madam, I hear nothing.

[*Enter the* SOOTHSAYER.]

Portia.
    Come hither, fellow. Which way hast thou been?

? Staging the Play
4. *Where should pauses be taken in these opening lines? How is Portia's servant standing while Portia debates what to do?*
6. constancy: determination.

9. counsel: a secret.

? Staging the Play
9. *Is there a clue in this speech that Portia knows Brutus's secret? In "stage time" (the time at which the play's events take place), could he have told her of the plot after their conversation in Scene 1?*

18. rumor: noise. **fray:** fight.

20. Sooth: in truth.

Ⓐ **Reading Focus** **Reading a Play** How does Portia's anxiety highlight the sense of impending doom in this scene?

Soothsayer.

At mine own house, good lady.

Portia.

What is't o'clock?

Soothsayer.   About the ninth hour, lady.

Portia.

Is Caesar yet gone to the Capitol?

Soothsayer.

25   Madam, not yet; I go to take my stand,

To see him pass on to the Capitol.

Portia.

Thou hast some suit to Caesar, hast thou not?

Soothsayer.

That I have, lady; if it will please Caesar

To be so good to Caesar as to hear me,

30   I shall beseech him to befriend himself.

Portia.

Why, know'st thou any harm's intended towards him?

Soothsayer.

None that I know will be, much that I fear may chance.

Good morrow to you. Here the street is narrow;

The throng that follows Caesar at the heels,

35   Of senators, of praetors,° common suitors,

Will crowd a feeble man almost to death.

I'll get me to a place more void,° and there

Speak to great Caesar as he comes along.   [*Exit.*]

Portia.

I must go in. Ay me, how weak a thing

40   The heart of woman is! O Brutus,

The heavens speed thee in thine enterprise!

Sure, the boy heard me—Brutus hath a suit

That Caesar will not grant—O, I grow faint.

Run, Lucius, and commend me to my lord;

45   Say I am merry; come to me again,

And bring me word what he doth say to thee.   **B**

[*Exeunt severally.*]

35. praetors (PREE turhz): magistrates; city officials.

37. void: empty.

B **Literary Focus** Tragedy What does this soliloquy reveal about Portia's state of mind?

Applying Your Skills

Respond and Think Critically

Reading Focus

Quick Check

1. In Brutus's soliloquy at the beginning of Act II, what reasons does he give for killing Caesar?

2. Who proposes the murder of Antony? Why does Brutus oppose it?

3. What does Portia want Brutus to do in Scene 1? How does Brutus respond?

4. In Scene 2, what does Calphurnia try to persuade Caesar to do? Why?

Read with a Purpose

5. Several characters in Act II experience internal conflicts. Choose two characters, and explain the <u>principal</u> reasons for their conflict.

Reading Skills: Reading a Play

6. Review the characters' actions and motivations in this act. At this point in the play, are there more people for or against Caesar? Whose feelings toward Caesar have changed the most?

Literary Focus

Literary Analysis

7. **Infer** Why won't Brutus swear an oath (Scene 1, lines 114–140)? What character traits does this speech reveal?

8. **Analyze** Describe the complexities of Caesar's character. How do you feel about him? Is he a monstrous tyrant or a sympathetic man? Does he deserve the public's love—or betrayal? Explain.

9. **Compare** Compare Portia and Calphurnia, and analyze their function in this act.

10. **Extend** In Scene 4, Portia appears to know that Brutus is involved in a plot to kill Caesar, although the play does not show her learning of the conspiracy. Is this a weakness in the play? If you were writing a scene, how would you have Portia react to her husband's news?

Literary Skills: Tragedy

11. **Interpret** Describe how Shakespeare builds suspense during the rising action of Act II (Scenes 3 and 4). What questions are you left with as this act ends?

Literary Skills Review: Mood

12. **Interpret** **Mood** is the atmosphere or feeling evoked in a work of literature. How would you describe the <u>predominant</u> mood of Act II?

Writing Focus

Think as a Reader/Writer

Use It in Your Writing Review your notes in your *Reader/Writer Notebook* about the complications introduced in Act II. Then, write a brief summary outlining the main events of the act.

 What Do You Think Now?

What circumstances can render an honorable person capable of betrayal?

Vocabulary Development

Vocabulary Skills: Elizabethan English

The English language classifies words as parts of speech, such as nouns and verbs. When someone mixes up the parts of speech, purists are outraged. (Today, for example, purists deplore the use of the noun *network* as a verb.) Shakespeare freely used the same words as different parts of speech.

1. Here he makes a verb out of the noun *conceit:*

   "You have right well conceited."

   —Act I, Scene 3, line 162

2. Here he uses an adjective (*vulgar*) as a noun (we'd say *vulgar people*):

   ". . . drive away the vulgar from the streets. . . ."

   —Act I, Scene 1, line 70

3. In some passages he omits words. What is understood in the following lines is "prevent him from doing it":

   "So Caesar may;

   Then lest he may, prevent."

   —Act II, Scene 1, lines 27–28

Your Turn

Use the sidenotes in Act II for help with these questions:

1. In Scene I, line 3 (page 869), Brutus says he cannot "Give guess how near to day." How would you clarify this phrase?

2. What word does Brutus omit after the word *general* in line 12 of Scene 1 (page 869)?

3. What do you think Lucius means in Scene I, line 73 (page 873), when he says the conspirators' "hats are plucked about their ears"?

4. In Scene 1, line 83 (page 873), what noun does Shakespeare use as a verb?

Language Coach

Shakespeare's English As you know, rephrasing a passage in your words is a good way to test your understanding of a text. Paraphrase the following lines. You may want to refer to the scene and line numbers for context.

1. Brutus: "Peace! Count the clock."
   —Act II, Scene I, line 192

2. Decius: "This dream is all amiss interpreted . . . ."
   —Act II, Scene 2, line 83

Academic Vocabulary

Talk About . . .

In groups of three or four, discuss the <u>principal</u> characters in this act: Brutus, Portia, Caesar, Calphurnia, and Cassius. Describe each character and point out the lines from the play that <u>highlight</u> each character's traits. Use the Academic Vocabulary in your discussion.

Learn It Online

Sharpen your word skills with *WordSharp*:

go.hrw.com   L10-893   Go

Act III

Casca and conspirators murder Caesar.

Act III

Scene 1. *Rome. Before the Capitol.*

Flourish. Enter CAESAR, BRUTUS, CASSIUS, CASCA, DECIUS,
    METELLUS CIMBER, TREBONIUS, CINNA, ANTONY,
    LEPIDUS, ARTEMIDORUS, PUBLIUS, POPILIUS, *and*
    the SOOTHSAYER.

Caesar.
    The ides of March are come.
Soothsayer.
    Ay, Caesar, but not gone.
Artemidorus.
    Hail, Caesar! Read this schedule.°
Decius.
    Trebonius doth desire you to o'er-read,
5   At your best leisure, this his humble suit.
Artemidorus.
    O Caesar, read mine first; for mine's a suit
    That touches° Caesar nearer. Read it, great Caesar.
Caesar.
    What touches us ourself shall be last served.
Artemidorus.
    Delay not, Caesar; read it instantly.
Caesar.
    What, is the fellow mad?
10 **Publius.**   Sirrah,° give place.
Cassius.
    What, urge you your petitions in the street?
    Come to the Capitol.

Staging the Play
Stage direction. *This scene takes place on Capitol Hill, where the temple of Jupiter is located. At the back of the stage are a few steps leading up to a throne. A statue of Pompey stands to one side. Where does Caesar go after he enters? Where do the others stand?*

3. **schedule:** scroll of paper.

7. **touches:** concerns.

Elements of Drama
9. *Why doesn't Caesar read the letter from Artemidorus? How will that affect events?*
10. **Sirrah** (SIHR uh): like *sir,* used to address an inferior, often indicating disrespect or anger.

[CAESAR *goes to the Capitol, the rest following.*]

Popilius.

I wish your enterprise today may thrive.

Cassius.

What enterprise, Popilius?

Popilius.   Fare you well.

[*Advances to* CAESAR.]

Brutus.

15   What said Popilius Lena?

Cassius.

He wished today our enterprise might thrive.
I fear our purpose is discoverèd.

Brutus.

Look how he makes to° Caesar; mark him.

Cassius.

Casca, be sudden, for we fear prevention.°

20   Brutus, what shall be done? If this be known,
Cassius or Caesar never shall turn back,°
For I will slay myself.

Brutus.   Cassius, be constant.°

Popilius Lena speaks not of our purposes;
For look, he smiles, and Caesar doth not change.

Cassius.

25   Trebonius knows his time; for look you, Brutus,
He draws Mark Antony out of the way.

[*Exeunt* ANTONY *and* TREBONIUS.]

Decius.

Where is Metellus Cimber? Let him go
And presently prefer his suit to Caesar.

Brutus.

He is addressed.° Press near and second him.

Cinna.

30   Casca, you are the first that rears your hand.

Caesar.

Are we all ready? What is now amiss
That Caesar and his Senate must redress?

18. makes to: makes his way toward.

19. prevention: being prevented from carrying out their deed.

21. turn back: come out alive.

22. constant: calm.

29. addressed: ready.

Staging the Play
29. *What is happening near Caesar now?*

Metellus.
> Most high, most mighty, and most puissant° Caesar,
> Metellus Cimber throws before thy seat
> An humble heart.   [*Kneeling.*]

35 **Caesar.**   I must prevent thee, Cimber.
> These couchings° and these lowly courtesies
> Might fire the blood of ordinary men,
> And turn preordinance and first decree°
> Into the law of children. Be not fond°
40 > To think that Caesar bears such rebel blood

33. puissant (PYOO ihs ehnt): powerful.

36. couchings: very low bows.
38. These were old Roman laws. Caesar warns that the laws might be changed at whim (just as the laws of children can be changed).
39. fond: so foolish as.

Analyzing Visuals   **Viewing and Interpreting** How does the actor's body language convey Caesar's attitude?

Metellus kneels before Caesar and is spurned.

> But I am constant as the Northern Star,
> Of whose true-fixed and resting quality
> There is no fellow in the firmament.

That will be thawed from the true quality°
With that which melteth fools—I mean sweet words,
Low-crookèd curtsies, and base spaniel fawning.
Thy brother by decree is banishèd.
45 If thou dost bend and pray and fawn for him,
I spurn thee like a cur out of my way.
Know, Caesar doth not wrong, nor without cause
Will he be satisfied.   **Ⓐ**

Metellus.
   Is there no voice more worthy than my own,
50 To sound more sweetly in great Caesar's ear
For the repealing of my banished brother?

Brutus.
   I kiss thy hand, but not in flattery, Caesar,
Desiring thee that Publius Cimber may
Have an immediate freedom of repeal.°

Caesar.
   What, Brutus?

55 **Cassius.**   Pardon, Caesar; Caesar, pardon!
As low as to thy foot doth Cassius fall
To beg enfranchisement° for Publius Cimber.   **Ⓑ**

Caesar.
   I could be well moved, if I were as you;
If I could pray to move,° prayers would move me;
60 But I am constant as the Northern Star,

---

41. true quality: that is, firmness.

? Staging the Play
48. *What is Caesar doing during this speech? What is Metellus doing in response to Caesar's words?*

54. freedom of repeal: permission to return to Rome from exile.

57. enfranchisement: restoration of the rights of citizenship.

59. pray to move: beg others to change their minds.

Ⓐ Literary Focus Tragedy What noble virtues does Caesar ascribe to himself? What character flaw does his speech reveal?

Ⓑ Reading Focus Making Inferences Brutus and Cassius are speaking on behalf of Publius Cimber, the exiled relative of Metellus Cimber. What can we infer about each character from Brutus's and Cassius's behavior toward Caesar?

Of whose true-fixed and resting° quality
There is no fellow° in the firmament.
The skies are painted with unnumb'red sparks,
They are all fire and every one doth shine;

65 But there's but one in all doth hold his place.
So in the world; 'tis furnished well with men,
And men are flesh and blood, and apprehensive;
Yet in the number I do know but one
That unassailable holds on his rank,°

70 Unshaked of motion; and that I am he,
Let me a little show it, even in this—
That I was constant° Cimber should be banished,
And constant do remain to keep him so. **C**

Cinna.
O Caesar—
Caesar.   Hence! Wilt thou lift up Olympus?°
Decius.
Great Caesar—
75 **Caesar.**   Doth not Brutus bootless° kneel?
Casca.
Speak hands for me!

[*They stab* CAESAR.]

Caesar.
Et tu, Brutè?° Then fall Caesar. **D**   [*Dies.*]
Cinna.
Liberty! Freedom! Tyranny is dead!
Run hence, proclaim, cry it about the streets.
Cassius.
80 Some to the common pulpits, and cry out
"Liberty, freedom, and enfranchisement!"
Brutus.
People, and senators, be not affrighted.
Fly not; stand still; ambition's debt is paid.

---

61. resting: unchanging.
62. fellow: equal.

69. rank: position.

? Staging the Play
70. *Stage direction.* During Caesar's speech the senators move in on Caesar and, in most productions, kneel before him. Casca works his way in back of Caesar. At what point in the speech would Caesar stand up?

72. constant: firmly determined.

74. Olympus: In Greek mythology, the mountain where the gods lived.

75. bootless: in vain.

77. *Et tu, Brutè?:* Latin for "And you also, Brutus?"

? Staging the Play
77. *Stage direction.* To stage the murder, directors often have conspirators standing at different places onstage—all points to which Caesar runs in his attempt to escape. Who strikes the first blow against Caesar?

? 83. *What is the immediate response of Cinna and Cassius to Caesar's death? How does Brutus try to counter their rash words?*

C **Literary Focus** **Tragedy** Caesar continues to reveal his flawed character. How does he respond when asked to change his mind?

D **Literary Focus** **Tragedy** Caesar's death is the turning point in the play. What final indignity does Caesar suffer?

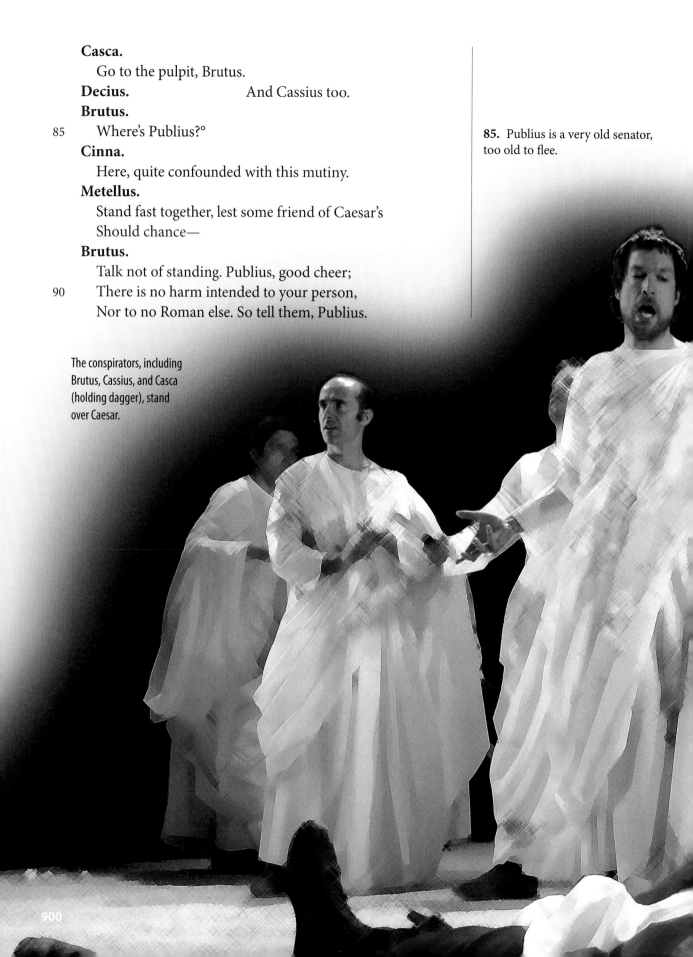

Casca.

Go to the pulpit, Brutus.

Decius.   And Cassius too.

Brutus.

85   Where's Publius?°

Cinna.

Here, quite confounded with this mutiny.

Metellus.

Stand fast together, lest some friend of Caesar's
Should chance—

Brutus.

Talk not of standing. Publius, good cheer;

90   There is no harm intended to your person,
Nor to no Roman else. So tell them, Publius.

85. Publius is a very old senator,
too old to flee.

The conspirators, including
Brutus, Cassius, and Casca
(holding dagger), stand
over Caesar.

Cassius.

And leave us, Publius, lest that the people
Rushing on us should do your age some mischief.

Brutus.

Do so; and let no man abide° this deed

95   But we the doers.

[*Enter* TREBONIUS.]

Cassius.

Where is Antony?

94. abide: take the consequences of.

Trebonius.　　　　Fled to his house amazed.
　　Men, wives, and children stare, cry out and run,
　　As it were doomsday.
Brutus.　　　　　　Fates, we will know your pleasures.
　　That we shall die, we know; 'tis but the time,
100　And drawing days out, that men stand upon.°　**E**
Casca.
　　Why, he that cuts off twenty years of life
　　Cuts off so many years of fearing death.
Brutus.
　　Grant that, and then is death a benefit.
　　So are we Caesar's friends, that have abridged
105　His time of fearing death. Stoop, Romans, stoop,
　　And let us bathe our hands in Caesar's blood
　　Up to the elbows, and besmear our swords.
　　Then walk we forth, even to the market place,°
　　And waving our red weapons o'er our heads,
110　Let's all cry "Peace, freedom, and liberty!"　**F**
Cassius.
　　Stoop then, and wash. How many ages hence
　　Shall this our lofty scene be acted over
　　In states unborn and accents yet unknown!
Brutus.
　　How many times shall Caesar bleed in sport,
115　That now on Pompey's basis° lies along°
　　No worthier than the dust!
Cassius.　　　　　　So oft as that shall be,
　　So often shall the knot of us be called
　　The men that gave their country liberty.
Decius.
　　What, shall we forth?
Cassius.　　　　　Ay, every man away.
120　Brutus shall lead, and we will grace his heels
　　With the most boldest and best hearts of Rome.

---

100. stand upon: wait for.

? **Staging the Play**
107. *Stage direction. What are the conspirators doing now?*
108. market place: the Forum, the center of public and commercial life in Rome.

115. basis: base (of Pompey's statue). **lies along:** stretches out.

E **Literary Focus** Tragedy Why do you think Brutus is so accepting of his fate?

F **Reading Focus** Reading Aloud How would you read this passage to convey Brutus's feelings here?

[*Enter a* SERVANT.]

Brutus.
　　Soft, who comes here? A friend of Antony's.

Servant.
　　Thus, Brutus, did my master bid me kneel;
　　Thus did Mark Antony bid me fall down;
125　And, being prostrate, thus he bade me say:
　　Brutus is noble, wise, valiant, and honest;
　　Caesar was mighty, bold, royal, and loving.
　　Say I love Brutus, and I honor him;
　　Say I feared Caesar, honored him, and loved him.
130　If Brutus will vouchsafe that Antony
　　May safely come to him and be resolved°
　　How Caesar hath deserved to lie in death,
　　Mark Antony shall not love Caesar dead
　　So well as Brutus living; but will follow
135　The fortunes and affairs of noble Brutus
　　Thorough° the hazards of this untrod state
　　With all true faith. So says my master Antony. **Ⓖ**

Brutus.
　　Thy master is a wise and valiant Roman;
　　I never thought him worse.
140　Tell him, so please him come unto this place,
　　He shall be satisfied and, by my honor,
　　Depart untouched.

Servant.　　　　　　I'll fetch him presently.°

　　　　　　　　　　　　　　　　[*Exit* SERVANT.]

Brutus.
　　I know that we shall have him well to friend.

Cassius.
　　I wish we may. But yet have I a mind
145　That fears him much; and my misgiving still
　　Falls shrewdly to the purpose.°

[*Enter* ANTONY.]

131. resolved: satisfied.

136. Thorough: through.

142. presently: immediately.

146. In other words, my doubts are usually justified.

Ⓖ **Reading Focus** **Paraphrasing** What does Antony ask of Brutus, and what does he promise in return? Paraphrase the servant's speech.

Brutus.

But here comes Antony. Welcome, Mark Antony.

Antony.

O mighty Caesar! Dost thou lie so low?
Are all thy conquests, glories, triumphs, spoils,
150   Shrunk to this little measure? Fare thee well.
I know not, gentlemen, what you intend,
Who else must be let blood,° who else is rank.°
If I myself, there is no hour so fit
As Caesar's death's hour, nor no instrument
155   Of half that worth as those your swords, made rich
With the most noble blood of all this world.
I do beseech ye, if you bear me hard,°
Now, whilst your purpled hands do reek and smoke,
Fulfill your pleasure. Live a thousand years,
160   I shall not find myself so apt to die;
No place will please me so, no mean of death,
As here by Caesar, and by you cut off,
The choice and master spirits of this age. **H**

Brutus.

O Antony, beg not your death of us!
165   Though now we must appear bloody and cruel,
As by our hands and this our present act
You see we do, yet see you but our hands
And this the bleeding business they have done.
Our hearts you see not; they are pitiful;°
170   And pity to the general wrong of Rome—
As fire drives out fire, so pity pity—
Hath done this deed on Caesar. For your part,
To you our swords have leaden° points, Mark Antony:
Our arms in strength of malice, and our hearts
175   Of brothers' temper, do receive you in
With all kind love, good thoughts, and reverence.

Cassius.

Your voice shall be as strong as any man's
In the disposing of new dignities.°

H **Literary Focus** Tragedy We've had a glimpse of Antony earlier in the play, but this scene is the first time he speaks at length. What heroic qualities does Mark Antony display?

> Our hearts you see not; they are pitiful;
> And pity to the general wrong of Rome—
> As fire drives out fire, so pity pity—
> Hath done this deed on Caesar.

Brutus.
    Only be patient till we have appeased
180   The multitude, beside themselves with fear,
    And then we will deliver you the cause
    Why I, that did love Caesar when I struck him,
    Have thus proceeded. ❶

Antony.   I doubt not of your wisdom.
    Let each man render me his bloody hand.
185   First, Marcus Brutus, will I shake with you;
    Next, Caius Cassius, do I take your hand;
    Now, Decius Brutus, yours; now yours, Metellus;
    Yours, Cinna; and, my valiant Casca, yours;
    Though last, not least in love, yours, good Trebonius.
190   Gentlemen all—alas, what shall I say?
    My credit° now stands on such slippery ground
    That one of two bad ways you must conceit° me,
    Either a coward or a flatterer.
    That I did love thee, Caesar, O, 'tis true!
195   If then thy spirit look upon us now,
    Shall it not grieve thee dearer than thy death
    To see thy Antony making his peace,
    Shaking the bloody fingers of thy foes,
    Most noble, in the presence of thy corse?°
200   Had I as many eyes as thou hast wounds,
    Weeping as fast as they stream forth thy blood,
    It would become me better than to close
    In terms of friendship with thine enemies.

? Elements of Drama
185. *This is a rather bold step on Antony's part. What is he doing? What is his motive?*

191. credit: reputation.
192. conceit: judge.

? Staging the Play
194. *What is Antony's position on stage now—is he standing or kneeling? Is he near the corpse or far away?*

199. corse (kawrs): corpse.

❶ **Reading Focus** **Making Inferences** Again, Cassius serves as foil to Brutus. What differences in character do Brutus and Cassius reveal here in replying to Antony?

Pardon me, Julius! Here wast thou bayed, brave hart;°
205 Here didst thou fall, and here thy hunters stand,
Signed in thy spoil and crimsoned in thy lethe.°
O world, thou wast the forest to this hart;
And this indeed, O world, the heart of thee.
How like a deer, stroken by many princes,
210 Dost thou here lie! 🟦**J**

Cassius.
Mark Antony—

Antony. Pardon me, Caius Cassius.
The enemies of Caesar shall say this;
Then, in a friend, it is cold modesty.°

Cassius.
I blame you not for praising Caesar so;
215 But what compact mean you to have with us?
Will you be pricked in number of° our friends,
Or shall we on, and not depend on you?

Antony.
Therefore I took your hands, but was indeed
Swayed from the point by looking down on Caesar.
220 Friends am I with you all, and love you all,
Upon this hope, that you shall give me reasons
Why, and wherein, Caesar was dangerous.

Brutus.
Or else were this a savage spectacle.
Our reasons are so full of good regard
225 That were you, Antony, the son of Caesar,
You should be satisfied.

Antony. That's all I seek;
And am moreover suitor that I may
Produce° his body to the market place,
And in the pulpit, as becomes a friend,
230 Speak in the order of his funeral.

Brutus.
You shall, Mark Antony.

Cassius. Brutus, a word with you.
(*Aside to* BRUTUS.) You know not what you do; do not consent
That Antony speak in his funeral.

204. Antony compares Caesar to a deer (hart) hunted down by barking (baying) hounds.

206. In other words, marked with the wounds of your slaughter and reddened like the river Lethe in the underworld.

? Elements of Drama
210. *Why is the **imagery** of the hunted deer appropriate here?*

213. modesty: moderation.

216. pricked in number of: counted with. In counting off a list of people, the Romans would prick a hole in a wax-coated tablet.

228. Produce: take.

? Elements of Drama
232. *An **aside** is words spoken by one character to another character or to the audience that others onstage are not supposed to hear. What is the function of Cassius's aside to Brutus?*

🟦 **J** **Reading Focus** **Reading Aloud** How would you read this monologue to <u>highlight</u> Mark Antony's feelings?

Antony kneels over the body of Caesar.

Know you how much the people may be moved
By that which he will utter?

235 **Brutus.**   By your pardon:
I will myself into the pulpit first,
And show the reason of our Caesar's death.
What Antony shall speak, I will protest
He speaks by leave and by permission,

240 And that we are contented Caesar shall
Have all true rites and lawful ceremonies.
It shall advantage more than do us wrong.

Cassius.
I know not what may fall;° I like it not.

243. fall: befall; happen.

Brutus.
Mark Antony, here, take you Caesar's body.

245 You shall not in your funeral speech blame us,
But speak all good you can devise of Caesar,
And say you do't by our permission;
Else shall you not have any hand at all
About his funeral. And you shall speak

250 In the same pulpit whereto I am going,
After my speech is ended.
Antony. Be it so;
I do desire no more.
Brutus.
Prepare the body then, and follow us. Ⓚ

[Exeunt all except ANTONY.]

Antony.
O pardon me, thou bleeding piece of earth,
255 That I am meek and gentle with these butchers!
Thou art the ruins of the noblest man
That ever livèd in the tide of times.
Woe to the hand that shed this costly blood!
Over thy wounds now do I prophesy
260 (Which like dumb mouths do ope their ruby lips
To beg the voice and utterance of my tongue),
A curse shall light upon the limbs of men;
Domestic fury and fierce civil strife
Shall cumber° all the parts of Italy;
265 Blood and destruction shall be so in use,
And dreadful objects so familiar,
That mothers shall but smile when they behold
Their infants quartered° with the hands of war,
All pity choked with custom of fell° deeds,
270 And Caesar's spirit, ranging for revenge,
With Atè° by his side come hot from hell,
Shall in these confines with a monarch's voice
Cry "Havoc,"° and let slip the dogs of war,
That this foul deed shall smell above the earth
275 With carrion° men, groaning for burial. Ⓛ

[Enter Octavius's SERVANT.]

You serve Octavius Caesar,° do you not?

? **Staging the Play**
254. *How should Antony immediately change his tone? To whom is he speaking?*

? **Staging the Play**
263. *Stage direction. Some directors let us hear a crowd offstage. At what moments in this speech would the offstage cries of the mob be appropriate?*
264. cumber: burden.

268. quartered: butchered; cut into four pieces.

269. fell: evil.
271. Atè (AY tee): Greek goddess of revenge.

273. Cry "Havoc": give the signal for the devastation to begin.

275. carrion: dead and rotting.
276. Octavius Caesar: Julius Caesar's great-nephew and heir, who is eighteen years old.

Ⓚ **Literary Focus** **Tragedy** Mark Antony asks to speak at Caesar's funeral, and Brutus and Cassius disagree about his request. Who do you think has the more accurate view of Antony?

Ⓛ **Reading Focus** **Reading a Play** What does Mark Antony think will be the result of Caesar's assassination?

> O pardon me, thou bleeding piece of earth,
> That I am meek and gentle with these butchers!
> Thou art the ruins of the noblest man
> That ever livèd in the tide of times.

Servant.
　　I do, Mark Antony.
Antony.
　　Caesar did write for him to come to Rome.
Servant.
　　He did receive his letters and is coming,
280　And bid me say to you by word of mouth—
　　O Caesar! .... [*Seeing the body*.]
Antony.
　　Thy heart is big;° get thee apart and weep.
　　Passion, I see, is catching, for mine eyes,
　　Seeing those beads of sorrow stand in thine,
285　Began to water. Is thy master coming?
Servant.
　　He lies tonight within seven leagues° of Rome.
Antony.
　　Post° back with speed, and tell him what hath chanced.
　　Here is a mourning Rome, a dangerous Rome,
　　No Rome of safety for Octavius yet.
290　Hie° hence and tell him so. Yet stay awhile;
　　Thou shalt not back till I have borne this corse
　　Into the market place; there shall I try°
　　In my oration how the people take
　　The cruel issue° of these bloody men;
295　According to the which, thou shalt discourse
　　To young Octavius of the state of things.
　　Lend me your hand. Ⓜ .... [*Exeunt*.]

282. big: full of grief.

❓ Staging the Play
284. *How might Antony act toward his servant to make us feel Antony's compassion?*

286. seven leagues: about twenty-one miles.

287. Post: ride on horseback (changing horses at posts along the way).

290. Hie: hurry.

292. try: test.

294. cruel issue: cruel deed; also, the outcome, or result, of cruelty.

Ⓜ **Reading Focus** **Paraphrase** What does Mark Antony hope to achieve by speaking at Caesar's funeral? Paraphrase this passage.

Scene 2. *The Forum.*

Enter BRUTUS *and goes into the pulpit,* and CASSIUS, *with the* PLEBEIANS.°

Plebeians.
We will be satisfied! Let us be satisfied!
Brutus.
Then follow me, and give me audience, friends.
Cassius, go you into the other street
And part the numbers.
5   Those that will hear me speak, let 'em stay here;
Those that will follow Cassius, go with him;
And public reasons shall be renderèd
Of Caesar's death.
First Plebeian.   I will hear Brutus speak.
Second Plebeian.
I will hear Cassius, and compare their reasons,
10   When severally we hear them renderèd.

[*Exit* CASSIUS, *with some of the* PLEBEIANS.]

Third Plebeian.
The noble Brutus is ascended. Silence!
Brutus. Be patient till the last.
Romans, countrymen, and lovers,° hear me for my cause,
and be silent, that you may hear. Believe me for mine
15   honor, and have respect to mine honor, that you may
believe. Censure° me in your wisdom, and awake your
senses,° that you may the better judge. If there be any in
this assembly, any dear friend of Caesar's, to him I say that
Brutus' love to Caesar was no less than his. If then
20   that friend demand why Brutus rose against Caesar, this is
my answer: Not that I loved Caesar less, but that I loved
Rome more. Had you rather Caesar were living, and die all
slaves, than that Caesar were dead, to live all free men? As
Caesar loved me, I weep for him; as he was fortunate,
25   I rejoice at it; as he was valiant, I honor him; but,
as he was ambitious, I slew him. There is tears, for his love;
joy, for his fortune; honor, for his valor; and death, for his
ambition. Who is here so base, that would be a bondman?°

Plebeians: common people.

? Staging the Play
Stage direction. *The Forum was the busy, crowded public meeting place of Rome. At one end was the Rostrum, a pulpit from which Rome's leaders spoke. In stage sets the pulpit is usually set on a platform with steps leading up to it. How might you use actors and sound effects to create a crowd of wild and noisy plebeians? What is Brutus's mood as he fights free of the mob and goes up to the pulpit?*

13. lovers: those who love Rome.

16. Censure: judge.
17. senses: reasoning powers.

28. bondman: slave.

If any, speak; for him have I offended.

30 Who is here so rude,° that would not be a Roman? If any, speak; for him have I offended. Who is here so vile, that will not love his country? If any, speak; for him have I offended. I pause for a reply. **Ⓐ**

All. None, Brutus, none!

35 **Brutus.** Then none have I offended. I have done no more to Caesar than you shall do to Brutus. The question of his death is enrolled° in the Capitol; his glory not extenuated,° wherein he was worthy, nor his offenses enforced,° for which he suffered death. **Ⓑ**

[*Enter* MARK ANTONY, *with Caesar's body.*]

40 Here comes his body, mourned by Mark Antony, who, though he had no hand in his death, shall receive the benefit of his dying, a place in the commonwealth, as which of you shall not? With this I depart, that, as I slew my best lover for the good of Rome, I have the same dagger for myself, when it shall please my country to need

45   my death.

All. Live, Brutus! Live, live!

First Plebeian.
Bring him with triumph home unto his house.

Second Plebeian.
Give him a statue with his ancestors.

Third Plebeian.
Let him be Caesar.

50 **Fourth Plebeian.**   Caesar's better parts°
Shall be crowned in Brutus. **Ⓒ**

First Plebeian.
We'll bring him to his house with shouts and clamors.

Brutus. My countrymen—

Second Plebeian.   Peace! Silence! Brutus speaks.

First Plebeian. Peace, ho!

---

30. **rude:** rough and uncivilized.

37. In other words, there is a record of reasons he was killed.
38. **extenuated:** lessened.
39. **enforced:** exaggerated.

50. **better parts:** better qualities.

? **Staging the Play**
52. *Stage direction. What do you think Antony should be doing while Brutus is talking? (Remember, he has brought Caesar's body to the Forum.)*

Ⓐ **Reading Focus** **Making Inferences** Why do you think Shakespeare has Brutus talk in common prose here?

Ⓑ **Literary Focus** **Tragedy** In this important monologue, what reasons does Brutus give for killing Caesar?

Ⓒ **Literary Focus** **Tragedy** Explain the irony in the crowd's reaction to Brutus's first speech.

Brutus.

55   Good countrymen, let me depart alone,

And, for my sake, stay here with Antony.

Do grace to Caesar's corpse, and grace his speech°

Tending to Caesar's glories, which Mark Antony

By our permission, is allowed to make.

60   I do entreat you, not a man depart,

Save I alone, till Antony have spoke.   [*Exit.*]

First Plebeian.

Stay, ho! And let us hear Mark Antony.

Third Plebeian.

Let him go up into the public chair;°

We'll hear him. Noble Antony, go up.

Antony.

65   For Brutus' sake, I am beholding to you.

Fourth Plebeian.

What does he say of Brutus?

Third Plebeian.   He says, for Brutus' sake,

He finds himself beholding to us all.

Fourth Plebeian.

'Twere best he speak no harm of Brutus here!

First Plebeian.

This Caesar was a tyrant.

Third Plebeian.   Nay, that's certain.

70   We are blest that Rome is rid of him.

Second Plebeian.

Peace! Let us hear what Antony can say.

Antony.

You gentle Romans—

All.   Peace, ho! Let us hear him.

Antony.

Friends, Romans, countrymen, lend me your ears; **Ⓓ**

I come to bury Caesar, not to praise him.

75   The evil that men do lives after them,

The good is oft interrèd with their bones;

So let it be with Caesar. The noble Brutus

Hath told you Caesar was ambitious.

---

57. grace his speech: listen respectfully to Antony's funeral oration.

63. public chair: the Rostrum (pulpit).

? **65.** *What will Mark Antony say to the people?*

? **Elements of Drama**
73. *Be sure to perform this famous funeral oration. What different **tones** do you hear in Antony's **monologue**?*

Ⓓ **Reading Focus** Paraphrasing In your own words, restate Antony's speech. Does he mean what he says here?

If it were so, it was a grievous fault,
80 And grievously hath Caesar answered° it.
Here, under leave of Brutus and the rest
(For Brutus is an honorable man,
So are they all, all honorable men),
Come I to speak in Caesar's funeral.
85 He was my friend, faithful and just to me;
But Brutus says he was ambitious,
And Brutus is an honorable man.
He hath brought many captives home to Rome,
Whose ransoms did the general coffers° fill;
90 Did this in Caesar seem ambitious?
When that the poor have cried, Caesar hath wept;
Ambition should be made of sterner stuff.
Yet Brutus says he was ambitious;
And Brutus is an honorable man.
95 You all did see that on the Lupercal
I thrice presented him a kingly crown,
Which he did thrice refuse. Was this ambition?
Yet Brutus says he was ambitious;
And sure he is an honorable man.
100 I speak not to disprove what Brutus spoke,
But here I am to speak what I do know.
You all did love him once, not without cause;
What cause withholds you then to mourn for him?
O judgment, thou art fled to brutish beasts,
105 And men have lost their reason! Bear with me;
My heart is in the coffin there with Caesar,
And I must pause till it come back to me.

First Plebeian.
Methinks there is much reason in his sayings.

Second Plebeian.
If thou consider rightly of the matter,
Caesar has had great wrong.

110 **Third Plebeian.**   Has he, masters?
I fear there will a worse come in his place.

Fourth Plebeian.
Marked ye his words? He would not take the crown,
Therefore 'tis certain he was not ambitious.

---

80. answered: paid the penalty for.

89. general coffers: public funds.

? Staging the Play
93. *Stage direction.* *How should the crowd be reacting to Antony's speech?*

First Plebeian.

If it be found so, some will dear abide it.°

Second Plebeian.

115   Poor soul, his eyes are red as fire with weeping.

Third Plebeian.

There's not a nobler man in Rome than Antony.

Fourth Plebeian.

Now mark him, he begins again to speak.

Antony.

But yesterday the word of Caesar might

Have stood against the world; now lies he there,

120   And none so poor to° do him reverence.

O masters! If I were disposed to stir

Your hearts and minds to mutiny and rage,

I should do Brutus wrong and Cassius wrong,

Who, you all know, are honorable men.

125   I will not do them wrong; I rather choose   **E**

To wrong the dead, to wrong myself and you,

Than I will wrong such honorable men.

But here's a parchment with the seal of Caesar;

I found it in his closet; 'tis his will.

130   Let but the commons hear this testament,

Which, pardon me, I do not mean to read,

And they would go and kiss dead Caesar's wounds,

And dip their napkins° in his sacred blood;

Yea, beg a hair of him for memory,

135   And dying, mention it within their wills,

Bequeathing it as a rich legacy

Unto their issue.°   **F**

Fourth Plebeian.

We'll hear the will; read it, Mark Antony.

All. The will, the will! We will hear Caesar's will!

Antony.

140   Have patience, gentle friends, I must not read it.

It is not meet you know how Caesar loved you.

You are not wood, you are not stones, but men;

And being men, hearing the will of Caesar,

114. dear abide it: pay dearly for it.

? **118.** *How has the opinion of the crowd shifted?*

120. so poor to: so low in rank as to.

133. napkins: handkerchiefs.

137. issue: children; heirs.

E **Literary Focus** **Tragedy** Why does Antony say he will not wrong Brutus and Cassius? What does he intend to do?

F **Reading Focus** **Making Inferences** Why does Antony bring up the will at this point? What does he seem to be promising the crowd?

Analyzing Visuals   **Viewing and Interpreting** According to the play, what might Antony be holding here?

Mark Antony.

It will inflame you, it will make you mad.
145 'Tis good you know not that you are his heirs;
For if you should, O, what would come of it?
Fourth Plebeian.
Read the will! We'll hear it, Antony!
You shall read us the will, Caesar's will!
Antony.
Will you be patient? Will you stay awhile?
150 I have o'ershot myself° to tell you of it.
I fear I wrong the honorable men
Whose daggers have stabbed Caesar; I do fear it.   **G**
Fourth Plebeian.
They were traitors. Honorable men!

Staging the Play
146. *How could an actor play Antony in this scene to make him seem manipulative?*

150. **o'ershot myself:** gone farther than I intended.

G **Literary Focus** Tragedy What are the signs that Antony, too, may have tragic flaws of character?

All. The will! The testament!

155 **Second Plebeian.** They were villains, murderers! The will!
Read the will!

Antony.
You will compel me then to read the will?
Then make a ring about the corpse of Caesar,
And let me show you him that made the will.

160 Shall I descend? And will you give me leave?

All. Come down.

Second Plebeian. Descend.

[ANTONY *comes down.*]

Third Plebeian. You shall have leave.

Fourth Plebeian. A ring! Stand round.

First Plebeian.
165 Stand from the hearse, stand from the body!

Second Plebeian.
Room for Antony, most noble Antony!

Antony.
Nay, press not so upon me; stand far off.

All. Stand back! Room! Bear back.

Antony.
If you have tears, prepare to shed them now.
170 You all do know this mantle; I remember
The first time ever Caesar put it on:
'Twas on a summer's evening, in his tent,
That day he overcame the Nervii.°
Look, in this place ran Cassius' dagger through;
175 See what a rent the envious° Casca made;
Through this the well-belovèd Brutus stabbed,
And as he plucked his cursèd steel away,
Mark how the blood of Caesar followed it,
As rushing out of doors, to be resolved
180 If Brutus so unkindly knocked, or no;
For Brutus, as you know, was Caesar's angel.
Judge, O you gods, how dearly Caesar loved him!
This was the most unkindest cut of all;
For when the noble Caesar saw him stab,
185 Ingratitude, more strong than traitors' arms,
Quite vanquished him. Then burst his mighty heart;
And, in his mantle muffling up his face,

? **Staging the Play**
162. *Stage direction.* How do you visualize the stage at this point? Where is Caesar's body? Where are the actors standing?

? **Staging the Play**
169. *What is Antony holding in his hand? How does he handle it for effect during the speech that follows?*

173. Nervii: one of the tribes conquered by Caesar, in 57 B.C.

175. envious: spiteful.

Roman Government: Rule by the Rich

The Roman Republic In a republic, the citizens elect representatives to govern on their behalf. The elected government body among Romans was the Senate. For centuries only patricians (aristocrats) could serve as senators or hold other high government posts. After about two centuries, a few wealthy men from the lower classes (the equestrians and plebeians) began entering public politics. Corruption was rampant, with public offices being openly bought and sold.

Roman Dictatorships At the time of Caesar and Cicero, the government of Rome was alternating between being a republic and being a dictatorship. In 59 B.C., Julius Caesar first shared the dictatorship, then fought a civil war, then became the sole ruler of Rome. Caesar and other popular leaders used the power of the mob to increase their own influence. Slaves, freed slaves, and other common people could be bribed and persuaded to make trouble.

Ask Yourself
Does our society resemble that of the Romans? Explain.

Cicero addressing Catiline in the Roman Senate.

	Even at the base of Pompey's statue°	**188. statue:** pronounced in three

Even at the base of Pompey's statue°
(Which all the while ran blood) great Caesar fell.
190 O, what a fall was there, my countrymen!
Then I, and you, and all of us fell down,
Whilst bloody treason flourished over us.
O, now you weep, and I perceive you feel
The dint° of pity; these are gracious drops.
195 Kind souls, what weep you when you but behold
Our Caesar's vesture° wounded? Look you here,
Here is himself, marred as you see with traitors.
  First Plebeian. O piteous spectacle!
  Second Plebeian. O noble Caesar!
200   **Third Plebeian.** O woeful day!
  Fourth Plebeian. O traitors, villains!
  First Plebeian. O most bloody sight!
  Second Plebeian. We will be revenged.

188. statue: pronounced in three syllables for meter's sake.

194. dint: stroke.

196. vesture: clothing.

? Staging the Play
197. *What might Antony do here with the mantle or the body?*

H **Literary Focus** Tragedy According to Antony, what crime has been committed against the state?

All. Revenge! About! Seek! Burn! Fire! Kill! Slay! Let not a
205   traitor live!

Antony. Stay, countrymen.

First Plebeian. Peace there! Hear the noble Antony.

Second Plebeian. We'll hear him, we'll follow him, we'll die
        with him!

Antony.
210   Good friends, sweet friends, let me not stir you up
        To such a sudden flood of mutiny.
        They that have done this deed are honorable.
        What private griefs° they have, alas, I know not,   **213. griefs:** grievances.
        That made them do it. They are wise and honorable,
215   And will, no doubt, with reasons answer you.   ❶
        I come not, friends, to steal away your hearts;
        I am no orator, as Brutus is;
        But (as you know me all) a plain blunt man
        That love my friend, and that they know full well
220   That gave me public leave to speak of him.
        For I have neither writ, nor words, nor worth,
        Action, nor utterance, nor the power of speech
        To stir men's blood; I only speak right on.
        I tell you that which you yourselves do know,   **223.** *How does Antony*
225   Show you sweet Caesar's wounds, poor poor dumb mouths, *characterize himself, as compared*
        And bid them speak for me. But were I Brutus,   *to Brutus? What is his motive?*
        And Brutus Antony, there were an Antony
        Would ruffle up your spirits, and put a tongue
        In every wound of Caesar that would move
230   The stones of Rome to rise and mutiny.

All.
        We'll mutiny.

First Plebeian. We'll burn the house of Brutus.

Third Plebeian.
        Away, then! Come, seek the conspirators.

Antony.
        Yet hear me, countrymen. Yet hear me speak.

All.
        Peace, ho! Hear Antony, most noble Antony!

---

❶ **Reading Focus** Making Inferences Why does Anthony imply that the conspirators have not given their reasons for killing Caesar?

> For I have neither writ, nor words, nor worth,
> Action, nor utterance, nor the power of speech
> To stir men's blood; I only speak right on.

Antony.

235   Why, friends, you go to do you know not what:
Wherein hath Caesar thus deserved your loves?
Alas, you know not; I must tell you then:
You have forgot the will I told you of.   **J**

All.

Most true, the will! Let's stay and hear the will.

Antony.

240   Here is the will, and under Caesar's seal.
To every Roman citizen he gives,
To every several° man, seventy-five drachmas.°

Second Plebeian.

Most noble Caesar! We'll revenge his death!

Third Plebeian. O royal Caesar!

245   **Antony.** Hear me with patience.

All. Peace, ho!

Antony.

Moreover, he hath left you all his walks,
His private arbors, and new-planted orchards,
On this side Tiber; he hath left them you,

250   And to your heirs forever: common pleasures,°
To walk abroad and recreate yourselves.
Here was a Caesar! When comes such another?

First Plebeian.

Never, never! Come, away, away!
We'll burn his body in the holy place,

255   And with the brands° fire the traitors' houses.
Take up the body.

242. several: separate; individual. **drachmas** (DRAK muhz): silver coins (Greek currency).

250. common pleasures: public recreation areas.

255. brands: torches.

J **Reading Focus** Making Inferences Notice how often Antony has pulled the crowd back with the promise of the will. How do you think he feels about the mob he has so cleverly manipulated?

Second Plebeian. Go fetch fire.

Third Plebeian. Pluck down benches.

Fourth Plebeian. Pluck down forms, windows,° anything!

[*Exeunt* PLEBEIANS *with the body.*]

Antony.
260   Now let it work: Mischief, thou art afoot,
    Take thou what course thou wilt.

[*Enter* SERVANT.]

                       How now, fellow?

Servant.
    Sir, Octavius is already come to Rome.

Antony. Where is he?

Servant.
    He and Lepidus are at Caesar's house.

Antony.
265   And thither will I straight to visit him;
    He comes upon a wish. Fortune is merry,
    And in this mood will give us anything.

Servant.
    I heard him say, Brutus and Cassius
    Are rid° like madmen through the gates of Rome. **Ⓚ**

Antony.
270   Belike° they had some notice of the people,
    How I had moved them. Bring me to Octavius.

                                [*Exeunt.*]

Scene 3. *A street.*

Enter CINNA *the poet, and after him the* PLEBEIANS.

Cinna.
    I dreamt tonight that I did feast with Caesar,
    And things unluckily charge my fantasy.°
    I have no will to wander forth of doors,
    Yet something leads me forth.

Ⓚ **Literary Focus** Tragedy   What has happened to Brutus and Cassius by the end of this scene?

---

259. forms, windows: long wooden benches and shutters.

❓ Staging the Play
260. *Stage direction.* Antony is alone onstage. How should he speak these lines? How would you create the sights and sounds of the offstage mob?

269. Are rid: have ridden.

270. Belike: probably.

❓ Staging the Play
Stage direction. What props would show that we are on an ordinary street in Rome?

2. That is, events fill his imagination with ominous ideas.

---

5 **First Plebeian.** What is your name?
Second Plebeian. Whither are you going?
Third Plebeian. Where do you dwell?
Fourth Plebeian. Are you a married man or a bachelor?
Second Plebeian. Answer every man directly.
10 **First Plebeian.** Ay, and briefly.
Fourth Plebeian. Ay, and wisely.
Third Plebeian. Ay, and truly, you were best.
Cinna. What is my name? Whither am I going? Where do I
dwell? Am I a married man or a bachelor? Then, to
15 answer every man directly and briefly, wisely and truly:
wisely I say, I am a bachelor.
Second Plebeian. That's as much as to say, they are fools that
marry; you'll bear me a bang° for that, I fear. Proceed
directly.
20 **Cinna.** Directly, I am going to Caesar's funeral.
First Plebeian. As a friend or an enemy?
Cinna. As a friend.
Second Plebeian. That matter is answered directly.
Fourth Plebeian. For your dwelling, briefly.
25 **Cinna.** Briefly, I dwell by the Capitol.
Third Plebeian. Your name, sir, truly.
Cinna. Truly, my name is Cinna.
First Plebeian. Tear him to pieces! He's a conspirator.
Cinna. I am Cinna the poet! I am Cinna the poet!
30 **Fourth Plebeian.** Tear him for his bad verses! Tear him for
his bad verses!
Cinna. I am not Cinna the conspirator.
Fourth Plebeian. It is no matter, his name's Cinna; pluck but
his name out of his heart, and turn him going.°
35 **Third Plebeian.** Tear him, tear him!

[*They attack him.*]

Come, brands, ho! Firebrands!° To Brutus', to Cassius'!
Burn all! Some to Decius' house, and some to Casca's;
some to Ligarius'! Away, go! **Ⓐ**

[*Exeunt all the* PLEBEIANS *with* CINNA.]

18. bear me a bang: get a punch from me.

? **Elements of Drama**
31. *What is the function of this scene, with its bits of comedy, at this point in the play? What does the mob end up doing to Cinna, an innocent poet?*

34. turn him going: send him packing.

36. Firebrands: torches used to start a bonfire; fiery people who make trouble. Shakespeare is punning here.

Ⓐ **Literary Focus** **Tragedy** How have events turned against the conspirators? What is now happening on the streets of Rome?

Applying Your Skills

The Tragedy of Julius Caesar, Act III

Respond and Think Critically

Reading Focus

Quick Check

1. In Scene 1, why does Cassius argue against allowing Antony to speak at Caesar's funeral? Why does Brutus overrule him?

2. What information concerning Caesar's will does Antony give the crowd? How do they react?

3. What do the plebeians do in Scene 3?

Read with a Purpose

4. What consequence of Caesar's murder is a surprise to his killers?

Reading Skills: Reading a Play

5. The third act of a Shakespearean tragedy usually contains the **turning point,** the moment when the action begins to spiral toward the tragic ending. Go back to the notes you made in your *Reader/Writer Notebook* and identify where you think the turning point is.

Literary Focus

Literary Analysis

6. **Analyze** Explain how Brutus and Cassius act as **character foils** (contrasting characters) in their responses to Antony in Scene 1.

7. **Analyze** How does Antony's soliloquy at the end of Scene I (lines 254–275) indicate his intentions regarding the assassins?

8. **Evaluate** Why do you think Shakespeare ends the act with the events of Scene 3?

Literary Skills: Tragedy

9. **Make Judgments** Who displays higher ideals, Brutus or Caesar? Who is the more **tragic hero?** Cite lines from the play to support your opinion.

10. **Predict** What social forces does Antony unleash by making his speech? What actions might be predicted as a result?

Literary Skills Review: Persuasion

11. Re-read the funeral orations of Brutus and Mark Antony and outline each speaker's argument. Find examples of **emotional appeals,** such as **loaded words** and **repetition.** Which argument is more convincing? Why?

Writing Focus

Think as a Reader/Writer

Use It in Your Writing Write a dialogue in which the cobbler from Act I tells another plebeian about the events he has witnessed in Act III. Perform your dialogue with a classmate.

What Do You Think Now? Who do you think has betrayed the Roman people more—Caesar or Brutus? Explain.

Vocabulary Development

Vocabulary Skills: Inverted Word Order and Paraphrasing

We are accustomed to using words in a certain order in a sentence. When writing or speaking, we tend to follow common patterns, such as:

subject–verb–object

They stabbed Caesar!

We normally place adjectives before the noun they modify (the *mighty* emperor); and we place adverbs after the verbs they modify (Brutus stood *regally*).

Shakespeare, however, often reversed, or **inverted** the usual order of words in characters' speeches. He did this to vary the rhythm and pace or to highlight certain words or phrases.

The best way to appreciate the effects of inverted word order in *Julius Caesar* is to read the speeches aloud and pay attention to the rhythm and flow of the words. Notice, too, how such unusual phrasing causes certain words to stand out. Here are examples from Act III:

1. "What touches us ourself shall be last served."
   (Scene 1, line 8)

   Normally, you would expect the sentence to end "...be served last." The inverted order calls attention to the word *last*.

2. "Here, under leave of Brutus and the rest...
   Come I to speak in Caesar's funeral."
   (Scene 2, lines 81, 84)

   Note the inverted word order in "Come I." Read the quote aloud to hear the rhythm of speech. Think about how the word order directs your attention.

One way to make sure you understand sentences with inverted word order (and Elizabethan English in general) is to **paraphrase.** By restating a sentence or passage in your own words, you clarify its meaning and confirm your understanding of the passage.

Your Turn

Read the excerpts below. Then, restate these lines in your own words, in normal word order.

1. "There is no harm intended to your person,
   Nor to no Roman else. So tell them, Publius."
   (Scene 1, lines 90–91)

2. "...yet see you but our hands
   And this the bleeding business they have done.
   Our hearts you see not; they are pitiful;"
   (Scene 1, lines 167–169)

3. "Who is here so base, that would be a bondman? If any, speak; for him have I offended. Who is here so rude, that would not be a Roman? If any, speak; for him have I offended. Who is here so vile, that will not love his country? If any, speak; for him have I offended. I pause for a reply."
   (Scene 2, lines 28–33)

4. "Look, in this place ran Cassius' dagger through;
   See what a rent the envious Casca made;
   Through this the well-belovèd Brutus stabbed,..."
   (Scene 2, lines 174–176)

Act IV

Brutus and Cassius.

Act IV

Scene 1. *A house in Rome.*

Enter ANTONY, OCTAVIUS, *and* LEPIDUS.

Antony.
   These many then shall die; their names are pricked.
Octavius.
   Your brother too must die; consent you, Lepidus?
Lepidus.
   I do consent—
Octavius.   Prick him down, Antony.
Lepidus.
   Upon condition Publius shall not live,
5   Who is your sister's son, Mark Antony.
Antony.
   He shall not live; look, with a spot I damn him.
   But, Lepidus, go you to Caesar's house;
   Fetch the will hither, and we shall determine
   How to cut off some charge in legacies.°
Lepidus.
10   What, shall I find you here?
Octavius.
   Or here or at the Capitol.   [*Exit* LEPIDUS.]
Antony.
   This is a slight unmeritable man,
   Meet to be sent on errands; is it fit,
   The threefold world° divided, he should stand
   One of the three to share it?°
15 **Octavius.**   So you thought him,
   And took his voice° who should be pricked to die
   In our black sentence and proscription.°   Ⓐ

9. In other words, cut down on some of the expenses by changing the will.

14. threefold world: three parts of the Roman Empire: Europe, Asia, and Africa.

15. Antony, Octavius, and Lepidus now govern the Roman Empire as a triumvirate, or three-member ruling body.

16. voice: vote.

17. proscription: death sentence. In Roman law a person under proscription could be killed by anyone, and the killer had no fear of murder charges being brought against him.

Ⓐ **Reading Focus** Making Inferences What details in this dialogue suggest that this triumvirate is showing signs of change? How has Antony changed since Act III?

Antony.

Octavius, I have seen more days than you;
And though we lay these honors on this man,
20 To ease ourselves of divers sland'rous loads,°
He shall but bear them as the ass bears gold,
To groan and sweat under the business,
Either led or driven, as we point the way;
And having brought our treasure where we will,
25 Then take we down his load, and turn him off,
(Like to the empty ass) to shake his ears
And graze in commons.°

Octavius.   You may do your will;
But he's a tried and valiant soldier.

Antony.

So is my horse, Octavius, and for that
30 I do appoint him store of provender.°
It is a creature that I teach to fight,
To wind, to stop, to run directly on,
His corporal motion governed by my spirit.
And, in some taste,° is Lepidus but so.
35 He must be taught, and trained, and bid go forth.
A barren-spirited fellow; one that feeds
On objects, arts, and imitations,
Which, out of use and staled by other men,
Begin his fashion.° Do not talk of him
40 But as a property.° And now, Octavius,
Listen great things. Brutus and Cassius
Are levying powers;° we must straight make head.°
Therefore let our alliance be combined,
Our best friends made, our means stretched;
45 And let us presently go sit in council
How covert matters may be best disclosed,
And open perils surest answerèd.

Octavius.

Let us do so; for we are at the stake,
And bayed about with many enemies;°
50 And some that smile have in their hearts, I fear,
Millions of mischiefs.   [*Exeunt.*]

---

20. divers sland'rous loads: blame that will be laid against them.

? **26.** *Who is compared to the ass?*

27. in commons: on pasture land that is commonly held, or shared by everyone.

30. appoint . . . provender: allot him a supply of food.

34. in some taste: in some measure.

39. In other words, he is always behind the times.

40. property: tool.

42. levying powers: gathering armies. **straight make head:** immediately gather troops.

49. A metaphor referring to the Elizabethan sport of bearbaiting, in which a bear was chained to a stake and attacked by dogs.

Scene 2. *Camp near Sardis.*

Drum. Enter BRUTUS, LUCILIUS, LUCIUS, *and the* ARMY.
*   *TITINIUS *and* PINDARUS *meet them.* **Ⓐ**

Brutus. Stand ho!
Lucilius. Give the word, ho! and stand.
Brutus.
    What now, Lucilius, is Cassius near?
Lucilius.
    He is at hand, and Pindarus is come
5   To do you salutation from his master.
Brutus.
    He greets me well.° Your master, Pindarus,
    In his own change, or by ill officers,°
    Hath given me some worthy cause to wish
    Things done undone; but if he be at hand,
    I shall be satisfied.°
10   **Pindarus.**   I do not doubt
    But that my noble master will appear
    Such as he is, full of regard and honor.
Brutus.
    He is not doubted. A word, Lucilius,
    How he received you; let me be resolved.°
Lucilius.
15   With courtesy and with respect enough,
    But not with such familiar instances,°
    Nor with such free and friendly conference
    As he hath used of old.
Brutus.   Thou hast described
    A hot friend cooling. Ever note, Lucilius,
20   When love begins to sicken and decay
    It useth an enforcèd ceremony.
    There are no tricks in plain and simple faith;
    But hollow men, like horses hot at hand,°
    Make gallant show and promise of their mettle;

[Low march within.]

6. He greets me well: He sends greetings with a good man.
7. In other words, either from a change of feelings or because of the bad advice or the bad deeds of subordinates.
10. be satisfied: get a satisfactory explanation.

14. resolved: informed.

16. familiar instances: friendly behavior.

23. hot at hand: very energetic at the start of the race.

Ⓐ **Reading Focus** **Making Inferences** Several months have passed since the assassination, and Brutus and Cassius are in Sardis, the capital of ancient Lydia, a kingdom in Asia Minor. Why did Brutus and Cassius flee from Rome with their armies?

25 But when they should endure the bloody spur,
They fall their crests, and like deceitful jades°
Sink in the trial. Comes his army on?   **B**

Lucilius.
They mean this night in Sardis to be quartered;
The greater part, the horse in general,°
Are come with Cassius.

[*Enter* CASSIUS *and his* POWERS.]

30 **Brutus.**   Hark! He is arrived.
March gently on to meet him.
Cassius. Stand, ho!
Brutus. Stand, ho! Speak the word along.
First Soldier. Stand!
35 **Second Soldier.** Stand!
Third Soldier. Stand!
Cassius.
Most noble brother, you have done me wrong.
Brutus.
Judge me, you gods! Wrong I mine enemies?
And if not so, how should I wrong a brother?
Cassius.
40 Brutus, this sober form of yours hides wrongs;
And when you do them—
Brutus.   Cassius, be content.°
Speak your griefs softly; I do know you well.
Before the eyes of both our armies here
(Which should perceive nothing but love from us)
45 Let us not wrangle. Bid them move away;
Then in my tent, Cassius, enlarge° your griefs,
And I will give you audience.   **C**
Cassius.   Pindarus,
Bid our commanders lead their charges off
A little from this ground.

26. **jades:** old horses.

29. **the horse in general:** all the cavalry.

? **Staging the Play**
36. *How do you picture Cassius and his men entering the stage? What might the soldiers do when they say, "Stand!"?*

41. **content:** calm.

46. **enlarge:** express in greater detail.

B **Reading Focus** Paraphrasing Restate Brutus's speech in your own words. Who are the "hollow men," and to what does he compare them?

C **Literary Focus** Tragedy What are Cassius's tragic flaws? Which is most predominant in this dialogue?

Pindarus (left), Lucilius, and a member of the army.

Brutus.

50 Lucilius, do you the like, and let no man
    Come to our tent till we have done our conference.
    Let Lucius and Titinius guard our door.

[*Exeunt all except* BRUTUS *and* CASSIUS.]

Scene 3. *Brutus' tent.*

Cassius.

That you have wronged me doth appear in this:
You have condemned and noted° Lucius Pella
For taking bribes here of the Sardians;
Wherein my letters, praying on his side,

5   Because I knew the man, was slighted off.

Brutus.

You wronged yourself to write in such a case.

Cassius.

In such a time as this it is not meet
That every nice offense should bear his comment.°

Brutus.

Let me tell you, Cassius, you yourself

10 Are much condemned to have an itching palm,
    To sell and mart° your offices for gold
    To undeservers.

Cassius.   I an itching palm?

You know that you are Brutus that speaks this,
Or, by the gods, this speech were else your last.

Brutus.

15 The name of Cassius honors° this corruption,
    And chastisement doth therefore hide his head.

Cassius. Chastisement!

Brutus.

Remember March, the ides of March remember.
Did not great Julius bleed for justice' sake?

20 What villain touched his body, that did stab,
    And not for justice? What, shall one of us,
    That struck the foremost man of all this world
    But for supporting robbers,° shall we now
    Contaminate our fingers with base bribes,

2. **noted:** publicly disgraced.

8. **That . . . comment:** that every trivial offense should be criticized.

11. **mart:** trade; traffic in.

? Elements of Drama
12. *Shakespeare complicates the plot by creating a rift between Brutus and Cassius. What offense does Brutus accuse Cassius of committing?*

15. **honors:** gives an air of respectability to.

23. **supporting robbers:** supporting or protecting dishonest public officials.

> Brutus, bait not me;
> I'll not endure it. You forget yourself
> To hedge me in.

25   And sell the mighty space of our large honors°
     For so much trash as may be graspèd thus?
     I had rather be a dog, and bay the moon,
     Than such a Roman. **Ⓐ**

Cassius.   Brutus, bait not me;
     I'll not endure it. You forget yourself
30   To hedge me in. I am a soldier, I,
     Older in practice, abler than yourself
     To make conditions.

Brutus.   Go to! You are not, Cassius.

Cassius. I am.

Brutus. I say you are not.

Cassius.
35   Urge° me no more, I shall forget myself;
     Have mind upon your health, tempt me no farther. **Ⓑ**

Brutus. Away, slight man!

Cassius.
     Is't possible?

Brutus.   Hear me, for I will speak.
     Must I give way and room to your rash choler?°
40   Shall I be frighted when a madman stares?

Cassius.
     O ye gods, ye gods! Must I endure all this?

Brutus.
     All this? Ay, more: fret till your proud heart break.
     Go show your slaves how choleric you are,
     And make your bondmen tremble. Must I budge?°
45   Must I observe° you? Must I stand and crouch

25. our large honors: capacity to be honorable and generous.

35. Urge: goad; bully.

39. choler: anger.

44. budge: defer.
45. observe: wait on.

Ⓐ **Reading Focus** **Making Inferences** What can you infer from this dialogue about Brutus's opinion of Cassius? How has it changed?

Ⓑ **Literary Focus** **Tragedy** What flaw (or flaws) does Cassius reveal in this dialogue with Brutus?

Under your testy humor? By the gods,
You shall digest the venom of your spleen,°
Though it do split you; for, from this day forth,
I'll use you for my mirth, yea, for my laughter,
When you are waspish.

50 **Cassius.**   Is it come to this?
Brutus.
You say you are a better soldier:
Let it appear so; make your vaunting° true,
And it shall please me well. For mine own part,
I shall be glad to learn of noble men.
Cassius.
55 You wrong me every way; you wrong me, Brutus;
I said, an elder soldier, not a better.
Did I say, better?
Brutus.   If you did, I care not.
Cassius.
When Caesar lived, he durst° not thus have moved° me.

47. spleen: fiery temper. (The spleen was believed to be the seat of the emotions.)

52. vaunting: boasting.

56–57. *What did Cassius say in lines 30–32?*

58. durst: dared. **moved:** exasperated.

Analyzing Visuals **Viewing and Interpreting** Who are the principal characters in this scene? What is happening here?

(left to right) Brutus, Casca, Cinna, Lucius, Cassius.

Brutus.

Peace, peace, you durst not so have tempted him.

60 **Cassius.** I durst not?

Brutus. No.

Cassius.

What? Durst not tempt him?

Brutus.   For your life you durst not.

Cassius.

Do not presume too much upon my love;

I may do that I shall be sorry for.

Brutus.

65 You have done that you should be sorry for.

There is no terror, Cassius, in your threats;

For I am armed so strong in honesty

That they pass by me as the idle wind,

Which I respect not. I did send to you

70 For certain sums of gold, which you denied me;

For I can raise no money by vile means.

By heaven, I had rather coin my heart

And drop my blood for drachmas than to wring

From the hard hands of peasants their vile trash

75 By any indirection.° I did send

To you for gold to pay my legions,

Which you denied me. Was that done like Cassius?

Should I have answered Caius Cassius so?

When Marcus Brutus grows so covetous

80 To lock such rascal counters° from his friends,

Be ready, gods, with all your thunderbolts,

Dash him to pieces! **C**

Cassius.   I denied you not.

Brutus.

You did.

Cassius.   I did not. He was but a fool

That brought my answer back. Brutus hath rived° my

heart.

85 A friend should bear his friend's infirmities;

But Brutus makes mine greater than they are.

75. **indirection:** illegal methods.

80. **counters:** coins.

84. **rived:** broken.

C **Reading Focus** **Paraphrasing** Paraphrase Brutus's speech in lines 65–82. What
do you think of Brutus's moral position here—is it honorable or hypocritical? Explain.

Brutus.

I do not, till you practice them on me.

Cassius.

You love me not.

Brutus.   I do not like your faults.

Cassius.

A friendly eye could never see such faults.

Brutus.

90   A flatterer's would not, though they do appear
     As huge as high Olympus.

Cassius.

     Come, Antony, and young Octavius, come,
     Revenge yourselves alone on Cassius,
     For Cassius is aweary of the world:

95   Hated by one he loves; braved° by his brother;
     Checked like a bondman; all his faults observed,
     Set in a notebook, learned and conned by rote°
     To cast into my teeth. O, I could weep
     My spirit from mine eyes! There is my dagger,

100 And here my naked breast; within, a heart
     Dearer than Pluto's mine,° richer than gold;
     If that thou be'st a Roman, take it forth.
     I, that denied thee gold,° will give my heart.
     Strike as thou didst at Caesar; for I know,
     When thou didst hate him worst, thou lovedst him

105   better
     Than ever thou lovedst Cassius.

Brutus.   Sheathe your dagger.
     Be angry when you will, it shall have scope.
     Do what you will, dishonor shall be humor.°
     O Cassius, you are yokèd with a lamb

110 That carries anger as the flint bears fire,
     Who, much enforcèd, shows a hasty spark,
     And straight is cold again.

Cassius.   Hath Cassius lived
     To be but mirth and laughter to his Brutus
     When grief and blood ill-tempered vexeth him?

Brutus.

115 When I spoke that, I was ill-tempered too.

Cassius.

     Do you confess so much? Give me your hand.

95. **braved:** defied.

97. **conned by rote:** learned by heart.

? Staging the Play
99. *What is Cassius doing here, and why?*

101. **Pluto's mine:** the riches under the earth. Pluto was the Roman god of the underworld (akin to the Greek god Hades); Shakespeare confuses him with Plutus, god of riches.

103. **that . . . gold:** that *you say* denied you gold.

108. In other words, dishonor or insults will be seen merely as the result of eccentric personality traits.

Brutus.

And my heart too.

Cassius.   O Brutus!   **D**

Brutus.   What's the matter?

Cassius.

Have not you love enough to bear with me
When that rash humor which my mother gave me
Makes me forgetful?

120 **Brutus.**   Yes, Cassius, and from henceforth,

When you are over-earnest with your Brutus,
He'll think your mother chides, and leave you so.

[*Enter a* POET, *followed by* LUCILIUS, TITINIUS, *and* LUCIUS.]

Poet.

Let me go in to see the generals;
There is some grudge between 'em; 'tis not meet
They be alone.

125 **Lucilius.**   You shall not come to them.

Poet. Nothing but death shall stay me.

Cassius. How now. What's the matter?

Poet.

For shame, you generals! What do you mean?
Love, and be friends, as two such men should be;
130   For I have seen more years, I'm sure, than ye.

Cassius.

Ha, ha! How vilely doth this cynic° rhyme!

Brutus.

Get you hence, sirrah! Saucy fellow, hence!

Cassius.

Bear with him, Brutus, 'tis his fashion.

Brutus.

I'll know his humor when he knows his time.°
135   What should the wars do with these jigging° fools?
Companion,° hence!

Cassius.   Away, away, be gone!

[*Exit* POET.]

? **Staging the Play**
122. *How could a humorous note be sounded here?*

131. cynic: rude person.

134. his time: the right time to speak.
135. jigging: rhyming.
136. Companion: lower-class fellow.

? **Elements of Drama**
136. *Remember that Shakespeare himself was a "jigging fool." What is the point of this scene with the poet?*

D **Reading Focus** Reading Aloud Read aloud lines 88–117, where a change occurs between Brutus and Cassius. What does this dialogue reveal about their characters and their feelings?

> **Speak no more of her. Give me a bowl of wine.**
> **In this I bury all unkindness, Cassius.**

Brutus.
Lucilius and Titinius, bid the commanders
Prepare to lodge their companies tonight.
Cassius.
And come yourselves, and bring Messala with you
Immediately to us.   [*Exeunt* LUCILIUS *and* TITINIUS.]
140 **Brutus.**   Lucius, a bowl of wine.

[*Exit* LUCIUS.]

Cassius.
I did not think you could have been so angry.
Brutus.
O Cassius, I am sick of many griefs.
Cassius.
Of your philosophy you make no use,
If you give place to accidental evils.
Brutus.
145 No man bears sorrow better. Portia is dead.
Cassius. Ha? Portia?
Brutus. She is dead.
Cassius.
How scaped I killing when I crossed you so?
O insupportable and touching loss!
Upon what sickness?
150 **Brutus.**   Impatient of my absence,
And grief that young Octavius with Mark Antony
Have made themselves so strong—for with her death
That tidings came—with this she fell distract,°
And (her attendants absent) swallowed fire.° **E**
Cassius.
And died so?
Brutus.   Even so.

? Staging the Play
144. *This refers to Brutus's philosophy of Stoicism, which taught that we should master our emotions, lead lives dictated by reason and duty, and submit to fate. How might Brutus deliver his next shocking line?*

? Staging the Play
145–160. *Which actor would show more emotion in this scene—Cassius or Brutus? Explain your reasoning. (Many fine actors have shown no emotion as they played Brutus in this scene.)*

153. fell distract: became distraught.
154. According to Plutarch, Portia killed herself by putting hot coals in her mouth.

E Literary Focus **Tragedy** At this point, Cassius and Brutus are left alone onstage. What has Brutus just revealed? How does this news contribute to the falling action of the play?

155 **Cassius.** O ye immortal gods!

[*Enter* LUCIUS, *with wine and tapers.*]

Brutus.
Speak no more of her. Give me a bowl of wine.
In this I bury all unkindness, Cassius.

[*Drinks.*]

Cassius.
My heart is thirsty for that noble pledge.
Fill, Lucius, till the wine o'erswell the cup;
160 I cannot drink too much of Brutus' love.

[*Drinks. Exit* LUCIUS.]

[*Enter* TITINIUS *and* MESSALA.]

Brutus.
Come in, Titinius! Welcome, good Messala.
Now sit we close about this taper here,
And call in question° our necessities.

163. call in question: consider.

Cassius.
Portia, art thou gone?
Brutus. No more, I pray you.
165 Messala, I have here receivèd letters
That young Octavius and Mark Antony
Come down upon us with a mighty power,
Bending their expedition toward Philippi.°

168. Philippi: ancient city in
northern Greece.

Messala.
Myself have letters of the selfsame tenure.°

169. tenure: tenor; meaning.

Brutus.
170 With what addition?

Messala.
That by proscription and bills of outlawry°
Octavius, Antony, and Lepidus
Have put to death an hundred senators.

171. bills of outlawry: lists of
proscribed people (people condemned to death or banishment).

Brutus.
Therein our letters do not well agree.
175 Mine speak of seventy senators that died
By their proscriptions, Cicero being one.

F **Reading Focus** **Reading a Play** How do Cassius's and Brutus's attitudes about
Portia's death seem to differ?

Cassius.

Cicero one?

Messala.   Cicero is dead,

And by that order of proscription.

Had you your letters from your wife, my lord?

180 **Brutus.** No, Messala.

Messala.

Nor nothing in your letters writ of her?

Brutus.

Nothing, Messala.

Messala.   That methinks is strange.

Brutus.

Why ask you? Hear you aught of her in yours?

Messala. No, my lord.

Brutus.

185   Now as you are a Roman, tell me true.

Messala.

Then like a Roman bear the truth I tell,

For certain she is dead, and by strange manner. **G**

Brutus.

Why, farewell, Portia. We must die, Messala.

With meditating that she must die once,°

190   I have the patience to endure it now.

Messala.

Even so great men great losses should endure.

Cassius.

I have as much of this in art° as you,

But yet my nature could not bear it so.

Brutus.

Well, to our work alive. What do you think

195   Of marching to Philippi presently?

Cassius.

I do not think it good.

Brutus.   Your reason?

Cassius.   This it is:

'Tis better that the enemy seek us;

So shall he waste his means, weary his soldiers,

G **Reading Focus** **Making Inferences** What does Brutus expect of Messala? What Stoic belief does he equate with Roman values? Explain.

Messala with the lutist Lucius behind him.

Doing himself offense, whilst we, lying still,
200   Are full of rest, defense, and nimbleness.

Brutus.
Good reasons must of force° give place to better.   **201. of force:** of necessity.
The people 'twixt Philippi and this ground
Do stand but in a forced affection;°   **203.** That is, they support us
For they have grudged us contribution.   only grudgingly.
205   The enemy, marching along by them,
By them shall make a fuller number up,
Come on refreshed, new-added and encouraged;
From which advantage shall we cut him off
If at Philippi we do face him there,
These people at our back.

H **Reading Focus** **Paraphrasing** Paraphrase Cassius's words in lines 196–200.
What are his reasons for not marching to Philippi?

210   **Cassius.**   Hear me, good brother.
           Brutus.
               Under your pardon. You must note beside
               That we have tried the utmost of our friends,
               Our legions are brimful, our cause is ripe.
               The enemy increaseth every day;
215   We, at the height, are ready to decline.
               There is a tide in the affairs of men
               Which, taken at the flood, leads on to fortune;
               Omitted,° all the voyage of their life
               Is bound in shallows and in miseries.
220   On such a full sea are we now afloat,
               And we must take the current when it serves,
               Or lose our ventures.   **❶**
           Cassius.   Then, with your will,° go on;
               We'll along ourselves and meet them at Philippi.
           Brutus.
               The deep of night is crept upon our talk,
225   And nature must obey necessity,
               Which we will niggard with a little rest.°
               There is no more to say?
           Cassius.   No more. Good night.
               Early tomorrow will we rise and hence.

           [*Enter* LUCIUS.]

           Brutus.
               Lucius, my gown.   [*Exit* LUCIUS.]
                          Farewell, good Messala.
230   Good night, Titinius. Noble, noble Cassius,
               Good night, and good repose.
           Cassius.   O my dear brother,
               This was an ill beginning of the night.
               Never come such division 'tween our souls!
               Let it not, Brutus.

           [*Enter* LUCIUS, *with the gown.*]

           Brutus.   Everything is well.
           Cassius.
               Good night, my lord.

218. Omitted: neglected.

? **222.** *Where does Brutus want to fight Antony, and why?*
222. with your will: as you wish.

226. niggard with a little rest: cheat with a short period of sleep.

? **Staging the Play**
231. *In some productions at this point in the scene, Brutus takes a letter out of his pocket and burns it. What letter are we to assume he is destroying, and what does his action demonstrate?*

---

❶ Reading Focus **Reading Aloud** Read aloud Brutus's speech. What tones and emotions would you use in these famous lines to bring them to life?

235 **Brutus.**   Good night, good brother.
Titinius, Messala.
    Good night, Lord Brutus.
Brutus.   Farewell, every one.

                                              [*Exeunt.*]

    Give me the gown. Where is thy instrument?°
Lucius.
    Here in the tent.
Brutus.   What, thou speak'st drowsily?
    Poor knave, I blame thee not; thou art o'erwatched.°
240 Call Claudius and some other of my men;
    I'll have them sleep on cushions in my tent.
Lucius. Varro and Claudius!

[*Enter* VARRO *and* CLAUDIUS.]

Varro. Calls my lord?
Brutus.
    I pray you, sirs, lie in my tent and sleep.
245 It may be I shall raise you by and by
    On business to my brother Cassius.
Varro.
    So please you, we will stand and watch your pleasure.°
Brutus.
    I will not have it so; lie down, good sirs;
    It may be I shall otherwise bethink me.

[VARRO *and* CLAUDIUS *lie down.*]

250 Look, Lucius, here's the book I sought for so;
    I put it in the pocket of my gown.
Lucius.
    I was sure your lordship did not give it me.
Brutus.
    Bear with me, good boy, I am much forgetful.
    Canst thou hold up thy heavy eyes awhile,
255 And touch thy instrument a strain or two?
Lucius.
    Ay, my lord, an't please you.   🄹
Brutus.   It does, my boy.

237. instrument: probably a lute.

239. o'erwatched: exhausted.

247. watch your pleasure: wait for your orders.

🄹 **Literary Focus** **Tragedy** Where does the change in mood in this scene occur? How is it suggested?

I trouble thee too much, but thou art willing.

Lucius. It is my duty, sir.

Brutus.

I should not urge thy duty past thy might;
260   I know young bloods look for a time of rest.

Lucius. I have slept, my lord, already.

Brutus.

It was well done, and thou shalt sleep again;
I will not hold thee long. If I do live,
I will be good to thee.

[*Music, and a song.*]

265   This is a sleepy tune. O murd'rous° slumber!
Layest thou thy leaden mace° upon my boy,
That plays thee music? Gentle knave, good night;
I will not do thee so much wrong to wake thee.
If thou dost nod, thou break'st thy instrument;
270   I'll take it from thee; and, good boy, good night.
Let me see, let me see; is not the leaf turned down
Where I left reading? Here it is, I think.

[*Enter the* GHOST *of Caesar.*]

How ill this taper burns. Ha! Who comes here?
I think it is the weakness of mine eyes
275   That shapes this monstrous apparition.
It comes upon° me. Art thou anything?
Art thou some god, some angel, or some devil,
That mak'st my blood cold, and my hair to stare?°
Speak to me what thou art.

Ghost.

Thy evil spirit, Brutus.

280 **Brutus.**   Why com'st thou?

Ghost.

To tell thee thou shalt see me at Philippi.

Brutus. Well; then I shall see thee again?

Ghost. Ay, at Philippi.

Brutus.

Why, I will see thee at Philippi then.

[*Exit* GHOST.]

? Staging the Play
Stage direction. How could lighting be used to suggest an intimate, drowsy, and nonmilitaristic scene?

265. murd'rous: deathlike.

266. mace: heavy club carried by public officials.

276. upon: toward.

278. stare: stand on end.

? Staging the Play
279. *Stage direction. How would you "stage" the Ghost? Would you have him in military dress, or maybe in his bloodied toga? Would you not show the Ghost at all, but merely project his voice onstage?*

? Elements of Drama
284. *What might the Ghost's appearance* **foreshadow?**

285   Now I have taken heart thou vanishest.
      Ill spirit, I would hold more talk with thee.
      Boy! Lucius! Varro! Claudius! Sirs, awake!
      Claudius! **Ⓚ**

Lucius. The strings, my lord, are false.°

Brutus.

290   He thinks he still is at his instrument.
      Lucius awake!

Lucius. My lord?

Brutus.

      Didst thou dream, Lucius, that thou so criedst out?

Lucius.

      My lord, I do not know that I did cry.

Brutus.

295   Yes, that thou didst. Didst thou see anything?

Lucius. Nothing, my lord.

Brutus.

      Sleep again, Lucius. Sirrah Claudius!
      (*To* VARRO.) Fellow thou, awake!

Varro. My lord?

300 **Claudius.** My lord?

Brutus.

      Why did you so cry out, sirs, in your sleep?

Both.

      Did we, my lord?

Brutus.   Ay. Saw you anything?

Varro.

      No, my lord, I saw nothing.

Claudius.   Nor I, my lord.

Brutus.

      Go and commend me to my brother Cassius;
305   Bid him set on his pow'rs betimes before,°
      And we will follow. **Ⓛ**

Both.   It shall be done, my lord.

[*Exeunt.*]

---

289. Lucius sleepily supposes that his instrument is out of tune.

? **Staging the Play**
293. *In one production, the Ghost scene was staged so that the Ghost's words seemed to come from the mouth of the sleeping Lucius. Would this explain Brutus's question to Lucius about "crying out"?*

305. That is, lead his forces out early in the morning, ahead of Brutus and his troops.

Ⓚ **Literary Focus** Tragedy Why might Brutus wish to speak more with Caesar's ghost?

Ⓛ **Reading Focus** Making Inferences Brutus decides that Cassius should go first into battle. What can you infer about Brutus from this decision?

Applying Your Skills

The Tragedy of Julius Caesar, Act IV

Respond and Think Critically

Reading Focus

Quick Check

1. Describe the military situation in this act.

2. Throughout the play, Brutus and Cassius have been **foils** (contrasting characters). What issues cause them to quarrel in Scene 3?

3. According to Brutus, why does Portia kill herself?

4. What vision appears to Brutus near the end of this act? How does he react?

Read with a Purpose

5. What does the stress of war bring out in the characters? Give examples from the text.

Reading Skills: Reading Dramas

6. At this point in the play, loyalties have begun to waver. In Scene 1, for example, Antony's loyalty to Lepidus begins to give way. With the chart you began on page 840, you may want to add a last column labeled "Loyalties." There, you can keep track of how the different characters' loyalties are changing.

Literary Focus

Literary Analysis

7. **Analyze** How is Antony characterized by his words and actions in Scene 1? In your opinion, is the Antony we see in this scene consistent with the Antony we saw earlier? Explain.

8. **Compare and Contrast** Compare and contrast the meeting of the triumvirate in Scene 1 with the meeting of the conspirators in Scene 3. How are the scenes parallel? How do they differ?

9. **Infer** Brutus and Cassius have been friends, with Cassius clearly being the subordinate one in the friendship. How does their relationship change as a result of their quarrel in Scene 3?

Literary Skills: Tragedy

10. **Analyze** In Act IV, we see the consequences of betrayal. How does Brutus's situation worsen after his betrayal of Caesar?

11. **Evaluate** With which character do you sympathize the most by the end of Act IV? Why?

Literary Skills Review: Setting

12. **Analyze** The time and place in which a story takes place, its **setting,** also reflects the values and beliefs of a culture. How does setting influence the mood of the play? Explain.

Writing Focus

Think as a Reader/Writer

Use It in Your Writing Using your *Reader/Writer Notebook* comments, summarize in two or three paragraphs the principal events in Act IV. Tell who and what has changed significantly since Act III, and why.

 What Do You Think Now

Which of Brutus's character traits is more predominant at this point in the play—ambition or honor? Explain.

Vocabulary Development

Vocabulary Skills: Recognizing Anachronisms

An **anachronism** (from *ana,* meaning "against," and *chronos,* meaning "time") is an event or a detail that is inappropriate for the time period. For example, a car in a story about the Civil War would be an anachronism because cars had not yet been invented. In a play set in the 1920s, the word *nerd* would be an anachronism because it was not used as slang until much later.

Your Turn

Remember that *Julius Caesar* is set in 44–42 B.C., in ancient Rome, and that Shakespeare wrote the play around A.D. 1600. Read the excerpts below. Identify the one detail in each excerpt that could not be found in ancient Rome. Suppose Shakespeare wanted to correct his errors. How could he eliminate these anachronisms? Rewrite each excerpt, and compare your changes with a partner's.

1. "... he plucked / me ope his doublet and offered them his throat to cut."
   —Act I, Scene 2, lines 261–262
2. "Peace! Count the clock."
       "The clock hath stricken three."
   —Act II, Scene 1, line 192
3. "Look, Lucius, here's the book I sought for so; I put it in the pocket of my gown."
   —Act IV, Scene 3, lines 250–251

Now, make a list of other details or situations that would be anachronistic. One example might be the conspirators' use of guns instead of daggers to kill Caesar, or Brutus receiving a telegram telling him of Portia's death.

Language Coach

Archaic Words and Meanings Many of the words in *Julius Caesar* are no longer in use. Other words have changed in meaning over time. Find four words from Act IV that are no longer in use today. List them in your *Reader/Writer Notebook,* along with the sentence in which each word appears. Then, rewrite each passage in modern English. Compare your lists and revisions in a small group.

Academic Vocabulary

Write About . . .

Use the Academic Vocabulary to answer the following questions about Act IV:

1. So far, what would you say are the predominant themes, or central ideas about human life, in *The Tragedy of Julius Caesar?*
2. Re-read Scene 3, lines 201–222. According to what criteria does Brutus decide to go and battle in Philippi?

Act V

Strato stands over the dead Brutus.

Act V

Scene 1. *The plains of Philippi.*

Enter OCTAVIUS, ANTONY, *and their* ARMY.

Octavius.
Now, Antony, our hopes are answerèd;
You said the enemy would not come down,
But keep the hills and upper regions.
It proves not so; their battles° are at hand;
5   They mean to warn us at Philippi here,
Answering before we do demand of them.
Antony.
Tut, I am in their bosoms,° and I know
Wherefore they do it. They could be content
To visit other places, and come down
10   With fearful bravery, thinking by this face
To fasten in our thoughts that they have courage;
But 'tis not so.

[*Enter a* MESSENGER.]

Messenger.   Prepare you, generals,
The enemy comes on in gallant show;
Their bloody sign° of battle is hung out,
15   And something to be done immediately.
Antony.
Octavius, lead your battle softly on
Upon the left hand of the even° field.
Octavius.
Upon the right hand I; keep thou the left.
Antony.
Why do you cross me in this exigent?°
Octavius.
20   I do not cross you; but I will do so.

? **Staging the Play**
Stage direction. *What props might be used to indicate that we are now on the plains of Philippi with Antony's and Octavius's army?*

4. battles: armies.

7. am in their bosoms: know their secret thoughts.

14. sign: flag.

17. even: level.

19. exigent (EHK sih jehnt): critical moment.
? **Staging the Play**
20. *Antony and Octavius argue in these lines. How might these lines be read?*

A **Reading Focus** **Making Inferences** Based on the dialogue between Antony and Octavius, what can you infer about their relationship?

[*March. Drum. Enter* BRUTUS, CASSIUS, *and their* ARMY; LUCILIUS, TITINIUS, MESSALA, *and others.*]

Brutus.
They stand, and would have parley.

Cassius.
Stand fast, Titinius, we must out and talk.

Octavius.
Mark Antony, shall we give sign of battle?

Antony.
No, Caesar, we will answer on their charge.
25   Make forth, the generals would have some words.

Octavius.
Stir not until the signal.

Brutus.
Words before blows; is it so, countrymen?

Octavius.
Not that we love words better, as you do.

Brutus.
Good words are better than bad strokes, Octavius.

Antony.
30   In your bad strokes, Brutus, you give good words;
Witness the hole you made in Caesar's heart,
Crying "Long live! Hail, Caesar!"

Cassius.   Antony,
The posture of your blows are yet unknown;
But for your words, they rob the Hybla° bees,
And leave them honeyless.

35   **Antony.**   Not stingless too.

Brutus.
O, yes, and soundless too;
For you have stol'n their buzzing, Antony,
And very wisely threat before you sting.

Antony.
Villains! You did not so, when your vile daggers
40   Hacked one another in the sides of Caesar.
You showed your teeth like apes, and fawned like hounds,
And bowed like bondmen, kissing Caesar's feet;
Whilst damnèd Casca, like a cur, behind
Struck Caesar on the neck. O you flatterers!

? **Staging the Play**
Stage direction. The armies should be placed at opposite sides of the stage, with a kind of no man's land between them. In the next lines, notice which man in which army speaks. They are taunting one another across the short distance that separates them.

34. Hybla: town in Sicily famous for its honey.

Cassius.

45 Flatterers! Now, Brutus, thank yourself;
This tongue had not offended so today,
If Cassius might have ruled.°

Octavius.

Come, come, the cause. If arguing make us sweat,
The proof of it will turn to redder drops.

50 Look,
I draw a sword against conspirators.
When think you that the sword goes up again?
Never, till Caesar's three and thirty wounds
Be well avenged; or till another Caesar°

55 Have added slaughter to the sword of traitors.

Brutus.

Caesar, thou canst not die by traitors' hands,
Unless thou bring'st them with thee.

47. ruled: gotten his way.

54. another Caesar: meaning Octavius himself.

B Literary Focus **Tragedy** What is Cassius referring to? What does this speech imply about Brutus's character?

The army listens to the calm before the storm.

Octavius.   So I hope.
　I was not born to die on Brutus' sword.
Brutus.
　O, if thou wert the noblest of thy strain,
60　Young man, thou couldst not die more honorable.
Cassius.
　A peevish schoolboy, worthless° of such honor,
　Joined with a masker and a reveler. **C**
Antony.
　Old Cassius still!
Octavius.   Come, Antony; away!
　Defiance, traitors, hurl we in your teeth.
65　If you dare fight today, come to the field;
　If not, when you have stomachs.

[*Exeunt* OCTAVIUS, ANTONY, *and* ARMY.]

Cassius.
　Why, now blow wind, swell billow, and swim bark!
　The storm is up, and all is on the hazard.°
Brutus.
　Ho, Lucilius, hark, a word with you.

[LUCILIUS *and* MESSALA *stand forth.*]

Lucilius.   My lord?

[BRUTUS *and* LUCILIUS *converse apart.*]

Cassius.
　Messala.
Messala.   What says my general?
70 **Cassius.**   Messala,
　This is my birthday; as this very day
　Was Cassius born. Give me thy hand, Messala:
　Be thou my witness that against my will
　(As Pompey was) am I compelled to set
75　Upon one battle all our liberties.
　You know that I held Epicurus strong,°
　And his opinion; now I change my mind,
　And partly credit things that do presage.°
　Coming from Sardis, on our former ensign°

61. **worthless:** unworthy.

68. **on the hazard:** at risk.

76. **held Epicurus strong:** believed in the philosophy of Epicurus, a philosopher of the third century B.C. who held that omens were worthless.
78. **presage** (pree SAYJ): foretell.
79. **former ensign:** foremost flag.

C **Reading Focus** **Reading a Play** What is Cassius saying about this "new Caesar"?

80 Two mighty eagles fell, and there they perched,
   Gorging and feeding from our soldiers' hands,
   Who to Philippi here consorted° us.
   This morning are they fled away and gone,
   And in their steads do ravens, crows, and kites
85 Fly o'er our heads and downward look on us
   As we were sickly prey; their shadows seem
   A canopy most fatal, under which
   Our army lies, ready to give up the ghost. **D**

Messala.
   Believe not so.

Cassius.   I but believe it partly,
90 For I am fresh of spirit and resolved
   To meet all perils very constantly.

Brutus.
   Even so, Lucilius.

Cassius.   Now, most noble Brutus,
   The gods today stand friendly, that we may,
   Lovers in peace, lead on our days to age!

82. consorted: accompanied.

? Staging the Play
92. *Remember that the two pairs of men have been talking separately. What action should now take place onstage?*

D **Reading Focus** **Making Inferences** Based on this monologue, what can you infer about how Cassius thinks the battle will go? Explain.

Brutus (left) and Octavius.

95 But since the affairs of men rests still incertain,
Let's reason with the worst that may befall.
If we do lose this battle, then is this
The very last time we shall speak together.
What are you then determinèd to do?

Brutus.
100 Even by the rule of that philosophy
By which I did blame Cato for the death
Which he did give himself; I know not how,
But I do find it cowardly and vile,
For fear of what might fall, so to prevent
105 The time° of life, arming myself with patience
To stay the providence of some high powers
That govern us below.

Cassius.   Then, if we lose this battle,
You are contented to be led in triumph°
Thorough the streets of Rome?   **E**

Brutus.
110 No, Cassius, no; think not, thou noble Roman,
That ever Brutus will go bound to Rome;
He bears too great a mind. But this same day
Must end that work the ides of March begun;
And whether we shall meet again I know not.
115 Therefore our everlasting farewell take.
Forever, and forever, farewell, Cassius!
If we do meet again, why, we shall smile;
If not, why then this parting was well made.

Cassius.
Forever, and forever, farewell, Brutus!
120 If we do meet again, we'll smile indeed;
If not, 'tis true this parting was well made.

Brutus.
Why then, lead on. O, that a man might know
The end of this day's business ere it come!
But it sufficeth that the day will end,
125 And then the end is known. Come, ho! Away!   **F**

[*Exeunt.*]

105. **time:** term, or natural span.

? 107. *Brutus refers again to his Stoic philosophy, which taught that he should be ruled by reason, not by emotion. What is Brutus saying about suicide?*
108. **in triumph:** as a captive in the victor's procession.

? **Staging the Play**
121. *Brutus and Cassius make their farewells in this dialogue. What actions or gestures might the two men make as they speak?*

E **Reading Focus** **Paraphrasing** Paraphrase lines 107–109. What does Cassius say will happen to the losing armies?

F **Literary Focus** **Tragedy** Brutus and Cassius say their goodbyes. What do you predict will happen to these two men?

Scene 2. *The field of battle.*

Alarum.° Enter BRUTUS *and* MESSALA.

Brutus.
Ride, ride, Messala, ride, and give these bills°
Unto the legions on the other side.

[*Loud alarum.*]

Let them set on at once; for I perceive
But cold demeanor° in Octavius' wing,
5   And sudden push° gives them the overthrow.
Ride, ride, Messala! Let them all come down.

[*Exeunt.*]

Scene 3. *The field of battle.*

Alarums. Enter CASSIUS *and* TITINIUS.

Cassius.
O, look, Titinius, look, the villains fly!
Myself have to mine own turned enemy.
This ensign° here of mine was turning back;
I slew the coward, and did take it° from him.

Titinius.
5   O Cassius, Brutus gave the word too early,
Who, having some advantage on Octavius,
Took it too eagerly; his soldiers fell to spoil,°
Whilst we by Antony are all enclosed.

[*Enter* PINDARUS.]

Pindarus.
Fly further off, my lord, fly further off!
10   Mark Antony is in your tents, my lord.
Fly, therefore, noble Cassius, fly far off!

Cassius.
This hill is far enough. Look, look, Titinius!
Are those my tents where I perceive the fire?

Alarum: call to arms by drum or trumpet.

1. bills: orders.

4. cold demeanor: lack of fighting spirit.
5. push: attack.

3. ensign: standard-bearer.
4. it: the flag (standard).

7. spoil: loot.
8. *What have Brutus's and Cassius's armies done?*

A **Reading Focus** **Paraphrasing** Paraphrase Brutus's words. What orders does he give his troops?

Titinius.

They are, my lord.

Cassius.   Titinius, if thou lovest me,

15   Mount thou my horse and hide thy spurs in him°
Till he have brought thee up to yonder troops
And here again, that I may rest assured
Whether yond troops are friend or enemy.

Titinius.

I will be here again even with a thought.°   [*Exit.*]

Cassius.

20   Go, Pindarus, get higher on that hill;
My sight was ever thick. Regard Titinius,
And tell me what thou not'st about the field.

[*Exit* PINDARUS.]

This day I breathèd first. Time is come round,
And where I did begin, there shall I end.

25   My life is run his compass.° Sirrah, what news?

Pindarus (*above*). O my lord!

Cassius. What news?

Pindarus (*above*).

Titinius is enclosèd round about
With horsemen that make to him on the spur;°

30   Yet he spurs on. Now they are almost on him.
Now, Titinius! Now some light. O, he lights too!
He's ta'en! (*Shout.*) And, hark! They shout for joy.

Cassius.

Come down; behold no more.
O, coward that I am, to live so long,

35   To see my best friend ta'en before my face!   **A**

[*Enter* PINDARUS.]

Come hither, sirrah.
In Parthia° did I take thee prisoner;
And then I swore thee, saving of° thy life,
That whatsoever I did bid thee do,

40   Thou shouldst attempt it. Come now, keep thine oath.
Now be a freeman, and with this good sword,
That ran through Caesar's bowels, search this bosom.

---

15. In other words, dig your spurs into him to make him go at top speed.

19. even with a thought: immediately.

24. *What is Cassius referring to here?*

25. is run his compass: has completed its appointed span.

Staging the Play
26. *Stage direction.* *Pindarus is supposed to be on higher ground, looking down on the battle, with Cassius standing below. How would you show this difference in height on the stage?*

29. on the spur: at top speed.

37. Parthia: ancient country (corresponding to part of modern Iran) that was the site of many Roman military campaigns.

38. saving of: sparing.

A **Reading Focus** **Making Inferences** What can you infer about Cassius's feelings about the news that Pindarus provides?

Stand not to answer. Here, take thou the hilts,
And when my face is covered, as 'tis now,
45   Guide thou the sword—Caesar, thou art revenged,
Even with the sword that killed thee. **B**   [*Dies.*]

Pindarus.
So, I am free; yet would not so have been,
Durst I have done my will. O Cassius!
Far from this country Pindarus shall run,
50   Where never Roman shall take note of him.   [*Exit.*]

[*Enter* TITINIUS *and* MESSALA.]

Messala.
It is but change,° Titinius; for Octavius   **51. change:** exchange of fortune.
Is overthrown by noble Brutus' power,
As Cassius' legions are by Antony.

Titinius.
These tidings will well comfort Cassius.

Messala.
Where did you leave him?

55 **Titinius.**   All disconsolate,
With Pindarus his bondman, on this hill.

Messala.
Is not that he that lies upon the ground?

Titinius.
He lies not like the living. O my heart!

Messala.
Is not that he?

Titinius.   No, this was he, Messala,
60   But Cassius is no more. O setting sun,
As in thy red rays thou dost sink to night,
So in his red blood Cassius' day is set.
The sun of Rome is set. Our day is gone;
Clouds, dews, and dangers come; our deeds are done!
65   Mistrust of° my success hath done this deed. **C**   **65. Mistrust of:** disbelief in.

Messala.
Mistrust of good success hath done this deed.
O hateful Error, Melancholy's child,   **68. apt:** credulous; easily
Why dost thou show to the apt° thoughts of men   impressed.

? Elements of Drama
58. *Titinius and Messala
enter from the wings and do not at
first see Cassius's body. What
irony do we in the audience feel
when we hear their conversation?*

B Literary Focus **Tragedy** What does Cassius have Pindarus do for him, and why?

C Reading Focus **Reading Aloud** Read aloud Titinius's words. Why does he think
Cassius killed himself?

The things that are not? O Error, soon conceived,
70 Thou never com'st unto a happy birth,
But kill'st the mother° that engend'red thee!
Titinius.
What, Pindarus! Where art thou, Pindarus?
Messala.
Seek him, Titinius, whilst I go to meet
The noble Brutus, thrusting this report
75 Into his ears. I may say "thrusting" it;
For piercing steel and darts envenomèd
Shall be as welcome to the ears of Brutus
As tidings of this sight.
Titinius.   Hie you, Messala,
And I will seek for Pindarus the while.

[*Exit* MESSALA.]

80 Why didst thou send me forth, brave Cassius?
Did I not meet thy friends, and did not they
Put on my brows this wreath of victory,
And bid me give it thee? Didst thou not hear their shouts?
Alas, thou hast misconstrued everything!
85 But hold thee, take this garland on thy brow;
Thy Brutus bid me give it thee, and I
Will do his bidding. Brutus, come apace,°
And see how I regarded Caius Cassius.
By your leave, gods.° This is a Roman's part:°
90 Come, Cassius' sword, and find Titinius' heart. **D**

[*Dies.*]

[*Alarum. Enter* BRUTUS, MESSALA, YOUNG CATO, STRATO,
    VOLUMNIUS, *and* LUCILIUS.]

Brutus.
Where, where, Messala, doth his body lie?
Messala.
Lo, yonder, and Titinius mourning it.
Brutus.
Titinius' face is upward.
Cato.   He is slain.

71. **the mother:** that is, Cassius, who conceived the error.

87. **apace:** quickly.

89. He asks the gods' permission to end his life before the time they have allotted him. **part:** role; duty.

D **Reading Focus** **Paraphrasing** Restate lines 80–90 in your own words. How does Titinius feel about Cassius and Brutus?

Brutus.

O Julius Caesar, thou art mighty yet!

95   Thy spirit walks abroad, and turns our swords

In our own proper entrails.   [*Low alarums.*]

Cato.   Brave Titinius!

Look, whe'r° he have not crowned dead Cassius.

Brutus.

Are yet two Romans living such as these?

The last of all the Romans, fare thee well!

100   It is impossible that ever Rome

Should breed thy fellow.° Friends, I owe moe tears

To this dead man than you shall see me pay.

I shall find time, Cassius; I shall find time.

Come, therefore, and to Thasos° send his body;

105   His funerals shall not be in our camp,

Lest it discomfort° us. Lucilius, come,

And come, young Cato; let us to the field.

Labeo and Flavius set our battles on.

'Tis three o'clock; and, Romans, yet ere night

110   We shall try fortune in a second fight.

                               [*Exeunt.*]

Scene 4. *The field of battle.*

Alarum. Enter BRUTUS, MESSALA, YOUNG CATO, LUCILIUS,
    and FLAVIUS.

Brutus.

Yet, countrymen, O, yet hold up your heads!

                [*Exit, with followers.*]

Cato.

What bastard° doth not? Who will go with me?

I will proclaim my name about the field.

I am the son of Marcus Cato,° ho!

5   A foe to tyrants, and my country's friend.

I am the son of Marcus Cato, ho!

[*Enter* SOLDIERS *and fight.*]

96. *How does Brutus think Caesar is resolving the issue of his murder?*

97. whe'r: whether.

101. fellow: equal.

104. Thasos: island in the Aegean Sea, near Philippi.

106. discomfort: discourage.

2. bastard: low fellow.

4. Thus he is Portia's brother.

Lucilius.

And I am Brutus, Marcus Brutus, I;
Brutus, my country's friend, know me for Brutus!

[YOUNG CATO *falls.*]

O young and noble Cato, art thou down?
10   Why, now thou diest as bravely as Titinius,
And mayst be honored, being Cato's son.
First Soldier.
Yield, or thou diest.
Lucilius.   Only I yield to die.
There is so much that thou wilt kill me straight;°
Kill Brutus, and be honored in his death.
First Soldier.
15   We must not. A noble prisoner!

[*Enter* ANTONY.]

Second Soldier.
Room, ho! Tell Antony, Brutus is ta'en.
First Soldier.
I'll tell the news. Here comes the general.
Brutus is ta'en, Brutus is ta'en, my lord.
Antony.
Where is he?
Lucilius.
20   Safe, Antony; Brutus is safe enough.
I dare assure thee that no enemy
Shall ever take alive the noble Brutus.
The gods defend him from so great a shame!
When you do find him, or alive or dead,
25   He will be found like Brutus, like himself.°   **A**
Antony.
This is not Brutus, friend, but, I assure you,
A prize no less in worth. Keep this man safe;
Give him all kindness. I had rather have
Such men my friends than enemies. Go on,
30   And see whe'r Brutus be alive or dead,
And bring us word unto Octavius' tent
How everything is chanced.°   [*Exeunt.*]

7. *Lucilius is impersonating Brutus. What are these young men doing, and why?*

13. That is, there is so much inducement to kill me that you will surely do so right away. (Some editors have interpreted this line to mean that Lucilius is offering his captors money to kill him rather than take him prisoner.)

25. like himself: true to his own noble nature.

32. chanced: turned out.
Staging the Play
32. *Antony tells his soldiers to be kind to Lucilius. This speech shows a change in Antony's attitude toward the traitors. How should it be read?*

A Reading Focus **Making Inferences** Based on Lucilius's words, what can you infer about his opinion of Brutus?

Scene 5. *The field of battle.*

Enter BRUTUS, DARDANIUS, CLITUS, STRATO, *and* VOLUMNIUS.

Brutus.
Come, poor remains of friends, rest on this rock.
Clitus.
Statilius showed the torchlight, but, my lord,
He came not back; he is or ta'en or slain.°
Brutus.
Sit thee down, Clitus. Slaying is the word;
5　It is a deed in fashion. Hark thee, Clitus.

[*Whispers.*]

Clitus.
What, I, my lord? No, not for all the world!
Brutus.
Peace then, no words.
Clitus.　　　　　　　I'll rather kill myself.
Brutus.
Hark thee, Dardanius.　　　　　　　　　[*Whispers.*]
Dardanius.　　　　Shall I do such a deed?
Clitus. O Dardanius!
10　**Dardanius.** O Clitus!
Clitus.
What ill request did Brutus make to thee?
Dardanius.
To kill him, Clitus. Look, he meditates.
Clitus.
Now is that noble vessel° full of grief,
That it runs over even at his eyes.　**A**
Brutus.
15　Come hither, good Volumnius; list° a word.
Volumnius.
What says my lord?
Brutus.　　　　　　　Why, this, Volumnius:
The ghost of Caesar hath appeared to me
Two several° times by night; at Sardis once,

3. According to Plutarch, Statilius volunteered to see what was happening at Cassius's camp. If all was well, he was to signal with his torchlight. He did signal but then was killed while returning to Brutus's camp.

? Staging the Play
8. *Stage direction.* *In this scene, Brutus whispers something to both Clitus and Dardanius. How would you stage this scene?*

13. **vessel:** figure of speech meaning "human being."

15. **list:** listen to.

18. **several:** separate.

A **Reading Focus** **Reading Aloud** Read aloud the conversation between Clitus and Dardanius. Why does Clitus think that Brutus gave the same request to both of them?

The army stands over the dead soldiers and Brutus's body.

And this last night here in Philippi fields.
I know my hour is come.
20 **Volumnius.** Not so, my lord.
Brutus.
Nay, I am sure it is, Volumnius.
Thou seest the world, Volumnius, how it goes;
Our enemies have beat us to the pit.°

[*Low alarums.*]

It is more worthy to leap in ourselves
25 Than tarry till they push us. Good Volumnius,
Thou know'st that we two went to school together;
Even for that our love of old, I prithee
Hold thou my sword-hilts whilst I run on it.

23. pit: trap for capturing wild animals; also, a grave.

Volumnius.
    That's not an office for a friend, my lord.

[*Alarum still.*]

Clitus.
30   Fly, fly, my lord, there is no tarrying here.
Brutus.
    Farewell to you; and you; and you, Volumnius.
    Strato, thou hast been all this while asleep;
    Farewell to thee too, Strato. Countrymen,
    My heart doth joy that yet in all my life
35   I found no man but he was true to me.
    I shall have glory by this losing day
    More than Octavius and Mark Antony

By this vile conquest shall attain unto.
So fare you well at once, for Brutus' tongue
40   Hath almost ended his life's history.
Night hangs upon mine eyes; my bones would rest,
That have but labored to attain this hour.

[*Alarum. Cry within,* "Fly, fly, fly!"]

Clitus.
    Fly, my lord, fly!
Brutus.   Hence! I will follow.

        [*Exeunt* CLITUS, DARDANIUS, *and* VOLUMNIUS.]

    I prithee, Strato, stay thou by thy lord,
45   Thou art a fellow of a good respect.°
    Thy life hath had some smatch° of honor in it;
    Hold then my sword, and turn away thy face,
    While I do run upon it. Wilt thou, Strato?
Strato.
    Give me your hand first. Fare you well, my lord.
Brutus.
50   Farewell, good Strato—Caesar, now be still;
    I killed not thee with half so good a will.   **Ⓑ**   [*Dies.*]

[*Alarum. Retreat. Enter* ANTONY, OCTAVIUS, MESSALA,
    LUCILIUS, *and the* ARMY.]

Octavius. What man is that?
Messala.
    My master's man. Strato, where is thy master?
Strato.
    Free from the bondage you are in, Messala;
55   The conquerors can but make a fire of him.
    For Brutus only overcame himself,
    And no man else hath honor by his death.
Lucilius.
    So Brutus should be found. I thank thee, Brutus,
    That thou hast proved Lucilius' saying true.

45. respect: reputation.
46. smatch: trace; taste.

? Staging the Play
51. *Stage direction.* *How many bodies now lie on the stage? It is important for a director of a Shakespearean tragedy to remember how many bodies are onstage. Getting rid of them is often a challenge.*

Ⓑ **Literary Focus** Tragedy How does Brutus meet his downfall?

> So fare you well at once,
> for Brutus' tongue
> Hath almost ended his life's history.

Octavius.

60   All that served Brutus, I will entertain them.
    Fellow, wilt thou bestow° thy time with me?   **C**

Strato.

    Ay, if Messala will prefer° me to you.

Octavius. Do so, good Messala.

Messala. How died my master, Strato?

Strato.

65   I held the sword, and he did run on it.

Messala.

    Octavius, then take him to follow thee,
    That did the latest service to my master.

Antony.

    This was the noblest Roman of them all.
    All the conspirators save only he

70   Did that they did in envy of great Caesar;
    He, only in a general honest thought
    And common good to all, made one of them.°
    His life was gentle, and the elements
    So mixed in him that Nature might stand up

75   And say to all the world, "This was a man!"   **D**

Octavius.

    According to his virtue, let us use° him
    With all respect and rites of burial.
    Within my tent his bones tonight shall lie,
    Most like a soldier ordered honorably.

80   So call the field to rest, and let's away
    To part° the glories of this happy day.

                      [Exeunt omnes.]

61. bestow: spend.

62. prefer: recommend.

72. made one of them: joined their group.

76. use: treat.

81. part: divide.

? Staging the Play
81. *Stage direction.* *Order has finally been restored, and healing will begin. Which actor would you have exit last?*

C **Literary Focus** **Tragedy** How does Octavius indicate to his former enemies that the strife is finally over?

D **Reading Focus** **Making Inferences** Based on Antony's words, what is his opinion of Brutus?

Applying Your Skills

 **RA.L.10.6** Explain how literary techniques, including foreshadowing and flashback, are used to shape the plot of a literary text. **RA.L.10.7** Recognize how irony is used in a literary text. *Also covered* **RA.L.10.5; RP.10.1; WP.10.9**

The Tragedy of Julius Caesar, Act V

Respond and Think Critically

Reading Focus

Quick Check

1. Which four characters finally confront each other in Scene 1?

2. What are the results of the first round of battle at Philippi? In the end, who triumphs?

3. What assumptions lead to Cassius's death?

4. Why does Brutus feel he must commit suicide?

5. How do Antony and Octavius react to Brutus's death?

Read with a Purpose

6. What events take place that finally restore order to Roman society? How do these events help define the play as a tragedy?

Reading Skills: Reading Dramas

7. Look back at the chart you began on page 840. In Act V, which characters do you believe would have changed the decisions they had made regarding Caesar? Why?

Literary Focus

Literary Analysis

8. **Interpret** In this tragedy, the plot's rising action peaks at the **climax,** the moment of greatest tension. What is the climax of the play?

9. **Analyze** How do Cassius and Brutus view Caesar's murder in Scenes 3 and 5? Do you think either had a choice other than suicide? Explain.

10. **Make Judgments** Describe your view of Brutus and the choices he made. Should he have betrayed a friend for the public good? Support your responses with evidence from the play.

Literary Skills: Tragedy

11. **Analyze** In the **resolution,** the last scene, why is it significant that Octavius delivers the play's final speech?

12. **Identify** In the *Poetics,* Aristotle describes a **tragic hero** as a person who is more noble than evil, whose fortunes go from good to bad, and who has a character flaw that leads to his or her downfall. Who is the tragic hero in this play, or do you think the play lacks one? Explain.

Literary Skills Review: Irony

13. **Identify** A turn of events that is contrary to our expectations is called **situational irony.** Identify three examples of situational irony in Cassius's death scene.

Writing Focus

Think as a Reader/Writer

Use It in Your Writing Write a dialogue between two Roman citizens. Have both citizens comment and give their views on the events that have occurred at Philippi. You may want to have one character in favor of the actions that happened and the other character against them.

 What Do **You Think Now** Is Caesar portrayed as truly ambitious? Is Brutus really honorable? Tell which of these characters you admire more, and explain why.

Wrap Up

The Tragedy of Julius Caesar, Act V

OH · WA.10.2 Write responses to literature that organize an insightful interpretation around several clear ideas, premises or images and support judgments with specific references to the original text, to other texts, authors and to prior knowledge. *Also covered* WP.10.8

CHOICES

As you respond to the Choices, use these **Academic Vocabulary** words as appropriate: highlight, predominant, principal, and criteria.

REVIEW
Analyze a Character

Timed └Writing In a brief essay, write a character analysis of Brutus. First, read the following critical comments. Then, become a critic yourself. Think about the criteria the critics use to judge Brutus. Evaluate the comments, and use them as you form your own **thesis statement,** a clear statement of your main idea or argument. Be sure to include details from the play to elaborate on and support your statements.

> Brutus is humorlessly good. If his duty is to know himself, his performance fails. Nobility has numbed him until he cannot see himself for his principles. . . . He is not mad or haunted or inspired or perplexed in the extreme. He is simply confused.
>
> —Mark Van Doren

> Brutus is an intellectual who can do things, who is not . . . hampered by doubts. . . . He cannot realize that men seek their own interests, for he has never sought his own, he has lived nobly among noble thoughts, wedded to a noble wife.
>
> —E. M. Forster

CONNECT
Create a Shooting Script

TechFocus Choose a short scene from the play that you would like to film. With a small group of classmates, create a shooting script for the scene. A shooting script tells exactly how a scene should be filmed. Include details about how you would film the scene: where you would use wide shots to show all the action and where you would use close-ups; where the actors should move and how they should be placed; what emotions the actors should convey through gestures and facial expressions; and what the predominant mood of the scene should be. If possible, perform and videotape the scene, using the script you created.

EXTEND
Write a Critical Review

Using what you've learned about the purposes and characteristics of drama, write a critical review of a movie or television drama you've watched recently. Begin by identifying the work's **genre** (tragedy, comedy, drama). Then, think about the criteria you will use to evaluate the work. Are the characters and plot believable? Is the action suspenseful? Is the ending satisfying? How effective are the scene designs, dialogue, and costumes? Cite details to support your points. Before you begin, you might want to read the review on pages 987–998.

Comparing Universal Themes Across Genres

CONTENTS

The Three Fates. Flemish tapestry depicting three women spinning. Early 16th century. Victoria & Albert Museum, London, Inv.: 65–186.

What Do You Think? Does life follow a fixed pattern, or do our choices determine our future?

QuickTalk
How do you see your life and your future? Talk with a partner about the role fate plays in our lives. Are we powerless to change our future, or are our destinies under our control?

Preparing to Read

The Seven Ages of Man / Demeter

 RA.L.10.4 Interpret universal themes across different works by the same author or by different authors. **RA.L.10.5** Analyze how an author's choice of genre affects the expression of a theme or topic.

Reader/Writer Notebook

Use your **RWN** to complete the activities for these selections.

Literary Focus

Universal Themes People throughout time have common emotions, concerns, and experiences—we all have hopes and dreams and cope with love, loss, death, and disappointment. These concerns are often reflected as **universal themes.** These themes, or ideas about life, are predominant in literature, yet each version is a bit different.

Myths Every society has its **myths,** stories that are connected to the traditions and religions of the culture that produced them. Myths often provide imaginative explanations for the origins of things.

Reading Focus

Comparing Themes Across Genres Sometimes two pieces of literature that at first seem very **different** turn out to have common themes. The selections that follow present different views of the role fate plays in our lives. The theme of a work is often too complicated to be stated in one word. As you read, look for similar subjects. For example, the idea of youth appears in both selections, but in one it is portrayed as relaxed and untroubled; in the other, anxious and bleak.

Into Action As you read, use a chart like the one below to help you pinpoint and compare subjects.

Subject	"The Seven Ages of Man"	"Demeter"
youth	"whining schoolboy," "unwillingly to school" —downtrodden, troubled time of life	"danced on her light feet, flowers sprang up" —lighthearted, fun time of life

Vocabulary

Demeter

discerned (duh ZURND) *v.*: recognized; detected. *The Greeks discerned Demeter's influence on the seasons.*

assent (uh SEHNT) *n.*: agreement. *The people nodded their assent to Celeus and vowed to build a temple to Demeter.*

manifest (MAN uh fehst) *adj.*: apparent; obvious. *The reasons for her disguise were manifest.*

Language Coach

Multiple-Meaning Words The word *manifest* is an adjective meaning "apparent," but it is also a noun referring to the list of the cargo carried by a ship. These lists are used by agents at ports of destination. How are the two meanings related?

Writing Focus

Think as a Reader/Writer

Find It in Your Reading Both selections use **sensory language**—words that appeal to the senses. Write examples of sensory words and expressions from the selections in your *Reader/Writer Notebook*.

 **Learn It Online**
There's more to words than just definitions. Get the whole story on:

go.hrw.com	L10-967	Go

The Seven Ages of Man

by **William Shakespeare**

Read with a Purpose

As you read the following speech, see if you agree with Jaques's view of life.

Build Background

The following selection is a **dramatic monologue**—a long speech delivered by a single character—in this case, the character of Jaques from Shakespeare's play *As You Like It*. This speech is considered one of the finest examples of extended metaphor ever written. An **extended metaphor** is a comparison developed over several lines of writing. Jaques opens with the metaphor "All the world's a stage" and goes on to compare the stages of our lives to seven acts, with seven different roles all played by the same character.

All the world's a stage,
And all the men and women merely players;
They have their exits and their entrances,
And one man in his time plays many parts,
5   His acts being seven ages. At first the infant,
Mewling and puking in the nurse's arms;
And then the whining schoolboy, with his satchel
And shining morning face, creeping like snail
Unwillingly to school. And then the lover, **A**
10   Sighing like furnace, with a woeful ballad
Made to his mistress' eyebrow. Then a soldier,
Full of strange oaths, and bearded like the pard,°   **12. pard:** leopard.
Jealous in honor, sudden and quick in quarrel,
Seeking the bubble reputation
15   Even in the cannon's mouth. And then the justice,°   **15. justice:** judge.
In fair round belly with good capon° lined,   **16. capon** (KAY pahn): fat chicken.
With eyes severe and beard of formal cut,
Full of wise saws° and modern instances;   **18. saws:** old sayings.
And so he plays his part. The sixth age shifts

A **Literary Focus** Universal Themes According to the speaker, what are the first three stages of a man's life?

The Ages of Man (late 16th century).
Oil on panel. English School.

20 Into the lean and slippered pantaloon,°
        With spectacles on nose and pouch on side;
    His youthful hose,° well saved, a world too wide
    For his shrunk shank; and his big manly voice,
    Turning again toward childish treble, pipes
25 And whistles in his sound. Last scene of all,
    That ends this strange eventful history,
    Is second childishness and mere oblivion,
    Sans° teeth, sans eyes, sans taste, sans everything. **B**

20. pantaloon (PAN tuh LOON):
silly old man.

22. hose: stockings.

28. sans (sanz): French for "without."

B **Literary Focus** Universal Themes How does Jaques describe the last
stage of life?

DEMETER

by **Edith Hamilton**

Read with a Purpose
Read this retelling of an ancient myth to learn how the Greeks explained one of the cycles of life.

Preparing to Read for this selection is on page 967.

Build Background
The origins of the myth of Demeter are believed to be from ancient Greece. In her book *Mythology,* from which this selection was taken, Edith Hamilton writes, "The original [story] has the marks of early Greek poetry, great simplicity and directness and delight in the beautiful world."

Demeter had an only daughter, Persephone (in Latin *Proserpine*), the maiden of the spring. She lost her and in her terrible grief she withheld her gifts from the earth, which turned into a frozen desert. The green and flowering land was icebound and lifeless because Persephone had disappeared. **A**

The lord of the dark underworld, the king of the multitudinous dead, carried her off when, enticed by the wondrous bloom of the narcissus,[1] she strayed too far from her companions. In his chariot drawn by coal-black steeds he rose up through a chasm in the earth, and grasping the maiden by the wrist set her beside him. He bore her away, weeping, down to the underworld. The high hills echoed her cry and the depths of the sea, and her mother heard it. She sped like a bird over sea and land seeking her daughter. But no one would tell her the truth, "no man nor god, nor any sure messenger from the birds." Nine days Demeter wandered, and all that time she would not taste of ambrosia[2] or put sweet nectar to her lips. At last she came to the Sun and he told her all the story: Persephone was down in the world beneath the earth, among the shadowy dead.

Then a still greater grief entered Demeter's heart. She left Olympus; she dwelt on earth, but so disguised that none knew her, and, indeed, the gods are not easily discerned by mortal men. In her desolate wanderings she came to Eleusis[3] and sat by the wayside near a wall. She seemed an aged woman, such as in great houses care for the children or guard the storerooms. Four lovely maidens, sisters, coming to draw water from the well, saw her and asked her pityingly what she did there. She answered that she had fled from pirates who had meant to sell her as a slave, and that she knew no one in this strange land to go to for help. They told her that any house in the town would welcome her, but that they would like best to bring her to their own if she would wait there while they went to ask their mother. The goddess bent her head, in assent, and the

---

1. **narcissus** (nahr SIHS uhs): type of flowering plant.
2. **ambrosia** (am BROH zhuh): in classical mythology, the food and drink of the gods.

3. **Eleusis**: ancient Greek city near Athens known for the Eleusinian Mysteries, secret rituals performed annually in honor of Demeter.

A **Literary Focus** Myths What do you think this myth is going to explain?

Vocabulary **discerned** (duh ZURND) *v.*: recognized; detected.
assent (uh SEHNT) *n.*: agreement.

The Return of Persephone (c.1891) by Frederic Leighton. Leeds Museums and Galleries (City Art Gallery), UK.

girls, filling their shining pitchers with water, hurried home. Their mother, Metaneira, bade them return at once and invite the stranger to come, and speeding back they found the glorious goddess still sitting there, deeply veiled and covered to her slender feet by her dark robe. She followed them, and as she crossed the threshold to the hall where the mother sat holding her young son, a divine radiance filled the doorway and awe fell upon Metaneira.

She bade Demeter be seated and herself offered her honey-sweet wine, but the goddess would not taste it. She asked instead for barley-water flavored with mint, the cooling draught of the reaper at harvest time and also the sacred cup given the worshipers at Eleusis. Thus refreshed she took the child and held him to her fragrant bosom and his mother's heart was glad. So Demeter nursed Demophoon, the son that Metaneira had borne to wise Celeus. And the child grew like a young god, for daily Demeter anointed him with ambrosia and at night she would place him in the red heart of the fire. Her purpose was to give him immortal youth. **B**

B **Literary Focus** Myths Why might Demeter want to give Demophoon eternal youth?

Something, however, made the mother uneasy, so that one night she kept watch and screamed in terror when she saw the child laid in the fire. The goddess was angered; she seized the boy and cast him on the ground. She had meant to set him free from old age and from death, but that was not to be. Still, he had lain upon her knees and slept in her arms and therefore he should have honor throughout his life.

Then she showed herself the goddess manifest. Beauty breathed about her and a lovely fragrance; light shone from her so that the great house was filled with brightness. She was Demeter, she told the awestruck women. They must build her a great temple near the town and so win back the favor of her heart.

Thus she left them, and Metaneira fell speechless to the earth and all there trembled with fear. In the morning they told Celeus what had happened and he called the people together and revealed to them the command of the goddess. They worked willingly to build her a temple, and when it was finished Demeter came to it and sat there—apart from the gods in Olympus, alone, wasting away with longing for her daughter.

That year was most dreadful and cruel for mankind over all the earth. Nothing grew; no seed sprang up; in vain the oxen drew the plowshare through the furrows. It seemed the whole race of men would die of famine. At last Zeus[4] saw that he must take the matter in hand. He sent the gods to Demeter, one after another, to try to turn her from her anger, but she listened to none of them. Never would she let the earth bear fruit until she had seen her daughter. Then Zeus realized that his brother must give way. He told Hermes[5] to go down to the underworld and to bid the lord of it let his bride go back to Demeter.

Hermes found the two sitting side by side, Persephone shrinking away, reluctant because she longed for her mother.

At Hermes' words she sprang up joyfully, eager to go. Her husband knew that he must obey the word of Zeus and send her up to earth away from him; but he prayed her as she left him to have kind thoughts of him and not be so sorrowful that she was the wife of one who was great among the immortals. And he made her eat a pomegranate seed, knowing in his heart that if she did so she must return to him.

He got ready his golden car and Hermes took the reins and drove the black horses straight to the temple where Demeter was. She ran out to meet her daughter as swiftly as a Maenad[6] runs down the mountainside. Persephone sprang into her arms and was held fast there. All day they talked of what had happened to them both, and Demeter grieved when she heard of the pomegranate seed, fearing that she could not keep her daughter with her. **C**

Then Zeus sent another messenger to her, a great personage, none other than his revered mother Rhea, the oldest of the gods. Swiftly she hastened down from the heights of Olympus to the barren, leafless earth, and standing at the door of the temple she spoke to Demeter.

---

4. **Zeus**: in classical mythology, the ruler of the gods.

5. **Hermes**: in classical mythology, the messenger of Zeus.

6. **Maenad**: in classical mythology, a female attendant.

C **Reading Focus** Comparing Themes Compare this description of loss to man's loss of youth in "The Seven Ages of Man." How are the two alike and different?

Vocabulary **manifest** (MAN uh fehst) *adj.*: apparent; obvious.

"Come, my daughter, for Zeus, far-seeing, loud-thundering, bids you. Come once again to the halls of the gods where you shall have honor, where you will have your desire, your daughter, to comfort your sorrow as each year is accomplished and bitter winter is ended. For a third part only the kingdom of darkness shall hold her. For the rest you will keep her, you and the happy immortals. Peace now. Give men life which comes alone from your giving." **Ⓓ**

Demeter did not refuse, poor comfort though it was that she must lose Persephone for four months every year and see her young loveliness go down to the world of the dead. But she was kind; the "Good Goddess," men always called her. She was sorry for the desolation she had brought about. She made the fields once more rich with abundant fruit and the whole world bright with flowers and green leaves. Also she went to the princes of Eleusis who had built her temple and she chose one, Triptolemus, to be her ambassador to men, instructing them how to sow the corn. She taught him and Celeus and the others her sacred rites, "mysteries which no one may utter, for deep awe checks the tongue. Blessed is he who has seen them; his lot will be good in the world to come."

Ⓓ **Literary Focus** **Myths** How does Zeus resolve the conflict and make Demeter happy again?

Analyzing Visuals **Viewing and Interpreting** What part of the myth does this sculpture depict?

Persephone abducted by one of the Dioscuri. Pinax relief. Greek. Museo Archeologico, Taranto, Italy.

Applying Your Skills

RA.L.10.4 Interpret universal themes across different works by the same author or by different authors. *Also covered* **RA.L.10.1; RA.L.10.5; RA.L.10.9; VO.10.6; VO.10.3; WP.10.9**

The Seven Ages of Man / Demeter

Respond and Think Critically

Reading Focus

Quick Check

1. In "The Seven Ages of Man," to what does Shakespeare compare the world? To what does he compare men and women?

2. What are the seven ages of man?

3. In "Demeter," why does Persephone have to stay in Hades for four months of the year?

Read with a Purpose

4. How do both selections show people trying to make sense of their world?

Reading Skills: Comparing Themes Across Genres

5. Review the graphic organizer you created comparing subjects in the selections. Then, come up with a theme statement for each selection. Consider your theme statements. What is universal about these themes? Use your notes as you respond to the Writing Focus on page 975.

✔ Vocabulary Check

Match each Vocabulary word below with its synonym, or word with a similar meaning.

6. **discerned**   a. show
7. **assent**   b. agreement
8. **manifest**   c. recognized

Literary Focus

Literary Analysis

9. **Infer** How does Zeus compromise with Hades to make Demeter content? What is the result of this compromise?

10. **Analyze** Which type of conflict—man versus man, man versus nature, man versus himself—do you think best describes "The Seven Ages of Man"? Explain.

Literary Skills: Monologue

11. **Evaluate** The **dramatic monologue** "The Seven Ages of Man" is very well known. Why do you think it is famous?

Literary Skills: Myths

12. **Interpret** Karen Armstrong, in her book *A Short History of Myth,* notes about "Demeter" that "This is not a simple nature allegory. . . . It is a myth about death." How does "Demeter" explain the patterns of life and death in the world?

Literary Skills Review: Symbols

13. **Analyze** Both selections use symbols that extend the literal meaning of the text. Choose three symbols and explain what each means.

Writing Focus

Think as a Reader/Writer

Review the examples of sensory language you wrote in your *Reader/Writer Notebook*. Think of some aspect of life or nature that could be explained by a myth and write a few paragraphs about it, using as much sensory language as you can.

RA.L.10.4 Interpret universal themes across different works by the same author or by different authors. **RA.L.10.5** Analyze how an author's choice of genre affects the expression of a theme or topic. *Also covered* **WA.10.2**

The Seven Ages of Man / Demeter

Writing Focus

A Comparison-Contrast Essay

Compare and contrast the universal themes in "The Seven Ages of Man" and "Demeter." Consider the following criteria when writing your essay. Be sure your essay includes

- an **introduction** containing the titles and authors of each selection as well as any necessary background information
- a **thesis statement** in the introduction that states how the themes are alike and different
- a **body** that explains in detail the similarities and differences between the treatment of the themes. Discuss at least two main points or ideas in the body. Elaborate on every general statement you make, using details, examples, and quotations from the selections. These details are your supporting information.
- a **conclusion** that sums up your major thoughts and offers a personal response to your findings.

Ask yourself these questions when gathering ideas for the body of your essay:

- How do the different genres contribute to the similarities and differences?
- What are the authors' attitudes toward their themes?
- What does each theme explain about the human experience?

What Do **You Think Now**

What do the selections say about what it means to be human? Explain your thoughts.

CHOICES

As you respond to the Choices, use these **Academic Vocabulary** words as appropriate: highlight, predominant, principal, and criteria.

REVIEW
Analyze a Theme

Timed └Writing Write a short essay responding to the universal theme presented in "The Seven Ages of Man." Tell whether you agree or disagree with Jaques's view on man's life cycle. Use details from the text as well as your own experience to support your opinion.

CONNECT
Write a Monologue

Respond to the speaker of "The Seven Ages of Man" with your own dramatic monologue. You can structure your monologue in the same way, choosing the same seven ages as Shakespeare did, or you may decide to define the ages differently. Give your own view of the stages of human life. Your monologue can be in blank verse or any other form you choose.

EXTEND
Explore More Myths

Find and read other myths that explain natural phenomena. These myths often deal with recurring themes from the human experience, such as our relationships with nature and each other. Choose a myth that interests you and write a short essay about what that myth says about human nature. You may present your findings to the class or share them with a small group of classmates.

Analyzing an Author's Argument

What Do You Think?

How do you decide which movies to see and which books to read?

QuickTalk

Find a partner and discuss a book or movie that you recently read or saw. How did you hear about it? What influenced your decision to read or see it? Was it a good experience? Tell your partner about it.

Preparing to Read

A Big-Name Brutus in a Caldron of Chaos

 **RA.I.10.5** Analyze an author's implicit and explicit argument, perspective or viewpoint in text.

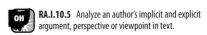 **Reader/Writer Notebook**

Use your **RWN** to complete the activities for this selection.

Informational Text Focus

Evaluating an Argument How do you decide what books to read or movies to see? When professional reviewers write about a book, play, movie, or anything else, they present the information in certain ways. They give their opinions, and they explain how and why they arrived at those opinions. Reviewers may also include their credentials; that is, the background and experience a reviewer has that makes his or her opinions worth reading.

Tips for Evaluating an Argument What does the author of a movie or theater review want to convince you to think and do? Use the following tips to determine a reviewer's **intent,** or purpose.

- Judge the writer's criteria, or standards, for quality. For example, what features or aspects of a performance make it "outstanding"? Which details does the reviewer highlight?

- What is the evidence? This could include informed and critical judgments, examples, or facts. The reviewer might discuss the elements of drama (plot and characters) as well as staging (sets, lighting, and acting).

- How comprehensive, or thorough, is the evidence? You can't prove an opinion; you can only support it. The more details you use to support that opinion, the more convincing it will be.

Into Action Use a chart like the one at the right to help you evaluate the reviewer's overall assessment of the play.

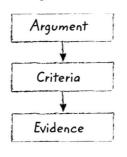

Vocabulary

carnage (KAHR nihj) *n.:* slaughter of a great number of people; butchery. *The survivors of the battle described the carnage on both sides.*

inaudible (ihn AW duh buhl) *adj.:* impossible to hear. *After yelling through three performances, the actor's voice was almost inaudible.*

conspirators (kuhn SPIHR uh tuhrz) *n.:* people who help plan a crime; traitors. *There were many conspirators in the plot to assassinate Caesar.*

Language Coach

Prefixes A **prefix** is a word part that, when added to the front of a word, changes the word's meaning. For example, the word *audible* is used to describe something that can be heard. The Vocabulary word *inaudible* means "impossible to hear." The prefix *in–* gives the word an opposite meaning. Find another word in the selection with the prefix *in–* and determine its meaning.

Writing Focus   Preparing for **Constructed Response**

As you read the following theater review, note the evidence the writer gives to support his opinion in your *Reader/Writer Notebook*.

 Learn It Online
Do pictures and animation help you learn? Try the *PowerNotes* version of this lesson on:

| go.hrw.com | L10-977 | Go |

A Big-Name Brutus in a Caldron of Chaos

by BEN BRANTLEY

from The New York Times

Read with a Purpose
Read the following selection to identify a reviewer's <u>criteria</u> for a good production of a play.

Build Background
The following review covered a 2005 Broadway production in New York City of the play *Julius Caesar*. Academy Award–winning actor Denzel Washington played the character of Brutus. It was the first time the play had been performed on Broadway in more than fifty years.

Those cruel forces of history known as the dogs of war are on a rampage at the Belasco Theater during a carnage-happy production of Shakespeare's *Julius Caesar*. Dripping blood and breathing smoke, these specters[1] are chewing up and spitting out everything in their path: friends, Romans, countrymen, blank verse, emotional credibility, a man who would be king and even the noblest movie star of them all, he whom the masses call Denzel.

That's Denzel Washington, the two-time Academy Award winner. He's the reason theater-goers are lining up to see this show. This play hasn't drawn such crowds in New York since Al Pacino gnawed his way through Mark Antony's funeral oration at the Public Theater seventeen years ago. Mr. Washington has taken on the quieter but meatier role of Brutus.

As the most important passenger on Daniel Sullivan's fast, bumpy ride of a production, Mr. Washington does not embarrass himself, as leading citizens of Hollywood have been known to do on Broadway. But even in the glow of fame, he can't help getting lost amid the mismatched crowd and the heavy topical artillery assembled here. **(A)**

This is regrettable, since Mr. Washington would appear an inspired choice. The character Brutus anticipates Hamlet in divided feelings about bloody deeds. And among leading American film actors, Mr. Washington has all but cornered the market on advanced ambivalence.[2] Whether playing smugly evil (*Training Day*) or raggedly heroic (*The Manchurian Candidate*), he gives off a grave, unsettled air. His world seems to be a symphony of mixed signals. Casting him as "poor Brutus, with himself at war," must have seemed like a no-brainer.

---

1. **specters** (SPEHK tuhrz): ghosts.

2. **ambivalence** (am BIHV uh luhns): uncertainty.

Vocabulary **carnage** (KAHR nihj) *n.*: slaughter of a great number of people; butchery.

(A) **Informational Focus** **Evaluating Argument** How would you describe the tone of this review at this point?

Actor Denzel Washington as Brutus in Daniel Sullivan's 2005 Broadway production of *Julius Caesar.*

In several shining sequences, Mr. Washington justifies his presence in this production. It is telling, however, that such moments usually occur during monologues. These scenes require little or no interaction with others. In the second-act soliloquy in which Brutus considers the planned assassination of the tyrant Caesar (William Sadler), Mr. Washington is filled with the uneasiness of a good man struggling against instinct. **Ⓑ**

He has the tired, open face of someone long battered by doubt. This same quality is surprisingly and affectingly carried over into the speech Brutus makes to the frightened mob after Caesar has been slain. You can sense why the people like Brutus. You can also understand why they will soon be putty in the hands of the more flamboyant and assured Mark Antony (Eamonn Walker).

This Brutus, however, so often seems plagued less by moral and philosophical uncertainty than by a kind of insecurity. Mr. Washington's voice becomes rushed and soft and sometimes inaudible. And when other characters are looking to the mighty Brutus for guidance amid chaos, Mr. Washington looks more apologetic than anything else.

Under the circumstances, it's hard to blame him. Mr. Sullivan is an agile director whose credits include

---

Ⓑ **Informational Focus** **Evaluating Argument** Why is it "telling" that Washington only shines during monologues?

Vocabulary **inaudible** (ihn AW duh buhl) *adj.:* impossible to hear.

Proof and *A Moon for the Misbegotten.* But he has populated his *Julius Caesar* with performers who seem to have arrived from different planets in the great galaxy of show business. On the one hand, you have the naturalistic actors[3] like Mr. Washington. They speak Shakespearean speech with the equivalent of an easygoing shrug. On the other hand, you have fiercely classical interpreters who are going for Tragedy with a capital *T*, such as the excellent Colm Feore (as Cassius) and Jessica Hecht (as Portia, Brutus's wife). **C**

Then there is Mr. Walker, whose Mark Antony combines fierceness with incomprehensibility. You have Jack Willis, who plays Casca as a jaunty backroom gossip. Mr. Sadler, a scrappy man with the air of a gangster, portrays the title character as if the play were titled *Little Caesar.* And Kelly AuCoin gives young Octavius Caesar (Julius's great nephew) the cockiness of a lead singer in a boy band.

The overall effect is bewildering, like a free-for-all concert in which opera, jazz, light rock and musical comedy are all performed. Points of emotional connection among the characters are mostly nonexistent.

There is little sense of the crucial, shifting relationships among the conspirators. When Mr. Feore's Cassius and Mr. Washington's Brutus fight and make up on the fields of battle, the impression is of scenes from different films spliced together. Everyone manages to convey intensity, but rarely with any specificity of character.

Mr. Sullivan, perhaps of necessity, shifts the burden of interpretation to the staging. Designed by Ralph Funicello (sets), Jess Goldstein (costumes), and Mimi Jordan Sherin (lighting), the production has a war-is-still-hell look. It will be familiar to anyone who has spent time at the National Theater in London or the New York Shakespeare Festival in Central Park.

The setting is a ravaged, vaguely Balkan-looking ancient city. Armed thugs lurk in shadows. Soldiers sport berets and guerrilla[4] fatigues. Plaster falls to the sound of exploding bombs. Accessories include photo I.D. tags and metal detectors. How the conspirators manage to bypass the latter in smuggling daggers becomes a matter of distracting stage business involving a battered briefcase.

Mr. Sullivan keeps things moving, though the general impression is blurry, like a landscape seen through the window of a speeding train. In the second half of the show, blood spurts in geysers. There is one especially grisly decapitation. And the suicides of Brutus and Cassius are rendered in gut-churning detail. But without having come to know these tragic losers, you may find it hard to work up sentiment about their demises, however grisly. **D**

Mr. Washington's Brutus bites the dust with convincing bravado. But it says much about this production that his final invocation of the ghost of Caesar ("I killed not thee with half so good a will") is muffled by the noise of his death throes.

Read with a Purpose What are the author's principal criteria in judging this performance of *Julius Caesar*?

---

3. **naturalistic actors:** Naturalistic acting tries to capture everyday ways of speaking and behaving.

4. **guerrilla:** a fighting technique that includes sudden raids and ambushes on the enemy.

C **Informational Focus** Evaluating Argument How does drawing attention to the different styles of acting support the reviewer's overall argument?

D **Informational Focus** Evaluating Argument What is the reviewer saying about the audience's reaction to the play?

Vocabulary **conspirators** (kuhn SPIHR uh tuhrz) *n.*: people who help plan a crime; traitors.

THEATER REVIEW
Applying Your Skills

RA.I.10.5 Analyze an author's implicit and explicit argument, perspective or viewpoint in text. VO.10.3 Infer the literal and figurative meaning of words and phrases and discuss the function of figurative language, including metaphors, similes, idioms and puns.

A Big-Name Brutus in a Caldron of Chaos

Practicing the Standards

Informational Text and Vocabulary

1. What is one <u>criterion</u> the reviewer uses to judge the actors' performances?

   A Fame

   B Success

   C Clear speaking

   D Physical strength

2. What **evidence** does the reviewer give to support his overall impression?

   A He says one actor is incomprehensible.

   B He writes about the set design.

   C He describes Denzel Washington's performance.

   D He describes the acting styles of the different actors.

3. What **argument** does the reviewer make about this production of *Julius Caesar*?

   A It has some good points but overall is poorly done.

   B It is terrible, with no redeeming qualities.

   C It is an excellent production in all respects.

   D It should have been staged in Central Park.

4. Which of the following statements does Brantley make about the production?

   A There is no finer play on Broadway.

   B The actors show a deep sense of connection with each other.

   C The deaths of some of the characters are overdone.

   D Mr. Washington would have been a good choice to play Brutus.

5. *Carnage* refers to —

   A embarrassment

   B intimidation

   C slaughter

   D mercy

6. A speaker who is *inaudible* is —

   A difficult to hear

   B confusing

   C clear-speaking

   D fascinating

7. A *conspirator* —

   A is a traveler

   B has spent time in jail

   C helps plan a crime

   D sells exotic items

Writing Focus Constructed Response

List three examples of evidence the author uses to support his opinion. Would these influence your decision whether or not to attend the play? Write a few sentences explaining your response.

What Do You Think Now

Are you more likely to read a review the next time you want to see a movie or find a good book? Why or why not?

Literary Skills Review

Elements of Drama   **Directions:** Read the following selection. Then, read and respond to the questions that follow.

from 12-1-A by **Wakako Yamauchi**

The following excerpt from *12-1-A* takes place in barracks 12-1-A of a Japanese internment camp during World War II. The main characters are Mrs. Tanaka (a widow) and her children Koko and Mitch. In this scene, Mitch is filling out a questionnaire from the U.S. government.

A February night, 1943. Inside 12-1-A. HAR-RY'S *chair is in the corner. The bowling trophy remains visible. It is bitter cold.* MITCH *sits at the table in a bathrobe, pajama tops, shoes, and socks.* MRS. TANAKA, *in a robe, crochets a muffler.* MITCH *fills out a questionnaire, squinting over the forms in the weak overhead light. There is quarreling in the Ichioka barrack.* MRS. TANAKA *looks at* MITCH.

Mrs. Ichioka *(offstage).* You writing again? *(No response.)* More better you write to President Roosevelt. Give him report of camp.

[KOKO *enters. She wears a pea coat[1] over her uniform. She shivers from the cold.*]

Mitch. Working overtime?
Mrs. Ichioka *(offstage).* Tell him come live with us. Sell everything for five dollars a piece and come live with us.

KoKo *(overlapping).* There was an emergency. Are those the questionnaires?

Mitch. You ought to come home after eight hours.

KoKo. Can't. Patients get sick regardless of the time. Well, I guess the experience will come in handy outside. I could get a job in a hospital. I guess they'll be paying more than sixteen dollars.

Mitch *(reading the form).* I should hope so. Ma, are we registered with the Japanese consul?[2]

Mrs. Tanaka. I don't think so. No. Papa died before. *(reminisces)* I told him every year, every year, "Register the kids; register the kids…" But he never did.

Mitch. Lucky for us now.

KoKo. Have we decided where to go?

Mitch. Lot of guys at the motor pool are talking 'bout Chicago. You wanta go there?

KoKo. I want to go back home.

Mitch. Forget that. They won't let us back there. *(reading the form)* Was Pa ever in the Japanese army? *(To* KOKO.*)* Plenty of bedpans in Chicago, Koko.

KoKo. Funny.

---

1. **pea coat:** a short, double-breasted, usually dark blue coat worn especially by sailors.

2. **consul:** an official appointed by a government to live in a foreign city. The consul looks after the business interests of his or her country and protects its citizens who are traveling or living in the city.

Mrs. Tanaka. Papa don't like army. That's why he came to America… so he won't have to go to army. He was peaceful man. He was eighteen then. Younger than you, Michio.

KoKo. There's a lot of army people… suddenly you see so many soldiers around. They're stepping up the recruiting.

Mitch *(contemptuously).* Fat chance they got! You'd have to have rocks in your head to volunteer. No one I know is… They'd have to sneak out in the middle of the night… *(still reading the questionnaire)* Look here. It says, "List all the addresses you have ever lived in for the period of as much as three months during the last twenty years." For crying out loud!

Mrs. Tanaka. We moved lots… lots. Mama had to live near work. Ah… can't remember addresses.

Mitch. I'll just put down some that I remember.

KoKo. Do them right, Mitch. You're filling out ours, too, aren't you? They should be consistent. Otherwise, they might not release us. *(removes her coat and quickly puts it back on after realizing the cold)* Or, worse yet, they might let us out one at a time.

[MITCH *stretches, yawns, and rubs his eyes.*]

Mitch. They'll be the same. They'll be perfect. We'll get out together or we won't go at all. Don't worry.

KoKo. Have we decided where to go?

Mitch. Let's get free first.

KoKo. We ought to go with friends. You or Ken. It'll be so lonely without friends. I wonder where the Ichiokas are planning to go.

Mrs. Tanaka. I don't know.

KoKo. Since I started working nights, I hardly see Ken anymore. I wonder if he's all right.

Mitch. I saw him in the mess hall tonight. He looks bad. Maybe he's sick. I hope he's not cracking up. Those types sometimes do, you know.

Mrs. Tanaka. Lots of fighting over there. *(meaning the Ichioka barrack)*

KoKo. Poor Ken.

Mrs. Tanaka. Yo-chan still going Montana?

KoKo. That's what she says. Gosh, I'm going to miss her.

Mrs. Tanaka. Can't go with everybody.

KoKo. When we make nice home, she will visit, ne?

[MITCH *returns to the questionnaire and suddenly springs to life.*]

Mitch. Holy mack! It says here… Boy, what a nerve!

KoKo. What? What?

Mitch. It says here. "Are you willing to serve in the armed forces of the United States on combat duty wherever ordered? That means…

[MITCH *stops. No one speaks. He slams the paper on the table.*]

Mitch. So that's why they're here.

KoKo. Who?

Mitch *(grimly).* That's why they're here. The recruiters. It's a frame-up…it's a trap! They need cannon fodder![3] *(slams his fist on the table)* They got us again. They got us again! What does it take for us to wise up? *(he grows stony)* Well, I'm not falling for it. No. I'll stay right here. I'll stay here 'til I rot.

[KOKO *takes the paper and reads it.*]

KoKo. But, Mitch, if you don't say yes, they might put you in jail!

Mrs. Tanaka. Jail!

Mitch. I don't care. If I say yes, they'll put me in the front line. They take away every right we have except the right to be shot at. No. I'll rot here first. I'll rot.

Mrs. Tanaka. What it say, Michio?

[MITCH *walks away from the table.*]

KoKo. It says if he says yes to the question, he goes to combat. If he says no, he's a traitor, Ma. A traitor is… Ma, Mitch might have to go jail or they might… Mitch! You can't say no!

Mitch. Hell, I'm not scared of no firing squad. I'm not afraid to die… not for what I believe in. I believe in freedom… equal rights for all men! I'm the real patriot! *(jumps on the table)* Look at me, Koko… I'm the true patriot!

I'm acting in the grand tradition of Patrick Henry.[4] Remember the guy? "Give me liberty or give me death!" *(makes a trumpet with his hands)* Tada-da-dum-to-da!

KoKo. Mitch, don't…

Mrs. Tanaka. Come down, Michio.

[*In his bathrobe* MITCH *marches in place on the table.*]

Mitch. Mine eyes have seen the glory of the coming of the Lord / He has trampled out the vintage where the grapes of wrath are stored…[5]

[KOKO *puts her hands on* MITCH's *legs.*]

KoKo. Stop… Shhh… Mitch. Make him stop, Mama.

Mrs. Tanaka. Shhh! Ichioka son's sick. Be quiet! Stop right now, Michio!

Mitch. Glory, glory hallelujah!/Glory, glory, hallelujah!/Glory, glory…

Mrs. Tanaka. Michio! No more! Koko is crying now!

[MITCH *jumps down.*]

Mrs. Tanaka *(trying to calm herself).* Calm down.

Mitch. It's okay, Koko. I'm not going crazy. But I'm not going to say yes. You have to

---

3. **fodder: coarse food for domestic animals;** here, it is used as a metaphor.

4. **Patrick Henry:** American **patriot who gained fame during the Revolutionary War by stating,** "… give me liberty or give me death."

5. **lyrics to "Battle Hymn of the Republic."**

understand that. You'll have to shoot me on the spot before I say yes.

KoKo. But, Mitch, I don't want to say no. I don't want to go to prison. I want to stay right here. I want to stay here!

Mitch. You can answer yes. There's no reason for you to say no. They can't take women for combat duty. It's all right. You and Ma, you'll be free. You can make it together.

Mrs. Tanaka. We stay together, Michio.

Mitch. I've made up my mind, Ma. You can't change it.

Mrs. Tanaka. If we separate now, we maybe never see each other again. We stay together.

Mitch. I made up my mind.

Mrs. Tanaka. Mama make up mind, too. *(more calmly)* Now. All questions same for everybody?

Mitch. The same for everybody. Everyone over seventeen.

Mrs. Tanaka. We say no then. Koko and Mama, too.

KoKo. No!

Mitch. No? But Ma, it won't hurt to say yes. You'll be free.

Mrs. Tanaka. We say no together.

Mitch. I'd rather do this alone, Ma. It might get pretty rough and…I can do it alone better. You can't tell what will happen.

Mrs. Tanaka. If they shoot, they shoot us together.

Mitch. I don't think they'll do that. They'll probably deport us. Send us to Tule Lake and then…

KoKo. Tule Lake!

Mrs. Tanaka. Tule Lake, this camp, that camp, all the same. Camp is camp, ne, Koko?

KoKo *(in protest).* We'll be leaving all our friends!

Mrs. Tanaka *(firmly).* We stand by Michio, ne, Koko? Together. One family. We live together or die together. We be together.

Mitch. It might get rough, Ma. We may starve out there.

Mrs. Tanaka. Then we be hungry together. Ne, Koko? Papa be proud of us.

[KOKO *straightens up.*]

Mitch. You really mean it, don't you?

Mrs. Tanaka. We mean it, Michio.

Mitch. I'm proud of you, too. I'm proud of our little family. Eh, Koko?

KoKo. Yes. *(reads the rest of the questionnaire)* Question twenty-eight: "Will you swear unqualified allegiance to…"

Mitch. Unqualified…

KoKo. "To the United States of America and faithfully defend the United States from any or all attack…" *(skims over couple of sentences)* "and foreswear any form of allegiance or obedience to the Japanese emperor, to any…

Mrs. Tanaka. That's okay, Koko. We go to Tule Lake. No-no to both questions. Michio, we go to Tule.

OH **RA.L.10.5** Analyze how an author's choice of genre affects the expression of a theme or topic. **RA.L.10.6** Explain how literary techniques, including foreshadowing and flashback, are used to shape the plot of a literary text. *Also covered:* **RA.L.10.1**

1. What is the primary <u>conflict</u> faced by the characters in this play?

   A. man vs. man

   B. man vs. himself

   C. man vs. nature

   D. man vs. family

2. How does Mitch's <u>character</u> change when his mother decides she and Koko will say no to all the questions too?

   A. He gets more defiant toward the government.

   B. He gets angry at the others.

   C. He becomes sad about their situation.

   D. He becomes proud of his family.

3. What do the <u>stage directions</u> indicate?

   A. where the props are placed

   B. why the family goes to Tule Lake

   C. how the characters are feeling

   D. what the characters look like

4. The <u>climax</u> of this scene occurs when

   A. Mitch realizes the purpose of the questionnaire.

   B. the Ichiokas are arguing.

   C. Mitch starts singing.

   D. Mrs. Tanaka says they will stay together as a family.

5. What does Mitch express in his <u>dramatic monologue</u>?

   A. his defiance

   B. His sorrow

   C. his love

   D. his sense of victory

6. Which of these statements is not true?

   A. The action takes place during World War II.

   B. The family wants to split up.

   C. Mitch wants to avoid becoming a soldier in the U.S. Army.

   D. Mrs. Tanaka believes Papa would be proud of the family.

Short Answer

7. What stage directions are given to Koko at the end of the excerpt? Explain what the directions indicate about Koko.

Extended Response

8. Write a paragraph describing a set you would design for this scene. Describe how your set design conveys the scene's conflict and allows the actors to perform the actions described in the play's stage directions.

Informational Skills Review

Analyzing an Author's Argument **Directions:** Read the following
selection. Then, read and respond to the questions that follow.

Julius Caesar in an Absorbing Production

from **The New York Post** by **John Mason Brown,** November 12, 1937

This is no funeral oration such as Miss Bankhead and Mr. Tearle forced me to deliver yesterday when they interred *Antony and Cleopatra*.[1] I come to praise *Caesar* at the Mercury, not to bury it. Of all the many new plays and productions the season has so far revealed, this modern-dress version of the mob mischief and demagoguery[2] which can follow the assassination of a dictator is by all odds the most exciting, the most imaginative, the most topical, the most awesome, and the most absorbing.

The astonishing, all-impressive virtue of Mr. Welles's *Julius Caesar* is that, magnificent as it is as theater, it is far larger than its medium. Something deathless and dangerous in the world sweeps past you down the darkened aisles at the Mercury and takes possession of the proud, gaunt stage. . . . It is an ageless warning, made in such arresting terms that it not only gives a new vitality to an ancient story but unrolls in your mind's eye a map of the world which is increasingly splotched with sickening colors.

Mr. Welles does not dress his conspirators and his Storm Troopers in Black Shirts or in Brown.[3] He does not have to. The antique Rome, which we had thought was securely Roman in Shakespeare's tragedy, he shows us to be a dateless state of mind.... To an extent no other director in our day and country has equaled, Mr. Welles proves in his production that Shakespeare was indeed not of an age but for all time. After this surly modern Caesar, dressed in a green uniform and scowling behind the mask-like face of a contemporary dictator, has fallen at the Mercury and new mischief is afoot, we cannot but shudder before the prophet's wisdom of those lines which read:

> "How many ages hence
> Shall this our lofty scene be acted over
> In states unborn and accents yet unknown!"[4]

---

1. Actors Tallulah Bankhead and Conway Tearle opened in *Antony and Cleopatra* on November 10, 1937. Mr. Brown reviewed the play, produced by Orson Welles, unfavorably.
2. demagoguery: method of appealing to the emotions of people in order to stir up discontent and gain power.
3. Storm . . . Brown: Storm troopers, members of Hitler's Nazi-party militia, wore brown shirts. In Italy, Mussolini's Fascist party members wore uniforms with black shirts.
4. Lines 111–113, spoken by Cassius in Act III, Scene 1.

To fit the play into modern dress and give it its fullest implication,[5] Mr. Welles has not hesitated to take his liberties with the script. Unlike Professor Strunk, however, who attempted to improve upon *Antony and Cleopatra,* he has not stabbed it through the heart. He has only chopped away at its body. You may miss a few fingers, even an arm and leg in the *Julius Caesar* you thought you knew. But the heart of the drama beats more vigorously in this production than it has in years. If the play ceases to be Shakespeare's tragedy, it does manage to become ours. That is the whole point and glory of Mr. Welles's unorthodox, but welcome, restatement of it.

He places it upon a bare stage, the brick walls of which are crimson[6] and naked. A few steps and a platform and an abyss[7] beyond are the setting. A few steps—and the miracle of enveloping shadows, knifelike rays, and superbly changing lights. . . .

His direction, which is constantly creative, is never more so than in its first revelation of Caesar hearing the warning of the soothsayer, or in the fine scene in which Cinna, the poet, is engulfed by a sinister crowd of ruffians.[8] Even when one misses Shakespeare's lines, Mr. Welles keeps drumming the meaning of his play into our minds by the scuffling of his mobs when they prowl in the shadows, or the herd-like thunder of their feet when they run as one threatening body. It is a memorable device. Like the setting in which it is used, it is pure theater: vibrant, unashamed, and enormously effective.

The theatrical virtues of this modern-dress *Julius Caesar* do not stop with its excitements as a stunt in showmanship. They extend to the performances. As Brutus Mr. Welles shows once again how uncommon is his gift for speaking great words simply. His

5. implication: suggested meaning.
6. crimson: deep red.
7. abyss: deep gulf or pit.

8. ruffians: tough people; hoodlums.

tones are conversational. His manner is quiet. The deliberation of his speech is the mark of the honesty which flames within him. His reticent Brutus is at once a foil to the staginess of the production as a whole and to the oratory[9] of Caesar and Antony. He is a perplexed liberal, this Brutus; an idealist who is swept by bad events into actions which have no less dangerous consequences for the state. His simple reading of the funeral oration is in happy contrast to what is usually done with the speech.

George Coulouris is an admirable Antony. So fresh is his characterization, so intelligent his performance that even "Friends, Romans, countrymen" sounds on his tongue as if it were a rabble-rousing harangue[10] which he is uttering for the first time. Joseph Holland's Caesar is an imperious[11] dictator who could be found frowning at you in this week's newsreels. He is excellently conceived and excellently projected. Some mention, however inadequate, must be made of Martin Gabel's capable Cassius, of John Hoysradt's Decius Brutus, of the conspirators whose black hats are pluck'd about their ears, and Norman Lloyd's humorous yet deeply affecting Cinna.

It would be easy to find faults here and there: to wonder about the wisdom of some of the textual changes even in terms of the present production's aims; to complain that the whole tragedy does not fit with equal ease into its modern treatment; and to wish this or that scene had been played a little differently. But such faultfindings strike me in the case of this *Julius Caesar* as being as picayune[12] as they are ungrateful. What Mr. Welles and his associates at the Mercury have achieved is a triumph that is exceptional from almost every point of view.

---

9. **oratory: skilled public speaking.**
10. **rabble-rousing harangue: scolding speech designed to arouse people to anger.**
11. **imperious: arrogant; domineering.**
12. **picayune: trivial; unimportant.**

Informational Skills Review

RA.I.10.5 Analyze an author's implicit and explicit argument, perspective or viewpoint in text. *Also covered:* **WA.10.2**

CONTINUED

1. "It is by odds the most exciting, the most imaginative, the most topical, the most awesome, and the most absorbing" is what kind of statement?

   A. evidence

   B. statement of criteria

   C. opinion statement

   D. summary

2. The reviewer argues that this version of the play presents a "dateless state of mind." What <u>evidence</u> does he use to support this claim?

   A. the changed dialogue

   B. the costume choices

   C. the bare stage

   D. the choice of actors

3. According to the reviewer, why does the director "take his liberties with the script"?

   A. to rewrite Shakespeare

   B. to be more relevant to the audience

   C. to show the play in modern dress

   D. to highlight the characters' flaws

4. What is the overall tone of the review?

   A. disappointed   C. excited

   B. negative   D. confused

5. The reviewer relies heavily on which of the following to make his points?

   A. debate

   B. description

   C. opinion

   D. quotations

6. Which statement is not an <u>opinion</u>?

   A. "It is a memorable device."

   B. "But the heart of the drama beats more vigorously in this production than it has in years."

   C. "George Coulouris is an admirable Antony."

   D. "He places it upon a bare stage, the brick walls of which are crimson and naked."

7. One aspect of the production that Brown does not discuss in this review is the

   A. actors' performances.

   B. set.

   C. costumes.

   D. audience's reaction.

Short Answer

8. Explain why the reviewer does not point out any faults in this production. Cite a quote from the review to support your explanation.

Extended Response

9. Write a paragraph evaluating the types of evidence Brown uses to support his positive opinion of Welles's production. Decide whether the evidence is convincing and discuss how credible you find his argument.

Vocabulary Skills Review

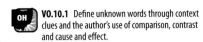

V0.10.1 Define unknown words through context clues and the author's use of comparison, contrast and cause and effect.

Synonyms **Directions:** Choose the best synonym for the underlined vocabulary word in each sentence.

1. In *Trifles,* the women look <u>abashed</u> when the sheriff and county attorney overhear them discussing the quilt that Mrs. Wright was sewing.
   A. scared
   B. embarrased
   C. amused
   D. upset

2. Mrs. Peters tells the county attorney that cats are <u>superstitious</u>.
   A. quick
   B. unpredictable
   C. fearful of the unknown
   D. unreliable

3. In *The Brute,* Luka tells Smirnov that Mrs. Popov is <u>indisposed</u>.
   A. angry
   B. impossible
   C. nervous
   D. unwell

4. Smirnov challenges Mrs. Popov to a duel, saying that no one, not even a woman, can insult him with <u>impunity</u>.
   A. embarrassment
   B. honor
   C. disrespect
   D. pity

5. In his review of *Julius Caesar,* Ben Brantley describes the production as "<u>carnage</u>-happy."
   A. slaughter
   B. dream
   C. war
   D. ego

6. In "Demeter," the goddess is not easily <u>discerned</u> by mortals.
   A. understood
   B. recognized
   C. liked
   D. desired

Academic Vocabulary

Directions: Choose the *best* synonym for each underlined Academic Vocabulary word below.

7. The <u>predominant</u> theme in *Julius Caesar* is the betrayal of trust.
   A. first
   B. main
   C. secondary
   D. domineering

8. Chekhov uses stage directions to <u>highlight</u> Mrs. Popov's agitated state of mind.
   A. emphasize
   B. conceal
   C. influence
   D. deny

Read On

DRAMA

A Raisin in the Sun

Lorraine Hansberry's stirring drama *A Raisin in the Sun* takes us inside the home of the Younger family—five larger-than-life personalities cramped but not crushed by their small, shabby living space. Each of the Youngers has big dreams—and no one's dreams are bigger than those of Walter, who thinks that money will solve his family's problems. You'll be moved by this story of an African American family's fortunes, losses, and hopes.

DRAMA

A Book of Plays

Some of the greatest plays ever to hit the stage are compiled in *A Book of Plays*. Here you'll have a front-row seat to drama that is astonishing in scope—featuring everything from a heartbreaking family story (Tennessee Williams's *The Glass Menagerie*) to a witty dialogue (Dorothy Parker's *Here We Are*). The Russian playwright Anton Chekhov and the Irish playwright John Millington Synge add a distinguished international flavor to the collection.

DRAMA

Macbeth

Julius Caesar is not the only assassinated leader featured in a Shakespearean tragedy. In 1040, a Scottish chieftain named Macbeth killed King Duncan I and seized the throne of Scotland. Shakespeare dramatized this story in his tragedy *Macbeth*—a play whose characters grapple with family loyalties, greed, and the price of ambition. You may find that this tale of medieval intrigue provides shocking contrasts to *The Tragedy of Julius Caesar*.

DRAMA

The Cherry Orchard

The Cherry Orchard is a 1903 play about a once-wealthy Russian family losing its ancestral home. In an attempt to face reality, Madame Ranevsky and her retinue arrive at the failing estate with its beloved cherry trees. Rather than let her land be sold off to build middle-class villas—and the orchard be destroyed—she plots other silly, heartless solutions. Anton Chekhov's last play contains hopeless love and loveless marriages, but it also displays his always-deepening understanding of human nature.

DRAMA
The Mousetrap

The Mousetrap by Agatha Christie is a classic whodunit set in an isolated manor during a snowstorm. The characters include the owners of the manor, the various guests, and a policeman who arrives to tell everyone that a killer is on his way there. Several of the characters are acting suspiciously and even match the description of the killer. The audience is kept guessing until the very end, when the killer turns out to be the least obvious character. Christie's play, which opened in London in 1952, is the longest continuously running stage play in history, with more than 22,000 performances.

DRAMA
The Twilight Zone Scripts

The Twilight Zone was a very popular TV show that originally aired from 1959 to 1964. Its stories often combined science fiction, horror, and eerie events in seemingly ordinary settings. The stories nearly always had a trick ending or twist that would leave viewers surprised and at times baffled. Here are eight of the scripts, including "The Invaders," in which a lone woman battles tiny spacemen; "Little Girl Lost," which shows that crawling under your bed can be dangerous; and "The Last Flight," in which a WWI biplane flies into a cloud and emerges in the future.

DRAMA
The Piano Lesson

Boy Willie wants to sell a family piano to buy some land that his family once worked as slaves. His sister Bernice opposes his plan because the piano's legs contain the family's history in elaborate carvings. Furthermore, Bernice has started seeing the ghost of Sutter, the landowner, and she thinks his appearance has something to do with the piano. In August Wilson's *The Piano Lesson*, the argument escalates until Bernice sees a way to exorcise Sutter's ghost and resolve the conflict.

DRAMA
Novio Boy

For ninth-grader Rudy, the good news is that he has managed to get a date with eleventh-grader Patricia. The bad news is that now he has to come up with the money, the poise, and the conversation to carry this off. Soto's one-act play, *Novio Boy*, is by turns heartwarming and heart-wrenching, as it follows Rudy from his desperate search for guidance through the hilarious date itself—all the way to its happy conclusion, despite interference from his mom, uncle, and best friend Alex.

Learn It Online
Explore other dramas with *NovelWise* online:

go.hrw.com | L10-993 | **Go**

Writing Workshop

Informative Essay

Write with a Purpose

Write an essay that provides information about a topic that interests you. The **purpose** of the essay is to inform an audience about your subject. Your **audience** may be teachers, students, or others in your community.

A Good Informative Essay

- presents a main idea, or thesis
- presents accurate and complete information
- provides evidence including facts and details
- follows a clear organizational structure
- presents information in an objective way, without the author's opinion

See page 1003 for complete rubric.

Reader/Writer Notebook

Use your **RWN** to complete the activities for this workshop.

Think as a Reader/Writer

In this collection, you've read several informative essays about a variety of topics. When writing your **informative essay,** think of what your audience needs to know. This excerpt from Salleh Buang's essay on new urbanism provides an excellent example of how to address the needs of the reader.

> In the late 1940s, just after the end of World War II, an American named William Levitt began a "revolution" in a potato field in Long Island, New York. He built 2,000 simple, standard houses for returning soldiers. In time, that small community grew to become known as Levittown. The "revolution" that it helped to bring about is now known as "suburbism"—in simple terms, the growth of suburbia.
>
> These suburbs are typically some distance away from the central business district of a city as well as work places. Residents of suburbia therefore have no choice but to rely on transportation to do just about anything and everything—leading to traffic jams on the roads, all day and even on most nights.
>
> Finding traditional suburbia no longer pleasant, a new movement has surfaced. Called "new urbanism," its advocates in the U.S. have established Seaside in Florida as their experimental community.
>
> Peter Gordon, a professor at the University of Southern California's Graduate School of Policy, Planning and Development, said new urbanism has one flaw: "People actually like suburbia."

← Buang puts the information in **historical perspective** by providing the date the first suburbs were built.

← He addresses several issues arising from suburbism.

← Buang clearly defines "new urbanism."

← He quotes an expert. This adds interest and suggests that he is a credible, reliable writer who did thorough research.

Think About the Professional Model

1. How does the author add interest to the opening paragraph and introduce the topic?

2. Where does the author state the thesis of the essay?

3. How does the author show that the topic has a broad audience?

WA.10.4.d Write informational essays or reports, including research that: support the main ideas with facts, details, examples and explanations from sources; and **WP.10.3** Establish and develop a clear thesis statement for informational writing or a clear plan or outline for narrative writing. **WP.10.8** Use paragraph form in writing, including topic sentences that arrange paragraphs in a logical sequence, using effective transitions and closing sentences and maintaining coherence across the whole through the use of parallel structures.

Prewriting

Choose Your Topic

When considering topics for any essay, start by thinking about subjects that interest you or that you already know something about. If you are excited and informed about a topic, try to convey that interest to your audience. Use the Idea Starters at the right to choose a topic.

Think About Purpose and Audience

The **purpose** of an informative essay is to provide information for the reader. Unlike a persuasive essay, an informative essay gives information in an objective, balanced manner. Think about what your **audience** needs to know, which might be different from what you like most about your topic. It could mean that you need to write about certain aspects of your topic before discussing others. For example, if you write about a historical event, your reader may first need to know about events leading up to that event. Ask yourself the following questions about your topic:

What do I already know about the topic?

What do I need to research about the topic?

What does my audience need to know?

What does my audience want to know?

Gather Information

Now that you have analyzed your audience and topic, begin to gather information. Look for the following kinds of evidence:

- **Fact**—information that can be proven
- **Example**—specific instances of an idea or situation
- **Expert Opinion**—statements by people considered to be experts
- **Statistic**—fact expressed as numerical information
- **Anecdote**—brief personal story that illustrates a point
- **Quotation**—someone's exact words

Choose Reliable Internet Sources

Although the World Wide Web is a great resource for information, anyone can create a Web site. This means that the information posted is not necessarily accurate or reliable. When choosing sources, consider where the information came from, who put it there, and why.

Idea Starters

- hobbies, sports, extracurricular activities
- favorite classes: art, history, political science, etc.
- places you've visited or want to visit
- interesting people
- historical events
- local landmarks such as buildings or famous places
- exotic animals
- global or climate issues

Peer Review

Share your topic with a small group of classmates. Ask them to write three questions they really want answered about your topic. If they don't have questions, your topic may be too broad, and you may want to reconsider your choice.

Your Turn _____

Get Started Make a list of possible topics for an informative essay in your **RWN**. Narrow your possibilities down to just a few. Then, make notes about sources you might use in your investigation. Consider the availability of information when making your final topic choice.

Learn It Online
Try an interactive graphic organizer at:

go.hrw.com   L10-995   **Go**

● Writing Tip

Narrow Your Scope One challenge in writing an informative essay is deciding how much information—or how little—to include. How do you decide? Considering the length of your paper is a good place to start. The following questions may also help:

- What is the most important aspect of this topic?
- How many points do I want or need to address?
- Can I write a whole paper on this topic? If your answer is "no," the topic may be too narrow.
- Could I write several papers on this topic? If your answer is "yes," the topic is probably too broad for a single paper.

Your Turn _____

Write Your Thesis and Organize Your Ideas Use your notes to formulate a thesis statement. Then, begin organizing your ideas into the different parts of a well-structured informative essay.

Write Your Thesis Statement

When you are writing an informative essay, the **thesis statement** is more than just your topic. The thesis statement announces what you want to say about the topic in a sentence or two. Found in the first paragraph, the thesis statement guides the reader to the main ideas in your essay. Notice the key words in the following thesis; they indicate the essay's focus: *urban sprawl, direct impact, economy,* and *health.*

Topic:	urban sprawl
Thesis Statement:	Urban sprawl has a direct impact on the whole nation's economy, affecting the health of cities and rural areas alike.

Use these pointers to write your thesis statement:

- Develop your thesis from your prewriting notes. What is the most important idea, the one that connects all of the information?
- Make your thesis clear and specific.
- Use your thesis statement as a guide as you plan and write. Remember, your essay should support and develop the central ideas expressed in your thesis.

Organize Your Essay

Once you have a thesis statement, it's time to start organizing your thoughts. Use the following chart to help you start organizing your essay. Jot down your ideas for each part in your *Reader/Writer Notebook.* This framework can also guide the drafting of your informative essay.

Framework for an Informative Essay

Introduction
- Grab the reader's attention.
- Include your topic and thesis statement.
- Provide basic background facts.

Body
- Provide additional definitions and background if necessary.
- Address issues related to thesis.
- Provide reliable evidence to support thesis.

Conclusion
- Summarize main points.
- Close with a final point for your reader to think about.

Drafting

Follow the Writer's Framework

The opening paragraph of your essay introduces the topic and thesis statement to your audience. Think of the **introduction** as a "hook." It provides enough information for the reader to know what your paper is about and interesting elements to make the reader want to continue reading.

The **body** of your informative essay must be both unified and coherent. **Unity** is the quality achieved when all of the sentences in a paragraph work together as a unit to express one main idea that supports the thesis statement. **Coherence** is achieved when all of the information, specific details, and other evidence are logically arranged and clearly connected to each other within and among the paragraphs. Direct references and transitions build coherence.

The **conclusion** summarizes or restates the main points and leaves the reader with some "final thoughts" to consider. Readers can then develop their own conclusions. Remember, an informative essay does not offer an opinion; it simply provides information. Readers are left to make up their own minds about the topic.

⬤ Writing Tip

Add Interest Think of how you can engage your reader from the beginning. Use the following tips to add interest to your paper:

- Open with a startling or interesting statistic or fact.
- Use a quote from an expert or one of your references.
- Include a story that illustrates, or shows the topic.
- Ask a rhetorical question about your topic.

The same techniques for a "hook" in the beginning can be used to end your informative essay.

Grammar Link Direct References and Transitional Phrases

Direct references can help you achieve coherence in your essay. They avoid choppiness and isolated information.

- Use a pronoun that refers to a noun or pronoun used earlier.
- Repeat a word used earlier.
- Use a word or phrase that means the same thing as a noun or pronoun used earlier.

Notice how Buang uses a direct reference to link one idea to another and one paragraph to another.

> . . . an American named William Levitt began a "revolution" in a potato field in Long Island, New York. He built 2,000 simple, standard houses for returning soldiers. In time, that small community grew to become known as Levittown. The "revolution" that it helped to bring about is known as "suburbism"—in simple terms, the growth of suburbia.
>
> These suburbs are typically some distance away from the central business district.

In addition to direct references, transitional expressions are essential in maintaining coherence. Transitional expressions are words that connect ideas and make relationships clear.

Common Transitional Expressions		
as a result	for example	in other words
at any rate	in addition	on the contrary
by the way	in fact	on the other hand

Your Turn _____

Write Your Draft Using your notes and thesis, and keeping in mind the framework of an informative essay, write your first draft. Be sure to carefully choose what information you will include and to use transitional expressions and direct references to reinforce coherence in your writing.

Writing Workshop **997**

Peer Review

Working with a peer, go over the chart to the right. Then review your draft. Answer each question in this chart to locate where and how your drafts could be improved. Be sure to take notes on what you and your partner discuss. Refer to these notes as you revise your draft.

Evaluating and Revising

Read the questions in the left column of the chart and then use the tips in the middle column to help you make revisions to your essay. The right column suggests techniques you can use to revise your draft.

Informative Essay: Guidelines for Content and Organization

Evaluation Questions	Tips	Revision Techniques
1. Does the paper open with a "hook" to grab the reader's attention?	**Put stars** next to statistics, facts, questions, quotes, or other attention-grabbing techniques.	If needed, **add** an attention-grabber to the beginning of your introduction.
2. Does the opening paragraph clearly state the topic of the paper?	**Underline** the topic of the paper.	**Narrow** the focus of the introduction to include information directly related to the topic. **Delete** anything unrelated.
3. Does the introduction include a clear thesis statement?	**Highlight** the thesis statement.	**Add** a thesis statement or, if necessary, **rewrite** your current one to make it more clear or interesting.
4. Does each body paragraph focus on one main idea?	**Circle** the main idea of each paragraph.	If there is not a main idea, **revise** and **add** one.
5. Does the paper provide specific information on the topic?	**Number** each fact, quote, or statistic that provides specific information.	If you do not have specific information in each paragraph, **add** some to support the main idea. **Consider reordering** evidence into a more logical order if necessary.
6. Does the conclusion restate the main points and leave a lasting impression?	**Put a check mark** next to the summarized information. **Underline** the final impression.	**Add** a statement that will leave a lasting impression.

Read this student draft. Note the comments on its structure and suggestions that could make the piece even stronger.

Urban Sprawl: Austin, Texas

by Rachel Langley, Lyndon Baines Johnson High School

Urban sprawl is the unplanned, uncontrolled spreading of urban development into areas adjoining the edge of a city. In basic terms, urban sprawl is when a city's developers use the spare land outlying city limits to build new residential areas, which soon become supported by strip malls, businesses, grocery stores, and much more. To most, urban sprawl is a part of the modern world, but unless the modern world started in the late 1800's after the Civil War, then they're wrong. Boston first had Concord, then New York had the Bronx and Staten Island, and from then on it was a trend that continued. These are all examples of America's very old version of urban sprawl that have now become widespread. By 1950 7 million Americans occupied these suburban areas. Urban sprawl has a direct impact on the nation's economy, affecting the health of cities and rural areas alike.

It is generally thought that urban sprawl creates growth within the economy, but in the long run, urban sprawl actually attacks a city's economy and human resources. As suburban areas explode in growth, urban areas lose population and jobs, a "brain drain," that leaves urban schools with the country's lowest test scores. Resources that could be used in the city are repurposed for clearing land, building roads, erecting new schools in order to accommodate new communites while the urban setting dies.

← Rachel clearly **defines** urban sprawl.

← She provides **background** and historical information on the topic.

Rachel establishes her **thesis statement.**

← In her first body paragraph, Rachel begins to examine issues and introduces **evidence** to support her thesis.

MINI-LESSON ▶ How to Open with Interesting Facts

Rachel defines urban sprawl for her reader in the first paragraph. She decides to add a startling statistic to hook her reader to the topic. She also adds a transitional sentence to lead smoothly into her definition.

Rachel's Revision of Paragraph One:

As of 2000, approximately 10.8 million people live in the suburbs of America's largest cities. This expansive growth has resulted in "urban sprawl," a problem for more than 50 years. ∧ Urban sprawl is the unplanned, uncontrolled spreading of urban development into areas adjoining the edge of a city. . . .

Your Turn _____

Revise Your Draft Read through your draft and ask yourself:

- Do you grab the reader's attention?
- Do you use smooth transitions between your introductory device and the rest of your introduction?

Student Draft continues

The **topic sentence** clearly states the focus of this paragraph. →

America's urban sprawl is endangering its farmland. According to Bob Winfield of the U.S. Department of Agriculture, the land being used to develop suburban housing and commercial areas is the country's finest farmland previously used for crops of high value. Texas lost 489,000 acres of good farmland to developers between 1982 and 1992—more than any other state. With the country's growing population, prime farmland cannot be sold for yet another strip mall and apartment complex.

Rachel includes another clear **definition** here. →

"Smart growth" is a very healthy solution to urban sprawl. It involves preserving the farmland with legislation before the developers can buy it, finding ways to improve public transportation which will allow people to get out of their cars and off of the roadways, and improving housing options in a city's downtown neighborhoods. There are bonuses, of course, in saving fuel and improving the environment.

She provides an **example** of a successful community. →

Rachel **quotes** a popular author and restates her thesis to leave the reader with a compelling thought. →

Portland, Oregon is a good example of a city and community that has, through legislation, community activism, and city growth, created a model of efficiency for curtailing urban sprawl. It can be done. Author Tom Clancy observes, "Terrorism is beyond our control, which is why it doesn't scare me. . . . We can control urban sprawl, but we choose not to; that is what is so frustrating." Our generation can preserve the farmland, honor our cities, and stop urban sprawl now.

MINI-LESSON ▶ How to Use Expert Testimony

One way to add interest to your essay is to use testimony from experts on the subject. In her third paragraph, Rachel decided to include quotations from a farmer to add credibility and a human voice to her information. She also had to add a transitional sentence to smoothly connect this addition to the rest of the paragraph.

Rachel's Revision of Paragraph Three:

. . . the country's finest farmland previously used for crops of high value. ∧*The owner of a family farm is under pressure from both sides. Tom Spellmire, a farmer in Dayton, Ohio, stated, "When I'm out there on my tractor, the subdivision kids are hanging over the fence watching me. And you know what their parents say to me, 'You're not going to sell to developers, are you?'" This problem is prevalent throughout the United States.* Texas lost 489,000 acres of good farmland to developers between 1982 and 1992, more than any other state. With the country's growing population, prime farmland cannot be sold for yet another strip mall and apartment complex.

Your Turn _____

Leave a Lasting Impression
Re-read your final paragraph and ask yourself, "Is it memorable?" If you have not left your reader with something to think about, consider revising your last few lines.

Proofreading and Publishing

Proofreading

Take time to proofread your essay to make it clear and error-free. Find and eliminate any errors in grammar, mechanics, and usage. Carefully review each body paragraph, ensuring that each focuses on one main idea. Does your conclusion restate your main points and leave your reader with some things to think about after finishing the essay? After you have checked the main structural and organizational issues, re-read your draft for specific grammar, punctuation, and usage issues.

> ### Grammar Link Using Commas with Cities and States
>
> Rachel's topic required her to use references to cities and their states. One often overlooked punctuation rule is placing a comma after the state as well as after the city. Rachel forgot to do that in her last paragraph. As she proofread, she found her error and corrected it.
>
> Portland, Oregon, is a good example of a city and community that has, through legislation, community activism, and city growth, created a model of efficiency curtailing urban sprawl.

Publishing

Share your work with an interested audience. In addition to the options provided in your class or school, you may want to submit your essay for publication outside the classroom. Here are a few ideas about where you might send your essay for possible publication:

- Local newspaper or periodical
- Journals or magazines (online or print) specializing in your topic or related topics
- Newsletters for businesses or organizations dealing with your topic
- Web sites devoted to the topic

Reflect on the Process Answer the following questions in your *Reader/Writer Notebook*.

1. What was the most difficult aspect of choosing a topic?
2. What information did you include to add interest to your essay?
3. Where else in your school-based writing can you apply the techniques of informative writing?

⬤ Proofreading Tip

When proofreading, make sure any changes you make are clear and legible. This can save time if you are rewriting or typing your essay later. It is also important during timed writing assignments when you will need to submit all your work to be reviewed. Your hard work can only pay off if it can be easily read.

Your Turn _____

Proofread and Publish Proofread your draft. Determine if you have omitted any important commas such as the ones used after cities and states. Carefully proofread your paper for errors in punctuation, usage, and spelling. Then, make a final copy of your informative essay and publish it.

Scoring Rubric

Use one of the following rubrics to evaluate your informative essay from the Writing Workshop or from the activity on the next page. Your teacher will tell you which rubric to use.

6-Point Scale

Score 6 *Demonstrates advanced success*
- focuses consistently on a clear thesis
- shows effective organization throughout, with smooth transitions
- offers thoughtful, creative ideas
- develops ideas thoroughly, using examples, details, and fully elaborated explanation
- exhibits mature control of written language

Score 5 *Demonstrates proficient success*
- focuses on a clear thesis
- shows effective organization, with transitions
- offers thoughtful ideas
- develops ideas competently, using examples, details, and well-elaborated explanation
- exhibits sufficient control of written language

Score 4 *Demonstrates competent success*
- focuses on a clear thesis, with minor distractions
- shows effective organization, with minor lapses
- offers mostly thoughtful ideas
- develops ideas adequately with a mixture of general and specific elaboration
- exhibits general control of written language

Score 3 *Demonstrates limited success*
- includes some loosely related ideas that distract from the writer's expository/informative focus
- shows some organization, with noticeable gaps in the logical flow of ideas
- offers routine, predictable ideas
- develops ideas with uneven elaboration
- exhibits limited control of written language

Score 2 *Demonstrates basic success*
- includes loosely related ideas that seriously distract from the writer's expository/informative focus
- shows minimal organization, with major gaps in the logical flow of ideas
- offers ideas that merely skim the surface
- develops ideas with inadequate elaboration
- exhibits significant problems with control of written language

Score 1 *Demonstrates emerging effort*
- shows little awareness of the topic and purpose for writing
- lacks organization
- offers unclear and confusing ideas
- develops ideas in only a minimal way, if at all
- exhibits major problems with control of written language

4-Point Scale

Score 4 *Demonstrates advanced success*
- focuses consistently on a clear thesis
- shows effective organization throughout, with smooth transitions
- offers thoughtful, creative ideas
- develops ideas thoroughly, using examples, details, and fully elaborated explanation
- exhibits mature control of written language

Score 3 *Demonstrates competent success*
- focuses on a clear thesis, with minor distractions
- shows effective organization, with minor lapses
- offers mostly thoughtful ideas
- develops ideas adequately, with a mixture of general and specific elaboration
- exhibits general control of written language

Score 2 *Demonstrates limited success*
- includes some loosely related ideas that distract from the writer's expository/informative focus
- shows some organization, with noticeable gaps in the logical flow of ideas
- offers routine, predictable ideas
- develops ideas with uneven elaboration
- exhibits limited control of written language

Score 1 *Demonstrates emerging effort*
- shows little awareness of the topic and purpose for writing
- lacks organization
- offers unclear and confusing ideas
- develops ideas in only a minimal way, if at all
- exhibits major problems with control of written language

Preparing for Timed Writing

Informative Essay

WA.10.4.d Write informational essays or reports, including research that: support the main ideas with facts, details, examples and explanations from sources; and *Also covered* **WP.10.3; WP.10.8**

You may be presented with an on-demand or timed writing task that asks you to write an informative essay about a topic of interest. Use the information you learned in the Writing Workshop, the rubric on the opposite page, and the following instructions to help you with this task.

Writing Prompt

Shakespeare's "Seven Ages of Man" speech describes the different parts people play as they go through life. Write an essay for parents informing them about the challenges teenagers face as individuals struggling to prove themselves as they "play the part" of an adolescent.

Study the Prompt

Begin by reading the prompt carefully. Notice that the **topic** is decided for you. Underline "the challenges teenagers face as individuals struggling to prove themselves." Circle the specific **audience:** "parents." Now circle your **purpose:** "informing them [parents] about the challenges teenagers face as they 'play the part' of an adolescent." It often helps to turn the words of the prompt into a question. You can ask, "What in adolescence creates challenges for teenagers?"

Remember that the purpose of the essay is to inform an audience that might not be familiar with your subject. **Tip:** Spend about five minutes analyzing the prompt.

Plan Your Response

Informative writing requires that you ask and answer the question *What*? The answers to this question become your **thesis statement** and **supporting points.** Ask: "What is the central issue of adolescence? As a result of this issue, what are the challenges for teenagers?"

The introductory paragraph should provide a clear statement of the thesis statement. Each **supporting point** should be addressed in its own paragraph. One effective way to plan an informative essay is to create an informal outline. As you complete your outline, keep the following in mind:

- Tailor your supporting details to your audience; provide them with any background information they will need to understand your topic.
- Link each main point to your central idea.
- Give facts, examples, expert opinions, statistics, anecdotes, and quotations.

Tip: Spend about ten minutes planning your essay.

Respond to the Prompt

Start by writing your thesis statements and supporting points. Consider adding an introduction after you have written the rest of your essay. With an outline to guide you, composing your essay is simply a matter of elaborating on your points. **Tip:** Spend about twenty minutes writing your essay.

Improve Your Response

Revising Go back to the prompt. Did you develop your thesis, linking each main point to it with transitions and direct references? Does your composition have an introduction, a body, and a conclusion?

Proofreading Take time to proofread. Correct errors in grammar, spelling, punctuation, and capitalization. Make sure that your paper is legible.

Checking Your Final Copy Read your paper over one final time. **Tip:** Save five or ten minutes to read and improve your response.

Listening & Speaking Workshop

Analyzing and Evaluating Speeches

Listen with a Purpose

Prepare to present an evaluation of the ideas, arguments, and rhetoric (choice of words) in a historically significant speech.

Think as a Reader/Writer

Earlier in this collection, you read Mark Antony's powerful eulogy presented at the funeral of Julius Caesar. Although his speech was full of sound reasoning, Antony turned the crowd into an angry mob through his passion and eloquence. Rhetoric—the art of speaking well—has played an important role in history as well as literature. Throughout history, speakers have used rhetoric to change people's minds, to sway their hearts, and to spur them into action. In this workshop you will have the opportunity to evaluate the impact of rhetoric in a historically significant speech.

Select a Speech

To find a speech to analyze, you can look through the speeches in this book or search your school and public libraries, history textbook, and the Internet. Think about topics that interest you, such as environmental protection, freedom of speech, or civil rights, and do a little research for speeches that have been made on those topics. You might also consider important historical events, such as the September 11 attacks, and find important speeches given during that time. If possible, find a speech that you can watch on video. While the words and ideas of a speech are important, the speaker's voice, gestures, and body language add to the speech's effectiveness.

Analyze Content and Organization

Most speeches—unless they are purely informational, like research presentations—contain elements of persuasion. That is, the speaker is trying to convince his or her listeners to believe an idea, support a cause, or take an action. Any analysis of a speech must include a look at the types of arguments and rhetorical devices a speaker can use to be persuasive. Before you evaluate a speech, identify the speech's content and organization as follows:

- **Supporting Points** Speakers offer reasons for accepting their viewpoint. Ask: *Why?* What reasons does the speaker give for believing or acting in a certain way? The main reasons are the arguments of the speech.

- **Evidence** Arguments need to be supported by evidence. Ask: *What?* What facts, statistics, examples, and expert testimony is the speaker using to prove his or her point?

Reader/Writer Notebook

Use your **RWN** to complete the activities for this workshop.

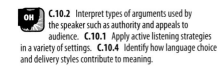

C.10.2 Interpret types of arguments used by the speaker such as authority and appeals to audience. **C.10.1** Apply active listening strategies in a variety of settings. **C.10.4** Identify how language choice and delivery styles contribute to meaning.

- **Organization** The arguments and evidence in a speech should be presented in a logical way and show connections between ideas. The speaker should make and support one point at a time. Ask: *How?* How is the speaker ordering his or her thoughts?
- **Audience** Ask: *Who?* Who are the listeners to whom the speaker is directing his or her comments?

Evaluate a Speech

The second task is to critique, or evaluate, the speech. The most important test of a good persuasive speech is your own reaction. The chart below lists criteria by which you can evaluate the elements of a speech as you listen or read.

Elements
Argument by causation: demonstrates how a cause-and-effect relationship support's the speaker's point
Analogy: illustrates a point by making a literal comparison between two unlike things
Appeal to authority: cites an expert on the subject
Appeal to emotion: uses an example or language that appeals to the emotional needs and values of the audience
Appeal to logic: gives facts, statistics, and examples that appeal to the listeners' sense of reason
Rhetorical devices: may include allusions, metaphors, repetition, or rhetorical questions to make the speech memorable and grab listeners' attention
Diction: words that create a certain tone or mood to make a lasting impression on the audience
Parallelism: repetition of the same syntax or sentence structure to point out similarities in ideas
Delivery: includes the effectiveness of the speaker's voice, gestures, and their effects on the tone or mood of speech

You should read the speech more than once to rate the effectiveness of each of its elements. If the speech is available on video or audio, make sure you also have a written transcript of the speech to follow along. After you have rated the effectiveness of each element in the chart, write a one-paragraph evaluation of the speech.

A Good Analysis of a Speech

- begins by identifying the speaker's topic, perspective, and purpose
- explains the types of arguments used in the speech and evaluates the reasoning of each
- points out the rhetorical devices and provides an analysis of how these devices add to or detract from the power of the speech
- describes the speaker's delivery and evaluates the speech's impact
- concludes with a statement about the overall effectiveness of the speech

Listening Tip

To discover a speaker's perspective, or what is important to the speaker, pay attention to ideas that are emphasized by means of tone, gesture, or repeated words. Speakers tend to emphasize what they believe.

Learn It Online
Pictures, music, and animation can make an argument more compelling. See how on *MediaScope* at:

go.hrw.com   L10-1005

Writing Skills Review

Informative Essay   **Directions:** Read the following paragraph from a student's informative essay. Then, answer the questions that follow.

(1) America has the ability and innovation to control and prevent urban sprawl. (2) Although urban sprawl may be the simplest way to grow in size and prevent population density. (3) In Portland, Oregon, they have controlled sprawl with boundaries and with a more densely packed society, and it is still cheaper to live there than in San Francisco. (4) This way of controlling sprawl helps the economy and solves the problem of sprawl altogether. (5) "Smart growth" is a very healthy solution to urban sprawl. (6) It involves preserving the countryside before developers reach it, finding ways to get people out of cars (improving public transportation), and fixing and filling up the older neighborhoods. (7) This isn't unrealistic being that Ohio voters voted yes for $400 billion going toward redevelopment of abandoned industrial sites. (8) Mayor Wynn of Austin, Texas, would like to have 25,000 downtown residents in the next ten years rather than the 5,200 that currently inhabit downtown Austin. (9) New York City can show a perfect example of smart growth, and how Austin can grow up instead of out. (10) If Mayor Wynn's plans follow through, the residential area downtown would be an amazing and convenient place to live. (11) And the public transportation would be a definite help in saving fuel and protecting our environment. (12) Supporters of smart growth in Austin, Texas, call for denser development in some areas.

1. Which of the following sentences is the *best* revision of the first two sentences?

   A. America has the ability and innovation to control and prevent urban sprawl: Although urban sprawl may be the simplest way to grow in size and prevent population density.

   B. America has the ability and innovation to control and prevent urban sprawl; although urban sprawl may be the simplest way to grow in size and prevent population density.

   C. America has the ability and innovation to control and prevent urban sprawl, although urban sprawl may be the simplest way to grow in size and prevent population density.

   D. America has the ability and innovation to control and prevent urban sprawl. Although urban sprawl may be the simplest way to grow in size and prevent population density, we need to balance growth with preservation.

2. Which of the following sentences could be deleted to keep the essay focused on presenting balanced information?

   A. sentence 2

   B. sentence 5

   C. sentence 8

   D. sentence 12

3. What type of information might the author include to keep the essay balanced?

A. additional examples of urban sprawl

B. information in support of urban sprawl

C. evidence that urban sprawl is a concern

D. additional definitions of related terms

4. What information could be moved near the beginning to grab the audience's interest and prove there is support for "smart growth"?

A. "Smart growth" is a very healthy solution to urban sprawl.

B. Ohio voters voted yes for $400 billion going toward redevelopment of abandoned industrial sites.

C. New York City is an example of smart growth and how Austin can grow up instead of out.

D. Supporters of smart growth in Austin, Texas, call for denser development in some areas.

5. What word in sentence 3 is too informal for an informative essay?

A. boundaries

B. packed

C. cheaper

D. controlled

6. Sentence 5 might better belong in what type of essay?

A. evaluative

B. cause and effect

C. persuasive

D. compare and contrast

7. What types of organizational changes would help the audience better understand the purpose of the paragraph?

A. including more examples of various cities

B. further defining *smart growth*

C. addressing the issue of preventing population density

D. keeping the paragraph focused on the situation in Austin

8. Which of the following topic sentences would help clarify the topic of the paragraph?

A. New York City, New York, and Portland, Oregon, have effectively addressed the problem of urban sprawl.

B. Urban sprawl has been addressed in many major cities.

C. Austin can prevent urban sprawl.

D. Austin, Texas, could model the methods used in other major cities to address the problem of urban sprawl.

9. What is the main idea of this paragraph?

A. Smart growth is an alternative to urban sprawl.

B. Urban sprawl prevents population density.

C. Cities should move out instead of up when possible.

D. *Smart growth* and *urban sprawl* have similar definitions.

UNIT 5

Myths and Legends
Writers on Writing

Madeleine L'Engle on Myths and Legends Madeleine L'Engle's popular books for adults and children often combine genres of fantasy and myth. One of her most famous books, *A Wrinkle in Time,* was rejected by twenty-six publishers before it was finally published; later, the book won a Newbery Medal. L'Engle died in 2007.

"And it came to pass."

"Once upon a time."

"Wonderful words! To be human is to be able to listen to a story, to tell a story, and to know that story is the most perfect vehicle of truth available to the human being. What is so remarkable about the stories—myths and legends and sacred texts—of ancient cultures is not their radical diversity, but their unity. We tell basically the same story in all parts of the world, over and over again in varying ways, but it is always the same story, of a universe created by God. One of my favorite authors, "anon," says that myth deals with those things which never were but always are. Myth is, for me, the vehicle of truth. Myth is where you look for reality. We're still hung up on the idea that myth is wrong, that myth is lie, but the only way we have to grope toward the infinite is through myth.

In fairy tales there are doors that should not be opened, and boxes that must remain closed, but human curiosity is such that we open doors, like Bluebeard's wife, and we open boxes, like Pandora. Now we have to live in a world that is irrevocably changed by what was in those secret rooms and by what has come out of the mysterious closed boxes. When we opened the heart of the atom we opened ourselves to the possibility of great destruction, but also—and we tend to forget this—to a vision of interrelatedness and unity.

The reader must see in his mind's eye the people and the pieces of the story, must make decisions, and argue, if necessary, with the author. I argue with authors violently with pencil. "No!" or "Yes!" in the margin. When I was a child, stories helped me find out who I was in a world staggering from the effects of that war which was meant to end all wars but which, alas, was the beginning of a century of continuing war. Stories helped me to accept that human beings do terrible things to other human beings, but that human beings also do marvelous things. Stories were a mirror in which I could be helped to find the image of God in myself and which demanded my participation. The reader plays an active and essential part in bringing words to life, and the reader, like the writer, must temporarily abandon his control and open himself to the aerial, underwater area of creativity. And this takes courage."

Think as a Writer

Madeleine L'Engle says that for her myth is "the vehicle of truth." Do you agree or disagree with this statement? Why?

The Hero's Story

INFORMATIONAL TEXT FOCUS
Generating Research Questions

"How important it is for us to recognize and celebrate our heroes and she-roes."

—**Maya Angelou**

What Do You Think

Why are some stories retold across generations and cultures?

Woman Super Hero by Robert Dale.

Learn It Online
Can you read images? Let *PowerNotes* show you at:

go.hrw.com   L10-1011   Go

Literary Focus

by **Carol Jago**

What Do Myths and Legends Teach Us About Society?

Angry gods and goddesses, brave heroes, monsters to be slain—these elements of myths and legends fuel our imagination. Although the particulars change, the challenge of slaying a monster and saving a damsel in distress continues to play out across movie and television screens. A good story never gets old!

Myths and Legends

Myths are traditional stories rooted in a particular culture that are basically religious in nature. They serve to explain beliefs, rituals, or natural phenomena. A myth reveals the ideals and values of the society that tells the story. The ancient Greeks, for example, invented stories to help explain the mysteries of nature: A stormy sea meant the god of the ocean was unhappy. Gods and goddesses were both observers and participants in human lives. **Folk tales** are similar to myths, but they are not religious. They are told to teach lessons and to entertain.

A **legend** is a story about extraordinary deeds based on a real historical event or person. Because legends are told and retold, they tend to take on fantastic, even supernatural, elements.

Heroes and Quests

In myths and legends, a **hero** (or a **heroine**) is a character, often descended from a god, who faces a seemingly impossible task that he or she accepts with courage, ingenuity, and often superhuman strength. Myths and legends of heroes often involve a **quest,** which is a journey or a test to find something of great significance. In Greek mythology, the hero Theseus goes on a quest to slay the Minotaur, which was devouring the youth of Athens.

> [Theseus] walked boldly into the maze, looking for the Minotaur. He came upon him asleep and fell upon him.
>
> from "Theseus" retold by Edith Hamilton

Norse Myths

Norse myths are the traditional stories of the people of ancient Scandinavia and Germany. Norse mythology includes hero tales, called *sagas,* which are part of an oral storytelling tradition. In the following excerpt, the hero Sigurd, the most famous Norse hero, gets help in his quest from Odin, the principal Norse god.

> "I gave your father a sword," said Odin as they watched the great creature breasting the flood. "Now I give you this horse. Ride out and win fame. . . . heroes shall rise to greet you as the greatest one of them all."
>
> from "Sigurd, the Dragon Slayer" retold by Olivia E. Coolidge

OH **RA.L.10.5** Analyze how an author's choice of genre affects the expression of a theme or topic.
RA.L.10.1 Compare and contrast an author's use of direct and indirect characterization, and ways in which characters reveal traits about themselves, including dialect, dramatic monologues and soliloquies.

Arthurian Legend

Arthurian legends are stories about King Arthur and the brave, powerful, and adventurous Knights of the Round Table. The medieval hero King Arthur was considered a great fighter and defender of his land. The legends are probably based on a fifth- or sixth-century Celtic chieftain who lived in Wales and led his people to victory against invaders from Germany. The following excerpt describes Arthur's first heroic task—pulling a sword out of a stone in which it had been lodged.

> "Why," said Arthur, "do you both kneel before me?"
>
> "My lord," Sir Ector replied, "there is only one man living who can draw the sword from the stone, and he is the true-born king of Britain."
>
> from "The Sword in the Stone" by Sir Thomas Malory

Romantic Literature

The legends of King Arthur are a part of the larger genre of **Romantic literature,** which developed in twelfth-century England and France and focuses on the adventures of knights and other heroes. The medieval romance celebrates the ideals of **chivalry**—the code of behavior a knight followed. He was to be brave, honorable, generous to his foes, respectful of women, and protective of the weak. Romantic literature features stories of love and loyalty, often with elements of magic or enchantment. In "The Tale of Sir Launcelot du Lake," the hero commits to helping the king's daughter.

> "God bless you, my lady; and when the time comes I promise I shall not fail you."
>
> from "The Tale of Sir Launcelot du Lake" by Sir Thomas Malory

Archetypes

An **archetype** is a plot pattern, image, or character type that appears throughout literature. Archetypes often reflect universal characters and themes. One example of an archetype is the hero, who faces formidable enemies and physical challenges or goes on a quest. As you read myths and legends, use a chart like the one below to track archetypal qualities.

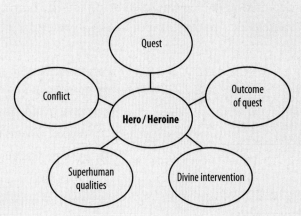

Your Turn   Analyze Myths and Legends

Think of a hero or heroine from literature or film and apply your knowledge of the archetypal hero. Use the following questions as a guide:

- What is the hero's or heroine's quest?
- What heroic qualities does the character possess to overcome the challenge(s)?
- What conflicts does the hero overcome?
- What is the outcome?

Learn It Online
Do pictures help you learn? Try the *PowerNotes* version of this lesson on:

go.hrw.com   L10-1013   **Go**

Analyzing Visuals

How Are Heroes Portrayed in Art?

Myths and legends from around the world are often similar—they usually tell stories of heroes who not only challenge and conquer evil, but are also prone to mistakes. Heroic figures in art are usually depicted in such a way as to bring out the hero's very best to reflect the values that are most important to a society.

Analyzing Heroes in Art

Use these guidelines to help you analyze heroes in art:

1. Who or what is the artwork about? Does it portray a myth or a hero?

2. How do you know who the hero is? How does he or she stand out?

3. Is the hero in action? Does the hero carry a weapon or accessory?

4. What qualities does the hero seem to embody? How might these qualities be important to a society?

The art on the facing page is from Benin, a West African kingdom from the early 1400s to the 1700s. The main character in the plaque is a high-ranking official, or *oba,* a warrior chief.

> Look at the details of the plaque to help you answer the questions on page 1015.

Details of Benin plaque.

OH **RA.L.10.1** Compare and contrast an author's use of direct and indirect characterization, and ways in which characters reveal traits about themselves, including dialect, dramatic monologues and soliloquies.

1. How would you describe the central figure in this artwork?

2. What do you think is the central figure's role? What is he holding?

3. Why is the central figure larger than the other people? What might this tell you about his role?

4. What qualities do you think the Edo people find important? What characteristics of the sculpture help you understand this?

Benin plaque with multiple figures (mid-16th to 17th century) by Edo peoples, Benin Kingdom, Nigeria. National Museum of African Art, Smithsonian Institution, Washington, D.C.

Your Turn Write About Heroes in Art

Find an image of a hero in popular media—from a movie, television show, or comic book. Describe how the hero is portrayed in relation to other elements in the image. Tell what qualities the hero embodies, referring to details from the image.

Reading Focus

by **Kylene Beers**

What Skills Help You Analyze Myths and Legends?

The myths and legends in this collection, filled with adventure and heroic actions, take many twists and turns. To follow the action, it is important to keep track of the sequence of events. No matter what you are reading, it's a good idea to monitor your reading to be sure you understand it. If you find you are not getting it, you can go back and check the sequence of events, summarize what you've read, or take some other action to keep your reading on track.

Understanding Sequence of Events

The specific order in which events unfold in a story is the **sequence of events.** Typically, story events occur in **chronological order,** or the order in which the events happen in time. Words such as *first, then, next, before, after,* and *finally* can signal the order of events, but not all stories include these words.

Have you ever told someone about an event you experienced and, in the middle of the telling, found you had to explain something that happened much earlier? A writer sometimes uses **flashback** to provide a significant scene or event from the past out of chronological order. Words and phrases like *long before this* or *years ago* might signal a flashback. Notice the words that signal the passage of time in "Sigurd, the Dragon Slayer."

> Years passed more slowly than ever, but at last he [Regin] saw Sigurd had become a tall, golden-haired lad. Then finally he went to King Alf.
>
> from "Sigurd, the Dragon Slayer"
> retold by Olivia E. Coolidge

Using a chart like the one below can help you identify the sequence of events. To identify sequence, look for words that show chronological order or signal a flashback.

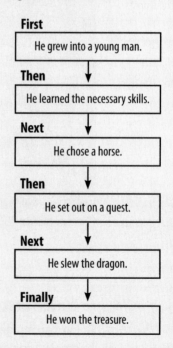

First
He grew into a young man.

Then
He learned the necessary skills.

Next
He chose a horse.

Then
He set out on a quest.

Next
He slew the dragon.

Finally
He won the treasure.

RA.I.10.1 Identify and understand organizational patterns and techniques, including repetition of ideas, syntax and word choice, that authors use to accomplish their purpose and reach their intended audience. **RP.10.1** Apply reading comprehension strategies, including making predictions, comparing and contrasting, recalling and summarizing and making inferences and drawing conclusions. **RP.10.3** Monitor own comprehension by adjusting speed to fit the purpose, or by skimming, scanning, reading on, looking back, note taking or summarizing what has been read so far in text.

Summarizing

How often have your friends asked you what you did over the weekend, and you answered by describing only the highlights? Whenever you describe highlights or main events, you are **summarizing.** When you summarize a story, you tell not only the main events but also the connections among them—not only what the hero did but why and what happened as a result. Filling in an outline like the one below will help you assemble the main points of a story from which to write a summary.

I. *Boy is born from peach and named Momotaro*

II. *Boy is raised by old woman and her husband*

III. _____

Monitoring Your Reading

Do you occasionally lose track of what you are reading? Then it's time to **monitor your reading,** or check to be sure you understand what is happening. Ask yourself questions such as "Is this making sense to me?" and "Do I understand why this is happening?" If a passage is not clear to you, you may need to re-read it or look up an unknown word.

Stopping periodically to summarize events is one way to monitor your reading. You can also ask yourself questions as you read. Use the *5W-HOW* strategy (*Who? What? Where? When? Why?* and *How?*) to monitor your understanding of the story. Ask yourself questions such as "Why is the king jealous of his son?"; "What happened after the god left the people?"; and "How does Arthur pull the sword from the stone?"

Your Turn   Apply Reading Skills

Read the following passage from "The Sword in the Stone," by Sir Thomas Malory. As you read, identify the sequence of events. Then, summarize the passage. As you write your summary, be sure to show how events are connected.

> When they arrived at the tournament, Sir Kay found to his annoyance that his sword was missing from his sheath, so he begged Arthur to ride back and fetch it from their lodging.
>
> Arthur found the door of the lodging locked and bolted, the landlord and his wife having left for the tournament. In order not to disappoint his brother, he rode on to St. Paul's, determined to get for him the sword which was lodged in the stone. The yard was empty, the guard also having slipped off to see the tournament, so Arthur strode up to the sword and, without troubling to read the inscription, tugged it free. He then rode straight back to Sir Kay and presented him with it.

Now go to the Skills in Action: Reading Model

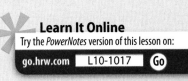

Learn It Online
Try the *PowerNotes* version of this lesson on:
go.hrw.com   L10-1017   **Go**

Reading Model

Build Background

Many of the gods and goddesses in Roman mythology have a counterpart (with a different name) in Greek mythology. Diana (known as Artemis to the Greeks) was the goddess of the moon and animals in the wild. She was often associated with the hunt. Venus (also known as Aphrodite) was the goddess of love.

Literary Focus

Myths The involvement of gods and goddesses in the lives of humans is a key element in Greek and Roman myths.

Read with a Purpose Read this story to learn what two young people will do for love—and what the gods will do for revenge.

The Golden Apples: The Story of Atalanta and Hippomenes

retold by **Mary Pope Osborne**

Long ago a baby girl named Atalanta was left on a wild mountainside because her father had wanted a boy instead of a girl. A kind bear discovered the tiny girl and nursed her and cared for her. And as Atalanta grew up, she lived as the bears lived: eating wild honey and berries and hunting in the woods. Finally as a young woman on her own, she became a follower of Diana, the goddess of wild things. Preferring to live on her own, Atalanta blissfully roamed the shadowy woods and sunlit fields.

The god Apollo agreed with Atalanta's choice to be alone. "You must never marry," he told her one day. "If you do, you will surely lose your own identity."

In spite of her decision never to marry, Atalanta was pursued by many suitors. As men watched her run through the fields and forest, they were struck by her beauty and grace.

Angry at the men for bothering her, Atalanta figured out how to keep them away. "I'll race anyone who wants to marry me!" she announced to the daily throng that pursued her. "Whoever is so swift that he can outrun me will receive the prize of my hand in marriage! But whomever I beat—will die."

Atalanta was certain these harsh conditions would discourage everyone from wanting to marry her. But she was wrong. Her strength and grace were so compelling that many men volunteered to race against her—and all of them lost their lives.

One day, a young stranger, wandering through the countryside, stopped to join a crowd that was watching a race between Atalanta and one of her suitors. When Hippomenes realized the terms of the contest, he was appalled. "No person could be worth such a risk!" he exclaimed. "Only an idiot would try to win her for his wife!"

But when Atalanta sped by, and Hippomenes saw her wild hair flying back from her ivory shoulders and her strong body moving as gracefully as a gazelle, even he was overwhelmed with the desire to be her husband.

"Forgive me," he said to the panting loser being taken away to his death. "I did not know what a prize she was."

When Atalanta was crowned with the wreath of victory, Hippomenes stepped forward boldly and spoke to her before the crowd. "Why do you race against men so slow?" he asked. "Why not race against me? If I defeat you, you will not be disgraced, for I am the great-grandson of Neptune, god of the seas!"

Atalanta and Hippomenes (1572) by Sebastiano Marsili. Palazzo della Signoria, Palazzo Vecchio, Florence, Italy.

Reading Model

"And if I beat you?" Atalanta asked.

"If you beat me . . . you will certainly have something to boast about!"

As Atalanta stared at the proud young man, she wondered why the gods would wish one as young and bold as Hippomenes to die. And for the first time, she felt she might rather lose than win. Inexperienced in matters of the heart, she did not realize she was falling in love. "Go, stranger," she said softly. "I'm not worth the loss of your life."

But the crowd, sensing a tremendous race might be about to take place, cheered wildly, urging the two to compete. And since Hippomenes eagerly sought the same, Atalanta was forced to give in. With a heavy heart, she consented to race the young man the next day.

In the pink twilight, alone in the hills, Hippomenes prayed to Venus, the goddess of love and beauty. He asked for help in his race against Atalanta. When Venus heard Hippomenes's prayer, she was only too glad to help him, for she wished to punish the young huntress for despising love.

As if in a dream, Venus led Hippomenes to a mighty tree in the middle of an open field. The tree shimmered with golden leaves and golden apples. Venus told Hippomenes to pluck three of the apples from the tree, and then she told him how to use the apples in his race against Atalanta.

The crowd roared as Atalanta and Hippomenes crouched at the starting line. Under his tunic, Hippomenes hid his three golden apples. When the trumpets sounded, the two shot forward and ran so fast that their bare feet barely touched the sand. They looked as if they could run over the surface of the sea without getting their feet wet—or skim over fields of corn without even bending the stalks.

The crowd cheered for Hippomenes, but Atalanta rushed ahead of him and stayed in the lead. When Hippomenes began to pant, and his chest felt as if it might burst open, he pulled one of the golden apples out from under his tunic and tossed it toward Atalanta.

The gleaming apple hit the sand and rolled across Atalanta's path. She left her course and chased after the glittering ball, and Hippomenes gained the lead. The crowd screamed with joy; but after Atalanta picked up the golden apple, she quickly made up for her delay and scooted ahead of Hippomenes.

Hippomenes tossed another golden apple. Again, Atalanta left her course, picked up the apple, then overtook Hippomenes.

Reading Focus

Summarizing This is a significant point in the story—a good point to add to your summary. Atalanta was raised by bears, followed the goddess Diana, and devised a plan to keep suitors from winning her hand in marriage. Now she seems interested in Hippomenes.

Reading Focus

Sequence of Events The events in the story are told in chronological order. The signal words *after, another, again,* and *then* move the action forward.

Hippomenes and Atalanta by Troy Howell. Illustration.

As Hippomenes pulled out his third golden apple, he realized this was his last chance. He reared back his arm and hurled the apple as far as he could into a field.

Atalanta watched the golden ball fly through the air; and she hesitated, wondering whether or not she should run after it. Just as she decided not to, Venus touched her heart, prompting her to abandon her course and rush after the glittering apple.

Atalanta took off into the field after the golden apple—and Hippomenes sped toward the finish line.

Hippomenes won Atalanta for his bride, but then he made a terrible mistake: He neglected to offer gifts to Venus to thank her for helping him.

Enraged by his ingratitude, the goddess of love and beauty called upon the moon goddess, Diana, and told her to punish Hippomenes and Atalanta.

Literary Focus

Myths A recurring event in many myths is the tragic mistake of the hero. Often, the hero forgets to pay tribute to the god or goddess who has helped him.

As the moon goddess studied the two proud lovers hunting in the woods and fields, she admired their strength and valor, and she decided to turn them into the animals they most resembled.

One night as Atalanta and Hippomenes lay side by side under the moonlight, changes began to happen to their bodies. They grew rough amber coats, and stiff, long claws. And when dawn came, they woke and growled at the early light. Then the thick tails of the two mighty lions swept the ground as they began hunting for their breakfast.

From then on, Atalanta and Hippomenes lived together as lions deep in the woods, and only the moon goddess could tame them.

Read with a Purpose What happened to Atalanta and Hippomenes? Why did the moon goddess punish them?

MEET THE WRITER

Mary Pope Osborne
(1949–)

A Writer on Adventures Near and Far

Mary Pope Osborne's love of adventure in faraway lands has led her to such places as the island of Crete, where she spent a short period camping in a cave after she graduated from college. Her journeys through sixteen Asian countries later influenced her love of mythology and religions, which led her to retell stories from Greek and Norse mythologies.

When she was growing up, Osborne's father was in the military, so her family moved frequently. When they finally planted roots in North Carolina, she was easily bored:

"I nearly went crazy with boredom. I craved the adventure and changing scenery of our military life. . . . Miraculously, one day I found these things, literally a block away—at the local community theater. From then on I spent nearly every waking hour after school there. . . . When I stepped from the sunny street into that musty-smelling little theater, all things seemed possible."

Think About the Writer How might Osborne's childhood have influenced her decision to travel later in life?

RA.L.10.5 Analyze how an author's choice of genre affects the expression of a theme or topic. RP.10.1 Apply reading comprehension strategies, including making predictions, comparing and contrasting, recalling and summarizing and making inferences and drawing conclusions. *Also covered* VO.10.6

SKILLS IN ACTION
Wrap Up

Into Action: Elements of Myths

In a table like the one below, describe the elements of myths you found in "The Golden Apples." Think about how the quest changes if you view Atalanta as the heroic character instead of Hippomenes.

Gods/Goddesses	Hero/Heroine	Quest

Talk About . . .

Get together in small groups to discuss the following questions about "The Golden Apples." Try to use each Academic Vocabulary word listed at the right at least once in your discussion.

1. What human traits and behaviors do the gods and goddesses exhibit in this myth?

2. Interaction between gods and humans is a recurring element in myths. Discuss both the benefits and the drawbacks of the gods' involvement in human lives, giving examples from "The Golden Apples" or another myth you know.

3. Describe the qualities Atalanta and Hippomenes retain after they become lions.

Write About . . .

4. What lesson does "The Golden Apples" teach? Recount details from the story that support your answer. Then, write a brief summary of the myth. When you are done, switch summaries with a partner and compare.

Writing Focus

Think as a Reader/Writer

Find it in Your Reading As you read the myths and legends in this collection, you'll learn about the enduring themes that connect people across centuries. On the Applying Your Skills pages, you will have an opportunity to explore these elements and make your own connections.

Academic Vocabulary for Collection 9

Talking and Writing About Myths and Legends

Academic Vocabulary is the language you use to write and talk about literature. Use these words to discuss the tales you read in this collection. The words are underlined throughout the collection.

recurring (rih KUR ihng) *v.* used as *adj.*: coming up again, being repeated. *The heroic quest is a recurring theme in literature.*

exhibit (ehg ZIHB iht) *v.*: show, display, or indicate. *Atalanta was reluctant at first to exhibit her feelings for Hippomenes.*

retain (rih TAYN) *v.*: continue to have or hold. *Atalanta was unable to retain her lead when Hippomenes threw out the golden apples.*

recount (rih KOWNT) *v.*: tell or give an account of. *The ability to recount a story accurately is a useful skill.*

Your Turn

Copy the words from the Academic Vocabulary list into your *Reader/Writer Notebook.* You may be familiar with some of them. As you read and discuss the myths and legends in the following collection, try to use each of these words at least once.

THESEUS

retold by **Edith Hamilton**

Theseus and the Minotaur: The Labyrinth (detail) (1510–1520) by Master of Campana Cassone

Reader/Writer Notebook

Use your **RWN** to complete the activities for this selection.

OH **RA.L.10.1** Compare and contrast an author's use of direct and indirect characterization, and ways in which characters reveal traits about themselves, including dialect, dramatic monologues and soliloquies. **RP.10.1** Apply reading comprehension strategies, including making predictions, comparing and contrasting, recalling and summarizing and making inferences and drawing conclusions.

Literary Focus

Myths and Heroes In ancient Greece, as in other places in the world, **myths**—traditional stories <u>recounted</u> over time about gods and heroes—were more than entertaining stories. They were part of the Greek religion, and they embodied the values of the people.

Though they often have supernatural powers, the **heroes** in the Greek myths are recognizably human. In a typical hero myth, a young man is sent on a quest to find something of great value and often finds qualities such as self-knowledge or self-control along the way. These hero stories reveal the qualities that the ancient Greeks valued.

Reading Focus

Summarizing When you **summarize** a narrative, you briefly retell it in your own words, including only the key points and events. Summarizing helps you recognize which parts of the story are most important to the plot and confirms your understanding of the story.

Into Action As you read "Theseus," jot down the principal events of the myth in a graphic organizer like the one below.

Theseus finds his father's sword.

TechFocus Imagine you are making a movie of this myth. Which scenes or parts of the story would best lend themselves to a short film?

Writing Focus

Think as a Reader/Writer

Find It in Your Reading Hamilton uses complex sentences and formal **diction,** or word choice, in her retelling of this myth. As you read, find examples of sentences with formal diction and copy these into your *Reader/Writer Notebook*.

Vocabulary

acknowledged (ak NAHL ihjd) *adj.:* admitted; recognized to be true. *Once Theseus proved he was King Aegeus's son, he became the acknowledged prince.*

endear (ehn DIHR) *v.:* inspire affection. *Theseus was able to endear himself to the Athenians by being a good and fair ruler.*

afflicted (uh FLIHKT ihd) *adj.:* upset; saddened. *King Aegeus was so afflicted at the sight of the black sail that he killed himself.*

prosperous (PRAHS puhr uhs) *adj.:* wealthy. *Citizens lived comfortably in the prosperous state of Athens.*

consent (kuhn SEHNT) *v.:* agree. *Theseus would not consent to becoming king.*

Language Coach

Suffixes When you add a suffix, such as *–ment* or *–ous,* to a base word, you change the meaning of the word. You can often guess the meaning of a word if you first consider the meanings of its base and suffix. Hamilton uses the word *prosperous* to describe Athens's wealth. *Prosper* means "to succeed," and *–ous* is a suffix meaning "full of." Think about the word *confinement.* The suffix *–ment* means "the act or state of." What does *confinement* mean?

 Learn It Online

See a good reader in action, and practice your own skills, at:

go.hrw.com   L10-1025   **Go**

Edith Hamilton
(1867–1963)

A Passion for Ancient Greece

The retellings of the Greek myths that many people first encounter as children are probably those by Edith Hamilton. When Hamilton retired from teaching the classics at the Bryn Mawr School in Baltimore, she decided she wanted to share her knowledge with a wider audience. Thus, she began writing *Mythology,* which soon became a bestseller. The miracle of Greek mythology, Hamilton said, is "a humanized world. . . . All the art and all the thought of Greece centered in human beings."

Raised on Classics

The classics—the literature of ancient Greece and Rome—had been part of Hamilton's life from the time she was seven years old. In later years, she became so identified with Greece that in 1957 she was named an honorary citizen of Athens.

Think About the Writer Why do you think Edith Hamilton felt so passionately about sharing the Greek myths with a wider audience?

Build Background

Although some people today believe that the myths about Theseus are based on the life of an actual early king, most scholars believe that Theseus is totally mythic. According to legend, when Theseus became king of Athens, he united several small independent kingdoms into a federation—the great city-state of Athens. Theseus is thus credited with beginning the first people's democracy. Athens became the home of liberty (at least for free males), and the first place in the world where people governed themselves.

Preview the Selection

In the following myth, **Theseus** is the son of **Aegeus,** king of Athens, and **Aethra,** princess of Troizen, a city in southern Greece.

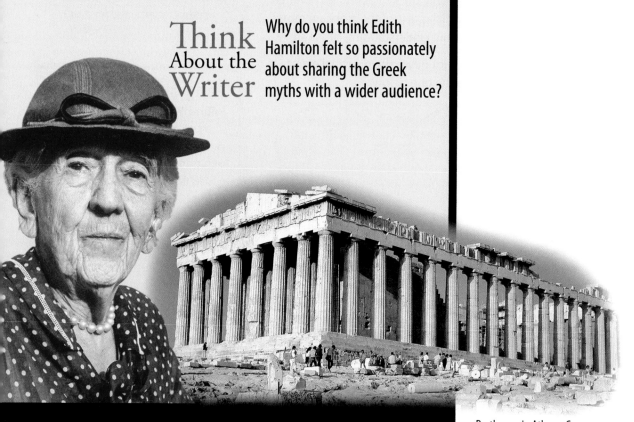

Parthenon in Athens, Greece.

CHARACTERS IN THE MYTH

Theseus (THEE see uhs): son of Aegeus and Aethra. He is brought up by his mother in Troizen, in southern Greece.

King Aegeus (ee JEE uhs): Theseus's father, king of Athens.

Aethra (EE thruh): Theseus's mother, princess of Troizen.

Medea (mee DEE uh): female magician from Corinth, now living with King Aegeus in Athens. Years earlier, Medea had used her magical powers to help the hero Jason steal the Golden Fleece.

Minos (MY nuhs): king of Crete, enemy of Athens.

Minotaur (MIHN uh tawr): offspring of Minos's wife and a bull. The Minotaur was a monstrous creature, half-man, half-bull, and confined by Minos to the labyrinth on Crete.

Ariadne (ar ee AHD nee): daughter of King Minos.

Dionysus (dy uh NY suhs): god of wine and pleasure.

THESEUS

retold by **Edith Hamilton**

The great Athenian hero was Theseus. He had so many adventures and took part in so many great enterprises that there grew up a saying in Athens, "Nothing without Theseus."

He was the son of the Athenian king, Aegeus. He spent his youth, however, in his mother's home, a city in southern Greece. Aegeus went back to Athens before the child was born, but first he placed in a hollow a sword and a pair of shoes and covered them with a great stone. He did this with the knowledge of his wife and told her that whenever the boy—if it was a boy—grew strong enough to roll away the stone and get the things beneath it, she could send him to Athens to claim him as his father. The child was a boy, and he grew up strong far beyond others, so that when his mother finally took him to the stone he lifted it with no trouble at all. She told him then that the time had come for him to seek his father, and a ship was placed at his disposal by his grandfather. But Theseus refused to go by water, because the voyage was safe and easy. His idea was to become a great hero as quickly as possible, and easy safety was certainly not the way to do that. Hercules, who was the most magnificent of all the heroes of Greece, was always in his mind, and the determination to be just as magnificent himself. This was quite natural, since the two were cousins.

He steadfastly refused, therefore, the ship his mother and grandfather urged on him, telling them that to sail on it would be a contemptible[1] flight from danger, and he set forth

---

1. **contemptible** (kuhn TEHMP tuh buhl): hateful; disgraceful.

Ⓐ Literary Focus Myths and Heroes What quest does Theseus undertake?

Theseus. Detail of a mural from Herculaneum, Italy.
Museo Archeologico Nazionale, Naples, Italy.

to go to Athens by land. The journey was long and very hazardous because of the bandits that beset the road. He killed them all, however; he left not one alive to trouble future travelers. His idea of dealing justice was simple but effective: What each had done to others, Theseus did to him. Sciron,[2] for instance, who had made those he captured kneel to wash his feet and then kicked them down into the sea, Theseus hurled over a precipice. Sinir, who killed people by fastening them to two pine trees bent down to the ground and letting the trees go, died in that way himself. Procrustes[3] was placed upon the iron bed which he used for his victims, tying them to it and then making them the right length for it by stretching those who were too short and cutting off as much as was necessary from those who were too long. The story does not say which of the two methods was used in his case, but there was not much to choose between them and in one way or the other Procrustes' career ended.

It can be imagined how Greece rang with the praises of the young man who had cleared the land of these banes[4] to travelers. When he reached Athens, he was an acknowledged hero, and he was invited to a banquet by the King, who of course was unaware that Theseus was his son. In fact, he was afraid of the young man's great popularity, thinking that he might win the people over to make him king, and he invited him with the idea of poisoning him. The plan was not his, but Medea's, the heroine of the Quest of the Golden Fleece, who knew through her sorcery who Theseus was. She had fled to

Athens when she left Corinth in her winged car, and she had acquired great influence over Aegeus, which she did not want disturbed by the appearance of a son. But as she handed him the poisoned cup, Theseus, wishing to make himself known at once to his father, drew his sword. The King instantly recognized it and dashed the cup to the ground. Medea escaped, as she always did, and got safely away to Asia.

Aegeus then proclaimed to the country that Theseus was his son and heir. The new heir apparent soon had an opportunity to endear himself to the Athenians. **B**

Years before his arrival in Athens, a terrible misfortune had happened to the city. Minos, the powerful ruler of Crete, had lost his only son, Androgenes,[5] while the young man was visiting the Athenian king. King Aegeus had done what no host should do: He had sent his guest on an expedition full of peril—to kill a dangerous bull. Instead, the bull had killed the youth. Minos invaded the country, captured Athens and declared that he would raze it to the ground unless every nine years the people sent him a tribute[6] of seven maidens and seven youths. A horrible fate awaited these young creatures. When they reached Crete they were given to the Minotaur to devour.

The Minotaur was a monster, half bull, half human, the offspring of Minos' wife Pasiphaë[7] and a wonderfully beautiful bull. Poseidon[8] had given this bull to Minos in order that he should

---

2. **Sciron** (SY rawn).
3. **Procrustes** (proh KRUHS teez).
4. **banes:** causes of destruction or ruin.

5. **Androgenes** (an DRAW juh neez).
6. **tribute:** something paid by one nation or ruler to another as an acknowledgment of submission.
7. **Pasiphaë** (puh SIF ay ee).
8. **Poseidon** (puh SY duhn): god of horses and of the sea; brother of Zeus.

B **Reading Focus** **Summarizing** What are the key events of this first part of the Theseus myth?

Vocabulary **acknowledged** (ak NAHL ihjd) *adj.*: admitted; recognized to be true.
endear (ehn DIHR) *v.*: inspire affection.

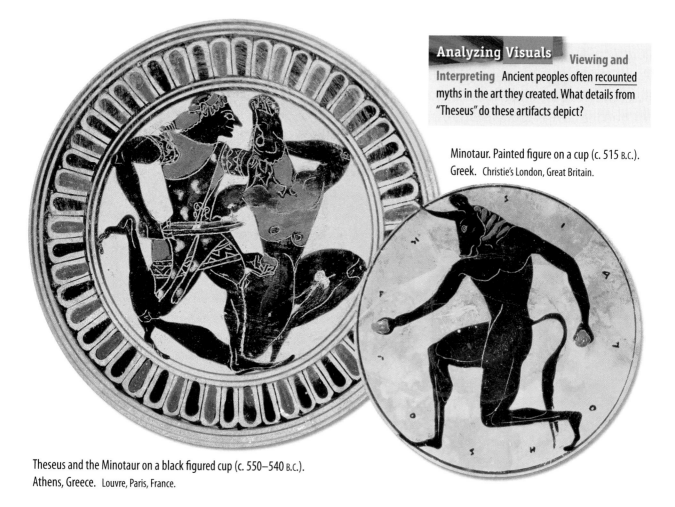

Minotaur. Painted figure on a cup (c. 515 B.C.). Greek. Christie's London, Great Britain.

Theseus and the Minotaur on a black figured cup (c. 550–540 B.C.). Athens, Greece. Louvre, Paris, France.

sacrifice it to him, but Minos could not bear to slay it and kept it for himself. To punish him, Poseidon had made Pasiphaë fall madly in love with it. **C**

When the Minotaur was born, Minos did not kill him. He had Daedalus,[9] a great architect and inventor, construct a place of confinement for him from which escape was impossible. Daedalus built the Labyrinth, famous throughout the world. Once inside, one would go endlessly along its twisting paths without ever finding the exit. To this place the young Athenians were each time taken and left to the

Minotaur. There was no possible way to escape. In whatever direction they ran, they might be running straight to the monster; if they stood still, he might at any moment emerge from the maze. Such was the doom which awaited fourteen youths and maidens a few days after Theseus reached Athens. The time had come for the next installment of the tribute.

At once Theseus came forward and offered to be one of the victims. All loved him for his goodness and admired him for his nobility, but they had no idea that he intended to try to kill the Minotaur. He told his father, however, and promised him that if he succeeded, he would have the black sail which the ship with its cargo

---

9. **Daedalus** (DEHD uh luhs).

C **Literary Focus** Myths and Heroes Why does Poseidon make Minos's wife fall in love with a bull?

of misery always carried changed to a white one, so that Aegeus could know long before it came to land that his son was safe.

When the young victims arrived in Crete, they were paraded before the inhabitants on their way to the Labyrinth. Minos' daughter Ariadne was among the spectators, and she fell in love with Theseus at first sight as he marched past her. She sent for Daedalus and told him he must show her a way to get out of the Labyrinth, and she sent for Theseus and told him she would bring about his escape if he would promise to take her back to Athens and marry her. As may be imagined, he made no difficulty about that, and she gave him the clue she had got from Daedalus, a ball of thread which he was to fasten at one end to the inside of the door and unwind as he went on. This he did and, certain that he could retrace his steps whenever he chose, he walked boldly into the maze, looking for the Minotaur. He came upon him asleep and fell upon him, pinning him to the ground; and with his fists—he had no other weapon—he battered the monster to death. **D**

> As an oak tree falls on the hillside
> Crushing all that lies beneath,
> So Theseus. He presses out the life,
> The brute's savage life, and now it lies dead.
> Only the head sways slowly, but the horns
> are useless now.

When Theseus lifted himself up from that terrific struggle, the ball of thread lay where he had dropped it. With it in his hands, the way out was clear. The others followed, and taking Ariadne with them they fled to the ship and over the sea toward Athens.

On the way there they put in at the island of Naxos, and what happened then is differently reported. One story says that Theseus deserted Ariadne. She was asleep, and he sailed away without her, but Dionysus found her and comforted her. The other story is much more favorable to Theseus. She was extremely seasick, and he set her ashore to recover while he returned to the ship to do some necessary work. A violent wind carried him out to sea and kept him there a long time. On his return he found that Ariadne had died, and he was deeply afflicted.

> They had no idea that he intended to try to kill the Minotaur.

Both stories agree that when they drew near to Athens, he forgot to hoist the white sail. Either his joy at the success of his voyage put every other thought out of his head, or his grief for Ariadne. The black sail was seen by his father, King Aegeus, from the Acropolis,[10] where for days he had watched the sea with straining eyes. It was to him the sign of his son's death, and he threw himself down from a rocky height into the sea and was killed. The sea into which he fell was called the Aegean ever after. **E**

---

10. **Acropolis** (uh KRAWP uh lihs): fortified heights in Athens. A huge temple to Athena stands on top of the hill.

D **Reading Focus** **Summarizing** How does Theseus defeat the Minotaur?

E **Literary Focus** **Myths and Heroes** What human qualities does Theseus exhibit after he kills the Minotaur, and what are the results of his actions?

Vocabulary **afflicted** (uh FLIHKT ihd) *adj.:* upset; saddened.

So Theseus became King of Athens, a most wise and disinterested king. He declared to the people that he did not wish to rule over them; he wanted a people's government where all would be equal. He resigned his royal power and organized a commonwealth, building a council hall where the citizens should gather and vote. The only office he kept for himself was that of commander in chief. Thus Athens became, of all earth's cities, the happiest and most prosperous, the only true home of liberty, the one place in the world where the people governed themselves. It was for this reason that in the great War of the Seven against Thebes,[11] when the victorious Thebans refused burial to those of the enemy who had died, the vanquished[12] turned to Theseus and Athens for help, believing that free men under such a leader would never consent to having the helpless dead wronged. They did not turn in vain. Theseus led his army against Thebes, conquered her, and forced her to allow the dead to be buried. But when he was victor, he did not return evil to the Thebans for the evil they had done. He showed himself the perfect knight. He refused to let his army enter and loot the city. He had come not to harm Thebes, but to bury the Argive[13] dead, and that duty done he led his soldiers back to Athens.

---

11. **Thebes** (theebz): chief city of Boeotia, a region in ancient Greece.

12. **vanquished:** conquered or defeated people.
13. **Argive** (AHR jyv): another word for "Greek." All of these people were Greek, but they gave allegiance to their separate small kingdoms.

F **Literary Focus** Myths and Heroes What heroic qualities does Theseus show as a leader?

Vocabulary **prosperous** (PRAHS puhr uhs) *adj.:* wealthy.
consent (kuhn SEHNT) *v.:* agree.

Ariadne (15th century) by L'Antico (1460–1528).
Partially gilded bronze bust.
Kunsthistorisches Museum, Vienna, Austria.

Applying Your Skills

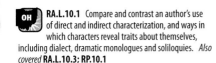
RA.L.10.1 Compare and contrast an author's use of direct and indirect characterization, and ways in which characters reveal traits about themselves, including dialect, dramatic monologues and soliloquies. *Also covered* **RA.L.10.3; RP.10.1**

Theseus

Respond and Think Critically

Reading Focus

Quick Check

1. Why does Medea try to prevent King Aegeus from recognizing his son?

2. Why does King Aegeus kill himself?

Read with a Purpose

3. What events in the myth show that Theseus has a human side? Is he a hero, despite his flaws?

Reading Skills: Summarizing

4. Use your graphic organizer to create a brief summary of the myth. Compare summaries with a partner. Did you cover the same points?

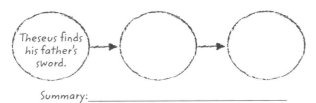

Theseus finds his father's sword.

Summary: _____

Literary Focus

Literary Analysis

5. **Infer** Why does Theseus insist on taking the land route to Athens? What does this suggest about his character?

6. **Infer** What does Androgenes' story tell you about the Greeks' view of kindness to strangers?

7. **Compare and Contrast** In what ways are Theseus and Aegeus different, as rulers and as men? In what ways are they similar?

8. **Infer** How does Theseus change the situation between Athens and Crete? What can you infer about the two city-states' relationship?

Literary Skills: Myths and Heroes

9. **Compare** What qualities of a hero does Theseus exhibit? What recurring themes exist in Theseus's tale and those of other heroes you've read about?

10. **Infer** Why do you think this myth is important to the Greeks? What values does this myth depict that Greeks thought were important?

Literary Skills Review: Conflict

11. **Analyze** A **conflict** is a struggle faced by a character and can be either internal or external. What internal conflicts does Theseus face in this myth?

Writing Focus

Think as a Reader/Writer

Use It in Your Writing Review the formal sentences you copied into your *Reader/Writer Notebook*. Then, rewrite the sentences in less formal, more conversational language. How does this change the tone of the narrative?

What Do You Think Now

What are the most important qualities of a hero?

Applying Your Skills

Theseus

Vocabulary Development

Vocabulary Check

Answer each of the questions below.

1. How might you **acknowledge** a new member of the student council?
2. If you wanted to **endear** yourself to your teacher, what would you do?
3. If you were **afflicted** with a sudden illness, where would you go for help?
4. In order to ensure a **prosperous** future, would you save your money or spend it?
5. How can you show someone that you **consent** to his or her plan?

Language Coach

Suffixes Practice using the suffixes *–ous* and *–ment*. Look up the following base words in the dictionary and write the definitions in the space. Then, without looking in the dictionary, write the definition of the word with the suffix.

1. **base word:** *indict* _____
   indictment _____
2. **base word:** *ridicule* _____
   ridiculous _____
3. **base word:** *murder* _____
   murderous _____

Vocabulary Skills: Words Derived from Greek and Roman Myths

The English language includes many words that come from characters and places in Greek and Roman myths. For example, the continent of Europe is named for Europa, a beautiful woman loved by Zeus in Greek myths, and the month of January is named for Janus, the Roman god of dates.

Your Turn

Answer the questions below. You might need to look up the derivations of words in a dictionary.

1. The **Furies** were wild female spirits who punished wrongdoers and avenged crimes. *How is the word* furious *related to the Furies?*
2. The Greek gods were said to live atop **Mount Olympus** in Greece. *What U.S. mountain range is named for this home of the gods?*
3. **Odysseus,** from Homer's *Odyssey*, took ten years to get home from the Trojan War. *How is the word* odyssey *related to Odysseus's journey?*

Academic Vocabulary

Write About . . .

Answer the following questions using the Academic Vocabulary words.

1. What is a recurring theme in the myth of Theseus? How do gods and humans interact?
2. Recount the story of the Minotaur. How did he come to be, and why does King Minos demand a tribute from the Athenians?

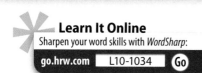

Learn It Online
Sharpen your word skills with *WordSharp*:

go.hrw.com   L10-1034   **Go**

V0.10.3 Infer the literal and figurative meaning of words and phrases and discuss the function of figurative language, including metaphors, similes, idioms and puns. *Also covered* **V0.10.5; V0.10.6; WA.10.2; WC.10.3; WP.10.17**

Grammar Link

Phrases

A **phrase** is a group of words that does not contain a verb and a subject. Phrases can be used as a part of speech. Three common types are prepositional, appositive, and participial phrases.

A **prepositional phrase** begins with a preposition, ends with the object of the preposition, and may include one or more descriptive words.

> Dad came *with me.*
> We went *to the doctor's office.*

An **appositive** is a noun or pronoun that describes another noun or pronoun. An **appositive phrase** consists of an appositive and its modifiers.

> Braulio, *the film's director*, shouted, "Cut!"
> Have you met my sister *Lin*?

A **participial phrase** consists of a **participle**—the *-ing* or *-ed* form of a verb used as an adjective—and related words.

> *Running to catch the bus*, I dropped my book.
> Roland, *amused by the story,* couldn't stop laughing.

Your Turn

Writing Applications Identify the type of phrase italicized in each sentence. Then, write three sentences of your own, using each type of phrase.

1. *Shocked and saddened*, the detective surveyed the crime scene.
2. I walked *around the puddle* to avoid getting my feet wet.
3. Mrs. Cepeda, *our social studies teacher,* gives really hard tests.

CHOICES

As you respond to the Choices, use these **Academic Vocabulary** words as appropriate: recurring, exhibit, retain, and recount.

REVIEW
Write About a Real Hero

Timed ⌐Writing Think about real people in sports, movies, or history who are considered to be heroes. Choose the person who most reminds you of Theseus. Could your hero's story be a modern-day myth? Write an essay explaining why this person is a hero and how he or she is similar to Theseus. Support your points with details from the selection and facts about your real-life hero.

CONNECT
Storyboard the Myth

TechFocus Many Greek myths have been made into films. Imagine you are writing a script about Theseus. With a partner, create a storyboard for one of the scenes from the myth. You might focus on the story of Androgenes, or the slaying of the Minotaur. Use details from the text in your storyboard. Exhibit your storyboard for the class.

EXTEND
Retell the Myth

The myth of Theseus is recounted in the third-person point of view, giving us few glimpses into the hero's feelings. Retell one of the major episodes from Theseus's point of view, recounting how he feels about the events and what motivates him to act as he does.

Learn It Online
There's more to this story than meets the eye. Expand your view with these Internet links:

go.hrw.com   L10-1035   **Go**

Momotaro:
Boy-of-the-Peach

retold by **Yoshiko Uchida**

The illustrations in this story are from "Momotaro" (1951), illustrated by Goro Arai, Koyosha Shuppan. Osaka, Japan. (Above) Momotaro shares his millet dumplings with a monkey, a dog, and a pheasant.

What Do You Think?

What qualities can help a hero succeed in a quest?

QuickWrite

Think about folk tales, fables, and fairy tales you have read. Who was the hero of each story, and how was he or she special? Write a few sentences describing these heroes.

 **Reader/Writer Notebook**

Use your **RWN** to complete the activities for this selection.

OH **RA.L.10.1** Compare and contrast an author's use of direct and indirect characterization, and ways in which characters reveal traits about themselves, including dialect, dramatic monologues and soliloquies.

RA.L.10.5 Analyze how an author's choice of genre affects the expression of a theme or topic. **RA.I.10.1** Identify and understand organizational patterns and techniques, including repetition of ideas, syntax and word choice, that authors use to accomplish their purpose and reach their intended audience.

Literary Focus

Heroes and Folk Tales A **hero** (or a **heroine**) is a character who faces a difficult situation and tries to overcome it using courage and ingenuity. Many folk tales involve a hero who goes on a **quest,** or a journey toward a goal. **Folk tales** are stories that have been handed down from generation to generation. Unlike myths, folk tales are not religious, but are told mostly to teach lessons and to entertain. As you read "Momotaro: Boy of the Peach," consider what makes the main character a hero and how he accomplishes his quest.

Reading Focus

Identifying a Sequence of Events When you look at the events in a story and the order in which they are told, you are **identifying the sequence of events.** As you read a narrative, ask yourself whether the events are <u>recounted</u> in **chronological order** (the order in which they happen over time), through **flashbacks** (references to an earlier time), or with a different sequence. When you understand the sequence of events, you can review them in order and analyze the importance of each event to the story.

Into Action As you read "Momotaro: Boy-of-the-Peach," note the main events of the story in the order in which they are told. Create a graphic like the one below and write each event in order from left to right.

The old woman brings the peach home.

Vocabulary

stalking (STAWK ihng) *v.:* approaching while trying not to be seen or heard. *The dog was stalking Momotaro because he did not know the boy's intentions.*

plundering (PLUHN duhr ihng) *v.* used as *adj.:* stealing; taking as much as possible. *The plundering ogres had left the people of the countryside with nothing to live on.*

Language Coach

Context Clues Often, you can use **context clues,** the words or phrases surrounding an unfamiliar word, to help you understand that word's meaning. For example, when Momotaro meets the pheasant, he calls it a "brave bird." Even without the footnote, then, you would have known that a pheasant is a type of bird. Find the words *stronghold* (when Momotaro comes to Ogre Island) and *laden* (near the end of the story). Use context clues to guess the meanings of these words; then look them up in the dictionary. Compare your guesses to the definitions.

Writing Focus

Think as a Reader/Writer

Find It in Your Reading Folk tales often contain magical elements—things that are not possible in real life. Find these elements in "Momotaro" and note them in your *Reader/WriterNotebook*.

 **Learn It Online**
Delve into vocabulary with Word Watch:

go.hrw.com | L10-1037 | **Go**

Yoshiko Uchida
(1921–1992)

An Outsider in Her Own Land

Born in California to Japanese parents, Yoshiko Uchida received a terrible shock when Japan and the United States went to war. After Japan attacked the United States at Pearl Harbor in December 1941, the U.S. government feared that Japanese Americans might be spying for the Japanese military. Thousands—many of them citizens like Uchida—were sent to live in makeshift relocation camps. In 1942, Uchida and her family were sent to live in a harsh relocation camp in the Utah desert. The experience affected Uchida strongly, and she wrote about it in several books, including *Journey to Topaz* (1971) and *Journey Home* (1978).

Sharing Japanese Culture

When she was a child, Uchida's father read Japanese folk tales to her and her sister. She included some of these stories in her first book, *The Dancing Kettle* (1949). As an adult, she studied in Japan for two years and collected more traditional stories. Through these tales, and her original children's stories, Uchida shared her experiences of Japanese culture with young people. About her work, she commented, "I feel that children need the sense of community that comes through knowing the past."

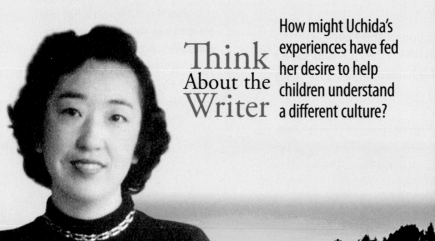

Think About the Writer — How might Uchida's experiences have fed her desire to help children understand a different culture?

Build Background

The story of Momotaro is very well known in Japan. It has been <u>recounted</u> countless times in books, films, and songs. The tale of Momotaro dates back to the Edo Period of Japan (1603–1868).

Preview the Selection

The main character of this tale is **Momotaro,** a boy born under unusual circumstances. When he undertakes a heroic quest, he is helped by three animals—a **dog,** a **monkey,** and a **bird.**

Momotaro:
Boy-of-the-Peach

retold by **Yoshiko Uchida**

Once long, long ago, there lived a kind old man and a kind old woman in a small village in Japan.

One fine day they set out from their little cottage together. The old man went toward the mountains to cut some firewood for their kitchen, and the old woman went toward the river to do her washing.

When the old woman reached the shore of the river, she knelt down beside her wooden tub and began to scrub her clothes on a round, flat stone. Suddenly she looked up and saw something very strange floating down the shallow river. It was an enormous peach, bigger than the round wooden tub that stood beside the old woman.

Rumbley-bump and a-bumpety-bump . . . Rumbley-bump and a-bumpety-bump. The big peach rolled closer and closer over the stones in the stream.

"My gracious me!" the old woman said to herself. "In all my long life I have never seen a peach of such great size and beauty. What a fine present it would make for the old man. I do think I will take it home with me."

Then the old woman stretched out her hand just as far as she could, but no matter how hard she stretched, she couldn't reach the big peach.

"If I could just find a long stick, I would be able to reach it," thought the old woman, looking around, but all she could see were pebbles and sand.

"Oh, dear, what shall I do?" she said to herself. Then suddenly she thought of a way to bring the beautiful big peach to her side. She began to sing out in a sweet, clear voice:

The deep waters are salty!
The shallow waters are sweet!
Stay away from the salty water,
And come where the water is sweet.

She sang this over and over, clapping her hands in time to her song. Then, strangely enough, the big peach slowly began to bob along toward the shore where the water was shallow. **Ⓐ**

Rumbley-bump and a-bumpety-bump . . . Rumbley-bump and a-bumpety-bump. The big peach came closer and closer to the old woman and finally came to a stop at her feet.

Ⓐ **Literary Focus** Heroes and Folk Tales Why does the old woman want to get the peach?

As he grows up, Momotaro becomes a fine strong youth. One day, he sets out to punish the *oni* (ogres) who are harassing people.

The old woman was so happy she picked the big peach up very carefully and quickly carried it home in her arms. Then she waited for the old man to return so she could show him her lovely present. Toward evening the old man came home with a big pack of wood on his back.

"Come quickly, come quickly," the old woman called to him from the house.

"What is it? What is the matter?" the old man asked as he hurried to the side of the old woman.

"Just look at the fine present I have for you," said the old woman happily as she showed him the big round peach.

"My goodness! What a great peach! Where in the world did you buy such a peach as this?" the old man asked.

The old woman smiled happily and told him how she had found the peach floating down the river.

"Well, well, this is a fine present indeed," said the old man, "for I have worked hard today and I am very hungry."

Then he got the biggest knife they had so he

could cut the big peach in half. Just as he was ready to thrust the sharp blade into the peach, he heard a tiny voice from inside.

"Wait, old man! Don't cut me!" it cried, and before the surprised old man and woman could say a word, the beautiful big peach broke in two, and a sweet little boy jumped out from inside. The old man and woman were so surprised they could only raise their hands and cry out, "Oh, oh! My goodness!"

Now the old man and woman had always wanted a child of their own, so they were very, very happy to find such a fine little boy, and decided to call him "Momotaro," which means boy-of-the-peach. They took very good care of the little boy and grew to love him dearly, for he was a fine young lad. They spent many happy years together, and before long Momotaro was fifteen years old. **B**

One day Momotaro came before the old man and said, "You have both been good and kind to me. I am very grateful for all you have done, and now I think I am old enough to do some good for others too. I have come to ask if I may leave you."

"You wish to leave us, my son? But why?" asked the old man in surprise.

"Oh, I shall be back in a very short time," said Momotaro. "I wish only to go to the Island of the Ogres, to rid the land of those harmful creatures. They have killed many good people, and have stolen and robbed throughout the country. I wish to kill the ogres so they can never harm our people again." **C**

"That is a fine idea, my son, and I will not stop you from going," said the old man.

So that very day Momotaro got ready to start out on his journey. The old woman prepared some millet[1] cakes for him to take along on his trip, and soon Momotaro was ready to leave. The old man and woman were sad to see him go and called, "Be careful, Momotaro! Come back safely to us."

"Yes, yes, I shall be back soon," he answered. "Take care of yourselves while I am away," he added, and waved as he started down the path toward the forest.

He hurried along, for he was anxious to get to the Island of the Ogres. While he was walking through the cool forest where the grass grew long and high, he began to feel hungry. He sat down at the foot of a tall pine tree and carefully unwrapped the *furoshiki*[2] which held his little millet cakes. "My, they smell good," he thought. Suddenly he heard the tall grass rustle and saw something stalking through the grass toward him. Momotaro blinked hard when he saw what it was. It was a dog as big as a calf! But Momotaro was not frightened, for the dog just said, "Momotaro-san,[3] Momotaro-san, what is it you are eating that smells so good?"

"I'm eating a delicious millet cake which my good mother made for me this morning," he answered.

The dog licked his chops and looked at the cake with hungry eyes. "Please, Momotaro-san," he said, "just give me one of your millet cakes, and I will come along with you to the Island of

---

1. **millet** (MIHL uht): a kind of grain.
2. *furoshiki*: a piece of cloth used to wrap and carry items.
3. **Momotaro-san:** In Japanese, adding *san* to the end of a person's name is a mark of respect, similar to addressing a person in English as Mr., Ms., or Mrs.

B **Reading Focus** **Sequence of Events** How many years have passed since the old woman found the peach?

C **Literary Focus** **Heroes and Folk Tales** What quest does Momotaro undertake here?

Vocabulary **stalking** (STAWK ihng) *v.*: approaching while trying not to be seen or heard.

the Ogres. I know why you are going there, and I can be of help to you." **D**

"Very well, my friend," said Momotaro, "I will take you along with me." And he gave the dog one of his millet cakes to eat.

As they walked on, something suddenly leaped from the branches above and jumped in front of Momotaro. He stopped in surprise and found that it was a monkey who had jumped down from the trees.

"Greetings, Momotaro-san!" called the monkey happily. "I have heard that you are going to the Island of the Ogres to rid the land of these plundering creatures. Take me with you, for I wish to help you in your fight."

When the dog heard this, he growled angrily. "Grruff," he said to the monkey. "I am going to help Momotaro-san. We do not need the help of a monkey such as you! Out of our way! Grruff, grruff," he barked angrily.

"How dare you speak to me like that?" shrieked the monkey, and he leaped at the dog, scratching with his sharp claws. The dog and the monkey began to fight each other, biting, clawing, and growling. When Momotaro saw this, he pushed them apart and cried, "Here, here, stop it, you two! There is no reason why you both cannot go with me to the Island of the Ogres. I shall have two helpers instead of one!" Then he took another millet cake from his *furoshiki* and gave it to the monkey. Now there were three of them going down the path to the edge of the woods—the dog in front, Momotaro in the middle, and the monkey walking in the rear. Soon they came to a big field, and just as they were about to cross it, a large pheasant[4]

hopped out in front of them. The dog jumped at it with a growl, but the pheasant fought back with such spirit that Momotaro ran over to stop the dog. "We could use a brave bird such as you to help us fight the ogres. We are on our way to their island this very day. How would you like to come along with us?"

"Oh, I would like that indeed, for I would like to help you rid the land of these evil and dangerous ogres," said the pheasant happily.

"Then here is a millet cake for you, too," said Momotaro, giving the pheasant a cake, just as he had the monkey and the dog.

Now there were four of them going to the Island of the Ogres, and as they walked down the path together, they became very good friends.

Before long they came to the water's edge and Momotaro found a boat big enough for all of them. They climbed in and headed for the Island of the Ogres. Soon they saw the island in the distance, wrapped in gray, foggy clouds. Dark stone walls rose up above towering cliffs, and large iron gates stood ready to keep out any who tried to enter.

Momotaro thought for a moment, then turned to the pheasant and said, "You alone can wing your way over their high walls and gates. Fly into their stronghold now, and do what you can to frighten them. We will follow as soon as we can." **E**

So the pheasant flew far above the iron gates and stone walls and down onto the roof of the ogres' castle. Then he called to the ogres,

---

4. **pheasant** (FEHZ uhnt): a kind of large bird.

D **Reading Focus** Sequence of Events What events occur after Momotaro sits down to eat a millet cake?

E **Literary Focus** Heroes and Folk Tales How does the pheasant help the hero in his quest?

Vocabulary **plundering** (PLUHN duhr ihng) *v.* used as *adj.*: stealing; taking as much as possible.

"Momotaro-san has come to rid the land of you and your many evil deeds. Give up your stolen treasures now, and perhaps he will spare your lives!"

When the ogres heard this, they laughed and shouted, "HO, HO, HO! We are not afraid of a little bird like you! We are not afraid of little Momotaro!"

The pheasant became very angry at this, and flew down, pecking at the heads of the ogres with his sharp, pointed beak. While the pheasant was fighting so bravely, the dog and monkey helped Momotaro to tear down the gates, and they soon came to the aid of the pheasant.  **F**

"Get away! Get away!" shouted the ogres, but the monkey clawed and scratched, the big dog growled and bit the ogres, and the pheasant flew about, pecking at their heads and faces. So fierce were they that soon the ogres began to run away. Half of them tumbled over the cliffs as they ran, and the others fell pell-mell[5] into the sea. Soon only the Chief of the Ogres remained.

---

5. **pell-mell** (PEHL MEHL): in a confused, rushing crowd.

F **Reading Focus** **Sequence of Events** What happens while the pheasant is attacking the ogres?

Analyzing Visuals **Viewing and Interpreting** What details in the painting resemble the descriptions in the story?

Mighty Momotaro defeats the *oni*.

Momotaro goes to the home of the old man and woman with his arms full of jewels and treasures from Ogre Island.

He threw up his hands, and then bowed low to Momotaro. "Please spare me my life, and all our stolen treasures are yours. I promise never to rob or kill anyone again," he said.

Momotaro tied up the evil ogre, while the monkey, the dog, and the pheasant carried many boxes filled with jewels and treasures down to their little boat. Soon it was laden with all the treasures it could hold, and they were ready to sail toward home.

When Momotaro returned, he went from one family to another, returning the many treasures which the ogres had stolen from the people of the land.

"You will never again be troubled by the ogres of Ogre Island!" he said to them happily.

And they all answered, "You are a kind and brave lad, and we thank you for making our land safe once again."

Then Momotaro went back to the home of the old man and woman with his arms full of jewels and treasures from Ogre Island. The old man and woman were so glad to see him once again, and the three of them lived happily together for many, many years. **G**

G Literary Focus Heroes and Folk Tales How does Momotaro's quest end?

Applying Your Skills

RA.L.10.1 Compare and contrast an author's use of direct and indirect characterization, and ways in which characters reveal traits about themselves, including dialect, dramatic monologues and soliloquies. *Also covered* **RA.L.10.5; RA.L.10.3; RA.I.10.1; VO.10.3; WA.10.1.c**

Momotaro: Boy-of-the-Peach

Respond and Think Critically

Reading Focus

Quick Check

1. Describe the quest Momataro undertakes. Why does he go to the land of the Ogres?

2. Explain how each of the animals helps Momotaro in his quest.

Read with a Purpose

3. Why do you think this folk tale is popular in Japan? What gives it a universal appeal? Explain.

Reading Skills: Identifying a Sequence of Events

4. Review the graphic you created showing the sequence of events in the story. Why are these events important to the final outcome of the story? Who benefits from Momotaro's quest?

✓ Vocabulary Check

Choose the Vocabulary word that *best* completes each sentence.

> stalking   plundering

5. The _____ armies had taken all the crops from the fields and the treasures from the houses.

6. Unseen and silent, the lion was _____ its prey.

Literary Focus

Literary Analysis

7. **Infer** What can you infer about the the old woman by her actions in the first part of the story? Explain.

8. **Compare and Contrast** What elements of the story are similar to events that could happen in real life? What elements could not happen in real life?

Literary Skills: Heroes and Folk Tales

9. **Analyze** What heroic qualities does Momotaro exhibit? Use details from the text to support your answer.

10. **Compare** Can you think of any other heroes or heroines who have mysterious origins? Do you recall other quest stories involving friends who help the hero or heroine accomplish a difficult task? Describe these recurring themes.

Literary Skills Review: Plot and Setting

11. **Analyze** Describe the setting of this folk tale. How does the setting contribute to the plot of the story?

Writing Focus

Think as a Reader/Writer

Use It in Your Writing Review the magical aspects of "Momotaro" that you recorded in your *Reader/Writer Notebook*. Think about why the details are important to the folk tale. Then, write a short story using at least one magical element. Be sure the magic is integral—important and vital—to the story.

What Do You Think Now

What are some qualities that all heroes possess?

Sigurd, the Dragon Slayer

retold by **Olivia E. Coolidge**

What Do You Think

How did myths help people explain their world?

QuickWrite

How would you describe a hero or heroine and a qu
today? What qualities would he or she have, and w
type of challenge would take extraordinary courag

Reader/Writer Notebook

Use your **RWN** to complete the activities for this selection.

OH **RA.L.10.5** Analyze how an author's choice of genre affects the expression of a theme or topic. **RP.10.3** Monitor own comprehension by adjusting speed to fit the purpose, or by skimming, scanning, reading on, looking back, note taking or summarizing what has been read so far in text.

Literary Focus

Norse Myths A **myth** is a traditional religious story that often explains the origins of natural phenomena and defines the values of the people who believe in them. **Norse mythology** consists of stories that were told in Scandinavia and Germany for thousands of years. Unlike the Greek myths, the Norse myths foretell a day of doom when the entire world will be consumed by fire and all life will end. Such being the tragic outlook of the Norse people, it is not surprising to find that the human heroes of their myths have much to endure.

Reading Focus

Monitoring Your Reading When you **monitor your reading,** you take note of what you do and do not understand about a story as you read. Ask yourself whether the events and vocabulary make sense, and periodically summarize while reading to help clarify your understanding of Norse myths.

Into Action Before you read "Sigurd, the Dragon Slayer," create a KWL chart like the one below. Then, skim the list of characters on page 1049, and begin to fill in the columns "What I Know" and "What I Want to Find Out." As you read, continue to fill in the chart.

What I Know (K)	What I Want to Find Out (W)	What I Learned (L)
Sigurd goes out to win fame.	How will he do it?	

Vocabulary

cunning (KUHN ihng) *adj.:* clever in a way that is intended to deceive. *The man was cunning in his old age as he tried to tempt the boy to tell his secret.*

wrath (rath) *n.:* fury often marked by a desire for revenge. *The king's wrath was enough to make every statue leap from its pedestal.*

writhed (rythd) *v.:* violently twisted and rolled, especially as a result of severe pain. *As the giant creature writhed in agony, the dragon slayer dealt the death blow.*

Language Coach

Multiple-Meaning Words Many words have multiple meanings. For example:

well — a hole dug for water
— to spring or rise
— good, right

When using the dictionary, look at *all* the meanings of a word and decide which one works for what you are reading. Look for multiple-meaning words in "Sigurd, the Dragon Slayer."

Writing Focus

Think as a Reader/Writer

Find It in Your Reading Pay attention to the dialogue between characters in "Sigurd, the Dragon Slayer." In your *Reader/Writer Notebook*, note what the dialogue reveals about the characters.

Learn It Online
Hear a professional actor read this myth, at:

go.hrw.com   L10-1047   **Go**

Olivia E. Coolidge
(1908–2006)

The Search for Home

Born in England in the early part of the twentieth century, Olivia Coolidge lived in a rural area without electricity or hot water. She retained good memories of her childhood, recalling the experience as "advantageous" because of the freedom living outside a city allowed her and her four siblings. Coolidge was thirty years old when she came to the United States for what she called "a good, long visit" during World War II, when her country was the target of German air strikes. She remained in the United States, where she became a citizen and began her long writing career.

A Picture of Life

Coolidge wrote mostly for young adults, both fiction and nonfiction. Of her subjects, she said, "I write about history, biography, and ancient legends for teens because I am more interested in values that always have been of concern to people than I am in the form we express them in at this moment. My general purpose . . . is to give a picture of life." Coolidge penned portraits of such historic figures as the leader of Indian independence, Mahatma Gandhi, in *Gandhi* (1971) and an important inspiration for American independence, Thomas Paine, in *Tom Paine* (1969). Coolidge taught Latin and Greek and wrote of many legends and historic adventures, including *The Trojan War* (1951), *Greek Myths* (1949), and *Egyptian Adventures* (1954).

Think About the Writer — What other topics might Coolidge write about to create a "picture of life" today?

Build Background

Norse mythology includes many hero tales, called *sagas,* which are part of the oral storytelling tradition. The story of Sigurd is part of the Volsunga saga, tales of a family of warriors very important to Norse myths.

Preview the Selection

The main character of this tale is **Sigurd,** the son of the great warrior **Sigmund** who dies before his son is born. Sigurd is raised by his mother and her new husband, **King Alf.** A dwarf named **Regin** teaches Sigurd many skills and sends him on his quest to kill the great dragon **Fafnir.**

Neptune's Horses, illustration for "The Greek Mythological Legend," published in London, 1910 by Walter Crane. Bibliothèque des Artes Decoratifs, Paris, France-Archives Charmet.

CHARACTERS IN THE MYTH

Regin (REE juhn): son of Reidmar, the dwarf king. In Norse mythology, dwarfs are a race of ugly, deceitful creatures who live under the earth and work as master craftsmen.

Sigurd (SIHG urd): son of Sigmund. He is brought up by his mother Hiordis and her new husband, King Alf, after Sigmund is killed in battle. Sigurd is the most famous hero in Norse mythology, the last of the Volsung family.

Sigmund (SIHG muhnd): Sigurd's father, who was killed in battle before Sigurd's birth.

Hiordis (HYAHR dihs): mother of Sigurd, who married King Alf after her husband Sigmund was killed in battle.

Fafnir (FAHV nihr): an evil dwarf who turned himself into a dragon. Fafnir is Regin's brother.

Reidmar (REED mahr): the dwarf king, father of Regin, Otter, and Fafnir.

Odin (OH dihn): leader of the gods and the god of war and wisdom. Odin assists Sigurd in his quest to kill Fafnir.

King Alf: king of Denmark, who married the widow Hiordis after her husband was killed in battle.

Sigurd, the Dragon Slayer

retold by **Olivia E. Coolidge**

Introduction

Sigurd's story is part of a cycle of hero sagas. Before this story opens, Loki, the cunning god of fire, thoughtlessly kills an otter sunning itself— but the otter is actually the son of Reidmar, the king of the dwarfs.

That night, Reidmar captures Loki and Odin, king of the gods. Furious, the dwarf king threatens to kill both of them in revenge for his son's death. Odin suggests a ransom instead. So Loki is sent off to steal the famous gold hoard of the elf Andvari.

When Reidmar receives the gold, he frees his hostages—but the lust for gold can result in evil. That night the dwarf king's son, Fafnir, kills his own father and seizes the elfin treasure for himself. The third son of the dwarf king, Regin, flees, terrified for his own life.

Many years pass. Fafnir, the brother who stole his father's gold, has changed his shape into that of a dragon. Fafnir now lies coiled jealously around his golden treasure in his dead father's crumbling hall. Meanwhile Regin, the third son, has wandered the world looking for a hero who can slay Fafnir and seize the treasure for Regin.

Vocabulary **cunning** (KUHN ihng) *adj.:* clever in a way that is intended to deceive.

One day a royal child is born in a peaceful kingdom. Regin recognizes the child as the one who will slay the dragon and get the gold. The baby, Sigurd, is the son of the great warrior Sigmund, who died in battle.

Now starts Sigurd's story.

The Dragon Slayer

Regin saw the baby, Sigurd, and his heart was wonderfully stirred, for he knew the dragon slayer was born after ages of time. He said nothing to Hiordis, who had borne this son to Sigmund, the Volsung, after that great hero had died. He kept his own counsel while the child was an infant, but he burned with secret desire. Years passed more slowly than ever, but at last he saw Sigurd had become a tall, golden-haired lad. Then finally he went to King Alf, who had wedded the widowed Hiordis. "My long life draws to a close," he said. "Grant me a pupil before I die, that I may teach him the skill of my hands, the words of my songs, and my herbs of healing, lest my wisdom perish with me and be forgotten."

"It is a good request," answered Alf, "and I grant it. Whom will you have?"

"Give me Sigurd," answered Regin quickly.

"It is done," declared the king, marveling at the beautiful boy who seemed to have touched the heart of this dark, secretive old man.

After this time the aged Regin appeared to recover the fire of his earlier days. The hand of Sigurd became cunning with the harp strings. His strong, young voice delighted the feasters with the legends of ancient time. He worked also with Regin in the smithy,[1] but there he could never rival his master, though among men he was a notable smith. He learned much of strange herbs and of the ways of the woodlands. Of the evil workings of Regin's mind, he understood nothing at all. Yet though other people spoke of the old man's love for his pupil, Sigurd felt the cold craft behind it. Though he admired his wise master, he had no affection for him. **Ⓐ**

Sigurd was wielding the hammer in the smithy one day when Regin, studying his mighty form, judged the awaited time was near. "Sigurd," he said when the din[2] ceased and the iron was thrust back in the fire, "you are the last of the Volsungs, who were a great warrior race. Are you content in this tame little country where Alf's sons, your brothers, grow up to be kings?"

Sigurd turned from the fire toward him. "I would ride into the world tomorrow," he answered, "were it not for my mother, and for King Alf, who has treated me well."

"So well," replied Regin drily, "that you have neither horse nor sword."

---

1. **smithy:** (SMIHTH ee): workplace of a smith, one who makes or repairs metal objects in a fiery forge. In former times, smiths used their hammers to shape the hot metal into armor, weapons, and shoes for horses.
2. **din:** noise.

Ⓐ **Literary Focus** Norse Myths What values are revealed in the skills that Sigurd learns?

"I ride what horse I please," retorted Sigurd, "as do the king's own sons."

"Your brothers are children. When they are men like you, they will have their own." **Ⓑ**

"I can have any horse for the asking," persisted Sigurd. This was true, for Alf was pleased by the youth's request.

"The horses are in the pasture at the head of the valley," said he. "Go up and choose which you will. It is time you had one of your own."

As Sigurd ran lightly toward the pasture, many a head turned after him. His bright hair shone in the sun, and in spite of his great size, he moved with the grace of a deer. "What will become of him," thought the elders. "Surely there was never before a young man so handsome and strong."

Odin himself stood in the way near the pasture, watching the young runner approach. The god seemed an old man in tattered garments

---

Ⓑ **Reading Focus** Monitor Your Reading What is Regin trying to get at here—what does he want Sigurd to do?

(detail) Carved portal of Hylestad stave church. Scene from the story of Sigurd: Sigurd kills the dragon Fafnir (12th century), Setesdal, Norway. Viking. Universitetets Oldsaksaming, University Collections, Oslo, Norway.

of gray which stirred, as if in a breeze, though the air was perfectly still. "Greetings," said he, fixing the youth with his one bright eye of blue. "Greetings, Sigurd. Why do you run?"

"To choose me a horse," panted Sigurd. "Are you the herdsman?"

"Do I look like a herdsman?"

"No. Like a warrior."

"You say well," said the god. "I am indeed a warrior, and I knew your father, Sigmund, all his days. Come with me, and let us test the strength of these horses by driving them through the stream."

The river was running in flood, for the snows had melted. Here at the head of the valley it came foaming down from the mountains with a roar. Sigurd and Odin collected the horses and drove them at a gallop down to the riverbank. Some wheeled to right or left when they saw the boiling water, and fled splashing along the shallows, whinnying with alarm. Some plunged full into the torrent, which carried them away, tossing, kicking, rolling, now under and now up. A few swam steadily, though these too were carried down. Only one great gray horse leapt far out into the water and made for the opposite bank. They saw him reach the shallows, climb up, and stand in the flowering meadow to shake his silvery sides. Finally with a snort he plunged back into the water to return.

"I gave your father a sword," said Odin as they watched the great creature breasting the flood. "Now I give you this horse. Ride out and win fame. When you come to the shield-roofed hall of Odin where your father sits, the heroes shall rise to greet you as the greatest one of them all. Look now how Grayfell stands in the shallows. He is of the tireless strain of Sleipner, the horse that Odin rides."

Sigurd leapt down into the water and swung himself onto Grayfell's back. Air whistled past them as they raced down the meadow. Drops sprayed from the mane of Grayfell. Turf flew up behind his heels. The two came thundering down the valley like an avalanche from the hills, huge horse and huge rider gleaming in the light of the evening sun. **Ⓒ**

"Who gave you that horse?" asked Regin when the young man slid off at his door.

"An old man with the wind in his garments and a single, bright blue eye. He spoke to me of my father."

"I know that old man," said Regin sourly. "He knew my father too. Why must he meddle now? But tell me, where will you ride with your fine horse?"

"Into the world."

"But whither? Will you serve some other king?"

"Never that!" cried Sigurd hotly. "I will win my own wealth and fame."

"I have an adventure for you," said Regin. "No man could achieve it till now. It is the winning of a fabulous treasure, enough to make both of us kings."

"What is the deed?"

"Come into the smithy," said Regin. "Blow up the fire, for my tale is long. Sit down by the bench while I tell you who I am, whence came the treasure, and where lies the hideous dragon who was my brother once. Kill him, for he is utterly evil, and take what you will. All I ask is the wisdom which he has stored in his heart for ages on ages, while I squandered[3] mine on men. Roast me the heart of the dragon, that I may eat, and be wise. Then take

---

3. **squandered:** (SKWAWN duhrd): used wastefully or extravagantly.

Ⓒ Literary Focus Norse Myths Why does Odin give Sigurd this horse?

1052 Unit 5 · Collection 9

Apprenticeship

Beginning in the thirteenth century in western Europe, craftsmen were organized into guilds, which regulated standards for each particular trade. A man who wanted to work in a particular craft, such as that of a smith, had to train as an apprentice with a craft master for a period of (typically) seven years. Only then was he likely to be allowed entrance into a guild. The master's shop was often part of his home, so he was always around to guide the apprentices.

Ask Yourself
What skills did Sigurd learn during his apprenticeship that might help him later on in his quest?

Cobbler's Shop (1874) by Giuseppe Constantini.

your fill of the treasure, and leave me what little you please."

Sigurd listened long to the tale of Reidmar and of the curse on Andvari's gold.[4] The fire grew low. The moon came up, as the quiet voice of Regin poured forth his long-stored hate. Each to the other in the darkness seemed only a vague, black shape, but the eyes of Regin gloated[5] on Sigurd, who peered back at his master with a half-formed feeling of doubt. At last silence fell. Sigurd burned for adventure, but Regin burned for the gold. "I will slay the dragon," said Sigurd slowly. "But first, you must make me a sword." **D**

---

4. **curse . . . gold:** Loki, the Norse fire god and master of cunning, forced the elf Andvari to give him all of his golden treasure hoard. Andvari placed a curse on his gold, saying that it would bring sorrow to anyone who owned it.

5. **gloated** (GLOH tuhd): looked at with spiteful pleasure.

"Get up and light me the torches," answered Regin. "I have made you a sword against this day. Open my chest there, and take it. All my skill went into the work."

Sigurd opened the chest by the wall and took out a gold-hilted sword. Down the dark blade ran strange signs of magic, and the hilt was studded with gems. He turned it over in his hands and scanned it, but the great blade had never a flaw. "Let us prove your skill, master of smiths," said he. With that, he swung it high and brought it down on the anvil with all his force. The blade broke with a fearful crash, and the point quivered past Regin's ear. Sigurd laughed at his master's frightened face as he threw the hilt on the floor. "I see this adventure is not for us, since your skill is too poor," he mocked.

"I will make you another," cried Regin. "This time it will never break, though you drive the anvil into the floor."

D **Reading Focus** **Monitor Your Reading** What words in this paragraph signify a change in Sigurd's relationship with Regin?

"When it is done, I will come back," said the hero, "but from this time on nobody is master to me."

It was many days later before Regin was ready. His eyes were red from peering into the fire, as they had been in the workshop of Reidmar. "Come into the smithy," said he. "I have your sword."

The sword lay on the bench dully shining. From hilt to point it was of bare steel unadorned. "Try this on the anvil," said Regin. "I am the master smith, and I tell you that if you break this, no steel that is forged on earth will serve your turn."

Again Sigurd lifted the sword. Again he swung it. Again he brought it down. There was a crack, and the shattered pieces lay strewn at Sigurd's feet. Regin stood astonished, for even he had never suspected the young man's giant strength. Sigurd laughed. "You say truly," he cried. "No sword will serve my turn but one which was not forged in an earthly fire." He cast the pieces from him and strode out. **E**

Queen Hiordis was in the dairy, where the women were making cheese. "Mother," said Sigurd coming to her as she carried a pail of whey. "Mother, where is my father's sword?"

Hiordis started, and a great splash of whey fell from the pan onto the dairy floor. "What need do you have of a sword?" asked she, putting her burden down.

"I am a man," said Sigurd, "and a mighty hero's son. This land is too quiet for me. I will go out and win fame."

"Before you were even born," said Hiordis, "I knew that this day would come. Two months after I was wed, great Sigmund fell, and with him my father and all the men of my house.

I alone hid in a thicket so that the plundering hosts of the enemy passed me by. Then I crept into the moonlight and found where my father lay, and mighty Sigmund with the dead heaped up before him like a wall. In his hand was the hilt of the sword that Odin gave, but the pieces of the shattered blade lay shining around him on the grass. Then I foresaw this day and gathered them up to be your inheritance." **F**

Hiordis went to her room and opened the chest where her clothes were always stored. There, under stiff mantles and robes of silver and blue lay a long piece of gold tissue with something heavy within.

"Your father was old when I wedded him," said she. "His sons had grown up, and won fame, and were dead. Then he wooed me, and I chose him gladly, for I thought, 'What woman will bear a greater hero than the wife of the most famous warrior alive?'"

"My stepfather is no warrior, however," remarked Sigurd.

"Alf is a good man and kind. This is a peaceful land, and I am happy here, but it is not the place for which you were born."

"That is true," said her son, "and I will say farewell, for when I go, I shall never return."

"Your fame will come back," she answered. "It will ring in my ears till I die." She gave him the sword, and he went down the stair and out over the flowering meadow. His mother watched him out of her window till the path hid him from sight.

Regin still sat in the smithy when Sigurd strode in and laid the bundle before him. "There is my sword," he said.

Regin opened the bundle and looked at the pieces, which glowed with a strange, pale

---

E Literary Focus Norse Myths What does this passage suggest about Sigurd's strength?

F Literary Focus Norse Myths What did Sigurd's mother see in her son's future, and how did she prepare for it?

1054 Unit 5 • Collection 9

light. "This was forged in heavenly fires," he said slowly, "and I am of the dwarf people. There is death to me in the steel."

"There is death to the dragon," replied Sigurd.

"Be it so. Leave me the pieces. I will remake the blade."

When Sigurd came again to the smithy, the great sword lay on the bench, and a pale light ran down the center from the hilt to the end of the blade. The edges, however, were dark and sharpened fine as a hair. Sigurd looked at the magic symbols which were carved in the steel. He fitted his hand to the jeweled hilt, and the sword stirred in his grip. He lifted it high and swung it. Suddenly he brought it down. With a crash the anvil fell shattered, while the blade sprung back unharmed. Then he cried, "I name this sword 'the Wrath of Sigurd.' No man shall feel it and live."

Regin said, "The long day is done. It is now a month that I have toiled for you. Tonight let us sleep. Tomorrow we will ride out against Fafnir, and the treasure shall be your own."

Fafnir's End

The hall of the dwarf king, Reidmar, no longer blazed in the sun. The gilt[6] had washed off its beams, the wide door was fallen from its hinges, and grass grew on the roof. "Look!" said Regin, pointing where a great track ran from the threshold[7] down to the riverbank. It was

"I name this sword 'the Wrath of Sigurd.' No man shall feel it and live."

Silver pendant representing Baldur on his horse.
Statens Historiska Museet, Stockholm, Sweden

ground through the dirt of the hillside to the depth of a tall man.

"That path must be made by Fafnir," said Sigurd, "and he uses it often, for no grass grows in it."

"Men say," answered Regin, "that the treasure still lies where my father piled it on the ground before his seat. Around it coils Fafnir, the serpent, gloating over it all day long. But when the moon shines down on him through the rents[8] in the ruined hall, he dreams of his youth, and the spring in the woodlands, and of the great gods he saw when the world was young. The gray morning wakens him early, and at that hour he loathes what he has become. He leaves his treasure and goes out to drink of the river, yet by dawn desire overcomes him once more, so that he returns to the gold." **G**

"When he goes down the path in the morning before it is yet quite light, I will meet him and smite[9] him," said Sigurd.

"His scales are as tough as steel, and it does no good to strike unless you can kill at a blow. Wound him, and he will crush you as you might step on an ant."

"I will dig a pit in the pathway and crouch there in the dark. When he comes, his eyes will be on the river and his mind still full of his dreams. Perhaps he will not see where I lie. Then as he rolls over me, I will thrust up through his belly where the scales are not so strong. This way I may reach his heart."

"But if he sees you?"

---

6. **gilt:** thin covering of gold.
7. **threshold** (THREHSH ohld): entrance; doorway.

8. **rents:** holes; gaps.
9. **smite:** kill.

G **Reading Focus** Monitor Your Reading What does Regin mean when he says Fafnir "loathes what he has become"?

Sigurd laughed. "You will wait another thousand years for a dragon slayer. That is all."

The moon was full and rose early. It took little time to dig the pit. Sigurd wrapped himself in his cloak and went to sleep while Regin stood on guard. He never stirred until Regin, weary of watching, touched his shoulder and whispered, "Hush! It is time."

Overhead at the edge of the mountains, the sky was pale gray by now, but a river mist hung in the valley and clung to the grassy slope, so that low in the depths of Fafnir's track, it was still dark as the grave.

Sigurd crouched, his sword under his cloak, for he feared lest its gleam should be seen. No wind stirred in the trees by the river. A fox barked. The little clouds overhead turned white with the approach of day.

Something moved in the house. There was a scraping sound as though a log were being pushed over the floor. The scales of the monster rattled. A stone rolled down the track. The sounds came closer, and with them a strong, damp, musty smell. Sigurd saw through the thinning mist that a dark shape was filling the sunken pathway from side to side. The dawn was very close. He could see the huge head now almost on the edge of his hole. It was flat and scaly like a snake's, but the weary eyes were human, though of monstrous size. They stared straight through the gloom at Sigurd, whose grip tightened on his sword. For a moment the two seemed to look at each other, eye to eye, yet the monster moved on, dull and unseeing, heavy with sleep.

Black darkness rolled over Sigurd. Stench stifled him. Loose earth filled up the pit. Inch by inch the creature slid over him. Sigurd shut his eyes, set his teeth, and waited. He dared not strike too soon.

After what seemed minutes, he thought, I must risk it now. With that he straightened his knees and drove the sword upward with all his force. It tore up through the cloak, through the loose earth, and on with the force of his arm until it buried itself to the hilt. A great cry came from the monster. The echoing hills threw back and forth to each another a long succession of cries. Fafnir writhed. His huge body arched like a bow. Sigurd leapt from the pit. The tail lashed wildly after its slayer. Blood rolled down the track to the stream.

The sun was up behind the mountains, but the valley was still cold and gray. When the long death struggles were over, Regin crept from the bushes to look at the endless monster, the color of weathered stone. He gave a great sigh. "You have killed him," he said to Sigurd. "He was my brother once."

Sigurd laughed shortly. "It is late to think of that."

"Yet he was my brother, and you killed him. The fire which burned within me is quenched now in his blood. The long years of my waiting are over, the days of work and the endless wakeful nights. Now let me sleep for an hour, since I watched all this night for you. Kindle me a fire while I rest, and roast me Fafnir's heart. I will eat it and be wise, and after that, we will look on the ancient treasure which has waited so long for us."

"I will gladly do that," replied Sigurd. "You are old, and our journey was long."

Regin lay on the bank by the river. Sigurd lighted a fire in the glade. He spitted[10] the monster's heart on a stick and thrust it into the

---

10. **spitted**: roasted on a thin, pointed rod or bar that is turned over a fire.

Vocabulary **writhed** (rythd) *v.*: violently twisted and rolled, especially as a result of severe pain.

flame. It hissed and crackled as he turned it from side to side. The sun came over the hills. Two woodpeckers sat in the trees calling to each other over his head. The meat blackened a little at the edges, and Sigurd thought it was nearly done. He put out his hand to turn it. It sputtered, and the hot fat seared his finger.

Sigurd put his hand to his mouth. As he tasted the fat with his tongue, all kinds of knowledge leapt suddenly into his head. The birds still chattered in the trees. Sigurd heard the first one say, "See how the hero, Sigurd, sits roasting Fafnir's heart."

"He roasts it for Regin," answered the other. "Does he not know that the wisdom and strength of the dragon go to him who eats?"

"Sigurd needs no strength from Fafnir, and he cares nothing for the wisdom of the dwarfs."

"Regin cares, but he covets[11] the wisdom, and he needs the strength to slay."

"To slay?"

"Fool! To slay Sigurd. Is not Sigurd his tool to kill Fafnir? Is not his use over? Regin planned this murder when he first saw the dragon slayer as a child in his mother's arms."

Sigurd turned from the fire to look at Regin. For the first time he understood the master of cunning who had reared him to this end. He saw how the love of gold burned in Regin, who must kill lest he have to divide. He understood

Analyzing Visuals

Viewing and Interpreting
What passage in the story does this carving depict?

Sigurd Burns His Finger. Sigurd roasting the dragon Fafnir's heart. Carved portal from the Hylestad church (12th century). Norway. Universitetets Oldsaksamling, University Collections, Oslo, Norway.

the cold dwarfs who knew neither conscience nor pity, and who despised mankind for feeling these things. **Ⓗ**

Regin opened his eyes. The two stared a moment, and the truth was open to each. Regin snatched at his belt for a dagger and leapt at the young man, who sprang up and away, fumbling for his long sword. The dwarf struck too soon, and his dagger whistled savagely through the air. Again he jumped, like a wildcat, but this time the sword met him halfway. He gave a great cry as it pierced him, and he dropped twisting on the grass.

Sigurd looked soberly down on the two evil brothers, great serpent and scheming dwarf. He left them on the grass by the river and turned up to the hill to the crumbling house which hid the treasure he had won.

---

11. **covets** (KUH vihts): envies.

Ⓗ **Literary Focus** Norse Myths What does Sigurd finally understand about Regin?

Applying Your Skills

Sigurd, the Dragon Slayer

Respond and Think Critically

Reading Focus

Quick Check

1. What is Sigurd's quest, and how does it end?

2. Why does Regin want to eat the dragon's heart? What happens when Sigurd eats it?

Read with a Purpose

3. What is Regin's motive, or reason, for taking Sigurd on as a pupil?

Reading Skills: Monitor Your Reading

4. Review the chart you made before you read. If a question remains unanswered, re-read the appropriate section. Look for clues in the dialogue between the characters.

What I Know (K)	What I Want to Find Out (W)	What I Learned (L)
Sigurd goes out to win fame.	How will he do it?	try to slay dragon and get treasure

Literary Focus

Literary Analysis

5. **Identify** What important role does Sigurd's sword play in this myth?

6. **Infer** Why does Hiordis tell Sigurd that King Alf's kingdom is not the place where he is destined to remain? Who else tells Sigurd about his future?

7. **Analyze** What images help you imagine what Fafnir looks, smells, and feels like?

8. **Interpret** What does Sigurd learn about Regin at the end of the tale? How are dwarfs described as being different from humans?

Literary Skills: Norse Myths

9. **Interpret** What qualities of a hero does Sigurd exhibit? Why might these qualities be important to the Norse people in the thirteenth century?

10. **Identify** The Norse hero sagas are full of magic. What examples of magic appear in this story?

Literary Skills Review: Characterization

11. **Analyze** An author helps a reader understand the characters through **characterization.** By describing a character's physical traits, explaining what the character is thinking, or showing his or her interactions with other characters, an author can reveal a lot about a character. Find examples of characterization in this myth.

Writing Focus

Think as a Reader/Writer

Use It in Your Writing Review the notes on the dialogue you copied into your *Reader/Writer Notebook*. Now, write a dialogue between Sigurd and Regin where the hero confronts his former master. What would Sigurd say to Regin? How would Regin try to convince Sigurd not to kill him? Make sure you try to match the dialogue with what you already know about each character.

What Do **You Think Now** Why might the Norse people have valued this myth? What does this myth explain about life?

Vocabulary Development

Vocabulary Check

cunning
wrath
writhed

Choose the Vocabulary word that *best* completes each sentence.

1. She _____ in severe pain after twisting her ankle so suddenly.

2. Only a _____ man could pull off such trickery.

3. It became apparent that his _____ could not be calmed with soothing words.

Language Coach

Multiple-Meaning Words Choose the answer in which the italicized word is used the same way it is used in the following sentence from "Sigurd, the Dragon Slayer."

"Hiordis *started*, and a great splash of whey fell from the pan onto the dairy floor."

a. Winona *started* her business when she was 25 years old.

b. The game *started* at three o'clock.

c. Jeb *started* to his feet when Sasha came in the room.

Academic Vocabulary

Talk About . . .
<u>Recount</u> a favorite film character who <u>exhibits</u> heroic qualities and compare him or her to Sigurd. Use the Academic Vocabulary words in your discussion.

Vocabulary Skills: Old Norse and Anglo-Saxon Word Origins

The Vikings were highly skilled sailors and warriors from Scandinavia who raided the coasts of Europe and the British Isles from the eighth to the tenth centuries. Many everyday words (such as *freckle, guess, sky, skirt,* and *ugly*) came into English from Old Norse, courtesy of the Vikings. A few of those words are directly tied to the Old Norse myths.

Your Turn

Answer these questions about words derived from Old Norse words. To answer some of the questions, you might need to look up word origins.

1. The Old Norse word that meant "roast on a spit" was **steik.** *What cut of beef today is often prepared over an open fire?*

2. The Old Norse word that meant "trouble, affliction, or grief" was **angr.** *What word do we use to show a strong feeling of displeasure or offense?*

3. When Norse people wanted to obtain something, they used the word **geta.** *What word do we use that means "obtain or acquire"?*

4. The Old Norse word for freely transferring something to someone was **gefa.** *What word do we use that means to "transfer something to another"?*

5. The Old Norse word **gunhildr** meant "war." *Give an example of something used in war today that comes from this word.*

Learn It Online
Use *WordSharp* to increase your skills:

go.hrw.com | L10-1059 | Go

e Sword in the Stone | The Tale of Sir Launcelot du

by **Sir Thomas Malory**

Arthur pulling the sword from the stone.   British Library, London, Great Britain.

What Do **You Think** What qualities do we look for in our heroes?

 QuickTalk

With a partner or small group, discuss what mak someone a hero.

Reader/Writer Notebook

Use your **RWN** to complete the activities for this selection.

OH **RA.L.10.5** Analyze how an author's choice of genre affects the expression of a theme or topic. **RA.I.10.1** Identify and understand organizational patterns and techniques, including repetition of ideas, syntax and word choice, that authors use to accomplish their purpose and reach their intended audience.

Literary Focus

Arthurian Legend A **legend** is a story about extraordinary deeds that has been <u>recounted</u> for generations among a group of people. King Arthur legends are probably based on a fifth- or sixth-century Celtic chieftain, or warlord, who lived in Wales and led his people to victory against Saxon invaders from northern Germany. **Arthurian legend,** as we know it today, emerged gradually over centuries as storytellers told and retold popular tales about a great chief who mysteriously disappeared but promised to return when his people needed him. When Sir Thomas Malory wrote *Le Morte d'Arthur* toward the end of the fifteenth century, the glory of the knights was past. Nonetheless, something in Malory's portrayal of those days answered a longing in his audience for the time of knights, lords, and castles—a time when "might fought for right."

Reading Focus

Understanding Sequence of Events The **sequence of events** is the order in which the events of the story are told. Stories generally follow a predictable, **chronological order.** Sometimes stories include a **flashback** that interrupts the present action to show events that happened at an earlier time. Flashbacks add important background information to the story.

Into Action As you read, use a chart to jot down the main events of the story. Pay particular attention to events that are mentioned out of chronological order, and add a box to fit each one into your chart.

Congregation sees the sword stuck in the stone			→	

Vocabulary

confronted (kuhn FRUHNT ehd) *v.:* faced. *The warriors were confronted with a fierce opponent.*

inscribed (ihn SKRYBD) *v.:* marked or written on a surface; engraved. *The ring was inscribed with my initials.*

tumultuous (too MUHL choo uhs) *adj.:* wild and noisy. *The tumultuous sea turned her face green.*

realm (rehlm) *n.:* kingdom. *The king's realm stretched as far as the sea.*

Language Coach

Prefixes Prefixes sometimes have more than one meaning. For example, the prefix *in–* can mean "in, into, within, or toward." Which meaning does it have in the Vocabulary word *inscribed?*

Writing Focus

Think as a Reader/Writer

Find It in Your Reading As you read, note the language used to portray the hero in your *Reader/Writer Notebook.*

 Learn It Online
There's more to words than just definitions. Get the whole story on:

go.hrw.com L10-1061   **Go**

MEET THE WRITER

Learn It Online
Learn more about the author at:
go.hrw.com L10-1062 Go

Sir Thomas Malory
(1405?–1471)

A Master of Escape

Though little is known about the life of Sir Thomas Malory, his title indicates that he was a knight. He was also a soldier and a member of the British Parliament for a brief time. We know that he spent most of the last twenty years of his life in prison, accused of some very unchivalrous crimes: assault, extortion, cattle rustling, poaching, jail breaking, plundering an abbey, and "waylaying the duke of Buckingham." Malory pleaded innocent to all charges, and it is likely that he was framed by political enemies. (It is also possible that Malory was something of a scoundrel.) During those miserable years in jail, Malory wrote his great romance.

The twelfth-century world of chivalrous knights in shining armor was almost as foreign to Malory as it is to us today. (For more about knights and chivalry, see page 1069.) The invention of gunpowder and the rise of the middle class had already broken down the feudal order. While Malory scribbled heroic tales in a dark jail cell, English political and social life was in a state of turmoil that no amount of chivalry seemed likely to cure.

Think About the Writer How might Malory's status as a knight (or a scoundrel) have shaped the Arthurian stories he wrote?

Build Background

According to legend, King Uther of England, who was unmarried, loved Igraine (ee GRAYN), another man's wife. In disguise the king deceived Igraine into thinking he was her husband. Arthur was the child born to Igraine as a result of that trick. The wise man Merlin knew the baby was in danger because many men wanted Uther's throne, so he asked Sir Ector and his wife to raise the infant Arthur with their own son Kay. When King Uther died, few aside from Merlin knew Arthur's true identity.

Preview the Selections

As "The Sword in the Stone" begins, many feuding lords of noble birth have assembled to participate in a great test to determine the next king of Britain. **Sir Ector,** his son **Sir Kay,** and **Arthur** come to London to attend the tournament that follows.

In the legend "The Tale of Sir Launcelot du Lake," **Launcelot** goes searching for adventure and runs into **Morgan le Fay,** King Arthur's evil half sister. Famous for her enchantments, Morgan continually plots to destroy Arthur.

"Le Morte D'Arthur" (1471) by Sir Thomas Malory, published 1927 by Aubrey Beardsley (1872–1898). Fairy Art Museum, Tokyo, Japan.

The Sword in the Stone

from **Le Morte d'Arthur**

by **Sir Thomas Malory** retold by **Keith Baines**

The archbishop held his service in the city's greatest church (St. Paul's), and when matins[1] were done, the congregation filed out to the yard. They were confronted by a marble block into which had been thrust a beautiful sword. The block was four feet square, and the sword passed through a steel anvil[2] which had been struck in the stone and which projected a foot from it. The anvil had been inscribed with letters of gold:

WHOSO PULLETH OUTE THIS
SWERD OF THIS STONE AND
ANVYLD IS RIGHTWYS KYNGE
BORNE OF ALL BRYTAYGNE **A**

The congregation was awed by this miraculous sight, but the archbishop forbade anyone to touch the sword before Mass had been heard. After Mass, many of the nobles tried to pull the sword out of the stone, but none was able to, so a watch of ten knights was set over the sword, and a tournament[3] proclaimed for New Year's Day, to provide men of noble blood with the opportunity of proving their right to the succession.

Sir Ector, who had been living on an estate near London, rode to the tournament with Arthur and his own son Sir Kay, who had been recently knighted. When they arrived at the tournament, Sir Kay found to his annoyance

---

1. **matins** (MAT uhnz): morning prayers.
2. **anvil** (AN vuhl): iron or steel block on which metal objects are hammered into shape.

3. **tournament** (TUR nuh muhnt): sport in which two knights compete on horseback, trying to unseat each other with long pole-like weapons called lances.

A **Literary Focus** Arthurian Legend What challenge does the congregation discover?

Vocabulary **confronted** (kuhn FRUHNT ehd) *v.*: faced.
inscribed (ihn SKRYBD ehd) *v.*: marked or written on a surface; engraved.

that his sword was missing from its sheath, so he begged Arthur to ride back and fetch it from their lodging.

Arthur found the door of the lodging locked and bolted, the landlord and his wife having left for the tournament. In order not to disappoint his brother, he rode on to St. Paul's, determined to get for him the sword which was lodged in the stone. The yard was empty, the guard also having slipped off to see the tournament, so Arthur strode up to the sword and, without troubling to read the inscription, tugged it free. He then rode straight back to Sir Kay and presented him with it. **Ⓑ**

Sir Kay recognized the sword and, taking it to Sir Ector, said, "Father, the succession falls to me, for I have here the sword that was lodged in the stone." But Sir Ector insisted that they should all ride to the churchyard, and once there, bound Sir Kay by oath[4] to tell how he had come by the sword. Sir Kay then admitted that Arthur had given it to him. Sir Ector turned to Arthur and said, "Was the sword not guarded?"

"It was not," Arthur replied.

"Would you please thrust it into the stone again?" said Sir Ector. Arthur did so, and first Sir Ector and then Sir Kay tried to remove it, but both were unable to. Then Arthur, for the second time, pulled it out. Sir Ector and Sir Kay both knelt before him.

"Why," said Arthur, "do you both kneel before me?"

---

4. **oath** (ohth): solemn promise or declaration; vow.

"My lord," Sir Ector replied, "there is only one man living who can draw the sword from the stone, and he is the true-born king of Britain." Sir Ector then told Arthur the story of his birth and upbringing. **Ⓒ**

"My dear father," said Arthur, "for so I shall always think of you—if, as you say, I am to be king, please know that any request you have to make is already granted."

Sir Ector asked that Sir Kay should be made royal seneschal,[5] and Arthur declared that while they both lived it should be so. Then the three of them visited the archbishop and told him what had taken place.

All those dukes and barons with ambitions to rule were present at the tournament on New Year's Day. But when all of them had failed, and Arthur alone had succeeded in drawing the sword from the stone, they protested against one so young, and of ignoble blood, succeeding to the throne.

The secret of Arthur's birth was known to only a few of the nobles surviving from the days of King Uther. The archbishop urged them to make Arthur's cause their own; but their support proved ineffective. The tournament was repeated at Candlemas[6] and at Easter, with the same outcome as before.

---

5. **seneschal** (SEHN uh shuhl): person in charge of the king's household. This was a powerful and respected position.

6. **Candlemas** (KAN duhl muhs): February 2, a Christian church festival that honors the purification of the Virgin Mary after the birth of Jesus.

Ⓑ Reading Focus Sequence of Events List the sequence of events that leads Arthur to the sword in the stone.

Ⓒ Literary Focus Arthurian Legend What does Sir Ector reveal to King Arthur here?

Finally, at Pentecost,[7] when once more Arthur alone had been able to remove the sword, the commoners arose with a tumultuous cry and demanded that Arthur should at once be made king. The nobles, knowing in their hearts that the commoners were right, all knelt before Arthur and begged forgiveness for hav-

ing delayed his succession for so long. Arthur forgave them and then, offering his sword at the high altar, was dubbed[8] first knight of the realm. The coronation took place a few days later, when Arthur swore to rule justly, and the nobles swore him their allegiance. **D**

---

7. **Pentecost** (PEHN tuh kawst): Christian festival celebrated on the seventh Sunday after Easter, commemorating the descent of the Holy Spirit upon the Apostles.

---

8. **dubbed** (duhbd): made a knight by striking his shoulder lightly with a sword.

D **Literary Focus** Arthurian Legend How and why do the nobles change their opinion of Arthur?

Vocabulary **tumultuous** (too MUHL choo uhs) *adj.:* wild and noisy.
realm (rehlm) *n.:* kingdom.

Applying Your Skills

The Sword in the Stone

Respond and Think Critically

Reading Focus

Quick Check

1. How does Sir Kay end up with the sword?

2. Why do the nobles protest Arthur's claim to the throne?

Read with a Purpose

3. What is the meaning of the inscription on the sword in the stone?

Reading Skills: Sequence of Events

4. Review the chart you created as you read the story. Which event is most important to the story, and why?

Literary Focus

Literary Analysis

5. **Infer** Considering Sir Kay's actions, what conclusions can you draw about him as a person? Where does he have the opportunity to <u>exhibit</u> heroic qualitites?

6. **Analyze** During Arthur's time, England operated on a feudal system with three distinct social classes: the nobility, the clergy, and the commoners. What role does each class play in this story? Why would the tale have special appeal to commoners?

Literary Skills: Arthurian Legends

7. **Analyze** What heroic qualities does Arthur <u>exhibit</u> when he responds to Sir Ector's request?

8. **Identify** In many legends, the hero's origins are mysterious—he is often raised in obscurity before taking his rightful place as leader. How does the story of Arthur reflect this pattern?

Literary Skills Review: Irony

9. **Analyze** Remember that **irony** is a discrepancy between what we expect to happen and what does happen. What is ironic about the first time Arthur removes the sword from the stone?

Writing Focus

Think as a Reader/Writer

Use It in Your Writing Review the notes you made in your *Reader/Writer Notebook*. Which qualities of an Arthurian knight would a hero of today <u>exhibit</u>? Write a short description of an ideal, modern hero.

What Do You Think Now

What qualities did Arthur show in this legend that we still value today? Explain.

Vocabulary Development

Vocabulary Check

Match each Vocabulary word with its definition.

1. **tumultuous**   a. kingdom
2. **realm**   b. engraved
3. **inscribed**   c. wild and noisy
4. **confronted**   d. faced

Vocabulary Skills: Etymology

A word's **etymology** is its origin. Knowing the etymology of words can help you understand other related words. You can use a dictionary to look up the etymology of a word. The etymologies for two of the Vocabulary words are listed below.

realm [< OFr. *reaume* < L. *regimen*, rule, influenced by L. *regalis*, regal.]

The letters *OFr* mean that the word originally comes from the Old French, which in turn came from the Latin (L) word *regimen*.

To find the origin of the adjective *tumultuous,* look at the entry for the noun *tumult*.

tumult [< ME. < *tumulte* < MFr. < L. *tumultus,* a swelling or surging up.]

This means that the word *tumult* comes from the Middle English, which in turn came from the Latin word *tumultus*.

Your Turn

Return to the story and pick out four unfamiliar words. Look up each word in a dictionary and write the word and its etymology in your *Reader/Writer Notebook*.

Language Coach

Prefixes The chart below shows some commonly used prefixes and their meanings.

Prefix	Meanings	Example
bi–	two	bimonthly
dis–	away, apart	disappear
ex–	from, out, away	exchange
re–	back, again, backward	rebuild
un–	not, reverse of	undone

Think of two more examples of words containing each prefix in the chart above and write them in your *Reader/Writer Notebook*.

Academic Vocabulary

Talk About . . .

What lessons or qualities might Arthur have <u>retained</u> from his relatively humble upbringing? How does he <u>exhibit</u> these qualities? Discuss your answers with a small group, using the underlined Academic Vocabulary words in your discussion.

Learn It Online
Focus on vocabulary with *WordSharp*:

go.hrw.com   L10-1067   **Go**

Applying Your Skills

The Sword in the Stone

RA.L.10.5 Analyze how an author's choice of genre affects the expression of a theme or topic.
RA.L.10.1 Compare and contrast an author's use of direct and indirect characterization, and ways in which characters reveal traits about themselves, including dialect, dramatic monologues and soliloquies. *Also covered* **WA.10.1.b; WA.10.2; WC.10.5**

Grammar Link

Modifiers

A **modifier** is a word or word group that limits the meaning of another word or word group. The two kinds of modifiers are adjectives and adverbs. Remember that adjectives modify nouns and pronouns, and adverbs modify verbs, adjectives, and other adverbs.

A **misplaced modifier** is a modifying word or word group that sounds awkward or unclear because it seems to modify the wrong word or word group. You can fix a misplaced modifier by placing the modifying word or word group as near as possible to the word(s) you intend to modify.

MISPLACED MODIFIER A light shone through the window *that was blinding.*

CLEAR A blinding light shone through the window.

A **dangling modifier** is a word or word group that does not sensibly modify any word or word group in the same sentence. One way to correct this is to add a word or words to the dangling modifier.

DANGLING While reading the novel, the plane took off.

CLEAR While *she was* reading the novel, the plane took off.

Your Turn

Writing Applications Find the misplaced or dangling modifier. Then, rewrite each sentence below.

1. Having overslept, my exam results were poor.
2. Before starting on his homework, his dad called.
3. The plate fell on the floor that was full of baked beans.

CHOICES

As you respond to the Choices, use these **Academic Vocabulary** words as appropriate: recount, recurring, exhibit, and retain.

REVIEW
Analyze Magical Elements

Timed ⌐Writing Which elements of "The Sword in the Stone" are magical, and which elements are more realistic? Write a brief essay in which you analyze the legend and your response to it. Do the legend's magical elements appeal to you, or do you prefer more realistic stories? Use examples from the story to support your response.

CONNECT
Write About a Modern Hero

Think about stories you have read or movies you have seen about other heroes, or consider other story versions of King Arthur and his Knights of the Round Table. Choose one hero and write a brief description of his or her talents. What makes this person a hero, and why? Do you think this hero will be remembered hundreds of years from now as King Arthur is today? Why or why not?

EXTEND
Research King Arthur

TechFocus Who was the real King Arthur? Do some research on the man behind the myth. Use the Internet to find some reliable sources with more information on the real King Arthur. Then, present your information to the class.

Preparing to Read

The Tale of Sir Launcelot du Lake

 RA.L.10.5 Analyze how an author's choice of genre affects the expression of a theme or topic. **RP.10.1** Apply reading comprehension strategies, including making predictions, comparing and contrasting, recalling and summarizing and making inferences and drawing conclusions.

Reader/Writer Notebook

Use your **RWN** to complete the activities for this selection.

Literary Focus

Romantic Literature Beginning in the twelfth century, **Romantic literature**—stories describing the adventures of knights and other heroes—became popular. These stories began as oral narratives that, by the fourteenth century, became written tales. They celebrated the ideals of **chivalry,** the code of behavior for the medieval knight. He was to be brave, honorable, loyal, pious, generous to foes, ready to help the weak, and a protector of women. Knights embarked on quests to prove their courage. The quest typically involved saving maidens, slaying dragons, and battling less noble persons.

Literary Perspectives Apply the literary perspective described on page 1070 as you read this legend.

Reading Focus

Summarizing When you **summarize,** you use your own words to recount the main points of a story. To help you find the main points, stop to ask yourself *Who, What, Where, When,* and *Why* questions.

Into Action As you read "Sir Launcelot du Lake," fill in a chart like the one below to answer *Who, What, Where, When,* and *Why* questions about the key events in the story.

Questions	Answers
Who?	Sir Launcelot, Morgan Le Fay
What?	

Writing Focus

Think as a Reader/Writer

Find It in Your Reading Descriptive words tell much about a knight's actions in a Romantic legend. In your *Reader/Writer Notebook* write down the descriptive words that stand out as you read.

Vocabulary

ignominiously (ihg nuh MIHN ee uhs lee) *adv.*: shamefully. *The two knights were ignominiously defeated by their lone opponent.*

adversary (AD vuhr sehr ee) *n.*: opponent. *Sir Launcelot easily defeated each adversary in the tournament.*

sovereign (SAHV ruhn) *n.*: the supreme ruler; king or queen. *King Arthur was crowned sovereign of Britain.*

vehemently (VEE uh muhnt lee) *adv.*: performed with unusual force or violence. *He vehemently fought for his freedom from the mouth of the dragon.*

Language Coach

Multiple-Meaning Words Some words have more than one meaning. For example, the word *cell* refers to both "a small room in a prison" and "an enclosed space in an organism." As you read the story, look for other multiple-meaning words.

 Learn It Online
There's more to words than just definitions. Get the whole story on:

go.hrw.com | L10-1069 | Go

The Tale of Sir Launcelot du Lake

from Le Morte d'Arthur

by **Sir Thomas Malory** retold by **Keith Baines**

Read with a Purpose
Read this tale to discover how one knight proves his heroism.

Build Background

Of the 150 knights who served King Arthur, Sir Launcelot is Arthur's favorite. Although Launcelot is devoted to Arthur, he falls in love with Arthur's wife, Queen Gwynevere, causing great suffering for the unfortunate trio. As this legend begins, Arthur has just returned from Rome, after conquering much of western Europe. Restless for adventure, he sets out on another journey and runs into his evil half sister, Morgan le Fay, who is famous for her enchantments.

When King Arthur returned from Rome he settled his court at Camelot, and there gathered about him his knights of the Round Table, who diverted themselves with jousting[1] and tournaments. Of all his knights one was supreme, both in prowess at arms and in nobility of bearing, and this was Sir Launcelot, who was also the favorite of Queen Gwynevere, to whom he had sworn oaths of fidelity.

One day Sir Launcelot, feeling weary of his life at the court, and of only playing at arms, decided to set forth in search of adventure. He asked his nephew Sir Lyonel to accompany him, and when both were suitably armed and mounted, they rode off together through the forest.

At noon they started across a plain, but the intensity of the sun made Sir Launcelot feel sleepy, so Sir Lyonel suggested that they should rest beneath the shade of an apple tree that

Literary Perspectives

Analyzing Archetypes An archetype is a recognizable pattern of character types, images, symbols, or genres that recurs throughout different kinds of literature. These patterns exist in different cultures at different times in history, giving archetypes a universal quality. The hero is a well-known character archetype. Though the characteristics of one hero might differ from those of another, certain similarities exist that help define each as a hero archetype. Other familiar archetypes include the damsel in distress, the villain, the trickster, and the wise man or woman. Archetypes can also be symbols, such as light as a symbol of hope and darkness as a symbol of despair. An author might reinterpret a story, but the archetypal conventions—those symbols of meaning we agree upon—remain fairly constant across time and place. As you read, use the notes and questions in the text to guide you in using this perspective.

---

1. **jousting** (JOWST ihng): fighting with lances—or long, wooden spears—on horseback.

grew by a hedge not far from the road. They dismounted, tethered their horses, and settled down.

"Not for seven years have I felt so sleepy," said Sir Launcelot, and with that fell fast asleep, while Sir Lyonel watched over him.

While Sir Launcelot still slept beneath the apple tree, four queens started across the plain. They were riding white mules and accompanied by four knights who held above them, at the tips of their spears, a green silk canopy, to protect them from the sun. The party was startled by the neighing of Sir Launcelot's horse and, changing direction, rode up to the apple tree, where they discovered the sleeping knight. And as each of the queens gazed at the handsome Sir Launcelot, so each wanted him for her own.

"Let us not quarrel," said Morgan le Fay. "Instead, I will cast a spell over him so that he remains asleep while we take him to my castle and make him our prisoner. We can then oblige[2] him to choose one of us for his paramour."[3]

Sir Launcelot was laid on his shield and borne by two of the knights to the Castle Charyot, which was Morgan le Fay's stronghold. He awoke to find himself in a cold cell, where a young noblewoman was serving him supper. B

"What cheer?" she asked.

"My lady, I hardly know, except that I must have been brought here by means of an

_____
2. **oblige** (uh BLYJ): to bind by promise.
3. **paramour** (PAR uh mawr): person who takes the place of a husband or wife illegally.

Miniature painting of Launcelot and Gwynevere playing chess (15th century). French.

enchantment."

"Sir, if you are the knight you appear to be, you will learn your fate at dawn tomorrow." And with that the young noblewoman left him. Sir Launcelot spent an uncomfortable night but at dawn the four queens presented themselves and Morgan le Fay spoke to him:

"Sir Launcelot, I know that Queen Gwynevere loves you, and you her. But now you are my prisoner, and you will have to choose: either to take one of us for your paramour, or

A **Literary Focus** Romantic Literature What elements of romantic literature are presented in this introduction to the story?

B **Reading Focus** Summarizing Summarize Launcelot's adventure so far.

to die miserably in this cell—just as you please. Now I will tell you who we are: I am Morgan le Fay, Queen of Gore; my companions are the Queens of North Galys, of Estelonde, and of the Outer Isles. So make your choice."

"A hard choice! Understand that I choose none of you, lewd sorceresses that you are; rather will I die in this cell. But were I free, I would take pleasure in proving it against any who would champion you that Queen Gwynevere is the finest lady of this land."

"So, you refuse us?" asked Morgan le Fay.

"On my life, I do," Sir Launcelot said finally, and so the queens departed.

Sometime later, the young noblewoman who had served Sir Launcelot's supper reappeared.

"What news?" she asked.

"It is the end," Sir Launcelot replied.

"Sir Launcelot, I know that you have refused the four queens, and that they wish to kill you out of spite. But if you will be ruled by me, I can save you. I ask that you will champion my father at a tournament next Tuesday, when he has to combat the King of North Galys, and three knights of the Round Table, who last Tuesday defeated him ignominiously."

"My lady, pray tell me, what is your father's name?"

"King Bagdemagus."

"Excellent, my lady, I know him for a good king and a true knight, so I shall be happy to serve him." **C**

"May God reward you! And tomorrow at dawn I will release you, and direct you to an abbey which is ten miles from here, and where the good monks will care for you while I fetch my father."

"I am at your service, my lady."

As promised, the young noblewoman released Sir Launcelot at dawn. When she had led him through the twelve doors to the castle entrance, she gave him his horse and armor, and directions for finding the abbey.

"God bless you, my lady; and when the time comes I promise I shall not fail you."

Sir Launcelot rode through the forest in search of the abbey, but at dusk had still failed to find it, and coming upon a red silk pavilion, apparently unoccupied, decided to rest there overnight, and continue his search in the morning.

He had not been asleep for more than an hour, however, when the knight who owned the pavilion returned, and got straight into bed with him. Having made an assignation[4] with his paramour, the knight supposed at first that Sir Launcelot was she, and taking him into his arms, started kissing him. Sir Launcelot awoke with a start, and seizing his sword, leaped out of bed and out of the pavilion, pursued closely by the other knight. Once in the open they set to with their swords, and before long Sir Launcelot had wounded his unknown adversary so seriously that he was obliged to yield.

The knight, whose name was Sir Belleus, now asked Sir Launcelot how he came to be sleeping in his bed, and then explained how he had an assignation with his lover, adding:

"But now I am so sorely wounded that I shall consider myself fortunate to escape with my life."

---

4. **assignation** (AS ihn NAY shuhn): secret meeting of lovers.

C **Literary Focus** Romantic Literature In your own words, explain how chivalry is <u>exhibited</u> in this exchange.

Vocabulary **ignominiously** (ihg nuh MIHN ee uhs lee) *adv.*: shamefully.
adversary (AD vuhr sehr ee) *n.*: opponent.

"Sir, please forgive me for wounding you; but lately I escaped from an enchantment, and I was afraid that once more I had been betrayed. Let us go into the pavilion and I will staunch[5] your wound."

Sir Launcelot had just finished binding the wound when the young noblewoman who was Sir Belleus' paramour arrived, and seeing the wound, at once rounded in fury[6] on Sir Launcelot.

"Peace, my love," said Sir Belleus. "This is a noble knight, and as soon as I yielded to him he treated my wound with the greatest care." Sir Belleus then described the events which had led up to the duel.

"Sir, pray tell me your name, and whose knight you are," the young noblewoman asked Sir Launcelot.

"My lady, I am called Sir Launcelot du Lake."

"As I guessed, both from your appearance and from your speech; and indeed I know you better than you realize. But I ask you, in recompense[7] for the injury you have done my lord, and out of the courtesy for which you are famous, to recommend Sir Belleus to King Arthur, and suggest that he be made one of the knights of the Round Table. I can assure you that my lord deserves it, being only less than yourself as a man-at-arms, and sovereign of many of the Outer Isles."

"My lady, let Sir Belleus come to Arthur's court at the next Pentecost. Make sure that you come with him, and I promise I will do what I can for him; and if he is as good a man-at-arms as you say he is, I am sure Arthur will accept him."

---

5. **staunch** (stawnch): to stop or check the flow of blood (from a wound).
6. **rounded in fury:** turned around in anger.

7. **recompense** (REHK uhm pehns): compensation.

Lancelot and the magic chessboard (left); Gwynevere and Arthur receiving the chessboard (center); Gwynevere playing chess (right). Detail from "Le Roman de Lancelot du Lac" (early 14th century). Northeastern France. The Pierpont Morgan Library, New York, NY.

Analyzing Visuals   **Viewing and Interpreting**   How does this painting help you visualize Launcelot's world?

Launcelot Enters a Tournament

As soon as it was daylight, Sir Launcelot armed, mounted, and rode away in search of the abbey, which he found in less than two hours. King Bagdemagus' daughter was waiting for him, and as soon as she heard his horse's footsteps in the yard, ran to the window, and, seeing that it was Sir Launcelot, herself ordered the servants to stable his horse. She then led him to her chamber, disarmed him, and gave him a long gown to wear, welcoming him warmly as she did so.

King Bagdemagus' castle was twelve miles away, and his daughter sent for him as soon as she had settled Sir Launcelot. The king arrived with his retinue[8] and embraced Sir Launcelot, who then described his recent enchantment, and the great obligation he was under to his daughter for releasing him.

"Sir, you will fight for me on Tuesday next?"

"Sire, I shall not fail you; but please tell me the names of the three Round Table knights whom I shall be fighting."

"Sir Modred, Sir Madore de la Porte, and Sir Gahalantyne. I must admit that last Tuesday they defeated me and my knights completely."

"Sire, I hear that the tournament is to be fought within three miles of the abbey. Could you send me three of your most trustworthy knights, clad in plain armor, and with no device, and a fourth suit of armor which I myself shall wear? We will take up our position just outside the tournament field and watch while you and the King of North Galys enter into combat with your followers; and then, as soon as you are in difficulties, we will come to your rescue, and show your opponents what kind of knights you command." **D**

This was arranged on Sunday, and on the following Tuesday Sir Launcelot and the three knights of King Bagdemagus waited in a copse,[9] not far from the pavilion which had been erected for the lords and ladies who were to judge the tournament and award the prizes.

The King of North Galys was the first on the field, with a company of ninescore[10] knights; he was followed by King Bagdemagus with fourscore knights, and then by the three knights of the Round Table, who remained apart from both companies. At the first encounter King Bagdemagus lost twelve knights, all killed, and the King of North Galys six.

With that, Sir Launcelot galloped onto the field, and with his first spear unhorsed five of the King of North Galys' knights, breaking the backs of four of them. With his next spear he charged the king, and wounded him deeply in the thigh. **E**

"That was a shrewd blow," commented Sir Madore, and galloped onto the field to challenge Sir Launcelot. But he too was tumbled from his horse, and with such violence that his shoulder was broken.

---

8. **retinue** (REHT uh noo): group of attendants or followers.

9. **copse** (kahps): thicket of shrubs.
10. **ninescore**: 180; *score* means a group of 20, so the total is 9 x 20.

D **Reading Focus** Summarizing Summarize the main events in the story so far.

E **Literary Perspective** Archetypes What qualities of an archetypal hero does Launcelot display in this passage?

Sir Modred was the next to challenge Sir Launcelot, and he was sent spinning over his horse's tail. He landed head first, his helmet became buried in the soil, and he nearly broke his neck, and for a long time lay stunned.

Finally, Sir Gahalantyne tried; at the first encounter both he and Sir Launcelot broke their spears, so both drew their swords and hacked vehemently at each other. But Sir Launcelot, with mounting wrath, soon struck his opponent a blow on the helmet which brought the blood streaming from eyes, ears, and mouth. Sir Gahalantyne slumped forward in the saddle, his horse panicked, and he was thrown to the ground, useless for further combat.

Sir Launcelot took another spear, and unhorsed sixteen more of the King of North Galys' knights, and with his next, unhorsed another twelve; and in each case with such violence that none of the knights ever fully recovered. The King of North Galys was forced to admit defeat, and the prize was awarded to King Bagdemagus.

That night Sir Launcelot was entertained as the guest of honor by King Bagdemagus and his daughter at their castle, and before leaving was loaded with gifts.

"My lady, please, if ever again you should need my services, remember that I shall not fail you." **F**

Analyzing Visuals Viewing and Interpreting Do you think the colors and textures the artist chose convey the same feelings as the words the author uses to describe each character in this scene? Explain.

Four Queens Find Lancelot Sleeping by Frank Cadogan Couper.

Arthur's kingdom thrived while the Round Table existed. However, several knights told King Arthur about the love between his wife and Launcelot, and Queen Gwynevere was sentenced to burn at the stake. At the last moment, Launcelot snatched Gwynevere from the flames. The resulting hostility between Arthur and Launcelot brought an end to the Round Table.

F **Literary Focus** Romantic Literature In what ways is Sir Launcelot proving his chivalry in this passage?

Vocabulary **vehemently** (VEE uh muhnt lee) *adv.*: performed with unusual force or violence.

Applying Your Skills

The Tale of Sir Launcelot du Lake

Respond and Think Critically

Reading Focus

Quick Check

1. What happens to Sir Launcelot each time he stops to sleep?

2. How does Launcelot escape Morgan le Fay?

Read with a Purpose

3. How does Sir Launcelot defend King Bagdemagus's honor without harming his own?

Reading Skills: Summarizing

4. Review the chart you created as you read. Use your notes to create a brief summary of the legend in your own words. Be sure you include only enough details to convey the story. Compare your summaries with those of a few classmates. Did you all cover the same points?

Questions	Answers
Who?	Sir Launcelot, Morgan Le Fay
What?	
Where?	
When?	
Why?	

Summary:

Literary Focus

Literary Analysis

5. **Identify** Who are the queens with Morgan le Fay? What is significant about one of them?

6. **Draw Conclusions** Why might the three Round Table knights set themselves apart from the knights with King Bagdemagus as they enter the tournament?

7. **Literary Perspectives** Sir Launcelot is the hero of this tale. What other archetypes can you identify in the legend?

Literary Skills: Romantic Literature

8. **Connect** How does Launcelot fit your image of a romantic hero? In what ways does he diverge from the image?

9. **Analyze** Describe the typical elements of a romance that you found in this tale.

Literary Skills Review: Tone

10. **Analyze** The **tone** of a story conveys the writer's attitude toward the subject. What is the tone of this legend? Support your answer with evidence from the story.

Writing Focus

Think as a Reader/Writer

Use It in Your Writing Review the descriptive words you copied into your *Reader/Writer Notebook*. Now write a paragraph in which you incorporate your observations, describing an ideal knight for today's audience.

 What Do You Think Now

What qualities of an Arthurian Knight do we still value today? Which chivalrous qualities may be outdated?

Vocabulary Development

Vocabulary Check

Choose the Vocabulary word that *best* completes each sentence.

> ignominiously
> adversary
> sovereign
> vehemently

1. Sir Launcelot _____ denied that he had intended any harm to Sir Belleus.

2. Morgan Le Fay was a(n) _____ of King Arthur's, often seeking to cause him trouble.

3. After the fateful battle, all knew that the unworthy knight had lost _____.

4. As the _____ of Britain, he commanded the best knights in the land.

Language Coach

Multiple-Meaning Words Work with a partner to find multiple-meaning words in the story. Write down each one you find, and look in a dictionary for two separate definitions of the word. Then choose the definition that matches the way the word is used in the story.

Academic Vocabulary

Write About . . .

What elements of Sir Launcelot's character have made people want to <u>recount</u> his story across generations? Write a paragraph explaining your answer. Use the underlined Academic Vocabulary word in your response.

Vocabulary Skills: English Word Origins

The English we use today derives from different languages—Germanic, Celtic, and Latin, to name a few. Much of English also comes from what is called Old English (OE) or Middle English (ME). Knowing the origin of a word helps you better understand its meaning when you look it up in a dictionary. For example, the word *hedge* comes from the Old English word *hecg* which means "thick row of bushes," but another, older meaning comes from the word *haw*, which means "hawthorn bush." Hawthorne bushes are found in hedges, which is specific to the original meaning.

Your Turn

Translate this passage from *Le Morte d'Arthur* into the kind of English spoken in the United States today. First, read the passage aloud. Then, take a guess at the meanings of unfamiliar-looking words. Check your guesses in a dictionary's **etymologies,** or word origins. Do you find the Middle English spellings included in the word's etymology?

> "A, Launcelot!" he sayd, "thou were hede of al Crysten knyghtes! And now I dare say," sayd syr Ector, "thou sir Launcelot, there thou lyest, that thou were never matched of erthely knyghtes hande. And thou werre the curtest knight that ever bare shelde!"
>
> —Sir Thomas Malory

Learn It Online
Sharpen your word skills with *WordSharp:*

go.hrw.com   L10-1077   **Go**

Comparing Archetypes

CONTENTS

A boy from Mali.

What Do You Think
Why do we experience both happiness and hardship in life?

⏱ **QuickWrite**
Think about a happy or troubling incident in your life or in the life of someone you know. What factors, such as a person's decision or luck, contributed to the outcome of the incident? Write about it.

Preparing to Read

from Sundiata / Quetzalcoatl

 RA.L.10.1 Compare and contrast an author's use of direct and indirect characterization, and ways in which characters reveal traits about themselves, including dialect, dramatic monologues and soliloquies. *Also covered* **RA.I.10.1**

Reader/Writer Notebook

Use your **RWN** to complete the activities for these selections.

Literary Focus

Archetypes An **archetype** is a <u>recurring</u> model or pattern found in literature throughout the ages. One archetypal story tells about a Golden Age when the world was filled with happiness and prosperity. Other archetypal stories <u>recount</u> the tale of a journey or quest in which the hero faces a series of ordeals before returning home. In contrast to the hero is the trickster archetype, or the "con artist" who creates trouble and disorder wherever he or she goes. Archetypes are helpful when reading works from other cultures because they help the reader recognize similarities among works.

Reading Focus

Analyzing a Sequence of Events Narratives are made up of a series of events, which are usually presented in chronological order. When you analyze a sequence of events, consider what causes events to occur and how one event leads to another.

Into Action As you read each selection, create a chart to record the sequence of events in the narrative. Add as many spaces as you need.

from "Sundiata"	*Sogolon's son can't walk.*		
"Quetzalcoatl"			

Writing Focus

Think as a Reader/Writer

Find It in Your Reading Writers *tell* us what characters are like (**direct characterization**) and *show* us characters' traits through their appearance, speech, and actions (**indirect characterization**). Keep a record in your *Reader/Writer Notebook* of what each writer's use of direct and indirect characterization reveals about the characters.

Vocabulary

from Sundiata

infirmity (ihn FUR muh tee) *n.:* defect; weakness. *Sogolon Djata's infirmity makes him different from other children.*

affront (uh FRUHNT) *n.:* intentional insult. *Sassouma's affront upsets Sogolon.*

efface (uh FAYS) *v.:* erase. *Sogolon thinks that nothing can efface her shame.*

Quetzalcoatl

abundant (uh BUHN duhnt) *adj.:* plentiful. *Food was abundant and no one went hungry during Quetzalcoatl's rule.*

strife (stryf) *n.:* bitter struggle. *There was no strife during Quetzalcoatl's rule.*

Language Coach

Parts of Speech Sometimes, words have different forms for different parts of speech. For example, *abundant* is an adjective while *abundance* is a noun, meaning "a great quantity." Some words, however, can be used as more than one part of speech, such as *affront*, which is not only a noun, but also a verb, meaning "to insult intentionally." Can you think of other words that can be used as more than one part of speech?

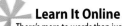 **Learn It Online**
There's more to words than just definitions. Get the whole story at:

go.hrw.com | L10-1079 | **Go**

D. T. Niane
(1932–   )

Ancestral Stories

D. T. Niane's connection to storytelling is rooted in his family tree. A historian and writer, Niane is a descendant of *griots* (gree OHZ), or African oral historians. Born in Conakry, Guinea, Niane received a degree in history from the University of Bordeaux in France.

The story of Sundiata was told to Niane by the griot Djeli Mamoudou Kouyaté of Guinea. Niane translated the story from Mandingo into French, and it subsequently was translated into English. Niane hopes that readers will learn to value "the words of the griots who teach wisdom and history."

Amy Cruse
(1870–?)

Favorite Stories

British writer Amy Cruse recognized that reading a variety of texts is part of people's everyday lives.

> "The books that figure largely in histories of literature are, in many households, those which are placed respectfully behind the glass doors of the best bookcase . . . while the family reads and re-reads old favourites in tattered covers. . . . From the point of view of their readers they are as important as those which take the higher rank."

Cruse recorded legends and tales that many people find meaningful and intriguing. The legend of Quetzalcoatl is one of these "favourite" tales that people have read and re-read.

Think About the Writers

Why might writers want to record stories from past societies?

Preview the Selections

The selection that follows is the first part of the epic of the hero **Sundiata.** (An epic is a long narrative that describes the deeds of a larger-than-life hero who embodies the values of a particular society.) Sundiata is called by three other names: **Sogolon Djata, Mari Djata,** and **Maghan.** He is the young son of the king and the king's second wife, **Sogolon** (also called **Sogolon Kedjou**). The jealous **Sassouma** is the king's first wife, who is also referred to as the queen mother. **Balla Fasséké** is Sundiata's griot—a storyteller who acts as an attendant and tutor.

In "Quetzalcoatl," the chief god of the Toltec people of Mexico, **Quetzalcoatl,** confronts a powerful enemy—**Tezcatlipoca**, the chief god of the neighboring states.

from *Sundiata*

told by **D. T. Niane**

translated by **G. D. Pickett**

Read with a Purpose
Read this section from the epic to learn how a young boy takes revenge against his mother's tormentor.

Build Background
Like most epics, *Sundiata* is a blend of history, legend, and myth. Sundiata was a real leader of the African people.

God has his mysteries, which none can fathom.[1] You, perhaps, will be a king. You can do nothing about it. You, on the other hand, will be unlucky, but you can do nothing about that either. Each man finds his way already marked out for him, and he can change nothing of it.

Sogolon's son had a slow and difficult childhood. At the age of three he still crawled along on all fours, while children of the same age were already walking. He had nothing of the great beauty of his father, Nare Maghan. He had a head so big that he seemed unable to support it; he also had large eyes, which would open wide whenever anyone entered his mother's house. He was taciturn and used to spend the whole day just sitting in the middle of the house. Whenever his mother went out, he would crawl on all fours to rummage about in the calabashes[2] in search of food, for he was very greedy.

---

1. **fathom** (FATH uhm): fully understand.
2. **calabashes** (KAL uh bash ihz): gourds used as bowls.

Malicious tongues began to blab. What three-year-old has not yet taken his first steps? What three-year-old is not the despair of his parents through his whims and shifts of mood? What three-year-old is not the joy of his circle through his backwardness in talking? Sogolon Djata (for it was thus that they called him, prefixing his mother's name to his), Sogolon Djata, then, was very different from others of his own age. He spoke little and his severe face never relaxed into a smile. You would have thought that he was already thinking, and what amused children of his age bored him. Often Sogolon would make some of them come to him to keep him company. These children were already walking, and she hoped that Djata, seeing his companions walking, would be tempted to do likewise. But nothing came of it. Besides, Sogolon Djata would brain the poor little things with his already strong arms, and none of them would come near him anymore.

The king's first wife was the first to rejoice at Sogolon Djata's infirmity. Her own son,

---

Vocabulary **infirmity** (ihn FUR muh tee) *n.:* defect; weakness.

Dankaran Touman, was already eleven. He was a fine and lively boy, who spent the day running about the village with those of his own age. He had even begun his initiation in the bush. The king had had a bow made for him, and he used to go behind the town to practice archery with his companions. Sassouma was quite happy and snapped her fingers at Sogolon, whose child was still crawling on the ground. Whenever the latter happened to pass by her house, she would say, "Come, my son, walk, jump, leap about. The jinni[3] didn't promise you anything out of the ordinary, but I prefer a son who walks on his two legs to a lion that crawls on the ground." She spoke thus whenever Sogolon went by her door. The innuendo would go straight home, and then she would burst into laughter, that diabolical laughter which a jealous woman knows how to use so well. **Ⓐ**

---

3. **jinni** (jih NEE): in Muslim folklore, supernatural being that can influence people's lives.

Her son's infirmity weighed heavily upon Sogolon Kedjou; she had resorted to all her talent as a sorceress to give strength to her son's legs, but the rarest herbs had been useless. The king himself lost hope. . . .

[*Four years pass and Sundiata is seven.*]

Sogolon Kedjou and her children lived on the queen mother's leftovers, but she kept a little garden in the open ground behind the village. It was there that she passed her brightest moments looking after her onions and gnougous.[4] One day she happened to be short of condiments and went to the queen mother to beg a little baobab[5] leaf.

"Look you," said the malicious Sassouma, "I have a calabash full. Help yourself, you poor

---

4. **gnougous:** root vegetables.
5. **baobab** (BAY oh bab): tree whose leaves are used in cooking.

Ⓐ **Literary Focus** Archetypes What does Sassouma's statement suggest about Sogolon Djata's future?

Tree in sandstorm on the Niger River.

woman. As for me, my son knew how to walk at seven, and it was he who went and picked these baobab leaves. Take them, then, since your son is unequal to mine." Then she laughed derisively with that fierce laughter which cuts through your flesh and penetrates right to the bone.

Sogolon Kedjou was dumbfounded. She had never imagined that hate could be so strong in a human being. With a lump in her throat, she left Sassouma's. Outside her hut Mari Djata, sitting on his useless legs, was blandly eating out of a calabash. Unable to contain herself any longer, Sogolon burst into sobs and, seizing a piece of wood, hit her son.

"Oh son of misfortune, will you never walk? Through your fault I have just suffered the greatest affront of my life! What have I done, God, for you to punish me in this way?"

Mari Djata seized the piece of wood and, looking at his mother, said, "Mother, what's the matter?"

"Shut up, nothing can ever wash me clean of this insult."

"But what, then?"

"Sassouma has just humiliated me over a matter of a baobab leaf. At your age her own son could walk and used to bring his mother baobab leaves."

"Cheer up, Mother, cheer up."

"No. It's too much. I can't."

"Very well, then, I am going to walk today," said Mari Djata. "Go and tell my father's smiths[6] to make me the heaviest possible iron rod. Mother, do you want just the leaves of the baobab, or would you rather I brought you the whole tree?" **Ⓑ**

---

6. **smiths:** shortened form of *blacksmiths*.

Vocabulary **affront** (uh FRUHNT) *n.*: intentional insult.

Ⓑ **Reading Focus** Sequence of Events What actions does Sundiata take after Sogolon is insulted?

"Ah, my son, to wipe out this insult, I want the tree and its roots at my feet outside my hut."

Balla Fasséké, who was present, ran to the master smith, Farakourou, to order an iron rod.

Sogolon had sat down in front of her hut. She was weeping softly and holding her head between her two hands. Mari Djata went calmly back to his calabash of rice and began eating again as if nothing had happened. From time to time he looked up discreetly at his mother, who was murmuring in a low voice, "I want the whole tree in front of my hut, the whole tree."

All of a sudden a voice burst into laughter behind the hut. It was the wicked Sassouma telling one of her serving women about the scene of humiliation, and she was laughing loudly so that Sogolon could hear. Sogolon fled into the hut and hid her face under the blankets so as not to have before her eyes this heedless boy, who was more preoccupied with eating than with anything else. With her head buried in the bedclothes, Sogolon wept, and her body shook violently. Her daughter, Sogolon Djamarou, had come and sat down beside her, and she said, "Mother, Mother, don't cry. Why are you crying?"

Mari Djata had finished eating, and dragging himself along on his legs, he came and sat under the wall of the hut, for the sun was scorching. What was he thinking about? He alone knew.

The royal forges were situated outside the walls, and over a hundred smiths worked there. The bows, spears, arrows, and shields of Niani's warriors came from there. When Balla Fasséké came to order the iron rod, Farakourou said to him, "The great day has arrived, then?" **Ⓒ**

Ⓒ **Reading Focus** Sequence of Events What does Farakourou's question suggest about his understanding of what is about to happen?

"Yes. Today is a day like any other, but it will see what no other day has seen."

The master of the forges, Farakourou, was the son of the old Nounfaïri, and he was a soothsayer[7] like his father. In his workshops there was an enormous iron bar wrought by his father, Nounfaïri. Everybody wondered what this bar was destined to be used for. Farakourou called six of his apprentices and told them to carry the iron bar to Sogolon's house.

When the smiths put the gigantic iron bar down in front of the hut, the noise was so frightening that Sogolon, who was lying down, jumped up with a start. Then Balla Fasséké, son of Gnankouman Doua, spoke.

"Here is the great day, Mari Djata. I am speaking to you, Maghan, son of Sogolon. The waters of the Niger can efface the stain from the body, but they cannot wipe out an insult. Arise, young lion, roar, and may the bush know that from henceforth it has a master."

The apprentice smiths were still there, Sogolon had come out, and everyone was watching Mari Djata. He crept on all fours and came to the iron bar. Supporting himself on his knees and one hand, with the other hand he picked up the iron bar without any effort and stood it up vertically. Now he was resting on nothing but his knees and held the bar with both his hands. A deathly silence had gripped all those present. Sogolon Djata closed his eyes, held tight; the muscles in his arms tensed. With a violent jerk he threw his weight onto the bar and his knees left the ground. Sogolon Kedjou

was all eyes and watched her son's legs, which were trembling as though from an electric shock. Djata was sweating, and the sweat ran from his brow. In a great effort, he straightened up and was on his feet at one go—but the great bar of iron was twisted and had taken the form of a bow! **(D)**

Then Balla Fasséké sang out the "Hymn to the Bow," striking up with his powerful voice:

Take your bow, Simbon,[8]
Take your bow and let us go.
Take your bow, Sogolon Djata.

When Sogolon saw her son standing, she stood dumb for a moment; then suddenly she sang these words of thanks to God, who had given her son the use of his legs:

Oh day, what a beautiful day,
Oh day, day of joy;
Allah[9] Almighty, you never created a finer day.
So my son is going to walk!

Standing in the position of a soldier at ease, Sogolon Djata, supported by his enormous rod, was sweating great beads of sweat. Balla Fasséké's song had alerted the whole palace; people came running from all over to see what had happened, and each stood bewildered before Sogolon's son. The queen mother had rushed there, and when she saw Mari Djata

---

7. **soothsayer:** a person who supposedly can predict future events.

8. **Simbon:** lion.
9. **Allah:** Arabic name for God.

Vocabulary   **efface** (uh FAYS) *v.:* erase.

(D) **Literary Focus** Archetypes What heroic qualities does Sogolon Djata display in this paragraph?

standing up, she trembled from head to foot. After recovering his breath, Sogolon's son dropped the bar and the crowd stood to one side. His first steps were those of a giant. Balla Fasséké fell into step, and pointing his finger at Djata, he cried:

Room, room, make room!
The lion has walked;
Hide, antelopes,
Get out of his way.

Behind Niani there was a young baobab tree, and it was there that the children of the town came to pick leaves for their mothers. With all his might the son of Sogolon tore up the tree and put it on his shoulders and went back to his mother. He threw the tree in front of the hut and said, "Mother, here are some baobab leaves for you. From henceforth it will be outside your hut that the women of Niani will come to stock up."

After the events related in this selection from the epic, the queen mother plots to have Sundiata killed. Sundiata escapes into exile and journeys from one kingdom to the other until he finds refuge with the king of Mema, who makes him his heir.

When Sundiata is eighteen years old, the people of Mali beg him to return. He raises an army, and with supernatural help from the same blacksmith-magician who aided him before, he defeats his enemies and unites the kingdom. Under Sundiata's rule, Mali, the "Bright Country," becomes one of the most powerful empires in Africa. Its rulers control the salt and gold trades and dominate western Sudan from about A.D. 1200 to A.D. 1500.

CULTURE LINK

African Storytellers

There are no written records from the thirteenth century of a king in Mali called Sundiata. Much of what we know has come to us from the oral tradition of storytelling through the African *griots*. However, historians have found written references to Sundiata that started in the fifteenth century.

Griots have been an important part of West African cultures for centuries, since long before the introduction of writing. These storytellers were the keepers of their people's history, <u>recounting</u> the great epics of the past, such as the tale of Sundiata. They also could recite family histories and acted as advisors to kings and other rulers. Nowadays, griots share their songs in media such as TV, the radio, and CDs, as well as through live performances, helping people who celebrate the tradition <u>retain</u> their cultural identity.

Ask Yourself

How might this story be different if it had been written down instead of told orally?

Applying Your Skills

from **Sundiata**

RA.L.10.1 Compare and contrast an author's use of direct and indirect characterization, and ways in which characters reveal traits about themselves, including dialect, dramatic monologues and soliloquies. *Also covered* **RA.I.10.1; VO.10.3; WA.10.1.c**

Respond and Think Critically

Reading Focus

Quick Check

1. Why does Sassouma make fun of Sogolon and her son?

2. Why does Sogolon Djata request that the smiths make him an iron rod?

3. When Sogolon Djata is eighteen years old, how does he gain power?

Read with a Purpose

4. How does Sogolon Djata "wipe out" the "insult" his mother received and enable her to triumph over Sassouma?

Reading Skills: Analyzing Sequence of Events

5. Review the chart you filled in as you read. Then, consider the narrator's statement at the beginning of the selection: "Each man finds his way already marked out for him, and he can change nothing of it." What role does fate play in the sequence of events in the story? Which characters seem not to understand the power of fate?

✔ Vocabulary Check

Match each Vocabulary word in the column on the left with its definition in the column on the right.

6. **infirmity**   a. insult
7. **affront**   b. erase
8. **efface**   c. defect

Literary Focus

Literary Analysis

9. **Analyze** What is Sogolon's attitude toward her son? Does it change during the story? Support your response with evidence from the text.

10. **Interpret** Why is it significant that the iron bar Sogolon Djata uses to support himself turns into a bow? What might the bow represent?

Literary Skills: Archetypes

11. **Summarize** Heroes often display evidence of their larger-than-life qualities at an early age. What makes Sogolon Djata different from other children? What heroic qualities does he fully exhibit at the end of the selection?

12. **Interpret** What is suggested by the comparison of Sogolon Djata to a lion?

Literary Skills Review: Subordinate Characters

13. **Analyze** Minor, or **subordinate,** characters are not central to a story but can play significant roles. How do Balla Fasséké and Farakourou contribute to the story's plot?

Writing Focus

Think as a Reader/Writer

Use It in Your Writing Write a short scene in your *Reader/Writer Notebook* in which a hero must prove him- or herself by overcoming an obstacle. Use direct and indirect characterization to develop your characters.

Quetzalcoatl

Retold by **Amy Cruse**

Read with a Purpose
Read this myth to explore why a Golden Age ends.

Preparing to Read for this selection is on page 1079.

Build Background
The Toltecs were the people who first brought civilization to Mexico; the Aztecs took over the Toltec religion. In 1519, when the Spanish explorer Hernando Cortés arrived in Mexico looking for gold, he was welcomed by the Aztec king Montezuma, much to his surprise. This myth explains why.

Long, long ago, hundreds of years before the people of Europe knew anything about the great land of America, a race of people called the Toltecs lived in the southern part of that country which we now call Mexico. They were ruled by Quetzalcoatl, the great god of the sun and the wind, who had left his home in the land of the Sunrise so that he might teach the Toltecs and help them to become a happy and prosperous nation. He was an old man with a flowing white beard, and he wore a long black robe fringed with white crosses. He was kind and wise, and while he reigned over them, the Toltecs were very happy. Everything in the country prospered. The maize crops were more abundant than they had ever been before; the fruits were larger and more plentiful. It is even said that the cotton grew in all sorts of colors, richer and rarer than could be produced by any dyes. The hills and valleys were gay with flowers, and bright-colored birds flitted through the air, filling the land with joyous song.

But the god Quetzalcoatl knew that if his people were to be really happy, they must not spend their days in the idle enjoyment of all this loveliness and plenty. They must work, and learn to take a pride in working as well as they possibly could. So he taught them many useful arts—painting and weaving and carving and working in metals. He taught them how to fashion the gold and silver and precious stones (which were found in great abundance throughout the country) into beautiful vessels and ornaments, and how to make marvelous many-tinted garments and hangings from the feathers of birds. Everyone was eager to work, and because each man did his share, there was plenty of leisure for all. No one was in want, and no one was unhappy. It seemed as if, for these fortunate Toltecs, the Golden Age had really come.

The people of the neighboring states, who were living almost like savages, were very jealous when they saw the prosperity of the Toltecs. The gods of these people were fierce and warlike, and they hated Quetzalcoatl because he was so unlike themselves. They plotted together to destroy the peace and good government which he had established.

Vocabulary **abundant** (uh BUHN duhnt) *adj.*: plentiful.

Tezcatlipoca, the chief of these gods, disguised himself as a very old man and went to the palace of Quetzalcoatl.

"I desire to speak with your master, the King," he said to the page who admitted him.

"That you cannot do," replied the page, "for the King is at present ill, and can see no one."

"Nevertheless, go and take my message," said Tezcatlipoca, "and come back and tell me what he says."

The page soon returned, saying that the King would see his visitor, and Tezcatlipoca went in. He bowed low and respectfully before the god, and said that he had come to bring him a drug that would at once cure him of his illness.

"I have been expecting you for some days," answered Quetzalcoatl, "and I will take your medicine, for my illness troubles me exceedingly."

Then Tezcatlipoca poured out a cupful of his medicine, which was really nothing but the strong wine of the country. Quetzalcoatl tasted it, and liked it very much; he did not know what it was, for he never drank wine. After drinking the cupful, he declared that he already felt better, so that it was easy to induce him to drink cupful after cupful of this new, pleasant-tasting medicine. Very soon the wine had its effect, and he could no longer think clearly or act wisely, or take his usual place as the ruler of the country. Tezcatlipoca took care to keep him supplied with plenty of the tempting drink, so that he remained for some time in this state of intoxication.[1] **A**

This was Tezcatlipoca's opportunity, and he used it to the full. He set to work to bring upon the happy Toltecs every kind of misery that he could devise. He stirred up strife between them and their neighbors, and in many cunning ways he used his magic arts to lure large numbers of them to destruction. He brought plagues upon them, and disasters in which many lost their lives; until at last, by his wicked devices, the once happy land was brought to a state even worse than that of its barbarous[2] neighbors. **B**

When Quetzalcoatl shook off the evil influence of the wine given to him by his enemy and came to his true self once more, the grief which he felt at seeing all his work undone made him resolve to leave the Toltecs and go back whence he had come. But first he determined to destroy what he could of the gifts he had given to the people. He burned the houses he had built, and changed the cacao trees[3] from which the Toltecs had obtained so much valuable food into useless mesquites.[4] He buried his treasures of gold and silver in one of the deep valleys. All the bright-plumaged birds he commanded to follow him back to his own country; and, full of anger and grief, he set out on his long journey, taking with him a train of pages and musicians to lighten the way with their flute playing. On the road, as he passed through the neighboring states, he was met by some of the gods of the land. These gods were his enemies, and were glad to see him depart; but before he went, they hoped to gain from him some of his secrets.

---

1. **intoxication** (ihn tahk suh KAY shuhn): state of being drunk.

2. **barbarous** (BAHR buhr uhs): mercilessly cruel.
3. **cacao** (kuh KAY oh) **trees:** Their seeds are used to make chocolate.
4. **mesquites** (mehs KEETS): thorny trees or shrubs found in the southwestern United States and in Mexico.

A **Literary Focus** Archetypes What characteristics of a trickster does Tezcatlipoca display?

B **Reading Focus** Sequence of Events How does Quetzalcoatl's state create an "opportunity" for Tezcatlipoca?

Vocabulary **strife** (stryf) *n.*: bitter struggle.

"Why are you going away," asked one, "and whither are you bound?"

"I am going back to my own country," Quetzalcoatl answered.

"But why?" the other asked again.

"Because my father, the Sun, has called for me."

"Go then," replied the gods. "But first tell us some of the secrets, which are known to you alone, concerning the arts you practice; for we know there is no one who can paint and weave and work in metals as you can."

"I will tell you nothing," replied Quetzalcoatl. He took all the treasures he had brought with him and cast them into a fountain nearby, which was called the Water of Precious Stones; and he went on his way, paying no heed to the entreaties of the disappointed gods. **C**

As they journeyed on, the road grew ever harder and more dangerous, but Quetzalcoatl, his staff in his hand, pressed steadily forward; and his train, though they were weary and nearly exhausted, followed him. Only once did they stop to rest, and that was when an enchanter met Quetzalcoatl and gave him a cup of wine. The wine sent the god into a deep sleep, but in the morning he had recovered from its effects and was ready to set out once more.

That day was a terrible one for the wayfarers. At each step, it grew colder and colder, and the poor pages, used to the sunny skies of their native land, felt their limbs gradually becoming numb and useless. At length, Quetzalcoatl led the way through a narrow valley between a volcano and the Sierra Nevada, or Mountain of Snow. Here the cold was so intense that the pages, one by one, sank down and died. Quetzalcoatl mourned over them with many tears and sang wild songs of lamentation;

Aztecs crying when they realize that Cortés is not Quetzalcoatl. From the Florentine Codex, Mexico (sixteenth century).

then sadly he went on his way, still weeping bitterly.

He had now to cross a great mountain. He climbed up one side, then, when he had reached the summit, he slid down the opposite slope to the bottom. After this, he soon reached the seashore, and there, awaiting him, was a raft. It was not made of timber, as most rafts are, but of serpents, twined together, with writhing bodies and lifted, hissing heads. Onto this strange raft Quetzalcoatl stepped, and was borne away back to his own land. The Mexicans believe that one day he will come again, and once more rule over his people and bring back to them the Golden Age. When Cortés[5] and his companions, in 1519, landed at Veracruz, which was the very place from which Quetzalcoatl was supposed to have departed centuries before, the people believed that here was their god returning to help them. Only slowly and reluctantly did they come to understand that he was a Spaniard, bent on conquest.

---

5. **Cortés:** Hernando Cortés (1485–1547) was a Spanish explorer who overthrew the Aztecs and conquered Mexico.

C **Literary Focus** Archetypes What human feelings are the causes for Quetzalcoatl's refusal to share his secrets?

Applying Your Skills

RA.L.10.1 Compare and contrast an author's use of direct and indirect characterization, and ways in which characters reveal traits about themselves, including dialect, dramatic monologues and soliloquies. *Also covered* **RA.L.10.11; RA.I.10.1; VO.10.3; WA.10.1.b**

Quetzalcoatl

Respond and Think Critically

Reading Focus

Quick Check

1. How do the Toltecs prosper under Quetzalcoatl's rule?

2. Who is Tezcatlipoca? How does he triumph over Quetzalcoatl?

3. How did the Mexicans' hope for Quetzalcoatl's return lead to their downfall?

Read with a Purpose

4. How did the Golden Age end?

Reading Skills: Comparing Texts

5. As you read the selections, you noted the sequence of events in a chart. Now ask yourself, "What different decisions or actions might have changed the sequence of events?"

from "Sundiata"	Sologon's son can't walk.		
"Quetzalcoatl"	Quetzalcoatl teaches the Toltecs to be prosperous.		

✓ Vocabulary Check

Tell whether each statement is true (T) or false (F).

6. When apple crops fail, there is **abundant** fruit.

7. A desire for land can lead to **strife** between countries.

Literary Focus

Literary Analysis

8. **Connect** Quetzalcoatl believes that in order for his people to be truly happy, they must not be idle but must work and take pride in their achievements. How does learning various arts lead to contentment for the Toltecs? Do you agree that work can lead to happiness? Why?

Literary Skills: Archetypes

9. **Identify** What key character traits of Quetzalcoatl make him a hero to the Toltecs? What makes Tezcatlipoca an archetypal trickster figure?

10. **Interpret** What might the myth suggest about Golden Ages? Can they last, or are they fated to end? Support your response with evidence from the text.

Literary Skills Review: Imagery

11. **Analyze** The storyteller uses **imagery**—language that appeals to the five senses—to describe Quetzalcoatl's journey and to convey its supernatural elements. Choose at least three images and explain the emotions they convey.

Writing Focus

Think as a Reader/Writer

Use It in Your Writing Do you know anyone (from real life or from a movie you've watched or a book you've read) who reminds you of the trickster Tezcatlipoca? Write a brief description of a modern-day trickster. Use direct and indirect characterization to convey the trickster's traits.

COMPARING TEXTS

Wrap Up

VO.10.6 Determine the meanings and pronunciations of unknown words by using dictionaries, glossaries, technology and textual features, such as definitional footnotes or sidebars. R.10.2 Identify appropriate sources and gather relevant information from multiple sources. *Also covered* WP.10.6; WA.10.4.c

from **Sundiata / Quetzalcoatl**

Writing Focus

Write a Comparison-Contrast Essay

Topic Both of the selections you've just read center on the archetypal conflict between good and evil. Write an essay in which you compare and contrast this conflict in the two works. Consider

- Sundiata's and Quetzalcoatl's character traits
- the nature and causes of the conflicts, including the characters' motivations
- the conflicts' resolutions, including their significance for the future

Organization Choose the method for organizing ideas that you find most helpful for creating a coherent, focused essay:

- If you prefer to consider one work at a time, use the block method. Present all your ideas about one work and then all your ideas about the second work.
- If you prefer to consider one point of comparison at a time, use the point-by-point method. Discuss each idea as it relates to both works.

Be sure to use one method consistently throughout your essay and create a balanced discussion by giving equal attention to each work.

What Do You Think Now What role does hardship play in our lives and the lives of others?

CHOICES

As you respond to the Choices, use the **Academic Vocabulary** words as appropriate: recurring, exhibit, retain, and recount.

REVIEW
Write a Movie Review

Think of a movie with archetypal characters, plots, or themes. Then, write a critical movie review. Is the treatment of these archetypes effective, fresh, or original? Why or why not? What elements of archetypes are similar to those you have just studied? Consider the screenplay, acting, direction, and the techniques used in shooting the film.

CONNECT
Write an Editorial

Timed └Writing What is your vision of a Golden Age? What would you do to make life happy, peaceful, and productive for people? Write an editorial discussing actions you would take to improve the world, the country, or your community. What rules or traditions would you retain? Focus on specific problems and solutions.

EXTEND
Deliver a Research Report

TechFocus With a partner, conduct research on the real leader Sundiata Keita, the historical events reflected in the conflict between Quetzalcoatl and Tezcatlipoca, or the Spanish conqueror Hernando Cortés. Present your findings to the class in a PowerPoint presentation.

Generating Research Questions

CONTENTS

What Do **You** **Think**? How does asking the right questions guide your research?

 QuickTalk

With a partner, brainstorm two lists of facts: those you know about the Loch Ness Monster and those you know about Pocahontas. Look at the facts and discuss where you got the information. How certain are you that your facts are true?

WEB ARTICLE
Preparing to Read

Birth of a Legend

R.10.1 Compose open-ended questions for research, assigned or personal interest, and modify questions as necessary during inquiry and investigation to narrow the focus or extend the investigation.

Reader/Writer Notebook

Use your **RWN** to complete the activities for this selection.

Informational Text Focus

Generating Research Questions The two articles you are about to read provide good opportunities for further research. The first step in researching a topic is generating specific, focused research questions. Use the tips below to help.

Tip 1: To focus your research, think of a specific question you have about the topic. For example, asking *What causes train accidents?* is too vague. You could be more specific by asking *What causes accidents at commuter train crossings?* As you form your research question, keep in mind that its purpose is to guide you in locating accurate information in a variety of reliable sources.

Tip 2: Use the **5W–How?** question strategy to come up with more questions. Make an organizer like the one here to record questions about the topic. Doing so will provide you with several different ideas to explore.

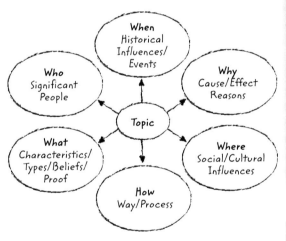

Tip 3: Write a few research questions. Then, choose the one that interests you the most. Try to choose one that you think you'll be able to find answers to given your available resources.

Writing Focus — Preparing for **Constructed Response**

As you read the following selection, think about what questions the author may have asked in order to gather information for the article, and write these down in your *Reader/Writer Notebook*.

Vocabulary

fidelity (fih DEHL ih tee) *n.:* exact rendering. *The animals were drawn with such fidelity that the researcher could identify them all.*

malevolent (muh LEHV uh luhnt) *adj.:* wishing evil to others. *The malevolent sea monster devoured swimmers in the lake.*

gullible (GUHL ih buhl) *adj.:* easily persuaded to believe. *Were the people gullible to believe in the monster?*

anecdotal (an ehk DOH tuhl) *adj.:* based on personal or casual observation. *Anecdotal evidence cannot prove scientific theories.*

skepticism (SKEHP tih sihz uhm) *n.:* tendency to question or doubt. *Her skepticism about the huge monster was understandable.*

dissuaded (dih SWAYD ihd) *v.:* persuaded not to do something. *Few will be dissuaded from their belief in the creature.*

Language Coach

Connotations Some words have emotional overtones, or **connotations,** that extend their literal meanings. Consider the word *fidelity.* Its literal meaning is "accuracy," but it carries an implied meaning of "faithfulness." Which word do you associate with the word *gullible*— *foolish* or *open-minded?*

Learn It Online
To read more articles like this, go to the interactive Reading Workshop on:

go.hrw.com | L10-1093 | Go

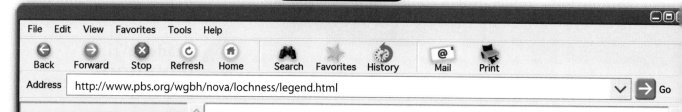

File   Edit   View   Favorites   Tools   Help

Back | Forward | Stop | Refresh | Home | Search | Favorites | History | Mail | Print

Address http://www.pbs.org/wgbh/nova/lochness/legend.html   Go

Read with a Purpose
Learn the history behind one of the most intriguing mysteries of our time.

Build Background
Loch Ness is a large, deep lake in northern Scotland. (*Loch* is the Scottish Gaelic word for "lake.") It has long been the source of mysterious sightings of a large aquatic creature, called the Loch Ness Monster.

Birth of a Legend
by Stephen Lyons

"Many a man has been hanged on less evidence than there is for the Loch Ness Monster." —G. K. Chesterton

When the Romans first came to northern Scotland in the first century A.D., they found the highlands occupied by fierce, tattoo-covered tribes they called the Picts, or painted people. From the carved, standing stones still found in the region around Loch Ness, it is clear the Picts were fascinated by animals and careful to render them with great fidelity. All the animals depicted on the Pictish stones are lifelike and easily recognizable—all but one. The exception is a strange beast with an elongated beak or muzzle, a head locket or spout, and flippers instead of feet. Described by some scholars as a swimming elephant, the Pictish beast is the earliest known evidence for an idea that has held sway in the Scottish Highlands for at least 1,500 years—that Loch Ness is home to a mysterious aquatic animal. **Ⓐ**

In Scottish folklore, large animals have been associated with many bodies of water, from small streams to the largest lakes, often labeled Loch-na-Beistie on old maps. These water-horses, or water-kelpies, are said to have magical powers and malevolent intentions. According to one version of the legend, the water-horse lures small children into the water by offering them rides on its back. Once the children are aboard, their hands become stuck to the beast and they are dragged to a watery death, their livers washing ashore the following day. **Ⓑ**

The earliest written reference linking such creatures to Loch Ness is in the biography of Saint Columba, the man credited with introducing Christianity to Scotland. In A.D. 565, according to this account, Columba was on his way to visit

> **Ⓐ** **Informational Focus** Generating Research Questions What research question does the writer answer in this paragraph?
>
> **Ⓑ** **Informational Focus** Generating Research Questions What research question would you ask about Scottish folklore and the Loch Ness creature?
>
> **Vocabulary** **fidelity** (fih DEHL ih tee) *n.*: exact rendering.
> **malevolent** (muh LEHV uh luhnt) *adj.*: wishing evil to others.

(above) Loch Ness. (inset) Newspaper article from the 1960s entitled "The Loch Ness Monster— Fact or Fancy?" by Peter Scott.

a Pictish king when he stopped along the shore of Loch Ness. Seeing a large beast about to attack a man who was swimming in the lake, Columba raised his hand, invoking the name of God and commanding the monster to "go back with all speed." The beast complied, and the swimmer was saved.

When Nicholas Witchell, a future BBC correspondent, researched the history of the legend for his 1974 book, *The Loch Ness Story,* he found about a dozen pre-20th-century references to large animals in Loch Ness, gradually shifting in character from these clearly mythical accounts to something more like eyewitness descriptions.

But the modern legend of Loch Ness dates from 1933, when a new road was completed along the shore, offering the first clear views of the loch from the northern side. One April afternoon, a local couple was driving home along this road when they spotted "an enormous animal rolling and plunging on the surface." Their account was written up by a correspondent for the *Inverness Courier,* whose editor used the word "monster" to describe the animal. The Loch Ness Monster has been a media phenomenon ever since. **C**

> **C** **Informational Focus** Generating Research Questions What was the primary cause for the modern legend of the Loch Ness Monster?

Public interest built gradually during the spring of 1933, then picked up sharply after a couple reported seeing one of the creatures on land, lumbering across the shore road. By October, several London newspapers had sent correspondents to Scotland, and radio programs were being interrupted to bring listeners the latest news from the loch. A British circus offered a reward of £20,000 for the capture of the beast. Hundreds of Boy Scouts and outdoorsmen arrived, some venturing out in small boats, others setting up deck chairs and waiting expectantly for the monster to appear.

The excitement over the monster reached a fever pitch in December, when the *London Daily Mail* hired an actor, film director, and big-game hunter named Marmaduke Wetherell to track down the beast. After only a few days at the loch, Wetherell reported finding the fresh footprints of a large, four-toed animal. He estimated it to be 20 feet long. With great fanfare, Wetherell made plaster casts of the footprints and, just before Christmas, sent them off to the Natural History Museum in London for analysis. While the world waited for the museum zoologists to return from holiday, legions of monster hunters descended on Loch Ness, filling the local hotels. Inverness was floodlit for the occasion, and traffic jammed the shoreline roads in both directions.

The bubble burst in early January, when museum zoologists announced that the footprints were those of a hippopotamus. They had been made with a stuffed hippo foot—the base of an umbrella stand or ashtray. It wasn't clear whether Wetherell was the perpetrator of the hoax or its gullible victim. Either way, the incident tainted the image of the Loch Ness Monster and discouraged serious investigation of the phenomenon. For the next three decades, most scientists scornfully dismissed reports of strange animals in the loch. Those sightings that weren't outright hoaxes, they said, were the result of optical illusions caused by boat wakes, wind slicks, floating logs, otters, ducks, or swimming deer. **ⓓ**

Saw Something, They Did

Nevertheless, eyewitnesses continued to come forward with accounts of their sightings—more than 4,000 of them, according to Witchell's estimate. Most of the witnesses described a large creature with one or more humps protruding above the surface like the hull of an upturned boat. Others reported seeing a long neck or flippers. What was most remarkable, however, was that many of the eyewitnesses were sober, level-headed people: lawyers and priests, scientists and schoolteachers, policemen and fishermen—even a Nobel Prize winner.

In the 1960s a group of dedicated amateurs formed the Loch Ness Investigation Bureau to keep a constant vigil on the loch.

ⓓ Informational Focus **Generating Research Questions** How could you make the following research question more specific: "Why do some people refuse to believe there is a creature in Loch Ness?"

Vocabulary **gullible** (GUHL ih buhl) *adj.:* easily persuaded to believe.

Illustration of the Loch Ness Monster and her young.

Eyewitness Accounts

While no hard evidence for the existence of the Loch Ness Monster has yet turned up, heaps of anecdotal evidence exist. Although such eyewitness accounts are of little value scientifically, they can be compelling nevertheless. Read the accounts by the following native Scots who swear they saw something in the loch. These tales were collected by the producers of the NOVA film *The Beast of Loch Ness*.

"I saw it, and nothing can take that away."

Well, we're talking about an incident that happened approximately 32 years ago, almost to the very day mid-summer, June 1965. I, along with a friend, was on the south shore of Loch Ness, fishing for brown trout, looking almost directly into Urquhart Bay, when I saw something break the surface of the water. I glanced there, and I saw it, and then it wasn't there, it had disappeared.

But while watching, keeping an eye, and fishing gently, I saw an object surface. It was a large, black object—a whale-like object, going from infinity up, and came round onto a block end—and it submerged, to reappear a matter of seconds later. But on this occasion, the block end, which had been on my right, was now on my left, so I realized immediately that while in the process of surfacing, as it may, it had rotated. And with the predominant wind, the south-west wind, it appeared to be, I would say, at that stage drifting easily across.

So I called to my friend Willie Frazer, who incidentally had a sighting of an object on the Loch almost a year ago to the very day. I called him, and he come up and joined me. We realized that it was drifting towards us, and, in fact, it came to within I would say about 250, 300 yards.

In no way am I even attempting to convert anybody to the religion of the object of Loch Ness. I mean, they can believe it but it doesn't upset me if they don't believe it. Because I would question very much if I hadn't the extraordinary experience of seeing this object. If I hadn't seen it I would have without question given a lot of skepticism to what it was. But I saw it, and nothing can take that away.

> **Vocabulary** **anecdotal** (an ehk DOH tuhl) *adj:* based on personal or casual observation.
> **skepticism** (SKEHP tih sihz uhm) *n.:* tendency to question or doubt.

—Ian Cameron, a retired superintendent of the Northern Police Force, lives with his wife Jessie in Inverness, Scotland, at the head of the loch. A keen angler, he is an authority on the Atlantic salmon.

"I'm gobsmacked°... I just didn't know what it was."

Right, I'm driving along the Loch side, glancing out of the window. You can see the rock formation, I was just down on the road there, it just rises. I saw this boiling in the water. I thought, "No, it can't be anything," and I carried on a wee bit. Then I looked again, and I saw three black humps. I mean, you know, there's the chance, I've seen something in the water. But what is it?

So I'm gobsmacked, I'm looking out the window, I just didn't know what it was. Then the people came behind me, and they obviously wanted me to move. But I didn't want to lose sight of this thing. So I just pulled over to the side, grabbed my camera, and I thought I was being very cool and very nonchalant and took two or three photos. In fact, as I say, I had taken nine or ten, without realizing, I just punched the button. It was just a pity it was a small camera.

NOVA: Did anybody else see anything?

WHITE: Yeah, the other two people who were there—I was just so excited I didn't get their name and address or anything—they saw it exactly the same as me. Because the wee wifey, who would have been a lady in her fifties, on holiday, she was Scottish, she said to me, "I've not been in the bar this morning!" And her husband said, "Ach, it's an eel! It's an eel!" And I said, "There's no eels that big!" And he said, "Ach, it's otters!" And I said, "You don't get otters swimming out like that!" **(E)**

I saw what I saw, and I'm not going to be dissuaded. It wasn't just an imagination. I'm a sane guy, and I've got no ax to grind. As I say I sell pet food! What use to me is the Loch Ness Monster? Unless I can invent a food called, I don't know, Monster Munchies perhaps?

—Richard White lives in the village of Muir of Ord, north of Inverness. He runs his own business selling pet food, and he also breeds dogs.

° **gobsmacked** (GAWB smakt): shocked, stunned (more commonly used in Great Britain).

Read with a Purpose   How has the mystery of the Loch Ness Monster deepened over time?

(E) Informational Focus Generating Research Questions   Why might it be a problem that White does not have the names or contact information for the other witnesses?

Vocabulary **dissuaded** (dih SWAYD ihd) *v.:* persuaded not to do something.

Internet

WEB ARTICLE
Applying Your Skills

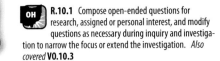

R.10.1 Compose open-ended questions for research, assigned or personal interest, and modify questions as necessary during inquiry and investigation to narrow the focus or extend the investigation. *Also covered* **VO.10.3**

Birth of a Legend

Respond and Think Critically

Informational Text and Vocabulary

1. Which of the following is the *most* focused **research question?**

  A Why do people try to catch the Loch Ness Monster?

  B How many people have seen the Loch Ness Monster?

  C Why has the number of reported sightings of the Loch Ness Monster declined in recent years?

  D Does the Loch Ness Monster exist?

2. What is the problem with the **research question** "Do the majority of Scots believe in sea monsters?"

  A The question could lead to local sources.

  B The question may offend some people.

  C The question does not go beyond a simple "yes" or "no" answer.

  D The question does not specify the Loch Ness Monster.

3. Which is the *best* follow-up **research question** to this article?

  A Could glacial changes in Scotland's geography have preserved the creature's habitat?

  B Where does the creature find its food?

  C Will global warming threaten the creature's existence?

  D Have people looked for similar creatures in other lochs?

4. Someone *dissuaded* by an argument —

  A has had a change of mind

  B tries to intimidate others

  C is anxious for a change

  D comes up with another argument

5. Someone with *skepticism* has —

  A doubts

  B no questions

  C a detailed report

  D strong beliefs

6. *Anecdotal* evidence is —

  A historical

  B unreliable

  C factual

  D thoughtful

7. A *gullible* person is —

  A critical of others

  B easy to fool

  C worried about the future

  D awkward in social situations

Writing Focus   Constructed Response

Write two research questions about the Loch Ness Monster. Where would you begin your research?

What Do You Think Now

What do you think is the most persuasive piece of evidence to support the existence of the Loch Ness Monster? Why?

MAGAZINE ARTICLE
Preparing to Read

Real Princess—A Portrait of Pocahontas

OH **R.10.1** Compose open-ended questions for research, assigned or personal interest, and modify questions as necessary during inquiry and investigation to narrow the focus or extend the investigation.

Reader/Writer Notebook

Use your **RWN** to complete the activities for this selection.

Informational Text Focus

Generating Research Questions Once you have come up with some viable research questions, your next step is to focus on your main points and evaluate potential sources.

Tip 1: Review your *5W–How?* questions. For which questions do you already have answers?

Tip 2: To narrow your topic, use a topic organizer like the one below to see how the author supports his or her central idea.

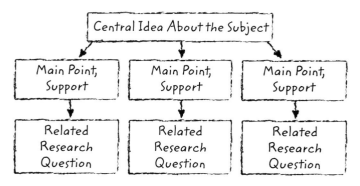

Tip 3: Evaluate the questions you've generated. Ask yourself if the question is answerable and if you know where you can begin your research to find answers.

Writing Focus   Preparing for **Constructed Response**

As you read the selection, note which aspects of the Pocahontas story seem factual and which seem questionable. Consider how these aspects can contribute to the development of a myth over time.

Vocabulary

obscurity (uhb SKYOOR ih tee) *n.:* state of being unknown. *As a young child, Pocahontas lived in obscurity.*

pretentious (prih TEHN shuhs) *adj.:* characterized by affecting greater importance than is actually possessed. *The pretentious colonist wanted to marry into royalty.*

deteriorating (dih TEER ee uhr ay tihng) *v.:* becoming worse. *Pocahontas's health was deteriorating rapidly when she reached the shore.*

entourage (AHN tuhr ahj) *n.:* group of people accompanying an important person. *Because the chief was an important man, he traveled with an entourage.*

Language Coach

Related Words The word *entourage* comes from the French word *entourer,* which means "to surround." A related word is *tour,* which comes from the French word *tourner,* "to turn." How many words can you think of that contain *tour?*

Real Princess
A Portrait of Pocahontas

by Jessica Cohn

Read with a Purpose
As you read this article about Pocahontas, think about what information you would like to research further.

Build Background
The story of Pocahontas is a good example of a story based on historical fact that has been embellished with each retelling.

As a friend to the Jamestown[1] settlers, Pocahontas was *"the instrument to pur-surve this colonie from death, famine, and utter confusion,"* wrote Captain John Smith, to Queen Anne of England, in 1616: quite an endorsement. In the years that followed, Pocahontas's reputation continued to grow, as a historical figure and, even later, as the Disney-marketed, two-dimensional cartoon character bearing her name.

Facts about this Native American princess have been clouded by imagination, however. Even before Jamestown was settled, America was represented in European art as a welcoming Indian woman, posed in an Eden-like garden. When Pocahontas entered the scene, it was as if her name were simply attached to an existing Indian icon. **Ⓐ**

---

1. **Jamestown:** In Virginia, the first permanent English settlement in North America.

Ⓐ Informational Focus Generating Research Questions
What is the author's main point in this paragraph?

Immortalized in stone monuments and eponymous[2] landmarks, Pocahontas became a shifting symbol in a stream of poetry and

---

2. **eponymous**: named for a certain person.

Pocahontas Saving the Life of Captain John Smith (c. 1836-40) by John Gadsby Chapman. Collection of the New York-Historical Society.

stories. Yet not a word written about her came from the woman herself.

Legend Has It

Pocahontas was a daughter of Powhatan, chief of the Algonquian, or Powhatan, Indians in the Tidewater area of what is now Virginia. Powhatan took many wives, and Pocahontas had many siblings, so some argue that her status as a "princess" is a stretch. Yet to the colonists, who viewed royalty by European standards, she was a daughter to a chief, and therefore a princess.

Her given name was Matoaka, but the pet name Pocahontas, meaning "spoiled child" or "the naughty one," according to Chief Roy Crazy Horse of the Powhatan Renape Nation, is what stuck.

In 1607, the young Pocahontas first met the English colonists, soon after they arrived on the shores of Virginia. The Indian princess leapfrogged from childhood obscurity to international history when she saved the life of early settler Captain John Smith—or at least, that's how the story goes. **Ⓑ**

Captain Smith's Role

According to Smith, he was captured by warriors in December 1607 and taken to Powhatan at a spot 12 miles outside Jamestown. The captain was welcomed with a feast, but was then made to stretch out on stone. Warriors stood over him with clubs, he said, as if ready to beat him. But suddenly, Pocahontas rushed to him.

He would later write that she took his "head in her arms and laid her owne upon his to save him from death." Then she pulled him upright.

In English circles, this story was interpreted as his rescue from savages. But mock executions and salvations were often dramatized in Native American ceremonies; so her display of affection could have been ritual. Interpretation of the event is complicated by the fact that the first time Smith described it in writing was in a letter to Queen Anne nearly a decade later, and he may have been trying to polish the story. Powhatan Chief Roy Crazy Horse remarks, in his essay "The Pocahontas Myth," that it "was one of three [stories] reported by the pretentious Smith that he was saved from death by a prominent woman." **Ⓒ**

The next development, however, is undisputed. The fun-loving Pocahontas started to visit Jamestown regularly.

White Man's World

Sometimes the young girl carried messages from her father. Or she and other tribal members traded fur and food. Several years after meeting her, Smith described her in those times: "a child of tenne yeares old, which not only for feature, countenance, and proportion much exceedeth any of the rest of [Powhatan's] people but for wit and spirit the only nonpareil[3] of his countrie."

Settlers took note of a friendship between the girl and the captain; some read more into it. Numerous fictional accounts, such as the 2005

---

3. **non-pareil:** unique or extraordinary person.

Ⓑ **Informational Focus** Generating Research Questions What questions come to mind as you read about Pocahontas?

Ⓒ **Informational Focus** Generating Research Questions If you wanted to research Crazy Horse's ideas about Pocahontas, what source would you consult?

Vocabulary **obscurity** (uhb SKYOOR ih tee) *n.*: state of being unknown.
pretentious (prih TEHN shuhs) *adj.*: characterized by affecting greater importance than is actually possessed.

Viewing and Interpreting Does this scene accurately reflect the story of Pocahontas? Why or why not?

The marriage of Pocahontas and John Rolfe at Jamestown, Virginia, in 1614.
The Granger Collection, New York.

film *The New World*, by Terrence Malick, dramatize a romance. What's certain is that Smith was injured in fall of 1609 when gunpowder exploded, and he returned to England. By that time, the colony was expanding farther into Powhatan's territory, and relations between whites and the tribes were deteriorating.

Sometime before 1613, the princess married a warrior named Kocoum. But no "happily ever after" followed. Pocahontas was targeted by Jamestown settlers in a kidnapping for ransom.

Playing the Pawn

The settlers wanted to exchange the princess for English prisoners being held by Powhatan, along with firearms and food. The plot was carried forth by Captain Samuel Argall, who lured Pocahontas to a ship. The English locked her away, then made their demands.

Powhatan sent back only part of what they asked for—and told them to treat his daughter well. In April 1613, Argall returned to shore, his plan yet unfulfilled.

Pocahontas was moved to a settlement called Henrico, run by Sir Thomas Dale, who tried to use her for barter as well. She was sent with a band of Englishmen to strike a deal with Powhatan, but the group was attacked. In response, the English destroyed villages, killing Indians. The situation turned explosive.

Vocabulary **deteriorating** (dih TEER ee uhr ay tihng) *v.*: becoming worse.

Pocahontas, daughter of Powhatan chief, by an unidentified artist. English school, after the 1616 engraving by Simon van de Passe. Oil on canvas. National Portrait Gallery, Smithsonian Institution, Washington, DC, USA.

Pocahontas went to her father and told him she planned to marry tobacco farmer John Rolfe, a merger that would encourage goodwill. By some accounts, she declared her love for the wealthy planter. But did she?

Rolfe's words about the impending union are the ones on record: "for the good of the plantation, the honor of our country, for the glory of God, for mine own salvation."

Chief Roy Crazy Horse characterizes this development as "a condition of her release." Whether it was a day of happiness or convenience—and without word from Pocahontas, we will never know—the wedding was held in April 1614, and Pocahontas became Rebecca Rolfe. **D**

Over the Sea

In 1616, Dale took a dozen or so Native Americans to England. The princess, her husband, and their young son Thomas were part of the entourage. Crazy Horse called it a "propaganda campaign" for the colony.

In London, she met King James I and the royal family, and she saw Captain John Smith, whom she had believed to be dead. He claimed she was overcome with emotion as they spoke—and that she referred to him as a "father." According to Crazy Horse, she turned her back on him and in a second encounter, called him a liar.

In 1617, the Rolfes boarded a return ship to Virginia, but Pocahontas fell ill at sea. When taken back to shore, in England, she died, taking her heart's secrets with her, at age twenty-one or twenty-two. **E**

"All must die," she supposedly said to her husband. "Tis enough that the child liveth." Yet Pocahontas lives on, larger than anyone's life.

Read with a Purpose Which aspects of the Pocahantas story would be most interesting to research?

D **Informational Focus** **Generating Research Questions** What research question would help you learn more about John Rolfe?

E **Informational Focus** **Generating Research Questions** What research question would help you learn more about the fateful trip to England?

Vocabulary **entourage** (AHN tuhr ahj) *n.*: group of people accompanying an important person.

MAGAZINE ARTICLE

Applying Your Skills

R.10.1 Compose open-ended questions for research, assigned or personal interest, and modify questions as necessary during inquiry and investigation to narrow the focus or extend the investigation. *Also covered* **VO.10.3**

Real Princess—A Portrait of Pocahontas

Respond and Think Critically

Informational Text and Vocabulary

1. Which is the *best* **research question** for learning whether parts of the Pocahontas myth are true?

A Why do people like romance stories?

B Was Captain Smith married?

C What were the prevailing beliefs about Native Americans during Pocahontas's lifetime?

D How did the relationship between Native Americans and settlers change over time?

2. What is the main problem with the question "Why did Pocahontas marry John Rolfe?"

A No records of Pocahontas's marriage exist.

B The question may not be answerable.

C The question is too general.

D The question is not relevant.

3. Which is the *most* focused question about Chief Roy Crazy Horse?

A Why does Crazy Horse have an interest in Pocahontas?

B What do Jamestown Colony documents reveal about Crazy Horse?

C Where does the chief live?

D What, if anything, does the chief have in common with John Smith?

4. Which question is *not* addressed in the article?

A Did the Powhatans intend to kill John Smith?

B Who was the real father of Pocahontas?

C Why did Pocahontas marry John Rolfe?

D Why did Pocahontas turn her back on Smith?

5. Someone who lives in *obscurity* is —

A influential

B isolated

C not well known

D famous

6. A *pretentious* person is someone who —

A seems unhappy

B is suspicious

C enjoys a challenge

D likes to feel important

7. An *entourage* is a kind of —

A village

B profession

C group

D talent

Writing Focus   Constructed Response

Choose a favorite, well-known person from the past. Imagine you have been asked to research this person's life, accomplishments, and contributions. Write a brief explanation of the steps you would follow to narrow your topic focus for your research.

What Do You Think Now

Why is it important to craft research questions that are specific and focused?

PREPARING FOR THE OHIO GRADUATION TEST

Literary Skills Review

Elements of Myth   **Directions:** Read the following selection. Then, read and respond to the questions that follow.

The Woman Who Fell from the Sky Seneca Traditional

A long time ago human beings lived high up in what is now called heaven. They had a great and illustrious chief. It so happened that this chief's daughter was taken very ill with a strange affliction. All the people were very anxious as to the outcome of her illness. Every known remedy was tried in an attempt to cure her, but none had any effect.

Near the lodge of this chief stood a great tree, which every year bore corn used for food. One of the friends of the chief had a dream, in which he was advised to tell the chief that in order to cure his daughter he must lay her beside this tree, and that he must have the tree dug up. This advice was carried out to the letter. While the people were at work and the young woman lay there, a young man came along. He was very angry and said: "It is not at all right to destroy this tree. Its fruit is all that we have to live on." With this remark he gave the young woman who lay there ill a shove with his foot, causing her to fall into the hole that had been dug.

Now, that hole opened into this world, which was then all water, on which floated waterfowl of many kinds. There was no land at that time. It came to pass that as these waterfowl saw this young woman falling they shouted, "Let us receive her," whereupon they, at least some of them, joined their bodies together, and the young woman fell on this platform of bodies. When these were wearied they asked, "Who will volunteer to care for this woman?" The great Turtle then took her, and when he got tired of holding her, he in turn asked who would take his place. At last the question arose as to what they should do to provide her with a permanent resting place in this world. Finally it was decided to prepare the earth, on which she would live in the future. To do this it was determined that soil from the bottom of the primal sea should be brought up and placed on the broad, firm carapace of the Turtle, where it would increase in size to such an extent that it would accommodate all the creatures that should be produced thereafter. After much discussion the toad was finally persuaded to dive to the bottom of the waters in search of soil. Bravely making the attempt, he succeeded in bringing up soil from the depths of the sea. This was carefully spread over the carapace of the Turtle, and at once both began to grow in size and depth.

After the young woman recovered from the illness from which she suffered when she was cast down from the upper world, she built herself a shelter, in which she lived quite contentedly. In the course of time she brought forth a girl baby, who grew rapidly in size and intelligence.

When the daughter had grown to young womanhood, the mother and she were accustomed to go out to dig wild potatoes. Her mother had said to her that in doing this she must face the West at all times. Before long the young daughter gave signs that she was about to become a mother. Her mother reproved her, saying that she had violated the injunction not to face the East, as her condition showed that she had faced the wrong way while digging potatoes. It is said that the breath of the West Wind had entered her person, causing conception. When the days of her delivery were at hand, she overheard twins within her body in a hot debate as to which should be born first and as to the proper place of exit, one declaring that he was going to emerge through the armpit of his mother, the other saying that he would emerge in the natural way. The first one born, who was of a reddish color, was called Othagwenda; that is, Flint. The other, who was light in color, was called Djuskaha; that is, the Little Sprout.

The grandmother of the twins liked Djuskaha and hated the other; so they cast Othagwenda into a hollow tree some distance from the lodge. The boy who remained in the lodge grew very rapidly, and soon was able to make himself bows and arrows and to go out to hunt in the vicinity. Finally, for several days he returned home without his bow and arrows. At last he was asked why he had to have a new bow and arrows every morning. He replied that there was a young boy in a hollow tree in the neighborhood who used them. The grandmother inquired where the tree stood, and he told her; whereupon then they went there and brought the other boy home again.

When the boys had grown to man's estate, they decided that it was necessary for them to increase the size of their island, so they agreed to start out together, afterward separating to create forests and lakes and other things. They parted as agreed, Othagwenda going westward and Djuskaha eastward. In the course of time, on returning, they met in their shelter or lodge at night, then agreeing to go the next day to see what each had made. First they went west to see what Othagwenda had made. It was found that he had made the country all rocks and full of ledges, and also a mosquito which was very large. Djuskaha asked the mosquito to run, in order that he might see whether the insect could fight. The mosquito ran, and sticking his bill through a sapling, thereby made it fall, at which Djuskaha said, "That will not be right, for you would kill the people who are about to come." So, seizing him, he rubbed him down in his hands, causing him to become very small; then he blew on the mosquito, whereupon

Literary Skills Review CONTINUED

he flew away. He also modified some of the other animals which his brother had made. After returning to their lodge, they agreed to go the next day to see what Djuskaha had fashioned. On visiting the east the next day, they found that Djuskaha had made a large number of animals which were so fat that they could hardly move; that he had made the sugar-maple trees to drop syrup; that he had made the sycamore tree to bear fine fruit; that the rivers were so formed that half the water flowed upstream and the other half down-stream. Then the reddish-colored brother, Othagwenda, was greatly displeased with what his brother had made, saying that the people who were about to come would live too easily and be too happy. So he shook violently the various animals—the bears, deer, and turkeys —causing them to become small at once, a characteristic which attached itself to their descendants. He also caused the sugar maple to drop sweetened water only, and the fruit of the sycamore to become small and useless; and lastly he caused the water of the rivers to flow in only one direction, because the origi-nal plan would make it too easy for the human beings who were about to come to navigate the streams.

The inspection of each other's work resulted in a deadly disagreement between the brothers, who finally came to grips and blows, and Othagwenda was killed in the fierce struggle.

1. What does this myth explain?
   A. who the writer is
   B. how people should relate to the universe
   C. the origin of the earth
   D. how a hero responds to obstacles in life

2. What characteristic does Djuskaha share with many other heroes of myth?
   A. He has a twin brother.
   B. He was born in magical circumstances.
   C. He is very unusual in appearance.
   D. His grandmother prefers him to his brother.

3. What human quality does the "Woman Who Fell from the Sky" display toward her grand-children?
   A. the ability to deceive herself
   B. the ability to hide her feelings
   C. the ability to feel deep sorrow
   D. the ability to love and hate

4. One natural phenomenon this myth explains is
   A. the appearance of the sky.
   B. the fact that some siblings are twins.
   C. the reason rivers flow in one direction.
   D. the creation of animals.

5. What conflict is at the heart of this myth?

   A. Djuskaha's disagreement with his brother over how the earth should be the created

   B. the mother and grandmother's disagreement over how the brothers should be treated

   C. the young man in the sky's disagreement with the great chief over digging up the great tree

   D. the debate over how the twins would be born

6. This myth is not a romance, but some of the characters display qualities that are associated with chivalry. Which one of the following characters exhibits qualities of chivalry?

   A. the grandmother

   B. Othagwenda

   C. the turtle

   D. the daughter

7. Which of the following would most likely not appear on a list of the main events of the story?

   A. The chief's daughter falls through a hole in the sky and lands on gathered waterfowl.

   B. The chief's daughter gives birth to a baby girl.

   C. A mosquito makes a tree fall.

   D. Djuskaha kills Othagwenda.

Short Answer

8. Explain what kind of world Djuskaha made. Cite an example from the myth to show why Djuskaha made the world this way.

Extended Response

9. Compare this tale to another heroic myth or legend you have read. In what ways are the heroes similar? In what ways are they different? What do their quests have in common?

Informational Skills Review

Generating Research Questions   **Directions:** Read the following selection. Then, read and respond to the questions that follow.

Legends and Lore

by **Peter Tyson**

Jacques Cousteau deemed it "the most beautiful island in the world." Michael Crichton wrote *Jurassic Park* with it in mind. Robert Louis Stevenson may have based his classic *Treasure Island* on it.

Cocos Island, 300 miles off the coast of Costa Rica, is legendary for its natural and man-made treasures. The largest uninhabited island in the world, this 10-square-mile tip of an ancient volcano is the only isle in the eastern Pacific that bears rainforest. From the precipitous cliffs towering over the craggy shoreline to the 2,079-foot summit of Mt. Iglesias, the island's highest peak, the luxuriant bed of jungle is riven only by scores of sparkling waterfalls that tumble out of the heights.

Yet it is for buried treasure that Cocos is perhaps most famous. Over the centuries before the Republic of Costa Rica assumed control of the island in 1869, pirates used Cocos as a buccaneer bank, secreting priceless artifacts and tons of gold bullion in its inaccessible hillsides. If the legends are to be believed, many of these pirates died from disease, battles, or execution before they could ever return to the island to claim their loot, and it remains there to this day, hidden in natural caves or long-forgotten trenches. One estimate puts the accumulated treasure, if it is indeed all still there, at over $1 billion.

Cocos' story begins in 1526, when the Spanish pilot Johan Cabeças first discovered the island. Sixteen years later, it appeared for the first time on a French map of the Americas, labeled as Ile de Coques (literally "Nutshell Island" or simply "Shell Island"). The Spanish apparently misunderstood the French name and called it Isla del Cocos ("Island of the Coconuts"), which proved apt enough. "'Tis thick set with Coco-nut Trees, which flourish here very finely," wrote Lionel Wafer, a surgeon who penned one of the earliest descriptions of this island after a visit in the late 1600s. So abundant were coconuts that Wafer's companions made a bit too merry with the milk one afternoon, drinking 20 gallons at a sitting: "[T]hat sort of Liquor had so chill'd and benumb'd their Nerves, that they could neither go nor stand; nor could they return on board the Ship, without the Help of those who had not been Partakers in the Frolick. . . ."

Over the next century, the island became a kind of oceanic truck-stop, where ships of all stripes could rest and take on freshwater, firewood—and coconuts. Whalers stopped there regularly until the mid-19th century, when their industry in the region collapsed due to overfishing. Captains with missions ranging from exploration to administration of justice dropped anchor in Chatham or Wafer Bays, the island's principal harbors. More than any, however, pirates made Cocos their home.

The Golden Age of treasure-burying on the island took place in just a few years on either side of 1820. It all began in 1818, when Captain Bennett Graham, a distinguished British naval officer put in charge of a coastal survey in the South Pacific aboard the H.M.S. *Devonshire*, threw up his mission for a life of piracy. He was eventually caught and executed along with his officers, the remainder of his crew being sent to a penal colony in Tasmania. Twenty years later, one of the crew, a woman named Mary Welch, was released from prison bearing a remarkable tale. She claimed to have witnessed the burial of Graham's fortune—350 tons of gold bullion stolen from Spanish galleons. (A recent estimate put the treasure's present-day value at $160 million). Moreover, she had a chart with compass bearings showing where the so-called "Devonshire Treasure" was buried. Graham had given it to her, she said, just before he was captured, thinking—rightly as it turned out—that it would be safer on her person than on his. Welch's story was believed, as much for her intimate knowledge of the island as for the chart, and an expedition was mounted to hunt for the treasure. Welch went along, of course, and as quite an old woman set foot once again on Cocos. In the decades since

she'd been there, however, the lay of the land had changed so much at the hands of visiting sailors that many of her identifying marks, including a huge cedar tree near which she had once camped for six months, had disappeared, and the expedition recovered nothing.

Another treasure that supposedly still lies buried somewhere on the island is that of Benito "Bloody Sword" Bonito. Bonito terrorized the west coast of the Americas beginning about 1818, looting and burning Spanish galleons and taking his hoardings to Cocos Island. In his most infamous exploit, Bonito, learning that Spanish gold was transported by uniformed guard from the Mexican cordillera to Acapulco, simply captured the guard, put their uniforms on his own men, and loaded the treasure onto his ship—without firing a shot. His most infamous mistake was to let two Englishmen from a British ship he hijacked join his band of pirates. Years later, these two Brits were arrested by the authorities and sentenced to hang, but were released after leading their captors to Bonito's West Indian hideout, where this notoriously blood-thirsty pirate was finally cut down. The two Englishmen apparently never managed to return to Cocos, and the "captain's cut" of Bonito's cache sits there to this day. Its estimated modern value: $300 million.

Informational Skills Review CONTINUED

The most famous Cocos hoard of all is the "Great Treasure of Lima." In 1820, as the revolutionary José de San Martín advanced on Lima, the Spanish Viceroy realized he had better remove the stores of gold and silver under his command. Officials of the more than 50 Spanish churches in the city came to the same conclusion about their ecclesiastical riches, which included a solid-gold, gem-encrusted, life-size image of the Virgin Mary. Figuring that hiding this wealth anywhere near Lima would be foolish, the Viceroy entrusted it to a British sea captain named William Thompson, a known and respected trader in the region. The Viceroy's plan was to have Thompson sail around for several months, with the treasure stowed aboard his merchantman, the *Mary Dear*, until the political situation improved. Big mistake. A load of such value—at the time, Spanish officials deemed it worth between $12 and $60 million—proved too great a temptation to Thompson and his men. Once out of sight of land, they cut the throats of the Viceroy's appointed guard, tossed their bodies overboard, and made haste to Cocos, where they duly buried the treasure.

Thompson and his crew decided to split up until things simmered down, then reconnoiter to divvy up the spoils. But not long after leaving Cocos, the *Mary Dear* was picked up by a Spanish man-of-war. The crew was put on trial for piracy, convicted, and hanged—all except for Thompson and his first mate, who agreed to lead their captors to the stolen goods if their lives were spared. Soon after they stepped on Cocos under an armed guard, however, Thompson and the mate suddenly hotfooted it into the jungle. Despite a protracted search, they were never found, and their frustrated captors finally left the island.

According to some versions of the story, the pair were later picked up by a whaler and taken to Puntarenas, in Costa Rica, where the mate contracted yellow fever and died. For his part, William Thompson seems to have vanished from the pages of history shortly thereafter, and there is no indication that he ever returned to Cocos Island.

Since that time, more than 300 expeditions have tried to locate these and other treasures on Cocos. American President Franklin Delano Roosevelt, visiting on three fishing trips between 1935 and 1940, even let his crew give it a whirl. Alas, all these efforts failed—or at least those that chose to make their findings public. (Would you, if you dug up a pot of gold?) The most earnest seeker was one Captain August Gissler, a German who lived on the island off and on for almost 20 years beginning in 1889. Gissler remained there so long scouring for the lost loot that the Costa Rican government made him governor of the island and granted him permission to establish a colony there. The colony failed, and in two decades of intense searching, Gissler turned up nothing more than a few Spanish pieces-of-eight.° He left the island in 1908, a broken man.

° **pieces-of-eight: a former Spanish peso (unit of money).**

Today, visitors to Cocos Island recognize that its real treasure lies in its natural wealth, both above and below water. The island is now part of Costa Rica's renowned national park system, and in 1997, UNESCO named it a World Heritage Site. It has become one of the world's top scuba-diving destinations, for the titanic schools of hammerhead sharks and other large oceanic fish that congregate in its tropical waters. With the Costa Rican government refusing to issue any more licenses for treasure-hunting, Cocos Island has returned to its sleepy, deserted self, just the way Johan Cabeças found it more than 450 years ago.

1. "Why has it been difficult to find buried treasure on Cocos Island?" is a more useful research question than "Why did whalers stop visiting Cocos Island?" because

   A. the question about difficulties is general.

   B. the question about whalers can be answered with only one fact.

   C. answering the question about difficulties would require interviewing historians in Costa Rica.

   D. answering the question about whalers would require special resources not found in most libraries.

2. Which of the following questions about Cocos Island is the *most* narrow and focused?

   A. What is the history of Cocos Island?

   B. What evidence supports the rumors of pirates' buried treasure on Cocos Island?

   C. What is the relationship between Cocos Island and piracy?

   D. What are some of the plants and animals that can be found on Cocos Island?

3. How could you revise the research question "What is interesting about Cocos Island?" so that it is both focused and likely to yield plenty of information?

   A. During what years did pirates bury treasure on Cocos Island?

   B. Why do people search for treasure?

   C. What have been the results of searches for treasure on Cocos Island?

   D. What are the directions to Cocos Island?

Short Answer

4. Read the first sentence of paragraph three. Write a focused research question using the information in that sentence.

Extended Response

5. Explain why and how reading a general article on your research topic can help you write a focused research question.

Vocabulary Skills Review

Context Clues **Directions:** Read the questions that follow and choose the correct answer.

1. In "The Woman Who Fell from the Sky," it was determined that soil from the bottom of the primal sea should be brought up and placed on the Turtle.

   In this passage, primal means

   A. primitive; from the earliest time in history.

   B. deep; from the great depths of the ocean.

   C. blue; the color of the ocean.

   D. pure; the unpolluted water.

2. The soil was carefully spread over the carapace of the Turtle.

   In this context, carapace means

   A. opening.

   B. property owned.

   C. hard upper shell.

   D. firm resting place.

3. "Legends and Lore" tells how the pirate Benito "Bloody Sword" Bonito was betrayed by two Englishmen who led authorities to Bonito's hideout. This notoriously bloodthirsty pirate was finally cut down.

   In this passage, what is (are) the context clue(s) that indicate(s) the word notoriously means "famous for some bad deed"?

   A. "was betrayed"

   B. "led authorities"

   C. "hideout" and "finally cut down"

   D. "Bloody Sword" and "bloodthirsty"

4. Sea captain William Thompson and his crew decided to split up until things simmered down, then reconnoiter a new hideout to divide the spoils.

   In this sentence, reconnoiter means to

   A. leave the area.

   B. explore, find.

   C. hide, stay out of sight.

   D. get reinforcements.

5. In "Sigurd, the Dragon Slayer," Regin knew Sigurd was the dragon slayer but kept his own counsel while the child was an infant because he had secrets to keep.

   What did Regin do?

   A. He stayed in his room.

   B. He did not share what he knew.

   C. He kept giving people advice.

   D. He met with a council of advisors.

6. In "Quetzalcoatl," the neighboring gods want Quetzalcoatl's secrets. Quetzalcoatl goes on his way, paying no heed to the entreaties of the disappointed gods.

   In this passage, entreaties means

   A. several questions.

   B. anxious begging and pleas.

   C. detailed directions.

   D. confused comments and insults.

7. In "Sundiata," the young hero was greedy for food. Whenever his mother went out, he would crawl on all fours to <u>rummage</u> in search of food.

   Which clue below indicates that the word <u>rummage</u> means "to look for something"?

   A. "crawl on all fours"

   B. "in search of"

   C. "greedy"

   D. "his mother went out"

8. In "Real Princess," the author explains, "When Pocahontas entered the scene, it was as if her name were simply attached to an existing Indian <u>icon</u>."

   In this passage, <u>icon</u> means

   A. a graphic representation.

   B. a person regarded as a representative symbol.

   C. a painting of a holy figure.

   D. a person who promises to deliver people from difficulties.

9. The author of "Sigurd, the Dragon Slayer" writes that Sigurd "understood the cold dwarfs who knew neither <u>conscience</u> nor pity."

   In this passage, <u>conscience</u> means

   A. an experience of confusion.

   B. a feeling of hatred.

   C. a sense of right and wrong.

   D. a desire to harm.

10. In "Legends and Lore," the author describes Cocos Island as having "<u>precipitous</u> cliffs towering over the craggy shoreline to the 2,079-foot summit of Mt. Iglesias, the island's highest peak."

    In this passage, which context clue below indicates that the word <u>precipitous</u> means "dangerously high" or "steep"?

    A. "towering over"

    B. "craggy shoreline"

    C. "summit"

    D. "highest peak"

Academic Vocabulary

Directions: Use your understanding of the Academic Vocabulary words to choose the best synonym for the underlined word.

11. People would <u>recount</u> the stories that became myths over and over again.

    A. relive

    B. number

    C. tell

    D. forget

12. Theseus <u>retained</u> his good qualitites throughout his many adventures.

    A. kept

    B. lost

    C. found

    D. retrieved

Read On

FICTION

The King Must Die

Mary Renault's mythical novel, *The King Must Die,* takes us through the boyhood and early life of the Greek hero Theseus, who would one day be famous for slaying the Minotaur. Bored with his uneventful life and filled with dreams of glory, young Theseus sets out on a journey to find his fate. He encounters a series of challenges beyond his expectations and returns to Athens a great hero.

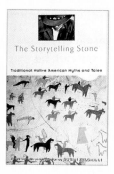

FICTION

The Storytelling Stone

According to a Seneca tale, a talking stone told the first stories about things that happened a long time ago. You'll meet this storytelling stone as well as Raven, Coyote, and the girl who wished to marry the stars in *The Storytelling Stone: Traditional Native American Myths and Tales*, a collection of Native American oral literature edited by Susan Feldmann.

FICTION

The Acts of King Arthur and His Noble Knights

If you'd like to know more about the Arthurian legend, John Steinbeck's *The Acts of King Arthur and his Noble Knights* is sure to please. Although this volume is focused on Arthur—older and more seasoned than he was when he first plucked the sword from the stone—it also features the adventures of such famous figures as Launcelot, Guinevere, and Gawain. John Steinbeck has converted their stories into clear, modern prose that opens the doors to the legendary city of Camelot.

FICTION

The Helmet of Horror

In Greek mythology, Ariadne, the daughter of King Minos of Crete, helps the hero Theseus escape from a man-eating monster called the Minotaur. In Victor Pelevin's retelling of this myth, *The Helmet of Horror*, a group of strangers are trapped in Internet chatrooms with someone who uses the screen name Ariadne. Their fate is controlled by a monster who is trying to keep them from returning to reality.

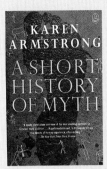

NONFICTION
A Short History of Myth

Karen Armstrong begins her book by asking, "What is a myth?" Part of the answer is that myths are stories meant to guide our lives and help us make sense of the world. Armstrong traces the development of myths and their meaning from the ancient to the present. According to Armstrong, we still need myths to guide us today. Read *A Short History of Myth,* written by a former nun, to find out what purpose myths serve in our world.

FICTION
Latin American Folktales

In *Latin American Folktales,* John Bierhorst has gathered more than one hundred folk tales from Spanish colonial times to the present. Early stories include legends of the Inca kings and omens predicting the arrival of the Conquistadores with their horses. Later tales include animal tricksters, hidden treasure, quests, tests, and clever deceptions. There are several variations of the Cinderella story and riddles with answers that lead to more questions. The stories often have ironic or unexpected endings.

FICTION
The Heart of the Ngoni

These heroic tales of kings, warriors, and sorcerers are from Segu, a seventeenth-century African kingdom along the Niger River that is now part of present-day Mali. The tales in *The Heart of the Ngoni* begin with the story of how Segu was founded at the site of a golden stone, and they tell what happens when a young man refuses to believe the stone is magically protected. Failure or refusal to believe in what has been prophesied is a major theme in these stories.

FICTION
Pocahontas

In 1607, when John Smith and his "Coatmen" arrive in Powhatan to begin settling the colony of Virginia, their relations with the village's inhabitants are anything but warm. Pocahontas, the beloved daughter of the Powhatan chief, is just eleven, but this astute, young girl plays a fateful, peaceful role in the destinies of two peoples. Drawing from the personal journals of John Smith, American Book Award winner Joseph Bruchac reveals an important chapter of history through the eyes of two legendary figures.

Learn It Online
Explore other novels—and find tips for choosing, reading, and studying works—at:
 L10-1117 **Go**

Writing Workshop

Research Paper

Write with a Purpose

Write a research paper about a topic that interests you. Your **purpose** is to research a topic thoroughly, draw conclusions about it, and then share your findings. Your **audience** is your classmates, teacher, and others who might be interested in the topic.

A Good Research Paper

- has an introduction that includes a clear thesis statement
- provides readers with background information on the topic
- fully develops each main point in the body, and supports each main point with evidence
- uses and gives credit to different, relevant, and reliable sources in correct format
- is objective and uses formal language
- restates the thesis at the conclusion and leaves readers with a closing thought

See page 1130 for complete rubric.

Think as a Reader/Writer

In this collection, you've read about the historical background to various legends and myths. Now it is your turn to write a **research paper** about the historical or biographical background surrounding a literary topic. Read the following excerpt from Stephen Fraser's "The Making of a Legend" to see some of the techniques he uses in his article.

Out of the mists of memory, the fogs of history, and the depths of imagination, hazy images slowly come into view. Knights on horseback thunder over the rolling green hills of an ancient land. Banners of purple and gold glow in the rosy dawn while sunlight glints off swords and shields and armor. Leading the charge is a great red-haired, bearded bear of a man. Hero. Warrior. King. Out of an age of darkness is born a legend. . . .

← Fraser's **introduction** grabs the reader's attention with evocative imagery.

[*The following is a later excerpt from Fraser's article.*]

The most influential version of the King Arthur legend, Sir Thomas Malory's *Le Morte d'Arthur* (The Death of Arthur), was published in 1485. Malory embellished the story with all the romantic flourishes of the era in which he lived. The author wove romantic tales of bravery, true love, and magic. "[The tales of Camelot] had something for everybody who read such things at all, and that included women, whose tastes in literature were becoming influential," says Geoffrey Ashe, an Arthurian scholar.

← He introduces the **main point** of this section.

← A **direct quotation** supports the main point.

Malory also integrated into the legend the religious search for the Holy Grail. The Holy Grail was said to have been the cup that Jesus Christ drank from during the Last Supper, before his crucifixion. According to Arthurian legend, the Holy Grail still existed. It fell to the morally superior, valiant knights of the Round Table to lead the quest to find it.

← This paragraph begins with another important **supporting detail.**

Reader/Writer Notebook

Use your **RWN** to complete the activities for this workshop.

Think About the Professional Model

With a partner, discuss the following questions about the model:

1. What details support the main point?

2. How does the author weave the quotation into the paragraph?

R.10.7 Use a variety of communication techniques, including oral, visual, written or multimedia reports, to present information that supports a clear position about the topic or research question and to maintain an appropriate balance between researched information and original ideas. **R.10.1** Compose open-ended questions for research, assigned or personal interest, and modify questions as necessary during inquiry and investigation to narrow the focus or extend the investigation. **R.10.2** Identify appropriate sources and gather relevant information from multiple sources. **R.10.6** Use style guides to produce oral and written reports that give proper credit for sources, and include an acceptable format for source acknowledgement.

Prewriting

Choose a Subject

Does something in particular fascinate you when you read a piece of literature? When choosing a subject for research, start with what interests you. Then, find a direction for your investigation by doing the following:

- **Skim books.** Skim your textbooks and the nonfiction section of the library for subjects related to your interests.
- **Watch films.** Watch documentaries or historical films with subjects that interest you.
- **Browse the Internet.** Search a subject and related terms on the Internet by using a search engine. Which results show a historical or biographical subject you want to explore?

Narrow Your Subject to Refine Your Topic

Once you have identified a subject, you will need to examine it in more detail in order to refine it to a manageable topic. Here are some ways to narrow your subject to a more specific research topic:

- **Read a few articles.** Search general reference materials, such as books or online encyclopedias. Consider using one of the articles' subheadings as your topic.
- **Look up your subject.** Check the *Readers' Guide to Periodical Literature* in your library's reference section or online.
- **Search the World Wide Web.** Search for sites that contain information relevant to your subject.
- **Discuss your subject with someone.** Talk with a teacher or librarian who has expert knowledge about your subject.

Think About Purpose and Audience

Your **purpose** is to uncover information about your topic and develop your own ideas about it. Your paper will inform readers about your findings. Consider what information will hold your **audience's** interest and give them a new understanding of the topic.

Idea Starters

- a historical figure or historical event that appears in a piece of literature
- an author's interests as revealed through literature
- the historical background of a piece of literature

Writing Tip

Ask the following questions to narrow your subject to a manageable topic:

- Is there enough information known about this topic to find research materials?
- Are there enough different resources available on the topic?
- Does my topic cover an interesting or new angle on the subject?

Your Turn

Get Started List three or four **topic** ideas in your **RWN,** and decide which one you would like to explore. Then, narrow your topic to direct your research as you examine sources. Keep your **purpose** and **audience** in mind as you select your topic.

Learn It Online
For an example of a complete, double-spaced historical investigation, visit:

go.hrw.com   L10-1119   **Go**

Library and Community Resources

Card or online catalog: Books listed by title, author, and subject; some libraries also include audio-visual materials

Readers' Guide to Periodical Literature: Subject and author index to magazine and journal articles; index to major newspapers

Online databases: Encyclopedias, biographical references, almanacs

General or specialized reference books or CD-ROMs: Indexes to major newspapers and back issues of newspapers; encyclopedias, dictionaries

World Wide Web and online services: Articles, interviews, bibliographies, pictures, videos, and sound recordings and access to the Library of Congress and other libraries

Develop Research Questions

As you narrow your topic, consider what you need to know about it for your paper. Then, develop **research questions** that will guide you as you search for sources and make it easier for you to sort through the information you find. Look at the following questions one student asked about her topic. Her research will provide answers to the questions.

Questions	Answers
Who is the real King Arthur, and how did the stories about him develop?	
Were the Knights of the Round Table real people? How did the quest for the Holy Grail come to be part of the story?	
Have the King Arthur stories always been the same, or have they changed?	

Find and Evaluate Sources

The first step in finding information on your topic is knowing where to look. Use the chart of resources to the left to get started on your research.

What types of sources provide the best information for your topic? You will need a variety of print and nonprint sources from which to gather information. Sources for research papers need to be objective so that the information is as **factual** as possible and not based on opinion.

You will use two types of sources for your research. **Primary sources** contain firsthand information that is typically unfiltered and unedited, such as a historical document, a letter, a speech, or a literary work. **Secondary sources** are derived from or about a primary source, such as an encyclopedia article, a documentary, or a history book.

Be sure each source meets the following requirements of the **4R** test:

- **Relevant** Make sure the source provides information directly relevant to your research questions. Check the table of contents or index (in print sources) before skimming through the book.

- **Reliable** Use only accurate and trustworthy sources. While magazines such as *Smithsonian* are well respected and objective, many others are opinion-based. The numerous online sources require added scrutiny.

- **Recent** At least some of your sources should be current so you have a modern perspective, but don't dismiss authoritative works on your topic just because they're old.

- **Representative** Provide a balanced and objective approach by addressing different sides of a controversial topic.

Your Turn _____

Get Ready to Research In your **RWN**, write a number of **research questions** as you think through your topic. List at least four **resources** you will use. As you begin your research, use the **4R test** to **evaluate** each source you locate.

Create Source Cards

Keeping track of all your sources is essential for giving credit within your paper as well as for preparing a *Works Cited* list in your final version. Cite each source on a source card, also called a bibliography card. Record information from your sources accurately. The format for recording source information shown at right and in the chart below is the format used by the Modern Language Association (MLA). Your teacher may prefer another style.

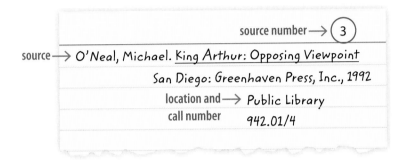

source number → ③

source → O'Neal, Michael. *King Arthur: Opposing Viewpoint*
San Diego: Greenhaven Press, Inc., 1992
location and → Public Library
call number   942.01/4

Guidelines for Recording Source Information

Books. Write author's name, last name first; book title; place of publication; name of publishing company; and year of publication.

Day, David. *The Search for King Arthur.* New York: Facts on File, 1995.

Magazine or Newspaper Articles. Write author's name, last name first; article title; magazine or newspaper name; day, month, and year of publication; edition; and beginning page number.

Ackroyd, Peter. "The Man Who Invented Arthur." *Times of London* 13 Aug. 2005: 12.

Online Sources. Write author's name, last name first (if listed); title of document; title of Web site or database; date of electronic publication (if available); name of sponsoring institution or organization; date information was accessed; <URL> or name of online service.

Snell, Melissa. "The Truth of Arthur." *Medieval History.* 2004. About, Inc. 5 Oct. 2009 <http://historymedren.about.com/od/historicalarthur/a/truthofarthur.htm>.

Encyclopedia Article. Write author's name, last name first (if provided); article title; encyclopedia name; and year of publication, followed by the abbreviation *ed.*

Reiss, Edmund. "Arthur, King." *The World Book Encyclopedia.* 2008 ed.

Radio or Television Program. Write episode or segment title; program name; series title (if any); network name; local station call letters and city (if any); and date of broadcast.

"King Arthur." *Biography Classroom.* Biography Channel. A&E Television Networks. 31 Oct. 2009.

Film, Audio, or Video. Write title; director or artist, first name first; distributor; and year of release. When citing an audio or video recording, include the original release date and the medium.

King Arthur's Britain. Dir. Francis Pryor. DVD. Acorn Media, 2005.

Preparing a *Works Cited* List

1. Center the words *Works Cited* on a separate page at the end of the draft.

2. List your sources in alphabetical order by the author's last names (or by the title), ignoring *A, An,* and *The.*

3. Follow the correct format for each type of source.

4. Begin each entry on a separate line, aligned with the left margin. Indent remaining lines of each entry one-half inch.

5. Double-space each entry. The *Works Cited* list on page 1128 is single-spaced because of limited space.

Your Turn

Create Source Cards Prepare a **source card** for each of the sources you have gathered. Use the format your teacher has approved.

Note-Taking Tips

To decide which note-taking technique to use, follow these tips:

- If the source succinctly states the information better than you can state it, quote it.
- If the source provides information you want to restate in your own words, paraphrase it.
- If the source provides a substantial amount of information you want to distill into a main idea, summarize it.

Writing Tip

To avoid **plagiarism,** a serious academic offense, always credit your sources—even when paraphrasing or summarizing the author's ideas in your own words.

Your Turn

Take Notes Create a **source card** for each of the sources you have gathered. (If you choose to make notes on a computer, record the information from each source in a separate file.) Take notes on each card by using **direct quotations, paraphrasing,** or **summarizing.** Be sure that your tone is **formal** in paraphrased and summarized notes.

Take Notes

When taking notes from sources, write only the information you think you will use. Gather facts and details—the **evidence** that you will use to develop your ideas. To keep track of all the information you gather, take notes on numbered 3 x 5 index cards or in separate files on your computer. The following three techniques are useful for writing only what you need on your notecards:

- A **direct quotation** uses the author's exact words. Copy the material word for word, and put **quotation marks** around it.
- A **paraphrase** restates a passage from the source in your own words. Paraphrase when you need to explain an idea in detail.
- A **summary** is a highly condensed passage in which you record (in your own words) only the most important ideas from your source.

The following shows a notecard one student made about the Saxon invasions into Britain, events that led to Arthur's leadership.

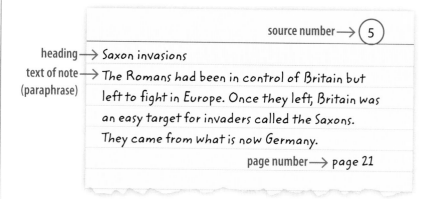

source number → 5

heading → Saxon invasions

text of note (paraphrase) → The Romans had been in control of Britain but left to fight in Europe. Once they left, Britain was an easy target for invaders called the Saxons. They came from what is now Germany.

page number → page 21

Consider Tone

Because a research paper is academic, it will have a **formal tone**—which uses the third-person pronouns *he, she,* and *they.* Be careful to avoid using informal language such as the first-person pronouns *I* and *we,* contractions, or slang. Try to use your own language to develop a formal voice without becoming stiff and boring. As difficult as this may sound, it becomes easier with practice.

When taking notes and writing your paper, be sure to distinguish information that is **fact** from that which is **opinion** by using phrases such as "Ms. Alexander says" or "according to Ms. Alexander."

Write a Thesis Statement

Describe your paper in one or two sentences. A **thesis statement** for a research paper states the main idea about your topic and lets your readers know immediately what main points you will cover. It will also help you identify what to emphasize and how best to organize the paper. Keep in mind that you will likely revise your thesis statement as you develop your paper, refining your ideas and developing your style and tone. The writer who chose the development of the legend of King Arthur as a topic drafted this preliminary thesis statement based on her research findings.

Topic:	The development of the legend of King Arthur
Thesis Statement:	Legends about King Arthur developed as storytellers, writers, and historians changed the story over time.

Organize Information

After you complete your research, you need to organize it. First, review your notecards, and divide them into groups based on their headings. Arrange the cards within each group according to your main idea and main points you plan to cover. Sorting your notes in this way helps you organize your main points and plan how you will support your thesis statement with your research and evidence. To show adequate development for each idea, use a coherent order by following one of the methods below or a combination of all three methods.

- **Chronological order** presents events in the order they happened.
- **Logical order** groups related ideas together.
- **Order of importance** places the most important ideas first and moves to the least important (or the reverse).

Try to limit your main points to three or four, so your paper will not be too long. Are there enough cards in each group to provide adequate support for each main point? If not, you need to do more research or omit a point.

Sometimes you may need to include complicated material in your research paper. In order to maintain a coherent organization, consider using visuals such as charts, maps, or graphs in your paper to present information that is technical or complicated. Provide a key to explain any technical terms or notations on your visuals.

Your Turn _____

Organize Your Research

Condense your thoughts on your topic into a **thesis statement,** and **organize** your notecards. Look for any big holes in your research. Determine what areas need further research and whether or not you need to delete any unnecessary points. Then, continue with your research until you are satisfied that you have what you need to begin writing a draft. Consider where to add visuals.

Research Paper

Create an Outline

The best way to develop a solid framework for your paper is to create an **outline** of your ideas before you begin writing. An outline will help you plan how to connect ideas. Begin with an **informal outline** based on your sorted notecards. The informal outline should include major headings and broad categories from your notes.

Use this informal outline to guide you as you create a more detailed **formal outline.** In a formal outline, you arrange specific information from your notes into a structured hierarchy of ideas, which includes an introduction, body, and conclusion. In the body, follow each **main point** with **supporting details** that include facts and examples. Use one or more paragraphs to support each main point.

> I. Introduction:
>   A. Grab attention with an interesting detail and include
>   a thesis statement.
>   B. Include background information or explanation of situation.
>
> II. Body:
>   A. Main point #1
>   1. Supporting detail
>   2. Supporting detail
>   B. Main point #2
>   1. Supporting detail
>   a. Supporting detail
>   b. Supporting detail
>   2. Supporting detail
>   C. Main point #3
>   1. Supporting detail
>   2. Supporting detail
>
> III. Conclusion:
>   A. Wrap up ideas and reword thesis in one paragraph.
>   B. Leave readers with a final thought about the topic.

Your Turn

Develop Your Outline First, create your informal outline by writing the basic structure in your **RWN**. Use this framework to create the formal outline from which you will draft your research paper. Add any important information you want to be sure to remember as you write your paper.

Drafting

Use your outline to guide your draft. Review the **Writer's Framework** at the right to be sure you include the key elements of a research paper.

Credit Your Sources

Give credit to each outside source from which you have gathered information for your paper. Specific data, such as facts, examples, and dates, always require citing. In addition, cite any original ideas, opinions, or insights from your sources. If you do not cite every source each time you use it, you will be plagiarizing the information.

How to Credit

Within the body of your paper, include **parenthetical citations,** or credit given within parentheses immediately following borrowed information. The intent of a parenthetical citation is to include only enough information to enable the reader to find the full citation in your *Works Cited* list at the end of your paper.

Guidelines for Parenthetical Citations	
Sources with one author	Last name of the author, followed by one page number (if any) of the work being cited: (Smith 25)
Sources with no author	Title, or shortened form of title, followed by the page number (if any): ("Quest for a King" 122)
Source with two or more authors	All authors' last names, followed by the page number (if any): (White and Barber 10)
An indirect source	Abbreviation *qtd in* [quoted in] before the source, followed by the page number: (qtd in Otero 99)
Author's name given in sentence	Page number only: (172)
An interview	Interviewee's full name: (Ellen Hayes)

As you draft, vary the ways in which you incorporate source material into your paper.

Grammar Link Weaving In Source Material

Introduce source material with your own words. Though there are many ways to do this, here are examples of using direct quotations and paraphrasing from the student model.

> Most scholars agree that Geoffrey's work is not real history but a "bizarre combination of fact and fiction" (Day 39).

> O'Neal explains that as England and France came out of the Dark Ages, the aristocrats became hungry for learning and history (14).

Framework for a Research Paper

Introduction
- Grab readers' attention.
- Include your thesis statement.
- Suggest the **main points** of the topic you will cover in your paper.

Body
- Develop each **main point** with related **supporting details.**
- Each paragraph should include a topic sentence and **supporting details** such as summaries, paraphrases, and quotations.
- Show how your research connects to your topic sentence.

Conclusion
- Reword your thesis.
- Leave readers with an insight.

Your Turn

Draft Your Research Paper
Using your **notes**, the **outline** you developed, and the **Writer's Framework,** write a first draft of your paper. Think about these questions:
- How will I grab the reader's attention?
- How will my main ideas and supporting details support my thesis?
- How can I connect points clearly?

Peer Review

Working with a partner, go over the chart by answering each question. Then, improve your draft based on how you answered each of the questions. Discuss with your partner any questions you have about improving your draft. Be sure to take notes as you and your peer reviewer go through your draft. You can refer to your noes when you revise your draft.

Evaluating and Revising

Read the questions in the left column of the chart and then use the tips in the middle column to help you make revisions to your research paper. The right column suggests techniques you can use to revise your draft.

Research Paper: Guidelines for Content and Organization

Evaluation Questions	Tips	Revision Techniques
1. Does the thesis statement appear in the introduction and identify the topic and main idea? Does it suggest which aspects of the topic are covered?	**Underline** the thesis statement. **Double underline** words that reveal aspects of the topic. If any part is missing, revise.	**Add** a thesis statement identifying your topic and main idea. **Elaborate** by consolidating the aspects of your topic into one thought.
2. Do relevant details support each main point, either by quotations, paraphrases, or summaries?	**Put a capital A** by the first main point and **put a lowercase a** by each supporting sentence. Continue with the next letter for each main point. If no lowercase letter follows a capital letter, revise.	**Elaborate** where necessary by adding direct quotations, paraphrases, or summaries. **Rearrange** information as needed for clarity.
3. Are direct quotations smoothly integrated into the paper?	**Draw an arrow** from each direct quotation to the words that introduce the quotation.	**Reword** the text around your quotations so that ideas flow smoothly.
4. Are all sources given proper credit in the body of the paper?	**Highlight** all direct quotes, paraphrases, and summaries. **Review** all highlighted sentences. **Place check marks** by parenthetical citations.	**Add** parenthetical citations for direct quotations, paraphrases, or summaries from sources.
5. Does the conclusion restate the paper's thesis and give the readers a closing thought?	**Underline** the restatement of the thesis. **Double underline** the closing thought.	**Add** a restatement of the thesis. **State** an idea or point for readers to ponder.
6. Does a Works Cited List indicate all sources referred to in the paper?	Place a **checkmark** next to each source listed in Works Cited and in parenthetical citations in the body of the paper.	**Add** sources cited in parenthetical citations to the list of Works Cited.

Read this student draft. Notice the comments on its strengths and the suggestions about how to improve its weaknesses.

A Legend Is Born
by Chris Camden, East Valley High School

Stories of King Arthur and his glorious kingdom of Camelot have been enchanting listeners for over 1,000 years. Scholars still cannot agree, however, whether Arthur was a real person. Most scholars believe that if a real Arthur lived, he probably was not the popular King Arthur most people think of today. Yet an elaborate and enduring legend developed around Arthur by the combination of a bit of history, a strong oral tradition, and writers who picked up and expanded the story.

The legend had many forms and variations, but the story that readers recognize tells of a young boy who pulls a sword from a stone, becomes a king, forms a fellowship of knights known as the Round Table, and lives in a kingdom called Camelot with his queen Guinevere and his advisor, the wizard Merlin. Arthur's knights devote themselves to good deeds and to the quest of finding the Holy Grail. Trouble befalls the kingdom when one of Arthur's closest knights, Lancelot, falls in love with Guinevere and Arthur is betrayed by Mordred, his rebellious son. Betrayal of loyalty and trust destroy Camelot and its golden age in a great final battle between Arthur and Mordred (Alexander).

← Chris provokes **reader interest** by immediately introducing the controversy over the existence of Arthur.

← His **thesis statement** clearly states the main idea about the topic and tells what **main points** he will cover.

← In the second paragraph, Chris provides information about the story of King Arthur.

MINI-LESSON ▶ How to Capture Reader Attention with Quotations

Unlike paraphrasing or summarizing, using **direct quotations** brings in an authoritative voice that might say best what you want to express about a topic. Chris's introduction twice refers to scholars' views, which sounds repetitive. He adds a direct quotation to his third sentence to prove his claim and lend more authority to what he writes.

Chris's Revision of Paragraph One:

Scholars still cannot agree, however, whether Arthur was a real person. Most scholars believe that if a real Arthur lived ~~he probably was not the popular King Arthur most people think of today~~, "he most certainly was not a king, did not wear shining armor, and in all probability was not accompanied by a band of noble knights who sat together at a round table" (Matthews and Stead 11).

Writing Tip

Research papers and their *Works Cited* lists are normally double-spaced. Because of limited space on these pages, the Student Model is single-spaced. To see a double-spaced version of a paper, go to go.hrw.com, keyword L10-1127.

Your Turn

Use Direct Quotations Read your introductory paragraph and then ask yourself:

- What can I add or change to emphasize the information in the introductory paragraph?
- Where would a direct quotation emphasize my main idea about the topic?

Student Draft *continues*

Chris's draft discusses the historical foundation of the Arthur legend in paragraphs 3 and 4. This excerpt resumes with paragraph 5.

Chris notes a potential controversy from the previous paragraph, and then backs up his position with **supporting details** and three **sources.**

This tiny historical seed, which may or may not be accurate, was watered and nurtured by the oral tradition. Andronik points out that very few people could read or write during the time of the Dark Ages, roughly A.D. 400–800, but that "the oral tradition was very strong among the Celts" (5–6). When Britain finally succumbed to Anglo-Saxon rule, many Celts fled overland to Wales and overseas to Europe. There they told stories and sang songs for centuries about their great leader Arthur (Alexander). O'Neal explains that as England and France came out of the Dark Ages, the aristocrats became hungry for learning and history (14). This hunger was satisfied by traveling storytellers, or minstrels, who told stories called "The Matter of Britain," which recapped Arthur's great victory and Britain's golden age (O'Neal 14–15). The oral tradition, however, is hard to count on, so the stories about Arthur may have been changed by storytellers to please their listeners. New details, characters, and events no doubt crept into the story, and many versions of Arthur's deeds probably existed (O'Neal 16–17).

The concluding thought rounds out the uncertainties that surround a historical figure becoming a legend.

Due to limited space, this *Works Cited* list shows only the sources used in the excerpt.

Works Cited

Alexander, Caroline. "A Pilgrim's Search for Relics of the Once and Future King." Smithsonian Feb. 1996: 32–41. Smithsonian Magazine. 2009. Smithsonian Institution. 24 Sept. 2009 <http://www.smithsonianmag.com>.

Andronik, Catherine M. Quest for a King: Searching for the Real King Arthur. New York: Atheneum, 1989.

Matthews, John, and Michael J. Stead. King Arthur's Britain: A Photographic Odyssey. New York: Sterling, 1995.

O'Neal, Michael. King Arthur: Opposing Viewpoints. San Diego: Greenhaven P, 1992.

Your Turn _____

Review Tone Read your draft and ask yourself these questions:

- Have I avoided first-person pronouns, contractions, and slang?
- Is my language formal enough to earn my reader's confidence?
- Is the tone consistent throughout the paper?

Revise your draft as necessary.

MINI-LESSON ▶ **How to Revise for a Formal Tone**

Because you are presenting facts and citing sources, you will want to use a formal tone in your report. Chris made the following revision to his draft.

Chris's Revision of Paragraph Five:

The oral tradition, however, is ~~hard to count on~~, so the stories about Arthur may have been changed by storytellers to please their listeners.

prone to exaggeration

Proofreading and Publishing

Proofreading

Now that you have evaluated and revised the content of your research paper, it is time to polish a final copy for publishing. Edit your paper by correcting any misspellings, punctuation errors, and problems in sentence structure. When appropriately used as a rhetorical style device, repetition can benefit your writing. However, unnecessary repetition used for no specific effect can make a paper seem dull and simplistic.

● Proofreading Tip

Swap papers with a classmate and proofread the paper for errors in grammar, punctuation, and spelling. Look for repetition that dulls the effect of the content, and offer suggestions for changing sentence structure where necessary.

> **Grammar Link Eliminating Repetition**
>
> Avoid frequent **repetition** of the definite article *the* by rephrasing some sentences. Because declarative sentences frequently begin with *the,* you can eliminate repetition and vary your sentence beginnings by using an introductory phrase. Chris revised one of his paragraphs as shown.
>
> Known as the Britons∧
> The Britons, as the people in Britain were known, came to appreciate the culture and protection that the Romans brought to their land during their long occupation (Andronik 5, 19). The Britons were from a race of Celtic people that had occupied the island of Britain for 1,000 years, but who in the first century A.D. thought of themselves as both Roman and Christian (Day 10).
>
> By beginning his first sentence with the introductory phrase *Known as the Britons,* Chris not only eliminated one *the,* but he also avoided repeating the same sentence beginning in his second sentence.

Publishing

Readers can learn from the findings of your research. Here are two ways to share your research:

- Post your research paper on a Web site dedicated to a similar subject. Find these Web sites by looking back at your source cards.
- Publish your paper along with the papers from the rest of your class in a bound book for the rest of the school to read.

Reflect on the Process
Think about your experience writing your research paper. What would you do differently? In your **RWN,** write short responses to the following questions:

1. What techniques helped you organize your thoughts as you conducted research?
2. What have you learned from this workshop to help you write research papers in the future?

Your Turn _____

Proofread and Publish Search your draft for repetitive words and sentence structures. Make changes that will vary the structure and word use. These changes will make your paper more interesting to read. Then, make a final copy of your research paper, and publish it.

Scoring Rubric

Use one of the rubrics below to evaluate your response to the prompt on the next page. Your teacher will tell you which to use.

6-Point Scale

Score 6 *Demonstrates advanced success:*
- focuses consistently on a process appropriate to the prompt
- shows effective, step-by-step organization throughout, with smooth transitions
- offers a thoughtful, creative explanation of the process
- explains each step of the assigned process thoroughly, using examples and specific, detailed instructions
- exhibits mature control of written language

Score 5 *Demonstrates proficient success:*
- focuses on a process appropriate to the prompt
- shows effective, step-by-step organization, with transitions
- offers a thoughtful explanation of the process
- explains the steps of the process competently, using examples and specific instructions
- exhibits sufficient control of written language

Score 4 *Demonstrates competent success:*
- focuses on an appropriate process, with minor distractions
- shows effective, step-by-step organization, with minor lapses
- offers a mostly thoughtful explanation of the process
- explains the process adequately, with a mixture of general and specific instructions
- exhibits general control of written language

Score 3 *Demonstrates limited success:*
- includes some loosely related material that distracts from the writer's focus
- shows some organization, with noticeable gaps in the step-by-step presentation of the process
- offers a routine, predictable explanation of the process
- explains the process with uneven elaboration
- exhibits limited control of written language

Score 2 *Demonstrates basic success:*
- includes loosely related material that seriously distracts from the writer's focus
- shows minimal organization, with major gaps in the step-by-step presentation of the process
- offers explanation that merely skims the surface
- explains the process with inadequate elaboration
- exhibits significant problems with control of written language

Score 1 *Demonstrates emerging effort:*
- shows little awareness of the topic and purpose for writing
- lacks organization
- offers unclear and confusing explanation
- develops the explanation in only a minimal way, if at all
- exhibits major problems with control of written language

4-Point Scale

Score 4 *Demonstrates advanced success:*
- focuses consistently on a process appropriate to the prompt
- shows effective, step-by-step organization throughout, with smooth transitions
- offers a thoughtful, creative explanation of the process
- explains each step of the assigned process thoroughly, using examples and specific, detailed instructions
- exhibits mature control of written language

Score 3 *Demonstrates competent success:*
- focuses on an appropriate process, with minor distractions
- shows effective, step-by-step organization, with minor lapses
- offers a mostly thoughtful explanation of the process
- explains the process adequately, with a mixture of general and specific instructions
- exhibits general control of written language

Score 2 *Demonstrates limited success:*
- includes some loosely related material that distracts from the writer's focus
- shows some organization, with noticeable gaps in the step-by-step presentation of the process
- offers a routine, predictable explanation of the process
- explains the process with uneven elaboration
- exhibits limited control of written language

Score 1 *Demonstrates emerging effort:*
- shows little awareness of the topic and purpose for writing
- lacks organization
- offers unclear and confusing explanation
- develops the explanation in only a minimal way, if at all
- exhibits major problems with control of written language

Preparing for **Timed Writing**

How-to Essay

When responding to a how-to prompt, use what you have learned from reading, writing your research paper, and studying the rubric on page 1130. Use the steps below to develop a response to the following prompt.

Writing Prompt

You have been assigned to write a research paper on a topic of your choice. Write an essay explaining how to conduct research that will provide the information needed for a paper. Describe the steps you will take as you research your topic.

Study the Prompt

Begin by reading the prompt carefully. Notice that the **type of essay** you are to write is determined for you. Circle important words in the prompt that tell you what you need to include: *explain, to research, conduct, information.* Re-read the prompt to see if there is any additional information that can help you.

Your purpose is to provide clear, step-by-step instructions about how to complete a task—in this case, how to conduct research. Organize your instructions in **chronological order,** from first step to last step. **Tip:** Spend about five minutes studying the prompt.

Plan Your Response

How-to instructions require that you ask the question *How?* Answer the question by giving details about each step. Ask yourself, *What is my main task? What will I do at each step?*

Keep your **audience** in mind. Your audience may not be familiar with the topic, so you need to be thorough. First, write a brief introduction explaining

the main task. For the body of the essay, list all of the things a person does when researching. Then, put the list in order by asking questions such as these:

- What should I do first?
- In order to _____, what do I need?
- What do I need before I _____?

Next, add details to each step. Make a quick note about points you will want to include in your conclusion. **Tip:** Spend about ten minutes planning your response.

Respond to the Prompt

Use your notes to start writing your essay. Introduce the task you are writing about. Then, write out your list of steps, adding details as you go. A brief conclusion should allow the reader to confirm that all steps have been taken. **Tip:** Spend about twenty minutes writing your explanation.

Improve Your Response

Revising Go back to the key aspects of the prompt. Did you give details for each step of research? Is each step clearly focused? Is your essay well organized, with an introduction, body, and conclusion?

Proofreading Take a few minutes to correct errors in grammar, spelling, punctuation, and capitalization. Make sure the paper is legible.

Checking Your Final Copy Read your response one more time to catch errors you may have missed. **Tip:** Save five or ten minutes to improve your response.

Presenting Research

Think as a Reader/Writer

When you read informative articles, such as a chapter from a textbook or a magazine article, you are probably in the habit of identifying the main points and essential information that you want to remember. Likewise, when preparing to present your research paper to the class, you will have to re-read your research paper and highlight the most interesting or compelling ideas. Although your research may have produced a wealth of fascinating material, you risk losing the attention of your listeners if you overwhelm them with too much information.

Adapt Your Research

The purpose of both an oral and a written research presentation is to inform others about your topic. For the oral presentation, simplify your written research paper by

- examining your thesis and selecting the most interesting points
- reviewing the primary evidence for your thesis and selecting the evidence that best supports your thesis
- selecting the details that you found most fascinating
- identifying information that will clarify any possible misunderstandings and will show your topic from different perspectives
- preparing how you will tell your listeners the sources for your evidence

Your presentation must include information from both primary and secondary sources. Since your presentation will not include a *Works Cited* list, tell your audience your sources within the text of your speech. Be accurate by correctly citing the author and source, and be coherent by inserting the source information into your text either directly before or after your evidence as in the following example.

| **Written Version** | For the Britons, "It was their heroic age and Arthur was their greatest hero" (Day 15). |
| **Spoken Version** | In *The Search for King Arthur,* writer David Day writes about the Britons, "It was their heroic age and Arthur was their greatest hero." |

Reader/Writer Notebook

Use your **RWN** to complete the activities for this workshop.

Deliver Your Presentation

- Introduce your research with a memorable quotation or anecdote that captures the essence of the topic.
- Identify your research question and your overall conclusions.
- State your thesis, and provide an overview of the evidence that supports your thesis. Then, indicate which evidence will be the focus of your presentation.
- As you present your ideas and supporting information, identify your sources, both primary and secondary. Research presents documented facts, and sources must be cited accurately.
- Enhance your presentation with visuals such as maps, pictures, photographs, or video clips. Graphics, such as charts, outlines, or posters, are also helpful. Computer slide-show presentations offer a way to present the text of your main points, visuals, and graphics in front of listeners.
- Conclude by restating your central idea. Listeners will remember what you say last, so tell them why knowing about your research is of value to them.

Speak with Authority

- You will deliver an **extemporaneous** speech, a speech that is outlined and rehearsed, but not memorized. Transfer information from your paper to notecards, and write one point or detail per card.
- Pause after important words and phrases. Look directly at listeners. Glance at notes to prompt your memory or to read a quotation.
- Connect one thought to the next with transitional expressions. Inform your listener how you will be presenting information. For example, you can say "The statistic clearly shows that . . ." or "Another reason I concluded that . . ."
- Think of yourself as a professor, someone who knows a great deal about a subject. Use a formal, mature voice to convey what you have learned. Speak slowly and distinctly, reminding yourself that your listeners will benefit from knowing about your research.

A Good Presentation of Research

- engages the audience's attention
- introduces the context of the research, the reasons for learning about the topic, and the central conclusion of the research
- includes enough supporting detail
- provides citations for all quoted, paraphrased, and summarized information
- guides listeners through the presentation with transitional words and phrases
- is spoken slowly, clearly, distinctly, and loudly enough for everyone to hear
- concludes by stating the significance of the research

● Speaking Tip

Refer to your sources in your written research paper to double-check that any **technical terms** or **notations**—documented sources of information—that you use for your speech are accurate.

Learn It Online
Pictures, music, and animation can make your presentation more compelling. See how on *MediaScope* at:

go.hrw.com L10-1133 Go

Writing Skills Review

Research Paper **Directions:** Read the following paragraph from a student research paper. Then, answer the questions that follow.

(1) Senator at age thirty-two, Julius Caesar was a historical figure who accomplished many things. (2) Known as "one of Rome's greatest generals and statesmen," Caesar used his brilliant leadership and "helped make Rome the center of an empire that stretched across Europe." (3) After studying oratory— the art of making speeches—in Greece, Caesar worked his way up through various political positions. (4) He first became the quaestor of Spain, then the aedile of Rome, then the pontifex maximus under the Consul (McGill 51). (5) Caesar was assassinated on March 15, 44 B.C. (6) Caesar's sharp political instincts greatly advanced his economic and military power, allowing him to become the sole dictator of Rome in 44 B.C. (McGill 52).

1. Which of the following sentences based on a secondary source could the student add to support the thesis?

   A. Caesar was captured by pirates on his way to study in Greece (McGill 51).

   B. Caesar's first marriage, against the wishes of his family, put his career at risk (Duggan 36).

   C. Caesar had a secret alliance with the First Triumvirate (McGill 52).

   D. Caesar won military prestige, losing only two battles in nine years (Gruen 12).

2. What should the student do to give credit for the quotations in sentence 2?

   A. omit the quotation marks since they are unnecessary.

   B. use appropriate documentation in the text and in the *Works Cited* list.

   C. expand the quotation to include the entire sentence from the source.

   D. cite the source in the text but do not include it in the *Works Cited* list.

3. To make sentence 4 more understandable for the reader, the student could

   A. define the technical terms that name Caesar's political positions.

   B. include visuals by employing appropriate technology.

   C. relate whether the facts came from a primary or secondary source.

   D. cite more examples of Caesar's political aspirations.

4. Which sentence should be deleted or moved to another paragraph?

   A. sentence 2

   B. sentence 4

   C. sentence 5

   D. sentence 6

5. To present the information in a research presentation, the student should

  A. read aloud the *Works Cited* list.

  B. answer listeners' potential questions by reading the entire paper aloud.

  C. include visuals, such as a representation of Caesar or a map.

  D. avoid citing primary or secondary sources.

6. Which of the following *best* states the writer's position?

  A. Julius Caesar was a formidable historical figure.

  B. Julius Caesar waged many wars.

  C. Julius Caesar was loved by all of Rome.

  D. Julius Caesar made Rome what it is today.

7. Based on the rest of sentence 4, what do you think the word *Consul* means?

  A. citizen

  B. religious leader

  C. leading government authority

  D. military

8. What information in sentence 6 is not alluded to anywhere else in the paragraph?

  A. Caesar's economic power

  B. Caesar's military power

  C. Caesar's political instincts

  D. Caesar's rule of Rome

9. Which would be the *best* source to research in order to learn what Rome was like when Caesar became dictator?

  A. a secondary source that describes Caesar's rise to power

  B. a secondary source that describes life in Rome in 50 B.C.

  C. a primary source written by Caesar

  D. a collection of drawings and paintings from 34 B.C.

10. What kinds of examples or evidence would help explain sentence 2?

  A. facts about each country Caesar conquered

  B. descriptions of Caesar's army and battle tactics

  C. examples of cultures that came under Caesar's control

  D. examples of how Caesar made Rome the "center of an empire"

11. Which sentence is the thesis statement?

  A. sentence 1

  B. sentence 3

  C. sentence 5

  D. sentence 6

Writing for Life
Writers on Writing

Carol Jago taught English for thirty-two years at Santa Monica High School in California. She also wrote an education column for the Los Angeles Times *and is the author of nine books for teachers.*

Carol Jago on Writing for Life

"Have you ever read a story in the newspaper that made you mad? The next time this happens, don't get angry. Write back!

I got my start as a journalist writing letters to the editor. It was such a thrill to see my ideas and name in print that I started sending short articles to the newspaper. When my pieces attracted letters from other readers—both positive and negative—the editor invited me to write a weekly column. It could happen to you, too.

My secret to success for having a letter printed? Make it short and sweet. Newspapers allot limited space to this feature. As a result, only rarely will they publish more than five sentences from any individual letter. Check this out for yourself on today's op-ed page. If you find a long letter, it is probably from someone famous. I think editors are nervous about cutting these people off. Rather than writing a long letter and having your best point cut, pare your response down to a few pithy comments.

Begin your letter with a reference to the person or article you are reacting to and then immediately state how you feel and why. Editors receive hundreds of letters every day. Make yours stand out from the others in their mailbox with a first sentence that compels a reader's attention. Use words that reveal you to be a reasonable human being who is knowledgeable on this topic. In terms of tone, you want to sound either authoritative or outraged. Both play well on the page.

Nowadays most letters to the editor are submitted via e-mail, but don't let the format you use every day with friends cause you to write casually or conversationally. The newspaper is a public forum. You have a right to be heard. Seize the day."

Think as a Writer

Can you think of any recent newspaper articles you have read that would make you want to write a letter to the editor? What would you say, and why?

Reading for Life

INFORMATIONAL TEXT FOCUS
Consumer and Workplace Documents

"I suppose leadership at one time meant muscles; but today it means getting along with people."

—Indira Gandhi

What Do
You
Think

What skills do you need to succeed in the world?

Learn It Online
Can you read pictures? Let *PowerNotes* show you how at:

go.hrw.com | L10-1139 | **Go**

Detail from *People Dancing on Tightrope Poles* by Todd Davidson.

Informational Text Focus

by **Carol Jago**

Documents for Life

Not everything we read has been written for our reading pleasure. Some texts are created solely to communicate information. Often these documents are dense and challenging to understand. They frequently include official-sounding language and assume a background knowledge you may or may not possess. The lessons that follow will help you learn how to tackle functional documents with confidence.

Functional Documents

A **functional document** provides information about how something works or performs. For example, a magazine article that reviews sound systems for cars (also called a **product review**) is a type of functional document.

To be successful, functional documents must meet two criteria:

- They must be clearly organized and easily understood.
- They must present information, procedures, or both in a logical sequence.

Logical Sequence

There are three ways to organize functional information logically:

- **step by step**—often used for instructions
- **point by point**—usually used for legal documents, such as contracts and agreements
- **highest to lowest,** or **lowest to highest**—usually used for product reviews that are based on price or quality standards

Consumer Documents

A **consumer document** is an informative text for consumers, such as a warranty, contract, or instruction manual. You encounter functional documents like these when buying new products such as cars, electronics, toys, or appliances. A consumer document may be as simple as a clothing tag with care instructions, or as complicated as a technical manual for setting up a computer. Listed below are five different types of consumer documents and the **elements** they may contain.

- **product information**—a pamphlet or book, often written in two or more languages, describing the product, its parts, and its functions.
- **contract**—a legal agreement spelling out the period of agreement and the rights and obligations of the purchaser, manufacturer, seller, or service agent.
- **product warranty**—a legal document stating the manufacturer's legal responsibilities if the product fails. A product warranty explains what the buyer can do to obtain service or replacement for the defective product.
- **instruction or owner's manual**—a book of instructions on using the product under specified conditions and troubleshooting problems.
- **technical directions**—directions for properly installing, or assembling, and using a product.

RA.I.10.7 Analyze the effectiveness of the features used in various consumer documents, functional or workplace documents and public documents. and techniques, including repetition of ideas, syntax and word choice, that authors use to accomplish their purpose and reach their intended audience.

RA.I.10.1 Identify and understand organizational patterns

Workplace Documents

A **workplace document** is any job-related text, such as an application, résumé, correspondence, policy manual, or employee handbook. Listed below are six common workplace documents and the **elements** they may contain.

- **job application**—usually the employer's form that an applicant completes and signs when applying for a position
- **résumé**—the applicant's list of qualifications and work experience, possibly including a specific job objective
- **business letter**—formal correspondence intended for conducting business, including an inquiry, a proposal, and a sales letter
- **contract**—a legal document outlining the terms of agreement between the employer and employee
- **employee handbook**—a procedural handbook describing the policies of a business entity, including benefits information
- **memorandum**—an official written or electronic communication between employees of a company

Technical Directions

Technical directions can help you assemble and operate electronic and mechanical devices, and perform scientific procedures. Well-written directions often have numbered steps and clear diagrams that make them easy to follow. These tips can help you follow technical directions:

1. Before you start, read *all* the directions to get the big picture.
2. Follow each instruction step by step.
3. Refer to the drawings and illustrations to be sure you are doing everything correctly.

Your Turn   Analyze Documents

1. What types of functional documents have you used? Were they easy to understand? Why or why not?
2. What type of logical sequence would make sense for a set of directions needed to assemble a bookshelf?
3. What kinds of functional documents should be organized point by point?
4. Which of the following are examples of consumer documents?
   - an agreement with a cell-phone service provider
   - a collection of short stories
   - an e-mail to a friend
   - instructions for filing income taxes
   - a rental agreement

Learn It Online
Do pictures help you learn? Try the *PowerNotes* version of this lesson on:

go.hrw.com   L10-1141   **Go**

Analyzing Visuals

How Can You Interpret Information on a Transit Map?

On a visit to a new city you decide that the best way to get around town is on public transportation. At the tourist bureau you pick up a transit map, which shows train and bus routes and includes the names of neighborhoods, waterways, thoroughfares, and destinations. Graphic artists and cartographers, or mapmakers, try to create maps that are logical and easy-to-use.

Analyzing a Transit Map

Use these guidelines to help you interpret a transit map:

1. Look at the title of the map to verify what information is being presented. The map at the right shows the subway lines in New York City.

2. Is there a map key to help you decipher symbols on the map? Is there a compass rose to help you determine the direction you wish to go?

3. Examine where the long lines that represent train or bus lines begin and end. Do they intersect with any other lines along the way? If so, can you transfer to another line at these points?

4. If you or someone you are traveling with requires a wheelchair, what stations allow for wheelchair access? How can you tell?

Look at the details of the map to help you answer the questions on page 1143.

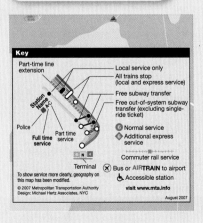

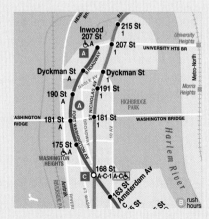

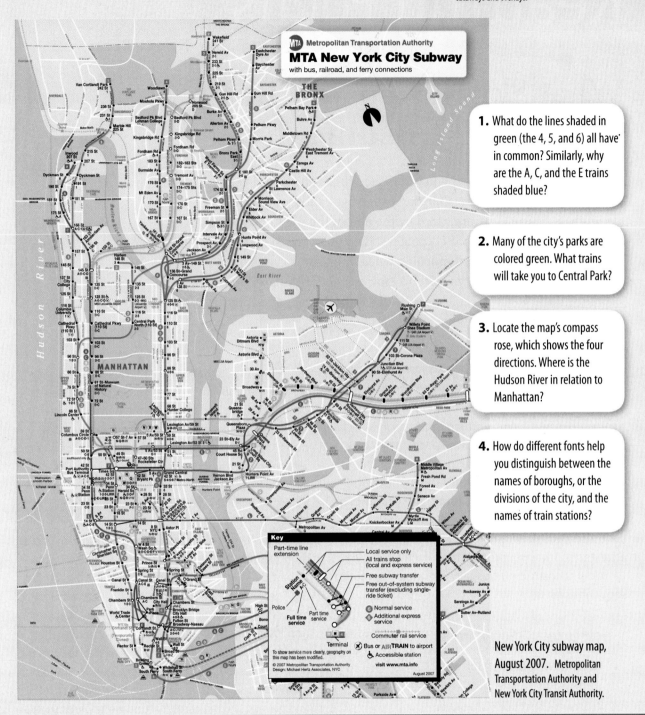

RA.I.10.3 Evaluate the effectiveness of information found in maps, charts, tables, graphs, diagrams, cutaways and overlays.

1. What do the lines shaded in green (the 4, 5, and 6) all have in common? Similarly, why are the A, C, and the E trains shaded blue?

2. Many of the city's parks are colored green. What trains will take you to Central Park?

3. Locate the map's compass rose, which shows the four directions. Where is the Hudson River in relation to Manhattan?

4. How do different fonts help you distinguish between the names of boroughs, or the divisions of the city, and the names of train stations?

New York City subway map, August 2007. Metropolitan Transportation Authority and New York City Transit Authority.

Your Turn   Talk About Transit Maps

With a partner take turns giving directions to the following locations using the map above: the Bronx Zoo, the United Nations, and Prospect Park. Your starting points should vary and begin from different boroughs.

Reading Focus

by **Kylene Beers**

What Skills Help You Read Functional Documents?

Let's flash forward ten years. You've finished high school and your post-high school education. One day your boss hands you a sales report that she wants summarized by the end of the week. Later you look up information on your computer's Help program to create tables in your document. The next morning when your hair dryer stops working, you jot a note to yourself to look online for the product warranty. Each scenario requires the skills to find, read, and interpret specific technical information.

Examining Structure and Format

While functional documents contain different information, they all have something in common—each will be organized according to a specific **structure** and **format**. When you read a functional document, it is important that you scan these elements first.

The **sequence, headers, fonts,** and **graphics** of a functional document provide clues about how its content is organized. Each functional document is arranged to transmit information effectively.

How-to instructions usually include a numbered sequence of steps.

How to Install Software

1. Remove the "Your Software" CD from packaging.
2. Insert CD in CD-ROM drive.

Other functional documents, such as contracts or legal papers, may use a numbered sequence and enlarged heads and subheads to organize important points.

Many functional documents also include visuals and graphics to illustrate the important points outlined in the document. Some written instructions for installation or assembly may contain illustrations. Other instructions may consist only of pictures arranged in easy-to-follow steps.

Finding the Main Idea

Readers often feel overwhelmed by functional documents containing **technical language.** The instruction booklet for a new sound system may state that the speakers are rated for 300 watts. The warranty for a computer upgrade component may mention RAM, gigabytes, and USB ports, among other details. Not knowing all the words in the document does not mean that the reader can't understand the main ideas. Good readers use the text's structure and format, paying careful attention to clues such as sequence, headers, fonts, and graphics to understand the technical terms and jargon.

When focusing on how the document is organized, think about the purpose of the document. If the **purpose** of the document is to provide step-by-step instructions, the reader should focus on the fol-

RA.I.10.7 Analyze the effectiveness of the features used in various consumer documents, functional or workplace documents and public documents.
RA.I.10.1 Identify and understand organizational patterns and techniques, including repetition of ideas, syntax and word choice, that authors use to accomplish their purpose and reach their intended audience.

lowing the steps. If the document is a warranty with rules for returning an item to the manufacturer, the reader should pay attention to any restrictions, such as the time allowed for a return and whether the manufacturer will take the merchandise back if the item is not in its original packaging.

Taking Notes

Sometimes **taking notes** while reading a complicated document will help clarify understanding. If you have a personal copy of the document, you may want to mark it up to highlight the most important steps or the answer to a problem you encountered. Here are several different options for marking up a document:

- Take notes in a separate notebook, such as your *Reader/Writer Notebook*.
- Write on the page or **highlight** important phrases, sentences, or paragraphs (if you own the document).
- Use **self-adhesive notes** to mark places in the document and clarify your understanding.

Using these techniques will help you customize a functional document, making it easier to use.

Your Turn   Apply Reading Skills

Visit the home page of your favorite Web site and then respond to these questions:

1. How is the information on the Web page organized?
2. How does the designer of the Web page use headers, fonts, and graphics?
3. What is the main idea and purpose of the Web page?
4. How could the Web page be improved?

If you do not have access to the Internet, analyze a magazine or newspaper article.

Now go to the Skills in Action: Reading Model

©The New Yorker Collection 1996.
Arnie Levin from cartoonbank.com.
All Rights Reserved.

"As I get older, I find I rely more and more on these sticky notes to remind me."

Learn It Online
Organize your thoughts! Use one of the interactive graphic organizers at:

 go.hrw.com   L10-1145   **Go**

Read with a Purpose Read the following magazine article to learn what you need to know before you shop for audio equipment.

AUDIO ASSERTIONS **The Expert Audio Magazine**

Multimedia Sound Card and Speakers: Buying Guide and Reviews

First Things First

Before you plunk down your hard-earned cash on a new sound card and speakers, know what you already own:

1. If your computer has expansion slots, check to see if one slot is free. If all your slots are in use, check to see if one of them is housing your current sound card. You can probably use that slot for a new card.

2. Your computer's user's manual will tell you its specific requirements, but here are some tips:

    A. Most of the newer sound cards use a PCI-X (peripheral component interface) bus, but some use an ISA (industry standard architecture) bus. Be sure that the card you choose fits the slot you have free. Also be sure that the new card can run at the speed required by your computer's free slot. PCI-X can run at clock speed of 66 or 133 MHz (megahertz). If the card you install will run at only 133 MHz and your computer requires 66 MHz, your computer can be damaged. Most cards run at both speeds, but check it out to be sure.

    B. Power consumption is important. Your computer has a maximum that all slots combined may use—for example, 45 watts. You risk damaging your computer if you exceed this limit by plugging power-hungry cards into all of your slots.

3. Regarding sound-card quality, keep the following points in mind:

    • **sampling rates:** Higher rates produce better-quality sound.
    • **signal-to-noise ratio:** Higher ratios (decibels, or dBs) produce clearer sound.
    • **voices:** More voices produce richer sound.

Informational Focus

Consumer Documents The author uses a point-by-point organizational method to convey key ideas. This is the first point.

Informational Focus

Consumer Documents The author supports the main point with smaller points to organize the information in a clear and easy-to-follow way.

- **wave-table synthesis:** This method produces sound that is far superior to the older FM synthesis.
- **MIDI** (musical-instrument digital interface) **input/output jacks:** These are necessary if you want to write or perform music and record your work.

4. Does your computer have expansion slots? Some computers of the all-in-one variety come with fixed sound capabilities pre-installed. If you own such a model, your best option for improved sound is to upgrade your speakers.

5. Finally, it's important to remember that your sound card and your speakers must work together. It will be useless to purchase top-of-the-line speakers if you do not have a sound card that can deliver the sound the speakers were built to accommodate, and the same goes the other way around. In general, the more you spend on speakers and sound cards, the more powerful your system will be. On the other hand, how much power do you really need?

Reading Focus

Analyzing Structure The information in this paragraph may have been better positioned at the top of the article, before item 1.

Buying Guide and Reviews

Multimedia Speakers	Price	Date*	Review
Scopia	$489	4/10	Best sub + satellite system to be heard, with an ultra clean sound that's a bit cerebral and bass light. A thinking person's choice.
InTune	$395	9/09	Worthwhile midprice system with clean, if hygienic sound. A can't-go-wrong choice.
Aurllogic	$280	12/09	Great value with a tight, punchy sound. Knockout bass.
Airtight	$159	12/09	Nicely built and nice musical sound. Good choice.

* The date indicates the month and year in which a full review of the product appeared in *Audio Assertions*.

Buying Guide and Reviews, continued

Sound Cards	Price	Date*	Review
Sonic Bombardier	$350	6/10	Excellent package, including almost everything you'll need to record your own music: SonicBoltblaster sound card (see below); full GS-compliant instrument set; great software bundle with award-winning MIDI sequencing software; cables.
SonicBoltblaster	$250	6/09	One of the best consumer-oriented cards on the market today, with MIDI input/output ; headphone jack; 5.1-channel output ; 1,024 wave-table voices, 64 of them hardware accelerated; >96-dB signal-to-noise ratio; sample at 2, 4, and 8 megabytes; wave-table or FM synthesis; minimal software bundle.
Sonic Bonanza	$150	6/09	Surprisingly affordable for its features: card supporting 2,4, or 6 speakers; wave-table synthesizer with capacity to support 64 hardware accelerated voices and 1,240 software voices; >96-dB signal-to-noise ratio; sample at 2, 4, and 8 megabytes. Good software bundle for MP3, MIDI, and WAV file conversion, playback, and rip to CD.
TD3S200	$50	4/09	Bargain basement 3-D sound. Card supporting 2 speakers; samples up to 48kHz; >96-dB signal-to-noise ratio; 320 voices; wave-table of FM synthesis, software limited to drivers. Look for a used model at auction for an even better price.

Reading Focus

Analyzing Structure Notice that the table is organized from the highest price to the lowest price.

Read with a Purpose What did you learn about buying audio equipment from reading this article?

OH **RA.I.10.7** Analyze the effectiveness of the features used in various consumer documents, functional or workplace documents and public documents. *Also covered* **RA.I.10.1; RA.I.10.3; VO.10.6**

Into Action: Functional Documents

Review the magazine article, "Multimedia Sound Card and Speakers: Buying Guide and Reviews." Notice how the author creates a helpful structure and format for the document by using a logical sequence, headers, bulleted lists, various fonts, and a table of information. Then, create the first page of your own magazine article about a product or process you know well that incorporates at least two of these elements.

Talk About...

1. With a partner, discuss the strengths of the magazine article and ways it could be improved. Is there anything in the article that seems confusing? Try to use each of the Academic Vocabulary words listed at the right at least once in your discussion.

Write About...

Answer the following questions about the magazine article:

2. What is the author's <u>objective</u>, and how is it accomplished?

3. How does the <u>format</u> of the article contribute to your understanding of the content? Consider why it is logical to place "First Things First" before "Buying Guide and Reviews."

4. What types of graphics could the author <u>insert</u> to increase reader understanding?

5. Using several examples from the article, explain how the author uses point-by-point organization to <u>illustrate</u> the main ideas.

Writing Focus

Think as a Reader/Writer

Find It in Your Reading In Collection 10, you will analyze many types of functional documents. The documents provide different information and ideas, but each one has a specific structure and format. In your *Reader/Writer Notebook,* track how each document is organized to express main ideas and increase reader understanding.

Academic Vocabulary for Collection 10

Writing and Talking About Functional Documents

Academic Vocabulary is the language you use to write and talk about functional documents. Use these words to discuss the documents you read in this collection. The words are underlined throughout the collection.

illustrate (IHL uh strayt) *v.:* show; demonstrate. *The author used a picture to illustrate how the task should be completed.*

objective (uhb JEHK tihv) *n.:* purpose; goal. *The objective of this article is to educate people about different types of stereo systems.*

insert (ihn SUHRT) *v.:* add; include; put in. *Insert a chart to show the different costs of stereo systems.*

format (FAWR mat) *n.:* design; arrangement. *Each functional document has a different format.*

Your Turn

Copy the words from the Academic Vocabulary list into your *Reader/Writer Notebook.* Practice using these words as you talk and write about functional documents.

Preparing to Read

Following Technical Directions

What tasks are more easily accomplished by following a set of directions?

QuickTalk

Think of a time when you had to follow a set of directions to accomplish a task. Did the directions seem confusing, or did they make the job easier? Why? Discuss your ideas with a partner.

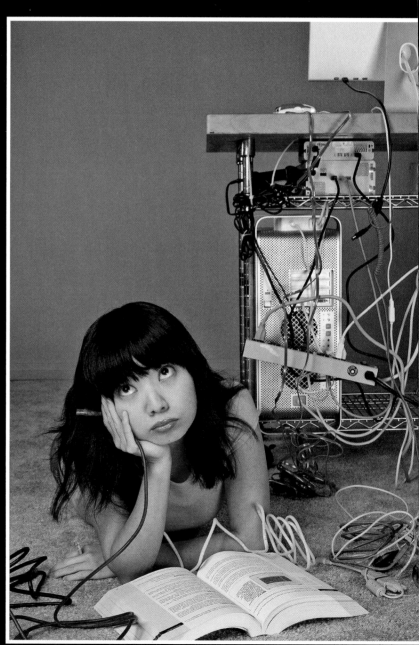

Reader/Writer Notebook

Use your **RWN** to complete the activities for this selection.

OH **RA.I.10.7** Analyze the effectiveness of the features used in various consumer documents, functional or workplace documents and public documents. *Also covered* **RA.I.10.1**

Informational Text Focus

Following Technical Directions The instructions for using electronic, mechanical, and scientific products and procedures are called **technical directions.** You follow technical directions whenever you program ring tones and phone numbers into your cell phone or when you do an experiment in science class.

When you first look at technical directions, they can seem hard to understand and maybe even a little overwhelming. How will you be able to sort through all that information? All you have to do is pay attention and follow each step carefully in the **sequence,** or order in which it is presented.

Into Action As you read "Installing a Computer Sound Card," think about the <u>format</u> of the document and how it helps the author achieve his or her purpose. What type of logical sequence does the author choose? Does the author use graphics to <u>illustrate</u> directions? Does he or she draw attention to certain parts of the document using headers or different fonts? Use a chart like the one below to describe your observations.

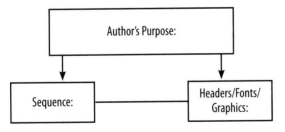

Vocabulary

discharge (dihs CHAHRJ) *v.:* release; let out. *Before opening the computer case, you should first discharge static electricity by touching something metal.*

pry (pry) *v.:* move or separate with force. *Do not pry the old sound card from its slot; instead, pull it out gently.*

obstructions (uhb STRUHK shuhnz) *n.:* things that are in the way or that block something else. *If the sound card does not fit in the slot, check for obstructions.*

correspond (kawr uh SPAWND) *v.:* match; be similar. *Find the connector pins that correspond with each end of the audio cables.*

Language Coach

Synonyms A word that has the same meaning as another word is a **synonym.** When writing a technical document, it is helpful to include synonyms for difficult words or technical terms the first time they appear in a text. This will make the document easier for readers to understand. What is a good synonym for the word *instructions*?

Writing Focus Preparing for **Constructed Response**

Installing a computer sound card, a device that lets your computer both play back and record sounds, could be a difficult task. In your *Reader/Writer Notebook,* note the parts of the directions that seem easiest to understand and where the author uses shorter sentences or simple language to create this understanding.

Learn It Online
There's more to words than just definitions. Get the whole story on:

go.hrw.com   L10-1151   **Go**

Installing a Computer Sound Card*

* Instructions for PC users.

Read with a Purpose
You will follow step-by-step instructions like these whenever you want to modify or improve a computer's capacity.

1. Be sure the computer is switched off.

2. To avoid damaging your computer, touch something metal on the outside of your computer with your fingers to discharge static electricity. Then, unplug your computer.

3. Open the computer case.

4. Locate the slot you want on the motherboard.[1] See the user's manual for specific instructions on the location and types of slots on the computer. Ⓐ

5a. If the slot is empty, remove the screw that holds the metal slot cover in place, slide the cover out, and set both the screw and the cover aside for later.

5b. If the slot currently contains the old sound card, remove the screw that holds the card in place and gently pull the card from the slot. It may need a firm yet careful tug. **CAUTION:** If rocked against the sides of the slot, the card might snap off in the slot or pry the slot from

---

1. **motherboard** (MUHTH uhr bawrd): a computer's main circuit board.

Ⓐ **Informational Focus** Technical Directions Why does the manual refer to a separate set of directions here?

Vocabulary **discharge** (dihs CHAHRJ) *v.:* release; let out.
pry (pry) *v.:* move or separate with force.

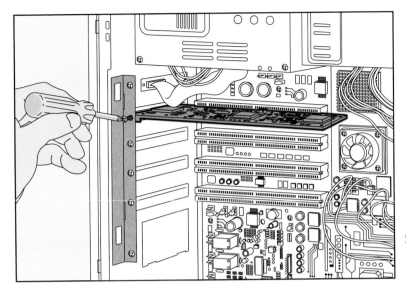

Step 5a

the motherboard. You will see an audio cable attached at one end
to the sound card and at the other end to the CD or DVD-ROM drive.
Disconnect this cable from the drive by pulling gently. **Ⓑ**

6. Plug the new sound card into the prepared slot by pressing down
   firmly until the connector is fully <u>inserted</u>. It should be a tight fit, but
   do not use undue force. If you encounter resistance, take the card
   out, check for alignment and possible obstructions, and try again.

7. To be sure the card is in place, give it a gentle tug. It should resist and
   stay in place. The connector strip's metal conductors should also be
   just barely visible when viewed at eye level.

Ⓑ **Informational Focus** Technical Directions Why is number 5 a two-part step in this
sequence?

Vocabulary **obstructions** (uhb STRUHK shuhnz) *n.*: things that are in the way or that block
something else.

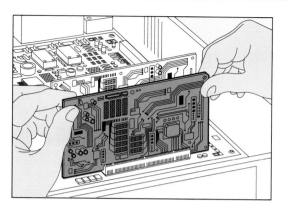

Step 7

8. Find the screw and the slot cover that were removed in step 5a. Both may need to be replaced. If the card is built with an integrated[2] slot cover, only the screw that will hold the new card in place will need to be replaced. Be sure the slot is covered. Then, tighten the screw to hold the new sound card in place.

9. Connect the audio cable to the sound card and to the CD- or DVD-ROM drive. Find connector pins on the sound card and on the back of the disk drive that correspond to the plugs on each end of the audio cable. Be sure to line these pins up carefully and press gently. As in step 6, if you encounter resistance, check to see that all pins are straight and that there are no other obstructions. Then, try again.

10. Close the computer case.

11. Connect the external speakers to their appropriate jacks.

12. Plug in the power cord and turn on the computer and monitor. Once the computer is up and running, <u>insert</u> the CD that accompanies the sound card and complete the software driver installation by following the on-screen instructions.

---

2. **integrated** (IHN tuh gray tihd): combined; not separate.

Read with a Purpose Did you find these instructions easy to follow? Why or why not?

Vocabulary **correspond** (kawr uh SPAWND) *v*.: match; be similar.

Applying Your Skills

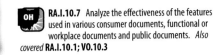

RA.I.10.7 Analyze the effectiveness of the features used in various consumer documents, functional or workplace documents and public documents. *Also covered* **RA.I.10.1; VO.10.3**

Following Technical Directions

Respond and Think Critically

Informational Text and Vocabulary

1. What will happen if you skip step number two in the technical directions?

  A The computer may be damaged.

  B The computer will still be receiving electricity.

  C The computer case will remain closed.

  D The computer may electrocute you.

2. Which of the following steps should be broken into several steps for improved clarity?

  A Step 3

  B Step 4

  C Step 7

  D Step 9

3. Which elements of <u>format</u> does the author use to draw attention to specific parts of the text?

  A Graphics

  B A header set in boldface type

  C A step-by-step sequence

  D Different font styles

4. What is this author's primary **purpose?**

  A Teaching people how to avoid damaging their computers

  B Providing an alternative to installing a computer sound card

  C Explaining how to install a sound card in a safe and effective way

  D Demonstrating how different sound cards may be installed

5. Ideas that *correspond* with each other —

  A clash

  B are unique

  C cancel each other out

  D match

6. If a person has to *pry* something loose, he or she must use —

  A a gentle touch

  B force

  C quick motions

  D agility

7. Which of the following is a type of *obstruction?*

  A A highway

  B A river

  C A house

  D A dam

Writing Focus   Constructed Response

Think about something that you know how to do well, such as doing research on the Internet or cooking a meal. What steps are involved? How might the steps be explained in a clear and concise way? Write a set of directions for accomplishing the task.

What Do You Think Now

How do detailed directions help you accomplish difficult tasks?

Preparing to Read

Analyzing Workplace Documents

 What Do **You Think**

How might an author organize different information into one document?

QuickWrite

Write about a time when you had a lot of information to share with a friend or relative, perhaps by letter or e-mail. How did you organize your information and ideas?

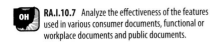

RA.I.10.7 Analyze the effectiveness of the features used in various consumer documents, functional or workplace documents and public documents.

Reader/Writer Notebook

Use your **RWN** to complete the activities for this selection.

Informational Text Focus

Analyzing Workplace Documents

The objective of a **functional workplace document** is to help people get things done effectively. Some types include **instructions for workplace procedures, business letters,** and **contracts.** The information may be different in each, but effective workplace documents share elements that make the information easier to understand.

Functional workplace documents are usually broken up into **sections,** each with its own **main idea** that is separated by a line or space. This makes it simple to locate a particular point and also increases the likelihood that the text will be both read and understood. **Headers** such as **titles** and **subtitles** help readers locate information.

Effective functional workplace documents also follow a certain **sequence,** in which ideas are ordered in a particular way to facilitate comprehension. Some common types of sequencing are **chronological, alphabetical, spatial,** and **logical.** Many functional documents follow a **logical sequence.** The **point-by-point** or **step-by-step** sequence often uses numbers or **roman numerals** to separate ideas.

Last, the format of functional effective workplace documents highlights important information and focuses the reader's attention on key words, sections, and ideas. Designers use these elements:
formatting—bold or italic type, margins, indentation, line spacing
graphics—drawings, photographs, and other illustrations
design—placement of the text and graphics on the page, color

Into Action As you read "Collaboration Agreement: Self-Published Musical Composition," use a table to analyze each element.

Structure/Design Element	How the Element Is Achieved
separating sections	using spaces between points

Vocabulary

composition (kahm puh ZIHSH uhn) *n.:* song or essay. *The songwriters created the composition together.*

administer (ad MIHN uh stuhr) *v.:* manage or control. *The songwriters can administer their rights to the song.*

provisions (pruh VIHZH uhnz) *n.:* requirements. *The songwriters must act according to the provisions of the agreement.*

Language Coach

Multiple-Meaning Words Some words have more than one meaning. For example, the word *shares* can be used to describe splitting something up (*I like it when he shares his candy with me*) or to describe a portion of something (*I own ten shares of stock in that music company*). Look up the list of Vocabulary words in the dictionary to see which ones have more than one meaning. Then, for each word that has multiple meanings, brainstorm how and when the different meanings might be used.

Writing Focus

Preparing for **Constructed Response**

In your *Reader/Writer Notebook,* summarize the main idea of each section of the collaboration agreement.

 Learn It Online
There's more to words than just definitions. Get the whole story on:

go.hrw.com L10-1157 **Go**

Read with a Purpose
Read this legal agreement to find out how songwriters establish and protect their rights to their musical creations.

Build Background
Songwriters, musicians, and other artists create legally binding documents to describe their rights to a piece of work. These documents may also describe how the proceeds, or money, from the work should be split. In this collaboration agreement, two songwriters agree to equally share the money they receive from selling their song.

Ⓐ Informational Focus Workplace Documents Why is this information separated from the text around it?

Ⓑ Informational Focus Workplace Documents What type of sequence does this document use?

Vocabulary composition (kahm puh ZIHSH uhn) *n.*: song or essay.
administer (ad MIHN uh stuhr) *v.*: manage or control.
provisions (pruh VIHZH uhnz) *n.*: requirements.

Collaboration Agreement
Self-Published Musical Composition

Date: _____

In a Collaboration Agreement dated _____, Sara Songster and Mike Melodic have agreed that they are equal co-authors of both the words and the music of the song titled "All Day," hereinafter called the Composition.

I. The worldwide copyrights[1] for the Composition, and any and all extensions and renewals thereof, are owned as follows:
> Sara Songster: undivided 50 percent
> Mike Melodic: undivided 50 percent Ⓐ

II. Sara Songster and Mike Melodic are entitled to administer their respective copyright shares in the Composition.

III. The Composition is to be registered with the U.S. Copyright Office, ASCAP, BMI, and/or SESAC, and other U.S. and foreign music agencies, in accordance with the provisions of this agreement.

IV. The Author's share of all royalties[2] and other earnings derived from the Composition are to be apportioned and paid as follows:
> Sara Songster: undivided 50 percent
> Mike Melodic: undivided 50 percent

V. The Publisher's share of all royalties and other earnings derived from the Composition are to be apportioned and paid as follows:
> Sara Songster: undivided 50 percent
> Mike Melodic: undivided 50 percent Ⓑ

Signed:
Sara Songster _____ Date _____

Mike Melodic _____ Date _____

---

1. **copyrights** (KAHP ee rytz): exclusive rights to publish, sell, and control an original piece of work.
2. **royalties** (ROY uhl teez): share of profits paid to an owner of a copyrighted work for its use.

Applying Your Skills

RA.I.10.7 Analyze the effectiveness of the features used in various consumer documents, functional or workplace documents and public documents. **V0.10.3** Infer the literal and figurative meaning of words and phrases and discuss the function of figurative language, including metaphors, similes, idioms and puns.

Analyzing Workplace Documents

Respond and Think Critically

Informational Text and Vocabulary

1. What type of **sequence** does the Collaboration Agreement use?

   A Chronological

   B Alphabetical

   C Spatial

   D Logical

2. What is the **main idea** of section I of the agreement?

   A Sara Songster and Mike Melodic share equal ownership of the song.

   B Sara Songster and Mike Melodic will split the song.

   C The song will be registered with the U.S. Copyright Office.

   D Royalty payments for use of the song will be equally divided between the song's authors.

3. The Collaboration Agreement uses all the following **formatting elements** *except* —

   A boldface headers

   B italics

   C indentations

   D line spacing

4. The **main points** in the Collaboration Agreement are indicated by —

   A roman numerals

   B a line of space

   C boldfaced key words

   D titles that summarize each main idea

5. One kind of *composition* is —

   A a price tag

   B a sentence

   C an essay

   D a label

6. People who *administer* their own finances can *best* be described as —

   A irresponsible

   B independent

   C wealthy

   D self-centered

7. Which of the following *provisions* would most likely appear in a workplace contract?

   A Salary to be paid

   B The employee's birthday

   C A company description

   D Computer passwords

Writing Focus   Constructed Response

Write an agreement you would like to have with your parents or guardians. Make sure that you include one main idea for each section. Think about provisions your parents or guardians might want to insert.

What Do You Think Now?

What are the most effective ways to structure a document that contains a great deal of information?

What Do You Think

What are some differences between conducting research using books and using the Internet?

 QuickTalk

Think of a topic you would like to resear Internet. Where would you look for info How would you keep track of the sites y Discuss your ideas with two classmates

Reader/Writer
Notebook
Use your **RWN** to complete the activities for these selections.

R.10.6 Use style guides to produce oral and written reports that give proper credit for sources, and include an acceptable format for source acknowledgement.

Informational Text Focus

Documenting Sources The Internet is a valuable tool for anyone researching a topic for a report. When you use information from the Internet, you must keep track of the sources you use and correctly **cite,** or name, them, at the end of your report.

Internet sources are frequently updated, thus requiring more documentation than print sources. Citations for each online source follow the same general <u>format</u> (see below).

> **GENERAL FORMAT FOR AN ONLINE SOURCE**
> Author's Last Name, Author's First Name (if known). "Title of Work."
> <u>Title of Web Site or Database</u>. Date of electronic publication. Name of Sponsoring Institution. Date information was accessed <URL>.
>
> Note: Enclose an electronic address, or URL, in angled brackets. If the URL must continue on a new line, divide the address immediately after one of the slash marks within it. Do not use a hyphen or any other mark of punctuation to divide the address.

A list of the sources used, or **Works Cited** list, appears at the end of a report. The list allows readers to follow the research trail. The list follows a specific <u>format</u>: alphabetize the sources, place the first line of each entry at the left margin, and indent succeeding lines five spaces.

Into Action As you read the instructions and examples for citing Internet sources, examine the <u>format</u> that is used for different sources. Then, record your observations in a chart like the one below.

What I Saw	Where I Saw It
The title of the work always appears in quotations with a period at the end.	"About the Latest Sound Cards" "Musical Notations"

Vocabulary

abbreviation (uh bree vee AY shuhn) *n.:* shortened form of a word or phrase. *"Ed." is an abbreviation for editor.*

commercial (kuh MUHR shuhl) *adj.:* having to do with trade or business. *The author visited a commercial Web site to get more information about computer sound cards.*

consumers (kuhn SOO muhrz) *n.:* people who use anything made or grown by producers. *The nonprofit magazine is written to protect consumers from buying bad products.*

archives (AHR kyvz) *n.:* public records or historical documents. *The University Library Web site contains archives of traditional music.*

Language Coach

Homonyms Homonyms are words with different meanings that have the same pronunciation or spelling. *Cite, site,* and *sight* are homonyms; one may *cite* Internet sources, visit a Web *site,* or have good *eyesight.* Use a dictionary to determine how these common homonyms are used:

- affect/effect
- accept/except
- write/right

Writing Focus
Preparing for **Constructed Response**

Look at the sample Works Cited list on page 1163. What do you think is the topic of the report? What kinds of sources did the author use? Write your ideas in your *Reader/Writer Notebook.*

Learn It Online
There's more to words than just definitions. Get the whole story on:

go.hrw.com   L10-1161   **Go**

Guidelines for an Internet Citation

Read with a Purpose
Read the selections to discover how to correctly cite Internet sources.

Build Background
The selections in this collection include citations from consumer and workplace sites, sources you might find when doing your own research on the Internet. All the sample citations in this collection follow the style of the Modern Language Association (MLA). Other styles for documenting sources are also acceptable and available, but it's important to choose one style and stick with it.

1. Author's Last Name [,] Author's First Name and Middle Initial (if given) [,] abbreviation such as Ed. (if appropriate) [.]

2. ["] Title of Work Found in Online Scholarly Project, on Database, or in Periodical[1] ["] or ["] Title of Posting to Discussion List or Forum (taken from the subject line) [.] ["] followed by the description Online posting [.]

3. Title of Book (underlined) [.]

4. The abbreviation Ed. followed by Name of Editor (if relevant and not cited earlier, as in Ed. Susan Smith) [.]

5. Publication information for any print version of the source: City of Publication [:] Name of Publisher [,] year of publication [.]

6. Title of Scholarly Project, Database, Magazine, Professional Site, or Personal Site (underlined) [.]

7. Name of Editor of Scholarly Project or Database (if available) [.]

8. Volume number, issue number, or other identifying number of the source (if available) [.]

9. Date of electronic publication, posting, or latest update (often found at the bottom of the site's home page) [.]

10. Name of Subscription Service [,] and, if a library, Name of Library [,] Name of City [,] and Abbreviation of State in which library is located [.]

11. For a posting to a discussion list or forum, Name of List or Forum [.]

12. If sections are numbered, number the range or total number of pages, paragraphs, or other sections (if information is available) [.]

13. Name of Institution or Organization Sponsoring or Associated with the Web site [.]

14. Date on which source was accessed [.]

15. [<] Electronic address (URL) of source [>] or if a subscription service, [<] URL of service's main page (if known) [>] and [[ ] Keyword: Keyword Assigned by Service [ ]] or [[ ] Path: sequence of topics followed to reach the page cited, as in first topic [;] second topic [;] third topic [;] and so on, ending with the page you are citing [ ]] [.] Ⓐ

---

1. **periodical** (pihr ee AHD uh kuhl): a magazine that appears regularly, but not daily.

Vocabulary **abbreviation** (uh bree vee AY shun) *n.:* shortened form of a word or phrase.

Ⓐ **Informational Focus** Citing Sources What seems to be the most important information in citations?

Sample Works Cited

Product Information from a Commercial Site

"About the Latest Sound Cards." Sound Cards Update Page. 10 Aug. 2009. New Sounds 4 Sept. 2009 <http://www.NewSoundsToday.com/article/index.asp>. **Ⓑ**

Article from an Online Nonprofit Magazine Dedicated to Protecting Consumers

Sleuthing, I. B. "Sound Cards and Speakers: Buying Guide and Reviews." Audio Assertions 7 Sept. 2009 <http://www.audioassertions.org/main/article/soundcard/l.html>.

Article from a Reference Database (Encyclopedia)

"Musical Notation." Electric Library Presents: Encyclopedia.com. The Columbia Electronic Encyclopedia, Sixth Ed. 2008. Columbia UP. 15 July 2009 <http://www.encyclopedia.com/articles/08892.html>.

Online Information from a University Library Site

The Hoagy Carmichael Collection. 1 Nov. 2005. Digital Library Program and The Archives of Traditional Music at Indiana U. 4 Sept. 2009 <http://www.dlib.indiana.edu/collections/hoagy/index.html>.

Copyright Forms from the Library of Congress (Government Office)

United States. Library of Congress. U.S. Copyright Office. Form PA—For a Work of the Performing Arts. Washington: GPO, 1999. 30 Sept. 2009 <http://www.loc.gov/copyright/forms/formpa.pdf>.

Information from a Company's FAQ[2] Page

"Supermusicnotation Software." The Music's Muse, Inc. 3 Jan. 2009 <http://www.themusicsmuse.com/corp/faqs/faqslist.html>.

Posting to a Discussion List (Message Board)

Chart Climbers. "Why Surfers Pause and Pass." Online posting. 3 June 2009. Way Kool Net. 19 Sept. 2001 <http://www.waykoolnet.com/mboards/boards.cgi?board=prgm&read=9218>.

Quotation from an E-mail Communication

Nguyen, W. "Re: 3-D sound, how to do it cheaply." E-mail to the author. 21 Aug. 2009. **Ⓒ**

---

2. **FAQ:** abbreviation for Frequently Asked Questions.

Ⓑ **Informational Focus** Citing Sources Why is this information placed in angled brackets?

Ⓒ **Informational Focus** Citing Sources What does this page tell you about the types of sources you can find on the Internet?

Vocabulary **commercial** (kuh MUHR shuhl) *adj.*: having to do with trade or business.
consumers (kuhn SOO muhrz) *n.*: people who use anything made or grown by producers.

Using Notecards

As you find sources on the Internet, it is a good idea to record the information you will need for your Works Cited list on three-by-five-inch notecards. You can also include other important information about your sources on these cards. Here are some examples. (Some of these are made-up sources.)

What it is: Online Interview
Author(s): none listed
Title: EMP Interviews: Nick Hornby
Other Information: Experience Music Project is a museum in Seattle, Washington, devoted completely to music. The site has last been updated on Sept. 14, 2009. That was the day I visited. A lot of what the site has is digital, so it's very useful for doing research. You could spend days on this site.
URL: http://www.emplive.com - I went to the home page, then to archives, then EMP interviews, then Nick Hornby.

What it is: Online consumer newsletter
Author(s): Stewart Cheifet
Title: Hardware Damage from Incorrect Clock Speed in PCI-X Cards
Other Information: from Inside the Internet newsletter, June 2008 [vol. 6, issue 8], page 3. Published by Superior Technical Data, Inc. A really clear explanation of the problem and how to avoid it. Accessed on Sept. 3, 2009.
URL: http://www.suptechdata.com/text/press/letter.html

What it is: Reference Source
Author(s): none listed, published by Mpeg.TV and edited by Tristan Savatier
Title: MPEG Audio Research and Software
Other Information: A good overview of MPEG audio and a place to start getting other resources. The page had last been updated May 31, 2008. I accessed it on August 31, 2009.
URL: http://www.mpeg.org/MPEG/audio.html **Ⓓ**

Read with a Purpose What have you learned about citing Internet sources correctly?

Ⓓ **Informational Focus** Citing Sources What types of notes go into the "Other Information" section?

Vocabulary **archives** (AHR kyvz) *n.*: public records or historical documents.

WORKS CITED
Applying Your Skills

R.10.6 Use style guides to produce oral and written reports that give proper credit for sources, and include an acceptable format for source acknowledgement. **V0.10.3** Infer the literal and figurative meaning of words and phrases and discuss the function of figurative language, including metaphors, similes, idioms and puns.

Citing Internet Sources

Respond and Think Critically

Informational Text and Vocabulary

1. What information should appear first in a **citation** with no author?

   A An abbreviation

   B Date of electronic publication

   C The title of the work

   D Name of sponsoring organization

2. Which of the following should be underlined in a **Works Cited** list?

   A Title of the database

   B Author's last name

   C URL address

   D Title of the work

3. The date on which a source is accessed appears —

   A after the author's name

   B before the author's name

   C after the URL

   D before the URL

4. The primary **purpose** of notecards is to —

   A come up with ideas for a research topic

   B exchange information with peers

   C maintain a correct sequence of sources for the Works Cited list

   D keep track of the sources and information used during research

5. An *abbreviation* is used to —

   A lengthen a word

   B shorten a word

   C organize information

   D simplify information

6. Which of the following publications targets *consumers?*

   A A medical journal

   B A school newsletter

   C A stereo buying guide

   D A book of essays

7. Important historical *archives* will most likely be found in —

   A museums

   B homes

   C periodicals

   D research papers

Writing Focus Constructed Response

Think of a topic you would like to know more about. How would you find Internet sources about this topic? Write a brief description of how you would find the sources online.

What Do You Think Now?

How does citing an Internet source differ from citing a book?

READING CONSUMER DOCUMENTS

What Do **You** Think? What type of information should be included with the purchase of a new electronic device?

QuickWrite

Write about a time when you or someone you know borrowed something from a friend. What were the conditions under which the item was borrowed? Did it have to be returned at a certain time? What would have to be done if the item were broken or lost?

Reader/Writer
Notebook
Use your **RWN** to complete the activities for
these selections.

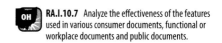
RA.I.10.7 Analyze the effectiveness of the features used in various consumer documents, functional or workplace documents and public documents.

Informational Text Focus

Reading Consumer Documents You just bought a new stereo. You open the box to find not only the new equipment, but also several **consumer documents.** Even though you may be anxious to hear your tunes blasting, it's important to take the time to read the **service contract, warranty, product information,** and **instruction manual.** These consumer documents are meant to serve you. They are an essential source of information that makes it easier for you to operate and enjoy the products you purchase.

Most consumer documents are made up of **elements,** or basic parts. Listed below are different types of consumer documents and the elements that each contains:

- **product information**—description of a product and what it does
- **service contract**—a legal agreement spelling out the rights and obligations of the purchaser and manufacturer, seller, or service agency
- **warranty**—a legal document stating what the manufacturer will do if the product fails to live up to the manufacturer's claims and what the purchaser must do to obtain service
- **instruction manual**—instructions on how to use the product and how to troubleshoot problems
- **technical directions**—directions for installation and use

Consumer documents may also outline the **features** of a product, or the things that make one product model different from other models.

Into Action As you read the consumer documents, keep track of the elements and features that you find.

Document	Elements	Features

Writing Focus   Preparing for **Constructed Response**

Consumer documents often use headers, various fonts, and graphics to emphasize main ideas. Use your *Reader/Writer Notebook* to make notes about how the different elements and features in these consumer documents are highlighted.

Vocabulary

claim (klaym) *n.:* demand for something due. *You can make a claim against the company if the product breaks.*

clause (klawz) *n.:* single provision of a law or agreement. *The contract contains a cancellation clause.*

void (voyd) *v.:* cancel legal force or effect. *If you use the product incorrectly, you will void the service contract.*

discretion (dihs KREHSH uhn) *n.:* ability to make a choice. *The contract may be renewed at the company's discretion.*

Language Coach

Word Definitions A word's meaning can depend on whether it is used as a noun or a verb. See how the definitions of these two Vocabulary words change:

claim *v.:* assert or affirm strongly. *They claim they are innocent.*

The meaning changes when used as a noun: *The service provider rejected my claim.*

void *n.:* empty space. *The spacecraft flew into the great void between the stars.*

The meaning changes when used as a verb: *Missing ballots meant the election was void.*

Write four sentences using these two Vocabulary words as both nouns and verbs.

 Learn It Online
There's more to words than just definitions. Get the whole story on:

go.hrw.com   L10-1167   **Go**

Aulsound Extended Service Contract

Read with a Purpose
Read the following selections to learn how to understand the paperwork that comes with the purchase of some electronic equipment.

ADMINISTRATOR
Aulsound Warranty Service Corporation
P.O. Box 840001 Century City, CA 90067
SERVICE CONTRACT AGREEMENT
Digital Multitrack Recorder DMR88

TERMS AND CONDITIONS
Details of coverage. This Service Contract provides coverage of any operating parts or labor required for the product listed above, for two years from date of original purchase. There will be no cost to the Purchaser for any authorized covered repair that is performed by one of our highly skilled service associates.

Limitations. This Service Contract covers product failures occurring during normal use. It does not cover misuse or abuse of the product during delivery, installation, or setup adjustments. It does not cover damage that occurs while adjusting consumer controls, loss of data or programming support, unauthorized repair, customer-sponsored specification changes, cosmetic damage, or simple maintenance as recommended in the product owner's guide. It also does not cover repairs that are necessary because of improper installation or improper electrical connections. Consequential or incidental damages are not covered. Damage due to acts of God is not covered. **Ⓐ**

Maintenance requirement. The Purchaser must maintain the product in accordance with the requirements or recommendations set forth by the manufacturer to keep this Service Contract in force. Evidence of proper maintenance and/or service, when required by the Administrator, must be submitted to validate a claim.

Unauthorized-repair clause. IMPORTANT: Unauthorized repairs may void this Service Contract. The cost of these repairs will be the responsibility of the Purchaser.

Transfer of ownership. This Service Contract is transferable with ownership of the product. Transfer may be accomplished only if the Purchaser mails or delivers to the Administrator a twenty-five dollar [$25.00] transfer fee and registers the name and address of the new owner within fifteen [15] days of change of ownership. **Ⓑ**

Cancellation clause. This Service Contract may be canceled by the Purchaser at any time, for any reason. In event of cancellation, we will provide a pro-rated refund minus reasonable handling costs and any claims that may have been paid. Any cancellation requested by the Purchaser within thirty [30] days of the Service Contract application date will be 100 percent canceled by the Administrator.

Contract insurance. Your Service Contract is fully insured by Aulquiet Insurance Company, 80 Sampler Way, Los Angeles, CA 90017. Purchasers who do not receive payment within sixty [60] days of submitting a pre-authorized covered claim may submit the claim directly to Aulquiet Insurance Company, Contractual Liability Claims Department, at the above address. **Ⓒ**

Renewal clause. This Service Contract may be renewed at the discretion of the Administrator. The renewal premium will be based on the age of the covered product, current service costs, the covered product's repair history, and actuarial data.

Ⓐ **Informational Focus** Consumer Documents Why does the service contract not cover some necessary repairs?

Ⓑ **Informational Focus** Consumer Documents According to the contract, how could you transfer ownership of the product?

Ⓒ **Informational Focus** Consumer Documents What does this section of the agreement direct consumers to do?

Vocabulary **claim** (klaym) *n.:* demand for something due.
clause (klawz) *n.:* single provision of a law or agreement.
void (voyd) *v.:* cancel legal force or effect.
discretion (dihs KREHSH uhn) *n.:* ability to make a choice.

Troubleshooting Guide

If you encounter problems operating your Aulsound DMR88 or if the product does not work as expected, look up the problem in this table and follow the advice provided. **Ⓓ**

PROBLEM	ADVICE
The DMR88 does not turn on.	• Make sure that the power cord is plugged into an AC wall outlet. • Check the AC IN connector at the rear of DMR88. • Make sure that the DMR88 power switch is in the ON position. • If there is still no power, contact your Aulsound dealer.
No sound is coming from the connected music source.	• Make sure that the MONITOR LEVEL control is raised. • Make sure that the FLIP and MONITOR SELECT switches are set correctly.
The DMR88 does not record.	• Make sure that the disc's write-protect tab is set to UNPROTECT. • Make sure that the PLAY function is not on. • Press a REC SELECT button, and make sure that the track is ready to record. • Make sure that the signal you wish to record has been selected at the recording source for the appropriate track. Use the CUE LEVEL control to determine whether the signal is being sent to the track.
Level meters do not indicate signal levels.	• Make sure that the track you wish to record has been selected. • Press the REC button, and make sure that the DMR88 is in RECORD-PAUSE mode.
Recordings play back at the wrong pitch.	• Make sure that the PITCH function is not set at VARIABLE. • Make sure that the 1.2 PLAY function is turned off.

Ⓓ **Informational Focus** Consumer Documents Where would you look in the Troubleshooting Guide for help if you were having trouble recording? What would you do first?

FCC* Information (USA)

1. IMPORTANT NOTICE: DO NOT MODIFY THIS UNIT!
This unit, when installed as indicated in the instructions contained in this manual, meets FCC requirements. Modifications not expressly approved by Aulsound may void your authority, granted by the FCC, to use this product.

2. IMPORTANT: When connecting this product to accessories and/or another product, the high-quality shielded cables supplied with this product MUST be used. Follow all installation instructions. Failure to follow instructions could void your FCC authorization to use this product in the United States.

3. NOTE: This product has been tested and found to comply with the requirements listed in FCC Regulations, Part 15 for Class "B" digital devices. Compliance with these requirements provides a reasonable level of assurance that your use of this product in a residential environment will not result in harmful interference with other electronic devices. This equipment generates and uses radio frequencies and, if not installed and used according to the instructions found in the user's manual, may cause interference harmful to the operation of other electronic devices. Compliance with FCC regulations does not guarantee that interference will not occur in all installations. If this product is found to be the source of interference, which can be determined by turning the unit OFF and ON, try to eliminate the problem by using one of the following measures:

- Relocate either this product or the device that is being affected by the interference.
- Utilize other outlets that are on different branch (circuit breaker or fuse) circuits, or install AC line filter(s). In the case of radio or TV interference, relocate or reorient the antenna.
- If the antenna lead-in is a 300-ohm ribbon lead, change the lead-in to a coaxial type cable.

If these corrective measures do not produce satisfactory results, contact the local retailer authorized to distribute this type of product. If you cannot locate the appropriate retailer, contact Aulsound Corporation of America, Electronic Service Division, 1000 Wilshire Blvd., Los Angeles, CA 90017. **E**

---

*FCC: Federal Communications Commission, U.S. agency that regulates communication by telegraph, telephone, radio, TV, cable TV, and satellite.

Read with a Purpose   How do documents like these help you, as a consumer, get the most out of a product?

E **Informational Focus**   Consumer Documents   How does the format of this FCC document highlight its main ideas?

OH **RA.I.10.7** Analyze the effectiveness of the features used in various consumer documents, functional or workplace documents and public documents. **VO.10.3** Infer the literal and figurative meaning of words and phrases and discuss the function of figurative language, including metaphors, similes, idioms and puns. *Also covered* **WA.10.3.a**

Reading Consumer Documents

Respond and Think Critically

Informational Text and Vocabulary

1. All the following features are described in the **service contract** *except* —

  A the time period in which defective parts will be replaced

  B FCC regulations and guidelines

  C the types of product failures that will be covered

  D the terms of a cancellation clause

2. The purpose of a **troubleshooting guide** is to —

  A help consumers understand the procedures for filing a claim

  B provide advice on how to operate a device that is not working properly

  C make a service contract easier to understand

  D provide instructions about transferring ownership of a product

3. The format for **consumer documents** draws attention to the main ideas by using all of the following *except* —

  A bold headers

  B numbered sequences

  C line spacing

  D smaller font sizes

4. A person who submits a *claim* with a company over a faulty product is submitting a —

  A demand for replacement or repair

  B description of the product

  C review of the product's features

  D complaint against the manufacturer

5. What is a synonym for *clause?*

  A Essay

  B Contract

  C Section

  D Law

6. A person with a great deal of *discretion* can best be described as —

  A needing guidance

  B unable to make a decision

  C power-hungry

  D having the power to choose

7. To *void* a contract is to make it —

  A no longer valid

  B submitted with a claim

  C legally binding

  D automatically renewed

Writing Focus Constructed Response

Write a brief service contract for an item you might lend to a friend or relative. Be sure your service contract includes and highlights the item's specific features.

What Do You Think Now

How can the information provided in consumer documents help you?

Informational Skills Review

Consumer and Workplace Documents   Directions: Read and respond to the following questions about consumer and workplace documents.

1. What is the most important thing to do when following technical directions?
   A. Read the directions quickly to get the best picture.
   B. Complete the project in one, uninterrupted session.
   C. Follow each step carefully and in the correct sequence.
   D. Decide in advance how much time to allow for the project.

2. Which type of sequence do many functional documents follow?
   A. random order
   B. logical, point by point
   C. spatial
   D. last to first

3. What type of functional document is best suited to a logical sequence that progresses from highest to lowest?
   A. a contract
   B. a recipe
   C. a product review
   D. a set of directions

4. The most logical way to organize a set of **instructions** is by
   A. chronological order.
   B. step-by-step order.
   C. order of importance.
   D. spatial order.

5. A set of technical directions is flawed if it
   A. omits a step.
   B. is logically sequenced.
   C. includes illustrations.
   D. does all of the above.

6. The purpose of a workplace document is to
   A. eliminate some jobs.
   B. increase paperwork.
   C. help people get things done.
   D. lessen people's dependence on computers.

7. Which type of document is a collaboration agreement?
   A. a warranty
   B. a contract
   C. a set of technical directions
   D. U.S. Copyright Office Registration form

8. In an Internet citation, the most crucial piece of information to reproduce is the
   A. author's name.
   B. title of the site.
   C. URL.
   D. date the site was accessed.

9. According to the MLA style, where in an Internet citation do you place the date a Web site was accessed?
   A. right after a URL
   B. just before a URL
   C. at the beginning of an entry
   D. at the end of an entry

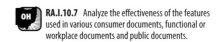

RA.I.10.7 Analyze the effectiveness of the features used in various consumer documents, functional or workplace documents and public documents.

10. According to the MLA style, which of the following URL citations is correct?

    A. <http:www.yourschool.edu

    B. www.yourschool.edu

    C. <http://www.yourschool.edu>

    D. http://www.yourschool.edu

11. In a Works Cited list, in what order are the entries listed?

    A. alphabetically, by the title of the work

    B. alphabetically, by the author's last name (when known)

    C. alphabetically, by the URL

    D. chronologically, by the date the source was accessed

12. Which consumer document is most likely to help you if you encounter problems operating a product?

    A. a contract

    B. a troubleshooting guide

    C. a warranty

    D. a safety guide

13. What is the purpose of an extended service contract?

    A. to provide a basic warranty for a product

    B. to give advice on how to repair a product if it breaks down

    C. to provide coverage for product repairs after the warranty expires

    D. to offer a money-back guarantee for a defective product

14. In which one of these consumer documents are you most likely to find out how powerful your new computer is?

    A. the warranty

    B. the product information brochure

    C. the technical directions

    D. the Quick-Start guide

Short Answer

15. Explain why information from the FCC (Federal Communications Commission) is included with certain products.

Extended Response

16. Explain the steps to take and the sources you might consult if you experience problems with a new purchase.

Vocabulary Skills Review

Context Clues   **Directions:** Use context clues from the sentences to respond to each question.

1. If the sound card appears to be stuck, do not attempt to <u>pry</u> it from the slot.

   In this sentence, <u>pry</u> means

   A. force.

   B. turn.

   C. release.

   D. erase.

2. The book was the result of <u>collaboration</u> between two writers, and the contract specifies that they will share the profits equally.

   In this sentence, <u>collaboration</u> means

   A. innovation.

   B. incorporation.

   C. cooperation.

   D. intuition.

3. FCC is the <u>abbreviation</u> for the Federal Communications Commission, a government agency.

   In this sentence, <u>abbreviation</u> means

   A. former name.

   B. alternate spelling.

   C. legal name.

   D. shortened form.

4. The manufacturer has the <u>discretion</u> to replace the faulty product or refund the purchase price.

   In this sentence, <u>discretion</u> means

   A. ability to choose.

   B. ability to keep a secret.

   C. ability to clarify.

   D. ability to inform.

5. If the plug will not fit into the socket, check for <u>obstructions</u> within the socket.

   In this sentence, <u>obstructions</u> means

   A. things that conduct electricity.

   B. things that block the way.

   C. things that speed progress.

   D. things that move easily.

6. Their contract contains several <u>provisions</u> that protect the rights of both the buyer and the seller.

   In this sentence, <u>provisions</u> means

   A. protections.

   B. requirements.

   C. sections.

   D. highlights.

7. <u>Consumers</u> should be sure to read all the documents that come with any new electronic product they purchase.

   In this sentence, <u>consumers</u> means

   A. people who sell products in stores.

   B. people who buy and use products.

   C. people who grow or create products.

   D. people who write articles about products.

8. Ines made a <u>claim</u> for a new MP3 player because the one she bought was defective.

   In this sentence, <u>claim</u> means

   A. denial.

   B. request.

   C. attempt.

   D. demand.

9. If you mistreat your new appliance and need service, the manufacturer could <u>void</u> the warranty.

   In this sentence, <u>void</u> means

   A. expand.

   B. repeat.

   C. cancel.

   D. forget.

10. As part of their new agreement, the song-writers maintain control of their rights to their songs and can <u>administer</u> their share of the profits as they see fit.

    In this sentence, <u>administer</u> means

    A. manage.

    B. divide.

    C. retain.

    D. give.

11. Static electricity can build up on your hands. To avoid damaging your computer, <u>discharge</u> any static electricity by touching something metal before you touch your computer.

    In this passage, <u>discharge</u> means

    A. obtain.

    B. release.

    C. repair.

    D. enhance.

12. Newspaper <u>archives</u> are a good source of information on local history.

    In this sentence, <u>archives</u> means

    A. Web sites.

    B. reporters.

    C. records.

    D. interviews.

Academic Vocabulary

Directions: Use context clues from the sentences to respond to each question.

13. To set apart the provisions of the contract, <u>insert</u> some extra space between them.

    In this sentence, <u>insert</u> means

    A. enlarge.

    B. add.

    C. remove.

    D. reduce.

14. The <u>objective</u> of the Quick-Start guide is to help you set up your computer quickly.

    In this sentence, <u>objective</u> means

    A. request.

    B. need.

    C. disagreement.

    D. purpose.

Read On

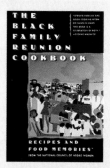

The Black Family Reunion Cookbook

The idea behind this book of more than 250 mouthwatering recipes is that good cooking can help families bond. The joy of eating a meal together can stimulate problem-solving conversation and remove barriers. Many of the recipes are accompanied with comments from the contributors. One contributor fondly remembers that as a child she could never get enough macaroni and cheese. When she was allowed to start cooking, her goal was to improve the recipe. Her sensational result: macaroni, cheese, and ground peanuts.

Home Tree Home

Building a tree house is the ultimate fantasy for many. *Home Tree Home,* which gives explicit directions for building a tree house, can help that fantasy become a reality. First, authors Peter Nelson and Gerry Hadden explain how to pick the right tree. The design of the house depends on the kind of tree you choose. The authors then guide you through the steps of building the platform, or floor, putting up the sides, and, finally, framing and covering the roof.

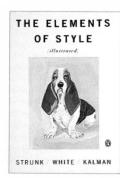

The Elements of Style

This classic reference book will improve your writing and warm your heart at the same time. William Strunk, Jr., was a professor of English at Cornell University. He first published *The Elements of Style* for his students in 1918. His one-time student E. B. White, author of the classic *Charlotte's Web,* updated and revised the book in 1959 and 1972. Today, the "little book" (so named by Strunk's students) has been updated with full-color illustrations by Maira Kalman. Read it and see how learning to write well can be fun.

Origami for the First Time

Origami is the art of paper folding that began in Asia thousands of years ago. In *Origami for the First Time,* Soonboke Smith introduces readers to the tools, supplies, papers, and terminology used in origami. She then shows readers how to make the basic origami folds and forms that are used in a number of designs. Numbered, four-color photos illustrate the step-by-step folds used in creating objects such as a box shaped like a swan, a lily, a flapping crane, and a pine tree.

NONFICTION
Send

If you use a computer, then you are probably writing more electronic mail than you ever thought possible. But are you writing effectively? That is the subject of this witty, practical book. Not surprisingly, the authors David Shipley and Will Schwalbe address the rules of writing, but they also spend time on what is appropriate to include in e-mails (especially within the workplace) and how to make writing concise. (Many business people receive hundreds of e-mails a day.) Most important, they explain how to make your writing factually correct.

FICTION
Test of Time

It's finals week for Orlando Garcia Ortiz and his friends at Hadleyburg University. Many years before, during that very same week, an eccentric writer in Hartford, Connecticut, put the finishing touches on a manuscript about a rebellious boy named Huck. Suddenly, the writer's manuscript disappeared and in its place appeared a strange contraption—a college student's laptop. As you read this exciting adventure by Charles Harrington Elster, you'll also be studying for the SAT, as the book includes hundreds of vocabulary words and their definitions.

WEB SITE
www.usps.com

Here is a Web site that contains everything you've ever wanted to know about the U.S. Postal Service. Suppose you have a great idea that will improve mail delivery. Look under the heading *Ideas* in the alphabetical list, and you'll find information about how to submit your idea. The official Web site of the United States Postal Service shows you how to start collecting stamps, ship live animals, buy stamps and envelopes, suspend mail delivery when you're away, and track and confirm delivery. It also includes a section on the history of the Postal Service.

NONFICTION
How to Study

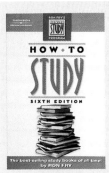

Hailed as "the best-selling study book of all time," *How to Study* by Ron Fry will help you ace your exams. This guide covers topics such as setting up a place to study, managing your time, and test-taking tips. The book also provides guidance on writing papers, remembering what you read, and using the library. Just when you thought you knew it all, this updated sixth edition provides you with proven strategies that will help you perform better in and out of the classroom.

Learn It Online
Explore other topics—and find tips for choosing, reading, and studying works—at

go.hrw.com | L10-1177 | **Go**

Writing Workshop

Business Communications

Write with a Purpose

Write a variety of business communications to an **audience** that includes a company, individual, group, or organization with whom you have a specific reason for communicating. Your **purpose** is to provide accurate information necessary for accomplishing your goals.

A Good Business Communication

- follows the specified format
- is purposeful, clear, and brief
- uses a respectful and formal tone
- provides all necessary information to the intended audience
- is grammatically correct and free of errors

See page 1186 for complete rubric.

Think as a Reader/Writer

Knowing how to write a variety of **business communications** is an important skill that you will use often. Below find examples of a business letter and a technical document.

440 Melody Lane
Rockville, CA 91112
June 2, 2009 ← Heading

Ms. Bettina Johnson, Editor ← Inside address
Doings in Town
1 Main Street
Rockville, CA 91112

Dear Ms. Johnson: ← Salutation

I am writing to submit a news item for inclusion in your magazine, *Doings in Town*. Our band, The DumpStar Gang, is giving a benefit performance on June 21 at 7:30 p.m. to raise money for the public library. Admission is $10. Thank you in advance for including us in your publication. ← Body includes purpose and supporting details. ← The tone of the letter is courteous.

Sincerely, ← Closing

Mike Musicano ← Signature

Mike Musicano

Rules for CAN-DO Conflict Resolution

Cease what you're doing. Count to ten. Cool down.
Assess the problem fairly.
Name the problem without placing blame.
Discover a problem-solving plan through compromise.
Operate the plan by cooperating with others involved.

Reader/Writer Notebook

Use your **RWN** to complete the activities for this workshop.

WA.10.3.a Write business letters, letters to the editor and job applications that: address audience needs, stated purpose and context in a clear and efficient manner; **WA.10.3.b** Write business letters, letters to the editor and job applications that: follow the conventional style appropriate to the text using proper technical terms; **WP.10.5** Use organizational strategies to plan writing.

Think About the Professional Models

With a partner, discuss the following questions about the model.

1. What is the goal of each of the communications?

2. How does each achieve its goal?

Prewriting

Organizing Your Ideas for a Business Communication

Business Letter The purpose of writing a business letter is to request that someone do something for you: hire you, provide you with information, donate money to a cause, handle a complaint, or publicize your event or ideas. Thus, it is important that you express your ideas and information in a clear, concise way. The reason for your letter should always appear in the first paragraph. Why are you writing the letter? What do you want to accomplish? Then, include any important information without repetition. What are the main ideas? What details do you need to include to support those ideas? Make a chart like the one below to help you organize your business letter.

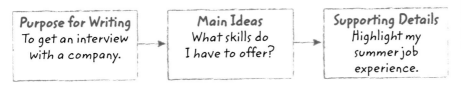

Technical Document Conflict-resolution rules are one type of technical document that may be used in the workplace. Other types of technical documents include workplace procedures, employee manuals, or how-to instructions. Like business letters, technical documents need to be well-organized, clear, and concise. In addition, technical documents should follow a logical order and may include definitions and examples to aid comprehension.

Think About Purpose and Audience

Before you draft any kind of business communication, think about your purpose and audience. It is important that you know as much as you can about your **audience.** This will not be personal information but rather facts about a business, group, or process you need to know before you begin. Your **purpose** is to convey or solicit needed information.

Idea Starters

Here are some ideas that might prompt a business communication:

- Write a business to inquire about a product or service.
- Write a company to inquire about a summer job or internship.
- Write a college or university about a scholarship or loan.
- Write a nonprofit organization about becoming a volunteer.
- Write an author, business leader, or government official requesting an interview.
- Write a city official requesting an improvement or change in services in your community.
- Take minutes at a meeting of your club, school organization, or another group to which you belong.

Your Turn

Getting Started In your **RWN**, brainstorm ideas for a **topic** for a business communication. List the **main ideas** and **details** you will include. As you brainstorm, think about your purpose and audience. Use your notes to write your draft.

Learn It Online
An interactive graphic organizer can help you generate and organize ideas. Try one at:

go.hrw.com   L10-1179

● **Writing Tip**

Business letters can use either of two formats:

- **block format,** in which all parts of the letter begin at the left margin, and no paragraphs are indented
- **modified block format,** in which the heading, the closing, and the signature begin to the right of the center of the page, and all paragraphs are indented

Formatting a Business Letter

Once you have your ideas in mind, you must organize them in a clear and concise way. To do this, use the conventional format of a business letter. The example below uses block format.

Your Address
Date

Name of Recipient and Business Title
Company Name
Company Address

Salutation:

The **opening paragraph** states the writer's purpose in clear, concise language.

The **body paragraphs** include relevant information and supporting details. They may include background information, examples, facts, or questions for the recipient.

The **final paragraph** briefly thanks the recipient in anticipation of a favorable and timely response.

Closing,
Sender's Signature
Sender's Full Name

Your Turn

Organize and Format Business Communications Each type of business communication has a purpose and a format. Gather information for a business letter and think about what information you will include in each paragraph and where you will place your supporting details.

Formatting a Technical Document

Ideas and information in other types of business communications must also be well-organized. These elements help the writer **format** the document and help the reader understand the information:

- Use numbers or Roman numerals, bulleted lists, and white space to separate information.
- Use words that are clear, concise, and easy to understand.
- Use short, well-written sentences to convey ideas and factual information effectively.
- Provide necessary examples and definitions for all technical terms.

Drafting

Business Letter Necessities

The format of a good business letter includes six main parts:

- heading: the sender's address and date
- inside address: the recipient's name and address
- salutation
- body
- closing
- signature

Business Communication: Consider Your Reader

One important component to writing a business communication, whether it is a business letter or a technical document, is to anticipate, or predict, reader understanding. Are any parts of your document confusing? Answering these questions will help you decide where to place appropriate definitions and examples. Thinking ahead about possible reader misunderstanding also provides a good reminder to write clearly and concisely. Your reader will expect clarity and precision in your business communication. **Parallelism** is one way to be more precise.

Grammar Link **Parallelism**

Parallelism is the use of similar grammatical forms in a sentence to express that the ideas are equal in importance. This can occur at the word, phrase, or clause level. Proper parallel structure makes sentences easy to understand and clarifies the connection between ideas in a sentence.

Not Parallel: We are seeking applicants with experience in the travel industry and selling.

Parallel: We are seeking applicants with experience in the travel industry and sales.

Not Parallel: The letter explains that the road needs repair, that the mayor is withholding money for this project, and the need for action.

Parallel: The letter explains that the road needs repair, that the mayor is withholding money for this project, and that action is needed.

Do your sentences have a parallel structure? Try these strategies:

Listen to the sounds of the words in a list. They should follow the same rhythm or have the same endings as this example: **I like writing, reading, and drawing.**

Check the wording on each side of *and* and *or*. Are the items parallel in structure? **I want to learn how to write poetry, speak Spanish, and play tennis.**

Writing Tip

Be proactive. Using verbs in the active voice helps make writing clear, concise, and crisp. Notice the difference between the following sentences. Which one sounds stronger? Why?

- I have had years of experience in sales that *have prepared* me for this job. (*passive verbs = passive voice*)
- My years of sales experience *prepared* me for this job. (*active verb = active voice*)

Your Turn _____

Writing Your Draft Use the notes you made in your **RWN** to draft a **business communication.** As you write, keep these questions in mind:

- What is my purpose for writing?
- What information does my audience need?
- How can I use parallelism to strengthen my letter or document?

Peer Review

Ask a writing partner to read your draft and state your purpose aloud. Also ask if anything seems unclear. Then, use this chart to locate where and how the draft could be improved. Be sure to make notes for revision.

Evaluating and Revising

Organizing your ideas and writing your draft are the beginning of the writing process. The next step is to examine your writing for places where improvements can be made. Use the chart below to revise your draft.

Business Communication: Guidelines for Content and Organization

Evaluation Questions	Tips	Revision Techniques
1. Is my purpose stated in the first paragraph of the letter or at the beginning of the technical document?	**Underline** the sentence that states the purpose.	**Add** a sentence in the first paragraph to state the purpose.
2. Do my ideas follow a logical order?	**Check** all elements that organize and separate ideas.	**Add** numbers, Roman numerals, bullets, or spaces where needed.
3. Do I use appropriate language and tone for a business communication?	**Draw a line** through slang expressions and any words that do not sound sincere or are not courteous.	**Replace** slang and casual language with formal English.
4. Are all of my ideas presented clearly and concisely?	**Bracket** any sentences that are lengthy or repetitive.	**Delete** repeated ideas and shorten overly long sentences.
5. Is my document free of errors in spelling, punctuation, and grammar?	**Circle** all errors.	**Correct** the errors. **Consult** a dictionary, a writing resource, or a peer editor.
6. Have I used an acceptable business format?	**Check** business documents for clear presentation of ideas and readability.	**Format** the letter or document so that it is easy to read and understand.

Read this student draft of a business communication; notice the comments on its strengths and suggestions about how it could be improved.

Student Draft

776 Brittany Trail
Florence, KY 41042
January 15, 2009

City Council Members
Florence Government Center
8100 Ewing Blvd.
Florence, KY 41042

Dear City Council Members:

As a teenage skateboarder, I often find myself going to the Yellow Pages to find the nearest skate park. Since there is an absence of a skate park in northern Kentucky, many avid skateboarders get totally bored. However, there is a way around this problem—open a skate park in Florence. To you, this may sound a bit crazy, but please share this letter at the next council meeting and consider a skate park.

← The writer includes the header and uses the **block format** for a business letter.

← The recipient's address correctly appears below the sender's address.

← Notice that the salutation is correctly followed by a colon.

← The writer states the purpose of the business letter in the opening paragraph.

MINI-LESSON ▶ How to Use Formal Diction

Diction is a writer's choice of words, phrases, and sentence structures. When writing a business communication, use formal diction and eliminate any slang. Doing so conveys your seriousness and sincerity to your recipient. To correct errors in diction, read your draft aloud. If a word or phrase sounds as if you would say it to a friend in casual conversation, eliminate it or replace it with a more appropriate word choice.

Andrew's Revision of Paragraph One:

. . . Since there ~~is an absence~~ of a skate park in northern Kentucky, many

      become bored
avid skateboarders ~~get totally bored~~. However, there is a way around this prob-

lem—open a skate park in Florence. ~~To you, this may sound a bit crazy, but~~

please share this letter at the next council meeting and consider a skate park.

Your Turn

Revising Informal Language
Revise your business letter and look for informal language. Replace informal language with language appropriate for a business communication.

Student Draft continues

The paragraphs in the body of the letter include details and facts that support the writer's purpose. →

A skate park will reduce crime and drug activity among the city's youth. Studies show that having an after-school activity will reduce the instances of vandalism and drugs. Yes, we have baseball, basketball, football, and many other sports. Not all kids are interested in these sports, but extreme sports like skateboarding, in-line rollerblading, and biking are increasing in popularity among teens.

Andrew can strengthen this part of the letter. →

The letter closes on a courteous, → respectful note.

The writer correctly includes a → closing and signature.

I hope that you will consider building a skate park. Just like a growing business needs to expand as it gains more employees, we need to build a skate park for the growing number of skateboarders in our area. Thank you for your time.

Sincerely,

Andrew McAlpin

Andrew McAlpin

MINI-LESSON ▶ How to Address a Counterargument

Andrew has researched the City Council's objections to the skate park and decides that his letter needs to address at least one of them. He revises his letter by politely negating the council's main objection, thus making his communication more persuasive. Addressing counterarguments also shows Andrew's careful preparation for writing to community leaders.

Marti's Revision

One problem that we might encounter is the location of the skate park. There are many plots of land suitable for construction of an outdoor park. If land is scarce, though, there are several vacant warehouses. With their high ceilings, these buildings would be perfect for an indoor park. Protected from the harsh weather, an indoor skate park would be utilized year-round.

∧I hope that you will consider building a skate park. Just like a growing business needs to expand as it gains more employees, we need to build a skate park for the growing number of skateboarders in our area. Thank you for your time.

Your Turn _____

Addressing Counterarguments

Could the recipient of your letter have an objection to what you are requesting? Be sure to address any counterarguments respectfully.

Proofreading and Publishing

Proofreading

Before you send your letter or publish your business communication, it is important to proofread carefully for any errors in spelling, grammar, and punctuation. If possible, ask two writing partners to help you edit. Ask one to check your spelling, and ask the other to proofread for grammar and punctuation. Using this strategy will help you find the errors that you may have overlooked. Reading your business communication aloud will help you to hear the repetition of nouns.

Grammar Link **Using Pronouns to Eliminate Repetition**

Repeating words can disrupt the flow of your writing and make it more difficult to read. The writer repeats the noun *skate park* in the sentence below. To correct this problem, he crosses out the repeated word and replaces it with the pronoun *it*.

A skate park will reduce crime and drug use among the youth of

this city because a ~~skate park~~ ^*it*^ will provide a place for teenagers to play.

Publishing

Once all of your revisions have been made, it is time to publish your document. Consider these strategies for sharing your document:

- Send the letter to the addressee.
- Display your document in school, or post it to a school-sponsored Web page.
- Make necessary changes and send it to your local or community newspaper.

Reflect on the Process
Think about the process you used to write the business communications in this workshop.

1. How did you adjust your use of language for the formality of a business communication?
2. What did you learn from writing business communications that could also apply to other types of writing?
3. What is unique to writing a business communication?

Your Turn ——————

Using Pronouns As you proofread and edit your work, replace repetitive nouns with appropriate pronouns. Share your business communication with an audience.

Scoring Rubric

Use this rubric to evaluate your business communication from the Writing Workshop or your response to the on-demand prompt on the next page. Your teacher will tell you which rubric to use.

6-Point Scale

Score 6 *Demonstrates advanced success*
- shows a clear sense of purpose and focused engagement with the topic
- shows effective organization throughout, with smooth transitions
- presents ideas that are meaningful and insightful
- supports ideas thoroughly, using fully elaborated explanations and specific examples
- displays a mature control of written language

Score 5 *Demonstrates proficient success*
- shows a clear sense of purpose and focus on the topic
- shows effective organization, with transitions
- presents ideas that are meaningful
- supports ideas competently, using well-elaborated explanations and specific examples
- displays sufficient control of written language

Score 4 *Demonstrates competent success*
- shows a sense of purpose and topic, but may include some loosely related ideas
- shows effective organization, with minor lapses
- presents ideas that are mostly meaningful
- elaborates on ideas with a mixture of the general and the specific
- displays general control of written language

Score 3 *Demonstrates limited success*
- includes some loosely related ideas that distract from the writer's ideas
- shows some organization, with noticeable gaps in the logical flow of ideas
- presents ideas that may be routine and predictable
- supports ideas with uneven elaboration
- displays limited control of written language

Score 2 *Demonstrates basic success*
- includes loosely related ideas that seriously distract from the writer's ideas
- shows minimal organization, with major gaps in the logical flow of ideas
- presents ideas that are mostly simplistic and superficial
- supports ideas with inadequate elaboration
- displays significant problems with control of written language

Score 1 *Demonstrates emerging effort*
- shows little awareness of the topic and purpose for writing
- lacks organization and a logical plan
- presents ideas that are mostly simplistic or that may be unclear or illogical
- develops ideas in only a minimal way, if at all
- displays major problems with control of written language

4-Point Scale

Score 4 *Demonstrates advanced success*
- shows a clear sense of purpose and focused engagement with the topic
- shows effective organization throughout, with smooth transitions
- presents ideas that are meaningful and insightful
- supports ideas thoroughly, using fully elaborated explanations and specific examples
- displays a mature control of written language

Score 3 *Demonstrates competent success*
- shows a sense of purpose and topic, but may include some loosely related ideas
- shows effective organization, with minor lapses
- presents ideas that are mostly meaningful
- elaborates on ideas with a mixture of the general and the specific
- displays general control of written language

Score 2 *Demonstrates limited success*
- includes some loosely related ideas that distract from the writer's ideas
- shows some organization, with noticeable gaps in the logical flow of ideas
- presents ideas that may be routine and predictable
- supports ideas with uneven elaboration
- displays limited control of written language

Score 1 *Demonstrates emerging effort*
- shows little awareness of the topic and purpose for writing
- lacks organization and a logical plan
- presents ideas that are mostly simplistic or that may be unclear or illogical
- develops ideas in only a minimal way, if at all
- displays major problems with control of written language

Preparing for **Timed** **Writing**

Business Communications

You may be presented with an on-demand or timed-writing task that asks you to write a business letter. Use the information you learned in the Writing Workshop, the rubric on the opposite page, and the instructions that follow to help you with this task.

Writing Prompt

Your club expected a shipment of bike helmets, which you were going to donate to young riders as part of a charity bike-a-thon. The helmets never arrived. Write a business letter to the helmet company, explaining the problem and describing the chain of events. Use specific details that will indicate the actions you need from the helmet company.

Study the Prompt

Circle the **writing task:** "write a business letter . . . explaining the problem and describing the chain of events," "use specific details," and "indicate the actions." Keep in mind your audience too: the helmet company.

Tip: Spend about five minutes studying the prompt.

Plan Your Response

The prompt requires that you explain the problem, outline the chain of events, and indicate what the helmet company should do to correct the problem. Use a chart like the one below to organize your ideas. **Tip:** Spend about ten minutes planning your response.

> Problem:
> Chain of events:
>
> Needed actions:

Respond to the Prompt

Your introduction should state your purpose for writing. Your body paragraphs should explain the problem and describe the chain of events. You'll probably want to list them in the order in which they occurred, using transitional words and phrases to connect them. Your conclusion should ask the company's representative to address the problem. **Tip:** Spend about twenty minutes writing your draft.

Improving Your Letter

Revising Go back to your notes in the prompt. Does your letter have an introduction, body, and conclusion? Did you include all the elements of a business letter (heading, inside address, salutation, body, closing, and signature)? Are your ideas clear and easy to follow? Does your tone sound sincere and courteous?

Proofreading Take the remaining time to proofread carefully and make a final copy.

Checking Your Final Copy Read your letter one more time to make sure all of your edits are neat and that your letter is legible. It always helps to review your writing one more time. **Tip:** Save ten minutes to improve your letter.

Listening & Speaking Workshop

Conducting an Interview

Speak with a Purpose

Prepare to interview someone by thinking about what you want to know and then phrasing questions that will elicit, or draw out, the most information. Conduct your interview so that a comfortable conversation occurs between you (the interviewer) and the person you are interviewing (the interviewee).

Think as a Reader/Writer

Consider how writers of editorials and informative articles elaborate on their ideas. Usually, they offer specific details about the who, what, when, where, why, and how of their subject. Sometimes, the best research involves interviewing an expert on a subject (or the person who might be the topic of your research). You can conduct interviews in person, over the phone, or via e-mail. Below are tips on how to get the most out of your interview.

Arrange an Interview

- Ask the person if he or she is willing to be interviewed.
- Arrange a mutually convenient time and place to meet.
- Make sure the place is quiet and there will be no interruptions.
- If you plan to tape-record the interview, ask for permission ahead of time from the interviewee.
- Remember to thank the person for the interview.

Plan for the Interview

- Before you interview someone, spend time thinking about what you hope to learn from this person.
- Write a few open-ended questions to start the conversation. Avoid creating a script.
- Remember to thank the person for the interview.

Conduct the Interview

- Listen carefully. Then, ask for elaboration, based on what the person has said. Keep your focus in mind.
- If the conversation seems to be moving away from what you want to know, re-direct it with a question that will return to your focus.
- Express sensitivity toward the person by backing away from topics that the person seems unwilling to discuss.
- Show respect by not interrupting. Sometimes you need to wait patiently for a person to get to the point.

Reader/Writer
Notebook

Use your **RWN** to complete the activities for this workshop.

- Even when taping an interview, take notes, including what you notice about the interviewee's gestures and attitudes.

- If you do not tape the interview, take the time to write down what the interviewee is saying in note form, listing key words and phrases. Make headings of the person's main points. Under each heading, list details and examples the person uses to explain his or her points.

- Write complete sentences when you are quoting what the person is saying. Quote information you consider important and statements that might be controversial or easily misunderstood. For accuracy, read back what you have quoted to the person you are interviewing.

- Conclude the interview by asking the person if there is anything else he or she wants to share. You can also ask what is the main thing he or she wants you to understand about the topic.

> ## A Good Interview
> - begins with an introduction that informs the interviewee about you and your purpose
> - expresses consideration and appreciation for the interview
> - has a focus; interviewers lead the interview toward what they want to learn
> - ends with a summary of how the conversation has been helpful

The following chart shows more tips for conducting your interview.

Interview Techniques	Question Frames
Use **open-ended** questions that invite the interviewee to describe, narrate, explain, evaluate, compare, and reveal.	• Please share the sequence of events that led you to ____. • I would appreciate a description of ____. • What can you tell me about ____? • Please explain your reasons for ____. • What is your opinion of ____?
Avoid questions that can be answered with "yes" or "no."	• Instead of asking, "Do you like your ____," ask the person to describe what he or she likes best (least) about ____. • What is most interesting (challenging, exciting, frustrating) about ____?
Ask for more detail about a point by using *who, what, when, where, why,* and *how* questions.	• Why did you decide to ____? • How do you feel about ____? • What was the result of ____? • What is a good example of ____?
Ask for clarification if you are having difficulty understanding something he or she said.	• What do you mean by ____? • I'm confused by ____. • I'm struggling to understand ____.
Pause to summarize periodically in order to prevent possible misunderstandings.	• Let me summarize what you said about ____. • I'd like to quote ____. • What I think you said about ____ is ____.

● Speaking Tip

Use gestures and eye contact to communicate interest in what the person is saying. People are more willing to share when they sense the interviewer is genuinely interested. Be sure to listen. Resist the temptation to think about what you will say next instead of paying attention to what the interviewee is saying.

 Learn It Online
Pictures, music, and animation can make your argument more compelling. See how on *MediaScope* at:

go.hrw.com | L10-1189 | **Go**

Writing Skills Review

Business Letter   **Directions:** Read the following business letter. Then, answer the questions that follow.

(1) Dear Mr. Musciano (2) We received your letter and will be happy to list your benefit performance in the, "Doings In Town" column in our June 17 edition. (3) In addition, in order to further support the library's children's bookmobile, we would like to help you publicize your event with a feature article on your band. (4) Our reporter Ritsa Lott will call you this Friday to arrange an interview. (5) I don't know very much about your band, so I will need you to help me out. (6) I am requesting that you send us some photographs and information about the DumpStar Gang that will interest our readers. (7) For example, it would be helpful to have information about the band members, your song list, and places where people can enjoy your music on other ocasions. (8) Please send the materials, a return envelope, and provide your contact information to Ritsa Lott. (9) Thank you for your prompt attention and for your awesome work in support of the library. (10) We are hopeful that the feature article will contribute to the success of your event.

1. What punctuation should appear after the salutation?
   A. comma
   B. colon
   C. period
   D. semicolon

2. Which sentence *best* states the author's purpose?
   A. sentence 1
   B. sentence 2
   C. sentence 3
   D. sentence 4

3. How should the writer revise sentence 2?
   A. correct the spelling of *received*
   B. capitalize *edition*
   C. delete the quotation marks
   D. delete the comma before *Doings*

4. In sentence 3, which of the following words are unnecessary?
   A. in order
   B. in addition
   C. further support
   D. would like to

5. Which of the following sentences is the correct revision for sentence 4?
   A. An interview will be arranged by our reporter Ritsa Lott.
   B. Ritsa Lott, who works as a reporter for our paper, will be contacting you for an interview.
   C. Arranged by our reporter, an interview will be arranged by Ritsa Lott.
   D. Our reporter, Ritsa Lott, will call to arrange an interview.

6. Which detail should be added to the body paragraph?

   A. information about the reporter

   B. a brief history of the newspaper

   C. when the information needs to be received

   D. a description of similar feature articles

7. Which of the following sentences should be deleted from the body paragraph to improve the flow?

   A. sentence 4

   B. sentence 5

   C. sentence 6

   D. sentence 7

8. How might the writer make sentence 6 more concise?

   A. delete the phrase *that will interest our readers* and insert the word *interesting* before *information*

   B. replace the phrase *I am requesting that you* with *I request*

   C. delete *about the DumpStar Gang*

   D. move *DumpStar Gang* before *photographs*

9. What revision is needed in sentence 7?

   A. replace *For example* with *Most of all*

   B. change the spelling of *ocasions* to *occasions*

   C. shorten the sentence by placing a period after *list*

   D. add another example of information that the band needs to provide

10. Which of the following revisions is the best correction for the faulty parallelism in sentence 8?

    A. Please send everything to Ritsa Lott.

    B. Please send the materials, a return envelope, and your contact information to Ritsa Lott.

    C. Please send the materials and a return envelope, and provide your contact information to Ritsa Lott.

    D. Please send the materials, send a return envelope, and send your contact information to Ritsa Lott.

11. How might the writer improve the diction of sentence 9?

    A. replace *thank you* with *I appreciate*

    B. replace *prompt* with *timely*

    C. replace *work* with *employment*

    D. replace *awesome* with *outstanding*

12. Which revision below sentence 10 creates a more active voice?

    A. We hope that the feature article contributes to the success of your event.

    B. We are hoping this article helps.

    C. Hopefully, the feature article will contribute to the success of your event.

    D. It is our hope that the feature article contributes to the success of your event.

13. Which is the best closing for this letter?

    A. love,

    B. from,

    C. sincerely,

    D. fondly,

Resource Center

Handbook of Literary Terms

For more information about a topic or to see related entries, turn to the page(s) indicated on a separate line at the end of most entries. For example, to learn more about *Allusion*, see page 657. On another line are cross-references to entries in this handbook that provide closely related information. For instance, at the end of *Alliteration* are cross-references to *Assonance* and *Rhythm*.

ALLEGORY **Narrative in which characters and settings stand for abstract ideas or moral qualities.** In addition to the literal meaning of the story, an allegory contains a symbolic, or **allegorical,** meaning. Characters and places in allegories often have names that indicate the abstract ideas they stand for: Justice, Deceit, Vanity. Many of Edgar Allan Poe's stories are allegories, including "The Masque of the Red Death" (page 369).

See pages 308, 367.

ALLITERATION **Repetition of the same or similar consonant sounds in words that are close together.** Although alliteration most often consists of sounds that begin words, it may also involve sounds that occur within words:

> Where the quail is whistling betwixt the woods
> and the wheat-lot.
> —Walt Whitman, from "Song of Myself"

See pages 647, 734, 739.
See also Assonance, Rhythm.

ALLUSION **Reference to a statement, a person, a place, an event, or a thing that is known from literature, history, religion, myth, politics, sports, science, or the arts.** Can you identify the literary allusion in the cartoon at the top of the next column? If not, turn to page 899.

See page 657.

"Et tu, Baxter?"

AMBIGUITY **Element of uncertainty in a text, in which something can be interpreted in a number of different ways.** Ambiguity adds a layer of complexity to a story, for it presents us with a variety of possible interpretations, all of which are valid. **Subtleties,** or fine distinctions, help create ambiguity.

ANALOGY **Comparison made between two things to show how they are alike.** In "The Man in the Water" (page 391), the writer draws an analogy between a man's struggle to stay alive in freezing water and a battle against "an implacable, impersonal enemy."

See also Metaphor, Simile.

ANECDOTE **Very brief account of a particular incident.** Like **parables,** anecdotes are often used by philosophers and teachers of religion to point out truths about life.

See also Fable, Folk Tale, Parable.

ASIDE **In a play, words spoken by a character directly to the audience or to another character but not overheard by others onstage.** In Act II, Scene 2 (page 889) of *Julius Caesar,* Trebonius and Brutus speak ominous asides that Caesar cannot hear.

See page 787.

ASSONANCE **Repetition of similar vowel sounds followed by different consonant sounds in words that are close together.** Like alliteration, assonance creates musical and rhythmic effects:

> And so all the night-tide, I lie down by the side,
> Of my darling, my darling, my life and my bride
>
> —Edgar Allan Poe, from "Annabel Lee"

See also *Alliteration, Rhythm.*

ATMOSPHERE **See Mood.**

AUTOBIOGRAPHY **Account by a writer of his or her own life.** "Typhoid Fever" (page 485) is a selection from a famous autobiography by Frank McCourt. An excerpt from Gordon Parks' autobiography *A Choice of Weapons* appears on page 471.

See also *Biography.*

BALLAD **Song or songlike poem that tells a story.** Ballads often tell stories that have tragic endings. Most ballads have a regular pattern of **rhythm** and **rhyme** and use simple language and repetition. Generally they have a **refrain**—lines or words repeated at regular intervals. **Folk ballads** (such as "Bonny Barbara Allan," page 722) were composed by unknown singers and passed on orally for generations before being written down. **Literary ballads** and some country-and-western songs imitate folk ballads.

See page 621.

BIOGRAPHY **Account of a person's life written or told by another person.** A classic American biography is Carl Sandburg's multivolume work about Abraham Lincoln. Today biographies of writers, actors, sports stars, and TV personalities are often bestsellers.

See pages 442, 453.
See also *Autobiography.*

BLANK VERSE **Poetry written in unrhymed iambic pentameter.** *Blank verse* means that the poetry is unrhymed. *Iambic pentameter* means that each line contains five iambs; an **iamb** is a type of **metrical foot** that consists of an unstressed syllable followed by a stressed syllable (˘ ′). Blank verse is the most important metrical form in English dramatic and epic poetry and the major verse line in Shakespeare's plays. One reason blank verse has been popular, even with some modern poets, is that it combines the naturalness of unrhymed verse and the structure of metrical verse.

> When I see birches bend to left and right
> Across the line of straighter darker trees,
> I like to think some boy's been swinging them.
>
> —Robert Frost, from "Birches"

See also *Iambic Pentameter, Meter.*

CHARACTER **Individual in a story, poem, or play.** A character always has human traits, even if the character is an animal, as in Aesop's fables. In myths the characters are divinities or heroes with super human powers, such as the hero Theseus in "Theseus"(page 1028) or Sigurd in "Sigurd, the Dragon Slayer" (page 1050). Most characters are ordinary human beings, however.

A writer can reveal a character's personality by doing the following:
1. telling us directly what the character is like (generous, deceitful, timid, and so on)
2. describing how the character looks and dresses
3. letting us hear the character speak
4. letting us listen to the character's inner thoughts and feelings
5. revealing what other people think or say about the character
6. showing the character's actions

The first method listed above is called **direct characterization:** The writer tells us directly what the character is like. The other five methods are **indirect characterization:** We have to put clues together to figure out what a character is like, just as we do in real life when we are getting to know someone.

Static and flat characters often function as **subordinate characters** in a story. This means that they may play important roles in a story, but they are not the main actors in the plot.

A **static character** does not change much in the course of a story. A **dynamic character,** on the other hand, changes in some important ways as a result of the story's action. **Flat characters** have only one or two personality traits and can be summed up in a single phrase. In contrast, **round characters** are complex and have many different traits. The needs or conflicts that drive a character are called **motivation.**

See pages 102–103, 106–107.
See also Protagonist.

COMEDY   **In general, a story that ends happily.** The hero of a comedy is usually an ordinary character who overcomes a series of obstacles that block what he or she wants. Many comedies have a boy-meets-girl (or girl-meets-boy) plot, in which young lovers must face figures from an older generation who do not want the young lovers to marry. At the end of such comedies, the lovers marry, and everyone celebrates the renewal of life and love, as in Shakespeare's play *A Midsummer Night's Dream.* In structure and characterization a comedy is the opposite of a **tragedy.**

In a serious literary work a humorous scene is said to provide **comic relief.**

See pages 784, 815.
See also Drama, Tragedy.

CONFLICT   **Struggle or clash between opposing characters, forces, or emotions.** In an **external conflict** a character struggles against an outside force, which may be another character, society as a whole, or something in nature. In "Into Thin Air" (page 508), mountain climbers find themselves in a fight with the harsh laws of nature.

An **internal conflict** is a struggle between opposing needs, desires, or emotions within a single character. Many works, especially longer ones, contain both internal and external conflicts, and an external conflict often leads to internal problems.

See pages 4–5, 103.

CONNOTATIONS   **All the meanings, associations, or emotions that a word suggests.** For example, an expensive restaurant might advertise its delicious "cuisine" rather than its delicious "cooking." *Cuisine* and *cooking* have the same **denotation** (literal meaning): "prepared food." However, *cuisine,* a word from French, has connotations of elegance and sophistication; *cooking,* a plain English word, suggests the plainness of everyday food. Connotations play an important role in creating **diction, mood,** and **tone.**

See pages 560, 575.
See also Diction, Mood, Tone.

COUPLET   **Two consecutive lines of poetry that form a unit, often emphasized by rhythm or rhyme.** Since the Middle Ages, the couplet has been used to express a completed thought or to provide a sense of closure, as in this final speech from Shakespeare's play *Julius Caesar:*

> So call the field to rest, and let's away
> To part the glories of this happy day.

DESCRIPTION   **Type of writing intended to create a mood or an emotion or to re-create a person, a place, a thing, an event, or an experience.** Description uses **images** that appeal to the senses, helping us imagine how a subject looks, sounds, smells, tastes, or feels. Description is used in fiction, nonfiction, drama, and poetry.

See also Imagery.

DIALECT   **Way of speaking that is characteristic of a particular region or group of people.** A dialect may have a distinct vocabulary, pronunciation system, and grammar. In the United States the dialect used in formal writing and spoken by most TV and radio announcers is known as standard English. This is the dialect taught in schools. To bring characters to life, writers often use dialects.

DIALOGUE   **Conversation between two or more characters.** Dramas are made up of dialogue, which is also important in novels and stories and in some poems and nonfiction.

See page 787.

DICTION   **Writer's or speaker's choice of words.** Diction is an essential element of a writer's **style.** A writer can choose words that are simple or flowery *(clothing/apparel),* modern or old-fashioned *(dress/frock),* general or specific *(pants/designer jeans).* Writers choose words for their connotations (emotional associations) as well as their literal meanings, or denotations.

See page 443.
See also Connotations, Tone.

DRAMA   **Story that is written to be acted for an audience.** The action of a drama is driven by a character who wants something and who takes steps to get it. The major elements of a dramatic plot are **exposition, complications, climax,** and **resolution.** The term *drama* is also used to refer to a serious play that is neither a **comedy** nor a **tragedy.**

See pages 784–787, 822.

DRAMATIC MONOLOGUE **A poem in which a speaker addresses one or more silent listeners, often reflecting on a specific problem or situation.** Although the person addressed in a dramatic monologue does not speak, we can often discover something about the listener or listeners by paying close attention to the speaker's words. The most famous dramatic monologues in English literature are those written by Robert Browning. Here are the opening lines of "My Last Duchess," spoken by a duke to his agent. The agent remains silent. As the monologue continues, we learn the duke's dark secret:

That's my last Duchess painted on the wall,
Looking as if she were alive. I call
That piece a wonder, now: Frà Pandolf's hands
Worked busily a day, and there she stands.
Will 't please you sit and look at her?

—Robert Browning, from
"My Last Duchess"

EPIC **Long narrative poem that relates the great deeds of a larger-than-life hero who embodies the values of a particular society.** Most epics include elements of myth, legend, folklore, and history; their tone is serious and their language grand. Epic heroes undertake quests to achieve something of tremendous value to themselves or their society. Homer's *Odyssey* and *Iliad* and Virgil's *Aeneid* are the best-known epics in the Western tradition. The great epic of India is the *Mahabharata;* Japan's is *The Tale of the Heike;* and Mali's is *Sundiata.*

ESSAY **Short piece of nonfiction that examines a single subject from a limited point of view.** Most essays can be classified as personal or formal. A **personal essay** (sometimes called **informal**) is generally subjective, revealing a great deal about the writer's personality and feelings. Its tone is conversational, sometimes even humorous.

A **formal essay** is usually serious, objective, and impersonal in tone. Because formal essays are often written to inform or persuade, they are expected to be factual, logical, and tightly organized.

EXPOSITION **Type of writing that explains, gives information, or clarifies an idea.** Exposition is generally objective and formal in tone (as in a magazine article on nutrition).

Exposition is also the term for the first part of a plot (also called the **basic situation**), which presents the main characters and their conflicts.

See also *Plot.*

FABLE **Brief story in prose or verse that teaches a moral, or a practical lesson about life.** The characters of most fables are animals that behave and speak like humans. Some of the most popular fables are those attributed to Aesop, who scholars believe was a slave in ancient Greece. Other widely read fables are those in the *Panchatantra,* ancient Indian tales about the art of ruling wisely.

See also *Folk Tale, Parable.*

FIGURE OF SPEECH **Word or phrase that describes one thing in terms of another and that is not meant to be understood on a literal level.** Figures of speech, or **figurative language,** always involve some sort of imaginative comparison between seemingly unlike things. The most common are the **simile** ("My heart is like a singing bird"), the **metaphor** ("Life's but a walking shadow"), and **personification** ("Death has reared himself a throne").

See pages 443, 645, 695.
See also *Metaphor, Personification, Simile, Symbol.*

FLASHBACK **Scene in a movie, play, short story, novel, or narrative poem that interrupts the present action of the plot to show events that happened at an earlier time.** In "Everyday Use" (page 117), the narrator uses a flashback to a house fire to explain family conflicts. Flashbacks are commonly used in movies.

See pages 4, 37.

FLASH-FORWARD **Scene in a movie, play, short story, novel, or narrative poem that interrupts the present action of the plot to shift into the future.** Writers may use a flash-forward to create dramatic irony. By means of the flash-forward, we know the future, but the story characters do not.

FOIL **Character who serves as a contrast to another character.** Writers use a foil to emphasize differences between two characters. In *Julius Caesar,* the solemn, self-controlled Octavius is a foil for the excitable, impetuous Antony.

See page 784.

FOLK TALE Anonymous traditional story originally passed down orally from generation to generation. Folk tales are told in every culture, and similar tales are told throughout the world. Many of these stories have been written down. Scholars draw a sharp distinction between folk tales and myths. **Myths,** unlike folk tales, are stories about humans and gods and are basically religious in nature. Examples of folk tales are fairy tales, fables, legends, ghost stories, tall tales, anecdotes, and even jokes. Folk tales tend to travel, so the same plot often appears in several cultures. For example, there are said to be nine hundred versions of the folk tale about Cinderella.

> See pages 61, 1037.
> See also *Fable, Myth, Tall Tale.*

FORESHADOWING The use of clues to hint at events that will occur later in the plot. Foreshadowing arouses the reader's curiosity and increases **suspense.** In Act I, Scene 3, of *Julius Caesar* (page 859), references to violent disturbances in the heavens foreshadow the turbulence and violence that will soon occur in the human world.

> See pages 5, 37.
> See also *Plot, Suspense.*

FREE VERSE Poetry that does not have a regular meter or rhyme scheme. Poets writing in free verse try to capture the natural rhythms of ordinary speech. To create musical effects, they may use **alliteration, assonance, internal rhyme,** and **onomatopoeia.** They also often repeat words or grammatical structures.

> Women sit or move to and fro, some old,
>   some young,
> The young are beautiful—but the old are more
>   beautiful than the young.
>
> —Walt Whitman, from
> "Beautiful Women"

> See also *Alliteration, Assonance, Meter, Onomatopoeia, Rhythm.*

GENRE The category that a work of literature is classified under. Five major genres in literature are **nonfiction, fiction, poetry, drama,** and **myth.** Collections 7 and 8 of this book are organized by genre: by poetry and by drama.

HAIKU Japanese verse form consisting of three lines and usually seventeen syllables (five in the first line, seven in the second, and five in the third). The writer of a haiku uses association and suggestion to describe a particular moment of discovery or enlightenment. A haiku often presents an image of daily life that relates to a particular season. Many modern American poets (such as William Carlos Williams, Amy Lowell, Ezra Pound, Richard Wright, and Gary Snyder) have tried to capture the spirit of haiku, although they have not always followed the form strictly.

HYPERBOLE Figure of speech that uses exaggeration to express strong emotion or create a comic effect. Writers often use hyperbole, also called **overstatement,** to intensify a description or to emphasize the essential nature of something. If you say that a limousine is as long as an ocean liner, you are using hyperbole.

IAMBIC PENTAMETER Line of poetry made up of five iambs. An **iamb** is a metrical foot consisting of an unstressed syllable followed by a stressed syllable, as in dĕný and ĕxpéct. Iambic pentameter is by far the most common meter in English poetry.

> See also *Blank Verse, Meter.*

IDIOM Expression peculiar to a particular language that means something different from the literal meaning of the words. "It's raining cats and dogs" and "We heard it straight from the horse's mouth" are idioms of American English. One of the difficulties of translating a work from another language is translating idioms.

IMAGERY Language that appeals to the senses. Imagery is used in all types of writing but is especially important in poetry. Most images are visual—that is, they create in the reader's mind pictures that appeal to the sense of sight. Imagery may also appeal to the senses of hearing, smell, touch, and taste, as in the lines on the next page about winter. (*Saw* in line 2 is a wise saying; *crabs* in line 5 are crab apples; and to *keel* is to cool by stirring.)

> When all aloud the wind doth blow,
>   And coughing drowns the parson's saw,
> And birds sit brooding in the snow,
>   And Marian's nose looks red and raw,
> When roasted crabs hiss in the bowl,
> Then nightly sings the staring owl—Tu whit,
> Tu-who, a merry note,
> While greasy Joan doth keel the pot.
>
> —William Shakespeare
> from *Love's Labor's Lost*

See pages 17, 644, 657, 677.

INCONGRUITY (IHN kuhn GROO uh tee) **A lack of fitness or appropriateness.** When someone goes to a formal dinner party dressed in a bathing suit, the situation is incongruous. Incongruity is often used to create situational irony in literature.

See also *Irony*.

INVERSION **Reversal of normal word order in a sentence.** The normal word order in an English sentence is subject-verb-complement (if there is a complement). Modifiers are usually placed immediately before or after the word they modify. Poets use inversion to give emphasis and variety and to create rhymes or accommodate a meter.

> Open here I flung the shutter, when, with many
>   a flirt and flutter,
> In there stepped a stately Raven of the saintly
>   days of yore;
> Not the least obeisance made he; not a minute
>   stopped or stayed he. . . .
>
> —Edgar Allan Poe, from
> "The Raven"

IRONY **Contrast or discrepancy between expectation and reality.** In **verbal irony** a speaker says one thing but means the opposite. In Shakespeare's *Julius Caesar*, Antony uses **verbal irony** during his funeral oration for Caesar. When he insists that "Brutus is an honorable man," he means precisely the opposite.

In **situational irony** what actually happens is the opposite of what is expected or appropriate. In Tim O'Brien's story "Where Have You Gone, Charming Billy?"

(page 131), we feel a strong sense of irony when Paul Berlin is overcome with laughter upon being told of the death of his fellow soldier, Billy Boy Watkins.

Dramatic irony occurs when the reader or the audience knows something important that a character does not know.

See pages 257, 308–309.
See also *Tone*.

LYRIC POETRY **Poetry that expresses a speaker's emotions or thoughts and does not tell a story.** The term **lyric** comes from ancient Greece, where such poems were recited to the accompaniment of a stringed instrument called a lyre. Most lyric poems are short, and they imply, rather than state directly, a single strong emotion. Li-Young Lee's "Eating Together" (page 663) and John Masefield's "Sea Fever" (page 719) are lyric poems.

See pages 644, 683.
See also *Sonnet*.

MAGIC REALISM **Style of fiction, commonly associated with contemporary Latin American writers, in which fantasy and reality are casually combined, producing humorous and thought-provoking results.** "A Very Old Man with Enormous Wings" (page 355), in which an old, winged, humanlike creature lands in a poor family's backyard, is an example of magic realism.

See pages 314, 353.

METAPHOR **Figure of speech that makes a comparison between two unlike things without using a connective word such as *like, as, than,* or *resembles.*** Some metaphors, such as Gerard Manley Hopkins's comparison "I am soft sift / In an hourglass," are **direct.** (If he had written, "I am *like* soft sift . . . ," he would have been using a **simile.**) Other metaphors are **implied,** such as the one in Walt Whitman's lines "O Captain! my Captain! our fearful trip is done, / The ship has weather'd every rack, the prize we sought is won." The images imply a comparison between a captain commanding his ship and a president leading his country (in this case, the president was Lincoln).

An **extended metaphor** is developed over several lines or throughout an entire poem. In the "The Seven Ages of Man" (page 968), which is a speech from Shakespeare's play *As You Like It,* an extended metaphor is used to compare the stages of a man's life to an actor playing many parts on the stage.

A **mixed metaphor** is the inconsistent combination of two or more metaphors. Mixed metaphors are usually unintentional and often humorous: "It's no use closing the barn door after the milk has been spilled."

See pages 274, 443, 645.
See also *Analogy, Figure of Speech, Personification, Simile, Symbol.*

METER **A generally regular pattern of stressed and unstressed syllables in poetry.** To indicate the metrical pattern of a poem, we mark the stressed syllables with the symbol (′) and the unstressed syllables with the symbol (‿). Analyzing the metrical pattern of a poem in this way is called **scanning** the poem, or **scansion**.

Meter is measured in units called feet. A **foot** usually consists of one stressed syllable and one or more unstressed syllables. Here are examples of the standard feet in English poetry:

1. **iamb** (iambic): an unstressed syllable followed by a stressed syllable, as in *forget, deceive*. This line from "The Eagle" by Alfred, Lord Tennyson, has four *iambic* feet:

   The wrinkled sea beneath him crawls

2. **trochee** (trochaic): a stressed syllable followed by an unstressed syllable, as in *listen, lonely*. This line from William Shakespeare's *Macbeth* is in trochees:

   Double, double, toil and trouble

3. **anapest** (anapestic): two unstressed syllables followed by one stressed syllable, as in *understand, luncheonette*. This line from "The Destruction of Sennacherib" by George Gordon, Lord Byron, is in anapests:

   The Assyrian came down like the wolf on the fold

4. **dactyl** (dactylic): one stressed syllable followed by two unstressed syllables, as in *excellent, temperate*. This extract from Shakespeare's *Macbeth* contains dactyls:

   . . . you murdering ministers . . .

5. **spondee** (spondaic): two stressed syllables, as in *heartbeat* and *football*. This foot is used for emphasis, as in these lines from *Leaves of Grass* by Walt Whitman:

   Come up here, bard, bard,
   Come up here, soul, soul. . . .

A metrical line is named for the type of foot and the number of feet in the line. (*Dimeter* is two feet, *trimeter* three feet, *tetrameter* four feet, and *pentameter* five feet.) Thus, a line of five iambs is called *iambic pentameter;* a line of four trochees is *trochaic tetrameter.*

See pages 646, 717.
See also *Blank Verse, Iambic Pentameter.*

MOOD **A story's atmosphere or the feeling it evokes.** Mood is often created by the story's setting. A story set on a dreary moor where cold water seeps into the hero's boots will probably convey a mood of suspense and uneasiness. A story set in a garden full of sunlight and the chirps of birds will probably create a mood of peace. Edgar Allan Poe's bizarre setting of "The Masque of the Red Death" (page 369) creates a dizzying atmosphere of horror.

See also *Setting.*

MYTH **Traditional story that is rooted in a particular culture, is basically religious, and usually serves to explain a belief, a ritual, or a mysterious natural phenomenon.** Most myths grew out of religious rituals; almost all of them involve the influence of gods on human affairs. Every culture has its own mythology. For centuries the myths of ancient Greece and Rome were influential in the Western world.

See pages 853, 898, 909, 926.

NARRATION **Type of writing that tells about a series of related events.** Narration can be long (an entire book) or short (a brief anecdote). Narration is most often found in fiction, drama, and narrative poetry (such as epics and ballads), but it also is used in nonfiction works (such as biographies and essays).

NARRATOR **The voice telling a story.** The choice of a narrator is very important in storytelling. For example, in "By the Waters of Babylon" (page 63), we know only what the narrator knows, and like him, we must figure out the mysteries of the Place of the Gods.

See pages 190–191, 199, 225.
See also *Point of View.*

NONFICTION **Prose writing that deals with real people, things, events, and places.** The most popular forms are biography and autobiography. Essays, newspaper stories, magazine articles, historical accounts, scientific reports, and even personal diaries and letters are also nonfiction.

NOVEL **Long fictional prose narrative, usually of more than fifty thousand words.** In general, the novel uses the same basic literary elements as the short story **(plot, character, setting, theme,** and **point of view),** but these elements are usually more fully developed in the novel. Many novels have several subplots, for instance. Some modern novels are basically character studies, with only the barest plot. Others concentrate on setting, tone, or even language itself.

ONOMATOPOEIA (ON uh MAT uh PEE uh) **Use of a word whose sound imitates or suggests its meaning.** *Buzz, splash,* and *bark* are examples of onomatopoeia. In poetry, onomatopoeia reinforces meaning and creates evocative and musical sound effects.

See pages 537, 627.

PARABLE **Brief story that teaches a lesson about life.** A parable has human characters, and its events are drawn from everyday life. Parables usually illustrate moral or religious lessons. A fable, in contrast, usually has animal characters and teaches a practical lesson about how to succeed in life. The most famous parables in Western literature are found in the Bible.

See also *Fable, Folk Tale.*

PARADOX **A statement or a situation that seems to be a contradiction but that reveals a truth.** Paradoxes are designed to make readers stop and think. They often express aspects of life that are mysterious, surprising, or difficult to describe. When the Ancient Mariner in Samuel Taylor Coleridge's poem cries, "Water, water everywhere, / Nor any drop to drink," he is expressing a paradox. He is dying of thirst adrift in the ocean, the water from which he cannot drink.

PARALLELISM **Repetition of words, phrases, or sentences that have the same grammatical structure or that state a similar idea.** Parallelism, or parallel structure, helps make lines rhythmic and memorable and heightens their emotional effect:

> Bring me my bow of burning gold!
> Bring me my arrows of desire!
> Bring me my spear! O clouds, unfold!
> Bring me my chariot of fire!
>
> —William Blake, from
> "Jerusalem"

PERSONA **Mask or voice assumed by a writer.** Authors often take on other identities in their works. In a short story a writer may assume a persona by using a first-person narrator. When a poet is not the speaker of a poem, the poet is creating a persona.

See also *Point of View, Speaker.*

PERSONIFICATION **Type of metaphor in which a nonhuman thing or quality is talked about as if it were human.** In the following example, trees are personified as women throwing off their robes.

> The trees are undressing, and fling in many
>   places—
> On the gray road, the roof, the window sill—
> Their radiant robes and ribbons and yellow
> laces.
>
> —Thomas Hardy
>   from "Last Week in October"

See pages 535, 583.
See also *Figure of Speech, Metaphor.*

PERSUASION **Type of writing designed to change the way a reader or listener thinks or acts.** Persuasive writing can be found in speeches, newspaper editorials, essays, and advertisements.

See page 459.

PLOT **Series of related events that make up a story or drama.** Plot is "what happens" in a story, novel, or play. A story map shows the parts of a plot.

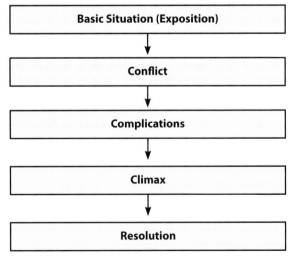

The **climax** is the most intense moment in the plot, the moment at which something happens that reveals how the conflict will turn out. In the **resolution,** or denouement, all the problems in the story are resolved, and the story is brought to a close.

See pages 4–5, 15.

POETRY Type of rhythmic, compressed language that uses figures of speech and imagery to appeal to the reader's emotions and imagination. The major forms of poetry are **lyric** and **narrative.** A popular type of lyric is the **sonnet.** Two major types of narrative are the **epic** and the **ballad.** Although poetry is one of the oldest forms of human expression, it is extremely difficult to define.

See pages 644–647, 650–651.
See also *Ballad, Epic, Lyric Poetry, Sonnet.*

POINT OF VIEW Vantage point from which a writer narrates, or tells, a story. The three main points of view are omniscient, third-person-limited, and first-person.

In the **omniscient** (or "all-knowing") **point of view,** the narrator plays no part in the story but can tell us what all the characters are thinking and feeling as well as what is happening in other places. For example, in "Through the Tunnel" (page 325), the storyteller can tell us what both Jerry and his mother are thinking and feeling.

In the **third-person-limited point of view,** the narrator, who plays no part in the story, zooms in on the thoughts and feelings of one character.

In the **first-person point of view,** the narrator (using the first-person pronoun *I*) is a character in the story. When we read a story told in the first person, we hear and see only what the narrator hears and sees. We must ask ourselves if the narrator is **credible,** or **reliable.** An **unreliable narrator** does not always know what is happening in the story, or he or she might be lying or telling us only part of the story. For example, in "By the Waters of Babylon" (see page 63), we cannot rely on the narrator to tell us the mystery of the Place of the Gods because he does not know it.

See also *Narrator.*

PROTAGONIST Main character in fiction or drama. The protagonist is the character we focus our attention on, the person who sets the plot in motion. The character or force that blocks the protagonist is called the **antagonist.** Most protagonists are round, dynamic characters who change in some important way by the end of the story, novel, or play. The antagonist is often, but not always, the villain in a story. Similarly, the protagonist is often, but not always, the hero.

See also *Character.*

PUN Play on the multiple meanings of a word or on two words that sound alike but have different meanings. Many jokes and riddles are based on puns. ("When is a doctor most annoyed?" Answer: "When he runs out of patients.") Shakespeare was one of the greatest punsters of all time. In Antony's speech to the conspirators after Caesar's murder in *The Tragedy of Julius Caesar* (page 904), Antony puns on the expression "to let blood." Doctors used to draw, or let, blood from sick people to cure them; murderers also "let blood."

REFRAIN Repeated word, phrase, line, or group of lines. Although refrains are usually associated with poetry and songs, they are sometimes used in prose, especially in speeches. Refrains create rhythm and may also build suspense or emphasize important words or ideas.

RHYME Repetition of accented vowel sounds and all sounds following them in words that are close together in a poem. *Heart* and *start* rhyme, as do *plaster* and *faster.* The most common type of rhyme, **end rhyme,** occurs at the ends of lines.

> When she I loved looked every day
> Fresh as a rose in June,
> I to her cottage bent my way,
> Beneath the evening moon.
>
> —William Wordsworth from
> "Strange Fits of Passion
> Have I Known"

The pattern of rhymed lines in a poem is called its **rhyme scheme.** You indicate a rhyme scheme by giving each new end rhyme a new letter of the alphabet. For example, the rhyme scheme in Wordsworth's stanza is *abab.*

Internal rhymes occur within lines.

> The warm sun is failing, the bleak wind is
> wailing,
> The bare boughs are sighing, the pale flowers
> are dying . . .
>
> —Percy Bysshe Shelley from
> "Autumn: A Dirge"

Words that sound similar but do not rhyme exactly are called **approximate rhymes** (or **half rhymes, slant rhymes,** or **imperfect rhymes**). The approximate rhymes at the ends of lines in this stanza from a poem about war keep the reader off balance and even uneasy, in keeping with the poem's subject:

> Let the boy try along this bayonet blade
> How cold steel is, and keen with hunger of
> blood;
> Blue with all malice, like a madman's flash;
> And thinly drawn with famishing for flesh.
>
> —Wilfred Owen, from "Arms
> and the Boy"

See pages 647, 717.

RHYTHM   **Musical quality in language, produced by repetition.** Rhythm occurs naturally in all forms of spoken and written language. Poems written in **meter** create rhythm by a strict pattern of stressed and unstressed syllables. Writers can also create rhythm by repeating grammatical structures, by using pauses, by varying line lengths, and by balancing long and short words or phrases.

See page 646.
See also *Meter*.

ROMANCE   **Centuries ago, in France and England, a romance was a verse narrative about the adventures of a hero who undertakes a quest for a high ideal.** The tales of King Arthur are typical romances. The term *romance* later came to mean any story set in a world of wish fulfillment, with larger-than-life characters having superhuman powers. Romances usually involve a series of adventures that end with good triumphing over evil. Fairy tales and western movies are often built on the old romance plots and use the characters typical of romantic literature.

See page 1069.

SATIRE   **Type of writing that ridicules human weakness, vice, or folly in order to reveal a weakness or to bring about social reform.** Satires often try to persuade the reader to do or believe something by showing the opposite view as absurd—or even as vicious and inhumane. One of the favorite techniques of the satirist is **exaggeration**—overstating something to make it look worse than it is.

See also *Hyperbole, Irony*.

SCENE DESIGN   **Sets, lights, costumes, and props, which bring a play to life onstage. Sets** are the furnishings and scenery that suggest the time and place of the action. **Props** (short for *properties*) are all the objects that the actors use onstage, such as books, telephones, or suitcases.

See page 786.

SETTING   **Time and place of a story or play.** Setting can function in several ways in a story. It can provide atmosphere, as the ice-coated world does in Jim Heynen's "What Happened During the Ice Storm" (page 214). Setting may provide conflict in a story, as it does in Tim O'Brien's "Where Have You Gone, Charming Billy?" (page 131). One of the most important functions of setting is to reveal character. In Alice Walker's "Everyday Use" (page 117), the narrator's home helps show us who she is and what her life is like.

See also *Mood*.

SHORT STORY   **Short piece of narrative fiction.** Edgar Allan Poe (see page 368), who lived and wrote during the first half of the nineteenth century, is often credited with writing the first short stories. He defined the short story (which he called the "prose tale") as a narrative that can be read in a single sitting and that creates a "single effect."

SIMILE   **Figure of speech that makes a comparison between two seemingly unlike things by using a connective word such as *like, as, than,* or *resembles*.** Here is a simile that creates a dramatic visual image; like any good figure of speech, Hardy's simile is original and vivid:

See pages 645, 705.
See also *Analogy, Figure of Speech, Metaphor.*

SOLILOQUY **Long speech in which a character who is alone onstage expresses private thoughts or feelings.** The soliloquy, especially popular in Shakespeare's day, is an old dramatic convention. Near the beginning of Act II in *Julius Caesar* (page 869), Brutus's speech in which he decides to join the conspiracy against Caesar is a soliloquy.

See page 787.

SONNET **Fourteen-line lyric poem, usually written in iambic pentameter.** There are two major types of sonnets. The **Italian sonnet,** also called the **Petrarchan sonnet,** is named after the fourteenth-century Italian poet Francesco Petrarch, who popularized the form. The Petrarchan sonnet has two parts: an eight-line **octave** with the rhyme scheme *abbaabba*, and a six-line **sestet** with the rhyme scheme *cdecde*. The octave usually presents a problem, poses a question, or expresses an idea, which the sestet then resolves, answers, or drives home.

The other major sonnet form is called the **Shakespearean sonnet,** or the **English sonnet.** It has three **quatrains** (four-line units) followed by a concluding **couplet** (two-line unit). The three quatrains often express related ideas or examples; the couplet sums up the poet's conclusion or message. The most common rhyme scheme for the Shakespearean sonnet is *abab cdcd efef gg*. The Shakespearean sonnet "Shall I Compare Thee to a Summer's Day?" can be found on page 691.

See pages 644, 690.
See also *Lyric Poetry.*

SPEAKER **The voice that is talking to us in a poem.** Sometimes the speaker is the same as the poet, but the poet may also create a different voice, speaking as a child, a woman, a man, a nation, an animal, or even an object.

See page 661.
See also *Dramatic Monologue, Persona.*

STANZA **Group of consecutive lines that form a single unit in a poem.** A stanza in a poem is something like a paragraph in prose: It often expresses a unit of thought. A stanza may consist of only one line or of any number of lines beyond that. John Updike's "Ex–Basketball Player" (page 736) consists of five six-line stanzas, each expressing a unit of thought.

See also *Sonnet.*

STYLE **The particular way in which a writer uses language.** Style is created mainly through diction (word choice), use of **figurative language,** and sentence patterns. Style can be described as plain, ornate, formal, ironic, conversational, sentimental, and so on.

See pages 355, 443, 453.

SUSPENSE **The uncertainty or anxiety we feel about what is going to happen next in a story.** Writers often create suspense by dropping hints or clues foreshadowing something—especially something bad—that is going to happen later. Writers also create suspense by setting up time limits, as in "R.M.S. Titanic" (page 398), where our suspense builds as we are shown the minutes ticking away.

See page 5.
See also *Foreshadowing, Plot.*

SYMBOL **Person, place, thing, or event that stands both for itself and for something beyond itself.** Many symbols have become so widely recognized that they are **public symbols:** In Western cultures, for example, most people recognize the heart as a symbol of love and the snake as a symbol of evil. Writers often invent new, personal symbols. For example, in this mysterious poem, "The Sick Rose," what might the rose and the worm symbolize?

> O Rose, thou art sick!
> The invisible worm,
> That flies in the night,
> In the howling storm,
> Has found out thy bed
> Of crimson joy:
> And his dark secret love
> Does thy life destroy.
>
> —William Blake

See pages 308, 377.
See also *Figure of Speech.*

TALL TALE **An outrageously exaggerated and obviously unbelievable humorous story.** In pre-TV days, the tall tale was a kind of oral entertainment. In the American Southwest, cowboys sat around their campfires telling stories about Pecos Bill, who invented the lariat, rode a bucking Kansas tornado, and dug the Rio Grande river. Other tall tale heroes include the Northwest logger Paul Bunyan (and Babe, his gigantic blue ox), the Pennsylvania steel man Joe Magarac, and the New England fisherman Captain Stormalong. Tall tales were told about real-life figures, too, such as Tennessee frontiersman Davy Crockett and sharpshooter Annie Oakley.

A modern **urban tall tale**—perennially rumored to be true—tells of a baby pet alligator someone flushed down a toilet in New York City. The result, according to this tale, is that monster alligators populate the sewers beneath the city.

See also *Folk Tale.*

THEME **The central idea or insight about human life revealed by a work of literature.** A theme is not the same as a work's subject, which can usually be expressed in a word or two: old age, ambition, love. The theme is the revelation the writer wishes us to discover about that subject. There is no single correct way to express a theme, and sometimes a work has several themes. Many works have **ambiguous themes;** that is, they have no clear single meaning but are open to a variety of interpretations, even opposing ones. Some themes are so commonly found in the literature of all cultures and all ages that they are called **universal themes.** Here are some universal themes found in stories throughout the ages: "Heroes must undergo trials and endure losses before they can claim their rightful kingdom." "Arrogance and pride can bring destruction." "When the rule of law is broken, chaos and anarchy will result." "Love will endure and triumph over evil."

Although a few stories, poems, and plays have themes that are stated directly, most themes are implied. The reader must piece together all the clues the writer has provided to arrive at a discovery of the work's total meaning. Two of the most important clues to consider are the way the main character has changed and the way the conflict has been resolved.

See pages 275, 522, 677, 967.

TONE **The attitude a writer takes toward a subject, a character, or the reader.** Tone is conveyed through the writer's choice of words and details. For example, Tim O'Brien's story "Where Have You Gone, Charming Billy?" (page 131) is ironic in tone. John Masefield's "Sea Fever" (page 719) has a nostalgic tone for a life that is now past.

See pages 186, 443.
See also *Connotations, Diction, Irony.*

TRAGEDY **Play, novel, or other narrative depicting serious and important events in which the main character comes to an unhappy end.** In a tragedy, the main character is usually dignified and courageous and often high ranking. This character's downfall may be caused by a **tragic flaw** (a serious character weakness) or by forces beyond the hero's control. The tragic hero usually wins self-knowledge and wisdom, even though he or she suffers defeat, possibly even death. Shakespeare's *The Tragedy of Julius Caesar* (page 843) is a tragedy. Tragedy is distinct from **comedy,** in which an ordinary character overcomes obstacles to get what he or she wants. At the end of most comedies, the characters are all happily integrated into society (comedies often end with weddings). Tragedies often end with death or separation or alienation.

See page 784.
See also *Comedy, Drama.*

VOICE **The writer's or speaker's distinctive use of language in a text.** Voice is created by a writer's **tone** and **diction,** or choice of words. Some writers have such a distinctive voice that you can identify their works on the basis of voice alone. Frank McCourt creates a distinctive voice in his memoir about growing up in Ireland, "Typhoid Fever" (page 485).

See page 209.

Handbook of Reading and Informational Terms

For more information about a topic, turn to the page(s) in this book indicated on a separate line at the end of most entries. To learn more about *Inference,* for example, turn to page 1209.

The words in **boldface** are other key terms, with definitions provided in context. On another line there are cross-references to entries in this *Handbook* that provide closely related information. For instance, *Logic* contains a cross-reference to *Logical Order.*

ARGUMENT A series of statements in a text designed to convince us of something. What the writer or speaker wants to prove is called the **claim** (or the **opinion**). An argument might appeal to both our reason and our emotions. An argument in a scientific or historical journal, for instance, would probably present only **logical appeals,** which include sound reasons and factual evidence. An argument in a political text would probably also include emotional appeals, which are directed more to our "hearts" than to our minds. Some arguments use **loaded words** (words loaded with emotional connotations) and **anecdotes** (brief, personal stories) that also appeal to our feelings. It is important to recognize emotional appeals used in arguments—and to be aware of how they can trick an audience.

Arguments may be found in editorials, magazine articles, political speeches, professional journals, and primary source material.

See pages 609, 977.

CAUSE AND EFFECT A text structure that shows how or why one thing leads to another. The **cause** is the reason that an action takes place. The **effect** is the result or consequence of the cause. A cause can have more than one effect, and an effect may have several causes. Writers may choose to explain only the causes or only the effects.

A text may be organized in a cause-effect chain. One cause leads to an effect, which causes another effect, and so on.

Writers use the cause-and-effect pattern in both narrative and informational texts. In most short stories, events in the plot are connected in a cause-effect chain. Some words and phrases that signal the cause-effect pattern are *because, depended on, inspired, produced, resulting in, led to,* and *outcome.* Never assume, either in your reading or in real life, that one event causes another just because it happened before it.

See pages 8, 17, 447.
See also *Text Structures.*

CHRONOLOGICAL ORDER The arrangement of details in time order, that is, in the order in which they occurred. Chronological order is used in a narrative, which describes a series of events, and in texts that explain the steps in a process.

See page 1016.
See also *Text Structures.*

CLAIM The idea or opinion that a writer tries to prove or defend in an argument. The claim can be stated as a **generalization,** a broad statement or conclusion that covers many situations (or follows from the evidence). The following statements are examples of claims stated as generalizations.

> We live in a society saturated with real-life violence—violence that is difficult to legislate away. (from "Target Real Violence, Not Video Games" page 610)
>
> Children are still learning the boundaries of good behavior, and the do's and don't of problem solving. (from "Harmless Fun?" page 613)

The author of the argument then supports the claim with either logical appeals (reasons backed by factual evidence), emotional appeals, or both.
See also *Argument, Generalization.*

COHERENT Logically integrated, consistent, and understandable. A text is **coherent** when its ideas are arranged in an order that makes sense to the reader. To aid in coherence, writers help readers follow a text by using **transitions,** words and phrases that show how ideas are connected.

Common Transitional Words and Phrases

Comparing Ideas	Contrasting Ideas
also, and, too, moreover, similarly, another	although, still, yet, but, on the other hand, instead
Showing Cause-Effect for, since, as a result, therefore, so that, because	**Showing Importance** first, last, to begin with, mainly, more important
Showing Location above, across, over, there, inside, behind, next to, through, near	**Showing Time** before, at last, now, when, eventually, at once, finally

COMPARISON AND CONTRAST A method of organizing information by showing similarities and differences among various groups of details.

See also *Text Structures.*

CONSUMER DOCUMENTS Informative texts directed to consumers, such as warranties, contracts, or instruction manuals. Here are some points to keep in mind when you read consumer documents:

1. Try to read the consumer document before you buy the product. Then you can ask the clerk to explain anything you don't understand.
2. Read all of the pages in whatever language comes most easily to you. (Many documents are printed in two or three languages.) You will often find important information where you least expect it, such as at the end of the document.
3. Read the fine print. Fine here means "tiny and barely readable." Some fine-print statements in documents are required by law. They are designed to protect you, the consumer, so the company may not be interested in emphasizing these points.
4. Don't expect the document to be interesting or easy to read. If you don't understand a statement, and you can't ask someone at the store that sold you the product, call or write to the company that made it. You should complain to the company if you find its consumer document confusing.
5. Before you sign anything, read everything on the page, and be sure you understand what you're agreeing to. Ask to take the document home, and have your parent or guardian read it. If you are not of legal age, an adult may be responsible for whatever you've signed. Make a copy of any document that you've signed—and keep the copy in a place where you can find it.

See pages 1146–1148.

CONTEXT CLUES The words and sentences surrounding a word. Context clues can sometimes help you guess at the meaning of an unfamiliar word. You will find examples below of three types of context clues. In the examples, the unfamiliar word appears in **boldface.** The context clue is underlined.

Definition: Look for words that define the unfamiliar word, often by giving a synonym or a definition for it.

> He was an EMS driver, **inured** to the sight of blood, accustomed to the carnage caused by traffic accidents.

Example: Look for examples that reveal the meaning of the unfamiliar word, as in the following sentence from "Two Kinds" (page 145).

> . . . I performed **listlessly,** my head propped on one arm. I pretended to be bored. And I was.

Contrast: Find words that contrast the unfamiliar word with a word or phrase you already know. Try this technique in the following passage from "A Very Old Man with Enormous Wings" (page 357).

> But when they went out into the courtyard with the first light of dawn, they found the whole neighborhood in front of the chicken coop having fun with the angel, without the slightest **reverence,** tossing him things to eat through the openings in the wire as if he weren't a supernatural creature but a circus animal.

See pages 61, 228.

CREDIBILITY The believability of a writer's argument. To evaluate credibility, you first need to determine the author's claim, or opinion. Then you need to look at the **reasons** (statements that explain *why* the author holds the opinion) and the **evidence** (information that supports each reason). To be credible, evidence must be **relevant,** that is, directly related to the argument; **comprehensive,** or sufficient to be convincing; and **accurate,** from a source that can be trusted as factually correct and reliable.

The writer's **intent** should also be considered. If you're reading an opinion essay, for instance, be sure to note any credentials or background information about the writer. Does the writer work for an institution that represents a particular point of view? Has the writer published a book on the same topic? Do emotional appeals and fallacious reasoning reveal a bias even though the writer pretends to be fair to both sides of the argument?

Notice the **tone** of the text. An argument that is based on logical appeals will usually have a serious, sincere tone. An angry or self-righteous tone might make you question the credibility of the argument.

See also *Argument.*

DICTIONARY You use a dictionary to find the precise meaning and usage of words. The elements of a typical entry are explained below.

① ② **Sample Dictionary Entry** ③ ④

in•dulge (in dulj´) **vt.** **-dulged´, -dulg´ing** vL
indulgere, to be kind to, yield to < *in-* + base prob.
⑤ akin to Gr *dolichos,* long & Goth *tulgus,* firmb **1** to
yield to or satisfy (a desire); give oneself up to [to
⑥ *indulge* a craving for sweets] **2** to gratify the wishes
of; be very lenient with; humor **3** [Archaic] to grant
⑦ as a kindness, favor, or privilege —*vi.* to give way
⑧ to one's own desires; indulge oneself (*in something*)
—**in•dulg´er** *n.*
⑨ *SYN.*—**indulge** implies a yielding to the wishes or
desires of oneself or another, as because of a weak
will or an amiable nature; **humor** suggests compliance with the mood or whim of another *[they humored the dying man]*; **pamper** implies overindul-
⑩ gence or excessive gratification; **spoil** emphasizes the harm done to the personality or character by overindulgence or excessive attention *[grandparents often spoil children]*; **baby** suggests the sort of pampering and devoted care lavished on infants and connotes a potential loss of self-reliance *[because he was sickly, his mother continued to baby him]* —*ANT.*
discipline, restrain

©1999 *Webster's New World College Dictionary,*
Fourth Edition.

1. **Entry word.** The entry word shows how the word is spelled and divided into syllables. It may also show capitalization and other spellings.
2. **Pronunciation. Phonetic symbols** (such as the *schwa, ə*) and **diacritical marks** (such as the *dieresis,* ä) show how to pronounce the entry word. A key to these symbols and marks usually appears at the bottom of every other page of a dictionary. In this book a pronunciation guide appears at the bottom of every other page of the *Glossary.*
3. **Part-of-speech label.** This label tells how the entry word is used. When a word can be used as more than one part of speech, definitions are grouped by part of speech. The sample entry shows three definitions of *indulge* as a transitive verb (*vt.*) and one as an intransitive verb (*vi.*).
4. **Other forms.** Sometimes the spellings of plural forms of nouns, principal parts of verbs, and comparative and superlative forms of adjectives and adverbs are shown.
5. **Word origin.** A word's origin, or **etymology,** shows where the word comes from. *Indulge* comes from the Latin *indulgere,* which probably comes from the prefix *in–,* meaning "not," added to the Greek *dolichos,* "long," and the Gothic *tulgus,* "firm."
6. **Examples.** Phrases or sentences show how the entry word is used.
7. **Definitions.** If a word has more than one meaning, the meanings are numbered or lettered.
8. **Special-usage labels.** These labels identify special meanings or special uses of the word. Here, *Archaic* indicates an outdated meaning.
9. **Related word forms.** Other forms of the entry word are listed. Usually these are created by the addition of suffixes.
10. **Synonyms and antonyms. Synonyms** (words similar in meaning) and **antonyms** (words opposite in meaning) may appear at the end of the entry.

A dictionary is available as a book or a CD-ROM or as part of a word-processing program or Web site.

EVIDENCE Specific information or proof that backs up the reasons in an argument. **Factual evidence** includes statements that can be proved by direct observation or by checking reliable reference sources. **Statistics** (facts in the form of numbers) and **expert testimony,** statements from people who are recognized as experts or authorities on an issue, may all be considered factual evidence.

In fields where discoveries are constantly being made, such as in astronomy and genetics, facts need to be checked in a recently published source. Remember that a Web site on the Internet may be current, but it may not always be reliable. If you suspect that a statement presented as a fact is not true, try to find the same fact in another source.

FALLACIOUS REASONING Faulty reasoning, or mistakes in logical thinking. The word *fallacious* comes from a Latin word meaning "deceptive; tricky." The word *false* comes from the same root word as does the word *fallacy*. Fallacious reasoning leads to false or incorrect conclusions. Here are some types of fallacious reasoning:

1. **Begging the question,** also called **circular reasoning,** assumes the truth of a statement before it has been proved. You appear to be giving a reason to support your opinion, but all you are doing is restating your opinion in different words.

> College graduates are financially successful because they can get high-paying jobs.

2. **Name-calling** uses labels to attack a person who holds an opposing view, instead of giving evidence to attack the opposing view itself. This fallacy includes criticizing the person's character, situation, or background.

> Computer geeks are out of touch with the real world.

3. **Stereotyping** gives all members of a group the same (usually undesirable) characteristics. It assumes that everyone (or everything) in that group is alike. (The word *stereotype* comes from the word for a metal plate that was used to print the same image over and over.) Stereotypes are often based on misconceptions about racial, social, religious, gender, or ethnic groups.

> Teenagers are too self-centered to participate in service programs.

4. **Hasty generalization** is a broad, general statement or conclusion that is made without sufficient evidence to back it up. A hasty generalization is often made on the basis of only one or two experiences or observations. If any exceptions to the conclusion can be found, the generalization is *not true*.

> **Insufficient evidence:** Jenna's cat has fleas, and she spends a lot of money on cat food.
>
> **Hasty generalization:** Cats don't make good pets.

5. **Either-or fallacy** assumes that there are only two possible choices or solutions (usually extremes), even though there may be many.

> I have to get a driver's license, or I'll lose all my friends.

6. **False cause and effect** occurs when one event is said to be the cause of another event just because the two events happened in sequence. You cannot assume that an event caused whatever happened afterward.

> As soon as I started jogging, my grades improved.

GENERALIZATION A broad statement that applies to or covers many individuals, experiences, situations, observations, or texts. A generalization can connect your own specific experiences and observations to a larger, general understanding.

A **valid generalization** is a type of conclusion that is drawn after considering as many of the facts as possible.

See pages 313, 339.

GRAPHS Graphic depiction of information. **Line graphs** generally show changes in quantity over time. **Bar graphs** usually compare quantities within categories. **Pie graphs,** or **circle graphs,** show proportions by dividing a circle into different-sized sections, like slices of a pie.

How to Read a Graph
1. **Read the title.** The title will tell you the subject and purpose of the graph.
2. **Read the headings and labels.** These will help you determine the types of information presented.

3. **Analyze the details.** Read numbers carefully. Note increases or decreases. Look for the direction or order of events and trends and for relationships.

INFERENCE A guess based on observation and prior experience. When you make inferences about a literary work, you use evidence from the text, from other texts you have read, and from your own prior experience. One way to analyze a character is to consider what the person says and how he or she interacts with other characters. For instance, what inferences might you make about the narrator in the following passage from "The Leap" (page 42)? The narrator says:

> Since my father's recent death, there is no one to read to her, which is why I returned, in fact, from my failed life where the land is flat. I came home to read to my mother, to read out loud, to read long into the dark if I must, to read all night.

Here are some clues to look for when making inferences:

Character. In a work of literature, look at a character's speech, actions, thoughts, and appearance. What do others think and say about the character?

Tone (the writer's attitude). In both literary and informational texts, look at the writer's choice of words and details.

Theme or **main idea.** Look for the writer's most important point, opinion, or message. What idea can you take from the text that extends beyond it to the world at large?

You infer, or predict, what will happen next in the plot of a story based on what the writer has already told you. You change your inferences as the writer gives you more information. Sometimes a writer will deliberately drop a clue that leads you, for a short time, to an incorrect inference. That's part of the fun of reading. Until you get to the end of a suspenseful story, you can never be sure how the plot will turn out.

When you're writing about a story or an informational text, you must be sure your inferences are supported by details in the text.

Supported inferences are based directly on evidence in a text and on reasonable prior knowledge. Some interpretation of the evidence is possible, but you cannot ignore or contradict facts that the writer gives you.

Unsupported inferences are conclusions that are not logical. They ignore the facts in the text or

misinterpret them. Whenever you're asked to write an essay about a text, it's a good idea to re-read the text before and after you write your essay. Check each inference you make against the text to make sure you can find evidence for it. For example, if you write an analysis of a character and you say that the character never answers a question directly, you should cite details from the text to support your inference.

See pages 106, 115, 790, 799.

INFORMATIVE TEXTS Texts that communicate information and data. When you're reading informative texts, you need to read slowly, looking for main ideas and important details. Slow and careful reading is especially important when you're trying to get meaning from consumer, workplace, and public documents. These documents are often not written by professional writers, so they may be difficult to read.

See also *Consumer Documents, Public Documents, Workplace Documents.*

LOGIC Correct reasoning. A logical text presents reasons supported by evidence (facts and examples). A text is illogical when it does not provide reasons backed by evidence. Notice how each sentence in this paragraph from "Kiss and Tell" (page 590) gives evidence that supports the idea that birds on the Galapagos Islands devoloped characteristics suited to life on each island.

> As a young naturalist, Charles Darwin was inspired by the variety of wildlife in the Galapagos Islands to formulate his theory of evolution by natural selection. He found thirteen species of finch, identical except for tiny differences precisely suiting them to the islands on which they lived. Birds living among flowers had long slender beaks for sipping nectar; those surrounded by seeds instead of blossoms had thick, tough beaks that worked as nutcrackers. Darwin reasoned that the animals changed over time, passing on characteristics that helped them successfully adapt to their surroundings.

See also *Logical Order.*

LOGICAL ORDER A method of organizing information by putting details into related groupings. Writers use logical order most often when they want to classify information, that is, to examine a subject and its relationship to other subjects. For example, when you classify, you can divide a subject into its parts. You can also use the comparison-contrast pattern to show similarities and differences among various groups.

See page 1140.
See also *Text Structures.*

MAIN IDEA The writer's most important point, opinion, or message. The main idea may be stated directly, or it may be only suggested or implied. If the idea is not stated directly, it's up to you to look at the details and decide on the idea that they all seem to support. Try to restate the writer's main idea in your own words.

In an argument the main idea (the generalization that the writer is trying to prove) is called the **claim,** or **opinion.**

See page 79.

MAP A drawing showing all or part of the earth's surface or of celestial bodies. Physical maps illustrate the natural landscape of an area, using shading, lines, and color to show landforms and elevation. **Political maps** show political units, such as states and nations. They usually also show borders and capitals and other major cities. **Special-purpose maps** present specific information, such as the location of Mount Everest in the Himalayas ("Into Thin Air," page 507).

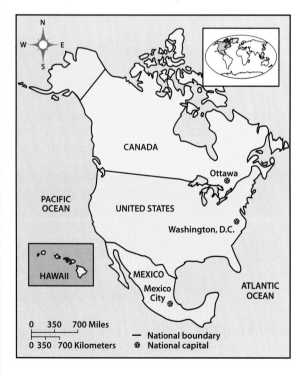

How to Read a Map
1. **Determine the focus of the map.** The map's title and labels tell you its focus—its subject and the geographical area it covers.
2. **Study the legend.** The **legend,** or **key,** explains the symbols, lines, colors, and shadings used in the map.
3. **Check directions and distances.** Maps often include a **compass rose,** a diagram that shows north, south, east, and west. If there isn't one, assume that north is at the top of the map, west to the left, and so on. Many maps also include a scale that relates distances on the map to actual distances.
4. **Look at the larger context.** The absolute **location** of any place on earth is given by its **latitude** (the number of degrees north or south of the equator) and its **longitude** (the number of degrees east or west of the **prime meridian,** or 0 degrees longitude). Some maps also include **locator maps,** which show the area depicted in relation to a larger area.

OPINION A statement of a person's belief, idea, or attitude. A **fact** is something that can be verified or proved by direct observation or by checking a reliable reference source. An **opinion** cannot be proved to be either true or false—even when it is supported by facts. The following statement is an unsupported opinion.

> *Julius Caesar* is an outstanding play.

A **valid opinion** is an opinion that is supported by verifiable facts. In the following example, the verifiable facts are underlined.

> *Julius Caesar* is an outstanding play because <u>it contains moral conflicts as well as ideas about power and politics that are still important today.</u>

When you read a persuasive text, remember that statements of opinion can't be proved, but they can and should be supported by facts and logical reasoning.

ORDER OF IMPORTANCE A means of organizing information by ranking details in the order of their importance. Writers of persuasive texts have to decide whether to give the strongest reason first or to present the weakest reason first and end with the strongest point. Informational texts such as news articles always begin with the most important details because they want to grab the reader's attention immediately. The structure of a news article looks like an upside-down triangle, with the least important details at the bottom.

See also *Text Structures*.

OUTLINING A way of organizing information to show relationships among key details in a text. You can use outlining as a writer and as a reader.

Outlining puts main ideas and details in a form that you can review quickly. An **informal outline,** sometimes called a working outline, should have at least three main ideas. You put supporting details under each main idea, like this:

> **Informal Outline**
> I. First main idea
>   A. Detail supporting first main idea
>   B. Another detail supporting first main idea
>   C. Third detail supporting first main idea
> II. Second main idea
>   [etc.]

A **formal outline** is especially useful if you're writing a research paper. You might start with a working outline and then revise it into a formal one. Your teacher may ask you to submit a formal outline with your completed research paper.

Formal outlines use Roman numerals (I, II, III), capital letters (A, B, C), and Arabic numerals (1, 2, 3) to show order, relationship, and relative importance of ideas. The headings in a formal outline should have the same grammatical structure, and you must be consistent in your use of either phrases or sentences. (You should not switch back and forth between them.) There should always be at least two divisions under each heading or none at all.

Here is the beginning of a formal outline of a textbook chapter on the Vietnam War:

> **Formal Outline**
> I. TV speech by Lyndon B. Johnson, 8/4/64
>   A. Destroyer *Maddox* attacked on 8/2 in Gulf of Tonkin
>   B. U.S. military forces ordered to take action against gunboats
> II. The Tonkin Gulf Resolution
>   A. In 1963, Johnson advised by McNamara to increase U.S. commitment to South Vietnam
>
>   B. Johnson's need for congressional support
>   1. The Gulf of Tonkin events an opportunity
>   2. Request for authorization of military force overwhelmingly passed

PARAPHRASING Restating each sentence of a text in your own words. Paraphrasing is often used when reading difficult texts. Paraphrasing a text helps you to be certain you understand it. When you paraphrase, you follow the author's sequence of ideas. You carefully reword each line (if it's a poem) or sentence (if it's prose) without changing the author's ideas or leaving anything out. You restate each figure of speech to be sure you understand the basis of the comparison. A paraphrase is longer than a **summary,** which is a brief statement of the main ideas in a text.

See pages 650, 790.

PRIMARY SOURCE An original, firsthand account. Primary sources may include an autobiography; an eyewitness testimony; a letter, speech, or literary work; a historical document; and information gathered from firsthand surveys or interviews. "A Fireman's Story" (page 411) is an example of a primary source. It's important to use primary sources whenever they are available on a topic, but you need to research widely to make sure that a primary source is not biased.

Be sure to keep track of your primary sources by numbering each source and recording the necessary publishing information. If you quote directly from the primary source, be sure to use quotation marks and to give credit to your source.

See pages 189, 397.
See also *Secondary Source*.

PUBLIC DOCUMENTS Informative texts put out by the government or public agencies. Public documents include political platforms, public policy statements, speeches, and debates. These documents inform the public about government policy, laws, municipal codes, records, schedules, and the like.

RESEARCH QUESTIONS Questions that are focused on a specific subject, which the researcher searches to answer. Questions are essential tools for focusing your research.

One way to generate research questions is to use a KWL chart as a research guide. This kind of chart is an easy way to organize questions and answers, especially if you know how to set up columns and rows on your computer. In the K column, you note what you already *know* about the subject. In the W column, you note *what* you'd like to find out. As you do your research, complete the L column by answering what you have *learned*.

Research questions can also be generated by brainstorming or by using the *5W-How* questions: *Who? What? When? Where? Why?* and *How?* As you seek primary and secondary source information at libraries and museums, in various electronic media (Internet, films, tapes), and from personal interviews, you will come up with more research questions. Always remember to keep your questions focused on the specific subject you have chosen.

See page 543.

ROOTS, PREFIXES, SUFFIXES English words are often made up of two or more word parts. These word parts include the following:

- **roots,** which carry a word's core meaning
- **prefixes,** added onto the beginning of a word or in front of a word root to form a new word
- **suffixes,** added onto the end of a word or after a word root to form a new word

Most word roots come from Greek and Latin. Prefixes and suffixes come from Greek, Latin, and Anglo-Saxon. *(See chart on roots, prefixes, and suffixes on pages 1214–1215.)*

SECONDARY SOURCE A secondhand account written by a writer who did not participate directly in the events he or she interprets, relates, or analyzes. Secondary sources may include encyclopedias, magazine articles, textbooks, biographies, and technical

journals. The historical article "R.M.S. Titanic" (page 398) is an example of a secondary source. A research paper may include both primary and secondary sources.

SPATIAL ORDER A means of organizing information by showing where things are located. (The word *spatial* is related to the word *space*. Spatial order shows where things are located in space.) Spatial order is often used in descriptive writing. Here is an example from the beginning of "Through the Tunnel" (page 325). Phrases showing spatial order are underlined.

> Going <u>to the shore</u> on the first morning of the vacation, the young English boy stopped <u>at a turning of the path</u> and looked <u>down at a wild and rocky bay</u> and then <u>over to the crowded beach</u> he knew so well from other years.

See also *Text Structures*.

SYNTHESIZING Putting all the different sources of information together in a process that gives you a better understanding of the whole subject. In order to synthesize information, you first gather information about a topic from several sources. Then, you find each writer's main ideas. Paraphrasing ideas, restating them in your own words, can help you understand difficult texts. Next, you examine the ideas in each source. You compare and contrast the ideas you've found. To synthesize what you have learned, you draw conclusions about the information you have gathered.

See page 189.
See also *Generalization*.

TEXT STRUCTURES Any organizational patterns that writers use to make their meaning clear. In imaginative literature, text structures range from the plot structures in stories and dramas to the sonnet structure in poetry.

In nonfiction and informational texts, the writer's **intent** or **purpose** in creating the text determines how the text will be organized. Don't expect writers of informational texts and nonfiction to use the same structure throughout an entire text. Most writers switch from one type of structure to another and may even combine structures. Here are four basic ways of arranging ideas or details in nonfiction and informational texts:

1. **Chronological order, time order,** or **sequence**—putting events or steps in the order in which they occur. Most narrative and historical texts are written in chronological order. Chronological order is also found in writing that explains a process, such as in technical directions and in recipes. This type of chronological order is called **step-by-step order.**

2. **Spatial order**—showing where things are located. This pattern is used in descriptive writing. It is especially useful in helping readers visualize setting. See the first paragraph of "From a Lifeboat" (page 412).

3. **Order of importance**—ranking details from most important to least important, or from least important to most important. Writers of persuasive texts in particular have to decide which order makes the strongest impact: putting the strongest reason first, and the weaker ones later, or saving the strongest reason for last. For an example of a text that uses order of importance, see the concluding section of "R.M.S. Titanic" (pages 409–410). News articles always begin with the most important details because they want to grab the reader's attention immediately.

4. **Logical order**—classifying details into related groups. One type of logical order is the **comparison and contrast** text structure, which shows similarities and differences among various groups.

Other methods used to organize texts include

- **enumeration**—also called **listing**—citing a list of details: first, second, and so on.
- **cause-and-effect**—showing how events happen as a result of other events.
- **problem-solution**—explaining how a problem may be solved.
- **question-answer**—asking questions, then giving the answers.

Recognizing these structures will help you understand the ideas in a text. The following guidelines can help you recognize text structures:

1. Search the text for the main idea. Look for clue words (**transitions**) that signal a specific pattern of organization. Also note colors, special type, headers, numbered lists, and icons that may be used to highlight terms or indicate text structure.

2. Analyze the text for other important ideas. Think about how the ideas connect, and look for an obvious pattern.

3. Remember that a writer might use one organizational pattern throughout a text or combine two or more patterns.

4. Draw a graphic organizer that maps how the text is structured. Some common graphic organizers are a **causal chain** (for the cause-effect text structure), a **flowchart** (showing chronological sequence), and a **Venn diagram** (showing similarities and differences).

See also *Chronological Order, Logical Order, Order of Importance, Spatial Order.*

WORKPLACE DOCUMENTS Job-related texts, such as job applications, memos, instructional manuals, and employee handbooks. When you read workplace documents, keep these points in mind (in addition to the points about reading consumer documents cited on page 1167):

1. Take all the time you need to read and understand the document. Don't let anyone rush you or tell you that a document is unimportant or just a formality.

2. Read technical directions carefully, including those that are posted on the side of a device you are supposed to operate. Read all of the directions before you start. Ask questions if you are not sure how to proceed. Don't try anything out before you know what will happen next.

3. The employee handbook contains the "rules of the game" at that particular business. It tells you about holidays, work hours, break times, vacations, and any other important company policies. Read the employee handbook from cover to cover.

See also *Consumer Documents.*

Handbook of Reading and Informational Terms

Greek Roots	Meaning	Examples
–astro–, –aster–	star	**astro**nomy, **aster**isk
–cosmo–	world; order	**cosmo**logy, **cosmo**politan
–eu–	good; well	**eu**phoria, **eu**phemism
–gno–, –kno–	know	**kno**wledge, a**gno**stic
–hypno–	sleep	**hypno**tize, **hypno**tic
–mis–	hatred of	**mis**anthrope, **mis**ology
–ortho–	straight	**ortho**pedics, **ortho**dontics
–pseudo–	false	**pseudo**nym, **pseudo**morph
–the–, –them–, –thet–	place; put	epi**thet**, anti**the**sis
–theo–	god	**theo**logy, **theo**cracy

Latin Roots	Meaning	Examples
–anima–, –anim–	life; mind	**anim**al, **anim**ate
–aqua–	water	**aqua**rium, **aqua**naut
–cid–, –cis–	cut off; kill	homi**cide**, con**cise**
–cor–, –card–	heart	**cor**onary, **card**iac
–fum–	smoke; scent	**fum**igate, per**fum**e
–gen–	race; family	**gen**ealogy, pro**gen**itor
–leg–	law	**leg**al, **leg**islate
–noc–, –nox–	night	equi**nox**, **noc**turne
–tract–	pull; draw	at**tract**, sub**tract**ion
–voc–, –vok–	voice; call	**voc**al, re**vok**e

Greek Prefixes	Meaning	Examples
anti–	against	**anti**body, **anti**social
dia–	through; across	**dia**gram, **dia**lectic
hypo–	under; below	**hypo**dermic, **hypo**allergenic
para–	beside; beyond	**para**legal, **para**llel
peri–	around	**peri**scope, **peri**phery

Latin Prefixes	Meaning	Examples
bene–	good	**bene**fit, **bene**diction
contra–	against	**contra**dict, **contra**st
extra–	outside	**extra**curricular, **extra**ordinary
intra–	within	**intra**venous, **intra**mural
trans–	across; over	**trans**atlantic, **trans**cend

Anglo-Saxon/Old English Prefixes	Meaning	Examples
be–	around	**be**dew, **be**get
for–	away; off; from	**for**get, **for**go
mis–	badly; not	**mis**hap, **mis**take
over–	above	**over**look, **over**coat
un–	not; reverse of	**un**sound, **un**kempt

Greek Suffixes	Meaning	Examples
–ess	female	poet**ess**, lion**ess**
–ic	having; showing	parapleg**ic**, ton**ic**
–ize	resemble; cause to be	American**ize,** ostrac**ize**
–meter	measure	thermo**meter**, baro**meter**
–oid	like; resembling	fact**oid**, andr**oid**

Latin Suffixes	Meaning	Examples
–age	act; result of	marri**age**, voy**age**
–fic	making; creating	horri**fic**, scienti**fic**
–ive	relating to; belonging to	inquisit**ive**, sport**ive**
–let	small	pig**let**, rivu**let**
–ure	act; state of being	leis**ure**, compos**ure**

Anglo-Saxon/Old English Suffixes	Meaning	Examples
–en	become	bright**en**, sull**en**
–ful	full of; marked by	cheer**ful**, fear**ful**
–ness	quality; state	kind**ness**, crazi**ness**
–ship	quality of	kin**ship**, relation**ship**
–ward	in the direction	for**ward**, sky**ward**

Writer's Handbook

Tip The writing process is **recursive,** meaning that writers go back and forth between the stages as necessary. For example, as you revise an essay you may realize that one paragraph contains no details to support your main idea. You can then go back to the prewriting stages, gathering and adding more information to the paragraph.

The Writing Process

There may be as many ways to write as there are kinds of texts. While individual writers' techniques may vary, successful writers do have one thing in common: the writing process. The writing process is made up of four stages, and each stage involves certain activities. The chart below summarizes what happens during each stage of the writing process.

Stages of the Writing Process	
Prewriting	• Choose your topic. • Identify your purpose and audience, and select form. • Begin to organize the information. • Decide the main point you want to express.
Drafting	• Grab your readers' attention in the introduction. • Provide background information. • State your main points, support, and elaboration. • Follow a plan of organization. • Wrap up with a conclusion.
Evaluating and Revising	• Evaluate your draft. • Revise the draft's content, organization, and style.
Proofreading and Publishing	• Proofread, or edit, your final draft. • Publish, or share, your finished writing with readers. • Reflect on your writing experience.

At every stage of the writing process, you'll need to stay focused on your goal, or purpose, for the piece of writing and on your specific audience. Use the following suggestions to keep your writing on track.

- **Keep your idea focused.** Every idea in a piece must clearly support your **thesis,** or the controlling impression, you want to create. Those ideas must also be **coherent,** or strongly connected to one another. Keep your thesis and purpose in mind every step of the way, eliminating any ideas that might take the reader's attention away from your distinct perspective or from a tightly reasoned argument.

- **Use a consistent tone.** Using the same tone throughout a piece will help to unify the ideas you present. Consider what tone—from slangy and joking to serious and formal—will best fit your audience and your topic, and stick with that tone.
- **Plan to publish.** Make publishing a piece—sharing it with an audience—easier by carefully revising and proofreading. Enlist the help of classmates to catch errors you might miss because you know the piece too well, and use the following proofreading guidelines. The numbers in parentheses indicate the sections in the *Language Handbook* in which instruction on each skill begins.

Guidelines for Proofreading

1. Is every sentence complete, not a fragment or a run-on? (9a, b)

2. Are punctuation marks used correctly? (12a–s, 13a–l, 14a–n)

3. Are the first letters of sentences and proper nouns and adjectives capitalized? (11a, 11d)

4. Does each verb agree in number with its subject? (2a) Are verb forms and tenses used correctly? (3a–f)

5. Are subject and object forms of personal pronouns used correctly? (4a–e) Do pronouns agree with clear antecedents in number and gender? (4i)

Symbols for Revising and Proofreading

Symbol	Example	Meaning of Symbol
≡	Maple High school	Capitalize a lowercase letter.
/	the First person	Lowercase a capitalized letter.
∧	on the fourth ^{of} May	Insert a missing word, letter, or punctuation mark.
⌒	in the East West	Replace a word.
℮	tell me the the plan	Delete a word, letter, or punctuation mark.
∽	recieve	Change the order of letters.
¶	¶"Help!" someone cried.	Begin a new paragraph.

Paragraphs

A **paragraph** is made up of sentences grouped together to present and support a single main idea, or central focus. In the same way, a composition is made up of a group of paragraphs working together to develop and support a thesis or controlling idea that makes the composition work as a whole.

Parts of a Body Paragraph

While paragraphs in narrative writing don't always have a central focus, paragraphs in most other types of compositions usually emphasize a main idea. These **body paragraphs** usually include a **topic sentence, supporting sentences,** and, sometimes, a **clincher sentence.**

Parts of Paragraphs	
Topic Sentence	• directly states the paragraph's main idea • is often the first sentence in the paragraph, but may occur at the end for emphasis or variety

Supporting Sentences	• support the main idea of a paragraph
	• use the following kinds of details
	
	  sensory details: information collected using sight, hearing, smell, touch, or taste
	
	  facts: information that can be proved
	
	  statistics: information in number form
	
	  examples: specific instances or illustrations of a general idea
	
	  anecdotes: extended examples or brief personal stories
	
	  scenarios: general descriptions of potential events or common situations
	
	  commonly held beliefs: ideas on which most people agree
	
	  hypotheses: unproven theories that serve as the basis for investigation
	
	  definitions: explanations of concepts

Clincher Sentence	• sometimes (but not always) found at the end of longer paragraphs • emphasizes or summarizes the main idea

PUTTING THE PARTS TOGETHER A typical paragraph that includes the parts listed in the chart above uses the following structure. Be aware, though, that you can use a different structure for effect—for example, you might occasionally leave out the clincher sentence and place your topic sentence at the end of the paragraph to drive home your point.

Typical Body Paragraph

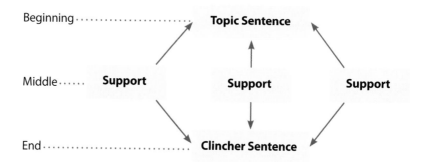

The following passage from an online magazine article shows how the parts of the paragraph work together to support a main idea—in this case, the idea that electric "bug zappers" do a poor job of protecting humans from insect bites.

> Electric insect traps, or "bug zappers," are effective killing machines, but they kill the wrong kind of insects, claims University of Delaware entomologist Doug Tallamy. Over the course of a summer, Tallamy and a high school student, Tim Frick, analyzed the victims of the electric traps installed in six yards in Newark, Delaware. Of the 13,789 insects killed, just 31— less than one-quarter of one percent—were biting insects. Tallamy and Frick estimate that the millions of traps employed in the U.S. needlessly kill 71 billion to 350 billion "nontarget insects" each year, causing untold damage to ecosystems. Bug zappers, they conclude, are "worthless" as well as "counterproductive."
>
> Steve Nadis, "Bug Zappers Miss Their Mark,"
> *Omni Online*

Topic Sentence

Supporting Sentences

(Facts and Statistics)

Clincher Sentence

Notice that the topic sentence immediately recalls the reader's attention to the paragraph's main idea: These traps kill the wrong insects. The rest of the paragraph maintains a consistent focus on this idea. Each supporting sentence contains evidence that supports this main idea, including facts and statistics. The final sentence, a clincher sentence, emphasizes the main idea by presenting a judgment based on the facts and statistics in the supporting sentences.

Qualities of Paragraphs

Having the parts of a paragraph in place is just the beginning of developing a good paragraph. The next step is to consider the **unity** and **coherence** of the ideas within the paragraph. Think of these qualities as the strong glue that holds the parts of a well-written paragraph together.

UNITY Unity is the quality achieved when all of the sentences in a paragraph work together as a unit to express or support one main idea and to maintain a consistent focus. Unrelated ideas spoil unity and distract the reader. Unity is present in a paragraph when all sentences relate to an implied or stated main idea or to a sequence of events. In a narrative paragraph, unity is achieved when all the sentences work together to narrate the event.

COHERENCE Along with unity, good paragraphs have coherence. Coherence is achieved when all of the details and ideas in a paragraph are both logically arranged and clearly connected.

To ensure that the ideas in a paragraph are arranged in a way that makes sense, pay attention to the structure or organizational pattern of the ideas. You will usually use one of the orders described in the chart on page 1220; in some cases, though, you may use a combination of two or even more of these orders.

Types of Order

Order	When to Use	How It Works
Chronological	• to tell a story • to explain a process	presents actions and events according to the order in which they occur
Spatial	• to describe a place or object	arranges details or ideas according to their location in space
Logical	• to explain or classify (by defining, dividing a subject into parts, or comparing and contrasting)	groups related details or ideas together to show their relationship
Order of Importance	• to inform or to persuade	arranges details or ideas from the most important to the least important, or vice versa

In addition to presenting details in an order that makes sense, a paragraph that has coherence should also show readers how those details are connected. You can show connections between ideas by using direct references or transitional expressions. **Direct references** refer to an idea presented earlier. **Transitional expressions** are words or phrases that take readers from one idea to the next, signaling the relationships between the ideas. The following chart explains how to use these two strategies for connecting ideas.

Connecting Strategies

Connecting Strategy	How to Use It
Direct References	• Use a noun or pronoun that refers to a noun or pronoun used earlier. • Repeat a word used earlier. • Use a word or phrase that means the same thing as a noun or pronoun used earlier.
Transitional Expressions	• Compare ideas (*also, and, besides, in addition, similarly, too*). • Contrast ideas (*although, but, however, instead, nevertheless, otherwise, yet*). • Show cause and effect (*as a result, because, consequently, so, therefore, thus*). • Show time (*after, before, eventually, finally, first, meanwhile, then, when*). • Show place (*above, across, around, beyond, here, in, on, over, there, to, under*). • Show importance (*first, last, mainly, then, to begin with*).

YOUR TURN Develop a paragraph on the topic of your choice. After identifying the main idea you will present, take the following steps to draft your paragraph.

- Plan your topic sentence, supporting sentences with a variety of types of support, and a clincher sentence.

- Create unity and coherence to maintain a consistent focus in your paragraph. Use an appropriate order, and connect your ideas using direct references and transitional expressions.

The Writer's Language

As part of revising a draft, fine-tune its **style** so that it will grab readers. To improve your paper's style, consider your **word choice** and use the **active voice.** Also, analyze the **tone** of your writing to make your style not only engaging but also appropriate.

GIVE IT FLAIR! Consider what is missing from the following passage.

> As I hiked around a bend, I saw a snake smack in the middle of the path. Its skin was being shed. It moved against the rocks. Eventually it got out of its old skin. Now it looked real different. It was smooth. There was a lot of sun. My forehead was covered in sweat. I couldn't hear nothing. I looked at the snakes eyes. They were black.

The passage poorly shares the writer's experience. The writer must improve word choice, using **precise language, sensory details, action verbs,** and **appropriate modifiers,** and use the **active voice** when possible.

Precise Language The passage above describes the snake in a vague way. Changing *moved* to *wriggled* or *slithered* would vividly show the snake's movement. Also, what kind of snake was it? What does the snake look like before, during, and after shedding its skin? Revise your own writing to show your subject vividly through precise language.

Sensory Details The statement "It was smooth" doesn't give readers much information about the snake. The description "smooth as silk" or "smooth as a stone" would explain how it feels to touch the snake. Words like *stone* and *silk* are the building blocks of sensory details, details that tell how things look, feel, taste, sound, or smell.

Action Verbs Which is more interesting—"They were black" or "They glittered like black stones"? Generally, *be* verbs (such as *were*) and other dull verbs such as *go, have* and *do* don't tell readers much. Action verbs such as *glittered* and *sparkled* bring a subject to life.

Appropriate Modifiers An appropriate modifier clearly relates to the correct word or phrase. For example, the word real in the passage in an adjective used incorrectly to modify the adjective *different*. The writer should use the adverb *really*, or even better, eliminate the tired word *really* altogether. Check that the modifier you use is both necessary and correct.

Active Voice In the **passive** voice, the action happens to the subject. For example, "Its skin was being shed" uses the passive voice. In the **active** voice, the subject does the action. The more forceful sentence "The snake was shedding its skin" uses the active voice.

TONING UP   Your **tone** expresses your attitude toward your audience and topic and comes through in the formality of your language, including your word choices. Consider these points.

- **Who is my audience?** When you speak, you adjust your tone based on listener reactions. For example, if listeners frown at a joke, you probably turn more serious. In writing, imagine your readers' attitude toward your topic and adopt a tone reflecting that attitude.

- **Why am I writing?** Your tone must fit your **purpose**. For example, if your purpose it to inform, avoid a sarcastic tone—even if your readers enjoy sarcasm—because irony could interfere with your goal.

- **For what context, or occasion, am I writing?** Are you writing for a school assignment or to share a story with a friend? The occasion that prompts your writing determines its formality. For a formal occasion, use standard English, avoiding contractions and slang.

Read the following revision of the passage on page 1221. Notice how revisions in word choice, voice, and tone bring the passage to life.

A Writer's Model

Active Voice
Precise Language

Action Verbs
Appropriate Modifiers
Sensory Details

Sensory Detail

As I hiked around a bend, I saw a gopher snake right in the middle of the path. The snake was shedding its skin. It wriggled and rubbed itself against the rough rocks. Eventually it slithered out of the flaky, dead layer of skin. Now it was as smooth as a polished apple, black and brown like shiny shoes. The morning sun was hot, and beads of sweat ran down my forehead. The world was silent—even the birds had stopped chirping. I looked right into the snake's eyes. They glittered like tiny chips of black stone.

YOUR TURN Revise the following paragraph for style, and use your imagination to add details.

Roosevelt Park is nice. People play softball there. Kids play on the playground, sliding down the slides and swinging on the swings. There's a petting zoo, too, with different kinds of animals that can be touched. There's a merry-go-round that first goes around slow and then fast. If you are hungry, there are places to eat. Or you can do nothing. I'm glad there's a place to go with my friends on the weekends.

Designing Your Writing

If you've ever tried to read a messy, confusing flier or a scientific report filled with statistics, you know how important design and visuals are in making documents readable. A document's design should help to communicate its information clearly and effectively. Visuals, such as a photograph or chart, should be used when needed to help readers grasp a point.

Page Design

EYE APPEAL Your page design, or **layout,** can influence your audience's desire and ability to read your document. When you design a document, make it as appealing and easy to read as possible, whether you create it by hand or use word-processing or publishing software. Use the following design elements to improve readability.

- **Columns** arrange text in separate sections printed side by side. Text in reference books and newspapers usually appear in columns. A **block** is a rectangle of text shorter than a page, such as a single newspaper story. Blocks are separated by white space.

- A **bullet** (•) is a dot or symbol used to make information stand out. Bullets often separate information into lists like this one. They attract attention and help readers remember the ideas listed.

- A **callout** is an important sentence from the text printed in a large font. Many magazine articles catch readers' attention with callouts.

- A **heading** tells what a section of text, such as a chapter, will be about. Headings appear at the beginning of a section of text. A **subheading** indicates a new idea or section within a heading. Several subheadings may appear under one heading. Headings and subheadings are often set in large letters, boldface type, or a different font.

- **White space** is any area on a page where there is little or no text or visuals. Usually, white space is limited to the margins and the spaces between words, lines, and columns. Advertisements have more white space than books or articles in newspapers or magazines.

- **Contrast** refers to the balance of light and dark areas on a page. Dark areas are those that contain blocks of text or graphics. Light areas have little type and few graphics. A page with high contrast, or balanced light and dark areas, is easier to read than a page with low contrast, such as one that is mostly light or that that is filled with text and images.

- **Emphasis** is how a page designer indicates to a reader what information on a page is most important. For example, the front page of a newspaper uses photographs and bold or large headlines to place emphasis on a particular story.

Type

BOLD AND BEAUTIFUL To enhance the readability of your documents, choose type carefully, considering especially the case and font of letters.

Case Most texts you read use mostly lowercase letters with capital letters at the beginning of sentences. However, you can use different cases for specific purposes within a document.

- **Uppercase Letters** All uppercase, or capital, letters may be used in headings or titles. Because words in all capital letters can be difficult to read, use all caps only for emphasis, not for large bodies of text.

- **Small Caps** Small capitals, or uppercase letters that are reduced in size. They appear in abbreviations of time, such as 9:00 A.M. and A.D. 1500.

Font A **font** is one complete set of characters (such as letters, numbers, and punctuation marks) of a given size and design.

- **Types of Fonts** All fonts belong to one of three categories:

Font Categories		
Category	**Explanation**	**How It Is Used**
decorative, or **script,** fonts	elaborately designed characters that convey a distinct mood or feeling	Decorative fonts are difficult to read and should be used in small amounts for artistic effect.
serif fonts	characters with small strokes (serifs) attached at each end	Because the strokes on serif characters help guide the reader's eyes from letter to letter, serif type is often used for large bodies of text.
sans serif fonts	characters formed of neat straight lines, with no serifs at the ends of letters	Sans serif fonts are easy to read and are used for headings, subheadings, callouts, and captions.

- **Font Size** The size of type is called the font size or point size. Most newspapers and textbooks use type measured at 12 points, with larger type for headings and headlines and smaller type for captions.
- **Font Styles** Most text is set in a roman style (not slanted). *Italic,* or slanted, type has special uses, as for captions or book titles. Underscored or boldface type can also be used for emphasis.

Visuals

GET THE PICTURE? Some information can be communicated much more effectively visually than in writing. Your visuals must meet the same standards as your text, and their design must also be uncluttered. Use only one or two colors for emphasis to keep your visuals clear. Here are some visuals you might find useful.

Charts Charts show relationships among ideas or data. A **flowchart** uses geometric shapes linked by arrows to show the sequence of events in a process. A **pie chart** is a circle divided into wedges, with each wedge representing a certain percentage of the total. As in the example below, a legend usually notes the concept each wedge color represents.

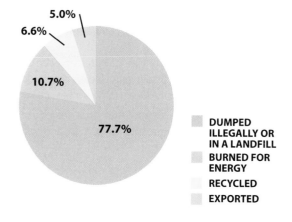

5.0%
6.6%
10.7%
77.7%

- DUMPED ILLEGALLY OR IN A LANDFILL
- BURNED FOR ENERGY
- RECYCLED
- EXPORTED

Diagrams Diagrams are simple drawings that show what something looks like, how something works, or how to do something. This diagram shows how water moves to create an ocean swell.

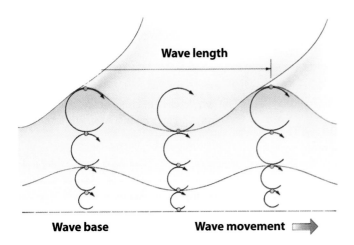

Wave length

Wave base

Wave movement

Graphs Graphs present numeric information visually and can show how one thing changes in relation to another. A **line graph** can show changes or trends over time, compare trends, or show how two or more variables interact. A **bar graph,** such as the one to the right, can compare quantities at a glance, show trends or changes over time, or indicate the parts of the whole.

Other Visuals Other visuals you might use in your documents include illustrations, time lines, and maps.

- **Illustrations** include drawings, photographs, and other artwork.

- **Time lines** identify events that have taken place over a given period of time. Usually, events are identified or described above the line, and the time demarcations are indicated below it.

- **Maps** represent part of the earth or space. Maps of the earth may show geographical features, roads, cities, and other important locations.

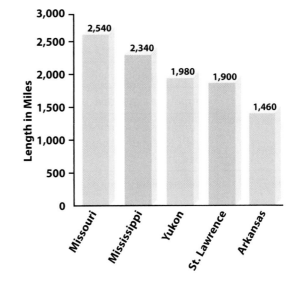

YOUR TURN Choose a visual to effectively communicate the following information. Then, use the guidelines in this section to create the visual.

One hundred students at Chavez High School are involved in team sports. Thirty-five students play soccer, twenty-three play softball, twenty-seven play football, and fifteen play volleyball.

Language Handbook

1. The Parts of Speech

Part of Speech	Definition	Examples
NOUN	Names person, place, thing, or idea	father, Peter Pan, crew, valley, poem, "With All Flags Flying," age, wisdom
PRONOUN	Takes the place of one or more nouns or pronouns	
Personal	Refers to one(s) speaking (first person), spoken to (second person), or spoken about (third person)	I, me, my, mine, we, us, our, ours you, your, yours he, him, his, she, her, hers, it, its they, them, their, theirs
Reflexive	Refers to subject and directs action of the verb back to the subject	myself, ourselves, yourself, yourselves, himself, herself, itself, themselves
Intensive	Refers to and emphasizes a noun or another pronoun	(See Reflexive.)
Demonstrative	Refers to specific one(s) of a group	this, that, these, those
Interrogative	Introduces a question	what, which, who, whom, whose
Relative	Introduces a subordinate clause and refers to a noun or pronoun outside the clause	that, which, who, whom, whose
Indefinite	Refers to one(s) not specifically named	all, any, anyone, both, each, either, everybody, many, none, nothing
ADJECTIVE	Modifies a noun or pronoun by telling *what kind, which one, how many,* or *how much*	**a young, self-assured** officer; **Mexican** tradition; **thirty** dollars; **that scary horror** story; **a two-thirds** majority
VERB	Shows action or state of being	
Action	Expresses physical or mental activity	read, dance, fly, care, pretend, argue
Linking	Connects subject with word identifying or describing it	appear, be, seem, become, feel, look, smell, sound, taste
Helping (Auxiliary)	Helps another verb express time or voice	be, have, may, can, shall, will, would
ADVERB	Modifies a verb, adjective, or adverb by telling *how, when, where,* or *to what extent*	drives **carefully,** spoke **loudly, very** old, **almost** ready, coming **here tomorrow**
PREPOSITION	Relates a noun or pronoun to another word	across, between, into, near, of, on, with, aside from, instead of, next to

CONJUNCTION	Joins words or word groups	
Coordinating	Joins words or word groups used in the same way	and, but, for, nor, or, so, yet
Correlative	A pair of conjunctions that joins parallel words or word groups	both . . . and, either . . . or, neither . . . nor, not only . . . but (also)
Subordinating	Begins a subordinate clause and connects it to an independent clause	as though, because, if, since, so that, than, when, where, while
INTERJECTION	Expresses emotion	hooray, yikes, ouch, wow

Determining Parts of Speech

The way a word is used in a sentence determines the word's part of speech. Many words can be used as different parts of speech.

The room was filled with **light.** [noun]
Let's **light** some candles. [verb]
A **light** snowfall covered the trees. [adjective]

What did you say? [pronoun]
I don't know **what** time it is. [adjective]
What! I won the contest? [interjection]

Have you ever been there **before**? [adverb]
Before they all died out, dinosaurs ruled the earth for millions of years. [conjunction]
The moon rose **before** sunset. [preposition]

Your Turn

Write three sentences using the words *play* and *right* as different parts of speech.

1. play [verb]
2. play [noun]
3. play [adjective]
4. right [adjective]
5. right [noun]
6. right [verb]

2. Agreement

Agreement of Subject and Verb

2a. A verb should always agree with its subject in number. Singular subjects take singular verbs. Plural subjects take plural verbs.

SINGULAR **She sings** in the school choir.
PLURAL **They sing** in the school choir.

SINGULAR **Mel is staying** home from school.
PLURAL His **friends are bringing** his homework to him.

2b. The number of the subject is not changed by a phrase following the subject.

SINGULAR **Friends** of the girl **are** sympathetic.
PLURAL **Tears,** absent in the day, **fall** at night.

SINGULAR The **aim** of her stories **is** to express truth.
PLURAL The **words** of their mother **reassure** them.

The number of the subject is not changed by a negative construction following the subject.

Miami, not the Florida Keys, **is** their home.

The number of the subject is also not affected when it is followed by a phrase beginning with *as well as, along with, in addition to,* or a similar expression.

The **teacher,** as well as her students, **looks** forward to spring break.

2c. The following indefinite pronouns are singular: *anybody, anyone, anything, each, either, everybody, everyone, everything, neither, nobody, no one, nothing, one, somebody, someone,* and *something.*

One of her mother's friends **asks** about Jim.
Somebody in the class **does** not **use** commas.

2d. The following indefinite pronouns are plural: *both, few, many,* and *several.*

> **Both** of the boys **want** to stay.
> **Several** of the students **offer** explanations.

2e. The indefinite pronouns *all, any, most, none,* and *some* are singular when they refer to singular words and are plural when they refer to plural words.

> SINGULAR **Most** of the garden still **needs** to be weeded.
> PLURAL **Most** of the plants also **need** to be watered.

> SINGULAR **All** of the kitchen **was** clean.
> PLURAL **All** of them **began** to run.

2f. A *compound subject,* which is two or more subjects that have the same verb, may be singular, plural, or either.

(1) Subjects joined by *and* usually take a plural verb.
> **Eddie** and **Lee sleep** in bunk beds.
> **Jean** and her **mother talk** in the car.

A compound subject that names only one person or thing takes a singular verb. A compound noun used as a subject also takes a singular verb.
> Jean's **friend** and **classmate was** Nancy Dryer.
> **Has law and order been** restored yet?

(2) Singular subjects joined by *or* or *nor* take a singular verb.
> **Eddie** or **Jean washes** dishes.
> Neither **Mother** nor **Roger wants** to return to Indiana with us.

(3) When a singular subject and a plural subject are joined by *or* or *nor,* the verb agrees with the subject nearer the verb.
> Neither the plot nor the **characters were** too complex.
> Neither the characters nor the **plot was** too complex.

NOTE: If such a construction sounds awkward, revise the sentence to give each part of the subject its own verb.
> The **plot wasn't** too complex, and neither **were** the **characters.**

2g. *Don't* and *doesn't* must agree with their subjects.

Use *don't (do not)* with the subjects *I* and *you* and with plural subjects.
> I **don't** agree. You **don't** sound well.
> Some people **don't** listen.

With other subjects, use *doesn't (does not).*
> She **doesn't** bring a lunch.
> It **doesn't** matter.

2h. A *collective noun* (such as *club, family,* or *swarm*) is singular in form but names a group of persons or things. A collective noun takes a singular verb when the noun refers to the group as a unit. However, a collective noun takes a plural verb when the noun refers to the parts or members of the group.

> SINGULAR The family **is** going home. [family = a unit]
> PLURAL The family **are** getting into the van. [family = individual family members]

Common Collective Nouns			
army	committee	flock	pair
audience	crew	group	public
band	crowd	herd	squad
choir	faculty	jury	staff
class	family	majority	swarm
club	fleet	number	team

2i. A verb agrees with its subject, not with its predicate nominative.

> SINGULAR The best **part** of her lunch **is** the **cheese and crackers.**
> PLURAL The **cheese and crackers are** the best **part** of her lunch.

2j. A verb agrees with its subject even when the verb precedes the subject, as in sentences beginning with *here* or *there* and in questions. Contractions such as *here's* and *there's* are used only with subjects that are singular in meaning.

> SINGULAR Here **is** [*or* **here's**] my **locker.**
> PLURAL Here **are** the **lockers.**

> SINGULAR Where **is** [*or* **where's**] the school **bus**?
> PLURAL Where **are** your gym **clothes**?

2k. An expression of an amount (a length of time, a statistic, or a fraction, for example) is singular when the amount is thought of as a unit or when it refers to a singular word. However, such an expression is plural when the amount is thought of as many parts or when it refers to a plural word.

> SINGULAR **Twenty-five cents is** the amount Dad gave my brother.
> PLURAL **Twenty-five cents were** jingling in his pocket.

SINGULAR   **One half** of the class **has** finished.

PLURAL   **A number** of students **have** transferred.

2l. The title of a creative work (such as a book, song, film, or painting) or the name of an organization, a country, or a city (even if it is plural in form) takes a singular verb.

"**Boys and Girls**" **was written** by Alice Munro.
The **United States is voting** in favor of the measure.

2m. Some nouns that are plural in form are singular in meaning.

Nouns that always take singular verbs include *civics, gymnastics, measles, news, electronics, mathematics, molasses,* and *physics.*

Mathematics is my favorite course.

Some nouns that end in *-s,* such as the following, take a plural verb even though they refer to single items: *binoculars, pants, shears, Olympics, eyeglasses, pliers, shorts,* and *scissors.*

The **scissors are** in the sewing basket.

2n. Subjects preceded by *every* or *many a* take singular verbs.

Many a [*or* Every] child **wants** a dog.

Agreement of Pronoun and Antecedent

A pronoun usually refers to a noun or another pronoun, which is called the pronoun's ***antecedent.***

2o. A pronoun agrees with its antecedent in number and gender. Singular pronouns refer to singular antecedents. Plural pronouns refer to plural antecedents.

A few singular pronouns indicate gender:

FEMININE   she, her, hers, herself

MASCULINE   he, him, his, himself

NEUTER   it, it, its, itself

The **man** decided **himself.** [singular, masculine]
His **daughter** wanted **her** father to stay with **her.**
    [singular, feminine]

2p. A singular pronoun is used to refer to *anybody, anyone, anything, each, either, everybody, everyone, everything, neither, nobody, no one, nothing, one, somebody, someone,* or *something.* The gender of any of these pronouns is determined by the gender of the pronoun's antecedent.

Each of the boys brought **his** uniform.

When the antecedent could be either masculine or feminine, use both the masculine and the feminine pronoun forms connected by *or.*

Not **everyone** gets a chance to know **his or her** grandparents.

2q. A singular pronoun is used to refer to two or more singular antecedents joined by *or* or *nor.*

Tim or Ahmad will read **his** poem next.
Neither **Heidi nor Laila** has read **hers** yet.

If a sentence sounds awkward when the antecedents are of different genders, revise it.

AWKWARD   Neither **Eric nor Sue** finished **his or her** part of the mural.

REVISED   **Eric** didn't finish **his** part of the mural, and **Sue** didn't finish **hers** either.

2r. A plural pronoun is used to refer to two or more antecedents joined by *and.*

The **man and his grandfather** have a good relationship despite the difference in **their** ages.
My **father and my brother** have **their** driver's licenses with **them.**

2s. The number of a relative pronoun (such as *who, whom, whose, which,* or *that*) depends on the number of its antecedent.

He is one **man who** goes **his** own way. [*Who* refers to the singular noun *man.* Therefore the singular form *his* is used to agree with *who.*]
Many who are older do **their** banking here. [*Who* refers to the plural pronoun *many.* Therefore, the plural form *their* is used to agree with *who.*]

Your Turn

In most of the following sentences, either a verb does not agree with its subject or a pronoun does not agree with its antecedent. Revise each incorrect sentence to correct the error.

1. Two students from each class is going to the state capital to attend a special conference on education.
2. Each of them are expected to bring back a report on the conference so that classmates can get firsthand information.
3. Since they will be on vacation next month, neither Miguel nor his sister are going to enter the tennis tournament.
4. This collection of Italian folk tales demonstrate the wisdom and humor of my ancestors.

3. Using Verbs

The Principal Parts of Verbs

3a. The four principal parts of a verb are the *base form,* the *present participle,* the *past,* and the *past participle.*

All verbs form the present participle by adding *–ing* to the base form. All verbs, however, do not form the past and past participle in the same way.

3b. A *regular verb* forms its past and past participle by adding *–d* or *–ed* to the base form.

3c. An *irregular verb* forms its past and past participle in some other way than by adding *–d* or *–ed* to the base form.

NOTE: The examples in the charts include *is* and *have* in parentheses to show that helping verbs (forms of *be* and *have*) are used with the present participle and past participle forms.

NOTE: If you are not sure about the principal parts of a verb, look in a dictionary. Entries for irregular verbs give the principal parts. If no principal parts are listed, the verb is a regular verb.

Common Regular Verbs			
BASE FORM	**PRESENT PARTICIPLE**	**PAST**	**PAST PARTICIPLE**
ask	(is) asking	asked	(have) asked
plan	(is) planning	planned	(have) planned
try	(is) trying	tried	(have) tried
use	(is) using	used	(have) used

Common Irregular Verbs			
BASE FORM	**PRESENT PARTICIPLE**	**PAST**	**PAST PARTICIPLE**
be	(is) being	was, were	(have) been
bring	(is) bringing	brought	(have) brought
catch	(is) catching	caught	(have) caught
drive	(is) driving	drove	(have) driven
eat	(is) eating	ate	(have) eaten
find	(is) finding	found	(have) found
go	(is) going	went	(have) gone
have	(is) having	had	(have) had
keep	(is) keeping	kept	(have) kept
lead	(is) leading	led	(have) led
pay	(is) paying	paid	(have) paid
ride	(is) riding	rode	(have) ridden
steal	(is) stealing	stole	(have) stolen
swim	(is) swimming	swam	(have) swum
tear	(is) tearing	tore	(have) torn

Tense

3d. The *tense* of a verb indicates the time of the action or the state of being that is expressed by the verb.

Every English verb has six tenses: *present, past, future, present perfect, past perfect,* and *future perfect.* The tenses are formed from the verb's principal parts.

Past	*Present*	*Future*
Existing or happening in the past	existing or happening now	existing or happening in the future

Past Perfect	*Present Perfect*	*Future Perfect*
existing or happening before a specific time in the past	existing or happening sometime before now	existing or happening before a specific time in the future

Each of the six tenses has an additional form called the *progressive form.* The progressive form expresses a continuing action or state of being. It consists of the appropriate tense of *be* followed by the verb's present participle. For the present tenses, the progressive form also includes one or more helping verbs.

Present Progressive	am, are, is singing
Past Progressive	was, were singing
Future Progressive	will (shall) be singing
Present Perfect Progressive	has, have been singing
Past Perfect Progressive	had been singing
Future Perfect Progressive	will (shall) have been singing

3e. Each of the six tenses has its own special uses.

(1) The *present tense* is used mainly to express an action or a state of being that is occurring now.

> Tara **knows** the answer.
> **Do** you **hear** the music?

The present tense is also used

• to show a customary or habitual action or state of being

> He **works** here.

• to express a general truth

> Basketball **entertains** millions.

• to make historical events seem current (such use is called the *historical present*)

> The Roman Empire **falls.**

• to discuss a literary work (such use is called the *literary present*)

> The poem **describes** summer.

• to express future time

> We **leave** on vacation next week.

(2) The *past tense* is used to express an action or a state of being that occurred in the past but that is not occurring now.

> Gerry once **scored** a hundred points.
> We **memorized** poetry in high school.

A past action or state of being can also be shown with the verb *used to* followed by the base form.

> My brother **used to ride** his bike to school.

(3) The *future tense* (formed with *will* or *shall* and the verb's base form) is used to express an action or a state of being that will occur.

> When he visits, he **will stay** in town.
> We **will read** Maya Angelou's poem next.

(4) The *present perfect tense* (formed with *have* or *has* and the verb's past participle) is used to express an action or a state of being that occurred at some indefinite time in the past.

> Her poems **have addressed** many situations.
> She **has published** widely.

The present perfect tense is also used to express an action or a state of being that began with the past and continues into the present.

> We **have shopped** at the market since May.

(5) The *past perfect tense* (formed with *had* and the verb's past participle) is used to express an action or a state of being that was completed in the past before some other past action or event.

> Other people remembered what he **had accomplished.** [The accomplishing occurred before the remembering.]
> I **had driven** for hours, and I arrived on time. [The driving occurred before the arriving.]

(6) The *future perfect tense* (formed with *will have* or *shall have* and the verb's past participle) is used to express an action or a state of being that will be completed in the future before some other future occurrence.

> After tonight, I **will have seen** the film twice.
> As of next Tuesday, we **will have lived** here two years.

3f. Do not change needlessly from one tense to another.

INCONSISTENT	Her family packed up and moves.
CONSISTENT	Her family **packed** up and **moved.**
CONSISTENT	Her family **packs** up and **moves.**

INCONSISTENT	They marry and bought a house.
CONSISTENT	They **married** and **bought** a house.
CONSISTENT	They **marry** and **buy** a house.

Using different verb tenses is often necessary to show the order of events that occur at different times.

NONSTANDARD	I wished that I wrote that poem.
STANDARD	I **wished** that I **had written** that poem. [Since the action of writing was completed before the action of wishing, the verb should be *had written,* not *wrote.*]

Active and Passive Voice

3g. A verb in the *active voice* expresses an action done by its subject. A verb in the *passive voice* expresses an action received by its subject.

ACTIVE VOICE	Inéz Romero **told** her story.
PASSIVE VOICE	The story **was told** by Inéz Romero.
ACTIVE VOICE	Patrick **instructed** them.
PASSIVE VOICE	They **were instructed** by Patrick.

3h. Use the passive voice sparingly.

The passive voice is not any less correct than the active voice, but it is less direct, less forceful, and less concise. As a result, a sentence in the passive voice can be wordy and sound awkward or weak.

AWKWARD PASSIVE	Instructions were given to them by the engineers.
ACTIVE	The engineers gave them instructions.

The passive voice is useful, however, in certain situations:

- when you do not know the performer of the action
  The First National Bank **was robbed** last night.
- when you do not want to reveal the performer of the action
  Police **were notified.**
- when you want to emphasize the receiver of the action
  Already, seven suspects **have been questioned.**

COMPUTER NOTE
Some software programs can identify verbs in the passive voice. If you use such a program, keep in mind that it can't tell *why* you used the passive voice. If you did so for a very good reason, you may want to leave the verb in the passive voice.

Your Turn

For each of the following sentences, correct the verb tenses to show the order of events.
1. After the clock had struck eight, Mr. Leonard Mead had gone for a walk.
2. For years, he had enjoyed the cool air and only occasionally has had trouble from roaming dogs.
3. Nothing moves on the street for an hour, and now he will hear no sounds.
4. While he was walking, a police car has approached him.
5. A voice had told him to stop, and he does so.

4. Using Pronouns

Case

Case is the form that a noun or pronoun takes to indicate its use in a sentence. In English, there are three cases: *nominative, objective,* and *possessive.*

The form of a noun is the same for both the nominative case and the objective case. For the possessive case, however, a noun changes its form, usually by adding an apostrophe and an –*s* to singular nouns and only an apostrophe to plural nouns.

NOMINATIVE	**Frank McCourt** told the story of his childhood.
OBJECTIVE	His family's poverty greatly affected **Frank McCourt.**
POSSESSIVE	**Frank McCourt's** story made me think.

Most personal pronouns, however, have a different form for each case.

The Nominative Case

4a. A subject of a verb is in the nominative case.

They knew that **he** was sincere. [*They* is the subject of *knew; he* is the subject of *was.*]
Has **he** or **she** visited New York City? [*He* and *she* are the subjects of *has visited.*]

4b. A predicate nominative is in the nominative case.

A ***predicate nominative*** follows a linking verb and explains or identifies the subject of the verb.

One of the witnesses was my **uncle.** [*Uncle* follows *was* and identifies the subject *one.*]

The narrators will be **Larry** and **I.** [*Larry* and *I* follow *will be* and identify the subject *narrators.*]

NOTE: Expressions such as *It's me, That's him,* and *Could it be her?* are examples of informal usage. Avoid using such expressions in formal speaking and writing.

PERSONAL PRONOUNS			
Singular			
	NOMINATIVE	OBJECTIVE	POSSESSIVE
First Person	I	me	my, mine
Second Person	you	you	your, yours
Third Person	he, she, it	him, her, it	his, her, hers, its
Plural			
	NOMINATIVE	OBJECTIVE	POSSESSIVE
First Person	we	us	our, ours
Second Person	you	you	your, yours
Third Person	they	them	their, theirs

NOTE: Notice in the chart that *you* and *it* are the only personal pronouns that have the same forms for the nominative and the objective cases. Notice also that only third-person singular pronouns indicate gender.

The Objective Case

4c. A direct object of a verb is in the objective case.

A **direct object** follows an action verb and tells *whom* or *what.*

Syha hasn't met **her** yet. [*Her* tells *whom* Syha hasn't met yet.]

They made **shirts** and painted **them.** [*Shirts* tells *what* they made, and *them* tells *what* they painted.]

4d. An indirect object of a verb is in the objective case.

An **indirect object** comes before a direct object and tells *to whom* or *to what* or *for whom* or *for what.*

The vision had given **them** hope. [*Them* tells *to whom* hope was given.]

Draw **me** a map. [*Me* tells *for whom* the map is drawn.]

4e. An object of a preposition is in the objective case.

An **object of a preposition** comes at the end of a phrase that begins with a preposition.

The sight of **him** haunts the narrator.

For **us,** such a sight is difficult to imagine.

Special Pronoun Problems

4f. The pronoun *who* (*whoever*) is in the nominative case. The pronoun *whom* (*whomever*) is in the objective case.

NOMINATIVE **Who** is John Krakauer? [*Who* is the subject of *is.*]

OBJECTIVE With **whom** was he traveling? [*Whom* is the object of *with.*]

When choosing between *who* and *whom* in a subordinate clause, do not be misled by a word outside the clause. Be sure to base your choice on how the pronoun functions in its own subordinate clause.

NOMINATIVE Do you know **who** the pool players are? [*Who* is the predicate nominative identifying the subject of the subordinate clause *who the pool players are.* The entire subordinate clause serves as the direct object of *do know.*]

OBJECTIVE Perhaps Gwendolyn Brooks knew the people **whom** she wrote about. [*Whom* is the object of *about.* The entire subordinate clause *whom she wrote about* modifies *people.*]

Often, *whom* is left out of a subordinate clause.

The poet [**whom**] I like best is Emily Dickinson. [*Whom* is the unstated direct object of *like.*]

Leaving out *whom* in such cases tends to make writing sound more informal. In formal situations, it is generally better to include *whom.*

NOTE: In spoken English, the use of *whom* is becoming less common. In written English, you should distinguish between *who* and *whom*.

| INFORMAL | **Who** did you see at the dance? |
| FORMAL | **Whom** did you see at the dance? |

4g. An appositive is in the same case as the noun or pronoun to which it refers.

An **appositive** is a noun or pronoun placed next to another noun or pronoun to identify or explain it.

| NOMINATIVE | They, **Lacy and she,** played the sisters. [The appositive *Lacy and she* is in the nominative case because it identifies the subject *they.*] |
| OBJECTIVE | The sisters were played by them, **Lacy and her.** [The appositive, *Lacy and her,* is in the objective case because it identifies *them*, the object of a preposition.] |

Sometimes the pronouns *we* and *us* are used with noun appositives.

We actors like to pretend. [The pronoun *we* is in the nominative case because it is the subject of *like*.]

Pretending is fun for **us** actors. [The pronoun *us* is in the objective case because it is the object of the preposition *for*.]

4h. A pronoun following *than* or *as* in an incomplete construction is in the same case as it would be if the construction were completed.

Notice how the meaning of each of the following sentences depends on the pronoun form in the incomplete construction.

NOMINATIVE	I liked Kim more than **he** [did].
OBJECTIVE	I liked Kim more than [I liked] **him.**
NOMINATIVE	You called Raquel more than **he** [called Raquel].
OBJECTIVE	You called Raquel more than [you called] **him.**

Clear Pronoun Reference

4i. A pronoun should refer clearly to its antecedent.

(1) Avoid an **ambiguous reference,** which occurs when a pronoun can refer to any one of two or more antecedents.

| AMBIGUOUS | Dee talked to Mama while she ate. [*She* can refer to either Mama or Dee.] |
| CLEAR | While **Mama** ate, Dee talked to **her.** |

(2) Avoid a **general reference,** which occurs when a pronoun refers to a general idea rather than to a specific antecedent.

GENERAL	Dee insisted on having the quilt. This did not surprise Maggie. [*This* has no specific antecedent.]
CLEAR	That Dee insisted on having the quilt did not surprise Maggie.
CLEAR	Maggie was not surprised that Dee insisted on having the quilt.

(3) Avoid a **weak reference,** which occurs when a pronoun refers to an implied antecedent.

| WEAK | She made quilts, but it was more than a hobby. [No antecedent is provided for *it*.] |
| CLEAR | Making quilts was more than a hobby for her. |

(4) Avoid using an **indefinite reference,** which occurs when a pronoun (such as *you, it,* or *they*) refers to no particular person or thing.

| INDEFINITE | In that museum, they display fine quilts. [*They* has no antecedent in the sentence.] |
| CLEAR | That museum displays fine quilts. |

NOTE: The indefinite use of *it* is acceptable in familiar expressions such as *It's snowing* and *It's late.*

Your Turn

Most of the following sentences contain errors in pronoun usage. Write the correct pronoun form for each error. If a sentence is already correct, write C (correct).

1. Us athletes have little time to spend watching television.
2. The one who organized the new filing system was she.
3. Ask Masha and he about the outcome of the race.
4. Ramona had not decided who she would vote for in the election.
5. Between you and I, that painting is worth much more.
6. We are willing to help whoever is in need.
7. Edna said that you speak Spanish better than her.
8. We can only guess whom it was.
9. Tell Christina and me what happened.
10. Is the meeting open to we students?

5. Using Modifiers

One-word Modifiers

A **modifier** is a word or group of words that limits the meaning of another word or group of words. The two kinds of modifiers are adjectives and adverbs.

Adjectives

5a. Use an *adjective* to limit the meaning of a noun or pronoun.

> Maggie was also a **skilled** quilter. [*Skilled* limits the meaning of the noun *quilter*.]
>
> **Arrogant** and **grasping,** she forfeited the quilts. [*Arrogant* and *grasping* limit the meaning of the pronoun *she*.]

Adverbs

5b. Use an *adverb* to limit the meaning of a verb, an adjective, or another adverb.

> **Suddenly,** Mama made her decision. [*Suddenly* limits the meaning of the verb *made*.]
>
> Mama was **not** talkative. [*Not* limits the meaning of the adjective *talkative*.]
>
> She **quite** abruptly gave the quilts to Maggie. [*Quite* limits the meaning of the adverb *abruptly*.]

NOTE: The adverbs *really, too, so,* and *very* are often overused. Replace these adverbs with: *completely, definitely, entirely, especially, extremely, generally, largely, mainly, mostly, particularly,* or *unusually.*

NOTE: Some modifiers can function as adjectives or as adverbs, depending on the word or words they modify.

| ADJECTIVE | That's a **hard** job. |
| ADVERB | We worked **hard.** |

Adjectives often follow linking verbs. Adverbs often follow action verbs. You can tell whether a verb is a linking or an action verb by replacing it with a form of *seem*. If the substitution makes sense, the original verb is a linking verb and should be followed by an adjective. If the substitution does not make sense, the original verb is an action verb and should be followed by an adverb.

| ADJECTIVE | Behind the mist, the sun appeared dim. [*The sun seemed dim* makes sense. In this case, *appeared* is a linking verb.] |

| ADVERB | From behind the mist, the sun appeared suddenly. [*The sun seemed suddenly* doesn't make sense. In this case, *appeared* is an action verb.] |

Comparison of Modifiers

5c. The forms of modifiers change to show comparison.

The three degrees of comparison are *positive, comparative,* and *superlative.*

(1) Most one-syllable modifiers form the comparative and superlative degrees by adding *–er* and *–est.*

(2) Some two-syllable modifiers form their comparative and superlative degrees by adding *–er* and *–est.* Other two-syllable modifiers form the comparative and superlative by using *more* and *most.*

(3) Modifiers of more than two syllables form the comparative and superlative degrees by using *more* and *most.*

(4) To show decreasing comparisons, all modifiers form their comparative and superlative degrees with *less* and *least.*

Positive	Comparative	Superlative
rude	ruder	rudest
happy	happier	happiest
skillful	more skillful	most skillful
quickly	more quickly	most quickly
artistic	more artistic	most artistic
carefully	more carefully	most carefully

(5) Some modifiers form the comparative and superlative degrees in other ways.

Positive	Comparative	Superlative
bad	worse	worst
good/well	better	best
little	less	least
many/much	more	most

5d. Use the comparative degree when comparing two things. Use the superlative degree when comparing more than two.

| COMPARATIVE | Maggie was **more respectful** than Dee. I liked this story **better** than that one. |
| SUPERLATIVE | Is this the **best** story of the ones you've read? |

5e. Include the word *other* or *else* when comparing one thing with others in the same group.

ILLOGICAL	This image is more vivid than any in the poem. [This image is in the poem. Logically, this image cannot be more vivid than itself.]
LOGICAL	This image is more vivid than any **other** in the poem.
ILLOGICAL	Rita understands plot better than everyone in class. [*Everyone* includes Rita. Logically, she cannot understand better than herself.]
LOGICAL	Rita understands plot better than everyone **else** in class.

5f. Avoid a *double comparison*—the use of both *–er* and *more* (or *less*) or both *–est* and *most* (or *least*) to modify the same word.

The test was **easier** [*not* more easier] than I thought it would be.
Our dog is the **noisiest** [*not* most noisiest] on the block.

5g. Be sure your comparisons are clear.

| UNCLEAR | The traffic here is faster than Detroit. [This sentence incorrectly compares traffic with a city.] |
| CLEAR | The traffic here is faster than **traffic in** Detroit. |

State both parts of an incomplete comparison if there is any chance of misunderstanding.

UNCLEAR	I see her more than Mark.
CLEAR	I see her more than Mark **sees her.**
CLEAR	I see her more than **I see** Mark.

Placement of Modifiers

5h. Avoid using a *dangling modifier*—a modifying word or word group that does not sensibly modify any word or word group in the same sentence.

You may correct a dangling modifier
- by adding a word or words that the dangling modifier can sensibly modify
- by adding a word or words to the dangling modifier
- by rewording the sentence

DANGLING	To understand Shakespeare's plays, some knowledge of his vocabulary is necessary.
CLEAR	To understand Shakespeare's plays, **readers** need some knowledge of his vocabulary.
DANGLING	While studying for the math test, my phone rang incessantly.
CLEAR	While **I was** studying for the math test, my phone rang incessantly.

5i. Avoid using a *misplaced modifier*—a modifying word or word group that sounds awkward or unclear because it seems to modify the wrong word or word group.

To correct a misplaced modifier, place the modifying word or word group as near as possible to the word you intend it to modify.

MISPLACED	A scrap from a uniform was part of the quilt that had been worn during the Civil War.
CLEAR	A scrap from a uniform **that had been worn during the Civil War** was part of the quilt.
MISPLACED	Made from pieces of old clothing, Dee held the quilts.
CLEAR	Dee held the quilts **made from pieces of old clothing.**

Your Turn

The following sentences contain errors in the use of modifiers. Rewrite each sentence, correcting the error.

1. Seeing that no damage had been done, their cars drove away in opposite directions.
2. The temperature in Houston is higher than Chicago.
3. The gift was more costlier than I had expected it to be.
4. The branches of the tree hung over the fence that we planted.
5. Balking, I quickly grew frustrated with the mule.

6. Phrases

6a. A *phrase* is a group of related words that is used as a single part of speech and that does not contain both a verb and its subject.

VERB PHRASE	have been writing
PREPOSITIONAL PHRASE	with you and me

Prepositional Phrases

6b. A *prepositional phrase* begins with a preposition and ends with the *object of the preposition,* a word or word group that functions as a noun.

They were covered **with golden fur.** [The noun *fur* is the object of the preposition *with*.]

According to Sari, her brother is a pest. [The noun *Sari* is the object of the preposition *according to*.]

(1) A prepositional phrase that modifies a noun or pronoun is called an ***adjective phrase***.

An adjective phrase tells *what kind* or *which one*.

Stories **of American Indians** sometimes feature coyotes. [The phrase *of American Indians* modifies *stories*, telling *what kind*.]

Stories **about coyotes** depict them as tricksters. [The phrase *about coyotes* modifies *stories*, telling *which ones*.]

An adjective phrase generally follows the word it modifies. That word may be the object of another preposition.

Did you see the film **about the coyotes of the desert?** [The phrase *of the desert* modifies *coyotes*, the object of the preposition *about*.]

More than one adjective phrase may modify the same noun or pronoun.

The sight **of them through the scope** startled the watchers. [The phrases *of them* and *through the scope* modify the noun *sight*.]

(2) A prepositional phrase that modifies a verb, an adjective, or an adverb is called an ***adverb phrase.*** An adverb phrase tells *when, where, how, why*, or *to what extent*.

In a moment, he reached for his camera. [*In a moment* modifies *reached*, telling *when*.]

The coyotes were not far **from him.** [*From him* modifies *far,* telling *where*.]

They were not afraid **of him.** [The phrase *of him* modifies *afraid,* telling *how*.]

An adverb phrase may come before or after the word it modifies.

To me, this was a wonderful story.
This was a wonderful story **to me.**

More than one adverb phrase may modify the same word or group of words.

In 1962, John Steinbeck received the Nobel Prize **at age sixty.** [Both *in 1962* and *at age sixty* modify *received*.]

Verbals and Verbal Phrases

A ***verbal*** is a form of a verb used as a noun, an adjective, or an adverb. A ***verbal phrase*** consists of a verbal and its modifiers and complements. The three kinds of verbals are *participles*, *gerunds*, and *infinitives*.

Participles and Participial Phrases

6c. A *participle* is a verb form that can be used as an adjective. A *participial phrase* consists of a participle and all the words related to the participle.

(1) ***Present participles*** end in –*ing*.

It was certainly an **embarrassing** moment. [The present participle *embarrassing* modifies the noun *moment*.]

Hammering loudly, Sobel took out his frustration in hard work. [The participial phrase *hammering loudly* modifies *Sobel*. The adverb *loudly* modifies the present participle *hammering*.]

(2) Most ***past participles*** end in –*d* or –*ed*. Others are irregularly formed.

The **injured** player did not return. [The past participle *injured* modifies the noun *player*.]

Feld, **dazzled by Max's college education,** thinks that the boy is a good match for Miriam. [The participial phrase modifies the noun *Feld*. The adverb phrase *by Max's college education* modifies the past participle *dazzled*.]

Read aloud, the story entertained the kindergarten class. [The participial phrase modifies the noun *story*. The adverb *aloud* modifies the past participle *read*.]

NOTE: Do not confuse a participle used as an adjective with a participle used as part of a verb phrase.

ADJECTIVE	What are **exploding** stars called?
VERB PHRASE	The fireworks **are exploding.**

Gerunds and Gerund Phrases

6d. A *gerund* is a verb form ending in *–ing* that is used as a noun. A *gerund phrase* consists of a gerund and all the words related to the gerund.

SUBJECT	**Reading** was Sobel's pastime. [The gerund *reading* is the subject of *was*.]
DIRECT OBJECT	She didn't like **speaking in class.** [The gerund phrase *speaking in class* is the direct object of the verb *did like*. The prepositional phrase *in class* modifies the gerund *speaking*.]
PREDICATE PREPOSITION	The best part was **winning the match.** [The gerund phrase *winning the match* is the predicate nominative identifying the subject *part*. *Match* is the direct object of *winning*.]
OBJECT OF A PREPOSITION	After **waiting for two years,** Sobel can propose to Miriam. [The gerund phrase *waiting for two years* is the object of the preposition *after*. The prepositional phrase *for two years* modifies *waiting*.]

A noun or pronoun should be in the possessive form when preceding a gerund.

Sobel's pounding bothered Feld because it interfered with his daydreaming.

NOTE: Do not confuse a gerund with a present participle used as an adjective or as part of a verb phrase.

Meddling, Feld was **arranging** for Max and Miriam to go out. [*Meddling* is a present participle modifying *Feld*. *Arranging* is part of the verb phrase *was arranging*.]

Infinitives and Infinitive Phrases

6e. An *infinitive* is a verb form, usually preceded by *to*, that can be used as a noun, an adjective, or an adverb. An *infinitive phrase* consists of an infinitive and all the words related to the infinitive.

NOUN	**To have friends** is important. [The infinitive phrase *to have friends* is the subject of *is*. *Friends* is the direct object of the infinitive *to have*.] Maggie did not want **to argue with Dee.** [The infinitive phrase *to argue with Dee* is the object of the verb *did want*. The prepositional phrase *with Dee* modifies the infinitive *to argue*.]

NOUN	Dee's plan was **to take the quilts.** [The infinitive phrase *to take the quilts* is the predicate nominative identifying the subject *plan*. *Quilts* is the direct object of the infinitive *to take*.]
ADJECTIVE	Her refusal **to answer questions** puzzled him. [The infinitive phrase *to answer questions* modifies the noun *refusal*. *Questions* is the direct object of the infinitive *to answer*.]
ADVERB	We were ready **to go to the game.** [The infinitive phrase *to go to the game* modifies the adjective *ready*. The prepositional phrase *to the game* modifies the infinitive *to go*.]

NOTE: Do not confuse an infinitive with a prepositional phrase that begins with *to*.

Eric went **to the gym** [prepositional phrase] **to meet Clint.** [infinitive phrase].

Sometimes the *to* of the infinitive is omitted.
Would you help me [to] proofread this?
Help me [to] bake a birthday cake for Leroy.

6f. An infinitive may have a subject, in which case it forms an *infinitive clause*.

He asked **the teacher to excuse him.** [The infinitive clause *the teacher to excuse him* is the direct object of *asked*. *The teacher* is the subject of the infinitive *to excuse*. *Him* is the direct object of the infinitive.]

NOTE: A *split infinitive* occurs when a word is placed between the word *to* and the verb in an infinitive. Although split infinitives are commonly used in informal speaking and writing, you should avoid using them in formal situations.

SPLIT	It was better **to** just **mind** his own business.
REVISED	It was better just **to mind** his own business.

Appositives and Appositive Phrases

6g. An *appositive* is a noun or a pronoun placed beside another noun or pronoun to identify or explain it. An *appositive phrase* consists of an appositive and its modifiers.

Janet Frame, **a resident of New Zealand,** wrote the essay. [The appositive phrase *a resident of New Zealand* identifies the subject *Janet Frame*.]

Have you seen *The Maltese Falcon,* **one of Humphrey Bogart's most famous films**? [The appositive phrase *one of Humphrey Bogart's most famous films* explains the direct object *The Maltese Falcon.*]

Who wrote the poem "**The Flying Cat**"? [The appositive *"The Flying Cat"* identifies the direct object *poem.*]

An appositive phrase usually follows the noun or pronoun it refers to. For emphasis, however, it may come at the beginning of a sentence.

A big brother all my life, I rushed to help the little girl who reminded me of my sister.

Appositives and appositive phrases are usually set off by commas. However, some appositives are necessary to identify or explain a noun or pronoun and therefore should not be set off by commas.

My cousin **Jim** lives in Alaska. [The appositive is not set off by commas because it is necessary to tell which of the writer's cousins lives in Alaska.]

My cousin, **Jim**, lives in Alaska. [The appositive is set off by commas because the writer has only one cousin, and the appositive is not necessary.]

Your Turn

Write five sentences, following the directions for each sentence. Underline the italicized phrase in each sentence you write. An example is given below.

Use *to get there from here* as an infinitive phrase acting as an adjective.

What is the best way *to get there from here?*

1. Use *for our English class* as an adverb phrase.
2. Use *walking in line* as a participial phrase.
3. Use *the new student in our class* as an appositive phrase.
4. Use *to hit a home run* as an infinitive phrase that is the direct object of a verb.
5. Use *playing the piano* as a gerund phrase that is the subject of a verb.

7. Clauses

7a. A *clause* is a group of words that contains a verb and its subject and that is used as part of a sentence.

SENTENCE	Lichens are small, rootless plants that are composed of both fungi and algae.
CLAUSE	Lichens are small, rootless plants. [complete thought]
CLAUSE	that are composed of both fungi and algae [incomplete thought]

Kinds of Clauses

7b. An *independent* (or *main*) *clause* expresses a complete thought and can stand by itself as a sentence.

The *Titanic* was the largest ship afloat, and **people were amazed by its size.**

When the ship left Southampton, **its passengers were looking forward to the voyage.**

7c. A *subordinate* (or *dependent*) clause does not express a complete thought and cannot stand alone.

When the ship left Southampton, its passengers were looking forward to the voyage.

7d. An *adjective clause* is a subordinate clause that modifies a noun or a pronoun.

An adjective clause, which usually follows the word it modifies, usually begins with a ***relative pronoun***—*who, whom, whose, which,* or *that*. Besides introducing an adjective clause, a relative pronoun has its own function within the clause.

J. Bruce Ismay, **who managed the White Star Line,** was on board. [The adjective clause modifies *J. Bruce Ismay. Who* serves as the subject of *managed.*]

The ship, **whose hold was filled to capacity,** set off into the Atlantic. [The adjective clause modifies the noun *ship. Whose* serves as an adjective modifying *hold.*]

A relative pronoun may sometimes be left out of an adjective clause.

Did the captain know [**that**] **icebergs were ahead?**

Occasionally an adjective clause begins with the relative adverb *where* or *when.*

It was after midnight **when the alarm sounded.**

The captain saw **where the iceberg hit the ship.**

Depending on how it is used, an adjective clause is either essential or nonessential. An ***essential clause*** provides information that is necessary to the meaning of a sentence. A *nonessential clause* provides additional information that can be omitted without changing the meaning of a sentence. A nonessential clause is always set off by commas.

ESSENTIAL	Students **who are going to the game** can take the bus at 4 P.M.
NONESSENTIAL	Austin Stevens, **whose mother is a pediatrician,** plans to study medicine.

7e. An *adverb clause* is a subordinate clause that modifies a verb, an adjective, or an adverb.

An adverb clause, which may come before or after the word it modifies, tells *how, when, where, why, to what extent* (*how much*), or *under what condition*. An adverb clause begins with a **subordinating conjunction,** such as *although, because, if, so that,* or *when.*

The passengers panicked **when they realized what had happened.** [The adverb phrase modifies the verb *panicked*, telling *when*.]

Although the ship had lifeboats, there were not enough. [The adverb clause modifies *were*, telling *under what condition*.]

Some passengers were more selfish **than others.** [The adverb clause modifies *selfish*, telling *to what extent*.]

7f. A *noun clause* is a subordinate clause used as a subject, a predicate nominative, a direct object, an indirect object, or an object of a preposition.

The words commonly used to begin noun clauses include *that, what, whether, who,* and *why.*

SUBJECT	**What the shipmates faced** was an impossible task.
PREDICATE NOMINATIVE	A major wonder was **that so many survived the disaster.**
DIRECT OBJECT	Who knows **whether the disaster could have been avoided?**

INDIRECT OBJECT	The story of the *Titanic* gives **whoever hears it** plenty to think about.

The word that introduces a noun clause may or may not have a function within the noun clause.

Later, he regretted **what he had done.** [*What* is the direct object of *had done*.]

Some people believe **that there is no excuse for bad manners.** [*That* has no function in the clause.]

Sometimes the word that introduces a noun clause is not stated, but its meaning is understood.

He is a **man [whom] you should respect.**

Although short sentences can be effective, your writing is more effective if you alternate between shorter sentences and longer ones. Often, you can combine short sentences by changing some of them into subordinate clauses and inserting them in other sentences.

CHOPPY	Malcolm X had a troubled youth. He landed in jail. There, he changed his life completely.
REVISED	Malcolm X, who had a troubled youth, landed in jail, where he changed his life completely.

Your Turn

The following paragraph consists mostly of short sentences. Change some of these sentences into subordinate clauses and then combine them to create longer, smoother sentences.

Some people have straight hair. They want curly hair. Some people have curly hair. They want straight hair. They spend millions of dollars. That money might be put to better use. These people discover something. Their appearance can't change who they really are.

8. Sentence Structure

Sentence or Sentence Fragment?

8a. A *sentence* is a group of words that contains a subject and a verb and that expresses a complete thought.

A sentence should begin with a capital letter and end with a period, a question mark, or an exclamation point. A group of words that either does not have a subject and a verb or does not express a complete thought is called a *sentence fragment.*

FRAGMENT	While his father was getting the wagon.
SENTENCE	While his father was getting the wagon, the boys got ready.
FRAGMENT	Their father up early on Saturday morning.
SENTENCE	Why was their father up early on Saturday morning?

Subject and Predicate

8b. A sentence consists of two parts: the subject and the predicate. The *subject* tells *whom* or *what* the sentence is about. The *predicate* tells something about the subject.

In the following examples, all the words labeled *subject* make up the **complete subject,** and all the words labeled *predicate* make up the **complete predicate.**

SUBJECT	PREDICATE
They	rode in the wagon.

SUBJECT	PREDICATE
A maze of streets and alleys	led to the dump.

PREDICATE	SUBJECT	PREDICATE
Doesn't	Brian's car	have a CD player?

The Simple Subject

8c. The *simple subject* is the main word or group of words that tells *whom* or *what* the sentence is about.

The railroad **crossing** south of 86th Street was noisy. [The complete subject is *the railroad crossing south of 86th Street.*]
The gifted **Frank McCourt** wrote "Typhoid Fever." [The complete subject is *the gifted Frank McCourt.*]

The Simple Predicate

8d. The *simple predicate*, or *verb*, is the main word or group of words that tells something about the subject.

He **ran** faster and faster up the hill. [The complete predicate is *ran faster and faster up the hill.*]
Have you ever **had** such a wild ride on a sled before? [The complete predicate is *have ever had such a wild ride on a sled before.*]

In this handbook, the term *subject* refers to the simple subject, and the term *verb* refers to the simple predicate unless otherwise indicated.

The Compound Subject and the Compound Verb

8e. A *compound subject* consists of two or more subjects that are joined by a conjunction and have the same verb.

He and his **brothers** were afraid of the storm.
Were the **boys or** their **father** hurt?

8f. A *compound verb* consists of two or more verbs that are joined by a conjunction and have the same subject.

They **ran** to the shack **and hid** inside.
Their father **protected** them **but was pelted** with hail himself.

A sentence may have a compound subject and a compound verb.

Both my **aunt** and my **uncle have** cars but rarely **drive** anywhere.

Finding the Subject of a Sentence

8g. To find the subject of a sentence, ask "Who?" or "What?" before the verb.

(1) The subject of a sentence is never in a prepositional phrase.
Piles of rotten garbage stood before them. [What stood? *Piles* stood, not *garbage*, which is the object of the preposition *of.*]
In the trash hid **rats.** [What hid? *Rats* hid. *Trash* is the object of the preposition *in.*]

(2) The subject of a sentence expressing a question usually follows the verb or a part of the verb phrase. Questions often begin with a verb, a helping verb, or a word such as *what, when, where, how,* or *why.*

Turning the question into a statement may help you find the subject.

QUESTION	Is hail dangerous to people?
STATEMENT	**Hail** is dangerous to people.

(3) The word *there* or *here* is never the subject of a sentence.
There is the **tarp.** [What is there? A *tarp* is there.]
Here is your **water.** [What is here? *Water* is here.]

(4) The subject of a sentence expressing a command or request is always understood to be *you* although *you* may not appear in the sentence.
[You] Pay attention to the writer's metaphors. [Who is to pay attention? *You* are.]

The subject of a command or request is *you* even when the sentence contains a **noun of direct address,** a word naming the one or ones spoken to.
Alistair, [you] please explain this story's ending.

Complements

8h. A *complement* is a word or group of words that completes the meaning of a verb.

Three kinds of complements are *subject complements* (predicate nominative and predicate adjective), *direct objects*, and *indirect objects*.

The Subject Complement

8i. A *subject complement* is a word or word group that completes the meaning of a linking verb or modifies the subject.

(1) A **predicate nominative** is a noun or pronoun that follows a linking verb and identifies the subject of the verb.

Their father was a powerful **man.** [*Man* identifies the subject *father*.]

Was the author the youngest **son?** [*Son* renames the subject *author*.]

(2) A **predicate adjective** is an adjective that follows a linking verb and modifies the subject of the verb.

Was their father **strong?** [The adjective *strong* modifies the subject *father*.]

The wagon was **sturdy** and **large.** [The adjectives *sturdy* and *large* modify the subject *wagon*.]

NOTE: A subject complement may precede the subject and the verb.

PREDICATE
ADJECTIVE   How **glad** they were to have the umbrella!

The Direct Object and the Indirect Object

8j. A *direct object* is a noun or pronoun that receives the action of a verb or that shows the result of the action. The direct object tells *whom* or *what* after a transitive verb.

Ice covered the **ground.** [covered what? *ground*]

How he admires his **father** and **mother!** [admires whom? *father* and *mother*]

8k. An *indirect object* is a noun or pronoun that precedes the direct object and usually tells *to whom* or *for whom* (or *to what* or *for what*) the action of the verb is done.

They brought their **mother** the apples they had picked. [brought apples for whom? *mother*]

He had given the **wheels** and **gears** some grease. [had given grease to what? *wheels* and *gears*]

Classifying Sentences by Purpose

8l. Sentences may be classified as *declarative*, *imperative*, *interrogative*, or *exclamatory*.

(1) A **declarative sentence** makes a statement. It is followed by a period.
They gazed out over the city.

(2) An **imperative sentence** makes a request or gives a command. It is usually followed by a period. A very strong command, however, is followed by an exclamation point.
Let me know when you are free. [request]
Be careful not to fall. [mild command]
Hurry! [strong command]

(3) An **interrogative sentence** asks a question. It is followed by a question mark.
What is the high point of the action?

(4) An **exclamatory sentence** expresses strong feeling. It is followed by an exclamation point.
Watch out!

Classifying Sentences by Structure

8m. Sentences may be classified as *simple*, *compound*, *complex*, or *compound-complex*.

(1) A **simple sentence** has one independent clause and no subordinate clauses.
Cora and Kareem bought party supplies.
Look at this!

(2) A **compound sentence** has two or more independent clauses but no subordinate clauses.
Cora hung streamers from the ceiling, and Kareem set party favors on the tables.
The lightning diminished; the storm was over.

NOTE: Do not confuse a compound sentence with a simple sentence that has a compound subject or a compound predicate.

COMPOUND
PREDICATE   S V V
Kareem yawned and **stretched** his arms.

COMPOUND
SENTENCE   S V S V
Kareem yawned, and **he stretched** his arms.

(3) A **complex sentence** has one independent clause and at least one subordinate clause.

After they got home, they unloaded the wagon. [The subordinate clause is *after they got home*; the independent clause is *they unloaded the wagon*.]

As he ran, sweat darkened the shirt that he was wearing. [The subordinate clauses are *as he ran* and *that he was wearing*.]

(4) A **compound-complex sentence** contains two or more independent clauses and at least one subordinate clause.

When the boys were ready, they piled into the car, and their father turned the key. [The independent clauses are *they piled into the car* and *their father turned the key*. The subordinate clause is *when the boys were ready*.]

Your Turn

The following paragraph contains only simple sentences. Revise the paragraph to create a variety of sentence structures.

Many people immigrate to the United States. Some bring children along. These children often face enormous difficulties. Many do not have the same cultural background as the other students at their new schools. The young immigrants may not speak English. They do not know the customs of their new home. Yet, their parents have high hopes for them. The children try to fulfill those hopes. Millions of immigrants have done so. Somehow these children adapt to life in the United States.

9. Writing Complete Sentences

Sentence Fragments

9a. Avoid using sentence fragments.

A **sentence** is a word group that has a subject and a verb and expresses a complete thought. A **sentence fragment** is a word group that does not have the basic parts of a complete sentence.

To find out whether a word group is a complete sentence or a sentence fragment, use this simple three-part test. If you answer *no* to any of these questions, the word group is a fragment.

1. Does the group of words have a subject?
2. Does it have a verb?
3. Does it express a complete thought?

SUBJECT MISSING	Was her dancing partner. [*Who* was her dancing partner?]
SENTENCE	**Geraldo** was her dancing partner.
VERB MISSING	Marin at the hospital. [*What* did she do at the hospital?]
SENTENCE	Marin **waited** at the hospital.
INCOMPLETE THOUGHT	When she was asked. [*What happened* when she was asked?]
SENTENCE	**She could not give his full name** when she was asked.

Phrase Fragments

A **phrase** is a group of words that does not have a subject and a verb.

FRAGMENT	Attending many dances.
SENTENCE	She enjoyed **attending many dances.**
FRAGMENT	In green pants and a fancy shirt.
SENTENCE	Emma bumped into the boy **in green pants and a fancy shirt.**
FRAGMENT	A writer of Mexican heritage.
SENTENCE	Sandra Cisneros, **a writer of Mexican heritage,** wrote this story.

Subordinate Clause Fragments

A **clause** is a group of words that has a subject and a verb. An **independent clause** expresses a complete thought and can stand on its own as a sentence.

| INDEPENDENT CLAUSE | She found her voice. |

However, a **subordinate clause** does not express a complete thought and can not stand by itself as a sentence.

| FRAGMENT | When Sandra Cisneros found her point of view. |
| SENTENCE | **When Sandra Cisneros found her point of view,** she found her voice. |

Run-on Sentences

9b. Avoid run-on sentences.

A **run-on sentence** is two or more complete sentences that are run together as one. Because a reader cannot tell where one idea ends and another begins, run-on sentences can be confusing.

There are two kinds of run-ons. In the first kind, called a **fused sentence,** the sentences have no punctuation at all between them.

| RUN-ON | He had no papers on him no one knew his identity. |

In the other kind of run-on, called a **comma splice,** only a comma separates the sentences from one another.

| RUN-ON | He had no papers on him, no one knew his identity. |

Revising Run-on Sentences

There are several ways that you can revise run-on sentences. Usually, the easiest way is to make two separate sentences. However, if the two thoughts are closely related and equally important, you may want to make a compound sentence. Here are three ways to make a compound sentence out of a run-on.

(1) You can use a comma and a coordinating conjunction – *and, but, or, yet, for, so,* or *nor.*

| REVISED | He had no papers on him, **and** no one knew his identity. |

(2) You can use a semicolon.

| REVISED | He had no papers on him; no one knew his identity. |

(3) You can use a semicolon and a **conjunctive adverb**—a word such as *therefore, instead, also, meanwhile, still, nevertheless,* or *however.* Follow a conjunctive adverb with a comma.

| REVISED | He had no papers on him; **consequently,** no one knew his identity. |

Your Turn

Revise each of the following run-on sentences by using a comma and a coordinating conjunction, a semicolon, or a semicolon and a conjunctive adverb.

1. I threw the dog toy into the air Charlie ran eagerly for it.
2. Charlie likes to chase things, he begs me to play with him every day after school.
3. Charlie is a gift from my parents I spotted him right away when we were at the shelter.
4. There were many other dogs at the shelter I knew instinctively that we were meant to be together.
5. I go to bed at night Charlie jumps up beside me and licks my face.

10. Writing Effective Sentences

Sentence Combining

10a. Combine short sentences by inserting a key word from one sentence into another sentence.

Sometimes you can simply insert a key word without changing its form. In many cases, however, you will need to change the form of the key word in some way before you can insert it smoothly into another sentence.

ORIGINAL   Gabriel García Márquez is a writer. He is from Colombia.

COMBINED   Gabriel García Márquez is a **Colombian** writer.

ORIGINAL   You will read one of his stories. It is compelling.

COMBINED   You will read one of his **compelling** stories.

Inserting Phrases

10b. Combine closely related sentences by taking a phrase from one sentence and inserting it into another sentence.

Prepositional Phrases

A **prepositional phrase,** a preposition with its object, can usually be inserted into another sentence without changing the phrase. All you have to do is leave out some of the words in one of the sentences.

ORIGINAL   Gabriel García Márquez uses fantasy. He uses it in his writing.

COMBINED   Gabriel García Márquez uses fantasy **in his writing.**

Participial Phrases

A **participial phrase** contains a participle and words related to the participle. The entire phrase acts as an adjective, modifying a noun or a pronoun. Sometimes, you can insert a participial phrase just as it is. At other times, you can change the verb from one sentence into a participle and insert it in the other sentence.

ORIGINAL   Pelayo and Elisenda were worried. They were trying to help their sick child.

COMBINED   **Trying to help their sick child,** Pelayo and Elisenda were worried.

ORIGINAL   The old man surprised them. He arrived without warning.

COMBINED   The old man surprised them, **arriving without warning.**

Appositive Phrases

An **appositive phrase** is placed next to a noun or pronoun to identify or explain it. Sometimes you can combine sentences by changing one of the sentences to an appositive phrase.

ORIGINAL   The old man had a pair of wings. He was a mystery.

COMBINED   The old man, **a mystery,** had a pair of wings.

Using Compound Subjects and Compound Verbs

10c. Combine sentences by making compound subjects and compound verbs.

Look for sentences that have the same subject or the same verb. Then, make the subject, verb, or both compound by using a coordinating conjunction.

ORIGINAL	The townspeople came to see the old man. The priest came to see the old man. [same verb with different subjects]
COMBINED	**The townspeople and the priest** came to see the old man. [compound subject]

ORIGINAL	The old man huddled in the courtyard. The old man said nothing. [same subject with different verbs]
COMBINED	The old man **huddled** in the courtyard and **said** nothing. [compound verb]

ORIGINAL	The priest waited to hear from the pope. The townspeople waited, too. They finally got the pope's answer. [same verb with different subjects and plural subject with a different verb]
COMBINED	**The priest and the townspeople waited and finally got** the pope's answer. [compound subject and compound verb]

Creating a Compound Sentence

10d. Combine sentences by creating a compound sentence.

A *compound sentence* is two or more simple sentences linked by

- a comma and a coordinating conjunction
  or
- a semicolon
  or
- a semicolon and a conjunctive adverb

ORIGINAL	The couple became rich. They built a new house.
COMBINED	The couple became rich, **and** they built a new house. [comma and coordinating conjunction]
	The couple became rich; they built a new house. [semicolon]
	The couple became rich; **therefore,** they built a new house. [semicolon and conjunctive adverb]

NOTE: Before linking two thoughts in a compound sentence, make sure that the thoughts are closely related to one another and equally important. Otherwise, you may confuse your readers.

UNRELATED IDEAS	García Márquez's stories have fantastic elements. Unusual events take place in a village.

CLOSELY RELATED IDEAS	García Márquez's stories have fantastic elements, and fantastic events take place in this story.

Creating a Complex Sentence

10e. Combine sentences by creating a complex sentence.

A *complex sentence* includes one independent clause and one or more subordinate clauses.

Adjective Clauses

You can change a sentence into an adjective clause by inserting *who, whom, which,* or *that* in place of the subject. Then you can use the adjective clause to give information about a noun or a pronoun in another sentence.

ORIGINAL	A carnival came to town. The carnival was amusing.
COMBINED	A carnival, **which was amusing,** came to town.

Adverb Clauses

You can turn a sentence into an adverb clause by placing a subordinating conjunction (such as *after, if, although, because, when,* or *where*) at the beginning of the sentence. Then you can use the clause to modify a verb, an adjective, or an adverb in another sentence.

ORIGINAL	The old man suffered. He survived the winter.
COMBINED	**Although the old man suffered,** he survived the winter.

Noun Clauses

You can make a sentence into a noun clause and insert it into another sentence, using it just as you would use a noun. You can create a noun clause by inserting a word such as *that, how, what,* or *who* at the beginning of a sentence. When you place the noun clause in the other sentence, you may have to change or remove some words or revise the sentence in other ways.

ORIGINAL	Elisenda looked up from chopping onions and saw. The old man was flying away.
COMBINED	Elisenda looked up from chopping onions and saw **that the old man was flying away.** [The word *that* introduces the noun clause, which becomes the object of the verb *saw.*]

Improving Sentence Style

Using Parallel Structure

10f. Use the same form to express equal ideas.

Using the same form for equal ideas creates balance in a sentence. For example, you balance a noun with a noun, a phrase with the same type of phrase, and a clause with a clause. This balance is called *parallel structure.*

NOT PARALLEL	I like reading, writing, and to draw. [two gerunds and an infinitive]
PARALLEL	I like **reading, writing,** and **drawing.** [three gerunds]
NOT PARALLEL	Some of these stories are funny, entertaining, and teach me a lot. [two adjectives and a complete predicate]
PARALLEL	Some of these stories are **funny, entertaining,** and **educational.** [three adjectives]
NOT PARALLEL	I knew that an airplane had crashed but not about the passenger's heroic rescue. [a clause and a phrase]
PARALLEL	I knew **that an airplane had crashed** but not **that a passenger had made a heroic rescue.** [two clauses]

Revising Stringy Sentences

10g. Avoid using stringy sentences.

A *stringy sentence* usually has too many independent clauses strung together with coordinating conjunctions like *and* or *but.* Since all the ideas are treated equally, the reader has trouble seeing how they are related. To fix a stringy sentence, you can break the sentence into two or more sentences or turn some of the independent clauses into subordinate clauses or phrases.

STRINGY	The water was freezing cold, and a few survivors clung to some wreckage, and a helicopter came, but it could only take one person at a time, and one man let the others go first.
REVISED	Although the water was freezing cold, a few survivors clung to some wreckage. A helicopter came, but it could only take one person at a time. One man let the others go first.

Revising Wordy Sentences

10h. Avoid using wordy sentences.

Extra words and unnecessarily difficult words clutter your writing and make it hard to follow. Compare the following sentences.

WORDY	I wonder if you would be so kind as to take the time to enlighten me as to the current weather conditions.
IMPROVED	What's the weather?

Here are three tips for avoiding wordy sentences.

- Don't use complicated words where simple ones will do.
- Don't repeat yourself unless repetition is absolutely necessary.
- Don't use more words than you need to.

Varying Sentence Structures

10i. Vary the structure of your sentences.

Using a variety of sentence structures makes your writing livelier. Instead of using all simple sentences, you can use a mix of simple, compound, complex, and compound-complex sentences.

ALL SIMPLE SENTENCES	I visited a friend on her grandparents' farm. I was about ten years old. There wasn't much room in the farmhouse. My friend and I begged. We got to sleep in the hayloft in the barn. It was wonderful. We lay awake at night. We counted shooting stars. We told each other our dreams and our hopes for the future.
VARIED SENTENCE STRUCTURE	When I was about ten years old, I visited a friend on her grandparents' farm. Because there wasn't much room in the farmhouse and because we begged, my friend and I got to sleep in the hayloft in the barn. It was wonderful. We counted shooting stars as we lay awake at night, and we told each other our dreams and our hopes for the future.

Varying Sentence Beginnings

10j. Vary the beginnings of your sentences.

The basic structure of an English sentence is a subject followed by a verb. But following this pattern all the time can make your writing dull. Compare the following paragraphs.

| SUBJECT-VERB PATTERN | The young girl's mother dies. Her father remarries. His new wife is beautiful but cruel. The girl grows up and becomes more beautiful. The new wife becomes jealous. She tells a woodsman to take the girl into the woods and kill her. The woodsman cannot bring himself to do so. He lets her go. The girl discovers a house in the forest. The house is inhabited by seven tiny men. |
| VARIED SENTENCE BEGINNINGS | After the young girl's mother dies, her father remarries. Although beautiful, his new wife is cruel. As the girl grows up and becomes more beautiful, the new wife becomes jealous. "Take the girl into the woods and kill her," she tells a woodsman. Unable to bring himself to do so, the woodsman lets the girl go. In the forest, the girl discovers a house inhabited by seven tiny men. |

You can use the methods given in the chart to vary sentence beginnings.

Varying Sentence Beginnings
SINGLE-WORD MODIFIERS
Courageously, the man remained behind. [adverb] **Cautious,** the copilot doubted an instrument reading. [adjective] **Iced,** the plane's wings were dangerous. [participle] **Laughing,** they dismissed their fear. [participle]
PHRASES
With haste, the rescue team rushed to the river. [prepositional phrase] **Writing of the incident,** Roger Rosenblatt says that people must fight back against nature. [participial phrase] **To operate safely,** wings must be clear of ice. [infinitive phrase]
SUBORDINATE CLAUSES
Because no one knew the hero's name, all people could identify with him. [adverb clause] **When Lenny Skutnik saw the injured woman,** he dragged her to shore. [adverb clause]

Your Turn

Using what you have learned about writing effective sentences, revise the following paragraph. Combine sentences and improve the sentence style to make it flow smoothly and be clear and direct.

   Roger Rosenblatt wrote "The Man in the Water." It took less than an hour for him to write it. However, any piece composed in this manner may be—and often, as practical experience indicates, is—flawed. Rosenblatt admits this possibility. He agrees. Writers, consequently, who are not far along in years should stop procrastinating, remembering one thing. Rosenblatt has spent many, many years, decades even, editing, revising, and has learned to perfect his skills.

11. Capitalization

11a. Capitalize the first word in every sentence.

   This poem has no title.
   Does the author say why?

(1) Capitalize the first word of a direct quotation.
   Roger answered, "**Y**es, I believe she does."

(2) Traditionally, the first word of a line of poetry is capitalized.
   He turned his face to the wall;
   She turned her back upon him;
            —Anonymous, "Bonny Barbara Allan"

11b. Capitalize the first word both in the salutation and in the closing of a letter.

   Dear Ann,   **D**ear Sir:
   Yours truly,   Sincerely,

11c. Capitalize the pronoun *I* and the interjection *O*.

The interjection *O* is always capitalized. The common interjection *oh* is not capitalized unless it is the first word in a sentence.

   "**O** Father, **O** Father, go dig my grave" is a line from "Bonny Barbara Allan."
   The play was a hit, but, **oh,** how nervous **I** was.
   Oh, I forgot my books again.

11d. Capitalize proper nouns and proper adjectives.

A **common noun** is a general name for a person, place, thing, or idea. A **proper noun** names a particular person, place, thing, or idea. **Proper adjectives** are formed from proper nouns. Common nouns are not capitalized unless they begin a sentence, begin a direct quotation, or are included in a title.

COMMON NOUNS	poet
	nation
PROPER NOUNS	Shakespeare
	Navajo
PROPER ADJECTIVES	Shakespearean sonnet
	Navajo art

In proper nouns with more than one word, do *not* capitalize

- articles (*a, an, the*)
- short prepositions (those with fewer than five letters, such as *at* and *with*)
- coordinating conjunctions (*and, but, for, nor, or, yet*)
- the sign of the infinitive (*to*)
  Attila **t**he Hun   "The Tale **of t**he Sands"

Notice in the second example above that articles are capitalized if they are the first word in a proper noun.

(1) Capitalize the names of persons and animals.

GIVEN NAMES	Oliver	Gwendolyn	Tomás
SURNAMES	Brown	Furuya	Muñoz
ANIMALS	Big Red	Bambi	Willy

Descriptive names and nicknames also should be capitalized.

Ivan the Terrible   Old Glory

Abbreviations such as Ms., Mr., Dr., and Gen. should always be capitalized. Capitalize the abbreviations Jr. (junior) and Sr. (senior) after a name, and set them off with commas.

Is **G**en. Daniel James**, Jr.,** still on active duty?

NOTE: Capitalization is part of the spelling for names with more than one word. Always check the spelling of such a name with the person whose name it is, or look in a reference source.

La Croix   DuPont   McEwen   O'Connor

(2) Capitalize geographical names.

Type of Name	Examples
Towns and Cities	Rio de Janeiro
Counties, Townships, and Parishes	Osceola County Parish Hayes Township

Type of Name	Examples
States	North Dakota
Countries	Mexico United States of America
Continents	North America
Islands	Cayman Islands
Mountains	Mesabi Range
Other Landforms and Features	Cape Horn Angel Falls
Bodies of Water	Dead Sea Lake Como
Parks	Williams Park
Regions	New England the South
Roads, Streets, and Highways	Interstate 4 Route 66

NOTE: words such as *north, western,* and *southeast* are not capitalized when they indicate direction.

western Iowa   driving south

NOTE: In a hyphenated number, the second word begins with a lowercase letter.

Forty-second Street

(3) Capitalize the names of organizations, teams, business firms, institutions, buildings and other structures, and government bodies.

Type of Name	Examples
Organizations	Greenpeace Chess Club
Teams	Los Angeles Lakers
Business Firms	Apple Computer, Inc. Walgreen Company
Institutions	Lakes High School
Buildings and Other Structures	Empire State Building the Great Wall of China
Government Bodies	Congress House of Commons

NOTE: Capitalize words such as *democratic* and *republican* only when they refer to a specific political party.

The new leaders promised **d**emocratic elections.
Was Abraham Lincoln a **R**epublican?

(4) Capitalize the names of historical events and periods, special events, holidays and other calendar items, and time zones.

Type of Name	Examples
Historical Events and Periods	Industrial **R**evolution **W**ar on **P**overty
Special Events	**R**ose **B**owl **P**arade **S**pring **F**ling
Holidays and Calendar Items	**S**unday June Election **D**ay **Y**om **K**ippur
Time Zones	**C**entral **D**aylight **T**ime (**CDT**) **P**acific **S**tandard **T**ime (**PST**)

NOTE: Do not capitalize the name of a season unless the season is personified or is used as part of a proper noun.

> Soon, **s**ummer will be here.
> Striding across the fields, **S**ummer scorched the crops.
> Are you going to the **S**ummer Spectacular?

(5) Capitalize the names of nationalities, races, and peoples.
> **G**reek, **C**aucasian, **A**frican **A**merican, **A**sian, **I**raqi, **R**oman, **C**herokee, **H**ispanic

NOTE: The words *black* and *white* may or may not be capitalized when they refer to people of African or Caucasian descent.

(6) Capitalize the brand names of business products.
> **H**onda, **T**eflon, **K**leenex, **S**ony

NOTE: Do not capitalize a common noun that follows a brand name.
> **H**onda hybrid, **T**eflon pan

(7) Capitalize the names of ships, trains, aircraft, spacecraft, monuments, awards, and planets, stars, and other heavenly bodies.

Type of Name	Examples
Ships and Trains	*Californian* ***TGV***
Aircraft and Spacecraft	*Concorde* *Spirit*
Monuments and Memorials	**S**tatue of Liberty **T**omb of the **U**nknown
Awards	**P**urple **H**eart
Planets, Stars, and other Heavenly Bodies	**S**aturn **A**ldebaran **O**rion 51 **P**egasi

NOTE: Do not capitalize the words *sun* and *moon*. Do not capitalize the word *earth* unless it is used along with the capitalized names of other heavenly bodies.

11e. Do *not* capitalize the names of school subjects, except for languages or course names followed by a number.

> You need not take **a**rt or a **f**oreign **l**anguage, but you must take **E**nglish, **c**ivics, and **M**athematics II.

11f. Capitalize titles.

(1) Capitalize the title of a person when it comes before the person's name.
> **P**resident Clinton   **P**rofessor Hayakawa

Do not capitalize a title that is used alone or following a person's name, especially if the title is preceded by *a* or *the*.

> Was the **r**everend at the concert?
> When did Cleopatra become **q**ueen of Egypt?

When a title is used alone in direct address, it is usually capitalized.

> Hurry, **D**octor!   Pardon me, **S**ir [*or* sir]?

(2) Capitalize words showing family relationship when used with a person's name but *not* when preceded by a possessive.
> my **m**other **A**untie Em **D**ad your **f**ather

(3) Capitalize the first and last words and all important words in titles of books, periodicals, poems, stories, essays, speeches, plays, historical documents, movies, radio and television programs, works of art, musical compositions, and cartoons. Unimportant words in a title are:

- articles: *a, an, the*
- short prepositions (fewer than five letters): *of, to, for, from, in, over,* and so on
- coordinating conjunctions: *and, but, so, nor, or, yet, for*

Type of Title	Examples
Books	***S**poon **R**iver **A**nthology*
Periodicals	***F**amily **C**omputing*
Poems	"**B**attle of the **L**andlord"
Stories	"**B**y the **W**aters of **B**abylon"
Essays and Speeches	"**W**here **I** **F**ind **M**y **H**eroes"
Plays	*The **B**rute*
Historical Documents	**D**eclaration of **I**ndependence
Movies	***D**ances with **W**olves*
Radio and Television Programs	***D**inosaurs!* *This **A**merican **L**ife*
Works of Art	***V**iew of **T**oledo*
Musical Compositions	"**G**reensleeves"
Cartoons	***C**alvin and **H**obbes*

(4) Capitalize the names of religions and their followers, holy days and celebrations, holy writings, and specific deities.

Type of Name	Examples	
Religions and Followers	**J**udaism **C**hristianity	**B**aptist **M**uslim
Holy Days and Celebrations	**P**assover **E**aster	**R**amadan **L**ent
Holy Writings	**B**ible **T**ao **T**e **C**hing	**U**panishads **K**oran
Specific Deities	**B**rahma **P**oseidon	**G**od **A**llah

NOTE: The word *god* is not capitalized when it refers to the gods of mythology. The names of such gods are capitalized, however.

The Egyptian **g**od of the sun was **R**a.

You may notice that various publications differ in the way they use capital letters. Nevertheless, making sure your own capitalization agrees with the rules and guidelines presented in this part of the Language Handbook will help you communicate clearly with nearly any audience.

Your Turn

Revise the capitalization in the following sentences.

1. Have you read the story "What happened during the ice storm"?
2. I asked, "isn't this a Prince Tennis Racket?"
3. That is professor John Luis nickol Bell, jr.
4. Most of the Senators were already present.
5. I enjoyed reading pablo neruda's "ode to my socks."

12. Punctuation

End Marks

End marks—periods, question marks, and exclamation points—are used to indicate the purpose of a sentence.

12a. A statement (or declarative sentence) is followed by a period.

Butterflies can symbolize rebirth.

12b. A question (or interrogative sentence) is followed by a question mark.

Who drew this picture of a butterfly? Did you?

12c. An exclamation (or exclamatory sentence) is followed by an exclamation point.

What a great idea!

12d. A command or request (or imperative sentence) is followed by either a period or an exclamation point.

When an imperative sentence makes a request, it is followed by a period. When an imperative sentence makes a command or shows strong feeling, it is followed by an exclamation point.

Let me see it.
Be quiet!

12e. An abbreviation is usually followed by a period.

If a statement ends with an abbreviation, do not use an additional period as an end mark. However, do use a question mark or an exclamation point if one is needed.

Abraham lived around the nineteenth century B.C.
Was the story written in the eighth century B.C.?

Type of Abbreviation	Examples		
Personal Names	Hanson W. Baldwin E.E. Cummings		
Organizations and Companies	Assn. Corp.	Co. Ltd.	Inc.
Titles Used with Names	Mr. Mrs.	Ms. Jr.	Dr.
Times of Day	A.M.	P.M.	
Years	B.C. (written after the date) A.D. (written before the date)		
Addresses	Ave. Blvd.	St. Hwy.	
States	Calif.	Mass.	Tex.

NOTE: Two-letter state abbreviations without periods are used only when the ZIP Code is included.
Cleveland Heights, OH 44118

Abbreviations for government agencies and official organizations and some other frequently used abbreviations are written without periods. Abbreviations for most units of measurement are usually written without periods, especially in science books.

CPR, FM, IQ, TV, USAF, cm, km, lb, ml, rpm

EXCEPTION To avoid confusion with the word *in*, use *in.* for *inch*.

Commas

12f. Use commas to separate words, phrases, or clauses in a series.

> Three major forms of poetry are the lyric, the epic, and the ballad.

(1) If all items in a series are joined by *and* or *or*, do not use commas to separate them.
> They need firestone **and** some sticks **or** twigs.

> Some words—such as *bread and butter* and *table and chairs*—are used in pairs and may be considered one item in a series.
> Get out the **bread and butter,** the tomatoes, and the cheese for the sandwiches.

(2) As a rule, independent clauses in a series are separated by semicolons. Short independent clauses, however, may be separated by commas.
> Lightning flashed, thunder boomed, and we hid.

12g. Use commas to separate two or more adjectives preceding a noun.

> What a strange, awesome, dramatic story this is!

> When the last adjective in a series is thought of as part of the noun (as in a compound noun), the comma before the adjective is omitted.
> These are great short stories.

NOTE: The comma may be omitted before a coordinating conjunction that joins the last two items in a series if the meaning is clear without the comma. However, using the comma is never wrong, and many writers prefer always to do so. Follow your teacher's instructions on this point.

12h. Use commas before *and, but, or, nor, for, so,* and *yet* when they join independent clauses.

> Cory raised his hand, **and** the teacher called on him.

> You may omit the comma before *and, but, or,* or *nor* if the clauses are very short and there is no chance of misunderstanding.

12i. Use commas to set off nonessential clauses and nonessential participial phrases.

A **nonessential** (or **nonrestrictive**) clause or phrase adds information that is not needed to understand the main idea in the sentence.

| NONESSENTIAL CLAUSE | Ray, **who is Gerald's son,** won the trophy. [Omitting the clause would not change the main idea of the sentence.] |

When a clause or phrase is necessary to the meaning of a sentence, the clause or phrase is **essential** (or **restrictive**), and commas are *not* used.

| ESSENTIAL CLAUSE | The cheers **given to the winning** team were numerous. [Omitting the clause would change the meaning of the sentence.] |

12j. Use commas after certain introductory elements.

(1) Use commas after words such as *next* and *no* and after introductory interjections such as *why* and *well*.
> **Yes,** Billy Collins wrote that poem.

(2) Use a comma after an introductory participial phrase.
> **Opening his notebook,** Jude showed us his story.

(3) Use a comma after one long introductory prepositional phrase or two or more short introductory prepositional phrases.
> **At the end of the story,** the son returns home.

(4) Use a comma after an introductory adverb clause.
> **When I call my dog,** she often ignores me.

12k. Use commas to set off elements that interrupt a sentence.

> The thief, **in fact,** later became a disciple.

(1) Appositives and appositive phrases are usually set off by commas.
> Shichiri, **a man of his word,** denied any theft.

(2) Words used in direct address are set off by commas.

What, **David,** is all the noise in the garage?

(3) Parenthetical expressions are set off by commas. **Parenthetical expressions** are side remarks that add minor information or that relate ideas to each other.

The party begins, **I think,** around 8 o'clock.

12l. Use commas in certain conventional situations.

(1) Use a comma to separate items in dates and addresses.

My sister was born in Akron, Ohio, on May 7, 1991.

Leon's new address is 945 Oak Drive, Covington, KY 41011.

(2) Use a comma after the salutation of a friendly letter and after the closing of any letter.

Dear Aunt Hazel,   Sincerely yours,

(3) Use a comma after a name followed by an abbreviation such as *Jr., Sr.,* or *M.D.* Follow such an abbreviation with a comma unless it ends the sentence.

My report is about Dr. Martin Luther King, Jr.

12m. Do not use unnecessary commas.

Too much punctuation is just as confusing as not enough punctuation, especially in the case of commas.

CONFUSING	A man thought that a girl, who was a neighbor, was a thief, but, to his surprise, he was wrong.
CLEAR	A man thought that a girl who was a neighbor was a thief, but to his surprise he was wrong.

Semicolons

12n. Use a semicolon between independent clauses in a sentence if they are not joined by *and, but, or, nor, for, so,* or *yet.*

The tiger was in a cage; a Brahman let him out.

Similarly, a semicolon can take the place of a period to join two sentences that are closely related.

TWO SIMPLE SENTENCES	The man opened the door. Then the tiger jumped out.
ONE COMPOUND SENTENCE	The man opened the door; then the tiger jumped out.

12o. Use a semicolon between independent clauses joined by a conjunctive adverb or a transitional expression.

The tiger thought the jackal was stupid; **however,** it was the jackal who outsmarted the tiger.

The tiger was angry; **in fact,** he yelled at the jackal.

Notice in the two examples above that a comma is placed after the conjunctive adverb and the transitional expression.

Commonly Used Conjunctive Adverbs			
besides	indeed	nevertheless	then
consequently	instead	therefore	next

Commonly Used Transitional Expressions		
as a result	for instance	in fact
for example	in addition	in other words

12p. Use a semicolon (rather than a comma) before a coordinating conjunction to join independent clauses that contain commas.

The tree, buffalo, and road were no help; but the jackal, pretending to be stupid, was.

12q. Use a semicolon between items in a series if the items contain commas.

We visited Lima, Peru; Rome, Italy; and Oslo, Norway.

Colons

12r. Use a colon to mean "note what follows."

(1) In some cases a colon is used before a list of items, especially after the expressions *the following* and *as follows.*

Discuss the following elements of the story: theme, plot, and conflict.

Do not use a colon before a list that follows a verb or a preposition.

INCORRECT	Additional figures of speech are: image, symbol, and metaphor.
CORRECT	Additional figures of speech are image, symbol, and metaphor.

(2) Use a colon before a long, formal statement or a long quotation.

Abraham Lincoln began his Gettysburg Address with these words: "Fourscore and seven years ago our fathers brought forth on this continent a new nation conceived in Liberty and dedicated to the proposition that all men are created equal."

12s. Use a colon in certain conventional situations.

(1) Use a colon between the hour and the minute.
7:30 P.M.   3:10 A.M.

(2) Use a colon between chapter and verse in referring to passages from the Bible.
Genesis 1:1   John 3:10-16

(3) Use a colon between a title and a subtitle.
The Brute: A Joke in One Act

(4) Use a colon after the salutation of a business letter.
Dear Ms. Ash:
Dear Sir:
To Whom It May Concern:

When you speak, your tone and pitch, your pauses in your speech, and your gestures and expressions all help make your meaning clear. In writing, marks of punctuation signal these verbal and nonverbal cues.

Your Turn

Correct any errors in punctuation in each of the following sentences.
1. Do you know about: Camelot, Arthur, and the sword Excalibur?
2. The sword the mighty Excalibur was in a stone.
3. Did anyone, in the region, pull the sword out.
4. No no one could; until Arthur did.
5. Aren't knights, and ladies, and magic in the tales?

13. Punctuation

Italics

When writing or typing, indicate italics by underlining. If your composition were to be printed, the typesetter would set the underlined words in italics, *like this*.

13a. Use underlining (italics) for titles of books, plays, long poems, films, periodicals, works of art, recordings, long musical works, television series, trains, ships, aircraft, and spacecraft.

Type of Title	Examples
Books	*Tales of King Arthur* *Into Thin Air*
Plays	*Julius Caesar* *Trifles*
Long Poems	*Paradise Lost* *Evangeline*
Films	*Pocahontas* *The Titanic*
Periodicals	*Rolling Stone* *The New York Times*

The articles *a, an,* and *the* written before a title are italicized only when they are part of the official title. The official title of a book appears on the title page. The official title of a newspaper or periodical appears on the masthead, which is usually found on the editorial page.

The *Wall Street Journal*   **the** *Miami Herald*

Type of Title	Examples
Works of Art	*Christina's World* *Guernica*
Recordings	*Into the Light* *The Bridge*
Long Musical Works	*Treemonisha* *Swan Lake*
Television Series	*Nova* *Avonlea*
Trains and Ships	*Orient Express* *Titanic*
Aircraft and Spacecraft	*Hindenburg* *Voyager 2*

13b. Use underlining (italics) for words, letters, and figures referred to as such and for foreign words not yet a part of English vocabulary.

There is only one *r* in *Kari*.
Put six *O*'s after that *5*.
Hawaiians say *aloha oe* as both a greeting and a farewell.

If you are not sure whether or not to italicize a foreign word or phrase, look it up in a current dictionary.

Quotation Marks

13c. Use quotation marks to enclose a *direct quotation*—a person's exact words.

I asked, "Where does Márquez get his ideas?"

"Apparently, from everywhere," answered Kathleen.

Do not use quotation marks for **indirect quotations,** which are rewordings of direct quotations.

DIRECT   She said, "I'll call them later."

INDIRECT   She said she will call them later.

An interrupting expression is not a part of a quotation and therefore should never be inside quotation marks.

"Let's go," Larry whispered, "right now."

When two or more sentences by the same speaker are quoted together, use one set of quotation marks.

Gerardo said, "Cassius was right. The fault is not in the stars."

13d. A direct quotation begins with a capital letter.

Ms. Wells asked, "**W**ho is Cassius?

If a direct quotation is obviously a fragment of the original quotation, it should begin with a lowercase letter.

Cassius is described as having "**a** lean and hungry look."

13e. When a quoted sentence is divided into two parts by an interrupting expression, the second part begins with a lowercase letter.

"The film version," he said, "**w**as great."

If the second part of a quotation is a new sentence, the second part begins with a capital letter.

"I enjoy seeing a stage play," Paul commented. "**I**t's more interesting than a movie."

13f. A direct quotation is set off from the rest of the sentence by commas, a question mark, or an exclamation point.

"I have to leave now," Alison said, "so that I will be on time."

"Wow!" he cried. "Wasn't that a great speech**?**"

13g. When used with quotation marks, other marks of punctuation are placed according to the following rules:

(1) A comma or a period is always placed inside the closing quotation marks.
After "Secrets**,**" we will read "Candles**.**"

(2) Semicolons or colons are always placed outside the closing quotation marks.
I've finally decided to title my paper "Caesar's March**"**; it's done now.

Study the following in "Mowing**"**: rhyme, meter, and image.

(3) Question marks or exclamation points are placed inside closing quotation marks if the quotation is a question or an exclamation; otherwise, they are placed outside.
"Margarita," Mr. Finn asked, "can you give us an example**?**"
Is the good in people really "oft interred with their bones"**?**
After lunch, the principal said, "All classes for the rest of the day are canceled"**!**
I shouted, "Hooray**!**"

13h. When you write dialogue (a conversation), begin a new paragraph every time the speaker changes.

"Hey, I've got a great idea! Why not do a modern version of *Julius Caesar?*" suggested Matt.
"What do you mean?" Ben replied. "We'd wear business suits and stuff?"
Matt seemed surprised and said, "Well, no, but that's a good idea."
"It sure is," Paula commented. "What were *you* thinking, Matt?"
"Well, let me explain."

13i. When a quoted passage consists of more than one paragraph, put quotation marks at the beginning of each paragraph and at the end of only the last paragraph.

"On Saturday, March 24," read the press release, "Hills High School will present *The Tragedy of Julius Caesar.*
"Tickets will be available at the box office. Advance tickets can be purchased by contacting the school at 555-0915.
"The performance will begin at 7 P.M. The box office will open at 6 P.M."

13j. Use single quotation marks to enclose a quotation within a quotation.

He asked, "What is the main theme in the story 'Through the Tunnel'?"

13k. Use quotation marks to enclose titles of articles, short stories, essays, poems, songs, individual episodes of TV shows, chapter titles, and other parts of books and periodicals.

Type of Title	Examples
Short Stories	"House Taken Over" "The Storyteller"
Poems	"We Real Cool" "After Apple-Picking"
Essays	"My Two Lives" "High Tide in Tucson"
Articles	"Harmless Fun?" "Pack of Lies"
TV Episodes	"The Sure Thing" "Monarch in Waiting"
Chapters and Other Parts of Books and Periodicals	"Medieval Life" "Index of Author" "All in a Day's Work"

13l. Use quotation marks to enclose slang words, technical terms, and other special uses of words.

I'm fresh out of "long green" (paper money).
She just "birdied" (shot one under par).

NOTE: Whenever you conduct an interview, always ask permission to quote the person, and always use the person's exact words. When quoting someone's exact words, be sure to enclose them in quotation marks.

Your Turn

You are a reporter for your school paper and have just conducted an interview with a local actor, Mr. Jones, who is playing the role of Mark Antony in *The Tragedy of Julius Caesar*. Use the following quotations from Mr. Jones to write a paragraph or two for your article. Be sure to use at least four direct quotations.

1. "Acting is more than playing dress-up."
2. "To learn to act is to learn to live."
3. "The plot of *Julius Caesar* is enacted all over the world every day."
4. "The main thing is to be able to see—no, to feel—events from anyone's point of view."
5. "Antony loved Caesar as the people did."

14. Punctuation

Apostrophes
Possessive Case

14a. The *possessive case* of a noun or pronoun shows ownership or relationship. To form the possessive case of a singular noun, add an apostrophe and an -*s*.

Malamud**'s** story   a shoemaker**'s** problem

Add only an apostrophe if adding -'*s* will make the name hard to pronounce.

Euripides**'** play   Mrs. Fuentes**'** class

14b. To form the possessive case of a plural noun ending in *s*, add only the apostrophe.

shoes**'** soles   fathers**'** hopes

To form the possessive case of a plural noun that does not end in -*s*, add an apostrophe and an -*s*.

children**'s** dreams   mice**'s** tails

14c. Possessive pronouns do not require an apostrophe.

Whose book is that?
That opinion is **yours.**
The dog chased **its** own tail.

14d. Indefinite pronouns in the possessive case require an apostrophe and an -*s*.

nobody**'s** fault   another**'s** help

14e. In compound words, names of organizations and businesses, and word groups showing joint possession, only the last word is possessive in form.

father-in-**law's** shop   Organic **Food's** staff
Mom and **Dad's** car   United **Way's** volunteers

14f. When two or more persons possess something individually, each name is possessive in form.

Pat Mora's and **Rita Dove's** poems

Contractions

14g. Use an apostrophe to show where letters, words, or numerals have been omitted in a contraction.

she will	= she**'ll**	I am	= I**'m**
who is	= who**'s**	Juan has	= Juan**'s**
is not	= isn**'t**	were not	= weren**'t**
1992	= **'**92	of the clock	= o**'**clock
EXCEPTION	will not = won**'t**		

Hyphens

14h. Use a hyphen to divide a word at the end of a line.

> At first, Feld did not consider the assistant shoe-maker suitable for his daughter.

When you divide a word at the end of a line, keep in mind the following rules:

(1) Do not divide one-syllable words.
  gasped [*not* gas-ped]

(2) Divide a word only between syllables.
  frag-ment [*not* fra-gment]

(3) Words with double consonants are usually divided between those two consonants.
  drum-mer   pres-sure

(4) Usually, a word with a prefix or a suffix may be divided between the prefix or suffix and the base word (or root).
  pre-judge   fall-ing

(5) Divide a hyphenated word only at a hyphen.
  mother-in-law [*not* moth-er-in-law]

(6) Do not divide a word so that one letter stands alone.
  elec-tricity [*not* e-lectricity]

14i. Use a hyphen with compound numbers from twenty-one to ninety-nine and with fractions used as adjectives.

> thirty-five years
> one-half pound [*One-half* is an adjective modifying *pound*.]
> one half of the flour [*Half* is a noun modified by the adjective *one*.]

14j. Use a hyphen with the prefixes *ex-*, *self-*, and *all-*; with the suffix *-elect*; and with all prefixes before a proper noun or proper adjective.

> ex-wife   all-star   self-employed
> governor-elect   pro-America

14k. Hyphenate a compound adjective when it precedes the noun it modifies.

> a **well-designed** engine
> an engine that is **well designed**
> a **world-famous** skier
> a skier who is **world famous**

Do not use a hyphen if one of the modifiers is an adverb that ends in *-ly*.

> a **partly finished** research paper

NOTE: Some compound adjectives are always hyphenated, whether they precede or follow the nouns they modify.

> an **up-to-date** dictionary
> a dictionary that is **up-to-date**
> a **self-reliant** person
> a person who is **self-reliant**

If you are unsure whether a compound adjective should always be hyphenated, look up the word in a current dictionary.

Dashes

14l. Use a dash to indicate an abrupt break in thought or speech or an unfinished statement or question.

> Jim—Tim, I mean—will show us his video.
> "But, I'm—" Tim began, and then stopped.

14m. Use a dash to mean *namely, that is, in other words,* and similar expressions that introduce an explanation.

> I know who wrote that story—Ray Bradbury.
> No, Arthur C. Clarke—he wrote *2001: A Space Odyssey*—was the author.

NOTE: In general, avoid using dashes in formal writing. When you evaluate your writing, make sure you haven't used dashes unnecessarily or in place of commas, semicolons, colons, or end marks. Using dashes only for special emphasis will make them more effective.

Parentheses

14n. Use parentheses to enclose explanatory or additional information.

> Richard Burton (as Mark Antony) appears in the film *Cleopatra.*
> Emily Dickinson (1830–1886) was a unique person.
> Fill in the application carefully. (Use a pen.)
> After reading the story (it was great), I ate.

Your Turn

Each of the following sentences has at least one error in punctuation. Correct the errors by adding apostrophes, hyphens, dashes, and parentheses where they are needed.

1. Trishs and Roberts presentation's were about Emily Dickinsons life and work.
2. They discovered and you would too that Dickinsons poems are quite complex.
3. Roberts brother in law read her poems in college as part of a self directed study.
4. One of her poems opening lines like all her works it has no title read, "Because I could not stop for Death, he kindly stopped for me."
5. Some people believe Dickinson was anti-social because she seldom left home, but Trish and Robert argues that she wasnt.

15. Spelling

Understanding Word Structure

Many English words are made up of word parts from other languages or earlier forms of English.

Roots

The **root** is the part of the word that carries the word's core meaning. Other word parts can be added to a root to create many different words.

Roots	Meanings	Examples
–aud–, –audit–	hear	audible, auditorium
–anthrop–	human	anthropology, misanthrope
–biblio–	book	bibliography, bibliophile
–chron–	time	chronological, synchronize
–vid–, –vis–	see	evidence, television

NOTE: Some word parts have alternate spellings. The spelling used in a particular word is influenced by how the word sounds. If you try pronouncing "televidion," for example, you'll see why –vis–, not –vid–, is the form used in *television*.

Prefixes

A **prefix** is a word part that is added before a root or base word. When a prefix is added, the new word combines the meanings of the prefix and the root or base word.

Prefixes	Meanings	Examples
bi–	two	bimonthly, bisect
re–	back, again, backward	revoke, reflect
trans–	across, beyond	transform, transport
un–	reverse of, not	untrue, unfold

Suffixes

A **suffix** is a word part that is added after a root or base word. Often, adding a suffix to a word changes the word's part of speech as well as its meaning.

Suffixes	Meanings	Examples
–dom	state, rank, condition	freedom, wisdom
–en	cause to be, become	deepen, darken
–ly	characteristic of, like	friendly, cowardly
–ness	quality, state	softness, shortness

Spelling Rules

ie and *ei*

15a. Write *ie* when the sound is long *e*, except after *c*.

| belief | achieve | thief | grief |
| deceive | receive | ceiling | conceit |

EXCEPTIONS

| leisure | protein | either | seize |

15b. Write *ei* when the sound is not long *e*.

| heifer | rein | beige | weight |

EXCEPTIONS

| view | ancient | patient | friend |

-cede, *-ceed*, and *-sede*

15c. Only one English word ends in *–sede: supersede*. Only three words end in *–ceed: exceed, proceed*, and *succeed*. Most other words with this sound end in *–cede*.

| accede | intercede | recede |
| concede | precede | secede |

Adding Prefixes

15d. When a prefix is added to a word, the spelling of the original word remains the same.

bi + monthly = **bi**monthly
un + natural = **un**natural
re + heat = **re**heat

Adding Suffixes

15e. When the suffix *-ness* or *-ly* is added to a word, the spelling of the original word remains the same.

careful + ly = careful**ly**
kind + ness = kind**ness**

EXCEPTIONS

Words ending in *y* usually change the *y* to *i* before adding *–ness* or *–ly*:

shady + ness = **shadi**ness   busy + ly = bus**ily**

NOTE: Most one-syllable adjectives ending in *y* follow rule **15e**.

coy + ness = coy**ness**   shy + ly = shy**ly**

15f. Drop the final silent *e* before adding a suffix that begins with a vowel.

tape + ing = tap**ing**
eliminate + ed = eliminat**ed**

EXCEPTIONS

Keep the final silent *e*

- in words ending in *–ce* or *–ge* before a suffix that begins with *a* or *o*: peac**eable**, knowledg**eable**, courag**eous**, outrag**eous**
- in *dye* and in *singe*, before *–ing*: dy**eing**, sing**eing**
- in *mile* before *–age*: mil**eage**

15g. Keep the final silent *e* before adding a suffix that begins with a consonant.

care + less = car**eless**   ease + ment = eas**ement**

EXCEPTIONS

argue + ment = argu**ment**   nine + th = nin**th**
true + ly = tru**ly**   whole + ly = whol**ly**

15h. When a word ends in *y* preceded by a consonant, change the *y* to *i* before any suffix except one beginning with *i*.

hurry + ed = hurr**ied**   tardy + ness = tard**iness**

EXCEPTIONS

1. some one-syllable words:
   shy + ness = shy**ness**   sky + ward = sky**ward**
2. *lady* and *baby* with suffixes:
   lady**like**   lady**ship**   baby**hood**

15i. When a word ends in *y* preceded by a vowel, simply add the suffix.

survey + ed = survey**ed**
gray + est = gray**est**

EXCEPTIONS

day + ly = da**ily**   say + ed = sa**id**

15j. When a word ends in a consonant, double the final consonant before a suffix that begins with a vowel only if the word

- has only one syllable or is accented on the last syllable
     and
- ends in a single consonant preceded by a single vowel.

wrap + ing = wra**pping**
occur + ence = occu**rrence**

Forming Plurals of Nouns

15k. To form the plurals of most English nouns, simply add *-s*.

SINGULAR	ship	pan	horse
	blacksmith	desk	Johnson
PLURAL	ship**s**	pan**s**	horse**s**
	blacksmith**s**	desk**s**	Johnson**s**

15l. To form the plurals of other nouns, follow these rules.

(1) If the noun ends in *s, x, z, ch,* or *sh,* add *–es.*

SINGULAR	guess	fox	buzz
	peach	wish	Hernandez
PLURAL	guess**es**	fox**es**	buzz**es**
	peach**es**	wish**es**	Hernandez**es**

NOTE: Proper nouns also usually follow rule **15l.**

the Jones**es**   the Sánchez**es**

(2) If the noun ends in *y* preceded by a consonant, change the *y* to *i* and add *–es.*

| SINGULAR | fly | city | quality | puppy |
| PLURAL | fli**es** | citi**es** | qualiti**es** | puppi**es** |

EXCEPTION

The plurals of proper nouns: the Darc**ys**, the Lac**ys**

(3) If the noun ends in *y* preceded by a vowel, add *–s.*

| SINGULAR | key | journey | Momaday |
| PLURAL | key**s** | journey**s** | Momaday**s** |

(4) For some nouns ending in *f* or *fe,* add *–s.* For other such nouns, change the *f* or *fe* to *v* and add *–es.*

| SINGULAR | thief | hoof | belief | roof |
| PLURAL | thie**ves** | hoo**ves** | belief**s** | roof**s** |

(5) If the noun ends in *o* preceded by *a* vowel, add *–s.*

| SINGULAR | curio | kangaroo | video |
| PLURAL | curio**s** | kangaroo**s** | video**s** |

(6) If the noun ends in *o* preceded by a consonant, add *–es.*

SINGULAR	potato	echo	torpedo
	hero	veto	tomato
PLURAL	potato**es**	echo**es**	torpedo**es**
	hero**es**	veto**es**	tomato**es**

EXCEPTIONS

Some common nouns ending in *o* preceded by a consonant, especially musical terms and some proper nouns, form the plural by adding only *–s.*

SINGULAR	taco	hairdo	alto	piano
	photo	Latino	Sakamoto	
PLURAL	taco**s**	hairdo**s**	alto**s**	piano**s**
	photo**s**	Latino**s**	Sakamoto**s**	

NOTE: Some nouns that end in *o* preceded by a consonant have two plural forms.

| SINGULAR | zero |
| PLURAL | zero**s** *or* zero**es** |

(7) The plurals of some nouns are formed irregularly.

| SINGULAR | foot | man | tooth | child |
| PLURAL | f**ee**t | m**e**n | t**ee**th | child**ren** |

(8) Some nouns have the same form in both the singular and the plural.

| SINGULAR | deer | species | Chinese |
| AND PLURAL | Iroquois | series | aircraft |

(9) If a compound noun is written as one word, form the plural by adding *–s* or *–es* to the end of the compound.

| SINGULAR | ballgame | background | bedroom |
| PLURAL | ballgame**s** | background**s** | bedroom**s** |

(10) If a compound noun is hyphenated or written as two words, make the main noun plural. The ***main noun*** is the noun that is modified.

| SINGULAR | mother-in-law | runner-up |
| PLURAL | mother**s**-in-law | runner**s**-up |

A few compound nouns form the plural in irregular ways.

| SINGULAR | go-between | mix-up | sixteen-year-old |
| PLURAL | go-between**s** | mix-up**s** | sixteen-year-old**s** |

(11) Some nouns borrowed from Latin and Greek form their plurals as they do in the original language.

SINGULAR	PLURAL
analysis	analys**es**
crisis	cris**es**
datum	dat**a**
phenomenon	phenomen**a**

Some nouns borrowed from other languages have two plural forms.

SINGULAR	PLURAL
cactus	cactus**es** *or* cact**i**
index	index**es** *or* ind**ices**
antenna	antenna**s** *or* antenn**ae**

(12) To form the plurals of numerals, most capital letters, symbols, and words used as words, add either an *–s* or an apostrophe and an *–s.*

These *R*'**s** [*or* R**s**] look like *K*'**s** [*or* K**s**].

Erase these *&*'**s** [*or* *&*'**s**] and write *and***s** [*or* *and*'**s**].

These *1*'**s** [*or* 1**s**] look like *7*'**s** [*or* 7**s**].

NOTE: Using both an apostrophe and an *–s* is never wrong. Therefore, if you have any doubt about whether or not to use the apostrophe, use it. To prevent confusion, get in the habit of using both an apostrophe and an *–s* to form the plurals of lowercase letters, certain capital letters, and some words used as words.

These *i*'**s** should be *e*'**s**. [Without an apostrophe, the plural of *i* would look like *is*.]

My sister always gets all *A*'**s**. [Without an apostrophe, the plural of *A* would look like *As*.]

Your Turn

Proofread the following sentences, and correctly write the misspelled words.

1. My brother Walter wieghs 180 pounds and stands six foot tall.
2. I can't beleive my wallet just droped out of my pocket.
3. How can those countrys improve health care for woman and children?
4. In the election, Darla received ninty votes, but her opponent won by doubleing that amount.
5. I tryd to explain the problem that had occured.

16. Glossary of Usage

The Glossary of Usage is an alphabetical list of words, expressions, and special terms with definitions, explanations, and examples. Some of the examples have specific labels. *Standard* or *formal* usages are appropriate in serious writing and speaking, such as compositions and speeches. *Informal* words and expressions are standard English usages and are generally appropriate in conversation and in everyday writing such as personal letters. *Nonstandard* usages do not follow the guidelines of standard English.

a lot Always write the expression *a lot* as two words. *A lot* may be used as a noun meaning "a large number or amount" or as an adverb meaning "a great deal; very much." Avoid using *a lot* in formal writing.

Ray Bradbury writes **a lot** of science fiction. [noun]
Your last draft is **a lot** more interesting. [adverb]

among See **between, among.**

and etc. The abbreviation *etc. (et cetera)* means "and other things." Do not use *and* with *etc.*

They sell CDs, videos, **etc.** [*not* and etc.]

anyways, anywheres Use these words (and others like them, such as *everywheres, somewheres,* and *nowheres*) without the final *s.*

She didn't like the movie **anyway** [*not* anyways].
They couldn't find the Grail **anywhere** [*not* anywheres].

as See **like, as.**

as if See **like, as if.**

at Do not use *at* after *where.*

NONSTANDARD   Where was the pendulum at?
STANDARD   **Where** was the pendulum?

bad, badly *Bad* is an adjective. *Badly* is an adverb. In standard English, only the adjective form, *bad,* should follow a linking verb, such as *feel, see, hear, taste,* or *smell,* or forms of the verb *be.*

Does that gas leak smell **bad** [*not* badly]?

NOTE: The expression *feel badly* has become acceptable in informal situations, but use *feel bad* in formal speaking and writing.

being as, being that Use *since* or *because* instead of these expressions.

Because [*not* being as] she was smart, she won a prize on the game show.

beside, besides *Beside* is a preposition that means "by the side of" or "next to." As a preposition, *besides* means "in addition to" or "other than." As an adverb, *besides* means "moreover."

People stood **beside** the coop.
Who **besides** Brutus killed Caesar? [preposition]
His wings were dirty; **besides,** he was almost toothless. [adverb]

between, among Use *between* when you are referring to two things at a time, even though they may be part of a group consisting of more than two.

She walked **between** her mother and father.
There were so many differences **between** the six poems. [Although there are more than two poems, each one is being compared separately with each of the others.]

Use *among* when you are thinking of a group rather than separate individuals.

Conflicts developed **among** the passengers. [The passengers are thought of as a group.]

bust, busted Avoid using these words as verbs. Use a form of either *burst* or *break,* depending on the meaning.

> The airtight compartments **burst** [*not* busted].
>
> A torrent of water **broke** [*not* busted] the doors.

could of See **of.**

done *Done* is the past participle of *do.* Avoid using *done* for *did,* which is the past form of *do* and which does not require a helping verb.

> | NONSTANDARD | The captain done all that he could do. |
> | STANDARD | The captain **did** all that he could do. |
> | STANDARD | The captain **had done** all that he could do. |

etc. See **and etc.**

everywheres See **anyways, anywheres.**

fewer, less *Fewer* tells "how many"; it is used with plural nouns. *Less* tells "how much"; it is used with singular nouns.

> We have **fewer** students in class this year.
>
> There is **less** emphasis on symbolism in this poem.

good, well *Good* is an adjective. *Well* may be used as an adjective or an adverb. Never use *good* to modify a verb; instead, use *well* as an adverb meaning "capably" or "satisfactorily."

> Julia Alvarez writes **well** [*not* good].

NOTE: *Feel good* and *feel well* mean different things. *Feel good* means "feel happy or pleased." *Feel well* simply means "feel healthy."

> I didn't feel **well** that day.
>
> Helping others always makes me feel **good** about myself.

had of See **of.**

had ought, hadn't ought Unlike other verbs, *ought* is not used with *had.*

> Her mother **ought** [*not* had ought] to come out of her room; She **ought not** [*not* hadn't ought] to stay in there so long.

he, she, it, they Do not use an unnecessary pronoun after the subject of a clause or a sentence. This error is called the *double subject.*

> | NONSTANDARD | Gary Soto he writes stories and poems. |
> | STANDARD | Gary Soto writes stories and poems. |

hisself, theirselves Do not use these words for *himself* and *themselves.*

> Phillip said that he would put up his tent **himself** [*not* hisself] and that they could put up their tents **themselves** [*not* theirselves].

imply, infer *Imply* means "suggest indirectly." *Infer* means "interpret" or "draw a conclusion [from a remark or an action]."

> This language **implies** a symbolic meaning.
>
> From this metaphor, we may **infer** his deep fear.

it See **he, she, it, they.**

kind of, sort of Avoid using these terms in formal situations. Instead, use *somewhat* or *rather.*

> | INFORMAL | Edgar Allan Poe's stories can be kind of scary. |
> | FORMAL | Edgar Allan Poe's stories can be **somewhat** [*or* **rather**] scary. |

kind of a, sort of a In formal situations, omit the *a.*

> | INFORMAL | What kind of a rhyme scheme does the poem have? |
> | FORMAL | What **kind of** rhyme scheme does the poem have? |

kind(s), sort(s), type(s) Use *this* or *that* with the singular form of each of these nouns. Use *these* or *those* with the plural form.

> **This kind** of guitar is cheaper than **those kinds.**

learn, teach *Learn* means "acquire knowledge." *Teach* means "instruct" or "show how."

> If you will **teach** me, I will **learn.**

leave, let *Leave* means "go away" or "depart from." *Let* means "allow" or "permit." Avoid using *leave* for *let.*

> The bus will **leave** at 7:40.
>
> **Let** [*not* leave] her stay if she wants to.

less See **fewer, less.**

like, as In informal English, the preposition *like* is often used as a conjunction meaning "as." In formal English, use *like* to introduce a prepositional phrase, and use *as* to introduce a subordinate clause.

> This song sounds **like** the other one.
>
> She should do **as** her mother says.

like, as if In formal situations, *like* should not be used for the compound conjunction *as if* or *as though.*

> It looked **as if** [*not* like] the crew would see them.

nowheres See **anyways, anywheres.**

of *Of* is a preposition. Do not use *of* in place of *have* after verbs such as *could, should, would, might, must,* and *ought* [*to*]. Also, do not use *had of* for *had.*

> | NONSTANDARD | They should of signaled. |
> | STANDARD | They **should have** [*or* **should've**] signaled. |

Do not use *of* after other prepositions such as *inside, off,* or *outside.*

> Hundreds jumped **off** [*not* off of] the ship.

off of See **of.**

ought See **had ought, hadn't ought.**

ought to of See **of.**

she See **he, she, it, they.**

some, somewhat In formal situations, do not use *some* to mean "to some extent." Instead, use *somewhat.*

| INFORMAL | Your advice helped some. |
| FORMAL | Your advice helped **somewhat.** |

somewheres See **anyways, anywheres.**

sort(s) See **kind(s), sort(s), type(s)** and **kind of a, sort of a.**

sort of See **kind of, sort of.**

teach See **learn, teach.**

than, then *Than* is a conjunction used in comparisons. *Then* is an adverb meaning "at that time" or "next."

I liked "Everyday Use" better **than** that other story.
Had you heard of Langston Hughes **then?**
I wrote a thesis statement; **then,** I made an outline.

them *Them* should not be used as an adjective. Use *those.*

I like **those** [*not* them] videos better than mine.

then See **than, then.**

this, that, these, those See **kind(s), sort(s), type(s).**

try and Use *try to,* not *try and.*

He would **try to** [*not* try and] send a message.

type(s) See **kind(s), sort(s), type(s).**

way, ways Use *way,* not *ways,* in referring to a distance.

| INFORMAL | The sisters walked a long ways to school each day. |
| FORMAL | The sisters walked a long **way** to school each day. |

well See **good, well.**

what Use *that,* not *what,* to introduce an adjective clause.

The poem **that** [*not* what] I studied was "A Valediction: Forbidding Mourning."

when, where Do not use *when* or *where* to begin a definition.

| NONSTANDARD | A "stanza" in poetry is when lines are grouped to form a unit. |
| STANDARD | A "stanza" in poetry is a group of lines that form a unit. |

where Do not use *where* for *that.*

I read **that** [*not* where] Alice Walker is speaking here.
Zilka saw on TV **that** [*not* where] the mayor has been reelected.

where . . . at See **at.**

who, which, that The relative pronoun *who* refers to persons only; *which* refers to things only; *that* may refer to either persons or things.

Isn't Louis L'Amour the man **who** [*or* that] writes westerns? [person]
Arthur's sword, **which** is called Excalibur, is legendary. [thing]
The poem **that** I memorized is beautiful. [thing]

would of See **of.**

Do not confuse contractions with possessive pronouns.

Possessive Pronouns	Contractions
This one is **theirs.**	**There's** [There is] Lana.
Their bus is here.	**They're** [They are] on the bus.
Your turn is next.	**You're** [You are] next.
Whose book is this?	**Who's** [Who is] your partner?
What is **its** title?	**It's** [It is] time to eat.

Your Turn

Revise the following sentences by correcting the errors in usage.

1. Elena should invite less people, but she inferred that she already sent the invitations.
2. We were supposed to meet Alexandra at eight o' clock, but I guess we could of gotten the time wrong.
3. Being as his grades were so good, he got a scholarship.
4. My uncle considers hisself an adequate cook, but we think he cooks bad.
5. The tasks were divided evenly among the two scouts.
6. Daryl had ought to take the job because she knows she could do the work good.
7. Anywheres you travel, you see the same kinds of hotel.
8. My sister she works at an office downtown.

Glossary

The glossary that follows is an alphabetical list of words found in the selections in this book. Use this glossary just as you would use a dictionary—to find out the meaning of unfamiliar words. (Some technical, foreign, and more obscure words in this book are not listed here but instead are defined for you in the footnotes that accompany many of the selections.)

Many words in the English language have more than one meaning. This glossary gives the meanings that apply to the words as they are used in the selections in this book. Words closely related in form and meaning are usually listed together in one entry (for instance, *cower* and *cowered*), and the definition is given for the first form.

The following abbreviations are used:

adj.	adjective
adv.	adverb
n.	noun
v.	verb

Each word's pronunciation is given in parentheses. For more information about the words in this glossary or for information about words not listed here, consult a dictionary.

A

abashed (uh BASHT) *adj.* embarrassed and confused.

abbreviation (uh bree vee AY shuhn) *n.* a shortened form of a word or phrase.

abhor (ab HAWR) *v.* strongly hate.

abstractions (ab STRAK shuhnz) *n.* ideas or concepts.

absurd (ab SURD) *adj.* plainly not logical, true, or sensible.

abundant (uh BUHN duhnt) *adj.* plentiful.

acknowledged (ak NAHL ihjd) *adj.* admitted; recognized to be true.

adjacent (uh JAY suhnt) *adj.* neighboring; next to each other.

administer (ad MIHN uh stuhr) *v.* manage or control.

adversary (AD vuhr sehr ee) *n.* opponent.

advocating (AD vuh kayt ihng) *v.* recommending; speaking in favor of.

affiliations (uh fihl ee AY shuhnz) *n.* connections; relationships.

afflicted (uh FLIHKT ihd) *adj.* upset; saddened.

affront (uh FRONT) *n.* intentional insult.

aggression (uh GREHSH uhn) *n.* habit of attacking; unfriendly, destructive behavior.

altruistic (al troo IHS tihk) *adj.* having an unselfish concern for others.

amplest (AM plehst) *adj.* most abundant; fullest.

anecdotal (an ehk DOH tuhl) *adj.* an account that cannot be proved.

archives (AHR kyvz) *n.* public records or historical documents.

ascertain (as uhr TAYN) *v.* find out with certainty; determine.

assent (uh SEHNT) *n.* agreement.

B

belligerent (buh LIHJ uhr uhnt) *adj.* warlike; fond of fighting.

benevolent (buh NEHV uh luhnt) *adj.* kind; generous toward others.

benign (bih NYN) *adj.* not dangerous.

blight (blyt) *n.* disease that causes plants to wither and die.

C

carnage (KAHR nihj) *n.* slaughter of a great number of people; butchery.

ceaseless (SEES lihs) *adj.* going all the time; never stopping.

censored (SEHN suhrd) *v.* examined for the purpose of removing anything objectionable.

chaotic (kay AHT ihk) *adj.* very confused; completely disordered.

cherish (CHEHR ihsh) *v.* treat with love and tenderness.

chide (chyd) *v.* to scold mildly.

claim (klaym) *n.* demand for something due.

clamor (KLAM uhr) *n.* loud uproar.

clause (klawz) *n.* single provision of a law or agreement.

coercion (koh UR shuhn) *n.* use of force or forceful persuasion.

collusion (kuh LOO zhuhn) *n.* secret agreement.

commercial (kuh MUHR shuhl) *adj.* having to do with trade or business.

compassionate (kuhm PASH uh niht) *adj.* sympathetic; willing to help others.

complexion (kuhm PLEHK shuhn) *n.* appearance of the skin, especially the face.

complied (kuhm PLYD) *v.* did as requested.

composition (kahm puh ZIHSH uhn) *n.* a song or essay.

confer (kuhn FUR) *v.* bestow or give.

confronted (kuhn FRUHNT ehd) *v.* faced.

consent (kuhn SEHNT) *v.* agree.

conspirators (kuhn SPIHR uh tuhrz) *n.* people who help plan a crime; traitors.

constricting (kuhn STRIHKT ihng) *v.* used as *adj.* limiting; confining.

consumers (kuhn SOO muhrz) *n.* people who use anything made or grown by producers.

contorted (kuhn TAWR tihd) *v.* twisted out of shape.

contradiction (kahn truh DIHK shuhn) *n.* a statement that opposes or disagrees with someone or something; disagreement.

contrition (kuhn TRIHSH uhn) *n.* regret or sense of guilt at having done wrong.

contrived (kuhn TRYVD) *adj.* planned; manipulated.

conviction (kuhn VIHK shuhn) *n.* strong belief; certainty.

correspond (kawr uh SPAHND) *v.* match; be similar.

corroborated (kuh RAHB uh rayt ihd) *v.* supported; upheld the truth of.

courted (KAWRT ihd) *v.* dated; wooed.

coveted (KUHV iht ehd) *v.* used as *adj.* very much desired.

cowering (KOW uhr ihng) *v.* used as *adj.* crouching or hiding in shame or fear.

crucial (KROO shuhl) *adj.* very important.

cunning (KUHN ihng) *adj.* clever in a way that is intended to deceive.

customs (KUHS tuhmz) *n.* habits; traditions.

D

decrepit (dih KREHP iht) *adj.* old and worn out.

defiant (dih FY uhnt): *adj.* challenging authority.

deflected (dih FLEHKT ihd) *v.* turned aside.

deftly (DEHFT lee) *adv.* quickly and skillfully.

degraded (dih GRAY dihd) *adj.* wicked; morally corrupted.

destinies (DEHS tuh neez) *n.* what becomes of people or things in the end; fates.

deteriorate (dih TIHR ee uh rayt) *v.* get worse.

devoid (dih VOYD) *adj.* completely missing; lacking.

devouring (dih VOWR ihng) *v.* eating hungrily.

diabetic (dy uh BEHT ihk) *adj.* having diabetes, a disease in which the body is unable to properly process sugar.

diffuse (dih FYOOS) *adj.* spread out; unfocused.

discern (dih SURN) *v.* recognize or distinguish.

discharge (dihs CHAHRJ) *v.* release; let out.

discordant (dihs KAWR duhnt) *adj.* clashing; not harmonious.

discretion (dihs KREHSH uhn) *n.* ability to make a choice.

discrimination (dihs krihm uh NAY shuhn) *n.* prejudiced, unfair treatment.

disdains (dihs DAYNZ) *v.* views something as lacking value or merit.

disinterested (dihs IHN tuhr ehs tihd) *adj.* fair; lacking bias.

dissuaded (dih SWAYD ihd) *v.* turned aside by persuasion.

dollop (DAHL uhp) *n.* a small serving.

drenched (drehncht) *v.* used as *adj.* soaked.

droll (drohl) *adj.* odd; wryly amusing.

drowsing (DROWZ ihng) *v.* falling half asleep, dozing.

E

earnest (UR nihst) *adj.* serious and sincere.

efface (uh FAYS) *v.* erase.

emanating (EHM uh nayt ihng) *v.* coming forth; emerging, as from a source.

emancipation (ih man suh PAY shuhn) *n.* liberation, the act of setting free.

empathy (EHM puh thee) *n.* ability to feel another's emotions.

endear (ehn DIHR) *v.* inspire affection.

engulfing (ehn GUHLF ihng) *v.* used as *adj.* swallowing up by surrounding completely.

entourage (AHN tuhr ahj) *n.* a group of people accompanying an important person.

equanimity (ee kwuh NIHM uh tee) *n.* calmness; composure.

eroded (ih ROHD ihd) *v.* used as *adj.* worn away.

exalted (ehg ZAWL tihd) *v.* held in high regard; glorified.

exasperate (ehg ZAS puh rayt) *v.* greatly irritate or disturb.

exasperated (ehg ZAS puh ray tihd) *v.* used as *adj.* irritated; annoyed.

exhalation (ehks huh LAY shuhn) *n.* breath; something breathed out.

exploited (ehk SPLOYT ihd) *v.* used selfishly for one's own advantage.

extenuating (ehk STEHN yoo ay tihng) *v.* used as *adj.* making something seem less severe by offering an excuse.

extraneous (ehk STRAY nee uhs) *adj.* external; not belonging.

extricate (EHKS truh kayt) *v.* set free; release.

extricating (EHKS truh kayt ihng) *v.* used as *n.* releasing or disentangling from something.

exudes (ehg ZOODZ) *v.* seems to radiate; oozes.

F

facetiously (fuh SEE shuhs lee) *adv.* in a joking way.

fiasco (fee AS koh) *n.* total failure.

fidelity (fih DEHL ih tee) *n.* an exact rendering.

firmament (FUR muh muhnt) *n.* the sky.

fortified (FAWR tuh fyd) *v.* strengthened.

fortitude (FAWR tuh tood) *n.* firm courage; strength to endure pain or danger.

frivolous (FRIHV uh luhs) *adj.* not properly serious; silly.

furtive (FUR tihv) *adj.* secretive; trying not to be seen.

G

generate (JEHN uhr ayt) *v.* cause to come into being.

gesture (JEHS chuhr) *n.* a movement, usually by part of the body; an action.

gorges (GAWRJ ehz) *n.* deep valleys with steep sides; ravines.

gullible (GUHL ih buhl) *adj.* easily persuaded to believe.

H

haphazard (hap HAZ uhrd) *adj.* lacking direction; unplanned.

hewn (hyoon) *v.* used as *adj.* shaped by cutting or chiseling.

hostile (HAHS tuhl) *adj.* very unfriendly.

I

ignominiously (ihg nuh MIHN ee uhs lee) *adv.* shamefully.

ignorant (IHG nuhr uhnt) *adj.* lacking knowledge; unaware.

immense (ih MEHNS) *adj.* very big; huge.

impeded (ihm PEED ihd) *v.* used as *adj.* obstructed; blocked, as by some obstacle.

imperceptibly (ihm puhr SEHP tuh blee) *adv.* in such a slight way as to be almost unnoticeable.

implacable (ihm PLAK uh buhl) *adj.* relentless; not affected by attempts at change.

impudence (IHM pyuh duhns) *n.* quality of being disrespectful.

impunity (ihm PYOO nih tee) *n.* freedom from punishment.

inaudible (ihn AW duh buhl) *adj.* impossible to hear.

incredulous (ihn KREHJ uh luhs) *adj.* disbelieving; skeptical.

indispensable (IHN dihs PEHN suh buhl) *adj.* absolutely necessary; essential.

indisposed (ihn dihs POHZD) *adj.* slightly ill.

induced (ihn DOOST) *v.* used as *adj.* persuaded; led on.

indulgently (ihn DUHL juhnt lee) *adv.* in a very easygoing manner.

inert (ihn URT) *adj.* motionless; here, dead.

infirmity (ihn FUHR mih tee) *n.* defect; weakness.

infuriated (ihn FYUR ee ay tihd) *v.* made very angry.

inquisitive (ihn KWIHZ uh tihv) *adj.* questioning or curious.

inscribed (ihn SKRYBD) *v.* marked or written on a surface; engraved.

insignificant (ihn sihg NIHF uh kuhnt) *adj.* having little importance or influence.

insinuate (ihn SIHN yoo ayt) *v.* to suggest.

integrated (IHN tuh gray tihd) *v.* used as *adj.* made up of elements that work together; combined.

integrity (ihn TEHG ruh tee) *n.* honesty or trustworthiness.

intermittent (ihn tuhr MIHT uhnt) *adj.* stopping and starting again.

internal (ihn TUR nuhl) *adj.* on the inside.

intimidation (ihn tihm uh DAY shuhn) *n.* inspiring fear; using threats or fear to influence behavior.

irrelevantly (ih REHL uh vuhnt lee) *adv.* in a way not relating to the point or situation.

J

jeopardize (JEHP uhr dyz) *v.* put in danger or at risk.

jutted (JUHT ihd) *v.* used as *adj.* sticking out.

L

latent (LAY tuhnt) *adj.* present but not active; concealed.

listlessly (LIHST lihs lee) *adv.* without energy or interest.

lurching (LURCH ihng) *v.* leaning or rolling suddenly to one side.

M

magnanimous (mag NAN uh muhs) *adj.* honorable; noble; generous and forgiving.

malevolent (muh LEHV uh luhnt) *adj.* wishing evil to others.

manifest (MAN uh fehst) *adj.* apparent; obvious.

meager (MEE guhr) *adj.* scanty; not full or rich.

mesmerizing (MEHS muh ryz ihng) *v.* used as *adj.* spellbinding; fascinating.

minute (my NOOT) *adj.* tiny; very small.

mirage (muh RAHZH) *n.* illusion; something that appears to be real but does not truly exist.

misgivings (mihs GIHV ihngz) *n.* feelings of doubt or dread.

misperceptions (mihs puhr SEHP shuhnz) *n.* incorrect ideas or understandings.

momentum (moh MEHN tuhm) *n.* force with which something moves.

N

nonchalantly (NAHN shuh luhnt lee) *adv.* without interest or concern; indifferently.

O

obligation (ahb luh GAY shuhn) *n.* duty.

obliterate (uh BLIHT uh rayt) *v.* destroy; wipe out.

obscurity (uhb SKYUHR ih tee) *n.* the fact of being not well known.

obstructions (uhb STRUHK shunz) *n.* things that are in the way or that block something else.

ominous (AHM uh nuhs) *adj.* unfavorable; threatening.

oppress (uh PREHS) *v.* hold down unjustly; burden.

P

parenthesis (puh REHN thuh sihs) *n.* a curved line used in pairs to set off words or phrases, usually comments or explanations, in a sentence.

perfunctory (puhr FUHNGK tuhr ee) *adj.* done with little care or thought; indifferent.

perplexed (puhr PLEHKST) *adj.* puzzled; confused.

persistent (puhr SIHS tuhnt) *adj.* continuing; stubborn.

pertinent (PUR tuh nuhnt) *adj.* having some association with the subject.

pervaded (puhr VAYD ihd) *v.* spread throughout.

petulant (PEHCH uh luhnt) *adj.* impatient; irritable; peevish.

plundering (PLUHN duhr ihng) *v.* used as *adj.* stealing; taking as much as possible.

pondered (PAHN duhrd) *v.* thought over; considered carefully.

potent (POH tuhnt) *adj.* powerful.

potential (puh TEHN shuhl) *adj.* possible; unrealized; undeveloped.

pretentious (prih TEHN shus) *adj.* attempting to impress by affecting greater importance than is

actually possessed.

primal (PRY muhl) *adj.* first in importance; essential.

principles (PRIHN suh puhlz) *n.* fundamental truths or beliefs.

prodigy (PRAHD uh jee) *n.* child having extraordinary talent.

profuse (pruh FYOOS) *adj.* abundant; plentiful.

prohibits (proh HIHB ihts) *v.* forbids; prevents.

projection (pruh JEHK shuhn) *n.* something that juts out from a surface.

propriety (pruh PRY uh tee) *n.* quality of being appropriate or proper.

prospects (PRAHS pehkts) *n.* things expected or looked forward to; outlook for the future.

prosperous (PRAHS puhr uhs) *adj.* thriving; doing well.

provisions (pruh VIHZH uhnz) *n.* requirements.

prudence (PROO duhns) *n.* good judgment; cautiousness.

pry (pry) *v.* move or separate with force.

punitive (PYOO nuh tihv) *adj.* punishing; seeking to punish.

putrid (PYOO trihd) *adj.* foul; decaying or rotten.

R

rationing (RASH uh nihng) *v.* used as *n.* distribution in small amounts.

realm (rehlm) *n.* kingdom.

rebounded (rih BOWND ihd) *v.* bounced back.

relapse (REE laps) *n.* process of slipping back into a former state.

remorse (rih MAWRS) *n.* deep regret for doing wrong.

replete (rih PLEET) *adj.* full of; abundant.

reprehensible (rehp rih HEHN suh buhl) *adj.* deserving of criticism.

repressive (rih PREHS ihv) *adj.* exerting strict control over; brutal.

reproach (rih PROHCH) *v.* blame; express disapproval.

resignation (rehz ihg NAY shuhn) *n.* passive acceptance; submission.

resolute (REHZ uh loot) *adj.* determined.

S

sated (SAYT ihd) *v.* used as *adj.* fully satisfied.

saturated (SACH uh rayt ihd) *adj.* filled completely.

searing (SIHR ihng) *v.* used as *adj.* burning; scorching.

sentiment (SEHN tuh muhnt) *n.* tender feeling.

serpentine (SUR puhn teen) *adj.* twisted or winding; like a snake.

severed (SEHV uhrd) *v.* cut; broke off.

sidle (SY duhl) *v.* move in a slow, sideways manner.

skeptical (SKEHP tuh kuhl) *adj.* doubting.

skepticism (SKEHP tuh sihz uhm) *n.* a tendency to question or doubt.

skirted (SKURT ihd) *v.* passed along the border or side of something.

slackened (SLAK uhnd) *v.* used as *adj.* made looser.

slighted (SLYT ihd) *v.* paid too little attention to.

sovereign (SAHV ruhn) *n.* the supreme ruler; king or queen.

spontaneous (spahn TAY nee uhs) *adj.* taking place without external cause or help.

stalking (STAWK ihng) *v.* approaching while trying not to be seen or heard.

stealth (stehlth) *n.* secretiveness; sly behavior.

stench (stehnch) *n.* offensive smell.

strife (stryf) *n.* bitter struggle.

submissive (suhb MIHS ihv) *adj.* obedient; under another's control.

sultry (SUHL tree) *adj.* hot and humid; sweltering.

superstitious (soo puhr STIHSH uhs) *adj.* having an irrational fear of the unknown, the mysterious, or the imaginary.

syntax (SIHN taks) *n.* sentence structure; relationship of words in a sentence.

T

tangible (TAN juh buhl) *adj.* capable of being touched or felt.

temperamental (tehm puhr uh MEHN tuhl) *adj.* moody; easily irritated.

temperate (TEHM puhr iht) *adj.* not too hot or too cold; mild; moderate in behavior; self-restrained.

tenacity (tih NAS uh tee) *n.* stubborn persistence and determination.

tentative (TEHN tuh tihv) *adj.* uncertain; hesitant.

tenuous (TEHN yoo uhs) *adj.* thin or slight; weak; fragile.

transfixed (trans FIHKST) *v.* used as *adj.* motionless.

trivial (TRIHV ee uhl) *adj.* unimportant; not significant.

tumultuous (too MUHL choo uhs) *adj.* wild and noisy.

tyrant (TY ruhnt) *n.* harsh, unjust ruler.

U

undisputed (uhn dihs PYOO tihd) *adj.* without doubt.

unprecedented (uhn PREHS uh dehn tihd) *adj.* never done before; new.

unscrupulous (uhn SKROO pyuh luhs) *adj.* unprincipled; not concerned with right and wrong.

utopian (yoo TOH pee uhn) *adj.* extremely idealistic but impractical.

V

vagrant (VAY gruhnt) *adj.* moving from place to place with no obvious means of support.

vain (vayn) *adj.* having too much pride in one's looks.

valiantly (VAL yuhnt lee) *adv.* bravely; courageously.

vehemently (VEE uh muhnt lee) *adv.* performed with unusual force or violence.

vigorously (VIHG uhr uhs lee) *adv.* in a strong, active, forceful way.

vitality (vy TAL uh tee) *n.* physical strength; energy for life.

void (voyd) *v.* cancel legal force or effect.

W

whetted (HWEHT ihd) *adj.* sharpened.

withered (WIHTH uhrd) *v.* used as *adj.* wrinkled and shrunken.

wrath (rath) *n.* fury often marked by a desire for revenge.

writhed (rythd) *v.* violently twisted and rolled, especially as a result of severe pain.

Spanish Glossary

A

abatido *adj.* avergonzado y confundido.

abogar *v.* recomendar; hablar en favor de alguien.

aborrecer *v.* detestar.

abrasar *adj.* quemar; tostar.

abreviatura *sust.* forma reducida de una palabra o una frase.

abstracción *sust.* idea o concepto.

absurdo *adj.* que es claramente ilógico, falso o poco razonable.

acechar *v.* acercarse tratando de no ser visto u oído.

acobardarse *v.* encogerse u ocultarse por miedo o vergüenza.

administrar *v.* dirigir o controlar.

admitido *adj.* reconocido como cierto.

adversario *sust.* oponente.

adyacente *adj.* vecino; cercano a algo.

afligido *adj.* triste, apenado.

afrenta *sust.* insulto intencional.

agresión *sust.* costumbre de atacar; comportamiento destructivo y poco amistoso.

aguzado *adj.* afilado.

altruista *adj.* que se preocupa por los demás de manera desinteresada.

anecdótico *adj.* versión que no se puede comprobar.

aniquilar *v.* destruir; borrar.

apreciar *v.* tratar con amor y cariño.

apropiado *adj.* adecuado o correcto.

archivo *sust.* registro público o documento histórico.

arrancar *v.* mover o separar con fuerza.

arriesgar *v.* poner en peligro.

artero *adj.* que usa la inteligencia para engañar.

artificioso *adj.* planificado; manipulado.

atenuar *v.* hacer que algo parezca menos grave con una excusa.

B

beligerante *adj.* agresivo; que le gusta pelear.

benévolo *adj.* amable; generoso con los demás.

benigno *adj.* que no es peligroso.

bordear *v.* moverse por la orilla de algo.

burlescamente *adv.* en tono de broma.

C

cañón *sust.* valle profundo con bordes empinados; barranco.

caótico *adj.* muy confuso; totalmente desordenado.

cavilar *v.* pensar detenidamente; considerar con cuidado.

censurar *v.* examinar con el objetivo de eliminar algo reprochable.

cercenar *v.* cortar; partir.

cerciorar *v.* saber con certeza; determinar.

clamar *v.* pedir a gritos; demandar.

clamor *sust.* griterío ruidoso.

cláusula *sust.* cada una de las disposiciones de una ley o acuerdo.

codiciar *v.* desear ansiosamente.

coerción *sust.* uso de la fuerza o de persuasión enérgica.

cólera *sust.* gran enfado, furia.

cólera *sust.* furia a menudo marcada por un deseo de venganza.

colusión *sust.* acuerdo secreto.

comercial *adj.* que tiene que ver con el mercado o los negocios.

compasivo *adj.* amable; que quiere ayudar a los demás.

composición *sust.* canción o ensayo.

concienzudo *adj.* serio y sincero.

concordar *v.* corresponder; ser similar.

condición *sust.* requerimiento.

conferir *v.* dar o conceder.

confrontar *v.* enfrentar.

consentimiento *sust.* aprobación.

consentir *v.* aceptar.

conspirador *sust.* persona que ayuda a planear un crimen; traidor.

consumidor *sust.* persona que usa lo que hace o cultiva un productor.

contienda *sust.* lucha furiosa.

contradicción *sust.* afirmación que se opone a algo o alguien; desacuerdo.

convicción *sust.* creencia firme; seguridad.

copioso *adj.* muy abundante o lleno.

corroborar *v.* apoyar; confirmar que algo es cierto.

cortejar *v.* galantear; enamorar.

costumbre *sust.* hábito; tradición.

crédulo *adj.* fácilmente convencido de creer algo.

criterio *sust.* capacidad de hacer una elección.

crucial *adj.* muy importante.

cumplir *v.* hacer lo que se pide.

D

decrépito *adj.* viejo y desgastado.
demanda *sust.* reclamación de algo que corresponde.
depravado *adj.* malvado; moralmente corrupto.
desafiante *adj.* que se enfrenta a la autoridad.
desdeñar *v.* pensar que algo no tiene valor o mérito.
desenmarañar *v.* liberar o desligar.
desenmarañar *v.* liberar; soltar.
desestimar *v.* prestar poca atención.
deslizarse *v.* moverse discretamente hacia un lado.
despreocupadamente *adv.* sin interés ni preocupación; de manera indiferente.
desprovisto *adj.* que carece completamente de algo.
destino *sust.* lo que espera a alguien o a algo; suerte.
desviar *v.* mover hacia un lado.
deteriorar *v.* empeorar.
deteriorar *v.* empeorar.
devorar *v.* comer con mucho apetito.
diabético *adj.* que padece de diabetes, una enfermedad que hace que el cuerpo sea incapaz de procesar cantidades grandes de azúcar.
diestramente *adv.* rápida y hábilmente.
difuso *adj.* extenso; fuera de foco.
diminuto *adj.* muy pequeño; mínimo.
discernir *v.* reconocer o distinguir.
discernir *v.* reconocer; detectar.
discriminación *sust.* prejuicio; tratamiento injusto.
disonante *adj.* contrario; que no concuerda.
dispensar *v.* liberar; soltar.
distender *v.* aflojar.
distorsionar *v.* torcer hasta cambiar de forma.
disuadir *v.* hacer desistir mediante la persuasión.
dolencia *sust.* defecto; debilidad.
dormitar *v.* quedarse medio dormido.

E

ecuanimidad *sust.* calma; serenidad.
emanar *v.* emerger; salir de una fuente.
emancipación *sust.* liberación, acto de liberar.
empapar *v.* humedecer totalmente.
empatía *sust.* capacidad de comprender las emociones de otra persona.
encolerizar *v.* enojar mucho.
envolver *v.* rodear algo completamente hasta absorberlo.
erosionar *v.* desgastar.
escepticismo *sust.* tendencia a cuestionar o dudar.
escéptico *adj.* que duda.
esculpir *v.* cortar o cincelar para dar forma.
espejismo *sust.* ilusión; algo que parece real pero que en realidad no existe.

espontáneo *adj.* que ocurre sin ayuda o causa externa.
exaltar *v.* tener en gran estima; glorificar.
exasperar *v.* irritar; enojar.
exasperar *v.* enojar o irritar mucho.
exhalación *sust.* aliento; lo que se deja salir al respirar.
exiguo *adj.* escaso; insuficiente.
expectativa *sust.* lo que alguien espera o desea hacer; proyecto de futuro.
explotar *v.* utilizar egoístamente en beneficio propio.
extrínseco *adj.* externo; que no pertenece a algo.

F

fascinar *v.* hipnotizar; hechizar.
fiasco *sust.* fracaso completo.
fidelidad *sust.* interpretación exacta.
firmamento *sust.* cielo.
fortaleza *sust.* fuerza para resistir el dolor o afrontar el peligro.
fortificar *v.* fortalecer.
fortuito *adj.* al azar; sin planificar.
frívolo *adj.* que no es serio; superficial.
funesto *adj.* desfavorable; amenazador.
furtivo *adj.* secreto, hecho a escondidas.
furtivo *adj.* secreto; que se hace a escondidas.

G

generar *v.* dar comienzo a algo.
gesto *sust.* movimiento, generalmente de una parte del cuerpo; acción.

H

hedor *sust.* olor desagradable.
hostil *adj.* muy poco amistoso.

I

ignominiosamente *adv.* de manera vergonzosa.
ignorante *adj.* que no tiene conocimientos o conciencia de algo.
imparcial *adj.* justo; neutral.
impedir *v.* obstruir; bloquear, por ejemplo con un obstáculo.
imperceptiblemente *adv.* de manera tan discreta que casi no se nota.
ímpetu *sust.* fuerza con la que se mueve algo.
impregnar *v.* esparcir por toda la superficie.
impunidad *sust.* falta de castigo.
inaudible *adj.* imposible de escuchar.
incesante *adj.* constante; que nunca se detiene.
incrédulo *adj.* que duda.
indiscutible *adj.* sin duda.

indispensable *adj.* absolutamente necesario; esencial.

indispuesto *adj.* algo enfermo.

inducir *v.* convencer; influir.

indulgentemente *adv.* de manera muy despreocupada.

inédito *adj.* que nunca se ha hecho antes; nuevo.

inerte *adj.* sin movimiento; falto de vida, muerto.

inescrupuloso *adj.* sin principios, que no se preocupa por lo que está bien y lo que está mal.

inexorable *adj.* inflexible; que no admite cambios.

inmenso *adj.* muy grande; enorme.

inquisitivo *adj.* curioso; que hace preguntas.

inscribir *v.* marcar o escribir en una superficie; grabar.

insignificante *adj.* que tiene poca importancia o influencia.

insinuar *v.* sugerir.

integración *sust.* el proceso de combinar o incluir.

integrar *v.* construir con elementos que funcionan en conjunto; combinar.

integridad *sust.* honestidad u honradez.

integridad *sust.* honestidad y sinceridad.

intermitente *adj.* que se interrumpe y vuelve a comenzar.

interno *adj.* en la parte de adentro de algo.

intimidar *v.* causar miedo; amenazar o atemorizar para influir en el comportamiento de alguien.

invalidar *v.* cancelar la fuerza o el efecto legal de algo.

irrelevantemente *adv.* de una manera que no tiene relación con el punto o la situación.

irreverencia *sust.* cualidad de ser irrespetuoso.

irritante *adj.* impaciente; fastidioso; malhumorado.

L

lánguidamente *adv.* sin energía ni interés.

latente *adj.* presente pero inactivo; oculto.

M

magnánimo *adj.* honorable; noble; generoso y compasivo.

malentendido *sust.* idea o interpretación equivocada.

malévolo *adj.* que desea el mal a otros.

manifiesto *adj.* evidente; obvio.

marchito *adj.* arrugado y encogido.

mortandad *sust.* matanza de una gran cantidad de personas; carnicería.

O

obligación *sust.* deber.

obstrucción *sust.* algo que se interpone a otra cosa o la obstaculiza.

oprimir *v.* reprimir injustamente, agobiar.

oscuridad *sust.* el hecho de no ser conocido.

P

paralizar *v.* inmovilizar.

parentesco *sust.* vínculo; relación.

paréntesis *sust.* par de líneas curvas que se usan para separar palabras o frases de una oración que por lo general expresan comentarios o explicaciones.

perplejo *adj.* sorprendido; confundido.

persistente *adj.* continuo; testarudo.

pertinente *adj.* que tiene relación con el tema.

pesar *sust.* arrepentimiento o sentimiento de culpa por haber hecho algo malo.

pizca *sust.* porción pequeña.

pletórico *adj.* abundante.

potencial *adj.* posible; no realizado; sin desarrollar.

potente *adj.* fuerte.

presumido *adj.* muy orgulloso de la apariencia física.

pretencioso *adj.* intentar impresionar fingiendo mayor importancia que la que se tiene.

primitivo *adj.* que pertenece a los primeros tiempos de algo; original.

primordial *adj.* primero en importancia; esencial.

principio *sust.* creencia o verdad fundamental.

prodigio *sust.* niño que tiene un talento extraordinario.

profuso *adj.* abundante; que existe en gran cantidad.

prominente *adj.* sobresaliente.

próspero *adj.* floreciente; que marcha bien.

próspero *adj.* rico.

prudencia *sust.* buen juicio; cautela.

punitivo *adj.* que castiga o busca castigar.

putrefacto *adj.* nauseabundo; en descomposición o podrido.

Q

querible *adj.* que inspira afecto.

R

racionar *v.* repartir en pequeñas cantidades.

rebotar *v.* volver hacia atrás.

recaída *sust.* proceso de volver al estado previo.

recelo *sust.* sentimiento de duda o desconfianza.

recriminar *v.* culpar; expresar desaprobación.

regañar *v.* reprender ligeramente.

reinado *sust.* reino.

remordimiento *sust.* profundo arrepentimiento por haber hecho una mala acción.

repleto *adj.* completamente lleno; que tiene algo en abundancia.

reprensible *adj.* que merece crítica.

represivo *adj.* que ejerce control severo sobre algo; brutal.

resignación *sust.* aceptación pasiva; sumisión.

restringir *v.* limitar; reducir.

resuelto *adj.* decidido.

retorcerse *v.* enroscarse violentamente, especialmente como resultado de un gran dolor.

rezumar *v.* irradiar; desprender.

risible *adj.* que causa risa; extravagante.

roya *sust.* enfermedad que hace que las plantas se marchiten y mueran.

S

saciar *v.* satisfacer plenamente.

saliente *sust.* algo que sobresale de una superficie.

saquear *v.* robar; tomar todo lo que se puede.

saturado *adj.* totalmente lleno.

sensibilidad *sust.* sentimiento tierno.

séquito *sust.* grupo de personas que acompañan a alguien importante.

serpentino *adj.* torcido o enroscado; similar a una serpiente.

sigilo *sust.* secreto, comportamiento discreto.

sintaxis *sust.* estructura de las oraciones; relación entre las palabras de una oración.

soberano *sust.* gobernante supremo; rey o reina.

sofocante *adj.* caliente y húmedo.

somero *adj.* hecho con poco cuidado o sin pensar; indiferente.

sumiso *adj.* obediente; bajo el control de otra persona.

supersticioso *adj.* que tiene un miedo irracional a lo desconocido, lo misterioso o lo imaginario.

suprimir *v.* borrar.

T

tambalear *v.* moverse repentinamente hacia un lado.

tangible *adj.* que se puede tocar o sentir.

temperamental *adj.* de humor variable; que se enoja fácilmente.

templado *adj.* ni muy caliente ni muy frío; suave; moderado en su comportamiento; contenido.

tenacidad *sust.* fuerte perseverancia y determinación.

tenue *adj.* fino o ligero; débil; frágil.

tez *sust.* apariencia de la piel, especialmente la de la cara.

tirano *sust.* gobernante severo e injusto.

trivial *adj.* sin importancia; insignificante.

tumultuoso *adj.* agitado y ruidoso.

U

utópico *adj.* extremadamente idealista pero irrealizable.

V

vacilante *adj.* incierto; indeciso.

vagabundo *adj.* que se mueve de un lugar a otro sin un oficio determinado.

valerosamente *adv.* con valentía; con coraje.

vedar *v.* prohibir; impedir.

vehementemente *adv.* hecho con fuerza o violencia inusual.

vigorosamente *adv.* de manera fuerte, activa y enérgica.

vitalidad *sust.* fuerza física; energía para vivir.

Academic Vocabulary Glossary

Academic Vocabulary Glossary English/ Spanish

The Academic Vocabulary Glossary in this section is an alphabetical list of the Academic Vocabulary words found in this textbook. Use this glossary just as you would use a dictionary—to find out the meanings of words used in your literature class to talk about and write about literary and informational texts and to talk about and write about concepts and topics in your other academic classes.

For each word, the glossary includes the pronunciation, part of speech, and meaning. A Spanish version of the glossary immediately follows the English version. For more information about the words in the Academic Vocabulary Glossary, please consult a dictionary.

ENGLISH

A

acquire (uh KWYR) *v.* get or gain.

aspects (AS pehkts) *n.* parts or features of a subject; facets.

attitude (AT uh tood) *n.* a state of mind or feeling about something.

C

challenge (CHAL uhnj) *v.* call to a contest or fight; dare.

complement (KAHM pluh muhnt) *v.* complete; fulfill a lack of any kind.

complex (kuhm PLEHKS) *adj.* made up of many parts; complicated.

component (kuhm POH nuhnt) *n.* necessary or essential part; element.

correspond (kawr uh SPAHND) *v.* agree or be in harmony; be similar.

credible (KREHD uh buhl) *adj.* believable; trustworthy.

criteria (kry TIHR ee uh) *n.* Rules or standards for making a judgment; test.

D

debate (dih BAYT) *n.* discussion of opposing arguments.

demonstrate (DEHM uhn strayt) *v.* show or prove by using evidence.

derive (dih RYV) *v.* obtain from a source or origin.

E

equivalent (ih KWIHV uh luhnt) *adj.* equal in value, strength, or force.

evaluation (ih val yoo AY shuhn) *n.* judgment; assessment.

evident (EHV uh duhnt) *adj.* easy to understand; obvious.

evoke (ih VOHK) *v.* bring out; call forth.

exhibit (ehg ZIHB iht) *v.* to show, display, or indicate.

F

format (FAWR mat) *n.* design; arrangement.

function (FUHNGK shuhn) *v.* act in a specific manner; work.

H

highlight (HY lyt) *v.* to make a subject or idea stand out so people will pay attention.

I

illustrate (IHL uh strayt) *v.* show; demonstrate.

incorporate (ihn KAWR puh rayt) *v.* make something a part of something else.

insert (ihn SUHRT) *v.* add; include; put in.

interact (ihn tuhr AKT) *v.* act upon each other.

L

literal (LIHT uhr uhl) *adj.* interpreting words the usual way.

O

objective (uhb JEHK tihv) *n.* purpose; goal.

P

perceive (puhr SEEV) *v.* be aware of; sense; observe.

predominant (pree DAHM uh nuhnt) *adj.* more powerful, common, or noticeable than others.

principal (PRIHN suh puhl) *adj.* most important.

R

recount (rih KOWNT) *v.* to tell or give an account of.

recurring (rih KUR ihng) *v.* used as *adj.* coming up again, being repeated.

retain (rih TAYN) *v.* to continue to have or hold.

reveal (rih VEEL) *v.* make known; show.

S

significant (sihg NIHF uh kuhnt) *adj.* meaningful; important.
subsequent (SUHB suh kwuhnt) *adj.* coming next; following.

T

technique (tehk NEEK) *n.* method used to accomplish something.
tension (TEHN shuhn) *n.* strained condition.
tradition (truh DIHSH uhn) *n.* handing down of beliefs, opinions, customs, and stories.
transform (trans FAWRM) *v.* change.

SPANISH

A

actitud *sust.* opinión o sentimiento sobre algo.
adquirir *v.* conseguir o ganar.
añadir *v.* agregar; incluir; poner.
aspecto *sust.* rasgo o característica; faceta.

C

coincidir *v.* estar de acuerdo o en armonía con algo; ser similar a algo.
complejo *adj.* hecho de varias partes o piezas; complicado.
complementar *v.* completar; agregar lo que falta.
componente *sust.* parte necesaria o fundamental; elemento.
controversia *sust.* debate entre argumentos opuestos.
criterio *sust.* reglas o normas para hacer un juicio.

D

demostrar *v.* enseñar o justificar con pruebas.
desafiar *v.* provocar a una lucha o competencia; retar.

E

equivalente *adj.* que tiene el mismo valor o fuerza.
evidente *adj.* fácil de comprender; obvio.
evocar *v.* traer; llamar.
exponer *v.* mostrar o indicar.

F

fidedigno *adj.* creíble; digno de confianza.

formato *sust.* diseño, arreglo.
funcionar *v.* trabajar de una manera determinada.

I

ilustrar *v.* mostrar; demostrar.
incorporar *v.* hacer que algo forme parte de otra cosa.
interactuar *v.* actuar juntos, uno con otro.

L

literal *adj.* que usa el significado común de las palabras.

N

narrar *v.* contar o dar una versión de algo.

O

objetivo *sust.* propósito; meta.
obtener *v.* conseguir de una determinada fuente u origen.

P

percibir *v.* ser consciente de algo; sentir; observar.
preponderante *adj.* más poderoso, común o perceptible que otras cosas.
principal *adj.* más importante.

R

realzar *v.* hacer que un tema o una idea resalte para que las personas le presten más atención.
recurrente *adj.* que ocurre de nuevo, que se repite.
retener *v.* seguir teniendo.
revelar *v.* dar a conocer; mostrar.

S

significativo *adj.* relevante; importante.
subsiguiente *adj.* que viene después; siguiente.

T

técnica *sust.* método que se usa para conseguir algo.
tensión *sust.* condición o situación tirante.
tradición *sust.* transmisión de creencias, opiniones, costumbres e historias.
transformar *v.* cambiar.

V

valoración *sust.* opinión; evaluación.

ACKNOWLEDGMENTS

Excerpt (retitled "Thinkin ' on Marryin'") from *The Quilters: Women and Domestic Art* by Norma Bradley Allen and Patricia Cooper. Published by Texas Tech University Press, Lubbock, TX. Copyright © 1999 by Patricia Cooper Baker and Norma Bradley Allen. Reproduced by permission of **Norma Bradley Allen.**

From "The Trip" from *Hope and Other Dangerous Pursuits* by Laila Lalami. Copyright 2005 © by Laila Lalami. Reproduced by permission of **Algonquin Books of Chapel Hill, a Division of Workman Publishing.**

From *On the Waterfront: The Final Shooting Script* by Budd Schulberg. Copyright © 1980 by Budd Schulberg. Reproduced by permission of **Miriam Altshuler Literary Agency on behalf of Budd Schulberg.**

From interview with Julie Otsuka by Andrew Duncan from *Booksense.com* Web site, accessed June 22, 2005, at http://www.booksense.com/people/archive/o/otsukajulie.jsp. Copyright © 2005 by the **American Booksellers Association**. Reproduced by permission of the publisher.

"Mint Snowball" from *Mint Snowball* by Naomi Shihab Nye. Copyright © 2001 by Naomi Shihab Nye. Reproduced by permission of **Anhinga Press.**

"The Brute" from *The Brute and Other Farces* by Anton Chekhov, English version by Eric Bentley. Copyright © 1956 and renewed © 1984 by Eric Bentley. Published by Samuel French, Inc. Reproduced by permission of **Applause Theatre & Cinema Books.**

"Same Song" from *Borders* by Pat Mora. Copyright © 1986 by Pat Mora. Published by **Arte Público Press–University of Houston, Houston, TX, 1986**. Reproduced by permission of the publisher.

"9/11 dogs seemed to escape illnesses" from *The Deseret News* (Salt Lake City), October 21, 2006. Copyright © 2006 by **The Associated Press.** All rights reserved. Reproduced by permission of the copyright holder.

From "Discourse of the Bear" (retitled "The Bear's Speech") from *Cronopios and Famas* by Julio Cortázar, translated by Paul Blackburn. Translation copyright © 1969 by Random House, Inc. Reproduced by permission **Agencia Literaria Carmen Balcells, S.A.**

"Momotaro: Boy-of-the-Peach" from *The Dancing Kettle and Other Japanese Folk Tales* by Yoshiko Uchida. Copyright © 1949 by Yoshiko Uchida. Reproduced by permission of **Bancroft Library, University of California, Berkeley.**

"The Possibility of Evil" from *Just an Ordinary Day: The Uncollected Stories* by Shirley Jackson. Copyright © 1965 by Stanley Edgar Hyman. Reproduced by permission of **Bantam Books, a division of Random House, Inc.**, and electronic format by permission of **Linda Allen Literary Agency for the Estate of Shirley Jackson.**

From interview with Julie Otsuka from *Barnes and Noble* Web site, accessed June 22, 2005, at http://www.barnesandnoble.com/writers/writerdetails.asp?userid=629jqKYAL4&cid=1020536. Copyright © 2005 by **Barnes and Noble**. Reproduced by permission of the publisher.

"All-American Girl" from *The Woman I Kept to Myself* by Julia Alvarez. Copyright © 2004 by Julia Alvarez. Published by Algonquin Books of Chapel Hill, 2004; first published in *Beauty's Nothing,* Arena Editions, 2001. Reproduced by permission of **Susan Bergholz, Literary Services, New York, NY and Lamy, NM.**

From "An American Childhood in the Dominican Republic" by Julia Alvarez from *The American Scholar*, vol. 56, no. 1, Winter 1987. Copyright © 1987 by Julia Alvarez. All rights reserved. Reproduced by permission of **Susan Bergholz Literary Services, New York, NY and Lamy, NM.**

"Antojos" by Julia Alvarez from *The Caribbean Writer Online*, Volume 4: pp. 68–73. Copyright © 2003 by Julia Alvarez. Reproduced by permission of **Susan Bergholz Literary Services, New York, NY and Lamy, NM.**

"Exile" from *The Other Side/El Otro Lado* by Julia Alvarez. Copyright © 1995 by Julia Alvarez. Published by Plume/Penguin, a division of Penguin Group (USA) Inc. Originally published in the *George Washington Review*. All rights reserved. Reproduced by permission of **Susan Bergholz Literary Services, New York, NY and Lamy, NM.**

"My First Free Summer" by Julia Alvarez from *Better Homes and Gardens*, August 2003. Copyright © 2003 by Julia Alvarez. Reproduced by permission of **Susan Bergholz Literary Services, New York.**

"Snow" from *How the García Girls Lost Their Accents* by Julia Alvarez. Copyright © 1991 by Julia Alvarez. Published by Plume, an imprint of Dutton Signet, a division of Penguin Group (USA) Inc., and originally in hardcover by Algonquin Books of Chapel Hill. All rights reserved. Reproduced by permission of **Susan Bergholz Literary Services, New York, NY and Lamy, NM.**

From "Ode to My Socks" by Pablo Neruda from *Neruda and Vallejo: Selected Poems,* edited and translated by Robert Bly. Copyright © 1971 by **Robert Bly**. Published by Beacon Press. Reproduced by permission of the translator.

"miss rosie" from *Good Woman: Poems and a Memoir 1969–1980* by Lucille Clifton. Copyright © 1987 by Lucille Clifton. Reproduced by permission of **BOA Editions, Ltd.**

"this morning" from *Good Woman: Poems and a Memoir 1969–1980* by Lucille Clifton. Copyright © 1987 by Lucille Clifton. Reproduced by permission of **BOA Editions, Ltd.**

"Eating Together" from *Rose: Poems* by Li-Young Lee. Copyright © 1986 by Li-Young Lee. Reproduced by permission of **BOA Editions, Ltd.**

From "Coming of age, Latino style special rite ushers girls into adulthood" by Cindy Rodriguez from *The Boston Globe,* January 5, 1997. Copyright © 1997 by **The Boston Globe**. Reproduced by permission of the publisher.

"By the Waters of Babylon" from *The Selected Works of Stephen Vincent Benét.* Copyright © 1937 by Stephen Vincent Benét; copyright renewed © 1965 by Thomas C. Benét, Stephanie B. Mahin, and Rachel Benét Lewis. Reproduced by permission of **Brandt & Hochman Literary Agents, Inc.**

"We Real Cool" from *Blacks* by Gwendolyn Brooks. Copyright © 1991 by Gwendolyn Brooks. Published by Third World Press, Chicago, 1991. Reproduced by permission of **Brooks Permissions**.

"R.M.S. Titanic" by Hanson W. Baldwin from *Harper's Magazine*, January 1934. Copyright © 1934 by Hanson W. Baldwin. Reproduced by permission of **Curtis Brown, Ltd.**

"Essay" by Jennifer Chang. Copyright © 2007 by **Jennifer Chang**. Reproduced by permission of the author.

"Obedience, or The Lying Tale" by Jennifer Chang. Copyright © 2005 by **Jennifer Chang**. Reproduced by permission of the author.

"Housepainting" by Lan Samantha Chang. Copyright © 1994 by **Lan Samantha Chang**. Reproduced by permission of the author.

From "Drunk and in Charge of a Bicycle" from *The Stories of Ray Bradbury*. Copyright © 1980 by Ray Bradbury. Reproduced by permission of **Don Congdon Associates, Inc.**

Quote, "You can't have 'plot' . . ." by Ray Bradbury. Reproduced by permission of **Don Congdon Associates, Inc.**

"The Pedestrian" by Ray Bradbury from *The Reporter*, August 7, 1951. Copyright © 1951 by the Fortnightly Publishing Co.; copyright renewed © 1979 by Ray Bradbury. Reproduced by permission of **Don Congdon Associates, Inc.**

From "Contents of the Dead Man's Pocket" (slightly adapted) by Jack Finney. Copyright © 1956 by Crowell-Collier Co.; copyright renewed © 1984 by Jack Finney. Reproduced by permission of **Don Congdon Associates, Inc.**

"The Summer I Was Sixteen" from *Province of Fire* by Geraldine Connolly. Copyright © 1998 by Geraldine Connolly. Reproduced by permission of **Iris Press, Oak Ridge, TN.**

"Power of the Pack" from *Cesar's Way* by Cesar Millan and Melissa Jo Peltier. Copyright © 2006 by Cesar Millan and Melissa Jo. Peltier. Reproduced by permission of **Crown Publishers, a division of Random House, Inc.**, and electronic format by permission of **Trident Media Group, LLC.**

From "Alice in Wonderland" by Toni Y. Joseph from *The Dallas Morning News*, May 27, 1992. Copyright © 1992 by **The Dallas Morning News**. Reproduced by permission of the publisher.

"Where Have You Gone, Charming Billy?" slightly adapted from *Going After Cacciato* by Tim O'Brien. Copyright © 1975, 1976, 1977, 1978 by Tim O'Brien. Reproduced by permission **Dell Publishing, a division of Random House, Inc.** and electronic format by permission of **Tim O'Brien.**

"Grape Sherbet" from *Museum* by Rita Dove. Copyright © 1983 by **Rita Dove**. Published by Carnegie-Mellon University Press. Reproduced by permission of the author.

"The Sword in the Stone" from *Le Morte D'Arthur* by Sir Thomas Malory, translated by Keith Baines. Translation copyright © 1962 by Keith Baines; copyright renewed © 1990 by Francesca Evans. Reproduced by permission of **Dutton Signet, a division of Penguin Group (USA) Inc., www.penguin.com.**

"The Tale of Sir Launcelot du Lake" from *Le Morte D'Arthur* by Sir Thomas Malory, translated by Keith Baines. Translation copyright © 1962 by Keith Baines; copyright renewed © 1990 by Francesca Evans. Reproduced by permission of **Dutton Signet, a division of Penguin Group (USA) Inc., www.penguin.com.**

"The Colomber" from *Restless Nights* by Dino Buzzati, translated by Lawrence Venuti. Copyright © 1983 by North Point Press. Reproduced by permission of **Guilio Enaudi Editore S.P.A.**

Entry for "vision quest" from *The New Encyclopaedia Britannica*, 15th Edition, vol. 12. Copyright © 1995 by **Encyclopaedia Britannica, Inc.** Reproduced by permission of the publisher.

"The First Seven Years" from *The Magic Barrel* by Bernard Malamud. Copyright © 1950, 1958 and renewed © 1977, 1986 by Bernard Malamud. Reproduced by permission of **Farrar, Straus & Giroux, LLC**, and electronic format by permission of **Russell & Volkening, Inc. as agents for the author**.

From "Man in the Drawer" from *Rembrandt's Hat* by Bernard Malamud. Copyright © 1973 by Bernard Malamud. Reproduced by permission of **Farrar, Straus and Giroux, LLC**.

"A Storm in the Mountains" from *Stories and Prose Poems* by Alexander Solzhenitsyn, translated by Michael Glenny. Translation copyright © 1971 by Michael Glenny. Reproduced by permission of **Farrar, Straus and Giroux, LLC**.

From "The Final Weeks" from *Team of Rivals: The Political Genius of Abraham Lincoln* by Doris Kearns Goodwin. Copyright © 2005 by Blithedale Productions, Inc. Reproduced by permission of **Simon and Schuster Adult Publishing Group**.

From "Introduction" to *Team of Rivals: The Political Genius of Abraham Lincoln* by Doris Kearns Goodwin. Copyright © 2005 by Blithedale Productions, Inc. Reproduced by permission of **The Free Press, a division of Simon & Schuster Adult Publishing Group**.

"Night Calls" by Lisa Fugard from *Outside*, vol. XX, no. 5, May 1995. Copyright © 1995 by **Lisa Fugard**. Reproduced by permission of the author.

"Sonnet for Heaven Below" from *Correspondence Between the Stonehaulers* by Jack Agüeros. Copyright © 1991 by Jack Agüeros. Reproduced by permission of **Hanging Loose Press**.

"Everyday Use" from *In Love & Trouble: Stories of Black Women* by Alice Walker. Copyright © 1973 by Alice Walker. Reproduced by permission of **Harcourt, Inc.**, and electronic format by permission of **Wendy Weil Agency, Inc.**

"The Writer" from *The Mind-Reader* by Richard Wilbur. Copyright © 1971 and © renewed 1999 by Richard Wilbur. Reproduced by permission of **Harcourt, Inc.**

"The Leap" by Louise Erdrich from *Harper's Magazine*, March 1990. Copyright © 1990 by **Harper's Magazine**. All rights reserved. Reproduced by permission of the publisher.

"A Very Old Man with Enormous Wings" from *Leaf Storm and Other Stories* by Gabriel García Márquez, translated by Gregory Rabassa. Copyright © 1971 by Gabriel García Márquez. Reproduced by permission of **HarperCollins Publishers, Inc.** and electronic format by permission of **Agencia Literaria Carmen Balcells, S.A.**

From *High Tide in Tucson: Essays from Now or Ever* by Barbara Kingsolver. Copyright ©1995 by Barbara Kingsolver. Reproduced by permission of **HarperCollins Publishers, Inc.**

"Through the Tunnel" from *The Habit of Loving* by Doris Lessing. Copyright © 1955 by Doris Lessing. Reproduced by permission of **HarperCollins Publishers, Inc.**, and electronic format by permission of **Jonathan Clowes Ltd., London, on behalf of Doris Lessing**.

From "Jackie Changed Face of Sports" by Larry Schwartz. Copyright © 1998 by Larry Schwartz. Reproduced by permission of the author.

"And of Clay Are We Created" from *The Stories of Eva Luna* by Isabel Allende, translated by Margaret Sayers Peden. Copyright © 1989 by Isabel Allende; English translation copyright © 1991 by Macmillan Publishing Company. Reproduced by permission of **Scribner, an imprint of Simon & Schuster Adult Publishing Group**.

From *Angela's Ashes* by Frank McCourt. Copyright © 1996 by Frank McCourt. Reproduced by permission of **Scribner, a division of Simon & Schuster Adult Publishing Group**.

"Kiss and Tell" by Judith Stone from *The Nature of Nature*, edited by William H. Shore. Copyright © 1994 by Judith Stone. Published by Harcourt Brace, 1994. Reproduced by permission of **Share Our Strength, Inc.**

From "Escape from Afghanistan" from *The Other Side of the Sky* by Farah Ahmedi with Tanim Ansary. Copyright © 2005 by Nestegg Productions LLC. Reproduced by permission of **Simon Spotlight Entertainment**.

From *The Other Side of the Sky* by Farah Ahmedi with Tanim Ansary. Copyright © 2005 by Nestegg Productions LLC. Reproduced by permission of **Simon Spotlight Entertainment**.

From "Interview with Tobias Wolff" by David Schrieberg from *Stanford Today*, September 1998. Copyright © 1998 by **Stanford University News Service**. Reproduced by permission of the publisher.

"A Young Boy's Stand on a New Orleans Streetcar" from *Story Corps: Recording America* from *National Public Radio*, January 24, 2007. Copyright © 2007 by **StoryCorps˚**. Reproduced by permission of the publisher.

From "Eating Poetry" from *Reasons for Moving* by Mark Strand. Copyright © 1968 by **Mark Strand**. Reproduced by permission of the author.

"Free Minds and Hearts at Work" by Jackie Robinson from *This I Believe: The Personal Philosophies of Remarkable Men and Women*. Copyright © 2006 by **This I Believe, Inc., thisibelieve. org.** Published by Henry Holt and Company. Reproduced by permission of the copyright holder.

"The Princess and the Tin Box" from *The Beast in Me and Other Animals* by James Thurber. Copyright © 1948 by James Thurber; copyright renewed © 1976 by Rosemary A. Thurber. All rights reserved. Reproduced by permission of **Rosemary A. Thurber and The Barbara Hogenson Agency**.

"The Man in the Water" by Roger Rosenblatt from *Time,* January 26, 1982. Copyright © 1982 by **Time Inc.** Reproduced by permission of the publisher.

"The Stayer" from *Palm Crows* by Virgil Suárez. Copyright © 2001 by Virgil Suárez. All rights reserved. Reproduced by permission of **The University of Arizona Press**.

"The Bass, the River, and Sheila Mant" from *The Man Who Loved Levittown* by W. D. Wetherell. Copyright © 1985 by W. D. Wetherell. All rights controlled by the **University of Pittsburgh Press**, Pittsburgh, PA 15260. Reproduced by permission of the publisher.

From *Into Thin Air* by Jon Krakauer. Copyright © 1997 by Jon Krakauer. Reproduced by permission of **Villard Books, a division of Random House, Inc.** and electronic format by permission of **John A. Ware Literary Agency.**

"How sad that I hope . . . ," "Should the world of love . . . ," and "Since my heart placed me . . . " by Ono No Komachi from *The Ink Dark Moon: Love Poems*, translated by Jane Hirshfield and Mariko Aratani. Copyright © 1990 by Jane Hirshfield and Mariko Aratani. Reproduced by permission of **Vintage Books, a division of Random House, Inc., www.randomhouse.com.**

From "What Your Pet is Thinking" by Sharon Begley from *The Wall Street Journal*, October 27, 2006. Copyright © 2006 by Dow Jones & Company, Inc. All rights reserved worldwide. Reproduced by permission of **The Wall Street Journal**.

From "Ill-Equipped Rescuers Dig Out Volcano Victims: Aid Slow to Reach Columbian Town" by Bradley Graham from *The Washington Post*, November 16, 1985. Copyright © 1985 by The Washington Post. Reproduced by permission **The Washington Post Writers Group**.

"Legends and Lore" by Peter Tyson from *Nova Online Adventure* Web site, accessed August 28, 2007, at http://www.pbs. org/wgbh/nova/sharks/island/legends.html. Copyright © 2007 by WGBH/Boston. Reproduced by permission of **WGBH Educational Foundation**.

From "Birth of a Legend" by Stephen Lyons from *NOVA Online* Web site, accessed August 28, 2007, at http://www.pbs.org/ wgbh/nova/lochness/legend.html. Copyright © 2000 by **WGBH Educational Foundation.** Reproduced by permission of the publisher.

"Pronunciation Key" from *World Book Online Reference Center* at www.worldbook.com. Reproduced by permission of **World Book, Inc.**

"12-1-A" by Wakako Yamauchi. Copyright © 1982 by **Wakako Yamauchi.** Reproduced by permission of the author.

Sources Cited:

From interview with Khaled Hosseini by Razeshta Sethna from *Newsline.com* Web site at http://www.newsline.com.pk/ newsnov2003/newsbeat4nov.htm. Published by Newsline.com, Karachi, Pakistan, 2003.

From "Whatever Is Really Yours: An Interview with Louise Erdrich" from *Survival This Way* by Joseph Bruchac. Published by The University of Arizona Press, Tucson, 1987.

Quote by Julia Alvarez from *Julia Alvarez* Web site, accessed August 29, 2005, at www.juliaalvarez.com/about/.

Quote by Julia Alvarez from *Julia Alvarez* Web site, accessed May 1, 2007, at www.juliaalvarez.com/books/.

Quote by Julia Alvarez from *Julia Alvarez* Web site, accessed May 1, 2007, at www.juliaalvarez.com/about

Quote by Steve Buscemi from *Guardian Unlimited*, July 16, 2001. Published by Guardian News and Media Limited, London, 2001.

From *Shakespeare Sisters: Feminist Essay on Women Poets,* edited by Sandra M. Gilbert and Susan Gubar. Published by Indian University Press, Bloomington, IN, 1979.

PICTURE CREDITS

The illustrations and photographs on the Contents pages are picked up from pages in the textbook. Credits for those can be found either on the textbook page on which they appear or in the listing below.

Rita Dove; **663,** Bridgeman Art Library; **667** (t), Shelly Withrow; (c), Steve Liss/Time Life Pictures/Getty Images; **668,** David Carlson/Alamy; **670,** Bridgeman Art Library; **673** (bl), Keystone/Getty Images; (br), Vassilis Constantineas/IML Image Group Ltd/Alamy; **674,** Punchstock; **678** (t), Connie Rieder/Courtesy Geraldine Connolly; (c), Heidi Fischer; **680,** Inman/www.artimagela.com; **684** (tl), Alexandra King/Albuquerque Journal; **685,** images.com/Corbis; **688,** Punchstock; **691,** Bridgeman Art Library; **696** (br), James Marshall/Corbis; **697** (c), Gerit Greve/Corbis; **701** (bl), J.S. Watson/Houghton Library/Harvard University; (br), MPI/Hulton Archive/Getty Images; **706** (t), Ulf Anderson/Getty Images; (c), Bettmann/Corbis; **707,** Art Resource, NY; **708,** Bridgeman Art Library; **711** (bl), Michael Glaser, St. Mary's College of Maryland; (br), Robert Francis/Robert Harding World Imagery/Corbis; **716,** Fernando Alvarado/EPA/Corbis; **718** (bl), BBC/Corbis; (br), Hirz/Hulton Archive/Getty Images; **719,** Atlantide Phototravel/Corbis; **722,** Bridgeman Art Library; **725,** Bridgeman Art Library; **729** (t), Ha Lam; (b), Gino Domenico/AP Photo; **730–731,** Images.com/Corbis; **732,** Bridgeman Art Library; **735** (t), Robert Spencer/The New York Times/Redux; (b), Jo McNulty/Courtesy Andrew Hudgins; **736,** Benjamin Rondel/zefa/Corbis; **737,** Julie Fisher/zefa/Corbis; **740** (br), Hulton Archive/Getty Images; **741,** Library of Congress, Rare Book and Special Collections Division; **744, 746** (all), Eric Schaal/Time & Life Pictures/Getty Images; **747,** Lee Snider/Photo Images/Corbis; **749,** superclic/Alamy; **750** (t), Bridgeman Art Library; **751,** Martin Ruegner/©Image State/Alamy; **755,** Art Rickerby/Time & Life Pictures/Getty Images; **757,** John F. Kennedy Library; **765** (tl), Cover image from *How to Read a Poem* by Edward Hirsch. Copyright ©1999 by Harcourt, Inc. Reproduced by permission of the publisher; (tr), Cover image from *Cool Salsa: Bilingual Poems on Growing Up Latino in the United States* by Lori M. Carlson. Copyright 1994 by Fawcett Publications, Inc., an imprint of Random House, Inc., www.randomhouse.com. Reproduced by permission of the publisher; (br) Cover image of *Platero and I* by Antonio de Nicolás. Illustration by Martin Hardy. Copyright ©2000 by Antonio de Nicolás. Reproduced by permission of the author; **770,** HRW Photo; **780** (bkgd), Marilys Ernst; (inset), Alia Malley; **782–783** (all), J.P. Zenobel/Bridgeman Art Library; **788, 789,** Donald Cooper/Photostage, UK; **793,** John Springer Collection/Corbis; **796** (tl), Everett Collection; (bl), Bassouls Sophie/Corbis Sygma; **798,** Dean Beason; **800** (b), Collection of the Pilgrim Monument and Provincetown Museum; **803, 806,** Bridgeman Art Library; **811,** Judith Collins/Alamy; **814** (bkgd), William Morris/Private Collection/Bridgeman Art Library; Rade Vranesh; **816** (bl), The Art Archive; (br), Mary Evans Picture Library/Alamy; **819, 822, 825, 827,** Rade Vranesh Photography; **830,** Donald Cooper/Photostage, UK; **831,** Erich Lessing/Art Resource, NY; **832** (t), Bridgeman Art Library; (b), Reinhard Saczewski/Bildarchiv Preussischer Kulturbesitz/Art Resource, NY; **833,** Bridgeman Art Library; **834,** Réunion des Musées Nationaux/Art Resource, NY; **836,** The Print Collector/Alamy; **837** (tr), Comedie Francaise, Paris, France/Archives Charmet/Bridgeman Art Library; (l), Universal/Everett Collection; (br), Andrea Pistolesi/Stone/Getty Images; **842** (bkgd), Siede Preis/Getty Images; (c), Pau Ros/Royal Shakespeare Company; **844,** Royal Shakespeare Company; **849,** Suzanne Worthington/Royal Shakespeare Company; **855,** Donald Cooper/Royal Shakespeare Company/Photostage; **860,** Royal Shakespeare Company; **863,** Massimo Listri/Corbis; **868** (bkgd), Siede Preis/Getty Images; (c), Royal Shakespeare Company; **871, 874, 880, 885,** Royal Shakespeare Company; **894** (bkgd), Siede Preis/Getty Images; (c), Suzanne Worthington/Royal Shakespeare Company; **897,** Royal Shakespeare Company; **900–901, 907, 915,** Royal Shakespeare Company/

Lebrecht Music Collection; **917,** Baldwin H. & Kathryn C. Ward/Corbis; **924** (bkgd), Siede Preis/Getty Images; (c), Suzanne Worthington/Royal Shakespeare Company; **929,** Suzanne Worthington/Royal Shakespeare Company; **932,** Donald Cooper/Royal Shakespeare Company/Photostage, UK; **939,** Royal Shakespeare Company; **946** (bkgd), Siede Preis/Getty Images; (c), Royal Shakespeare Company; **949, 951, 960–961,** Royal Shakespeare Company/Lebrecht Music Collection; **966,** Art Resource, NY; **969, 971,** Bridgeman Art Library; **973,** Scala/Art Resource, NY; **976,** Jupiter Images/Creatas/Alamy; **979,** UPI Photo/Ezio Petersen/Landov; **993** (tl), Cover image from *The Mousetrap and Other Plays* by Agatha Christie. Copyright ©1978 by Dutton Signet, a division of Penguin Group (USA) INC., www.penguin.com. Reproduced by permission of the publisher; **998,** Erich Lessing/Art Resource, NY; **1008** (bkgd), images.com/Corbis; (inset), Courtesy Wheaton College Archives and Special Collections; **1010–1011** (all), Robert Dale/Images.com/Corbis; **1014, 1015** (all), Aldo Tutino/Art Resource, NY; **1019,** Bridgeman Art Library; **1021,** ©Troy Howell, published by Scholastic; **1022** (t), Macduff Everton/Corbis; (b), AP Photo/Jessica Hill; **1024,** R.G. Ojeda/Reunion des Musees Nationaux/Art Resource, NY; **1026** (bl), James Whitmore/Time Life Pictures/Getty Images; (br), Pictor International/ImageState/Alamy; **1027,** M. Angelo/Westlight Stock/Corbis; **1030** (l), Réunion des Musées Nationaux/Art Resource, NY; (r), Werner Forman/Art Resource, NY; **1032,** Erich Lessing/Art Resource, NY; **1038** (l), Courtesy the Bancroft Library, University of California; (r), Galen Rowell/Corbis; **1040, 1043, 1044,** National Diet Library, Japan; **1046,** Réunion des Musées Nationaux/Art Resource, NY; **1048** (l), Houghton Mifflin Company, Boston; (r), Bridgeman Art Library; **1049,** M. Angelo/Westlight Stock/Corbis; **1051,** Werner Forman/Art Resource, NY; **1053,** Bridgeman Art Library; **1055, 1057,** Werner Forman/Art Resource, NY; **1060,** HIP/Art Resource, NY; **1062,** Bridgeman Art Library; **1063,** David Crausby/Alamy; **1065,** The Everett Collection; **1071,** Johansen Krause/Archivo Iconografico, SA/Corbis; **1073,** Art Resource, NY; **1075** (t), Francesco Venturi/Corbis; **1078,** Paul W. Liebhardt/Corbis; **1082,** Remi Benali/Corbis; **1085,** Marc & Evelyne Bernheim/Woodfin Camp/IPN Stock; **1087,** Laurie Platt Winfrey, Inc.; **1089,** Mireille Vautier/The Art Archive; **1092,** Najlah Feanny/Corbis; **1095** (t), Vo Trung Dung/Corbis Sygma; (inset), John Frost Newspapers; **1096,** Topham/The Image Works; **1097,** Mary Evans Picture Library/Alamy; **1101,** Bridgeman Art Library; **1104** (t), Art Resource, NY; **1116,** (tl) From *The King Must Die* (book cover) by Mary Renault, copyright ©1958 by Mary Renault. Used by permission of Vintage Books, a division of Random House, Inc.; (bl) Cover image from *The Helmet of Horror: The Myth of Theseus and the Minotaur* by Victor Pelevin. Copyright 2006 by Canongate Books. Reproduced by permission of the publisher; (br) Jacket design by Louise Fili from *The Acts of King Arthur and his Noble Knights.* Copyright ©1976 by Elaine Steinbeck. Reprinted by permission of Farrar, Straus and Giroux LLC; **1117** (tl), Cover image from *A Short History of Myth* by Karen Armstrong. Copyright 2005 by Canongate Books. Reproduced by permission of the publisher; (br) Cover image from *Pocahontas* by Joseph Bruchac. Copyright ©2003 by Harcourt, Inc. Reproduced by permission of the publisher; **1126,** HRW Photo; **1136** (bkgd), moodboard/Punchstock; (inset), HRW Photo; **1138–1139** (all), Todd Davidson/Illustration Works/Corbis; **1150,** Lawrence Manning/Corbis; **1156,** Image Bank/Getty Images; **1160,** Frederic Lucano/Stone/Getty Images; **1166,** Reggie Casagrande/Graphistock/Jupiter Images; **1182,** HRW Photo; **1192,** BananaStock/age Fotostock.

INDEX OF SKILLS

The Index of Skills is divided into the following categories:

LITERARY SKILLS

Allegory, **308, 367,** 370, 371, 373, 374, 375
Alliteration, **647,** 731, 732, 737, 740, 751, 754
Allusion, 63, 540, **657,** 659, 660
Analysis. See Literary analysis.
Analyzing style, **355,** 356, 358, 362
Analyzing Visuals
  character in paintings, **104–105**
  heroes in art, **1014–1015**
  interpreting characters, **788–789**
  persuasion in artwork, **562–563**
  setting and mood in art, **6–7**
  similar subjects in painting, **210–211**
  style in art, **444–445, 648–649**
  symbolism and irony in art, **310–311**
  transit maps, **1142–1143**
Anecdote, **560, 571**
Antagonist, **103, 785**
Appeal. *See* Persuasion.
Approximate rhyme, **647**
Archetype, **1013, 1070,** 1074, 1076, **1079,** 1082, 1084, 1086, 1088, 1089, 1090
Argument
  faulty reasoning, **609,** 610, 611, 612, 613, 615
  generalizations, **609,** 613, 614, 615
  pro and con, **593,** 595, 598, 601, 602, 605, 606
  structure and tone, **583,** 585, 586, 587, 589, 590, 591
  See also Persuasion.
Art, visual
  heroes in, **1014–1015**
  paintings, **104–105, 210–211**
  persuasion in, **562–563**
  setting and mood in, **6–7**
  style in, **444–445, 648–649**
  symbolism and irony in, **310–311**

Arthurian legend, **1012–1013, 1061,** 1063, 1065, 1066
Aside, **787**
Assonance, **734**
Autobiography, **442**
Ballad, **644, 721,** 723, 724, 725
Basic situation, **4**
Biographical approach, **261,** 264, 266, 267, 270, 273, 274
Biographical context, **131,** 135, 139, **577,** 579
Biography, **442, 453**
Character, **102–107**
  and conflict, **103,** 108, 125, 153, **171,** 175, 176, 177, 178, 179, 181, 183, 186, 197
  interactions, **141,** 153, 198
  minor, 1116
  and motivation, **103,** 113, 141, 144, 145, 150, 151, 152, 153, 198, 227
  in paintings, **104–105**
  traits, **102,** 115, 118, 120, 121, 122, 123, 124, 125, 197, 198
  types of, **103**
Characterization, **102,** 108, 198, 493, 660, 827
  direct/indirect, **102, 157,** 198, 493, 1109
  in myth, 1088, 1109
  in short story, **129,** 131, 134, 136, 138, 139, **157,** 159, 160, 162, 164, 165, 168, 169
Chivalry, **1043**
Chronological sequence, **4, 17,** 33, 93
Climax, 93, 375, **785,** 975
Comedy, **784, 815,** 817, 818, 821, 823, 824, 825, 826, 828, 829
Comparing across genres
  characters, **171,** 186
  plot and setting, **61,** 76
  themes, 275, 276, 277, 280, 281, 283, 284, 967, 972, 974
Complications, plot, **4, 785**

Conflict, **4–5,** 57
  and character, **103,** 108, 125, 153, **171,** 175, 176, 177, 178, 179, 181, 183, 186, 197
  in drama, **785,** 792
  and historical context, **171,** 178
  internal/external, **5,** 33, 73, 93, 197, 284, **785**
  in myth, 1033
Connotations, **560, 571**
Constructed Response, 93, 198, 299, 416, 551, 618, 759, 986, 1109
Couplet, **690**
Credibility
  of argument, 593
  character, **143,** 151, 153
  of evidence, **560,** 567
Cross-curricular links, 55, 123, 165, 265, 372, 458, 487, 511, 589, 688, 861, 917, 1053, 1085
Description, 467
Dialogue, **787**
Diction, 209, **443,** 453, 483, 497, 676
Direct characterization, **102, 157,** 198, 493, 1079
Direct metaphor, **645**
Drama, **784–787,** 986
  characterization in, 829
  comedy, **784, 815,** 817, 818, 821, 823, 824, 825, 826, 828, 829
  conflict in, **785,** 792
  dialogue, **787**
  setting of, 813, 864, 932
  stage directions, **786**
  theme in, **967,** 968, 969
  tragedy, **784,** 795, **840,** 842, 844, 846, 848, 849, 850, 851, 853, 856, 857, 858, 861, 864, 878, 883, 886, 890, 893, 894, 896, 897, 899, 902, 904, 908, 911, 914, 915, 917, 920, 921, 922, 928, 931, 936, 941, 942, 944, 949, 952, 9553, 963, 964
Dramatic irony, **309, 339,** 377, **799,** 804, 805, 810, 812, 813

READING SKILLS

INDEX OF AUTHORS AND TITLES

Page numbers in italic type refer to the pages on which author biographies appear.